# STATUTORY INSTRUMENTS 1969

## PART I
### (in two Sections)

### SECTION 2

*Published by Authority*

*LONDON*
HER MAJESTY'S STATIONERY OFFICE
1969

2a

SBN 11 840030 4

# Contents of the Volume

## PART I, Section 1

## PART I, Section 2

## PART II

## PART III

# STATUTORY INSTRUMENTS

## 1969 No. 330

## SUGAR

## The Sugar Beet (Research and Education) Order 1969

| | | |
|---|---|---|
| Made - - - - | | 12th March 1969 |
| Laid before Parliament | | 20th March 1969 |
| Coming into Operation | | 1st April 1969 |

The Minister of Agriculture, Fisheries and Food and the Secretary of State in exercise of the powers conferred upon them by section 18(1) and (2) of the Sugar Act 1956(a), and of all other powers them enabling in that behalf, after consultation with the British Sugar Corporation Limited and with such bodies as in their opinion are substantially representative of growers of home-grown beet and having prepared a programme for carrying out research and education in matters affecting the growing of home-grown beet, hereby jointly make the following order:—

1.—(1) This order may be cited as the Sugar Beet (Research and Education) Order 1969; and shall come into operation on 1st April 1969.

(2) The Interpretation Act 1889(b), shall apply to the interpretation of this order as it applies to the interpretation of an Act of Parliament.

2. The programme of research and education set out in the Schedule to this order together with the expenditure estimated to be incurred in carrying it out shall be the programme for the year beginning on 1st April 1969.

3. The contributions from the British Sugar Corporation Ltd. (hereinafter referred to as "the Corporation") and every grower of home-grown beet who delivers beet to the Corporation during the year beginning on 1st April 1969, towards defraying the expenditure to be incurred in carrying out the aforesaid programme shall be assessed as follows:—

   (a) in the case of any grower of home-grown beet, the contribution shall be at the rate of threepence halfpenny for every ton of home-grown beet sold by him for delivery to the Corporation in that year;

   (b) in the case of the Corporation the contribution shall be at the rate of threepence halfpenny for every ton of home-grown beet purchased by them for delivery in that year.

4.—(1) All contracts made between the Corporation and any grower for the sale of home-grown beet for delivery to the Corporation during the year beginning on 1st April 1969 shall provide that the total amount of the grower's contribution assessed in accordance with the foregoing provisions of this order shall be payable by the grower to the Corporation out of any sums standing to the credit of that grower in account with the Corporation and be deducted by the Corporation from the amount payable to the grower.

(2) The Corporation shall pay the proceeds, together with the amount of the contribution from the Corporation assessed in accordance with sub-

---

(a) 1956 c. 48.     (b) 1889 c. 63.

paragraph (*b*) of Article 3 of this order, to the Minister of Agriculture, Fisheries and Food within that year.

**5.** The amount of any contribution which has not been paid to the Minister of Agriculture, Fisheries and Food during the year within which it is due shall become a debt due to that Minister.

In witness whereof the Official Seal of the Minister of Agriculture, Fisheries and Food is hereunto affixed on 14th March 1969.

(L.S.) *Cledwyn Hughes,*
Minister of Agriculture, Fisheries and Food.

Given under the Seal of the Secretary of State for Scotland on 12th March 1969.

(L.S.) *William Ross,*
Secretary of State for Scotland.

## SCHEDULE

Projects of research and education in matters affecting the growing of home-grown beet to be carried out by the persons or bodies described in relation thereto and estimates of expenditures to be incurred in carrying them out.

| A. RESEARCH | £ | £ |
|---|---|---|
| 1. Plant Breeding: Plant Breeding Institute, Cambridge ... ... ... ... ... | | 55,431 |
| 2. Variety Trials: National Institute of Agricultural Botany ... ... ... ... ... | | 19,104 |
| 3. Diseases Investigations, Fertilizer and Seed Production Experiments: Broom's Barn Experimental Station ... ... ... ... | | 81,561 |
| 4. Crop Husbandry: Norfolk Agricultural Station | | 11,321 |
| 5. Machinery and Cultivation Experiments: National Institute of Agricultural Engineering | | 8,782 |
| 6. Scottish Trials and Experiments ... ... | | 3,850 |
| 7. Agronomic Experiments: School of Agriculture, University of Nottingham ... ... | | 2,550 |
| 8. Physiology:— | | |
| (*a*) Imperial College of Science and Technology, London ... ... ... ... ... ... | 3,907 | |
| (*b*) Rothamsted Experimental Station ... | 3,500 | |
| (*c*) School of Agricultural Sciences, University of Leeds ... ... ... ... ... | 1,243 | 8,650 |

B.  EDUCATION                                        £          £

 9.  British Sugar Corporation Ltd.:—

  Publicity:

  (a)  British Sugar Beet Review ...    ...    ...    3,570

  (b)  Films ...    ...    ...    ...    ...    ...    750

  (c)  Virus Yellows    ...    ...    ...    ...    2,085        6,405

  Demonstrations:

  (a)  Cultivation    ...    ...    ...    ...    ...    16,800

  (b)  Harvest Machinery ...    ...    ...    ...    960

  (c)  Spring Mechanisation    ...    ...    ...    3,320        21,080

 10.  Scottish Demonstrations ...    ...    ...    ...                  500

C.  GENERAL

 11.  Travelling and Subsistence Expenses of Members and Officers of the Sugar Beet Research and Education Committee and its sub-committees    ...    ...    ...    ...    ...                  410

 12.  Administrative Charges:—

  (a)  Ministry of Agriculture, Fisheries and Food    1,620

  (b)  Department of Agriculture and Fisheries for Scotland    ...    ...    ...    ...    ...    100

  (c)  Exchequer and Audit Department...    ...    100        1,820

 13.  Institut International de Recherches Betteravières:—

  (a)  Subscriptions    ...    ...    ...    ...    1,400

  (b)  Expenses and Visits ...    ...    ...    ...    1,350

  (c)  Visit of American Society of Sugar Beet Technologists    ...    ...    ...    ...    ...    1,100        3,850

 14.  Other Items:—

  (a)  Docking Disorder, Aerial Photographic Survey    ...    ...    ...    ...    ...    ...    1,000

  (b)  Visits Abroad    ...    ...    ...    ...    250

  (c)  Contingencies    ...    ...    ...    ...    1,436        2,686

        Total                  228,000

## EXPLANATORY NOTE
*(This Note is not part of the Order.)*

This order provides for the assessment and collection of contributions in 1969 from the British Sugar Corporation Ltd. and growers of home-grown beet towards the programme of research and education set out in the Schedule to the order. The contributions in 1969 remain at $3\frac{1}{2}$d. per ton.

# STATUTORY INSTRUMENTS

## 1969 No. 339

## SOCIAL SECURITY

### The National Insurance (Claims and Payments) Amendment (No. 2) Regulations 1969

| | | |
|---|---|---|
| *Made* - - - | *14th March* 1969 |
| *Laid before Parliament* | *19th March* 1969 |
| *Coming into Operation* | *20th March* 1969 |

The Secretary of State for Social Services, in exercise of his powers under section 30 of the National Insurance Act 1965(**a**) and of all other powers enabling him in that behalf, after considering the report of the National Insurance Advisory Committee on the preliminary draft submitted to them in accordance with section 108 of that Act, hereby makes the following regulations :—

*Citation, interpretation and commencement*

**1.** These regulations, which may be cited as the National Insurance (Claims and Payments) Amendment (No. 2) Regulations 1969, shall be read as one with the National Insurance (Claims and Payments) Regulations 1948(**b**) as amended (**c**) (hereinafter referred to as "the principal regulations") and shall come into operation on 20th March 1969.

*Substitution of paragraph 8(2), (2A) and (3) of Part II of Schedule 2 to the principal regulations*

**2.** For paragraph 8(2), (2A) and (3) of Part II of Schedule 2 to the principal regulations (which schedule is included by virtue of the National Insurance (Claims and Payments) Amendment Regulations 1952(**d**) as amended (**e**) and which sub-paragraphs relate to notice of retirement) there shall be substituted the following sub-paragraphs—

"(2) A notice for the purpose of section 30(3) of the National Insurance Act 1965(**a**) (which relates to retirement pensions) shall be given to the Secretary of State for Social Services in writing and shall specify a date being a date not earlier than the date on which the person giving the notice attains pensionable age and not later than the expiration of 4 months after the date on which the notice is given, as the date of that person's retirement.

(3) For the purposes of paragraph (*a*) of the said section 30(3) the prescribed period shall be the period of 1 month :

Provided that the prescribed period shall be extended to the commencement of any continuous period immediately preceding the said period of 1 month throughout which the person giving the notice proves that there was good cause for the delay in giving such notice so, however, that the prescribed period shall in no case exceed 12 months.

---

(**a**) 1965 c. 51.   (**b**) S.I. 1948/1041 (Rev. XVI, p. 313: 1948 I, p. 2709).
(**c**) The relevant amending regulations are S.I. 1952/1207, 1957/1357 (1952 II, p. 2122; 1957 I, p. 1518).   (**d**) S.I. 1952/1207 (1952 II, p. 2122).   (**e**) S.I. 1957/1357 (1957 I, p. 1518).

(4) For the purpose of facilitating the determination of a subsequent claim for retirement pension, a person may at any time not more than 4 months before the date on which he will attain pensionable age, and notwithstanding that he does not intend to retire from regular employment at that date, submit particulars in writing to the Secretary of State for Social Services in a form approved by him for that purpose with a view to the determination (in advance of a claim) of any questions under the National Insurance Act 1965 relating to that person's title to a retirement pension other than the question of retirement, and subject to the necessary modifications, the provisions of Part II of these regulations shall apply to any such particulars."

*R. H. S. Crossman,*
Secretary of State for Social Services.

14th March 1969.

## EXPLANATORY NOTE
### (*This Note is not part of the Regulations.*)

These Regulations amend the National Insurance (Claims and Payments) Regulations 1948 by providing that, in cases in which a person giving notice of retirement proves that there was good cause for delay in giving the notice, the period of giving notice may be extended to 12 months, instead of 6 months. Other changes are of a minor and technical nature.

The report of the National Insurance Advisory Committee, dated 10th March 1969, on the preliminary draft of these Regulations is contained in the House of Commons Paper No. 190 (Session 1968-69) published by Her Majesty's Stationery Office.

## STATUTORY INSTRUMENTS

## 1969 No. 344

## ROAD TRAFFIC

### The Motor Vehicles (Authorisation of Special Types) General Order 1969

*Made* - - - - 12th March 1969

*Coming into Operation* 1st May 1969

### ARRANGEMENT OF THE ORDER

Marking of projecting loads and fixed appliances or apparatus which
project ... ... ... ... ... ... ... ... ... 25
Approval of the Minister as to the time, date and route of a journey by
a vehicle or a vehicle and its load exceeding 14 feet in width ... 26
Notice to police ... ... ... ... ... ... ... ... 27
Notice to highway and bridge authorities ... ... ... ... 28
Restriction on the passage over bridges of vehicles carrying abnormal
indivisible loads ... ... ... ... ... ... ... 29

## SCHEDULES

The Minister of Transport, in exercise of his powers under section 64(4) of
the Road Traffic Act 1960(a) as amended by section 51 of and Schedule 4 to
the Road Traffic Act 1962(b) and under subsections (5) and (6) of the said section
64 and of all other powers him enabling in that behalf, hereby makes the
following Order:—

### PART I
### PRELIMINARY

*Commencement and Citation*

**1.** This Order shall come into operation on the 1st May 1969 and may be
cited as the Motor Vehicles (Authorisation of Special Types) General
Order 1969.

*Revocation*

**2.** The Orders specified in Schedule 3 to this Order are hereby revoked.

*Interpretation*

**3.**—(1) In this Order, unless the context otherwise requires, the following
expressions have the meanings hereby assigned to them respectively, that is to
say—

"Construction and Use Regulations" means the Motor Vehicles (Construction and Use) Regulations 1969(c);

"Track Laying Regulations" means the Motor Vehicles (Construction
and Use) (Track Laying Vehicles) Regulations 1955(d);

"bank holiday", in relation to any provision of this Order requiring notice
to be given of the intended use of a vehicle on a road, means a day which is,
or is to be observed as, a bank holiday, or a holiday under the Bank Holidays
Act 1871(e) or the Holidays Extension Act 1875(f), either generally or in the
locality in which that road is situated;

"controlled by a pedestrian" has the same meaning as in section 254(2)
of the Road Traffic Act 1960;

"chief officer of police", and "police area", in relation to England and
Wales, have respectively the same meanings as in the Police Act 1964(g),
and, in relation to Scotland, have respectively the same meanings as in the
Police Pensions Act 1921(h);

---

(a) 8 & 9 Eliz. 2. c. 16.                    (b) 10 &11 Eliz. 2. c. 59.
(c) S.I. 1969/321 (1969 I, p. 829).          (d) S.I. 1955/990 (1955 II, p. 2287).
(e) 34 & 35 Vict. c. 17.                      (f) 38 & 39 Vict. c. 13.
(g) 1964 c. 48.                               (h) 11 & 12 Geo. 5. c. 31.

"the Minister" means the Minister of Transport;

"articulated vehicle", "land locomotive", "land tractor", "overall length", "overall width", "overhang", "registered", "straddle carrier", "track laying" and "wheeled" have the same meanings respectively as in the Construction and Use Regulations.

(2) Any reference in this Order to the Construction and Use Regulations shall be construed as a reference to those Regulations as for the time being amended by any regulations made under the Road Traffic Act 1960 after the coming into operation of this Order.

(3) Any reference in this Order to the Track Laying Regulations shall be construed as a reference to those Regulations as for the time being amended by any regulations made under the Road Traffic Act 1930(a) before the coming into operation of this Order or by any regulations made under the Road Traffic Act 1960 after the coming into operation of this Order.

(4) The Interpretation Act 1889(b) shall apply for the interpretation of this Order as it applies for the interpretation of an Act of Parliament, and as if for the purposes of section 38 of that Act this Order were an Act of Parliament and the Orders revoked by Article 2 of this Order were Acts of Parliament thereby repealed.

(5) In so far as any consent, notice, indemnity or dispensation given or any other thing done under a provision of any of the Orders revoked by this Order could have been given or done under a corresponding provision of this Order it shall not be invalidated by the revocation effected by Article 2 of this Order but shall have effect as if given or done under that corresponding provision.

*Speed limits*

**4.** Nothing in this Order relating to the speed of vehicles shall be taken to authorise any speed which is in excess of any other speed limit imposed by or under any enactment.

## PART II
### MISCELLANEOUS VEHICLES

*Track laying vehicles*

**5.** The Minister authorises the use on roads of track laying motor vehicles and track laying trailers notwithstanding that such vehicles do not comply in all respects with the requirements of the Construction and Use Regulations or the Track Laying Regulations, subject to the following restrictions and conditions:—

(*a*) a vehicle shall be used only for the purpose of—
  (i) demonstration, or
  (ii) enabling it to proceed to the nearest suitable railway station for conveyance to a port for shipment or to proceed to a port for shipment from a place in the immediate vicinity of that port where suitable railway facilities are not available;

(*b*) before a vehicle is so used the consent of every highway authority or every person responsible for the maintenance and repair of any road on which it is proposed that the vehicle shall be used shall in each case be obtained in writing; and

(*c*) a vehicle shall not be used for the carriage of goods or burden for hire or reward.

---

(a) 20 & 21 Geo. 5. c. 43.        (b) 52 & 53 Vict. c. 63.

*Naval, military, air force and aviation vehicles*

**6.** The Minister authorises the use on roads of the vehicles specified in Column 1 of Schedule 1 to this Order notwithstanding that such vehicles do not comply in all respects with the requirements of the Regulations of the Construction and Use Regulations or the Track Laying Regulations respectively specified opposite thereto in Column 2 of the said Schedule, subject to the vehicles being the property of, or for the time being under the control of, the persons respectively specified opposite thereto in Column 3 of the said Schedule.

*Vehicles used in connection with the saving of life at sea*

**7.** The Minister authorises the use on roads of track laying motor vehicles and track laying trailers notwithstanding that such vehicles do not comply in all respects with the requirements of the Construction and Use Regulations or the Track Laying Regulations, subject to the vehicles being used only for drawing or in connection with the launching of lifeboats the property of the Royal National Lifeboat Institution.

*Grass cutting machines and hedge trimmers*

**8.** The Minister authorises the use on roads of motor tractors constructed or adapted for use as grass cutters or hedge trimmers (not, in either case, being vehicles controlled by a pedestrian) notwithstanding that such vehicles do not comply with Regulation 39 of the Construction and Use Regulations, subject to the condition that all other relevant requirements of those Regulations are complied with as respects the vehicle and also subject to the following conditions:—

    (*a*) the overall width of a vehicle, except when it is actually engaged in grass cutting or hedge trimming operations, must not exceed 7 feet 6 inches; and

    (*b*) except when a vehicle is actually engaged in such operations as aforesaid, all cutting or trimming blades which form part of the machinery fitted to the vehicle must be effectively guarded so that no danger is caused or is likely to be caused to any person.

**9.** The Minister authorises the use on roads of hedge trimmers being vehicles controlled by a pedestrian notwithstanding that such vehicles do not comply in all respects with the requirements of the Construction and Use Regulations, subject to the following conditions:—

    (*a*) the requirements of Regulations 16, 22, 24, 76, 82, 84, 87, 88, 90, 95, 96, and 111 of the said Regulations, so far as applicable, must be complied with as respects a vehicle;

    (*b*) the unladen weight of a vehicle must not exceed 8 hundredweight;

    (*c*) the overall width of a vehicle, except when it is actually engaged in hedge trimming operations, must not exceed 7 feet 6 inches; and

    (*d*) except when a vehicle is actually engaged in such operations as aforesaid all trimming blades which form part of the machinery fitted to the vehicle must be effectively guarded so that no danger is caused or is likely to be caused to any person.

**10.** The Minister authorises the use on roads of trailers constructed or adapted for use as grass cutters or hedge trimmers notwithstanding that such trailers do not comply in all respects with such of the requirements of the

Construction and Use Regulations as apply to trailers, subject to the following restrictions and conditions:—

(a) the requirements of Regulations 31, 32, 83, and 87 of the said Regulations, so far as they apply to trailers, must be complied with;

(b) the unladen weight of such a trailer must not exceed—

    (i) 1 ton, if drawn by a locomotive, a motor tractor or a heavy motor car, or

    (ii) 16 hundredweight, in any other case;

(c) the overall width of the motor vehicle by which such a trailer is drawn and, except when it is actually engaged in grass cutting or hedge trimming operations, the overall width of such a trailer must not exceed 8 feet 6 inches;

(d) except when such a trailer is actually engaged in such operations as aforesaid, where it is being drawn in such a manner that its longitudinal axis and that of the drawing vehicle are parallel but lie in different vertical planes, the width of road occupied by both vehicles must not exceed 8 feet 6 inches.

    For the purposes of this paragraph, the width aforesaid shall be taken as a distance equivalent to the distance which, if both vehicles were treated as if they were one vehicle at a time when the one is drawing the other in the manner aforesaid, would fall to be measured as its overall width;

(e) except when such a trailer is actually engaged in such operations as aforesaid, all cutting or trimming blades which form part of the machinery fitted to the trailer must be effectively guarded so that no danger is caused or is likely to be caused to any person; and

(f) such a trailer must not be drawn at a speed exceeding 20 miles per hour.

## Rotary ploughs

**11.** The Minister authorises the use on roads of land locomotives specially designed and constructed as rotary ploughs notwithstanding that such vehicles do not comply with the requirements of Regulations 25 and 26 of the Track Laying Regulations, subject to the condition that all other relevant requirements of those Regulations are complied with as respects a vehicle and also subject to the following restrictions and conditions:—

(a) the overall width of a vehicle shall not exceed 11 feet 6 inches;

(b) the unladen weight of a vehicle shall not exceed 26 tons;

(c) no vehicle shall draw a trailer other than a living van or a trailer or trailers carrying the necessary gear and equipment of or fuel for the vehicle;

(d) where a vehicle exceeds 8 feet in overall width, and

    (i) is not drawing a trailer, three persons inclusive of the driver or drivers shall be in attendance upon it, one of whom shall whenever necessary by reason of the width of the road or otherwise proceed at a reasonable distance in front of the vehicle and another of whom shall whenever so necessary as aforesaid proceed at a reasonable distance behind the vehicle in each case to give warning to other traffic on the road, or

    (ii) is drawing one or more trailers, two persons shall drive or attend the vehicle and in addition at least one person shall be in attendance upon each trailer and such person or one of such persons in attendance upon the trailer or trailers as the case may be shall whenever necessary by reason of the width of the road or otherwise proceed at a reasonable distance behind the trailer or rearmost trailer to give warning to other traffic on the road;

(e) save in so far as the chief officer of police of any police area in which it is proposed that a vehicle will be used dispenses, as respects the use of the vehicle in that area, with any of the requirements contained in this and the following paragraph as to length of notice or particulars to be given, and save in so far as the highway authority for any road on which it is proposed that the vehicle will be used dispenses, as respects the use of the vehicle on that road, with any of the said requirements, the owner of the vehicle, before using it on a road for a journey exceeding 5 miles, shall give at least four clear days' notice (excluding Sundays, any bank holiday, Christmas Day or Good Friday) to the chief officer of police of any such area as aforesaid and to the highway authority for any such road as aforesaid;

(f) the notice referred to in the foregoing paragraph shall contain particulars of the vehicle concerned, of its overall width and of the time, date and route of the proposed journey; and

(g) subject to any variation in the time, date or route of the journey which the owner may be directed to make by any such chief officer of police as aforesaid, the vehicle shall be used only in circumstances which accord with the particulars given in compliance with the foregoing paragraph as to the time, date and route of the journey and only if the overall width of the vehicle does not exceed the width of which particulars have been given as aforesaid:

Provided that if, by reason of adverse weather conditions or other special circumstances, the surface of any road comprised in the route of the proposed journey is abnormally susceptible to damage the highway authority for that road may require the owner of the vehicle to postpone that journey until such time as they notify him that the journey may be undertaken and in such a case the vehicle shall not be used for the purpose of making the journey until that time.

### Vehicles used for experiments or trials

**12.** The Minister authorises the use on roads of vehicles in or in connection with the conduct of experiments or trials under section 6 of the Roads Improvement Act 1925(a) or section 249 of the Highways Act 1959(b) notwithstanding that such vehicles do not comply in all respects with the requirements of the Construction and Use Regulations or the Track Laying Regulations.

### Straddle carriers

**13.** The Minister authorises the use on roads of straddle carriers notwithstanding that such vehicles do not comply in all respects with the requirements of Regulations 10, 11(2) (b)(ii), 43, 44, 45(5), (6) and (7) and 79 (other than those in paragraph (1)(a) thereof) of the Construction and Use Regulations, subject to the condition that all other relevant requirements of those Regulations are complied with as respects a vehicle and also subject to the following restrictions and conditions:—

(a) a vehicle shall not be used otherwise than for the purpose of demonstration or in the course of delivery on sale or when proceeding to or returning from a manufacturer or repairer for the purpose of repair or overhaul and, when so used, shall carry no load other than its necessary gear or equipment:

(a) 15 & 16 Geo. 5. c. 68.          (b) 7 & 8 Eliz. 2. c. 25.

Provided that a vehicle which does not comply with the said Regulation 44 may, if it complies with the said Regulations 10 and 43, be used whether laden or unladen in passing from one part of any private premises to any other part thereof or to other private premises in the immediate neighbourhood;

(*b*) no vehicle shall travel at a speed exceeding 12 miles per hour;

(*c*) the overall width of a vehicle shall not exceed 9 feet 6 inches;

(*d*) no vehicle shall be used if the overall length of the vehicle or, where the vehicle is carrying a load, if the overall length of the vehicle together with the length of any forward projection and of any rearward projection of its load exceeds 30 feet except with the consent of the chief officer of police of every police area in which it is proposed that the vehicle will be used.

For the purposes of this and the following paragraph the expressions "forward projection" and "rearward projection" have the same meanings respectively as in Regulation 110(1) of the Construction and Use Regulations and the provisions of sub-paragraph (*e*) of the said Regulation 110(1) shall apply accordingly; and

(*e*) save in so far as the chief officer of police of any police area in which it is proposed that a vehicle will be used dispenses, as respects the use of the vehicle in that area, with any of the requirements contained in this paragraph, the owner of the vehicle shall, not less than two clear days (excluding Sundays, any bank holiday, Christmas Day or Good Friday) before the day on which it is proposed that the vehicle will be used, apply to the chief officer of police of any such area as aforesaid for his consent to the use of the vehicle, and shall, when making the application, furnish to him particulars of the vehicle concerned, of its overall length, of the length of any forward projection or rearward projection of any load proposed to be carried, and of the roads on which it is proposed that the vehicle will be used.

*Land tractors used for reaping and threshing*

**14.** The Minister authorises the use on roads of land tractors constructed for the combined purpose of reaping and threshing notwithstanding that such vehicles do not comply with the requirements of Regulations 39 and 40 of the Construction and Use Regulations, subject to the condition that all other relevant requirements of those Regulations are complied with as respects a vehicle and also subject to the following restrictions and conditions:—

(*a*) no vehicle shall draw a trailer other than a two-wheeled trailer used solely for the carriage of the necessary gear and equipment of the vehicle;

(*b*) the overall width of a vehicle shall not exceed 14 feet;

(*c*) where the overall width of a vehicle—

(i) exceeds 9 feet 6 inches but does not exceed 11 feet, one person in addition to the driver shall be in attendance, or

(ii) exceeds 11 feet, two persons in addition to the driver shall be in attendance, one of whom shall whenever necessary proceed at a reasonable distance in front of the vehicle and the other of whom shall whenever necessary proceed at a reasonable distance behind the vehicle, in each case to give warning to other traffic on the road;

(*d*) no vehicle the overall width of which exceeds 11 feet shall travel at a speed exceeding 5 miles per hour and no other vehicle shall travel at a speed exceeding 10 miles per hour;

(*e*) all cutting blades which form part of the machinery fitted to the vehicle must be effectively guarded so that no danger is caused or is likely to be caused to any person;

(*f*) the three following paragraphs shall apply to the use of a vehicle of which the overall width exceeds 9 feet 6 inches;

(*g*) save in so far as the chief officer of police of any police area in which it is proposed that the vehicle will be used dispenses, as respects the use of the vehicle in that area, with any of the requirements contained in this and the following paragraph as to length of notice or particulars to be given, the owner of the vehicle, before using it on a road for a journey exceeding 5 miles, shall give at least twenty-four hours' notice to the chief officer of police of any such area as aforesaid;

(*h*) the notice referred to in the foregoing paragraph shall contain particulars of the vehicle concerned, of its overall width, and of the time, date and route of the proposed journey; and

(*i*) subject to any variation in the time, date or route of the journey which the owner may be directed to make by any such chief officer of police as aforesaid, the vehicle shall be used only in circumstances which accord with the particulars given in compliance with the foregoing paragraph as to the time, date and route of the journey and only if the overall width of the vehicle does not exceed the width of which particulars have been given as aforesaid.

### Mechanically propelled hay and straw balers

**15.** The Minister authorises the use on roads of motor tractors constructed for the purpose of picking up, baling and binding hay or straw notwithstanding that such vehicles do not comply with the requirements of Regulation 40 of the Construction and Use Regulations, subject to the condition that all other relevant requirements of those Regulations are complied with as respects a vehicle and also subject to the following restrictions and conditions:—

(*a*) the overall width of a vehicle shall not exceed 8 feet;

(*b*) the overhang of a vehicle shall not exceed 8 feet; and

(*c*) no vehicle shall travel on a road at a speed exceeding 10 miles per hour.

### Vehicles for moving excavated material

**16.** The Minister authorises the use on roads of moveable plant or equipment (other than engineering plant as defined in Article 19 of this Order) being a heavy motor car, trailer or articulated vehicle specially designed and constructed for use in private premises for the primary purpose of moving excavated material and fitted with a tipping body, moving platform or other similar device for discharging its load, and which cannot, owing to the requirements of that purpose, comply in all respects with the requirements of the Construction and Use Regulations, subject to the following restrictions and conditions:—

(*a*) a vehicle shall only be used in proceeding to and from private premises or between private premises and a port in either direction and shall carry no load other than its necessary gear or equipment;

(*b*) a heavy motor car not forming part of an articulated vehicle shall not draw any trailer;

(*c*) where a trailer is drawn by a motor vehicle the motor vehicle shall not draw any other trailer;

(*d*) in the case of a heavy motor car not forming part of an articulated vehicle all the Regulations of the Construction and Use Regulations, other than Regulations 10, 11(2)(*b*)(ii), 43, 45(5), (6) and (7), 47, 71, 75 and 79 (with the exception of paragraph (1)(*a*) thereof) shall apply;

(*e*) in the case of a trailer not forming part of an articulated vehicle all the Regulations of the Construction and Use Regulations, other than Regulations 10, 60, 61, 65 and 79 (with the exception of paragraph (1)(*a*) thereof) shall, subject as provided in paragraph (*h*) of this Article, apply;

(*f*) in the case of an articulated vehicle all the Regulations of the Construction and Use Regulations, other than Regulations 7(1), 10, 11(2)(*b*) (ii), 43, 45(5),(6) and (7), 47, 61, 65, 71, 72, 74, 75 and 79 (with the exception of paragraph (1)(*a*) thereof) shall, subject as provided in paragraph (*h*) of this Article, apply;

(*g*) in the case of a heavy motor car not forming part of an articulated vehicle and in the case of an articulated vehicle the sum of the weights transmitted to the road surface by any two wheels in line transversely shall not exceed 15 tons and the sum of the weights so transmitted by all the wheels shall not exceed 25 tons;

(*h*) in the case of a trailer, whether or not forming part of an articulated vehicle, sub-paragraphs (*b*) and (*c*) of paragraph (1) or paragraph (2) of Regulation 62 of the Construction and Use Regulations shall not apply if the trailer is equipped with an efficient brake or with suitable scotches or similar devices to hold it stationary when necessary;

(*i*) the overall length of a trailer shall not exceed 28 feet and the overall length of an articulated vehicle shall not excceed 44 feet;

(*j*) no vehicle the overall width of which exceeds 9 feet 6 inches shall travel at a speed exceeding 8 miles per hour and no other vehicle shall travel at a speed exceeding 12 miles per hour;

(*k*) every wheel of the vehicle shall be equipped with a pneumatic tyre;

(*l*) where the overall width of a vehicle exceeds 9 feet 6 inches at least two persons, or where the overall width of a vehicle exceeds 8 feet but does not exceed 9 feet 6 inches, at least one person, in addition to the person or persons employed as respects a motor vehicle in driving that vehicle, shall be employed in attending to that vehicle and any load carried thereby and any trailer drawn by that vehicle and any load carried on the trailer and to give warning to the driver of the said motor vehicle and to any other person of any danger likely to be caused to any such other person by reason of the presence of the vehicle or the vehicle and trailer on the road;

(*m*) the three following paragraphs shall apply to the use of a vehicle of which the overall width exceeds 8 feet on a road on which a tramcar is operated and to the use of a vehicle of which the overall width exceeds 9 feet 6 inches on any other road;

(*n*) save in so far as the chief officer of police of any police area in which it is proposed that the vehicle will be used dispenses, as respects the use of the vehicle in that area, with any of the requirements contained in this and the following paragraph as to length of notice or particulars to be given, the owner of the vehicle, if its overall width exceeds 8 feet, before using it on a road on which a tramcar is operated or, if its overall width exceeds 9 feet 6 inches, before using it on any road, shall give at least two clear days' notice (excluding Sundays, any bank holiday, Christmas Day or Good Friday) to the chief officer of police of any such area as aforesaid;

(*o*) the notice referred to in the foregoing paragraph shall contain particulars of the vehicle concerned, of its overall width, and of the time, date and route of the proposed journey;

(*p*) subject to any variation in the time, date or route of the journey which may be directed by any such chief officer of police as aforesaid, the vehicle shall be used only in circumstances which accord with the particulars given in compliance with the foregoing paragraph as to the time, date and route of the journey and only if the overall width of the vehicle does not exceed the width of which particulars have been given as aforesaid;

(*q*) the four following paragraphs shall apply to the use of a vehicle in respect of which any of the requirements of the Construction and Use Regulations with respect to the weights of vehicles whether laden or unladen or the weights transmitted to the road surface by all or any of the wheels is not complied with or, where a combination of vehicles is used, if any of the said requirements as respects any or all of the vehicles comprised in the combination is not complied with.

For the purposes of this paragraph the reference to a combination of vehicles shall be construed in the same manner as is provided in Regulation 110(1)(*g*) of the Construction and Use Regulations for the purposes of Regulation 111 thereof;

(*r*) save in so far as the highway authority for any road or the bridge authority for any bridge on which it is proposed that the vehicle or, as the case may be, the vehicles will be used dispenses, as respects the use of the vehicle or vehicles on that road or, as the case may be, on that bridge, with the requirements contained in this paragraph as to length of notice or with any of the requirements applicable by virtue of the following paragraph as respects the form of notice or the particulars to be given, the owner of the vehicle, or, as the case may be, of the vehicles, before using the vehicle or vehicles on that road or that bridge, shall give at least two clear days' notice (excluding Sundays, any bank holiday, Christmas Day or Good Friday) as provided by the following paragraph to the highway authority for any such road and to the bridge authority for any such bridge;

(*s*) the notice referred to in the foregoing paragraph shall, subject to any necessary modification, be in the form and shall contain the particulars specified in Part II of Schedule 2 to this Order and the provisions of Article 28(6) and (7) thereof shall apply as respects any such notice;

(*t*) before using the vehicle or, as the case may be, the vehicles on any road or bridge the owner of the vehicle or vehicles shall give to the highway authority for the road and to the bridge authority for the bridge an indemnity as provided by the following paragraph; and

(*u*) the indemnity referred to in the foregoing paragraph shall be in the form specified in Part III of Schedule 2 to this Order and the provisions of Article 28(6) and (7) thereof shall apply as respects any such indemnity.

*Motor vehicles and trailers constructed for use outside the United Kingdom and new or improved types of motor vehicles and trailers constructed for tests or trials and motor vehicles and trailers equipped with new or improved equipment or types of equipment.*

**17.**—(1) This Article applies to wheeled motor vehicles and trailers not falling within any description of motor vehicle or trailer specified in Article 20 or 21 of this Order and references in this Article to motor vehicles and trailers shall be construed accordingly.

(2) The Minister authorises the use on roads—

(A) of motor vehicles and trailers, or types of motor vehicles and trailers, constructed for use outside the United Kingdom and of new or improved types of motor vehicles and trailers constructed for tests or trials notwithstanding that such vehicles do not comply in all respects with the requirements of the Construction and Use Regulations, and

(B) of motor vehicles and trailers equipped with new or improved equipment or types of equipment notwithstanding that such vehicles do not comply in all respects with such of the requirements of the Construction and Use Regulations as cannot, by reason only of the said equipment, be complied with,

subject, in all cases, to the following restrictions and conditions:—

(a) no vehicle shall be used otherwise than—

(i) for or in connection with the testing or demonstration of the vehicle, or

(ii) in the course of delivery on sale, or

(iii) for proceeding to or returning from a manufacturer or repairer for the purpose of construction, repair or overhaul;

(b) a vehicle shall comply with Regulations 6, 11, 16, 19, 21, 67, 76, 78, 79(1)(a), 80 and 83 to 86 (inclusive) of the Construction and Use Regulations and Regulations 87 to 98 (inclusive), 100 to 104 (inclusive), 106 and 109 to 113 (inclusive) of the said Regulations shall apply thereto;

(c) no vehicle shall be used for the carriage of any load other than its necessary gear or equipment or such apparatus or ballast as may be necessary for the purpose of carrying out a test or trial of that vehicle;

(d) the three following sub-paragraphs shall apply to the use of a vehicle of which the overall width exceeds 9 feet 6 inches or of a vehicle which has an overall length exceeding that specified by any provision of Regulation 7 or 60 of the Construction and Use Regulations as the maximum length for that vehicle;

(e) save in so far as the chief officer of police of any police area in which it is proposed that the vehicle will be used dispenses, as respects the use of the vehicle in that area, with any of the requirements contained in this and the following sub-paragraph as to length of notice or particulars to be given, the owner of the vehicle, before using it on a road, shall give at least two clear days' notice (excluding Sundays, any bank holiday, Christmas Day or Good Friday) to the chief officer of police of any such area as aforesaid;

(f) the notice referred to in the foregoing sub-paragraph shall contain particulars of the vehicle concerned, of its overall width and overall length, of the width and length of any load proposed to be carried, and of the time, date and route of the proposed journey;

(g) subject to any variation in the time, date or route of the journey which may be directed by any such chief officer of police as aforesaid, the vehicle shall be used only in circumstances which accord with the particulars given in compliance with the foregoing sub-paragraph as to the time, date and route of the journey and only if the overall width and overall length of the vehicle and the width and length of any load carried thereon do not exceed the width and length of which particulars have been given as aforesaid;

(h) the four following sub-paragraphs shall apply to the use of a vehicle in respect of which any of the requirements of the Construction and

Use Regulations with respect to the weights of vehicles whether laden or unladen or the weights transmitted to the road surface by all or any of the wheels is not complied with or, where a combination of vehicles is used, if any of the said requirements as respects any or all of the vehicles comprised in the combination is not complied with.

For the purposes of this sub-paragraph the reference to a combination of vehicles shall be construed in the same manner as is provided in Regulation 110(1)(*g*) of the Construction and Use Regulations for the purposes of Regulation 111 thereof;

(*i*) save in so far as the highway authority for any road or the bridge authority for any bridge on which it is proposed that the vehicle or, as the case may be, the vehicles will be used dispenses, as respects the use of the vehicle or vehicles on that road or, as the case may be, on that bridge, with the requirements contained in this sub-paragraph as to length of notice or with any of the requirements applicable by virtue of the following sub-paragraph as respects the form of notice or the particulars to be given, the owner of the vehicle or, as the case may be, of the vehicles, before using the vehicle or vehicles on that road or that bridge, shall give at least two clear days' notice (excluding Sundays, any bank holiday, Christmas Day or Good Friday) as provided by the following sub-paragraph to the highway authority for any such road and to the bridge authority for any such bridge;

(*j*) the notice referred to in the foregoing sub-paragraph shall, subject to any necessary modification, be in the form and shall contain the particulars specified in Part II of Schedule 2 to this Order and the provisions of Article 28(6) and (7) thereof shall apply as respects any such notice;

(*k*) before using the vehicle or, as the case may be, the vehicles on any road or bridge the owner of the vehicle or vehicles shall give to the highway authority for the road and to the bridge authority for the bridge an indemnity as provided by the following sub-paragraph; and

(*l*) the indemnity referred to in the foregoing sub-paragraph shall be in the form specified in Part III of Schedule 2 to this Order and the provisions of Article 28(6) and (7) thereof shall apply as respects any such indemnity.

### Vehicles fitted with moveable platforms

**18.**—(1) The Minister authorises the use on roads of a vehicle fitted with a moveable platform notwithstanding that the vehicle does not comply in all respects with the requirements of Regulations 6, 7, 9, 34, 39, 40, 43, 44, 48, 49 or 111 of the Construction and Use Regulations, subject to the condition that all other relevant requirements of those regulations are complied with as respects the vehicle and also subject to the following restrictions and conditions:—

(*a*) no vehicle shall be used on a road unless its special equipment is fully retracted except when the vehicle is at a place where it is being used to facilitate overhead working,

(*b*) any jacks with which the vehicle is fitted for stabilising it while the moveable platform is in use and which project from the sides of the vehicle shall be clearly visible to persons using the road within a reasonable distance of the vehicle, and

(*c*) the vehicle, except in respect of its special equipment when the vehicle is at a place where it is being used to facilitate overhead working, shall—

(i) as respects its overall length, comply with Regulation 7 of the said Regulations,

(ii) as respects its overall width, comply with Regulation 34, 39, 43 or 48 (as the case may be) of the said Regulations,

(iii) in the case of a vehicle other than a locomotive, as respects its overhang, comply with Regulation 40, 44 or 49 (as the case may be) of the said Regulations.

(2) In this Article the expression "moveable platform" means a platform which is attached to, and may be moved by means of, an extensible boom, and the expression "special equipment" means a moveable platform, the apparatus for moving the platform and any jacks fitted to the vehicle for stabilising it while the moveable platform is in use.

## Part III

### Abnormal Indivisible Loads, Engineering Plant and other Vehicles carrying Wide Loads

*Interpretation*

**19.** In this Part of the Order, unless the context otherwise requires, the following expressions have the meanings hereby assigned to them respectively, that is to say—

"abnormal indivisible load" means a load—

(a) which cannot without undue expense or risk of damage be divided into two or more loads for the purpose of carriage on roads, and

(b) which—

(i) owing to its dimensions, cannot be carried by a heavy motor car or trailer or a combination of a heavy motor car and trailer complying in all respects with the requirements of the Construction and Use Regulations, or

(ii) owing to its weight cannot be carried by a heavy motor car or trailer or a combination of a heavy motor car and trailer having a total laden weight of less than 24 tons and complying in all respects with the requirements of the Construction and Use Regulations;

"engineering plant" means—

(a) moveable plant or equipment being a motor vehicle or trailer (not constructed primarily to carry a load) specially designed and constructed for the special purposes of engineering operations, and which cannot, owing to the requirements of those purposes, comply in all respects with the requirements of the Construction and Use Regulations or the Track Laying Regulations, or

(b) a mobile crane which does not comply in all respects with the requirements of the Construction and Use Regulations or the Track Laying Regulations;

"special road" means a special road which is open for use as a special road;

"lateral projection", "forward projection" and "rearward projection" have the same meanings respectively as in Regulation 110(1) of the Construction and Use Regulations and references in this Part of this Order to a special appliance or apparatus in relation to a vehicle, to a forward projection or a rearward projection in relation to a vehicle, to the distance between vehicles in relation to vehicles carrying a load, and to a combination of vehicles in relation to a motor vehicle which is drawing one or more trailers, shall be construed respectively in the same manner as is provided in the said Regulation 110(1) for the purposes of Regulation 111 of the said Regulations, and the provisions of sub-paragraphs (*b*), (*e*), (*h*), (*i*) and (*j*) of the said Regulation 110(1) shall apply for the purposes of this Part of this Order as they apply for the purposes of the said Regulations 110(1) and 111;

"tractor" means a motor tractor;

"locomotive" has the same meaning as in the Construction and Use Regulations.

*Vehicles for carrying or drawing abnormal indivisible loads*

**20.** The Minister authorises the use on roads of heavy motor cars and trailers specially designed and constructed for the carriage of abnormal indivisible loads and of locomotives and tractors specially designed and constructed to draw trailers specially so designed and constructed notwithstanding that such vehicles do not comply in all respects with the requirements of the Construction and Use Regulations, subject to the restrictions and conditions contained in Articles 23(1) and 29 of this Order and, in a case where Article 24, 25, 27 or 28 of this Order applies, to the restrictions and conditions contained in such of those Articles as are applicable to that case and, in a case where the overall width of a vehicle or of a vehicle together with the width of any lateral projection or projections of its load exceeds 14 feet, to the restrictions and conditions contained in Article 26 of this Order and also, in any case, to the following further restrictions and conditions:—

(*a*) a heavy motor car or trailer which does not comply with Part II of the Construction and Use Regulations shall be used only, save as provided in paragraph (*p*) of this Article, for or in connection with the carriage of an abnormal indivisible load;

(*b*) a locomotive or tractor which does not comply with Part II of the Construction and Use Regulations shall be used only for or in connection with the drawing of trailers the use of which on roads is authorised by this Article;

(*c*) in the case of a heavy motor car all the Regulations of the Construction and Use Regulations, other than Regulations 10, 11(2)(*b*)(ii), 43, 45(5), (6) and (7), 46, 47, 71, 73 to 75 (inclusive), 79 (with the exception of paragraph (1)(*a*) thereof), 111 and 121 shall apply;

(*d*) in the case of a trailer all the Regulations of the Construction and Use Regulations, other than Regulations 7, 10, 14, 61, 62(2), 63 to 65 (inclusive), 69, 72 to 75 (inclusive), 79 (with the exception of paragraph (1)(*a*) thereof), 111 and 121 shall, subject as provided in paragraph (*e*) of this Article, apply:

Provided that it shall not be necessary for a trailer constructed before 15th January 1931 to comply with Regulation 9 of the Construction and Use Regulations;

(*e*) in the case of a trailer whether manufactured before 1st January 1968 or on or after that date, Regulation 62(1) of the Construction and Use Regulations shall apply as it applies to trailers manufactured before 1st January 1968;

(*f*) in the case of a locomotive or tractor all the Regulations of the Construction and Use Regulations, other than Regulations 10, 34, 39, 69 and 73 shall apply;

(*g*) the overall width of a heavy motor car shall not exceed 9 feet 6 inches unless it is used for or in connection with the carriage of a load which can only safely be carried on a heavy motor car which exceeds that overall width;

(*h*) the overall width of a locomotive or tractor shall not exceed 9 feet 6 inches unless it is used for or in connection with the carriage of a load on a trailer which exceeds that overall width, being a load which can only be safely carried on such a trailer;

(*i*) the overall width of a trailer shall not exceed 9 feet 6 inches unless it is drawn by a locomotive or tractor and is used for or in connection with the carriage of such a load as is mentioned in the foregoing paragraph;

(*j*) notwithstanding anything in any of the three foregoing paragraphs the overall width of a heavy motor car, locomotive, tractor or trailer shall not exceed 20 feet;

(*k*) where, in relation to the load carried by a vehicle, there is a lateral projection on one or both sides of the vehicle the overall width of the vehicle together with the width of the projection, or as the case may be, of both projections shall not exceed 20 feet;

(*l*) the overall length of a vehicle or of a vehicle together with the length of any forward projection and of any rearward projection of its load or, where a load is carried in such a manner that part of its weight rests on more than one vehicle, of the vehicles together with the distance between vehicles and the length of any forward projection and of any rearward projection of the load shall not exceed 90 feet;

(*m*) a vehicle shall be so constructed that it is a wheeled vehicle;

(*n*) every wheel of a vehicle shall be equipped with a pneumatic tyre or a tyre of soft or elastic material;

(*o*) the following restrictions on weight shall apply to vehicles, including articulated vehicles, carrying an abnormal indivisible load:—

  (i) the sum of the weights transmitted to the road surface by all the wheels of the vehicle or vehicles carrying the load shall not exceed 150 tons,

  (ii) the weight transmitted to the road surface by any one wheel shall not exceed $11\frac{1}{2}$ tons,

  (iii) the weight transmitted to any strip of road surface upon which the wheels rest contained between any two parallel lines drawn on that surface at right angles to the longitudinal axis of the vehicle or vehicles carrying the load shall not exceed, if the parallel lines are not more than 2 feet apart, 45 tons and, thereafter, additional weight shall be permitted, for any distance apart of the parallel lines in excess of 2 feet but not exceeding a total distance apart of 7 feet, at a rate of 9 tons per foot and, thereafter, additional weight shall be permitted, for any distance apart of the parallel lines in excess of 7 feet, at a rate of 3 tons per foot, and

  (iv) the total weight transmitted to the road surface by any wheels in line transversely not fitted with pneumatic tyres shall be such that the average weight per inch width of tyre in contact with the road surface shall not exceed 15 hundredweight:

Provided that the restrictions contained in item (ii) of this paragraph shall not apply to any heavy motor car registered on or before 31st December 1951 or any trailer manufactured before the 1st January 1952.

For the purposes of item (ii) of this paragraph any two wheels shall be regarded as one wheel if the distance between the centres of the areas of contact between such wheels and the road surface is less than 2 feet; and (*p*) no vehicle or combination of vehicles shall carry more than one abnormal indivisible load at any one time:

Provided that, subject to compliance with all the requirements of the Construction and Use Regulations with respect to the laden weights of vehicles and the weights transmitted to the road surface by all or any of the wheels, it shall be permissible for a vehicle or any vehicles comprised in a combination of vehicles to carry more than one abnormal indivisible load of the same character and, where any abnormal indivisible load is carried, to carry any articles of a similar character.

*Engineering Plant*

**21.** The Minister authorises the use on roads of engineering plant notwithstanding that such vehicles do not comply in all respects with the requirements of the Construction and Use Regulations or the Track Laying Regulations, subject to the restriction contained in Article 23(2) of this Order and, in a case where Article 24, 25, 27 or 28 of this Order applies, to the restrictions and conditions contained in such of those Articles as are applicable to that case and, in a case where the overall width of a vehicle or of a vehicle together with the width of any lateral projection or projections of its load exceeds 14 feet, to the restrictions and conditions contained in Article 26 of this Order and also, in any case, to the following further restrictions and conditions:—

(*a*) engineering plant other than a mobile crane shall only be used on a road for the purpose of proceeding to or from the site of engineering operations or when actually engaged in such operations and shall carry no load other than its necessary gear or equipment or, in the case of plant when actually engaged on the construction, maintenance and repair of roads, materials which it is specially designed to treat while carried on the vehicle;

(*b*) a mobile crane shall only be used on a road for the purpose of proceeding from one place to another and not for the purpose of the lifting or transportation of goods or burden otherwise than when actually engaged in engineering operations;

(*c*) no engineering plant other than a mobile crane shall draw any trailer other than a trailer which is engineering plant or a living van or office hut used in connection with the construction, maintenance and repair of roads;

(*d*) no mobile crane shall draw a trailer;

(*e*) a vehicle shall be so constructed that it is either a wheeled vehicle or a track laying vehicle;

(*f*) in the case of a wheeled motor vehicle Regulations 4, 9, 15, 16, 18 to 26 (inclusive), 31 to 33 (inclusive), 76, 78, 79(1)(*a*), 80 to 84 (inclusive), 87 to 98 (inclusive), 100 and 101 of the Construction and Use Regulations shall apply:

Provided that—

(i) in the case of a motor vehicle registered on or before 31st December 1951 Regulations 18 and 19 of the said Regulations shall not apply, and

(ii) in the case of a machine designed for use and used solely for the purpose of laying materials for the repair or construction of road surfaces if the weight transmitted to the road surface by any two wheels in line transversely does not exceed 11 tons the said Regulation 9 shall not apply;

(iii) in the case of a motor vehicle designed for use in work of construction or repair of road surfaces, the wheels of which are equipped with pneumatic tyres specially provided with smooth treads for such use and which is incapable by reason of its construction of exceeding a speed of 20 miles per hour on the level under its own power, Regulation 83(1)($f$) of the said Regulations shall not apply;

(g) in the case of a wheeled trailer Regulations 4, 9, 31, 32, 67, 76, 79(1)($a$), 80, 83, 87, 95 and 100 of the Construction and Use Regulations shall apply;

Provided that in the case of a trailer designed for use in work of construction or repair of road surfaces and the wheels of which are equipped with pneumatic tyres specially provided with smooth treads for such use, the said Regulation 83(1)($f$) shall not apply;

(h) in the case of a track laying motor vehicle Regulations 4, 6, 9, 13, 14, 16 to 24 (inclusive), 51, 53 to 69 (inclusive) 71, 72 and 78 of the Track Laying Regulations shall apply:

Provided that—

(i) in the case of a motor vehicle registered on or before 31st December 1951 Regulations 16 and 17 of the said Regulations shall not apply, and

(ii) in the case of a motor vehicle which is a road roller the said Regulation 9 shall not apply;

(i) in the case of a track laying trailer Regulations 4, 6, 9, 22, 23, 44, 51, 54, 56, 57, 59, 67 and 71 of the Track Laying Regulations shall apply:

Provided that in the case of a trailer which is a road roller the said Regulation 9 shall not apply;

(j) all the wheels of a vehicle which are not equipped with pneumatic tyres or tyres of soft or elastic material shall be equipped with smooth tyres and have the edges rounded to a radius of not less than ½ inch and not more than 1 inch:

Provided that in the case of gritting machines designed for use and used for gritting frosted and icebound roads all or any of the tyres may be shod with diagonal cross bars of equal width of not less than 1 inch, extending the full breadth of the tyre and so arranged that the distance between adjacent cross bars is not greater than the width of the cross bars;

(k) in the case of any vehicle the weight transmitted to the road surface by any one wheel not equipped with pneumatic tyres where no other wheel is in the same line transversely or by all the wheels not equipped with pneumatic tyres in line transversely shall be such that the average weight per inch width of tyre in contact with such surface does not exceed 15 hundredweight;

(l) a motor vehicle shall be equipped with an efficient brake:

Provided that—

(i) in the case of a motor vehicle propelled by steam the engine shall be deemed to be an efficient brake if the engine is capable of being reversed, and

(ii) in the case of a motor vehicle registered on or after 1st January 1952 any brake required by this paragraph shall be capable of being set so as to hold the vehicle when stationary unless another brake fitted to the vehicle is capable of being so set;

(*m*) a trailer shall be equipped with an efficient brake or with suitable scotches or other similar devices to hold the vehicle stationary when necessary;

(*n*) no motor vehicle which exceeds 26 feet in overall length shall draw a trailer:

Provided that this paragraph shall not apply to any broken down vehicle which is being drawn by a motor vehicle in consequence of the breakdown;

(*o*) the sum of the weights transmitted to the road surface by all the wheels and tracks of a vehicle shall not exceed 150 tons:

(*p*) the overall length of a vehicle shall not exceed 90 feet; and

(*q*) the overall width of a vehicle shall not exceed 20 feet.

### Other vehicles carrying loads exceeding 14 feet in width

**22.** The Minister authorises the use on roads of motor vehicles and trailers carrying loads where the overall width of the vehicle on which the load is carried together with the width of any lateral projection or projections of the load exceeds 14 feet but does not exceed 20 feet, subject to the restrictions and conditions contained in Articles 23(3), 24, 26 and 27 of this Order and also to the condition that the vehicle complies in all respects with the requirements of the Construction and Use Regulations (other than Regulation 111(1) and (2) thereof).

### Speed limits for vehicles authorised by Article 20, 21 or 22

**23.**—(1) A vehicle the use of which on roads is authorised by Article 20 of this Order shall not travel on any road, other than a special road,—

(*a*) in the case of a vehicle—

(i) which is not carrying a load,

(ii) which has an overall width not exceeding 9 feet 6 inches, and

(iii) which complies with all the relevant requirements of the Construction and Use Regulations with respect to the springs, wings, brakes and tyres with which a vehicle is required to be fitted or equipped, to the weights of vehicles and to the weights transmitted to the road surface by the wheels of vehicles,

at a speed exceeding 20 miles per hour; and

(*b*) in any other case, at a speed exceeding 12 miles per hour.

(2) A vehicle the use of which on roads is authorised by Article 21 of this Order shall not travel on any road, other than a special road, at a speed exceeding 12 miles per hour.

(3) A vehicle the use of which on roads is authorised by Article 22 of this Order shall not travel on any road, other than a special road, at a speed exceeding 20 miles per hour.

### Attendants

**24.**—(1) This Article applies in the case of a vehicle the use of which on roads is authorised by Article 22 of this Order and in a case where—

(*a*) the overall width of a vehicle the use of which on roads is authorised by Article 20 or 21 of this Order or of the vehicle together with the width of any lateral projection or projections of its load exceeds 9 feet 6 inches, or

(*b*) the overall width of a vehicle the use of which on roads is authorised by the said Article 20 or 21 or of the vehicle together with the width of any lateral projection or projections of its load exceeds 2.5 metres but does not exceed 9 feet 6 inches, or

(c) the overall length of a vehicle the use of which on roads is authorised by the said Article 20 or 21 or of the vehicle together with the length of any forward projection and of any rearward projection of its load exceeds 60 feet, or

(d) as respects a motor vehicle (whether or not its use is authorised by the said Article 20 or 21) which is drawing a trailer or trailers the use of which is so authorised a load is carried in such a manner that part of its weight rests on more than one of the vehicles and the overall length of the vehicles by which the load is carried together with the distance between vehicles and the length of any forward projection and of any rearward projection of the load exceeds 60 feet, or

(e) a motor vehicle (whether or not its use is authorised by the said Article 20 or 21) is drawing a trailer or trailers the use of which is so authorised and the overall length of the combination of vehicles together with the length of any forward projection of any load extending beyond the foremost point of the drawing vehicle comprised in the combination and the length of any rearward projection of any load extending beyond the rearmost point of the rearmost vehicle comprised therein exceeds 85 feet, or

(f) a vehicle the use of which is authorised by the said Article 20 or 21 is carrying a load having a forward projection exceeding 6 feet in length or a rearward projection exceeding 10 feet in length or is fitted with any special appliance or apparatus having such a projection as aforesaid.

(2) In a case mentioned in sub-paragraph (a) of the foregoing paragraph, at least two persons and in a case where the use of the vehicle on roads is authorised by the said Article 22 and in any of the cases mentioned in sub-paragraphs (b) to (f) of that paragraph, at least one person, in addition to the person or persons employed as respects a motor vehicle in driving that vehicle, shall be employed in attending to that vehicle and its load and any other vehicle or vehicles drawn by that vehicle and the load carried on the vehicle or vehicles so drawn and to give warning to the driver of the said motor vehicle and to any other person of any danger likely to be caused to any such other person by reason of the presence of the said vehicle or vehicles on the road:

Provided that where, in a case mentioned in the said sub-paragraph (a), a vehicle is engaged in engineering operations and moves on a road only to the extent necessary for the efficient performance of such operations it shall be sufficient compliance with this paragraph if one person in addition to the driver or drivers is employed in attending to the vehicle for the purposes aforesaid.

(3) For the purposes of the foregoing paragraph—

(a) in a case where a motor vehicle is drawing a trailer or trailers any person employed in pursuance of section 72 of the Road Traffic Act 1960 in attending that vehicle or any such trailer shall be treated as being an attendant required by that paragraph so long as he is also employed to discharge the duties mentioned in that paragraph, and

(b) in a case where a motor vehicle is drawing a trailer or trailers and another motor vehicle is used for the purpose of assisting in their propulsion on the road, the person or persons employed in driving that other motor vehicle shall not be treated as a person or persons employed in attending to the first-mentioned vehicle or any vehicle or vehicles drawn thereby.

*Marking of projecting loads and fixed appliances or apparatus which project*

**25.**—(1) This Article applies in a case where a load carried by a vehicle the use of which is authorised by Article 20 or 21 of this Order or where a special appliance or apparatus fitted to a vehicle the use of which is so authorised—

(*a*) has a forward projection exceeding 6 feet in length or a rearward projection exceeding 10 feet in length, or

(*b*) has a rearward projection exceeding 3 feet 6 inches in length but not exceeding 10 feet in length.

(2) Subject to the provisions of paragraphs (3) and (4) of this Article—

(*a*) as respects a projection mentioned in sub-paragraph (*a*) of the foregoing paragraph the conditions specified in paragraph 3 of Schedule 8 to the Construction and Use Regulations shall be complied with, and accordingly the provisions of the said paragraph 3 shall apply in relation to that projection as they apply in relation to a relevant projection as mentioned in that paragraph, and

(*b*) as respects a projection mentioned in sub-paragraph (*b*) of the foregoing paragraph the conditions specified in paragraph 4 of the said Schedule 8 shall be complied with, and accordingly the provisions of the said paragraph 4 shall apply in relation to that projection as they apply in relation to a relevant projection as mentioned in that paragraph.

(3) Where, in any of the cases mentioned in paragraph (1) of this Article, a vehicle is carrying a load or is fitted with a special appliance or apparatus and the load or the appliance or apparatus has, in relation to the vehicle, a forward projection or a rearward projection, and another vehicle is attached to that end of the vehicle from which the load or, as the case may be, the appliance or apparatus projects and is attached to that vehicle in such a manner that—

(*a*) in the case where there is a forward projection, the foremost point of that other vehicle extends beyond the foremost part of the projection or, in the case where there is a rearward projection, the rearmost point of that other vehicle extends beyond the rearmost part of the projection, or

(*b*) in the case where there is a forward projection, the foremost part of the projection extends beyond the foremost point of that other vehicle or, in the case where there is a rearward projection, the rearmost part of the projection extends beyond the rearmost point of that other vehicle, then—

(i) in either of the cases mentioned in sub-paragraph (*a*) of this paragraph, the provisions of paragraph (2) of this Article shall not apply as respects any such projection, and

(ii) in either of the cases mentioned in sub-paragraph (*b*) of this paragraph, the provisions of the said paragraph (2) shall apply as if each of the references in paragraph (1) of this Article to a rearward projection were treated as a reference to so much of a rearward projection as extends beyond the rearmost point of that other vehicle and as if the reference in the said paragraph (1) to a forward projection were treated as a reference to so much of a forward projection as extends beyond the foremost point of that other vehicle measured, in either case, when the longitudinal axis of each vehicle lies in the same vertical plane between vertical planes at right angles to the said longitudinal axis and passing, in the case of a rearward projection, through the rearmost point of the said other vehicle and that part of the projection furthest from that point or, in the case of a forward projection, through the foremost point of the said other vehicle and that part of the projection furthest from that point.

(4) This Article shall not apply to any motor vehicle or trailer being used—

    (a) for fire brigade, ambulance or police purposes or for defence purposes (including civil defence purposes), or

    (b) in connection with the removal of any obstruction to traffic

if, in any such case, compliance with any provision of this Article would hinder or be likely to hinder the use of the vehicle for the purpose for which it is being used on that occasion.

*Approval of the Minister as to the time, date and route of a journey by a vehicle or a vehicle and its load exceeding 14 feet in width*

**26.**—(1) This Article applies in the case of a vehicle the use of which on roads otherwise falls to be authorised—

    (a) by Article 22 of this Order, or

    (b) by Article 20 or 21 of this Order where the overall width of the vehicle or, if it is used for carrying a load, where the overall width of the vehicle together with the width of any lateral projection or projections of its load exceeds 14 feet.

(2) Subject to the provisions of paragraph (3) of this Article, a vehicle mentioned in the foregoing paragraph shall be used only

    (a) for the purpose of making such a journey between specified places as the Minister may have approved by notice in writing given to the owner of the vehicle and only at such times (if any), on such a date or dates (if any) and on such a route (if any) as the Minister may have specified in the said notice or as the chief officer of police of any police area in which it is proposed that the vehicle shall be used may have specified, in relation to the use of the vehicle in that area, in a direction given to the owner of the vehicle, and

    (b) if the notice referred to in the foregoing sub-paragraph is carried on the vehicle at all times while it is being used for the purpose of making the journey for which the Minister's approval has been given.

(3) Where the effect of any such direction as is mentioned in sub-paragraph (a) of the foregoing paragraph is to vary, in relation to a time, a date or a route of the journey approved by the Minister under that sub-paragraph, the time, the date or dates or the route of the said journey, the vehicle shall not be used in accordance with that direction unless the Minister has given his further approval that the vehicle shall be so used.

*Notice to police*

**27.**—(1) This Article applies in the case of a vehicle the use of which on roads is authorised by Article 22 of this Order and in a case where—

    (a) the overall width of a vehicle the use of which on roads is authorised by Article 20 or 21 of this Order or of the vehicle together with the width of any lateral projection or projections of its load exceeds—

        (i) if the vehicle is to be used on a road on which a tramcar is operated, 8 feet, or

(ii) if the vehicle is not to be used on such a road, 9 feet 6 inches, or

(*b*) the overall length of a vehicle the use of which on roads is authorised by the said Article 20 or 21 or of the vehicle together with the length of any forward projection and of any rearward projection of its load exceeds 50 feet, or

(*c*) as respects a motor vehicle (whether or not its use on roads is authorised by the said Article 20 or 21) which is drawing a trailer or trailers the use of which is so authorised a load is carried in such a manner that part of its weight rests on more than one of the vehicles and the overall length of the vehicles by which the load is carried together with the distance between vehicles and the length of any forward projection and of any rearward projection of the load exceeds 50 feet, or

(*d*) a motor vehicle (whether or not its use on roads is authorised by the said Article 20 or 21) is drawing a trailer or trailers the use of which is so authorised and the overall length of the combination of vehicles together with the length of any forward projection of any load extending beyond the foremost point of the drawing vehicle comprised in the combination and the length of any rearward projection of any load extending beyond the rearmost point of the rearmost vehicle comprised therein exceeds 85 feet, or

(*e*) a vehicle the use of which on roads is authorised by the said Article 20 or 21 is carrying a load having a forward projection or a rearward projection exceeding 10 feet in length or is fitted with any special appliance or apparatus having such a projection as aforesaid, or

(*f*) the total weight of a vehicle the use of which on roads is authorised by the said Article 20 or 21 or of such a vehicle and its load or, in a case where a motor vehicle (whether or not its use is so authorised) is drawing a trailer or trailers the use of which is so authorised, the total weight of the combination of vehicles or of the said combination and of any load carried by any vehicle or vehicles comprised therein exceeds 75 tons.

(2) Save in so far as the chief officer of police of any police area in which it is proposed that the vehicle or, as the case may be, the vehicles, will be used dispenses, as respects the use of the vehicle or vehicles in that area, with the requirements contained in this paragraph as to length of notice or with any of the requirements applicable by virtue of the following paragraph as respects the form of notice or the particulars to be given, the owner of the vehicle or, as the case may be, of the vehicles, before using the vehicle or vehicles on a road, shall give at least two clear days' notice (excluding Sundays, any bank holiday, Christmas Day or Good Friday) as provided by the following paragraph to the chief officer of police of any such area as aforesaid.

(3) The notice referred to in the foregoing paragraph shall, subject to any necessary modification, be in the form and shall contain the particulars specified in Part I of Schedule 2 to this Order.

(4) Subject to any variation in the time, date or route of the journey which may be directed by any such chief officer of police as aforesaid, the vehicle or vehicles shall be used only in circumstances which accord with the particulars given in compliance with the foregoing paragraph as to the time, date and route of the journey and only if any dimension or measurement relating to the vehicle or the vehicles (including that relating to a combination of vehicles) or to a special appliance or apparatus or to a load to be carried, being a dimension or measurement of which particulars have been given as aforesaid, is not exceeded.

*Notice to highway and bridge authorities*

**28.**—(1) This Article applies in a case where—

    (*a*) the total weight of a vehicle the use of which on roads is authorised by Article 20 or 21 of this Order or of such a vehicle and its load or, in a case where a motor vehicle (whether or not its use is so authorised) is drawing a trailer or trailers the use of which is so authorised, the total weight of the combination of vehicles or of the said combination and of any load carried by any vehicle or vehicles comprised therein exceeds 75 tons, or

    (*b*) as respects any vehicle the use of which is authorised as aforesaid any of the requirements of the Construction and Use Regulations or the Track Laying Regulations with respect to the weights of vehicles whether laden or unladen or the weights transmitted to the road surface by all or any of the wheels or tracks or, as the case may be, the wheels and tracks, is not complied with or, where a combination of vehicles is used, if any of the said requirements as respects any or all of the vehicles comprised in the combination is not complied with.

(2) Subject to the provisions of paragraphs (6), (7), (8), (9) and (10) of this Article, save in so far as the highway authority for any road or the bridge authority for any bridge on which it is proposed that the vehicle or, as the case may be, the vehicles, will be used dispenses, as respects the use of the vehicle or vehicles on that road or, as the case may be, on that bridge, with the requirements contained in this paragraph as to length of notice or with any of the requirements applicable by virtue of the following paragraph as respects the form of notice or the particulars to be given, the owner of the vehicle or, as the case may be, of the vehicles, before using the vehicle or vehicles on that road or that bridge, shall give, in a case mentioned in sub-paragraph (*a*) of the foregoing paragraph, at least six clear days' notice as provided by the following paragraph and, in a case mentioned in sub-paragraph (*b*) of the foregoing paragraph, at least two clear days' notice as so provided (in either case excluding Sundays, any bank holiday, Christmas Day or Good Friday) to the highway authority for any such road and to the bridge authority for any such bridge.

(3) The notice referred to in the foregoing paragraph shall, subject to any necessary modification, be in the form and shall contain the particulars specified in Part II of Schedule 2 to this Order.

(4) Before using the vehicle or, as the case may be, the vehicles on any road or bridge the owner of the vehicle or vehicles shall give to the highway authority for the road and to the bridge authority for the bridge an indemnity as provided by the following paragraph.

(5) The indemnity referred to in the foregoing paragraph shall be in the form specified in Part III of Schedule 2 to this Order.

(6) In the case of any part of a trunk road where, by virtue of the provisions of section 10 of the Highways Act 1959, the functions of the Minister with respect to maintenance are exercised in England (excluding Monmouthshire) by the council of a county (including the Greater London Council) the council of a borough (including a London borough) or the council of an urban district or the functions of the Secretary of State with respect to maintenance are exercised in Wales (including Monmouthshire) by the council of a county, borough or urban district or where, by virtue of the provisions of section 5 of the Trunk

Roads Act 1936(a), as amended or modified by the Trunk Roads Act 1946(b), the functions of the Secretary of State with respect to maintenance and repair are exercised in Scotland by the council of a county or large burgh or where by virtue of an agreement between or having effect under paragraph 2 of Schedule 6 to the Transport Act 1962(c) as if between the Minister or the Secretary of State and either the British Railways Board, the London Transport Board, the British Transport Docks Board or the British Waterways Board, the maintenance or, as the case may be, the maintenance and repair of that part are carried out by any such Board, the notice and indemnity required to be given to the Minister or, as the case may be, the Secretary of State by paragraphs (2) and (4) respectively of this Article shall be treated as given in accordance with paragraph (2) of this Article (as respects the said notice) and paragrah (4) thereof (as respects the said indemnity) only if addressed to, or included in any notice and indemnity given to, such Council or Board as the case may be.

(7) Any notice and indemnity in respect of any part of a trunk road required by the foregoing paragraph to be addressed to, or included in any notice and indemnity given to, the British Railways Board shall be addressed to, or included in a notice and indemnity given to, the Board at the Headquarters of the Regional Railways Board responsible for the part of the railway system which is affected by any such agreement as is mentioned in that paragraph by virtue of the agreement applying to that part of the trunk road.

(8) Where in the case of any trailer, being a vehicle falling within a case mentioned in sub-paragraph (a) of paragraph (1) of this Article, at least six days' notice has been given in accordance with paragraph (2) of this Article and it is found impracticable to use any vehicle specified in the notice (not being a vehicle the use of which upon roads is authorised by Article 20 or 21 of this Order) as a vehicle intended to draw the trailer, then any other vehicle similar in type to the vehicle so specified may be substituted for that vehicle if at least two clear days' notice of the substitution is given to every authority to whom the previous notice was given, and thereupon the last-mentioned notice shall have effect as if the substituted vehicle and not the replaced vehicle had always been specified therein as the vehicle intended to draw the trailer.

(9) In the case of a vehicle the use of which on roads is authorised by Article 20 of this Order, being a vehicle in relation to the use of which notice and an indemnity is required respectively by paragraphs (2) and (4) of this Article to be given to any authority but, in connection with a particular journey, cannot be given to that authority in accordance with the said paragraphs (2) and (4) on account of the urgency of the journey in the national interest, it shall be sufficient compliance with the provisions of the said paragraph (2) (as respects the said notice) and of the said paragraph (4) (as respects the said indemnity) as respects that authority if the notice and indemnity be given so as to be received by that authority or, if sent by post, be posted, before the vehicle is used on any road or bridge for the maintenance and repair of which that authority is responsible:

Provided that the provisions of this paragraph shall only apply if—

> (a) the vehicle is used solely for carrying any of the vehicles specified in paragraph 1 or 2 in column 1 of Schedule 1 to this Order, being the property of, or for the time being under the control of, the persons respectively specified opposite thereto in column 3 of that Schedule;

---

(a) 1 Edw. 8 & 1 Geo. 6. c. 5.     (b) 9 & 10 Geo. 6. c. 30.
(c) 10 & 11 Eliz. 2. c. 46.

(b) the owner of the carrying vehicle has previously consulted the Minister on the route proposed to be followed; and

(c) it is certified in writing by the proper naval, military or air force authority that the journey is urgent in the national interest.

(10) Notwithstanding anything in the foregoing provisions of this Order, nothing in this Article shall apply to the use on roads of any vehicle which is the property of, or for the time being under the control of, the Secretary of State for Defence.

*Restriction on the passage over bridges of vehicles carrying abnormal indivisible loads*

**29.** Where a motor vehicle the use of which on roads is authorised by Article 20 of this Order is so used or where a motor vehicle (whether or not its use is so authorised) is drawing a trailer or trailers the use of which is so authorised and an abnormal indivisible load is being carried by any such vehicle, the driver of the motor vehicle shall not cause or permit either that vehicle or, in the case of a combination of vehicles, any vehicle comprised in the combination—

(a) to enter on any bridge whilst there is on that bridge any other vehicle which is either carrying an abnormal indivisible load or is being used to draw a trailer carrying such a load the presence of which is known to or could reasonably be ascertained by him, or

(b) to remain stationary on any bridge except in circumstances beyond his control.


Given under the Official Seal of the Minister of Transport the 12th March 1969.


(L.S.)

*J. R. Madge,*
An Under Secretary of the
Ministry of Transport.

## SCHEDULE 1

(see Article 6)

### SERVICE AND AVIATION VEHICLES

| Column 1 | Column 2 | Column 3 |
|---|---|---|
| 1. Motor vehicles or trailers constructed either for actual combative purposes or for naval, military or air force training in connection therewith or for use with, or for the carriage or drawing of, instruments of war, including guns and machine guns. | Construction and Use Regulations—All. Track Laying Regulations—All. | The Secretary of State for Defence, Minister of Technology or President of the Board of Trade or any contractor making such vehicles for the said Secretary of State, the said Minister or the said President or any sub-contractor of such contractor. |
| 2. Track laying motor vehicles or track laying trailers constructed either for actual combative purposes or for use with, or for the carriage or drawing of, instruments of war, including guns and machine guns, ammunition, equipment or stores in connection therewith. | Construction and Use Regulations—All. Track Laying Regulations—All. | The Secretary of State for Defence, Minister of Technology or President of the Board of Trade or any contractor making such vehicles for the said Secretary of State, the said Minister or the said President or any sub-contractor of such contractor. |
| 3. Motor vehicles or trailers constructed for the carriage of tanks. | Construction and Use Regulations—All. Track Laying Regulations—All. | The Secretary of State for Defence, Minister of Technology or President of the Board of Trade or any contractor making such vehicles for the said Secretary of State, the said Minister or the said President or any sub-contractor of such contractor. |
| 4. Motor vehicles or trailers constructed for the carriage of searchlights or the necessary equipment therefor. | Construction and Use Regulation 10. Track Laying Regulation 7. | The Secretary of State for Defence, Minister of Technology or President of the Board of Trade or any contractor making such vehicles for the said Secretary of State, the said Minister or the said President or any sub-contractor of such contractor. |
| 5. Motor vehicles or trailers constructed for the carriage of aircraft or aircraft parts. | Construction and Use Regulations 7, 43, 44, 61 and 111. Track Laying Regulations 5, 30 and 75. | The Secretary of State for Defence, Minister of Technology or President of the Board of Trade or any contractor making such vehicles for the said Secretary of State, the said Minister or the said President or any sub-contractor of such contractor. |

| Column 1 | Column 2 | Column 3 |
|---|---|---|
| 6. Motor tractors, heavy motor cars and trailers constructed for naval, military, air force or aviation purposes before 1st January 1949. | Construction and Use Regulations 39, 43, 44, 61 and 62. | The Secretary of State for Defence, Minister of Technology or President of the Board of Trade or any contractor making such vehicles for the said Secretary of State, the said Minister or the said President or any sub-contractor of such contractor. |
| 7. Heavy motor cars or trailers constructed for use and used only in connection with flying operations where the additional width is made necessary by the design of the equipment or its installation on the vehicle. | Construction and Use Regulations 43 and 61. | The Secretary of State for Defence or President of the Board of Trade or Minister of Technology or any contractor making such vehicles for the said Secretary of State or for the said President or for the said Minister or any sub-contractor of such contractor. |
| 8. Aircraft drawn by motor vehicles. | Construction and Use Regulations 10 and 60 to 62 (inclusive). | The Secretary of State for Defence. |

## SCHEDULE 2

PART I (see Article 27)

*Form of Notice to Police*

The Motor Vehicles (Authorisation of Special Types) General Order 1969

In pursuance of Article 27 of the above-mentioned Order I/We................................
................................of.................................................................being the owner(s) of
the under-mentioned vehicle(s) to which the Order applies hereby give notice that
it is my/our intention to use the said vehicle(s) on the roads specified below from
.................................................to.................................................starting at
approximately.......................a.m./p.m. on the...................day of.......................and
completing the journey at approximately.................a.m./p.m. on the.....................
day of.......................The route proposed to be followed is:—

.......................to.......................................          Ministry of Transport
.......................to.......................................          Classification No.   .......................
                                                                          ,,          ,,         .......................

Note:—Any further particulars of route necessary to define it clearly are to be given
overleaf and where a road is unclassified sufficient information is to be given to enable
it to be identified.

*Particulars*
(to be given in respect of each vehicle)

1. Vehicle(s) to which the Order applies.
Index mark and registered number (if any)................................................
Carrier's licence number (if any)................................................
Type................................................
Description of load (if any)................................................
Dimensions of vehicle(s) and of load (if any)—
Maximum height of vehicle(s) or of vehicle(s) and load................................................

Overall width of vehicle(s) inclusive, where a load is to be carried having a lateral projection, of the width of any such projection................................................
Overall length of vehicle(s)................................................
Length of any projection of special appliance or apparatus or load—
forward projection................................................
rearward projection................................................
Distance between vehicles where load is to be carried by more than one vehicle

Overall length of any combination of vehicles (inclusive of load)................................................
Total weight of vehicle(s) (inclusive of load, if any)................................................
2. Other vehicle(s) (if any) drawing or drawn by the above-mentioned vehicle(s).
Index mark and registration number (if any)................................................
Carrier's licence number (if any)................................................
Type................................................
Laden weight................................................

Date................................................ Signed................................................

PART II (see Articles 16, 17 and 28)
*Form of Notice to Highway and Bridge Authorities*

The Motor Vehicles (Authorisation of Special Types) General Order 1969

In pursuance of Article 16/17/28 of the above-mentioned Order I/We
................................................of ................................................
being the owner(s) of the under-mentioned vehicle(s) to which the Order applies hereby give notice that it is my/our intention to use the said vehicle(s) on the roads specified below from................................................to................................................
starting at approximately................a.m./p.m. on the................day of................
and completing the journey at approximately................a.m./p.m. on the................
day of................................. The route proposed to be followed is:—

|  |  |
|---|---|
| ................................to................................ | Ministry of Transport |
| ................................to................................ | Classification No. ................................ |
|  | ,, ,, ................................ |

Note:—Any further particulars of route necessary to define it clearly are to be given overleaf and where a road is unclassified sufficient information is to be given to enable it to be identified.

*Particulars*
(to be given in respect of each vehicle)

1. Total number of vehicles to be used including not only vehicles the use of which is authorised only by the Order but also other vehicles to be used in conjunction therewith................................................

2. Number of such vehicles the use of which is authorised only by the Order................

3. Vehicle(s) to which the Order applies.

*(Particulars to be given in respect of each vehicle)

*All particulars in respect of an articulated vehicle should be included under 3 as if it were a single vehicle.

Index mark and registration number (if any).............................................
Carrier's licence number (if any)...........................................................
Type............................................................................................................
Description of load (if any)..................................................................

Overall dimensions of vehicle(s) (inclusive of load, if any):—
    Maximum height............................................................................
    Maximum width...............................................................................
    Maximum length.............................................................................

Weight of vehicle(s) (inclusive of load, if any)...................................

Spacing and weight of load carrying axles—

    (a) first load carrying axle:
        (i) number of wheels......................................................
        (ii) approximate weight on axle...................................
        (iii) distance to second load carrying axle.................

    (b) second load carrying axle:
        (i) number of wheels......................................................
        (ii) approximate weight on axle...................................
        (iii) distance to third load carrying axle...................

Repeat for all load carrying axles.

In the case of track laying vehicles a dimensioned sketch plan is to be attached showing the number and disposition of all wheels (if any) and tracks in contact with the road surface indicating the weights transmitted by the wheels or tracks of the vehicle(s).

4. Other vehicle(s) (if any) drawing or drawn by the above-mentioned vehicle(s).
Index mark and registration number (if any).......................................
Carrier's licence number (if any)...........................................................
Type............................................................................................................
Laden weight..............................................................................................

## PART III (see Articles 16, 17 and 28)

### Form of Indemnity

I/We hereby agree to indemnify you and each and every highway or bridge authority responsible for the maintenance and repair of any road or bridge on the journey to which the above notice relates in respect of any damage which may be caused to any such road or bridge—

    (a) by [any of] the above-mentioned vehicle[s]—
        (i) by reason of the construction of or weight transmitted to the road surface by [any of] the said vehicle[s], or
        (ii) by reason of the dimensions, distribution or adjustment of the load carried by [any of] the said vehicle[s]; or

    (b) by any other vehicle by reason of the use of [any of] the above-mentioned vehicle[s] on the road or, as the case may be, the bridge except to the extent that the damage was caused or contributed to by the negligence of the driver of the other vehicle:

Provided that any claim in respect of damage so caused by any vehicle shall be made in writing within twelve months from the date on which the vehicle is last used on the journey to which the above notice relates, stating the occasion and place of the damage.

    Date.................................................        Signed.................................................

Note:—Paragraph (a)(ii) above only applies where vehicles are carrying an abnormal indivisible load and in other cases should be omitted.

## SCHEDULE 3

ORDERS REVOKED BY ARTICLE 2

| Title | Year and Number |
|-------|-----------------|
| The Motor Vehicles (Authorisation of Special Types) General Order 1966 | S.I. 1966/1289 (1966 III, p. 3579). |
| The Motor Vehicles (Authorisation of Special Types) (Amendment) Order 1968 | S.I. 1968/438 (1968 I, p.1146). |
| The Motor Vehicles (Authorisation of Special Types) (Amendment) (No. 2) Order 1968 | S.I. 1968/839 (1968 II, p.2251). |

## EXPLANATORY NOTE

### (*This Note is not part of the Order.*)

This Order re-enacts with amendment the Motor Vehicles (Authorisation of Special Types) General Order 1966 and the amending Orders specified in Schedule 3 to this Order. The Order provides for authorising, subject to specified restrictions and conditions, the use on roads of special vehicles constructed for special purposes or equipped with special equipment, notwithstanding that such vehicles do not comply either with all the requirements of the Motor Vehicles (Construction and Use) Regulations 1969 or the Motor Vehicles (Construction and Use) (Track Laying Vehicles) Regulations 1955, as amended, or, as the case may be with such of those requirements as are specified in the Order.

The principal changes made by this Order are:

1. Article 20 (*c*) and (*d*) have been amended so as to exclude compliance by vehicles used for the conveyance of abnormal indivisible loads with Regulation 121 of the Motor Vehicles (Construction and Use) Regulations 1969 (which relates to weight restrictions on goods vehicles for which plating certificates have been issued.).
2. The previous references to the Minister of Aviation in column 3 of Schedule 1 have now been amended to references to the Minister of Technology or the President of the Board of Trade.

## STATUTORY INSTRUMENTS

### 1969 No. 349

### PENSIONS

### The Superannuation (Monopolies Commission) Order 1969

| | |
|---|---|
| *Made* - - - | *12th March* 1969 |
| *Laid before Parliament* | *20th March* 1969 |
| *Coming into Operation* | *1st May* 1969 |

The Minister for the Civil Service, in exercise of the powers conferred on him by section 98(5) and (9) of the Superannuation Act 1965(a) and article 2(1)(c) of the Minister for the Civil Service Order 1968(b), hereby makes the following Order:—

**1.** This Order may be cited as the Superannuation (Monopolies Commission) Order 1969, and shall come into operation on 1st May 1969.

**2.** The Interpretation Act 1889(c) shall apply for the interpretation of this Order as it applies for the interpretation of an Act of Parliament.

**3.**—(1) Employment by the Monopolies Commission shall be added to the employments listed in Schedule 8 to the Superannuation Act 1965.

(2) This article shall have effect as from 1st January 1949.

Given under the official seal of the Minister for the Civil Service on 12th March 1969.

(L.S.)

*J. E. Herbecq,*
Authorised by the Minister
for the Civil Service.

### EXPLANATORY NOTE
(*This Note is not part of the Order.*)

Section 98(4) of the Superannuation Act 1965 provides that service in employments of the kinds listed in Schedule 8 to that Act shall be treated as service in the civil service of the State for the purposes of pensions and other superannuation benefits. This Order adds employment by the Monopolies Commission to the list in that Schedule. Under the powers of Section 98(9) of that Act the Order has retrospective effect as from 1st January 1949.

(a) 1965 c. 74.        (b) S.I. 1968/1656 (1968 III, p. 4485).        (c) 1889 c. 63.

## STATUTORY INSTRUMENTS

### 1969 No. 351

## NATIONAL HEALTH SERVICE, ENGLAND AND WALES
### The National Health Service (General Ophthalmic Services) (Amendment) Regulations 1969

|  |  |  |
|---|---|---|
| *Made* - - - | *14th March* 1969 |
| *Laid before Parliament* | *26th March* 1969 |
| *Coming into Operation* | *1st April* 1969 |

The Secretary of State for Social Services in exercise of his powers under sections 41 and 74 of the National Health Service Act 1946(a) and sections 17, 18 and 20 of the Health Services and Public Health Act 1968(b) and of all other powers enabling him in that behalf, hereby makes the following regulations :—

**1.** These regulations may be cited as the National Health Service (General Ophthalmic Services) (Amendment) Regulations 1969 and shall come into operation on the 1st April 1969.

**2.** In these regulations—

    (i) "the principal regulations" means the National Health Service (Supplementary Ophthalmic Services) Regulations 1956(c) as amended (d).

    (ii) The Interpretation Act 1889(e) applies to the interpretation of these regulations as it applies to the interpretation of an Act of Parliament.

**3.** The principal regulations shall be further amended as follows :—
    (1) In regulation 2(1)—

        (*a*) the definition "Committee" shall be deleted ;

        (*b*) the definitions "dispensing optician" and "ophthalmic optician" shall be deleted.

    (2) In the principal regulations any reference to the "Committee" or "Ophthalmic Services Committee" however expressed and wheresoever it occurs shall be read as a reference to the Council.

    (3) In regulation 4 paragraph (4) and (5) shall be deleted.

    (4) In regulation 6(3) the words "and the Committee" shall be deleted ;

    (5) In regulation 6(4)—

        (*a*) the words "to the Council and" shall be deleted ;

        (*b*) for the words "each of them" where they first occur there shall be substituted the word "him".

---

(a) 1946 c. 81.       (b) 1968 c. 46.       (c) S.I. 1956/1078 (1956 I, p. 1524).
(d) S.I. 1958/2024, 1961/908, 947 (1958 II, p. 1548; 1961 II, p. 1752; II, p. 1843).
(e) 1889 c. 63.

(6) In regulation 7(4)(*b*)—

(*a*) for the words from "is called up" to the words "national emergency" there shall be substituted the words "is called into whole-time service in the armed forces of the Crown in a national emergency as a volunteer or otherwise, or compulsory whole-time service in those forces, including service resulting from any reserve liability, or any equivalent service by a person liable for compulsory whole-time service in those forces" ;

(*b*) for the words "the completion of his service" there shall be substituted the words "he has completed that service".

(7) In regulation 11(2) the words "together with a note confirming the Council's decision" shall be deleted.

(8) In regulation 18(8)—

(*a*) the words "on form No. 3 set out in the third schedule to these regulations" shall be deleted ;

(*b*) for the words "The form" there shall be substituted the words "The authority".

(9) Regulation 21 shall be deleted.

(10) In Schedule 3. Form No. 3 shall be deleted.

*R. H. S. Crossman,*
Secretary of State for Social Services.

14th March 1969.

---

## EXPLANATORY NOTE

*(This Note is not part of the Regulations.)*

These Regulations amend the National Health Service (Supplementary Ophthalmic Services) Regulations 1956 by transferring to Executive Councils the functions of Ophthalmic Services Committees which are dissolved by the Health Services and Public Health Act 1968 ; definitions now in the Act are removed, as also is an unnecessary form ; and the description of Crown Service which protects a practitioner or optician against the removal of his name from the ophthalmic list is revised.

## STATUTORY INSTRUMENTS

### 1969 No. 352

## NATIONAL HEALTH SERVICE, ENGLAND AND WALES

### The National Health Service (Executive Councils) Regulations 1969

| | | |
|---|---|---|
| *Made* - - - - | | *14th March* 1969 |
| *Laid before Parliament* | | *26th March* 1969 |
| *Coming into Operation* | | *1st April* 1969 |

The Secretary of State for Social Services, in exercise of his powers under section 31 of, and Schedule 5 to, the National Health Service Act 1946(a), as substituted by section 16 of and Schedule 1 to, the Health Services and Public Health Act 1968(b) and of all other powers enabling him in that behalf, hereby makes the following regulations:—

### PART I

#### GENERAL

*Short title, commencement and extent*

**1.**—(1) These regulations may be cited as the National Health Service (Executive Councils) Regulations 1969 and shall come into operation on 1st April 1969.

(2) These regulations shall not apply to the Isles of Scilly.

*Interpretation*

**2.**—(1) In these regulations, unless the context otherwise requires, the following expressions have the respective meanings hereby assigned to them:—
"the Act" means the National Health Service Act 1946.
"council" means the Executive Council constituted for any area.
"enactment" includes regulations.

(2) Unless the context otherwise requires, references in these regulations to any enactment shall be construed as references to that enactment as amended or re-enacted by any subsequent enactment.

(3) References in any other regulations to the regulations revoked by these regulations or to any provision thereof shall be construed as references to these regulations or to the corresponding provision thereof as the case may be.

(4) The Interpretation Act 1889(c), applies to the interpretation of these regulations as it applies to the interpretation of an Act of Parliament.

*Appointment of members, term of office, casual vacancies, etc.*
*Notice of appointment of members*

**3.**—(1) A local health authority, local medical committee, local pharmaceutical committee, or local dental committee shall forthwith give notice in writing

---

(a) 1946 c. 81.   (b) 1968 c. 46.   (c) 1889 c. 63.

to the clerk of the council of the name and address of any person appointed by them to be a member of the council and the local optical committee shall give such notice of such particulars of the persons so appointed by the members of that committee who are respectively ophthalmic opticians and dispensing opticians.

(2) The clerk of the council shall forthwith inform the Secretaty of State of the names and addresses of any members so notified to him.

*Term of office*

**4.** The term of office of members of a council shall be three years:

Provided that at the expiration of his term of office a member shall be eligible for re-appointment.

*Chairman*

**5.**—(1) The council shall appoint a member to be chairman.

(2) The following provisions shall have effect with regard to the appointment of the chairman:—
  (a) The chairman shall be appointed at a meeting of the members of the council to be specially summoned for the purpose;
  (b) The members present at the meeting shall appoint a person to preside at the meeting.

*Vice-chairman*

**6.** A council shall appoint a member to be vice-chairman, and any person so appointed shall, so long as he remains a member of that council, hold office for such period as may be specified in the resolution under which he is appointed.

*Resignation or removal of members*

**7.**—(1) A member of the council who desires to resign his membership shall give notice in writing to the clerk of the council.

(2) If a member of the council has not attended any meeting of the council or of any committee for a period of six months, the clerk of the council shall inform the council, and unless the council are satisfied that his absence was due to illness or other reasonable cause, they shall declare that his seat on the council has become vacant.

*Vacation of office*

**8.** If a member of the council, being a member appointed by the local health authority, is also a member or officer of that authority, he shall upon ceasing to be a member or officer of the authority, also cease to be a member of the council:

Provided that for the purpose of this regulation a person shall not be deemed to have ceased to be a member of the local health authority, if he has been re-elected a member thereof not later than the day of his retirement.

*Disqualification for membership*

**9.** Subject to paragraphs (ii), (iii) and (v) of the proviso to subsection (1) of section 59 of the Local Government Act 1933(a), the provisions of paragraphs (b) and (e) of that subsection (which disqualify a person for being elected or being a member of a local authority if he has been adjudged bankrupt or made a composition or arrangement with his creditors or has been sentenced to imprisonment for not less than three months without the option of a fine) shall apply as if the section related to membership of a council.

---

(a) 1933 c. 51

*Notification and filling of casual vacancies*

**10.**—(1) If a casual vacancy occurs by reason of the death, vacation of office or disqualification of any member of the council appointed by the Secretary of State the clerk of the council shall forthwith inform the Secretary of State, and if the person whose seat is vacated was other than one appointed by the Secretary of State, he shall inform the clerk or secretary of the appointing body.

(2) If a casual vacancy occurs amongst the persons appointed by the Secretary of State, he shall inform the clerk of the council of the name and address of the person appointed to fill the vacancy.

(3) If a casual vacancy occurs amongst the persons appointed by one of the bodies specified in regulation 3, it shall be filled by the same body.

*Term of office of persons filling casual vacancies*

**11.** Any person appointed to fill a casual vacancy shall hold office for the remainder of the term of office of the person in whose place he is appointed.

## PART II

### PROCEDURE OF EXECUTIVE COUNCILS

*Meetings*

**12.**—(1) At every meeting of the council, the chairman, if present, shall preside.

(2) If the chairman is absent from any meeting, the vice-chairman shall, if present, preside, and if the chairman and vice-chairman are both absent the members present at the meeting shall elect from among themselves a person to act as chairman for that meeting.

(3) Every question at a meeting of the council shall be determined by a majority of the votes of the members of the council present and voting on the question, and, in case of an equal division of votes, the chairman of the meeting shall have a second or casting vote.

*Minutes*

**13.** Minutes of the proceedings at every meeting of the council and a record of the attendance of the members of the council shall be duly kept by the clerk.

*Officers*

**14.**—(1) The council shall appoint a person approved by the Secretary of State to act as clerk of the council and shall also appoint such other officers as may be necessary. The resolution appointing the clerk shall embody the terms on which the appointment is made.

(2) When an officer has attained the age of 65 years he shall cease to hold office unless the council, with the consent of the officer, and also, in the case of the clerk, of the Secretary of State, by resolution extend his period of service, in his existing capacity or in some other capacity, for one year or any less period, and so on from time to time:

Provided that when the officer attains the age of 70 years, further extensions of service shall be given only in special circumstances.

(3) The council shall pay to the clerk and to their other officers remuneration in accordance with scales from time to time approved by the Secretary of State, or such remuneration as the Secretary of State may in special circumstances authorise.

(4) No member of the council or person who has at any time in the prevoius twelve months been a member of the council shall be appointed to the office of clerk or any other paid office under the council.

*Committees*

**15.**—(1) The council shall appoint a committee to be called the finance committee which shall consist wholly of members of the council, and may appoint such further committees as they think fit which shall consist either wholly or partly of members of the council as the council may determine, provided that at least a majority of the members of the committee shall be members of the council.

(2) Subject to the provisions of any regulations relating to the finance committee, the council may delegate to any committee any of the powers and duties of the council, and any resolution of the council appointing a committee shall define the powers and duties delegated to them and the term of office of the members:

Provided that—

    (i) No expenditure shall be incurred by any committee without the consent of the council; and

    (ii) Every committee shall report their proceedings to the council at such times and in such manner as the council may direct.

(3) Every committee shall appoint a chairman and subject as aforesaid and to any standing orders of the council relating to committees the provisions of these regulations relating to the duties of the chairman and the provisions relating to the vice-chairman, and proceedings of council shall apply to committees as they apply to councils, with the substitution of the committee for the council.

*Power to make standing orders*

**16.** The council may make, vary, and revoke standing orders for the regulation of the proceedings and business of the council and of the committees and in particular—

    (*a*) for the times and places of the meetings of the council or committee which in the case of the council shall be held not less often than once in every three months;

    (*b*) for due notice of the time and place of each meeting of the council or any committee and, subject to any exceptions which may be mentioned in the standing orders, of the business to be transacted thereat, to be given to members;

    (*c*) for the suspension of a member who is guilty of persistent disorder;

    (*d*) for providing that, subject to such exceptions and qualifications as may be specified in the standing orders, if a member has any pecuniary interest, direct or indirect, in any contract or proposed contract or other matter (not being a contract for the provision of one of the services mentioned in Part IV of the Act) and is present at a meeting of the council or committee at which the contract or other matter is the subject of consideration, he shall at the meeting, as soon as practicable after the commencement thereof, disclose the fact, and shall not take part in the consideration or discussion of, or vote on any question with respect to, the contract or other matter;

    (*e*) for such number of members of the council or committee, not being less than one-third of the whole number, as the standing order may specify to form a quorum.

*Committees authorised or required to be appointed by other provisions*

**17.** Nothing in this part of these regulations shall apply (except so far as it may be specifically applied) to a committee constituted for any purpose for which a committee is authorised or required to be appointed by any other provisions for the time being in force.

*Offices*

**18.** The council may provide itself with offices and in the case of a joint committee established under subsection (4) of section 31 of the Act, the constituent councils may provide the joint committee with offices.

## PART III

### SUBSCRIPTIONS TO AN ASSOCIATION OF EXECUTIVE COUNCILS

**19.** A council may pay any sum, not exceeding in respect of any year £20 or such higher amount as the Secretary of State approves not exceeding £50, as a subscription to the funds of any association of councils whose objects are approved by the Secretary of State.

## PART IV

### REVOCATION OF REGULATIONS

**20.** The regulations named in the Schedule to these regulations are hereby revoked;

Provided that—

    (*a*) such revocation shall not affect any right, privilege, obligation or liability acquired, accrued or incurred, or anything duly done or suffered, under those regulations;

    (*b*) such revocation shall not affect any legal proceedings commenced before the revocation, or the commencement of any proceedings to enforce any such right, privilege, obligation or liability as aforesaid, but any such proceedings may be continued or commenced as if these regulations had not been made;

    (*c*) such revocation shall not affect any appointment, approval, arrangement, authority, condition, consent, delegation of powers, minutes, notice, recognition, requirement, or standing orders, made, prepared, issued or given under the regulations so revoked and every such appointment, approval, arrangement, authority, condition, consent, delegation of powers, minutes, notice, recognition, requirement or standing order shall so far as it could have been made, prepared, issued or given under these regulations, have effect as if it had been so made, prepared, issued or given.

## SCHEDULE

### REGULATIONS REVOKED

The National Health Service (Executive Councils) Regulations 1954(a)
The National Health Service (Executive Councils) Amendment Regulations 1956(b)
The National Health Service (Executive Councils) Amendment Regulations 1967(c)

|  |  |
|---|---|
| 14th March 1969. | *R. H. S. Crossman,* <br> Secretary of State for Social Services. |

(**a**) S.I. 1954/224 (1954 I, p. 1270).    (**b**) S.I. 1956/1075 (1956 I, p. 1552).
(**c**) S.I. 1967/278 (1967 I, p. 998).

# EXPLANATORY NOTE

## (*This Note is not part of the Regulations.*)

These Regulations consolidate with amendments the National Health Service (Executive Councils) Regulations 1954, as amended, and give effect to the changes in the constitution and responsibilities of Executive Councils introduced by the Health Services and Public Health Act, 1968. The main change is the repeal of Part III of the previous regulations, which is no longer required because the ophthalmic services are to be directly administered by Executive Councils instead of by separately constituted Ophthalmic Services Committees.

# STATUTORY INSTRUMENTS

## 1969 No. 353

## NATIONAL HEALTH SERVICE, ENGLAND AND WALES

### The National Health Service (Executive Councils London) Order 1969

| | | |
|---|---|---|
| *Made* - - - | | 14th *March* 1969 |
| *Coming into Operation* | | 1st *April* 1969 |

The Secretary of State for Social Services in exercise of his powers under section 31 of the National Health Service Act 1946(a) and of all other powers enabling him in that behalf, and after consulting the Executive Councils for Inner London, North-East London, South-East London and Kent and South-West London and Surrey, hereby makes the following order:—

1.—(1) This order may be cited as the National Health Service (Executive Councils London) Order 1969 and shall come into operation on 1st April 1969.

(2) The Interpretation Act 1889(b) shall apply to the interpretation of this order as it applies to the interpretation of an Act of Parliament.

2. Schedule 2 to the London Government (Executive Councils) Order 1964(c) shall be amended as follows:—

    (1) Under the heading "*Inner London*" for the figures "7" and "11" in column (2) against the words in column (1) "The Minister" and "The local medical committee" there shall be respectively substituted the figures "9" and "12".

    (2) Under the heading *North-East London* for the figures "5" and "8" in column (2) against the words in column (1) "The Minister" and "The local medical committee" there shall be respectively substituted the figures "7" and "9".

    (3) Under the headings *South-East London and Kent* and *South-West London and Surrey* for the figures "6" and "9" in column (2) against the words in column (1) "The Minister" and "The local medical committee" there shall be respectively substituted in each case the figures "8" and "10".

    (4) Under the headings *Inner London, North-East London, South-East London and Kent* and *South-West London and Surrey:*—

        (*a*) Under the figure in column (2) against the words in column (1) "The local medical committee" there shall be added in each case the words:—

        "of whom one, but no more, shall be a medical practitioner having the qualifications prescribed for the purposes of section 41 of the Act of 1946".

        (*b*) At the end of column (1) and column (2) there shall be added in each case:—

---

(a) 1946 c. 81.     (b) 1889 c. 63.     (c) S.I. 1964/1771 (1964 III, p. 3914).

| (1) | (2) |
| --- | --- |
| The members of the Local Optical Committee who are ophthalmic opticians | 1. who shall be an ophthalmic optician. |
| The members of the Local Optical Committee who are dispensing opticians | 1. who shall be a dispensing optician. |

*R. H. S. Crossman,*
Secretary of State for Social Services.

14th March 1969.

## EXPLANATORY NOTE

(*This Note is not part of the Order.*)

The Health Services and Public Health Act 1968 (c.46) increased the membership of Executive Councils by 2 persons appointed by the Secretary of State and 3 persons qualified to provide ophthalmic services. This order effects a similar increase in the constitutions of those Executive Councils for which a special constitution was provided by the London Government (Executive Councils) Order 1964.

## STATUTORY INSTRUMENTS

### 1969 No. 354

## NATIONAL HEALTH SERVICE, ENGLAND AND WALES

### The National Health Service (Service Committees and Tribunal) (Amendment) Regulations 1969

|  |  |
|---|---|
| *Made* - - - | *14th March* 1969 |
| *Laid before Parliament* | *26th March* 1969 |
| *Coming into Operation* | *1st April* 1969 |

The Secretary of State for Social Services in exercise of his powers under sections 32, 33, 38, 40, 41 and 42 of, and Schedules 5 and 7 to, the National Health Service Act 1946(a), as amended by the National Health Service (Amendment) Act 1949(b) and the Health Services and Public Health Act 1968(c) and of all other powers enabling him in that behalf and after consultation with the Council on Tribunals in accordance with section 8 of the Tribunals and Inquiries Act 1958(d) hereby makes the following regulations:—

**1.** These regulations may be cited as the National Health Service (Service Committees and Tribunal) (Amendment) Regulations 1969, and shall come into operation on 1st April 1969.

**2.** The Interpretation Act 1889(e) applies to the interpretation of these regulations as it applies to the interpretation of an Act of Parliament.

**3.** The National Health Service (Service Committees and Tribunal) Regulations 1956 (f) as amended (g) shall be further amended as follows:—

(1) In regulation 2(1)—

    (*a*) in the definition "service committee" for the words "or dental" there shall be substituted the words "dental or ophthalmic" and the words "an ophthalmic investigation committee" shall be deleted;

    (*b*) the definitions "dispensing optician", "ophthalmic optician" and "Ophthalmic Services Committee" shall be deleted.

(2) (*a*) In regulations 3(1), 3(2)(*d*), 3(2)(*f*), 3(3)(*c*), 3(3)(*d*), 4(1), 4(5)(*a*), 4(7A), 48(*b*) and schedule 1 paragraphs 1(1), 1(1)(*i*), 1(2) and 2(3) for the words "ophthalmic investigation committee" there shall be substituted the words "ophthalmic service committee".

    (*b*) in regulation 3(1) for the words "ophthalmic investigation committees" there shall be substituted the words "ophthalmic service committees".

(3) For regulation 3(2)(*d*)(I) there shall be substituted:—
    "(I) four appointed by and from the lay members of the Council".

(4) In regulation 3(3)(*b*) the words after "optician" shall be deleted.

---

(a) 1946 c. 81.   (b) 1949 c. 93.   (c) 1968 c. 46.   (d) 1958 c. 66.   (e) 1889 c. 63.
(f) S.I. 1956/1077 (1956 I, p. 1554).
(g) The relevant amending instrument is S.I. 1965/1366 (1965 II, p. 3878).

(5) In regulation 3(3) in the definition of "lay members" for the words after "local health authority" there shall be substituted "or the Secretary of State and in relation to a service committee means members of the committee appointed by the lay members of the Council".

(6) In regulations 4(1)(a), 4(5)(a), 20(1) and 22(1) for the words "supplementary ophthalmic services" there shall be substituted the words "general ophthalmic services".

(7) In regulation 20(1) for the words "Ophthalmic Services Committee" there shall be substituted the word "Council".

(8) In regulation 20 for the word "Committee" wherever it occurs there shall be substituted the words "service committee".

(9) At the end of regulation 21 there shall be added:—

"(4) The Local Optical Committee shall have power to consider any complaint made to them by any optician against an optician practising in the area for which the committee is constituted involving any question of the efficiency of the general ophthalmic services."

(10) In regulation 48(a) for the words "or Dental" in each place where they occur, there shall be substituted the words "Dental or Optical".

(11) In schedule 1 paragraph 3 for the definition "lay member" there shall be substituted:—

"lay member" in relation to a service committee means a member appointed by and from the members of the Council who were appointed by the local health authority or the Secretary of State.

(12) In schedule 3:—

(a) the words "[Ophthalmic Services Committee]" wherever they occur shall be deleted;

(b) for the words "supplementary ophthalmic" wherever they occur there shall be substituted the words "general ophthalmic".

*R. H. S. Crossman,*
Secretary of State for Social Services.
**14th March 1969.**

---

## EXPLANATORY NOTE
*(This Note is not part of the Regulations.)*

These Regulations further amend the National Health Service (Service Committees and Tribunal) Regulations 1956, in consequence of the dissolution by the Health Services and Public Health Act 1968, of the Ophthalmic Services Committees and the cessation of the exercise by them on behalf of Executive Councils of functions in respect of ophthalmic services.

## 1969 No. 355

## NATIONAL HEALTH SERVICE, ENGLAND AND WALES
### The Isles of Scilly (National Health Service) Order 1969

| | |
|---|---|
| *Made* - - - | 14*th March* 1969 |
| *Coming into Operation* | 1*st April* 1969 |

The Secretary of State for Social Services in exercise of his powers under section 80(3) of the National Health Service Act 1946(a) hereby orders as follows:—

**1.**—(1) This order may be cited as the Isles of Scilly (National Health Service) Order 1969 and shall come into operation on 1st April 1969.

(2) The Interpretation Act 1889(b) applies to the interpretation of this order as it applies to the interpretation of an Act of Parliament.

**2.** In the Schedule to the Isles of Scilly (National Health Service) Order 1948(c) as amended(d), after the words "and registered pharmacist" there shall be inserted the words "and such ophthalmic medical practitioner, such ophthalmic optician and such dispensing optician".


*R. H. S. Crossman,*
Secretary of State for Social Services.
14th March 1969.

---

### EXPLANATORY NOTE
(*This Note is not part of the Order.*)

The Health Service and Public Health Act 1968 (c. 46) increased the membership of Executive Councils in order to provide representation thereon of persons qualified to provide ophthalmic services. This Order effects a comparable provision for the Executive Council for the Isles of Scilly.

---

(a) 1946 c. 81.                  (b) 1889 c. 63.
(c) S.I. 1948/167 (Rev. XV, p. 807: 1948 I, p. 2304).
(d) S.I. 1950/1835 (1950 I, p. 1315).

# STATUTORY INSTRUMENTS

## 1969 No. 359

## LONDON GOVERNMENT

### The London Authorities (Rate Fund Liabilities) Order 1969

| | | |
|---|---|---|
| *Made* - - - - | | *17th March* 1969 |
| *Laid before Parliament* | | *25th March* 1969 |
| *Coming into Operation* | | *28th March* 1969 |

The Minister of Housing and Local Government, in exercise of his powers under section 84 of the London Government Act 1963(a) and of all other powers enabling him in that behalf, hereby makes the following order:—

*Title, commencement and interpretation*

**1.** This order may be cited as the London Authorities (Rate Fund Liabilities) Order 1969 and shall come into operation on 28th March 1969.

**2.**—(1) The Interpretation Act 1889(b) applies to the interpretation of this order as it applies to the interpretation of an Act of Parliament.

(2) In this order—

"relevant liabilities" means any liabilities falling upon the general fund of the Greater London Council, the county fund of the county council of Essex, Hertfordshire, Kent or Surrey or the general rate fund of the London borough council of Croydon or Newham, as the case may be—

(*a*) in relation to the superannuation fund of such council;

(*b*) in relation to any pension not payable out of such superannuation fund;

(*c*) by virtue of the Pensions (Increase) Acts 1920 to 1965;

(*d*) in relation to any gratuity, payable under any enactment;

(*e*) by virtue of any provision for the payment of compensation for loss of employment or loss or diminution of emoluments; or

(*f*) by virtue of the Workmen's Compensation Acts 1925 to 1945, the enactments repealed by the Workmen's Compensation Act 1925(c), the enactments repealed by the Workmen's Compensation Act 1906(d), the Workmen's Compensation (Supplementation) Act 1951(e) and the Workmen's Compensation and Benefit (Amendment) Act 1965(f);

"the Minister" means the Minister of Housing and Local Government; and

"the year 1964-65", "the year 1965-66" and "the year 1966-67" mean the year ending on the 31st day of March in the year secondly-mentioned in each case.

In the application of articles 3, 6 and 7, the words "or any extension thereof" shall be deemed to be added to item (*c*) in the definition of "relevant liabilities".

| | |
|---|---|
| (a) 1963 c. 33. | (b) 1889 c. 63. |
| (c) 1925 c. 84. | (d) 1906 c. 58. |
| (e) 1951 c. 22. | (f) 1965 c. 79. |

(3) In this order, unless the context otherwise requires, references to any enactment shall be construed as references to that enactment as amended, extended or applied by or under any other enactment, and in this paragraph "enactment" includes any instrument made under any Act.

*Payments to the county councils of Essex, Hertfordshire, Kent and Surrey*

**3.** Any liability of a London borough council to the county council of Essex, Hertfordshire, Kent or Surrey in respect of relevant liabilities consequential on any transfer of property, liabilities, contracts, etc., actions and proceedings and causes of action or proceeding or of any officer (including the holder of any place, situation or employment) made by or under any provision of the London Government Act 1963 shall cease.

**4.**—(1) The Greater London Council shall make to the county council of Essex, Hertfordshire, Kent or Surrey, in respect of the relevant liabilities in relation to the county fund of such council, otherwise than in respect of fire services, such payments as may be agreed by the councils concerned, or in default of agreement determined by an arbitrator agreed upon by such councils, or in the absence of agreement appointed by the Minister, to be proper by reason of the inclusion of part of the county in Greater London.

(2) Any agreement made under the preceding paragraph may be varied from time to time, in particular on any extension of the Pensions (Increase) Acts 1920 to 1965, by agreement between the councils concerned.

*Payments to the Greater London Council*

**5.**—(1) In this article—

"the aggregate liabilities" means the aggregate of the amounts payable by the Greater London Council under article 4 of this order and the amount of £20,430,000, such amount being that calculated, upon the best information available at 31st December 1967, as representing the sum of—

    (*a*) the aggregate amount of assessed deficiency charges in respect of the superannuation funds of the London County Council and the county council of Middlesex outstanding against the county funds of such councils on 31st March 1965;

    (*b*) ten times the total paid out of such county funds in respect of the year 1964-65 as pensions increases and augmentations of pensions paid out of the superannuation funds aforesaid,

less such payments as have been made in respect of such liabilities in the years 1965-66 and 1966-67;

"relevant authority" means the Greater London Council or any authority named in column (1) of the Schedule; and

"the Schedule" means the Schedule to this order.

(2) Subject to paragraph (3) of this article, any authority named in column (1) of the Schedule shall pay to the Greater London Council, towards the aggregate liabilities—

    (*a*) before or on 31st March 1969, twice the amount specified in respect of that authority in column (2);

    (*b*) on 1st January 1970 and each following 1st January until 1st January 1980, the amount so specified in column (2),

the amount in column (2) being that defined in column (3).

(3) The Minister, on the representations of any relevant authority, on any variation of an agreement under article 4 of this order or in the light of any material circumstances becoming known after 31st December 1967, and after consultation with all other relevant authorities concerned, may make such variation as he considers expedient of—

 (a) the amount of £20,430,000 contained in the definition of "the aggregate liabilities";

 (b) any fraction specified in column (3) of the Schedule or any amount specified in column (2).

**6.** The county council of Hertfordshire or Surrey shall, in relation to the urban district of Potters Bar or the urban districts of Staines and Sunbury-on-Thames, being parts of the former county of Middlesex transferred to the said counties respectively, make to the Greater London Council such payments towards the relevant liabilities in relation to the general fund of the Greater London Council as may be agreed between the county council and the Greater London Council, or in default of agreement determined by an arbitrator agreed upon by such councils, or in the absence of agreement appointed by the Minister.

*Payments to the London borough councils of Croydon and Newham*

**7.** The Greater London Council shall make to the London borough council of Croydon or Newham, in respect of relevant liabilities of such council in relation to persons employed by the councils of the county boroughs of Croydon, East Ham and West Ham in services not now provided by that London borough council, such payments as may be agreed by the councils concerned, or in default of agreement determined by an arbitrator agreed upon by such councils, or in the absence of agreement appointed by the Minister.

*Saving for adjustments*

**8.** The provision made in article 4, 6 or 7 of this order is without prejudice to any adjustment under section 151 of the Local Government Act 1933(a) in respect of any matter other than the liabilities in relation to which provision is made in such article.

*Consolidation of equal annual charges payable by the Greater London Council*

**9.** The Greater London Council may by resolution provide for the consolidation and discharge by 31st March 1980 of any equal annual charges which they are required to pay by article 4(6) of the London Authorities (Superannuation) Order 1965(b).

---

(a) 1933 c. 51.        (b) S.I. 1965/621 (1965 I, p. 1970).

SCHEDULE

| (1) | (2) | (3) |
|---|---|---|
| | £ | |
| The council of the London borough of Barking | 22,850 | |
|     ,,  ,,  ,,  ,, Barnet | 48,116 | |
|     ,,  ,,  ,,  ,, Bexley | 23,596 | |
|     ,,  ,,  ,,  ,, Brent | 44,812 | |
|     ,,  ,,  ,,  ,, Bromley | 34,510 | |
|     ,,  ,,  ,,  ,, Ealing | 51,724 | 56/100ths of the relevant rate product for the area of the authority. |
|     ,,  ,,  ,,  ,, Enfield | 39,528 | |
|     ,,  ,,  ,,  ,, Haringey | 29,926 | |
|     ,,  ,,  ,,  ,, Harrow | 25,038 | |
|     ,,  ,,  ,,  ,, Havering | 26,362 | |
|     ,,  ,,  ,,  ,, Hillingdon | 36,904 | |
|     ,,  ,,  ,,  ,, Hounslow | 34,862 | |
| The council of the Royal borough of Kingston upon Thames | 21,480 | |
| The council of the London borough of Merton | 24,974 | |
|     ,,  ,,  ,,  ,, Redbridge | 28,282 | |
|     ,,  ,,  ,,  ,, Richmond upon Thames | 23,358 | |
|     ,,  ,,  ,,  ,, Sutton | 20,842 | |
|     ,,  ,,  ,,  ,, Waltham Forest | 25,828 | |
| The council of the London borough of Croydon | 8,583 | 56/100ths of the relevant rate product for the relevant area. |
|     ,,  ,,  ,,  ,, Newham | 1,880 | |

| (1) | (2) | (3) |
|---|---|---|
| | £ | |
| The Common Council of the City of London | 41,312 | |
| The council of the London borough of Camden | 30,837 | |
| " " " " " Greenwich | 12,353 | |
| " " " " " Hackney | 13,587 | |
| " " " " " Hammersmith | 13,388 | |
| " " " " " Islington | 18,273 | 24/100ths of the relevant rate product for the area of the authority, 32/100ths of such product being borne by the Inner London Education Authority. |
| The council of the Royal borough of Kensington and Chelsea | 23,974 | |
| The council of the London borough of Lambeth | 18,702 | |
| " " " " " Lewisham | 11,347 | |
| " " " " " Southwark | 16,937 | |
| " " " " " Tower Hamlets | 13,705 | |
| " " " " " Wandsworth | 14,858 | |
| The council of the city of Westminster | 99,610 | |
| The Sub-Treasurer of the Inner Temple | 95 | |
| The Under-Treasurer of the Middle Temple | 60 | |

"The relevant rate product", in relation to any area, means the product of a rate of one penny in the pound for the year 1964-65, being—

(a) in a case where that product has been ascertained by the rating authority for the purposes of section 9(2) of the Rating and Valuation Act 1925(a), that product as so ascertained;

(b) in the case of any other part of a rating area, that product estimated by the council of the London borough concerned in accordance with the principles of the Rate-product Rules 1959(b); or

(c) such aggregate of the products defined in (a) and (b) as may be appropriate.

"The relevant area" means—

in the case of the council of the London borough of Croydon, the urban district of Coulsdon and Purley;

in the case of the council of the London borough of Newham, the areas of the borough of Barking and the metropolitan borough of Woolwich included in the London borough.

(a) 1925 c. 90.        (b) S.I. 1959/258 (1959 II, p 2288).

Given under the official seal of the Minister of Housing and Local Government on 17th March 1969.


(L.S.)

*Anthony Greenwood,*
Minister of Housing and Local Government.

## EXPLANATORY NOTE

*(This Note is not part of the Order.)*

This Order makes provision consequential on the London Government Act 1963 in relation to liabilities falling on general funds in relation to super-annuation funds, pensions, etc.

# STATUTORY INSTRUMENTS

## 1969 No. 362

## SUGAR

## The Sugar (Rates of Surcharge and Surcharge Repayments) (No. 3) Order 1969

| | |
|---|---|
| *Made* - - - | 17*th March* 1969 |
| *Laid before Parliament* | 18*th March* 1969 |
| *Coming into Operation* | 19*th March* 1969 |

The Minister of Agriculture, Fisheries and Food, in exercise of the powers conferred on him by sections 7(4), 8(6) and 33(4) of the Sugar Act 1956(a) having effect subject to the provisions of section 3 of, and Part II of Schedule 5 to, the Finance Act 1962(b), and section 58 of the Finance Act 1968 (c) and of all other powers enabling him in that behalf, with the concurrence of the Treasury, on the advice of the Sugar Board, hereby makes the following order:—

1.—(1) This order may be cited as the Sugar (Rates of Surcharge and Surcharge Repayments) (No. 3) Order 1969; and shall come into operation on 19th March 1969.

(2) The Interpretation Act 1889(d) shall apply for the interpretation of this order as it applies for the interpretation of an Act of Parliament.

2. Notwithstanding the provisions of Article 2 of the Sugar (Rates of Surcharge and Surcharge Repayments) (No. 2) Order 1969(e), the rates of surcharge payable under and in accordance with the provisions of section 7 of the Sugar Act 1956, having effect as aforesaid, in respect of sugar and invert sugar imported or home produced or used in the manufacture of imported composite sugar products shall on and after 19th March 1969 be those rates specified in Schedule 1 to this order.

3. For the purpose of section 8(3)(*b*) of the Sugar Act 1956, having effect as aforesaid, the rates of surcharge repayments in respect of invert sugar produced in the United Kingdom from materials on which on or after 19th March 1969 sugar duty has been paid or, by virtue of paragraph 1 of Part II of Schedule 5 to the Finance Act 1962, is treated as having been paid shall, notwithstanding the provisions of Article 3 of the Sugar (Rates of Surcharge and Surcharge Repayments) (No. 2) Order 1969 be those specified in Schedule 2 to this order.

| | |
|---|---|
| (a) 1956 c. 48. | (b) 1962 c. 44. |
| (c) 1968 c. 44. | (d) 1889 c. 63. |
| (e) S.I. 1969/279 (1969 I, p. 759). | |

In Witness whereof the Official Seal of the Minister of Agriculture, Fisheries and Food is hereunto affixed on 14th March 1969.

(L.S.)

> R. P. Fraser,
>
> Authorised by the Minister.

We concur.

17th March 1969.

> J. McCann,
> Joseph Harper,
>
> Two of the Lords Commissioners of
> Her Majesty's Treasury.

## SCHEDULE 1

### PART I

#### SURCHARGE RATES FOR SUGAR

| Polarisation | Rate of Surcharge per cwt. | |
|---|---|---|
| | s. | d. |
| Exceeding— | | |
| 99° ... ... ... ... ... ... ... ... | 18 | 8·0 |
| 98° but not exceeding 99° ... ... ... ... ... | 17 | 7·2 |
| 97° ,, ,, ,, 98° ... ... ... ... ... | 17 | 2·0 |
| 96° ,, ,, ,, 97° ... ... ... ... ... | 16 | 8·7 |
| 95° ,, ,, ,, 96° ... ... ... ... ... | 16 | 3·3 |
| 94° ,, ,, ,, 95° ... ... ... ... ... | 15 | 9·9 |
| 93° ,, ,, ,, 94° ... ... ... ... ... | 15 | 4·5 |
| 92° ,, ,, ,, 93° ... ... ... ... ... | 14 | 11·2 |
| 91° ,, ,, ,, 92° ... ... ... ... ... | 14 | 5·8 |
| 90° ,, ,, ,, 91° ... ... ... ... ... | 14 | 0·4 |
| 89° ,, ,, ,, 90° ... ... ... ... ... | 13 | 7·0 |
| 88° ,, ,, ,, 89° ... ... ... ... ... | 13 | 1·6 |
| 87° ,, ,, ,, 88° ... ... ... ... ... | 12 | 9·2 |
| 86° ,, ,, ,, 87° ... ... ... ... ... | 12 | 4·7 |
| 85° ,, , ,, 86° ... ... ... ... ... | 12 | 0·7 |
| 84° ,, ,, ,, 85° ... ... ... ... ... | 11 | 8·6 |
| 83° ,, ,, ,, 84° ... ... ... ... ... | 11 | 4·6 |
| 82° ,, ,, ,, 83° ... ... ... ... ... | 11 | 0·6 |
| 81° ,, ,, ,, 82° ... ... ... ... ... | 10 | 9·0 |
| 80° ,, ,, ,, 81° ... ... ... ... ... | 10 | 5·4 |
| 79° ,, ,, ,, 80° ... ... ... ... ... | 10 | 1·8 |
| 78° ,, ,, ,, 79° ... ... ... ... ... | 9 | 10·2 |
| 77° ,, ,, ,, 78° ... ... ... ... ... | 9 | 6·6 |
| 76° ,, ,, ,, 77° ... ... ... ... ... | 9 | 3·1 |
| Not exceeding 76° ... ... ... ... ... ... | 9 | 0·0 |

## PART II

### SURCHARGE RATES FOR INVERT SUGAR

| Sweetening matter content by weight | Rate of Surcharge per cwt. |
|---|---|
| | s.   d. |
| 70 per cent. or more ... ... ... ... ... | 11   10 |
| Less than 70 per cent. and more than 50 per cent. ... ... ... | 8   6 |
| Not more than 50 per cent. ... ... ... ... ... ... | 4   2 |

## SCHEDULE 2

### SURCHARGE REPAYMENT RATES FOR INVERT SUGAR

| Sweetening matter content by weight | Rate of Surcharge Repayment per cwt. |
|---|---|
| | s.   d. |
| More than 80 per cent. ... ... ... ... ... ... | 14   0 |
| More than 70 per cent. but not more than 80 per cent. ... ... | 11   10 |
| More than 60 per cent. but not more than 70 per cent. ... ... | 8   6 |
| More than 50 per cent. but not more than 60 per cent. ... ... | 6   9 |
| Not more than 50 per cent. and the invert sugar not being less in weight than 14 lb. per gallon ... ... ... ... ... | 4   2 |

## EXPLANATORY NOTE

*(This Note is not part of the Order.)*

This order prescribes—

(a) reductions equivalent to 2s. 4d. per cwt. of refined sugar in the rates of surcharge payable on sugar and invert sugar which become chargeable with surcharge on or after 19th March 1969;

(b) correspondingly reduced rates of surcharge repayment in respect of invert sugar produced in the United Kingdom from materials on which surcharge has been paid.

## STATUTORY INSTRUMENTS

### 1969 No. 363

### SUGAR

## The Composite Sugar Products (Surcharge and Surcharge Repayments—Average Rates) (No. 3) Order 1969

|  |  |
|---|---|
| *Made* - - - - | 17*th March* 1969 |
| *Laid before Parliament* | 18*th March* 1969 |
| *Coming into Operation* | 19*th March* 1969 |

Whereas the Minister of Agriculture, Fisheries and Food (hereinafter called "the Minister") has on the recommendation of the Commissioners of Customs and Excise (hereinafter called "the Commissioners") made an order(a) pursuant to the powers conferred upon him by sections 9(1) and 9(4) of the Sugar Act 1956(b), having effect subject to the provisions of section 3 of, and Part II of Schedule 5 to, the Finance Act 1962(c), to the provisions of section 52(2) of the Finance Act 1966(d), and to the provisions of Section 58 of the Finance Act 1968(e), providing that in the case of certain descriptions of composite sugar products surcharge shall be calculated on the basis of an average quantity of sugar or invert sugar taken to have been used in the manufacture of the products, and that certain other descriptions of composite sugar products shall be treated as not containing any sugar or invert sugar, and that in the case of certain descriptions of goods in the manufacture of which sugar or invert sugar is used, surcharge repayments shall be calculated on the basis of an average quantity of sugar or invert sugar taken to have been so used:

Now, therefore, the Minister, on the recommendation of the Commissioners and in exercise of the powers conferred upon him by sections 9(1), 9(4) and 33(4) of the Sugar Act 1956, having effect as aforesaid, and of all other powers enabling him in that behalf, hereby makes the following order:—

1.—(1) This order may be cited as the Composite Sugar Products (Surcharge and Surcharge Repayments—Average Rates) (No. 3) Order 1969; and shall come into operation on 19th March 1969.

(2) The Interpretation Act 1889(f) shall apply for the interpretation of this order as it applies for the interpretation of an Act of Parliament.

2. Surcharge payable on or after 19th March 1969 under and in accordance with the Sugar Act 1956, having effect as aforesaid, in respect of sugar and invert sugar used in the manufacture of the descriptions of imported composite sugar products specified in column 2 of Schedule 1 to this order shall, notwithstanding the provisions of the Sugar (Rates of Surcharge and Surcharge Repayments) (No. 3) Order 1969(g) and the Composite Sugar Products (Surcharge and Surcharge Repayments—Average Rates) (No. 2) Order 1969(a), be calculated by reference to the weight or value, as the case may be, of the products at the rates specified in relation thereto in column 3 of the said Schedule.

(a) S.I. 1969/280 (1969 I, p. 762).   (b) 1956 c. 48.   (c) 1962 c. 44.
(d) 1966 c. 18.   (e) 1968 c. 44.   (f) 1889 c. 63.
(g) S.I. 1969/362 (1969 I, p. 997).

**3.** Imported composite sugar products other than those of a description specified in Schedules 1 and 2 to this order shall be treated as not containing any sugar or invert sugar for the purposes of surcharge payable on or after 19th March 1969.

**4.** Surcharge repayments payable on and after 19th March 1969 under and in accordance with the provisions of section 8 of the Sugar Act 1956, having effect as aforesaid, in respect of sugar and invert sugar used in the manufacture of the descriptions of goods specified in column 1 of Schedule 3 to this order shall, notwithstanding the provisions of the Sugar (Rates of Surcharge and Surcharge Repayments) (No. 3) Order 1969(**a**) and the Composite Sugar Products (Surcharge and Surcharge Repayments—Average Rates) (No. 2) Order 1969(**b**), be calculated by reference to the quantity of the goods at the rates specified in relation thereto in column 2 of the said Schedule.

In Witness whereof the Official Seal of the Minister of Agriculture, Fisheries and Food is hereunto affixed on 17th March 1969.

(**L.S.**)　　　　　　　　　　　　　　　*R. P. Fraser,*

　　　　　　　　　　　　　　Authorised by the Minister.

### SCHEDULE 1

In this Schedule:—

" Tariff heading " means a heading or, where the context so requires, a subheading of the Customs Tariff 1959 (see paragraph (1) of Article 1 of the Import Duties (General) (No. 4) Order 1968(**c**)).

" Per cent." means, where it occurs in relation to any rate of surcharge, per cent. of the value for customs duty purposes of the product to which it relates.

| Tariff heading | Description of Imported Composite Sugar Products | Rate of Surcharge |
|---|---|---|
| | | per cwt. s. d. |
| 04.02 ... ... | Milk and cream, preserved, concentrated or sweetened, containing more than 10 per cent. by weight of added sweetening matter ... ... | 8 3 |
| 17.02 (B) (2) and 17.05 (B) | Syrups containing sucrose sugar, whether or not flavoured or coloured, but not including fruit juices containing added sugar in any proportion:— | |
| | containing 70 per cent. or more by weight of sweetening matter ... ... ... ... | 11 10 |
| | containing less than 70 per cent., and more than 50 per cent., by weight of sweetening matter... | 8 6 |
| | containing not more than 50 per cent. by weight of sweetening matter ... ... ... ... | 4 2 |

(**a**) S.I. 1969/362.(1969 I, p. 997).　　　　(**b**) S.I. 1969/280 (1969 I, p. 762).

(**c**) S.I. 1968/679 (1968 I, p. 1519).

| Tariff heading | Description of Imported Composite Sugar Products | Rate of Surcharge |
|---|---|---|
| | | per cwt. <br> s. d. |
| 17.02 (F) ... | Caramel:— | |
| | Solid ... ... ... ... ... ... ... | 18 8 |
| | Liquid ... ... ... ... ... ... | 13 1 |
| 17.04 ... ... | Sugar confectionery, not containing cocoa ... ... | 15 2 |
| 18.06 ... ... | Chocolate and other food preparations containing cocoa:— | |
| | Chocolate couverture not prepared for retail sale; chocolate milk crumb, liquid ... ... | 8 3 |
| | Chocolate milk crumb, solid ... ... ... | 10 3 |
| | Solid chocolate bars or blocks, milk or plain, with or without fruit or nuts; other chocolate confectionery consisting wholly of chocolate or of chocolate and other ingredients not containing added sugar, but not including such goods when packed together in retail packages with goods liable to surcharge at a higher rate | 8 5 |
| | Other ... ... ... ... ... ... | 10 10 |
| | | per cent. |
| 19.08 ... ... | Pastry, biscuits, cakes and other fine bakers' wares containing added sweetening matter:— | |
| | Biscuits ... ... ... ... ... ... | 4 |
| | Other ... ... ... ... ... ... | 2⅖ |
| 20.01 ... ... | Vegetables and fruit, prepared or preserved by vinegar or acetic acid, containing added sweetening matter ... ... ... ... ... ... | 5¾ |
| 20.03 ... ... | Fruit preserved by freezing, containing added sugar | 2 |
| | | per cwt. <br> s. d. |
| 20.04 ... ... | Fruit, fruit-peel and parts of plants, preserved by sugar (drained, glacé or crystallised) ... ... | 12 3 |
| 20.05 ... ... | Jams, fruit jellies, marmalades, fruit purée and fruit pastes, being cooked preparations, containing added sweetening matter ... ... ... ... | 11 9 |
| | | per cent. |
| 20.06 ... ... | Fruit otherwise prepared or preserved, containing added sweetening matter:— | |
| | Ginger ... ... ... ... ... ... | 8 |
| | Other ... ... ... ... ... ... | 2 |

## SCHEDULE 2

| Tariff heading | Description of Imported Composite Sugar Products |
|---|---|
| 17.05 (A) and (B) | Sugar and invert sugar, flavoured or coloured. |

## SCHEDULE 3

| Description of goods | Rate of surcharge repayment per bulk barrel of 36 gallons |
|---|---|
| Lager  ...  ...  ...  ...  ... | 9 ·3d. |
| All beer other than lager  ...  ... | 8 ·3d. |

## EXPLANATORY NOTE

### (*This Note is not part of the Order.*)

This order provides for reductions on and after 19th March 1969 in the average rates of surcharge payable on imported composite sugar products of the descriptions specified in Schedule 1 and in the average rates of surcharge repayment in respect of exported goods of the descriptions specified in Schedule 3. These correspond to the reductions in surcharge rates effected by the Sugar (Rates of Surcharge and Surcharge Repayments) (No. 3) Order 1969 (S.I. 1969/362). Provision is also made for certain imported composite sugar products to be treated as not containing any sugar or invert sugar.

## STATUTORY INSTRUMENTS

### 1969 No. 364 (C.8) (S.30)

## NATIONAL HEALTH SERVICE, SCOTLAND

### The Health Services and Public Health Act 1968 (Commencement No. 3) (Scotland) Order 1969

*Made - - - -*         *17th March* 1969

In exercise of the powers conferred on me by section 79(2) of the Health Services and Public Health Act 1968(a) and of all other powers enabling me in that behalf, I hereby make the following order:—

**1.** This order, which shall extend to Scotland only, may be cited as the Health Services and Public Health Act 1968 (Commencement No. 3) (Scotland) Order 1969.

**2.** The provisions of the Health Services and Public Health Act 1968 specified in the Schedule to this order shall come into operation on 1st April 1969.

*William Ross,*
One of Her Majesty's Principal
Secretaries of State.

St. Andrew's House,
Edinburgh, 1.
17th March 1969.

---

(a) 1968 c. 46.

## SCHEDULE

PROVISIONS COMING INTO FORCE ON 1ST APRIL 1969

| Provisions of the Act | Subject matter of provisions |
|---|---|
| Section 1 | Accommodation and treatment, at hospitals providing hospital and specialist services, of persons as private resident patients. |
| Section 2 | Accommodation and treatment, at hospitals providing hospital and specialist services, of persons as private non-resident patients. |
| Section 4 | Amendment as to fixing of charges for accommodation made available on part payment. |
| Section 78(2) and Schedule 4 to the extent set out in the Appendix hereto | Repeal. |

## APPENDIX TO SCHEDULE

REPEAL TAKING EFFECT ON 1ST APRIL 1969

| Chapter | Short Title | Extent of Repeal |
|---|---|---|
| 10 & 11 Geo. 6 c.27. | The National Health Service (Scotland) Act 1947 | Section 5 |

## EXPLANATORY NOTE

*(This Note is not part of the Order.)*

This Order brings into force on 1st April 1969 those provisions of the Health Services and Public Health Act 1968 which are set out in the Order. The Order extends only to Scotland.

# STATUTORY INSTRUMENTS

## 1969 No. 365

## JUDICIAL COMMITTEE

### PROCEDURE

## The Judicial Committee Rules (Amendment) Order 1969

| | |
|---|---|
| *Made* - - - - | 18*th March* 1969 |
| *Coming into Operation* | 14*th April* 1969 |

At the Court at Buckingham Palace, the 18th day of March 1969

Present,

The Queen's Most Excellent Majesty in Council

Whereas there was this day read at the Board a representation from the Judicial Committee of the Privy Council recommending that the rules set out in the Schedule to the Order in Council of 20th December 1957(a) ought to be amended:

Now, therefore, Her Majesty, having taken the said representation into consideration, and in exercise of the powers conferred on Her by section 24 of the Judicial Committee Act 1833(b), or otherwise in Her vested, is pleased, by and with the advice of Her Privy Council, to approve thereof and to order, as it is hereby ordered, as follows:—

**1.** The rules set out in the Schedule to the Order in Council of 20th December 1957 are hereby amended in the manner and to the extent set out in the Schedule to this Order.

**2.** This Order shall come into operation on 14th April 1969 and may be cited as the Judicial Committee Rules (Amendment) Order 1969.

Whereof all persons whom it may concern are to take notice and govern themselves accordingly.

*W. G. Agnew.*

### SCHEDULE

(1) After Rule 11 in the Arrangement of Rules there shall be inserted the following new entry—" 11A. Record produced on hearing of petition for special leave ".

(2) In Rule 11 after the words " special leave to appeal " where those words first occur there shall be inserted the words " (unless in such case the said Order in Council otherwise provides)".

(3) After Rule 11 there shall be inserted the following new Rule—

" 11A. Where an Appeal has been admitted by Order of Her Majesty in Council granting special leave to appeal and an authenticated copy of the Record was produced upon the hearing of the Petition for such special leave, then, if the Order in Council so provides, such copy may be accepted as the Record proper to be laid before Her Majesty on the hearing of the Appeal and the provisions of Rule 14 shall not apply."

(a) S I. 1957/2224 (1957 I, p. 1205).
(b) 1833 c. 41.

(4) In Rule 22 after the word " arrival " there shall be inserted the words and figures " or, in a case to which the provisions of Rule 11A apply, within a period of one month from the date of the Order in Council granting special leave to appeal ".

(5) In Rule 29 at the end of paragraph (b) there shall be inserted the words and figures " or, in a case to which the provisions of Rule 11A apply, within a period of fourteen days from the date of the completion of the printing or duplicating of the Record: ".

(6) In Rule 34 after the word " England " there shall be inserted the words and figures " or, in a case to which the provisions of Rule 11A apply, within a period of one month from the date of the Order in Council granting special leave to appeal ".

(7) In Rules 22, 23 and 24 the word " typewritten " shall be omitted.

---

## EXPLANATORY NOTE

### (*This Note is not part of the Order.*)

This Order amends certain provisions in the Judicial Committee Rules 1957 dealing with the record, so as to reduce delay in the hearing of appeals where special leave to appeal is granted.

STATUTORY INSTRUMENTS

## 1969 No. 366

# FOREIGN COMPENSATION

## The Foreign Compensation (Financial Provisions) Order 1969

| | |
|---|---|
| *Made* - - - - | 18*th March* 1969 |
| *Laid before Parliament* | 24*th March* 1969 |
| *Coming into Operation* | 25*th March* 1969 |

At the Court at Buckingham Palace, the 18th day of March 1969

Present,

The Queen's Most Excellent Majesty in Council

Her Majesty, by virtue and in exercise of the powers in that behalf by section 7(2) of the Foreign Compensation Act 1950(a) and section 3(3) of the Foreign Compensation Act 1962(b) or otherwise in Her Majesty vested, is pleased, by and with the advice of Her Privy Council, to order, and it is hereby ordered, as follows:

**1.** The Foreign Compensation Commission shall pay into the Exchequer not later than 30th March 1969 out of each of the Funds named in column 1 of the Schedule to this Order the amount specified in respect of that Fund in column 2 of the Schedule which is hereby determined to be the amount of the expenses of the Commission during the period 1st October 1967 to 30th September 1968 attributable to the discharge by the Commission of their functions in relation to the distribution of sums from that Fund.

**2.** This Order shall come into operation on 25th March 1969 and may be cited as the Foreign Compensation (Financial Provisions) Order 1969.

*W. G. Agnew.*

### SCHEDULE

| Column 1<br>*Name of Fund* | Column 2<br>*Amount* |
|---|---|
| | £ |
| The Egyptian Compensation Fund ... | 183,775 |
| The Hungarian Compensation Fund ... | 514 |
| The Roumanian Compensation Fund ... | 3,875 |

### EXPLANATORY NOTE

*(This Note is not part of the Order.)*

This Order, which is made under section 7(2) of the Foreign Compensation Act 1950 and section 3(3) of the Foreign Compensation Act 1962, directs the Foreign Compensation Commission to pay into the Exchequer, out of

(a) 1950 c. 12.　　　　　　　　　　(b) 11 & 12 Eliz. 2. c. 4.

sums paid to the Commission for the purpose of being distributed under the said Acts, amounts in respect of the Commission's expenses during the period 1st October 1967 to 30th September 1968 in relation to the distribution of those sums.

## STATUTORY INSTRUMENTS

### 1969 No. 367

### JUDICIAL COMMITTEE

## The Botswana (Procedure in Appeals to Judicial Committee of Privy Council) (Amendment) Order 1969

| | |
|---|---|
| Made - - - - | 18*th March* 1969 |
| *Coming into Operation* | 14*th April* 1969 |

At the Court at Buckingham Palace, the 18th day of March 1969

Present,

The Queen's Most Excellent Majesty in Council

Her Majesty, by virtue and in exercise of the powers conferred on Her by section 24 of the Judicial Committee Act 1833(**a**) as applied by section 5 of the Botswana Independence Act 1966(**b**) or otherwise in Her Majesty vested, is pleased, by and with the advice of Her Privy Council, to order, and it is hereby ordered, as follows :—

Citation, commencement and construction.

**1.**—(1) This Order may be cited as the Botswana (Procedure in Appeals to Judicial Committee of Privy Council) (Amendment) Order 1969 and shall come into operation on 14th April 1969.

(2) This Order shall be construed as one with the Botswana (Procedure in Appeals to Judicial Committee of Privy Council) Order 1966(**c**) (hereinafter referred to as " the principal Order ") and that Order and this Order may be cited together as the Botswana (Procedure in Appeals to Judicial Committee of Privy Council) Orders 1966 and 1969.

Amendment of section 3 of principal Order.

**2.** Section 3 of the principal Order is amended by the deletion of the words " as amended by the Judicial Committee (Fees) Rules 1963 " and the substitution therefor of the words " as from time to time amended ".

Amendment of Schedule 1 to principal Order.

**3.** The heading to Schedule 1 to the principal Order is amended by deleting the words " as amended by the Judicial Committee (Fees) Rules 1963 " ; and that schedule is amended—

(*a*) by the addition at the end of paragraph 1 of the words " and any reference to an Order of Her Majesty in Council or to an Order in Council shall, without prejudice to the provisions of paragraphs 9 and 10 of this schedule, be construed accordingly " ; and

(*b*) by the insertion after paragraph 5 of the following paragraph—

' 5A. For the words " Her Majesty " in Rule 11A where those words secondly occur there shall be substituted the words " the Judicial Committee ".'

*W. G. Agnew.*

---

(**a**) 1833 c. 41.    (**b**) 1966 c. 23.    (**c**) S.I. 1966/1174 (1966 III, p. 3037).

# EXPLANATORY NOTE

*(This Note is not part of the Order.)*

The Judicial Committee of the Privy Council exercises its jurisdiction in respect of appeals from the Court of Appeal for Botswana in accordance with the Judicial Committee Rules 1957 as amended by the Judicial Committee (Fees) Rules 1963.  This Order makes provision for such exercise to be in accordance with the 1957 Rules as from time to time amended.

# STATUTORY INSTRUMENTS

## 1969 No. 368

## JUDICIAL COMMITTEE

### The Lesotho (Procedure in Appeals to Judicial Committee of Privy Council) (Amendment) Order 1969

|  |  |
|---|---|
| *Made* - - - - | 18*th March* 1969 |
| *Coming into Operation* | 14*th April* 1969 |

At the Court at Buckingham Palace, the 18th day of March 1969

**Present,**

**The Queen's Most Excellent Majesty in Council**

Her Majesty, by virtue and in exercise of the powers conferred on Her by section 24 of the Judicial Committee Act 1833(a) as applied by section 5 of the Lesotho Independence Act 1966(b) or otherwise in Her Majesty vested, is pleased, by and with the advice of Her Privy Council, to order, and it is hereby ordered, as follows:—

Citation, commencement and construction.

**1.**—(1) This Order may be cited as the Lesotho (Procedure in Appeals to Judicial Committee of Privy Council) (Amendment) Order 1969 and shall come into operation on 14th April 1969.

(2) This Order shall be construed as one with the Lesotho (Procedure in Appeals to Judicial Committee of Privy Council) Order 1966(c) (hereinafter referred to as "the principal Order") and that Order and this Order may be cited together as the Lesotho (Procedure in Appeals to Judicial Committee of Privy Council) Orders 1966 and 1969.

Amendment of section 3 of principal Order.

**2.** Section 3 of the principal Order is amended by the deletion of the words "as amended by the Judicial Committee (Fees) Rules 1963" and the substitution therefor of the words "as from time to time amended".

Amendment of Schedule 1 to principal Order.

**3.** The heading to Schedule 1 to the principal Order is amended by deleting the words "as amended by the Judicial Committee (Fees) Rules 1963"; and that schedule is amended—

(*a*) by the addition at the end of paragraph 1 of the words "and any reference to an Order of Her Majesty in Council or to an Order in Council shall, without prejudice to the provisions of paragraphs 9 and 10 of this schedule, be construed accordingly"; and

(*b*) by the insertion after paragraph 5 of the following paragraph—

'5A. For the words "Her Majesty" in Rule 11A where those words secondly occur there shall be substituted the words "the Judicial Committee".'

*W. G. Agnew.*

---

(a) 1833 c. 41.     (b) 1966 c. 24.     (c) S.I. 1966/1176 (1966 III, p. 3045).

# EXPLANATORY NOTE

*(This Note is not part of the Order.)*

The Judicial Committee of the Privy Council exercises its jurisdiction in respect of appeals from the Court of Appeal for Lesotho in accordance with the Judicial Committee Rules 1957 as amended by the Judicial Committee (Fees) Rules 1963. This Order makes provision for such exercise to be in accordance with the 1957 Rules as from time to time amended.

## STATUTORY INSTRUMENTS

### 1969 No. 369

### JUDICIAL COMMITTEE

### The Malaysia (Appeals to Privy Council) (Amendment) Order 1969

Made - - - - 18*th March* 1969
*Coming into Operation* 14*th April* 1969

At the Court at Buckingham Palace, the 18th day of March 1969

**Present,**

The Queen's Most Excellent Majesty in Council

Her Majesty, by virtue and in exercise of the powers conferred on Her by section 3 of the Federation of Malaya Independence Act 1957(**a**), and section 5 of the Malaysia Act 1963(**b**) or otherwise in Her Majesty vested, is pleased, by and with the advice of Her Privy Council, to order, and it is hereby ordered, as follows:—

Citation, commencement and construction.

**1.**—(1) This Order may be cited as the Malaysia (Appeals to Privy Council) (Amendment) Order 1969 and shall come into operation on 14th April 1969.

(2) This Order shall be construed as one with the Federation of Malaya (Appeals to Privy Council) Order in Council 1958(**c**) (hereinafter referred to as " the principal Order ") and the Malaysia (Appeals to Privy Council) Order in Council 1963(**d**), and those Orders and this Order may be cited together as the Malaysia (Appeals to Privy Council) Orders 1958 to 1969.

Amendment of article 5 of principal Order.

**2.** Article 5 of the principal Order is amended by the deletion of the words " but the said Rules " and the substitution therefor of the words " as from time to time amended, but the said Rules, as so amended,".

Amendment of Second Schedule to principal Order.

**3.** The Second Schedule to the principal Order is amended by the insertion after paragraph 9 of the following paragraph—

' 9A. For the words " Her Majesty " in Rule 11A where those words secondly occur there shall be substituted the words " the Judicial Committee ".'

*W. G. Agnew.*

### EXPLANATORY NOTE

(*This Note is not part of the Order.*)

The Judicial Committee of the Privy Council exercises its jurisdiction in respect of appeals from the Federal Court of Malaysia in accordance with the Judicial Committee Rules 1957. This Order makes provision for such exercise to be in accordance with those Rules as from time to time amended.

(**a**) 1957 c. 60.  (**b**) 1963 c. 35.  (**c**) S.I. 1958/426 (1958 I, p. 1322).
(**d**) S.I. 1963/2086 (1963 III, p. 4529).

## STATUTORY INSTRUMENTS

### 1969 No. 370

### JUDICIAL COMMITTEE

## The Republic of Singapore (Appeals to Judicial Committee) (Amendment) Order 1969

*Made* - - - - 18*th March* 1969
*Coming into Operation* 14*th April* 1969

At the Court at Buckingham Palace, the 18th day of March 1969

**Present,**

The Queen's Most Excellent Majesty in Council

Her Majesty, by virtue and in exercise of the powers conferred on Her by section 3 of the Singapore Act 1966(**a**) or otherwise in Her vested, is pleased, by and with the advice of Her Privy Council, to order, and it is hereby ordered, as follows:—

**1.**—(1) This Order may be cited as the Republic of Singapore (Appeals to Judicial Committee) (Amendment) Order 1969 and shall come into operation on 14th April 1969. *(Citation, commencement and construction.)*

(2) This Order shall be construed as one with the Republic of Singapore (Appeals to Judicial Committee) Order 1966(**b**) (hereinafter referred to as "the principal Order") and that Order and this Order may be cited together as the Republic of Singapore (Appeals to Judicial Committee) Orders 1966 and 1969.

**2.** Article 5 of the principal Order is amended by the deletion of the words "but the said Rules" and the substitution therefor of the words "as from time to time amended, but the said Rules, as so amended,". *(Amendment of article 5 of principal Order.)*

*W. G. Agnew.*

---

### EXPLANATORY NOTE

*(This Note is not part of the Order.)*

In respect of the Republic of Singapore, the Judicial Committee of the Privy Council exercises in accordance with the Judicial Committee Rules 1957 its jurisdiction in respect of appeals from an Appellate Court. This Order makes provision for such exercise to be in accordance with those Rules as from time to time amended.

---

(**a**) 1966 c. 29.     (**b**) S.I. 1966/1182 (1966 III, p. 3067).

## STATUTORY INSTRUMENTS

### 1969 No. 371

### ASSOCIATED STATES

### The Anguilla (Temporary Provision) Order 1969

| | |
|---|---|
| *Made* - - - | 18*th March* 1969 |
| *Coming into Operation* | *On a date to be appointed under section* 1(2). |

At the Court at Buckingham Palace, the 18th day of March 1969

Present,

The Queen's Most Excellent Majesty in Council

Whereas Her Majesty's Government in the United Kingdom and the Government of the Associated State of St. Christopher Nevis and Anguilla (hereinafter called " the Associated State ") have consulted together concerning the situation that now exists in Anguilla and have agreed that appropriate measures should be taken to restore law and order in Anguilla and to preserve the territorial integrity of the Associated State in order to ensure that the discharge of the responsibilities of Her Majesty's Government in the United Kingdom under the West Indies Act 1967(a) relating to defence and external affairs is not prejudiced:

And Whereas it appears to Her Majesty that, in the interests of the responsibilities of Her Majesty's Government in the United Kingdom relating to defence and external affairs, a change should be made in the law of the Associated State whereby provision is made for the exercise in Anguilla of certain functions by Her Majesty's Commissioner in Anguilla:

And Whereas the Government of the Associated State who, subject to the provisions of the West Indies Act 1967, are responsible for the peace, order and good government of Anguilla have signified their agreement that such provision should be made by Order of Her Majesty in Council:

Now, therefore, Her Majesty in exercise of the powers conferred upon Her by section 7(2) of the West Indies Act 1967 is pleased, by and with the advice of Her Privy Council, to order, and it is hereby ordered, as follows:—

**1.**—(1) This Order may be cited as the Anguilla (Temporary Provision) Order 1969.

(2) This Order shall come into operation on such date as a Secretary of State may by order appoint.

(3) This Order shall cease to have effect on such date as a Secretary of State may by order appoint.

**2.**—(1) In this Order—

" the Commissioner " means such person as Her Majesty may appoint by instrument under Her Sign Manual and Signet to be Her Majesty's Commissioner in Anguilla for the purposes of this Order and includes any person appointed by Her Majesty to act in that office;

" the Constitution " means the Constitution of the Associated State(b); and

" the Courts Order " means the West Indies Associated States Supreme Court Order 1967(c).

---

(a) 1967 c. 4.　　　　(b) Schedule 2 to S.I. 1967/228 (1967 I, p. 594).
(c) S.I. 1967/223 (1967 I, p. 364).

(2) The Interpretation Act 1889(**a**) shall apply, with the necessary adaptations, for the purpose of interpreting this Order and otherwise in relation thereto as it applies for the purpose of interpreting and in relation to Acts of the United Kingdom Parliament.

**3.**—(1) The Commissioner shall have such powers and other functions as may be conferred upon him by this Order or any other law for the time being in force in Anguilla.

(2) In the exercise of the functions conferred upon him by this Order or any other law as aforesaid the Commissioner shall act in accordance with such instructions as may from time to time be given to him by Her Majesty through a Secretary of State.

(3) The question whether the Commissioner has complied with any such instructions as aforesaid shall not be enquired into in any court of law.

**4.**—(1) The Commissioner may by regulations make provision for securing and maintaining public safety and public order in Anguilla and generally for securing and maintaining within Anguilla, as part of the Associated State, such conditions as are required in the interests of the responsibilities of Her Majesty's Government in the United Kingdom relating to defence and external affairs.

(2) Regulations under the foregoing subsection may amend, suspend or revoke any law for the time being in force in Anguilla other than the Constitution or the Courts Order.

**5.** So long as this Order is in operation and subject to any regulations made under section 4 of this Order, all laws for the time being in force in Anguilla (except the Constitution and the Courts Order) shall have effect as if any function conferred thereby upon the Governor, the Cabinet or any Minister of the Associated State were exercisable by the Commissioner to such extent as he may consider necessary for the purposes mentioned in section 4(1) of this Order.

*W. G. Agnew.*

---

## EXPLANATORY NOTE

*(This Note is not part of the Order.)*

This Order provides that a Commissioner appointed by Her Majesty may exercise certain functions in Anguilla in the interests of the responsibilities of Her Majesty's Government in the United Kingdom relating to defence and external affairs.

---

(**a**) 1889 c. 63.

## STATUTORY INSTRUMENTS

## 1969 No. 372

## POLICE

## The Police (Overseas Service) (Anguilla) Regulations 1969

| | |
|---|---|
| *Made* - - - - | 18*th March* 1969 |
| *Coming into Operation* - | 19*th March* 1969 |
| *To be laid before Parliament* | 19*th March* 1969 |

In pursuance of the powers conferred on me by section 1 of the Police (Overseas Service) Act 1945(**a**), I, the Right Honourable Michael Stewart, Her Majesty's Principal Secretary of State for Foreign and Commonwealth Affairs, hereby make the following Regulations:—

**1.** These Regulations may be cited as the Police (Overseas Service) (Anguilla) Regulations 1969, and shall come into operation on 19th March 1969.

**2.** The Anguilla Police Unit (hereinafter referred to as " the Unit ") shall consist of persons nominated by the Secretary of State to serve as members of the Unit for the purpose of performing police duties on behalf of Her Majesty's Commissioner in Anguilla.

**3.**—(1) A member of the Unit may be dismissed by the Secretary of State or required by the Secretary of State to resign, as an alternative to dismissal, if he is found guilty of serious misconduct or a serious offence against discipline: Provided that where some person authorised by the Secretary of State in that behalf exercises the powers conferred by this Regulation, an appeal against dismissal shall lie to the Secretary of State.

(2) An Appeal under this Regulation shall be brought within one month of the date of dismissal and a successful appellant shall be re-instated as a member of the Unit as from the date of that dismissal.

**4.** A member of the Unit—

(*a*) may resign subject to his giving to the Secretary of State three months' notice or such shorter period of notice as may be agreed;

(*b*) may be discharged by the Secretary of State subject to his being given three months' notice or such shorter period of notice as may be agreed.

---

(**a**) 9 & 10 Geo. 6. c. 17.

**5.** Any function conferred on the Secretary of State by these Regulations (other than the consideration of an appeal under Regulation 3 of these Regulations) may be performed by any other person or authority acting under his authorisation in that behalf.

Dated the 18th March 1969.

*Michael Stewart,*
Secretary of State for Foreign and
Commonwealth Affairs.

---

## EXPLANATORY NOTE

*(This Note is not part of the Regulations.)*

The Police (Overseas Service) Act 1945 empowers the Secretary of State to make regulations for the government and discipline of persons engaged under his control in the performance of police duties in any territory outside the United Kingdom.

The Anguilla Police Unit has been established under the control of the Secretary of State for Foreign and Commonwealth Affairs for police duties in Anguilla.

These regulations provide for the appointment, discipline, resignation and discharge of members of the Unit.

## STATUTORY INSTRUMENTS

### 1969 No. 376 (C.9)

### JUSTICES OF THE PEACE

### The Justices of the Peace Act 1968 (Commencement No. 2) Order 1969

| | |
|---|---|
| *Made* - - - - | 18*th March* 1969 |
| *Laid before Parliament* | 24*th March* 1969 |
| *Coming into Operation—* | |
| *for the purposes of Article* 3(1) | 1*st October* 1969 |
| *for all other purposes* | 1*st April* 1969 |

At the Court at Buckingham Palace, the 18th day of March 1969

Present,

The Queen's Most Excellent Majesty in Council

Her Majesty, in exercise of the powers conferred on Her by section 7 of the Justices of the Peace Act 1968(a) and of all other powers enabling Her in that behalf, is pleased, by and with the advice of Her Privy Council, to order, and it is hereby ordered, as follows:—

**1.** This Order may be cited as the Justices of the Peace Act 1968 (Commencement No. 2) Order 1969.

**2.**—(1) In this Order, unless the context otherwise requires—

"the appointed day" means 1st April 1969 except that in relation to the Staffordshire Potteries stipendiary magistrate or his district it means 1st October 1969;

"petty sessions area" has the same meaning as in the Magistrates' Courts Act 1952(b);

"probation order" means an order made or having effect as if made under section 3 of the Criminal Justice Act 1948(c);

"South Staffordshire stipendiary magistrate" means the stipendiary magistrate who, immediately before the appointed day, held office for the district comprising the county boroughs of Wolverhampton and West Bromwich and "South Staffordshire stipendiary magistrate's district" shall be construed accordingly;

"Staffordshire Potteries stipendiary magistrate" means the stipendiary magistrate who, immediately before the appointed day, held office for the district as defined in the Staffordshire Potteries Stipendiary Justice Act 1895(d) as amended by the Stoke-on-Trent Order 1964(e) and "Staffordshire Potteries stipendiary magistrate's district" shall be construed accordingly;

(a) 1968 c. 69.  (b) 1952 c. 55.
(c) 1948 c. 58.  (d) 1895 c. cvii.
(e) S.I. 1964/1113.

"Stoke-on-Trent stipendiary magistrate" means the stipendiary magistrate who, on and after the appointed day, holds office for the area consisting of the city of Stoke-on-Trent;

"supervision order" means an order made under any provision of the Children and Young Persons Act 1933(a) placing a child or young person under the supervision of a probation officer or of some other person appointed for the purpose by the court;

"Wolverhampton stipendiary magistrate" means the stipendiary magistrate who holds office, on and after the appointed day, for the area consisting of the county borough of Wolverhampton.

(2) The Interpretation Act 1889(b) applies to the interpretation of this Order as it applies to the interpretation of an Act of Parliament.

3.—(1) Section 1(8) of the Justices of the Peace Act 1968, Parts II and III of Schedule 3 to that Act and so much of Schedule 5 to that Act as is set out in the Schedule hereto shall, in so far as they relate to the Staffordshire Potteries stipendiary magistrate or his district, come into operation on 1st October 1969.

(2) Subject to paragraph (1), the said provisions shall, except in relation to the City of London, come into operation on 1st April 1969.

4. Every proceeding which before the appointed day has been begun before the South Staffordshire stipendiary magistrate or the Staffordshire Potteries stipendiary magistrate may be continued and completed in like manner and with the like incidents and consequences as nearly as may be as if this Order had not been made and as if the said stipendiary magistrates continued in office after the appointed day for the same areas for which they held office before the appointed day.

5. Any thing done by or in relation to the South Staffordshire stipendiary magistrate or his clerk as respects an offence committed within the area of the county borough of Wolverhampton or as respects a complaint arising in relation to that area shall, for the purposes of any subsequent proceedings in relation to that thing or any other thing subsequently done in relation thereto, be deemed to have been done by or in relation to the Wolverhampton stipendiary magistrate or his clerk or the magistrates' court for the county borough of Wolverhampton and any other thing done by or in relation to the first-mentioned magistrate or his clerk shall, for the purposes aforesaid, be deemed to have been done by or in relation to the magistrates' court for the county borough of West Bromwich, and, in the case of a thing in process of being done, may accordingly be continued by or in relation to the Wolverhampton stipendiary magistrate, the magistrates' court for the county borough of Wolverhampton or the magistrates' court for the county borough of West Bromwich, as the case may be.

6.—(1) Any thing done by or in relation to the Staffordshire Potteries stipendiary magistrate or his clerk as respects an offence committed in any part of the county of Stafford other than the city of Stoke-on-Trent or as respects a complaint arising in relation to that area shall, for the purposes of any subsequent proceedings in relation to that thing or any other thing subsequently done in relation thereto, be deemed to have been done by or in relation to a magistrates' court for the petty sessional division of the county of Stafford in whose area the offence was committed or in relation to whose area the complaint arose, and, in the case of a thing in process of being done, may accordingly be continued by or in relation to a magistrates' court for the said petty sessional division.

---

(a) 1933 c. 12.                   (b) 1889 c. 63.

(2) Any other thing done by or in relation to the Staffordshire Potteries stipendiary magistrate or his clerk shall, for the purposes of any subsequent proceedings in relation to that thing or any other thing subsequently done in relation thereto, be deemed to have been done by or in relation to the Stoke-on-Trent stipendiary magistrate or the magistrates' court for the city of Stoke-on-Trent, and, in the case of a thing in process of being done, may accordingly be continued by or in relation to the Stoke-on-Trent stipendiary magistrate or the magistrates' court for the city of Stoke-on-Trent.

7. Where the South Staffordshire stipendiary magistrate's district or the Staffordshire Potteries stipendiary magistrate's district is named in a probation order or supervision order—

  (i) the powers and functions of the South Staffordshire stipendiary magistrate as supervising court shall vest in and be discharged by the justices for the county borough of Wolverhampton if the person subject to the probation order or supervision order resides in the county borough of Wolverhampton;

  (ii) the powers and functions of the Staffordshire Potteries stipendiary magistrate as supervising court shall vest in and be discharged by the justices for the city of Stoke-on-Trent if the person subject to the probation order or supervision order resides in the city of Stoke-on-Trent;

  (iii) the powers and functions of the South Staffordshire stipendiary magistrate or the Staffordshire Potteries stipendiary magistrate, as the case may be, as supervising court shall vest in and be discharged by the justices for the petty sessions area in which the person subject to the probation order or supervision order resides if such person does not reside in the county borough of Wolverhampton or the city of Stoke-on-Trent;

and such orders, unless amended in regard to the district named therein, shall have effect in all respects as if the relevant area, as set out in sub-paragraphs (i) to (iii) above, were named therein.

8. Where immediately before the appointed day, a probation order or supervision order is in force and the person subject thereto is residing in an area which is no longer comprised in the district named in the order, the supervising court may amend the order as if the said person had changed his residence.

9.—(1) Any process, record or other document in the custody, by virtue of his office as such, of the clerk to the South Staffordshire stipendiary magistrate shall be transferred, if such documents relate to any matter arising in or concerning the county borough of Wolverhampton, to the clerk to the justices for the said county borough or, if such documents relate to any matter arising in or concerning the county borough of West Bromwich, to the clerk to the justices for the last-mentioned county borough.

(2) Any process, record or other document in the custody, by virtue of his office as such, of the clerk to the Staffordshire Potteries stipendiary magistrate shall be transferred to the clerk to the justices for the city of Stoke-on-Trent.

(3) Copies of or extracts from any such record or document made or certified by the clerk to the justices to whom the documents are transferred shall be of the same effect as if they had been made or certified by the clerk to the stipendiary magistrate from whom the documents are transferred.

*W. G. Agnew.*

## SCHEDULE

Article 3

EXTRACT FROM SCHEDULE 5 TO JUSTICES OF THE PEACE ACT 1968 (REPEALS)

| Chapter | Title or Short Title | Extent of Repeal |
| --- | --- | --- |
| 2 & 3 Vict. c. 15. | The Staffordshire Potteries Stipendiary Justice Act 1839. | The whole Act, so far as unrepealed. |
| 6 & 7 Vict. c. xliv. | An Act to provide for the more effectual execution of the office of the justice of the peace within the parish of Merthyr Tydfil and certain adjoining parishes. | The whole Act, so far as unrepealed. |
| 31 & 32 Vict. c. xxxvi. | An Act to extend the limits of the Act for appointing a stipendiary justice of the peace for the parish of Merthyr Tydfil and adjoining places; and for other purposes. | The whole Act, so far as unrepealed. |
| 34 & 35 Vict. c. xc. | The Staffordshire Potteries Stipendiary Justice Act 1871. | The whole Act, so far as unrepealed. |
| 41 & 42 Vict. c. lv. | The Manchester Division and Borough of Salford (Stipendiary Justices) Act 1878. | The whole Act, so far as unrepealed. |
| 57 & 58 Vict. c. xxvii. | The Merthyr Tydfil Stipendiary Justice Act 1894. | The whole Act, so far as unrepealed. |
| 58 & 59 Vict. c. cvii. | The Staffordshire Potteries Stipendiary Justice Act 1895. | The whole Act, so far as unrepealed. |
| 62 & 63 Vict. c. xc. | The South Staffordshire Stipendiary Justice Act 1899. | The whole Act, so far as unrepealed. |
| 7 Edw. 7. c. cxxviii. | The Merthyr Tydfil Stipendiary Justice Act 1907. | The whole Act, so far as unrepealed. |

| Chapter | Title or Short Title | Extent of Repeal |
| --- | --- | --- |
| 10 & 11 Geo. 5. c. lxxxvi. | The Pontypridd Stipendiary Magistrate Act 1920. | The whole Act, so far as unrepealed. |
| 11 & 12 Geo. 5. c. ciii. | The Ministry of Health Provisional Order Confirmation (Stoke-on-Trent Extension) Act 1921. | In the Schedule, Article 16. |
| 16 & 17 Geo. 5. c. cvi. | The Wolverhampton Corporation Act 1926. | Section 19. |
| 17 & 18 Geo. 5. c. lxxxvi. | The West Bromwich Corporation Act 1927. | Section 18. |
| 20 & 21 Geo. 5. c. cxx. | The West Bromwich Corporation Act 1930. | Section 20. |
| 20 & 21 Geo. 5. c. cxxv. | The Wednesbury Corporation Act 1930. | Section 23. |
| 20 & 21 Geo. 5. c. clxx. | The Walsall Corporation Act 1930. | Section 14. |
| 22 & 23 Geo. 5. c. xc. | The Wolverhampton Corporation Act 1932. | Section 15. |
| 26 Geo. 5. & 1 Edw. 8. c. cxi. | The Wolverhampton Corporation Act 1936. | Section 101, so far as unrepealed. |
| 11 & 12 Geo. 6. c. 58. | The Criminal Justice Act 1948. | Section 45(2)(c) and (3). |
| 12, 13 & 14 Geo. 6. c. 101. | The Justices of the Peace Act 1949. | In section 27(10), in paragraph (c) the words from "to a stipendiary magistrate" to "and a clerk", in paragraph (d) the words from "and" onwards, and paragraph (e). |
| | | In section 29(8), the words from "act as" to "nor". |
| | | Section 30. |
| | | Section 31(1) and (4). |
| | | Schedule 6. |
| 4 & 5 Eliz. 2. c. 34. | The Criminal Justice Administration Act 1956. | In Schedule 2, paragraph 6. |
| 10 & 11 Eliz. 2. c. 15. | The Criminal Justice Administration Act 1962. | Section 11(2). |
| 1964 c. 42. | The Administration of Justice Act 1964. | In section 27(5), the words "a clerk to a stipendiary magistrate". |

## EXPLANATORY NOTE

*(This Note is not part of the Order.)*

This Order brings into force section 1(8) of the Justices of the Peace Act 1968 (continuance in office of local Act stipendiary magistrates) and certain provisions in the Schedules to that Act and makes transitional provisions which are consequential on the alteration in areas of certain local Act stipendiary districts.

## STATUTORY INSTRUMENTS

## 1969 No. 377

## MINISTERS OF THE CROWN

### The Transfer of Functions (Refreshment House Licences) Order 1969

|  |  |
|---|---|
| *Made* - - - - | 18*th March* 1969 |
| *Laid before Parliament* | 24*th March* 1969 |
| *Coming into Operation* | 1*st April* 1969 |

At the Court at Buckingham Palace, the 18th day of March 1969

Present,

The Queen's Most Excellent Majesty in Council.

Her Majesty, in pursuance of section 1 of the Ministers of the Crown (Transfer of Functions) Act 1946(**a**) is pleased, by and with the advice of Her Privy Council, to order, and it is hereby ordered, as follows:—

*Citation, interpretation and commencement*

**1.**—(1) This Order may be cited as the Transfer of Functions (Refreshment House Licences) Order 1969.

(2) The Interpretation Act 1889(**b**) applies for the interpretation of this Order as it applies for the interpretation of an Act of Parliament.

(3) This Order shall come into operation on 1st April 1969.

*Transfer of power to vary duty on refreshment house licence*

**2.** There is hereby transferred to the Secretary of State the power of the Treasury under section 35(2) of the Local Government Act 1966(**c**) to make orders amending section 9 of the Revenue (No. 2) Act 1861(**d**).

*W. G. Agnew.*

### EXPLANATORY NOTE

(*This Note is not part of the Order.*)

This Order in Council transfers from the Treasury to the Secretary of State the power, under section 35(2) of the Local Government Act 1966, to alter the amount payable to a local authority on the grant of a licence under the Refreshment Houses Act 1860.

(**a**) 1946 c. 31.     (**b**) 1889 c. 63.     (**c**) 1966 c. 42.     (**d**) 1861 c. 91.

## STATUTORY INSTRUMENTS

## 1969 No. 378

## INCOME TAX

## The Double Taxation Relief (Air Transport Profits) (Spain) Order 1969

*Laid before the House of Commons in draft*

Made - - - 18*th March* 1969

At the Court at Buckingham Palace, the 18th day of March 1969

Present,

The Queen's Most Excellent Majesty in Council

Whereas a draft of this Order was laid before the Commons House of Parliament in accordance with the provisions of section 347(6) of the Income Tax Act 1952(**a**), and an Address has been presented to Her Majesty by that House praying that an Order may be made in the terms of this Order :

Now, therefore, Her Majesty, in exercise of the powers conferred upon Her by section 347(1) of the said Income Tax Act 1952, as amended by section 39 and section 64 of the Finance Act 1965(**b**), and of all other powers enabling Her in that behalf, is pleased, by and with the advice of Her Privy Council, to order, and it is hereby ordered, as follows :—

**1.** This Order may be cited as the Double Taxation Relief (Air Transport Profits) (Spain) Order 1969.

**2.** It is hereby declared—

(*a*) that the arrangements specified in the Schedule to this Order have been made with the Government of Spain with a view to affording relief from double taxation in relation to income tax, corporation tax, or capital gains tax and taxes of a similar character imposed by the laws of Spain ; and

(*b*) that it is expedient that those arrangements should have effect.

*W. G. Agnew.*

---

(**a**) 15 & 16 Geo. 6 & 1 Eliz. 2. c. 10.     (**b**) 1965 c. 25.

## SCHEDULE

(1) The Government of Spain shall exempt United Kingdom undertakings devoted to the business of air transport from the corporation tax, and shall exempt members of the boards of administration of the said undertakings from the taxes on the earnings of personal work, and the dividends and interest which according to Spanish law are considered to be earned in Spain, from the taxes on income from capital.

(2) The Government of the United Kingdom shall exempt from income tax, corporation tax, and capital gains tax all profits derived by Spanish undertakings from the business of air transport.

(3) The expression "the business of air transport" means the business of transporting persons, goods or mail carried on by the owner, hirer or charterer of aircraft.

(4) The expression "United Kingdom undertakings" means the Government of the United Kingdom, and corporations and partnerships constituted under the laws in force in the United Kingdom and managed and controlled in the United Kingdom.

(5) The expression "Spanish undertakings" means the Government of Spain, and corporations and partnerships constituted under the laws in force in Spain and managed and controlled in Spain.

(6) By mutual consent this Agreement shall also apply to any identical or substantially similar taxes which are imposed by either Contracting State after 21st December 1968 in addition to or in place of the existing taxes referred to above.

(7) The exemption provided for in paragraphs (1) and (2) above shall apply to all profits earned as from 1st January 1968.

(8) The Agreement may be terminated by either Contracting Government by giving six months' notice in writing to the other.

---

## EXPLANATORY NOTE

*(This Note is not part of the Order.)*

The Schedule to this Order sets out the arrangements made with Spain, in Notes exchanged between the Contracting Governments on 21st December 1968, under which air transport undertakings of one country are to be exempt from tax in the other country.

The arrangements apply to profits earned from 1st January 1968.

# STATUTORY INSTRUMENTS

## 1969 No. 379

## INCOME TAX

## The Double Taxation Relief (Taxes on Income) (Seychelles) Order 1969

*Laid before the House of Commons in draft*

*Made* - - - 18*th March* 1969

At the Court at Buckingham Palace, the 18th day of March 1969

Present,

The Queen's Most Excellent Majesty in Council

Whereas a draft of this Order was laid before the Commons House of Parliament in accordance with the provisions of section 347(6) of the Income Tax Act 1952(**a**), and an Address has been presented to Her Majesty by that House praying that an Order may be made in the terms of this Order:

Now, therefore, Her Majesty, in exercise of the powers conferred upon Her by section 347(1) of the said Income Tax Act 1952, as amended by section 64 of the Finance Act 1965(**b**), and of all other powers enabling Her in that behalf, is pleased, by and with the advice of Her Privy Council, to order, and it is hereby ordered, as follows:—

**1.** This Order may be cited as the Double Taxation Relief (Taxes on Income) (Seychelles) Order 1969.

**2.** It is hereby declared—

(*a*) that the arrangements specified in the Arrangement set out in the Schedule to this Order have been made with the Government of Seychelles with a view to affording relief from double taxation in relation to income tax or corporation tax and taxes of a similar character imposed by the laws of Seychelles varying the arrangements set out in the Schedule to the Double Taxation Relief (Taxes on Income) (Seychelles) Order 1947(**c**); and

(*b*) that it is expedient that those arrangements should have effect.

*W. G. Agnew.*

---

(a) 15 & 16 Geo. 6 & 1 Eliz. 2. c. 10.       (b) 1965 c. 25.
(c) S.R. & O. 1947/1778 (Rev. X, p. 486: 1947 I, p. 1165).

## SCHEDULE

ARRANGEMENT BETWEEN HER MAJESTY'S GOVERNMENT AND THE GOVERNMENT OF SEYCHELLES TO AMEND THE EXISTING ARRANGEMENT FOR THE AVOIDANCE OF DOUBLE TAXATION AND THE PREVENTION OF FISCAL EVASION WITH RESPECT TO TAXES ON INCOME

1. The Arrangement made in 1947 between His Majesty's Government and the Government of Seychelles for the avoidance of double taxation and the prevention of fiscal evasion with respect to taxes on income (hereinafter referred to as "the existing Arrangement") shall be amended—

(a) by the substitution for paragraph 1(1) (b) of the following—

"(b) in Seychelles:

The income tax and land sales tax (hereinafter referred to as "Colonial tax").

Provided that paragraph 3 of this Arrangement shall not apply to the land sales tax."

(b) by the addition at the end of paragraph 6 of the following new sub-paragraph—

"(3) If the recipient of a dividend is a company which owns 10 per cent. or more of the class of shares in respect of which the dividend is paid then sub-paragraph (1) shall not apply to the dividend to the extent that it can have been paid only out of profits which the company paying the dividend earned or other income which it received in a period ending twelve months or more before the relevant date. For the purposes of this sub-paragraph the term "relevant date" means the date on which the beneficial owner of the dividend became the owner of 10 per cent. or more of the class of shares in question. Provided that this sub-paragraph shall not apply if the beneficial owner of the dividend shows that the shares were acquired for *bona fide* commercial reasons and not primarily for the purpose of securing the benefit of this paragraph."; and

(c) by the substitution for sub-paragraphs (1) and (2) of paragraph 13 of the following two new sub-paragraphs—

"(1) Subject to the provisions of the law of the United Kingdom regarding the allowance as a credit against United Kingdom tax of tax payable in a territory outside the United Kingdom (which shall not affect the general principle hereof)—

(a) Colonial tax payable under the laws of the Colony and in accordance with this Arrangement, whether directly or by deduction, on profits or income from sources within the Colony shall be allowed as a credit against any United Kingdom tax computed by reference to the same profits or income by reference to which the Colonial tax is computed. Provided that in the case of a dividend the credit shall only take into account such tax in respect thereof as is additional to any tax payable by the company on the profits out of which the dividend is paid and is ultimately borne by the recipient without reference to any tax so payable.

(b) Where a company which is a resident of the Colony pays a dividend to a company resident in the United Kingdom which controls directly or indirectly at least 10 per cent. of the voting power in the first-mentioned company, the credit shall take into account (in addition to any Colonial tax for which credit may be allowed under (a) of this sub-paragraph) the Colonial tax payable by that first-mentioned company in respect of the profits out of which such dividend is paid.

(2) Subject to the provisions of the law of the Colony regarding the allowance as a credit against Colonial tax of tax payable in a territory outside the Colony (which shall not affect the general principle hereof)—

(a) United Kingdom tax payable under the laws of the United Kingdom and in accordance with this Arrangement, whether directly or by deduction, on profits or income from sources within the United Kingdom shall be allowed as a credit against any Colonial tax computed by reference to the same profits or income by reference to which the United Kingdom tax is computed. Provided that in the case of a dividend the credit shall only take into account such tax in respect thereof as is additional to any tax payable by the company on the profits out of which the dividend is paid and is ultimately borne by the recipient without reference to any tax so payable.

(b) Where a company which is a resident of the United Kingdom pays a dividend to a company resident in the Colony which controls directly or indirectly at least 10 per cent. of the voting power in the first-mentioned company, the credit shall take into account (in addition to any United Kingdom tax for which credit may be allowed under (a) of this sub-paragraph) the United Kingdom tax payable by that first-mentioned company in respect of the profits out of which such dividend is paid."

2. This Arrangement shall enter into force when the last of all such things shall have been done in the United Kingdom and the Colony as are necessary to give them the force of law in the United Kingdom and the Colony respectively and shall thereupon have effect—

(a) in the case of the new sub-paragraph (1) (b) of paragraph 1 from the date the land sales tax becomes effective;

(b) in the case of the new sub-paragraph (3) of paragraph 6 immediately;

(c) in the case of the new sub-paragraphs (1) and (2) of paragraph 13—

(i) in the United Kingdom:

(aa) as respects income tax (including surtax), for any year of assessment beginning on or after 6 April, 1968; and

(bb) as respects corporation tax, for any financial year beginning on or after 1 April, 1968;

(ii) in the Colony:
as respects income tax, for any year of assessment beginning on or after 1 January, 1969.

## EXPLANATORY NOTE

*(This Note is not part of the Order.)*

This Arrangement makes three amendments to the Arrangement between the United Kingdom and Seychelles which is scheduled to the Double Taxation Relief (Taxes on Income) (Seychelles) Order 1947.

First it provides that, in addition to income tax, "Colonial tax" shall include Seychelles land sales tax from such date as the proposed new tax becomes effective. Paragraph 3 of the 1947 Arrangement which concerns the treatment of certain trading profits will not, however, apply to the land sales tax.

Secondly, it provides that the exemption of dividends from any tax chargeable in addition to the tax on the paying company's profits is not to be allowed in certain cases where the shareholder is a company having a substantial holding in the paying company. The restriction does not apply to dividends on shares acquired for *bona fide* commercial reasons.

Thirdly, it amends paragraph 13 of the 1947 Arrangement in its application to dividends by providing that credit for tax on the profits out of which dividends are paid, whether that tax is deducted from the dividends or not, is to be given only where the recipient is a company which holds not less than 10 per cent of the voting power in the paying company. So far as United Kingdom income tax is concerned this provision takes effect from the year of assessment 1968/69.

## STATUTORY INSTRUMENTS

### 1969 No. 380

### INCOME TAX

## The Double Taxation Relief (Taxes on Income) (Swaziland) Order 1969

*Laid before the House of Commons in draft*

*Made* - - - 18th March 1969

At the Court at Buckingham Palace, the 18th day of March 1969

Present,

The Queen's Most Excellent Majesty in Council

Whereas a draft of this Order was laid before the Commons House of Parliament in accordance with the provisions of section 347(6) of the Income Tax Act 1952(**a**), and an Address has been presented to Her Majesty by that House praying that an Order may be made in the terms of this Order :

Now, therefore, Her Majesty, in exercise of the powers conferred upon Her by section 347(1) of the said Income Tax Act 1952, as amended by section 39 and section 64 of the Finance Act 1965(**b**), and of all other powers enabling Her in that behalf, is pleased, by and with the advice of Her Privy Council, to order, and it is hereby ordered, as follows :—

**1.** This Order may be cited as the Double Taxation Relief (Taxes on Income) (Swaziland) Order 1969.

**2.** It is hereby declared—

(*a*) that the arrangements specified in the Agreement set out in the Schedule to this Order have been made with the Government of the Kingdom of Swaziland with a view to affording relief from double taxation in relation to income tax, corporation tax or capital gains tax and taxes of a similar character imposed by the laws of Swaziland ; and

(*b*) that it is expedient that those arrangements should have effect.

*W. G. Agnew.*

---

(**a**) 15 & 16 Geo. 6 & 1 Eliz. 2. c. 10.    (**b**) 1965 c.25.

## SCHEDULE

AGREEMENT BETWEEN THE GOVERNMENT OF THE UNITED KINGDOM OF GREAT BRITAIN AND NORTHERN IRELAND AND THE GOVERNMENT OF THE KINGDOM OF SWAZILAND FOR THE AVOIDANCE OF DOUBLE TAXATION AND THE PREVENTION OF FISCAL EVASION WITH RESPECT TO TAXES ON INCOME

The Government of the United Kingdom of Great Britain and Northern Ireland and the Government of the Kingdom of Swaziland ;

Desiring to conclude an Agreement for the avoidance of double taxation and the prevention of fiscal evasion with respect to taxes on income ;

Have agreed as follows:

### ARTICLE 1

#### Persons Covered

This Agreement shall apply to persons who are residents of one or both of the Contracting States.

### ARTICLE 2

#### Taxes Covered

(1) The taxes which are the subject of this Agreement are—

(a) in the United Kingdom of Great Britain and Northern Ireland—
   (i) the income tax (including surtax) ;
   (ii) the corporation tax ; and
   (iii) the capital gains tax ;

(b) in Swaziland—
   (i) the normal tax ;
   (ii) the non-resident shareholders' tax ; and
   (iii) the non-residents' tax on interest.

(2) This Agreement shall also apply to any identical or substantially similar taxes which are imposed by either Contracting State after the date of signature of this Agreement in addition to, or in place of, the existing taxes. The competent authorities of the Contracting States shall notify to each other any changes which are made in their respective taxation laws.

### ARTICLE 3

#### General Definitions

(1) In this Agreement, unless the context otherwise requires—

(a) the term "United Kingdom" means Great Britain and Northern Ireland, including any area outside the territorial sea of the United Kingdom which in accordance with international law has been or may hereafter be designated, under the laws of the United Kingdom concerning the Continental Shelf, as an area within which the rights of the United Kingdom with respect to the sea-bed and sub-soil and their natural resources may be exercised ;

(b) the term "Swaziland" means the Kingdom of Swaziland ;

(c) the term "nationals" means—
   (i) in relation to the United Kingdom, all citizens of the United Kingdom and Colonies who derive their status as such from their connection with the United Kingdom and all legal persons, partnerships and associations deriving their status as such from the law in force in the United Kingdom ;
   (ii) in relation to Swaziland, all Swaziland citizens and all legal persons, partnerships and associations deriving their status as such from the law in force in Swaziland ;

(*d*) the term "United Kingdom tax" means tax imposed by the United Kingdom being tax to which this Agreement applies by virtue of Article 2 ; the term "Swaziland tax" means tax imposed by Swaziland being tax to which this Agreement applies by virtue of Article 2 ;

(*e*) the term "tax" means United Kingdom tax or Swaziland tax, as the context requires ;

(*f*) the terms "a Contracting State" and "the other Contracting State" mean the United Kingdom or Swaziland, as the context requires ;

(*g*) the term "person" comprises an individual, a company and any other body of persons ;

(*h*) the term "company" means any body corporate or any entity which is treated as a body corporate for tax purposes ;

(*i*) the terms "enterprise of a Contracting State" and "enterprise of the other Contracting State" mean respectively an enterprise carried on by a resident of a Contracting State and an enterprise carried on by a resident of the other Contracting State ;

(*j*) the term "competent authority" means, in the case of the United Kingdom the Commissioners of Inland Revenue or their authorised representative, and in the case of Swaziland, the Collector of Income Tax or his authorised representative.

(2) As regards the application of this Agreement by a Contracting State any term not otherwise defined shall, unless the context otherwise requires, have the meaning which it has under the laws of that Contracting State relating to the taxes which are the subject of this Agreement.

### ARTICLE 4
### Fiscal Domicile

(1) For the purposes of this Agreement, the term "resident of a Contracting State" means, subject to paragraphs (2) and (3) of this Article, any person who, under the law of that State, is liable to taxation therein by reason of his domicile, residence, place of management or any other criterion of a similar nature ; the term does not include any individual who is liable to tax in that Contracting State only if he derives income from sources therein. The terms "resident of the United Kingdom" and "resident of Swaziland" shall be construed accordingly.

(2) Where by reason of the provisions of paragraph (1) of this Article an individual is a resident of both Contracting States, then his status shall be determined in accordance with the following rules—

(*a*) he shall be deemed to be a resident of the Contracting State in which he has a permanent home available to him. If he has a permanent home available to him in both Contracting States, he shall be deemed to be a resident of the Contracting State with which his personal and economic relations are closest (centre of vital interests) ;

(*b*) if the Contracting State in which he has his centre of vital interests cannot be determined, or if he has not a permanent home available to him in either Contracting State, he shall be deemed to be a resident of the Contracting State in which he has an habitual abode ;

(*c*) if he has an habitual abode in both Contracting States or in neither of them, he shall be deemed to be a resident of the Contracting State of which he is a national ;

(*d*) if he is a national of both Contracting States or of neither of them, the competent authorities of the Contracting States shall settle the question by mutual agreement.

(3) Where by reason of the provisions of paragraph (1) of this Article a person other than an individual is a resident of both Contracting States, then it shall be deemed to be a resident of the Contracting State in which its place of effective management is situated.

## ARTICLE 5

### Permanent Establishment

(1) For the purposes of this Agreement, the term "permanent establishment" means a fixed place of business in which the business of the enterprise is wholly or partly carried on.

(2) The term "permanent establishment" shall include especially—

(a) a place of management ;

(b) a branch ;

(c) an office ;

(d) a factory ;

(e) a workshop ;

(f) a mine, quarry or other place of extraction of natural resources ;

(g) a building site or construction or assembly project which exists for more than twelve months.

(3) The term "permanent establishment" shall not be deemed to include—

(a) the use of facilities solely for the purpose of storage, display or delivery of goods or merchandise belonging to the enterprise ;

(b) the maintenance of a stock of goods or merchandise belonging to the enterprise solely for the purpose of storage, display or delivery ;

(c) the maintenance of a stock of goods or merchandise belonging to the enterprise solely for the purpose of processing by another enterprise ;

(d) the maintenance of a fixed place of business solely for the purpose of purchasing goods or merchandise, or for collecting information, for the enterprise ;

(e) the maintenance of a fixed place of business solely for the purpose of advertising, for the supply of information, for scientific research or for similar activities which have a preparatory or auxiliary character, for the enterprise.

(4) An enterprise of a Contracting State shall be deemed to have a permanent establishment in the other Contracting State if it carries on the activity of providing the services within that other Contracting State of public entertainers or athletes referred to in Article 15.

(5) A person acting in a Contracting State on behalf of an enterprise of the other Contracting State—other than an agent of an independent status to whom paragraph (6) of this Article applies—shall be deemed to be a permanent establishment in the first-mentioned State if he has, and habitually exercises in that State, an authority to conclude contracts in the name of the enterprise, unless his activities are limited to the purchase of goods or merchandise for the enterprise.

(6) An enterprise of a Contracting State shall not be deemed to have a permanent establishment in the other Contracting State merely because it carries on business in that other State through a broker, general commission agent or any other agent of an independent status, where such persons are acting in the ordinary course of their business.

(7) The fact that a company which is a resident of a Contracting State controls or is controlled by a company which is a resident of the other Contracting State, or which carries on business in that other State (whether through a permanent establishment or otherwise), shall not of itself constitute either company a permanent establishment of the other.

## ARTICLE 6

### Limitation of Relief

Where under any provision of this Agreement income is relieved from tax in one of the Contracting States and, under the law in force in the other Contracting State, an individual, in respect of the said income is subject to tax by reference to the amount thereof which is remitted to or received in that other Contracting State and not by reference to the full amount thereof, then the relief to be allowed under this Agreement in the first-mentioned Contracting State shall apply only to so much of the income as is remitted to or received in that other Contracting State.

## ARTICLE 7

### Income from Immovable Property

(1) Income from immovable property may be taxed in the Contracting State in which such property is situated.

(2)—(a) The term "immovable property" shall, subject to sub-paragraph (b) below, be defined in accordance with the law of the Contracting State in which the property in question is situated ;

(b) the term "immovable property" shall in any case include property accessory to immovable property, livestock and equipment used in agriculture and forestry, rights to which the provisions of general law respecting landed property apply, usufruct of immovable property and rights to variable or fixed payments as consideration for the working of, or the right to work, mineral deposits, sources and other natural resources ; ships, boats and aircraft shall not be regarded as immovable property.

(3) The provisions of paragraph (1) of this Article shall apply to income derived from the direct use, letting, or use in any other form of immovable property, including income from agricultural or forestry enterprises.

(4) The provisions of paragraphs (1) and (3) of this Article shall also apply to the income from immovable property of any enterprises other than agricultural or forestry enterprises and to income from immovable property used for the performance of professional services.

## ARTICLE 8

### Business Profits

(1) The profits of an enterprise of a Contracting State shall be taxable only in that State unless the enterprise carries on business in the other Contracting State through a permanent establishment situated therein. If the enterprise carries on business as aforesaid, the profits of the enterprise may be taxed in the other State but only so much of them as is attributable to that permanent establishment.

(2) Where an enterprise of a Contracting State carries on business in the other Contracting State through a permanent establishment situated therein, there shall in each Contracting State be attributed to that permanent establishment the profits which it might be expected to make if it were a distinct and separate enterprise engaged in the same or similar activities under the same or similar conditions and dealing at arm's length with the enterprise of which it is a permanent establishment.

(3) In the determination of the profits of a permanent establishment, there shall be allowed as deductions expenses of the enterprise (other than expenses which would not be deductible if the permanent establishment were a separate enterprise) which are incurred for the purposes of the permanent establishment, including executive and general administrative expenses so incurred, whether in the State in which the permanent establishment is situated or elsewhere.

(4) In so far as it has been customary in a Contracting State, according to its law, to determine the profits to be attributed to a permanent establishment on the basis of an apportionment of the total income of the enterprise to its various parts, nothing in paragraph (2) of this Article shall preclude that Contracting State from determining the profits to be taxed by such an apportionment as may be

customary ; the method of apportionment adopted shall, however, be such that the result shall be in accordance with the principles of this Article.

(5) No profits shall be attributed to a permanent establishment by reason of the mere purchase by that permanent establishment of goods or merchandise for the enterprise.

(6) For the purposes of the preceding paragraphs, the profits to be attributed to the permanent establishment shall be determined by the same method year by year unless there is good and sufficient reason to the contrary.

(7) Where profits include items which are dealt with separately in other Articles of this Agreement, then the provisions of those Articles shall not be affected by the provisions of this Article.

## ARTICLE 9

### Shipping and Air Transport

A resident of a Contracting State shall be exempt from tax in the other Contracting State on profits from the operation of ships or aircraft other than profits from voyages of ships or aircraft confined solely to places in the other Contracting State.

## ARTICLE 10

### Associated Enterprises

Where—

(a) an enterprise of a Contracting State participates directly or indirectly in the management, control or capital of an enterprise of the other Contracting State ; or

(b) the same persons participate directly or indirectly in the management, control or capital of an enterprise of a Contracting State and an enterprise of the other Contracting State ;

and in either case conditions are made or imposed between the two enterprises in their commercial or financial relations which differ from those which would be made between independent enterprises, then any profits which would, but for those conditions, have accrued to one of the enterprises, but, by reason of those conditions, have not so accrued, may be included in the profits of that enterprise and taxed accordingly.

## ARTICLE 11

### Dividends

(1) Dividends paid by a company being a resident of a Contracting State which are beneficially owned by a resident of the other Contracting State may be taxed in that other Contracting State.

(2) However, such dividends may also be taxed in the Contracting State of which the company paying the dividends is a resident, and according to the law of that State, but the tax so charged shall not exceed 15 per cent. of the gross amount of the dividends.

(3) The term "dividends" as used in this Article means income from shares, or other rights, not being debt-claims, participating in profits, as well as income from other corporate rights assimilated to income from shares by the taxation law of the Contracting State of which the company making the distribution is a resident and also includes any other item (other than royalties relieved from tax under Article 12 of this Agreement) which, under the law of the Contracting State of which the company paying the dividend is a resident, is treated as a dividend or distribution of a company.

(4) The provisions of paragraphs (1) and (2) of this Article shall not apply if the

beneficial owner of the dividends, being a resident of a Contracting State, has in the other Contracting State, of which the company paying the dividends is a resident, a permanent establishment and the holding by virtue of which the dividends are paid is effectively connected with a business carried on through that permanent establishment. In such a case, the provisions of Article 8 shall apply.

(5) If the beneficial owner of a dividend being a resident of a Contracting State owns 10 per cent. or more of the class of shares in respect of which the dividend is paid then the relief from tax provided for in paragraph (2) of this Article shall not apply to the dividend to the extent that it can have been paid only out of profits which the company paying the dividend earned or other income which it received in a period ending twelve months or more before the relevant date. For the purposes of this paragraph the term "relevant date" means the date on which the beneficial owner of the dividend became the owner of 10 per cent. or more of the class of shares in question. Provided that this paragraph shall not apply if the beneficial owner of the dividend shows that the shares were acquired for *bona fide* commercial reasons and not primarily for the purpose of securing the benefit of this Article.

(6) Where a company which is a resident of a Contracting State derives profits or income from the other Contracting State, that other State may not impose any tax on the dividends paid by the company and beneficially owned by persons who are not residents of that other State, or subject the company's undistributed profits to a tax on undistributed profits, even if the dividends paid or the undistributed profits consist wholly or partly of profits or income arising in that other State.

## ARTICLE 12

### Royalties

(1) Royalties derived and beneficially owned by a resident of a Contracting State shall be taxable only in that State.

(2) The term "royalties" as used in this Article means payments of any kind received as a consideration for the use of, or the right to use, any copyright of literary, artistic or scientific work (including cinematograph films, and films or tapes for radio or television broadcasting), any patent, trade mark, design or model, plan, secret formula or process, or for the use of, or the right to use, industrial, commercial or scientific equipment, or for information concerning industrial, commercial or scientific experience.

(3) The provisions of paragraph (1) of this Article shall not apply if the beneficial owner of the royalties, being a resident of a Contracting State, has in the other Contracting State a permanent establishment and the right or property giving rise to the royalties is effectively connected with a business carried on through that permanent establishment. In such a case, the provisions of Article 8 shall apply.

(4) Any provision of the law of a Contracting State which requires royalties paid by a company to be left out of account as a deduction in computing the company's taxable profits as being a distribution shall not operate in relation to royalties paid to a resident of the other Contracting State. The preceding sentence shall not however apply to royalties derived and beneficially owned by a company which is a resident of that other Contracting State where—

(a) the same persons participate directly or indirectly in the management or control of the company paying the royalties and the company beneficially owning the royalties ; and

(b) more than 50 per cent. of the voting power in the company beneficially owning the royalties is controlled directly or indirectly by a person or persons resident in the Contracting State in which the company paying the royalties is resident.

(5) Where, owing to a special relationship between the payer and the beneficial owner or between both of them and some other person, the amount of the royalties

paid, having regard to the use, right or information for which they are paid, exceeds the amount which would have been agreed upon by the payer and the beneficial owner in the absence of such relationship, the provisions of this Article shall apply only to the last-mentioned amount. In that case, the excess part of the payments shall remain taxable according to the law of each Contracting State, due regard being had to the other provisions of this Agreement.

## ARTICLE 13

### Independent Personal Services

(1) Income derived by a resident of a Contracting State in respect of professional services or other independent activities of a similar character shall be taxable only in that State unless he has a fixed base regularly available to him in the other Contracting State for the purpose of performing his activities. If he has such a fixed base, the income may be taxed in the other Contracting State but only so much of it as is attributable to that fixed base.

(2) The term "professional services" includes especially independent scientific, literary, artistic, educational or teaching activities as well as the independent activities of physicians, lawyers, engineers, architects, dentists and accountants.

## ARTICLE 14

### Employments

(1) Subject to the provisions of Articles 16, 17 and 19, salaries, wages and other similar remuneration derived by a resident of a Contracting State in respect of an employment shall be taxable only in that State unless the employment is exercised in the other Contracting State. If the employment is so exercised, such remuneration as is derived therefrom may be taxed in that other State.

(2) Notwithstanding the provisions of paragraph (1) of this Article, remuneration derived by a resident of a Contracting State in respect of an employment exercised in the other Contracting State shall be taxable only in the first-mentioned State if—

    (a) the recipient is present in the other State for a period or periods not exceeding in the aggregate 183 days in the fiscal year concerned ; and

    (b) the remuneration is paid by, or on behalf of, an employer who is not a resident of the other State ; and

    (c) the remuneration is not borne by a permanent establishment or a fixed base which the employer has in the other State.

(3) Notwithstanding the preceding provisions of this Article, remuneration in respect of an employment exercised aboard a ship or aircraft in international traffic may be taxed in the Contracting State of which the person deriving the profits from the operation of the ship or aircraft is a resident.

(4) In relation to remuneration of a director of a company derived from the company the preceding provisions of this Article shall apply as if the remuneration were remuneration of an employee in respect of an employment and as if references to "employer" were references to the company.

## ARTICLE 15

### Artistes and Athletes

Notwithstanding the provisions of Articles 13 and 14, income derived by public entertainers, such as theatre, motion picture, radio or television artistes, and musicians, and by athletes, from their personal activities as such may be taxed in the Contracting State in which those activities are exercised.

ARTICLE 16

**Pensions**

(1) Subject to the provisions of paragraph (1) of Article 17, pensions and other similar remuneration paid in consideration of past employment to a resident of a Contracting State and any annuity paid to such a resident shall be taxable only in that State.

(2) The term "annuity" means a stated sum payable periodically at stated times during life or during a specified or ascertainable period of time under an obligation to make the payments in return for adequate and full consideration in money or money's worth.

ARTICLE 17

**Governmental Functions**

(1) Remuneration, including pensions, paid by one of the Contracting Governments to any individual in respect of services rendered to that Government in the discharge of governmental functions shall be exempt from tax in the territory of the other Contracting Government, if the individual is not ordinarily resident in that other territory or (where the remuneration is not a pension) is ordinarily resident in that other territory solely for the purpose of rendering those services.

(2) The provisions of this Article shall not apply to payments in respect of services rendered in connection with any trade or business carried on by either of the Contracting Governments for purposes of profit.

ARTICLE 18

**Students**

Payments which a student or business apprentice who is or was immediately before visiting a Contracting State a resident of the other Contracting State and who is present in the first-mentioned Contracting State solely for the purpose of his education or training receives for the purpose of his maintenance, education or training shall not be taxed in the first-mentioned State, provided that such payments are made to him from sources outside that State.

ARTICLE 19

**Teachers**

A professor or teacher who visits a Contracting State for a period not exceeding two years for the purpose of teaching at a university, college, school or other educational institution in that Contracting State and who is, or was immediately before that visit, a resident of the other Contracting State shall be exempt from tax in the first-mentioned Contracting State on any remuneration for such teaching in respect of which he is subject to tax in the other Contracting State.

ARTICLE 20

**Income not Expressly Mentioned**

Items of income of a resident of a Contracting State being income of a class or from sources not expressly mentioned in the foregoing Articles of this Agreement shall be taxable only in that State. Provided that this Article shall not apply to interest derived by a resident of one of the Contracting States from sources in the other Contracting State.

ARTICLE 21

**Elimination of Double Taxation**

(1) Subject to the provisions of the law of the United Kingdom regarding the allowance as a credit against United Kingdom tax of tax payable in a territory

outside the United Kingdom (which shall not affect the general principle hereof)—

(a) Swaziland tax payable under the laws of Swaziland and in accordance with this Agreement, whether directly or by deduction, on profits, income or chargeable gains from sources within Swaziland (excluding in the case of a dividend, tax payable in respect of the profits out of which the dividend is paid) shall be allowed as a credit against any United Kingdom tax computed by reference to the same profits, income or chargeable gains by reference to which the Swaziland tax is computed ;

(b) in the case of a dividend paid by a company which is a resident of Swaziland to a company which is a resident of the United Kingdom and which controls directly or indirectly at least 10 per cent. of the voting power in the company paying the dividend, the credit shall take into account (in addition to any Swaziland tax creditable under sub-paragraph (a) of this paragraph) the Swaziland tax payable by the company in respect of the profits out of which such dividend is paid.

(2) Where United Kingdom tax is payable under the laws of the United Kingdom and in accordance with this Agreement, whether directly or by deduction, in respect of profits, income or chargeable gains derived from sources within the United Kingdom by a resident of Swaziland, and that tax is borne by him, Swaziland shall either impose no tax on such profits, income or chargeable gains or, subject to such provisions (which shall not affect the general principle hereof) as may be enacted in Swaziland, shall allow the United Kingdom tax as a credit against any Swaziland tax payable in respect of such profits, income or chargeable gains. Where such income is a dividend paid by a company which is a resident of the United Kingdom to a company which is a resident of Swaziland and which controls directly or indirectly at least 10 per cent. of the voting power in the United Kingdom company, any such credit shall take into account (in addition to any United Kingdom tax creditable under the preceding provisions of this paragraph) the United Kingdom tax payable by the company in respect of the profits out of which such dividend is paid.

(3) For the purposes of paragraphs (1) and (2) of this Article income, profits and capital gains owned by a resident of a Contracting State which may be taxed in the other Contracting State in accordance with this Agreement shall be deemed to arise from sources in that other State.

(4) Where profits on which an enterprise of a Contracting State has been charged to tax in that State are also included in the profits of an enterprise of the other Contracting State and the profits so included are profits which would have accrued to that enterprise of the other Contracting State if the conditions made between the enterprises had been those which would have been made between independent enterprises dealing at arm's length, the amount included in the profits of both enterprises shall be treated for the purposes of this Article as income from a source in the other Contracting State of the enterprise of the first-mentioned State and relief shall be given accordingly under paragraph (1) or paragraph (2) of this Article.

## ARTICLE 22
### Personal Allowances

(1) Individuals who are residents of Swaziland shall be entitled to the same personal allowances, reliefs and reductions for the purposes of United Kingdom tax as British subjects not resident in the United Kingdom.

(2) Individuals who are residents of the United Kingdom shall be entitled to the same personal allowances, reliefs and reductions for the purposes of Swaziland tax as those to which Swaziland citizens not resident in Swaziland may be entitled.

## ARTICLE 23
### Non-discrimination

(1) The nationals of a Contracting State shall not be subjected in the other

Contracting State to any taxation or any requirement connected therewith which is other or more burdensome than the taxation and connected requirements to which nationals of that other State in the same circumstances are or may be subjected.

(2) The taxation on a permanent establishment which an enterprise of a Contracting State has in the other Contracting State shall not be less favourably levied in that other State than the taxation levied on enterprises of that other State carrying on the same activities.

(3) Enterprises of a Contracting State, the capital of which is wholly or partly owned or controlled, directly or indirectly, by one or more residents of the other Contracting State, shall not be subjected in the first-mentioned Contracting State to any taxation or any requirement connected therewith which is other or more burdensome than the taxation and connected requirements to which other similar enterprises of that first-mentioned State are or may be subjected.

(4) Nothing contained in this Article shall be construed as obliging either Contracting State to grant to individuals not resident in that State any of the personal allowances, reliefs and reductions for tax purposes which are granted to individuals so resident, nor as conferring any exemption from tax in a Contracting State in respect of dividends paid to a company which is a resident of the other Contracting State.

(5) In this Article the term "taxation" means the taxes which are the subject of this Agreement.

## ARTICLE 24

### Mutual Agreement Procedure

(1) Where a resident of a Contracting State considers that the actions of one or both of the Contracting States result or will result for him in taxation not in accordance with this Agreement, he may, notwithstanding the remedies provided by the national laws of those States, present his case to the competent authority of the Contracting State of which he is a resident.

(2) The competent authority shall endeavour, if the objection appears to it to be justified and if it is not itself able to arrive at an appropriate solution, to resolve the case by mutual agreement with the competent authority of the other Contracting State, with a view to the avoidance of taxation not in accordance with the Agreement.

(3) The competent authorities of the Contracting States shall endeavour to resolve by mutual agreement any difficulties or doubts arising as to the interpretation or application of the Agreement.

(4) The competent authorities of the Contracting States may communicate with each other directly for the purpose of reaching an agreement in the sense of the preceding paragraphs.

## ARTICLE 25

### Exchange of Information

The competent authorities of the Contracting States shall exchange such information (being information which is at their disposal under their respective taxation laws in the normal course of administration) as is necessary for carrying out the provisions of this Agreement or for the prevention of fraud or the administration of statutory provisions against legal avoidance in relation to the taxes which are the subject of this Agreement. Any information so exchanged shall be treated as secret but may be disclosed to persons (including a court or administrative body) concerned with assessment, collection, enforcement or prosecution in respect of taxes which are the subject of this Agreement. No information shall be exchanged which would disclose any trade, business, industrial or professional secret or any trade process.

## Article 26

### Territorial Extension

(1) This Agreement may be extended, either in its entirety or with modifications, to any territory for whose international relations the United Kingdom is responsible and which imposes taxes substantially similar in character to those to which this Agreement applies. Any such extension shall take effect from such date and subject to such modifications and conditions, including conditions as to termination, as may be specified and agreed between the Contracting States in letters to be exchanged through diplomatic channels.

(2) Unless otherwise agreed by both Contracting States, the termination of this Agreement shall terminate the application of this Agreement to any territory to which it has been extended under this Article.

## Article 27

### Entry into Force

(1) This Agreement shall come into force on the date when the last of all such things shall have been done in the United Kingdom and Swaziland as are necessary to give the Agreement the force of law in the United Kingdom and Swaziland respectively, and shall thereupon have effect—

    (a) in the United Kingdom—

        (i) as respects income tax (including surtax) and capital gains tax, for any year of assessment beginning on or after 6 April, 1968 ; and

        (ii) as respects corporation tax, for any financial year beginning on or after 1 April, 1968 ;

    (b) in Swaziland—

        (i) as respects normal tax, for any year of assessment ending after 30 June, 1968 ;

        (ii) as respects non-resident shareholders' tax on dividends declared after 30 June, 1968 ; and

        (iii) as respects non-residents' tax on interest, on interest payable after 30 June, 1968.

(2) Subject to paragraphs (3) and (4) of this Article the Arrangement for the avoidance of double taxation and the prevention of fiscal evasion with respect to taxes on income which was made in 1949(a) between the Government of the United Kingdom of Great Britain and Northern Ireland and the Government of Swaziland shall cease to have effect as respects taxes to which this Agreement in accordance with paragraph (1) of this Article applies.

(3) Subject to paragraph (4) of this Article, where any provision of the Arrangement referred to in paragraph (2) of this Article would have afforded any greater relief from tax any such provision as aforesaid shall continue to have effect for any year of assessment or financial year beginning before the entry into force of this Agreement.

(4) Where any greater relief from Swaziland tax would have been afforded by sub-paragraph (1) of paragraph 6 of the Arrangement referred to in paragraph (2) of this Article than is afforded by Article 11 of this Agreement, the aforesaid sub-paragraph (1) of paragraph 6 shall continue to have effect in respect of dividends declared on or before the day following the date of signature of this Agreement.

(5) The Arrangement referred to in paragraph (2) of this Article shall terminate on the last date on which it has effect in accordance with the foregoing provisions of this Article.

---

(a) S.I. 1949/2199 (1949 I, p. 2309).

ARTICLE 28

**Termination**

This Agreement shall remain in force until denounced by one of the Governments. Either Government may denounce the Agreement, through diplomatic channels, by giving notice of termination at least six months before the end of any calendar year after the year 1971. In such event, the Agreement shall cease to have effect—

(a) in the United Kingdom—
  (i) as respects income tax (including surtax) and capital gains tax, for any year of assessment beginning on or after 6 April in the calendar year next following that in which the notice is given ; and
  (ii) as respects corporation tax, for any financial year beginning on or after 1 April in the calendar year next following that in which the notice is given ;

(b) in Swaziland—
  (i) as respects taxes on income, for any year of assessment ending after 30 June in the calendar year next following that in which the notice is given ;
  (ii) as respects non-resident shareholders' tax, on dividends declared after 30 June in the calendar year next following that in which the notice is given ; and
  (iii) as respects non-residents' tax on interest, on interest payable after 30 June in the calendar year next following that in which the notice is given.

IN WITNESS WHEREOF the undersigned, duly authorised thereto, have signed this Agreement.

DONE in duplicate at London this 26th day of November 1968.

For the Government of
the United Kingdom of
Great Britain and
Northern Ireland:
  MAURICE FOLEY

For the Government of the
Kingdom of Swaziland:
  L. LOVELL

---

# EXPLANATORY NOTE

*(This Note is not part of the Order.)*

The Agreement with Swaziland scheduled to this Order replaces the Arrangement made in 1949. As in the earlier Arrangement, shipping and air transport profits, certain trading profits not arising through a permanent establishment, royalties, pensions (other than Government pensions), purchased annuities and earnings of temporary business visitors are (subject to certain conditions) to be taxed only in the country of the taxpayer's residence. Government salaries are to be taxed in general by the paying Government only. Remuneration of visiting professors and teachers and payments made for the maintenance of visiting students are (subject to certain conditions) to be exempt in the country visited.

There are a number of new or substantially different provisions. Dividends may now be taxed in the country of which the paying company is a resident, but subject to a maximum of 15 per cent of the gross amount of the dividends. Where income is taxable in both countries, credit continues to be given by the country of the taxpayer's residence for the tax payable in the country of origin of the income, but in the case of dividends credit for the tax on the profits out of which the dividends are paid is to be given only where the recipient of the dividends is a company which holds not less than 10 per cent of the voting power in the paying company. Residents of Swaziland are to be entitled to the same personal allowances and reliefs for United Kingdom tax purposes as British subjects not resident in the United Kingdom, and residents of the United Kingdom to the same personal allowances and reliefs for Swaziland tax purposes as Swaziland citizens not resident in Swaziland.

In addition to a provision for exchange of information between the tax authorities of the two countries, which is similar to that in the earlier Arrangement, the Agreement includes provisions for consultation between those authorities to implement the provisions of the Agreement. There is also a new provision safeguarding residents and enterprises of one country against discriminatory taxation in the other country.

The Agreement is in general to take effect in the United Kingdom for 1968/69 and subsequent years.

## STATUTORY INSTRUMENTS

### 1969 No. 383

## MINISTERS OF THE CROWN

## The Transfer of Functions (Scottish Royal Parks and Ancient Monuments) Order 1969

| | | |
|---|---|---|
| *Made* - - - | | *18th March* 1969 |
| *Laid before Parliament* | | *24th March* 1969 |
| *Coming into Operation* | | *1st April* 1969 |

At the Court at Buckingham Palace, the 18th day of March 1969

Present,

The Queen's Most Excellent Majesty in Council

Her Majesty, in pursuance of the Ministers of the Crown (Transfer of Functions) Act 1946(a), is pleased, by and with the advice of Her Privy Council, to order, and it is hereby ordered, as follows :—

*Citation, interpretation and commencement*

**1.**—(1) This Order may be cited as the Transfer of Functions (Scottish Royal Parks and Ancient Monuments) Order 1969.

(2) The Interpretation Act 1889(b) applies for the interpretation of this Order as it applies for the interpretation of an Act of Parliament.

(3) In this Order the following expressions shall have the meanings hereby respectively assigned to them, that is to say—

"instrument" (without prejudice to the generality of that expression) includes in particular an Order in Council, order, rule, regulation, byelaw, judgment, decree, award, contract, agreement, scheme, certificate, licence or other document, and "made" in relation to an instrument shall be construed accordingly ;

"the Minister" means the Minister of Public Building and Works.

(4) Any reference in this Order to an enactment or instrument shall be construed as a reference thereto as amended by or under any other enactment or instrument.

(5) This Order shall come into operation on 1st April 1969.

---

(a) 1946 c. 31.                         (b) 1889 c.63.

*Transfer of functions*

**2.** The functions of the Minister under the enactments described in Part I of the Schedule to this Order in so far as conferred by those enactments in relation to the parks described in Part II of the said Schedule are hereby transferred to the Secretary of State.

**3.**—(1) The functions of the Minister under the Ancient Monuments Acts 1913 to 1953(**a**) (except section 16 of the Ancient Monuments Consolidation and Amendment Act 1913) together with—

(*a*) his functions under subsections (2) to (5) of section 5 and section 7 of the Historic Buildings and Ancient Monuments Act 1953 so far as relating to buildings mentioned in paragraph (*b*) of subsection (2) of section 5, and his functions under section 8 of that Act so far as relating to the upkeep of buildings mentioned in paragraph (*c*) of subsection (1) of section 8 (with or without other property), and

(*b*) his functions under section 9 of the Coal-Mining (Subsidence) Act 1957(**b**), and

(*c*) his functions under paragraph 12 of the First Schedule to the Acquisition of Land (Authorisation Procedure) (Scotland) Act 1947(**c**)

are in relation to Scotland hereby transferred to the Secretary of State.

(2) Accordingly (without prejudice to Article 5) in the following enactments that is to say (*a*) subsection (2) of section 34 of the Finance Act 1956(**d**) and (*b*) subsection (8) of section 7 of the Mines (Working Facilities and Support) Act 1966(**e**), any reference to the Minister (including any reference which is to be construed as such a reference) shall include a reference to the Secretary of State.

*Transfer of property etc.*

**4.** With the functions transferred under the foregoing provisions of this Order there are also hereby transferred to the Secretary of State for Scotland all property, rights and liabilities to which the Minister is entitled or subject at the coming into operation of this Order in connection only with those functions.

*Supplementary and consequential provisions*

**5.**—(1) Any enactment or instrument shall have effect, so far as may be necessary for or in consequence of the transfers effected by this Order as if references to, or which are to be construed as references to, the Minister were references to the Secretary of State.

(2) This Order shall not affect the validity of anything done in the exercise of powers transferred by this Order by or in relation to the Minister before the coming into operation of this Order ; and anything which at the time of the coming into operation of this Order, is in process of being done by or in relation to the Minister as aforesaid may be continued by or in relation to the Secretary of State.

---

(a) 1913 c. 32; 1931 c. 16; 1953 c. 49.
(b) 1957 c. 59.   (c) 1947 c. 42.
(d) 1956 c. 54.   (e) 1966 c. 4.

(3) Any approval, authority, notice or licence given, scheme prepared or confirmed, order made or other thing done by the Minister in the exercise of the powers transferred by this Order shall, if in force at the time of the coming into operation of this Order, continue in force as if given or done by the Secretary of State.

*W. G. Agnew.*

SCHEDULE      *Article* 2

PART I

The Crown Lands Act 1851 (1851 c. 42)

The Parks Regulation Act 1872 (1872 c. 15)

The Works and Public Buildings Act 1874 (1874 c. 84)

Universities (Scotland) Act 1889 (1889 c. 55)

The Parks Regulation (Amendment) Act 1926 (1926 c. 36)

PART II

Holyrood Park

The Peel or Park and Loch of Linlithgow

Royal Botanic Garden, Edinburgh

EXPLANATORY NOTE

(*This Note is not part of the Order.*)

Under this Order the functions of the Minister of Public Building and Works, in so far as they relate to Royal Parks and Ancient Monuments in Scotland, are transferred to the Secretary of State for Scotland.

# STATUTORY INSTRUMENTS

## 1969 No. 384

## SOCIAL SECURITY

## The Family Allowances, National Insurance and Industrial Injuries (Switzerland) Order 1969

*Made - - - -* 18*th March* 1969

At the Court at Buckingham Palace, the 18th day of March 1969

Present,

The Queen's Most Excellent Majesty in Council

Whereas at Berne on 21st February 1968, a Convention on social security between the Government of the United Kingdom of Great Britain and Northern Ireland and the Swiss Federal Council (which Convention is set out in Schedule I to this Order and is hereinafter referred to as "the Convention") was signed on behalf of the said Government and Council:

And Whereas by Article 26 of the Convention it is provided that the Convention shall enter into force on the first day of the second month following the month in which the instruments of ratification are exchanged:

And Whereas the said instruments of ratification were exchanged on 19th February 1969 and, accordingly, the Convention enters into force on 1st April 1969:

And Whereas by section 105(1) of the National Insurance Act 1965(a), as extended by section 22(1) of the Family Allowances Act 1965(b), and section 84(1) of the National Insurance (Industrial Injuries) Act 1965(c), it is provided that Her Majesty may, by Order in Council, make provision for modifying or adapting the said Acts of 1965 in their application to cases affected by agreements with other governments providing for reciprocity in matters specified in those sections:

Now, therefore, Her Majesty, in pursuance of the said section 105(1), as so extended, and the said section 84(1), and of all other powers enabling Her in that behalf, is pleased, by and with the advice of Her Privy Council, to order, and it is hereby ordered, as follows:—

*Citation and interpretation*

**1.**—(1) This Order may be cited as the Family Allowances, National Insurance and Industrial Injuries (Switzerland) Order 1969.

(2) The rules for the construction of Acts of Parliament contained in the Interpretation Act 1889(d) shall apply in relation to this Order and in relation to the Orders revoked by it as if this Order and the Orders revoked by it were Acts of Parliament, and as if each revocation were a repeal.

(a) 1965 c. 51.    (b) 1965 c. 53.
(c) 1965 c. 52.    (d) 1889 c. 63.

*Modification of Acts*

**2.** The provisions contained in the Convention shall have full force and effect, so far as the same relate to England, Wales and Scotland and provide by way of agreement with the Swiss Federal Council for reciprocity with the said Council in any matters specified in either section 105(1) of the National Insurance Act 1965, as extended by section 22(1) of the Family Allowances Act 1965, or section 84(1) of the National Insurance (Industrial Injuries) Act 1965; and the Family Allowances Acts 1965 to 1969, the National Insurance Acts 1965 to 1969 and the National Insurance (Industrial Injuries) Acts 1965 to 1969, shall have effect subject to such modifications as may be required therein for the purpose of giving effect to any such provisions.

*Revocation of Orders*

**3.** The Orders specified in Schedule 2 to this Order are hereby revoked.

*W. G. Agnew.*

---

## SCHEDULE I

### CONVENTION
### ON SOCIAL SECURITY BETWEEN THE UNITED KINGDOM OF GREAT BRITAIN AND NORTHERN IRELAND AND SWITZERLAND

The Government of the United Kingdom of Great Britain and Northern Ireland and the Swiss Federal Council,

HAVING established reciprocal arrangements in the field of social security by means of the Conventions which were signed on their behalf at Berne on the 16th January 1953(a) and the 12th November 1959(b), respectively,

DESIRING to widen the scope of those arrangements and, in particular, to give more complete effect to the principal that nationals of the two Contracting Parties should receive equal treatment under the social insurance legislation of each Party,

HAVE AGREED as follows:—

### PART I

#### Definitions and Legislation

##### ARTICLE 1

For the purpose of the present Convention—

(a) "territory" means, in relation to the United Kingdom, England, Scotland, Wales, Northern Ireland, the Isle of Man, Jersey, Guernsey, Alderney, Herm and Jethou, and, in relation to Switzerland, the territory of the Swiss Confederation;

(b) "national" means, in relation to the United Kingdom, a citizen of the United Kingdom and Colonies, and, in relation to Switzerland, a person having Swiss nationality;

(c) "legislation" means, according to the context, the laws and regulations of one or the other Contracting Party which are mentioned in Article 2 of the Convention;

(d) "Swiss pensions insurance" means Swiss legislation on old age and survivors' insurance and invalidity insurance;

(e) "Swiss accident insurance" means Swiss legislation on accident insurance;

(a) "Treaty Series No. 36 (1954)", Cmnd. 9157.
(b) "Treaty Series No. 43 (1960)", Cmnd. 1108.

(*f*) "competent authority" means, in relation to the United Kingdom, the Minister of Social Security, the Ministry of Health and Social Services for Northern Ireland, the Isle of Man Board of Social Services, the Social Security Committee of the States of Jersey or the States Insurance Authority of Guernsey, as the case may require, and in relation to Switzerland, the Federal Office of Social Insurance;

(*g*) "social insurance authority" means, in relation to the United Kingdom, the competent authority of the United Kingdom, and, in relation to Switzerland, the appropriate compensation fund for old age and survivors' insurance or the Swiss National Institute for Accident Insurance, as the case may require;

(*h*) "Swiss sickness insurance fund" means an institute approved by the Swiss competent authority under the Federal Sickness and Accidents Insurance Act of the 13th June 1911;

(*i*) "the former Conventions" means the Convention on Social Insurance and the Supplementary Convention on Social Insurance which were signed on behalf of the Contracting Parties at Berne on the 16th January 1953 and the 12th November 1959, respectively;

(*j*) "employed person" means a person who comes within the definition of an employed person or a person who is treated as an employed person in the legislation which is being applied; "employment" means employment as an employed person, and the words "employ" and "employer" refer to such employment;

(*k*) "contribution period" means, in relation to the United Kingdom, a period for which contributions appropriate to the benefit in question have been paid under the legislation of the United Kingdom, and, in relation to Switzerland, a period during which contributions have been paid under Swiss pensions insurance or a period which is treated as such period under that insurance;

(*l*) "equivalent period" means a period for which contributions appropriate to the benefit in question have been credited under the legislation of the United Kingdom;

(*m*) "benefit" and "pension" mean, according to the context, any benefit or pension provided under the legislation of one or the other Party, other than a family allowance, and include any increase in the benefit or pension and any additional allowances payable therewith under that legislation;

(*n*) "period of interruption of employment" has the meaning assigned to it in the legislation of the United Kingdom;

(*o*) other words and expressions have the meanings respectively assigned to them in the legislation of the United Kingdom or Switzerland, as the case may require.

## ARTICLE 2

(1) The present Convention shall apply—

    (*a*) in relation to the United Kindom, to—

        (i) the National Insurance Act 1965, the National Insurance Act (Northern Ireland) 1966, the National Insurance (Isle of Man) Act 1948, and the legislation which was consolidated by, or repealed by legislation consolidated by, those Acts;

        (ii) the National Insurance (Industrial Injuries) Act 1965, the National Insurance (Industrial Injuries) Act (Northern Ireland) 1966, and the National Insurance (Industrial Injuries) (Isle of Man) Act 1948;

        (iii) the Insular Insurance (Jersey) Law 1950;

(iv) the Social Insurance (Guernsey) Law 1964 and the legislation repealed by that Law;

(v) the Family Allowances Act 1965, the Family Allowances Act (Northern Ireland) 1966, the Family Allowances (Isle of Man) Act 1945, the Family Allowances (Guernsey) Law 1950, and the Family Allowances (Jersey) Law 1951.

(b) in relation to Switzerland to—

(i) the Federal Old Age and Survivors' Insurance Act of the 20th December 1946;

(ii) the Federal Invalidity Insurance Act of the 19th June 1959;

(iii) the Federal Act on Family Allowances for Agricultural Workers and Small Farmers of the 20th June 1952;

(iv) the Federal Sickness and Accidents Insurance Act of the 13th June 1911; provided that none of the Articles of Parts II, III and IV of the Convention, except Article II, shall apply to Part I of the last-mentioned Act (which Part concerns sickness insurance).

(2) Subject to the provisions of paragraph (3) of this Article, the Convention shall apply also to any law or regulation which amends, supplements or consolidates the legislation specified in paragraph (1) of this Article.

(3) The Convention shall apply, only if the Contracting Parties so decide, to laws and regulations which amend the legislation specified in paragraph (1) of this Article for the purpose of giving effect to a reciprocal agreement on social security with a third Party.

# PART II

### Provisions concerning Equality of Treatment

#### ARTICLE 3

(1) Subject to the provisions of the present Convention, a national of one Contracting Party shall be entitled to enjoy the advantages, and shall be subject to the obligations, of the legislation of the other Party, under the same conditions as a national of the latter Party.

(2) Where a person, not being a national of either Party, has claimed, by virtue of the contributions of a national of either Party or in respect of the death of a national of either Party, any benefit under the legislation of either Party, other than a special pension under Swiss pensions insurance, any provision of the Convention which applies to nationals of either Party shall apply also to him in relation to his claim.

(3) Paragraph (1) of this Article shall not apply to those provisions of Swiss legislation which concern emergency allowances for Swiss invalids resident abroad, the Swiss pensions insurance of Swiss nationals working abroad in the service of employers in Switzerland, or the voluntary Swiss pensions insurance of Swiss nationals resident abroad.

#### ARTICLE 4

No provision of any of the Articles 3, 9, 11 and 16 of the present Convention shall be construed as affecting any provision of the legislation of either Contracting Party which is more favourable to the person concerned.

## PART III

### Provisions concerning Contributions

#### ARTICLE 5

(1) Subject to the provisions of paragraphs (3), (5) and (6) of this Article and of Articles 6 and 7 of the present Convention, where a national of either Contracting Party is gainfully occupied in the territory of one Party, either as an employed person or otherwise, the legislation of that Party shall apply to him, and, for the purpose of calculating any contributions payable under that legislation, no account shall be taken of any income he may receive from a gainful occupation in the territory of the other Party.

(2) Where a national of one Party is ordinarily resident in the territory of the other Party and not gainfully occupied in the territory of either Party, the legislation of the latter Party shall apply to him.

(3) Where a person, in the service of an employer having a place of business in the territory of one Party, is sent by that employer to the territory of the other Party immediately after a contribution period or equivalent period under the legislation of the former Party, that legislation shall continue to apply to him as if he were employed in the territory of the former Party, provided that his employment in the territory of the latter Party is not expected to last for more than twenty-four months or such longer period as may be agreed by the competent authorities of the two Parties in any particular case; and no contributions shall be payable in respect of his employment under the legislation of the latter Party.

(4) Where a national of Switzerland is employed as a member of the crew of a British ship or vessel which is registered in the United Kingdom or of which the owner is resident in the United Kingdom, the legislation of the United Kingdom shall apply to him as if he were domiciled or had a place of residence in the United Kingdom.

(5) (a) Subject to the provisions of sub-paragraph (b) of this paragraph, where a person, ordinarily resident in the territory of either Party, is employed as a member of the crew of an aircraft registered in the United Kingdom, the legislation of the United Kingdom shall apply to him as if any conditions relating to residence or domicile in the United Kingdom were satisfied in his case.

(b) Where a person is employed as a member of the crew of an aircraft which is managed by an air transport undertaking whose principal place of business is in Switzerland, Swiss legislation shall apply to him unless he is in the service of an undertaking whose principal place of business is in the United Kingdom.

(c) Where a person, to whom none of the provisions of sub-paragraphs (a) and (b) of this paragraph apply, is in the service of an air transport undertaking whose principal place of business is in the territory of one Party and is sent by that undertaking to the territory of the other Party immediately after a contribution period or equivalent period under the legislation of the former Party, that legislation shall continue to apply to him as if he were employed in the territory of the former Party.

(6) Subject to the provisions of sub-paragraph (b) of paragraph (5) of this Article, where a person, ordinarily resident in the United Kingdom and in the service of a person or undertaking having a place of business there, is employed on board an aircraft which is owned by a person or undertaking whose principal place of business is in Switzerland, the legislation of the United Kingdom shall apply to him as if the aircraft were registered in the United Kingdom.

ARTICLE 6

(1) The provisions of this Part of the present Convention shall not apply—

    (*a*) in relation to the United Kingdom, to established members of the Diplomatic Service; and

    (*b*) in relation to Switzerland, to established members of the Diplomatic or Consular Service.

(2) Subject to the provisions of paragraph (1) of this Article, where a national of one Contracting Party, in the government service of that Party, is sent to the territory of the other Party, the legislation of the former Party shall apply to him as if he were employed in its territory.

(3) Subject to the provisions of paragraph (1) of this Article, where a national of one Party is engaged in the territory of the other Party for employment in that territory in the government service of the former Party, the legislation of the latter Party shall apply to him unless, within three months after his engagement, he chooses that the legislation of the former Party shall apply to him.

(4) Where a national of one Party is employed in the territory of the other Party in the private service of a national of the former Party who is employed in its government service, the provisions of paragraphs (2) and (3) of this Article shall apply to him in the same way as they apply to a national of the former Party who is employed in its government service.

(5) Where a person who is not a national of either Party is employed in Switzerland in the private service of a national of the United Kingdom who is employed in the government service of the United Kingdom, the legislation of Switzerland shall apply to him unless, within three months after that employment in Switzerland begins, he chooses that the legislation of the United Kingdom shall apply to him.

(6) The competent authorities may provide by agreement that, where a national of either Party is employed by a public corporation or official body of one Party in the territory of the other Party, the legislation of the former Party shall apply to him as if he were employed in its territory.

ARTICLE 7

The competent authorities of the two Contracting Parties may, by agreement with one another, modify the provisions of Articles 5 and 6 of the present Convention in relation to particular persons or classes of persons where this is in the interest of those persons or classes of persons.

ARTICLE 8

Where a person is ordinarily resident in the territory of the United Kingdom or has, since his last arrival in that territory, become liable to pay contributions under the legislation of the United Kingdom as an employed person or as a self-employed person and applies, on grounds of incapacity for work, confinement or unemployment, for exception from liability to pay contributions for any period, and for contributions to be credited to him for that period, then, for the purpose of that application—

    (*a*) any period during which he was employed in Switzerland shall be treated as a period during which he was employed in the United Kingdom and for which he paid contributions as an employed person under the legislation of the United Kingdom;

    (*b*) any period during which he was gainfully occupied on his own account in Switzerland shall be treated as a period during which he was self-employed in the United Kingdom and for which he paid contributions as a self-employed person under the legislation of the United Kingdom.

## PART IV

### Provisions concerning Benefit

*Benefits for employed persons sent from one country to the other*

#### ARTICLE 9

(1) Where a person is employed in the United Kingdom, and Swiss legislation applies to him in accordance with the provisions of the present Convention, he shall be treated, for the purpose of any right to receive benefit under that legislation for an accident, industrial accident or industrial disease, as if the accident or industrial accident had occurred or the disease had been contracted in Switzerland.

(2) Where a person is employed in Switzerland, and the legislation of the United Kingdom applies to him in accordance with the provisions of the present Convention, he shall be treated—

(a) for the purpose of any right to receive sickness or maternity benefit under that legislation, as if he were in the United Kingdom;

(b) for the purpose of any right to receive benefit under that legislation for an industrial accident occurring or an industrial disease contracted in the course of that employment, as if the accident had occurred or the disease had been contracted in the United Kingdom.

(3) If an accident happens to an insured person after he leaves the territory of one Contracting Party to go, in the course of his employment, to the territory of the other Party, and before he arrives in the latter territory, and the legislation of the United Kingdom was expected to apply to him in the latter territory, then, for the purpose of any claim to receive benefit in respect of that accident under that legislation—

(a) the accident shall be treated as if it had happened in the United Kingdom; and

(b) his absence from the territory of either Party shall be disregarded in determining whether his employment was insurable under that legislation.

### Family Allowances

#### ARTICLE 10

For the purpose of any condition requiring persons who claim family allowances under the legislation of the United Kingdom to have been in the United Kingdom for a prescribed period, a national of either Contracting Party, who is ordinarily resident in the United Kingdom or is required to pay contributions under that legislation as an employed or self-employed person shall, be treated—

(a) as if his place of birth were in the United Kingdom, if it is in Switzerland;

(b) as if he had been in the United Kingdom during any period during which he was in Switzerland.

### Sickness Benefit in case of transfer from one country to the other

#### ARTICLE 11

(1) The Swiss competent authority shall designate those Swiss sickness insurance funds which have undertaken responsibility for giving effect to the provisions of paragraphs (2) and (3) of this Article.

(2) Where a national of either Contracting Party—

(a) has paid contributions under the legislation of the United Kingdom or had contributions credited to him under that legislation or is entitled to a retirement pension or widow's benefit under that legislation, and furnishes evidence of this; and

(b) applies for membership of a Swiss sickness insurance fund designated in accordance with the provisions of paragraph (1) of this Article within three months—

    (i) of the end of the week for which his last contribution was paid or credited; or

    (ii) of his departure from the United Kingdom if he is entitled to one of the benefits mentioned in sub-paragraph (a) of this paragraph;

he shall be treated as if he satisfied any condition concerning age which that fund imposes on persons applying for membership, and he shall be admitted, provided that—

    (i) he satisfies the other statutory conditions for membership; and

    (ii) he has not come to Switzerland solely for the purpose of receiving medical or curative treatment;

and, if he is admitted to membership of the fund, he shall be treated, for the purpose of any claim to receive the benefits of the fund, as if any period for which he paid contributions under the legislation of the United Kingdom or had contributions credited to him under that legislation were a period of membership of the fund, provided that, if the national concerned is a woman claiming maternity benefits, she has been a member of the fund for a continuous period of at least three months immediately before her confinement.

(3) Where a national of either Party satisfies the conditions (a) and (b) specified in paragraph (2) of this Article, the provisions of that paragraph shall apply, in relation to benefits in kind, to his wife also and to any child of his who has not reached the age of twenty.

(4) Where a national of either Party is ordinarily resident in the United Kingdom or has, since his last arrival in the United Kingdom, become liable to pay contributions as an employed person or as a self-employed person under the legislation of the United Kingdom, he shall, for the purpose of any claim to receive sickness benefit under that legislation, be treated as if—

    (a) he had so paid a contribution for every week during which he was a member of a Swiss sickness insurance fund and was gainfully occupied;

    (b) he had had a contribution so credited to him for every week during which he was a member of such a fund and was prevented by illness or unemployment from being gainfully occupied; and

    (c) he satisfied the contribution conditions for receiving that benefit throughout the first six months after the time when he last ceased to be a member of a Swiss sickness insurance fund by which he was insured for benefits in cash;

provided that he shall not be entitled, by virtue of this paragraph, to receive sickness benefit:—

    (i) for any day for which he is entitled to receive a daily allowance under Swiss accident insurance or a pension, under Swiss pensions insurance, in respect of any invalidity which is assessed under that insurance at not less than two-thirds;

    (ii) for more than 312 days in any period of interruption of employment;

and the amount of any sickness benefit which is payable by virtue of this paragraph shall be reduced by the amount of any Swiss benefit payable for the same period other than an invalidity pension payable under Swiss accident insurance.

*United Kingdom Retirement Pensions, Widow's Benefit and*
*Long-term Sickness Benefit*

ARTICLE 12

(1) For the purpose of determining whether sickness benefit, widow's benefit or retirement pension is payable under the legislation of the United Kingdom, any contribution period which an insured person has completed under Swiss pensions

insurance shall be treated as if it were a contribution period which he had completed under the legislation of the United Kingdom; and, where such benefit is so payable, the rate of that benefit shall be a part of the rate at which it would have been payable if all the contribution periods completed by the insured person under Swiss pensions insurance had been completed under the legislation of the United Kingdom, namely, that part which bears the same relation to the whole as the total of all the contribution periods and equivalent periods completed by him under the legislation of the United Kingdom bears to the total of all the contribution periods and equivalent periods completed by him under the legislation of the two Contracting Parties, provided that, if the relation which the former total bears to the latter has been determined on a claim to sickness benefit for any day, it shall not be determined afresh on any claim for a later day which is part of the same period of interruption of employment.

(2) For the purpose of applying the provisions of paragraph (1) of this Article—

(a) no account shall be taken of any contribution period completed under Swiss pensions insurance in so far as that period, together with contribution periods completed under the legislation of the United Kingdom, raises the total number of contributions paid or credited in any contribution year under the legislation of the United Kingdom above the total number of weeks in that year;

(b) if the claim is for sickness benefit, no account shall be taken of any contribution period completed under Swiss pensions insurance during which the insured person was neither gainfully occupied nor prevented by illness or unemployment from being gainfully occupied;

(c) no account shall be taken of any contributions paid under the legislation of the United Kingdom which are calculated by reference to taxable earnings, or of any benefit payable under that legislation which is so calculated, but the rate of any benefit, determined in accordance with the provisions of that paragraph, shall be increased by any benefit which is so calculated;

(d) in those cases where the person concerned is—

(i) a woman claiming a retirement pension by virtue of her husband's insurance; or

(ii) a woman whose husband's contributions are taken into account in determining her right to receive a retirement pension by virtue of her own insurance, her marriage having been terminated by the death of her husband or otherwise;

any reference to a contribution period or equivalent period completed by the person shall be construed, for the purpose of ascertaining her husband's yearly average of contributions paid or credited, as including a reference to a contribution period or equivalent period completed by the husband.

(3) The provisions of paragraph (1) of this Article shall apply—

(a) only where the contribution periods and equivalent periods completed by the insured person under the legislation of each of the two Parties amount to one year or more;

(b) in the case of sickness benefit, only where—

(i) the competent authority of the United Kingdom is satisfied that the insured person is likely to remain incapable of work for a period of at least three months; and

(ii) the contribution periods completed by the insured person under the legislation of the two Parties, other than periods which are ignored in accordance with the provisions of paragraph (2) of this Article, amount in the aggregate to three years or more; and

(iii) either—

(aa) the insured person is not entitled to sickness benefit under the legislation of the United Kingdom by virtue of the provisions of paragraph (4) of Article 11 of the present Convention or otherwise; or (*bb*) he is receiving benefit in cash under Swiss legislation, other than an invalidity pension payable under Swiss accident insurance or a lump sum, and has received sickness benefit under the legislation of the United Kingdom for one hundred and fifty six days in any period of interruption of employment which includes the day for which benefit is claimed;

    (*c*) in the case of retirement pension or widow's benefit, only where the insured person does not wholly or partially satisfy the contribution conditions for that benefit solely by virtue of contribution periods and equivalent periods completed under the legislation of the United Kingdom.

(4) Where a person is entitled to receive benefit under the legislation of the United Kingdom in accordance with the provisions of paragraph (1) of this Article, he shall be entitled to receive under that legislation any amount also by which the sum of that benefit and any benefit in cash which he is receiving under Swiss legislation is less than the benefit which would be payable to him under the legislation of the United Kingdom if the provisions of that paragraph were not applied in his case.

### *Rehabilitation*
### ARTICLE 13

A national of the United Kingdom shall be entitled to take advantage of the rehabilitation measures provided under Swiss pensions insurance only so long as he maintains his domicile in Switzerland and only—

    (*a*) if, immediately before the onset of invalidity—

        (i) he has completed a contribution period of at least one year under that legislation; or

        (ii) being a married woman or widow who is not gainfully occupied, she has lived in Switzerland for a continuous period of at least one year; and

        (iii) being a child, he has lived in Switzerland for a continuous period of at least one year; or

    (*b*) if, being a child, he was born an invalid in Switzerland or has lived there continuously since his birth.

### *Ordinary Invalidity Pensions under Swiss Pensions Insurance*
### ARTICLE 14

For the purpose of any claim to receive an ordinary invalidity pension under Swiss pensions insurance, a national of the United Kingdom who has ceased to be insured under that insurance shall be treated as if he were so insured if, immediately before the onset of invalidity, he was paying contributions under the legislation of the United Kingdom or having contributions credited to him under that legislation.

### *Special Pensions under Swiss Pensions Insurance*
### ARTICLE 15

A national of the United Kingdom who is resident in Switzerland shall be entitled to receive a special pension under Swiss pensions insurance only if, immediately before the month from which he claims the pension, he has resided in Switzerland for a continuous period of not less than—

    (*a*) ten years in the case of an old age pension;

    (*b*) five years in the case of an invalidity pension or survivor's pension or an old age pension which replaces an invalidity or survivor's pension;

and, for this purpose—

        (i) no account shall be taken of any period during which he was exempt from liability to pay contributions under Swiss pensions insurance;

        (ii) a period of residence in Switzerland shall be treated as continuous if any spells of absence from Switzerland during that period do not amount in the aggregate to more than three months in any calendar year.

*Payment of Benefit Abroad*

ARTICLE 16

(1) Where a national of the United Kingdom would be entitled to receive any benefit under Swiss legislation if he were resident in Switzerland, he shall be entitled to receive that benefit if he is resident outside Switzerland, provided that he shall not be entitled, under Swiss pensions insurance, to receive a special pension, a helpless person's allowance or an ordinary pension in respect of any invalidity which is assessed under that insurance at less than one-half unless he is resident in Switzerland.

(2) Where a person would be entitled to receive sickness benefit, widow's benefit, guardian's allowance, retirement pension, injury benefit, disablement benefit or death benefit under the legislation of the United Kingdom if he were in the United Kingdom or resident there, he shall be entitled to receive that benefit while he is, respectively, in Switzerland or resident there, provided that—

(a) in the case of sickness benefit, he—

(i) can wholly or partially satisfy the contribution conditions for receiving that benefit without taking advantage of the provisions of Article 11 of the present Convention; and

(ii) (aa) is receiving, under Swiss legislation, a pension in respect of any invalidity which is assessed under that legislation at not less than two-thirds; or

(bb) before leaving the United Kingdom, has notified the competent authority of the United Kingdom of his intention to reside in Switzerland and satisfied that authority that he is likely to remain permanantly incapable of work; or

(cc) is temporarily absent from the United Kingdom for the purpose of receiving treatment for an incapacity which began before he left the United Kingdom;

(b) in the case of guardian's allowance, the person by virtue of whose insurance the benefit is claimed has completed contribution periods under the legislation of the United Kingdom which amount in the aggregate to at least five years.

(3) Where a person claims any benefit under the legislation of the United Kingdom, no provision of that legislation which would affect his claim by reason of the absence of a child, adult dependant or other person from the United Kingdom shall apply to him if the child, adult dependant or other person, as the case may be, is, or was at the time in question, in Switzerland.

PART V

**Miscellaneous Provisions**

ARTICLE 17

The competent authorities—

(a) shall make such administrative arrangements as may be required for the application of the present Convention;

(b) shall communicate to each other information regarding any measure taken by them for the application of the Convention;

(c) shall communicate to each other, as soon as possible, information regarding any changes made under their national legislation which affect the application of the Convention.

## ARTICLE 18

(1) The competent authorities and the social insurance authorities of the two Contracting Parties shall furnish assistance to one another with regard to any matter relating to the application of the present Convention as if the matter were one affecting the application of their own national legislation.

(2) The competent authorities shall, in particular, agree upon the measures to be adopted for the medical and administrative supervision of persons entitled to benefit by virtue of the present Convention.

## ARTICLE 19

(1) Where any benefit in cash is payable by a social insurance authority of one Contracting Party to a person who is resident in the territory of the other Party, the payment may be made by a social insurance authority of the latter Party as agent for the authority of the former Party in accordance with any arrangements which may be made by the competent authorities of the two Parties.

(2) Where payment of any benefit is made by a social insurance authority of one Party as agent for a social insurance authority of the other, in accordance with the provisions of paragraph (1) of this Article, payment may be made, except in the case of a lump sum, in arrear at intervals of two months.

## ARTICLE 20

(1) Any exemption from, or reduction of, legal dues, charges and fees provided for in the legislation of one Contracting Party in connexion with the issue of any certificate or document required to be produced for the purposes of that legislation, shall be extended to certificates and documents required to be produced for the purposes of the legislation of the other Party.

(2) Where any certificate or other document has to be produced to the competent authority or social insurance authority of one or the other Party for the purpose of applying the present Convention, that authority shall not require the certificate or other document to be legalized by a diplomatic or consular authority.

## ARTICLE 21

(1) Any claim, notice or appeal which should, for the purposes of the legislation of one Contracting Party, have been presented within a prescribed period to the social insurance authority of that Party, but which is in fact presented within the same period to the social insurance authority of the other Party, shall be treated as if it had been presented to the social insurance authority of the former Party. In such cases, the social insurance authority of the latter Party shall, as soon as possible, send the claim, notice or appeal to the social insurance authority of the former Party.

(2) Any appeal which should, for the purposes of the legislation of Switzerland, have been presented within a prescribed period to a tribunal specified in that legislation, but which is in fact presented within the same period to a tribunal established under the legislation of the United Kingdom, shall be treated as if it had been presented to the former tribunal. In such cases, the social insurance authority of the United Kingdom shall, as soon as possible, send the appeal to the social insurance authority of Switzerland, which shall send it to the appropriate tribunal.

(3) Any appeal which should, for the purposes of the legislation of the United Kingdom, have been presented within a prescribed period to a tribunal established under that legislation, but which is in fact presented within the same period to a tribunal specified in the legislation of Switzerland, shall be treated as if it had been presented to the former tribunal. In such case, the latter tribunal shall, as soon as possible, send the appeal through the social insurance authority of Switzerland to the social insurance authority of the United Kingdom.

ARTICLE 22

The amount of any benefit due in accordance with the provisions of the present Convention shall be calculated in the currency of the Contracting Party whose social insurance authority is responsible for such benefit.

ARTICLE 23

(1) Any dispute concerning the interpretation or application of the present Convention shall, as far as possible, be resolved by the competent authorities of the Contracting Parties.

(2) If a dispute cannot be resolved in this way, it shall be submitted, at the request of either Party, to an arbitration tribunal.

(3) The arbitration tribunal shall be determined when the occasion arises, as follows: each Party shall appoint a representative and the two representatives shall choose, in agreement with one another, among nationals of a third State, a chairman who shall be appointed by the Governments of the two Parties. The representatives shall be appointed within two months, and the chairman within three months of the day on which one of the Parties informs the other that it proposes to submit the dispute to the arbitration tribunal.

(4) If any of the time limits prescribed in paragraph (3) of this Article is not observed, either Party may ask the President of the European Court of Human Rights to make the requisite appointments. If the President is a national of either Party or if he is prevented for any other reason, the Vice-President shall make the nominations. If the Vice-President also is a national of either Party or if he is likewise prevented, the most senior member of the Court of Justice who is not a national of either Party shall make the appointments.

(5) The arbitration tribunal shall act by majority vote. Its decision shall be binding. Each Party shall bear the expenses of its representative on the arbitration tribunal. This shall apply also to the expenses of its representation in the arbitration. The expenses of the chairman, as well as any other expenses, shall be borne equally by the two Parties. The arbitration tribunal may decide on another distribution of the expenses. Apart from these provisions, the arbitration tribunal shall itself determine its rules of procedure.

# PART VI

## Transitional and Final Provisions

### ARTICLE 24

(1) No provision of the present Convention shall confer any right to receive any payment of benefit for a period before the date of the entry into force of the Convention.

(2) No provision of the Convention shall diminish any right which a person has acquired under the legislation of either Contracting Party before the date of the entry into force of the Convention, whether by virtue of the former Conventions or otherwise.

(3) Any contribution period or equivalent period which a person has completed before the date of the entry into force of the Convention shall be taken into account for the purpose of determining the right to receive benefit under the Convention, provided that no account shall be taken of a contribution period if the contributions paid for that period have been refunded to the insured person or transferred under the former conventions or if supplementary allowances have been paid in respect of those contributions under those conventions.

(4) Subject to the provisions of paragraphs (1), (2) and (3) of this Article, any benefit, other than lump sum payments, shall be payable under the present Convention in respect of events which happened before the date of the entry into force of the Convention, provided that any claim which a national of the United Kingdom makes, under Swiss pensions insurance, in respect of an event which happened before the 1st January 1960, shall be determined under the former Conventions and not not under the present Convention.

(5) Any benefit which has been determined before the date of the entry into force of the Convention shall, if necessary, be determined afresh in accordance with the provisions of paragraph (4) of this Article.

(6) Any benefit which is payable, in accordance with the foregoing provisions of this Article, shall be paid or determined and paid, as the case may be, as from the date of the entry into force of the Convention, and, for this purpose—

(a) in the case of any benefit payable under Swiss legislation, any time limit for claiming that benefit shall be deemed to run from that date at the earliest;

(b) in the case of any benefit payable under the legislation of the United Kingdom, any relevant claim may be submitted and any relevant notice of retirement may be given within twelve months of that date.

## ARTICLE 25

In the event of the termination of the present Convention, any right acquired by a person in accordance with its provisions shall be maintained, and negotiations shall take place for the settlement of any rights then in course of acquisition by virtue of those provisions.

## ARTICLE 26

(1) The present Convention shall be ratified and the instruments of ratification shall be exchanged in London as soon as possible. The Convention shall enter into force on the first day of the second month following the month in which the instruments of ratification are exchanged.

(2) Subject to the provisions of Article 24, the former Conventions shall be terminated on the date of entry into force of the present Convention.

## ARTICLE 27

The present Convention shall remain in force for a period of one year from the date of its entry into force. Thereafter, it shall continue in force from year to year unless it is denounced in writing three months before the expiry of any such yearly period.

IN WITNESS WHEREOF the undersigned, duly authorised by their respective Governments, have signed the present Convention.

DONE in duplicate at Berne, this twenty-first day of February 1968, in the English and French languages, both tests being equally authoritive.

For the Government of the United Kingdom     For the Swiss Federal Council:
of Great Britain and Northern Ireland:

H. A. F. HOHLER                          CRISTOFORO MOTTA

## SCHEDULE 2

**Orders Revoked**

The National Insurance and Industrial Injuries (Switzerland) Order 1954(a)

The National Insurance (Switzerland) Order 1960(b)

---

## EXPLANATORY NOTE

*(This Note is not part of the Order.)*

This Order gives effect in England, Wales and Scotland to the Convention (set out in Schedule I) made between the United Kingdom and the Swiss Federal Council in so far as it relates to the matters for which provision is made by the Family Allowances Acts 1965 to 1969, the National Insurance Acts 1965 to 1969 and the National Insurance (Industrial Injuries) Acts 1965 to 1969.

---

**(a)** S.I. 1954/641 (1954 I, p. 1422).     **(b)** S.I. 1960/1064 (1960 II, p. 2340).

# STATUTORY INSTRUMENTS

## 1969 No. 385

## ROAD TRAFFIC

## The Carriage of Goods by Road (Parties to Convention) (Amendment) Order 1969

*Made* - - - 18*th March* 1969

At the Court at Buckingham Palace, the 18th day of March 1969

Present,

The Queen's Most Excellent Majesty in Council

Her Majesty, in exercise of the powers conferred upon Her by section 2(1) of the Carriage of Goods by Road Act 1965(**a**) (which provides that Her Majesty may by Order in Council from time to time certify who are the High Contracting Parties to the Convention on the Contract for the International Carriage of Goods by Road signed at Geneva on 19th May 1956 and in respect of what territories they are respectively parties) is pleased, by and with the advice of Her Privy Council, to order, and it is hereby ordered, as follows :—

**1.** It is hereby certified that Gibraltar is a territory in respect of which the United Kingdom of Great Britain and Northern Ireland is a party to the said Convention, and accordingly the Schedule to the Carriage of Goods by Road (Parties to Convention) Order 1967(**b**) is amended by inserting in the second column thereof, between the entry "The United Kingdom of Great Britain and Northern Ireland" and the entry "Austria", the word "Gibraltar", and by inserting in the third column of the said Schedule, opposite the said word, the date "29th January 1969".

**2.** This Order may be cited as the Carriage of Goods by Road (Parties to Convention) (Amendment) Order 1969.

*W. G. Agnew.*

---

### EXPLANATORY NOTE

*(This Note is not part of the Order.)*

The Carriage of Goods by Road Act 1965 gave effect in the United Kingdom to the Convention signed at Geneva on 19th May 1956 on the Contract for the International Carriage of Goods by Road. The Carriage of Goods by Road (Parties to Convention) Order 1967 certified who are the High Contracting

---

(**a**) 1965 c. 37.  (**b**) S.I. 1967/1683 (1967 III, p. 4599).

Parties to the Convention and in respect of what territories they are respectively parties. This Order amends that Order by certifying Gibraltar as a territory in respect of which the United Kingdom is a party to the Convention. The Order is, except in so far as it may be superseded by a subsequent Order, conclusive evidence of the matters so certified.

# STATUTORY INSTRUMENTS

## 1969 No. 386

## MERCHANT SHIPPING

### The Merchant Shipping (Light Dues) Order 1969

*Laid before Parliament in draft*

| | |
|---|---|
| *Made* - - - - | 18*th March* 1969 |
| *Laid before Parliament* | 24*th March* 1969 |
| *Coming into Operation* | 1*st April* 1969 |

At the Court at Buckingham Palace, the 18th day of March 1969

Present,

The Queen's Most Excellent Majesty in Council.

Her Majesty in exercise of the powers conferred upon Her by section 5 of the Merchant Shipping (Mercantile Marine Fund) Act 1898(a), and of all other powers enabling Her in that behalf, is pleased, by and with the advice of Her Privy Council, to order, and it is hereby ordered, as follows:—

**1.**—(1) This Order shall come into operation on the 1st April 1969 and may be cited as the Merchant Shipping (Light Dues) Order 1969.

(2) The Interpretation Act 1889(b) shall apply to the interpretation of this Order as it applies to the interpretation of an Act of Parliament and as if this Order and the Order hereby revoked were Acts of Parliament.

**2.** The scale of payments and rules relating to the levying of light dues contained in Schedule 2 to the Merchant Shipping (Mercantile Marine Fund) Act 1898, as altered(c), shall be further altered as follows:—

(*a*) for the scale of payments set out therein there shall be substituted the scale set out in the Schedule to this Order ;

(*b*) in the proviso to Rule 1 for " 7s. 2·625d." and " 5s. 10·875d." there shall be substituted respectively " 8s. 7·95d." and " 7s. 1·05d." ; and

(*c*) in the proviso to Rule 7 for " 5·25d." there shall be substituted " 6·3d."

**3.** The following shall be added to the exemptions set out in the said Schedule 2:—

" Dredgers and hoppers for the time being employed solely in dredging channels or deepening water for or on behalf of a harbour authority or a conservancy authority, within the area in which that authority has jurisdiction, or in disposing within or without such area, otherwise than by way of sale or exchange, of the spoil from such operations."

**4.** The Merchant Shipping (Light Dues) Order 1968(d) is hereby revoked.

*W. G. Agnew.*

---

(**a**) 1898 c. 44.  (**b**) 1889 c. 63.
(**c**) S.I. 1953/392, 1968/580 (1953 I, p. 1065; 1968 I, p. 1347).
(**d**) S.I. 1968/580 (1968 I, p. 1347).

## SCHEDULE

### SCALE OF PAYMENTS

*(Substituted for the scale set out in Schedule 2 to the Merchant Shipping (Mercantile Marine Fund) Act 1898)*

1. Home-trade sailing ships: 6·3d. per ton per voyage.

2. Foreign-going sailing ships: 1s. 2·175d. per ton per voyage.

3. Home-trade steamers: 9·45d. per ton per voyage.

4. Foreign-going steamers:

   *Full rate :* 1s. 5·325d. per ton per voyage.

   *Reduced rate (visiting cruise ships)*: 9·6d. per ton per voyage.

A ship shall be treated as a visiting cruise ship if and only if it makes a call at one or more ports in the United Kingdom, Isle of Man or Republic of Ireland for the purpose of disembarking passengers for a visit ashore and for subsequent re-embarkation (whether or not at the same port) and at no time during that cruise does the ship—

   (*a*) embark or disembark any other passengers ; or

   (*b*) load or discharge any cargo or mails—

at any such port.

5. In the place of payments per voyage, the following payments: —

   (*a*) for pleasure yachts which the general lighthouse authority is satisfied are ordinarily kept or used outside any of the following countries and territories (including the territorial waters adjacent thereto), namely the United Kingdom, Isle of Man, Republic of Ireland, a payment in respect of any visit of 6·3d. per ton for every period of 30 days or less comprised in such visit ;

   (*b*) for tugs and pleasure yachts not included in sub-paragraph (*a*) of this paragraph an annual payment of 6s. 3·6d. per ton.

---

## EXPLANATORY NOTE

*(This Note is not part of the Order.)*

The Order increases by 20 per cent. the scale of light dues set out in the Merchant Shipping (Light Dues) Order 1968.

The Order also exempts from light dues dredgers and hoppers when employed solely in dredging channels or deepening water for or on behalf of a harbour or conservancy authority or in disposing of the spoil otherwise than by sale or exchange.

## STATUTORY INSTRUMENTS

### 1969 No. 387

### MERCHANT SHIPPING

### The Oil in Navigable Waters (Convention Countries) (Syria) Order 1969

| | |
|---|---|
| *Made* - - - | *18th March* 1969 |
| *Laid before Parliament* | *24th March* 1969 |
| *Coming into Operation* | *1st April* 1969 |

At the Court at Buckingham Palace, the 18th day of March 1969

Present,

The Queen's Most Excellent Majesty in Council

Whereas by section 18(3) of the Oil in Navigable Waters Act 1955(a) it is enacted that for the purposes of that section Her Majesty may, if satisfied that the government of any country has accepted the International Convention for the Prevention of Pollution of the Sea by Oil 1954, by Order in Council make a declaration to that effect :

And whereas Her Majesty is satisfied that the Government of the Syrian Arab Republic has accepted the said Convention :

Now, therefore, Her Majesty, in pursuance of the powers conferred upon Her by the said section 18(3) and of all other powers enabling Her in that behalf, is pleased, by and with the advice of Her Privy Council, to order, and it is hereby ordered, as follows :—

**1.** This Order may be cited as the Oil in Navigable Waters (Convention Countries) (Syria) Order 1969 and shall come into operation on 1st April 1969.

**2.** For the purposes of section 18 of the Oil in Navigable Waters Act 1955 it is hereby declared that the Government of the Syrian Arab Republic has accepted the International Convention for the Prevention of Pollution of the Sea by Oil 1954.

*W. G. Agnew.*

(a) 1955 c. 25.

## STATUTORY INSTRUMENTS

### 1969 No. 388

### MINISTERS OF THE CROWN

## The Transfer of Functions (Wales) Order 1969

| | |
|---|---|
| *Made -   -   -   -* | *18th March* 1969 |
| *Laid before Parliament* | *24th March* 1969 |
| *Coming into Operation* | *1st April* 1969 |

At the Court at Buckingham Palace, the 18th day of March, 1969

Present,

The Queen's Most Excellent Majesty in Council

Her Majesty, in pursuance of section 1 of the Ministers of the Crown (Transfer of Functions) Act 1946(a), is pleased by and with the advice of Her Privy Council to order, and it is hereby ordered, as follows :—

*Citation, interpretation and commencement*

**1.**—(1) This Order may be cited as the Transfer of Functions (Wales) Order 1969.

(2) The Interpretation Act 1889(b) applies for the interpretation of this Order as it applies for the interpretation of an Act of Parliament.

(3) In this Order references to Wales include, and references to England do not include, Monmouthshire.

(4) Any reference in this Order to an enactment or instrument is a reference to that enactment or instrument as amended or extended by or under any other enactment or instrument ; and in this Order " instrument " includes the judgment, decree or order of any court or tribunal.

(5) This Order shall come into operation on 1st April 1969.

*Transfer of health functions*

**2.**—(1) It shall be for the Secretary of State for Wales, instead of the Secretary of State for Social Services, to discharge in matters only affecting Wales the general duties of the Secretary of State under section 2 of the Ministry of Health Act 1919(c) and section 1 of the National Health Service Act 1946(d), and the functions of the Secretary of State under the National Health Service Acts 1946 to 1968(e) in relation to the provision of hospital and specialist services and other services.

(2) In the enactments mentioned in Schedule 1 to this Order there shall be made the amendments provided for by that Schedule, being amendments arising out of paragraph (1) above or making further provision for transferring to the Secretary of State for Wales responsibility in matters relating to health or welfare.

(3) There are hereby transferred to the Secretary of State for Wales all property, rights and liabilities to which the Secretary of State for Social

---

(a) 1946 c. 31.     (b) 1889 c. 63.     (c) 1919 c. 21.     (d) 1946 c. 81.
(e) 1946 c. 81;   1949 c. 93;   1951 c. 31:   1952 c. 25;   1961 c. 19;   1966 c. 8;
1967 c. 39;   1968 c. 46.

Services is entitled or subject at the coming into operation of this Order in connection only with the provision of hospital and specialist services for Wales (but not including any part of the Hospital Endowments Fund).

*Transfer of functions relating to agriculture, fisheries etc.*

**3.**—(1) Subject to the provisions of this Article, the functions of the Minister of Agriculture, Fisheries and Food which are mentioned in Parts I and II of Schedule 2 to this Order, including the share of that Minister in any such functions exercisable by him jointly with any other Minister or Ministers, are to the extent so mentioned hereby transferred to that Minister and the Secretary of State jointly or, where so provided in Part II of the Schedule, to the Secretary of State alone.

(2) The discharge of any functions as functions exercisable by virtue of paragraph (1) above by the Secretary of State shall belong to the Secretary of State for Wales, but without prejudice to the responsibilities of any other Secretary of State for functions hitherto shared jointly by the Minister of Agriculture, Fisheries and Food and the Secretary of State or for functions with which a Secretary of State is otherwise concerned apart from this Article.

(3) Subject to paragraph (4) below, where the functions transferred by this Article to the Minister of Agriculture, Fisheries and Food and the Secretary of State jointly involve the making, receipt or recovery of any payments, it shall continue to be for the Minister of Agriculture, Fisheries and Food, without the Secretary of State, to make, receive or recover those payments and, in connection with the receipt or recovery of any payment, to give a discharge or accept a less payment.

(4) Paragraph (3) above shall not apply to the recovery from any person of expenses borne by the Secretary of State; but any expenses which by virtue of this Article are incurred by or under the authority of the Minister of Agriculture, Fisheries and Food and the Secretary of State jointly in such circumstances as to be recoverable from any other person shall be defrayed by the Minister of Agriculture, Fisheries and Food.

(5) Part III of Schedule 2 to this Order shall have effect to make consequential provision in relation to or for purposes of functions transferred by this Article.

*Transfer of functions relating to ancient monuments*

**4.**—(1) The functions of the Minister of Public Building and Works under the Ancient Monuments Acts 1913 to 1953(**a**) (except section 16 of the Ancient Monuments Consolidation and Amendment Act 1913(**b**)), together with—

(*a*) his functions under sections 5(2) and 8(1) of the Historic Buildings and Ancient Monuments Act 1953(**c**), in so far as the like functions are not exercisable in relation to Wales by the Secretary of State by virtue of Article 4 of the Transfer of Functions (Building Control and Historic Buildings) Order 1966(**d**); and

(*b*) his functions under section 9 of the Coal-Mining (Subsidence) Act 1957(**e**); and

(*c*) his functions under paragraph 12 of Schedule 1 to the Acquisition of Land (Authorisation Procedure) Act 1946(**f**);

are, in relation to Wales, hereby transferred to the Secretary of State, and the discharge of those functions as functions exercisable by virtue of this

(a) 1913 c. 32; 1931 c. 16; 1953 c. 49.　　(b) 1913 c. 32.　　(c) 1953 c. 49.
(d) S.I. 1966/692 (1966 II p. 1558).　　(e) 1957 c. 59.　　(f) 1946 c. 49.

paragraph by the Secretary of State shall belong to the Secretary of State for Wales.

(2) Accordingly (without prejudice to Article 5 below) in the following enactments, that is to say,—

(a) section 34(2) of the Finance Act 1956(**a**) ;

(b) section 7(8) of the Mines (Working Facilities and Support) Act 1966(**b**) ; and

(c) sections 41(1)(*c*), 48(2)(*c*) and 50(3)(*c*) of the Town and Country Planning Act 1968(**c**) ;

any reference to the Minister of Public Building and Works (including any reference which is to be construed as such a reference) shall include a reference to the Secretary of State ; and in sections 5(2) and 8(1) of the Historic Buildings and Ancient Monuments Act 1953(**d**) any such reference to the Minister, except the first reference in section 8(1)(*a*), shall not apply to him in relation to Wales.

(3) There are hereby transferred to the Secretary of State for Wales any ancient monument in Wales, or land held with such a monument, which at the coming into operation of this Order is vested in the Minister of Public Building and Works, and any rights and liabilities to which that Minister is then entitled or subject in or in relation to any ancient monument in Wales or land held therewith.

*Supplementary*

**5.**—(1) This Order shall not affect the validity of anything done by or in relation to any Minister or Ministers before the coming into operation of this Order ; and anything which, at the time of the coming into operation of this Order, is in process of being done by or in relation to any Minister or Ministers other than the Secretary of State for Wales may, if it relates to any functions, property, rights or liabilities transferred by this Order, be continued by or in relation to that Secretary of State, with or without the other Minister or Ministers as may be appropriate.

(2) Any authority, approval, consent or direction given or other thing whatsoever done by any Minister or Ministers for the purpose of any functions transferred by this Order shall, if in force at the coming into operation of this Order, have effect as if made or done by the Secretary of State for Wales in so far as that is required for continuing its effect after the coming into operation of this Order.

(3) Subject to the provisions of this Order, any enactment or instrument passed or made before the coming into operation of this Order shall have effect, so far as may be necessary for the purpose or in consequence of the transfers effected by this Order, as if any reference to the Secretary of State for Social Services, to the Minister of Agriculture, Fisheries and Food or to the Minister of Public Building and Works, or to the department or an officer of any of them (including any reference which is to be construed as such a reference) were or included a reference to the Secretary of State for Wales or to his department or an officer of his, as the case may require.

(4) Nothing in this Order shall be taken to prejudice any powers exercisable in relation to the functions of Ministers of the Crown and government departments by virtue of Her Majesty's prerogative, or to affect the power of any Secretary of State to perform any functions of that office in place of the Secretary of State entrusted with the discharge of those functions.

*W. G. Agnew.*

(**a**) 1956 c. 54.   (**b**) 1966 c. 4.   (**c**) 1968 c. 72.   (**d**) 1953 c. 49.

## SCHEDULES

### Schedule 1

#### Amendments of Enactments relating to Health Functions

| Enactment | Amendment |
|---|---|
| The Ministry of Health Act 1919 (c. 21). | Section 5 shall cease to have effect. |
| The Radioactive Substances Act 1948 (c. 37). | In sections 3(7)(*a*) and 4(2)(*a*) for the words " England and Wales " there shall in each case be substituted the words " England or Wales "; in sections 3(7) and (9) and 4(2) and (4), as amended by the Secretary of State for Social Services Order 1968(a), after the words " Secretary of State for Social Services " there shall in each case be inserted the words " the Secretary of State for Wales "; and in section 12 there shall be added at the end the words " and in this Act references to Wales include, and references to England do not include, Monmouthshire ". |
| The Therapeutic Substances Act 1956 (c. 25). | In sections 4(1) and (2), section 8(1) and section 9(3) there shall be made, in place of the amendments made by the Secretary of State for Social Services Order 1968(a), the following amendments:–<br>(*a*) for the words " the Minister of Health " there shall be substituted the words " the Secretary of State for Social Services "; and<br>(*b*) for the words " the Secretary of State " there shall, except in section 4(2), be substituted the words " the Secretary of State for Wales, the Secretary of State for Scotland " and, in section 4(2), be substituted the words " the Secretary of State for Wales and one by the Secretary of State for Scotland ". |
| The Dentists Act 1957 (c. 28) | In Schedule 1, in paragraph 14(3) as amended by the Secretary of State for Social Services Order 1968(a), for the words " Secretaries of State respectively concerned with health in England and Wales and in Scotland " there shall be substituted the words " Secretaries of State respectively concerned with health in England, in Wales and in Scotland ". |
| The Professions Supplementary to Medicine Act 1960 (c. 66). | In Schedule 1, in paragraph 1(1)(*b*) as amended by the Secretary of State for Social Services Order 1968(a), after the words " Secretary of State for Social Services " there shall be inserted the words " the Secretary of State for Wales ". |
| The Commonwealth Immigrants Act 1962 (c. 21). | In section 16, as amended by the Secretary of State for Social Services Order 1968(a), after the words " the Secretary of State for Social Services ", wherever occurring, there shall be inserted the words " or Secretary of State for Wales ". |

(a) S.I. 1968/1699 (1968 III, p. 4585).

| Enactment | Amendment |
|---|---|
| The Health Visiting and Social Work (Training) Act 1962 (c. 33). | In section 7(2), as amended by the Secretary of State for Social Services Order 1968(a), for the words " Secretaries of State respectively concerned with health in England and Wales and in Scotland " there shall be substituted the words " Secretaries of State respectively concerned with health in England, in Wales and in Scotland ". |
| The Weights and Measures Act 1963 (c. 31). | In section 10(7), as amended by the Secretary of State for Social Services Order 1968(a), for the words " Secretaries of State respectively concerned with health in England and Wales and in Scotland " there shall be substituted the words " Secretaries of State respectively concerned with health in England, in Wales and in Scotland ". |
| The National Health Service Contributions Act 1965 (c. 54). | In section 1(4) and (5), as substituted by the Secretary of State for Social Services Order 1968(a), for the words " towards the cost of the national health service in England and Wales " there shall in each case be substituted the words " towards the cost of the national health service in England, except Monmouthshire, and towards the cost of the national health service in Wales and Monmouthshire ". |
| The National Health Service Act 1966 (c. 8). | In section 4, in subsection (2) for the words " or the Secretary of State " there shall be substituted the words " the Secretary of State for Wales or the Secretary of State for Scotland "; for subsection (4)(b) there shall be substituted— <br> " (b) by the Secretary of State for Scotland or the Secretary of State for Wales, as the case may be, if the directions concern the performance of functions in Scotland only or Wales only, and whether the directions are of a general or of a particular character; and <br> (c) by the Minister in other cases "; <br> and at the end of subsection (4) there shall be added the words " In paragraph (b) of this subsection the reference to Wales includes Monmouthshire ". |
| The Abortion Act 1967 (c. 87). | In section 2(2) for the words " Chief Medical Officers of the Ministry of Health and the Scottish Home and Health Department respectively " there shall be substituted the words " Chief Medical Officer of the Department of Health and Social Security, or of the Welsh Office, or of the Scottish Home and Health Department ". |
| The Health Services and Public Health Act 1968 (c. 46). | In section 59(1) as amended by the Secretary of State for Social Services Order 1968 (a), and in section 61(1) as so amended, for the words " Secretaries of State respectively concerned with health in England and Wales and in Scotland " there shall in each case be substituted the words " Secretaries of State respectively concerned with health in England, in Wales and in Scotland ". |

(a) S.I. 1968/1699 (1968 III, p. 4585).

| Enactment | Amendment |
|---|---|
| The Medicines Act 1968 (c. 67). | In section 1(1)(*a*) and in section 5(2), in place of the amendments made by the Secretary of State for Social Services Order 1968(**a**), there shall be made the following amendments:—<br>(*a*) for the words " the Minister of Health, the Secretary of State concerned with health in Scotland " in section 1(1)(*a*) there shall be substituted the words " the Secretaries of State respectively concerned with health in England, in Wales and in Scotland "; and<br>(*b*) for the words " the Minister of Health, the Secretary of State " in section 5(2) there shall be substituted the words " the Secretaries of State ". |
| The Aliens Order 1953 (S.I. 1953/1671 (1953 I, p. 94)). | In Articles 30(3), 32(*b*) and 33(*e*), as amended by the Secretary of State for Social Services Order 1968(**a**), after the words " Secretary of State for Social Services " wherever occurring, there shall be inserted the words " or Secretary of State for Wales ". |

SCHEDULE 2

FUNCTIONS RELATING TO AGRICULTURE, FISHERIES, ETC., AND EXTENT OF TRANSFER TO SECRETARY OF STATE

PART I

*Establishment of and appointments to authorities, boards, etc.*

1. The functions of the Minister of Agriculture, Fisheries and Food which are by Article 3 of this Order transferred to that Minister and the Secretary of State jointly shall include the making and termination of appointments, and other functions in connection with appointments, under or by virtue of the enactments listed below, subject to any limitation expressed in relation to any of those enactments: —

(*a*) as regards drainage boards for areas wholly or partly in Wales, paragraph 2 of Part II of Schedule 3 to the Land Drainage Act 1930 (c. 44) ;

(*b*) sections 1 and 2 of the Herring Industry Act 1938 (c. 42), together with paragraph 6 of Schedule 1 to the Herring Industry Act 1935 (c. 9) ;

(*c*) section 11(2) of the Agriculture (Miscellaneous Provisions) Act 1941 (c. 50) ;

(*d*) section 32 of the Hill Farming Act 1946 (c. 73) ;

(*e*) sections 1(2) and 3(2) of the Sea Fish Industry Act 1951 (c. 30) ;

(*f*) as regards any committee or commission for England and Wales, with or without another part or parts of the United Kingdom, sections 19(1), 23, 26(1) and (4) and 32(1) of the Agricultural Marketing Act 1958 (c. 47), and as regards any board or committee under a scheme applicable in Wales, or in England and Wales (with or without another part or parts of the United Kingdom), paragraph 2 of Schedule 2 to that Act ;

(*g*) as regards Welsh river authorities and Anglo-Welsh river authorities, sections 6(3) and 8(4) of the Water Resources Act 1963 (c. 38), together with paragraph 6 of Schedule 4 to that Act ;

(*h*) section 1 of the Cereals Marketing Act 1965 (c. 14) ;

(**a**) S.I. 1968/1699 (1968 III, p. 4585).

(*i*) as regards local fisheries committees for sea fisheries districts comprising any part of the coast of Wales or of the sea adjacent thereto, section 2 of the Sea Fisheries Regulation Act 1966 (c. 38) ;

(*j*) sections 1(3) and (4) and 2(1) of the Agriculture Act 1967 (c. 22), together with paragraphs 1 to 3 of Part III of Schedule 1 to that Act ;

(*k*) section 58(4) to (7) of the Agriculture Act 1967 (c. 22) ;

(*l*) Articles 9 and 11 of the Saundersfoot Harbour Order 1958(**a**) ;

(*m*) as regards areas wholly or partly in Wales, Part I of the Schedule to the Milk and Dairies (General) Regulations 1959(**b**) and Part I of Schedule 4 to the Milk (Special Designation) Regulations 1963(**c**).

2. The functions of the Minister of Agriculture, Fisheries and Food which are by Article 3 of this Order transferred to that Minister and the Secretary of State jointly shall include, as regards County Agricultural Executive Committees for any county in Wales (or for a joint county including a county in Wales), any functions under section 71 of the Agriculture Act 1947 (c. 48), together with paragraphs 7 to 12 and 21 of Schedule 9 to that Act.

3. The functions of the Minister of Agriculture, Fisheries and Food which are by Article 3 of this Order transferred to that Minister and the Secretary of State jointly shall include the selection of the persons to be nominated by that Minister as directors of the Agricultural Mortgage Corporation in accordance with the provisions referred to in section 2(3) of the Agriculture (Miscellaneous Provisions) Act 1944 (c. 28).

## PART II

### *Other transferred functions, and extent of transfer to Secretary of State*

4. The functions of the Minister of Agriculture, Fisheries and Food which are by Article 3 of this Order transferred to that Minister and the Secretary of State jointly shall include the functions of that Minister under section 2 of the Agriculture Act 1947 (c. 48).

5. The functions of the Minister of Agriculture, Fisheries and Food which are by Article 3 of this Order transferred to that Minister and the Secretary of State jointly shall include any power of that Minister which is exercisable by statutory instrument in relation to England and Wales under the enactments listed below, and also in relation to Wales any other functions of that Minister under the enactments so listed, or under any scheme, regulations, rules, order, bye-laws or similar instrument having effect under any of the enactments so listed, subject to any limitation expressed in relation to any of those enactments: —

(*a*) sections 1, 2 and 10 of the Destructive Imported Animals Act 1932 (c. 12) ;

(*b*) Part I of the Agriculture Act 1937 (c. 70) and section 97 of the Agriculture Act 1947 (c. 48) ;

(*c*) section 15 of the Agriculture (Miscellaneous War Provisions) Act 1940 (c. 14) ;

(*d*) section 11(1) of the Agriculture (Miscellaneous Provisions) Act 1941 (c. 50) ;

(*e*) the Hill Farming Act 1946 (c. 73) (so far as not comprised in Part I of this Schedule) ;

(*f*) sections 98 and 99 of the Agriculture Act 1947 (c. 48) ;

(*g*) section 2 of the Agricultural Holdings Act 1948 (c. 63) ;

(*h*) section 17(5) of the Sea Fish Industry Act 1951 (c. 30) ;

(*i*) the Agriculture (Fertilisers) Act 1952 (c. 15) ;

(*j*) the Agriculture (Ploughing Grants) Act 1952 (c. 35) ;

---

**(a)** S.I. 1958/886.     **(b)** S.I. 1959/277 (1959 I, p. 1351).
**(c)** S.I. 1963/1571 (1963 III, p. 2937).

(*k*) the Agriculture (Calf Subsidies) Act 1952 (c. 62), together with section 11 of the Agriculture Act 1967 (c. 22);

(*l*) sections 1, 5 and 6 of the White Fish and Herring Industries Act 1953 (c. 17);

(*m*) section 10 of the Protection of Birds Act 1954 (c. 30);

(*n*) section 1(1) of the Pests Act 1954 (c. 68);

(*o*) section 2 of the Fisheries Act 1955 (c. 7);

(*p*) section 3 of the White Fish and Herring Industries Act 1957 (c. 22);

(*q*) Part I of the Agriculture Act 1957 (c. 57), together with sections 61(7) and 64(6) of the Agriculture Act 1967 (c. 22);

(*r*) the Agriculture (Small Farmers) Act 1959 (c. 12);

(*s*) the Agricultural Improvement Grants Act 1959 (c. 31);

(*t*) the Weeds Act 1959 (c. 54);

(*u*) Part I of the Horticulture Act 1960 (c. 22);

(*v*) sections 5, 10 and 11 of the Agriculture (Miscellaneous Provisions) Act 1963 (c. 11);

(*w*) sections 2 and 3 of the Agriculture and Horticulture Act 1964 (c. 28);

(*x*) sections 14, 15, 16, 31 and 33 of, and paragraph 6 of Schedule 3 to, the Harbours Act 1964 (c. 40);

(*y*) the Cereals Marketing Act 1965 (c. 14) (so far as not comprised in Part I of this Schedule);

(*z*) in the Agriculture Act 1967 (c. 22)—

    (i) in Part I, sections 3, 12, 13, 16 and 17;

    (ii) Part II, together with Schedule 3 so far as it has effect for purposes of section 26, and together also with sections 82 and 90 of the Agriculture Act 1947 (c. 48) as they apply for the purposes specified in section 29(1), but not including section 28;

    (iii) in Part III, sections 41, 49(5) and 50(2);

    (iv) Part IV;

    (v) in Part V, section 65;

(*aa*) sections 1, 4(5) and (7) and 5 of the Sea Fisheries (Shellfish) Act 1967 (c. 83), together with section 15 of the Sea Fisheries Act 1968 (c. 77);

(*bb*) section 40 of the Agriculture (Miscellaneous Provisions) Act 1968 (c. 34);

(*cc*) any local enactment referring to the confirmation of byelaws made under the Harbours, Docks and Piers Clauses Act 1847 (c. 27) or under any Act incorporating it in whole or in part;

(*dd*) Article 38(2) of the Saundersfoot Harbour Order 1958(**a**).

6. The functions of the Minister of Agriculture, Fisheries and Food which are by Article 3 of this Order transferred to that Minister and the Secretary of State jointly shall include the functions of that Minister under the enactments listed below, or under any scheme, regulations, rules, order, byelaws or similar instrument having effect under any of the enactments so listed, subject to the limitations expressed in relation to those enactments:—

(*a*) Parts IV and VII of the Salmon and Freshwater Fisheries Act 1923 (c. 16), so far as relates to river authority areas wholly or partly in Wales or to river authorities for any such area, but excluding as regards Part IV sections 38(3) and 40(6) and functions under any provision made by virtue of section 38(1)(*e*);

(*b*) so much of the Agricultural Marketing Act 1958 (c. 47) as is not comprised in Part I of this Schedule, and section 45 of the Agriculture (Miscellaneous Provisions) Act 1968 (c. 34), so far as relates to Wales or to any scheme applicable in England and Wales (with or without another part or

(a) S.I. 1958/886.

parts of the United Kingdom), but excluding, as regards the Agricultural Marketing Act 1958 (c. 47), section 22, section 24(1) and so much of section 25 as provides for the making of loans (but not so much as authorises the making of regulations), and also any functions under the following provisions having effect under that Act: —

(i) regulation 9 of the Agricultural Marketing (Facilities Committee) Regulations 1932(a) ;

(ii) regulation 13 of the Agricultural Marketing (Consumers' Committee) Regulations 1932(b) ;

(iii) regulation 19 of the Agricultural Marketing (Committee of Investigation) Regulations 1949(c) ;

(iv) regulation 14 of the Agricultural Marketing (Re-organisation Commission) Regulations 1950(d) ;

(v) in the Milk Marketing Scheme(e) (as amended(f)) sub-paragraph (c) of the paragraph inserted as paragraph 59 by the Milk Marketing Scheme (Amendment) Order 1955(g) and the proviso in the paragraph renumbered as paragraph 60 by that Order ;

and so that, as regards section 45 of the Agriculture (Miscellaneous Provisions) Act 1968 (c. 34), no notice served for purposes of that section need be served on the Secretary of State by reason of this Order ;

(c) Schedule 12 to the Water Resources Act 1963 (c. 38), so far as relates to byelaws of river authorities for areas wholly or partly in Wales and functions exercisable by the Minister of Agriculture, Fisheries and Food by reason of his being concerned with fisheries ;

(d) sections 1, 7, 8 and 13(1) and (2) of the Sea Fisheries Regulation Act 1966 (c. 38), so far as relates to sea fisheries districts comprising any part of the coast of Wales or of the sea adjacent thereto or to local fisheries committees for any such district, and section 18(2) of that Act, so far as relates to areas wholly or partly in Wales.

7. There shall be included among the functions of the Minister of Agriculture, Fisheries and Food transferred by Article 3 of this Order any functions under section 70(9) of the Finance Act 1965 (c. 25) or section 44(2) of the Agriculture (Miscellaneous Provisions) Act 1968 (c. 34), in relation to associations concerned with forestry in Wales, and those functions shall be transferred—

(a) in the case of functions under the said section 44(2) in relation to an association concerned only with forestry in Wales, to the Secretary of State ; and

(b) in any other case, to the Minister of Agriculture, Fisheries and Food and the Secretary of State jointly.

## PART III
### Application of supplementary provisions

8. Where, in connection with any functions which by Article 3 of this Order are made exercisable by the Secretary of State jointly with the Minister of Agriculture, Fisheries and Food, provision is made by or under any enactment (whether mentioned or not mentioned in Part I or II of this Schedule) for matters falling within any sub-paragraph of this paragraph, then in connection with those functions as so exercisable the provision shall have effect in accordance with that sub-paragraph, that is to say—

(a) any provision conferring power on the Minister to give directions to any authority or body as to the discharge of their functions by that authority or body or any matter connected therewith shall apply to the Minister and the Secretary of State jointly ;

---

(a) S.R. & O. 1932/560 (Rev. I p. 160; 1932, p. 15).
(b) S.R. & O. 1932/715 (Rev. I p. 158; 1932, p. 8).     (c) S.I. 1949/2452 (1949 I, p. 32).
(d) S.I. 1950/1869 (1950 I, p. 16).     ,     (e) S.R. & O. 1933/789 (Rev. I, p. 224: 1933, p. 20).
(f) S.R. & O. 1936/767, 1937/228, 744, 1939/324 (Rev. I, at p. 225: 1936 I, p. 22; 1937, pp. 1, 2; 1939 I, p. 30); S.I. 1950/1029 (1950 I, p. 43); S.I. 1955/946 (1955 I, p. 128).
(g) S.I. 1955/946 (1955 I, p. 128).

(*b*) any provision relating to the making or submission to the Minister of any report or accounts, or (except as otherwise provided in Part II of this Schedule) providing for notice to be given to the Minister, shall apply to the Minister and the Secretary of State jointly ;

(*c*) any provision conferring power, or enabling power to be conferred, on the Minister to delegate functions shall apply to the Minister and the Secretary of State jointly ;

(*d*) any provision conferring any default power on the Minister, or conferring any power on a person authorised by the Minister, shall apply to confer that power on the Minister and the Secretary of State or either of them, or on a person authorised by them or either of them, as the case may be ;

(*e*) any provision authorising the disclosure of information by or to the Minister or to a person authorised or appointed by him shall apply also to the Secretary of State or to a person authorised or appointed by him, as the case may be ;

(*f*) any provision requiring or authorising prosecutions to be brought by the Minister shall require or authorise them to be brought either by the Minister or by the Secretary of State ;

and where before the coming into operation of this Order the Minister has delegated any functions made exercisable as aforesaid, the delegation shall have effect as a joint delegation by him and the Secretary of State.

---

## EXPLANATORY NOTE

### (*This Note is not part of the Order.*)

This Order in Council transfers functions in relation to Wales and Monmouthshire under a number of enactments to the Secretary of State for Wales or, in the case of functions relating to agriculture and fisheries, to the Secretary of State and the Minister of Agriculture, Fisheries and Food acting jointly.

Article 2(1) of the Order transfers to the Secretary of State for Wales, in relation to Wales and Monmouthshire, the general duties of the Secretary of State for Social Services regarding the health of the people and the provision of a comprehensive health service, together with his specific functions in connection with that service. Where a function relates to the whole of England and Wales it will be exercised by the Secretary of State for Social Services in consultation with the Secretary of State for Wales.

Article 2(2) and Schedule 1 make amendments to certain enactments. These are consequential on the allocation of new health and welfare responsibilities to the Secretary of State for Wales.

Article 2(3) transfers from the Secretary of State for Social Services to the Secretary of State for Wales property held for the purpose of the provision of hospital and specialist services. This consists in the main of hospitals administered by the Welsh Hospital Board and the Board of Governors of the United Cardiff Hospitals.

Article 3 of the Order transfers in relation to Wales and Monmouthshire the functions of the Minister of Agriculture, Fisheries and Food under the enactments specified in Parts I and II of Schedule 2 ; except in one instance (see paragraph 7(*a*) of the Schedule), the transfer is to the Minister and the Secretary of State jointly. Part I of this Schedule concerns the making of appointments, establishment of Committees, etc. ; Part II relates to grant and subsidy schemes and other statutory responsibilities and the functions arising therefrom. Part III of Schedule 2 sets out general provisions applicable in connection with the transferred functions.

Article 3(3) reserves to the Minister of Agriculture, Fisheries and Food financial responsibility for the functions which will otherwise be exercised jointly.

Under Article 4 the functions of the Minister of Public Building and Works in so far as they relate to ancient monuments in Wales are transferred to the Secretary of State for Wales.

# STATUTORY INSTRUMENTS

## 1969 No. 398

## JUSTICES OF THE PEACE

### The Justices of the Peace Act 1968 (Compensation) Regulations 1969

*Made* - - - 18*th March* 1969

*Coming into Operation* 1*st April* 1969

### ARRANGEMENT OF REGULATIONS

#### PART I

##### PRELIMINARY

#### PART II

##### ENTITLEMENT TO COMPENSATION

#### PART III

##### RESETTLEMENT COMPENSATION

#### PART IV

##### LONG-TERM COMPENSATION FOR LOSS OF EMPLOYMENT OR LOSS OR DIMINUTION OF EMOLUMENTS

## Part V

### Retirement Compensation and Payments on Death

## Part VI

### Adjustment, Review and Compounding of Compensation

## Part VII

### Procedure and Miscellaneous

In pursuance of the powers conferred on me by paragraph 16 of Schedule 3 to the Justices of the Peace Act 1968(**a**), I hereby make the following Regulations :—

## PART I

### PRELIMINARY

#### Citation and commencement

**1.** These Regulations may be cited as the Justices of the Peace Act 1968 (Compensation) Regulations 1969 and shall come into operation on 1st April 1969.

#### Interpretation

**2.**—(1) In these Regulations, unless the context otherwise requires, the following expressions have the meanings hereby respectively assigned to them, that is to say :—

"accrued pension", in relation to a pensionable officer who has suffered loss of employment, means—

  (*a*) if his last relevant pension scheme provided benefits in which he had a right to participate, the pension to which he would have become entitled in respect of his pensionable service according to the method of calculation, modified where necessary in accordance with Regulation 18(2), prescribed by that scheme if, at the date on which he ceased to be subject to that scheme, he had attained normal retiring age and complied with any requirement of that scheme as to a minimum period of qualifying service or contribution and completed any additional contributory payments or payments in respect of added years which he was in the course of making ; and

  (*b*) in any other case, such portion of the pension (if any) of which he had reasonable expectations as the determining authority consider equitable, having regard to his age, the length of his employment at the date of loss and all the other circumstances of the case ;

"accrued retiring allowance", in relation to a pensionable officer who has suffered loss of employment, means—

  (*a*) if his last relevant pension scheme provided benefits in which he had a right to participate, any lump sum payment to which he would have become entitled in respect of his pensionable service according to the method of calculation, modified where necessary in accordance with Regulation 18(2), prescribed by that scheme if, at the date on which he ceased to be subject to that scheme, he had attained normal retiring age and complied with any requirement of that scheme as to a minimum period of qualifying service or contribution and completed any additional contributory payments or payments in respect of added years which he was in the course of making ; and

  (*b*) in any other case, such portion of the lump sum payment (if any) of which he had reasonable expectations as the determining authority consider equitable, having regard to his age, the length of his employment at the date of loss and all the other circumstances of the case ;

"accrued incapacity pension" and "accrued incapacity retiring allowance" have the same respective meanings as "accrued pension" and "accrued retiring allowance" except that the reference to a person's attaining normal retiring age shall be construed as a reference to his becoming incapable of

---

(a) 1968 c. 69.

discharging efficiently the duties of his employment by reason of permanent ill-health or infirmity of mind or body ;

"added years" in relation to a person who suffers loss of employment means—

(a) in the case of a contributory employee or local Act contributor any additional years of service reckonable by him in his employment immediately prior to the loss in question under Regulation 12 of the Local Government Superannuation (Benefits) Regulations 1954(a) as amended (b), or any corresponding provision of a local Act scheme, or that Regulation or any such provision as aforesaid as applied by or under any enactment, and includes any additional years of service which, having been granted under any such provision or under any similar provision contained in any other enactment or scheme, have subsequently become and are reckonable under or by virtue of rules made under section 2 of the Superannuation (Miscellaneous Provisions) Act 1948(c), or any other enactment ; and

(b) in the case of any other person, any additional years of service, similar to those mentioned in sub-paragraph (a) of this definition, reckonable by him under the pension scheme associated with the employment he has lost ;

"additional contributory payments" means—

(a) additional contributory payments of the kind referred to in section 2(3) and (4) of the Local Government Superannuation Act 1953(d) ; or

(b) any similar payments made under a local Act scheme or other pension scheme as a condition of reckoning any period of employment as service or as a period of contribution for the purposes of the scheme, or, where the scheme provides for the reckoning of non-contributing service, as contributing service for the purposes of the scheme ; or

(c) any payments made for the purpose of increasing the length at which any period of service or of contribution would be reckonable for the purpose of calculating a benefit under a local Act scheme ; or

(d) any payments similar to any of those mentioned in the foregoing sub-paragraphs made in pursuance of rules made under section 2 of the Superannuation (Miscellaneous Provisions) Act 1948 or in pursuance of any arrangements in that behalf made by an officer of a local authority in respect of a person employed under such an officer for the purposes of the functions of the local authority ;

"compensation question" means a question—

(a) as to a person's entitlement to compensation for loss of employment, or for loss or diminution of emoluments ; or

(b) as to the manner of a person's employment or the comparability of his duties ;

"contributory employee" and "local Act contributor" have the same meaning as in the Local Government Superannuation Act 1937(e) ;

---

(a) S.I. 1954/1048 (1954 II, p. 1595).     (b) S.I. 1955/1041 (1955 II, p. 1825).
(c) 1948 c. 33.     (d) 1953 c. 25.
(e) 1937 c. 68.

"determining authority" means—

(a) in relation to the South Staffordshire Stipendiary Justice Act 1899(**a**), the councils of the county boroughs of Wolverhampton and West Bromwich acting jointly ;

(b) in any other case, the paying authority ;

"emoluments" means all salary, wages, fees and other payments paid or made to an officer as such for his own use, and also the money value of any apartments, rations or other allowances in kind appertaining to his employment, but does not include payments for overtime, other than payments which are a usual incident of his employment, or any allowances payable to him to cover the cost of providing office accommodation or clerical or other assistance, or any travelling or subsistence allowance or other moneys to be spent, or to cover expenses incurred, by him for the purposes of his employment ; and "net emoluments", in relation to any employment, means the annual rate of the emoluments of that employment less such part of those emoluments as the officer was liable to contribute under a pension scheme, and in relation to any employment which has been lost or the emoluments of which have been diminished, the expression means the annual rate of emoluments as aforesaid immediately before the loss or diminution, as the case may be :

Provided that, where fees or other variable payments were paid to an officer as part of his emoluments during any period immediately preceding the loss or diminution, the amount in respect of fees or other variable payments to be included in the annual rate of emoluments shall be the annual average of the fees or other payments paid to him during the period of five years immediately preceding the loss or diminution, or such other period as the determining authority may think reasonable in the circumstances ;

"enactment" means any Act or any instrument made under an Act ;

"justices' clerk" includes a clerk to a stipendiary magistrate, a clerk to a metropolitan stipendiary court and a clerk to the justices of a liberty ;

"local authority" means the council of a county, county borough, metropolitan borough, London borough, county district, rural parish or borough included in a rural district, the Greater London Council, the Common Council of the City of London and the council of the Isles of Scilly, any two or more of those authorities acting jointly and any joint committee, combined authority or joint board and a police authority for a county, a borough or a combined police area ;

"long-term compensation" means compensation payable in accordance with the provisions of Part IV of these Regulations for loss of employment or loss or diminution of emoluments ;

"material date" means—

(a) in relation to the South Staffordshire Stipendiary Justice Act 1899, 1st April 1969 ;

(b) in relation to the Staffordshire Potteries Stipendiary Justice Acts 1839 to 1895(**b**), 1st October 1969 ; and

(c) in relation to the City of London, the day appointed in relation thereto under section 7(1) of the Justices of the Peace Act 1968 ;

---

(**a**) 1899 c. xc.             (**b**) 1839 c. 15; 1871 c. xc; 1895 c. cvii.

"minimum pensionable age" means, in relation to a pensionable officer, the earliest age at which, under his last relevant pension scheme, he could have become entitled to a pension, other than a pension payable in consequence of his redundancy or the termination of his employment in the interests of efficiency or his incapacity to discharge efficiently the duties of his employment by reason of permanent ill-health or infirmity of mind or body ;

"national service" means service which is relevant service within the meaning of the Reserve and Auxiliary Forces (Protection of Civil Interests) Act 1951(a), and includes service immediately following such service as aforesaid, being service in any of Her Majesty's naval, military or air forces pursuant to a voluntary engagement entered into with the consent of the authority or person under whom an officer held his last relevant employment or by whom he was appointed ;

"normal retiring age" means, in the case of a pensionable officer to whom an age of compulsory retirement applied by virtue of any enactment to which he was subject in the employment which he has lost or the emoluments of which have been diminished or by virtue of the conditions of that employment, that age, and, in any other case—

  (a) in relation to a person claiming compensation in respect of the office of justices' clerk or of employment by the South Staffordshire Stipendiary Justice Commissioners or the Staffordshire Potteries Stipendiary Justice Commissioners, the age of seventy years, and

  (b) in relation to any other person, the age of sixty-five years if the officer is a male, or sixty years if the officer is a female ;

"officer" includes the holder of any place, situation or employment ;
"paying authority" means—

  (a) in relation to the City of London, the Corporation thereof ;

  (b) in relation to the South Staffordshire Stipendiary Justice Act 1899—

    (i) in the case of the stipendiary magistrate, the council of the county borough of West Bromwich ; and

    (ii) in any other case, the councils of the county boroughs of Wolverhampton and West Bromwich acting jointly ;

  and

  (c) in relation to the Staffordshire Potteries Stipendiary Justice Acts 1839 to 1895, the council of the city of Stoke-on-Trent ;

"pensionable officer", in relation to a person who has suffered loss of employment or loss or diminution of emoluments, means a person who immediately before such loss or diminution was subject to a pension scheme ;

"pension scheme", in relation to a pensionable officer, means any form of arrangement associated with his employment for the payment of superannuation benefits, whether subsisting by virtue of Act of Parliament, trust, contract or otherwise ; and "last relevant pension scheme", in relation to a pensionable officer, means the pension scheme to which he was last subject before suffering loss of employment or loss or diminution of emoluments ;

"reckonable service", in relation to a person, means any period of wholetime or part-time employment in any relevant employment and includes any period of war service or national service undertaken on his ceasing to hold any such employment but does not include employment of which account

---

(a) 1951 c. 65.

has been taken, or is required to be taken, in calculating the amount of any superannuation benefit to which he has become entitled ;

"relevant employment" means employment in any of the following offices or employments, that is to say : —

(a) stipendiary magistrate,

(b) clerk of the peace,

(c) deputy clerk of the peace,

(d) justices' clerk,

(e) employment in assisting the holder of an office mentioned in any of the foregoing paragraphs of this definition in the performance of the duties of that office,

(f) employment by the South Staffordshire Stipendiary Justice Commissioners or the Staffordshire Potteries Stipendiary Justice Commissioners,

(g) service as collecting officer or in the employment of a collecting officer,

(h) employment under the Crown or in the service of a local authority in Great Britain,

(i) employment by any authority or body for the purposes of the Crown or of local government in Great Britain,

(j) employment under any officer employed as mentioned in paragraph (h) or (i) of this definition for the purposes of the functions of the employing authority or body,

(k) employment preceding any of the foregoing offices or employments which was reckonable for the purposes of any pension scheme associated with the office which has been lost, or

(l) such other employment as the Secretary of State may, in the case of any named officer, approve,

but, except as provided in Regulations 6(1) and 12(1), does not include service in the armed forces of the Crown ;

"resettlement compensation" means compensation payable in accordance with Part III of these Regulations for loss of employment ;

"retirement compensation" means compensation payable in accordance with the provisions of Regulation 19, 20, 21 or 22 ;

"tribunal" means a tribunal established under section 12 of the Industrial Training Act 1964(a) ;

"war service" means war service within the meaning of the Local Government Staffs (War Service) Act 1939(b), the Teachers Superannuation (War Service) Act 1939(c), the Police and Firemen (War Service) Act 1939(d) or employment for war purposes within the meaning of the Superannuation Schemes (War Service) Act 1940(e) and includes any period of service in the First World War in the armed forces of the Crown or in the forces of the Allied or Associated Powers if such service immediately followed a period of relevant employment and was undertaken either compulsorily or with the permission of the authority or person by whom the holder of that employment was appointed or employed.

(a) 1964 c. 16.                    (b) 1939 c. 94.
(c) 1939 c. 95.                    (d) 1939 c. 103.
(e) 1940 c. 26.

(2)(*a*) Where under any provision of these Regulations an annual value is to be assigned to a capital sum or a capital value to an annual amount, the annual or capital value shall be ascertained in accordance with the tables set out in the Schedule to these Regulations in so far as they provide for the particular case.

(*b*) For the purpose of determining the application of the said tables the headings and the note to each table shall be treated as a part of the table.

(*c*) Where the said tables do not provide for a case in which an annual value is to be assigned to a capital sum or a capital value to an annual amount, the annual or capital value shall be such as may be agreed between the determining authority and the person to whom the capital sum or annual amount is payable.

(3) Where any compensation is payable under these Regulations by the councils of the county boroughs of Wolverhampton and West Bromwich acting jointly as paying authority, the compensation shall be borne by those councils—

(*a*) in such proportions as may be agreed between those councils ;

or

(*b*) failing agreement as aforesaid, in the same proportions as those in which the expenses of carrying the South Staffordshire Stipendiary Justice Act 1899 into execution were, in accordance with section 33 of that Act, borne by them immediately before the material date.

(4) The holder of an office shall, for the purposes of these Regulations, be regarded as employed in that office, and the expression "employment" shall be construed accordingly.

(5) Unless the context otherwise requires, references in these Regulations to the provisions of any enactment shall be construed as references to those provisions as amended, re-enacted or modified by any subsequent enactment.

(6) References in these Regulations to a numbered Regulation shall, unless the reference is to a regulation of specified regulations, be construed as references to the Regulation bearing that number in these Regulations.

(7) References in any of these Regulations to a numbered paragraph shall, unless the reference is to a paragraph of a specified Regulation, be construed as references to the paragraph bearing that number in the first mentioned Regulation.

(8) The Interpretation Act 1889(**a**) shall apply for the interpretation of these Regulations as it applies for the interpretation of an Act of Parliament.

## Part II

### Entitlement to Compensation

*Persons to whom the Regulations apply*

**3.** These Regulations shall apply to any person who is at the material date, for the whole or for part only of his time—

(*a*) the holder of an office or employment in respect of which he is paid a salary by the Corporation of the City of London or by the South Staffordshire Stipendiary Justice Commissioners or the Staffordshire Potteries Stipendiary Justice Commissioners ; or

(**a**) 1889 c. 63.

(b) employed by the holder of such an office or employment to assist him in the performance of the duties of that office or employment.

## Grounds of entitlement to compensation

**4.** Subject to the provisions of these Regulations, any person to whom these Regulations apply and who suffers any loss of office or employment, or loss or diminution of emoluments, which is attributable to the operation of section 1 of the Justices of the Peace Act 1968 in relation to the City of London or in relation to the South Staffordshire Stipendiary Justice Act 1899 or the Staffordshire Potteries Stipendiary Justice Acts 1839 to 1895, shall be entitled to have his case considered for the payment of compensation under these Regulations, and such compensation shall be determined in accordance with these Regulations.

## PART III

### RESETTLEMENT COMPENSATION

### Resettlement compensation for loss of employment

**5.** The paying authority shall, subject to the provisions of these Regulations, pay resettlement compensation to any person to whom these Regulations apply and who satisfies the conditions set out in Regulation 6.

### Conditions for payment of resettlement compensation

**6.**—(1) Without prejudice to any other requirement of these Regulations, the conditions for the payment of resettlement compensation to any person are that—

(a) he has, not later than ten years after the material date, suffered loss of employment attributable to the operation of section 1 of the Justices of the Peace Act 1968 in any of the circumstances mentioned in Regulation 4 ;

(b) he had not at the date of the loss attained normal retiring age ;

(c) he had been for a period of three years immediately before the material date continuously engaged (disregarding breaks not exceeding in the aggregate six months) for the whole or part of his time in relevant employment ; and for this purpose the expression "relevant employment" includes any period of national service immediately following such employment ;

(d) he has made a claim for such compensation in accordance with the provisions of Part VII of these Regulations not later than thirteen weeks after the loss of employment which is the cause of his claim ;

(e) the loss of employment which is the cause of his claim has occurred for some reason other than misconduct or incapacity to perform such duties as, immediately before the loss, he was performing or might reasonably have been required to perform ; and

(f) he has not, subject to paragraph (3), been offered, in the case of a person holding the office of stipendiary magistrate or justices' clerk, any reasonably comparable employment under the Crown or in the service of a local authority or in the office of justices' clerk, clerk of the peace or deputy clerk of the peace or, in any other case, any reasonably comparable employment as aforesaid or in assisting a holder of the office of justices' clerk, clerk of the peace or deputy clerk of the peace.

(2) In ascertaining for the purposes of this Regulation whether a person has been offered employment which is reasonably comparable with the employ-

ment which he has lost, no account shall be taken of the fact that the duties of the employment offered are in relation to a different service from that in connection with which his employment was held or are duties which involve a transfer of his employment from one place to another within England and Wales.

(3) No account shall be taken for the purposes of this Regulation of an offer of employment where the determining authority is satisfied—

(a) that acceptance would have involved undue hardship to the person, or

(b) that he was prevented from accepting the offer by reason of ill-health or other circumstances beyond his control.

## Amount of resettlement compensation

**7.**—(1) The amount of resettlement compensation which may be paid to a person shall, for each week for which such compensation is payable, be a sum ascertained by taking two-thirds of the weekly rate of the net emoluments which that person has lost and deducting therefrom, in addition to the items mentioned in Regulation 32(3) and (4), such of the following items as may be applicable—

(a) unemployment, sickness or injury benefit under any Act relating to National Insurance claimable by him in respect of such week (excluding any amount claimable by him in respect of a dependant) ; and

(b) two-thirds of the net emoluments received by him in respect of such week from work or employment undertaken as a result of the loss of employment.

(2) For the purposes of this Regulation the weekly rate of a person's net emoluments shall be deemed to be seven three hundred and sixty-fifths of those emoluments.

## Period for payment of resettlement compensation

**8.** Subject to the provisions of these Regulations, resettlement compensation shall be payable to a person only in respect of the period of thirteen weeks next succeeding the week in which he lost the employment in respect of which his claim has been made or, in the case of a person who has attained the age of forty-five years, the said thirteen weeks and one additional week for every year of his age after attaining the age of forty-five years and before the date of the loss of employment, subject to a maximum addition of thirteen such weeks.

## Additional provisions relating to resettlement compensation

**9.**—(1) Resettlement compensation shall be payable to a person at intervals equivalent to those at which the emoluments of his employment were previously paid or at such other intervals as may be agreed between the person and the paying authority.

(2) Resettlement compensation shall be terminated by the determining authority—

(a) if without reasonable cause the recipient fails to comply with any of the provisions of Regulation 10, or

(b) if on being requested to do so, he fails to satisfy the determining authority that, so far as he is able, he is seeking suitable employment.

*Claimant for resettlement compensation to furnish particulars of employment*

**10.** Every person claiming or in receipt of resettlement compensation shall (after as well as before the compensation begins to be paid)—

(*a*) forthwith supply the determining authority in writing with particulars of any employment which he obtains or of any change in his earnings from any such employment, and

(*b*) if the determining authority so requires, so long as he is out of employment and is not receiving sickness or injury benefit, register with the Department of Employment and Productivity.

## PART IV

### LONG-TERM COMPENSATION FOR LOSS OF
### EMPLOYMENT OR LOSS OR DIMINUTION OF EMOLUMENTS

*Long-term compensation*

**11.** The paying authority shall, subject to the provisions of these Regulations, pay long-term compensation to any person to whom these Regulations apply and who satisfies the conditions set out in Regulation 12.

*Conditions for payment of long-term compensation*

**12.**—(1) Without prejudice to any other requirement of these Regulations, the conditions for the payment of long-term compensation to any person are that—

(*a*) he has, not later than ten years after the material date, suffered loss of employment or loss or diminution of emoluments attributable to the operation of section 1 of the Justices of the Peace Act 1968 in any of the circumstances mentioned in Regulation 4;

(*b*) he had not, save as is provided in Regulation 28, at the date of the loss or diminution attained normal retiring age;

(*c*) he had been, for a period of not less than eight years immediately before the material date, continuously engaged (without a break of more than twelve months at any one time) for the whole or part of his time in relevant employment; and for this purpose the expression "relevant employment" includes any period of national service immediately following such employment;

(*d*) he has made a claim for such compensation in accordance with the provisions of Part VII of these Regulations not later than two years after the loss or diminution which is the cause of the claim; and

(*e*) if the cause of the claim for compensation is loss of employment—

(i) the loss has occurred for some reason other than misconduct or incapacity to perform such duties as, immediately before the loss, he was performing or might reasonably have been required to perform; and

(ii) he has not been offered, in the case of a person holding the office of stipendiary magistrate or justices' clerk, any reasonably comparable employment under the Crown or in the service of a local authority or in the office of justices' clerk, clerk of the peace or deputy clerk of the peace or, in any other case, any reasonably comparable employment as aforesaid or in assisting a holder of the office of justices' clerk, clerk of the peace or deputy clerk of the peace.

(2) Regulation 6(2) and (3) (which relate to offers of employment) shall apply for the purposes of this Regulation in ascertaining whether a person has been offered reasonably comparable employment.

(3) Claims for long-term compensation for loss of employment shall in all respects be treated as claims for such compensation for the loss of emoluments occasioned thereby and the provisions of these Regulations shall apply to all such claims accordingly.

*Factors to be considered in determining payment of long-term compensation*

**13.**—(1) For the purpose of determining whether long-term compensation for loss or diminution of emoluments is payable to any person and, if so, the amount of the compensation (subject to the limits set out in these Regulations), the determining authority shall have regard to such of the following factors as may be relevant, that is to say—

(*a*) the conditions upon which the person held the employment which he has lost, including in particular its security of tenure, whether by law or practice;

(*b*) the emoluments and other conditions, including security of tenure, whether by law or practice, of any work or employment undertaken by the person as a result of the loss of employment;

(*c*) the extent to which he has sought suitable employment and the emoluments which he might have acquired by accepting other suitable employment offered to him;

(*d*) all the other circumstances of his case.

(2) In ascertaining for the purposes of paragraph (1)(*c*) whether a person has been offered suitable employment, Regulation 6(2) and (3) shall apply as they apply for the purpose of ascertaining whether employment is reasonably comparable with employment which has been lost.

*Amount of long-term compensation payable for loss of emoluments*

**14.**—(1) Long-term compensation for loss of emoluments shall, subject to the provisions of these Regulations, be payable until the normal retiring age or death of a person to whom it is payable, whichever first occurs, and shall not exceed a maximum annual sum calculated in accordance with the provisions of paragraphs (2) to (4).

(2) The said maximum annual sum shall, subject as hereinafter provided, be the aggregate of the following sums, namely—

(*a*) for every year of the person's reckonable service, one-sixtieth of the net emoluments which he has lost; and

(*b*) in the case of a person who has attained the age of forty years at the date of the loss, a sum calculated in accordance with the provisions of paragraph (3) appropriate to his age at that date,

but the said maximum annual sum shall in no case exceed two-thirds of the net emoluments which the person has lost.

(3) The sum referred to in paragraph (2)(*b*) shall be—

(*a*) in the case of a person who has attained the age of forty years but has not attained the age of fifty years at the date of the loss, the following fraction of the net emoluments which he has lost—

(i) where his reckonable service is less than ten years, one-sixtieth for each year of such service after attaining the age of forty years; or

    (ii) where his reckonable service amounts to ten years but is less than fifteen years, one-sixtieth for each year of such service after attaining the age of forty years and one additional sixtieth; or

    (iii) where his reckonable service amounts to fifteen years but is less than twenty years, one-sixtieth for each year of such service after attaining the age of forty years and two additional sixtieths; or

    (iv) where his reckonable service amounts to twenty years or more, one-sixtieth for each year of such service after attaining the age of forty years and three additional sixtieths;

but the sum so calculated shall not in any case exceed one-sixth of the said net emoluments;

    (b) in the case of a person who has attained the age of fifty years but has not attained the age of sixty years at the date of the loss, one-sixtieth of the said net emoluments for each year of his reckonable service after attaining the age of forty years, up to a maximum of fifteen such years; and

    (c) in the case of a person who has attained the age of sixty years at the date of the loss, one-sixtieth of the said net emoluments for each year of his reckonable service after attaining the age of forty-five years.

(4) Where a person has become entitled (whether immediately or prospectively on attaining some greater age) to a superannuation benefit by way of annual amounts under a pension scheme associated with the employment which he has lost, the maximum annual sum referred to in paragraph (1) shall be the maximum sum calculated under paragraphs (2) and (3) as if he had not become so entitled.

(5) Where long-term compensation is payable in respect of any period and resettlement compensation has also been paid in respect of that period, the long-term compensation shall be limited to the amount (if any) by which it exceeds the resettlement compensation paid as aforesaid.

(6) Long-term compensation shall be payable to a person at intervals equivalent to those at which the emoluments of his employment were previously paid or at such other intervals as may be agreed between the person and the paying authority.

*Long-term compensation for diminution of emoluments*

**15.** Long-term compensation for diminution of emoluments in respect of any employment shall, subject to the provisions of these Regulations, be awarded and paid in accordance with the following provisions:—

    (a) the compensation shall consist of an annual sum which shall be payable to a person at intervals equivalent to those at which the emoluments of his employment are or were previously paid or at such other intervals as may be agreed between the person and the paying authority, and shall, subject to the provisions of these Regulations, be payable until normal retiring age or death, whichever first occurs; and

    (b) the said annual sum shall not exceed the maximum annual sum which could have been awarded under Regulation 14 if the person had suffered loss of employment and of emoluments equivalent to the amount of the diminution:

Provided that no compensation shall be payable if the emoluments have been diminished by less than 2½ per cent.

*Date from which long-term compensation is to be payable*

**16.**—(1) Long-term compensation shall be payable with effect from the date of the claim or from any earlier date permitted by the succeeding provisions of this Regulation.

(2) Where a claim for long-term compensation is duly made within thirteen weeks of the occurrence of the loss or diminution which is the cause of the claim, the award shall be made retrospective to the date on which the loss or diminution occurred.

(3) Where a claim for long-term compensation is made after the expiry of the period mentioned in paragraph (2), the award may, at the discretion of the determining authority, be made retrospective to a date not earlier than thirteen weeks prior to the date on which the claim was made:

Provided that if the determining authority is satisfied that the failure to make the claim within the period mentioned in paragraph (2) was due to ill-health or other circumstances beyond the claimant's control, the award may be made retrospective to a date not earlier than that on which the loss or diminution occurred.

## PART V

### RETIREMENT COMPENSATION AND PAYMENTS ON DEATH

*Entitlement to retirement compensation and other payments*

**17.**—(1) The paying authority shall, subject to the provisions of these Regulations, pay retirement compensation to any person to whom this Part of these Regulations applies, and shall make the other payments for which provision is made in Regulations 25 to 29.

(2) Save as is provided in Regulation 28, this Part of these Regulations applies to a pensionable officer who satisfies the conditions set out in Regulation 12.

(3) Regulation 13 shall apply in relation to retirement compensation as it applies in relation to long-term compensation.

*Additional factors governing payment of retirement compensation*

**18.**—(1) Where retirement compensation is payable under any one of Regulations 19, 20, 21 and 22, such compensation shall not be payable under any other of those Regulations.

(2) If a person has attained the age of forty years at the date on which he lost his employment or suffered a diminution of his emoluments, the determining authority, in calculating the amount of the retirement compensation payable to him, shall credit him with additional years of service or an additional period of contribution on the following basis, namely—

    (*a*) two years, whether or not he has completed any years of service after attaining the age of forty years, and

    (*b*) two years for each of the first four completed years of his reckonable service between the date when he attained the age of forty years and the date of the loss or diminution, and

    (*c*) one year for each such year of service after the fourth,
but the additional years of service or period of contribution so credited shall not exceed the shortest of the following periods, namely—

      (i) such number of years as, when added to his pensionable service, would amount to the maximum period of such service which would have been reckonable by him had he continued in his employment until attaining normal retiring age, or

(ii) the number of years of his reckonable service, or

(iii) fifteen years;

and in calculating the amount of any retirement compensation payable to him any period so added shall be aggregated with any years of service or period of contribution entailing reduction of the relevant pension or retiring allowance because of a retirement pension payable under section 30 of the National Insurance Act 1965(a).

(3) When retirement compensation is awarded, or when an award is reviewed under Regulation 34, the additional compensation payable in consequence of any years of service or period of contribution credited to a person under paragraph (2) may be reduced or withheld to such an extent as the determining authority may think reasonable having regard to the pension scheme (if any) associated with any further employment obtained by him.

(4) If under his last relevant pension scheme the amount of any benefit to which a person might have become entitled could have been increased at the discretion of the authority administering the pension scheme or of any other body, the determining authority may increase, to an extent not exceeding that to which his accrued pension, accrued retiring allowance, accrued incapacity pension or accrued incapacity retiring allowance might have been increased or supplemented, the corresponding component of any retirement compensation payable to him; and in this connection the determining authority shall have regard to the terms of any relevant resolutions of the authority or body with regard to the increase of benefits and to the provision of any enactment protecting the interests of that person.

(5) If under his last relevant pension scheme a person would have been entitled to surrender a proportion of any pension which might have become payable to him in favour of his spouse or any dependant, then, if he so desires and informs the determining authority by notice in writing accordingly within one month after becoming entitled to retirement compensation under these Regulations, he may surrender a proportion of so much of the said compensation as is payable by way of an annual sum on the like terms and conditions and in consideration of the like payments by the paying authority as if the said annual sum were a pension to which he had become entitled under the said pension scheme.

(6) In calculating for the purposes of Regulation 19, 20 or 21 the amount of the annual sum which is equal to a person's accrued pension, no account shall be taken of any reduction falling to be made in that pension by reason of the provisions of any Act relating to National Insurance until the person reaches the age at which under his last relevant pension scheme the pension would have been so reduced.

(7) In paragraph (2) the expression "reckonable service" includes any period of employment of which account has been taken or is required to be taken in calculating the amount of any superannuation benefit to which a person has become entitled under a pension scheme associated with the employment which he has lost or, as the case may be, the employment in which his emoluments were diminished.

_____

(a) 1965 c. 51.

*Retirement compensation for loss of emoluments payable to pensionable officer on attainment of normal retiring age*

**19.** Subject to the provisions of these Regulations, when a person to whom this Part of these Regulations applies reaches normal retiring age, the retirement compensation payable to him for loss of emoluments shall be—

(*a*) an annual sum equal to the amount of his accrued pension, and

(*b*) a lump sum equal to the amount of his accrued retiring allowance (if any).

*Retirement compensation payable to pensionable officer on his becoming incapacitated or reaching minimum pensionable age*

**20.**—(1) Where a person to whom this Part of these Regulations applies and who has suffered loss of employment before attaining what would have been his normal retiring age—

(*a*) becomes incapacitated in circumstances in which, if he had continued in the employment which he has lost, he would have become entitled to a pension under his last relevant pension scheme; or

(*b*) attains the age which, had he continued to serve in the employment which he has lost, would have been his minimum pensionable age,

he shall be entitled on the happening of either event to claim, in lieu of any compensation to which he would otherwise be entitled under these Regulations—

(i) in the case mentioned in head (*a*) of this paragraph, an annual sum equal to the amount of his accrued incapacity pension and a lump sum equal to the amount of his accrued incapacity retiring allowance (if any), and

(ii) in the case mentioned in head (*b*) of this paragraph, an annual sum equal to the amount of his accrued pension and a lump sum equal to the amount of his accrued retiring allowance (if any),

subject however to the conditions specified in paragraph (5).

(2) On receipt of a claim under paragraph (1) the determining authority shall consider whether the claimant is a person to whom that paragraph applies, and within thirteen weeks after the date of the receipt of the claim—

(*a*) if it is satisfied that he is not such a person, it shall notify him in writing accordingly; or

(*b*) if it is satisfied that he is such a person, it shall assess the amount of compensation payable to him and notify him in writing accordingly,

and any such notification shall, for the purposes of these Regulations, be deemed to be a notification by the authority of a decision on a claim for compensation.

(3) A determining authority may require any person who makes a claim under head (*a*) of paragraph (1) to submit himself to a medical examination by a registered medical practitioner selected by that authority, and, if it does so, it shall also offer the person an opportunity of submitting a report from his own medical adviser as a result of an examination by him, and the authority shall take that report into consideration together with the report of the medical practitioner selected by it.

(4) If a person wishes to receive compensation under this Regulation, he shall so inform the determining authority in writing within one month from the receipt of a notification under paragraph (2) or, where the claim has been the subject of an appeal, from the decision of the tribunal thereon; and the compensation shall be payable as from the date on which the determining authority received the claim.

(5) The calculation of compensation under this Regulation shall be subject to the following conditions—

   (a) where the determining authority, by virtue of Regulation 18, has credited the person with additional years of service or an additional period of contribution, no account shall be taken of any additional years or period beyond the number of years which he could have served, had he not lost his employment, before the date on which the claim was received by the determining authority; and

   (b) if, by reason of any provision of the relevant pension scheme for a minimum benefit, the amount of any such pension or retiring allowance is in excess of that attributable to the person's actual service, no account shall be taken of any such additional years or period except to the extent (if any) by which they exceed the number of years represented by the difference between his actual service and the period by reference to which the minimum benefit has been calculated; and

   (c) if the number of years by reference to which an accrued incapacity pension or accrued incapacity retiring allowance is to be calculated is less than any minimum number of years of qualifying service prescribed by the relevant pension scheme, the amount of such pension or retiring allowance shall, notwithstanding any minimum benefit prescribed by the pension scheme, not exceed such proportion of such minimum benefit as the number of years of pensionable service bears to the minimum number of years of qualifying service.

*Option to take retirement compensation prematurely*

**21.**—(1) If a person to whom this Part of these Regulations applies has suffered loss of employment after attaining the age of fifty years and so requests the determining authority by notice in writing, he shall be entitled, as from the date on which the determining authority receives such notice, to an annual sum equal to the amount of his accrued pension and a lump sum equal to the amount of his accrued retiring allowance (if any), and in that event he shall not be entitled to receive any further payment of long-term compensation after that date:

Provided that—

   (i) in calculating the amount of the compensation payable to a person who has given such notice as aforesaid no account shall be taken of any additional years of service or period of contribution credited to him under Regulation 18; and

   (ii) where the person has claimed long-term compensation the said notice shall be given not later than two years after the determination of the claim or, where the determination has been reviewed under Regulation 34(3), not later than two years after the review.

(2) Regulation 20(2) shall apply in relation to a notice given under the last foregoing paragraph as it applies to a claim made under paragraph (1) of that Regulation.

(3) Where an annual sum is payable under this Regulation in respect of any period and resettlement compensation is also payable in respect of that period, the said annual sum shall be limited to the amount (if any) by which it exceeds the resettlement compensation payable as aforesaid.

*Retirement compensation for diminution of emoluments*

**22.** Regulations 19 and 20 shall apply to a person to whom this Part of these Regulations applies and who has suffered a diminution of his emoluments, as if

2f

he had suffered loss of employment and of emoluments equivalent to the amount of the diminution:

Provided that no compensation shall be payable—

(i) if the emoluments have been diminished by less than $2\frac{1}{2}$ per cent.; or

(ii) if the person has continued to pay superannuation contributions as if his emoluments had not been diminished.

*Superannuation contributions*

**23.**—(1) A person entitled to retirement compensation under Regulation 19, 20 or 21 shall pay to the paying authority an amount equal to any sum which was paid to him by way of return of superannuation contributions, including any interest, after ceasing to be employed, and the paying authority may at his request repay that amount to him at any time before he becomes entitled as aforesaid, but if that amount is not paid to the paying authority, or is repaid by them to the person, the compensation shall be reduced by an annual amount the capital value of which is equal to the amount of the said superannuation contributions.

(2) For the purposes of this Regulation the expression "superannuation contributions" shall include payments made by the person in respect of added years and any additional contributory payments made by him.

(3) Any sums paid to a paying authority under this Regulation in respect of returned contributions shall, except in so far as they are repaid to the officers concerned, be applied for the payment of compensation which the authority is liable to pay under this Part of these Regulations.

*Retirement compensation of a person who obtains further pensionable employment*

**24.**—(1) Where a person to whom this Part of these Regulations applies, after suffering loss of employment or diminution of emoluments, enters employment in which he is subject to a pension scheme and thereafter becomes entitled to reckon for the purposes of that scheme any service or period of contribution which falls to be taken into account for the purpose of assessing the amount of any retirement compensation payable to him, his entitlement to retirement compensation shall be reviewed and no retirement compensation shall be payable in respect of such service or period unless the annual rate of the emoluments to which he was entitled immediately before such loss or diminution exceeds the annual rate on entry of the emoluments of the new employment by more than $2\frac{1}{2}$ per cent. of such first mentioned emoluments, and any retirement compensation so payable to him shall, in so far as it is calculated by reference to remuneration, be calculated by reference to the difference between the said annual rates:

Provided that this paragraph shall not operate to increase the amount of any retirement compensation payable in respect of diminution of emoluments beyond the amount which would have been payable if the person had attained normal retiring age immediately before he ceased to hold the employment in which he suffered the diminution of emoluments.

(2) No retirement compensation shall be payable in the circumstances mentioned in paragraph (1) if the person has continued to pay superannuation contributions as if his emoluments had not been diminished.

*Compensation payable to widow or dependants of a claimant*

**25.**—(1) Payments in accordance with this Regulation and Regulations 26 and 27 shall be made to or for the benefit of the widow, child or other dependant or to the personal representatives of a person to whom this Part of these Regulations applies.

(2) If the widow, child or other dependant of that person might have become entitled to a pension under his last relevant pension scheme, the widow, child or other dependant, as the case may be, shall be entitled to receive an annual sum equal to the prescribed proportion of any retirement compensation by way of annual amounts payable to the person under Regulation 19, 20 or 21 immediately before his death or, if he dies before becoming entitled to receive compensation under any of those Regulations, the prescribed proportion of the compensation by way of annual amounts which he would have received under Regulation 20 had he become entitled thereto immediately before his death:

Provided that—

    (i) where any retirement compensation has been surrendered under Regulation 18(5) or compounded under Regulation 35, any sum payable under this Regulation shall be calculated as if such surrender or compounding had not taken place;

    (ii) where the pension scheme provides for payment of the pension to any person on behalf of a child or other dependant, any annual sum payable as aforesaid to a child or other dependant shall be paid to that person on behalf of the child or dependant in the like manner and for the like period as is provided in the pension scheme;

    (iii) in calculating the sum payable as aforesaid, it shall be assumed that the retirement compensation payable, or which would have been payable, to a person under Regulation 19, 20 or 21 was such sum as would have been payable if the accrued pension or accrued incapacity pension had not been reduced by reason of the provisions of any Act relating to National Insurance.

(3) Any annual sum payable to or for the benefit of a widow, child or other dependant under this Regulation shall cease to be payable in any circumstances in which a corresponding pension under the pension scheme referred to in paragraph (2) would have ceased to be payable.

(4) Except where the compensation has been reduced under Regulation 23, compensation payable under this Regulation and Regulation 26 shall in the aggregate be reduced by an amount the capital value whereof is equal to the amount of any superannuation contributions as defined in Regulation 23(2) returned to the person in respect of whom the compensation is payable and either not paid to the paying authority or repaid to him by the paying authority, the compensation under each such Regulation being reduced in proportion to the capital value of each amount.

(5) This Regulation shall apply in the case of a person who has suffered a diminution of emoluments with the substitution of references to diminution of emoluments for references to loss of employment, and the annual sum payable to a widow, child or other dependant of such a person shall be calculated as if he had lost emoluments equivalent to the amount of the diminution:

Provided that no sum shall be payable under this paragraph—

    (i) if the emoluments have been diminished by less than 2½ per cent.; or

    (ii) if the person has continued to pay superannuation contributions as if his emoluments had not been diminished.

(6) In this Regulation "prescribed proportion" means the proportion which, under the relevant pension scheme, the pension payable to the widow, child or other dependant of any person, as the case may be, bears to the person's pension.

*Compensation where death grant would have been payable*

**26.**—(1) If the widow or the personal representatives of a person to whom this Part of these Regulations applies, or trustees empowered by such a person to stand possessed of any benefit under his last relevant pension scheme, might have become entitled to a death grant under that scheme, she or they, as the case may be, shall be entitled to receive a sum calculated in accordance with the provisions of Regulation 25(4) and paragraph (2) of this Regulation.

(2) The amount of the sum referred to in paragraph (1) shall be ascertained in accordance with the method of calculation prescribed by the last relevant pension scheme for the ascertainment of death grant as if the person had died immediately before losing his employment, subject to the following modifications—

(*a*) except where the person had been in receipt of retirement compensation under Regulation 21, account shall be taken of any additional years of service or period of contribution credited to him under Regulation 18(2)—

(i) in the case of a person who had been in receipt of retirement compensation under Regulation 20, to the extent of the period between the loss of employment and the date of the claim made under that Regulation; and

(ii) in any other case, to the extent of the period between the loss of employment and the person's death;

(*b*) if the number of years of the person's service or period of contribution is less than the minimum number of years of qualifying service or period prescribed by the pension scheme for the receipt of a death grant, the said sum shall not exceed such proportion of the death grant calculated as aforesaid as the number of years of the person's pensionable service or period of contribution bears to the minimum number of years of qualifying service or period prescribed by the pension scheme; and

(*c*) there shall be deducted from such sum the amount of any retirement compensation paid to the person under Regulation 19, 20 or 21, or, where any part of the compensation had been surrendered under Regulation 18(5), the amount which would have been so paid but for any such surrender.

(3) For the purpose of calculating such death grant, an annual sum payable to or for the benefit of a widow, child or other dependant under Regulation 25 shall be deemed to be a pension payable to or for the benefit of the widow, child or dependant, as the case may be.

(4) This Regulation shall apply in the case of a person who has suffered a diminution of emoluments with the substitution of references to diminution of emoluments for references to loss of employment, and the sum payable to the widow or personal representatives of such a person shall be calculated as if he had lost emoluments equivalent to the amount of the diminution:

Provided that no sum shall be payable under this paragraph—

(i) if the emoluments have been diminished by less than $2\frac{1}{2}$ per cent.; or

(ii) if the person has continued to pay superannuation contributions as if his emoluments had not been diminished.

*Balance payable to a claimant's widow or personal representatives*

**27.**—(1) If no annual sum is payable to the widow, child or other dependant of any person under Regulation 25 and no sum is payable under Regulation 26 and the person dies before he has received in the aggregate by way of retirement compensation a sum equivalent to the amount of any contributions repaid by him under Regulation 23, together with compound interest thereon calculated at the rate of 3 per cent. per annum with half-yearly rests up to the date of his death as from the 1st April or the 1st October following the half year in which the amount was paid, there shall be paid to his personal representatives the difference between the aggregate amount received by way of retirement compensation as aforesaid and the said equivalent sum.

(2) If an annual sum becomes payable to a widow under Regulation 25 and on her re-marriage or death the sum ceases to be payable, and any sum payable to a child or other dependant under that Regulation has ceased to be payable, and if the aggregate amount of the payments which were made as aforesaid, to her husband by way of retirement compensation and to the widow or personal representatives under Regulation 26 is less than a sum equivalent to the amount which would have been payable to the personal representatives under that Regulation if no annual sum had been payable under Regulation 25, there shall be paid to her or her personal representatives the difference between such aggregate amount and the said equivalent sum.

(3) For the purposes of this Regulation a person who has surrendered any part of his retirement compensation under Regulation 18(5) shall be deemed to have received during any period the amount of compensation for that period which he would have received but for any such surrender.

*Compensation payable to non-pensionable officer on reaching retiring age*

**28.**—(1) Where a person who is not a pensionable officer is receiving long-term compensation for loss of employment and attains normal retiring age, the determining authority may, if satisfied that the person would, but for the loss, have continued in the employment he has lost for a substantial period beyond that age, determine that compensation shall continue to be paid to him for the remainder of his life at half its former rate.

(2) Where a person who is not a pensionable officer suffers loss of employment on or after attaining normal retiring age, the determining authority may, if satisfied that the person would in the normal course have continued in the employment he has lost for a further substantial period, determine that compensation shall be paid to him for the remainder of his life at half the rate to which he would have been entitled under Regulation 14 had he not attained normal retiring age at the date on which he lost his employment.

*Persons subject to policy schemes*

**29.**—(1) Regulations 19, 20, 21, 22 and 26 shall not apply to a person (in this Regulation referred to as a "policy scheme participant") who had been participating in a scheme associated with his employment for providing superannuation benefits by means of contracts or policies of insurance, and who, after the loss of his employment or the diminution of his emoluments, continued to participate in that scheme, or became entitled to a benefit or prospective benefit thereunder other than a return of contributions.

(2) If a policy scheme participant has lost his employment, the determining authority may, if the relevant scheme so permits, determine that such payments shall be made to or in respect of him, whether by way of the payment of premiums or otherwise, as are actuarially equivalent to the amounts by which his retirement compensation might have been increased under Regulation 18(2) or (4) had he been a person to whom Regulation 19, 20 or 21 applied.

(3) If a policy scheme participant has suffered a diminution of his emoluments, the determining authority may, if the relevant scheme so permits,

determine that such payments shall be made to or in respect of him, whether by way of the payment of premiums or otherwise, as will secure to him the like benefits as if his emoluments had not been diminished.

(4) If a policy scheme participant becomes entitled to a benefit under such a scheme as is mentioned in paragraph (1) before reaching normal retiring age, the determining authority may reduce any long-term compensation payable to him by the amount of such benefit.

*Intervals for payment of compensation under Part V*

**30.** Any compensation awarded as an annual sum under this Part of these Regulations to or in respect of any person shall be payable at intervals equivalent to those at which the corresponding benefit would have been payable under the person's last relevant pension scheme or at such other intervals as may be agreed between the person entitled to receive the compensation and the paying authority.

## PART VI

### ADJUSTMENT, REVIEW AND COMPOUNDING OF COMPENSATION

*Adjustment of compensation where superannuation benefit is also payable*

**31.**—(1) Where any period of service of which account was taken in calculating the amount of any compensation payable under Part IV or V of these Regulations is subsequently taken into account for the purpose of calculating the amount of any superannuation benefit payable to or in respect of any person in accordance with a pension scheme associated with any employment undertaken subsequent to the loss of employment or diminution of emoluments which was the subject of the claim for compensation, the determining authority may in accordance with this Regulation withhold or reduce the compensation payable in respect of any period for which such superannuation benefit is being received.

(2) If the part of any superannuation benefit by way of annual amounts which is attributable to a period of service mentioned in paragraph (1) equals or exceeds the part of any compensation by way of annual amounts which is attributable to the same period, that part of the compensation may be withheld, or, if such part of the superannuation benefit is less than such part of the compensation, the compensation may be reduced by an amount not exceeding such part of the superannuation benefit.

(3) In the case of a death benefit payable in respect of any person, the sum payable under Regulation 26 may be reduced by an amount not greater than the proportion of the death benefit which the period of service mentioned in paragraph (1) bears to the total period of service of which account was taken in the calculation of the death benefit.

(4) In addition to any reduction authorised by paragraph (2) or (3), if, in the circumstances mentioned in paragraph (1), compensation by way of annual amounts is attributable in part to any provision of the relevant pension scheme for a minimum benefit, the compensation may be reduced by an amount not exceeding that part.

(5) Where any additional years of service or period of contribution have been credited to a person under Regulation 18(2), if the number of such years or such period is equal to or less than the period spent in the subsequent employment mentioned in paragraph (1), the compensation by way of annual amounts may be reduced (in addition to any other reduction authorised by this Regulation) by an amount not exceeding that attributable to the additional years or period

so credited or, if the number of such years or such period is greater than the period spent in the subsequent employment, by such proportion of that amount as the period spent in the subsequent employment bears to the number of additional years or the period so credited.

(6) Where compensation has been calculated in accordance with Regulation 24, the provisions of this Regulation shall apply only in relation to such part (if any) of the superannuation benefit as is attributable to annual emoluments in excess of those to which the person was entitled on entering the new employment referred to in Regulation 24.

(7) Where compensation is payable in respect of diminution of emoluments, the provisions of this Regulation shall apply only in relation to such part (if any) of the superannuation benefit as is attributable to annual emoluments in excess of those to which the person was entitled immediately prior to the diminution.

### Reduction of compensation in certain cases

**32.**—(1) If under a person's last relevant pension scheme any benefit for which the scheme provided would have been subject to reduction or suspension on his taking up other specified employment, any retirement compensation to which he is entitled for loss of employment or diminution of emoluments shall, where such employment is taken up, be reduced or suspended in the like manner and to the like extent:

Provided that in calculating the amount of the reduction there shall be aggregated with the emoluments of the employment taken up the amount of any superannuation benefit by way of annual amounts payable to the person under a pension scheme associated with the employment which he has lost or, as the case may be, the employment in which the emoluments were diminished.

(2) There shall be deducted from the retirement compensation payable to any person any additional contributory payments remaining unpaid at the date when he suffered loss of employment; and any such payments not recovered at the date of his death shall be deducted from any compensation payable in respect of that person under Regulation 25, 26 or 27.

(3) Where a person is entitled to compensation under these Regulations and the circumstances are such that he is also entitled to—

(a) a redundancy payment under the Redundancy Payments Act 1965(a), or

(b) any similar payment in consequence of the loss of his employment under any contract or arrangement with the authority or person by whom he was appointed or employed (other than payments by way of a return of contributions under a pension scheme), or

(c) any payment under or by virtue of the provisions of any enactment relating to the reinstatement in civil employment of persons who have been in the service of the Crown,

the compensation which would, apart from this paragraph become due to the person, whether by instalments or lump sum or both, shall in the aggregate be reduced by the amount of the payments referred to in this paragraph.

(4) Where compensation under these Regulations is payable to or in respect of any person, and that person or his widow, child or other dependant or his personal representatives is or are also entitled (whether immediately or on the person's attaining some greater age) to a superannuation benefit under a pension scheme associated with the employment which he has lost—

(a) any instalment of such compensation which is payable in respect of any period shall be reduced by the amount of the instalment of such

---

(a) 1965 c. 62.

superannuation benefit which is payable in respect of the same period; and

(b) any such compensation which is payable as a lump sum shall be reduced by the amount of any lump sum superannuation benefit.

(5) For the purposes of paragraph (4) no account shall be taken of any sum payable in consequence of the surrender by any person of part of his superannuation benefit under any provision in that behalf in the relevant pension scheme with a view to obtaining or increasing allowances for his widow, child or other dependant; and the person shall be deemed to have received during any period the amount of superannuation benefit which he would have received but for any such surrender.

(6) Where in any week a person is entitled to long-term compensation for loss or diminution of emoluments and is also entitled to unemployment, sickness or injury benefit under any Act relating to National Insurance, other than a benefit claimable by him in respect of a dependant, there shall be deducted from the long-term compensation payable for that week a sum equal to the amount by which the aggregate of such National Insurance benefits claimable in respect of that week and the weekly rate at which the long-term compensation would be payable but for this Regulation exceeds two-thirds of the weekly rate of the net emoluments of the employment which he has lost or in which the emoluments have been diminished:

Provided that this paragraph shall not apply in relation to any such sickness or injury benefit in so far as—

(i) an equivalent sum is deducted from the emoluments of his current employment, and

(ii) such deduction from those emoluments has not occasioned an increase in his long-term compensation.

(7) In paragraph (6) the expression "weekly rate" means seven three hundred and sixty-fifths of the relevant annual rate.

*Notification of change of circumstances*

**33.** Where—

(a) a pensionable officer after suffering loss of employment or diminution of emoluments enters any employment referred to in Regulation 24 or becomes entitled to any superannuation benefit on ceasing to hold such employment, or

(b) a person entitled to long-term compensation enters employment the remuneration whereof is payable out of public funds, or ceases to hold such employment, or receives any increase in his remuneration in such employment, or

(c) a person entitled to retirement compensation enters employment in which the compensation is subject to reduction or suspension under Regulation 32, or ceases to hold such employment, or receives any increase in his remuneration in such employment, or

(d) a person entitled to long-term compensation is receiving or starts to receive any benefit, any increase in benefit or any further benefit under any Act relating to National Insurance,

he shall forthwith inform the determining authority in writing of that fact.

*Review of awards of long-term or retirement compensation*

**34.**—(1) The determining authority shall, within a period of two years after the date on which any decision on a claim for long-term or retirement compensation for loss of employment (other than compensation payable under Regulation 21) is notified to a claimant under Regulation 36, or within such longer period as is specified in the subsequent provisions of this Regulation, and at intervals of not more than six months, review its decision or, where the claim has been the subject of an appeal, the decision of the tribunal, and these Regulations shall apply in relation to any such review as they apply in relation to the initial determination of the claim; and on such review, in the light of any material change in the circumstances of the case, compensation may be awarded, or compensation previously awarded may be increased, reduced or discontinued, subject to the limits set out in these Regulations.

(2) The person to whom the decision relates may require the determining authority to carry out the review mentioned in paragraph (1) at any time within the period of two years mentioned in that paragraph if he considers that there has been a change in the circumstances of his case which is material for the purposes of these Regulations.

(3) The determining authority shall carry out a review in accordance with paragraph (1), notwithstanding the expiration of the period mentioned in that paragraph, if—

(a) the emoluments of employment or work undertaken as a result of the loss of employment were taken into account in determining the amount of any compensation awarded, and

(b) such employment or work has been lost or the emoluments thereof reduced, otherwise than by reason of misconduct or incapacity to perform such duties as the person might reasonably have been required to perform, and

(c) the determining authority is satisfied that such loss or reduction is causing him hardship,

and where any decision is so reviewed, the decision shall be subject to further review in accordance with paragraph (1) as if the review carried out under this paragraph had been the initial determination of the claim.

(4) Paragraphs (1) and (2) shall apply in relation to any decision on a claim for long-term or retirement compensation in respect of diminution of emoluments as they apply in relation to any decision mentioned in paragraph (1):

Provided that—

(i) where the person to whom the decision relates ceases to hold the employment in which his emoluments were diminished, a review shall be held within three months after that date, but no further review shall be held after the expiry of that period, and

(ii) while that person continues to hold that employment, there shall be no limit to the period within which a review may take place.

(5) Notwithstanding anything contained in the foregoing provisions of this Regulation, the determining authority shall review a decision (whether of the authority or the tribunal) on a claim for long-term compensation for loss of employment or diminution of emoluments after the expiration of any period within which a review is required to be made if at any time—

(a) the person to whom the decision relates becomes engaged in employment (hereinafter referred to as his "current employment") the remuneration whereof is payable out of public funds and which he has undertaken subsequent to the loss or diminution, and

(b) the aggregate of the net emoluments of his current employment, any superannuation benefit by way of annual amounts payable to him in respect of the employment which he has lost or the employment in which his emoluments have been diminished and the long-term compensation payable to him exceeds the net emoluments of the employment which he has lost or, as the case may be, in which the emoluments have been diminished.

(6) The determining authority shall further review any decision reviewed under paragraph (5) whenever the net emoluments of the person's current employment are increased.

(7) If on any review under paragraph (5) or (6) the compensation is reduced, it shall not be reduced below the amount by which the net emoluments of the person's current employment, together with any superannuation benefit by way of annual amounts payable to him in respect of the employment which he has lost or the employment in which his emoluments have been diminished, falls short of the net emoluments of the employment he has lost or, as the case may be, in which the emoluments have been diminished.

(8) The determining authority shall give to a person to whom a decision relates not less than fourteen days' notice of any review of that decision to be carried out under this Regulation unless the review is carried out at his request.

(9) Nothing in this Regulation shall preclude the making of any adjustment of compensation required by Regulation 31 or 32.

*Compounding of awards*

35.—(1) In a case where an annual sum which has been or might be awarded under these Regulations does not exceed £26, the determining authority may, at its discretion, determine that the liability of the paying authority in respect thereof shall be compounded by payment of a sum equivalent to the capital value of the annual sum and, if any lump sum payment has been or might be awarded in addition to such annual sum under Regulation 19, 20, 21 or 22, the determining authority may likewise determine that the liability of the paying authority in respect thereof shall be discharged by an immediate payment.

(2) In any other case, if the person who has been awarded long-term or retirement compensation requests them to do so, the determining authority may, after having regard to the state of health of that person and the other circumstances of the case, determine that up to one quarter of the liability of the paying authority to make payments under the award (other than payments to a widow, child or other dependant under Regulation 25) shall be compounded by the payment of an equivalent amount as a lump sum or, where any compensation has been awarded as a lump sum, by increasing that compensation to such equivalent amount; and in calculating for this purpose the liability of the paying authority to make such payments, account shall be taken of the annual value of lump sum payments of compensation.

(3) The making of a composition under paragraph (2) in relation to an award of long-term or retirement compensation shall not prevent the subsequent making of a composition under paragraph (1) in relation to that award, but, subject as aforesaid, not more than one composition may be made in relation to any award.

## PART VII

### PROCEDURE AND MISCELLANEOUS

*Procedure on making claims*

36.—(1) Every claim for compensation under these Regulations and every request for a review of an award of long-term or retirement compensation shall be made in accordance with this Regulation.

(2) Every such claim and request shall be made to the determining authority in a form approved by the Secretary of State, and shall state whether any other claim for compensation has been made by the claimant under these Regulations.

(3) Resettlement compensation shall be claimed separately from any other form of compensation claimable under these Regulations.

(4) The determining authority shall consider any such claim or request in accordance with the relevant provisions of these Regulations and shall notify the person making the claim or request in writing of its decision—

(a) in the case of a claim for resettlement compensation, not later than one month after the receipt of the claim, and

(b) in the case of a claim for, or request for the review of an award of, compensation under Part IV or V of these Regulations, not later than thirteen weeks after the receipt of the claim or request, and

(c) in any other case, as soon as possible after the decision;

but the decision of a determining authority shall not be invalidated by reason of the fact that notice of the decision is given after the expiry of the period mentioned in this paragraph.

(5) Every notification of a decision by the determining authority (whether granting or refusing compensation or reviewing an award, or otherwise affecting any compensation under these Regulations) shall contain a statement—

(a) giving reasons for the decision;

(b) showing how any compensation has been calculated and, in particular, if the amount is less than the maximum which could have been awarded under these Regulations, showing the factors taken into account in awarding that amount; and

(c) directing the attention of the claimant to his right under Regulation 42, if he is aggrieved by the decision, to institute proceedings before a tribunal and giving him the address to which the application instituting such proceedings should be sent.

### Claimants to furnish information

37.—(1) Any person claiming or receiving compensation or whose award of compensation is being reviewed shall furnish all such information as the determining authority may at any time reasonably require; and he shall verify the same in such manner, including the production of books or of original documents in his possession or control, as may be reasonably so required.

(2) Any such person shall, on receipt of reasonable notice, present himself for interview at such place as the determining authority may reasonably require; and any person who attends for interview may, if he so desires, be represented by his adviser.

### Procedure on death of claimant

38.—(1) In the event of the death of a claimant or of a person who, if he had survived, could have been a claimant, a claim for compensation under these Regulations may be continued or made, as the case may be, by his personal representatives.

(2) Where any such claim is continued or made as aforesaid by personal representatives, the personal representatives shall, as respects any steps to be taken or thing to be done by them in order to continue or make the claim, be deemed for the purposes of these Regulations to be the person entitled to

claim, but, save as aforesaid, the person in whose right they continue or make the claim shall be deemed for the purposes of these Regulations to be such person, and the relevant provisions of these Regulations shall be construed accordingly:

Provided that the determining authority may in any such case extend the period within which a claim is required to be made by Regulation 6 or 12.

*Calculation of service*

**39.**—(1) For the purpose of determining the amount of any compensation payable in respect of the loss of an office to which, or of any two or more offices to which in the aggregate, a person devoted substantially the whole of his time, any previous period of part-time employment shall be treated as though it were whole-time employment for a proportionately reduced period.

(2) For the purpose of making any calculation under these Regulations in respect of a person's reckonable service, all periods of such service shall be aggregated and, except where reference is made to completed years of service, if the aggregated service includes a fraction of a year, that fraction shall, if it equals or exceeds six months, be treated as a year, and shall in any other case be disregarded.

*Emoluments of part-time employments*

**40.** In ascertaining for the purposes of these Regulations whether, and how far, the remuneration of alternative employment falls short of emoluments which have been lost where those emoluments were payable in respect of two or more part-time employments, the remuneration of the alternative employment or of the aggregate of two or more such employments shall be apportioned in the proportion which the emoluments of the part-time employments bore to each other.

*Compensation not assignable*

**41.** Subject to any statutory provision in that behalf, any compensation to which a person becomes entitled under these Regulations shall be paid by the paying authority and shall be payable to, or in trust for, the person who is entitled to receive it, and shall not be assignable:

Provided that, without prejudice to any other right of recovery, any compensation paid in error may be recovered by the paying authority by deduction from any compensation payable under these Regulations.

*Right of appeal from decision of determining authority*

**42.**—(1) Every person who is aggrieved by any decision of the determining authority with respect to a compensation question or by any failure on the part of the determining authority to notify him or, if required by these Regulations, the paying authority of any such decision within the appropriate time prescribed by these Regulations, may within thirteen weeks of the notification to him of the decision or the expiry of the prescribed time, as the case may be, institute proceedings for the determination of the question by a tribunal in accordance with the Industrial Tribunals (Employment and Compensation) Regulations 1967(a) and these Regulations; and the tribunal shall determine the question accordingly.

(2) A local authority (unless it is itself the sole determining authority) which is or forms part of the paying authority and which is aggrieved by any decision of the determining authority with respect to a compensation question may, within thirteen weeks of the notification to it of the decision, institute

---

(a) S.I. 1967/361 (1967 I, p. 1205).

proceedings for the determination of the question by a tribunal in accordance with the said Regulations; and the tribunal shall determine the question accordingly.

(3) For the purpose of any proceedings instituted under this Regulation a person or persons may be appointed to sit with the tribunal as assessor or assessors.

(4) The paying authority shall give effect to the decision of a tribunal subject to any modifications that may be required in consequence of any appeal from that decision on a point of law.

*George Thomas,*
One of Her Majesty's Principal
Secretaries of State.

Whitehall.
18th March 1969.

Regulation 2(2)          SCHEDULE

## TABLES OF ANNUAL AND CAPITAL VALUES

### TABLE I

Table showing the capital value of an annual amount of £1 payable for life

| Age | Capital value of £1 per annum payable for life | |
|---|---|---|
| | Female | Male |
| | £ s. d. | £ s. d. |
| Under 35 ... ... ... ... ... ... ... | 15 11 0 | 15 3 0 |
| 35 and under 40 ... ... ... ... ... ... | 15 2 0 | 14 12 0 |
| 40 and under 45 ... ... ... ... ... ... | 14 11 0 | 13 19 0 |
| 45 and under 50 ... ... ... ... ... ... | 13 18 0 | 13 2 0 |
| 50 ... ... ... ... ... ... ... | 13 9 0 | 12 11 0 |
| 51 ... ... ... ... ... ... ... | 13 5 0 | 12 7 0 |
| 52 ... ... ... ... ... ... ... | 13 2 0 | 12 3 0 |
| 53 ... ... ... ... ... ... ... | 12 18 0 | 11 18 0 |
| 54 ... ... ... ... ... ... ... | 12 14 0 | 11 14 0 |
| 55 ... ... ... ... ... ... ... | 12 10 0 | 11 9 0 |
| 56 ... ... ... ... ... ... ... | 12 6 0 | 11 5 0 |
| 57 ... ... ... ... ... ... ... | 12 2 0 | 11 0 0 |
| 58 ... ... ... ... ... ... ... | 11 18 0 | 10 15 0 |
| 59 ... ... ... ... ... ... ... | 11 13 0 | 10 10 0 |
| 60 ... ... ... ... ... ... ... | 11 8 0 | 10 5 0 |
| 61 ... ... ... ... ... ... ... | 11 4 0 | 10 0 0 |
| 62 ... ... ... ... ... ... ... | 10 19 0 | 9 14 0 |
| 63 ... ... ... ... ... ... ... | 10 14 0 | 9 9 0 |
| 64 ... ... ... ... ... ... ... | 10 8 0 | 9 3 0 |
| 65 ... ... ... ... ... ... ... | 10 3 0 | 8 18 0 |
| 66 ... ... ... ... ... ... ... | 9 18 0 | 8 12 0 |
| 67 ... ... ... ... ... ... ... | 9 12 0 | 8 7 0 |
| 68 ... ... ... ... ... ... ... | 9 7 0 | 8 1 0 |
| 69 ... ... ... ... ... ... ... | 9 1 0 | 7 16 0 |
| 70 ... ... ... ... ... ... ... | 8 15 0 | 7 10 0 |

NOTE:—This table is for use in connection with Regulation 35(1) and (2) for the compounding of annual retirement compensation which a person is currently entilted to receive under Regulation 19, 20, 21 or 22. Where the compensation is payable before age 60 (females), 65 (males) but will be reduced on the attainment of that age (in connection with National Insurance pension) the table should be used in conjunction with Table II, i.e. Table II should be used for valuing that part of the compensation which ceases to be payable at 60 (65) and this table should be used for valuing the remainder.

## TABLE II

Table showing the capital value of an amount of £1 per annum ceasing
at age 60 (females), 65 (males)

| Age | | | | | | | Capital Value | | | | | |
|---|---|---|---|---|---|---|---|---|---|---|---|---|
| | | | | | | | Female | | | Male | | |
| | | | | | | | £ | s. | d. | £ | s. | d. |
| Under 35 | ... | ... | ... | ... | ... | ... | 13 | 8 | 0 | 14 | 2 | 0 |
| 35 and under 40 | ... | ... | ... | ... | ... | ... | 12 | 5 | 0 | 13 | 3 | 0 |
| 40 and under 45 | ... | ... | ... | ... | ... | ... | 10 | 14 | 0 | 11 | 19 | 0 |
| 45 and under 50 | ... | ... | ... | ... | ... | ... | 8 | 13 | 0 | 10 | 8 | 0 |
| 50 | ... | ... | ... | ... | ... | ... | 7 | 3 | 0 | 9 | 6 | 0 |
| 51 | ... | ... | ... | ... | ... | ... | 6 | 12 | 0 | 8 | 18 | 0 |
| 52 | ... | ... | ... | ... | ... | ... | 6 | 0 | 0 | 8 | 9 | 0 |
| 53 | ... | ... | ... | ... | ... | ... | 5 | 7 | 0 | 7 | 19 | 0 |
| 54 | ... | ... | ... | ... | ... | ... | 4 | 13 | 0 | 7 | 10 | 0 |
| 55 | ... | ... | ... | ... | ... | ... | 3 | 18 | 0 | 6 | 19 | 0 |
| 56 | ... | ... | ... | ... | ... | ... | 3 | 3 | 0 | 6 | 8 | 0 |
| 57 | ... | ... | ... | ... | ... | ... | 2 | 6 | 0 | 5 | 17 | 0 |
| 58 | ... | ... | ... | ... | ... | ... | 1 | 9 | 0 | 5 | 4 | 0 |
| 59 | ... | ... | ... | ... | ... | ... | | 10 | 0 | 4 | 11 | 0 |
| 60 | ... | ... | ... | ... | ... | ... | | — | | 3 | 17 | 0 |
| 61 | ... | ... | ... | ... | ... | ... | | — | | 3 | 2 | 0 |
| 62 | ... | ... | ... | ... | ... | ... | | — | | 2 | 6 | 0 |
| 63 | ... | ... | ... | ... | ... | ... | | — | | 1 | 8 | 0 |
| 64 | ... | ... | ... | ... | ... | ... | | — | | | 10 | 0 |

NOTE:—This table is for use in connection with Regulation 35(1) and (2) for the compounding of any part of annual retirement compensation which will cease to be payable on the attainment of age 60 (females), 65 (males). Table I should be used in relation to the remainder of such compensation, i.e. the part which is payable for life—see note on that table.

## TABLE III

Table showing the capital value of an annual amount of £1 payable to a widow until death or remarriage

| Age of widow at date of widowhood | Capital value of £1 per annum as at date of widowhood | Age of widow at date of widowhood | Capital value of £1 per annum as at date of widowhood |
|---|---|---|---|
| | £   s.   d. | | £   s.   d. |
| 20 | 6   0   0 | 45 | 11 18   0 |
| 21 | 6   0   0 | 46 | 12   1   0 |
| 22 | 6   0   0 | 47 | 12   3   0 |
| 23 | 6   0   0 | 48 | 12   5   0 |
| 24 | 6   0   0 | 49 | 12   6   0 |
| 25 | 6   5   0 | 50 | 12   6   0 |
| 26 | 6 12   0 | 51 | 12   6   0 |
| 27 | 6 19   0 | 52 | 12   5   0 |
| 28 | 7   6   0 | 53 | 12   4   0 |
| 29 | 7 13   0 | 54 | 12   3   0 |
| 30 | 8   0   0 | 55 | 12   1   0 |
| 31 | 8   8   0 | 56 | 11 19   0 |
| 32 | 8 15   0 | 57 | 11 16   0 |
| 33 | 9   2   0 | 58 | 11 13   0 |
| 34 | 9   8   0 | 59 | 11 10   0 |
| 35 | 9 15   0 | 60 | 11   6   0 |
| 36 | 10   1   0 | 61 | 11   3   0 |
| 37 | 10   6   0 | 62 | 10 19   0 |
| 38 | 10 11   0 | 63 | 10 14   0 |
| 39 | 10 16   0 | 64 | 10   8   0 |
| 40 | 11   1   0 | 65 | 10   3   0 |
| 41 | 11   5   0 | 66 | 9 18   0 |
| 42 | 11   9   0 | 67 | 9 12   0 |
| 43 | 11 12   0 | 68 | 9   7   0 |
| 44 | 11 15   0 | 69 | 9   1   0 |
| | | 70 | 8 15   0 |

NOTE:—This table is for use in connection with Regulation 35(1) for compounding annual compensation payable to a widow under Regulation 25. It should also be used, where a reduction of compensation under Regulation 25(4) falls to be apportioned between the compensation payable under that Regulation and under Regulation 26, for ascertaining the capital value of annual compensation to a widow.

## TABLE IV

Table showing the annual amount payable for life equivalent in value
to a lump sum of £100

| Age | | | | | | | Annual sum, payable for life, equal in value to a lump sum of £100 | | | | | |
|---|---|---|---|---|---|---|---|---|---|---|---|---|
| | | | | | | | Female | | | Male | | |
| | | | | | | | £ | s. | d. | £ | s. | d. |
| Under 35 ... | ... | ... | ... | ... | ... | ... | 6 | 8 | 7 | 6 | 12 | 0 |
| 35 and under 40 ... | ... | ... | ... | ... | ... | ... | 6 | 12 | 5 | 6 | 17 | 0 |
| 40 and under 45 ... | ... | ... | ... | ... | ... | ... | 6 | 17 | 5 | 7 | 3 | 4 |
| 45 and under 50 ... | ... | ... | ... | ... | ... | ... | 7 | 3 | 11 | 7 | 12 | 8 |
| 50 ... | ... | ... | ... | ... | ... | ... | 7 | 8 | 8 | 7 | 19 | 4 |
| 51 ... | ... | ... | ... | ... | ... | ... | 7 | 10 | 11 | 8 | 1 | 11 |
| 52 ... | ... | ... | ... | ... | ... | ... | 7 | 12 | 8 | 8 | 4 | 7 |
| 53 ... | ... | ... | ... | ... | ... | ... | 7 | 15 | 0 | 8 | 8 | 1 |
| 54 ... | ... | ... | ... | ... | ... | ... | 7 | 17 | 6 | 8 | 10 | 11 |
| 55 ... | ... | ... | ... | ... | ... | ... | 8 | 0 | 0 | 8 | 14 | 8 |
| 56 ... | ... | ... | ... | ... | ... | ... | 8 | 2 | 7 | 8 | 17 | 9 |
| 57 ... | ... | ... | ... | ... | ... | ... | 8 | 5 | 3 | 9 | 1 | 10 |
| 58 ... | ... | ... | ... | ... | ... | ... | 8 | 8 | 1 | 9 | 6 | 0 |
| 59 ... | ... | ... | ... | ... | ... | ... | 8 | 11 | 8 | 9 | 10 | 6 |
| 60 ... | ... | ... | ... | ... | ... | ... | 8 | 15 | 5 | 9 | 15 | 1 |
| 61 ... | ... | ... | ... | ... | ... | ... | 8 | 18 | 7 | 10 | 0 | 0 |
| 62 ... | ... | ... | ... | ... | ... | ... | 9 | 2 | 8 | 10 | 6 | 2 |
| 63 ... | ... | ... | ... | ... | ... | ... | 9 | 6 | 11 | 10 | 11 | 8 |
| 64 ... | ... | ... | ... | ... | ... | ... | 9 | 12 | 4 | 10 | 18 | 7 |
| 65 ... | ... | ... | ... | ... | ... | ... | 9 | 17 | 0 | 11 | 4 | 9 |
| 66 ... | ... | ... | ... | ... | ... | ... | 10 | 2 | 0 | 11 | 12 | 7 |
| 67 ... | ... | ... | ... | ... | ... | ... | 10 | 8 | 4 | 11 | 19 | 6 |
| 68 ... | ... | ... | ... | ... | ... | ... | 10 | 13 | 11 | 12 | 8 | 5 |
| 69 ... | ... | ... | ... | ... | ... | ... | 11 | 1 | 0 | 12 | 16 | 5 |
| 70 ... | ... | ... | ... | ... | ... | ... | 11 | 8 | 7 | 13 | 6 | 8 |

NOTE:—This table is for use in connection with Regulation 23(1) for ascertaining the annual amount by which retirement compensation under Regulation 19, 20 or 21 is to be reduced where a claimant has not paid to the paying authority an amount equal to any sum paid to him by way of superannuation contributions or that amount has been repaid to him by the paying authority at his request. It should also be used in connection with Regulation 35(2) for calculating for the purposes of that paragraph the annual value of retirement compensation awarded as a lump sum.

## TABLE V

Table showing the annual amount payable to a widow until death or
remarriage equivalent in value to a lump sum of £100

| Age of widow at date of widowhood | Annual amount equal in value to a lump sum of £100 | Age of widow at date of widowhood | Annual amount equal in value to a lump sum of £100 |
|---|---|---|---|
| | £  s.  d. | | £  s.  d. |
| 20 | 16 13  4 | 45 | 8  8  1 |
| 21 | 16 13  4 | 46 | 8  6  0 |
| 22 | 16 13  4 | 47 | 8  4  7 |
| 23 | 16 13  4 | 48 | 8  3  3 |
| 24 | 16 13  4 | 49 | 8  2  7 |
| 25 | 16  0  0 | 50 | 8  2  7 |
| 26 | 15  3  0 | 51 | 8  2  7 |
| 27 | 14  7  9 | 52 | 8  3  3 |
| 28 | 13 14  0 | 53 | 8  3 11 |
| 29 | 13  1  5 | 54 | 8  4  7 |
| 30 | 12 10  0 | 55 | 8  6  0 |
| 31 | 11 18  1 | 56 | 8  7  4 |
| 32 | 11  8  7 | 57 | 8  9  6 |
| 33 | 10 19  9 | 58 | 8 11  8 |
| 34 | 10 12  9 | 59 | 8 13 11 |
| 35 | 10  5  2 | 60 | 8 17  0 |
| 36 | 9 19  0 | 61 | 8 19  5 |
| 37 | 9 14  2 | 62 | 9  2  8 |
| 38 | 9  9  7 | 63 | 9  6 11 |
| 39 | 9  5  2 | 64 | 9 12  4 |
| 40 | 9  1  0 | 65 | 9 17  0 |
| 41 | 8 17  9 | 66 | 10  2  0 |
| 42 | 8 14  8 | 67 | 10  8  4 |
| 43 | 8 12  5 | 68 | 10 13 11 |
| 44 | 8 10  3 | 69 | 11  1  0 |
| | | 70 | 11  8  7 |

NOTE:—This table is for use in connection with Regulation 25(4) for ascertaining the annual amount by which compensation to a widow is to be reduced in the circumstances described in that paragraph. If a reduction is required to be apportioned between compensation payable under Regulations 25 and 26, the capital value of annual compensation to a widow should be ascertained by reference to Table III.

## TABLE VI

Table showing, according to the outstanding period of long-term compensation, the capital value of each £100 of the total amount of long-term compensation compounded

| Outstanding number of complete years of long-term compensation | | | | | | Capital value of each £100 of the total amount of long-term compensation | | |
|---|---|---|---|---|---|---|---|---|
| | | | | | | Female | | Male |
| | | | | | | £ s. d. | | £ s. d. |
| 0 | ... | ... | ... | ... | ... | 98 8 0 | | 98 4 0 |
| 1 | ... | ... | ... | ... | ... | 95 4 0 | | 94 16 0 |
| 2 | ... | ... | ... | ... | ... | 92 2 0 | | 91 10 0 |
| 3 | ... | ... | ... | ... | ... | 89 4 0 | | 88 6 0 |
| 4 | ... | ... | ... | ... | ... | 86 8 0 | | 85 8 0 |
| 5 | ... | ... | ... | ... | ... | 83 16 0 | | 82 14 0 |
| 6 | ... | ... | ... | ... | ... | 81 6 0 | | 80 2 0 |
| 7 | ... | ... | ... | ... | ... | 78 18 0 | | 77 14 0 |
| 8 | ... | ... | ... | ... | ... | 76 14 0 | | 75 8 0 |
| 9 | ... | ... | ... | ... | ... | 74 12 0 | | 73 4 0 |
| 10 | ... | ... | ... | ... | ... | 72 12 0 | | 71 4 0 |
| 11 | ... | ... | ... | ... | ... | 70 12 0 | | 69 6 0 |
| 12 | ... | ... | ... | ... | ... | 68 16 0 | | 67 10 0 |
| 13 | ... | ... | ... | ... | ... | 67 0 0 | | 65 14 0 |
| 14 | ... | ... | ... | ... | ... | 65 6 0 | | 64 2 0 |
| 15 | ... | ... | ... | ... | ... | 63 14 0 | | 62 10 0 |
| 16 | ... | ... | ... | ... | ... | 62 2 0 | | 61 0 0 |
| 17 | ... | ... | ... | ... | ... | 60 12 0 | | 59 12 0 |
| 18 | ... | ... | ... | ... | ... | 59 4 0 | | 58 4 0 |
| 19 | ... | ... | ... | ... | ... | 57 16 0 | | 56 18 0 |
| 20 | ... | ... | ... | ... | ... | 56 10 0 | | 55 12 0 |
| 21 | ... | ... | ... | ... | ... | 55 4 0 | | 54 8 0 |
| 22 | ... | ... | ... | ... | ... | 54 0 0 | | 53 4 0 |
| 23 | ... | ... | ... | ... | ... | 52 16 0 | | 52 0 0 |
| 24 | ... | ... | ... | ... | ... | 51 12 0 | | 50 18 0 |
| 25 | ... | ... | ... | ... | ... | 50 10 0 | | 49 18 0 |
| 26 | ... | ... | ... | ... | ... | 49 8 0 | | 48 18 0 |
| 27 | ... | ... | ... | ... | ... | 48 8 0 | | 47 18 0 |
| 28 | ... | ... | ... | ... | ... | 47 8 0 | | 46 18 0 |
| 29 | ... | ... | ... | ... | ... | 46 8 0 | | 45 18 0 |
| 30 | ... | ... | ... | ... | ... | 45 10 0 | | 45 0 0 |

NOTE:—This table is for use in connection with Regulation 35(1) and (2) for compounding awards of long-term compensation under Part IV of these Regulations. The total amount of the annual long-term compensation which is to be compounded must first be calculated, i.e. the amount which the person would receive on account of that compensation or the part of it which is to be compounded, if it were paid until "normal retiring age" (as defined in these Regulations). For each £100 so calculated, the lump sum payment will be the amount shown in the table according to the number of complete years in the period between the date of compounding and "normal retiring age".

## EXPLANATORY NOTE
### (*This Note is not part of the Regulations.*)

1. These Regulations, made under paragraph 16 of Schedule 3 to the Justices of the Peace Act 1968, provide for the payment of compensation in respect of persons who suffer loss of office or employment or loss or diminution of emoluments which is attributable to the operation of section 1 of that Act in relation to the City of London or to the South Staffordshire Stipendiary Justice Act 1899 or the Staffordshire Potteries Stipendiary Justice Acts 1839 to 1895.

2. Part I of the Regulations contains definitions. Part II specifies the persons to whom the Regulations apply and the grounds of entitlement to compensation. The Regulations apply to persons who hold office or employment in respect of which a salary is paid by the Corporation of the City of London or by the South Staffordshire or Staffordshire Potteries Stipendiary Justice Commissioners and to the assistants of such persons.

3. The compensation payable is—

   (*a*) resettlement compensation for loss of employment (Part III of the Regulations) ;

   (*b*) long-term compensation for loss of employment or loss or diminution of emoluments (Part IV) ;

   (*c*) retirement compensation for loss of employment or loss or diminution of emoluments (Part V) ;

   (*d*) compensation to the widow, child or other dependant or to the personal representatives of a claimant who was a pensionable officer (Part V).

4. Resettlement compensation is payable for a period not exceeding 26 weeks to officers with at least three years' service in relevant employment. The qualifying conditions and factors to be considered are set out in Regulation 6. The method of calculating the amount of compensation is contained in Regulation 7.

5. Long-term and retirement compensation is payable to officers with at least eight years' service in relevant employment. The qualifying and other conditions are set out in Regulation 12.

6. The method of calculating the maximum amount of long-term compensation is laid down in Regulation 14 (loss of employment) and 15 (diminution of emoluments). This amount is a proportion, not exceeding two-thirds, of the net emoluments lost or of the amount by which emoluments have been diminished, as the case may be. This compensation is payable from a date determined under Regulation 16 and can be payable up to normal retiring age. In the case of a non-pensionable officer, compensation not exceeding one-half of the rate of long-term compensation may be paid beyond normal retiring age (Regulation 28).

7. Retirement compensation payable to a pensionable officer is based upon his accrued pension rights (Regulations 19 and 22) supplemented in the case of persons aged 40 or over at the date of loss by the addition of notional years of service (Regulation 18). Special provision is made for any persons whose pension arrangements are by way of policies of insurance (Regulation 29). Retirement compensation is ordinarily payable from normal retiring age but in certain circumstances is payable earlier (Regulations 20 and 21).

8. Compensation is payable to the widow, child or other dependant or to the personal representatives or trustees of a claimant who dies where such persons would have benefited under the relevant pension scheme (Regulations 25 to 27).

9. Part VI of the Regulations provides for long-term and retirement compensation to be reviewed and for awards to be varied in the light of changing circumstances (Regulation 34). It also contains provisions for the adjustment, suspension and compounding of compensation in certain circumstances.

10. Part VII contains provisions relating to the procedure for making claims and notifying decisions. It also confers upon a person claiming compensation and local authorities required to pay compensation the right to refer compensation questions for determination by a tribunal established under section 12 of the Industrial Training Act 1964.

# STATUTORY INSTRUMENTS

## 1969 No. 399

# NATIONAL HEALTH SERVICE, ENGLAND AND WALES

## The National Health Service (General Dental Services) Amendment (No. 2) Regulations 1969

| | |
|---|---|
| *Made* - - - | 19*th March* 1969 |
| *Laid before Parliament* | 27*th March* 1969 |
| *Coming into Operation* | 1*st April* 1969 |

The Secretary of State for Social Services, in exercise of the powers conferred on him by section 40 of the National Health Service Act 1946(a), as amended by the National Health Service (Amendment) Act 1949(b) hereby makes the following regulations :—

1.—(1) These regulations may be cited as the National Health Service (General Dental Services) Amendment (No. 2) Regulations 1969 and shall come into operation on 1st April 1969.

(2) The Interpretation Act 1889(c) applies to the interpretation of the regulations as it applies to the interpretation of an Act of Parliament.

2. The National Health Service (General Dental Services) Regulations 1967(d) (hereinafter referred to as the principal regulations) as amended (e) shall be further amended as follows :—

(1) Regulation 31 (additional payment to practitioners) shall cease to have effect.

(2) In paragraph 8(2)(*a*) of Part I, Schedule 1 (which deals with "occasional treatment"), for the words "repairs to dentures at a scale cost not exceeding £1 18s. 0d. per denture" there shall be substituted the words "repairs to dentures at a scale cost not exceeding £2 0s. 0d. per denture".

(3) For Parts I to VI of Schedule 5 (scale of fees for treatment) there shall be substituted the following :—

---

(a) 1946 c. 81.  (b) 1949 c.93.
(c) 1889 c. 63.  (d) S.I. 1967/937 (1967 II, p.2816).
(e) The amending Regulations are not relevant to the subject matter of this Regulation.

"PART I. DIAGNOSIS

1. Clinical examination and report: 8s. 0d.
   Provided that—
   (1) only one fee shall be payable during a course of treatment;
   (2) no fee shall be payable for:—
   (*a*) an examination in respect of repairs to dentures for edentulous patients,
   (*b*) a group examination in schools or institutions,
   (*c*) an examination of a person aged 21 years or over if the same practitioner† has been paid or is entitled to be paid for an examination and report on that person at any time during any of the 5 months preceding the month during which a further examination is made,
   (*d*) an examination of a person under 21 years of age if the same practitioner† has been paid or is entitled to be paid for an examination and report on that person made on or after the preceding 1st March, 1st July or 1st November, whichever of these dates last occurred;
   (3) in the case of a woman who is, or has been, pregnant and who is not edentulous, a fee shall be payable for one examination during the period of pregnancy and 12 months thereafter, additional to the examinations for which payment may otherwise be made under this item and all such examinations may be carried out at any time during the said period.

2. Radiological examination and report:
   Fees per course of treatment—
   (*a*) Intra-oral films:

| | | | | |
|---|---|---|---|---|
| 1 film | ... | ... | ... | ... 8s. 0d. |
| 2 films | ... | ... | ... | ... 10s. 0d. |
| *Each additional film | | ... | ... | 2s. 6d. up to a maximum of £1 15s. 0d. |

   (*b*) Extra-oral films:

| | | | | |
|---|---|---|---|---|
| 1 film | ... | ... | ... | ... 11s. 0d. |
| *Each additional film | | ... | ... | 6s. 6d. up to a maximum of £1 4s. 0d. |

Provided that a fee shall not be payable, in cases in which the Board have required the submission of the films, or in which the Board's prior approval was required, unless the films or duplicates thereof are submitted to the Board.

---

† Reference in this scale of fees to dental treatment by the same practitioner shall include also dental treatment by his principal or the partner of either, or by the assistant of any of them and where the practitioner is employed by a body corporate shall include treatment by another employee of that body.
* See schedule 2 for treatment requiring prior approval.

## PART II. CONSERVATIVE TREATMENT

A. *Periodontal Treatment*

3. Scaling, including the removal of calculus and other deposits from the teeth, and the provision of prophylactic or other necessary treatment for all ordinary or simple disorders of the gums, for persons aged 16 or over at the beginning of a course of treatment:—

| | |
|---|---|
| (*a*) Scaling and gum treatment (except cases under (*b*)). | 13s. 6d. |
| *(*b*) Scaling and gum treatment to be followed by extraction of the teeth charted for scaling, gum treatment and extraction during the same course of treatment: | Such fee as the Board may approve, not exceeding 13s. 6d. |

*Provided that no fee shall be payable where the last course of treatment in respect of which provision was made for payment under item 3 (*a*) or (*b*) to the same practitioner† commenced at any time during any of the 5 months preceding the month in which the further treatment is to be done, unless the prior approval of the Board has been obtained.

4. Treatment urgently required for acute infective conditions of the gingivae/oral mucosa: Fee per course of treatment—      8s. 0d.

*5. Other periodontal treatment including where necessary protracted scaling and gingivectomy (estimates to include an outline of proposed treatment):      Such fee as the Board may approve up to a maximum of £4 10s. 0d. (or such higher fee as they may in special circumstances approve).

Provided that where gingivectomy and associated aftercare is involved an additional fee shall be allowed—

| | |
|---|---|
| For treatment relating to the first 2 adjacent teeth in one jaw   ... | £1 2s. 0d. |
| For treatment relating to additional teeth, per tooth   ...   ... | 5s. 0d. |

B. *Restorative Treatment*

6. Fillings (including any dressings, pulp capping and other necessary preparatory treatment), except fillings in deciduous teeth of children under 16 years. The fillings to which this scale applies shall be permanent in character. Fee per filling:—

(*a*) amalgam filling in:

| | |
|---|---|
| (i) a single surface cavity ...   ... | 13s. 6d. with a maximum of 13s. 6d. for 2 or more such fillings in any one surface of a tooth and a maximum of 19s. 0d. for 2 or more such fillings per tooth not all in one surface. |
| (ii) a mesial-occlusal-distal cavity inclusive of any extension of such a cavity in a molar or pre-molar tooth. | £1 16s. 0d. |
| (iii) a mesial-occlusal or distal-occlusal cavity inclusive of any extension of such a cavity into the lingual or buccal surfaces or both in a molar or pre-molar tooth. | £1 4s. 0d. with a maximum for a combination of such fillings of £1 16s. 0d. per tooth. |
| (iv) a compound cavity other than a cavity covered by (ii) or (iii) above. | 19s. 0d. with a maximum of £1 6s. 0d. for 2 or more such fillings per tooth. |

*See schedule 2 for treatment requiring prior approval.

†Reference in this scale of fees to dental treatment by the same practitioner shall include also dental treatment by his principal of the partner of either, or by the assistant of any of them and where the practitioner is employed by a body corporate shall include treatment by another employee of that body    .

(b) silicate, silico-phosphate or synthetic resin filling:

19s. 0d. with a maximum for 2 or more such fillings per tooth of £1 9s. 0d.

Provided that—
(a) for combinations of the types of fillings set out below in the same tooth no fee shall be payable in excess of the amount shewn opposite:—

1 or more of (a) (i) with 1 of (a) (iii) £1 10s. 0d.
1 or more of (a) (i) with 1 of (a) (iv) £1 4s. 0d.
1 or more of (a) (i) with 2 or more of (a) (iv) £1 11s. 0d.
1 of (a) (iii) with 1 or more of (a) (iv). £1 11s. 0d.

(b) no fee in excess of £2 2s. 0d. shall be payable for any combination of any of the types of fillings necessary in one tooth.

7. Root treatment of permanent teeth, including all attention in connection therewith but not including the provision of X-rays or the insertion of any filling in the crown of the tooth:
(a) treatment comprising either the devitalisation of the pulp of a tooth and the subsequent removal of the pulp followed by the necessary treatment and filling of each root canal of the tooth, or the treatment of septic root canals and the subsequent filling of each canal—

Fee per single rooted non-septic tooth. £1 15s. 0d.

Fee per multi-rooted or septic tooth. £3 0s. 0d.

(b) vital pulpotomy consisting of removal of the coronal portion of the pulp, including any necessary dressing—

Fee per tooth ... ... ... £1 10s. 0d.
(c) apicectomy, fee per tooth ... ... £2 0s. 0d.

*8. Gold fillings (other than inlays) ... ... £3 0s. 0d. per filling with a maximum for 2 or more such fillings per tooth of £4 10s. 0d.

9. Inlays (including any dressings):

| | A. | B. |
| --- | --- | --- |
| *(a) metal inlay ... ... ... ... | Alloys containing 60 per cent. or more fine gold. | Any other alloys. |
| (i) a single surface cavity ... ... | £4 5s. 0d. | £4 0s. 0d. |
| (ii) a compound cavity ... ... | £6 5s. 0d. | £5 0s. 0d. |
| (iii) a compound cavity involving the incisal angle. | £6 0s. 0d. | £5 0s. 0d. |
| (iv) a confluent compound cavity | £8 0s. 0d. | £6 0s. 0d. |

*(b) fused porcelain inlay ... ... Such fee as the Board may approve within a range of £5 0s. 0d. to £9 0s. 0d.

*(c) provision or renewal of a facing of silicate or synthetic resin. 15s. 0d. per inlay.

---

*See schedule 2 for treatment requiring prior approval.

(d) refixing or recementing an inlay ...　15s. 0d. per inlay.

*(e) renewal or replacement by another　Such fee as the Board may approve
inlay.　not exceeding the fee for a new
inlay of the type being provided.

10. Crowning of permanent teeth, including
any dressings but excluding root treatment:

*(a) Full veneer or jacket crown (on a
vital or non-vital tooth):
   (i) gold　...　...　...　...　£7 15s. 0d.
   (ii) gold with facing of silicate or　£8 10s. 0d.
   synthetic resin.

*(b) Three-quarter crown gold, cast　...　£9　0s. 0d.

*(c) Full veneer or jacket crown:
   (i) synthetic resin on a vital tooth　£5 10s. 0d.
   (ii) synthetic resin on a non-vital　£4　5s. 0d.
   tooth
   (iii) synthetic resin constructed on a　£8　0s. 0d.
   cast gold core or thimble on a
   vital tooth.

*(d) Full veneer or jacket crown:
   (i) porcelain on a vital tooth　...　£10　0s. 0d.
   (ii) porcelain on a non-vital tooth　£8　0s. 0d.
   (iii) porcelain constructed on a cast　£12 15s. 0d.
   gold core or thimble on a vital
   tooth.

*(e)　(i) Synthetic resin veneer or jacket　£7　0s. 0d.
   constructed on a cast gold core
   and post
   (ii) Porcelain veneer or jacket con-　£10　0s. 0d.
   structed on a cast gold core and
   post.

*(f) Synthetic resin post or dowel crown:
   (i) without diaphragm　...　...　£4　0s. 0d.
   (ii) with diaphragm　...　...　£7　0s. 0d.
   (iii) with gold post, diaphragm and　£8　0s. 0d.
   backing.

*(g) Modifications to the above crowns,　Such fee as the Board may approve
and other forms of crown not in the　not exceeding £12 15s. 0d.
opinion of the Board included in the
above items.

(h) Refixing or recementing a crown ...　15s. 0d. per crown.

*(i) Repair of a crown:
   (i) Renewal of the coronal portion　£2　4s. 0d.
   only of a post or dowel crown
   appropriate to item 10(f) (i)
   or 10 (f) (ii).
   (ii) Other repair of a crown　...　Such fee as the Board may approve
   not exceeding two-thirds of the
   fee for a new crown of the type
   being repaired.

*(j) Renewal by a similar type of crown　Such fee as the Board may approve
   not exceeding the fee for a new
   crown of the type being provided.

*(k) Replacement by a different type of　Such fee as the Board may approve
crown.　not exceeding the fee for a new
   crown of the type being provided.

Provided that, where the Board approve the use of a special bonding technique in
connection with a porcelain crown, the Board may increase the fee by an amount
not exceeding £5 0s. 0d.

---

*See schedule 2 for treatment requiring prior approval.

PART III. SURGICAL TREATMENT

*11. Extractions:

Fee per course of treatment:—

| | | |
|---|---|---|
| 1 tooth ... ... ... ... | 11s. 0d. | |
| 2 teeth ... ... ... ... | 12s. 0d. | |
| 3, 4 or 5 teeth ... ... ... | 13s. 6d. | With an additional fee of 2s. 0d. for each quadrant of the mouth involved other than the first. |
| 6, 7 or 8 teeth ... ... ... | 18s. 0d. | |
| 9, 10 or 11 teeth ... ... ... | £1 2s. 6d. | |
| 12, 13 or 14 teeth ... ... ... | £1 7s. 0d. | |
| 15, 16 or 17 teeth ... ... ... | £1 11s. 6d. | |
| 18, 19 or 20 teeth ... ... ... | £1 16s. 0d. | |
| over 20 teeth ... ... ... ... | £2 0s. 6d. | |

Provided that where an exceptional number of visits is necessary because of the abnormal systemic condition of the patient the Board may allow an additional fee not exceeding £2 0s. 0d. per course.

*12

(a) Alveolectomy, in either upper or lower jaw.

Such fee as the Board may approve up to a maximum of £3 10s. 0d. (or such higher fee as they may in special circumstances approve).

(b) Removal of a cyst, buried root, impacted tooth or grossly exostosed tooth, or other similar operation, including attention in connection therewith.

Such fee as the Board may approve up to a maximum of £8 5s. 0d. (or such higher fee as they may in special circumstances approve).

(c) Surgery on soft tissue, other than periodontal surgery appropriate to item 5.

Such fee as the Board may approve up to a maximum of £1 15s. 0d. (or such higher fee as they may in special circumstances approve).

13. Administration of a general anaesthetic:—

(a) In connection with treatment under Item 11:

(i) where a doctor or dentist other than the dentist carrying out the extraction administers the anaesthetic:

Fee per visit—

| | |
|---|---|
| 1 to 3 teeth extracted ... | 15s. 0d. |
| 4 to 11 teeth extracted ... | £1 1s. 0d. |
| 12 to 19 teeth extracted... | £1 11s. 6d. |
| 20 teeth or over extracted | £2 2s. 0d. |

(ii) where the anaesthetic is administered by the dentist carrying out the extraction:

Fee per patient per course of treatment.

8s. 0d.

*(iii) where the Board are satisfied that the anaesthetist would be faced with special difficulties owing to the medical condition of the patient and the anaesthetic is to be administered by a doctor or dentist other than the dentist carrying out the extraction:

Such fee as the Board may approve not exceeding £4 14s. 6d. per course of treatment.

*See schedule 2 for treatment requiring prior approval.

Provided that no fee exceeding £2 2s. 0d. per course of treatment shall be payable under (i) or under (i) and (ii) combined, and no fee exceeding £5 10s. 0d. per course of treatment shall be payable for any combination of (iii) with (i), or with both (i) and (ii).

*(b) In connection with treatment under Items 5, 7 (c) and 12 where a doctor or dentist other than the dentist carrying out the treatment administers the anaesthetic:

Such fee as the Board may approve not exceeding £2 2s. 0d.

Provided that in cases presenting special clinical difficulty the fee will be such fee as the Board may approve not exceeding £4 14s. 6d.

### PART IV. DENTURES, BRIDGES AND SPECIAL APPLIANCES OTHER THAN ORTHODONTIC APPLIANCES

**A.** *Dentures*

Fees for the provision of dentures cover the provision of all necessary clasps, rests and strengtheners and all adjustments needed within a reasonable period of time after completion.

*14. Dentures in vulcanite or synthetic resin:

| | |
|---|---|
| (a) full upper and full lower dentures... | £12  5s. 0d. |
| (b) denture bearing 1, 2 or 3 teeth  ... | £5  10s. 0d. |
| denture bearing 4 to 8 teeth  ... | £6  10s. 0d. |
| denture bearing 9 to 14 teeth  ... | £7  5s. 0d. |

Provided that no fee for upper and lower dentures shall exceed £12 5s. 0d.

(c) additional fee for lingual or palatal bar—

(i) stainless steel ...    ...    ...    £1  5s. 0d.

(ii) gold or other approved material    Such fee as the Board may approve not exceeding £3 10s. 0d.

15. Relining or rebasing of dentures, or provision of soft linings to dentures, including all adjustments needed within a reasonable period of time after completion:

(a) relining or rebasing dentures:

(i) not accompanied by repairs or additions.    £2  8s. 0d.

*(ii) accompanied by repairs and/or additions.    Such fee as the Board may approve.

*(b) Addition of soft lining or soft partial lining to a new or existing vulcanite or synthetic resin denture where this is required on account of the abnormal anatomical condition of the patient's alveolus.    Such fee as the Board may approve not exceeding £2 10s. 0d. per denture.

*(c) Replacement or refitting of soft lining or soft partial lining which has been provided on account of the abnormal anatomical condition of the patient's alveolus.    Such fee as the Board may approve not exceeding £2 10s. 0d. per denture.

16. Repairs (except repairs accompanying relining or rebasing which are appropriate to item 15 (a) (ii)):

(a) (i) repairing a crack or fracture (including provision of any strengthener), or

---

*See schedule 2 for treatment requiring prior approval.

    (ii) refixing a tooth, or providing
      and fixing a replacement for a
      missing tooth (including any
      gum associated therewith), or
    (iii) refixing a clasp, or providing
      and fixing a replacement for a
      missing clasp (including any
      gum associated therewith) or
    (iv) covering exposed pins.

| | | |
|---|---|---|
| One repair under (a) | ... | 17s. 0d. |
| (b) each additional repair under (a) (i)-(iv). | | 5s. 0d. |
| (c) renewal of gum not associated with repair under (a). | | 17s. 0d. per denture. |

Provided that no fee in excess of £2 0s. d. per denture shall be payable under item 16 or for any combination of treatment under items 16 and 17.

17. Additions (except additions accompanying relining or rebasing, which are appropriate to item 15 (a)(ii)):

| | |
|---|---|
| (a) addition of a clasp or tooth (including any gum associated therewith). | £1 10s. 0d. |
| (b) addition of new gum not associated with addition under item 17 (a). | £1 10s. 0d. per denture. |

Provided that no fee in excess of £2 0s. 0d. per denture shall be payable under item 17 or for any combination of treatment under items 16 and 17.

*18. Backing or posting and tagging of teeth on non-metallic based dentures:
Fee per tooth in addition to the appropriate fee for a non-metallic based denture:—

| | | |
|---|---|---|
| (i) stainless steel ... | ... ... | 12s. 0d. |
| (ii) chrome cobalt or a precious metal alloy containing less than 60 per cent. fine gold | ... | £1 6s. 0d. |
| (iii) precious metal alloy containing 60 per cent. or more fine gold. | | £2 6s. 0d. |

*19. Metal dentures. These dentures may not be provided until such period after extraction (normally not less than three months) as the dentist thinks fit:
(a) Fee per denture in—

| | A. Stainless steel. | B. Chrome cobalt |
|---|---|---|
| (i) Base metal alloys: | | |
| partial denture bearing 1, 2 or 3 teeth. | £10 0s. 0d. | £12 10s. 0d. |
| partial denture bearing 4, 5 or 6 teeth. | £12 0s. 0d. | £14 5s. 0d. |
| partial denture bearing 7, 8 or 9 teeth. | £12 10s. 0d. | £15 10s. 0d. |
| partial denture bearing 10 or more teeth. | £12 15s. 0d. | £16 0s. 0d. |
| full denture ... ... ... | £11 10s. 0d. | £14 5s. 0d. |
| Additional fee where teeth are backed in any metal. | £1 0s. 0d. per tooth up to a maximum of £4 0s. 0d. per denture. | £1 0s. 0d. per tooth up to a maximum of £4 0s. 0d. per denture. |

---

*See schedule 2 for treatment requiring prior approval.

| | A.<br>Containing less than 60 per cent. fine gold. | B.<br>Containing 60 per cent. or more fine gold. |
|---|---|---|
| (ii) Precious metal alloys: | | |
| partial denture bearing 1, 2 or 3 teeth. | £12  5s.  0d. | Such fee as the Board may approve. |
| partial denture bearing 4, 5 or 6 teeth. | £14  5s.  0d. | |
| partial denture bearing 7, 8 or 9 teeth. | £15 15s.  0d. | |
| partial denture bearing 10 or more teeth. | £16  0s.  0d. | |
| Full denture ...    ...    ... | £15 10s.  0d. | |
| Additional fee where teeth are backed in any metal. | £1  5s.  0d. per tooth up to a maximum of £5 0s. 0d. per denture. | |
| (b) Repairs and<br>(c) Additions | Fee appropriate to similar treatment to synthetic resin or vulcanite dentures as covered by items 16 and/or 17 together with such additional fee, if any, as the Board may approve. | |

B. *Bridges and Special Appliances*

| | |
|---|---|
| *20. Bridges    ...    ...    ...    ... | Such fee as the Board may approve. |
| *21.  (a) Obturators, fee per case in addition to appropriate denture fee. | Such fee as the Board may approve within a range of £3 10s. 0d. to £6 0s. 0d. or such additional fee as may be approved in special circumstances. |
| (b) Repairs to obturators    ...    ... | Such fee as the Board may approve. |
| (c) Treatment involving splints or other appliances (other than in connection with periodontal treatment). | Such fee as the Board may approve. |

PART V.  TREATMENT SPECIAL TO CHILDREN

*22. Conservative treatment of deciduous teeth of children under 16 years of age at the beginning of a course of treatment:

   (a) by filling with amalgam, oxyphosphate cement or other similar materials (including any dressings, pulp capping and other necessary preparatory treatment):

| | |
|---|---|
| (i) single surface cavity, per filling | 11s.  6d. |
| (ii) any other cavity, per filling ... | 16s.  0d. |
| (b) by conservation of a molar with a preformed metal cap: | 16s.  0d. per tooth. |

     Provided that no fee in excess of 16s. 0d. shall be payable for any combination of the above types of conservation necessary in one tooth.

   (c) by conservation by other means:

      (i) by preparing self-cleansing areas followed by applications of silver nitrate or similar medicaments:

| | |
|---|---|
| per tooth    ...    ...    ... | 8s.  0d. |
| maximum per patient    ... | £1  0s.  0d. |

\*Provided that no fee shall be payable under (i) where the treatment occurs within 12 months of similar treatment to the same surface by the same practitioner† unless, in exceptional circumstances, the approval of the Board is first obtained.

    (ii) by topical applications of obtundents and coagulants:
        per patient ...    ...    ...    **8s. 0d.**

    \*Provided that no fee shall be payable under (ii) where the treatment occurs within 12 months of similar treatment by the same practitioner† unless, in exceptional circumstances, the approval of the Board is first obtained.

(*d*) by vital pulpotomy, including any  **11s. 0d.**
necessary dressing, per tooth.

23.    (*a*) Removal of calculus and other de-  **6s. 0d.**
        posits from the teeth of children under 16 years at the beginning of a course of treatment and the provision of necessary treatment for all ordinary or simple disorders of the gums.

    \*Provided that no fee shall be payable under item 23(*a*)—

    (i) where the last course of treatment in respect of which provision was made for payment under item 23(*a*) or (*b*) to the same practitioner† commenced at any time during any of the 5 months preceding the month in which the further treatment is to be done;

    (ii) in respect of a patient under 9 years at the beginning of a course of treatment,
unless the prior approval of the Board has been obtained.

\*(*b*) Removal of calculus, where in ex-  **13s. 6d.**
ceptional cases calculus is present to an abnormal degree, from the teeth of children under 16 years at the beginning of a course of treatment, and the provision of necessary treatment for all ordinary or simple disorders of the gums.

(*c*) Removal of stain including any  **6s. 0d.**
necessary polishing:

---

\*See schedule 2 for treatment requiring prior approval.
†Reference in this scale of fees to dental treatment by the same practitioner shall include also dental treatment by his principal or the partner of either, or by the assistant of any of them and where the practitioner is employed by a body corporate shall include treatment by another employee of that body.

Provided that no fee shall be payable under item 23 (c)—

*(i) where the last course of treatment in respect of which provision was made for payment under item 23 (c) to the same practitioner† commenced at any time during any of the 11 months preceding the month in which the further treatment is to be done unless the prior approval of the Board has been obtained;

(ii) during a course of treatment where a fee is paid under item 23 (a) or (b).

24. *(a) Orthodontic treatment of children and young persons under 18 years at the beginning of a course of treatment.    Such fee as the Board may approve.

(b) Repairs to orthodontic appliances...    Such fee as the Board may approve.

PART VI.  GENERAL ITEMS

25. Dressing of teeth in respect of a casual patient.

Fee for one tooth ... ... ...    9s. 0d.
Fee for two or more teeth ... ...    12s. 0d.

26. Domiciliary visits where a patient's condition so requires:

Fee per visit to one or more patients at one address.    15s. 0d.

27. Treatment of sensitive cementum or dentine:

Fee per course ... ... ... ...    5s. 6d.

28. Taking of material for pathological or bacteriological examination, etc.:

Fee per course ... ... ... ...    8s. 0d.

29. Treatment for arrest of abnormal haemorrhage, including abnormal haemorrhage following dental treatment provided otherwise than as part of general dental services:

Fee per visit for arrest of bleeding or for administration of associated after care:    17s. 6d.

Provided that—

(i) the same practitioner† who arrests bleeding may not also be paid for the administration of aftercare.

(ii) where the treatment consists solely of the removal of plugs and/or stitches the fee shall be only 10s. 0d.

(iii) the maximum fee per course of treatment shall be £2 5s. 0d. or such higher sum as the Board may in special circumstances approve.

*30. Fee for any other treatment not included in this scale.    Such fee as the Board may approve.

---

* See schedule 2 for treatment requiring prior approval.
† Reference in this scale of fees to dental treatment by the same practitioner shall include also dental treatment by his principal or the partner of either, or by the assistant of any of them and where the practitioner is employed by a body corporate shall include treatment by another employee of that body".

3. Where an advice of payment from the Board to a Council is in respect of a contract or arrangement entered into or made on or after 1st April 1969, the Council shall pay to a practitioner in addition to the fees authorised under regulation 28 of the principal regulations a sum equal to 3 per cent. of the amount of these fees.

4.—(1) Subject to the following provisions of this regulation, these regulations shall not apply to general dental services provided under a contract or arrangement entered into or made before 1st April 1969, and such services shall continue to be subject to the provisions of the regulations in force immediately before that date.

(2) Where an advice of payment from the Board to a Council dated on or after 1st April 1969 is in respect of a contract or arrangement entered into or made on or after 1st July 1966 and before 1st April 1969, the Council shall pay to a practitioner in addition to the fees authorised under regulation 28 of the principal regulations a sum equal to 5·6 per cent. of the amount of these fees.

(3) Where an advice of payment from the Board to a Council dated on or after 1st April 1969 is in respect of a contract or arrangement entered into or made before 1st July 1966, the Council shall pay to a practitioner in addition to the fees authorised under regulation 28 of the principal regulations a sum equal to 16·7 per cent. of the amount of these fees.

(4) In respect of an advice of payment from the Board to a Council dated during the period beginning with 1st January 1969 and ending with 31st March 1969, the Council shall pay to a practitioner an additional sum equal to 5·6 per cent. of the amounts payable under regulations 28 and 31 of the principal regulations.

*R. H. S. Crossman,*
Secretary of State for Social Services.
19th March 1969.

---

## EXPLANATORY NOTE

*(This Note is not part of the Regulations.)*

These Regulations further amend the National Health Service (General Dental Services) Regulations 1967 by providing for a new scale of fees and for certain additional payments for practitioners, other than salaried practitioners, providing general dental services. They also make a minor amendment in respect of the definition of denture repairs which may be provided as "occasional treatment".

## STATUTORY INSTRUMENTS

## 1969 No. 400

## INDIA

## The Indian Military Service Family Pension Fund (Amendment) Rules 1969

Made - - - - 14*th March* 1969

The Minister of Overseas Development, in exercise of the powers conferred on the Secretary of State by section 273(1) of the Government of India Act 1935(a) and paragraph 14(1) of the Government of India (Family Pension Funds) Order 1936(b) and transferred to the Minister by the Transfer of Functions (Overseas Pensions) Order 1965(c), hereby makes the following Rules:—

1. The Indian Military Service Family Pension Fund Rules(d), as amended(e), are hereby further amended as follows:—

(1) The following sub-rule shall be substituted for Rule 14(1):—

"(1) (*a*) Subject to paragraph (*b*) of this sub-rule, an officer who ceases to subscribe under the provisions of Rules 10, 11 or 13 may, if married or a widower with children, be granted a refund in respect of the portion, if any, of the contributions paid by him for his living dependants still eligible for pension which is in excess of the risk previously borne by the Fund in respect of such dependants.

(*b*) An officer who, under the provisions of Rule 13, ceases to subscribe on or after 1st April 1969 may, if he was subscribing at the unmarried rate immediately before he ceased to subscribe and was not then subscribing for any dependants, be granted the following refund of his contributions, that is to say:—

(i) if he has never been married, a refund of all the contributions that he has made ; or

(ii) in any other case, a refund of all the contributions that he has made after the date on which he ceased to subscribe for dependants,

together, in each case, with compound interest of $2\frac{1}{2}$ per cent. per annum."

(2) The following new Rule shall be inserted immediately after Rule 14A as Rule 14B :—

"14B (1) Where an officer dies on or after 1st April 1969, having subscribed at the unmarried rate at all times up to his death, there may be granted to his estate a refund of all the contributions that he has made, together with compound interest of $2\frac{1}{2}$ per cent. per annum.

---

(a) 26 Geo. 5 & 1 Edw. 8. c. 2.
1936 I, p. 1385).
(d) S.R. & O. 1937/1226 (Rev. X, p. 632: 1937 p. 1374).
(e) The relevant amending instrument is S.I. 1952/1502 (1952 I, p. 1228).

(b) S.R. & O. 1936/1310 (Rev. X, p. 624: 1936 I, p. 1385).
(c) S.I. 1965/1528 (1965 II, p. 4435).

(2) Where an officer dies on or after 1st April 1969, having formerly subscribed at the married rate but having been, immediately before his death, a subscriber at the unmarried rate who was not then subscribing for dependants, there may be granted to his estate a refund of all the contributions that he has made as from the time when he last became a subscriber at the unmarried rate who was not subscribing for dependants, together with compound interest of 2½ per cent. per annum.

**2.** These Rules may be cited as the Indian Military Service Family Pension Fund (Amendment) Rules 1969.

Given under my hand this 14th day of March 1969.

*R. E. Prentice.*

## EXPLANATORY NOTE
*(This Note is not part of the Rules.)*

These Rules provide for the refund of contributions, with interest, in certain cases where subscribers withdraw on or after 1st April 1969 and also provide for the refund of contributions, with interest, in certain cases where subscribers die on or after 1st April 1969.

## STATUTORY INSTRUMENTS

### 1969 No. 401

### AGRICULTURE

#### GUARANTEED PRICES AND ASSURED MARKETS

### The Eggs (Guaranteed Prices) Order 1969

| | | |
|---|---|---|
| *Made* - - - | *17th March* 1969 |
| *Laid before Parliament* | *26th March* 1969 |
| *Coming into Operation* | *30th March* 1969 |

The Minister of Agriculture, Fisheries and Food and the Secretaries of State respectively concerned with agriculture in Scotland and Northern Ireland acting jointly in exercise of the powers conferred upon them by sections 1 and 35(3) of the Agriculture Act 1957(a) and of all other powers enabling them in that behalf, with the consent of the Treasury and after consultation with such bodies of persons as appear to the said Ministers to represent the interests of the producers of eggs, hereby make the following order :—

*Citation and commencement*

**1.** This order may be cited as the Eggs (Guaranteed Prices) Order 1969 ; and shall come into operation on 30th March 1969.

*Interpretation*

**2.**—(1) In this order, unless the context otherwise requires—

"average selling price" means the average selling price ascertained in accordance with article 5 hereof ;

"the Board" means the British Egg Marketing Board constituted by the British Egg Marketing Scheme 1956(b) which has effect as if made under the Agricultural Marketing Act 1958(c) ;

"determined" means determined from time to time by the Minister, subject to such terms and conditions as he may specify, with the approval of the Treasury and in the light of the conclusions of the Ministers from a review held under section 2 of the Agriculture Act 1947(d) ;

"duck eggs" means eggs in shell laid by domestic ducks in the United Kingdom ;

"guaranteed price", "indicator price" and "standard quantity" mean respectively the prices and quantity determined pursuant to article 4 hereof ;

"hen eggs" means eggs in shell laid by domestic fowls in the United Kingdom ;

---

(a) 1957 c.57.                       (b) S.I. 1956/2082 (1956 I, p.66).
(c) 1958 c.47.                       (d) 1947 c.48.

"packed" means packed on behalf of the Board by any person appointed by the Board to purchase, grade and pack hen eggs on their behalf or packed by the Board in the course of exercising those functions themselves :
"the Ministers" means the Minister of Agriculture, Fisheries and Food and the Secretaries of State respectively concerned with agriculture in Scotland and Northern Ireland, acting jointly ;

"the Minister", in relation to any part of the United Kingdom, means either that one of the Ministers who is concerned with agriculture in that part, or that Minister and either or both of the others acting jointly ;

"year" means a period of 52 or 53 weeks commencing with the Sunday nearest to 31st March in any calendar year.

(2) The Interpretation Act 1889(a) shall apply to the interpretation of this order as it applies to the interpretation of an Act of Parliament, and as if this order and the orders hereby revoked were Acts of Parliament.

*Guarantee standards*

**3.** This order shall apply to such hen eggs and duck eggs respectively as conform to the standards and conditions specified by the Ministers from time to time in the light of their conclusions from a review held under section 2 of the Agriculture Act 1947.

*Guarantee prices and payments*

**4.**—(1) In respect of each year there shall be determined for hen eggs and duck eggs respectively—

(a) a guaranteed price ;

(b) an indicator price, being an estimate by the Minister of the average price to be received by the Board on the sale of hen eggs or duck eggs, as the case may be, on the basis that production thereof is sufficient but not excessive having regard to the national demand therefor and, in the case of hen eggs, to normal imports into the United Kingdom during the year of hen eggs produced outside ;

being in each case a price per dozen :

Provided that, in the case of hen eggs, the Minister may in the light of the conclusions of the Ministers from a review held under section 2 of the Agriculture Act 1947 make such reduction in the indicator price as appears to the Minister, with the approval of the Treasury, to be appropriate having regard to any increase above a normal level of imports into the United Kingdom, during any part of the year, of hen eggs produced outside and to the prices received by the Board during the same period and throughout the year.

(2) In respect of each year a standard quantity shall be determined for hen eggs.

**5.** After 28th March 1970 an average selling price of hen eggs and duck eggs respectively for the year ending on that day shall be ascertained by the Minister in accordance with arrangements agreed with the Board or in default of agreement in accordance with such principles as the Minister shall decide.

**6.** Subject to the provisions of article 8 hereof and to such terms and conditions as he may with the approval of the Treasury prescribe, the Minister may pay to the Board in respect of each dozen hen eggs packed or each dozen duck eggs purchased by the Board, as the case may be, in any year the difference between the guaranteed price and the indicator price.

---

(a) 1889 c. 63.

7.—(1) If for the year ending on 28th March 1970 the average selling price of hen eggs or duck eggs respectively is higher than the indicator price thereof, then, subject to the provisions of article 8 hereof, the Board shall pay to the Minister two thirds of the difference in respect of each dozen hen eggs packed or each dozen duck eggs purchased by the Board, as the case may be, in that year:

Provided that in the case of hen eggs or duck eggs, as the case may be, the total amount payable by the Board to the Minister under this paragraph shall not exceed the total amount which may be paid by the Minister to the Board in respect of those eggs under article 6 hereof in respect of the same year.

(2) If for the aforesaid year the indicator price of hen eggs or duck eggs, as the case may be, is higher than the average selling price thereof, then, subject to the provisions of article 8 hereof, the Minister may pay to the Board one tenth of the difference in respect of each dozen hen eggs packed or each dozen duck eggs purchased by the Board, as the case may be, in that year.

8. As respects any year in which the number of hen eggs packed exceeds the standard quantity for that year, any reference in articles 6 and 7 hereof to the difference between the guaranteed price and the indicator price and the difference between the average selling price and the indicator price respectively shall in each case, insofar as each of the said provisions relates to hen eggs, be taken to be a reference to the respective difference divided by the proportion which the number of hen eggs packed in that year bears to the standard quantity.

9. Subject to such terms and conditions as he may with the approval of the Treasury prescribe, the Minister may make available by way of advance to the Board such sums as he may from time to time think fit.

*Keeping of records*

10. The Board shall maintain such books of account, records and documents as the Minister may from time to time direct and shall ensure that such books of account, records and documents are available for inspection at all reasonable times by any duly authorised officer, servant or agent of the Minister or of the Comptroller and Auditor General.

*Revocation*

11. The Eggs (Guaranteed Prices) Order 1963(a), the Eggs (Guaranteed Prices) (Amendment) Order 1964(b) and the Eggs (Guaranteed Prices) (Amendment) Order 1966(c) are hereby revoked.

In Witness whereof the Official Seal of the Minister of Agriculture, Fisheries and Food is hereunto affixed on 13th March 1969.

(L.S.)                                   *Cledwyn Hughes,*
                          Minister of Agriculture, Fisheries and Food.

Given under the Seal of the Secretary of State for Scotland on 14th March 1969.

(L.S.)                                   *William Ross,*
                             Secretary of State for Scotland.

(a) S.I. 1963/569 (1963 I, p.655).          (b) S.I. 1964/462 (1964 I, p.743).
(c) S.I. 1966/479 (1966 I, p.987).

Given under the hand of the Secretary of State for the Home Department
on 12th March 1969.

*James Callaghan,*
Secretary of State for the Home Department.

We consent
17th March 1969.

*Joseph Harper,*
J. *McCann,*
Two of the Lords Commissioners of
Her Majesty's Treasury.

---

## EXPLANATORY NOTE

*(This Note is not part of the Order.)*

This order, which comes into operation on 30th March 1969, supersedes the
Eggs (Guaranteed Prices) Order 1963, as amended, and provides for changes
in the arrangements for guaranteed prices for hen eggs and duck eggs following the determinations of the Ministers after a review held under section 2 of
the Agriculture Act 1947.

The principal changes are :—

   (*a*) in the case of hen eggs, provision is made for the determination each
      year of a standard quantity which is used for the calculation of
      guarantee payments in certain circumstances ;

   (*b*) supplementary provisions which apply if the Board's average selling
      price of hen eggs or duck eggs is higher or lower than the indicator
      price thereof are to cease after the end of the year 1969/70, and for
      that year the proportion of the difference to be borne by the Minister
      if the Board's average selling price is lower than the indicator price is
      fixed at one tenth.

## STATUTORY INSTRUMENTS

## 1969 No. 402

## PENSIONS

## The Superannuation (Pool of Soil Scientists and Civil Service) Transfer Rules 1969

| | | |
|---|---|---|
| *Made* - - - - | | 17th March 1969 |
| *Laid before Parliament* | | 25th March 1969 |
| *Coming into Operation* | | 26th March 1969 |

The Minister for the Civil Service, in exercise of the powers conferred upon him by section 33 of the Superannuation Act 1965(a) and article 2(1)(c) of the Minister for the Civil Service Order 1968(b), and of all other powers enabling him in that behalf, hereby makes the following Rules:—

1.—(1) Where a person was, at some time after 30th June 1965 and before 1st October 1966, taken into the civil service of the State as an officer of the Ministry of Overseas Development after having been employed as a member of the staff of the Rothamsted Experimental Station or the Macaulay Institute for Soil Research engaged on soil survey work, and his employment by the body by whom he was so employed was, in the opinion of the Minister for the Civil Service, of the same nature and for the same purpose as his employment in the service of the State, his service in employment by that body, not being service before he attained the age of eighteen years, may be reckoned for the purposes of the Superannuation Acts 1965 and 1967(c) as employment in an unestablished capacity within the meaning of section 99(1) of the Superannuation Act 1965.

(2) Where a person to whom the foregoing paragraph applies was, before he was taken into the civil service of the State, subject to a superannuation scheme operated under the Federated Superannuation System for Universities, it shall be a condition of the making of any payment under the Superannuation Acts 1965 and 1967 in respect of that person's service, so far as that payment is dependent on the provisions of the foregoing paragraph, that any policies of insurance purchased in respect of him under that superannuation scheme have, within three months after the coming into operation of these Rules or within such longer period as the Minister for the Civil Service may allow in any particular case, been assigned to such person and in such manner as the Minister may direct.

(3) These Rules shall not have effect so as to authorise an increase in an annual superannuation allowance or pension so far as the allowance or pension is payable in respect of a period before the coming into operation of these Rules.

2. The Interpretation Act 1889(d) shall apply for the interpretation of these Rules as it applies for the interpretation of an Act of Parliament.

---

(a) 1965 c. 74.  (b) S.I. 1968/1656 (1968 III, p. 4485).
(c) 1965 c. 74; 1967 c. 28.  (d) 1889 c. 63.

**3.** These Rules may be cited as the Superannuation (Pool of Soil Scientists and Civil Service) Transfer Rules 1969, and shall come into operation on 26th March 1969.

Given under the official seal of the Minister for the Civil Service on 17th March 1969.

(L.S.)                                 *J. E. Herbecq,*
                                          **Authorised by the Minister**
                                               **for the Civil Service.**

17th March 1969.

---

# EXPLANATORY NOTE

*(This Note is not part of the Rules.)*

These Rules provide for service (after the age of 18) in the Rothamsted Experimental Station and the Macaulay Institute for Soil Research of certain employees, who were taken into the Civil Service between 1st July 1965 and 30th September 1966, to be reckoned on certain conditions as unestablished civil service for the purposes of the Superannuation Acts 1965 and 1967.

# STATUTORY INSTRUMENTS

## 1969 No. 403

## EDUCATION, ENGLAND AND WALES

## LOCAL GOVERNMENT, ENGLAND AND WALES

### The Further Education Regulations 1969

| | |
|---|---|
| *Made* - - - | 18*th March* 1969 |
| *Laid before Parliament* | 27*th March* 1969 |
| *Coming into Operation* | 1*st April* 1969 |

The Secretary of State for Education and Science, in exercise of the powers conferred upon him by section 100(1)(*b*) and (3) of the Education Act 1944(**a**), as amended by the Secretary of State for Education and Science Order 1964(**b**), section 3(4) of the Local Government Act 1958(**c**) and section 4(2) of, and paragraph 13 of Schedule 1 to, the Local Government Act 1966(**d**), hereby makes the following regulations :—

## PART I

### GENERAL

*Citation, commencement and interpretation*

**1.**—(1) These regulations may be cited as the Further Education Regulations 1969 and shall come into operation on 1st April 1969.

(2) The Interpretation Act 1889(**e**) shall apply for the interpretation of these regulations as it applies for the interpretation of an Act of Parliament.

*Definitions*

**2.**—(1) In these regulations, unless the context otherwise requires—

"adult" means a person who has attained the age of eighteen years and references to courses of adult education shall be construed accordingly ;

"authority" means a local education authority ;

"establishment" means an establishment of further education other than a college of education but, in its application to voluntary institutions, does not include any institution to which grants in aid of university education are paid out of moneys provided by Parliament or a college of a university ;

"maintained" means maintained by an authority ;

"national association" means a voluntary national association having as one of its principal objects the promotion of liberal education for adults ;

"premises" includes a hostel or other residential accommodation ;

---

| | |
|---|---|
| (**a**) 1944 c.31. | (**b**) S.I. 1964/490 (1964 I, p.800). |
| (**c**) 1958 c.55. | (**d**) 1966 c.42. |
| (**e**) 1889 c.63. | |

"responsible body" means a university, a university college, a committee of a university or university college, a national association or a district committee of a national association ;

"Secretary of State" means the Secretary of State for Education and Science ; and

"voluntary" means maintained by a body other than an authority.

(2) References to expenditure incurred in connection with the provision of an institution shall, in relation to the power to pay grants in respect of such expenditure, be construed as references to expenditure incurred in the provision, replacement, extension, impovement, furnishing or equipment of the premises of the institution.

## Revocations, savings and consequential amendment

**3.**—(1) The regulations specified in Schedule 3 are hereby revoked.

(2) Any approval, direction or other authorisation or order however described given under a provision of the regulations revoked by paragraph (1) which is reproduced with or without amendment by these regulations shall have effect as if it had been given under the relevant provision of these regulations.

(3) In regulation 2(2)(c)(i) of the Rate Support Grants (Pooling Arrangements) Regulations 1967(**a**), for the reference to regulation 10(2)(a), (b) and (c) of the Further Education (Local Education Authorities) Regulations 1959(**b**) as amended (**c**) there shall be substituted a reference to paragraph (a), (b) or (d) of schedule 1 to these regulations.

## PART II

### MAINTAINED ESTABLISHMENTS

## Application of Part II

**4.** This Part, except regulations 15 and 16, applies to maintained establishments.

## Co-ordination with neighbouring authorities

**5.** Every authority shall in consultation where appropriate with the Regional Advisory Council for Further Education secure that so far as may be reasonable—

(a) the courses provided by the authority do not duplicate the courses provided in the areas of neighbouring authorities ; and

(b) the fees charged by them do not differ substantially from the corresponding fees charged in those areas.

## Provision of courses

**6.** The provision of the courses specified in Schedule 1 shall be subject to the approval of and (where approval is granted subject to conditions) in accordance with conditions imposed by the Secretary of State.

(a) S.I. 1967/467 (1967 I, p.1407).    (b) S.I. 1959/393 (1959 I, p.1577).
(c) The relevant amending instruments are S.I. 1965/2, 1966/1432 (1965 I, p.3; 1966 III, p.3789).

*Instruction involving use of radioactive materials, etc.*

**7.** No instruction which involves the use of—

(a) radioactive material, other than a compound of potassium, thorium or uranium used as a chemical agent ; or

(b) apparatus in which electrons are accelerated by a potential difference of not less than five kilovolts, other than apparatus used only for the purpose of receiving visual images by way of television and sounds connected therewith

shall be given without the approval of the Secretary of State.

*Premises*

**8.**—(1) Premises shall be suitable for the purposes of the establishment.

(2) Without prejudice to the generality of paragraph (1), effective and suitable provision shall in particular be made with regard to—

(a) the lighting, heating, sanitation and ventilation of the premises ;

(b) the provision of safeguards against danger from fire and accident ;

(c) the maintenance of the premises in good repair and their cleanliness ; and

(d) the equipment of the premises.

*Provision of premises and equipment*

**9.**—(1) The provision of new premises and the alteration of existing premises shall be subject to the approval of the Secretary of State.

(2) No installation or article of equipment costing £1,000 or more shall be provided for teaching or research without the approval of the Secretary of State.

*Teaching Staff*

**10.** The teachers shall be sufficient in number and have the qualifications necessary for the adequate instruction of the students in the courses provided.

*Employment of teachers*

**11.**—(1) A teacher, not being an occasional teacher or a teacher employed for not more than a year as a part-time teacher, shall be employed under a written agreement or a minute of the authority appointing him to a post specified in the agreement or minute.

(2) The agreement or minute shall define the conditions of service of the teacher and shall in particular specify whether the teacher is employed in full-time service in the capacity of a teacher, in part-time service in the capacity of a teacher or partly in the capacity of a teacher and partly in another capacity.

*Restriction on employment of teachers on grounds of misconduct*

**12.**—(1) A person who is on grounds of misconduct or conviction of a criminal offence determined by the Secretary of State to be unsuitable for employment as a teacher or suitable for employment as such only to a limited extent, shall not be employed as a teacher or, as the case may be, shall be employed as such only to the extent determined by the Secretary of State.

(2) In this regulation the expression "teacher" includes warden of a community centre, leader of a youth club or similar institution and youth worker.

## Restriction on employment of teachers on medical grounds

**13.** A teacher shall not be employed, or as the case may be shall be employed upon conditions approved by the Secretary of State, if, after consulting the authority and offering the teacher an opportunity of making representations to him, the Secretary of State is satisfied that it is on medical grounds desirable that the teacher should not be employed or should be employed on such conditions.

## Reporting of termination of employment of teachers

**14.** If the engagement of a teacher, warden, club leader or youth worker is terminated whether by dismissal or resignation on account of misconduct or conviction of a criminal offence, the facts shall be reported to the Secretary of State.

## Assistance to voluntary institutions

**15.**—(1) Where an authority assist a voluntary establishment by means of recurrent grants or other regular payments, they shall require as a condition of their assisting the establishment that—

(a) the preceding provisions of these regulations ; and

(b) the provisions of Section 68 (reasonable exercise of functions), 77 (inspection) and 92 (reports and returns) of the Education Act 1944—

are, subject to the necessary modifications, treated as having effect as if the governing body of that establishment were an authority and the establishment a maintained establishment.

(2) This regulation shall not apply to any voluntary establishment in respect of which grants are paid under Part III.

## Extension of regulations 12 and 14

**16.** Regulations 12 and 14 shall apply to youth workers employed by an authority otherwise than on the staff of an establishment as they apply to youth workers so employed on such staff.

## PART III

### VOLUNTARY ESTABLISHMENTS

## Grants to voluntary establishments

**17.**—(1) The Secretary of State may pay to the governing body of any voluntary establishment—

(a) a grant not exceeding any expenditure incurred by them in connection with the provision of the establishment ;

(b) grants not exceeding the expenditure incurred by them in maintaining the establishment.

(2) Regulation 18 and, subject to paragraph (3), regulations 19 to 23 shall apply to any establishment in respect of which grants are paid under this regulation.

(3) The payment of a grant to the governing body of any institution named in Schedule 2 shall be subject to such conditions as the Secretary of State may direct ; and accordingly regulations 19 to 24 shall not apply to those institutions.

*General conditions of grant*

**18.** If the Secretary of State is satisfied that the governing body are not conducting the establishment efficiently or are in default in respect of any duty imposed upon them by or under these regulations, he may withhold or reduce the grant otherwise payable to them.

*Application of regulations*

**19.** Regulations 7 to 14 shall apply to voluntary establishments as they apply to maintained establishments.

*Conduct of voluntary establishments*

**20.** The provisions relating to the reasonable exercise of functions and the making of reports and returns respectively contained in sections 68 and 92 of the Education Act 1944 shall apply to the governing bodies of voluntary establishments as they apply to authorities ; and the provisions relating to inspection contained in section 77 of that Act shall apply to voluntary establishments as they apply to maintained establishments.

*Provision of courses*

**21.** The governing body shall comply with any direction given by the Secretary of State requiring his approval to the provision of any course of instruction.

*Fees*

**22.** The governing body shall comply with any direction given by the Secretary of State as to the approval by him of arrangements for the charging and remission of fees.

*Religious instruction*

**23.** Courses of instruction in religious subjects distinctive of any particular religious denomination shall not be included as part of the general programme of full-time instruction.

*Particular requirements relating to capital grant*

**24.**—(1) The governing body of an establishment in respect of which grant is paid under regulation 17(1)(a) shall comply with any requirement of the Secretary of State to which this regulation applies.

(2) This regulation applies to—

　(a) a requirement imposing conditions for securing the continuity of the institution ;

　(b) a requirement that an assessor appointed by the Secretary of State shall attend the meetings of the body maintaining the establishment, with power to require that any matter coming before that body be referred to the Secretary of State before action is taken thereon ;

(c) a requirement that the books and other documents relating to the accounts of the establishment shall be open to inspection by persons appointed for the purpose by the Secretary of State ;

(d) a requirement that, in the event of the discontinuance of the use of any premises, plant or equipment provided wholly or mainly out of grant paid under regulation 17(1)(a), no interest in such premises, plant or equipment shall be disposed of without the approval of the Secretary of State ;

(e) a requirement to undertake in writing to repay to the Secretary of State such portion of the grant as he may require if the establishment ceases to be carried on as an establishment in accordance with these regulations.

## PART IV

### OTHER VOLUNTARY INSTITUTIONS AND ORGANISATIONS

*Grants to responsible bodies*

**25.**—(1) Subject to the provisions of this regulation, the Secretary of State may pay a grant to a responsible body towards the cost of providing tuition in any course of liberal adult education included in a programme approved by him for the purposes of these regulations.

(2) The amount of any such grant shall be determined by reference to the general standard of the courses included in the programme (having regard to the syllabuses, the quality of teaching, the length of courses and the arrangements for written work, reading under guidance and other forms of private study to be carried out between meetings), the needs of the area, the activities of other bodies providing further education in the area and the fees paid by students.

(3) It shall be a condition of grant under this regulation that the appointment of full-time lecturers and tutor organisers for any such programme shall be subject to the approval of the Secretary of State ; and regulation 20 shall apply in respect of any course included in the programme as it applies in respect of courses provided by voluntary establishments.

*Grants to national associations*

**26.** The Secretary of State may pay to any national association grants towards expenditure incurred by them in providing educational services otherwise than in or in connection with the provision of courses to which regulation 25(1) applies.

*Grants for village halls and community centres*

**27.** The Secretary of State may pay a grant to the trustees or other persons responsible for the management of any village hall or community centre in respect of capital expenditure incurred by them in connection with the provision of any such hall or centre.

*Grants for training youth leaders*

**28.** The Secretary of State may pay grants to the governing body of any university department of education or college of education in respect of expenditure incurred by them in providing courses for the training of youth leaders and community centre wardens.

*Grants to other organisations*

**29.** The Secretary of State may pay grants to any other voluntary organisation, and in particular to any youth organisation, in respect of expenditure incurred by them, whether as part of wider activities or not, in providing, or in connection with the provision of, facilities for further education within the meaning of section 41(*b*) of the Education Act 1944.

*Conditions of grant under Part IV*

**30.**—(1) Regulation 18 shall apply to institutions and organisations in respect of which grants are paid under this Part as it applies to establishments in respect of which grants are paid under Part III.

(2) The payment of grant under regulation 26, 27, 28 or 29 shall be subject to such conditions as the Secretary of State may direct.

*Regulation 6*                    SCHEDULE 1

COURSES SUBJECT TO APPROVAL

This Schedule applies to any full-time course of more than one month's duration and any part-time course occupying more than forty hours, being—

(*a*) a course of post-graduate or post-diploma instruction;

(*b*) a course of study in preparation for a degree, a Higher National Diploma, a Higher National Certificate, a Diploma in Management Studies, a Diploma in Art and Design or a final professional examination of a standard above that of the examination for the Ordinary National Certificate or General Certificate of Education (advanced level);

(*c*) a course of study of at least two years' duration if part-time other than block release or of equivalent length if full-time or block release, following an initial course of not less than one years' duration or equivalent length respectively, in preparation for an Advanced or Final Certificate or a Full Technological Certificate of the City and Guilds of London Institute or any other course for which the possession of such an Advanced or Final Certificate is a minimum qualification for entry;

(*d*) any other course in preparation for an examination of a standard above that of the examination for the Ordinary National Certificate or General Certificate of Education (advanced level) for which the normal age of entry is not less than 18 years and the normal minimum qualification for entry is, or is of a standard not below, one of the following:—

(i) an Ordinary National Certificate;

(ii) five passes in examinations for Certificates of Education being passes at the ordinary level in the examination for the General Certificate of Education or at the grade 1 level in the examination for the Certificate of Secondary Education;

(iii) two passes in the examination for the General Certificate of Education, one of which is at the advanced level.

*Regulation 17(3)*                 SCHEDULE 2

NAMED INSTITUTIONS

College of Aeronautics
Royal Academy of Music
Royal College of Art
Royal College of Music

## SCHEDULE 3

*Regulation* 3(1)

## REVOCATIONS

| Regulations Revoked | References |
|---|---|
| Further Education (Local Education Authorities) Regulations 1959 | S.I. 1959/393 (1959 I, p.1577). |
| Further Education (Grant) Regulations 1959 | S.I. 1959/394 (1959 I, p.1041). |
| Further Education (Local Education Authorities) Amending Regulations 1961 | S.I. 1961/1582 (1961 II, p.3245). |
| Further Education (Local Education Authorities) Amending Regulations 1964 | S.I. 1964/1309 (1964 II, p.2982). |
| Further Education (Grant) Amending Regulations 1964 | S.I. 1964/1310 (1964 II, p.2983). |
| Further Education (Grant) Second Amending Regulations 1964 | S.I. 1964/1514 (1964 III, p.3475). |
| Further Education (Local Education Authorities) Second Amending Regulations 1964 | S.I. 1964/1515 (1964 III, p.3476). |
| Further Education (Local Education Authorities) Amending Regulations 1965 | S.I. 1965/2 (1965 I, p.3). |
| Further Education (Local Education Authorities) Amending Regulations 1966 | S.I. 1966/1432 (1966 III, p.3789). |

Given under the Official Seal of the Secretary of State for Education and Science on 18th March 1969.

(L.S.)

*Edward Short,*
Secretary of State for Education
and Science.

## EXPLANATORY NOTE

*(This Note is not part of the Regulations.)*

These Regulations consolidate with amendments all the Regulations relating to the provision of full-time and part-time education for persons over compulsory school age. Part II prescribes standards and general requirements for the administration of establishments maintained by local education authorities. Part III provides for the payment of grants to bodies other than local education authorities which maintain establishments and prescribes the conditions to be satisfied by those bodies. Part IV provides for the payment of grants to bodies maintaining other institutions and organisations and prescribes conditions to be satisfied by those bodies.

The principal changes are the following :—

(*a*) the power to restrict the employment of teachers on medical grounds (regulation 13) ;

(*b*) the power to restrict the employment of certain youth workers (regulation 16) ;

(*c*) the special provision for the four institutions listed in schedule 2 (regulation 17).

Regulations 27 to 29 make new provision for the payment of grants, subject to conditions determined under the Regulations, in connection with the provision of facilities for leisure time occupation.

## 1969 No. 407

## AGRICULTURE

## The Price Stability of Imported Products (Rates of Levy No. 6) Order 1969

| | | | | |
|---|---|---|---|---|
| *Made* - | - | - | - | *18th March* 1969 |
| *Coming into Operation* | | | | *19th March* 1969 |

The Minister of Agriculture, Fisheries and Food, in exercise of the powers conferred upon him by section 1(2), (4), (5), (6) and (7) of the Agriculture and Horticulture Act 1964(a) and of all other powers enabling him in that behalf, hereby makes the following order:—

**1.** This order may be cited as the Price Stability of Imported Products (Rates of Levy No. 6) Order 1969 ; and shall come into operation on 19th March 1969.

**2.**—(1) In this order—

" the Principal Order " means the Price Stability of Imported Products (Levy Arrangements) Order 1966(b), as amended by any subsequent order and if any such order is replaced by any subsequent order the expression shall be construed as a reference to such subsequent order ;

AND other expressions have the same meaning as in the Principal Order.

(2) The Interpretation Act 1889(c) shall apply to the interpretation of this order as it applies to the interpretation of an Act of Parliament and as if this order and the order hereby revoked were Acts of Parliament.

**3.** In accordance with and subject to the provisions of Part II of the Principal Order (which provides for the charging of levies on imports of certain specified commodities)—

(a) the rate of general levy for such imports into the United Kingdom of any specified commodity as are described in column 2 of Part I of the Schedule to this order in relation to a tariff heading indicated in column 1 of that Part shall be the rate set forth in relation thereto in column 3 of that Part ;

(b) the rate of country levy for such imports into the United Kingdom of any specified commodity as are described in column 2 of Part II of the Schedule to this order in relation to a tariff heading indicated in column 1 of that Part shall be the rate set forth in relation thereto in column 3 of that Part.

**4.** The Price Stability of Imported Products (Rates of Levy No. 5) Order 1969(d) is hereby revoked.

In Witness whereof the Official Seal of the Minister of Agriculture, Fisheries and Food is hereunto affixed on 18th March 1969.

(L.S.)

*R. J. E. Taylor,*
Assistant Secretary.

---

(a) 1964 c. 28.    (b) S.I. 1966/936 (1966 II, p. 2271).    (c) 1889 c. 63.
(d) S.I. 1969/329. (1969 I, p. 938).

## SCHEDULE

### Part 1

| 1.<br>Tariff<br>Heading | 2.<br>Description of Imports | 3.<br>Rate of<br>General Levy |
|---|---|---|
| | | per ton<br>£  s.  d. |
| | Imports of:— | |
| 10·01 | Denatured wheat ...      ...      ...      ...      ...      ... | 15  0 |
| 10·01 | Any wheat (other than seed wheat the value of which is not less than £34 per ton, denatured wheat and durum wheat) for which a minimum import price level is precsribed      ...      ...      ...      ...      ... | 1  10  0 |
| 10·03 | Barley      ...      ...      ...      ...      ...      ... | 1  0  0 |
| 11·02 | Cereal meal—<br>of maize ...      ...      ...      ...      ...      ... | 5  10  0 |
| 11·02 | Rolled, flaked, crushed or bruised cereals—<br>barley      ...      ...      ...      ...      ... | 5  15  0 |

### Part II

| 1.<br>Tariff<br>Heading | 2.<br>Description of Imports | 3.<br>Rate of<br>Country Levy |
|---|---|---|
| | | per ton<br>£  s.  d. |
| | Imports of:— | |
| 10·01 | Denatured wheat which has been grown in and consigned to the United Kingdom from Belgium, the French Republic, the Kingdom of the Netherlands or the Kingdom of Sweden      ...      ...      ... | 15  0 |
| 10·01 | Any wheat (other than seed wheat the value of which is not less than £34 per ton, denatured wheat and durum wheat) for which a minimum import price level is prescribed and which is grown in and consigned to the United Kingdom from the French Republic or the Kingdom of the Netherlands ...      ...      ...      ... | 1  10  0 |
| 10·03 | Barley which has been grown in and consigned to the United Kingdom from Canada      ...      ...      ... | 1  0  0 |
| 10·03 | Barley which has been grown in and consigned to the United Kingdom from the Commonwealth of Australia      ...      ...      ...      ...      ... | 15  0 |
| 10·03 | Barley which has been grown in and consigned to the United Kingdom from Belgium, the Kingdom of Denmark, Finland, the French Republic, the Kingdom of the Netherlands or the Kingdom of Sweden... | 5  0 |

# EXPLANATORY NOTE

*(This Note is not part of the Order.)*

This order which comes into operation on 19th March 1969 supersedes the Price Stability of Imported Products (Rates of Levy No. 5) Order 1969. It :—

(*a*) increases to 30s. per ton the general levy on imports of wheat (other than seed wheat the value of which is not less than £34 per ton, denatured wheat and durum wheat) ;

(*b*) increases to 30s. per ton the country levy on imports of such wheat which is grown in and consigned to the United Kingdom from France or the Netherlands ;

(*c*) fixes a rate of country levy at 5s. per ton on imports of barley which has been grown in and consigned to the United Kingdom from Belgium, Denmark, Finland, France, the Netherlands or Sweden ; and

(*d*) retains unchanged the other rates of general and country levy prescribed by the above mentioned order.

## STATUTORY INSTRUMENTS

### 1969 No. 408

### POLICE

### The Police Cadets (Amendment) Regulations 1969

| | | |
|---|---|---|
| *Made* - - - | *19th March* 1969 |
| *Laid before Parliament* | *28th March* 1969 |
| *Coming into Operation* | *31st March* 1969 |

In exercise of the powers conferred on me by section 35 of the Police Act 1964(**a**), and after consulting the Police Council for Great Britain in accordance with section 45(4) of that Act, I hereby make the following Regulations :—

*Citation*

**1.** These Regulations may be cited as the Police Cadets (Amendment) Regulations 1969.

*Operation and effect*

**2.**—(1) These Regulations shall come into operation on 31st March 1969 and, subject to paragraph (2) of this Regulation, shall have effect—

 (*a*) for the purposes of Regulation 3 thereof, as from 1st September 1968 ;

 (*b*) for the purposes of Regulation 4 thereof, as from 31st March 1969;

 (*c*) for the purposes of Regulation 5 thereof, as from 1st January 1969.

(2) A travel allowance payable to a police cadet under Regulation 14 of the Police Cadets Regulations 1968(**b**), in respect of a return journey made on or after 1st January 1969 but before 31st March 1969, shall be calculated in accordance with the said Regulation 14 as originally made and not as amended by Regulation 5 of these Regulations, if it is more favourable in his case so to calculate the allowance.

*Pay*

**3.** For the Table in Schedule 1 to the said Regulations of 1968 (which contains scales of pay) there shall be substituted the following Table :—

"TABLE

| Age | City of London and metropolitan police forces | Other police forces |
|---|---|---|
| Under 17 years | £420 a year | £390 a year |
| 17 years | £455 a year | £425 a year |
| 18 years | £500 a year | £470 a year |
| 19 years | £535 a year | £505 a year" |

(**a**) 1964 c. 48.    (**b**) S.I. 1968/25 (1968 I, p. 31).

*Charge for board and lodging*

**4.** For paragraph 2 of Schedule 2 to the said Regulations of 1968 (which relates to charges for board and lodging) there shall be substituted the following paragraph :—

"2. The annual rate of charge shall be—
  (*a*) in the case of a police cadet attached to the City of London or metropolitan police force, £103 10s. 0d.;
  (*b*) in any other case, £93 10s. 0d.".

*Travel allowances*

**5.** For Regulation 14(2) of the said Regulations of 1968 (which relates to the amount of the travel allowance) there shall be substituted the following provision :—

"(2) An allowance payable under this Regulation shall not in any case exceed whichever is the less of the two following amounts, namely : —

  (*a*) the reasonable cost of the return journey actually made ;

  (*b*) the reasonable cost of a return journey to the parent's or guardian's usual place of abode ;

and, without prejudice to the said limitation, an allowance payable in respect of a return journey to a place outside the British Isles shall not exceed £15.

In computing the amount referred to in sub-paragraph (*a*) or (*b*) of this paragraph, any question as to reasonable cost shall be determined by the police authority.".

*George Thomas,*
One of Her Majesty's Principal
Secretaries of State.

Whitehall.
19th March 1969.

---

### EXPLANATORY NOTE
*(This Note is not part of the Regulations.)*

These Regulations amend the Police Cadets Regulations 1968.

Regulation 3 increases the pay of a police cadet by £15 or £20 a year, depending on his age.

Regulation 4 increases charges for board and lodging by £3 10s 0d. a year.

Regulation 5 makes new provision as regards the maximum amount of a travel allowance when a police cadet visits a parent or guardian outside the British Isles.

By virtue of Regulation 2(1)(*a*) and (*c*) the increases in pay have effect from 1st September 1968 and the changes in the maximum amount of a travel allowance have effect from 1st January 1969. This is provided in exercise of the power conferred by section 33(4), as applied by section 35(2), of the Police Act 1964. Regulation 2(2) contains a safeguard against any retrospective reduction in a travel allowance.

## STATUTORY INSTRUMENTS

### 1969 No. 409

### MERCHANT SHIPPING

**SAFETY**

### The Merchant Shipping (Life-Saving Appliances) (Second Amendment) Rules 1969

| | |
|---|---|
| *Made* - - - | 20*th March* 1969 |
| *Laid before Parliament* | 28*th March* 1969 |
| *Coming into Operation* | 1*st May* 1969 |

The Board of Trade in exercise of their powers under section 427 of the Merchant Shipping Act 1894(**a**), as substituted by section 2 of the Merchant Shipping (Safety Convention) Act 1949(**b**) and amended by section 9 of the Merchant Shipping Act 1964(**c**) and as having effect by virtue of the Transfer of Functions (Shipping and Construction of Ships) Order 1965(**d**), and of all other powers enabling them in that behalf hereby make the following Rules:—

1.—(1) These Rules shall come into operation on 1st May 1969 and may be cited as the Merchant Shipping (Life-Saving Appliances) (Second Amendment) Rules 1969.

(2) The Interpretation Act 1889(**e**) shall apply to the interpretation of these Rules as it applies to the interpretation of an Act of Parliament.

2. The Merchant Shipping (Life-Saving Appliances) Rules 1965(**f**) as amended (**g**) shall be further amended as follows:—

(*a*) in Rule 9(4) the words "at least 70 per cent of" in the penultimate line shall be deleted; and

(*b*) in Schedule 12, Part I, paragraph 5(*d*) the following shall be substituted for the final sentence:—

"The sewing shall be carried out with thread of undyed linen yarn having a count of 25 lea, 3 cord reverse twist (resultant Tex count 66), satin finish and complying with the specifications in Clauses 2, 3 and 4 (except subparagraph 4(*a*)) of British Standards Specification No. BS 4F 34: 1960: for thread of that count."

*William Rodgers,*
Minister of State,
Board of Trade.

20th March 1969.

---

(a) 1894 c. 60.   (b) 1949 c. 43.   (c) 1964 c. 47.
(d) S.I. 1965/145 (1965 I, p. 438).   (e) 1889 c. 63.
(f) S.I. 1965/1105 (1965 II, p. 2940).   (g) The amendment is not relevant to the subject matter of these Rules.

# EXPLANATORY NOTE

*(This Note is not part of the Rules.)*

These Rules amend the Merchant Shipping (Life-Saving Appliances) Rules 1965 in two respects :—

(1) They require that ships of Class VI of less than 70 ft. in length and plying not more than 3 nautical miles from their starting point in any direction shall carry liferafts, buoyant apparatus or lifebuoys sufficient for the total number of persons the ship is certified to carry, instead of, as previously, sufficient for only 70% of that total.

(2) The thread for the sewing of kapok lifejackets must now comply with a British Standards Specification.

## STATUTORY INSTRUMENTS

## 1969 No. 410

## EDUCATION, ENGLAND AND WALES

### The Special Schools and Establishments (Grant) (Amendment) Regulations 1969

| | |
|---|---|
| *Made* - - - | *19th March* 1969 |
| *Laid before Parliament* | *27th March* 1969 |
| *Coming into Operation* | *1st April* 1969 |

The Secretary of State for Education and Science, in exercise of the powers conferred upon him by section 100(1)(*b*) and (3) of the Education Act 1944(a) as amended by the Secretary of State for Education and Science Order 1964(b), hereby makes the following regulations:—

*Citation, commencement and interpretation*

**1.**—(1) These regulations may be cited as the Special Schools and Establishments (Grant) (Amendment) Regulations 1969 and shall come into operation on 1st April 1969.

(2) The Interpretation Act 1889(c) shall apply for the interpretation of these regulations as it applies for the interpretation of an Act of Parliament.

*Amendment of 1959 Regulations*

**2.** Regulation 5 of the Special Schools and Establishments (Grant) Regulations 1959(d) (grant in respect of employer's superannuation contribution) is hereby revoked.

Given under the Official Seal of the Secretary of State for Education and Science on 19th March 1969.

(L.S.)

*Edward Short,*
Secretary of State for Education
and Science.

### EXPLANATORY NOTE

*(This Note is not part of the Regulations.)*

These regulations terminate the Secretary of State's power to pay grants towards the employer's superannuation contribution in respect of teachers who are in contributory service in a special school or establishment for the further education and training of disabled persons.

| | |
|---|---|
| (a) 1944 c. 31. | (b) S.I. 1964/490 (1964 I, p. 800). |
| (c) 1889 c. 63. | (d) S.I. 1959/366 (1959 I, p. 1051). |

## STATUTORY INSTRUMENTS

### 1969 No. 411

### CLEAN AIR

## The Clean Air (Height of Chimneys) (Exemption) Regulations 1969

| | | |
|---|---|---|
| *Made* - - - | *20th March* 1969 |
| *Laid before Parliament* | *27th March* 1969 |
| *Coming into Operation* | *1st April* 1969 |

The Minister of Housing and Local Government, in exercise of the powers conferred on him by sections 6(11) and 13(1) of the Clean Air Act 1968(a), and of all other powers enabling him in that behalf, hereby makes the following regulations :—

*Title and commencement*

**1.** These regulations may be cited as the Clean Air (Height of Chimneys) (Exemption) Regulations 1969 and shall come into operation on 1st April 1969.

*Interpretation*

**2.** The Interpretation Act 1889(b) shall apply for the interpretation of these regulations as it applies for the interpretation of an Act of Parliament.

*Exempted boilers and plant*

**3.**—(1) The purposes set out in paragraph (2) below shall be prescribed purposes in relation to section 6(11) of the Clean Air Act 1968 (which section relates to the height of chimneys serving new or enlarged furnaces connected with boilers or industrial plant, but exempts from certain of its provisions any boiler or plant used or to be used wholly for a prescribed purpose).

(2) The said purposes are—

  (a) temporarily replacing any other boiler or plant which is—
    (i) under inspection, maintenance or repair ;
    (ii) being rebuilt ; or
    (iii) being replaced by a permanent boiler or plant ;

  (b) providing a temporary source of heat or power during any building operation or work of engineering construction (within the meaning of section 176 of the Factories Act 1961(c)) ;

  (c) providing a temporary source of heat or power for investigation or research ;

  (d) providing products of combustion to heat other plant (whether directly or indirectly) to an operating temperature ;

---

(a) 1968 c. 62.       (b) 1889 c. 63.
(c) 1961 c. 34.

(e) providing heat or power by mobile or transportable plant for the purposes of agriculture (within the meaning of section 109(3) of the
Agriculture Act 1947(**a**)).

Given under the official seal of the Minister of Housing and Local Government on 20th March 1969.

(L.S.)

*Anthony Greenwood*,
**Minister of Housing and
Local Government.**

## EXPLANATORY NOTE

*(This Note is not part of the Regulations.)*

Under section 6(2) of the Clean Air Act 1968, a person having possession
of a boiler or industrial plant attached to a building or for the time being
fixed to or installed on any land (other than an exempted boiler or plant)
is required to obtain the approval of the local authority to the height of the
chimney if he proposes to construct a new chimney or to enlarge the furnace.
By section 6(11), exempted boilers and plant mean those used or to be used
wholly for any purpose prescribed by regulations ; and these regulations prescribe the purposes which carry exemption. They include temporary or local
provision of heat or power during replacement or maintenance, building
operations, engineering construction, investigation or research, and agricultural operations.

---

(a) 1947 c. 48.

## 1969 No. 412

## CLEAN AIR

## The Clean Air (Height of Chimneys) (Prescribed Form) Regulations 1969

| | |
|---|---|
| *Made* - - - | *20th March* 1969 |
| *Laid before Parliament* | *27th March* 1969 |
| *Coming into Operation* | *1st April* 1969 |

The Minister of Housing and Local Government, in exercise of the powers conferred on him by sections 6(3) and 13(1) of the Clean Air Act 1968(a), and of all other powers enabling him in that behalf, hereby makes the following regulations:—

*Title and commencement*

**1.** These regulations may be cited as the Clean Air (Height of Chimneys) (Prescribed Form) Regulations 1969 and shall come into operation on 1st April 1969.

*Interpretation*

**2.** The Interpretation Act 1889(b) shall apply for the interpretation of these regulations as it applies for the interpretation of an Act of Parliament.

*Prescribed form for purposes of section 6(3) of Clean Air Act 1968*

**3.** For the purposes of section 6(3) of the Clean Air Act 1968 (which requires an application for approval of the height of a chimney to be made to the local authority on the prescribed form and to be accompanied by the prescribed particulars), the prescribed form shall be the form set out in schedule 1 to these regulations and the prescribed particulars shall be the particulars set out in schedule 2.

---

(a) 1968 c. 62.                    (b) 1889 c. 63.

## SCHEDULE 1

### CLEAN AIR ACT 1968

### Section 6—CHIMNEY HEIGHTS (Note 1)

*Application for approval by the local authority
of the height of a chimney serving a
furnace or furnaces*

*Name and address of local authority*

A. *Full name and address of applicant.*

   *Telephone No.*

   *Address of premises where chimney is or will be constructed (if different from above).*

   *Name and address of consultant, contractor or other agent (if employed).*

   *Telephone No.*

B. *Brief description of proposed works.*

C. *Category under which chimney height approval is sought* (Note 2)

|  |  |  |
|---|---|---|
| (a) Construction of new chimney. | | Insert |
| (b) Increase of combustion space of existing furnace. (Note 3) | | YES |
| | | or |
| (c) Replacement of furnace by one having larger combustion space. | | NO |


**(Signed by or on behalf of the applicant)**

**Date (Note 4)**


*Notes* 1 *to* 4

1.   An Explanatory Memorandum on the Clean Air Act 1968, with notes on Section 6, is contained in a Joint Circular (Ministry of Housing and Local Government 69/68, Welsh Office 62/68) available from H.M.S.O. price 1s. 9d. net.

2.   The exact terms of section 6(10) of the Clean Air Act 1968 are—

"This section applies to the following furnaces:—

(a)   any furnace served by a chimney other than a chimney the construction of which was begun or the plans for which were passed before the commencement of this section;

(b)   any furnace the combustion space of which has been increased since the commencement of this section; and

(c)   any furnace the installation of which was begun after the commencement of this section and which replaces a furnace which had a smaller combustion space;

not being a furnace forming part of a generating station as defined in the Electricity (Supply) Act 1919, other than a private generating station as so defined."

The commencement date referred to is 1st April 1969.

An application may cover more than one category.

3.   Including addition of a new furnace to an existing installation.

4.   Section 6(6) of the Clean Air Act 1968 provides as follows:

"If a local authority to whom an application is duly made for approval under this section fail to determine the application and to give a written notification of their decision to the applicant within four weeks of receiving the application or such longer period as may be agreed in writing between the applicant and the authority, the approval applied for shall be deemed to have been granted without qualification".

## SCHEDULE 2

*Particulars to accompany application for approval*

A. *Description and use of furnace(s)*

**1.** Intended use of furnace(s) (e.g. boiler plant, metal melting or reheating, calcining, drying etc.) (Note 5)

**2.** Type and description of furnace(s) (Note 5)

**3.** (*a*)  Particulars of furnaces to be installed.

(*b*)  Particulars of changes intended to existing furnaces.

(*c*)  Particulars of furnaces to be removed.

B. *Rating and fuel consumption (Note 5)*

**4.** (*a*)  Maximum continuous rating of boiler(s) (pounds steam per hour from and at 100°C., or B.t.u.'s per hour).

(*b*)  Maximum rate of fuel consumption in pounds per hour (separately for different fuels).

**5.** Type(s) of fuel to be used (Note 6)

**6.** Sulphur content of fuel %.

C. *Particulars of emissions*

**7.** Quantity and quality of emission (if any) from the material being heated e.g. fume, sulphur trioxide, hydrogen sulphide.

**8.** (*a*) Volume of chimney gases at working temperature (cubic ft. per second, calculated from paragraph 4(*b*) above).

(*b*) Working temperature of chimney gases in degrees C. (State point of measurement).

(*c*) Efflux velocity of chimney gases at working temperature and at maximum loading of plant (ft. per sec.).

D. *Particulars of buildings*

**9.** Height of building to which the chimney is attached.

**10.** Length of building to which the chimney is attached.

**11.** Height(s) of adjacent building(s).

**12.** Distance of adjacent buildings from proposed chimney.

E. *Particulars of chimney for which approval required*

**13.** Height of chimney above ground level.

**14.** Details of construction of chimney (materials, insulation, single or multi-flue, internal diameter of chimney top).

F. *Supplementary information*

**15.** Brief description and/or sketch plan of other emission sources on same site with heights of chimneys and approximate distances from chimney for which approval is sought.

**16.** Any other information relevant to the application.

*Notes 5 and 6*

5. The information should relate to the total furnace or boiler plant which the proposed chimney will serve after all the works have been completed.

6. If oil specify type and viscosity. If solid fuel give Coal Board specification, or colliery source, if known.

Given under the official seal of the Minister of Housing and Local Government on 20th March 1969.

(L.S.)                                                        *Anthony Greenwood,*
                                                    **Minister of Housing**
                                                **and Local Government.**

---

## EXPLANATORY NOTE

*(This Note is not part of the Regulations.)*

These Regulations prescribe (i) the form of application for the approval of the local authority to the height of a chimney serving a furnace to which section 6 of the Clean Air Act 1968 applies, and (ii) the particulars to accompany that form. The section applies to furnaces which are being enlarged, or the chimneys serving which are being constructed, after 1st April 1969.

# STATUTORY INSTRUMENTS

## 1969 No. 413

## LONDON GOVERNMENT

### The London Authorities (Superannuation) (Amendment)

### Order 1969

| | | |
|---|---|---|
| Made - - - | | 20th March 1969 |
| Laid before Parliament | | 27th March 1969 |
| Coming into Operation | | 1st April 1969 |

The Minister of Housing and Local Government, in exercise of his powers under sections 77(3), 84 and 90 of the London Government Act 1963(a), and of all other powers enabling him in that behalf, hereby makes the following order :—

### PART I

#### PRELIMINARY

*Title and commencement*

**1.**—(1) This order may be cited as the London Authorities (Superannuation) (Amendment) Order 1969 and shall come into operation on 1st April 1969.

(2) The London Authorities (Superannuation) Orders 1965 and 1967(**b**) and this order may be cited together as the London Authorities (Superannuation) Orders 1965 to 1969.

*Interpretation*

**2.**—(1) In this order, unless the context otherwise requires, "the principal order" means the London Authorities (Superannuation) Order 1965(**c**) as amended (**d**), and other expressions which have meanings assigned to them by the Local Government Superannuation Act 1937(**e**) or the principal order have the same respective meanings for the purposes of this order.

(2) In this order, unless the context otherwise requires, references to the provisions of any enactment or instrument shall be construed as references to those provisions as amended or re-enacted by any subsequent enactment or instrument.

(3) The Interpretation Act 1889(**f**) shall apply for the interpretation of this order as it applies for the interpretation of an Act of Parliament.

---

(a) 1963 c. 33.    (b) S.I. 1965/621, 1967/1330 (1965 I, p. 1970; 1967 III p. 3975).
(c) S.I. 1965/621 (1965 I, p. 1970).
(d) The relevant amending instrument is S.I. 1967/1330 (1967 III, p. 3975).
(e) 1937 c. 68.    (f) 1889 c. 63.

## PART II

### PROTECTION OF INTERESTS

*Amendment of the principal order*

**3.**—(1) For article 14(1) of the principal order (which prescribes the appropriate superannuation fund in relation to certain former employees of the county council of London or Middlesex becoming employed on or after 1st April 1965 by the council of a London borough) there shall be substituted the following :—

> "(1) For the purposes of the Act of 1937, the appropriate superannuation fund in relation to a person to whom this article applies shall be the superannuation fund maintained by the Greater London Council, so long as he continues to enjoy the protection conferred by article 21(6)."

(2) In article 15(1) of the principal order (which prescribes the appropriate superannuation fund in relation to certain former employees of the county council of London or Middlesex becoming employed on or after 1st April 1965 by the Common Council of the City of London) for the words "as long as he continues without a break in the employment of the Common Council" there shall be substituted the words "so long as he continues to enjoy the protection conferred by article 21(6)".

(3) In article 21 of the principal order (which protects superannuation rights and obligations of transferred employees, and provides for their duration)—

> (*a*) in paragraph (6) the words "without a break of twelve months or more" shall be omitted ; and
>
> (*b*) there shall be added the following paragraph :—
>> "(7) For the purposes of the preceding paragraph, if an employee leaves the employment of the authority or body but re-enters their employment within twelve months without any intervening period of employment under any local authority, he shall be deemed for purposes of this article to have continued in their employment".

*Amendment of the order of 1967*

**4.** For article 8 of the London Authorities (Superannuation) (Amendment) Order 1967(a) (which provides that where a person who is within the Greater London Council's fund by virtue of article 14 or 15 of the principal order loses the protection of article 21, he shall be treated for superannuation purposes as if he had just entered the employment of the authority by whom he is employed) there shall be substituted the following article :—

*"Deemed transfer, following loss of protection*

**8.**—(1) This article applies to any transferred employee who by virtue of article 14 or 15 of the principal order is on or after 1st April 1969 entitled to participate in the benefits of the Greater London Council's superannuation fund and to whom article 21(2) of the principal order applies.

(2) Where an employee to whom this article applies—

> (*a*) continues in the employment of the authority referred to in article 21(2) of the principal order, or
>
> (*b*) leaves their employment and re-enters it,

but in such circumstances that he loses the protection conferred by the said

---

(a) S.I. 1967/1330 (1967 III, p. 3975).

article 21(2), he shall be treated for the purposes of the provisions mentioned in paragraph (3) of this article—

    (i) in the case described in sub-paragraph (*a*), as if at the date when he lost the said protection he were entering the employment of the authority immediately after ceasing to be employed by another local authority, or

    (ii) in the case described in sub-paragraph (*b*), as if at the date when he left the employment of the authority he had ceased to be employed by another local authority.

(3) The provisions referred to in the preceding paragraph are—

    (i) the Acts of 1937 to 1953 and the regulations made thereunder ;

    (ii) the local Act scheme of the Common Council ;

    (iii) article 21(4) of the principal order.".

*Transitional provisions*

**5.** Article 3 of this order shall not apply so as to alter the appropriate superannuation fund in relation to any person or to affect the rights of any person under article 21(2) of the principal order in consequence of a change in that person's employment, or a change in the circumstances of that person's employment, which occurred before the commencement of this order.

PART III

TRANSFER OF CERTAIN PENSION LIABILITIES

*Liabilities in respect of teachers in former poor law schools*

**6.** Where after the commencement of this order a liability arises under section 124(5) of the Local Government Act 1929(**a**) (which subsection provides for the superannuation of teachers transferred from poor law schools) in respect of an officer who was immediately before 1st April 1930 serving in an establishment which was subsequently transferred to the corporation of a London borough by the London Authorities (Property etc.) Order 1964(**b**), the liability shall be discharged by the council of that borough and not by the Greater London Council as provided by that order.

*Liabilities in respect of increases of pension payable to certain employees in health and education services*

**7.** As from the commencement of this order article 8(3) of the principal order shall cease to apply to any liability which was transferred to an authority by virtue of a transfer of functions effected by or under the Education Act 1944(**c**) or the National Health Service Act 1946(**d**).

*Liabilities in respect of certain justices' clerks, etc., and probation officers*

**8.**—(1) This article applies to any liability existing on 31st March 1965 with respect to the payment of superannuation benefit to or in respect of a person whose last employing authority was the magistrates' courts committee or the probation committee for the borough of Croydon, East Ham or West Ham.

(2) As from the commencement of this order any liability to which this article applies shall be discharged by the Greater London Council out of the superannuation fund maintained by them, and not by the council of the London borough of Croydon or Newham, as the case may be, as provided by the principal order ; but each of those councils shall pay from their superannuation fund into the superannuation fund of the Greater London Council

(**a**) 1929 c. 17.         (**b**) S.I. 1964/1464 (1964 III, p. 3392).

(**c**) 1944 c. 31.         (**d**) 1946 c. 81.

an amount equivalent to the value, as certified by an actuary, of the liability of which their fund has been relieved by virtue of this article.

*Liabilities in respect of certain hospital employees*

**9.**—(1) This article applies to any liability existing on 31st March 1965 of the council of the county borough of Croydon, East Ham or West Ham to pay to the Minister of Health, under superannuation regulations made by the said Minister under section 67(1) of the National Health Service Act 1946, instalments of transfer value in respect of any person formerly subject to the Asylums Officers' Superannuation Act 1909(a).

(2) As from the commencement of this order any liability to which this article applies shall be discharged by the Greater London Council and not by the council of the London borough of Croydon or Newham, as the case may be, as provided by the London Authorities (Property etc.) Order 1964.

Given under the official seal of the Minister of Housing and Local Government on 20th March 1969.

(L.S.)                                          *Anthony Greenwood,*
                                               Minister of Housing and
                                               Local Government.

---

### EXPLANATORY NOTE
*(This Note is not part of the Order.)*

This Order effects a group of linked amendments to the London Authorities (Superannuation) Orders 1965 and 1967, and transfers the obligation to discharge certain minor liabilities in respect of pensions from the Greater London Council to London borough councils and vice versa. (The actual pensions are not affected.)

The linked amendments are these. Articles 14 and 15 of the Order of 1965 enabled former employees of the county councils of London and Middlesex to participate in the Greater London Council's superannuation fund even if they were transferred to the employment of some other authority. Article 21 protected their existing superannuation rights and obligations. The present order—

(i) relates the right to participate in the Greater London Council's fund specifically to continuation of protected rights ;

(ii) re-defines the circumstances in which protected rights can survive a break in service ;

(iii) extends article 8 of the Order of 1967 (which provides for a deemed transfer for superannuation purposes in the case where a person loses his protected rights although remaining in the employment of the same authority) to cover the case where a person re-enters their employment after a break.

---

**(a)** 1909 c. 48.

## 1969 No. 414

## ROAD TRAFFIC
### The Motor Vehicles (Competitions and Trials) Regulations 1969

| | |
|---|---|
| *Made* - - - | 19*th March* 1969 |
| *Laid before Parliament* | 28*th March* 1969 |
| *Coming into Operation* | 1*st April* 1969 |

The Secretary of State and the Minister of Transport in exercise of their powers under section 36 of the Road Traffic Act 1962(**a**), as read with the Secretary of State for Wales and Minister of Land and National Resources Order 1965(**b**), and of all other enabling powers, and after consultation with representative organisations in accordance with section 260(2) of the Road Traffic Act 1960(**c**), hereby make the following Regulations :—

*Commencement and citation*

**1.** These Regulations shall come into operation on the 1st April 1969 and may be cited as the Motor Vehicles (Competitions and Trials) Regulations 1969.

*Revocation*

**2.** The Regulations specified in Schedule 1 to these Regulations are hereby revoked.

*Transitional provisions*

**3.**—(1) An event which was authorised before the coming into force of these Regulations by the Royal Automobile Club, a chief officer or officers of police, or a chief constable or constables, under such of the Regulations revoked by Regulation 2 of these Regulations as relate thereto, shall be treated, in so far as it is held after the coming into force of these Regulations, as authorised in accordance with these Regulations.

(2) Where an application for the authorisation of an event was made to the Royal Automobile Club, a chief officer or officers of police, or a chief constable or constables before the coming into force of these Regulations, being an event which is proposed to be held after the coming into force of these Regulations, but the event was not authorised before the coming into force of these Regulations, the Royal Automobile Club, chief officer or officers of police, or chief constable or constables may authorise such event in accordance with such of the Regulations revoked by Regulation 2 of these Regulations as relate thereto, as though the same had not been revoked.

(3) Where under the Regulations revoked by Regulation 2 of these Regulations an application for the authorisation of an event could be made to a chief officer or officers of police or a chief constable or constables, but no such application has been made before the coming into force of these Regulations,

---

(a) 10 & 11 Eliz. 2. c.59.
(c) 8 & 9 Eliz. 2. c.16.
(b) S.I. 1965/319 (1965 I, p.785).

an application for the authorisation of such an event which is proposed to be held or to begin on or before the 14th June 1969 may be made on or before the 14th April 1969, under such of the Regulations revoked as aforesaid as relate thereto, and the said chief officer or officers of police or chief constable or constables may authorise the event in accordance with such Regulations as aforesaid, as though the same had not been revoked.

(4) Where an application for the authorisation of an event which is proposed to be held after the coming into force of these Regulations was received by the Royal Automobile Club before the coming into force of these Regulations, the fee payable shall be the fee specified in such of the Regulations revoked by Regulation 2 of these Regulations as relate thereto, and Regulation 8 of these Regulations shall not apply in relation to such an event.

(5) An event which is authorised or treated as authorised under this Regulation shall be held in accordance with the conditions applying thereto specified in such of the Regulations revoked by Regulation 2 of these Regulations as relate thereto, subject to any modifications thereof made under those Regulations, and in accordance with any additional conditions imposed under those Regulations, as though the same had not been revoked, and Regulation 9 of these Regulations shall not apply in relation to such an event.

*Interpretation*

**4.**—(1) In these Regulations, unless the contrary intention appears, the following expressions have the meanings hereby respectively assigned to them, that is to say :—

" "A" road" means a road to which has been allocated a route number commencing with the letter "A" by the Minister of Transport in England excluding Monmouthshire, or by the Minister of Transport or the Secretary of State in Scotland, Wales and Monmouthshire ;

"control point" means a place other than at the start or finish of an event where the route being followed by the competitors or the times being kept by them are checked ;

"event" means a competition or trial (other than a race or trial of speed) involving the use of motor vehicles on a public highway ;

"motorway" means a special road which (save as otherwise provided by or under regulations made or having effect as if made under section 13 of the Road Traffic Regulation Act 1967(a) can only be used by traffic of Class I or II of the classes of traffic set out, as respects England and Wales, in Schedule 4 to the Highways Act 1959(b), as amended by the Special Roads (Classes of Traffic) Order 1961(c) and the Special Roads (Classes of Traffic) (England and Wales) Order 1968(d), and, as respects Scotland, in Schedule II to the Special Roads Act 1949(e) as amended by the Special Roads (Classes of Traffic) (Scotland) Order 1964(f) and the Special Roads (Classes of Traffic) (Scotland) Order 1968(g) ;

"night event" means an event a part or the whole of which is intended to take place between the hours of 10 p.m. and 7 a.m. ;

"overall average speed on the public highway" in relation to a vehicle driven by a competitor in an event means the average speed calculated by reference to the interval between the time when the competitor commenced to drive that vehicle on the public highway in the event and the time when

---

(a) 1967 c.76.                              (b) 7 & 8 Eliz. 2. c.25.
(c) S. I. 1961/1210 (1961 II, p.2408).     (d) S.I. 1968/1966 (1968 III, p. 5372).
(e) 12, 13 & 14 Geo. 6. c.32.              (f) S.I. 1964/1084 (1964 II, p. 2398).
(g) S.I. 1968/1982 (1968 III, p. 5396).

he finished so to drive and the total distance travelled on the public highway, but there shall be excluded from such interval any period during which the vehicle driven by the competitor was off the public highway or at a rest halt between such times ;

"performance test" means a test in which merit is attached to a competitor's skill in manoeuvring or controlling the vehicle, including maintaining the forward motion of the vehicle in adverse conditions ;

"problem" means a problem given to a competitor the setting or solution of which is necessary to enable him or assists him to complete the event, or which he is required by the rules of the event to set or solve, and in this context "problem" shall include any instruction given to a competitor to collect information or an object and "solution" shall be construed accordingly ;

"problem solving event" means an event in which the competitors are required by the rules of the event to travel the route by a fixed time and are given before that time the task of setting or solving a number of set problems, whether the problems are required to be set or solved before or after that time, and in which there is an average of more than one set problem for each three miles of route ;

"promoter" means the person who is primarily responsible for the organisation or arrangements of the event ;

"requirement" in relation to the rules of an event includes a requirement or an instruction to a competitor in the event compliance with which carries merit in the event or non-compliance with which carries demerit in the event, and cognate expressions shall be construed accordingly ;

"rest halt" means a place specified in the rules of the event as a place where the competitors are required to stop during the course of the event, or may stop during the course of the event without incurring a penalty or demerit in the event, in either case for the purpose of obtaining rest or refreshment ;

"route" in relation to an event means a route which the rules of the event require or are likely to cause the competitors taking part in the event to travel ;

"rules" in relation to an event includes any instruction given by or on behalf of the promoter of the event to a competitor in the event ;

"specified event" means an event, held not more than once each calendar year, specified in Schedule 4 to these Regulations ;

"standard conditions" has the meaning assigned to it in Regulation 9(1) of these Regulations ;

"time limit event" means an event in which the competitors are required by the rules of the event to travel the route of the event by a fixed time such that they will be caused to maintain an overall average speed on the public highway exceeding 10 miles per hour ;

"time schedule event" means an event in which individual competitors or groups of competitors are required by the rules of the event to arrive at or depart from control points at or between specific times or to arrive at the finish of the event at or between specific times.

(2) Any reference in these Regulations to any enactment or instrument shall be construed, unless the context otherwise requires, as a reference to that enactment or instrument as amended, re-enacted or replaced by any subsequent enactment or instrument.

(3) The Interpretation Act 1889(a) shall apply for the interpretation of these Regulations as it applies for the interpretation of an Act of Parliament, and as if for the purposes of Section 38 of that Act these Regulations were an Act of Parliament and the Regulations revoked by Regulation 2 of these Regulations were Acts of Parliament thereby repealed.

*Authorisation of certain events*

5. Any event of one of the following descriptions, that is to say :—

(*a*) an event in which the total number of vehicles driven by the competitors does not exceed 12, being an event no part of which takes place within 8 days of any part of any other event in which the total number of vehicles driven by the competitors does not exceed 12 and where either the other event has the same promoter or the promoters of both events are members of the same club in connection with which the events are promoted ;

(*b*) an event in which no merit is attached to completing the event with the lowest mileage and in which, as respects such part of the event as is held on a public highway, there are no performance tests and no route and competitors are not timed or required to visit the same places, except that they may be required to finish at the same place by a specified time ;

(*c*) an event in which, as respects such part of the event as is held on a public highway, merit attaches to a competitor's performance only in relation to good road behaviour and compliance with the Highway Code ;

(*d*) an event in which all the competitors are members of the armed forces of the Crown and which is designed solely for the purposes of their service training ;

is hereby authorised.

*Authorisation of other events*

6.—(1) Events not authorised by the last preceding Regulation may be authorised by the Royal Automobile Club in accordance with these Regulations.

(2) An authorisation of an event given by the Royal Automobile Club under paragraph (1) of this Regulation may be varied or revoked by the Royal Automobile Club at any time before the event is held or begins.

*Applications for authorisation*

7.—(1) Applications for authorisation of an event shall be made to the Royal Automobile Club on a form (which may be obtained from the Royal Automobile Club) containing the particulars specified in Schedule 2 to these Regulations.

(2) Applications for such authorisation shall be made not less than 2 months before the date on which the event is proposed to be held, or if it is to be held on more than one date, the date on which the event is to begin, and, except in the case of a specified event, shall not be made more than 6 months before such date.

*Fees*

8.—(1) It shall be a condition of any authorisation of an event by the Royal Automobile Club that a fee, to be calculated in accordance with the next following paragraph of this Regulation, shall be paid.

---

(a) 52 & 53 Vict. c. 63.

(2) The fee referred to in the last preceding paragraph of this Regulation shall be a basic fee of £5 increased by £3 for each 50 miles or part thereof of the length of the route of the event on the public highway.

*Other conditions*

**9.**—(1) Subject to paragraph (2) of this Regulation an event, other than an event authorised by Regulation 5 of these Regulations, shall be held subject to such of the conditions specified in column 1 of Schedule 3 to these Regulations (in these Regulations referred to as "the standard conditions") as apply to the event in question in accordance with column 2 of that Schedule.

(2) The Royal Automobile Club to the exent specified in column 3 of Schedule 3 to these Regulations shall, subject to the provisions of the next following paragraph, have power to modify the standard conditions, and where this power is exercised in relation to a competition or trial the event shall be held subject to the standard conditions as modified.

(3) The Royal Automobile Club in exercising its power to modify the standard conditions applying to an event shall have regard to the need for securing the safety and preserving amenity for, and minimising the inconvenience suffered by, members of the public.

(4) Without prejudice to the foregoing provisions of this Regulation the Royal Automobile Club shall have, when authorising an event, power to impose such additional conditions as it may think fit for the purpose of securing the safety or preserving amenity for, or minimising the inconvenience suffered by, members of the public.

**10.**—(1) Before authorising an event the Royal Automobile Club shall not less than 6 weeks before the date on which the event is proposed to be held, or, if it is to be held on more than one date, the date on which the event is to begin, notify, in England and Wales, the chief officer of police and, in Scotland, the chief constable of any police area in which the route of the event on the public highway lies, whether partially or wholly.

(2) Before authorising an event the route of which lies in whole or in part along a road in England and Wales used as a public path shown on a definitive map prepared by the council of a county or county borough or a joint planning board pursuant to section 32 of the National Parks and Access to the Countryside Act 1949(a) the Royal Automobile Club shall consult with the highway authority for that road.

(3) Before authorising an event the route of which on the public highway lies in whole or in part in an area in England and Wales comprised in a National Park the Royal Automobile Club shall consult with the appropriate planning authority for the area concerned.

(4) In the last preceding paragraph of this Regulation the expression "appropriate planning authority" has the meaning assigned to it in section 6(6) of the National Parks and Access to the Countryside Act 1949.

*Grant of authorisations*

**11.** In exercising their discretion to authorise an event the Royal Automobile Club shall have regard to the following considerations—

(*a*) whether in all the circumstances it is likely that the conditions, subject to which the event if authorised would be required to be held, will be observed,

---

(a) 12, 13 & 14 Geo. c.97.

(b) the extent to which the holding of the event might prejudicially affect the safety, amenity or convenience of members of the public,

(c) the number of and the intervals between the events which have recently been held or are due to be held on or adjacent to the route of the proposed event on the public highway or in the locality where the proposed event is planned to take place, and

(d) the nature and suitability of the route of the proposed event on the public highway and the class or description of vehicles taking part in the event.

*Measurement of distance*

**12.** The length of the route, or any part thereof, of an event and the distance from such route of any point shall for the purposes of these Regulations be calculated by reference to the most recent edition of the one-inch Ordnance Survey Map of the area concerned.

Dated the 18th March 1969.

*William Ross,*
One of Her Majesty's Principal
Secretaries of State.

Dated the 18th March 1969.

*George Thomas,*
One of Her Majesty's Principal
Secretaries of State.

Given under the Official Seal of the Minister of Transport the 19th March 1969.

(L.S.)                                        *Richard Marsh,*
Minister of Transport.

# SCHEDULE 1

## REGULATIONS REVOKED BY REGULATION 2

| Title | Year and Number |
|---|---|
| The Motor Vehicles (Competitions and Trials) (England) Regulations 1965. | S.I. 1965/1400 (1965 II, p.4118). |
| The Motor Vehicles (Competitions and Trials) (Wales) Regulations 1965. | S.I. 1965/1414 (1965 II, p.4179). |
| The Motor Vehicles (Competitions and Trials) (Scotland) Regulations 1966. | S.I. 1966/1069 (1966 II, p.2629). |
| The Motor Vehicles (Competitions and Trials) (Wales) (Amendment) Regulations 1967. | S.I. 1967/176 (1967 I, p.307). |
| The Motor Vehicles (Competitions and Trials) (England) (Amendment) Regulations 1967. | S.I. 1967/415 (1967 I, p.1356). |
| The Motor Vehicles (Competitions and Trials) (Wales) (Amendment) (No. 2) Regulations 1967. | S.I. 1967/439 (1967 I, p.1373). |
| The Motor Vehicles (Competitions and Trials) (Scotland) (Amendment) Regulations 1967. | S.I. 1967/706 (1967 II, p.2139). |

## SCHEDULE 2 (see Regulation 7)

PARTICULARS TO BE GIVEN IN THE APPLICATION FOR AUTHORISATION

(1) Name of promoter of the event.

(2) Name of event.

(3) Full name and address of applicant and daytime telephone number (if any).

(4) Date(s) of event.

(5) Maximum number of competing vehicles.

(6) Interval at which competitors will be despatched from starting points.

(7) Type of competing vehicles.

(8) Mileage of the route of the event on the public highway.

(9) Indicate the number of each current one-inch Ordnance Survey sheet traversed by the route of the event on the public highway.

(10) Will the event be a (i) time schedule event, (ii) time limit event, (iii) a problem solving event?

(11) Is the event a Specified Event under Schedule 4 of the Regulations?

(12) Describe exactly (in words) the location of each starting and finishing point, and state whether it is on the public highway.

(13) Will the rules of the event require or be likely to cause any competitor to traverse any length of public highway (other than a motorway) more than once? If yes, give the reasons why Standard Condition No. 6 should be modified.

(14) Provide two identical tracings of the route of the event from each current one-inch Ordnance Survey sheet traversed by the route omitting any part of the route which is not on a public highway. Each tracing should show:—

    (i) the number of the Ordnance sheet;

    (ii) two intersecting grid lines appropriately numbered;

    (iii) the location of any starting and finishing points;

    (iv) the times when the first competitor is expected to leave any starting point and arrive at any finishing point (use the 24 hour clock for all times);

    (v) the time and date when the first competitor is expected to arrive at any point where the route enters or leaves a map;

    (vi) (with the letter "C") the location of any control point on a public highway and of any other point on such highway at which the rules of the event require or are likely to cause competitors to stop for any purpose or to slow down for the purpose of solving a problem;

    (vii) (with the letter "R") the location of each rest halt and also the length of time it is expected to be open;

    (viii) (with a cross (X)) any point where the route leaves or rejoins the public highway and also the time when the first competitor is expected to reach any such point. If the route leaves and rejoins the pulbic highway at the same point, show both the time then the first competitor is expected to leave the public highway and the time when he is expected to rejoin it at that point;

    (ix) (with arrows marked "F" or "B") lengths of any public highway which are footpaths or bridleways forming part of the route.

Send the completed application form with the tracings to the Royal Automobile Club, 31 Belgrave Square, LONDON, S.W.1.

*Declaration*

I declare that the event if authorised will be held in accordance with such of the standard conditions contained in the Motor Vehicles (Competitions and Trials) Regulations 1969 as apply to the event, subject to any modifications which may be made by the Royal Automobile Club, and in accordance with any additional conditions imposed by the Royal Automobile Club.

Signature of Applicant.................................................

Date....................................

SCHEDULE 3 (see Regulation 9)

STANDARD CONDITIONS

| 1.<br>Standard conditions | 2.<br>Application | 3.<br>Power to modify |
|---|---|---|
| 1. Each event shall be held in accordance with the particulars of the event given in the application for authorisation of the event, except that an event may be held subject to such modifications of the particulars—<br>(a) as may have been agreed with or required by the Royal Automobile Club, and<br><br>(b) as may be necessary to permit the event to take place in a case where part of the route of the event is closed or becomes impassable after the event is authorised. | All events. | None. |
| 2. The total number of vehicles driven by competitors in any night event shall not exceed 120 and the total number of such vehicles in any other event shall not exceed 180. | All events. | The Royal Automobile Club has power to modify in respect of specified events. |
| 3. The competitors shall be required by the rules of the event to observe a time-table such that:—<br><br>(i) the interval between the times of departure from the start of the event of the first and last competitors,<br><br>(ii) the interval between the time of arrival of the first competitor at and the time of departure of the last competitor from any control point on a public highway, other than a control point at which there is provided a rest halt,<br><br>(iii) the interval between the times at which the first and last competitors may be expected to pass any point on the route on a public highway, other than a point on a motorway, and<br><br>(iv) the interval between the times of arrival of the first and last competitors at the finish of the event,<br><br>shall not exceed 2 hours in the case of a night event, or 3 hours in the case of any other event. | All time schedule events, except events in which all the vehicles driven by competitors were registered under the Roads Act 1920 (a) before the 1st January 1930. | The Royal Automobile Club has power to modify<br><br>(i) in respect of the intervals specified in paragraph (iii) of this condition to the extent that the modification is necessary or expedient either in connection with a modification of standard condition No. 6 permitted in relation to an event or to permit the competitors to use private property on which part of the event is being held, and<br><br>(ii) in respect of specified events. |

(a) 10 & 11 Geo. 5.c.72.

Schedule 3—continued

| 1.<br>Standard conditions | 2.<br>Application | 3.<br>Power to modify |
|---|---|---|
| 4. No person at a starting point or finishing point of an event or control point, other than a control point at which there is provided a rest halt, shall check or record for the purpose of the event the times being kept by the competitors after 2½ hours in the case of any night event or 3½ hours in the case of any other event from the time when the first competitor departed from tnat point, in the case of a starting point, or arrived at that point, in the case of any other point. | All time schedule events, except events in which all the vehicles driven by competitors were registered under the Roads Act 1920 before the 1st January 1930. | The Royal Automobile Club has power to modify in respect of specified events. |
| 5. No competitor shall be dispatched from a starting point of an event at an interval less than one minute from the dispatch of the previous competitor. | All time schedule events, time limit events and problem solving events. | The Royal Automobile Club has power to modify in respect of specified events. |
| 6. The rules of an event shall not require or be such as are likely to cause any length of public highway (other than a motorway) to be traversed more than once by a vehicle driven by a competitor during the course of the event. | All events. | The Royal Automobile Club has power to modify:— <br><br>(i) the extent that the modification is to permit the competitors to travel twice the same length of "A" road, or to reach a finishing point in the same place as a starting point, or to use a rest halt, private property on which part of the event is being held or a filling station, and<br><br>(ii) in respect of specified events. |
| 7. No starting point or finishing point of an event shall be on a public highway. | All events. | The Royal Automobile Club has power to modify. |
| 8. The rules of an event shall not require, or be such as are likely to cause, a competitor to stop or to slow down for the purpose of setting or solving a problem, a vehicle he is driving in the event on a public highway within 500 yards of any occupied dwelling, unless an adult occupant of the dwelling has given his consent in writing. | All events | None. |
| 9. No point on a public highway at which the times being kept by competitors in an event are checked or recorded for the purposes of the event shall be situated less than two miles measured along the route of the event from any other point at which such times are so checked or recorded. | All time schedule events. | None. |

Schedule 3—continued

| 1.<br>Standard conditions | 2.<br>Application | 3.<br>Power to modify |
|---|---|---|
| 10.   The rules of an event shall be such that no greater merit accrues to a competitor for visiting certain control points rather than others or for reaching one finishing point rather than another. | All events. | None. |
| 11.   The rules of an event shall be such that once a competitor has been penalised for arriving at, or departing from a control point along the route of the event after the time at or by which he was required by the rules to arrive at or depart from that point, the times at or by which he is required to arrive at or depart from subsequent control points along the route and to arrive at the finish of the event are adjusted so that he will not incur further penalties for failing to make up the time by which he was late and for which he has incurred a penalty. | All time schedule events. | None. |
| 12.   A person who is acting as an official of an event shall not set up or place on the carriageway or footway of any public highway any equipment to be used in connection with the event, nor shall he park any vehicle he is using on the carriageway of any public highway forming part of the route of the event, except at a place provided for the parking of vehicles. | All events. | None. |
| 13.   Where the route of an event contains roads across which there are gates or cattle grids:—<br><br> (a)   the promoter of the event shall before the event takes place notify the occupiers of the land, other than any common land in England and Wales or land which is fenced off from the road, adjoining either side of the road between the gates, cattle grids, or a gate and a cattle grid of the holding of the event,<br><br> (b)   competitors shall not be required to leave their vehicles in order to open or close a gate, and<br><br> (c)   a person shall be posted at each gate until the last competitor has passed through the gateway for the purpose of ensuring that cattle do not pass through the gateway and closing the gate after the last competitor has | All events. | None. |

Schedule 3—continued

| 1.<br>Standard conditions | 2.<br>Application | 3.<br>Power to modify |
|---|---|---|
| passed through the gateway:<br>  Provided that where the interested occupiers consent in writing a person may be posted for the above purpose in respect of more than one gate, not being in England and Wales a gate across a road on any common land or a gate across a road leading to any common land where there is not another gate or a cattle grid across the road between the gate and the common land. In this proviso the expression "interested occupiers" in relation to a gate means the occupiers of the land adjoining such lengths of road on either side of the gate as extend to another gate or a cattle grid across the road, other than land which is fenced off from the road. | | |
| 14. The average speed, calculated by reference to the distance travelled by a vehicle being driven by a competitor on the public highway and the time during which it is being so driven, which the competitors in an event are required by the rules of the event or may reasonably be expected having regard to the rules of the event to maintain over a part or the whole of the route of the event on the public highway shall— | All events. | None. |
| (a) be such as is not likely to cause competitors to exceed any speed limit imposed by or under any enactment in respect of any vehicle or on any public highway which forms part of the route of the event or drive at a speed which might be dangerous having regard to the nature of the route, and | | |
| (b) without prejudice to the foregoing, not exceed— | | |
| (i) in the case of vehicles of a class or description for which no speed limit is specified in Schedule 5 to the Road Traffic Regulation Act 1967, 50 miles per hour in so far as the route consists of a motorway, and 30 miles per hour in all other cases; | | |
| (ii) in the case of goods vehicles and large passenger | | |

Schedule 3—continued

| 1.<br>Standard conditions | 2.<br>Application | 3.<br>Power to modify |
|---|---|---|
| vehicles, 50 miles per hour in so far as the route consists of a motorway, and 25 miles per hour in all other cases; | | |
| (iii) in the case of a vehicle constructed solely for the carriage of passengers and their effects, being a motor car adapted to carry not more than seven passengers exclusive of the driver, which is towing a caravan, in so far as the route does not consist of a motorway, 25 miles per hour. | | |
| In this condition "goods vehicle" means a vehicle of the description of vehicles to which paragraph 2(1) of Schedule 5 to the Road Traffic Regulation Act 1967 applies, and "large passenger vehicle" means a vehicle of the description of vehicles to which paragraph 1(1) and (2) of that Schedule applies. | | |
| 15.  The rules of an event shall be such as to require each competitor to take a rest period at intervals not exceeding each 200 miles which he drives whether continuously or not. The rest period shall not be less than one hour and may be taken as a passenger in a vehicle taking part in the event. | All events. | None. |
| 16.  The promoter of an event shall require each competitor driving in the event as a condition of entry to declare that there will be in force in relation to the user of the vehicle which he intends to drive during the event such a policy of insurance or such a security in respect of third party risks as complies with the requirements of Part VI of the Road Traffic Act 1960. | All events. | None. |
| 17.  The promoter of an event shall record the name and address of each competitor driving a vehicle in the event and the registered number and make of each such vehicle, and he shall send this information to the Royal Automobile Club if so requested. | All events. | None. |

## SCHEDULE 4 (see Regulation 4)

### SPECIFIED EVENTS

| Country in which event held | Title of Event | Promoter |
|---|---|---|
| Great Britain. | British Caravan Road Rally. | Caravan Club Ltd. |
| | International Rally of Great Britain. | Royal Automobile Club. |
| | International Six Days' Trial. | Auto-Cycle Union. |
| | London Rally. | London Motor Club Ltd. |
| England (excluding Monmouthshire) and Scotland. | Scoot to Scotland and Edinburgh Run. | Motor Cycling Club Ltd. |
| England and Wales. | Auto-Cycle Union National Rally. | Auto-Cycle Union. |
| England (excluding Monmouthshire). | Auto-Cycle Union International Training Trial. | Auto-Cycle Union. |
| | Banbury Run. | Vintage Motor Cycle Club. |
| | Exeter Trial. | Motor Cycling Club Ltd. |
| | Land's End Trial. | Motor Cycling Club Ltd. |
| | Pioneer Run. | Sunbeam Motor Cycle Club. |
| | Veteran Car Run. | Royal Automobile Club. |
| Scotland. | International Scottish Rally. | Royal Scottish Automobile Club. |
| | Scottish Six Days' Reliability Trial. | Edinburgh & District Motor Club Ltd. |
| Wales and Monmouthshire. | Welsh Three Days' Trial. | Auto-Cycle Union. |
| | International Welsh Rally. | South Wales Automobile Club Ltd. |

## EXPLANATORY NOTE

*(This Note is not part of the Regulations.)*

These Regulations consolidate with modifications the Regulations specified in Schedule 1.

The principal changes are:—

1.    An event involving not more than 12 vehicles is only authorised unconditionally if it does not take place within 8 days of any other similar event, where the promoters of each event are either the same person or members of the same club (Regulation 5(*a*)).

2.    All events, other than those authorised unconditionally by Regulation 5, which were previously authorised by the Royal Automobile Club, or by the chief officer of police in England and Wales or the chief constable in Scotland of the appropriate area, are now to be authorised by the Royal Automobile Club (Regulation 6).

3.    A revised form of particulars to be given in the application for authorisation of an event is prescribed (Regulation 7 and Schedule 2).

4.    The fee to be paid for the authorisation of an event by the Royal Automobile Club is increased to £5 plus £3 for each 50 miles or part thereof of the length of the route of the event on the public highway (Regulation 8).

5.    A new condition subject to which events, other than those authorised by Regulation 5, are to be held, requires each driver to have one hour's rest after each 200 miles which he drives (Regulation 9 and Schedule 3 paragraph 15).

6.    The list of events specified in Schedule 4 has been increased by the addition of two events.

# STATUTORY INSTRUMENTS

## 1969 No. 415

## PENSIONS

# The Superannuation (Local Government and Membership of the House of Commons) Interchange Rules 1969

| | |
|---|---|
| *Made* - - - - | *20th March* 1969 |
| *Laid before Parliament* | *27th March* 1969 |
| *Coming into Operation* | *1st April* 1969 |

### ARRANGEMENT OF RULES

PART IV

MISCELLANEOUS

16. Extension of time
17. Interest on returned contributions

The Minister of Housing and Local Government, in exercise of his powers under sections 2 and 15 of the Superannuation (Miscellaneous Provisions) Act 1948(a), as extended by section 13(6) of the Ministerial Salaries and Members' Pensions Act 1965(b) and amended by section 11(6) of the Superannuation (Miscellaneous Provisions) Act 1967(c), and of all other powers enabling him in that behalf, hereby makes the following rules:—

PART I

PRELIMINARY

*Title and commencement*

**1.** These rules may be cited as the Superannuation (Local Government and Membership of the House of Commons) Interchange Rules 1969, and shall come into operation on 1st April 1969.

*Interpretation*

**2.**—(1) In these rules, unless the context otherwise requires—

"the Act of 1937" means the Local Government Superannuation Act 1937(d);

"the Act of 1948" means the Superannuation (Miscellaneous Provisions) Act 1948;

"the Act of 1953" means the Local Government Superannuation Act 1953(e);

"added years", in relation to a person in local government employment, means any additional years of service reckonable by him under regulation 12 of the benefits regulations or that regulation as applied by or under any enactment, and includes any additional years of service which, having been granted thereunder, have subsequently become reckonable under or by virtue of any other enactment;

"benefit" means any superannuation benefit payable to or in respect of any person;

"the benefits regulations" means the Local Government Superannuation (Benefits) Regulations 1954(f);

"contributing service" and "contributory employee" have the same meanings as in the Act of 1937;

"enactment" includes any instrument made under any enactment;

"fund authority" means a local authority maintaining a superannuation fund to which a person either became a contributor after ceasing to be a Member of the House of Commons or, as the case may be, was last a contributor before he became such a Member;

"interchange rules" means rules made under section 2 of the Act of 1948;

"local authority" has the same meaning as in the Act of 1937;

---

(a) 1948 c. 33.
(c) 1967 c.28.
(e) 1953 c. 25.

(b) 1965 c.11.
(d) 1937 c. 68.
(f) S.I. 1954/1048 (1954 II, p.1595).

"local government employment" means employment by virtue of which the person employed is or is deemed to be a contributory employee;

"the Minister" means the Minister of Housing and Local Government;

"national service", in relation to any person, means service which is relevant service within the meaning of the Reserve and Auxiliary Forces (Protection of Civil Interests) Act 1951(a), and any similar service immediately following relevant service, entered into with the consent of the authority or person by whom he was employed before undertaking that service or, in the case of a person who holds an appointment to an office and is not employed under a contract of employment, with the consent of the authority by whom he was appointed;

"non-contributing service" has the same meaning as in the Act of 1937;

"prescribed period" has the meaning assigned to it by rule 3;

"transfer value regulations" means the Local Government Superannuation (Transfer Value) Regulations 1954(b);

"the Trustees" means the Trustees of the Members' Contributory Pension Fund established under Part II of the Ministerial Salaries and Members' Pensions Act 1965;

"voluntary contributions" means payments made voluntarily by a person while in local government employment or in overseas employment within the meaning of the Superannuation (Local Government and Overseas Employment) Interchange Rules 1958(c) for the purpose of securing benefits for his widow, children or other dependants and payments (other than payments made in respect of a liability which has been wholly discharged) of any of the following categories:—

(i) additional contributory payments of the kind referred to in section 2(3) and (4) of the Act of 1953;

(ii) any similar payments made under a local Act scheme as a condition of reckoning any period of employment as service or as a period of contribution for the purposes of the scheme or, where the local Act scheme provides for the reckoning of non-contributing service, as contributing service for the purposes of the scheme;

(iii) any payments made for the purpose of increasing the length at which any period of service or of contribution would be reckonable for the purpose of calculating a benefit under a local Act scheme;

(iv) any payments made in respect of added years.

(2) For the purposes of these rules a justices' clerk shall be deemed to be in the employment of the magistrates' courts committee or committee of magistrates by whom he is, or under the provisions of any enactment is deemed to have been, appointed, and in relation to any such person references to "employment" shall be construed accordingly.

(3) Any references in these rules to a person as a contributory employee, or to contributing service, or to the Act of 1937, the Act of 1953, the benefits regulations, or any provision in any of those enactments in their application to that person shall be deemed to include references to a person as a local Act contributor within the meaning of the Act of 1937 and to a person entitled to participate in the benefits of a superannuation fund maintained under a local Act scheme, or to service for the purposes of a local Act scheme, or to any corresponding local Act or scheme or provision therein in their application to that person.

---

(a) 1951 c.65.                                    (b) S.I. 1954/1212 (1954 II, p.1723).
(c) S.I. 1958/1416 (1958 II, p.1845).

(4) References in these rules to a numbered rule shall, unless the reference is to a rule of a specified enactment, be construed as references to the rule bearing that number in these rules.

(5) Unless the context otherwise requires, references in these rules to the provisions of any enactment shall be construed as references to those provisions as amended, extended, modified, applied or re-enacted by any subsequent enactment.

(6) The Interpretation Act 1889(a) shall apply for the interpretation of these rules as it applies for the interpretation of an Act of Parliament.

*Meaning of "prescribed period"*

**3.**—(1) Subject to the provisions of these rules, the expression "prescribed period" in rules 4 and 8 means a period of 12 months after the date on which a person left local government employment or, as the case may be, ceased to be a Member of the House of Commons, and in the case of a person who immediately after leaving local government employment become engaged in national service, a period of 6 months after the termination of that service.

(2) The reference in the preceding paragraph to a period of 12 months shall be construed in relation to a person to whom section 6 of the Act of 1948 applies (which makes special provision as to local government superannuation during periods of emergency) as a reference to a period of 5 years or such longer period as the Minister may in any particular case allow.

## PART II

### TRANSFER FROM LOCAL GOVERNMENT EMPLOYMENT TO MEMBERSHIP OF THE HOUSE OF COMMONS

*Persons to whom part II applies*

**4.**—(1) Subject to the provisions of these rules and subject to the conditions specified in rule 5 being satisfied, this part of these rules shall apply—

(a) to a person who on or after the commencement of these rules becomes a Member of the House of Commons within the prescribed period, having left local government employment not earlier than 4th February 1948, and

(b) if the fund authority consent, to a person who before the commencement of these rules became a Member of the House of Commons within the prescribed period, having left local government employment not earlier than 4th February 1948 and having been elected such a member on or after 15th October 1964.

(2) This part of these rules shall not apply to any person—

(a) who has become entitled to and received payment of any benefit (other than a return of contributions) in respect of his local government employment; or

(b) in respect of whom a transfer value has been paid by the fund authority since he left his local government employment.

*Conditions for application of part II*

**5.** The conditions referred to in rule 4 are that the person shall within 3 months after becoming a Member of the House of Commons or, if he became a Member

(a) 1889 c.63.

before the commencement of these rules, within 6 months after their commencement—

(a) notify the Trustees in writing that he desires these rules to apply to him;

(b) furnish the Trustees with particulars in writing of any national service in which he has been engaged since leaving local government employment; and

(c) pay to the fund authority an amount equal to any sum paid to him by way of return of contributions (other than voluntary contributions) on or after leaving local government employment, together with any further sum by way of interest required under rule 17.

*Payment of transfer value*

**6.**—(1) The fund authority shall, when this part of these rules becomes applicable to a person—

(a) pay to the Trustees, subject to the provisions of these rules, the same transfer value as would have been payable under the transfer value regulations if that person had become a contributory employee under another local authority in the circumstances described in section 29 of the Act of 1937, less an amount equal to any sum which the fund authority may become liable to pay by way of income tax in respect of the amount transferred by way of transfer value; and

(b) furnish the Trustees and the person with the same particulars as to previous pensionable service as would have been furnished to the person if instead of becoming a Member of the House of Commons he had become a contributory employee under another local authority.

(2) The transfer value payable in respect of a person who left local government employment before 1st April 1968 and who became a Member of the House of Commons before 1st April 1969 shall be calculated by reference to his age at 1st April 1969.

(3) The transfer value payable in respect of a person who becomes a Member of the House of Commons on or after 1st April 1969 and more than 12 months after leaving local government employment shall be calculated by reference to his age on becoming a Member of the House of Commons.

(4) The transfer value payable in respect of a person who had been an established officer or servant within the meaning of the Asylums Officers' Superannuation Act 1909(a) (in this rule called "the Act of 1909") shall be calculated as if paragraph (c) had been omitted from the definition of "service" in paragraph 1 of Schedule 1 to the transfer value regulations.

(5) Where—

(a) a transfer value is payable by a fund authority in respect of a person who before entering local government employment had been subject to the Act of 1909 and

(b) the body by whom he was last employed while subject to that Act (in this rule called "the hospital body") would, if he had become entitled to a superannuation allowance on leaving local government employment, have been liable to contribute to that allowance,

the hospital body shall pay to the fund authority a sum equal to the transfer value which they would have been liable to pay to the Minister of Health under

(a) 1909 c.48.

regulation 56(4) of the National Health Service (Superannuation) Regulations 1950(a) if that regulation had become applicable to the person when he became a Member of the House of Commons.

(6) Where the hospital body would have had in respect of any such contribution as aforesaid a right of contribution from any other body, that other body shall pay to the fund authority a sum equal to the transfer value which they would have been liable to pay to the Minister of Health under paragraph (5) of the said regulation 56 if that regulation had become applicable to the person when he became a Member of the House of Commons.

(7) Where any body referred to in paragraph (5) or (6) hereof has been dissolved or has ceased to exercise functions as such, references to that body shall be construed as references to the appropriate authority as defined in paragraph (15) of the said regulation 56.

(8) Notwithstanding anything in the Act of 1937, when this part of these rules becomes applicable to a person, he shall cease to be entitled to any payment out of the superannuation fund administered by the fund authority other than a payment by way of return of voluntary contributions.

*Exercise by local authority of discretionary powers to increase benefits*

7.—(1) Where a person becomes, or before the commencement of these rules became, a Member of the House of Commons after leaving local government employment and these rules have become applicable to him, the authority or body by whom he was employed may, within 6 months after the date on which they are informed by the Trustees of his notification that he desires these rules to apply to him, exercise any discretion which, with a view to increasing the benefits payable to him, they could have exercised at the time when he left their employment if he had then retired and had been entitled to a retirement pension under regulation 5 of the benefits regulations or (if that regulation was not applicable to him) to any corresponding benefit provided under the superannuation provisions which were applicable to him in that employment.

(2) A decision in the exercise of any discretion under this rule shall be subject to the limitations and restrictions (if any) and to the right of appeal (if any) to which it would have been subject if the discretion had been exercised on the person's retirement in the circumstances aforesaid.

(3) Where a discretion has been exercised under this rule, the service reckonable immediately before he left his former employment by the person in whose favour the discretion has been exercised shall be deemed to have been correspondingly increased, and the transfer value payable in respect of him shall be calculated accordingly.

(4) Any increase in service, if attributable to a decision under this rule to increase benefit otherwise than by any notional increase or extension of the service reckonable for the purpose of calculating benefit, or by treating any specified period of non-contributing service as contributing service or, under a local Act scheme, by similarly converting service of one category to service of another category, shall be ascertained by converting the service in respect of which the higher rate of benefit is payable into contributing service in the manner in which non-contributing service is converted into contributing service under section 2(4) of the Act of 1953.

---

(a) S.I. 1950/497 (1950 I, p. 1327).

(5) Where the amount of any transfer value payable under rule 6 is increased in consequence of the exercise by an authority or body of any power conferred upon them by this rule, that authority or body shall repay the amount of the said increase to the superannuation fund out of which the transfer value is payable.

## PART III

### TRANSFER FROM MEMBERSHIP OF THE HOUSE OF COMMONS TO LOCAL GOVERNMENT EMPLOYMENT

*Persons to whom part III applies*

**8.** Subject to the provisions of these rules and subject to the conditions specified in rule 9 being satisfied, this part of these rules shall apply—

(a) to a person who on or after the commencement of these rules enters local government employment within the prescribed period, having ceased to be a Member of the House of Commons after 15th October 1964, and

(b) if the Trustees consent, to a person who before the commencement of these rules entered local government employment within the prescribed period, having ceased to be a Member of the House of Commons after 15th October 1964.

*Conditions for application of part III*

**9.** The conditions referred to in rule 8 are that—

(a) the person shall, before or within 3 months after entering local government employment or, if he entered that employment before the commencement of these rules, within 6 months thereafter, notify the fund authority in writing that he desires these rules to apply to him; and

(b) the fund authority shall receive from the Trustees sums certified or calculated under section 13(1) of the Ministerial Salaries and Members' Pensions Act 1965 as representing the value of the person's accrued pension rights in the Members' Contributory Pension Fund, less any sum which the Trustees become liable to pay by way of income tax.

*Reckoning of service*

**10.**—(1) Subject to the provisions of this rule, a person to whom this part of these rules applies shall be entitled to reckon as contributing service such number of completed years and months as having regard to his age and re-muneration at the date when he entered local government employment would have produced a transfer value of the amount received under rule 9(b) had he left local government employment in the circumstances described in section 29 of the Act of 1937 at that date.

(2) The reference in the preceding paragraph to a transfer value shall be construed as a reference to a transfer value which is not subject to reduction under regulation 6 of the transfer value regulations or under any regulations made or having effect as if made under section 110 of the National Insurance Act 1965(a).

(3) A person to whom this part of these rules applies shall not be entitled under section 12(2) of the Act of 1937 to reckon as non-contributing service

(a) 1965 c.51.

any service as referred to therein before the date he became a Member of the House of Commons if—

    (a) a transfer value in respect of that service has been paid under rule 6, or

    (b) a transfer value in respect of that service has been paid under the corresponding provision of any other interchange rules, or

    (c) a transfer of assets in respect of his accrued pension rights has been made out of a local authority's superannuation fund under any enactment.

*Computation of contributions*

**11.**—(1) Where any enactment relating to local government superannuation refers, in connection with assessing a return of contributions or a benefit, to the amount of the contributions paid by a person, the amount of the contributions paid by a person to whom this part of these rules applies shall be deemed to be increased, in accordance with the provisions of this rule, to take account of earlier periods of service which became reckonable under rule 10.

(2) Subject to the provisions of this rule, the amount of the increase shall be the amount which would have been payable to him if, on ceasing to be a member of the House of Commons, he had been entitled to a return of contributions without interest.

(3) Where an amount described in paragraph (1) of this rule is the amount of a person's contributions with interest thereon, interest shall also be payable on the amount by which those contributions are increased under paragraph (2), calculated—

    (a) as respects the period ending immediately before he entered local government employment, at the rate at which it would have been calculated if after ceasing to be a Member of the House of Commons he had been entitled to a return of contributions with interest; and

    (b) as respects the period beginning on his entry into local government employment, in the manner described in section 10(1) of the Act of 1937.

*Calculation of "average remuneration" for periods of less than three years*

**12.** Where a person to whom this part of these rules applies dies or leaves local government employment within 3 years after entering such employment, and in such circumstances that a benefit (other than a return of contributions) is payable, his average remuneration for the purposes of calculating any such benefit shall be deemed to be the annual average of his remuneration during such period of employment.

*Modification of benefits and obligations in relation to National Insurance*

**13.**—(1) In this rule "person retaining unmodified status" means a person whose contributions and pension are, by virtue of regulation 9, 9A or 10 of the National Insurance (Modification of Local Government Superannuation Schemes) Regulations 1947(a) or of interchange rules, not subject to reduction to take into account his entitlement to a retirement pension referred to in section 30 of the National Insurance Act 1965.

(2) Where a person to whom this part of these rules applies was before becoming a member of the House of Commons a person retaining unmodified status in local government employment, and after he became a Member of the

    (a) S.R. & O. 1947/1245 (Rev. XVI, p.273: 1947 I, p.1498).

House of Commons the Trustees received in respect of preceding local government employment a transfer value which had not been reduced pursuant to regulation 6 of the transfer value regulations, he shall re-enter local government employment as a person retaining unmodified status.

### Application of section 11 of the Act of 1953

**14.** The provisions of section 11 of the Act of 1953 (which enables persons who would otherwise be debarred from becoming contributory employees on grounds of age to reckon, in relation to local government employment, previous service reckonable under a pension scheme) shall apply in relation to a person who before the commencement of these rules entered local government employment after ceasing to be a Member of the House of Commons; and the references in subsection (3) of that section to the passing of the Act shall be construed as including references to the commencement of these rules.

### Right of appeal

**15.** The provisions of section 35 of the Act of 1937 (which provides for decision of questions and appeals to the Minister) shall have effect in relation to a person who enters local government employment in circumstances in which these rules apply as if the reference in that section to regulations made under that Act included a reference to these rules:

Provided that this rule shall not apply in relation to a person who is a local Act contributor.

## PART IV

### MISCELLANEOUS

### Extension of time

**16.**—(1) A fund authority and the Trustees may at any time, on the application of a person who desires these rules to apply to him, agree to extend any of the following periods, namely—

(a) the periods of 6 and of 12 months referred to in rule 3(1);

(b) the periods of 3 and of 6 months referred to in rules 5 and 9 within which a person must notify in writing that he desires these rules to apply to him;

(c) the periods of 3 and of 6 months during which a person must pay to the fund authority any sum described in rule 5(c).

(2) The Trustees may, in respect of a person required to furnish them with particulars in writing of national service, at any time extend, on the application of that person, the period of 3 or of 6 months referred to in rule 5(b) within which he must take such action.

### Interest on returned contributions

**17.**—(1) Where a period longer than 12 months is allowed, pursuant to rule 16(1)(a), in respect of any person who has left local government employment, the fund authority may require that person to pay compound interest on any sum paid to him by way of return of contributions (other than voluntary contributions) on or after leaving that employment at a rate of 3% per annum with half-yearly rests for a period beginning either with the date 12 months after the date on which he left that employment or, where this is later, the date on which he received such sum, and ending with the date on which he notified in writing that he desired these rules to apply to him.

(2) The interest payable under this rule shall not exceed a sum equal to one-half of the difference between the transfer value payable under these rules and the transfer value which would be payable if calculated by reference to the person's age on leaving local government employment.

Given under the official seal of the Minister of Housing and Local Government on 20th March 1969

(L.S.)

*Anthony Greenwood,*
Minister of Housing and
Local Government.

## EXPLANATORY NOTE

*(This Note is not part of the Rules.)*

These Rules provide for the preservation of the superannuation rights of persons who transfer from pensionable employment with a local authority in England or Wales to Membership of the House of Commons or vice versa. Where such a transfer is made, the person is enabled, subject to the payment of an appropriate transfer value, to reckon previous service for pension under the superannuation scheme to which he transfers.

Under the powers conferred by section 2(5) of the Superannuation (Miscellaneous Provisions) Act 1948, the Rules apply to persons who have transferred before the coming into operation of the Rules. But a person who transfers to Membership of the House of Commons must have become a Member not earlier than 15th October 1964, and a person who transfers to a local authority must have ceased to be a Member after that date.

## STATUTORY INSTRUMENTS

### 1969 No. 417

### PENSIONS

# The Superannuation (Local Government and Federated Schemes Employment) Interchange Rules 1969

| | |
|---|---|
| Made - - - | 21st March 1969 |
| Laid before Parliament | 27th March 1969 |
| Coming into Operation | 1st April 1969 |

## ARRANGEMENT OF RULES

## Part IV

### Miscellaneous

16. Extension of time
17. Interest on returned contributions

The Minister of Housing and Local Government, in exercise of his powers under sections 2 and 15 of the Superannuation (Miscellaneous Provisions) Act 1948(a), as amended by section 11(6) of the Superannuation (Miscellaneous Provisions) Act 1967(b), and of all other powers enabling him in that behalf, hereby makes the following rules :—

## Part I

### Preliminary

*Title and commencement*

**1.** These rules may be cited as the Superannuation (Local Government and Federated Schemes Employment) Interchange Rules 1969, and shall come into operation on 1st April 1969.

*Interpretation*

**2.**—(1) In these rules, unless the context otherwise requires—

"the Act of 1937" means the Local Government Superannuation Act 1937(c);

"the Act of 1948" means the Superanuation (Miscellaneous Provisions) Act 1948 ;

"the Act of 1953" means the Local Government Superannuation Act 1953(d) ;

"added years" means—

(*a*) in relation to a person in local government employment, any additional years of service reckonable by him under regulation 12 of the benefits regulations or that regulation as applied by or under any enactment. and includes any additional years of service which, having been granted thereunder, have subsequently become reckonable under or by virtue of any other enactment, and

(*b*) in relation to a person in Federated Schemes Employment. any additional years of service of the nature of the additional years of service referred to in (*a*) of this definition which have been granted in, or have otherwise become reckonable in, that employment ;

"benefit" means any superannuation benefit payable to or in respect of any person ;

"the benefits regulations" means the Local Government Superannuation (Benefits) Regulations 1954(e) ;

"contributing service" and "contributory employee" have the same meanings as in the Act of 1937 ;

"enactment" includes any instrument made under any enactment ;

"Federated Schemes Employment" means employment in which a person is a member of the Federated Group Pension Scheme or a Federated Pension Scheme established under a trust deed made between the Trustee and an employer ;

(a) 1948 c. 33.                 (b) 1967 c. 28.                 (c) 1937 c. 68.
(d) 1953 c. 25.                 (e) S.I. 1954/1048 (1954 II, p. 1595).

2i

"fund authority" means a local authority maintaining a superannuation fund to which a person either became a contributor after he left Federated Schemes Employment or, as the case may be, was last a contributor before he entered Federated Schemes Employment ;

"interchange rules" means rules made under section 2 of the Act of 1948 ;

"local authority" has the same meaning as in the Act of 1937 ;

"local government employment" means employment by virtue of which the person employed is or is deemed to be a contributory employee ;

"the Minister" means the Minister of Housing and Local Government ;

"national service", in relation to any person, means service which is relevant service within the meaning of the Reserve and Auxiliary Forces (Protection of Civil Interests) Act 1951(a), and any similar service immediately following relevant service, entered into with the consent of the authority or person by whom he was employed before undertaking that service or, in the case of a person who holds an appointment to an office and is not employed under a contract of employment, with the consent of the authority by whom he was appointed ;

"non-contributing service" has the same meaning as in the Act of 1937 ;

"prescribed period" has the meaning assigned to it by rule 3 ;

"relevant scheme" means the pension scheme of which a person is or was a member in his Federated Schemes Employment ;

"transfer value regulations" means the Local Government Superannuation (Transfer Value) Regulations 1954(b) ;

"the Trustee" means the incorporated body known as the Federated Pension Schemes ;

"voluntary contributions" means—

(a) in relation to a person who enters Federated Schemes Employment after leaving local government employment, payments made voluntarily by him, while in local government employment or in overseas employment within the meaning of the Superannuation (Local Government and Overseas Employment) Interchange Rules 1958(c), for the purpose of securing benefits for his widow, children or other dependants and payments (other than payments made in respect of a liability which has been wholly discharged) of any of the following categories:—

(i) additional contributory payments of the kind referred to in section 2(3) and (4) of the Act of 1953 ;

(ii) any similar payments made under a local Act scheme as a condition of reckoning any period of employment as service or as a period of contribution for the purposes of the scheme or, where the local Act scheme provides for the reckoning of non-contributing service, as contributing service for the purposes of the scheme ;

(iii) any payments made for the purpose of increasing the length at which any period of service or of contribution would be reckonable for the purpose of calculating a benefit under a local Act scheme ;

(iv) any payments made in respect of added years ; and

(b) in relation to a person who enters local government employment after leaving Federated Schemes Employment, any payments similar in character to those referred to in (a) of this definition for which provision was made in the relevant scheme.

---

(a) 1951 c. 65.      (b) S.I. 1954/1212 (1954 II, p. 1723).
(c) S.I. 1958/1416 (1958 II, p. 1845).

(2) For the purposes of these rules a justices' clerk shall be deemed to be in the employment of the magistrates' courts committee or committee of magistrates by whom he is, or under the provisions of any enactment is deemed to have been, appointed, and in relation to any such person references to "employment" shall be construed accordingly.

(3) Any references in these rules to a person as a contributory employee, or to contributing service, or to the Act of 1937, the Act of 1953, the benefits regulations, or any provision in any of those enactments in their application to that person shall be deemed to include references to a person as a local Act contributor within the meaning of the Act of 1937 and to a person entitled to participate in the benefits of a superannuation fund maintained under a local Act scheme, or to service for the purposes of a local Act scheme, or to any corresponding local Act or scheme or provision therein in their application to that person.

(4) References in these rules to a numbered rule shall, unless the reference is to a rule of a specified enactment, be construed as references to the rule bearing that number in these rules.

(5) Unless the context otherwise requires, references in these rules to the provisions of any enactment shall be construed as references to those provisions as amended, extended, modified, applied or re-enacted by any subsequent enactment.

(6) The Interpretation Act 1889(a) shall apply for the interpretation of these rules as it applies for the interpretation of an Act of Parliament.

*Meaning of "prescribed period"*

**3.**—(1) Subject to the provisions of these rules, the expression "prescribed period" in rules 4 and 8 means a period of 12 months after the date on which a person left local government employment or, as the case may be, Federated Schemes Employment, and in the case of a person who immediately after leaving such employment became engaged in national service, a period of 6 months after the termination of that service.

(2) The reference in the preceding paragraph to a period of 12 months shall be construed in relation to a person to whom section 6 of the Act of 1948 applies (which makes special provision as to local government superannuation during periods of emergency) as a reference to a period of 5 years or such longer period as the Minister may in any particular case allow.

## PART II

### TRANSFER FROM LOCAL GOVERNMENT EMPLOYMENT TO FEDERATED SCHEMES EMPLOYMENT

*Persons to whom part II applies*

**4.**—(1) Subject to the provisions of these rules and subject to the conditions specified in rule 5 being satisfied, this part of these rules shall apply—

    (*a*) to a person who on or after the commencement of these rules enters Federated Schemes Employment within the prescribed period, having left local government employment not earlier than 4th February 1948, and

    (*b*) if the fund authority consent, to a person who before the commencement of these rules entered Federated Schemes Employment within the prescribed period, having left local government employment not earlier than 4th February 1948.

(a) 1889 c. 63.

(2) This part of these rules shall not apply to any person—

　(*a*) who has become entitled to and received payment of any benefit (other than a return of contributions) in respect of his local government employment ; or

　(*b*) in respect of whom a transfer value has been paid by the fund authority since he left his local government employment.

## Conditions for application of part II

**5.** The conditions referred to in rule 4 are that the person shall, before or within 3 months after entering Federated Schemes Employment or, if he entered that employment before the commencement of these rules, within 6 months after their commencement—

　(*a*) notify the Trustee in writing that he desires these rules to apply to him ;

　(*b*) furnish the Trustee with particulars in writing of any national service in which he has been engaged since leaving local government employment ; and

　(*c*) pay to the fund authority an amount equal to any sum paid to him by way of return of contributions (other than voluntary contributions) on or after leaving local government employment, together with any further sum by way of interest required under rule 17.

## Payment of transfer value

**6.**—(1) The fund authority shall, when this part of these rules becomes applicable to a person—

　(*a*) pay to the Trustee, subject to the provisions of these rules, the same transfer value as would have been payable under the transfer value regulations if that person had become a contributory employee under another local authority in the circumstances described in section 29 of the Act of 1937, less an amount equal to any sum which the fund authority may become liable to pay by way of income tax in respect of the amount transferred by way of transfer value ; and

　(*b*) furnish the Trustee and the person with the same particulars as to previous pensionable service as would have been furnished to the person if instead of entering Federated Schemes Employment he had become a contributory employee under another local authority.

(2) The transfer value payable in respect of a person who left local government employment before 1st April 1968 and who entered Federated Schemes Employment before 1st April 1969 shall be calculated by reference to his age at 1st April 1969.

(3) The transfer value payable in respect of a person who enters Federated Schemes Employment on or after 1st April 1969 and more than 12 months after leaving local government employment shall be calculated by reference to his age on entering Federated Schemes Employment.

(4) The transfer value payable in respect of a person who had been an established officer or servant within the meaning of the Asylums Officers' Superannuation Act 1909(**a**) (in this rule called "the Act of 1909") shall be calculated as if paragraph (*c*) had been omitted from the definition of "service" in paragraph 1 of Schedule 1 to the transfer value regulations.

---

(**a**) 1909 c. 48.

(5) Where—

(a) a transfer value is payable by a fund authority in respect of a person who before entering local government employment had been subject to the Act of 1909, and

(b) the body by whom he was last employed while subject to that Act (in this rule called "the hospital body") would, if he had become entitled to a superannuation allowance on leaving local government employment, have been liable to contribute to that allowance,

the hospital body shall pay to the fund authority a sum equal to the transfer value which they would have been liable to pay to the Minister of Health under regulation 56(4) of the National Health Service (Superannuation) Regulations 1950(a) if that regulation had become applicable to the person when he entered Federated Schemes Employment.

(6) Where the hospital body would have had in respect of any such contribution as aforesaid a right of contribution from any other body, that other body shall pay to the fund authority a sum equal to the transfer value which they would have been liable to pay to the Minister of Health under paragraph (5) of the said regulation 56 if that regulation had become applicable to the person when he entered Federated Schemes Employment.

(7) Where any body referred to in paragraph (5) or (6) hereof has been dissolved or has ceased to exercise functions as such, references to that body shall be construed as references to the appropriate authority as defined in paragraph (15) of the said regulation 56.

(8) Notwithstanding anything in the Act of 1937, when this part of these rules becomes applicable to a person, he shall cease to be entitled to any payment out of a superannuation fund administered by the fund authority other than a payment by way of return of voluntary contributions.

*Exercise by local authority of discretionary powers to increase benefits*

7.—(1) Where a person enters, or before the commencement of these rules entered, Federated Schemes Employment after leaving local government employment and these rules have become applicable to him, the authority or body by whom he was employed may, within 6 months after the date on which they are informed by the Trustee of his notification that he desires these rules to apply to him, exercise any discretion which, with a view to increasing the benefits payable to him, they could have exercised at the time when he left their employment if he had then retired and had been entitled to a retirement pension under regulation 5 of the benefits regulations or (if that regulation was not applicable to him) to any corresponding benefit provided under the superannuation provisions which were applicable to him in that employment.

(2) A decision in the exercise of any discretion under this rule shall be subject to the limitations and restrictions (if any) and to the right of appeal (if any) to which it would have been subject if the discretion had been exercised on the person's retirement in the circumstances aforesaid.

(3) Where a discretion has been exercised under this rule, the service reckonable immediately before he left his former employment by the person in whose favour the discretion has been exercised shall be deemed to have been correspondingly increased, and the transfer value payable in respect of him shall be calculated accordingly.

(a) S.I. 1950/497 (1950 I, p. 1327).

(4) Any increase in service, if attributable to a decision under this rule to increase benefit otherwise than by any notional increase or extension of the service reckonable for the purpose of calculating benefit, or by treating any specified period of non-contributing service as contributing service or, under a local Act scheme, by similarly converting service of one category to service of another category, shall be ascertained by converting the service in respect of which the higher rate of benefit is payable into contributing service in the manner in which non-contributing service is converted into contributing service under section 2(4) of the Act of 1953.

(5) Where the amount of any transfer value payable under rule 6 is increased in consequence of the exercise by an authority or body of any power conferred upon them by this rule, that authority or body shall repay the amount of the said increase to the superannuation fund out of which the transfer value is payable.

## Part III

### Transfer from Federated Schemes Employment to Local Government Employment

*Persons to whom part III applies*

**8.** Subject to the provisions of these rules and to the conditions specified in rule 9 being satisfied, this part of these rules shall apply—

(*a*) to a person who on or after the commencement of these rules enters local government employment within the prescribed period, having left Federated Schemes Employment not earlier than 1st April 1966, and

(*b*) if the Trustee consents, to a person who before the commencement of these rules entered local government employment within the prescribed period having left Federated Schemes Employment not earlier than 1st April 1966.

*Conditions for application of part III*

**9.** The conditions referred to in rule 8 are that—

(*a*) the person shall, before or within 3 months after entering local government employment or, if he entered that employment before the commencement of these rules, within 6 months thereafter—

(i) notify the fund authority in writing that he desires these rules to apply to him ;

(ii) furnish the fund authority with particulars in writing of any national service in which he has been engaged since leaving Federated Schemes Employment ; and

(iii) pay to the Trustee an amount equal to any sum paid to him by way of return of contributions (other than voluntary contributions) on or after leaving Federated Schemes Employment, together with any further sum by way of interest required under rule 17, and

(*b*) the fund authority shall receive from the Trustee a transfer value, calculated under the rules of the relevant scheme, in respect of the service which the person was entitled to reckon for purposes of the relevant scheme immediately before leaving Federated Schemes Employment.

*Reckoning of service*

**10.**—(1) Subject to the provisions of this rule, a person to whom this part of these rules applies shall be entitled to reckon as contributing service such number of completed years and months as having regard—

(*a*) to his age and remuneration at the date when he left Federated Schemes Employment and

(*b*) to the class to which he belonged or the description under which he fell as an officer or a servant on entering local government employment,

would have produced a transfer value of the amount received under rule 9(*b*) had he left local government employment in the circumstances described in section 29 of the Act of 1937 at that date.

(2) The reference in the preceding paragraph to the person's age shall be construed—

(*a*) where he left Federated Schemes Employment before 1st April 1968 and entered local government employment before 1st April 1969, as a reference to his age at 1st April 1969 ;

(*b*) where he enters local government employment on or after 1st April 1969 and more than 12 months after leaving Federated Schemes Employment, as a reference to his age on entering local government employment.

(3) The reference in paragraph (1) of this rule to a transfer value shall be construed as a reference to a transfer value which is not subject to reduction under regulation 6 of the transfer value regulations or under any regulations made or having effect as if made under section 110 of the National Insurance Act 1965(**a**).

(4) A person to whom this part of these rules applies shall not be entitled under section 12(2) of the Act of 1937 to reckon as non-contributing service any service as referred to therein before the date he entered Federated Schemes Employment if—

(*a*) a transfer value in respect of that service has been paid under rule 6, or

(*b*) a transfer value in respect of that service has been paid under the corresponding provision of any other interchange rules, or

(*c*) a transfer of assets in respect of his accrued pension rights has been made out of a local authority's superannuation fund under any enactment.

(5) Any service which would have been reckonable under the relevant scheme by a person to whom this part of these rules applies for the purpose of determining whether he was entitled to receive a benefit thereunder shall be reckonable to the same extent for the purpose of determining whether he is entitled to receive a benefit as a contributory employee.

*Continuation of voluntary contributions*

**11.**—(1) The provisions of this rule shall have effect for the purpose of enabling a person to whom this part of these rules applies to continue any voluntary contributions which are described herein and which he was in course of paying immediately before leaving Federated Schemes Employment.

(2) Where a person elects to continue any such contributions, he shall—

(*a*) when notifying the fund authority under rule 9(*a*)(i), notify them also that he wishes to continue the payment of voluntary contributions ;

---

(**a**) 1965 c. 51.

(b) within the period specified in rule 9(a), or allowed under rule 16, pay to the fund authority a sum equal to the sum (if any) paid to him by way of return of any such contributions ; and

(c) make the payments required by this rule.

(3) Where the voluntary contributions were paid in respect of added years, the person shall pay the outstanding amounts as they would have been payable in his Federated Schemes Employment ; and thereupon having regard to the total amount of voluntary contributions there shall be added to the service which he is entitled to reckon under rule 10 such period as may be certified by an actuary to be appropriate.

(4) Where the voluntary contributions were paid by way of—

    (i) instalments in discharge of a fixed sum or

    (ii) contributions of a fraction or percentage of emoluments,

as a condition of being entitled to reckon any period of service for the purposes of the relevant scheme, or as a condition of increasing the length at which any period of service would be reckoned for those purposes, the person shall be entitled to continue making those payments to the fund authority ; and thereupon having regard to the total amount of voluntary contributions there shall be added to the service which he is entitled to reckon under rule 10 such period as may be certified by an actuary to be appropriate.

(5) Notwithstanding the provisions of this rule, the person shall not be required to make payments between the date on which he retires from local government employment and the date on which he would ordinarily have expected to retire from Federated Schemes Employment if he had continued therein.

## Computation of contributions

**12.**—(1) Where any enactment relating to local government superannuation refers, in connection with assessing a return of contributions or a benefit, to the amount of the contributions paid by a person, the amount of the contributions paid by a person to whom this part of these rules applies shall be deemed to be increased, in accordance with the provisions of this rule, to take account of earlier periods of service which became reckonable under rule 10.

(2) Subject to the provisions of this rule, the amount of the increase shall be the amount which would have been payable to him if, on leaving Federated Schemes Employment, he had been entitled to a return of contributions without interest.

(3) Where an amount described in paragraph (1) of this rule is the amount of a person's contributions with interest thereon, interest shall also be payable on the amount by which those contributions are increased under paragraph (2), calculated—

(a) as respects the period ending immediately before he entered local government employment, at the rate at which it would have been calculated under the relevant scheme if on leaving Federated Schemes Employment he had been entitled to a return of contributions with interest ; and

(b) as respects the period beginning on his entry into local government employment, in the manner described in section 10(1) of the Act of 1937.

(4) For the purposes of this rule no account shall be taken of—

(a) payments made voluntarily for securing family benefits ;

(b) any sum in respect of contributions which were returned to and retained by the person who paid them ;

(c) any voluntary contributions described in rule 11 which have not been continued under that rule.

*Application of section 11 of the Act of 1953*

**13.** The provisions of section 11 of the Act of 1953 (which enables persons who would otherwise be debarred from becoming contributory employees on grounds of age to reckon, in relation to local government employment, previous service reckonable under a pension scheme) shall apply in relation to a person who entered the employment of a local authority from Federated Schemes Employment before the commencement of these rules ; and the references in subsection (3) of that section to the passing of the Act shall be construed as including references to the commencement of these rules.

*Period of Federated Schemes Employment : effect on later period of local government employment and on transfer values*

**14.** Where a person to whom this part of these rules applies—

(a) had entered, and then left, local government employment before the commencement of these rules, and then

(b) had entered, or enters, further employment in such circumstances that a transfer value is paid under section 29 of the Act of 1937 or by virtue of interchange rules,

then if the fund authority to whom the person first paid contributions after leaving Federated Schemes Employment receive a transfer value under rule 9(b), they shall—

(i) treat the service which becomes reckonable under rule 10 as though it had been reckonable at the time when he ceased to participate in their fund and

(ii) re-calculate the transfer value which they paid in respect of him.

*Right of appeal*

**15.** The provisions of section 35 of the Act of 1937 (which provides for decision of questions and appeals to the Minister) shall have effect in relation to a person who enters local government employment in circumstances in which these rules apply as if the reference in that section to regulations made under that Act included a reference to these rules :

Provided that this rule shall not apply in relation to a person who is a local Act contributor.

## PART IV

### MISCELLANEOUS

*Extension of time*

**16.**—(1) A fund authority and the Trustee may at any time, on the application of a person who desires these rules to apply to him, agree to extend any of the following periods, namely—

(a) the periods of 6 and of 12 months referred to in rule 3(1) and (*b*) the periods of 3 and of 6 months referred to in rules 5 and 9 within which the person must notify in writing that he desires these rules to apply to him.

(2) A fund authority or the Trustee may, in respect of a person required to furnish particulars in writing of national service or pay any sum described in rule 5(*c*) or 9(*a*)(iii) at any time extend, on the application of that person, the period of 3 or of 6 months referred to in rule 5 or 9, as the case may be, within which he must take such action.

*Interest on returned contributions*

**17.**—(1) Where a period of 12 months is extended pursuant to rule 16(1)(*a*), the fund authority in respect of a person who has left local government employment, or the Trustee in respect of a person who has left Federated Schemes Employment, may require that person to pay compound interest on any sum paid to him by way of return of contributions (other than voluntary contributions) on or after leaving that employment, at a rate of 3% per annum with half-yearly rests for a period beginning either with the date 12 months after the date on which he left that employment or, where this is later, the date on which he received such sum, and ending with the date on which he notified in writing that he desired these rules to apply to him.

(2) The interest payable under this rule shall not exceed a sum equal to one-half of the difference between the transfer value payable under these rules or the rules of the relevant scheme, as the case may be, and the transfer value which would be payable if calculated by reference to the person's age on leaving such employment.

Given under the official seal of the Minister of Housing and Local Government on 21st March 1969.

(L.S.)                                          *Anthony Greenwood,*
                              Minister of Housing and Local Government.

---

## EXPLANATORY NOTE
### (*This Note is not part of the Rules.*)

These Rules provide for the aggregation of service and for a single superannuation award in cases where persons transfer within the prescribed period (generally 12 months) from pensionable employment with a local authority in England or Wales to employment entailing membership of the Federated Group Pension Scheme or of a Federated Pension Scheme for Individual Employers, and vice versa. Where such a transfer is made the person is enabled, subject to the payment of an appropriate transfer value, to reckon previous service for pension under the superannuation scheme to which he transfers.

The Rules are given retrospective effect to a limited extent under the express powers of, and subject to the safeguards required by, section 2(5) of the Superannuation (Miscellaneous Provisions) Act 1948.

## STATUTORY INSTRUMENTS

### 1969 No. 418

## ROAD TRAFFIC

### The Motor Vehicles (Production of Test Certificates) Regulations 1969

| | |
|---|---|
| *Made* - - - | 18*th March* 1969 |
| *Laid before Parliament* | 31*st March* 1969 |
| *Coming into Operation* | 1*st May* 1969 |

The Minister of Transport, in exercise of his powers under section 66(6) of the Road Traffic Act 1960(**a**) and section 4(3) of the Road Traffic (Amendment) Act 1967(**b**), and of all other powers him enabling in that behalf, and after consultation with representative organisations in accordance with the provisions of section 260(2) of the said Act of 1960 and of that section as applied by section 9(3) of the said Act of 1967, hereby makes the following Regulations :—

**1.** These Regulations shall come into operation on the 1st May 1969 and may be cited as the Motor Vehicles (Production of Test Certificates) Regulations 1969.

**2.** The Motor Vehicles (Production of Test Certificates) Regulations 1962(**c**) are hereby revoked.

**3.** The Interpretation Act 1889(**d**) shall apply for the interpretation of these Regulations as it applies for the interpretation of an Act of Parliament, and as if for the purpose of section 38 of that Act these Regulations were an Act of Parliament and the Regulations revoked by Regulation 2 of these Regulations were an Act of Parliament thereby repealed.

**4.** Where an application is made for a licence under the Vehicles (Excise) Act 1962(**e**) for a vehicle to which section 66 of the Road Traffic Act 1960 applies (not being a vehicle to which that section applies by virtue of section 4(1) of the Road Traffic (Amendment) Act 1967), the licence shall not be granted except after either—

(*a*) the production of an effective test certificate, or

(*b*) the making of such a declaration as is specified in the Schedule to these Regulations by the person making the application.

**5.**—(1) This Regulation applies to a vehicle which—

(*a*) is not a vehicle to which section 66 of the Road Traffic Act 1960 applies, unless that section applies by virtue of section 4(1) of the Road Traffic (Amendment) Act 1967, and

---

(**a**) 8 & 9 Eliz. 2. c. 16.  (**b**) 1967 c. 70.  (**c**) S.I. 1962/1127 (1962 II, p. 1294).
(**d**) 52 & 53 Vict. c. 63.  (**e**) 10 & 11 Eliz. 2. c. 13.

(*b*) has been used on roads (whether in Great Britain or elsewhere), but excluding for this purpose any use of the vehicle before it is sold or supplied by retail.

(2) Where an application is made for a licence under the Vehicles (Excise) Act 1962 for a vehicle to which this Regulation applies, and it appears from the application that the vehicle has been used on roads (whether in Great Britain or elsewhere) before the date of the application, the licence shall not be granted unless—

(*a*) there is produced an effective test certificate ; or

(*b*) the owner of the vehicle declares in writing the year in which the vehicle was manufactured, and a period of ten years or such shorter period as may be specified in an order under section 66(3) of the Road Traffic Act 1960 from the date of manufacture has not expired ; or

(*c*) the person making the application makes such a declaration as is specified in the Schedule to these Regulations.

Given under the Official Seal of the Minister of Transport the 18th March 1969.

(L.S.)                                                *Richard Marsh,*
                                                    Minister of Transport.

## SCHEDULE
### FORM OF DECLARATION

I DECLARE that the vehicle, of which the registration mark is..............
and for which I have made application for a licence for the period commencing
................. and ending ................., is not intended to be used during
the period for which the licence is to be in force except—

(*a*) for a purpose prescribed in Regulation 5(2) of the Motor Vehicles (Tests) (Exemption) Regulations 1969(a), or

(*b*) in an area prescribed in Regulation 6 of the Motor Vehicles (Tests) (Exemption) Regulations 1969, being an area to which that Regulation applies.

Usual signature ...............................

Name (in full) ...............................

Address .......................................

Date ..........................................

## EXPLANATORY NOTE
### (*This Note is not part of the Regulations.*)

These Regulations revoke and re-enact the Motor Vehicles (Production of Test Certificates) Regulations 1962, and provide that where an application is made for an excise licence for a vehicle which was registered more than three years previously the applicant must, before the licence will be granted, produce a current test certificate or declare that the proposed use of the vehicle does not need a test certificate. (Regulations 2 and 4).

Under section 4 of the Road Traffic (Amendment) Act 1967 obligatory test certificates are needed as from 1969 for motor vehicles which have been used

(a) S.I. 1969/419 (1969 I, p. 1206).

before being registered and which were manufactured more than three years previously. These Regulations also provide that where an application is made for an excise licence for a vehicle which has not been registered more than three years previously, but which has been used before being registered, the applicant must, before the licence will be granted, produce a current test certificate, declare that the vehicle was manufactured not more than three years previously, or declare that its proposed use does not need a test certificate. (Regulation 5).

## STATUTORY INSTRUMENTS

## 1969 No. 419

## ROAD TRAFFIC

### The Motor Vehicles (Tests) (Exemption) Regulations 1969

| | |
|---|---|
| *Made* - - - | *18th March* 1969 |
| *Laid before Parliament* | *31st March* 1969 |
| *Coming into Operation* | *1st May* 1969 |

The Minister of Transport in exercise of his powers under section 66 of the Road Traffic Act 1960(a), and of all other powers him enabling in that behalf, and after consultation with representative organisations in accordance with the provisions of section 260(2) of the said Act of 1960, hereby makes the following Regulations:—

*Commencement and Citation*

**1.** These Regulations shall come into operation on the 1st May 1969, and may be cited as the Motor Vehicles (Tests) (Exemption) Regulations 1969.

*Revocation*

**2.** The Regulations specified in the Schedule hereto are hereby revoked.

*Interpretation*

**3.**—(1) In these Regulations, except where the context otherwise requires, the following expressions have the meanings hereby respectively assigned to them:—

"1960 Act" means the Road Traffic Act 1960;

"articulated vehicle", "dual-purpose vehicle" and "works truck" have the same meanings respectively as in the Motor Vehicles (Construction and Use) Regulations 1969(b);

"goods vehicle" means a motor vehicle constructed or adapted for use for the carriage of goods or burden of any description, but does not include a dual-purpose vehicle;

"pedestrian controlled vehicle" means a motor vehicle which is controlled by a pedestrian and is not constructed or adapted for use for the carriage of a driver or passenger;

"statutory test", in relation to a vehicle, means an examination for the purposes of section 65 of the 1960 Act;

(a) 8 & 9 Eliz 2. c. 16.      (b) S.I. 1969/321  (1969 I, p. 829).

"the prescribed statutory requirements" has the same meaning as in the Motor Vehicles (Tests) Regulations 1968(a); and

"track-laying", in relation to a vehicle, means that the vehicle is so designed and constructed that the weight thereof is transmitted to the road surface either by means of continuous tracks or by a combination of wheels and continuous tracks.

(2) For the purposes of these Regulations the unladen weight of a motor vehicle shall be computed in accordance with the provisions of Schedule 6 to the Vehicles (Excise) Act 1962(b) as amended by section 8(1) of the Finance Act 1966(c).

(3) Any reference in these Regulations to any enactment or instrument shall be construed as a reference to that enactment or instrument as amended re-enacted or replaced by any subsequent enactment or instrument.

(4) The Interpretation Act 1889(d) shall apply for the interpretation of these Regulations as it applies for the interpretation of an Act of Parliament, and as if for the purpose of section 38 of that Act these Regulations were an Act of Parliament and the Regulations revoked by Regulation 2 of these Regulations were Acts of Parliament thereby repealed.

*Exemption of certain vehicles from test*

**4.** Section 66 of the 1960 Act shall not apply to motor vehicles of the following classes or descriptions, that is to say—

(*a*) heavy locomotives, light locomotives and motor tractors;

(*b*) track-laying vehicles;

(*c*) goods vehicles the unladen weight of which exceeds thirty hundredweight;

(*d*) articulated vehicles or vehicles constructed or adapted for the purpose of forming part of an articulated vehicle;

(*e*) works trucks;

(*f*) pedestrian controlled vehicles;

(*g*) vehicles (including cycles with an attachment for propelling them by mechanical power) which do not exceed six hundredweight in weight unladen and are adapted, and used or kept on a road, for invalids;

(*h*) hackney carriages in respect of which there are in force licences granted under section 6 of the Metropolitan Public Carriage Act 1869(e);

(*i*) vehicles to which any of the prescribed statutory requirements do not apply by virtue of any of the following provisions of the Motor Vehicles (Construction and Use) Regulations 1969, namely—

   (i) Regulation 4(3) (which relates to vehicles proceeding to a port for export);

   (ii) Regulation 4(7) (which relates to vehicles in the service of a visiting force or of a headquarters);

   (iii) Regulation 5 (which relates to land tractors);

(*j*) vehicles temporarily in Great Britain to which a registration mark is assigned under Regulation 2(1) of the Motor Vehicles (International Circulation) Regulations 1965(f), or under provisions applying in Northern Ireland and corresponding to the provisions of that paragraph or under Regulation 4(2) of the said Regulations, a period of one year not having elapsed since the mark was so assigned;

---

(a) S.I. 1968/1714 (1968 III, p. 4607).     (b) 10 & 11 Eliz. 2. c. 13.       (c) 1966 c. 18.
(d) 52 & 53 Vict. c. 63.                (e) 32 & 33 Vict. c. 115.
(f) S.I. 1965/329 (1965 I, p. 1067).

(*k*) vehicles for the time being licensed under the Vehicles (Excise) Act (Northern Ireland) 1954(a);

(*l*) vehicles exempted from duty under section 6(6) of the Vehicles (Excise) Act 1962;

(*m*) Hackney carriages or cabs in respect of which there are in force licences granted under—

    (i) section 37 of the Town Police Clauses Act 1847(b) by the Council of the County Borough of Birkenhead, Birmingham, Cardiff, Kingston upon Hull, Leeds, Manchester, Nottingham, Oldham, Preston, Salford, Sheffield, Sunderland or Swansea or the Council of the Borough of Batley, Chatham, Gillingham, Harrogate, Ilkeston, Ripon, Rochester or Sudbury or the Urban District Council of Bingley: or

    (ii) Part XXIV F of the Edinburgh Corporation Order 1967(c); or

    (iii) Part V A of the Glasgow Corporation Consolidation (General Powers) Order 1960(d); or

    (iv) Part XXVII of the Dundee Corporation (Consolidated Powers) Order 1957(e); or

    (v) Part VI B of the Aberdeen Corporation (General Powers) Order 1938(f), and sections 67 and 68 of the Aberdeen Corporation Order 1955(g); or

    (vi) Schedule V of the Burgh Police (Scotland) Act 1892(h) by the Council of the Burgh of Paisley;

(*n*) vehicles provided for police purposes and maintained in workshops approved by the Minister of Transport as suitable for such maintenance, being vehicles provided in England and Wales by a police authority or the Receiver for the metropolitan police district, or, in Scotland, by a police authority or a joint police committee; and

(*o*) vehicles imported into Great Britain and to which section 66 of the Road Traffic Act 1960 applies by virtue of section 4(1) of the Road Traffic (Amendment) Act 1967(i), being vehicles owned by or in the service of the naval, military or air forces of Her Majesty raised in the United Kingdom and used for naval, military or air force purposes.

*Exemption of the use of vehicles for certain purposes from test*

**5.** The use of a motor vehicle for any of the following purposes is exempted from section 66(1) of the 1960 Act:—

(1) The use of a vehicle—

(*a*) for the purpose of submitting it by previous arrangement for, or bringing it away from, a statutory test; or

(*b*) in the course of a statutory test, for the purpose of taking it to, or bringing it away from, any place where a part of the test is to be or, as the case may be, has been carried out, or of carrying out any part of the test, the person so using it being either—

    (i) a person authorised as an examiner or appointed as an inspector under section 65 of the 1960 Act, or acting on behalf of a person so authorised, or

(a) 1954 c. 17 (N.I.)     (b) 10 & 11 Vict. c. 89.     (c) See 1967 c.v.
(d) See 8 & 9 Eliz. 2. c. iii.     (e) See 6 & 7 Eliz. 2. c. iv.     (f) See 2 & 3 Geo. 6. c. iii.
(g) See 4 & 5 Eliz. 2. c. iii.     (h) 55 & 56 Vict. c. 55.     (i) 1967 c. 70.

    (ii) a person acting under the personal direction of such a person as aforesaid, or

  (c) where a test certificate is refused on a statutory test—

    (i) for the purpose of delivering it by previous arrangement at, or bringing it away from, a place where work is to be or has been done on it to remedy for a further statutory test the defects on the ground of which the test certificate was refused; or

    (ii) for the purpose of delivering it, by towing it, to a place where the vehicle is to be broken up.

(2) The use of a vehicle for any purpose for which it is authorised to be used on roads by an order under section 64 (4) of the 1960 Act being an order authorising that vehicle or any class or description of vehicles comprising that vehicle to be so used notwithstanding that it does not comply with the prescribed statutory requirements or with such of the said requirements as are specified in the said order.

(3) The use of a vehicle imported into Great Britain and to which section 66 of the Road Traffic Act 1960 applies by virtue of section 4 (1) of the Road Traffic (Amendment) Act 1967 whilst it is being driven after arrival in Great Britain on the journey from the place where it has arrived in Great Britain to a place of residence of the owner or driver of the vehicle.

(4) The use of a vehicle for the purpose of removing it in pursuance of section 20 of the Civic Amenities Act 1967(a), of moving or removing it in pursuance of regulations under section 20 of the Road Traffic Regulation Act 1967(b) as altered by the Removal and Disposal of Vehicles (Alteration of Enactments) Order 1967(c), or of removing it from a parking place in pursuance of an order under section 31 (1) of the Road Traffic Regulation Act 1967, an order relating to a parking place designated under section 35 thereof, or a provision of a designation order having effect by virtue of section 39 (2) thereof.

(5) The use of a vehicle, which has been detained or seized by a police constable, for police purposes connected with such detention or seizure.

(6) The use by an Officer of Customs and Excise, or by any other person authorised generally or specially in that behalf in writing by the Commissioners of Customs and Excise, of any vehicle removed, detained, seized or condemned as forfeited under any provision of the Customs and Excise Act 1952(d).

(7) The use of a vehicle for the purpose of testing it by a motor trader as defined in section 12 (10) of the Vehicles (Excise) Act 1962, to whom a trade licence has been issued under that section, during the course of, or after completion of repairs carried out to that vehicle by that motor trader.

*Exemption of the use of vehicles in certain areas from test*

  **6.**—(1) The use of a motor vehicle in any area to which this Regulation applies is exempted from section 66 (1) of the 1960 Act.

(2) This Regulation applies to any island and to any area mainly surrounded by water, being an island or area from which motor vehicles not constructed for special purposes can at no time be conveniently driven to a road in any other part

---

(a) 1967 c. 69.          (b) 1967 c. 76.
(c) S.I. 1967/1900 (1967 III, p. 5191).  (d) 15 & 16 Geo. 6 & 1 Eliz. 2. c. 44.

of Great Britain by reason of the absence of any bridge, tunnel, ford or other way suitable for the passage of such motor vehicles;

Provided that this Regulation does not apply to any of the following islands, namely, the Isle of Wight, the islands of Arran, Bute, Great Cumbrae, Islay, Lewis, Mainland (Orkney), Mainland (Shetland), Mull, North Uist and Skye or to any other island or area from which motor vehicles not constructed for special purposes can either at all times or at some times be conveniently driven to a road in any of the aforesaid islands by reason of the existence of a bridge, tunnel, ford, or other way suitable for the passage of such motor vehicles.

Given under the Official Seal of the Minister of Transport the 18th March 1969.

(L.S.)

*Richard Marsh,*
**Minister of Transport.**

## SCHEDULE
### REGULATIONS REVOKED BY REGULATION 2

| Column 1<br>Regulations Revoked | Column 2<br>References |
|---|---|
| The Motor Vehicles (Tests) (Exemption) Regulations 1961 | S.I. 1961/209 (1961 I, p.358). |
| The Motor Vehicles (Tests) (Exemption) (Amendment) Regulations 1961 | S.I. 1961/2108 (1961 III, p. 3860). |
| The Motor Vehicles (Tests) (Exemption) (Amendment) Regulations 1966 | S.I. 1966/1240 (1966 III, p. 3372). |
| The Motor Vehicles (Tests) (Exemption) (Amendment) Regulations 1967. | S.I. 1967/261 (1967 I, p. 966). |

## EXPLANATORY NOTE
*(This Note is not part of the Regulations.)*

These Regulations consolidate with amendments the Motor Vehicles (Tests) (Exemption) Regulations 1961 and the amending Regulations specified in the Schedule to these Regulations, which create exemptions from the prohibition in section 66 of the Road Traffic Act 1960 against certain vehicles being used on roads unless test certificates have been issued in respect of them. The principal changes are:—

(1) certain vehicles licensed to ply for hire in Leicester and in Liverpool which were previously exempt from the requirement to have a test certificate are no longer exempt;

(2) the exemption from the requirement to have a test certificate for certain vehicles provided for police purposes is extended to include, in Scotland, vehicles provided by a joint police committee (Regulation 4);

(3) certain imported vehicles which will need test certificates after section 4 of the Road Traffic (Amendment) Act 1967 is brought into operation will on 1st

May 1969 be exempt from the requirement to have a test certificate while they are being used for the purpose of being driven from the place of their arrival in Great Britain to the residence of the owner or driver of the vehicle (Regulation 5(3));

(4) certain vehicles are exempted for the purpose of testing them by a motor trader during the course of, or after completion of repairs carried out to those vehicles by that motor trader (Regulation 5(7)).

## STATUTORY INSTRUMENTS

## 1969 No. 420

## ROAD TRAFFIC

## The Goods Vehicles (Licences and Prohibitions) (Amendment) Regulations 1969

| | |
|---|---|
| *Made* - - - | 17*th March* 1969 |
| *Laid before Parliament* | 31*st March* 1969 |
| *Coming into Operation* | 9*th May* 1969 |

The Minister of Transport, in exercise of his powers under section 190 of the Road Traffic Act 1960(a), as amended by section 22 of the Road Traffic Act 1962(b), and of all other enabling powers, and after consultation with representative organisations in accordance with the provisions of section 260(2) of the Road Traffic Act 1960, and with the Council on Tribunals in accordance with the requirements of section 8 of the Tribunals and Inquiries Act 1958(c), hereby makes the following Regulations :—

**1.**—(1) These Regulations shall come into operation on the 9th May 1969, and may be cited as the Goods Vehicles (Licences and Prohibitions) (Amendment) Regulations 1969.

(2) The Interpretation Act 1889(d) shall apply for the interpretation of these Regulations as it applies for the interpretation of an Act of Parliament.

**2.** The Goods Vehicles (Licences and Prohibitions) Regulations 1960(e), as amended (f), shall have effect as though, in Regulation 8(2) thereof, for the words "one shilling", there were substituted the words "two shillings and sixpence".

Given under the Official Seal of the Minister of Transport the 17th March 1969.

(L.S.)

*Richard Marsh,*
Minister of Transport.

---

### EXPLANATORY NOTE

*(This Note is not part of the Regulations.)*

These Regulations amend Regulation 8(2) of the Goods Vehicles (Licences and Prohibitions) Regulations 1960 by increasing from one shilling to two shillings and sixpence the maximum price which may be charged for a copy of a statement of "Applications and Decisions" issued by a licensing authority.

---

(a) 8 & 9 Eliz. 2. c. 16.
(c) 6 & 7 Eliz. 2. c. 66.
(e) S.I. 1960/1505 (1960 III, p. 3020).

(b) 10 & 11 Eliz. 2. c. 59.
(d) 52 & 53 Vict. c. 63.
(f) There is no relevant amending instrument.

STATUTORY INSTRUMENTS

1969 No. 425

ACQUISITION OF LAND

The Compulsory Purchase of Land (General Vesting Declaration) Regulations 1969

| | |
|---|---|
| *Made* - - - - | *20th March* 1969 |
| *Laid before Parliament* | *28th March* 1969 |
| *Coming into Operation* | *1st April* 1969 |

The Minister of Housing and Local Government, in exercise of the powers conferred on him by section 217 of the Town and Country Planning Act 1962(a) and sections 30 and 104 of, and paragraphs 1, 2 and 4 of Schedule 3 to, the Town and Country Planning Act 1968(b), and of all other powers enabling him in that behalf, hereby makes the following regulations:—

*Citation and commencement*

**1.** These regulations may be cited as the Compulsory Purchase of Land (General Vesting Declaration) Regulations 1969 and shall come into operation on 1st April 1969.

*Interpretation*

**2.**—(1) In these regulations:—

"the Act" means the Town and Country Planning Act 1968;

"acquiring authority" has the meaning assigned to it by section 30(2) of the Act;

"general vesting declaration" has the meaning assigned to it by paragraph 1 of Schedule 3 to the Act.

(2) The Interpretation Act 1889(c) applies for the interpretation of these regulations as it applies for the interpretation of an Act of Parliament.

*General vesting declarations*

**3.**—(1) For the purposes of paragraph 1 of Schedule 3 to the Act (by virtue of which an acquiring authority may execute a general vesting declaration in respect of land which they are authorised to acquire by a compulsory purchase order), a general vesting declaration shall be in the form specified in Part I of Schedule 1 to these regulations or in a form substantially to the like effect.

(a) 1962 c. 38.  (b) 1968 c. 72.
(c) 1889 c. 63.

(2) For the purposes of paragraph 4 of Schedule 3 to the Act, a notice specifying the land specified in a general vesting declaration and stating the effect of the declaration (which notice is required by that paragraph to be served by an acquiring authority on the persons referred to in sub-paragraphs (*a*) and (*b*) thereof as soon as may be after the authority have executed a general vesting declaration) shall be in the form specified in Part II of Schedule 1 to these regulations or in a form substantially to the like effect.

**4.** For the purposes of sub-paragraph (1) of paragraph 2 of Schedule 3 to the Act (which requires an acquiring authority, before making a general vesting declaration, to publish or serve a statement of the effect of paragraphs 1 to 8 of that Schedule and a notification inviting interested persons to give information to them with respect to their interest in the relevant land) the statement set out in Part I of Schedule 2 to these regulations, or a statement substantially to the like effect, shall be the statement prescribed under sub-paragraph (1)(*a*), and the form set out in Part II of the said Schedule 2, or a form substantially to the like effect, shall be the form prescribed under sub-paragraph (1)(*b*), of the said paragraph 2.

(Regulation 3)                    SCHEDULE 1

PART I

FORM OF GENERAL VESTING DECLARATION

THIS GENERAL VESTING DECLARATION is made the                    day
of                    19          by                                        (*a*)
(hereinafter called "the Authority").

WHEREAS:

(1) On                    19          an order entitled "The
        Compulsory Purchase Order 19          "(hereinafter called "the order")
was [made] [confirmed] by                              (*b*) under the powers conferred
on him by section          of the                                        (*c*)
authorising the Authority to acquire certain land specified in the Schedule hereto.

(2) Notice of the [making] [confirmation] of the order was first published in accordance with [paragraph 6 of Schedule 1 to the Acquisition of Land (Authorisation Procedure) Act 1946(*d*)] on                    19    .

(3) (*e*) [The said notice included a statement and a notification complying with paragraph 2(1) of Schedule 3 to the Town and Country Planning Act 1968.]

*or*

[A subsequent notice given on                    19          before the service of any notice to treat in respect of any of the land described in the Schedule hereto included a statement and a notification complying with paragraph 2(1) of Schedule 3 to the Town and Country Planning Act 1968.]

(4) (*e*) [The said [subsequent] notice did not specify any period longer than two months beginning with the date of the first publication thereof as the period before the end of which this general vesting declaration could not be executed.]

*or*

[The said [subsequent] notice specified the period of          months beginning with the date of the first publication thereof as the period before the end of which this general vesting declaration could not be executed.]

*or*

[The consent in writing of every occupier of any of the land described in the Schedule hereto was obtained for the execution on the date above mentioned of this general vesting declaration.]

NOW THIS DEED WITNESSETH that in exercise of the power conferred on them by section 30 of the Town and Country Planning Act 1968 (hereinafter called "the Act") the Authority hereby declare as follows:

1. The land described in the Schedule hereto (being [the whole] [part] of the land authorised to be acquired by the order) and more particularly delineated on the plan annexed hereto together with the right to enter upon and take possession of the same shall vest in the Authority as from the end of the period of [*insert period of* 28 *days or longer*] from the date on which the service of notices required by paragraph 4 of Schedule 3 to the Act is completed.

2. For the purposes of paragraph 16(1) of Schedule 3 to the Act (which defines "long tenancy about to expire" in relation to a general vesting declaration as meaning a tenancy granted for an interest greater than a minor tenancy as therein defined but having at the date of the declaration a period still to run which is not more than the specified period, that is to say, such period, longer than one year, as may be specified in the declaration in relation to the land in which the tenancy subsists) the Authority hereby specify that [in relation to the land comprised in this declaration that period shall be            years and            months] [in relation to each area of land specified in column 1 of Part II of the Schedule hereto that period shall be the period stated with respect to that area in column 2 thereof].

IN WITNESS, etc.

## THE SCHEDULE above referred to

### *Notes*

(*a*) Insert the name of the acquiring authority.

(*b*) Insert the name of the confirming authority or, where the order was made by a Minister, that Minister.

(*c*) Insert the section and Act authorising compulsory purchase.

(*d*) Where the notice was published under a procedure prescribed by some enactment other than the Acquisition of Land (Authorisation Procedure) Act 1946, insert the relevant provision of that enactment in place of these words.

(*e*) Delete any alternative which does not apply.

### PART II

#### FORM OF NOTICE STATING EFFECT OF GENERAL VESTING DECLARATION

#### TOWN AND COUNTRY PLANNING ACT 1968

The                                    Compulsory Purchase Order 19

To:

of:

NOTICE IS HEREBY GIVEN that the
(hereinafter called "the Authority") on                                    19            made a general vesting declaration under section 30 of the Town and Country Planning Act 1968 (hereinafter called "the Act") vesting the land described in the Schedule to this notice (hereinafter called "the said land") in themselves as from the end of the period of            days from the date on which the service of notices required by paragraph 4 of Schedule 3 to the Act is completed.

(Paragraph 4 of Schedule 3 to the Act requires notice to be served on every occupier of any of the land specified in the declaration (other than land in which there subsists a "minor tenancy" or a "long tenancy which is about to expire"—these expressions are defined in Appendix A to this notice) and on every other person who has given information to the Authority with respect to any of that land in pursuance of the invitation published and served under paragraph 2(1) of Schedule 3 to the Act).

The Authority will in due course specify in a certificate the date on which the service of the said notices is completed.

The effect of the general vesting declaration is as follows:—

On the date of vesting (as determined in accordance with the first paragraph of this notice) the said land, together with the right to enter upon and take possession of it, will vest in the Authority as if the Authority had on that date exercised their powers to execute a deed poll under Part I of the Compulsory Purchase Act 1965.

Also, on the date of vesting the Acts providing for compensation will apply as if, on the date on which the general vesting declaration was made (namely          19   ) a notice to treat had been served on every person on whom the Authority could have served such a notice (other than any person entitled to an interest in the land in respect of which such a notice had actually been served before that date and any person entitled to a minor tenancy or a long term tenancy which is about to expire).

If the land includes any land in which there is a minor tenancy or a long tenancy which is about to expire, the right of entry will not be exercisable in respect of that land unless, after serving a notice to treat in respect of that tenancy, the Authority have served on every occupier of any of the land in which the tenancy subsists a notice stating that, at the end of a specified period (not being less than fourteen days) from the date of service of the notice they intend to enter upon and take possession of the land specified in the notice, and that period has expired: the vesting of the land will then be subject to the tenancy until that period expires, or the tenancy comes to an end, whichever happens first.

Schedule 3 to the Land Commission Act 1967 as applied by the Act of 1968 contains supplementary provisions as to general vesting declarations executed under the Act. These provisions as so applied are set out in Appendix B to this notice.

A copy of the general vesting declaration to which this notice refers and of the plan annexed to the declaration can be inspected at
and may be seen there at all reasonable hours.

This notice is issued on behalf of the                                                          by

    Signed


                          authorised by the
                          to act in that behalf.


                          THE SCHEDULE above referred to
                    [*Description of the land vested in the Authority
                          by the general vesting declaration*]


                                APPENDIX A

                    [*Here set out paragraph 16 of Schedule 3 to the
                          Town and Country Planning Act 1968*]


                                APPENDIX B

                    [*Here set out Schedule 3 to the Land Commission Act 1967
                    as applied by paragraph 9 of Schedule 3 to the
                          Town and Country Planning Act 1968*]

## SCHEDULE 2                    (Regulation 4)

### PART I

*Statement of the effect of paragraphs 1 to 8 of Schedule 3 to the Town and Country Planning Act 1968 for the purposes of paragraph 2(1)(a) of that Schedule.*

#### Power to make a general vesting declaration

1. The [insert the name of the acquiring authority] (hereinafter called "the Authority") may acquire any of the land to which this notice relates (hereinafter called "the relevant land") by making a general vesting declaration under section 30 of the Town and Country Planning Act 1968, which has the effect, subject to paragraph 4 below, of vesting the land in the Authority at the end of the period mentioned in paragraph 2. Generally a declaration may not be made before the end of the period of two months from the order's becoming operative; but the order may prescribe a longer period. In either case, the Authority may make a declaration before the end of the period with the consent of every occupier of the land affected.

#### Notice, etc., preliminary to general vesting declaration

2. If the Authority make a general vesting declaration, they must serve notice of it on every occupier of any of the land affected (except where there is one of the short tenancies described in paragraph 3) and on every person who gives them information relating to the land in pursuance of the invitation contained in this or any similar notice. When the service of notices of the general vesting declaration is completed, an intermediate period before vesting begins to run. This period, which must not be less than 28 days, will be specified in the declaration. At the end of the period the land described in the declaration will, subject to paragraph 4, vest in the Authority together with the right to enter on the land and take possession of it. At the same time every person on whom the Authority could have served a notice to treat in respect of his interest in the land (other than a tenant under one of the short tenancies described in paragraph 3) will be entitled to compensation for the acquisition of his interest in the land and to interest on the compensation from the date of vesting.

#### Tenancies with only a short time to run

3. Where a person's interest arises under a tenancy which has only a short time to run, the position stated above is subject to modification. For the modifications to apply the tenancy must be either a "minor tenancy", i.e. a tenancy for a year or a yearly tenancy or a tenancy for a lesser interest, or a "long tenancy which is about to expire". The latter expression means a tenancy granted for an interest greater than a minor tenancy but having at the date of the general vesting declaration a period still to run which is not more than the period specified in the declaration for this purpose (which must be more than a year). In calculating how long a tenancy has to run where any option to renew or to terminate it is available to either party, it is assumed that the landlord will take every opportunity open to him to terminate the tenancy while the tenant will use every opportunity to retain or extend his interest.

#### Notice of entry

4. The Authority may not exercise the right of entry referred to in paragraph 2 in respect of land subject to one of the short tenancies described in paragraph 3 unless they first serve notice to treat in respect of the tenancy and then serve every occupier of the land with a notice of their intention to enter and take possession after the period (not less than 14 days) specified in the notice. The right of entry will be exercisable at the end of that period. The effect of the general vesting declaration will be subject to the tenancy until it comes to an end.

*Severance*

5. If the effect of the general vesting declaration will be to sever a house, building or factory, or a park or garden belonging to a house, by vesting part of it in the Authority and leaving part of it with the person who is entitled to, and is in a position to sell, the whole, that person may serve on the Authority a notice of objection to severance. A notice of objection to severance, in order to be effective, must be served by that person within 28 days of the service on him by the Authority of the notice of the general vesting declaration referred to in paragraph 2 (save in the exceptional cases referred to in paragraph 13 of Schedule 3 to the Land Commission Act 1967, as applied by paragraph 9 of Schedule 3 to the Town and Country Planning Act 1968). This (save in those exceptional cases) stops the objector's interest from vesting in the Authority until his rights in the matter have been settled. The Authority have (save in those exceptional cases) three courses open to them:

(1) they may serve the objector with a notice which in effect excludes the objector's land from the scope of the declaration (and, if he receives no notice from the Authority under one of the other two alternatives within three months after he has served them with his notice of objection to severance, they will be treated as having done this); or

(2) they may serve him with notice that the declaration shall have effect in relation to the whole of the land (in which case the declaration will take effect in accordance with the notice); or

(3) they may refer the objection to the Lands Tribunal and give him notice that they have done so.

*Powers of the Lands Tribunal in severance cases*

6. If the Lands Tribunal determine that the part of the objector's property comprised in the declaration can be taken without material detriment (where the objection concerns the taking of part of a house, building or factory) or (where the objection concerns the taking of part of a park or garden) can be taken without seriously affecting the amenity or convenience of the house, the notice of objection ceases to have effect, so that the land affected, i.e. the part of the property comprised in the declaration, will vest in the Authority. If the Lands Tribunal do not decide in that way, they must decide what part (if any) of the objector's land the Authority ought to be required to take in addition to the part comprised in the declaration. The declaration will then take effect as if both these parts had been comprised in the declaration.

*Apportionment of rentcharge*

7. If any of the relevant land forms part of property subject to a rentcharge, and the rentcharge is apportioned between the relevant land and the remainder of the property by agreement or by award of the Lands Tribunal under section 18 of the Compulsory Purchase Act 1965, the part apportioned to the relevant land will be treated as extinguished on the vesting of that land in the Authority, and after that the owner of the land will only be liable to pay the part apportioned to the remainder of the property. Compensation for the extinguishment will be payable to the person entitled to the rentcharge, and may be settled by agreement between him and the Authority or determined by the Lands Tribunal. Alternatively the owner of the land and the person entitled to the rentcharge may agree that the part of the property which is comprised in the relevant land shall be released from the rentcharge and that the whole rentcharge shall be charged on the remainder of the property. This will operate to release the relevant land from the rentcharge and to charge the whole rentcharge on the remainder of the property.

*Apportionment of rent*

8. Where any of the relevant land forms part of property subject to a tenancy, the rent will be apportioned between the relevant land and the remainder of the property on the vesting in the Authority of the tenancy of the relevant land. After that, the tenant will only be liable for that part of the rent which is apportioned to the remainder of the property. Any compensation to which he may be entitled for severance of his property will be assessed with reference to the severance caused by that vesting.

## PART II

*Form for the giving of information to an acquiring authority in response to an invitation required to be notified under paragraph 2(1)(b) of Schedule 3 to the Town and Country Planning Act 1968*

### TOWN AND COUNTRY PLANNING ACT 1968

The                                       Compulsory Purchase Order 19

To:                                          (*a*)

[I] [We]* being [a person] [persons]* who, if a general vesting declaration were made under paragraph 1 of Schedule 3 to the Town and Country Planning Act 1968 in respect of all the land comprised in the compulsory purchase order cited above in respect of which notice to treat has not been given, would be entitled to claim compensation in respect of [all] [part of]* that land, hereby give you the following information, pursuant to the provisions of paragraph 2(1)(b) of the said Schedule 3:—

1. Name and address   ......................................................................... (*b*)
   of claimant(s)   .........................................................................

2. Land in which an   ......................................................................... (*c*)
   interest is held by   .........................................................................
   claimant(s)   .........................................................................
     .........................................................................

3. Nature of interest   ......................................................................... (*d*)
   (including particulars   .........................................................................
   of any mortgage or   .........................................................................
   charge thereon)   .........................................................................

Signed ...........................................................................................

[On behalf of................................................................]*

Date ...........................................................................

### Notes

(*a*) Insert name of acquiring authority.

(*b*) In the case of a joint interest, insert the names and addresses of all the claimants.

(*c*) The land should be described as concisely as possible.

(*d*) If the interest is leasehold, the date of commencement and length of term should be given.

*Delete where inappropriate.

Given under the official seal of the Minister of Housing and Local Government on 20th March 1969.

(L.S.)                                  *Anthony Greenwood,*
Minister of Housing and Local Government.

## EXPLANATORY NOTE

*(This Note is not part of the Regulations.)*

These regulations prescribe the form of general vesting declaration which may be made by an acquiring authority under the Town and Country Planning Act 1968 and the form of other documents required to be published or served before or after the making of such a declaration.

Regulation 3, with Schedule 1, prescribes the form of general vesting declaration, and the form of notice stating the effect thereof, for the purposes of paragraphs 1 and 4 of Schedule 3 to the Act, under which an acquiring authority may by means of such a declaration vest in themselves land which they are authorised to acquire by a compulsory purchase order.

Paragraph 2(1)(*a*) of Schedule 3 to the Act requires an acquiring authority, before they make a general vesting declaration, to include in the notice which they give of the making or confirmation of the relevant compulsory purchase order (or in a notice given subsequently) a statement of the effect of paragraphs 1 to 8 of that Schedule. Such a statement is set out in Part I of Schedule 2 to these regulations.

Paragraph 2(1)(*b*) of Schedule 3 to the Act requires the same notice also to contain an invitation to any person who will be entitled to compensation if a general vesting declaration is made, to inform the acquiring authority of his name and address and his interest in any land affected by the declaration: the giving of this information then entitles him under paragraph 4 of the Schedule to receive notice of the making of any general vesting declaration so that he may make a claim for compensation. Part II of Schedule 2 to these regulations sets out the form in which the information is to be given.

# STATUTORY INSTRUMENTS

## 1969 No. 428

## WAGES COUNCILS

## The Wages Regulation (Boot and Shoe Repairing) Order 1969

| | |
|---|---|
| *Made* - - - - | *20th March* 1969 |
| *Coming into Operation* | *23rd April* 1969 |

Whereas the Secretary of State has received from the Boot and Shoe Repairing Wages Council (Great Britain) the wages regulation proposals set out in the Schedules 1 and 2 hereof;

Now, therefore, the Secretary of State in exercise of her powers under section 11 of the Wages Councils Act 1959(a), and of all other powers enabling her in that behalf, hereby makes the following Order:—

**1.** This Order may be cited as the Wages Regulation (Boot and Shoe Repairing) Order 1969.

**2.**—(1) In this Order the expression "the specified date" means the 23rd April 1969, provided that where, as respects any worker who is paid wages at intervals not exceeding seven days, that date does not correspond with the beginning of the period for which the wages are paid, the expression "the specified date" means, as respects that worker, the beginning of the next such period following that date.

(2) The Interpretation Act 1889(b) shall apply to the interpretation of this Order as it applies to the interpretation of an Act of Parliament and as if this Order and the Orders hereby revoked were Acts of Parliament.

**3.** The wages regulation proposals set out in the Schedules 1 and 2 hereof shall have effect as from the specified date and as from that date the Wages Regulation (Boot and Shoe Repairing) Order 1967(c) and the Wages Regulation (Boot and Shoe Repairing) (Amendment) Order 1967(d) shall cease to have effect.

Signed by order of the Secretary of State,
20th March 1969.

*A. A. Jarratt,*
Deputy Under Secretary of State,
Department of Employment and Productivity.

---

(a) 1959 c. 69.             (b) 1889 c. 63.
(c) S.I. 1967/640 (1967 I, p. 1923).      (d) S.I. 1967/1898 (1967 III, p. 5185).

## ARRANGEMENT OF SCHEDULE

Article 3             SCHEDULE 1

The following minimum remuneration shall be substituted for the statutory minimum remuneration fixed by the Wages Regulation (Boot and Shoe Repairing) Order 1967 (Order D. (144)), as amended by the Wages Regulation (Boot and Shoe Repairing) (Amendment) Order 1967 (Order D. (147)).

## STATUTORY MINIMUM REMUNERATION

### PART I

### APPLICATION

1.—(1) Subject to the provisions of this Schedule, the minimum remuneration payable to a worker to whom this Schedule applies for all work except work to which a minimum overtime rate applies under Part VI of this Schedule is:—

    (a) in the case of a time worker, the hourly general minimum time rate applicable to the worker under the provisions of this Schedule;

    (b) in the case of a worker employed on piece work,

        (i) where a general minimum piece rate applies under Part VIII of this Schedule, that piece rate;

        (ii) where no general minimum piece rate applies, piece rates each of which would yield, in the circumstances of the case, to an ordinary worker at least the same amount of money as the hourly general minimum time rate which would be applicable if the worker were a time worker:

    Provided that where a guaranteed time rate is applicable to the worker under paragraph 3 or 5 and the worker's minimum remuneration calculated on a time work basis at the hourly guaranteed time rate exceeds the minimum remuneration calculated under the provisions of (b) of this subparagraph, the worker shall be paid at not less than the hourly guaranteed time rate.

(2) In this Schedule, the expressions "hourly general minimum time rate" and "hourly guaranteed time rate" mean respectively the general minimum time rate and the guaranteed time rate applicable to the worker under Part II, Part III or Part IV of this Schedule divided by 41.

2.—(1) Subject to the provisions of sub-paragraph (2) of this paragraph, this Schedule applies to workers in relation to whom the Boot and Shoe Repairing Wages Council (Great Britain) operates, that is to say, workers employed in Great Britain in the circumstances specified in the Schedule to the Boot and Shoe Repairing Wages Council (Great Britain) (Variation) Order 1948(a), namely:—

(i) all workers employed in Great Britain in a boot and shoe repairing undertaking as defined in sub-paragraph (3) of this paragraph on any of the following work:—

(a) the repairing, altering or dyeing of boots, shoes, slippers and all other similar kinds of footwear;

(b) the making of bespoke footwear;

(c) work incidental or ancillary to any of the above-mentioned operations;

(d) shop duties in connection with the above operations, including attending to customers and sale by retail of boot and shoe laces and materials and articles used in connection with the cleaning or repair of boots or shoes;

(e) collection or despatch in connection with the operations in (a) and (b) above, and work ancillary thereto;

(f) canvassing for boot or shoe repairs and the collection of accounts in connection with the undertaking;

(g) clerical or other office work in connection with the undertaking, including costing and the work of a cashier;

(ii) all outworkers employed by way of trade in Great Britain on any of the operations specified in (a), (b) or (c) of (i) above.

(2) Notwithstanding the provisions of sub-paragraph (1) of this paragraph, this Schedule does not apply:—

(i) to workers employed in any shop or in any department in a shop, being a shop or department which is wholly or mainly engaged in the sale by retail of footwear (including operations in connection with such sale), in respect of their employment:—

(a) on retail sales at such shop and operations incidental thereto; or

(b) on transport or clerical work relating to such sales; or

(ii) to workers employed in or in connection with a factory which is wholly or mainly engaged on the manufacture of leather footwear on a large scale, in respect of their employment:—

(a) on the making of bespoke footwear and work incidental or ancillary thereto; or

(b) on transport or clerical work relating to bespoke footwear; or

(iii) to workers who are persons registered as handicapped by disablement in pursuance of the Disabled Persons (Employment) Acts 1944 and 1958(b), in respect of their employment by Remploy Limited.

(3) For the purpose of this Schedule a "boot and shoe repairing undertaking" means any undertaking or any part of an undertaking which is wholly or mainly engaged by way of trade on any of the following operations, including operations incidental or ancillary thereto, that is to say—

(i) the repairing of leather footwear;

(ii) the making of bespoke footwear:

Provided that as regards trainees who, under the Government Vocational Training Scheme for resettlement training, have been placed by the Department of Employment and Productivity with, and are being trained by, an employer for a period of approved training, this Schedule shall not (subject to the condition that the requirements of the Training Scheme are complied with) apply during the period in respect of which the trainees are in receipt of allowances as provided under the Scheme.

(a) S.I. 1948/706 (Rev. XXIII, p. 453: 1948 I, p. 4398).
(b) 1944 c. 10 and 1958 c. 33.

PART II

MALE OR FEMALE WORKERS AGED 21 YEARS OR OVER

GENERAL MINIMUM TIME RATE AND GUARANTEED TIME
RATE FOR FOREMEN OR MANAGERS

Per week of
41 hours

3.—(1) The general minimum time rate applicable to all male or female   s.  d.
workers aged 21 years or over and employed as foremen or managers is   *255*  *6*

(2) The guaranteed time rate applicable to the workers specified in
sub-paragraph (1) when employed on piece work is   ...   ...   ...   *255*  *6*

(3) For the purposes of this paragraph,

   (*a*) a foreman or manager is a male or female worker who either—

      (i) exercises sole supervisory authority over all journeyworkers who must
exceed three in number (excluding himself) working in the same shop or
department, or

      (ii) (whether working alone or with any other worker) under the terms of
his employment and, in addition to any work which may be required of
him as a journeyworker, fits up or supervises the fitting up, of the work
and has control of the repairing or making and the technical direction
thereof;

   (*b*) a journeyworker is a male or female worker to whom there applies under
this Schedule either a general minimum piece rate or a general minimum time
rate of not less than *225s. 0d.* per week of 41 hours or to whom such a general
minimum time rate would be applicable if he were a time worker.

GENERAL MINIMUM TIME RATES

4. The general minimum time rates applicable to all male or female workers aged
21 years or over, except (i) the foremen or managers specified in paragraph 3 and
(ii) learners to whom the minimum rates specified in Part IV of this Schedule apply,
are as follows:—

Per week of
41 hours

   (*a*) sewing or stitching machine operators employed in operating—   s.  d.

      (i)  power sole stitchers or both power sole stitchers and Blake
or other sole sewing machines on the Blake principle   ...   *246*  *0*

      (ii) Blake or other sole sewing machines on the Blake principle
or edge trimming machines   ...   ...   ...   ...   ...   *237*  *6*

      Provided that where the worker, for the purpose of training
thereon, is employed on such machines for one probationary
period not exceeding four months, the general minimum time rate
applicable during the said period shall be ...   ...   ...   ...   *228*  *6*

   (*b*)   (i)  press cutters responsible for cutting and costing ...   ...   *245*  *0*

      (ii) press cutters other than those responsible for cutting and
costing   ...   ...   ...   ...   ...   ...   ...   ...   *228*  *6*

   (*c*) workers employed—

      (i)  as makers of bespoke (which term includes surgical)
footwear ...   ...   ...   ...   ...   ...   ...   ...   *257*  *0*

      (ii) as repairers engaged in sewing down caps, re-welting, welt
repairs, linking or any other hand stitching operation   ...   *234*  *0*

      (iii) in clicking   ...   ...   ...   ...   ...   ...   ...   *234*  *0*

      (iv) in clicking and closing   ...   ...   ...   ...   ...   *234*  *0*

|  | Male workers | Female workers |
|---|---|---|
|  | Per week of 41 hours | |
|  | s. d. | s. d. |

(v) as closers (that is, in fitting and machining) in the making of uppers for bespoke (which term includes surgical) footwear and not employed in clicking    ...    ...    ...    ...    *234  0*    *169  0*

All workers
Per week of 41 hours

(*d*) workers employed in altering footwear or on benching or finishing operations (whether performed by hand or machine) in repairing leather footwear ...    ...    ...    ...    ...    ...

s.  d.
*228  0*

|  | Male workers | Female workers |
|---|---|---|
|  | Per week of 41 hours | |

(*e*) all other workers to whom this paragraph applies    s.  d.     s.  d.
                                                          *225  0*    *164  0*

PART III
## MALE OR FEMALE WORKERS AGED UNDER 21 YEARS
### GENERAL MINIMUM TIME RATES AND GUARANTEED TIME RATE

5.—(1) The general minimum time rates applicable to all male or female workers aged under 21 years, being—

(*a*) foremen or managers as defined in paragraph 3 (3),

(*b*) press cutters responsible for cutting and costing, or

(*c*) workers who have worked at least five years in the trade under a contract of apprenticeship,

are the general minimum time rates which would be applicable to those workers under paragraph 3 or 4 if they were aged 21 years or over.

Per week of
41 hours

(2) The guaranteed time rate applicable to the workers specified in sub-paragraph (1)(*a*) of this paragraph when employed on piece work is

s.  d.
*255  6*

### GENERAL MINIMUM TIME RATES

6.—(1) The general minimum time rates applicable to all male or female workers aged under 21 years except (i) the workers specified in paragraph 5 and (ii) learners or apprentices to whom the minimum rates specified in Part IV of this Schedule apply are those specified in the following Table.

|  | Column 1 | Column 2 | Column 3 |
|---|---|---|---|
|  | The workers specified in sub-para. (2) of this paragraph | Other male workers | Other female workers |
|  | Per week of 41 hours | | |
|  | s.  d. | s.  d. | s.  d. |
| Aged 20 and under 21 years    ...    ...    ... | *182  0* | *182  0* | *145  0* |
| „  19  „    „  20  „ ...    ...    ...    ... | *162  0* | *162  0* | *128  6* |
| „  18  „    „  19  „ ...    ...    ...    ... | *148  0* | *148  0* | *118  0* |
| „  17  „    „  18  „ ...    ...    ...    ... | *122  3* | *122  3* | *99  3* |
| „  16  „    „  17  „ ...    ...    ...    ... | *113  3* | *113  3* | *90  9* |
| Under 16 years    ...    ...    ...    ...    ... | *106  3* | *106  3* | *83  9* |

2j

(2) The workers referred to in Column 1 of the foregoing Table are male or female workers who are—

    (*a*) operators of sole stitching, sole sewing or edge trimming machines,

    (*b*) press cutters not responsible for cutting and costing,

    (*c*) employed as makers of bespoke (which term includes surgical) footwear,

    (*d*) repairers engaged in sewing down caps, re-welting, welt repairs, linking or any other hand stitching operation,

    (*e*) employed in clicking,

    (*f*) employed in clicking and closing,

    (*g*) employed in altering footwear or on benching operations (whether performed by hand or machine) in repairing leather footwear, or

    (*h*) employed in finishing operations (whether performed by hand or machine) in repairing leather footwear.

## PART IV

### GENERAL MINIMUM TIME RATES FOR LEARNERS AND APPRENTICES

### LEARNERS

7.—(1) The following general minimum time rates are applicable to male or female learners employed in accordance with the conditions set out in paragraph 9.

| | Learners to bespoke hand sewn making | All others learners |
|---|---|---|
| | Per week of 41 hours | |
| | s.   d. | s.   d. |
| Aged under 16 years ... ... ... ... ... | 100  3 | 99  3 |
| „ 16 and under 17 years ... ... ... ... | 106  3 | 105  3 |
| „ 17 „ „ 18 „ ... ... ... ... | 116  3 | 115  3 |
| „ 18 „ „ 19 „ ... ... ... ... | 142  0 | 141  0 |
| „ 19 „ „ 20 „ ... ... ... ... | 156  0 | 155  0 |
| „ 20 „ „ 21 „ ... ... ... ... | 176  0 | 175  0 |

(2) The general minimum time rate applicable to a learner to bespoke hand sewn making who is aged 21 years or over and who has not completed a period of five years in such learnership shall, until he attains the age of 22 years or until he completes the said period of learnership (whichever period is the less), be the rate applicable to a learner aged 20 and under 21 years, increased by 5s. 0d. weekly.

### APPRENTICES

8. The following general minimum time rates are applicable to male or female apprentices—

    (*a*) who are employed under contracts of apprenticeship in writing to be taught one or more of the following sections of the trade—

        (i) bespoke hand sewn making including hand finishing,

        (ii) boot and shoe repairing in all its operations as performed in the establishment, including benching by hand and by such benching machines as are used in the establishment, hand sewing, re-stitching, re-welting, finishing by hand, by any finishing machine used in the establishment, by hand and such machine, patching by hand, by machine and by solution, and all other upper repairing,

        (iii) clicking (including pattern cutting) and closing (including fitting and machining) of uppers for bespoke work or either of such operations, and

    (*b*) in whose case the conditions specified in paragraph 10 are fulfilled.

|  | Per week of 41 hours |
|---|---|
|  | s.  d. |
| Aged under 16 years ... ... ... ... ... ... ... | 99   3 |
| „ 16 and under 17 years ... ... ... ... ... ... | 104   3 |
| „ 17 „ „ 18 „ ... ... ... ... ... ... | 114   3 |
| „ 18 „ „ 19 „ ... ... ... ... ... ... | 139   0 |
| „ 19 „ „ 20 „ ... ... ... ... ... ... | 153   0 |
| „ 20 „ „ 21 „ ... ... ... ... ... ... | 173   0 |

PART V

CONDITIONS AS TO LEARNERS AND APPRENTICES

LEARNERS

9.—(1) The general minimum time rates specified in paragraph 7 apply only to a male or female learner in whose case the conditions following are fulfilled—

(a) if he is a learner to bespoke hand sewn making, he shall be employed for not less than two-thirds of his time in learning the bespoke hand sewn making branch of the trade and shall, during the whole or a substantial part of such time, receive adequate instruction in either (i) bespoke hand sewn making, (ii) clicking, or (iii) clicking and closing of uppers for bespoke work;

(b) if he is a learner employed in a factory in which machinery driven by mechanical power is used for benching or finishing operations, he shall be employed, during the whole or a substantial part of his time, as a learner in the trade and shall receive, during such time, adequate instruction in a progressive manner in either—

(i) benching by hand and all operations of benching by machine which are carried out in the factory, or

(ii) benching by hand or machine and finishing by hand or machine, not less than one-third of the learner's time being spent in benching:

Provided that where the learner has been so employed for not less than three years he may be employed thereafter, in conjunction with a journeyworker finisher, as a learner to finishing by machine, and in such case the learner shall be employed for at least one-third of his time in learning the operations of edge trimming, edge setting and heel scouring;

(c) any other learner shall be employed during the whole or a substantial part of his time, as a learner in the trade and shall receive during such time adequate instruction in a progressive manner in either—

(i) benching by hand, throughout the whole period of his employment, or

(ii) benching by hand and finishing by hand or machine, not less than one-third of the learner's time being spent in benching;

(d) in the establishment in which the learner is employed the proportion of learners to journeyworkers shall not exceed that of one learner to two journeyworkers:

Provided that one learner of each of the classes specified at (a), (b) or (c) of this sub-paragraph may be employed in an establishment in which only one journeyworker is employed on the operation or group of operations in which the learner is receiving instruction.

(2) For the purposes of sub-paragraph (1) of this paragraph,

    (a) the "bespoke hand sewn making branch of the trade" shall mean that branch in which workers are employed for not less than two-thirds of their time on bespoke hand sewn making, clicking or closing of uppers or on one or more of such operations for bespoke work;

    (b) the expression "journeyworker" shall, save as is hereinafter provided in this sub-paragraph, have the same meaning as in paragraph 3 (3);

    (c) a worker aged under 21 years to whom a general minimum time rate specified in paragraph 6 applies shall not be reckoned as a learner, apprentice or journeyworker;

    (d) where an employer is wholly or mainly performing the work of a journeyworker he shall be reckoned as a journeyworker.

(3) For the purposes of determining the proportion of learners to journeyworkers in accordance with condition (d) of sub-paragraph (1) of this paragraph,

    (a) a casual absence of a journeyworker or a casual vacancy for a short period in the number of journeyworkers employed shall not be treated as a failure to comply with the said condition;

    (b) an apprentice shall be reckoned as a learner notwithstanding that the general minimum rates set out in paragraph 7 do not apply to him.

## APPRENTICES

10.—(1) The general minimum time rates specified in paragraph 8 apply only to a male or female apprentice employed under a contract of apprenticeship in writing in whose case the conditions following are fulfilled:—

    (a) The apprentice shall be employed under a written contract of apprenticeship which has been duly executed and which contains the following provisions (which the Wages Council considers necessary for the effective instruction of the apprentice) or provisions substantially to the like effect and no provisions contrary thereto;

        (i) A description of the section or sections of work in the trade to which the worker is apprenticed;

        (ii) The date of the commencement of the apprenticeship and a provision for its continuance until the date on which the apprentice shall have completed five years' apprenticeship or reached his 21st birthday whichever is the earlier;

        (iii) A term that during the period of apprenticeship the employer will pay to the apprentice not less than the appropriate statutory minimum remuneration from time to time;

        (iv) A covenant or agreement by the employer that, throughout the period of apprenticeship, he will keep the apprentice under his supervision and instruct the apprentice himself, or place him in the hands of one or more competent journeyworkers for instruction, so that in either case the apprentice shall receive throughout the period of apprenticeship and in a progressive manner effective instruction in the section or sections of work in the trade to which he is apprenticed;

        (v) A covenant or agreement by the apprentice whereby, throughout the period of apprenticeship, he binds himself to the employer to learn the section or sections of work in the trade to which he is apprenticed;

        (vi) A term, in the case of an apprentice who is apprenticed to the boot and shoe repairing section of work in the trade, that the employment of the apprentice on benching shall alternate regularly with his employment on finishing, so that not more than one-third of his time is spent on finishing operations;

(vii) A provision that, during the apprenticeship, the apprentice shall not be put on piece work and shall not be employed on any work to which any minimum overtime rate applies under Part VI of this Schedule.

(b) In the establishment in which the apprentice is employed the proportion of apprentices to journeyworkers in either branch of the trade shall not at any time exceed that of one apprentice to two journeyworkers:

Provided that

(i) one apprentice may be employed in each branch of the trade if only one journeyworker is employed in the same branch;

(ii) where an employer who works personally at the trade and does not employ a journeyworker has one apprentice who has completed at least four years' apprenticeship, he may employ a second apprentice during the last year of the apprenticeship of the first apprentice, and for the purpose of calculating the proportion of apprentices to journeyworkers the first apprentice shall not be taken into account.

(c) The apprentice shall be the holder of a certificate of registration as an apprentice issued by, or on behalf of, the Wages Council or shall have made application for such a certificate which has been duly acknowledged and is still under consideration:

Provided that the certification of an apprentice may be cancelled by the Wages Council if the other conditions of apprenticeship are not complied with.

(2) For the purpose of determining the proportion of apprentices to journeyworkers in accordance with condition (b) of the last preceding sub-paragraph,

(a) one of the said branches of the trade shall be that branch in which workers are employed for not less than two-thirds of their time on one or more of the operations of (i) bespoke hand sewn making, (ii) hand sewn repairing, (iii) clicking (cutting), and (iv) the closing of uppers for bespoke work, and the other branch shall be any other section of the trade;

(b) a casual absence of a journeyworker or a casual vacancy for a short period in the number of journeyworkers employed shall not be treated as a failure to comply with the said condition;

(c) where an employer is wholly or mainly performing the work of a journeyworker he shall be reckoned as a journeyworker;

(d) a learner shall be reckoned as an apprentice notwithstanding that the general minimum time rates set out in paragraph 8 do not apply to him;

(e) a worker aged under 21 years to whom a general minimum time rate specified in paragraph 6 applies shall not be reckoned as a learner, apprentice or journeyworker;

(f) save as aforesaid, the expression " journeyworker " shall have the same meaning as in paragraph 3 (3).

(3) Notwithstanding the foregoing provisions of this Schedule, where an employer employs a worker as a prospective apprentice for a probationary period not exceeding three months and the conditions of apprenticeship set out in sub-paragraph (1) of this paragraph, other than employment under a written contract of apprenticeship and certification by the Wages Council are fulfilled, the minimum remuneration payable to that worker during the said period shall be that applicable to an apprentice employed in accordance with the condition specified in sub-paragraph (1) of this paragraph, and, in the event of the worker being continued thereafter at his employment as an apprentice, the said probationary period shall, for the purposes of this Schedule, be treated as part of the period of apprenticeship, whether or not it is included therein:

Provided that where the employer does not, on or before the last day of the said probationary period, enter into with the worker such a contract of apprenticeship as is mentioned in sub-paragraph (1) of this paragraph, the employer shall pay to the worker a sum equal to the difference between the minimum remuneration payable to him as a prospective apprentice and the amount that would have been payable to him had the provisions of this sub-paragraph not applied.

## PART VI

### OVERTIME AND WAITING TIME

### MINIMUM OVERTIME RATES

11. Minimum overtime rates are payable to a worker to whom this Schedule applies as follows:—

(1) on any day other than a Sunday or customary holiday or a day on which a rest period occurs,

    (a) for the first 2 hours worked in excess of 10 hours   ...   time-and-a-quarter

    (b) thereafter  ...  ...  ...  ...  ...  ...  time-and-a-half

(2) in any week for all time worked during rest periods,

    (a) for the first 2 hours worked  ...  ...  ...  ...  time-and-a-quarter

    (b) thereafter  ...  ...  ...  ...  ...  time-and-a-half

(3) on a Sunday or customary holiday, for all time worked ... double time

(4) in any week, for all time worked in excess of 41 hours, exclusive of any time for which a minimum rate is payable under the foregoing provisions of this paragraph,

    (a) for the first 3 hours so worked  ...  ...  ...  time-and-a-quarter

    (b) thereafter  ...  ...  ...  ...  ...  time-and-a-half

12. In this Schedule

(1) the expressions " time-and-a-quarter ", " time-and-a-half " and " double time " mean respectively—

    (a) in the case of a time worker, one and a quarter times, one and a half times and twice the hourly general minimum time rate otherwise applicable to the worker,

    (b) in the case of a worker employed on piece work

        (i) a time rate equal respectively to one quarter, one half and the whole of the hourly general minimum time rate which would be applicable to the worker if he were a time worker and a minimum overtime rate did not apply, and in addition thereto,

        (ii) the minimum remuneration otherwise applicable to the worker under paragraph 1(1)(b).

(2) the expression "customary holiday" means—

    (a) in England and Wales

        (i) Christmas Day, Boxing Day, Good Friday, Easter Monday, Whit Monday (or where another day is substituted therefor by national proclamation, that day), August Bank Holiday and any day proclaimed as a public holiday or additional bank holiday, or

        (ii) in the case of each of the named holidays, such other day (not being a day on which a rest period occurs) as may be substituted therefor by the employer by a notice posted in the factory throughout the three weeks immediately preceding the holiday for which it is substituted;

    (b) in Scotland

        (i) New Year's Day, Good Friday, the local Spring holiday, the day observed as Victoria Day or Queen's Birthday, the local Autumn holiday, Christmas Day and any day proclaimed as a public holiday or additional bank holiday, or

(ii) in the case of each of the named holidays, such other day (not being a day on which a rest period occurs) as may be substituted therefor by the employer by a notice posted in the factory throughout the three weeks immediately preceding the holiday for which it is substituted:

Provided that notification of days of holiday made by the employer for the purpose of Section 94 of the Factories Act 1961(a), shall be treated for the purposes of this sub-paragraph as effective notice of substitution.

(3) the expression "rest period" means—

(a) a day (other than a Sunday or customary holiday) in each week of employment (or where one or more customary holidays fall in any such week either in that week or at the employer's option in the next succeeding week), appointed by the employer by giving at least three weeks notice to the worker as the day upon which the worker will not normally be required to work, or

(b) each of the periods during which a worker will not normally be required to work on two days (other than Sundays or customary holidays) in each week of employment (or where one or more customary holidays fall in any such week either in that week or at the employer's option in the next succeeding week) similarly appointed by the employer as days upon which the worker will not normally be required to work for more than 5 hours, or

(c) in default of any such appointment by the employer as is mentioned in the preceding sub-paragraphs (a) and (b) hereof, Saturday or if Saturday is a customary holiday the last working day preceding it.

## WAITING TIME

13.—(1) A worker is entitled to payment of the minimum remuneration specified in this Schedule for all time during which he is present on the premises of his employer, unless he is present thereon in any of the following circumstances:—

(a) without the employer's consent, express or implied,

(b) for some purpose unconnected with his work and other than that of waiting for work to be given to him to perform,

(c) by reason only of the fact that he is resident thereon,

(d) during normal meal times in a room or place in which no work is being done and he is not waiting for work to be given to him to perform.

(2) The minimum remuneration payable under sub-paragraph (1) of this paragraph to a piece worker when not engaged on piece work is that which would be applicable if he were a time worker.

## Part VII
## GUARANTEED REMUNERATION
## GUARANTEED WEEKLY REMUNERATION

14.—(1) This paragraph applies to a worker (other than a casual worker) who ordinarily works for the employer for at least 36 hours weekly on work to which this Schedule applies.

(2) Notwithstanding anything in this Schedule contained, where in any week:—

(a) no remuneration is payable to the worker under the foregoing provisions of this Schedule or by way of holiday remuneration under any wages regulation order made by the Secretary of State to give effect to the proposals of the Wages Council, or

(b) the total amount of any such remuneration is less than the guaranteed weekly remuneration provided for by this paragraph,

the minimum remuneration payable to that worker for that week in lieu any amount aforesaid shall, subject to the provisions of this paragraph, be of the guaranteed weekly remuneration.

(3) Subject to the provisions of the next following sub-paragraph the amount of the guaranteed weekly remuneration is as follows:—

(a) 1961 c. 34.

(a) in the case of a worker who ordinarily works for the employer on work to which this Schedule applies for at least 41 hours weekly, 32 hours' pay calculated at the general minimum time rate ordinarily applicable to the worker, or

(b) in the case of a worker who ordinarily works for the employer for less than 41 but not less than 36 hours weekly on such work, 32/41sts of the amount payable at the said rate for the hours ordinarily worked by the worker in a week for the employer on such work.

(4) Payment of the guaranteed weekly remuneration in any week is subject to the condition that the worker throughout the period of his ordinary employment in that week, excluding any day allowed to him as a holiday, is (a) capable of and available for work and (b) willing to perform such duties outside his normal occupation as the employer may reasonably require if his normal work is not available to him in the establishment in which he is employed:

Provided that guaranteed weekly remuneration shall not cease to be payable to a worker in respect of any week by reason only of the fact that he is absent during any part of that week by reason of proved illness or with the consent of the employer but, in the case of any such absence (other than absence on a holiday with pay allowed under the provisions of a wages regulation order) the amount of the guaranteed weekly remuneration shall be reduced by the amount to which he would have been entitled under this Schedule as a time worker had he worked the number of hours ordinarily worked by him during the period of such absence in that week.

(5) If the employer is unable to provide the worker with work by reason of a strike, failure of supplies or any cause (other than shortage of work) outside the control of the employer, guaranteed weekly remuneration shall not be payable in respect of any week during which, or part of which, the employer is unable to provide work as aforesaid.

(6) The amount of the guaranteed weekly remuneration applicable to a piece worker shall be the sum to which he would be entitled if he were a time worker.

(7) In this paragraph the expression "week" means "pay week".

## GUARANTEED DAILY REMUNERATION FOR CASUAL WORKERS

15.—(1) Notwithstanding anything in this Schedule contained, where the time worked by a casual worker on work to which this Schedule applies is less than 5 hours on a weekly short day (not being a customary holiday) or 8 hours on any other day, he shall be treated for the purposes of this Schedule (except Part VI) as if he had worked on such work 5 and 8 hours respectively.

(2) A casual worker who, in accordance with his employer's instructions, reports on any day for work to which this Schedule applies, but does not perform any such work, shall be treated as if the provisions of sub-paragraph (1) of this paragraph applied in respect of that day.

(3) For the purposes of this paragraph:—

(a) A casual worker is a worker who undertakes short engagements on an hourly or a day to day basis.

(b) A piece worker shall be treated as though he were a time worker.

## PART VIII

## GENERAL MINIMUM PIECE RATES FOR MALE OR FEMALE WORKERS

16.—(1) The general minimum piece rates applicable to male or female workers employed on repairing are the piece rates set out in Part IX of this Schedule increased by 100 per cent.

(2) The general minimum piece rates applicable to male or female workers employed on bespoke making are the piece rates set out in Part X of this Schedule increased by 100 per cent.

## Part IX

## PIECE RATES FOR MALE OR FEMALE WORKERS EMPLOYED ON REPAIRING

### A.—SOLES—COMPLETED WORK

17.—(1) Subject to the provisions of paragraph 19 and the provisions as to extras and reductions specified in paragraphs 20 to 29 inclusive, the piece rates for male or female workers employed on repairing soles (completed work) are set out in the following Table.

(2) "Benching throughout" means the performance by a single worker of all the separate operations of benching, the appropriate rates for which, in paragraph 42, amount to the appropriate rate for benching throughout, and includes in the case of riveted work the operations of riveting round soles by machine when the riveting machine is operated by the benchman but does not include the sewing or stitching of the new soles where the work is sewn or stitched.

(3) The piece rates for "benching throughout" shall be increased by 2d. per pair where nails have to be removed from full nailed or bradded work.

(4) The piece rates for "hand stitching (with square awl)" shall be increased by one-third when old stitches are taken out from welts before restitching.

| | RIVETED WORK | | | | | | | | SEWN OR STITCHED WORK | | | | | | | |
|---|---|---|---|---|---|---|---|---|---|---|---|---|---|---|---|---|
| | Men's | Ladies' | Youths' | Boys' | | Girls' and infants' | | | Men's | Ladies' | Youths' | Boys' | | Girls' and infants' | | |
| Size ... ... | 6–11 | 2–8 | 2–5½ | 11–1½ | 7–10½ | 11–1½ | 7–10½ | Under 7 | 6–11 | 2–8 | 2–5½ | 11–1½ | 7–10½ | 11–1½ | 7–10½ | Under 7 |
| Column ... | 1 | 2 | 3 | 4 | 5 | 6 | 7 | 8 | 9 | 10 | 11 | 12 | 13 | 14 | 15 | 16 |
| | Per pair s. d. | Per pair s. d. | Per pair s. d. | Per pair s. d. | Per pair s. d. | Per pair s. d. | Per pair s. d. | Per pair s. d. | Per pair s. d. | Per pair s. d. | Per pair s. d. | Per pair s. d. | Per pair s. d. | Per pair s. d. | Per pair s. d. | Per pair s. d. |
| (*a*) (i) HALF SOLE (other than pumps and slippers):— | | | | | | | | | | | | | | | | |
| Benching throughout ... ... | 7½ | 6½ | 7 | 6½ | 5½ | 5½ | 5½ | 4¾ | 8¼ | 7¼ | 7¾ | 7¼ | 6¼ | 6¼ | 6¼ | 5½ |
| Hand sewing ... ... ... | — | — | — | — | — | — | — | — | 1 0¾ | 10¼ | 11¼ | 10¼ | 9¼ | 9¼ | 8 | 8 |
| Hand stitching (with square awl) | — | — | — | — | — | — | — | — | 1 5½ | 1 2¼ | 1 3¾ | 1 2½ | 1 0½ | 1 0½ | 10 | 9 |
| Hand finishing ... ... | 7 | 6 | 6½ | 5 | 4 | 4 | 3½ | 3 | 7 | 6 | 6½ | 5 | 4 | 4 | 3½ | 3 |

| | RIVETED WORK | | | | | | | | SEWN OR STITCHED WORK | | | | | | | |
|---|---|---|---|---|---|---|---|---|---|---|---|---|---|---|---|---|
| | Men's | Ladies' | Youths' | Boys' | | Girls' and infants' | | | Men's | Ladies' | Youths' | Boys' | | Girls' and infants' | | |
| Size ... | 6–11 | 2–8 | 2–5½ | 11–1½ | 7–10½ | 11–1½ | 7–10½ | Under 7 | 6–11 | 2–8 | 2–5½ | 11–1½ | 7–10½ | 11–1½ | 7–10½ | Under 7 |
| Column ... | 1 | 2 | 3 | 4 | 5 | 6 | 7 | 8 | 9 | 10 | 11 | 12 | 13 | 14 | 15 | 16 |
| | Per pair s. d. | Per pair s. d. | Per pair s. d. | Per pair s. d. | Per pair s. d. | Per pair s. d. | Per pair s. d. | Per pair s. d. | Per pair s. d. | Per pair s. d. | Per pair s. d. | Per pair s. d. | Per pair s. d. | Per pair s. d. | Per pair s. d. | Per pair s. d. |
| (ii) SOLE UNDER HEEL (other than pumps and slippers):— | | | | | | | | | | | | | | | | |
| Benching throughout ... ... | 1 2 | 1 1 | 1 1½ | 1 1 | 10½ | 10½ | 10 | 9 | 1 3 | 1 2 | 1 2½ | 1 2 | 11½ | 11½ | 11 | 9¾ |
| Hand sewing ... ... ... | — | — | — | — | — | — | — | — | 1 5 | 1 1 | 1 2½ | 1 1 | 11 | 11 | 9 | 8½ |
| Hand stitching (with square awl) | — | — | — | — | — | — | — | — | 1 11 | 1 5½ | 1 7½ | 1 5½ | 1 2 | 1 2 | 1 0 | 11 |
| Hand finishing (whether heeled or not) ... ... ... | 1 1 | 10½ | 1 0 | 10½ | 9 | 9 | 8 | 8 | 1 1 | 10½ | 1 0 | 10½ | 9 | 9 | 8 | 8 |
| (*b*) HALF SOLE, SLIPPERS (other than pumps):— | | | | | | | | | | | | | | | | |
| Benching ... ... ... | 6½ | 5½ | 6 | 5½ | 4½ | 4½ | 4 | 3 | 7¼ | 6¼ | 6¾ | 6¼ | 5¼ | 5¼ | 4¾ | 3¾ |
| Hand sewing ... ... ... | — | — | — | — | — | — | — | — | 10¾ | 8¾ | 9½ | 8½ | 7¼ | 7¼ | 6¼ | 6 |
| Hand finishing ... ... | 6 | 5 | 5½ | 4 | 3 | 3 | 2½ | 2 | 6 | 5 | 5½ | 4 | 3 | 3 | 2½ | 2 |

| | PUMPS TURNED | | | | | | | | PUMPS TURNED AND GRAFTED | | | | | | | |
|---|---|---|---|---|---|---|---|---|---|---|---|---|---|---|---|---|
| | Men's | Ladies' | Youths' | Boys' | | Girls' and infants' | | | Men's | Ladies' | Youths' | Boys' | | Girls' and infants' | | |
| Size ... | 6–11 | 2–8 | 2–5½ | 11–1½ | 7–10½ | 11–1½ | 7–10½ | Under 7 | 6–11 | 2–8 | 2–5½ | 11–1½ | 7–10½ | 11–1½ | 7–10½ | Under 7 |
| Column ... | 1 | 2 | 3 | 4 | 5 | 6 | 7 | 8 | 9 | 10 | 11 | 12 | 13 | 14 | 15 | 16 |
| | Per pair s. d. | Per pair s. d. | Per pair s. d. | Per pair s. d. | Per pair s. d. | Per pair s. d. | Per pair s. d. | Per pair s. d. | Per pair s. d. | Per pair s. d. | Per pair s. d. | Per pair s. d. | Per pair s. d. | Per pair s. d. | Per pair s. d. | Per pair s. d. |
| (*c*) HALF SOLE, PUMPS (other than slippers):— | | | | | | | | | | | | | | | | |
| Benching and hand sewing of soles complete ... | 2 1 | 1 9 | 1 10 | 1 9 | 1 7 | 1 7 | 1 6 | 1 5 | 2 5 | 2 1 | 2 2 | 2 1 | 1 10 | 1 10 | 1 9 | 1 8 |
| Hand finishing ... ... | 7 | 6 | 6½ | 5 | 4 | 4 | 3½ | 3 | 7 | 6 | 6½ | 5 | 4 | 4 | 3½ | 3 |
| Pumps which are slippers— | | | | | | | | | | | | | | | | |
| Benching and hand sewing of soles complete ... | 1 10½ | 1 6¼ | 1 7½ | 1 6¼ | 1 4¼ | 1 4¼ | 1 3¼ | 1 2¼ | 2 2½ | 1 10¼ | 1 11¼ | 1 10¼ | 1 7¼ | 1 7¼ | 1 6¼ | 1 5½ |
| Hand finishing ... ... | 7 | 6 | 6½ | 5 | 4 | 4 | 3½ | 3 | 7 | 6 | 6½ | 5 | 4 | 4 | 3½ | 3 |

(*d*) FITTING LADIES' BREASTED SOLES

(i) Where splitting and butting is completed by benchman by hand and cemented to heel breasts ... ... ... ... ... 1s. 0d. per pair

(ii) Where splitting and butting is completed by benchman by machine and cemented to heel breasts ... ... ... ... 6d. per pair

18. LEATHER SOLES CEMENTED ON

| | MEN'S | | LADIES' | |
|---|---|---|---|---|
| | By Hand | Machine only | By Hand | Machine only |
| | Per pair d. | Per pair d. | Per pair d. | Per pair d. |
| (*a*) Stripping and levelling, including filling ... ... ... | 2¾ | 2¾ | 2¼ | 2¼ |
| (*b*) Skiving and securing old soles at waist ... ... ... | 1½ | 1¼ | 1 | 1 |
| (*c*) Rolling and moulding soles ... ... ... ... ... | ¼ | ¼ | ¼ | ¼ |
| (*d*) Skiving new soles ... ... ... ... ... ... ... | ¼ | ¼ | ¼ | ¼ |
| (*e*) Roughing upper or welt ... ... ... ... ... | 1¼ | 1¼ | 1¼ | 1¼ |
| (*f*) Roughing new soles ... ... ... ... ... ... | 1¼ | 1¼ | 1¼ | ¾ |
| (*g*) Applying cement to upper or welt ... ... ... ... | ¾ | ¾ | ¾ | ¾ |
| (*h*) Applying cement to soles ... ... ... ... ... | ¾ | ¾ | ¾ | ¾ |
| (*i*) Attaching new soles and hammering down by hand ... | 1¼ | — | 1¼ | — |
| (*j*) Fixing new soles in press (including use of activator) ... | — | ¾ | — | ½ |
| (*k*) Securing with rivets at waist and toe as necessary ... ... | ½ | ¼ | ½ | ¼ |
| (*l*) Rounding ... ... ... ... ... ... ... ... ... | 1 | ½ | 1 | ½ |
| | 11½ | 10 | 10½ | 8½ |

19.—The piece rates for benching set out in paragraphs 17 and 18 do not include payment for:—

(*a*) Pegging the waists,

(*b*) Repairing insoles of welted work,

(*c*) In the case of sole under heel, the sewing or repairing of hand sewn or welted seats.

Where the benchman performs any of these operations, he shall be paid in respect of such work the piece rates specified in paragraph 1 (1) (*b*) (ii).

## 20. SOLEING MATERIAL NOT CUT TO SHAPE

The piece rates for benching throughout set out in paragraphs 17 and 18 in respect of soles apply where the soleing material is cut into separate soles shaped rights and lefts. If the soleing material is not given out in this form, 1d. per pair extra is payable.

## 21. OUTSIZES

For men's work over size 11 the piece rates provided in paragraph 17 for soleing men's work sizes 6–11 and in paragraph 18 for men's work and for ladies' work over size 8 the piece rates provided in paragraph 17 for soleing ladies' work sizes 2–8 and in paragraph 18 for ladies' work shall be respectively payable, with the following additions:—

Per pair

(a) Hand sewn or hand stitched work where the benching and the sewing (or stitching) are done by the same worker    1½d.

(b) Benching of riveted work, machine sewn work or machine stitched work ... ... ... ... ... ... ...    ½d.

(c) Hand sewing or hand stitching only... ... ... ...    1d.

(d) Hand finishing ... ... ... ... ... ... ...    ½d.

## 22. LONG WORK

(a) Repairing men's or youths' Napoleon, jockey or riding boots, long Wellingtons, short Wellingtons, field boots or sea boots which reach to the knee or above—

(i) Sole only, men's (all sizes) and youths' (sizes 2–5½): 1½d. per pair extra to the rates for benching;

(ii) Soleing and heeling (or half heeling) when done together, men's (all sizes) and youths' (sizes 2–5½): 2½d. per pair extra to the rates for benching;

(b) Repairing ladies' long work—

(i) Sole only, or

(ii) Soleing and heeling (or half heeling) when done together: ¾d. per pair extra to the rates for benching.

## 23. RIVETING SOLES ON WELTED BOOTS OR SHOES

Riveting soles by hand on welted boots or shoes, 1d. per pair extra to the rates for benching riveted work. This extra does not apply when the new sole is riveted on the top of the old sole or middle sole.

## 24. SEWING THROUGH (SOLES OR CLUMPS)

Soles or clumps, sewn through by hand on Blake principle, 5d. per pair extra to the rates for hand sewing.

## 25. SOLEING WITH LEATHER SUBSTITUTES

Soleing with leather substitutes, but excluding the work for which rates are provided in paragraphs 67 and 68:—

(a) Where the worker has to prepare or roughen or prepare and roughen both the new sole and the bottom and to apply an adhesive for the purpose of fixing the new sole before sewing or riveting ... ... ... ... ... ...    4d. per pair extra.

(b) Where the worker has no preparatory work to perform to the new sole but prepares or roughens or prepares and roughens the bottom and applies an adhesive for the purpose of fixing the new sole before sewing or riveting ...    2d. per pair extra.

## 26. SOLEING WITH WATERPROOF LEATHERS OTHER THAN CHROME

Benching throughout ... ... ... ... ... ¾d. per pair extra.
Hand finishing ... ... ... ... ... ... 1¼d. per pair extra.

## 27. WOOD PEGGING BY HAND

Soleing, 5¼d. per pair extra to the rates for benching riveted work.

## 28. FINISHING (PART ONLY), EXCLUDING LEATHER SUBSTITUTES

Finishing edges only, bottoms not touched, 25 per cent. less.
Finishing edges and finishing waist from heel to joint, foreparts of bottoms not touched, 12½ per cent. less.

## 29. FINISHING (PART ONLY), LEATHER SUBSTITUTES

Finishing edges only by hand, 12½ per cent. less.
Finishing edges and surface of the waist by hand, 7½ per cent. less.

## B.—HEELING OR HALF HEELING, TOE BITS, SIDE BITS, UNDERLAYS AND CROSS PIECES

30.—Subject to the provisions of paragraph 31 and to the provisions as to addition and subtraction set out in paragraphs 32 to 41, the piece rates specified in the following Table apply to male or female workers employed on repairing.

| | Men's | Ladies' | Youths' | Boys' | | Girls' and infants' | | |
|---|---|---|---|---|---|---|---|---|
| Size ... ... ... | 6–11 | 2–8 | 2–5½ | 11–1½ | 7–10½ | 11–1½ | 7–10½ | Under 7 |
| Column ... ... | 1 | 2 | 3 | 4 | 5 | 6 | 7 | 8 |
| | Per pair d. | Per pair d. | Per pair d. | Per pair d. | Per pair d. | Per pair d. | Per pair d. | Per pair d. |
| (*a*) HEELING OR HALF HEELING WITH LEATHER OR LEATHER SUBSTITUTES | | | | | | | | |
| (1) WORK OTHER THAN SLIPPERS | | | | | | | | |
| BENCHING— | | | | | | | | |
| (*a*) Stripping top piece, removing old grindery, levelling and securing under lifts ... ... ... ... ... ... ... | 2 | 1¼ | 1¾ | 1¾ | 1¾ | 1¼ | 1¼ | 1¼ |
| (*b*) Tacking on top pieces ... ... ... ... ... | ¼ | ¼ | ¼ | ¼ | ¼ | ¼ | ¼ | ¼ |
| (*c*) Rounding by hand ... ... ... ... ... ... | ¼ | ¼ | ¼ | ¼ | ¼ | ¼ | ¼ | ¼ |
| (*d*) Nailing round by hand ... ... ... ... ... | ¾ | ½ | ½ | ½ | ½ | ½ | ½ | ½ |
| (*e*) Hammering down and filing nails ... ... ... | ¼ | ¼ | ¼ | ¼ | ¼ | ¼ | ¼ | ¼ |
| HAND FINISHING ... ... ... ... ... ... ... | 3½ | 2 | 2½ | 2 | 1½ | 2 | 1 | 1 |
| (2) SLIPPERS | | | | | | | | |
| Benching, including nailing by machine when the nailing or slugging machine is operated by the benchman ... ... ... ... | 3 | 2 | 2½ | 2½ | 2 | 2½ | 2 | 1½ |
| Hand finishing ... ... ... ... ... ... ... ... | 2½ | 2 | 2 | 2 | 1½ | 1½ | 1 | 1 |

Benching for nailing round or slugging by machine when the nailing or slugging machine is not operated by the benchman ...

The rates for benching set out above, subject to the following reductions:—

(i) Boys' (size 11 and over), youths' (sizes 2 to 5½) and men's work... ... ... ... ¾d. per pair

(ii) All other sizes ... ... ... ... ½d. per pair

When the work is returned to the same benchman for hammering down and filing the heels after nailing round or slugging by machine the rates for benching shall be subject in respect of all sizes to a reduction of ¼d. per pair only.

|  | HAND SEWN | | | | | | | | RIVETED | | | | | | | |
|---|---|---|---|---|---|---|---|---|---|---|---|---|---|---|---|---|
|  | Men's Ladies' | | Youths' | Boys' | | Girls' and infants' | | | Men's Ladies' | | Youths' | Boys' | | Girls' and infants' | | |
| Size ... | 6–11 | 2–8 | 2–5½ | 11–1½ | 7–10½ | 11–1½ | 7–10½ | Under 7 | 6–11 | 2–8 | 2–5½ | 11–1½ | 7–10½ | 11–1½ | 7–10½ | Under 7 |
| Column ... | 1 | 2 | 3 | 4 | 5 | 6 | 7 | 8 | 9 | 10 | 11 | 12 | 13 | 14 | 15 | 16 |
|  | Per pair d. | Per pair d. | Per pair d. | Per pair d. | Per pair d. | Per pair d. | Per pair d. | Per pair d. | Per pair d. | Per pair d. | Per pair d. | Per pair d. | Per pair d. | Per pair d. | Per pair d. | Per pair d. |
| **(b) TOE BITS, SIDE BITS OR UNDERLAYS** Benching, exclusive of hand sewing ... | 3½ | 2½ | 3 | 3 | 2½ | 2½ | 2 | 1½ | 3½ | 2½ | 3 | 3 | 2½ | 2½ | 2 | 1½ |
| Hand sewing ... | 4½ | 4 | 4 | 4 | 3½ | 3½ | 3 | 3 |  |  |  |  |  |  |  |  |
| Hand finishing ... | 3½ | 2 | 2½ | 2 | 1½ | 2 | 1 | 1 | 3½ | 2 | 2½ | 2 | 1½ | 2 | 1 | 1 |

**(c) FIXING MOULDED RUBBER HEELS WHERE NO PARING REQUIRED** ... ... MEN'S, 3d. per pair. All other sizes, 2d. per pair.

### (d) CROSS PIECES

All rates are "Per pair d."

| Size | HAND SEWN | | | | | | | | RIVETED | | | | | | | |
|---|---|---|---|---|---|---|---|---|---|---|---|---|---|---|---|---|
| | Men's 6–11 | Ladies' 2–8 | Youths' 2–5½ | Boys' 11–1½ | Boys' 7–10½ | Girls' and infants' 11–1½ | Girls' and infants' 7–10½ | Girls' and infants' Under 7 | Men's 6–11 | Ladies' 2–8 | Youths' 2–5½ | Boys' 11–1½ | Boys' 7–10½ | Girls' and infants' 11–1½ | Girls' and infants' 7–10½ | Girls' and infants' Under 7 |
| Column | 1 | 2 | 3 | 4 | 5 | 6 | 7 | 8 | 9 | 10 | 11 | 12 | 13 | 14 | 15 | 16 |
| Benching, exclusive of hand sewing | 5½ | 4 | 5 | 3½ | 3 | 3½ | 3 | 2½ | 5½ | 4 | 5 | 3½ | 3 | 3½ | 3 | 2½ |
| Benching, cemented work | 7½ | 6 | 7 | 5½ | 5 | 5½ | 5 | 4½ | 7½ | 6 | 7 | 5½ | 5 | 5½ | 5 | 4½ |
| Hand sewing | 7 | 6 | 6½ | 5½ | 5 | 5 | 4 | 4 | — | — | — | — | — | — | — | — |
| Hand finishing | 3½ | 2½ | 3 | 2 | 1½ | 2 | 1 | 1 | 3½ | 2½ | 3 | 2 | 1½ | 2 | 1 | 1 |

31.—As respects the work specified in paragraph 30:—

(i) If benching (other than hand sewing) is not completed by one worker, the piece rates specified in paragraph 1 (1) (b) (ii) apply.

(ii) The piece rates for benching are payable to the benchman whether his work includes or does not include the filing of heels, toe plates and metal tips.

(iii) The piece rates for benching heels do not apply to the removing of old heels and the fixing (including knifing up) of new ready made heels of pulp or leather. If the benchman performs these operations he shall be paid the piece rates specified in paragraph 1 (1) (b) (ii).

## 32. TOP PIECES CUT TO SHAPE AND SIZE

The piece rates for benching heels set out in paragraph 30 shall be reduced by ¼d. per pair where no knifing up is required before the top pieces are nailed or riveted round.

## 33. OUTSIZES, HEEL OR HALF HEEL

For men's work over size 11, the piece rate provided in paragraph 30 for men's work sizes 6–11, and for ladies' work over size 8, the piece rate provided in paragraph 30 for ladies' work sizes 2–8 shall be payable respectively with the following additions:—

| | |
|---|---|
| For benching (whether complete or in preparation for the riveting or slugging machine) ... ... ... | ¼d. per pair. |
| For hand finishing ... ... ... ... ... ... | ¼d. per pair. |

## 34. NEW LIFTS AND PART LIFTS

(1) (*a*) New lifts—for each quarter of an inch or part thereof, 1d. per pair extra;

(*b*) Part lifts—where parts of heels have to be cut out to the depth of ½ inch or more for the purpose of levelling the heels, although complete new lifts may not be inserted, 1d. per pair extra.

(2) Where heels are stripped down to the seat piece, the piece rates for re-building heels and heeling (benching) set out in paragraph 64 shall apply.

## 35. QUARTER OR HALF-TIPS

(1) (*a*) Inserted iron quarter or half-tips ... ... ... 1d. per pair extra.

(*b*) Inserted rubber tips:

    (i) When solutioned ... ... ... ... 2d. per pair extra.

    (ii) When not solutioned ... ... ... ... 1d. per pair extra.

(*c*) Where the top piece has a quarter rubber tip already attached when the top piece is given out:

    (i) For solutioning on the quarter rubber tip in the process of fixing the top piece to the heel ... ... ... ... ... ... 1d. per pair extra.

    (ii) For attaching any additional leather to the top piece to make up the difference between the thickness of the quarter rubber tip and the top piece ... ... ... ... ½d. per pair extra.

(2) No extra is payable for affixing the top piece which has a quarter rubber tip already attached.

## 36. ELONGATED HEELS

Repairing elongated heels (where waists already filled in):

| | |
|---|---|
| Men's (all sizes) and youths' (sizes 2 to 5½) | 1¾d. per pair extra to the rates for benching. |
| All other sizes ... ... | ¾d. per pair extra to the rates for benching. |

## 37. LONG WORK—HEELING

(*a*) Repairing men's and youths' Napoleon, jockey, or riding boots, long Wellingtons, short Wellingtons, field boots or sea boots which reach to the knee or above—

    (i) Heeling or half heeling:

    1d. per pair extra to the rates for benching;

(ii) Toe bits, side bits, underlays, and cross pieces or any of them:
1d. per pair extra to the rates for benching.

(b) Repairing ladies' long work—
(i) Heeling or half heeling:
½d. per pair extra to the rates for benching;

(ii) Heeling or half heeling when done together with toe bits, side bits, underlays, and cross pieces or any of them:
¾d. per pair extra to the rates for benching;

(iii) Toe bits, side bits, underlays, and cross pieces or any of them:
½d. per pair extra to the rates for benching.

## 38. TOE PIECES (SHAPED)

Shaped toe pieces:

Hand sewn and benched, 3½d. per pair extra;
Riveted, 1d. per pair extra.

## 39. WOOD PEGGING BY HAND

Heeling, 1¾d. per pair extra to the rates for benching riveted work.

## 40. FINISHING (PART ONLY), EXCLUDING LEATHER SUBSTITUTES

Finishing edges only, bottoms not touched, 25 per cent. less.

## 41. FINISHING (PART ONLY), LEATHER SUBSTITUTES

Finishing edges only by hand 12½ per cent. less.

## C.—PIECE RATES FOR SEPARATE OPERATIONS OF BENCHING SOLES

42.—(1) Subject to the provisions of paragraphs 43 and 44 and to the provisions as to extras set out in paragraphs 47 to 50, the piece rates for separate operations of benching soles set out in the following Table apply to male or female workers employed on repairing.

(2) If benching throughout is not performed by a single worker, the piece rates for any of the separate operations of benching specified in the said Table are the rates for the individual operations or, where more than one of these operations is performed by a single worker, the sum of the appropriate rates for the individual operations involved.

| | RIVETED WORK | | | | | | | | SEWN OR STITCHED WORK | | | | | | | |
|---|---|---|---|---|---|---|---|---|---|---|---|---|---|---|---|---|
| | Men's | Ladies' | Youths' | Boys' | | Girls' and infants' | | | Men's | Ladies' | Youths' | Boys' | | Girls' and infants' | | |
| Size ... ... | 6–11 | 2–8 | 2–5½ | 11–1½ | 7–10½ | 11–1½ | 7–10½ | Under 7 | 6–11 | 2–8 | 2–5½ | 11–1½ | 7–10½ | 11–1½ | 7–10½ | Under 7 |
| Column ... | 1 | 2 | 3 | 4 | 5 | 6 | 7 | 8 | 9 | 10 | 11 | 12 | 13 | 14 | 15 | 16 |
| | Per pair d. | Per pair d. | Per pair d. | Per pair d. | Per pair d. | Per pair d. | Per pair d. | Per pair d. | Per pair d. | Per pair d. | Per pair d. | Per pair d. | Per pair d. | Per pair d. | Per pair d. | Per pair d. |
| (a) HALF SOLE (other than pumps and slippers):— | | | | | | | | | | | | | | | | |
| 1. Stripping and levelling, including filling ... | 2¾ | 2¼ | 2½ | 2¼ | 1¾ | 1¾ | 1¾ | 1¾ | 2½ | 2 | 2¼ | 2¼ | 1¾ | 1¾ | 1¾ | 1¾ |
| 2. Skiving old soles at waist | 1 | ½ | ¾ | ½ | ½ | ½ | ½ | ½ | 1 | ½ | ¾ | ½ | ½ | ½ | ½ | ½ |
| 3. Tacking on new soles ... | ½ | ½ | ½ | ½ | ½ | ½ | ½ | ½ | ½ | ½ | ½ | ½ | ½ | ½ | ½ | ½ |
| 4. Rolling or moulding ... | ¼ | ¼ | ¼ | ¼ | ¼ | ¼ | ¼ | ¼ | ¼ | ¼ | ¼ | ¼ | ¼ | ¼ | ¼ | ¼ |
| 5. Skiving new soles by hand or machine ... ... | ¼ | ¼ | ¼ | ¼ | ¼ | ¼ | ¼ | ¼ | ¼ | ¼ | ¼ | ¼ | ¼ | ¼ | ¼ | ¼ |
| 6. Riveting across waist by hand ... ... ... | ¼ | ¼ | ¼ | ¼ | ¼ | ¼ | ¼ | ¼ | ½ | ½ | ½ | ¼ | ¼ | ¼ | ¼ | ¼ |
| 7. Rounding by hand ... | ¾ | ¾ | ¾ | ¾ | ½ | ½ | ½ | ¼ | 1 | 1 | 1 | 1 | ¾ | ¾ | ¾ | ½ |
| 8. Riveting round soles by hand ... ... ... | 1¼ | 1¼ | 1¼ | 1¼ | 1 | 1 | 1 | ¾ | — | — | — | — | — | — | — | — |
| 9. Hammering down rivets... | ½ | ½ | ½ | ½ | ½ | ½ | ½ | ¼ | — | — | — | — | — | — | — | — |
| 10. Cutting channels by hand | — | — | — | — | — | — | — | — | ½ | ½ | ½ | ½ | ½ | ½ | ½ | ½ |
| 11. Opening channels by hand | — | — | — | — | — | — | — | — | ½ | ½ | ½ | ½ | ½ | ½ | ½ | ½ |
| 12. Laying channels by hand | — | — | — | — | — | — | — | — | ¾ | ¾ | ¾ | ¾ | ½ | ½ | ½ | ¼ |
| 13. Hammering down bottoms | — | — | — | — | — | — | — | — | ½ | ½ | ½ | ½ | ½ | ½ | ½ | ¼ |

| | RIVETED WORK | | | | | | | | SEWN OR STITCHED WORK | | | | | | | |
|---|---|---|---|---|---|---|---|---|---|---|---|---|---|---|---|---|
| | Men's | Ladies' | Youths' | Boys' | | Girls' and infants' | | | Men's | Ladies' | Youths' | Boys' | | Girls' and infants' | | |
| Size ... ... | 6–11 | 2–8 | 2–5½ | 11–1½ | 7–10½ | 11–1½ | 7–10½ | Under 7 | 6–11 | 2–8 | 2–5½ | 11–1½ | 7–10½ | 11–1½ | 7–10½ | Under 7 |
| Column ... | 1 | 2 | 3 | 4 | 5 | 6 | 7 | 8 | 9 | 10 | 11 | 12 | 13 | 14 | 15 | 16 |
| | Per pair d. | Per pair d. | Per pair d. | Per pair d. | Per pair d. | Per pair d. | Per pair d. | Per pair d. | Per pair d. | Per pair d. | Per pair d. | Per pair d. | Per pair d. | Per pair d. | Per pair d. | Per pair d. |
| (*b*) SOLE UNDER HEEL (other than pumps and slippers):— | | | | | | | | | | | | | | | | |
| 1. Stripping and levelling, including filling ... | 4½ | 3½ | 4 | 3½ | 3 | 3 | 2½ | 2¼ | 4½ | 3½ | 4 | 3½ | 3 | 3 | 2½ | 2¼ |
| 2. Tacking on ... ... | 1¼ | 1¼ | 1¼ | 1¼ | 1¼ | 1¼ | 1¼ | 1¼ | 1¼ | 1¼ | 1¼ | 1¼ | 1¼ | 1¼ | 1¼ | 1¼ |
| 3. Removing old heels ... | 1¾ | 1¾ | 1¾ | 1¾ | 1¼ | 1¼ | 1¼ | 1¼ | 1¾ | 1¾ | 1¾ | 1¾ | 1¼ | 1¼ | 1¼ | 1¼ |
| 4. Rolling or moulding ... | ¼ | ¼ | ¼ | ¼ | ¼ | ¼ | ¼ | ¼ | ¼ | ¼ | ¼ | ¼ | ¼ | ¼ | ¼ | ¼ |
| 5. Fitting new sole to seat ... | ¼ | ¼ | ¼ | ¼ | ¼ | ¼ | ¼ | ¼ | ¼ | ¼ | ¼ | ¼ | ¼ | ¼ | ¼ | ¼ |
| 6. Securing seat by hand riveting ... ... ... | ¼ | ¼ | ¼ | ¼ | ¼ | ¼ | ¼ | ¼ | ¼ | ¼ | ¼ | ¼ | ¼ | ¼ | ¼ | ¼ |
| 7. Rounding by hand ... | 1½ | 1½ | 1½ | 1½ | 1 | 1 | 1 | ¾ | 1¾ | 1¾ | 1¾ | 1¾ | 1¼ | 1¼ | 1¼ | ¾ |
| 8. Riveting round soles by hand ... ... ... | 1¾ | 1¾ | 1¾ | 1¾ | 1¼ | 1¼ | 1¼ | 1 | — | — | — | — | — | — | — | — |
| 9. Hammering down rivets... | ¾ | ¾ | ¾ | ¾ | ¾ | ¾ | ¾ | ½ | — | — | — | — | — | — | — | — |
| 10. Replacing old heels by hand ... ... ... | 1¾ | 1¾ | 1¾ | 1¾ | 1¼ | 1¼ | 1¼ | 1¼ | 1¾ | 1¾ | 1¾ | 1¾ | 1¼ | 1¼ | 1¼ | 1¼ |
| 11. Cutting channels by hand | — | — | — | — | — | — | — | — | ¾ | ¾ | ¾ | ¾ | ½ | ½ | ½ | ½ |
| 12. Opening channels by hand | — | — | — | — | — | — | — | — | ¾ | ¾ | ¾ | ¾ | ½ | ½ | ½ | ½ |
| 13. Laying channels by hand | — | — | — | — | — | — | — | — | 1 | 1 | 1 | 1 | 1 | 1 | 1 | ¾ |
| 14. Hammering down bottoms | — | — | — | — | — | — | — | — | ¾ | ¾ | ¾ | ¾ | ¾ | ¾ | ¾ | ½ |

43.—(1) The piece rates for stripping and levelling including filling set out at (*a*) and (*b*) of the last foregoing Table shall be increased by 1d. per pair where nails have to be removed from full nailed or bradded work.

(2) Where new lifts are required, the piece rate for replacing old heels by hand set out at (*b*) of the said Table shall be increased as if paragraph 34 applied.

(3) Where piece rates for riveting round soles by hand, hammering down rivets, laying channels by hand and hammering down bottoms set out at (*a*) and (*b*) of the said Table are payable and:—

(*a*) the operation of riveting round soles is performed by hand, the worker shall also be paid the appropriate rate for hammering down rivets;

(*b*) the channels have not been laid by machine and hammering down bottoms is performed, the worker shall also be paid the appropriate rate for laying channels by hand.

44. The piece rates for benching set out in paragraphs 42 and 43 do not include payment for:—
    (a) Pegging the waists,
    (b) Repairing insoles of welted work,
    (c) In the case of sole under heel, the sewing or repairing of hand sewn or welted seats,

    Where the benchman performs any of these operations, he shall be paid in respect of such work the piece rates specified in paragraph 1 (1) (b) (ii).

    (d) Fitting ladies' breasted through soles—see paragraph 45.

## 45. FITTING LADIES' BREASTED THROUGH SOLES

(a) Where splitting and butting is completed by benchman by hand and cemented to heel breasts ... ... ... ... 1s. per pair.

(b) Where splitting and butting is completed by benchman by machine and cemented to heel breasts ... ... ... 6d. per pair.

## 46. LADIES' PLATFORM THROUGH SOLES

| | By Hand Per pair s. d. | Machine only s. d. |
|---|---|---|
| 1. Stripping and levelling, including securing and filling ... | 4¾ | 4¾ |
| 2. Roughing uppers ... ... ... ... ... ... | 2¼ | 1¼ |
| 3. Roughing new soles ... ... ... ... ... | 2 | 1¼ |
| 4. Cementing uppers ... ... ... ... ... ... | 1½ | 1 |
| 5. Cementing soles ... ... ... ... ... ... | 1½ | 1 |
| 6. Attaching bottoms (including use of activator) ... ... | 2¼ | 2 |
| 7. Rounding ... ... ... ... ... ... ... | 1½ | ¾ |
| | 1 4 | 1 0 |

## 47. SOLEING MATERIAL NOT CUT TO SHAPE

The piece rates for stripping and levelling including filling set out in paragraph 42 apply where soleing material is cut into separate soles shaped rights and lefts. If the soleing material is not given out in this form, an addition of 1d. per pair is payable.

## 48. OUTSIZES

For men's work over size 11, the piece rates provided in paragraph 42 for soleing men's work size 6–11 and for ladies' work over size 8 the piece rates provided in paragraph 42 for soleing ladies' work size 2–8 shall be payable respectively, with the following addition:—

Riveted work, machine sewn work or machine stitched work:

For stripping, levelling and tacking-on ... ... ... ½d. per pair.

## 49. RIVETING SOLES ON WELTED BOOTS OR SHOES

Riveting soles by hand on welted boots or shoes—

1d. per pair extra to the appropriate rate for riveting round soles.

This extra does not apply when the new sole is riveted on the top of the old sole or middle sole.

## 50.  SOLEING WITH LEATHER SUBSTITUTES

Soleing with leather substitutes, but excluding the work for which rates are provided in paragraphs 67 and 68:—

(*a*) Where the worker has to prepare or roughen or prepare and roughen both the new sole and the bottom and to apply an adhesive for the purpose of fixing the new sole before sewing or riveting,
4d. per pair extra.

(*b*) Where the worker has no preparatory work to perform to the new sole but prepares or roughens or prepares and roughens the bottom and applies an adhesive for the purpose of fixing the new sole before sewing or riveting,
2d. per pair extra.

## D.—PIECE RATES FOR OTHER REPAIRS TO SOLES

## 51.—(1) INSOLES OR HALF INSOLES—SHAPING AND SLIPPING IN

(excluding welted insoles).

| | |
|---|---|
| Men's (all sizes) and youths' (sizes 2 to 5½) ... ... ... | 4d. per pair. |
| Ladies' ... ... ... ... ... ... ... ... | 3d. per pair. |
| Boys' and girls' (up to size 1½)... ... ... ... ... | 2d. per pair. |

(2) Where either the whole or half of the present insole has to be removed and a new insole (either whole or half) is fitted and the upper is lasted in, the above piece rates do not apply, and a piece worker doing such work shall be paid the piece rates specified in paragraph 1 (1) (*b*) (ii).

## 52.  MIDDLES, (TOE TO JOINT) SECURELY ATTACHED BY EITHER GRINDERY OR SOLUTION, AND ROUNDING BY HAND

| | |
|---|---|
| Men's (all sizes) and youths' (sizes 2 to 5½) ... ... ... | 4d. per pair. |
| Ladies' ... ... ... ... ... ... ... ... | 3d. per pair. |
| Boys' and girls' (up to size 1½)... ... ... ... ... | 2d. per pair. |
| Fitting of press cut slip middles, being a reinforcement and not separately attached or rounded, by hand ... ... | 1d. per pair. |

## 53.  HALF MIDDLES (slotted and fitted)

Where half middles are slotted and fitted into the old middles:—

| | |
|---|---|
| Men's (all sizes) and youths' (sizes 2 to 5½) ... ... ... | 2d. per pair. |
| Ladies' ... ... ... ... ... ... ... ... | 1½d. per pair. |
| Boys' and girls' (up to size 1½)... ... ... ... ... | 1d. per pair. |

## 54.  TOE PLATES OR TOE TIPS (separate job)

| | |
|---|---|
| Nailed on... ... ... ... ... ... ... ... | 1d. per pair. |
| Nailed on and sunk or inserted ... ... ... ... | 3½d. per pair. |
| Screwed on ... ... ... ... ... ... ... | 2d. per pair. |
| Screwed on and sunk or inserted ... ... ... ... | 4½d. per pair. |

Provided that these rates shall not apply to toe plates or toe tips when combined with nailing to which the rates in paragraph 55 apply.

## 55. NAILS OR BRADS

(1) (a) Nailing or bradding foreparts (with or without toe plates or toe tips nailed on): the piece rates specified in the following Table:—

| Column 1 | Column 2 | Column 3 | Column 4 | Column 5 |
|---|---|---|---|---|
| — | Men's | Youths' (sizes 2 to 5½) | Ladies' | Children's (i.e., all under size 2) |
| | Per pair d. | Per pair d. | Per pair d. | Per pair d. |
| **NAILS:** | | | | |
| Full rows round, each row ... ... | 1¾ | 1½ | 1¼ | 1 |
| Rows up middle, each row ... | ¾ | ½ | ½ | ¼ |
| Toe and joint:—One row ... | 1¼ | 1 | 1 | — |
| Two rows ... | 2 | 1¾ | 1¾ | — |
| **BRADS** | | | | |
| Full rows round, each row ... | 2 | 1¾ | 1½ | 1¼ |
| Rows up middle, each row ... | 1 | 1 | ¾ | ¾ |
| Toe and joint:—One row ... | 1½ | 1¼ | 1 | — |
| Two rows ... | 2½ | 2¼ | 2 | — |

If toe plates or toe tips screwed on, 1d. per pair extra.
If toe plates or toe tips sunk or inserted, 2½d. per pair extra.
  (b) Nailing waists:—1¾d. per pair.

(2) The rates for nailing or bradding foreparts and for nailing waists set out in this paragraph do not include payments for fitters, clinkers, ice, climbing, cricket or golf nails, the removing of old nails or the filling up of old holes with wood pegs. If the benchman performs any of these operations, he shall be paid in respect thereof the piece rates specified in paragraph 1 (1) (b) (ii).

## 56. RE-SEWING

(a) Re-sewing old soles or waists:—
  Up to 4 inches, 3d.; ¾d. per inch thereafter.
(b) Re-sewing old pumps:—
  Joint to joint:—
    Men's (all sizes) and youths' (sizes 2 to 5½), 1s. 6d. per pair.
    Ladies' and other sizes, 1s. 2d. per pair.
    Turning and re-turning, 6d. per pair extra.
  Heel to heel:—
    8d. per pair additional to the rates for re-sewing from joint to joint set out above.
  Part re-sewing only:—
    Sewing, 2d. per inch with a minimum of 2d.
    Turning and re-turning, 6d. per pair extra.

## 57. LINK STITCHING OR LOOPING

1½d. per inch with a minimum of 3d.

## 58. STIFFENERS (NEW)

New stiffeners (Blake or riveted work) lasted in:
  Men's (all sizes) and youths' (sizes 2 to 5½), 1s. 6d. per pair.
  Ladies' and boys' and girls' (sizes 11 to 1½), 1s. 3d. per pair.
  Boys' and girls' (sizes 7 to 10½ and 4 to 6), 10d. per pair.
If welted:
  With tingled or braced seats, 6d. per pair extra.
  With sewn seats, 1s. 0d. per pair extra.

59. WELTS

    (a) Re-welting (including taking out old welts):—

        Heel to heel—

| | |
|---|---|
| Men's (all sizes) ... ... ... ... ... | 3s. 0d. per pair. |
| Youths' (sizes 2 to 5½) ... ... ... ... | 2s. 6d. per pair. |
| Ladies' and other sizes ... ... ... ... | 2s. 0d. per pair. |

        Joint to joint—

| | |
|---|---|
| Men's (all sizes) ... ... ... ... ... | 2s. 0d. per pair. |
| Youths' (sizes 2 to 5½) ... ... ... ... | 1s. 9d. per pair. |
| Ladies' and other sizes ... ... ... ... | 1s. 8d. per pair. |
| New pieces of welt on a job (that is on one boot or shoe or on a pair of boots or shoes) ... ... | Up to one inch 3¼d., with 1¼d. per inch thereafter. |

    (b) Re-sewing of old welts:—

        Joint to joint—

| | |
|---|---|
| Men's (all sizes) ... ... ... ... ... | 1s. 8d. per pair. |
| Youths' (sizes 2 to 5½) ... ... ... ... | 1s. 4d. per pair. |
| Ladies' and other sizes ... ... ... ... | 1s. 2d. per pair. |
| Re-sewing old welts whether of one boot or shoe or of a pair of boots or shoes ... ... ... ... | Up to 2 inches 2d., with 1d. per inch thereafter. |

### E.—PIECE RATES FOR OTHER REPAIRS TO HEELS

60. HAND FINISHING NEW HEELS

| | |
|---|---|
| Ladies' French ... ... ... ... ... ... ... | 5½d. per pair. |
| Ladies' Cuban ... ... ... ... ... ... ... | 4d. per pair. |
| Ladies' Square ... ... ... ... ... ... ... | 3d. per pair. |
| Men's ... ... ... ... ... ... ... ... | 3½d. per pair. |

61. HEEL SUPPORTS

    Metal or other ready made heel breast supports, 2d. per pair.

62. HEELING WITH LEATHER SUBSTITUTES

    The piece rates appropriate under paragraph 67 and 68.

63. NAILING HEELS

    (1) Nailing heels when boots are not heeled or when performed as a job additional to complete heeling:
        Less than two rows, 1d. per pair.
        Two or more rows, 2d. per pair.

    (2) The rates for nailing heels set out in this paragraph do not include payment for fitters, clinkers, ice, climbing, cricket or golf nails, the removing of old nails or the filling up of old holes with wood pegs. If the benchman performs any of these operations, he shall be paid in respect thereof the piece rates specified in paragraph 1 (1) (b) (ii).

64.—(1) REBUILDING HEELS AND HEELING (BENCHING)

| | |
|---|---|
| (i) Ladies' French ... ... ... | 1s. 2d. per pair up to 2 inches. |
| Ladies' Cuban ... ... ... ... | 10½d. per pair up to 1½ inches. |
| Ladies' Square ... ... ... ... | 7d. per pair up to 1¼ inches. |
| Men's ... ... ... ... ... | 9d. per pair up to 1¼ inches. |

    The measurement of the height of the heel is to be taken from the upper at the breast of the heel.

    (ii) For every quarter inch or part thereof higher, 1d. per pair extra.

    (iii) When sole seat piece is required, 2d. per pair extra.

  (2) The above rates do not apply to sewn seats.

## 65. REFASTENING HEELS

Refastening heels with pieced insoles and nailing through seat by hand, 3d. each.

## 66. WOOD HEELS

Turning back covers and lowering heels, 1d. per pair.
Replacing covers, 1d. per pair.

## F.—PIECE RATES FOR FIXING COMPLETE RUBBER SETS, RUBBER FOREPARTS AND RUBBER OR LEATHER SUBSTITUTE HEELS

67.—(1) The piece rates for fixing complete rubber sets, rubber foreparts, and rubber or leather substitute heels are set out in the following Table:—

| Column 1 | Column 2 | Column 3 | Column 4 |
|---|---|---|---|
| — | Men's (all sizes) | Ladies' (all sizes) and youths' (sizes 2 to 5½) | Children's (i.e., all sizes under 2) |
| | Per pair d. | Per pair d. | Per pair d. |
| (a) REMOVING RUBBER SETS | | | |
| Removing old rubber sets and plugging holes: | | | |
| (i) Foreparts... ... ... ... ... ... | 2 | 1½ | 1½ |
| (ii) Heels ... ... ... ... ... ... | 1 | 1 | 1 |
| (b) FIXING COMPLETE RUBBER SETS | | | |
| (i) Solutioning complete rubber sets (when nails or screws also used) additional to the rates in (ii) below... ... ... ... ... ... | 2 | 2 | 2 |
| (ii) Fixing complete rubber sets (that is, heels and two or more parts or sections on each sole) by screwing or nailing ... ... ... ... | 6 | 4 | 4 |
| (c) FIXING RUBBER FOREPARTS | | | |
| (i) Solutioning rubber foreparts (when nails or screws also used) additional to the rates in (ii) and (iii) below ... ... ... ... ... | 1 | 1 | 1 |
| (ii) Fixing rubber foreparts (one piece) by screwing or nailing... ... ... ... ... ... | 3 | 2 | 1½ |
| (iii) Fixing rubber foreparts (two or more parts or sections on each sole) by screwing or nailing... | 4 | 3 | 3 |
| (d) FIXING RUBBER FOREPARTS BY SOLUTION (with or without screws or nails) where the new or old soles are roughened by the worker in preparation for fixing by any adhesive process ... ... | 8 | 6 | 4 |
| (e) RUBBER OR LEATHER SUBSTITUTE HEELS | | | |
| (i) Where rubber shaped to the heels or leather substitute is used in conjunction with heeling and no lift is placed underneath, the piece rates for heeling shall apply ... ... ... ... | (see paragraph 30) | | |
| (ii) Fixing rubbers or leather substitute already shaped to the heel when there is no removal of lift or top piece and no building up ... ... | 2 | 1½ | 1½ |
| (iii) Solutioning rubber or leather substitute heels (when nails or screws also used), additional to the rates for the work specified in (i) and (ii) above ... ... ... ... ... ... | 1 | 1 | 1 |
| (iv) Attaching revolving rubber heels without removing lifts or top piece ... ... ... | 1 | 1 | 1 |
| (v) Finishing heels when fixing of rubbers or leather substitute is not combined with heeling | 1 | 1 | 1 |

(2) The rates set out in this paragraph do not apply to (a) other rubber soles for which the worker shall be paid the piece rates specified in paragraph 1 (1) (b) (ii), or (b) rubber tips, the rates for which are set out in paragraph 35.

## G.—PIECE RATES FOR CREPE WORK

68. The piece rates for crepe work are set out in the following Table:—

| | Men's | Ladies' | Youths' 2–5½ | Boys' and Girls' 11–1½ | Boys' and Girls' 7–10½ |
|---|---|---|---|---|---|
| Column ... | 1 | 2 | 3 | 4 | 5 |
| | Per pair s. d. | Per pair s. d. | Per pair s. d. | Per pair s. d. | Per pair s. d. |
| (1) THROUGH SOLE | | | | | |
| (*a*) Stripping, levelling and filling ... | 5½ | 4½ | 4½ | 3¼ | 3 |
| (*b*) Preparing and solutioning bottoms | 2½ | 2½ | 2½ | 2 | 1¾ |
| (*c*) Solutioning new middle soles ... | 1¾ | 1¼ | 1¼ | 1 | 1 |
| (*d*) Fixing and hammering down middles ... ... ... ... | 2¾ | 1¾ | 1¾ | 1¼ | 1 |
| (*e*) Solutioning outsoles and middles | 2½ | 2¼ | 2¼ | 1½ | 1¼ |
| (*f*) Fixing and hammering down outsoles ... ... ... ... | 2½ | 2¼ | 2¼ | 2 | 1½ |
| (*g*) Rounding both middles and outsoles ... ... ... ... | 4 | 3½ | 3½ | 2½ | 2 |
| | 1 9½ | 1 6 | 1 6 | 1 1½ | 11½ |
| (2) HALF-SOLE | | | | | |
| (*a*) Stripping, levelling, filling and skiving ... ... ... ... | 4½ | 3½ | 3½ | 2¾ | 2¼ |
| (*b*) Preparing and solutioning bottoms | 1¾ | 1¼ | 1¼ | 1 | 1 |
| (*c*) Solutioning crepe middle soles ... | 1 | 1 | 1 | ¾ | ¾ |
| (*d*) Fixing and hammering down middles ... ... ... ... | 1¾ | 1¼ | 1¼ | 1¼ | 1 |
| (*e*) Solutioning outsoles and middles | 2¼ | 1¾ | 1¾ | 1¼ | 1 |
| (*f*) Fixing and hammering down outsoles ... ... ... ... | 1¾ | 1¾ | 1¾ | 1¼ | 1 |
| (*g*) Rounding outsoles and middles... | 3 | 3 | 3 | 2½ | 2 |
| | 1 4 | 1 1½ | 1 1½ | 10¾ | 9 |
| (3) HEEL | | | | | |
| (*a*) Scouring and levelling old heel... | 2½ | 2 | 2 | 1¼ | 1 |
| (*b*) Solutioning old heel ... ... | ¾ | ½ | ½ | ½ | ¼ |
| (*c*) Solutioning new top pieces ... | ¾ | ½ | ½ | ½ | ¼ |
| (*d*) Fixing and hammering down top pieces ... ... ... ... | ½ | ½ | ½ | ½ | ½ |
| (*e*) Rounding by hand ... ... | ¾ | ¾ | ¾ | ¾ | ¾ |
| | 5¼ | 4¼ | 4¼ | 3½ | 2¾ |
| (4) TOE PIECES OR SIDE PIECES | | | | | |
| (*a*) Stripping, levelling and skiving old soles ... ... ... ... | 2¾ | 2¼ | 2¼ | 2 | 1½ |
| (*b*) Fitting piece of new middle sole | 1¼ | 1 | 1 | 1 | ¾ |
| (*c*) Attaching toe or side piece ... | 1½ | 1½ | 1½ | 1½ | 1¼ |
| (*d*) Rounding by hand ... ... | ¾ | ¾ | ¾ | ½ | ½ |
| (*e*) Hammering down by hand ... | ¾ | ¾ | ¾ | ½ | ½ |
| | 7 | 6¼ | 6¼ | 5½ | 4½ |

| | Per pair d. |
|---|---|
| (5) EXTRAS ON CREPE WORK | |
| (*a*) Rands, joint to joint, solutioned, fixed and pared to sole ... ... | 7 |
| (*b*) Rands, joint to joint, frictioned, fixed and pared to sole ... ... | 4 |
| (*c*) Rands, full, solutioned, fixed and pared to sole ... ... ... ... | 10½ |
| (*d*) Rands, full, frictioned, fixed and pared to sole ... ... ... ... | 7 |
| (*e*) All round welts, solutioned, turned down and pared to sole ... ... | 10½ |
| (*f*) Building heels by single press cut lifts ... ... ... ... ... | 2 |
| (*g*) Wedge shape lifts ... ... ... ... ... ... ... | 2 |
| (*h*) Attaching ready-built heels (solutioned) ... ... ... ... ... | 2 |

## H.—REPAIRS TO UPPERS

### 69. BACK STRAPS

(a) Completed work machined:
  (i) When not put under seat:
  Up to 4 inches, 2½d. each.
  Over 4 inches, 1d. each per inch or part thereof extra.

  (ii) When put under seat:
  Up to 4 inches, 4d. each.
  Over 4 inches, 1d. each per inch or part thereof extra.

  (iii) When stabbed to seat:
  Up to 4 inches, 5d. each.
  Over 4 inches, 1d. each per inch or part thereof extra.

(b) Completed work solutioned:
  2d. each additional to the rates for machined work set out in (a) of this paragraph.

70. The piece rates for PATCHES (other than seat patches) are set out in the following Table:—

|  | Each |
|---|---|
|  | d. |
| (a) Patches machined (when not soled): | |
| (i) If neither sewn to sole nor put under ... ... | 4 |
| (ii) If put under sole ... ... ... ... ... | 6 |
| (iii) If sewn down to sole or welt ... ... ... | 7 |
| (b) Patches machined (when to be soled): | |
| (i) If neither sewn to sole nor put under ... ... | 4 |
| (ii) If put under sole ... ... ... ... ... | 4½ |
| (iii) If sewn down to sole or welt ... ... ... | 7 |
| (c) Patches solutioned: to be paid at the rates for machined work in (a) and (b) of this Table with the addition of | 2 |
| (d) Lasted in or put under (when to be soled) ... ... | 1 |
| (e) Put under (when not soled) ... ... ... | 2 |
| (f) Sewn down to sole or welt only ... ... ... | 3 |

(g) Hand stabbed on, 2½d. each extra to the rates for machined work set out in this Table.

(h) Saddle or cross patches to be paid for as two patches.

71. The piece rates for SEAT PATCHES are set out in the following Table:—

| Column 1 | Column 2 | Column 3 |
|---|---|---|
| — | Men's (all sizes) and youths' (sizes 2 to 5½) | Ladies' and other sizes |
| | Each s. d. | Each s. d. |
| Completed work: | | |
| (a) Machined and lasted in: | | |
|   (i) Half way round heel or less | 7 | 6 |
|   (ii) Over half way round heel ... | 1　1 | 11 |
| (b) Machined and sewn down to seat: | | |
|   (i) Half way round heel or less | 9 | 7 |
|   (ii) Over half way round heel ... | 1　4 | 1　1 |
| (c) Solutioned on and lasted in: | | |
|   (i) Half way round heel or less | 9 | 8 |
|   (ii) Over half way round heel ... | 1　5 | 1　3 |
| (d) Solutioned on and sewn down to seat: | | |
|   (i) Half way round heel or less | 11 | 9 |
|   (ii) Over half way round heel ... | 1　8 | 1　5 |
| Separate operations: | | |
| (e) Shaping, fitting and machining: | | |
|   (i) Half way round heel or less | 3½ | 3½ |
|   (ii) Over half way round heel ... | 6 | 6 |
| (f) Shaping, fitting and solutioning: | | |
|   (i) Half way round heel or less | 6 | 6 |
|   (ii) Over half way round heel ... | 10 | 10 |
| (g) Lasting-in: | | |
|   (i) Half way round heel or less | 4 | 4 |
|   (ii) Over half way round heel ... | 8 | 7 |
| (h) Sewing down to seat: | | |
|   (i) Half way round heel or less | 6 | 4 |
|   (ii) Over half way round heel ... | 1　3 | 1　0 |

Hand stabbed on, 5d. each extra to the rates for machined work set out in this Table.

72. The piece rates for TOE CAPS are set out in the following Table:—

| Column 1 | Column 2 | Column 3 |
|---|---|---|
| — | Men's (all sizes) and youths' (sizes 2 to 5½) | Ladies' and other sizes |
| | Per pair s. d. | Per pair s. d. |
| (a) Toe caps machined and lasted in: | | |
|   (i) When boots are soled | 10 | 8 |
|   (ii) When boots are not soled | 1　3 | 1　0 |
|   (iii) When boots are made longer (including piecing the insoles) | 1　10 | 1　6 |
| (b) Toe caps, solutioned: to be paid at the rates for machined work in (a) of this Table with the addition of | 2 | 2 |
| (c) Lasted in only: | | |
|   (i) When boots are soled | 6 | 4½ |
|   (ii) When boots are not soled | 1　2 | 9 |
|   (iii) When boots are made longer (including piecing the insoles) | 1　6 | 1　0 |
| (d) When sewn down to sole or welt, machined ... | 1　0 | 10 |
| (e) When sewn down to sole or welt, solutioned... | 1　5 | 1　2 |
| (f) Sewn down only | 9 | 6 |

(g) When caps are sewn in under welt, the appropriate rates specified in paragraph 59 are to be paid in addition to the rates in (a), (b) and (c) of this Table.

(h) Toe caps fitted and machined only, 3½d. per pair; if solutioned only, 5½d. per pair.

(i) All work when uppers are pulled up to joint for re-capping is to be paid for as lasting vamps with caps as set out in paragraph 74.

(j) Toe caps of waxed kips, waxed splits and heavy chrome leathers, 2d. each extra.

## 73. TOE PUFFS

(a) Toe puffs when not re-capped to be paid for as toe caps.

(b) When toe puffs are put in and the material is not prepared for the worker, an extra of 2d. per pair shall apply in addition to the rates for toe caps.

74. The piece rates for VAMPS (re-vamping) are set out in the following Table:—

| Column 1 | Column 2 | Column 3 | Column 4 |
|---|---|---|---|
| — | Men's (all sizes) and youths' (sizes 2 to 5½) | Ladies' | Other sizes |
| | Per pair<br>s. d. | Per pair<br>s. d. | Per pair<br>s. d. |
| (a) Vamps machined and fitted ... | 11 | 9 | 7 |
| If solutioned, extra ... ... | 6 | 6 | 5 |
| (b) Lasting ... ... ... ... | 11 | 10 | 8 |
| (c) Sewing down to sole or welt ... | 1 4 | 1 2 | 1 0 |

(d) When vamps are sewn in under welt, the appropriate rates specified in paragraph 59 are to be paid in addition to the rates in (a), (b) and (c) of this Table.

(e) Toe capped vamps:
Machined and fitted, 1d. per pair ... ... ⎫ extra to the rates in (a), (b) and
Lasted in, 1d. per pair ... ... ... ... ⎬ (c) of this Table.
Sewn down through welt, 2½d. per pair ... ⎭

(f) Lasting vamps of single soled boots, when being soled, 2½d. per pair less.

## I.—SURGICAL REPAIRING AND EXTRAS

75. The piece rates for repairing set out in this Part of this Schedule apply to surgical repairing. The additional extras provided in paragraphs 77 and 78 for bespoke hand sewn surgical making apply also to bespoke hand sewn surgical repairing.

## PART X

### PIECE RATES FOR MALE OR FEMALE WORKERS EMPLOYED ON BESPOKE MAKING BESPOKE HAND SEWN WORK (INCLUDING BESPOKE HAND SEWN SURGICAL WORK)

76.—(1) Subject to the provisions of this Part of this Schedule, the piece rates applicable to male or female workers employed on the bespoke making of bespoke hand sewn work (including bespoke hand sewn surgical work) are set out in the following Table.

(2) Where surgical work is not hand stitched by the maker, the rates for completed work shall be reduced by an amount equal to the appropriate rate for "hand stitching" specified in Column 7 of the said Table.

(3) Where surgical work is not finished by the maker, the rates for completed work shall be reduced by an amount equal to the appropriate rate for "finishing by hand alone" specified in Column 8 of the said Table.

(4) In this Part of this Schedule, the expression "groundwork" includes the making of all boots and shoes of black leathers (other than patent) whether made with or without toecaps, puffs, or box, block or stiffened toes.

### GROUND WORK

| Column 1 | Column 2 | Column 3 | Column 4 | Column 5 | Column 6 | Column 7 | Column 8 |
|---|---|---|---|---|---|---|---|
| | | | Work on sectional system | | | | |
| | Completed work | Lasting-up (tacking on, rounding and holeing insoles, including preparing stiffeners and toe puffs and trimming uppers out (for sewer) | Hand sewing (including preparing and setting up of welts) | Rounding (fill up bottom, round sole, channel) | Heeling, closing channels, building heel, getting ready for finishing | Hand stitching | Finishing by hand alone |
| | Per pair s. d. | Per pair s. d. | Per pair s. d. | Per pair s. d. | Per pair s. d. | Per pair s. d. | Per pair s. d. |
| (a) MEN'S, LADIES' AND YOUTHS' LONG WORK: Napoleon, jockey or riding boots, Long Wellingtons, Short Wellingtons, Field Boots ... ... | 40  2 | 6  2 | 5  8 | 4  3½ | 3  9½ | 8  1 | 7  6 |

| Column 1 | Column 2 | Column 3 | Column 4 | Column 5 | Column 6 | Column 7 | Column 8 |
|---|---|---|---|---|---|---|---|
| | | Work on sectional system | | | | | |
| | Completed work | Lasting-up (tacking on, rounding and holeing insoles, including preparing stiffeners and toe puffs and trimming uppers out for sewer) | Hand sewing (including preparing and setting up of welts) | Rounding (fill up bottom, round sole, channel) | Heeling, closing channels, building heel, getting ready for finishing | Hand stitching | Finishing by hand alone |
| | Per pair s. d. | Per pair s. d. | Per pair s. d. | Per pair s. d. | Per pair s. d. | Per pair s. d. | Per pair s. d. |
| (b) MEN'S, LADIES' AND YOUTHS' SHORT WORK: | | | | | | | |
| Boots and Shoes ... ... ... | 33 4 | 4 10 | 4 10 | 3 0 | 3 3 | 6 6 | 7 6 |
| (c) BOYS' AND GIRLS': | | | | | | | |
| Boots and Shoes ... ... ... | 23 1 | 3 5½ | 3 3½ | 2 1 | 2 5 | 4 0½ | 5 1 |
| (d) INFANTS': | | | | | | | |
| Boots and Shoes under size 9 ... ... | 20 1¾ | 2 10 | 2 10 | 1 7 | 2 3 | 3 7 | 4 10 |
| (e) Chrome leather soles in hand stitched work, extra | 2 0 | — | — | 6¼ | — | 1 0 | 5¼ |
| (f) Outsizes (i.e. men's size 11 and over, ladies' size 8 and over), extra ... ... ... | 1 8 | 3 | 3 | 3 | 3 | 3 | 3 |

# EXTRAS TO GROUND WORK

77. The extras set out in the following Table apply to the piece rates specified in paragraph 76:—

| Column 1 | Completed work — Column 2 | Work on sectional system | | | | | |
|---|---|---|---|---|---|---|---|
| | | Lasting — Column 3 | Hand sewing — Column 4 | Rounding — Column 5 | Heeling — Column 6 | Hand stitching — Column 7 | Finishing by hand — Column 8 |
| | Per pair s. d. | Per pair s. d. | Per pair s. d. | Per pair s. d. | Per pair s. d. | Per pair s. d. | Per pair s. d. |
| **(a) MEN'S LONG WORK:** | | | | | | | |
| (1) Ham or thigh boots | 2 3½ | 8 | 5½ | 3½ | 3½ | 3½ | 3½ |
| (2) Patent uppers or fronts: | | | | | | | |
|    When patent calf used | 3 6 | 2 1½ | 9 | — | — | — | 7½ |
|    When patent leathers other than patent calf used | 3 1½ | 1 11 | 9 | — | — | — | 5½ 1 |
| (3) Spur boxes | 4 11½ | — | — | — | 3 10½ | — | 1 |
| (4) Stabbing seats | 2 4 | — | — | — | — | 1 1 | 2 |
| (5) Middles to field boots | 1 8½ | — | — | 5½ | — | — | — |
| (6) Stiff leg | 1 11½ | — | — | — | — | — | — |
| (7) White, coloured or velvet finished leathers, whether covers are used or not (employer to find material for covers) | 3 5½ | 8 | 4½ | 4½ | 4½ | 10 | 10 |
| (8) Other extras as set out in paragraphs 78 and 81 | | | | | | | |
| **(b) MEN'S SHORT WORK:** | | | | | | | |
| (1) Patent uppers: | | | | | | | |
|    When patent calf used | 2 11½ | 10 | 5½ | 2½ | 2½ | 7½ | 7½ |
|    When patent leathers other than patent calf used | 2 6½ | 9 | 5½ | 2 | 2 | 6½ | 5½ 2 |
| (2) Crupp uppers | 1 0 | 2½ | 2 | 1 | 1 | 3½ | 2 |
| (3) Patent golosh: | | | | | | | |
|    When patent calf used | 2 5½ | 10 | 3½ | 2½ | 2½ | 5½ | 5½ |
|    When patent leathers other than patent calf used | 1 11 | 7½ | 3½ | 2½ | 2½ | 3½ | 3½ |

| Column 1 | Completed work<br>Column 2<br>Per pair s. d. | Work on sectional system: Lasting<br>Column 3<br>Per pair s. d. | Hand sewing<br>Column 4<br>Per pair s. d. | Rounding<br>Column 5<br>Per pair s. d. | Heeling<br>Column 6<br>Per pair s. d. | Hand stitching<br>Column 7<br>Per pair s. d. | Finishing by hand<br>Column 8<br>Per pair s. d. |
|---|---|---|---|---|---|---|---|
| (4) Patent vamp: | | | | | | | |
| When patent calf used ... ... ... | 1 4 | 9 | 3½ | — | — | 3½ | — |
| When patent leathers other than patent calf used... ... ... ... | 1 2½ | 7½ | 3½ | — | — | 3½ | — |
| (5) Patent toe cap: | | | | | | | |
| When patent calf used ... ... ... | 11½ | 6½ | 2½ | — | — | 2½ | — |
| When patent leathers other than patent calf used... ... ... ... | 8½ | 4½ | 2 | — | — | 2 | — |
| (6) Patent back golosh: | | | | | | | |
| When patent calf used ... ... ... | 1 0½ | 6½ | 2 | — | — | 2 | 2 |
| When patent leathers other than patent calf used... ... ... ... | 8½ | 2½ | 2 | — | — | 2 | 2 |
| (7) Cloth leg ... ... ... ... | 1 0½ | 2½ | 2 | 2 | 2 | 2 | 2 |
| (8) Wing toe cap ... ... ... ... | 11½ | 8 | 3½ | — | — | — | — |
| (9) Middle soles, through ... ... ... | 2 4 | — | — | 9 | — | 1 1½ | 5½ |
| (10) Middle soles to joint ... ... ... | 1 4½ | — | — | 5½ | — | 9 | 2 |
| (11) Welts from ¼ inch to ⅜ inch in width ... | 1 0 | — | 4½ | 2 | — | 2 | 3½ |
| (12) Welts over ⅜ inch in width ... ... ... | 1 11½ | — | 9 | 3½ | — | 3½ | 7½ |
| (13) Bevel clumps ... ... ... ... | 2 11½ | — | — | 1 11½ | — | — | 1 0 |
| (14) Square clumps ... ... ... ... | 2 4 | — | — | 1 6 | — | — | 10 |
| (15) Heels, for each ¼ inch over and above 1¼ inches per pair ... ... ... ... | 6½ | — | — | — | 4½ | — | 2 |
| (16) Seats welted or sewn ... ... ... | 2 8 | — | 1 0 | 5½ | — | 9 | 5½ |
| (17) Seats braced ... ... ... ... | 6 | — | 6 | — | — | — | — |
| (18) Heels seats sewn down ... ... ... | 6 | — | — | — | 6 | — | — |
| (19) Seats randed ... ... ... ... | 2 8 | — | 1 0 | 5½ | — | 9 | 5½ |
| (20) German seats... ... ... ... | 2 6 | — | 1 0 | — | 9 | 5½ | 3½ |
| (21) Spur boxes ... ... ... ... | 4 11½ | — | — | — | 3 10½ | — | 1 1 |
| (22) Sock linings sewn in ... ... ... | 2 4½ | 1 3½ | 1 1 | — | — | — | — |
| (23) Arched insoles ... ... ... ... | 2 0 | 2 0 | — | — | — | — | — |
| (24) Inserted rubberettes or iron tips ... | 6½ | — | — | — | 4½ | — | 2 |
| (25) Stitching aloft and bunked ... ... ... | 1 3 | — | — | — | — | 7½ | 7½ |
| (26) French corks ... ... ... ... | 6 11 | 6 0 | 11 | — | — | — | — |

| Column 1 | Completed work<br>Column 2 | Work on sectional system<br>Lasting<br>Column 3 | Hand sewing<br>Column 4 | Rounding<br>Column 5 | Heeling<br>Column 6 | Hand stitching<br>Column 7 | Finishing by hand<br>Column 8 |
|---|---|---|---|---|---|---|---|
| | Per pair<br>s. d. | Per pair<br>s. d. | Per pair<br>s. d. | Per pair<br>s. d. | Per pair<br>s. d. | Per pair<br>s. d. | Per pair<br>s. d. |
| (27) Mock corks ... ... ... ... ... | 5 11 | 5 0 | 11 | — | — | — | — |
| (28) Inside corks, not surgical ... ... | 2 6 | 2 6 | — | — | — | — | — |
| (29) White, coloured or velvet finished leathers whether covers are used or not (employer to find material for covers) ... ... | 2 0 | 5½ | 2 | 2 | 3½ | 5½ | 5½ |
| (30) Full bradding or nailing ... ... ... | 1 2½ | — | — | — | — | — | — |
| (31) Bradding or nailing toe and joint ... ... | 7½ | — | — | — | — | — | — |
| (32) Clinkered round ... ... ... ... | 1 2½ | — | — | — | — | — | — |
| (33) Clinkered round toes ... ... ... | 7½ | — | — | — | — | — | — |
| (34) Other extras as set out in paragraphs 78 and 81. | | | | | | | |
| (*c*) LADIES' LONG WORK: | | | | | | | |
| (1) Patent uppers or fronts: | | | | | | | |
| When patent calf used ... ... ... | 2 8 | 1 11 | 4½ | — | — | — | 4½ |
| When patent leathers other than patent calf used... ... ... ... ... ... | 2 4 | 1 7 | 4½ | — | — | — | 4½ |
| (2) Other extras the same as for "Men's long work" as set out in this paragraph and in paragraphs 78 and 81. | | | | | | | |
| (*d*) LADIES' SHORT WORK: | | | | | | | |
| (1) Cloth leg up to 7 inches ... ... ... | 1 0½ | 2½ | 2 | 2 | 2 | 2 | 2 |
| (2) Cloth leg over 7 inches ... ... ... | 1 6½ | 3½ | 4½ | 2 | 2 | 2 | 4½ |
| (3) Middle soles ... ... ... ... | 1 0 | — | — | 3½ | — | 6½ | 2 |
| (4) Welts above ½ inch in width ... ... | 1 0 | — | 4½ | 2 | — | 2 | 3½ |
| (5) Heels above 1⅜ inches in height, for each ¼ inch or part of ¼ inch ... ... ... | 6½ | — | — | — | 4½ | — | 2 |
| (6) French corks ... ... ... ... ... | 5 11 | 5 0 | 11 | — | — | — | — |
| (7) Mock corks ... ... ... ... ... | 4 8 | 4 0½ | 7½ | — | — | — | — |
| (8) Inside corks, not surgical ... ... | 1 11½ | 1 11½ | — | — | — | — | — |
| (9) White, coloured or velvet finished leathers whether covers are used or not (employer to find material for covers) ... ... | 1 4½ | 3½ | 2 | 2 | 2 | 3½ | 3½ |

78.—(1) Additional extras to ground work for bespoke hand sewn surgical work (including repairing) are set out in the following Table.

(2) For the purposes of (a) to (f) all measurements of the heights of corks are to be taken from the centre of the heel base or under the joint, whichever is the greater.

| Column 1 | Column 2 | Column 3 | Column 4 | Column 5 | Column 6 | Column 7 |
|---|---|---|---|---|---|---|
| | Completed work | Work on sectional system | | | | |
| | | Preparing work ready for lasting (excluding covering) | Covering | Lasting | Sewing | Finishing by hand |
| | Each s. d. | Each s. d. | Each d. | Each s. d. | Each s. d. | Each d. |
| (a) Outside through cork (box randed): | | | | | | |
| (1) Rising to 1 inch | 18 8 | 6 10 | — | 4 6½ | 7 3½ | — |
| (2) For every additional half-inch or part thereof | 1 8 | 1 1 | — | 3½ | 3½ | 3½ |
| (3) Bridge or arched waists, add | 1 2½ | — | — | — | 11 | — |
| (4) Steel bridge plate, fixing | 5½ | — | — | — | — | — |
| (b) Outside through cork (randed other than box randed): | | | | | | |
| (1) Rising to 1 inch | 14 7 | 4 10½ | — | 2 11 | 6 9½ | — |
| (2) For every additional half-inch or part thereof | 1 8 | 1 1 | — | 3½ | 3½ | 3½ |
| (3) Bridge or arched waists, add | 1 2½ | — | — | — | 11 | 3½ |
| (4) Steel bridge plate, fixing | 5½ | — | — | — | — | — |
| c) Outside cork forepart: | | | | | | |
| (1) Rising from joint to 1 inch | 10 6 | 3 2½ | — | 2 1½ | 5 2 | — |
| (2) For every additional half-inch or part thereof | 1 0 | 8 | — | 2 | 2 | — |
| (d) Outside heel cork, cased: | | | | | | |
| (1) Rising to 1 inch | 3 6 | 1 8 | — | 9 | 1 1 | — |
| (2) For every additional half-inch or part thereof | 8½ | 4½ | — | 2 | 2 | — |
| (e) Through inside corks, covered: | | | | | | |
| (1) Rising to 1 inch: | | | | | | |
| (i) Loose | 8 8 | 5 5½ | 11 | 1 10 | 5½ | — |
| (ii) Sewn in | 9 4½ | 3 10½ | 11 | 2 9 | 1 10 | — |
| (2) For every additional half-inch or part thereof | 2 3½ | 1 1 | 2 | 9 | 3½ | — |

| Column 1 | Completed work | Work on sectional system | | | | |
|---|---|---|---|---|---|---|
| | | Preparing work ready for lasting (excluding covering) | Covering | Lasting | Sewing | Finishing by hand |
| | Column 2 | Column 3 | Column 4 | Column 5 | Column 6 | Column 7 |
| | Each s. d. | Each s. d. | Each d. | Each s. d. | Each s. d. | Each d. |
| (f) Inside heel cork, covered: | | | | | | |
| (1) Rising to 1 inch: | | | | | | |
| (i) Loose | 5 11 | 3 2½ | 9 | 1 8 | 3½ | — |
| (ii) Sewn in | 6 10½ | 3 3 | 9 | 1 11½ | 11 | — |
| (2) For every additional half-inch or part thereof | 1 0 | 4½ | 2 | 3½ | 2 | — |
| (g) Extra heel, loose cork fitted inside up to joint | 3 6 | — | — | — | — | — |
| (h) Cork fillers for Chopart's boots or false toe parts: | | | | | | |
| (1) 2 inches long and over | 3 0 | 2 3 | 9 | — | — | — |
| (2) Under 2 inches long | 1 5 | 9 | 8 | — | — | — |
| (i) Fitting in brace or tack | 2 6 | — | — | 1 6 | 1 0 | — |

*(Column 7 below: Each s. d.)*

| Column 1 | Column 2 | Column 3 | Column 4 | Column 5 | Column 6 | Column 7 Each s. d. |
|---|---|---|---|---|---|---|
| (j) Fitting heel round fixed iron heel stop (exclusive of riveting) | | | | | | 1 0 |
| (k) Stiffeners: | | | | | | |
| (1) High stiffeners carried above ankle | | | | | | 1 2½ |
| (2) Double high stiffeners to cover each side of ankle | | | | | | 1 9 |
| (3) Long stiffeners | | | | | | 5½ |
| (l) Completely filled in waist from heel to joint, completed job (if not finished by maker, 7d. each less) | | | | | | 3 6 |
| (m)(1) Meta bars (outside) | | | | | | 10 |
| (2) Meta bars (concealed) | | | | | | 1 2½ |
| (n)(1) Wedges or layers (either forepart or heel), sewn in | | | | | | 5½ |
| (2) Wedges or layers riveted on or sewn in made-up boot, on forepart, when not soled | | | | | | 10 |
| (3) Wedges or layers in made-up boot, on heel, when not heeled | | | | | | 7½ |
| (4) Through wedges or layers from forepart to heel (including making up waist on stock boots) | | | | | | 2 8 |
| (5) Where the wedge or layer sewn in is over ¼ inch thick at the thickest point, 2¼d. additional to above rates. | | | | | | |

|  |  | Each s. d. |
|---|---|---|
| (o) (1) "T" straps | ... | 5½ |
| (2) "T" straps if stabbed on to finished boot | ... | 10 |
| (p) "D" straps | ... | 5½ |
| (q) Buckles | ... | 4½ |
| (r) Sponge rubber insoles, cut, cemented to sock, inserted and, if required, cemented to leather insole | ... | 1 6 |
| (s) Valgus or Meta rubber pads with socks, fixing | ... | 10 |
| (t) Mechanical appliances: | | |
| (1) Concealed ankle support springs (exclusive of riveting, see item (8) below) | ... | 1 9 |
| (2) Inserted metal arch supports (exclusive of riveting, see item (8) below) | ... | 1 9 |
| (3) Single or double sockets and fixed shoe pieces (exclusive of riveting, see item (8) below) | ... | 1 9 |
| (4) Sole or foot springs (exclusive of riveting, see item (8) below) | ... | 10 |
| (5) Fixing to heel and building round undetachable leg appliance | ... | 3 6 |
| (6) Riveting in socket, single or double | ... | 9 |
| (7) Taking down heel, fixing in socket by riveting, rebuilding heel and working over socket | ... | 2 6 |
| (8) For the work of riveting referred to in items (1) to (4) above, the worker must be paid the piece rates specified in paragraph 1 (1) (b) (ii). | | |

|  | Benching Each s. d. | Finishing Each d. |
|---|---|---|
| (u) Shaped oblique or elongated heels: | | |
| (1) For an elongation up to and including ¼ inch ... (No extra) | | |
| (2) For an elongation exceeding ¼ inch but not exceeding 1 inch | 4½ | 2 |
| (3) For an elongation exceeding 1 inch but not extending more than half-way from the position of the ordinary heel to the joint | 1 1 | 3½ |
| (4) For an elongation extending more than half-way from the position of the ordinary heel to the joint | 2 1½ | 7½ |
| (v) For any extra work involved in the building or re-building of a heel from the seat which is necessitated by the floating out of the heel above ¼ inch from the ordinary contour of the heel | 4½ | 2 |

(w) Converting stock boot into surgical boot to be paid for on the basis of new work.

|  | Each Side d. |
|---|---|
| (x) Sewing waist by hand where foreparts are stitched by machine | 2 |

## BESPOKE PEGGED WORK

79. The piece rates for all completed bespoke pegged work are 2s. 0d. per pair less than the rates for completed bespoke hand sewn work as set out in paragraph 76. The piece rates for extras to bespoke pegged work are the same as those set out in paragraphs 77 and 78 for the extras to hand sewn work.

## BESPOKE RIVETED WORK

80. The piece rates for bespoke riveted work are set out in the following Table:—

| Column 1 | Men's | Ladies' and youths' | Boys' and girls', sizes 11 to 1½ | Boys' and girls', sizes 7 to 10½ |
|---|---|---|---|---|
| | Column 2 | Column 3 | Column 4 | Column 5 |
| | Per pair s. d. | Per pair s. d. | Per pair s. d. | Per pair s. d. |
| (a) Benched (stuff cut by machinery) ... ... | 2  4 | 2  1 | 1  9 | 1  6 |
| (b) Finished by hand throughout | 1  4 | 10 | 7 | 6 |
| (c) Finished by hand (edges and heels only) ... ... | 10 | 7 | 5 | 4½ |
| (d) Extras:— | | | | |
| (i) Nailing or bradding soles by hand ... | 7 | 7 | 5 | 5 |
| (ii) Stuff not press cut ... | 4½ | 4½ | 3½ | 3½ |

(e) Light Bluchers (no cap):—
    (i) Putting-up ... ... ... ... ... ...   1s. 9d. per pair.
    (ii) Nailing or bradding ... ... ... ... ...   5d. per pair.
    (iii) Finishing by hand (edges and heels only) ... ...   9½d. per pair.

## PART XI

## GENERAL

81.—(1) For each try on, or re-try on, outworkers shall be paid 1s. 4d. extra for one boot or shoe or pair of boots or shoes, and indoor workers, 8d. extra for one boot or shoe or pair of boots or shoes. These rates do not include bracing. Alterations (other than operations to which general minimum piece rates are applicable) are to be paid at the piece rates specified in paragraph 1 (1) (b) (ii).

(2) Scafe or similar soles, 2s. 6d. per pair extra to the rates for completed work set out in paragraphs 76, 77 and 78.

(3) The minimum rates of wages specified in this Schedule do not include the cost of grindery.

82. Rates per pair—where a piece rate is specified in this Schedule as a rate per pair one-half of such rate shall be payable where only one boot or shoe is involved.

## DEFINITIONS

83. (a) " German seat " is a piece of butt leather sewn round the heel.

(b) " Inside corks " are extra insoles of cork which are made with the boot.

(c) " Shaped toe piece " is a toe piece that is larger than the ordinary toe bit and extends along the side up to the joint.

(d) " Underlays " are inserted and slotted toe bits or side bits.

(e) " Grindery " is all material apart from tools used by the worker in the making or repairing of leather footwear.

(f) " Box randed "—a box rand is a rand which is made from a piece of bend, butt, fore-end, shoulder or belly leather.

Article 3 **SCHEDULE 2**

**HOLIDAYS AND HOLIDAY REMUNERATION**

The Wages Regulation (Boot and Shoe Repairing) (Holidays) Order 1967**(a)** (Order D. (145)) shall have effect as if in the Schedule thereto for sub-paragraph (2)(a) of paragraph 2 (which relates to customary holidays) there were substituted the following:—

"(2) The said customary holidays are:—
(a) in England and Wales

(i) Christmas Day, Boxing Day, Good Friday, Easter Monday, Whit Monday (or where another day is substituted therefor by national proclamation, that day), August Bank Holiday and any day proclaimed as a public holiday or additional bank holiday, or

(ii) in the case of each of the named holidays, such other day (not being a day on which a rest period occurs) as may be substituted therefor by the employer by a notice posted in the factory throughout the three weeks immediately preceding the holiday for which it is substituted;"

---

## EXPLANATORY NOTE

*(This Note is not part of the Order.)*

This Order has effect from 23rd April 1969. Schedule 1 sets out the statutory minimum remuneration payable in substitution for that fixed by the Wages Regulation (Boot and Shoe Repairing) Order 1967 (Order D. (144)), as amended by the Wages Regulation (Boot and Shoe Repairing) (Amendment) Order 1967 (Order D. (147)) which Orders are revoked.

Schedule 2 repeats without alteration the amendment to the Wages Regulation (Boot and Shoe Repairing) (Holidays) Order 1967 (Order D. (145)), which was contained in Order D. (147).

New provisions are printed in italics.

---

**(a)** S.I. 1967/641 (1967 I, p. 1967).

STATUTORY INSTRUMENTS

## 1969 No. 429

## OVERSEAS AID

## The International Development Association (Additional Payments) Order 1969

*Laid before the House of Commons in draft*
*Made - - - -* 18*th March* 1969
*Coming into Operation* 19*th March* 1969

Whereas it is provided in section 1(5) of the Overseas Aid Act 1968(a) that if Her Majesty's Government in the United Kingdom becomes bound by arrangements for the making of additional payments to the International Development Association, the Minister of Overseas Development may with the approval of the Treasury by order made by Statutory Instrument provide for the payment out of moneys provided by Parliament of any sums required by him for any of the purposes specified in that subsection :

Now, therefore, the Minister of Overseas Development in exercise of the powers conferred upon him by section 1 of the Overseas Aid Act 1968 and with the approval of the Treasury, hereby makes the following Order :—

**1.**—(1) This Order may be cited as the International Development Association (Additional Payments) Order 1969 and shall come into operation on 19th March 1969.

(2) In this Order—

" the Association " means the International Development Association established by the Agreement ;

" the Agreement " means the Articles of Agreement of the International Development Association dated 29th January 1960 and accepted on behalf of Her Majesty's Government in the United Kingdom on 14th September 1960 ;

the " Minister " means the Minister of Overseas Development.

(3) The Interpretation Act 1889(b) shall apply to the interpretation of, and otherwise in relation to, this Order as it applies to the interpretation of, and otherwise in relation to, an Act of Parliament.

**2.** The Minister may make payment on behalf of Her Majesty's Government in the United Kingdom out of moneys provided by Parliament of an additional contribution to the Association of a sum equivalent to fifty-one million eight hundred and forty thousand United States dollars in the weight and fineness in effect on 1st January 1960, in accordance with arrangements made between Her Majesty's said Government and the Association.

**3.** The Minister may make on behalf of Her Majesty's said Government out of moneys provided by Parliament any payment to the Association which may become payable under paragraph (*a*) of Section 2 of Article IV of the Agreement, as applied by the said arrangements.

---

(a) 1968 c. 57.  (b) 1889 c. 63.

**4.** The Minister may redeem out of moneys provided by Parliament any non-interest-bearing and non-negotiable notes or other obligations which may be issued or created by him and accepted by the Association in accordance with the said arrangements or any provision of the Agreement applied by the said arrangements.

**5.** Any sums received by Her Majesty's said Government from the Association in pursuance of the Agreement as applied by the said arrangements shall be paid into the Consolidated Fund.

18th March 1969.

*R. E. Prentice,*
**Minister of Overseas Development.**

We approve,

*Joseph Harper,*
*E. Alan Fitch,*
**Two of the Lords Commissioners**
**of Her Majesty's Treasury.**

18th March 1969.

---

## EXPLANATORY NOTE

*(This Note is not part of the Order.)*

The Overseas Aid Act 1968 section 1(5) provides that if the Government of the United Kingdom becomes bound by arrangements for the making of additional payments to the International Development Association, the Minister of Overseas Development may, with the approval of the Treasury, provide by order for the payment out of moneys provided by Parliament of any sums required by him for any of the purposes specified in that subsection.

This Order provides for the payment of a sum equivalent to U.S. $51,840,000 as an additional contribution to the Association, for the payment of any sum which may be required to maintain the foreign exchange value of that contribution, and for the redemption of non-interest-bearing and non-negotiable notes issued by the Minister in payment of that contribution. The Order further provides that certain sums which may be received by the Government of the United Kingdom from the Association shall be paid into the Consolidated Fund.

## STATUTORY INSTRUMENTS

### 1969 No. 430 (C.10) (S.31)

## SOCIAL WORK, SCOTLAND

### The Social Work (Scotland) Act 1968 (Commencement No. 1) Order 1969

*Made* - - - -                    20*th March* 1969

In exercise of the powers conferred on me by section 98 of the Social Work (Scotland) Act 1968(a) I hereby make the following order:—

**1.** This order may be cited as the Social Work (Scotland) Act 1968 (Commencement No. 1) Order 1969.

**2.** The provisions of the Social Work (Scotland) Act 1968 specified in Schedules 1 and 2 to this order shall come into operation on the dates and to the extent specified therein.

*William Ross,*
One of Her Majesty's Principal
Secretaries of State.

St. Andrew's House,
Edinburgh, 1.
20th March 1969

---

(a) 1968 c. 49.

## SCHEDULE 1

PROVISIONS COMING INTO FORCE ON 1ST APRIL 1969

| Provisions of the Act | Subject matter of provisions |
|---|---|
| Section 1(1), (2), (3) and (6) | Local authorities for the administration of the Act. |
| Section 2(1) and (3) | Establishment of social work committee. |
| Section 5 | Powers of Secretary of State. |
| Section 19 | Amendment of Children Act 1958(a). |
| Section 27(2) to (5) | Probation schemes. |
| Section 84 | Transfer of assets and liabilities. |
| Section 85 | Transfer and compensation of officers. |
| Section 90 | Orders, regulations etc. |
| Section 94 | Interpretation. |
| Section 95(2) | Repeals. |
| Section 96 | Power of Parliament of Northern Ireland to make consequential amendments of the Act. |
| Section 97(2) to the extent that it extends to Northern Ireland the application of the provisions of section 96 of the Act. | Extension of certain provisions of the Act to Northern Ireland. |
| Section 99 | Short title. |
| Schedule 1 | Amendment of Children Act 1958. |
| Schedule 6 | Transfer of assets and liabilities. |
| Schedule 9 to the extent set out in the Appendix hereto. | Repeals. |

## APPENDIX TO SCHEDULE 1

REPEALS TAKING EFFECT ON 1ST APRIL 1969

| Chapter | Short Title | Extent of Repeal |
|---|---|---|
| 12, 13 & 14 Geo. 6 c.94. | The Criminal Justice (Scotland) Act 1949 | Section 4(2) and (3). |
| 6 & 7 Eliz. 2 c.65. | The Children Act 1958 | Section 1.<br>Section 2(6) and (7). |

(a) 1958 c. 65.

## SCHEDULE 2

PROVISIONS COMING INTO FORCE ON 1st JULY 1969

| Provisions of the Act | Subject matter of provisions |
|---|---|
| Section 3(1) to (8) | The director of social work. |
| Section 7 | Advisory Council on Social Work. |
| Section 8 | Research. |
| Section 9 | Training courses and grants for training in social work. |
| Section 10 | Financial and other assistance to voluntary organisations, etc., for social work. |
| Section 60 | Control of residential and other establishments. |
| Section 62(2) | Form of application for registration. |
| Section 63 | Special provisions for registration by Secretary of State. |
| Section 87(5) | Charges for services and accommodation. |
| Section 91 | Expenses. |
| Schedule 9 to the extent set out in the Appendix hereto. | Repeals. |

## APPENDIX TO SCHEDULE 2

REPEALS TAKING EFFECT ON 1ST JULY 1969

| Chapter | Short Title | Extent of Repeal |
|---|---|---|
| 11 & 12 Geo. 6 c.43. | The Children Act 1948 | Section 44. |
| 15 & 16 Geo. 6 &1 Eliz. 2 c.61. | The Prisons (Scotland) Act 1952 | Section 18(1) to (3A). |
| 1963 c.39. | The Criminal Justice (Scotland) Act 1963 | Section 15(2). |

## EXPLANATORY NOTE

*(This Note is not part of the Order.)*

This Order brings into force the provisions of the Social Work (Scotland) Act 1968 which are set out in the Schedules to the Order. These include provisions dealing with child protection, research, training and grants to voluntary organisations and those requiring local authorities to appoint social work committees and directors of social work.

# STATUTORY INSTRUMENTS

## 1969 No. 433

## EDUCATION, ENGLAND AND WALES

### The Standards for School Premises (Middle Schools and Minor Amendments) Regulations 1969

| | |
|---|---|
| *Made* - - - | *21st March* 1969 |
| *Laid before Parliament* | *28th March* 1969 |
| *Coming into Operation* | *1st April* 1969 |

The Secretary of State for Education and Science, in exercise of the powers conferred upon him by section 10(1) of the Education Act 1944(**a**), as amended by the Secretary of State for Education and Science Order 1964(**b**), hereby makes the following regulations:—

*Citation, commencement and interpretation*

**1.**—(1) These regulations may be cited as the Standards for School Premises (Middle Schools and Minor Amendments) Regulations 1969 and shall come into operation on 1st April 1969.

(2) The Interpretation Act 1889(**c**) shall apply for the interpretation of these regulations as it applies for the interpretation of an Act of Parliament.

*Definitions*

**2.** In these regulations—

" middle school " means a school in respect of which the Secretary of State has given a direction under section 1(2) of the Education Act 1964(**d**) (classification of schools with special age limits); and

" the principal regulations " means the Standards for School Premises Regulations 1959(**e**) and references to regulations shall, except where the context otherwise requires, be construed as references to those regulations.

*Amendment of principal regulations*

**3.** The principal regulations shall have effect subject to the amendments specified in Schedule 1 to these regulations.

*Middle schools*

**4.** The principal regulations as amended by these regulations shall apply—

(*a*) to middle schools which do not admit pupils under the age of ten years as they apply to secondary schools;

(*b*) subject to Schedule 2, to other middle schools as they apply to primary schools.

---

(**a**) 1944 c. 31.
(**c**) 1889 c. 63.
(**e**) S.I. 1959/890 (1959 I, p. 1006).

(**b**) S.I. 1964/490 (1964 I, p. 800).
(**d**) 1964 c. 82.

*Regulation 3* SCHEDULE 1

AMENDMENT OF PRINCIPAL REGULATIONS

*Definitions*

1. In regulation 2 (interpretation) the definitions in paragraph (1) of " school year " and " teaching space " shall be omitted and for the words " at the beginning of the school year " in paragraph (3) there shall be substituted the words " on 1st September ".

*Primary schools*

2. In regulation 3 (sites) the proviso to paragraph (1) shall be omitted.

3. In regulation 5 (teaching accommodation) there shall be omitted—

(a) the provisos to paragraph (1); and

(b) paragraph (2).

*Secondary schools*

4. In regulation 15 (sites) paragraph (2) shall be omitted.

5. In regulation 16 (playing field accommodation)—

(a) there shall be omitted the words " aged 11–15 years inclusive " in every place where they occur;

(b) the first proviso shall be omitted; and

(c) for the fourth proviso there shall be substituted—

" Provided also that the area of the playing field accommodation may be reduced to such extent as may be approved in each case where—

(i) approved facilities for regular instruction in swimming are provided;

(ii) buildings are provided for instruction in outdoor sports."

6. In regulation 17 (teaching accommodation)—

(a) for the table there shall be substituted—

| Number of pupils aged under 16 for which the school is designed* | Appropriate teaching area per pupil (in square feet) according to the ages of pupils for whom the school is designed | | | |
| --- | --- | --- | --- | --- |
| | Aged under 11 | Aged 11 and 12 | Aged 13 and 14 | Aged 15 and over |
| Not more than 150 | | 40 | 50 | 56 |
| 151– 300... ... | 23 | | | |
| 301– 450... ... | 22 | 39 | 49 | 55 |
| 451– 520... ... | 21 | | | |
| 521– 700... ... | 20 | 38 | 48 | 54 |
| 701– 800... ... | | 37·5 | 47·5 | 53·5 |
| 801– 900... ... | | 36·5 | 46·5 | 52·5 |
| 901–1,050... ... | | 35 | 45 | 51 |
| 1,051–1,200... ... | | 34·5 | 44·5 | 50·5 |
| 1,201–1,350... ... | | 34 | 44 | 50 |
| 1,351–1,500... ... | | 33·3 | 43·3 | 49·3 |
| 1,501–1,650... ... | | 33 | 43 | 49 |
| 1,651–1,800... ... | | 32·7 | 42·7 | 48·7 |
| 1,801–1,950... ... | | 32·2 | 42·2 | 48·2 |
| 1,951–2,100... ... | | 32 | 42 | 48 |

*In the application of this table to a school designed mainly for pupils who have

attained the age of 16 this heading is to be read without the words ' aged under 16 ';"
and

(b) the provisos shall be omitted.

*Nursery schools and classes*

7. In regulation 30(1) (playroom accommodation) the proviso shall be omitted.

8. In regulation 31 (storage of clothing) there shall be omitted everything after the word " clothing ".

9. In regulation 32(1) (washing and sanitary accommodation) after the words " for every 5 children under five years of age " there shall be inserted the words " in a school or class where more than half the number of children regularly stay for a midday meal and for every 10 such children in any other school or class ".

*General requirements*

10. In regulation 51 (precautions for health and safety) after the word " construction " there shall be inserted the words " the limitation of surface flame spread ".

11. At the end of regulation 52(2) (lighting) there shall be added the following proviso—

" Provided that if in the case of any particular teaching room or space the Secretary of State is satisfied that, regard being had to its proposed use, sufficient lighting can be provided by a combination of permanent supplementary artificial lighting and daylight at less than a 2 per cent daylight factor, the minimum daylight factor shall be such lower percentage as may be approved ".

12. In regulation 56 (gas and electric power) for the words " supplies of gas and electricity are available " there shall be substituted the following words—

" it is reasonable for gas and electricity to be supplied, the premises shall be connected to such supplies and ".

## SCHEDULE 2                                    *Regulation 4(b)*

### MODIFICATION OF PRINCIPAL REGULATIONS AS AMENDED

1. The following provisions of this Schedule shall have effect for the modification of the principal regulations as amended by Schedule 1 in their application to middle schools which admit pupils under the age of ten years.

2.—(1) Regulation 3(1) shall apply for the calculation of the area of the school site subject to the addition to the appropriate area of ⅛ acre for every 60 pupils over the age of eleven years or part thereof.

(2) In regulation 3(2), after the entry relating to junior schools there shall be inserted the following—

" (d) middle schools which admit pupils under the age of ten years

| | | |
|---|---|---|
| Not more than 140 | ... | 6,600 |
| 141–280 | ... ... | 12,100 |
| 281–360 | ... ... | 18,700 |
| 361–420 | ... ... | 24,200 |
| 421–600 | ... ... | 34,200 |
| More than 600 | ... | 34,200 plus 5,000 for every 150 pupils or part thereof." |

3. Regulation 4 shall apply for the calculation of the appropriate area of playing field accommodation subject to the substitution of the following table—

" *Number of pupils aged 8 or over*     *Appropriate area*

| | | | |
|---|---|---|---|
| Not more than 150 | ... | ... | $1\frac{1}{2}$ acres |
| 151–200 | ... | ... ... | $2\frac{1}{4}$ acres |
| 201–280 | ... | ... ... | $3\frac{1}{2}$ acres |
| 281–320 | ... | ... ... | $4\frac{1}{2}$ acres |
| 321–480 | ... | ... ... | 6 acres |
| 481–600 | ... | ... ... | 7 acres |
| 601 or more | ... | ... ... | $8\frac{1}{2}$ acres" |

4. Regulation 5 shall not apply, but regulation 17 shall apply for the calculation of the area of teaching accommodation.

5. Regulation 14(1) shall apply for the calculation of the area of accommodation for meals subject to the substitution, in respect of each senior pupil, of a reference to 5 square feet for the reference to $4\frac{1}{2}$ square feet and of a reference to 10 square feet for the reference to 9 square feet.

Given under the Official Seal of the Secretary of State for Education and Science on 21st March 1969.

(L.S.)

*Edward Short,*
Secretary of State for Education and Science.

---

## EXPLANATORY NOTE

*(This Note is **not** part of the Regulations.)*

These regulations make minor amendments to the Standards for School Premises Regulations 1959 and apply those regulations to middle schools, i.e. schools which provide both primary and secondary education.

# STATUTORY INSTRUMENTS

## 1969 No. 434 (C.11)

## ROAD TRAFFIC

## The Road Traffic (Amendment) Act 1967 (Commencement No. 2) Order 1969

*Made* - - - *18th March* 1969

The Minister of Transport, in exercise of his powers under section 10(3) of the Road Traffic (Amendment) Act 1967(**a**) and of all other powers him enabling in that behalf, hereby makes the following Order :—

**1.** Section 4 of the Road Traffic (Amendment) Act 1967 shall come into operation on the 1st May 1969.

**2.** This Order may be cited as the Road Traffic (Amendment) Act 1967 (Commencement No. 2) Order 1969.

Given under the Official Seal of the Minister of Transport the 18th March 1969.

(L.S.)             *J. R. Madge,*
An Under Secretary of the
Ministry of Transport.

---

## EXPLANATORY NOTE

(*This Note is not part of the Order.*)

This Order brings into operation on 1st May 1969 section 4 of the Road Traffic (Amendment) Act 1967, which extends the requirements for certain vehicles to have test certificates, to certain vehicles which have been used on roads in Great Britain or elsewhere before being registered in Great Britain.

---

(**a**) 1967 c. 70.

## STATUTORY INSTRUMENTS

### 1969 No. 436 (S.32)

## NATIONAL HEALTH SERVICE, SCOTLAND

### The National Health Service (General Dental Services) (Scotland) Amendment (No. 2) Regulations 1969

| | | |
|---|---|---|
| *Made* - - - | *21st March* 1969 |
| *Laid before Parliament* | *28th March* 1969 |
| *Coming into Operation* | *1st April* 1969 |

In exercise of the powers conferred on me by section 39 of the National Health Service (Scotland) Act 1947(a), as amended by section 11 of the National Health Service (Amendment) Act 1949(b), and of all other powers enabling me in that behalf, I hereby make the following regulations :—

**1.**—(1) These regulations may be cited as the National Health Service (General Dental Services) (Scotland) Amendment (No. 2) Regulations 1969 and shall come into operation on 1st April 1969.

(2) The Interpretation Act 1889(c) applies for the interpretation of these regulations as it applies for the interpretation of an Act of Parliament.

(3) Expressions used in these regulations shall have the same meanings as in the principal regulations.

**2.** The National Health Service (General Dental Services) (Scotland) Regulations 1966(d) as amended (e) (referred to in these regulations as "the principal regulations") shall be further amended as follows :—

(1) Regulation 30 (which provides for additional payments to practitioners) shall cease to have effect.

(2) For Parts I to VI of Schedule 5 (which prescribe the scale of fees for treatment) there shall be substituted the provisions set out in the Schedule to these regulations.

**3.** Where an advice of payment from the Board to a Council is in respect of a contract or arrangement entered into or made on or after 1st April 1969, the Council shall pay to a practitioner in addition to the fees authorised under regulation 27 of the principal regulations a sum equal to 3 per cent of the amount of these fees.

---

(a) 1947 c. 27.  (b) 1949 c. 93.
(c) 1889 c. 63.  (d) S.I. 1966/1449 (1966 III, p. 3802).
(e) S.I. 1967/947, 1969/254 (1967 II, p. 2898; 1969 I, p. 644).

**4.**—(1) Subject to the following provisions of this regulation, these regulations shall not apply to general dental services provided under a contract or arrangement entered into or made before 1st April 1969, and such services shall continue to be subject to the provisions of the regulations in force immediately before that date.

(2) Where an advice of payment from the Board to a Council dated on or after 1st April 1969 is in respect of a contract or arrangement entered into or made on or after 1st July 1966 and before 1st April 1969, the Council shall pay to a practitioner in addition to the fees authorised under regulation 27 of the principal regulations a sum equal to 5.6 per cent of the amount of these fees.

(3) Where an advice of payment from the Board to a Council dated on or after 1st April 1969 is in respect of a contract or arrangement entered into or made before 1st July 1966, the Council shall pay to a practitioner in addition to the fees authorised under regulation 27 of the principal regulations a sum equal to 16.7 per cent of the amount of these fees.

(4) In respect of an advice of payment from the Board to a Council dated during the period beginning with 1st January 1969 and ending with 31st March 1969, the Council shall pay to a practitioner an additional sum equal to 5.6 per cent of the amounts payable under regulations 27 and 30 of the principal regulations.


*William Ross,*
One of Her Majesty's Principal
Secretaries of State.

St. Andrew's House,
Edinburgh, 1.
21st March 1969.

## SCHEDULE
### PART I—DIAGNOSIS

1. Clinical examination and report:          ... 8s. 0d.
   Provided that:—
   (1) Only one fee shall be payable during a
       course of treatment.
   (2) No fee shall be payable:—
       (a) for an examination in respect of
           repairs to dentures for edentulous
           patients,
       (b) where the special form is used,
       (c) where treatment is restricted to
           the treatment referred to in para-
           graph 3 (2) of Part I of Schedule 1,
       (d) for a group examination in
           schools or institutions,
       (e) for an examination of a person
           aged 21 years or over if the same
           practitioner† has been paid or is
           entitled to be paid for an exami-
           nation and report on that person
           at any time during any of the
           5 months preceding the month
           during which a further examina-
           tion is made,
       (f) for an examination of a person
           under 21 years of age if the same
           practitioner† has been paid or is
           entitled to be paid for an exami-
           nation and report on that person
           made within the preceding three
           months.
   (3) in the case of a woman who is, or
       has been, pregnant and who is not
       edentulous, a fee shall be payable for
       one examination during the period of
       pregnancy and 12 months thereafter,
       additional to the examinations for
       which payment may otherwise be
       made under this item and all such
       examinations may be carried out at
       any time during the said period.

2. Radiological examination and report:
   Fees per course of treatment:—
   (a) Intra-oral films:
       1 film          ...     ...     ...     ...          8s. 0d.
       *2 films        ...     ...     ...     ...          10s. 0d.
       *Each additional film     ...     ...     2s. 6d. up to a maximum of
                                                          £1 15s. 0d.
   (b) Extra-oral films:
       *1 film         ...     ...     ...     ...          11s. 0d.
       *Each additional film     ...     ...     6s. 6d. up to a maximum of £1 4s. 0d.

Provided that a fee shall not be payable in cases in which the Board have required
the submission of the films, or in which the Board's prior approval was required
unless the films or duplicates thereof are submitted to the Board.

---

† Reference in this scale of fees to dental treatment by the same practitioner shall include
also dental treatment by his principal or the partner of either, or by the assistant of any of
them and where the practitioner is employed by a body corporate shall include treatment
by another employee of that body.

* See schedule 2 for treatment requiring prior approval.

## Part II—CONSERVATIVE TREATMENT

### A.　PERIODONTAL TREATMENT

3. Scaling, including the removal of calculus and other deposits from the teeth, and the provision of prophylactic or other necessary treatment for all ordinary or simple disorders of the gums, for persons aged 16 or over at the beginning of a course of treatment:—

    (a) Scaling and gum treatment (except cases under (b)).　　13s. 6d.

    *(b) Scaling and gum treatment to be followed by extraction of the teeth charted for scaling, gum treatment and extraction during the same course of treatment:　　Such fee as the Board may approve, not exceeding 13s. 6d.

*Provided that no fee shall be payable where the last course of treatment in respect of which provision was made for payment under item 3 (a) or (b) to the same practitioner† commenced at any time during any of the 5 months preceding the month in which the further treatment is to be done, unless the prior approval of the Board has been obtained.

4. Treatment urgently required for acute infective conditions of the gingivae/oral mucosa: fee per course of treatment.　　8s. 0d.

5. *Other periodontal treatment, including where necessary protracted scaling and gingivectomy (estimates to include an outline of proposed treatment):　　Such fee as the Board may approve up to a maximum of £4 10s. 0d. (or such higher fee as they may in special circumstances approve).

Provided that where gingivectomy and associated aftercare is involved an additional fee shall be allowed:—

For treatment relating to the first 2 adjacent teeth in one jaw £1 2s. 0d.

For treatment relating to additional teeth, per tooth 5s. 0d.

### B.　RESTORATIVE TREATMENT

6. Fillings (including any dressings, pulp capping and other necessary preparatory treatment) except fillings in deciduous teeth of children under 16 years. The fillings to which this scale applies shall be permanent in character.　Fee per filling:—

    (a) amalgam filling in:

      (i) a single surface cavity ...　　...　　13s. 6d. with a maximum of 13s. 6d. for 2 or more such fillings in any one surface of a tooth and a maximum of 19s. 0d. for 2 or more such fillings per tooth not all in one surface.

      (ii) a mesial-occlusal-distal cavity inclusive of any extension of such a cavity in a molar or premolar tooth.　　£1 16s. 0d.

---

\* See schedule 2 for treatment requiring prior approval.

† Reference in this scale of fees to dental treatment by the same practitioner shall include also dental treatment by his principal or the partner of either, or by the assistant of any of them and where the practitioner is employed by a body corporate shall include treatment by another employee of that body.

(iii) a mesial-occlusal or distal-occlusal cavity inclusive of any extension of such a cavity into the lingual or buccal surfaces or both in a molar or pre-molar tooth.

£1 4s. 0d. with a maximum for a combination of such fillings of £1 16s. 0d. per tooth.

(iv) a compound cavity other than a cavity covered by (ii) or (iii) above.

19s. 0d. with a maximum of £1 6s. 0d. for 2 or more such fillings per tooth.

(b) silicate, silico-phosphate or synthetic resin filling.

19s. 0d. with a maximum for 2 or more such fillings per tooth of £1 9s. 0d.

Provided that:—

(a) for combinations of the types of fillings set out below in the same tooth no fee shall be payable in excess of the amount shown opposite:—

| | |
|---|---|
| 1 or more of (a) (i) with 1 of (a) (iii) | £1 10s. 0d. |
| 1 or more of (a) (i) with 1 of (a) (iv) | £1  4s. 0d. |
| 1 or more of (a) (i) with 2 or more of (a) (iv). | £1 11s. 0d. |
| 1 of (a) (iii) with 1 or more of (a) (iv). | £1 11s. 0d. |

(b) no fee in excess of £2 2s. 0d. shall be payable for any combination of any of the types of fillings necessary in one tooth.

7. Root treatment of permanent teeth, including all attention in connection therewith but not including the provision of X-rays or the insertion of any filling in the crown of the tooth:—

(a) treatment comprising either the devitalisation of the pulp of a tooth and the subsequent removal of the pulp followed by the necessary treatment and filling of each root canal of the tooth, or the treatment of septic root canals and the subsequent filling of each canal—

Fee per single rooted non-septic tooth.

£1 15s. 0d.

Fee per multi-rooted or septic tooth.

£3 0s. 0d.

(b) Vital pulpotomy consisting of removal of the coronal portion of the pulp, including any necessary dressing, fee per tooth.

£1 10s. 0d.

(c) apicectomy, fee per tooth ...　　...

£2 0s. 0d.

*8. Gold fillings (other than inlays) ...　　...

£3 0s. 0d. per filling with a maximum for 2 or more such fillings per tooth of £4 10s. 0d.

* See schedule 2 for treatment requiring prior approval.

9. Inlays (including any dressings):

|  | A. | B. |
|---|---|---|
| *(a) metal inlay ... ... ... ... | Alloys containing 60% or more fine gold. | Any other alloys. |
|     (i) a single surface cavity ... ... | £4 5s. 0d. | £4 0s. 0d. |
|     (ii) a compound cavity ... ... | £6 5s. 0d. | £5 0s. 0d. |
|     (iii) a compound cavity involving the incisal angle. | £6 0s. 0d. | £5 0s. 0d. |
|     (iv) a confluent compound cavity | £8 0s. 0d. | £6 0s. 0d. |

*(b) fused porcelain inlay ... ... Such fee as the Board may approve within a range of £5 0s. 0d. to £9 0s. 0d.

*(c) provision or renewal of a facing of silicate, or synthetic resin. 15s. 0d. per inlay.

(d) refixing or recementing an inlay ... 15s. 0d. per inlay.

*(e) renewal or replacement by another inlay. Such fee as the Board may approve not exceeding the fee for a new inlay of the type being provided.

10. Crowning of permanent teeth, including any dressings, but excluding root treatment:—

*(a) Full veneer or jacket crown (on a vital or non-vital tooth):—
    (i) gold ... ... ... ... £7 15s. 0d.
    (ii) gold with facing of silicate or synthetic resin £8 10s. 0d.

*(b) Three-quarter crown gold, cast ... £9 0s. 0d.

*(c) Full veneer or jacket crown:—
    (i) synthetic resin on a vital tooth £5 10s. 0d.
    (ii) synthetic resin on a non-vital tooth £4 5s. 0d.
    (iii) synthetic resin constructed on a cast gold core or thimble on a vital tooth £8 0s. 0d.

*(d) Full veneer or jacket crown:—
    (i) porcelain on a vital tooth ... £10 0s. 0d.
    (ii) porcelain on a non-vital tooth £8 0s. 0d.
    (iii) porcelain constructed on a cast gold core or thimble on a vital tooth £12 15s. 0d.

*(e) (i) Synthetic resin veneer or jacket constructed on a cast gold core and post £7 0s. 0d.
    (ii) Porcelain veneer or jacket constructed on a cast gold core and post £10 0s. 0d.

*(f) Synthetic resin post or dowel crown:—
    (i) without diaphragm ... ... £4 0s. 0d.
    (ii) with diaphragm ... ... £7 0s. 0d.
    (iii) with gold post, diaphragm and backing £8 0s. 0d.

* See schedule 2 for treatment requiring prior approval.

*(g) Modifications to the above crowns, and other forms of crown not in the opinion of the Board included in the above items — Such fee as the Board may approve not exceeding £12 15s. 0d.

(h) Refixing or recementing a crown ... — 15s. 0d. per crown.

*(i) Repair of a crown:—

(i) Renewal of the coronal portion only of a post or dowel crown appropriate to item 10 (f) (i) or 10 (f) (ii) — £2 4s. 0d.

(ii) Other repair of a crown ... — Such fee as the Board may approve not exceeding two-thirds of the fee for a new crown of the type being repaired.

*(j) Renewal by a similar type of crown — Such fee as the Board may approve not exceeding the fee for a new crown of the type being provided.

*(k) Replacement by a different type of crown: — Such fee as the Board may approve not exceeding the fee for a new crown of the type being provided.

Provided that where the Board approve the use of a special bonding technique in connection with a porcelain crown the Board may increase the fee by an amount not exceeding £5 0s. 0d.

## PART III—SURGICAL TREATMENT

*11. Extractions:—

Fee per course of treatment:—

| | | | | | | |
|---|---|---|---|---|---|---|
| 1 tooth ... | ... | ... | ... | ... | 11s. 0d. | With an additional fee of 2s. 0d. for each quadrant of the mouth involved other than the first. |
| 2 teeth ... | ... | ... | ... | ... | 12s. 0d. | |
| 3, 4 or 5 teeth ... | ... | ... | ... | 13s. 6d. | |
| 6, 7 or 8 teeth ... | ... | ... | ... | 18s. 0d. | |
| 9, 10 or 11 teeth | ... | ... | ... | £1 2s. 6d. | |
| 12, 13 or 14 teeth | ... | ... | ... | £1 7s. 0d. | |
| 15, 16 or 17 teeth | ... | ... | ... | £1 11s. 6d. | |
| 18, 19 or 20 teeth | ... | ... | ... | £1 16s. 0d. | |
| over 20 teeth: ... | ... | ... | ... | £2 0s. 6d. | |

Provided that where an exceptional number of visits is necessary because of the abnormal systemic condition of the patient the Board may allow an additional fee not exceeding £2 0s. 0d. per course.

*12 (a) Alveolectomy, in either upper or lower jaw — Such fee as the Board may approve up to a maximum of £3 10s. 0d. (or such higher fee as they may in special circumstances approve).

(b) Removal of a cyst, buried root, impacted tooth or grossly exostosed tooth, or other similar operation, including attention in connection therewith — Such fee as the Board may approve up to a maximum of £8 5s. 0d. (or such higher fee as they may in special circumstances approve).

(c) Surgery on soft tissue, other than periodontal surgery appropriate to item 5 — Such fee as the Board may approve up to a maximum of £1 15s. 0d. (or such higher fee as they may in special circumstances approve).

---

* See schedule 2 for treatment requiring prior approval.

13. Administration of a general anaesthetic:—

(a) In connection with treatment under Item 11:—

    (i) where a doctor or dentist other than the dentist carrying out the extraction administers the anaesthetic:

        Fee per visit—

| | |
|---|---|
| 1 to 3 teeth extracted ... | 15s. 0d. |
| 4 to 11 teeth extracted ... | £1  1s. 0d. |
| 12 to 19 teeth extracted... | £1 11s. 6d. |
| 20 teeth or over extracted | £2  2s. 0d. |

    (ii) where the anaesthetic is administered by the dentist carrying out the extraction:

        Fee per patient per course of treatment.    8s. 0d.

    *(iii) where the Board are satisfied that the anaesthetist would be faced with special difficulties owing to the medical condition of the patient and the anaesthetic is to be administered by a doctor or dentist other than the dentist carrying out the extraction:    Such fee as the Board may approve not exceeding £4 14s. 6d. per course of treatment.

Provided that no fee exceeding £2 2s. 0d. per course of treatment shall be payable under (i) or under (i) and (ii) combined, and no fee exceeding £5 10s. 0d. per course of treatment shall be payable for any combination of (iii) with (i), or with both (i) and (ii).

    *(b) In connection with treatment under Items 5, 7 (c) and 12 where a doctor or dentist other than the dentist carrying out the treatment administers the anaesthetic:    Such fee as the Board may approve not exceeding £2 2s. 0d.

Provided that in cases presenting special clinical difficulty the fee will be such fee as the Board may approve not exceeding £4 14s. 6d.

## Part IV—DENTURES, BRIDGES AND SPECIAL APPLIANCES OTHER THAN ORTHODONTIC APPLIANCES

### A.  DENTURES

Fees for the provision of dentures cover the provision of all necessary clasps, rests and strengtheners and all adjustments needed within a reasonable period of time after completion.

*14.  Dentures in vulcanite or synthetic resin:—

| | |
|---|---|
| (a) full upper and full lower dentures... | £12  5s. 0d. |
| (b) denture bearing 1, 2 or 3 teeth    ... | £5 10s. 0d. |
|     denture bearing 4 to 8 teeth    ... | £6 10s. 0d. |
|     denture bearing 9 to 14 teeth    ... | £7  5s. 0d. |

Provided that no fee for upper and lower dentures shall exceed £12 5s. 0d.

(c) additional fee for lingual or palatal bar:—

| | |
|---|---|
| (i) stainless steel ...    ...    ... | £1  5s. 0d. |
| (ii) gold or other approved material | Such fee as the Board may approve not exceeding £3 10s. 0d. |

---

* See schedule 2 for treatment requiring prior approval.

15. Relining or rebasing of dentures, or provision of soft linings to dentures, including all adjustments needed within a reasonable period of time after completion:—

    (a) relining or rebasing dentures:—

        (i) not accompanied by repairs or additions     £2 8s. 0d. per denture.

        *(ii) accompanied by repairs and/or additions     Such fee as the Board may approve.

    *(b) Addition of soft lining or soft partial lining to a new or existing vulcanite or synthetic resin denture where this is required on account of the abnormal anatomical condition of the patient's alveolus     Such fee as the Board may approve not exceeding £2 10s. 0d. per denture.

    *(c) Replacement or refitting of soft lining or soft partial lining which has been provided on account of the abnormal anatomical condition of the patient's alveolus     Such fee as the Board may approve not exceeding £2 10s. 0d. per denture.

16. Repairs (except repairs accompanying relining or rebasing which are appropriate to item 15 (a) (ii)):—

    (a) (i) repairing a crack or fracture (including provision of any strengthener), or

        (ii) refixing a tooth, or providing and fixing a replacement for a missing tooth (including any gum associated therewith), or

        (iii) refixing a clasp, or providing and fixing a replacement for a missing clasp (including any gum associated therewith), or

        (iv) covering exposed pins:
        One repair under (a) (i)-(iv)     17s. 0d.

    (b) each additional repair under (a) (i)-(iv).     5s. 0d.

    (c) renewal of gum not associated with repair under (a):     17s. 0d. per denture.

Provided that no fee in excess of £2 0s. 0d. per denture shall be payable under item 16 or for any combination of treatment under items 16 and 17.

17. Additions (except additions accompanying relining or rebasing, which are appropriate to item 15 (a)(ii)):—

    (a) addition of a clasp or tooth (including any gum associated therewith).     £1 10s. 0d.

---

* See schedule 2 for treatment requiring prior approval.

(b) addition of new gum not associated with addition under item 17 (a): £1 10s. 0d. per denture.

Provided that no fee in excess of £2 0s. 0d. per denture shall be payable under item 17 or for any combination of treatment under items 16 and 17.

\*18. Backing or posting and tagging of teeth on non-metallic based dentures:—

Fee per tooth in addition to the appropriate fee for a non-metallic based denture:—

(i) stainless steel ... ... ... 12s. 0d.

(ii) chrome cobalt or a precious metal alloy containing less than 60 per cent. fine gold ... £1 6s. 0d.

(iii) precious metal alloy containing 60 per cent. or more fine gold £2 6s. 0d.

\*19. Metal dentures. These dentures may not be provided until such period after extraction (normally not less than 3 months) as the dentist thinks fit:—

(a) Fee per denture in:—

|  | A. | B. |
|---|---|---|
| (i) Base metal alloys: | Stainless steel. | Chrome cobalt. |
| partial denture bearing 1, 2 or 3 teeth | £10 0s. 0d. | £12 10s. 0d. |
| partial denture bearing 4, 5 or 6 teeth | £12 0s. 0d. | £14 5s. 0d. |
| partial denture bearing 7, 8 or 9 teeth | £12 10s. 0d. | £15 10s. 0d. |
| partial denture bearing 10 or more teeth | £12 15s. 0d. | £16 0s. 0d. |
| full denture ... ... ... | £11 10s. 0d. | £14 5s. 0d. |
| Additional fee where teeth are backed in any metal | £1 0s. 0d. per tooth up to a maximum of £4 0s. 0d. per denture. | £1 0s. 0d. per tooth up to a maximum of £4 0s. 0d. per denture. |

|  | A. | B. |
|---|---|---|
| (ii) Precious metal alloys: | Containing less than 60 per cent. fine gold. | Containing 60 per cent. or more fine gold. |
| partial denture bearing 1, 2 or 3 teeth | £12 5s. 0d. | Such fee as the Board may approve. |
| partial denture bearing 4, 5 or 6 teeth | £14 5s. 0d. | |
| partial denture bearing 7, 8 or 9 teeth | £15 15s. 0d. | |
| partial denture bearing 10 or more teeth | £16 0s. 0d. | |
| Full denture ... ... ... | £15 10s. 0d. | |
| Additional fee where teeth are backed in any metal | £1 5s. 0d. per tooth up to a maximum of £5 0s. 0d. per denture. | |

\* See schedule 2 for treatment requiring prior approval.

| | |
|---|---|
| (b) Repairs and<br>(c) Additions | Fee appropriate to similar treatment to synthetic resin or vulcanite dentures as covered by items 16 and/or 17 together with such additional fee, if any, as the Board may approve. |

## B. BRIDGES AND SPECIAL APPLIANCES

| | |
|---|---|
| *20. Bridges ... ... ... ... ... | Such fee as the Board may approve. |
| *21. (a) Obturators, fee per case in addition to appropriate denture fee | Such fee as the Board may approve within a range of £3 10s. 0d. to £6 0s. 0d. or such additional fee as may be approved in special circumstances. |
| (b) Repairs to obturators ... ... | Such fee as the Board may approve. |
| (c) Treatment involving splints or other appliances (other than in connection with periodontal treatment). | Such fee as the Board may approve. |

## PART V—TREATMENT SPECIAL TO CHILDREN

22. Conservative treatment of deciduous teeth of children under 16 years of age at the beginning of a course of treatment:—

    (a) By filling with amalgam, oxyphosphate cement, or other similar materials (including any dressings, pulp capping and other necessary preparatory treatment):—

| | |
|---|---|
| (i) single surface cavity, per filling ... | 11s. 6d. |
| (ii) any other cavity, per filling ... | 16s. 0d. |
| (b) By conservation of a molar with a preformed metal cap: | 16s. 0d. per tooth. |

        Provided that no fee in excess of 16s. 0d. shall be payable for the conservation of one tooth by the above types of consevation.

    (c) by conservation by other means:—

        (i) By preparing self-cleansing areas followed by applications of silver nitrate or similar medicaments:

| | |
|---|---|
| per tooth ... ... ... | 8s. 0d. |
| maximum per patient ... | £1 0s. 0d. |

        *Provided that no fee shall be payable under (i) where the treatment occurs within 12 months of similar treatment to the same surface by the same practitioner† unless, in exceptional circumstances, the approval of the Board is first obtained.

---

\* See schedule 2 for treatment requiring prior approval.

   † Reference in this scale of fees to dental treatment by the same practitioner shall include also dental treatment by his principal or the partner of either, or by the assistant of any of them and where the practitioner is employed by a body corporate shall include treatment by another employee of that body.

(ii) By topical applications of ob-
tundents and coagulants:

per patient ...        ...        ...        8s. 0d.

*Provided that no fee shall be pay-
able under (ii) where the treatment
occurs within 12 months of similar
treatment by the same practitioner†
unless, in exceptional circumstances,
the approval of the Board is first
obtained.

(d) By vital pulpotomy, including any        11s. 0d.
necessary dressing, per tooth.

23.    (a) Removal of calculus and other de-        6s. 0d.
posits from the teeth of children under
16 years at the beginning of a course
of treatment and the provision of
necessary treatment for all ordinary
or simple disorders of the gums:

*Provided that no fee shall be pay-
able under item 23(a)—

(i) where the last course of treatment in respect of which provision was made for payment
under item 23(a) or (b) to the
same practitioner† commenced
at any time during any of the 5
months preceding the month in
which the further treatment is
to be done

(ii) in respect of a patient under 9
years at the beginning of a
course of treatment

unless the prior approval of the Board
has been obtained.

*(b) Removal of calculus, where in ex-        13s. 6d.
ceptional cases calculus is present to
an abnormal degree, from the teeth
of children under 16 years at the
beginning of a course of treatment,
and the provision of necessary treatment for all ordinary or simple disorders of the gums

(c) Removal of stain including any        6s. 0d.
necessary polishing:

Provided that no fee shall be payable under item 23 (c)—

---

* See schedule 2 for treatment requiring prior approval.

† Reference in this scale of fees to dental treatment by the same practitioner shall include
also dental treatment by his principal or the partner of either, or by the assistant of any of
them and where the practitioner is employed by a body corporate shall include treatment by
another employee of that body.

*(i) where the last course of treat-
ment in respect of which provision was made for payment
under item 23 (c) to the same
practitioner† commenced at
any time during any of the 11
months preceding the month in
which the further treatment is
to be done unless the prior
approval of the Board has been
obtained

(ii) during a course of treatment
where a fee is paid under item
23 (a) or (b).

24. *(a) Orthodontic treatment of children    Such fee as the Board may approve.
and young persons under 18 years at
the beginning of a course of treatment

(b) Repairs to orthodontic appliances    Such fee as the Board may approve.

## Part VI—GENERAL ITEMS

25. Dressing of teeth in respect of a casual
patient:—
Fee for one tooth    ...    ...    ...    9s. 0d.
Fee for two or more teeth    ...    ...    12s. 0d.

26. Treatment of sensitive cementum or
dentine:—
Fee per course    ...    ...    ...    ...    5s. 6d.

27. Taking of material for pathological or
bacteriological examination, etc.:—
Fee per course    ...    ...    ...    ...    8s. 0d.

28. Treatment for arrest of abnormal haemorrhage, including abnormal haemorrhage
following dental treatment provided otherwise than as part of general dental
services:—
Fee per visit for arrest of bleeding or for    17s. 6d.
administration of associated after-
care:

Provided that:   (i) the same practitioner† who arrests bleeding may not also be
paid for the administration of after-care;   (ii) where the treatment consists solely
of the removal of plugs and/or stitches the fee shall be only 10s. 0d.; (iii) the maximum
fee per course of treatment shall be £2 5s. 0d. or such higher sum as the Board may in
special circumstances approve.

*29. Fee for any other treatment not included    Such fee as the Board may approve
in this scale.

---

* See schedule 2 for treatment requiring prior approval.

† Reference in this scale of fees to dental treatment by the same practitioner shall include
also dental treatment by his principal or the partner of either, or by the assistant of any of
them and where the practitioner is employed by a body corporate shall include treatment by
another employee of that body.

## EXPLANATORY NOTE

*(This Note is not part of the Regulations.)*

These Regulations further amend the National Health Service (General Dental Services) (Scotland) Regulations 1966 by providing for a new scale of fees and for certain additional payments for practitioners, other than salaried practitioners, providing general dental services.

## STATUTORY INSTRUMENTS

### 1969 No. 437 (S.33)

## NATIONAL HEALTH SERVICE, SCOTLAND

### The National Health Service (Functions of Regional Hospital Boards) (Scotland) Amendment Regulations 1969

| | |
|---|---|
| *Made* - - - - | *20th March* 1969 |
| *Laid before Parliament* | *31st March* 1969 |
| *Coming into Operation* | *1st April* 1969 |

In exercise of the powers conferred on me by section 12 of the National Health Service (Scotland) Act 1947(a), and of all other powers enabling me in that behalf I hereby make the following regulations:—

**1.** These regulations may be cited as the National Health Service (Functions of Regional Hospital Boards) (Scotland) Amendment Regulations 1969, and shall come into operation on 1st April 1969.

**2.** The Interpretation Act 1889(b) applies for the interpretation of these regulations as it applies for the interpretation of an Act of Parliament.

**3.** The National Health Service (Functions of Regional Hospital Boards) (Scotland) Regulations 1948(c), as amended(d), shall be amended as follows:—

(1) In regulation 2(1) after the definition of "the Act" there shall be added the following:—

" 'the 1968 Act' means the Health Services and Public Health Act 1968" (e).

(2) In regulation 4 after the words "the Act" there shall be inserted the words "and of the 1968 Act".

(3) For paragraph (6) of regulation 4 there shall be substituted the following paragraph:

"(6) Under sections 1 and 2 of the 1968 Act with respect to the making available of accommodation and services for resident and non-resident patients who undertake to pay charges determined by the Secretary of State, the recovery of such charges and the making of arrangements by medical or dental practitioners for the treatment of their private patients."

**4.** For paragraph (b) of the proviso to regulation 4 there shall be substituted the following paragraph:—

"(b) A Regional Hospital Board shall not, except with the consent of the Secretary of State, undertake any building or civil engineering project or scheme, the estimated cost of which exceeds £250,000."

---

(a) 1947 c. 27.        (b) 1889 c. 63.
(c) S.I. 1948/594 (Rev. XV, p. 841; 1948 I, p. 2449).
(d) S.I. 1956/1809, 1961/125, 1963/993 (1956 I, p. 1599; 1961 I, p. 179; 1963 II, p. 1633).
(e) 1968 c. 46.

**5.** There shall be added to the proviso to regulation 4, the following paragraphs:—

"(c) The charges to be recovered under section 4 of the Act and under sections 1 and 2 of the 1968 Act shall be determined by the Secretary of State.

(d) The maximum extent of accommodation and services 'to be made available under sections 1 and 2 of the 1968 Act shall be subject to the approval of the Secretary of State."

*William Ross,*
One of Her Majesty's Principal
Secretaries of State.

St. Andrew's House,
Edinburgh, 1.
20th March 1969.

## EXPLANATORY NOTE

*(This Note is not part of the Regulations.)*

These Regulations further amend the National Health Service (Functions of Regional Hospital Boards) (Scotland) Regulations 1948. Apart from the amendment to paragraph (b) of the proviso to paragraph 4, the amendments are in consequence of the coming into operation on 1st April 1969 of sections 1, 2 and 4 of the Health Services and Public Health Act 1968. These amendments contain the necessary references to the new statutory provisions (which relate to the accommodation and treatment of private in-patients and of private out-patients, and also the provision of accommodation on part payment), and provide (a) for the charges for accommodation available on part payment, and for accommodation and services made available for private in-patients and for private out-patients, to be determined by the Secretary of State, and (b) for the maximum extent of the accommodation and services which can be made available in hospitals for private in-patients and for private out-patients to be subject to the approval of the Secretary of State.

The amendment to paragraph (b) of the proviso to paragraph 4 raises from £120,000 to £250,000 the limit on a building or civil engineering project or scheme that a Regional Hospital Board may undertake without the consent of the Secretary of State.

## STATUTORY INSTRUMENTS

### 1969 No. 438

### LAND DRAINAGE

### The River Authorities (Precepts on Internal Drainage Boards) Regulations 1969

| | |
|---|---|
| *Made* - - - | *21st March* 1969 |
| *Laid before Parliament* | *31st March* 1969 |
| *Coming into Operation* | *1st April* 1969 |

The Minister of Agriculture, Fisheries and Food, in exercise of the powers conferred on him by Sections 22(3) and 74 of the Land Drainage Act 1930(a), as applied by section 5 of the Water Resources Act 1963(b), and of all other powers enabling him in that behalf, hereby makes the following regulations:—

*Citation, Commencement and Interpretation*

1.—(1) These regulations may be cited as the River Authorities (Precepts on Internal Drainage Boards) Regulations 1969 and shall come into operation on the 1st April 1969.

(2) The Interpretation Act 1889(c) shall apply to the interpretation of these regulations as it applies to the interpretation of an Act of Parliament, and as if these regulations and the regulations hereby revoked were Acts of Parliament.

*Form of Statement of Purposes*

2. Any statement prepared under section 22(3) of the Land Drainage Act 1930, as applied by section 5 of the Water Resources Act 1963 (which requires a river authority to prepare a statement of the purposes to which the amount demanded by any precept issued by the authority under that section is intended to be applied, and of the basis upon which it is calculated), shall be in the form set out in the schedule to these regulations, or in a form substantially to the like effect.

*Revocation*

3. The River Authorities (Precepts) Regulations 1965(d) are hereby revoked.

In witness whereof the official seal of the Minister of Agriculture, Fisheries and Food is hereunto affixed on 21st March 1969.

(L.S.)

*Cledwyn Hughes,*
Minister of Agriculture, Fisheries and Food.

---

(a) 1930 c. 44. For change of title of the Minister see S.I. 1955/554 (1955 I, p. 1200).
(b) 1963 c. 38.    (c) 1889 c. 63.    (d) S.I. 1965/542 (1965 I, p. 1675).

## SCHEDULE
### FORM OF STATEMENT

| I. Statement of the purposes to which the amount demanded by precept is intended to be applied.<br><br>PURPOSE | Total expenditure<br><br>(2) | Government grants<br><br>(3) | Defrayed from replacement fund (i)<br><br>(4) | Relevant expenditure (Col. (2) less Cols. (3) and (4) )<br><br>(5) |
|---|---|---|---|---|
| 1. Expenses under enactments relating to land drainage—<br>(1) Capital expenditure from revenue—<br>(a) grant-aided works<br>(b) non grant-aided items ... ...<br>(2) Other expenditure—<br>(a) Loan charges ...<br>(b) Works of maintenance ... ...<br>(c) Administration and general charges ... ...<br>(d) Contributions to internal drainage boards ... ...<br>(e) Contributions to water resources account. ... ...<br>(f) Other items (ii) | | | | |
| 2. Expenses (including administration) under enactments relating to rivers pollution prevention (ii) ... ... ... | | | | |
| 3. Expenses (including administration) under enactments relating to fisheries (ii)—<br>(a) Contributions to water resources account ... ...<br>(b) All other expenses, including administration ... ... ... | | | | |
| 4. Payments into any replacement fund (i) (other than payments from the water resources account of the Authority) ... ... ... | | | | |
| 5. Provision for working capital ... ... ... ... ... | | | | |
| 6. Debit balances brought forward in respect of transferred functions (iii) ... ... ... ... ... ... ... ... | | | | |
| 7. Debit balances brought forward in respect of new functions (iii) and (iv) ... ... ... ... ... ... ... ... | | | | |
| | | | | £ |

II. (1) Statement of income in respect of transferred functions under enactments other than section 87 of the Water Resources Act 1963—
    (a) Contributions from internal drainage boards (see statement III) ... ... ... ...
    (b) General drainage charge ... ... ...
    (c) Fishery revenues ... ... ... ...
    (d) Contributions from Water Resources account
    (e) Sundry general receipts ... ... ...
  (2) Credit balances brought forward in respect of transferred functions (iii) ... ... ...
  (3) Credit balances brought forward in respect of new functions (iii) and (iv) ... ... ...
  (4) Amount to be met under section 87 of the Water Resources Act 1963 by precepts on the councils of counties, county boroughs and London boroughs.

Total revenues     £

| III. Statement of the amounts demanded by precepts from internal drainage boards and of the basis on which they are calculated including amounts specified under section 21(1) of the Land Drainage Act 1961 as corresponding to contributions. | Amount of precept | Basis on which the precept is calculated |
|---|---|---|
| | £ s. d. | |
| ............................................................ | | |
| ............................................................ | | |
| ............................................................ | | |

Under section 21(1) of the Land Drainage Act 1930, which is made applicable to river authorities by virtue of section 5 of, and Schedule 3 to, the Water Resources Act 1963, a river authority shall by resolution require each internal drainage board to make towards the expenses of the river authority such contribution as the river authority may consider to be fair. By section 21(5) of the Land Drainage Act 1930 as applied to river authorities, an internal drainage board, if it is aggrieved by a resolution of a river authority determining the amount of the contribution, may, within six weeks after the date on which notice of the resolution is given by the river authority to the internal drainage board, appeal to the Minister of Agriculture, Fisheries and Food against the resolution, and the Minister may, after considering any objections made to him and, if he thinks fit, holding a local public inquiry, make such an order as he thinks just.

*Notes*

(i) "Replacement fund" means a fund authorised by section 85(1) of the Water Resources Act 1963.

(ii) Excluding payments into any replacement fund which are to be entered in paragraph 4 of section I.

(iii) The terms "transferred functions" and "new functions" have the meaning assigned to them by section 3(5) of the Water Resources Act 1963.

(iv) This will only be applicable when precepting for the first and possibly the second year during which a charging scheme is in force.

# EXPLANATORY NOTE

*(This Note is not part of the Regulations.)*

River Authorities may raise money towards defraying their expenses by issuing precepts to internal drainage boards. These regulations, which come into operation on the 1st April 1969, prescribe a form of statement to be sent with every precept setting out the purposes to which the amount demanded is to be applied and the basis on which it is calculated.

## STATUTORY INSTRUMENTS

### 1969 No. 440

## LAND COMMISSION
### The Betterment Levy (Rate of Interest) Order 1969

| | |
|---|---|
| *Made* - - - | *21st March* 1969 |
| *Laid before the House of Commons* | *31st March* 1969 |
| *Coming into Operation* | *1st April* 1969 |

The Treasury, in exercise of the powers conferred upon them by section 51(2) of the Land Commission Act 1967(a) and of all other powers enabling them in that behalf, hereby make the following Order :—

**1.** This Order may be cited as the Betterment Levy (Rate of Interest) Order 1969, and shall come into operation on 1st April 1969.

**2.** The Interpretation Act 1889(b) shall apply for the interpretation of this Order as it applies for the interpretation of an Act of Parliament.

**3.** The rate of interest for the purposes of section 51 of the Land Commission Act 1967 shall be 8 per cent. per annum.

**4.** The Betterment Levy (Rate of Interest) (No. 2) Order 1968(c) is hereby revoked.

*Joseph Harper,*
*Walter Harrison,*
Two of the Lords Commissioners
of Her Majesty's Treasury.

21st March 1969.

---

### EXPLANATORY NOTE
*(This Note is not part of the Order.)*

Section 51 of the Land Commission Act 1967 provides that interest shall be paid on unpaid or overpaid betterment levy. This Order increases the rate of interest from 7 per cent. to 8 per cent. per annum and revokes the Betterment Levy (Rate of Interest) (No. 2) Order 1968.

---

(a) 1967 c. 1.    (b) 1889 c. 63.    (c) S.I. 1968/1591 (1968 III, p. 4394).

STATUTORY INSTRUMENTS

## 1969 No. 451

# NATIONAL HEALTH SERVICE, ENGLAND AND WALES

### HOSPITAL AND SPECIALIST SERVICES

## The National Health Service (Regional Hospital Areas) Order 1969

| | | |
|---|---|---|
| *Made* - - - | | *24th March* 1969 |
| *Coming into Operation* | | *1st April* 1969 |
| *Laid before Parliament* | | *24th April* 1969 |

The Secretary of State for Social Services, in exercise of his powers under sections 11(1) and 75 of the National Health Service Act 1946(a) and of all other powers enabling him in that behalf, and after consulting with such bodies and organisations as appear to him to be concerned, hereby orders and determines as follows :—

**1.** This order may be cited as the National Health Service (Regional Hospital Areas) Order 1969, and shall come into operation on 1st April 1969.

**2.** The Interpretation Act 1889(b) shall apply to the interpretation of this order as it applies to the interpretation of an Act of Parliament.

**3.** In column (3) of Schedule 1 to the National Health Service (Regional Hospital Areas) Order 1965(c) (which Schedule determines regional hospital areas), in the description of the Liverpool Regional Hospital Area, there shall be substituted for the word "Skelmersdale" the words "Skelmersdale and Holland".

Signed by authority of the Secretary of State for Social Services.

*H. M. Hedley,*
Assistant Under Secretary of State,
Department of Health and Social Security.
24th March 1969.

---

### EXPLANATORY NOTE

*(This Note is not part of the Order.)*

This Order amends the National Health Service (Regional Hospital Areas) Order 1965 by varying the Liverpool Regional Hospital Area to include the newly-formed urban district of Skelmersdale and Holland.

---

(a) 1946 c. 81.     (b) 1889 c. 63.     (c) S.I. 1965/527 (1965 I, p. 1382).

STATUTORY INSTRUMENTS

## 1969 No. 453

## BORROWING AND SECURITIES

## The New Towns (Scotland) Act 1968 National Loans Fund Substitution Order 1969

*Laid before the House of Commons in draft*
Made - - - *25th March* 1969
*Coming into Operation* *1st April* 1969

The Treasury, in exercise of the powers conferred upon them by section 20 of the National Loans Act 1968(a), and of all other powers enabling them in that behalf, hereby make the following Order, a draft of which has been laid before the Commons House of Parliament and has been approved by resolution of that House :—

**1.**—(1) This Order may be cited as The New Towns (Scotland) Act 1968 National Loans Fund Substitution Order 1969 and shall come into operation on 1st April 1969.

(2) The Interpretation Act 1889(b) shall apply for the interpretation of this Order as it applies for the interpretation of an Act of Parliament.

**2.**—(1) The provisions of the New Towns (Scotland) Act 1968(c) specified in the Schedule to this Order shall have effect subject to the amendments specified therein.

(2) Section 38(2) and (4) of the New Towns (Scotland) Act 1968 and in section 39(5) of that Act the words "out of the Consolidated Fund" shall be repealed.

*E. Alan Fitch,*
*Joseph Harper,*
Two of the Lords Commissioners of
Her Majesty's Treasury.

25th March 1969.

---

(a) 1968 c. 13.      (b) 1889 c. 63.      (c) 1968 c. 16.

SCHEDULE      Article 2

New Towns (Scotland) Act 1968

| Section | Subject Matter | Amendment |
|---|---|---|
| 37(1) | Advances to development corporations | Rate of interest to be fixed in accordance with National Loans Act 1968. |
| 38(1) | Advances to development corporations | For "Consolidated Fund" read "National Loans Fund". |
| 38(3), 39(5) | Repayment into Exchequer | For "Exchequer" read "National Loans Fund". |

EXPLANATORY NOTE

(*This Note is not part of the Order.*)

This Order substitutes references to the National Loans Fund for references to the Consolidated Fund in the New Towns (Scotland) Act 1968, and makes certain related amendments, and repeals certain provisions of that Act which, in view of the provisions of the National Loans Act 1968, are not necessary.

# STATUTORY INSTRUMENTS

## 1969 No. 456

## PENSIONS

### The Superannuation (Local Government and National and Local Government Officers Association) Interchange Rules 1969

| | | |
|---|---|---|
| *Made* - - - | *25th March* 1969 |
| *Laid before Parliament* | *31st March* 1969 |
| *Coming into Operation* | *1st April* 1969 |

### ARRANGEMENT OF RULES

#### PART I
##### PRELIMINARY

#### PART II
##### TRANSFER FROM LOCAL GOVERNMENT EMPLOYMENT TO ASSOCIATION EMPLOYMENT

#### PART III
##### TRANSFER FROM ASSOCIATION EMPLOYMENT TO LOCAL GOVERNMENT EMPLOYMENT

## PART IV

### MISCELLANEOUS

17. Extension of time

18. Interest on returned contributions

Schedule. Transfer values receivable from the Staff Superannuation Fund.

The Minister of Housing and Local Government, in exercise of his powers under sections 2 and 15 of the Superannuation (Miscellaneous Provisions) Act 1948(a), as amended by section 11(6) of the Superannuation (Miscellaneous Provisions) Act 1967(b), and of all other powers enabling him in that behalf, hereby makes the following rules:—

## PART I

### PRELIMINARY

*Title and commencement*

**1.** These rules may be cited as the Superannuation (Local Government and National and Local Government Officers Association) Interchange Rules 1969, and shall come into operation on 1st April 1969.

*Interpretation*

**2.**—(1) In these rules, unless the context otherwise requires—

"the Act of 1937" means the Local Government Superannuation Act 1937(c);

"the Act of 1948" means the Superannuation (Miscellaneous Provisions) Act 1948;

"the Act of 1953" means the Local Government Superannuation Act 1953(d);

"added years" means—

(*a*) in relation to a person in local government employment, any additional years of service reckonable by him under regulation 12 of the benefits regulations or that regulation as applied by or under any enactment, and includes any additional years of service which, having been granted thereunder, have subsequently become reckonable under or by virtue of any other enactment, and

(*b*) in relation to a person in Association employment, any additional years of service of the nature of the additional years of service referred to in (*a*) of this definition which have been granted in, or have otherwise become reckonable in, that employment;

"the Association" means the National and Local Government Officers Association;

"Association employment", in relation to any person, means employment in which the person is subject to the Staff Superannuation Fund;

"benefit" means any superannuation benefit payable to or in respect of any person;

"the benefits regulations" means the Local Government Superannuation (Benefits) Regulations 1954(e);

"contributing service" and "contributory employee" have the same meanings as in the Act of 1937;

---

(a) 1948 c. 33.　　　　(b) 1967 c. 28.　　　　(c) 1937 c. 68.
　　(d) 1953 c. 25.　　　　(e) S.I. 1954/1048 (1954 II, p. 1595).

"the Council" means the National Executive Council of the Association;

"enactment" includes any instrument made under any enactment;

"fund authority" means a local authority maintaining a superannuation fund to which a person either became a contributor after he left Association employment or, as the case may be, was last a contributor before he entered Association employment;

"interchange rules" means rules made under section 2 of the Act of 1948;

"local authority" has the same meaning as in the Act of 1937;

"local government employment" means employment by virtue of which the person employed is or is deemed to be a contributory employee;

"the Minister" means the Minister of Housing and Local Government;

"national service", in relation to any person, means service which is relevant service within the meaning of the Reserve and Auxiliary Forces (Protection of Civil Interests) Act 1951(a), and any similar service immediately following relevant service, entered into with the consent of the authority or person by whom he was employed before undertaking that service or, in the case of a person who holds an appointment to an office and is not employed under a contract of employment, with the consent of the authority by whom he was appointed;

"non-contributing service" has the same meaning as in the Act of 1937;

"prescribed period" has the meaning assigned to it by rule 3;

"the Staff Superannuation Fund" means the Staff Superannuation Fund of the Association;

"transfer value regulations" means the Local Government Superannuation (Transfer Value) Regulations 1954(b);

"voluntary contributions" means—

(a) in relation to a person who enters Association employment after leaving local government employment, payments made voluntarily by him, while in local government employment or in overseas employment within the meaning of the Superannuation (Local Government and Overseas Employment) Interchange Rules 1958(c), for the purpose of securing benefits for his widow, children or other dependants and payments (other than payments made in respect of a liability which has been wholly discharged) of any of the following categories:—

(i) additional contributory payments of the kind referred to in section 2(3) and (4) of the Act of 1953;

(ii) any similar payments made under a local Act scheme as a condition of reckoning any period of employment as service or as a period of contribution for the purposes of the scheme or, where the local Act scheme provides for the reckoning of non-contributing service, as contributing service for the purposes of the scheme;

(iii) any payments made for the purpose of increasing the length at which any period of service or of contribution would be reckonable for the purpose of calculating a benefit under a local Act scheme;

(iv) any payments made in respect of added years; and

(a) 1951 c. 65.  (b) S.I. 1954/1212 (1954 II, p. 1723).
(c) S.I. 1958/1416 (1958 II, p. 1845).

(b) in relation to a person who enters local government employment after leaving Association employment, any payments similar in character to those referred to in (a) of this definition for which provision was made by the rules of the Staff Superannuation Fund.

(2) For the purposes of these rules a justices' clerk shall be deemed to be in the employment of the magistrates' courts committee or committee of magistrates by whom he is, or, under the provisions of any enactment is deemed to have been, appointed, and in relation to any such person references to "employment" shall be construed accordingly.

(3) Any references in these rules to a person as a contributory employee, or to contributing service, or to the Act of 1937, the Act of 1953, the benefits regulations, or any provision in any of those enactments in their application to that person shall be deemed to include references to a person as a local Act contributor within the meaning of the Act of 1937 and to a person entitled to participate in the benefits of a superannuation fund maintained under a local Act scheme, or to service for the purposes of a local Act scheme, or to any corresponding local Act or scheme or provision therein in their application to that person.

(4) References in these rules to a numbered rule shall, unless the reference is to a rule of a specified enactment, be construed as references to the rule bearing that number in these rules.

(5) Unless the context otherwise requires, references in these rules to the provisions of any enactment shall be construed as references to those provisions as amended, extended, modified, applied or re-enacted by any subsequent enactment.

(6) The Interpretation Act 1889(a) shall apply for the interpretation of these rules as it applies for the interpretation of an Act of Parliament.

*Meaning of "prescribed period"*

**3.**—(1) Subject to the provisions of these rules, the expression "prescribed period" in rules 4 and 8 means a period of 12 months after the date on which a person left local government employment or, as the case may be, Association employment, and in the case of a person who immediately after leaving such employment became engaged in national service, a period of 6 months after the termination of that service.

(2) The reference in the preceding paragraph to a period of 12 months shall be construed in relation to a person to whom section 6 of the Act of 1948 applies (which makes special provision as to local government superannuation during periods of emergency) as a reference to a period of 5 years or such longer period as the Minister may in any particular case allow.

PART II

TRANSFER FROM LOCAL GOVERNMENT EMPLOYMENT
TO ASSOCIATION EMPLOYMENT

*Persons to whom part II applies*

**4.**—(1) Subject to the provisions of these rules and subject to the conditions specified in rule 5 being satisfied, this part of these rules shall apply—

(a) to a person who on or after the commencement of these rules enters Association employment within the prescribed period, having left local government employment not earlier than 4th February 1948, and

_____
(a) 1889 c. 63.

(b) if the fund authority consent, to a person who before the commencement of these rules entered Association employment within the prescribed period, having left local government employment not earlier than 4th February 1948.

(2) This part of these rules shall not apply to any person—

(a) who has become entitled to and received payment of any benefit (other than a return of contributions) in respect of his local government employment; or

(b) in respect of whom a transfer value has been paid by the fund authority since he left his local government employment.

### Conditions for application of part II

5. The conditions referred to in rule 4 are that the person shall, before or within 3 months after entering Association employment or, if he entered that employment before the commencement of these rules, within 6 months after their commencement—

(a) notify the Council in writing that he desires these rules to apply to him;

(b) furnish the Council with particulars in writing of any national service in which he has been engaged since leaving local government employment; and

(c) pay to the Staff Superannuation Fund an amount equal to any sum paid to him by way of return of contributions (other than voluntary contributions) on or after leaving local government employment, together with any further sum by way of interest required under rule 18.

### Payment of transfer value

6.—(1) The fund authority shall, when this part of these rules becomes applicable to a person—

(a) pay to the Staff Superannuation Fund, subject to the provisions of these rules, the same transfer value as would have been payable under the transfer value regulations if that person had become a contributory employee under another local authority in the circumstances described in section 29 of the Act of 1937, less—

(i) an amount equal to any sum which the fund authority may become liable to pay by way of income tax in respect of the amount transferred by way of transfer value; and

(ii) an amount equal to any interest required under rule 18; and

(b) furnish the Council and the person with the same particulars as to previous pensionable service as would have been furnished to the person if instead of entering Association employment he had become a contributory employee under another local authority.

(2) The transfer value payable in respect of a person who left local government employment before 1st April 1968 and who entered Association employment before 1st April 1969 shall be calculated by reference to his age at 1st April 1969.

(3) The transfer value payable in respect of a person who enters Association employment on or after 1st April 1969 and more than 12 months after leaving local government employment shall be calculated by reference to his age on entering Association employment.

(4) The transfer value payable in respect of a person who had been an established officer or servant within the meaning of the Asylums Officers' Superannuation Act 1909(a) (in this rule called "the Act of 1909") shall be calculated as if paragraph (c) has been omitted from the definition of "service" in paragraph 1 of Schedule 1 to the transfer value regulations.

(5) Where—

(a) a transfer value is payable by a fund authority in respect of a person who before entering local government employment had been subject to the Act of 1909, and

(b) the body by whom he was last employed while subject to that Act (in this rule called "the hospital body") would, if he had become entitled to a superannuation allowance on leaving local government employment, have been liable to contribute to that allowance,

the hospital body shall pay to the fund authority a sum equal to the transfer value which they would have been liable to pay to the Minister of Health under regulation 56(4) of the National Health Service (Superannuation) Regulations 1950(b) if that regulation had become applicable to the person when he entered Association employment.

(6) Where the hospital body would have had in respect of any such contribution as aforesaid a right of contribution from any other body, that other body shall pay to the fund authority a sum equal to the transfer value which they would have been liable to pay to the Minister of Health under paragraph (5) of the said regulation 56 if that regulation had become applicable to the person when he entered Association employment.

(7) Where any body referred to in paragraph (5) or (6) hereof has been dissolved or has ceased to exercise functions as such, references to that body shall be construed as references to the appropriate authority as defined in paragraph (15) of the said regulation 56.

(8) Notwithstanding anything in the Act of 1937, when this part of these rules becomes applicable to a person, he shall cease to be entitled to any payment out of the superannuation fund administered by the fund authority other than a payment by way of return of voluntary contributions.

*Exercise by local authority of discretionary powers to increase benefits*

7.—(1) Where a person enters, or before the commencement of these rules entered, Association employment after leaving local government employment and these rules have become applicable to him, the authority or body by whom he was employed may, within 6 months after the date on which they are informed by the Council of his notification that he desires these rules to apply to him, exercise any discretion which, with a view to increasing the benefits payable to him, they could have exercised at the time when he left their employment if he had then retired and had been entitled to a retirement pension under regulation 5 of the benefits regulations or (if that regulation was not applicable to him) to any corresponding benefit provided under the superannuation provisions which were applicable to him in that employment.

(2) A decision in the exercise of any discretion under this rule shall be subject to the limitations and restrictions (if any) and to the right of appeal (if any) to which it would have been subject if the discretion had been exercised on the person's retirement in the circumstances aforesaid.

---

(a) 1909 c. 48.         (b) S.I. 1950/497 (1950 I, p. 1327).

(3) Where a discretion has been exercised under this rule, the service reckonable immediately before he left his former employment by the person in whose favour the discretion has been exercised shall be deemed to have been correspondingly increased, and the transfer value payable in respect of him shall be calculated accordingly.

(4) Any increase in service, if attributable to a decision under this rule to increase benefit otherwise than by any notional increase or extension of the service reckonable for the purpose of calculating benefit, or by treating any specified period of non-contributing service as contributing service or, under a local Act scheme, by similarly converting service of one category to service of another category, shall be ascertained by converting the service in respect of which the higher rate of benefit is payable into contributing service in the manner in which non-contributing service is converted into contributing service under section 2(4) of the Act of 1953.

(5) Where the amount of any transfer value payable under rule 6 is increased in consequence of the exercise by an authority or body of any power conferred upon them by this rule, that authority or body shall repay the amount of the said increase to the superannuation fund out of which the transfer value is payable.

## Part III

### Transfer from Association Employment To Local Government Employment

*Persons to whom part III applies*

**8.** Subject to the provisions of these rules and to the conditions specified in rule 9 being satisfied, this part of these rules shall apply—

(a) to a person who on or after the commencement of the rules enters local government employment within the prescribed period, having left Association employment not earlier than 4th February 1948, and

(b) if the Council consent, to a person who before the commencement of these rules entered local government employment within the prescribed period, having left Association employment not earlier than 4th February 1948.

*Conditions for application of part III*

**9.** The conditions referred to in rule 8 are that—

(a) the person shall, before or within 3 months after entering local government employment or, if he entered that employment before the commencement of these rules, within 6 months thereafter—

(i) notify the fund authority in writing that he desires these rules to apply to him;

(ii) furnish the fund authority with particulars in writing of any national service in which he has been engaged since leaving Association employment; and

(iii) pay to the fund authority an amount equal to any sum paid to him by way of return of contributions (other than voluntary contributions) on or after leaving Association employment, together with any further sum by way of interest required under rule 18, and

(b) the fund authority shall receive from the Staff Superannuation Fund a transfer value, calculated in accordance with the schedule to these rules, in respect of the service which the person was entitled to reckon for purposes of the Staff Superannuation Fund immediately before leaving Association employment.

*Reckoning of service*

**10.**—(1) Subject to the provisions of these rules, a person to whom this part of these rules applies shall be entitled to reckon—

(a) the pensionable service he was entitled to reckon at full length for the purposes of the Staff Superannuation Fund, as contributing service; and

(b) any other service he was entitled to reckon for such purposes as contributing service for a period reduced by the fraction by which it would have been reduced under the Staff Superannuation Fund.

(2) Where a person had been engaged in national service before entering local government employment, the period of service which he becomes entitled to reckon under this rule shall, if the transfer value received under rule 9 (b) is calculated so as to include the liability from which the Staff Superannuation Fund was relieved in respect of the period of national service, be treated as increased by so much of that period as would have been reckonable as pensionable service had the person returned to Association employment on the termination of his national service.

(3) Any service which would have been reckonable under the Staff Superannuation Fund by a person to whom this part of these rules applies for the purpose of determining whether he was entitled to receive a benefit thereunder shall be reckonable to the same extent for the purpose of determining whether he is entitled to receive a benefit as a contributory employee.

(4) Where any part of the service of a person to whom this part of these rules applies is attributable to service, before he entered Association employment, which was non-contributing service for the purpose of these rules or of regulations made under section 67 of the National Health Service Act 1946(a), such service shall be reckonable in the manner and to the extent to which it would have been reckonable if instead of entering Association employment he had become a contributory employee.

(5) A person to whom this part of these rules applies shall not be entitled under section 12(2) of the Act of 1937 to reckon as non-contributing service any service as referred to therein before the date he entered Association employment if—

(a) a transfer value in respect of that service has been paid under rule 6, or

(b) a transfer value in respect of that service has been paid under the corresponding provision of any other interchange rules, or

(c) a transfer of assets in respect of his accrued pension rights has been made out of a local authority's superannuation fund under any enactment.

(6) Where at any time after a transfer value has been received under rule 9(b), any further period of employment has become reckonable as service for purposes of the Staff Superannuation Fund, and the Council remit to the fund authority a further transfer value in respect of it, that further period shall be reckonable as it would have been if the further transfer value had been received under rule 9(b).

*Continuation of voluntary contributions*

**11.**—(1) The provisions of this rule shall have effect for the purpose of enabling a person to whom this part of these rules applies to continue any voluntary contributions which are described herein and which he was in course of paying immediately before leaving Association employment.

---

(a) 1946 c. 81.

(2) Where a person elects to continue any such contribution, he shall—

    (a)  when notifying the fund authority under rule 9(a)(i), notify them also that he wishes to continue the payment of voluntary contributions;

    (b)  within the period specified in rule 9(a)(iii) or allowed under rule 17, pay to the fund authority a sum equal to the sum (if any) paid to him by way of return of any such contributions; and

    (c)  make the payments required by this rule.

(3) Where the voluntary contributions were paid in respect of added years, the person shall pay the outstanding amounts as they would have been payable in his Association employment; and thereupon in respect of the added years to which the voluntary payments relate he shall enjoy rights and be subject to liabilities as if those years were added years in respect of which payments were being made under regulation 12 of the benefits regulations.

(4) Where the voluntary contributions were paid by way of—

    (i)  instalments in discharge of a fixed sum or

    (ii)  contributions of a fraction or percentage of emoluments,

as a condition of being entitled to reckon any period of service for the purposes of the Staff Superannuation Fund, or as a condition of increasing the length at which any period of service would be reckoned for those purposes, the person shall pay in the former case a sum or sums equivalent to the aggregate amount or value of the unpaid instalments, and in the latter case a sum or sums equivalent to the capital value of the outstanding liabilities (as certified by an actuary appointed by the Staff Superannuation Fund trustees), as if paragraphs 2, 4(a) and 4(b) of Schedule 2 to the benefits regulations applied to the payment of any such sum or sums; and thereupon his service shall for purposes of rule 10 be affected as nearly as may be in the same manner as it would have been affected in his Association employment if he had completed those payments before leaving that employment.

(5) Notwithstanding the provisions of this rule, the person shall not be required to make payments between the date on which he retires from local government employment and the date on which he would ordinarily have expected to retire from Association employment if he had continued therein.

### Computation of contributions

**12.**—(1) Where any enactment relating to local government superannuation refers, in connection with assessing a return of contributions or a benefit, to the amount of the contributions paid by a person, the amount of the contributions paid by a person to whom this part of these rules applies shall be deemed to be increased, in accordance with the provisions of this rule, to take account of earlier periods of service which became reckonable under rule 10.

(2) Subject to the provisions of this rule, the amount of the increase shall be the amount which would have been payable to him if, on leaving Association employment, he had been entitled to a return of contributions without interest.

(3) Where an amount described in paragraph (1) of this rule is the amount of a person's contributions with interest thereon, interest shall also be payable on the amount by which those contributions are increased under paragraph (2), calculated—

    (a)  as respects the period ending immediately before he entered local government employment, at the rate at which it would have been calculated under the Staff Superannuation Fund if on leaving Association employment he had been entitled to a return of contributions with interest; and

(b) as respects the period beginning on his entry into local government employment, in the manner described in section 10(1) of the Act of 1937.

(4) For the purposes of this rule no account shall be taken of—

(a) payments made voluntarily for securing family benefits;

(b) any sum in respect of contributions which were returned to and retained by the person who paid them;

(c) any voluntary contributions described in rule 11 which have not been continued under that rule; or

(d) any sum paid by way of interest under rule 9(a)(iii).

*Modification of benefits and obligations in relation to National Insurance*

**13.**—(1) In this rule—

"insured person" means an insured person within the meaning of the National Insurance Act 1965(**a**) or, if the person left Association employment before 5th July 1948, an insured person under the National Health Insurance Acts 1936 to 1938 or the Widows', Orphans' and Old Age Contributory Pensions Act 1936(**b**);

"local government modification provisions" means the provisions of the National Insurance (Modification of Local Government Superannuation Schemes) Regulations 1947(**c**) and of Part III of and Schedule 3 to the benefits regulations;

"pension scheme modification provisions" means any provisions contained in or relating to the Staff Superannuation Fund, whereby the benefits provided under the Fund are modified in pursuance of any enactment re-enacted in the National Insurance Act 1965, whether directly, or indirectly, by adjustment of remuneration by reference to which benefits are calculated, or otherwise;

"unreduced" in relation to a transfer value, means without reduction under regulation 6 of the transfer value regulations, or under that regulation as applied by paragraph 8(1) of the schedule to these rules.

(2) Where the following conditions are satisfied in relation to a person to whom this part of these rules applies, namely—

(a) that he was an insured person in Association employment, and

(b) that a transfer value is received which is unreduced in respect of the whole of the period of employment which he becomes entitled to reckon under these rules,

the local government modification provisions shall not apply to him.

(3) Where the conditions specified in paragraph (2) above are not satisfied in relation to such a person, the local government modification provisions shall apply to him, and shall so apply as if any period of employment which he becomes entitled to reckon under these rules were service rendered on or after 5th July 1948:

Provided that—

(a) if part of the transfer value is received unreduced, the period of employment to which that part relates shall be treated as service before 1st September 1947; and

---

(**a**) 1965 c. 51.  (**b**) 1936 c. 33.
(**c**) S.R. & O. 1947/1245 (Rev. xvi, p. 273; 1947 I, p. 1498).

(b) if on or before 5th July 1948 the pension scheme modification provisions (or any corresponding provisions contained in any scheme to which he was formerly subject in employment which was reckonable as service for the purposes of the Staff Superannuation Fund) modified benefit by reference to a table and to age at a given date, the local government modification provisions shall have effect as if any provision therein modifying benefit by reference to a table and age at a given date applied to him, except that the reference to age at that date shall be construed as a reference to his age at that date which was relevant for the purpose of the pension scheme modification provisions.

(4) Nothing in this rule shall affect the application of regulation 18 of the National Insurance (Modification of Local Government Superannuation Schemes) Regulations 1963(a) (which provides for reduction of local government pensions in respect of certain former employments).

*Application of section 11 of the Act of 1953*

**14.** The provisions of section 11 of the Act of 1953 (which enables persons who would otherwise be debarred from becoming contributory employees on grounds of age to reckon, in relation to local government employment, previous service reckonable under a pension scheme) shall apply in relation to a person who entered the employment of a local authority from Association employment before the commencement of these rules; and the references in subsection (3) of that section to the passing of the Act shall be construed as including references to the commencement of these rules.

*Period of Association employment: effect on later period of local government employment and on transfer values*

**15.** Where a person to whom this part of these rules applies—

(a) had entered, and then left, local government employment before the commencement of these rules, and then

(b) had entered, or enters, further employment in such circumstances that a transfer value is paid under section 29 of the Act of 1937 or by virtue of interchange rules,

then, if the fund authority to whom the person first paid contributions after leaving Association employment receive a transfer value under rule 9(b), they shall—

(i) treat the service which becomes reckonable under rule 10 as though it had been reckonable at the time when he ceased to participate in their fund and

(ii) re-calculate the transfer value which they paid in respect of him.

*Right of appeal*

**16.** The provisions of section 35 of the Act of 1937 (which provides for decision of questions and appeals to the Minister) shall have effect in relation to a person who enters local government employment in circumstances in which these rules apply as if the reference in that section to regulations made under that Act included a reference to these rules:

Provided that this rule shall not apply in relation to a person who is a local Act contributor.

---

(a) S.I. 1963/2060 (1963 III, p. 4363).

## PART IV
### MISCELLANEOUS
*Extension of time*

**17.**—(1) A fund authority and the Council may at any time, on the application of a person who desires these rules to apply to him, agree to extend any of the following periods, namely—

(*a*) the periods of 6 and of 12 months referred to in rule 3(1) and

(*b*) the periods of 3 and of 6 months referred to in rules 5 and 9 within which the person must notify in writing that he desires these rules to apply to him.

(2) A fund authority or the Council may, in respect of a person required to furnish particulars in writing of national service or pay any sum described in rule 5(*c*) or 9(*a*)(iii), at any time extend, on the application of that person, the period of 3 or of 6 months referred to in rule 5 or 9, as the case may be, within which he must take such action; and when the person receives notice in writing of their approval of his application he shall be deemed to have complied with the relevant condition specified in that rule.

*Interest on returned contributions*

**18.**—(1) Where a period of 12 months is extended pursuant to rule 17(1)(*a*), the fund authority in respect of a person who has left local government employment, or the Council in respect of a person who has left Association employment, may require that person to pay compound interest on any sum paid to him by way of return of contributions (other than voluntary contributions) on or after leaving that employment, at a rate of 3% per annum with half-yearly rests for a period beginning either with the date 12 months after the date on which he left that employment or, where this is later, the date on which he received such sum, and ending with the date on which he notified in writing that he desired these rules to apply to him.

(2) The interest payable under this rule shall not exceed a sum equal to one-half of the difference between the transfer value payable under these rules and the transfer value which would be payable if calculated by reference to the person's age on leaving such employment.

---

SCHEDULE                                        Rule 9 (*b*)

### TRANSFER VALUES RECEIVABLE FROM THE STAFF SUPERANNUATION FUND

*Method of calculation*

**1.** The transfer value receivable under these rules in respect of a person who leaves Association employment shall be an amount equal to the transfer value which would have been payable under the transfer value regulations if—

(*a*) the person, at the date when he left Association employment, had ceased to be a contributory employee under one local authority and had become such an employee under another local authority in the circumstances described in section 29 of the Act of 1937 and

(*b*) the transfer value regulations had, at that date, been subject to the modifications set out in this schedule and to such incidental and consequential modifications as might have been necessary.

*Contributing service*

**2.** References to contributing service shall be construed as references to service which—

    (*a*)  would have been reckonable for the purpose of calculating a benefit under the Staff Superannuation Fund and

    (*b*)  is not non-contributing service:

Provided that where such service would not have been reckonable at full length, it shall be reckonable as service for a period reduced by the fraction by which it would have been reduced under the Staff Superannuation Fund.

*Non-contributing service*

**3.** References to non-contributing service shall be construed as references to service which—

    (*a*)  would have been reckonable for the purpose of calculating a benefit under the Staff Superannuation Fund and

    (*b*)  is attributable to service, before entering Association employment, which was non-contributing service for the purpose of the Act of 1937 or of regulations made under section 67 of the National Health Service Act 1946.

*Voluntary contributions*

**4.** Where the person was formerly in local government employment and was making voluntary contributions which he had continued but not completed while in Association employment, or where the person was making similar payments originating in Association employment or any other employment, and in either case has elected to continue payments under rule 11, then—

    (*a*)  the period in respect of which the payments are being made shall be treated as if the payments had been completed before he left Association employment; and

    (*b*)  the transfer value shall be reduced by the amount of the payments outstanding at the date of leaving Association employment.

*Added years*

**5.** References to added years shall be construed as references to added years as defined in rule 2(1).

*Age*

**6.**—(1) Where the person left Association employment before 1st April 1968 and entered local government employment before 1st April 1969, references to his age shall be construed as references to his age at 1st April 1969.

(2) Where the person enters local government employment on or after 1st April 1969 and more than 12 months after leaving Association employment, his age shall be taken to mean his age at the date of entering local government employment.

(3) The transfer value payable in respect of a further period of employment described in rule 10(6) shall be calculated by reference to the person's age at the date on which the Council notify the fund authority that such a transfer value has become payable.

*Remuneration*

**7.** References to a person's remuneration shall be construed as references to his annual remuneration for the purpose of the Staff Superannuation Fund immediately before leaving Association employment.

*National Insurance*

**8.**—(1) Where a person's benefits under the Staff Superannuation Fund would have been reduced in respect of any period of Association employment by reason of the provisions for flat-rate retirement pension in the National Insurance Act 1965, the amount of the transfer value shall be reduced by the sum shown in the appropriate column of the Table in Schedule 5 to the transfer value regulations in relation to an age which corresponds—

(a) in the case of a person referred to in paragraph 6 of this schedule, with the age specified therein and

(b) in any other case, with his age at the date of leaving Association employment,

in respect of each one pound of the amount by which any benefit by way of annual amounts to which he may become entitled under the Staff Superannuation Fund may be reduced thereunder in respect of any service of which account is taken in the calculation of the transfer value (excepting service referred to in sub-paragraph (2) hereof), and by a proportionate sum in respect of any fraction of a pound included in the said amount.

(2) Where either—

(a) a person's benefits under the Staff Superannuation Fund would have been reduced in respect of any period of Association employment by reason of the provisions for graduated retirement benefit in the National Insurance Act 1965 or

(b) on or after leaving Association employment a payment in lieu of contributions has been made or equivalent pension benefits have been assured,

regulation 11 of the National Insurance (Modification of Local Government Superannuation Schemes) No. 2 Regulations 1961(a) (which relates to the reduction of transfer values) shall apply as if that period of employment were mentioned in paragraph (1) thereof; and for this purpose—

(i) references in the said regulation 11 to Part IV of the transfer value regulations shall be construed as references to sub-paragraph (1) hereof; and

(ii) references in the said regulation 11 to persons mentioned in regulation 5 of the said regulations of 1961 shall be construed as references to persons who have not been subject to reduction as mentioned in the said sub-paragraph (1).

*Interest on returned contributions*

**9.** The transfer value shall be reduced by an amount equal to that paid under rule 18 by the person in respect of interest on the contributions returned to him on or after he left Association employment.

*Income tax*

**10.** The transfer value shall be reduced by an amount equal to any income tax which the Staff Superannuation Fund may have become liable to pay in respect of the transfer value.

Given under the official seal of the Minister of Housing and Local Government on 25th March 1969.


(L.S.) *Anthony Greenwood,*
Minister of Housing and
Local Government.

---

(a) S.I. 1961/405 (1961 I, p. 1031).

## EXPLANATORY NOTE

*(This Note is not part of the Rules.)*

These Rules provide for the aggregation of service and for a single superannuation award in cases where persons transfer within the prescribed period (generally 12 months) from pensionable employment with a local authority in England or Wales to employment entailing membership of the Staff Superannuation Fund of the National and Local Government Officers Association, and vice versa. Where such a transfer is made the person is enabled, subject to the payment of an appropriate transfer value, to reckon previous service at its actual length for pension under the superannuation scheme to which he transfers.

The Rules are given retrospective effect to a limited extent under the express powers of, and subject to the safeguards required by, section 2(5) of the Superannuation (Miscellaneous Provisions) Act 1948.

## STATUTORY INSTRUMENTS

## 1969 No. 458

## ACQUISITION OF LAND
### COMPENSATION
## The Acquisition of Land (Rate of Interest after Entry) Regulations 1969

| | |
|---|---|
| *Made* - - - - - | *24th March* 1969 |
| *Laid before Parliament* | *2nd April* 1969 |
| *Coming into Operation* | *3rd April* 1969 |

The Treasury, in exercise of the powers conferred upon them by section 32(1) of the Land Compensation Act 1961(a), and of all other powers enabling them in that behalf, hereby make the following Regulations:—

**1.** These Regulations may be cited as the Acquisition of Land (Rate of Interest after Entry) Regulations 1969, and shall come into operation on 3rd April 1969.

**2.** The Interpretation Act 1889(b) shall apply for the interpretation of these Regulations as it applies for the interpretation of an Act of Parliament.

**3.** The rate of interest on any compensation in respect of the compulsory acquisition of an interest in any land on which entry has been made before the payment of the compensation shall be 9 per cent. per annum.

**4.** The Acquisition of Land (Rate of Interest after Entry) (No. 3) Regulations 1967(c) are hereby revoked.

*E. Alan Fitch,*
*Joseph Harper,*
Two of the Lords Commissioners
of Her Majesty's Treasury.

24th March 1969

---

### EXPLANATORY NOTE
*(This Note is not part of the Regulations.)*

These Regulations increase from 8 per cent. to 9 per cent. per annum the rate of interest payable where entry is made, before payment of compensation, on land in England and Wales which is being purchased compulsorily, and revoke the Acquisition of Land (Rate of Interest after Entry) (No. 3) Regulations 1967.

---

(a) 1961 c. 33.  (b) 1889 c. 63  (c) S.I. 1967/1854 (1967 III, p. 4973).

## STATUTORY INSTRUMENTS

### 1969 No. 459

### ACQUISITION OF LAND

#### COMPENSATION

### The Acquisition of Land (Rate of Interest after Entry) (Scotland) Regulations 1969

|  |  |
|---|---|
| *Made* - - - - | *24th March* 1969 |
| *Laid before Parliament* | *2nd April* 1969 |
| *Coming into Operation* | *3rd April* 1969 |

The Treasury, in exercise of the powers conferred upon them by section 40(1) of the Land Compensation (Scotland) Act 1963(a), and of all other powers enabling them in that behalf, hereby make the following Regulations:—

**1.**—(1) These Regulations may be cited as the Acquisition of Land (Rate of Interest after Entry) (Scotland) Regulations 1969, and shall come into operation on 3rd April 1969.

(2) These Regulations shall extend to Scotland only.

**2.** The Interpretation Act 1889(b) shall apply for the interpretation of these Regulations as it applies for the interpretation of an Act of Parliament.

**3.** The rate of interest on any compensation in respect of the compulsory acquisition of an interest in any land on which entry has been made before the payment of the compensation shall be 9 per cent. per annum.

**4.** The Acquisition of Land (Rate of Interest after Entry) (Scotland) (No. 3) Regulations 1967(c) are hereby revoked.

*E. Alan Fitch,*
*Joseph Harper,*
Two of the Lords Commissioners
of Her Majesty's Treasury.

24th March 1969.

---

### EXPLANATORY NOTE

*(This note is not part of the Regulations.)*

These Regulations increase from 8 per cent. to 9 per cent. per annum the rate of interest payable where entry is made, before payment of compensation, on land in Scotland which is being purchased compulsorily, and revoke the Acquisition of Land (Rate of Interest after Entry) (Scotland) (No. 3) Regulations 1967.

---

(a) 1963 c. 51.  (b) 1889 c. 63.  (c) S.I. 1967/1853 (1967 III, p. 4972).

## STATUTORY INSTRUMENTS

## 1969 No. 460

## COAL INDUSTRY

## The Opencast Coal (Rate of Interest on Compensation) Order 1969

| | |
|---|---|
| *Made -    -    -    -* | *24th March* 1969 |
| *Laid before Parliament* | *2nd April* 1969 |
| *Coming into Operation* | *3rd April* 1969 |

The Treasury, in exercise of the powers conferred upon them by sections 35(8) and 49(4) of the Opencast Coal Act 1958(a) and of all other powers enabling them in that behalf, hereby make the following Order:—

**1.** This Order may be cited as the Opencast Coal (Rate of Interest on Compensation) Order 1969, and shall come into operation on 3rd April 1969.

**2.** The Interpretation Act 1889(b) shall apply for the interpretation of this Order as it applies for the interpretation of an Act of Parliament.

**3.** The rate of interest for the purposes of section 35 of the Opencast Coal Act 1958 shall be 8¾ per cent. per annum.

**4.** The Opencast Coal (Rate of Interest on Compensation) (No. 4) Order 1967(c) is hereby revoked.

*E. Alan Fitch,*

*Joseph Harper,*

Two of the Lords Commissioners
of Her Majesty's Treasury.

24th March 1969.

### EXPLANATORY NOTE

*(This Note is not part of the Order.)*

Section 35 of the Opencast Coal Act 1958 provides that interest shall be payable in addition to compensation in certain circumstances. This Order increases the rate of interest from 8 per cent. to 8¾ per cent. per annum and revokes the Opencast Coal (Rate of Interest on Compensation) (No. 4) Order 1967.

(a) 1958 c. 69.          (b) 1889 c. 63.          (c) S.I. 1967/1855 (1967 III, p. 4974).

## STATUTORY INSTRUMENTS

## 1969 No. 463

## ROAD TRAFFIC

## The Local Authorities' Traffic Orders (Procedure) (England and Wales) Regulations 1969

| | | |
|---|---|---|
| *Made* - - - | | *25th March* 1969 |
| *Laid before Parliament* | | *3rd April* 1969 |
| *Coming into Operation* | | *20th April* 1969 |

The Minister of Transport (as respects England and Wales in relation to orders under section 15 or 33 of the Road Traffic Regulation Act 1967(**a**), and as respects England excluding Monmouthshire in relation to all other matters) and the Secretary of State (as respects Wales and Monmouthshire in relation to all matters other than orders under the said section 15 or 33) make these Regulations in exercise of their powers under section 84C of, and Schedule 8 to, the said Act, as amended by Part IX of the Transport Act 1968(**b**) and as read with section 32 of the Countryside Act 1968(**c**), and (for Regulation 1(2) below only) of their powers under sections 4, 26 and 32 of the said Act of 1967, and of all other enabling powers, after consultation with representative organisations in accordance with section 107(2) of the said Act of 1967 :—

### PART I

#### GENERAL

*Citation, Commencement, Revocation*

**1.**—(1) These Regulations may be cited as the Local Authorities' Traffic Orders (Procedure) (England and Wales) Regulations 1969, and shall come into operation on the 20th April 1969.

(2) The Traffic Regulation Orders (Procedure) (England and Wales) Regulations 1968(**d**), the Parking Places Orders (Procedure) (England and Wales) Regulations 1961(**e**) and the Street Playground Orders (Procedure) (England and Wales) Regulations 1961(**f**) are hereby revoked.

*Interpretation*

**2.**—(1) In these Regulations the following expressions have the meanings hereby respectively assigned to them :—

"the Act" means the Road Traffic Regulation Act 1967 as amended by Part IX of the Transport Act 1968 and as read with section 32 of the Countryside Act 1968 ;

---

| | |
|---|---|
| (a) 1967 c.76. | (b) 1968 c.73. |
| (c) 1968 c.41. | (d) S.I. 1968/172 (1968 I, p.406). |
| (e) S.I. 1961/411 (1961 I, p.1051). | (f) S.I. 1961/1242 (1961 II, p.2440). |

"the appropriate Minister", in relation to any order under section 15 or 33 of the Act, means the Minister of Transport, and in relation to any other order to which these Regulations apply, means the Minister of Transport where the order has, or will have, effect in England (excluding Monmouthshire), and the Secretary of State where the order has, or will have, effect in Wales (including Monmouthshire) ;

"the authority", in relation to any order, means the local authority making, or proposing to make, the order under the Act ;

"consolidation order" means an order which revokes provisions of two or more existing orders and reproduces the unspent provisions of those orders without any change in substance ;

"Crown road" and "the appropriate Crown authority" have the same meanings as in section 32 of the Countryside Act 1968 ;

"London local authority" means the Greater London Council, the Council of a London Borough, or the Common Council of the City of London ;

"the notice of proposals" and "the notice of making", in relation to an order, mean respectively the notices required to be published under Regulations 5 and 17 of these Regulations ;

"the objection period" means the period within which objections to an order may be made in accordance with Regulation 6 of these Regulations ;

"the order" means, in relation to anything occurring or falling to be done before its making, the order as proposed to be made, and in relation to anything occurring or falling to be done on or after its making, the order as made ; and

"relevant map", in relation to an order, means the map required to be prepared and kept in connection with that order by Regulation 14 of these Regulations.

(2) Any reference in these Regulations to an order under any particular section of the Act includes a reference to an order varying or revoking an order made, or having effect as if made, under that section.

(3) Any reference in these Regulations to any enactment shall be construed as a reference to that enactment as amended by or under any subsequent enactment.

(4) The Interpretation Act 1889(a) shall apply for the interpretation of these Regulations as it applies for the interpretation of an Act of Parliament.

*Application of Regulations*

3.—(1) These Regulations apply to orders made or proposed to be made by a local authority (other than a London local authority) under any of the following provisions of the Act, that is to say, sections 1(1) to (7), 5, 9, 15, 26, 28, 31, 33, 35, 36, 37(2) and (3), 73(3) and 74.

(2) Except where otherwise stated, each Regulation applies to every such order.

(3) Except where otherwise stated, these Regulations apply to an order under any of the above-mentioned provisions of the Act made or proposed to be made by such a local authority in pursuance of a direction of the appropriate Minister under section 84A(1) of the Act in the same way as it applies to an order in relation to which no such direction has been given.

(4) Where in connection with any order to which these Regulations apply some, but not all, of the necessary procedural steps have been taken before the coming into operation of these Regulations, then the remaining procedural steps in connection with that order shall be determined by, and carried out in accordance with, these Regulations, as nearly as may be.

---

(a) 1889 c.63.

## PART II

### PROCEDURE BEFORE MAKING THE ORDER

*Consultation*

**4.**—(1) Before making the order the authority shall :—

(a) where they are not the highway authority for any road to which the order relates, consult with the highway authority for that road, and

(b) where the order relates to a Crown road, consult with the appropriate Crown authority for that road, and

(c) in all cases consult with one or more organisations representing persons who use any road to which the order relates or are likely to be otherwise affected by any provisions of the order, unless it appears to the authority that there is no such organisation which can appropriately be consulted.

(2) The consultations referred to in paragraph (1) of this Regulation are additional to the consultation with the chief officer of police required by section 84C(1) of the Act and any other consultation required by the Act.

(3) This Regulation has effect subject to Regulation 18 below.

*Publication of proposals*

**5.**—(1) After the consultations referred to in Regulation 4 above but before making the order the authority shall :—

(a) publish once at least in a local newspaper circulating in the area in which any road or other place to which the order relates is situated a notice of proposals containing the particulars specified in Part I of Schedule 1 to these Regulations ;

(b) publish a similar notice in the London Gazette ;

(c) comply with the relevant requirements of Schedules 2 and 3 to these Regulations as to the notices to be displayed in each road or other place to which the order relates and as to the availability of documents for inspection.

(2) This Regulation has effect subject to Regulations 18 and 19 below.

*Objections*

**6.**—(1) The period during which objections to the order can be made shall begin not earlier than the date on which the authority have complied with the requirements of paragraph (1)(a) and (b), and have begun to display the notices required by paragraph (1)(c), of the last foregoing Regulation, and shall continue, in the case of orders under section 73(3) or 74 of the Act, for not less than 28 days, and in the case of all other orders, for not less than 21 days.

(2) Any person desiring to object to the authority's proposal to make the order shall send within the period, and to the address, specified in the notice of proposals published as required by the last foregoing Regulation a written statement of his objection and of the grounds thereof.

(3) This Regulation has effect subject to Regulations 18 and 19 below.

*Public Inquiries*

**7.**—(1) Before making any order to which these Regulations apply the authority may hold a public inquiry in connection with that order and the authority shall hold such an inquiry before making the order in the following cases :—

(a) where the order is :—

(i) an order under section 1, 5 or 35 of the Act which contains a provision for prohibiting the loading or unloading of vehicles in any road, or

(ii) an order under section 9 of the Act which contains a provision for prohibiting the loading or unloading of vehicles in any road and which is proposed to be made within 6 months of the date on which a previous order under section 9 of the Act containing a similar provision as respects that road ceased to be in force,

and an objection to that provision in the order is made by any person in accordance with Regulation 6 above and is not withdrawn ;

(b) where the order is :—

(i) an order under section 1, 5 or 35 of the Act which contains a provision for requiring vehicular traffic generally, or vehicular traffic of any class, to proceed on a road in a specified direction, or for prohibiting such traffic from so proceeding, or

(ii) an order under section 9 of the Act which contains a provision for requiring vehicular traffic generally, or vehicular traffic of any class, to proceed on a road in a specified direction, or for prohibiting such traffic from so proceeding, and which is proposed to be made within 6 months of the date on which a previous order under section 9 of the Act containing a similar provision as respects that road ceased to be in force,

and an objection to that provision in the order is made in accordance with Regulation 6 above by a person who provides a service of stage or express carriages on any road to which the order relates, and is not withdrawn ; and

(c) where the order is one which requires the consent of the appropriate Minister under section 84B of the Act, or under paragraph 17 of Schedule 8 to the Act, and that Minister has notified the authority that he will not be willing to give his consent to the making of the order until a public inquiry has been held by the authority in connection with it.

(2) The authority shall appoint as the person to hold the public inquiry a person selected by them from a panel of persons chosen by the appropriate Minister for the purpose of holding public inquiries under these Regulations.

*Notice of public inquiry*

**8.**—(1) Where the authority decide, before publishing the notice of proposals under Regulation 5 above, to hold a public inquiry, the notice of proposals shall contain, in addition to the particulars required by that Regulation, the particulars specified in Part II of Schedule 1 to these Regulations.

(2) In all other cases where, in connection with an order to which these Regulations apply, a public inquiry is to be held (whether as a result of the authority's decision or the requirements of Regulation 7 above) the authority shall, after complying with the requirements of Regulation 5 above :—

(a) publish once at least in a local newspaper circulating in the area in which any road or other place to which the order relates is situated a notice of the inquiry containing the particulars specified in Part III of Schedule 1 to these Regulations ;

2m

(b) publish a similar notice in the London Gazette ;

(c) comply with the relevant requirements of Schedules 2 and 3 to these Regulations as to the display of notices in each road or other place to which the order relates and as to the availability of documents for inspection ;

(d) not later than the date of the first publication of the notice required by sub-paragraph (a) of this paragraph, inform in writing any person who has objected to the order in accordance with Regulation 6 above and who has not withdrawn the objection, of the date, time and place of the inquiry.

(3) Where the notice of proposals announces the holding of a public inquiry, there shall be at least 42 days between the date on which the publication of that notice in the local newspaper and the London Gazette under the foregoing provisions of these Regulations is completed and the date on which the inquiry is due to begin, and in all other cases there shall be at least 21 days between the date on which the publication as aforesaid of the notice announcing the holding of the public inquiry is completed or the date of the expiration of the objection period (whichever is later) and the date on which the inquiry is due to begin.

*Procedure at public inquiry*

**9.**—(1) Any person interested in the subject matter of a public inquiry may appear at the inquiry either in person or by counsel, solicitor or other representative.

(2) Any person so interested may, whether or not he proposes to appear at the inquiry, send to the person appointed to hold the inquiry, at the address given in the notice of proposals for the receipt of objections, such written representations as he may wish to make in relation to the subject matter of the inquiry with a view to their consideration by that person at the inquiry.

(3) The person holding the inquiry may refuse to hear any person, or to consider any objection or representation made by any person, if he is satisfied that the views of that person or the objection or representation are frivolous or that such views have already been adequately stated by some other person at the inquiry.

(4) Subject as aforesaid, the procedure at the inquiry shall be in the discretion of the person holding it.

*Consent of the appropriate Minister*

**10.** Where the order is one which under section 84B of, or under paragraph 17 of Schedule 8 to, the Act requires the consent of the appropriate Minister, the authority's application to that Minister for such consent shall be accompanied by copies of such of the documents specified in Schedule 4 to these Regulations as may be applicable.

*Consideration of objections*

**11.** Before making the order the authority shall consider all objections duly made in accordance with Regulation 6 above and not withdrawn and also the report and recommendations (if any) of the person holding any public inquiry in connection with the order.

*Modifications*

**12.**—(1) The authority shall not make the order with modifications where :—

(*a*) any of the modifications would involve a departure from the order in the form to which the appropriate Minister or Crown authority have given their consent, or

(*b*) in a case where under section 84A(1) of the Act the appropriate Minister has directed the authority to make the order, any of the modifications would involve a departure from the form in which that Minister has directed the order to be made, or

(*c*) in a case where the consent of the appropriate Minister is not required by or under section 84B of, or under paragraph 17 of Schedule 8 to, the Act, any of the modifications would extend the application of the order or increase the stringency of any prohibition or restriction contained in it,

but subject as aforesaid the authority may make the order with modifications (whether in consequence of any objections or otherwise).

(2) Where the appropriate Minister proposes to consent to the order with modifications which appear to him substantially to affect the character of the order as submitted to him, the authority shall, before making the order, take such steps as that Minister may require for informing the persons likely to be concerned of the effect of the modifications, for giving to those persons an opportunity to make representations in connection therewith and for ensuring that any such representations are duly considered by the authority and (if the appropriate Minister so requests) by that Minister.

*Special provisions for transmission of documents to Minister in certain cases*

**13.** Where the order is one in connection with which the holding of a public inquiry is required by Regulation 7(1)(*a*) or (*b*) above and the authority decide to make the order in a form which includes any provision at variance with the recommendations of the person who held the inquiry, they shall :—

(*a*) before making the order, send to the appropriate Minister a copy of the order as proposed to be made, a copy of the relevant map, a copy of the report and recommendations of the person who held the inquiry and a statement of the authority's reasons for not accepting the relevant recommendations of that person ;

(*b*) at the same time as they send to the appropriate Minister the documents specified above, give written notification of this fact to each person who has duly objected to the order in accordance with Regulation 6 above and has not withdrawn his objection ;

(*c*) not make the order before the expiration of one month from the date on which the said documents were sent to the appropriate Minister, unless that Minister gives the authority earlier notification that he has no observations to make about the order.

## PART III

### THE FORM OF THE ORDER

*The relevant map*

**14.**—(1) The authority shall prepare and keep in connection with the order a map on a scale of not less than 6 inches to 1 mile which clearly indicates by distinctive colours, symbols or markings :—

(*a*) each road to which the order relates,

(*b*) in a case where any provision of the order prohibits the use of a road by all vehicles, or by all vehicles of a particular class, the alternative route available for the vehicles to which the provision applies, and

(*c*) in a case where the order does not relate to a road, the location of the site or other place to which the order applies and the relationship of that site or place to adjacent roads and premises.

(2) Except in the case of an order under section 33 of the Act, it shall not be obligatory for the text of the order to make any specific reference to the relevant map or for that map to be made a part of the order.

(3) Where the relevant map is neither specifically referred to in the text of the order nor made a part of the order, the map shall be for purposes of illustration only and the matter indicated on it shall not prevail over the actual text of the order in the event of any discrepancy between the map and the text.

(4) None of the foregoing paragraphs of this Regulation applies to :—

(*a*) an order which provides only for the revocation of the provisions of any previous order, or

(*b*) an order which relates only to a parking place and provides only for the variation of any one or more of the following matters, namely :—

(i) the charges for the use of the parking place,

(ii) the time limits applicable to such use,

(iii) the classes of vehicle which may use the parking place,

(iv) the conditions applicable to the use of the parking place by vehicles.

### Operative date of Order

**15.**—(1) The order shall specify the date on which it comes into operation or, in a case where different operative dates are provided for different provisions of the order, each of the dates on which a provision of the order comes into operation.

(2) No date on which an order, or a provision of an order, comes into operation shall be earlier than the date on which the notice of the making of the order is published in the local newspaper under Regulation 17 below.

## PART IV

### MAKING THE ORDER AND SUBSEQUENT PROCEDURE

### Making the Order

**16.** Subject to the foregoing provisions of these Regulations the authority may make the order and the order as made shall bear the authority's seal duly authenticated in accordance with the relevant Standing Orders of the authority.

### Notice of the making of the Order

**17.**—(1) When the authority have made the order, they shall :—

(*a*) forthwith give notice in writing of the making of the order to the chief officer of police for the police area in which any road or other place to which the order relates is situated ;

(*b*) notify in writing each person who has duly objected to the order in accordance with Regulation 6 above and has not withdrawn his objection, of the authority's reasons for making the order in spite of the objection ;

(c) within 14 days of the making of the order publish once in a local newspaper circulating in the area in which any road or other place to which the order relates is situated a notice of the making of the order containing the particulars specified in Part IV of Schedule 1 to these Regulations ;

(d) within the same period publish a similar notice in the London Gazette;

(e) comply with the relevant requirements of Schedule 3 to these Regulations as to the availability of documents for inspection ;

(f) where the order relates to any road, forthwith take such steps as are necessary to secure : —

  (i) the erection on or near the road of such traffic signs in such positions as the authority may consider requisite for the purpose of securing that adequate information as to the effect of the order is given to persons using the road, and

  (ii) in a case where the order contains provisions for revoking, or altering the application of, a previous order, such removal or replacement of existing traffic signs as the authority may consider requisite for the purpose of avoiding confusion to users of the road or the continuance of traffic signs in incorrect positions,

but where the road is a Crown road only after consultation with the appropriate Crown authority.

(2) This Regulation has effect subject to Regulation 18 below.

## PART V
### SPECIAL PROCEDURAL PROVISIONS FOR CERTAIN ORDERS

*Special provisions for consolidation orders*

**18.**—(1) Regulations 4(1)(a) and (c), 5 and 6 above shall not apply to a consolidation order and Regulation 17 above shall have effect in relation to such an order with the following modifications, namely, that the particulars to be contained in the notice of the making of the order shall consist only of : —

  (i) the name of the authority ;

  (ii) the title of the order ;

  (iii) a statement of the titles of the orders the provisions of which are reproduced in the consolidation order ;

  (iv) the operative date or dates of the order ; and

  (v) the items numbered 7 and (if appropriate) 8 in Part IV of Schedule 1 to these Regulations.

(2) A consolidation order shall be framed so as to come into operation on a date not less than 14 days after the publication in the local newspaper of the notice of the making of the order.

*Special provisions for certain experimental traffic orders*

**19.**—(1) This Regulation applies to the following orders, that is to say :—

(a) an order under section 9(1) of the Act which provides only for one or more of the following matters : —

  (i) the revocation of an order made, or having effect as if made, under the said section 9(1) ;

    (ii) the variation of an order made, or having effect as if made, under the said section 9(1) so as to reduce the extent of its application or the stringency of any prohibition or restriction imposed by it ;

(*b*) an order under section 9(3) of the Act.

(2) Regulations 5 and 6 above shall not apply to any order to which this Regulation applies.

Sealed with the Official Seal of the Minister of Transport the 25th March 1969.

(L.S.)

*Richard Marsh,*
Minister of Transport.

Dated the 25th March 1969.

*George Thomas,*
One of Her Majesty's Principal
Secretaries of State.

## SCHEDULE 1

### PARTICULARS TO BE INCLUDED IN PRESS NOTICES

### PART I—PARTICULARS TO BE INCLUDED IN THE NOTICE OF PROPOSALS

1. The name of the authority.

2. The title of the order.

3. A statement of the general nature and effect of the order.

4. Where the order relates to any road, the name or other brief description of the road and, in a case where the order is an order under section 73(3) or 74 of the Act, a statement of the approximate length of that road to which the order will apply.

5. Where the order relates to an off-street parking place, a brief description of that place and of its location.

6. Where the order relates to a parking place, a statement of all the charges (if any) proposed to be made for the use of the parking place and of the time limits and the classes of vehicle for which the parking place will be available.

7. Each address at which a copy of the order, as drafted, a copy of the relevant map, and a copy of the authority's statement of reasons for proposing to make the order can be inspected, and the times when inspection can take place at each such address.

8. The period during which, and the address to which, objections to the order can be made, and a statement that all objections must be made in writing and must specify the grounds thereof.

### Part II—Additional Particulars to be Included in the Notice of Proposals Which Announces the Holding of a Public Inquiry

1. A statement that a public inquiry will be held in connection with the order.
2. The date, time and place of the inquiry.
3. The name of the person appointed to hold the inquiry.

### Part III—Particulars to be Included in the Separate Notice of a Public Inquiry

1. The name of the authority.
2. The title of the order.
3. A statement which refers to the published notice of proposals for the order and which indicates that a public inquiry will be held in connection with the order.
4. A brief statement of the general nature and effect of the order and of the name or other brief description of any road or other place to which the order will apply.
5. The date, time and place of the inquiry and the name of the person appointed to hold the inquiry.
6. Each address at which a copy of the order, as drafted, a copy of the relevant map, and a copy of the authority's statement of reasons for proposing to make the order can be inspected, and the times when inspection can take place at each such address.

### Part IV—Particulars to be Included in the Notice of Making the Order

1. The name of the authority.
2. The title of the order.
3. A statement of the general nature and effect of the order and of its operative date or dates.
4. Where the order relates to any road, the name or other brief description of the road.
5. Where the order relates to an off-street parking place, a brief description of that place and of its location.
6. Where the order relates to a parking place, a statement of all the charges (if any) proposed to be made for the use of the parking place and of the time limits and the classes of vehicle for which the parking place will be available.
7. Each address at which a copy of the order, as made, and a copy of the relevant map can be inspected, and the times when inspection can take place at each such address.
8. In the case of an order under section 1, 5, 9, 15, 28, 33 or 35 of the Act, a statement that any person who desires to question the validity of the order or of any provision contained in the order on the ground that it is not within the powers of the relevant section of the Act or on the ground that any requirement of that section or of section 84A, 84B or 84C of the Act or any regulations made under the said section 84C has not been complied with in relation to the order, may, within 6 weeks of the date on which the order is made (such date being stated in the notice) make application for the purpose to the High Court.

## SCHEDULE 2

### Requirements as to Notices to be Displayed in a Road or Other Place

#### Part I—Particulars to be Included in the Notice

1. The name of the authority.
2. The title of the order.

3. A brief statement of the effect of the order in relation to the road or other place where it is displayed.

4. An address at which a copy of the order, a copy of the relevant map and a copy of the authority's statement of reasons for proposing to make the order can be inspected, and the times when such inspection can take place.

5. Where the notice is a notice of proposals, the address to which, and the period during which, objections to the order can be made, and a statement that all objections must be made in writing and must specify the grounds thereof.

6. Where the notice announces the holding of a public inquiry, the date, time and place of the inquiry and the name of the person appointed to hold the inquiry.

PART II—OTHER REQUIREMENTS AS TO THE DISPLAY OF THE NOTICE

1. Where the order relates to any road, the notice shall be displayed in a prominent position at or near each end of the road and in such other positions as the authority think requisite for securing that adequate information about the subject matter of the notice is given to persons using the road.

2. Where the order relates to an off-street parking place, the notice shall be displayed in one or more prominent positions in the road or roads giving access to the parking place, and, where the parking place is in public use, in the parking place itself.

3. The notice shall first be displayed as aforesaid at the same time as the corresponding notice is first published in the local newspaper and the authority shall take all reasonable steps to ensure that it remains in a legible condition and continues to be so displayed:—

    (a) in the case of a notice of proposals not announcing the holding of a public inquiry, until the end of the objection period;

    (b) in the case of a notice announcing the holding of a public inquiry, until the date on which the inquiry begins.

## SCHEDULE 3

REQUIREMENTS AS TO THE AVAILABILITY OF DOCUMENTS FOR INSPECTION

1. There shall be available for inspection at the authority's offices during normal office hours, and (if the authority think fit) at such other places within the authority's area and during such times respectively at those places as the authority may determine, the following documents:—

    (a) a copy of the order as drafted or made (as the case may be);

    (b) a copy of the relevant map;

    (c) in the case of an order which varies or revokes a previous order, a copy of that order and of its relevant map;

    (d) in the case of a proposed order, a copy of a statement setting out the authority's reasons for proposing to make the order; and

    (e) in the case of an order made after the holding of a public inquiry, a copy of the report and the recommendations (if any) of the person appointed to hold the inquiry.

2. The said documents shall be made available as aforesaid on the date of the first publication in the local newspaper of the notice in connection with which they are required to be made available, and they shall continue to be so available:—

    (a) where the notice is a notice of proposals not announcing the holding of a public inquiry, until the end of the objection period;

    (b) where the notice is one announcing the holding of a public inquiry, until the date on which the inquiry begins, and

    (c) where the notice is a notice of making the order, until the end of 6 weeks from the date on which the order is made.

## SCHEDULE 4

DOCUMENTS TO ACCOMPANY THE APPLICATION FOR THE APPROPRIATE
MINISTER'S CONSENT

1. The order as proposed to be made.

2. The relevant map.

3. The statement of the authority's reasons for proposing to make the order.

4. The issues of each local newspaper and of the London Gazette containing the notice of proposals.

5. Each unwithdrawn objection or, in a case where there are no objections or no unwithdrawn objections, a statement to this effect.

6. Copies of the reply or replies sent to each objector.

7. A list of the persons and organisations consulted by the authority and a statement of the views (if any) expressed by each such person or organisation.

8. In a case where a public inquiry has been held, the report and recommendations (if any) of the person holding the inquiry.

9. In a case where the order relates to a Crown road, the consent of the appropriate Crown authority.

10. In a case where the order relates to a Crown road and will apply to persons or vehicles in the service of the Crown, particulars of the Crown authority or authorities whose persons and vehicles are known to be involved.

---

## EXPLANATORY NOTE

*(This Note is not part of the Regulations.)*

These Regulations lay down the procedure to be followed by local authorities in England (outside Greater London) and Wales in connection with the making by them of the main types of traffic and parking place orders under the Road Traffic Regulation Act 1967, as amended by Part IX of the Transport Act 1968. The Regulations replace the Traffic Regulation Orders (Procedure) (England and Wales) Regulations 1968 (S.I. No. 172), the Parking Places Orders (Procedure) (England and Wales) Regulations 1961 (S.I. No. 411), and the Street Playground Orders (Procedure) (England and Wales) Regulations 1961 (S.I. No. 1242), all of which are revoked.

Regulation 3 specifies the Orders to which the Regulations apply. These include traffic regulation orders, experimental traffic orders, orders relating to the use of roads by public service vehicles, street playground orders, orders relating to parking places both on and off the highway (including bus station and parking meter orders) and orders relating to speed limits.

Regulations 4 to 13 lay down the procedure to be followed before the order is made. They provide for preliminary consultations (Regulation 4), publication of proposals (Regulation 5), objections to the order (Regulations 6 and 11), public inquiries (Regulations 7 to 9), the modification of proposals (Regulation 12) and for certain cases where the appropriate Minister's consent is required or where the appropriate Minister has to be notified of the local authority's proposals (Regulations 10 and 13).

Regulations 14 and 15 contain certain requirements about the order itself, in particular about the use of a map to illustrate the order and about the operative date of the order.

Provisions as to the manner of making the order and as to the giving notice of its making are contained in Regulations 16 and 17.

Certain of the above requirements are modified in relation to consolidation orders and some experimental traffic orders by Regulations 18 and 19.

Schedules 1 to 3 contain particulars of the details to be included in the press notices of an order, of the requirements as to display of notices of an order in the road itself, and of the requirements about making documents relating to an order available for public inspection. Schedule 4 lists the documents which must accompany an application for the appropriate Minister's consent.

STATUTORY INSTRUMENTS

## 1969 No. 464 (S.37)

## SHERIFF COURT, SCOTLAND

### Act of Sederunt (Alteration of Sheriff Court Fees) 1969

| | |
|---|---|
| *Made* - - - | *25th March* 1969 |
| *Laid before Parliament* | *31st March* 1969 |
| *Coming into Operation* | *1st April* 1969 |

The Lords of Council and Session, under and by virtue of the powers conferred upon them by section 2 of the Courts of Law Fees (Scotland) Act 1895(a), and by section 40 of the Sheriff Courts (Scotland) Act 1907(b), as amended, and of all other powers competent to them in that behalf, and with the approval and concurrence of the Treasury, do hereby enact as follows :—

**1.** In Section A Part I of the Table of Fees for the Sheriff Clerks of Scotland annexed to the Act of Sederunt (Alteration of Sheriff Court Fees) 1963(c), sub-paragraph (*a*) of paragraph 3 shall be deleted and there shall be substituted therefor a new sub-paragraph (*a*) as set forth in the Schedule hereto.

**2.** In the Act of Sederunt (Alteration of Sheriff Court Fees) 1963 each and every reference to the table of fees annexed thereto shall be construed as a reference to the said table as amended by this or any other enactment.

**3.** This Act of Sederunt may be cited as the Act of Sederunt (Alteration of Sheriff Court Fees) 1969, and shall come into operation on 1st April 1969.

And the Lords appoint this Act of Sederunt to be inserted in the Books of Sederunt.

*J. L. Clyde,*
I.P.D.

Edinburgh,
25th March 1969.

---

(a) 1895 c.14.                 (b) 1907 c.51.
(c) S.I. 1963/133 (1963 I, p.128).

## SCHEDULE

When the amount of the estate vested in or belonging beneficially to the deceased, of which confirmation is required, is as shown in Column A hereunder, the fee shall be as shown for that amount in Column B hereunder:—

| A Estate not exceeding | B Fee | A Estate not exceeding | B Fee | A Estate not exceeding | B Fee | A Estate not exceeding | B Fee | A Estate not exceeding | B Fee |
|---|---|---|---|---|---|---|---|---|---|
| £ | £ s. | £ | £ s. | £ | £ s. | £ | £ s. | £ | £ s. |
| 50 | 0 5 | 15,000 | 23 7 | 57,000 | 51 7 | 99,000 | 79 7 | 141,000 | 107 7 |
| 100 | 0 11 | 16,000 | 24 0 | 58,000 | 52 0 | 100,000 | 80 0 | 142,000 | 108 0 |
| 150 | 0 16 | 17,000 | 24 13 | 59,000 | 52 13 | 101,000 | 80 13 | 143,000 | 108 13 |
| 200 | 1 1 | 18,000 | 25 7 | 60,000 | 53 7 | 102,000 | 81 7 | 144,000 | 109 7 |
| 250 | 1 7 | 19,000 | 26 0 | 61,000 | 54 0 | 103,000 | 82 0 | 145,000 | 110 0 |
| 300 | 1 12 | 20,000 | 26 13 | 62,000 | 54 13 | 104,000 | 82 13 | 146,000 | 110 13 |
| 350 | 1 17 | 21,000 | 27 7 | 63,000 | 55 7 | 105,000 | 83 7 | 147,000 | 111 7 |
| 400 | 2 3 | 22,000 | 28 0 | 64,000 | 56 0 | 106.000 | 84 0 | 148,000 | 112 0 |
| 450 | 2 8 | 23,000 | 28 13 | 65,000 | 56 13 | 107,000 | 84 13 | 149,000 | 112 13 |
| 500 | 2 13 | 24,000 | 29 7 | 66,000 | 57 7 | 108,000 | 85 7 | 150,000 | 113 7 |
| 550 | 2 19 | 25,000 | 30 0 | 67,000 | 58 0 | 109,000 | 86 0 | 151,000 | 114 0 |
| 600 | 3 4 | 26,000 | 30 13 | 68,000 | 58 13 | 110,000 | 86 13 | 152,000 | 114 13 |
| 650 | 3 9 | 27,000 | 31 7 | 69,000 | 59 7 | 111,000 | 87 7 | 153,000 | 115 7 |
| 700 | 3 15 | 28,000 | 32 0 | 70,000 | 60 0 | 112,000 | 88 0 | 154,000 | 116 0 |
| 750 | 4 0 | 29,000 | 32 13 | 71,000 | 60 13 | 113,000 | 88 13 | 155,000 | 116 13 |
| 800 | 4 5 | 30,000 | 33 7 | 72,000 | 61 7 | 114,000 | 89 7 | 156,000 | 117 7 |
| 850 | 4 11 | 31,000 | 34 0 | 73,000 | 62 0 | 115,000 | 90 0 | 157,000 | 118 0 |
| 900 | 4 16 | 32,000 | 34 13 | 74,000 | 62 13 | 116,000 | 90 13 | 158,000 | 118 13 |
| 950 | 5 1 | 33,000 | 35 7 | 75,000 | 63 7 | 117,000 | 91 7 | 159,000 | 119 7 |
| 1,000 | 5 7 | 34,000 | 36 0 | 76,000 | 64 0 | 118,000 | 92 0 | 160,000 | 120 0 |
| 1,500 | 6 7 | 35,000 | 36 13 | 77,000 | 64 13 | 119,000 | 92 13 | 161,000 | 120 13 |
| 2,000 | 7 7 | 36,000 | 37 7 | 78,000 | 65 7 | 120,000 | 93 7 | 162,000 | 121 7 |
| 2,500 | 8 7 | 37,000 | 38 0 | 79,000 | 66 0 | 121,000 | 94 0 | 163,000 | 122 0 |
| 3,000 | 9 7 | 38,000 | 38 13 | 80,000 | 66 13 | 122,000 | 94 13 | 164,000 | 122 13 |
| 3,500 | 10 7 | 39,000 | 39 7 | 81,000 | 67 7 | 123,000 | 95 7 | 165,000 | 123 7 |
| 4,000 | 11 7 | 40,000 | 40 0 | 82,000 | 68 0 | 124,000 | 96 0 | 166,000 | 124 0 |
| 4,500 | 12 7 | 41,000 | 40 13 | 83,000 | 68 13 | 125,000 | 96 13 | 167,000 | 124 13 |
| 5,000 | 13 7 | 42,000 | 41 7 | 84,000 | 69 7 | 126,000 | 97 7 | 168,000 | 125 7 |
| 5,500 | 14 0 | 43,000 | 42 0 | 85,000 | 70 0 | 127,000 | 98 0 | 169,000 | 126 0 |
| 6,000 | 14 13 | 44,000 | 42 13 | 86,000 | 70 13 | 128,000 | 98 13 | 170,000 | 126 13 |
| 6,500 | 15 7 | 45,000 | 43 7 | 87,000 | 71 7 | 129,000 | 99 7 | 171,000 | 127 7 |
| 7,000 | 16 0 | 46,000 | 44 0 | 88,000 | 72 0 | 130,000 | 100 0 | 172,000 | 128 0 |
| 7,500 | 16 13 | 47,000 | 44 13 | 89,000 | 72 13 | 131,000 | 100 13 | 173,000 | 128 13 |
| 8,000 | 17 7 | 48,000 | 45 7 | 90,000 | 73 7 | 132,000 | 101 7 | 174,000 | 129 7 |
| 8,500 | 18 0 | 49,000 | 46 0 | 91,000 | 74 0 | 133,000 | 102 0 | 175,000 | 130 0 |
| 9,000 | 18 13 | 50,000 | 46 13 | 92,000 | 74 13 | 134,000 | 102 13 | 176,000 | 130 13 |
| 9,500 | 19 7 | 51,000 | 47 7 | 93,000 | 75 7 | 135,000 | 103 7 | 177,000 | 131 7 |
| 10,000 | 20 0 | 52,000 | 48 0 | 94,000 | 76 0 | 136,000 | 104 0 | 178,000 | 132 0 |
| 11,000 | 20 13 | 53,000 | 48 13 | 95,000 | 76 13 | 137,000 | 104 13 | 179,000 | 132 13 |
| 12,000 | 21 7 | 54,000 | 49 7 | 96,000 | 77 7 | 138,000 | 105 7 | exceeding | |
| 13,000 | 22 0 | 55,000 | 50 0 | 97,000 | 78 0 | 139,000 | 106 0 | ing | |
| 14,000 | 22 13 | 56,000 | 50 13 | 98,000 | 78 13 | 140,000 | 106 13 | 179,000 | 133 7 |

## EXPLANATORY NOTE
### (This Note is not part of the Act of Sederunt.)

This Act of Sederunt prescribes a new scale of fees chargeable by Sheriff Clerks for receiving and examining certain inventories of estates in Commissary proceedings.

STATUTORY INSTRUMENTS

## 1969 No. 465 (S.38)

## CLEAN AIR

## The Clean Air (Height of Chimneys) (Exemption) (Scotland) Regulations 1969

| | |
|---|---|
| *Made* - - - | *25th March* 1969 |
| *Laid before Parliament* | *31st March* 1969 |
| *Coming into Operation* | *1st April* 1969 |

In exercise of the powers conferred on me by sections 6(11) and 13(1) of the Clean Air Act 1968(a), and of all other powers enabling me in that behalf, I hereby make the following regulations :—

*Title and commencement*

**1.** These regulations may be cited as the Clean Air (Height of Chimneys) (Exemption) (Scotland) Regulations 1969, and shall come into operation on 1st April 1969.

*Interpretation*

**2.** The Interpretation Act 1889(b) shall apply for the interpretation of these regulations as it applies for the interpretation of an Act of Parliament.

*Exempted boilers and plant*

**3.**—(1) The purposes set out in paragraph (2) of this regulation shall be purposes prescribed in terms of section 6(11) of the Clean Air Act 1968 (which section relates to the height of chimneys serving new or enlarged furnaces connected with boilers or industrial plant, but exempts from certain of its provisions any boiler or plant used or to be used wholly for a prescribed purpose).

(2) The said purposes are—

(a) temporarily replacing any other boiler or plant which is—

(i) under inspection, maintenance or repair ;

(ii) being rebuilt ; or

(iii) being replaced by a permanent boiler or plant ;

(b) providing a temporary source of heat or power during any building operation or work of engineering construction (within the meaning of section 176 of the Factories Act 1961(c)) ;

(c) providing a temporary source of heat or power for investigation or research ;

(d) providing products of combustion to heat other plant (whether directly or indirectly) to an operating temperature ;

---

(a) 1968 c. 62.　　(b) 1889 c. 63.　　(c) 1961 c. 34.

(*e*) providing heat or power by mobile or transportable plant for the purposes of agriculture (within the meaning of section 86(3) of the Agriculture (Scotland) Act 1948(**a**)).

*William Ross,*
One of Her Majesty's Principal
Secretaries of State.

St. Andrew's House,
Edinburgh, 1.
25th March 1969.

---

## EXPLANATORY NOTE

### (*This Note is not part of the Regulations.*)

Under Section 6(2) of the Clean Air Act 1968, a person having possession of a boiler or industrial plant attached to a building or for the time being fixed to or installed on any land (other than an exempted boiler or plant) is required to obtain the approval of the local authority to the height of the chimney if he proposes to construct a new chimney or enlarge the furnace. By Section 6(11), exempted boilers and plant mean those used or to be used wholly for any purpose prescribed by Regulations ; and these Regulations prescribe the purposes which carry exemption. They include temporary or local provision of heat or power during replacement or maintenance, building operations, engineering construction, investigation or research, and agricultural operations.

---

(**a**) 1948 c. 45.

## 1969 No. 466 (S.39)

## CLEAN AIR

## The Clean Air (Height of Chimneys) (Prescribed Form) (Scotland) Regulations 1969

| | | | |
|---|---|---|---|
| *Made* | - | - | - | *25th March* 1969 |
| *Laid before Parliament* | | | *31st March* 1969 |
| *Coming into Operation* | | | *1st April* 1969 |

In exercise of the powers conferred on me by sections 6(3) and 13(1) of the Clean Air Act 1968(a), and of all other powers enabling me in that behalf, I hereby make the following regulations :—

*Title and commencement*

**1.** These regulations may be cited as the Clean Air (Height of Chimneys) (Prescribed Form) (Scotland) Regulations 1969, and shall come into operation on 1st April 1969.

*Interpretation*

**2.** The Interpretation Act 1889(b) shall apply for the interpretation of these regulations as it applies for the interpretation of an Act of Parliament.

*Prescribed form for purposes of section* 6(3) *of Clean Air Act* 1968

**3.** For the purposes of section 6(3) of the Clean Air Act 1968 (which requires an application for approval of the height of a chimney to be made to the local authority on the prescribed form and to be accompanied by the prescribed particulars), the prescribed form shall be the form set out in Schedule 1 to these regulations and the prescribed particulars shall be the particulars set out in Schedule 2.

*William Ross,*
One of Her Majesty's Principal
Secretaries of State.

St. Andrew's House,
Edinburgh, 1.
25th March 1969.

(a) 1968 c. 62.  (b) 1889 c. 63.

# SCHEDULE 1

## CLEAN AIR ACT 1968

### SECTION 6—CHIMNEY HEIGHTS (Note 1)

Application for approval by the local authority
of the height of a chimney serving a
furnace or furnaces

Name and address of local authority.

A. Full name and address of applicant.

Telephone No.

Address of premises where chimney is or will be constructed (if different from above).

Name and address of consultant, contractor or other agent (if employed).

Telephone No.

B. Brief description of proposed works.

C. Category under which chimney height approval is sought (Note 2)

|  |  |
|---|---|
| (a) Construction of new chimney | Insert |
| (b) Increase of combustion space of existing furnace (Note 3) | YES or |
| (c) Replacement of furnace by one having larger combustion space | NO |

(Signed by or on behalf of the applicant)

Date                                          (Note 4)

# SCHEDULE 2

Particulars to accompany application for approval

A. Description and use of furnace(s).

1. Intended use of furnace(s) (e.g. boiler plant, metal melting or reheating, calcining, drying, etc.) (Note 5).

2. Type and description of furnace(s) (Note 5).

3. (a) Particulars of furnaces to be installed.

   (b) Particulars of changes intended to existing furnaces.

   (c) Particulars of furnaces to be removed.

B. Rating and fuel consumption (Note 5).

4. (a) Maximum continuous rating of boiler(s) (pounds steam per hour from and at 100°C., or B.t.u.s. per hour).

   (b) Maximum rate of fuel consumption in pounds per hour (separately for different fuels).

5.   Type(s) of fuel to be used (Note 6).

6.   Sulphur content of fuel %.

C.  Particulars of emissions.

   7.   Quantity and quality of emission (if any) from the material being heated, e.g., fume, sulphur trioxide, hydrogen sulphide.

   8.   (a) Volume of chimney gases at working temperature (cubic ft. per second, calculated from paragraph 4(b) above).

      (b) Working temperature of chimney gases in degrees C. (State point of measurement).

      (c) Efflux velocity of chimney gases at working temperature and at maximum loading of plant (ft. per sec.).

D.  Particulars of buildings.

   9.   Height of building to which the chimney is attached.

  10.   Length of building to which the chimney is attached.

  11.   Height(s) of adjacent building(s).

  12.   Distance of adjacent buildings from proposed chimney.

E.  Particulars of chimney for which approval required.

  13.   Height of chimney above ground level.

  14.   Details of construction of chimney, i.e., materials, insulation, single or multi-flue, internal diameter of chimney top.

F.  Supplementary information.

  15.   Brief description and/or sketch plan of other emission sources on same site with heights of chimneys and approximate distances from chimney for which approval is sought.

  16.   Any other information relevant to the application.

*Notes*

1. An Explanatory Memorandum on the Clean Air Act Act 1968, with notes on Section 6, is contained in Scottish Development Department Circular No. 8/1969, available from H.M.S.O. price 1s. 9d. net.

2. The exact terms of section 6(10) of the Clean Air Act 1968 are—

"This section applies to the following furnaces:—

(a) any furnace served by a chimney other than a chimney the construction of which was begun or the plans for which were passed before the commencement of this section;

(b) any furnace the combustion space of which has been increased since the commencement of this section; and

(c) any furnace the installation of which was begun after the commencement of this section and which replaces a furnace which had a smaller combustion space;

not being a furnace forming part of a generating station as defined in the Electricity (Supply) Act 1919, other than a private generating station as so defined."

The commencement date referred to is 1st April 1969.

An application may cover more than one category.

3. Including addition of a new furnace to an existing installation.

4. Section 6(6) of the Clean Air Act 1968 provides as follows:

"If a local authority to whom an application is duly made for approval under this section fail to determine the application and to give a written notification of their decision to the applicant within four weeks of receiving the application or such longer period as may be agreed in writing between the applicant and the authority, the approval applied for shall be deemed to have been granted without qualification".

5. The information should relate to the total furnace or boiler plant which the proposed chimney will serve after all the works have been completed.

6. If oil specify type and viscosity. If solid fuel give Coal Board specification, or colliery source, if known.

---

## EXPLANATORY NOTE

*(This Note is not part of the Regulations.)*

These Regulations prescribe (i) the form of application for the approval of the local authority to the height of a chimney serving a furnace to which Section 6 of the Clean Air Act 1968 applies, and (ii) the particulars to accompany that form. The Section applies to furnaces which are being enlarged, or the chimneys serving which are being constructed, after 1st April 1969.

STATUTORY INSTRUMENTS

# 1969 No. 469

# LAND DRAINAGE

## The Drainage Charges (Forms) Regulations 1969

Made - - - 24th March 1969

Coming into Operation 1st April 1969

### ARRANGEMENT OF REGULATIONS

1. Citation, commencement and revocation.
2. Interpretation.
3. Forms of drainage charges.
4. Forms of demand for general drainage charges.
5. Forms of demand for special drainage charges.
6. Comprehensive demands.
7. Special cases.

### SCHEDULE

Form 1. General drainage charge raised on acreage basis.

Form 2. General drainage charge raised on annual value basis.

Form 3. Special drainage charge.

Form 4. Demand for general drainage charge raised on acreage basis when assessed on occupier.

Form 5. Demand for general drainage charge raised on acreage basis when assessed on owner.

Form 6. Demand for general drainage charge raised on annual value basis when assessed on occupier.

Form 7. Demand for general drainage charge raised on annual value basis when assessed on owner.

Form 8. Demand for special drainage charge when assessed on occupier.

Form 9. Demand for special drainage charge when assessed on owner.

The Minister of Agriculture, Fisheries and Food, in exercise of the powers conferred on him by section 5(3) of the Land Drainage Act 1961(a) and by that section as applied by section 7 of the Isle of Wight River and Water Authority Act 1964(b), and of all other powers enabling him in that behalf, hereby makes the following regulations :—

*Citation, commencement and revocation*

1.—(1) These regulations may be cited as the Drainage Charges (Forms) Regulations 1969 and shall come into operation on 1st April 1969.

(2) The Drainage Charges (Forms) Regulations 1962(c) are hereby revoked.

(a) 1961 c.48.
(c) S.I. 1962 / 347 (1962 I, p.317).

(b) 1964 c.xxv.

*Interpretation*

**2.**—(1) In these regulations, in relation to the raising of a general drainage charge by a river authority, the following expressions have the meanings hereby assigned to them respectively, that is to say :—

"the acreage basis" means the basis described in section 21 of the Agriculture (Miscellaneous Provisions) Act 1968(**a**) on which such a charge may be raised ; and

"the annual value basis" means the basis described in section 1 of the Land Drainage Act 1961 subject to such modifications as may be applicable by virtue of any determination made by that authority under section 28(3) of the said Act of 1968 on which that authority may raise such a charge.

(2) Any reference in these regulations to a form denoted by a number is a reference to the form so numbered in the Schedule to these regulations, and any requirement that any charge raised or any demand for payment shall be in one of those forms shall be treated as a requirement that it shall be in that form adapted as required in accordance with the notes to that form or in a form substantially to the like effect.

(3) The Interpretation Act 1889(**b**) shall apply to the interpretation of these regulations as it applies to the interpretation of an Act of Parliament.

*Forms of drainage charges*

**3.**—(1) Every general drainage charge raised by a river authority on the acreage basis shall be in Form 1.

(2) Every general drainage charge raised by a river authority on the annual value basis shall be in Form 2.

(3) Every special drainage charge raised by a river authority shall be in Form 3.

*Forms of demand for general drainage charges*

**4.**—(1) Every demand for payment of a general drainage charge raised by a river authority on the acreage basis shall be in Form 4 if it is assessed on an occupier and in Form 5 if it is assessed on an owner.

(2) Every demand for payment of a general drainage charge raised by a river authority on the annual value basis shall be in Form 6 if it is assessed on an occupier and in Form 7 if it is assessed on an owner.

*Forms of demand for special drainage charges*

**5.** Every demand for a special drainage charge shall be in Form 8 if it is assessed on an occupier and in Form 9 if it is assessed on an owner.

*Comprehensive demands*

**6.** Where a general and a special drainage charge are payable by the same person, the amount of the special drainage charge may be included in the general drainage charge demand if the additional information required to be given by the appropriate form of special drainage charge demand is also included.

---

   (a) 1968 c. 34.                           (b) 1889 c.63.

*Special cases*

**7.**—(1) Subject to paragraph (2) below the foregoing regulations shall apply to the Conservators of the River Thames and the Lee Conservancy Catchment Board as they apply to a river authority.

(2) Such modifications shall be made in the forms specified in those regulations when used by the said Conservators or the said Catchment Board or by the Isle of Wight River and Water Authority as may be necessary to meet the circumstances of the case.

In Witness whereof the Official Seal of the Minister of Agriculture, Fisheries and Food is hereunto affixed on 24th March 1969.

(L.S.) *Cledwyn Hughes,*
Minister of Agriculture, Fisheries and Food.

---

## SCHEDULE

### FORM I

#### GENERAL DRAINAGE CHARGE RAISED ON ACREAGE BASIS

The                                    River Authority, in exercise of the powers conferred on them by section 1 of the Land Drainage Act 1961, as amended by the Agriculture (Miscellaneous Provisions) Act 1968, hereby raise for the year ending on 31st March 19      a general drainage charge of              per acre of chargeable land in the                                    River Authority Area.

The Common Seal of the                                    River Authority is hereunto affixed on                              19      pursuant to a resolution of the Authority dated                              19      .

### FORM 2

#### GENERAL DRAINAGE CHARGE RAISED ON ANNUAL VALUE BASIS

The                                    River Authority, who have determined that *subsections (2) and (3)* of section 28 of the Agriculture (Miscellaneous Provisions) Act 1968 shall apply to the Authority for the year ending on 31st March 19      , in exercise of the powers conferred on them by section 1 of the Land Drainage Act 1961, hereby raise for that year a general drainage charge of              per pound on the annual value of each chargeable hereditament in the River Authority Area.

The Common Seal of the                                    River Authority is hereunto affixed on                  19      pursuant to a resolution of the Authority dated                  19      .

*Note.* Delete the matter in italics where no determination has been made under subsection (3) of the section above referred to.

FORM 3

SPECIAL DRAINAGE CHARGE

The                                    River Authority, in exercise of the powers
conferred on them by a scheme made by them and confirmed by the
                                    Order 19    , hereby raise, for the year
ending on 31st March 19    , a special drainage charge of                per
acre of chargeable land in *such part of* the                    River
Authority Area *as is specified in the said scheme.*

The Common Seal of the                         River Authority is
hereunto affixed on            19     pursuant to a resolution of the
Authority dated            19   .

*Note.* Delete the words in italics where the scheme designates the whole of the river authority
area for the purpose of the special drainage charge.


FORM 4

DEMAND FOR GENERAL DRAINAGE CHARGE RAISED ON
ACREAGE BASIS WHEN ASSESSED ON OCCUPIER

THE                         RIVER AUTHORITY

GENERAL DRAINAGE CHARGE

LAND DRAINAGE ACT 1961

AGRICULTURE (MISCELLANEOUS PROVISIONS) ACT 1968

To                ..................................................(a)

Address            ................................................

                   ................................................

The                                    River Authority have raised a general drainage charge of                    per acre for the year ending on 31st March 19    .
Payment of this charge and of the arrears (if any) of former charges as shown below
is now due from you.

| Assessment No. | Description of chargeable land | Acreage of commercial woodlands | Assessable acreage of commercial woodlands | Assessable acreage of other chargeable land | Total assessable acreage | Amount of charge |
|---|---|---|---|---|---|---|
|  |  |  |  |  |  | £   s.   d. |

Arrears (if any) of former charges

Total amount now due

The amount due should be paid                (b). Cheques, money orders
and postal orders should be made payable to the
River Authority and crossed. They should not be made payable to any individual
officer.

By order of the Authority

Treasurer.

*Notes.*
(a) Where the name of the occupier is not known to the river authority, insert "The occupier".
(b) Insert instructions as to place, time and method of payment.

FORM 5

DEMAND FOR GENERAL DRAINAGE CHARGE RAISED ON
ACREAGE BASIS WHEN ASSESSED ON OWNER

THE                  RIVER AUTHORITY

GENERAL DRAINAGE CHARGE

LAND DRAINAGE ACT 1961

AGRICULTURE (MISCELLANEOUS PROVISIONS) ACT 1968

To           ........................................................

Address      ........................................................

                 ........................................................

The                          River Authority have raised a general
drainage charge of              per acre for the year ending on 31st March
19     .   Payment of this charge and of the arrears (if any) of former charges as
shown below is now due from you.

| Assessment No. | Description of chargeable land | Acreage of commercial woodlands | Assessable acreage of commercial woodlands | Assessable acreage of other chargeable land | Total assessable acreage | Amount of charge |
|---|---|---|---|---|---|---|
| | | | | | | £  s.  d. |
| | | | | | | |

Arrears (if any) of former charges

Total amount now due

This charge has been assessed upon you, as owner of the land described above,
in accordance with the arrangements made with you by the Authority under section
25(1) of the Agriculture (Miscellaneous Provisions) Act 1968. If the amount of the
charge for the current year is paid within two months beginning with the date of
service of this demand upon you or before 1st October 19     (if this is later), the
Authority will make an allowance equal to ten per cent of the amount of that charge.

The amount due should be paid                 (a).   Cheques,
money orders and postal orders should be made payable to the
River Authority and crossed.   They should not be made payable to any individual
officer.

By order of the Authority

Treasurer.

Note.

(a) Insert instructions as to place, time and method of payment.

FORM 6

DEMAND FOR GENERAL DRAINAGE CHARGE RAISED ON
ANNUAL VALUE BASIS WHEN ASSESSED ON OCCUPIER

THE                                        RIVER AUTHORITY

GENERAL DRAINAGE CHARGE

LAND DRAINAGE ACT 1961

AGRICULTURE (MISCELLANEOUS PROVISIONS) ACT 1968

To                    ....................................................(a)

Address               ....................................................

                      ....................................................

The                              River Authority have raised a general
drainage charge of                in the pound for the year ending on 31st
March 19    . Payment of this charge and of the arrears (if any) of former charges
as shown below is now due from you.

| Assessment No. | Name or description of hereditament | Annual value for drainage charge purposes | Amount of charge |
|---|---|---|---|
| | | | £   s.   d. |
| | | | |
| | Arrears (if any) of former charges | | |
| | Total amount now due | | |

The amount due should be paid                    (b). Cheques, money orders
and postal orders should be made payable to the
River Authority and crossed,  They should not be made payable to any individual
officer.

By order of the Authority

Treasurer.

*Notes.*
(a) Where the name of the occupier is not known to the river authority, insert "The occupier".
(b) Insert instructions as to place, time and method of payment.

FORM 7

DEMAND FOR GENERAL DRAINAGE CHARGE RAISED ON
ANNUAL VALUE BASIS WHEN ASSESSED ON OWNER

THE ............................................ RIVER AUTHORITY

GENERAL DRAINAGE CHARGE

LAND DRAINAGE ACT 1961

AGRICULTURE (MISCELLANEOUS PROVISIONS) ACT 1968

To ......................................................

Address ......................................................

......................................................

The ............................. River Authority have raised a general drainage charge
of ............................. in the pound for the year ending on 31st March 19    .
Payment of this charge and of the arrears (if any) of former charges as shown below
is now due from you.

| Assessment No. | Name or description of hereditament | Annual value for drainage charge purposes | Amount of charge |
|---|---|---|---|
| | | | £      s.      d. |
| | | Arrears (if any) of former charges | |
| | | Total amount now due | |

This charge has been assessed upon you, as owner of the land described above,
in accordance with the arrangements made with you by the Authority under section
25(1) of the Agriculture (Miscellaneous Provisions) Act 1968. If the amount of
the charge for the current year is paid within two months beginning with the date
of service of this demand upon you or before 1st October 19    (if this is later),
the Authority will make an allowance equal to ten per cent of the amount of that
charge.

The amount due should be paid ............................. (a). Cheques, money orders
and postal orders should be made payable to the .............................
River Authority and crossed. They should not be made payable to any individual
officer.

By order of the Authority

............................. Treasurer.

Note.

(a) Insert instructions as to place, time and method of payment.

Form 8

Demand for Special Drainage Charge when Assessed on Occupier

THE                            RIVER AUTHORITY

SPECIAL DRAINAGE CHARGE

LAND DRAINAGE ACT 1961

AGRICULTURE (MISCELLANEOUS PROVISIONS) ACT 1968

To             ...................................................(a)

Address        ..................................................

                  ..................................................

     The                              River Authority have raised a special drainage charge of                  per acre for the year ending on 31st March 19     to meet the expenses of drainage works in connection with the watercourses designated in the scheme confirmed by the                  Order 19      and any expenses arising from such works. Payment of this charge and of the arrears (if any) of former charges as shown below is now due from you.

| Assessment No. | Descrip-tion of chargeable land | Acreage of commer-cial wood-lands | Assessable acreage of commer-cial wood-lands | Assessable acreage of other chargeable land | Total assessable acreage | Amount of charge |
|---|---|---|---|---|---|---|
| | | | | | | £   s.   d. |
| | | | | | | |

Arrears (if any) of former charges

Total amount now due

     The amount due should be paid                 (b). Cheques, money orders and postal orders should be made payable to the River Authority and crossed. They should not be made payable to any individual officer.

By order of the Authority

Treasurer.

*Notes.*

(a) Where the name of the occupier is not known to the river authority, insert "The occupier".

(b) Insert instructions as to place, time and method of payment.

FORM 9

DEMAND FOR SPECIAL DRAINAGE CHARGE WHEN ASSESSED ON OWNER

THE                                    RIVER AUTHORITY

SPECIAL DRAINAGE CHARGE

LAND DRAINAGE ACT 1961

AGRICULTURE (MISCELLANEOUS PROVISIONS) ACT 1968

To          .................................................

Address     .............................................

            .............................................

The                                    River Authority have raised a special drainage charge of                          per acre for the year ending on 31st March
19      to meet the expenses of drainage works in connection with the watercourses
designated in the scheme confirmed by the                          Order 19
and any expenses arising from such works.   Payment of this charge and of the arrears
(if any) of former charges as shown below is now due from you.

| Assessment No. | Description of chargeable land | Acreage of commercial woodlands | Assessable acreage of commercial woodlands | Assessable acreage of other chargeable land | Total assessable acreage | Amount of charge |
|---|---|---|---|---|---|---|
|  |  |  |  |  |  | £   s.   d. |
|  |  |  |  |  |  |  |

Arrears (if any) of former charges

Total amount now due

This charge has been assessed upon you, as owner of the land described above,
in accordance with the arrangements made with you by the Authority under section
25(1) of the Agriculture (Miscellaneous Provisions) Act 1968.   If the amount of
the charge for the current year is paid within two months beginning with the date
of service of this demand upon you or before 1st October 19      (if this is later),
the Authority will make an allowance equal to ten per cent of the amount of that
charge.

The amount due should be paid                          (a). Cheques, money orders
and postal orders should be made payable to the
River Authority and crossed.   They should not be made payable to any individual
officer.

By order of the Authority

Treasurer.

*Note.*

(a) Insert instructions as to place, time and method of payment.

# EXPLANATORY NOTE

*(This Note is not part of the Regulations.)*

These Regulations, which supersede the Drainage Charges (Forms) Regulations 1962, prescribe the forms to be used for raising drainage charges, whether general or special, and the forms of demands for such charges. The forms, based on those scheduled to the 1962 Regulations, have been adapted to meet the altered basis on which drainage charges may be raised, which is provided by the Agriculture (Miscellaneous Provisions) Act 1968.

The Regulations apply to England and Wales.

## STATUTORY INSTRUMENTS

## 1969 No. 471

## SEA FISHERIES

# The White Fish and Herring Subsidies (United Kingdom) (Amendment) Scheme 1969

| | |
|---|---|
| *Made* - - - | *17th February* 1969 |
| *Laid before Parliament* | *25th February* 1969 |
| *Coming into Operation* | *26th March* 1969 |

The Minister of Agriculture, Fisheries and Food and the Secretary of State for Scotland (being the Secretary of State concerned with the sea fishing industry in Scotland) in exercise of the powers conferred on them by section 5 of the White Fish and Herring Industries Act 1953(**a**) (as amended by section 2 of the White Fish and Herring Industries Act 1957(**b**), section 37 of and paragraph 18 of Schedule 2 to the Sea Fish Industry Act 1962(**c**) and section 22 of and paragraphs 10 to 13 inclusive of Schedule 1 to the Sea Fisheries Act 1968(**d**)), section 1 of the Sea Fish Industry Act 1962 and sections 1 and 2 of the Sea Fisheries Act 1968, and of all other powers enabling them in that behalf, with the approval of the Treasury, hereby make the following scheme :—

*Citation, extent, commencement and interpretation*

**1.**—(1) This scheme, which may be cited as the White Fish and Herring Subsidies (United Kingdom) (Amendment) Scheme 1969, shall apply to the United Kingdom and shall come into operation on the day following the day on which it is approved by Parliament.

(2) The Interpretation Act 1889(**e**) shall apply for the interpretation of this scheme as it applies for the interpretation of an Act of Parliament.

*Amendment of White Fish and Herring Subsidies (United Kingdom) Scheme 1968*

**2.** The White Fish and Herring Subsidies (United Kingdom) Scheme 1968(**f**) shall have effect—

(*a*) in relation to grants which may be paid in respect of white fish landed from a vessel in the United Kingdom after the date of the coming into operation of this scheme as if in Part I of Schedule 2 the words "of a kind normally sold for human consumption" were omitted ;

---

(a) 1953 c. 17.      (b) 1957 c. 22.      (c) 1962 c. 31.
(d) 1968 c. 77.      (e) 1889 c. 63.      (f) S.I. 1968/1235 (1968 II, p. 3336).

(*b*) in relation to grants which may be paid in respect of a voyage made by a vessel, terminating after the coming into operation of this scheme, as if paragraph 13 were omitted.

In Witness whereof the official seal of the Minister of Agriculture, Fisheries and Food is hereunto affixed on 11th February 1969.

(L.S.) *Cledwyn Hughes,*
Minister of Agriculture, Fisheries and Food.

Given under the seal of the Secretary of State for Scotland on 13th February 1969.

(L.S.) *William Ross,*
Secretary of State for Scotland.

*Walter Harrison,*
*Joseph Harper,*
Two of the Lords Commissioners of Her Majesty's Treasury.

Approved on 17th February 1969.

---

## EXPLANATORY NOTE

*(This Note is not part of the Scheme.)*

This scheme amends the White Fish and Herring Subsidies (United Kingdom) Scheme 1968 by removing the restrictions whereby subsidy is payable only for voyages made for the purpose of catching and landing fish of a kind normally sold for human consumption or in respect of the landing of such fish.

# STATUTORY INSTRUMENTS

## 1969 No. 472

## SEA FISHERIES

## The White Fish Subsidy (Deep Sea Vessels) (United Kingdom) Scheme 1969

| | | |
|---|---|---|
| *Made* - - - | | *17th February* 1969 |
| *Laid before Parliament* | | *25th February* 1969 |
| *Coming into Operation* | | *26th March* 1969 |

The Minister of Agriculture, Fisheries and Food and the Secretary of State for Scotland (being the Secretary of State concerned with the sea fishing industry in Scotland) in exercise of the powers conferred on them by section 5 of the White Fish and Herring Industries Act 1953(**a**) (as amended by section 2 of the White Fish and Herring Industries Act 1957(**b**), section 37 of and paragraph 18 of Schedule 2 to the Sea Fish Industry Act 1962(**c**) and section 22 of and paragraphs 10 to 13 inclusive of Schedule 1 to the Sea Fisheries Act 1968(**d**)), section 1 of the Sea Fish Industry Act 1962 and sections 1 and 2 of the Sea Fisheries Act 1968, and of all other powers enabling them in that behalf, with the approval of the Treasury, hereby make the following scheme :—

### Citation, extent and commencement

**1.** This scheme, which may be cited as the White Fish Subsidy (Deep Sea Vessels) (United Kingdom) Scheme 1969, shall apply to the United Kingdom and shall come into operation on the day following the day on which it is approved by Parliament.

### Interpretation

**2.**—(1) In this scheme, unless the context otherwise requires—

"aggregate operating profits" has the meaning assigned to it by paragraph 8 ;

"the appropriate Minister" means, in relation to England, Wales or Northern Ireland, the Minister of Agriculture, Fisheries and Food, and, in relation to Scotland, the Secretary of State for Scotland ;

"approved" means approved by the appropriate Minister ;

"the exclusive fishery limits" does not include waters within the fishery limits of the British Islands which are adjacent to the Isle of Man or any of the Channel Islands ;

"fish" includes shellfish ;

---

| | |
|---|---|
| (**a**) 1953 c. 17. | (**b**) 1957 c. 22. |
| (**c**) 1962 c. 31. | (**d**) 1968 c. 77. |

"length", in relation to a vessel, means the length in relation to which its registered tonnage was calculated for the purposes of registration under the Merchant Shipping Act 1894(a) ;

"the Ministers" means the Minister of Agriculture, Fisheries and Food and the Secretary of State for Scotland ;

"paragraph" means a paragraph of this scheme ;

"products", in relation to fish, means anything produced by processing the fish and "processing" includes preserving or preparing fish, or producing any substance or article wholly or partly from fish, by any method for human or animal consumption ;

"reference period" has the meaning assigned to it by paragraph 8 ;

"subsidy period" has the meaning assigned to it by paragraph 4 ;

"white fish" means fish of any kind found in the sea, except herring, salmon, migratory trout and shellfish.

(2) In this scheme, in relation to a vessel to which this scheme applies which has completed a voyage, being a voyage for such a purpose as is mentioned in paragraph 3(2), terminating during any reference period :—

"gross proceeds" means the gross proceeds from the first hand sale of the fish caught by the vessel on that voyage or the products of such fish together with, in any case where during the voyage the vessel was employed for a purpose other than that mentioned in paragraph 3(2) and a payment has been or will be received as a result of such employment, the whole or such part of such payment to the extent to which the appropriate Minister shall consider appropriate having regard to the loss of fishing time resulting from such employment :

Provided that where the first-hand sale of any of the said fish or products landed as aforesaid takes place at a time other than immediately after they were landed the gross proceeds of such fish or products shall for the purposes of this scheme be taken to be such a sum as shall appear to the appropriate Minister to be that which would have been received had such fish or products been sold immediately after they were landed ;

"operating costs" means the total of all approved costs incurred in respect of that voyage including such proportion of the costs of management, of the training of officers and crew and of overhead expenses (or provision for such expenses) as the appropriate Minister may approve as referable to the voyage but excluding the payment of interest on, and the depreciation of, capital ;

"operating loss" means any amount by which the gross proceeds of that voyage are less than the operating costs of the voyage ;

"operating profit" means any amount by which the gross proceeds of that voyage exceed the operating costs of the voyage.

(3) The Interpretation Act 1889(b) shall apply for the interpretation of this scheme as it applies for the interpretation of an Act of Parliament.

*General conditions of grant*

**3.**—(1) This scheme applies to every fishing vessel of 80 feet or over in length, registered in the United Kingdom, being a vessel engaged on voyages falling within sub-paragraph (2) of this paragraph, the owner or charterer of which has employed it or another such vessel on such a voyage terminating on or after 1st August 1968.

---

(a) 1894 c. 60.                          (b) 1889 c. 63.

(2) The voyages to which sub-paragraph (1) of this paragraph relates are voyages made for the purpose of catching white fish where it is part of the purpose that the fish or the products of the fish are to be landed in the United Kingdom whether by the vessel which caught them or by another vessel or are to be trans-shipped in a port in the United Kingdom or within the exclusive fishery limits by the vessel which caught them or by another vessel.

4. A grant may be paid by the appropriate Minister in accordance with the following provisions of this scheme to the owner (or his agent) or, where there is a charter-party, to the charterer (or his agent), of a vessel to which this scheme applies in respect of each such period (hereinafter referred to as "the subsidy period") as the Ministers may determine, being a period not exceeding 12 months in duration, which commences—

(a) in the case of the first subsidy period, on 1st August 1968 ;

(b) in the case of subsequent subsidy periods, on the termination of the immediately preceding subsidy period

and which, in the case of the last subsidy period, terminates on 31st July 1971.

5.—(1) Application for payment of a grant under this scheme shall be made by the owner or charterer or his duly authorised agent in such form and within such period as the appropriate Minister may from time to time require and shall be completed and certified in all respects as so required and shall be delivered to the appropriate Minister at such address as he may specify for the purpose.

(2) Notice that a person is authorised to make application for and receive payment of grants under this scheme on behalf of an owner or charterer shall be given in writing signed by the owner or charterer in such form as the appropriate Minister may from time to time require and shall be sent to the address specified by the appropriate Minister for the purpose of this paragraph.

6. The owner or charterer of a vessel to which this scheme applies (or his duly authorised agent) who applies for payment of a grant under this scheme shall, within such time, in such form and for such period, as may be specified by the appropriate Minister, supply such information as may be required by the appropriate Minister including returns concerning fishing operations, costs and trading results and detailed accounts of the financial results of the operation of all such vessels of which he is the owner or charterer, and shall make any relevant books and records open to examination by any person authorised by the appropriate Minister.

7. Without prejudice to the discretion of the appropriate Minister in the payment of grants under this scheme, if any owner or charterer or any person acting on his behalf makes a statement or produces a document which is false in a material particular or refuses to supply any information, make any return or produce any document in respect of any of the matters required to be disclosed either in connection with an application for payment of grant under this scheme or in accordance with the provisions of paragraph 6 or if any of the conditions relating to the payment of grants under this scheme are not complied with by any owner or charterer or person acting on behalf of an owner or charterer, the payment of grants to that owner, charterer or person at any time may be refused.

*Total amount of grant*

**8.** The Ministers may in respect of any subsidy period make available for payment of grant a sum (hereinafter referred to as "the total amount of grant") calculated in accordance with the next following paragraph related to the aggregate operating profits of all vessels to which this scheme applies from all voyages which terminated during the relevant reference period.

In this and the succeeding paragraphs of this scheme the "reference period" in relation to any subsidy period means such period, having the same duration as that subsidy period, as the Ministers may determine, and "aggregate operating profits" for a reference period means the sum, if any, by which the total operating profits of all such vessels from the voyages which terminated during that reference period exceed the total operating losses of such vessels from such voyages.

**9.**—(1) Subject to the following provisions of this paragraph, the total amount of grant made available in respect of a subsidy period, being a subsidy period of 12 months, shall be—

    (*a*) if the aggregate operating profits for the relevant reference period do not exceed £4,000,000, the sum representing the total of the sum of £2,000,000 and one half of the amount by which the aggregate operating profits are less than £4,000,000 ;

    (*b*) if the aggregate operating profits for the relevant reference period exceed £4,000,000, the sum remaining after deducting from the sum of £2,000,000 one half of the amount by which the aggregate operating profits exceed the sum of £4,000,000 :

Provided that the total amount of grant in respect of such a subsidy period shall not exceed such sum as taken together with the aggregate operating profits for the relevant reference period will exceed the sum of £7,000,000.

(2) Subject to the following provisions of this paragraph, where the duration of a subsidy period is less than 12 months the provisions of the last foregoing sub-paragraph shall have effect as if for the sums of £2,000,000, £4,000,000 and £7,000,000 mentioned therein there were substituted respectively such sums as bear the same proportion to £2,000,000, £4,000,000 and £7,000,000 as the subsidy period bears to a period of 12 months.

(3) Where grants have been paid under the White Fish and Herring Subsidies (United Kingdom) Scheme 1968(**a**) (hereinafter in this paragraph referred to as "1968 Scheme grants") in respect of voyages made by vessels to which this scheme applies which have terminated during a subsidy period, the total amount of grant made available in respect of that subsidy period shall be the sum calculated in accordance with sub-paragraph (1) or, as the case may be, sub-paragraph (2), of this paragraph reduced by such amount in respect of the 1968 Scheme grants as the Ministers may determine :

Provided that the amount deducted under this sub-paragraph in respect of any subsidy period shall not, taken together with deductions made under this sub-paragraph in respect of any previous subsidy period, exceed the total of all sums payable by way of 1968 Scheme grants in respect of that and any previous subsidy period.

*Grant payable in respect of each vessel*

**10.** The amount of grant payable in respect of a vessel to which this scheme applies in respect of any subsidy period shall be a sum equal to the relevant

---

(a) S.I. 1968/1235 (1968 II, p. 3336).

fraction of the added value, if any, attributable to the employment of the vessel during the relevant reference period.

In this paragraph—

(*a*) the "relevant fraction" means the fraction which represents the proportion which the total amount of grant made available in respect of the subsidy period bears to the total amount of added value attributable to the employment during the relevant reference period of all vessels to which this scheme applies ;

(*b*) the added value attributable to the employment of a vessel during any reference period shall be the sum, if any, by which the total of the gross proceeds from the employment of the vessel on all the voyages which terminated during that reference period exceeds the total of the operating costs of the vessel in respect of such voyages other than—

(i) wages, holiday pay and other remuneration or benefits paid to or on behalf of the officers and crew of the vessel ;

(ii) national insurance payments made by the owner or charterer in respect of the officers and crew of the vessel ;

(iii) victualling expenses, and

(iv) the approved costs of the training of officers and crew.

**11.** The appropriate Minister may during the course of any subsidy period make a payment on account of grant in respect of a vessel in relation to such period and if, after the expiration of that period, the payment so made exceeds the amount payable under this scheme in respect of the vessel in respect of the subsidy period the amount of the overpayment shall be repaid to the appropriate Minister by the person to whom it was paid.

**12.** In the event of a dispute as to the purpose of a voyage undertaken by a vessel to which this scheme applies, as to the day on which such a voyage terminated or as to the ascertainment of the amount of any gross proceeds or operating costs the determination of the appropriate Minister shall be conclusive.

**13.** If, at the time when they propose to make a calculation for any reference period of the aggregate operating profits for the purposes of paragraph 9 or of the total amount of added value for the purposes of paragraph 10, there shall not be available to the Ministers any return, or a return appearing to the appropriate Minister to be adequate for the purpose, of the gross proceeds or any of the costs of any vessel to which this scheme applies for that reference period the appropriate Minister may estimate the gross proceeds or, as the case may be, costs from such information as is available to him and the amounts so estimated may be treated by the Ministers as the gross proceeds or, as the case may be, costs of that vessel for the purposes of either of the calculations aforesaid.

**14.** If at any time after 1st August 1968 any structural alteration shall be made or shall have been made to any vessel which increases or has increased its length to 80 feet or over, such vessel shall not be treated as one to which this scheme applies unless the appropriate Minister is satisfied that the alteration was likely to be conducive to the increased fishing efficiency of the vessel.

In witness whereof the official seal of the Minister of Agriculture, Fisheries and Food is hereunto affixed on 11th February 1969.

(L.S.)                         *Cledwyn Hughes,*
             Minister of Agriculture, Fisheries and Food.

Given under the seal of the Secretary of State for Scotland on 13th February 1969.

(L.S.)                          *William Ross,*
            Secretary of State for Scotland.

Approved on 17th February 1969.

                         *Walter Harrison,*
                         *Joseph Harper,*
          Two of the Lords Commissioners of
                         Her Majesty's Treasury.

---

## EXPLANATORY NOTE

*(This Note is not part of the Scheme.)*

This scheme is made in exercise of the powers given by the White Fish and Herring Industries Act 1953, as amended, for the payment of grants to the owners and charterers of fishing vessels of 80 feet or over in length registered in the United Kingdom and engaged in catching white fish. It provides for grants for the three years from the 1st August 1968 to 31st July 1971.

The grants payable will be calculated by reference to the results of fishing during specified periods, for which vessel owners will make returns.

The total amount of grant to be paid in respect of a period of one year will be calculated by reference to the aggregate operating profits of all vessels to which the scheme applies. A basic grant of £2m. will be increased by one half of the amount by which those profits, in any one year, fall short of £4m. or reduced by one half of the amount by which the profits exceed £4m. The total amount of grant will in no case exceed £4m. and the scheme provides that the total amount of grant shall be limited to ensure that the grant plus the aggregate operating profits shall not exceed £7m. In respect of a period of less than one year the sums referred to will be reduced proportionately.

The amount payable to individual owners or charterers will be assessed on the basis of the added value contributed by each vessel towards the aggregate added value of all the vessels. The added value will be the total of the operating profits and the costs of officers' and crews' remuneration and training.

Provision is made for the making of returns by the owners and charterers of vessels and the scheme provides which receipts and expenditure are to be taken into account in assessing the gross proceeds and operating costs of a vessel.

Payments under the White Fish and Herring Subsidies (United Kingdom) Scheme 1968 (S.I. 1968 No. 1235), which provides for the payment of grant in respect of voyages made for the purpose of catching white fish during the year beginning on the 1st August 1968, will be taken into account when the total amount of grant is calculated under the present scheme.

This scheme was approved by resolutions of the House of Lords on the 13th March 1969 and of the House of Commons on the 25th March 1969 and came into operation on the 26th March 1969.

## STATUTORY INSTRUMENTS

## 1969 No. 473

## AGRICULTURE

## The Price Stability of Imported Products (Rates of Levy No. 7) Order 1969

| | | |
|---|---|---|
| Made - - - - | | 25th March 1969 |
| Coming into Operation | | 26th March 1969 |

The Minister of Agriculture, Fisheries and Food, in exercise of the powers conferred upon him by section 1(2), (4), (5), (6) and (7) of the Agriculture and Horticulture Act 1964(a) and of all other powers enabling him in that behalf, hereby makes the following order :—

**1.** This order may be cited as the Price Stability of Imported Products (Rates of Levy No. 7) Order 1969 ; and shall come into operation on 26th March 1969.

**2.**—(1) In this order—

" the Principal Order " means the Price Stability of Imported Products (Levy Arrangements) Order 1966(b), as amended by any subsequent order and if any such order is replaced by any subsequent order the expression shall be construed as a reference to such subsequent order ;

AND other expressions have the same meaning as in the Principal Order.

(2) The Interpretation Act 1889(c) shall apply to the interpretation of this order as it applies to the interpretation of an Act of Parliament and as if this order and the order hereby revoked were Acts of Parliament.

**3.** In accordance with and subject to the provisions of Part II of the Principal Order (which provides for the charging of levies on imports of certain specified commodities)—

(a) the rate of general levy for such imports into the United Kingdom of any specified commodity as are described in column 2 of Part I of the Schedule to this order in relation to a tariff heading indicated in column 1 of that Part shall be the rate set forth in relation thereto in column 3 of that Part ;

(b) the rate of country levy for such imports into the United Kingdom of any specified commodity as are described in column 2 of Part II of the Schedule to this order in relation to a tariff heading indicated in column 1 of that Part shall be the rate set forth in relation thereto in column 3 of that Part.

**4.** The Price Stability of Imported Products (Rates of Levy No. 6) Order 1969(d) is hereby revoked.

In Witness whereof the Official Seal of the Minister of Agriculture, Fisheries and Food is hereunto affixed on 25th March 1969.

(L.S.)

R. J. E. Taylor,
Assistant Secretary.

---

(a) 1964 c. 28.     (b) S.I. 1966/936 (1966 II, p. 2271).     (c) 1889 c. 63.
(d) S.I. 1969/407 (1969 I, p. 1147).

# SCHEDULE
## PART I

| 1.<br>Tariff<br>Heading | 2.<br>Description of Imports | 3.<br>Rate of<br>General Levy |
|---|---|---|
| | | per ton<br>£ s. d. |
| | Imports of:— | |
| 10.01 | Denatured wheat .. .. .. .. .. | 15 0 |
| 10.01 | Any wheat (other than seed wheat the value of which is not less than £34 per ton, denatured wheat and durum wheat) for which a minimum import price level is prescribed .. .. .. .. .. | 1 10 0 |
| 10.03 | Barley .. .. .. .. .. .. .. | 1 0 0 |
| 11.02 | Cereal meal—<br>of maize .. .. .. .. .. .. | 5 10 0 |
| 11.02 | Rolled, flaked, crushed or bruised cereals—<br>barley .. .. .. .. .. .. .. | 5 15 0 |

## PART II

| 1.<br>Tariff<br>Heading | 2.<br>Description of Imports | 3.<br>Rate of<br>Country Levy |
|---|---|---|
| | | per ton<br>£ s. d. |
| | Imports of:— | |
| 10.01 | Denatured wheat which has been grown in and consigned to the United Kingdom from Belgium, the French Republic, the Kingdom of the Netherlands or the Kingdom of Sweden.. .. .. .. | 15 0 |
| 10.01 | Any wheat (other than seed wheat the value of which is not less than £34 per ton, denatured wheat and durum wheat) for which a minimum import price level is prescribed and which is grown in and consigned to the United Kingdom from the French Republic or the Kingdom of the Netherlands .. | 1 10 0 |
| 10.03 | Barley which has been grown in and consigned to the United Kingdom from Canada .. .. .. | 1 0 0 |
| 10.03 | Barley which has been grown in and consigned to the United Kingdom from the Commonwealth of Australia .. .. .. .. .. .. | 15 0 |
| 10.03 | Barley which has been grown in and consigned to the United Kingdom from Belgium, the Kingdom of Denmark, Finland, the French Republic, the Kingdom of the Netherlands or the Kingdom of Sweden .. .. .. .. .. .. | 15 0 |

## EXPLANATORY NOTE
*(This Note is not part of the Order.)*

This order, which comes into operation on 26th March 1969, re-enacts with amendments the Price Stability of Imported Products (Rates of Levy No. 6) Order 1969.

It:—

(a) increases to 15s. per ton the country levy on imports of barley which has been grown in and consigned to the United Kingdom from Belgium, Denmark, Finland, France, the Netherlands or Sweden; and

(b) reimposes unchanged the other rates of general and country levy prescribed by the above-mentioned order.

## STATUTORY INSTRUMENTS

### 1969 No. 474 (S.40)

## COURT OF SESSION, SCOTLAND
### Act of Sederunt (Rules of Court Amendment No. 1) 1969

*Made* - - - 14*th February* 1969
*Coming into Operation* 15*th February* 1969

The Lords of Council and Session, under and by virtue of the powers conferred upon them by section 16 of the Administration of Justice (Scotland) Act 1933(a) and of all other powers competent to them in that behalf, do hereby enact and declare as follows :—

**1.** The Rules of Court (*b*) are hereby amended by deleting paragraph (*b*) of Rule 166 and by substituting a new paragraph (*b*) of Rule 166 as follows :— "Where a final decree containing such reservation is not reclaimed against, or where (a final decree being reclaimed against) any reservation shall ultimately be affirmed or shall ultimately be made, the process shall continue to be in dependence until the date stated in the reservation, to the effect that either the pursuer or the defender or any other party showing an interest may apply to the court anent the custody, maintenance or education of any child continuing to be under the age of sixteen years."

**2.** This Act of Sederunt may be cited as the Act of Sederunt (Rules of Court Amendment No. 1) 1969 and shall come into operation on 15th February 1969.

*J. L. Clyde,*
I.P.D.

Edinburgh,
14th February 1969.

---

### EXPLANATORY NOTE
*(This Note is not part of the Act of Sederunt.)*

This Act of Sederunt amends the Rules of Court by empowering any party showing an interest to apply to the Court in terms of a direction reserving leave to apply anent the custody, maintenance or education of a child in a consistorial action.

---

(a) 1933 c. 41.  (b) S.I. 1965/321 (1965 I, p. 803).

## STATUTORY INSTRUMENTS

### 1969 No. 475 (S.41)

## COURT OF SESSION, SCOTLAND

### Act of Sederunt (Rules of Court Amendment No. 2) 1969

| | | |
|---|---|---|
| *Made* - - - | | *25th March* 1969 |
| *Coming into Operation* | | *1st April* 1969 |

The Lords of Council and Session, under and by virtue of the powers conferred upon them by section 2 of the Courts of Law Fees (Scotland) Act 1895(a) and section 16 of the Administration of Justice (Scotland) Act 1933(b) and of all other powers competent to them in that behalf, with the approval of the Treasury for the exercise of the said powers under section 2 of the Courts of Law Fees (Scotland) Act 1895(a), do hereby enact and declare as follows :—

**1.** In the case of any Summons lodged on or after 1st April 1969, or of any Petition lodged on or after the said date, or of any proceedings commenced on or after the said date by a Minute lodged in a process in which leave to apply to the Court has been reserved by the Court or by virtue of an Act of Parliament, or of any other action commenced on or after the said date, the Rules of Court(c) shall apply subject to the following amendments :—

(1) In Rule of Court 169 the words "and on payment of a fee of seven shillings and six pence" shall be deleted and a comma shall be substituted therefor.

(2) Rule of Court 346 shall be deleted and a new Rule 346 shall be substituted therefor as set forth in the Schedule annexed hereto.

(3) In Rule of Court 347 as substituted by the Act of Sederunt (Rules of Court Amendment No. 1) 1966(d), Chapter III, Part I, the figure "£15 15s." shall be deleted and "£18 15s." shall be substituted.

(4) In each of Forms 22, 24 and 26 appended to the Rules the words "seven shillings and sixpence" shall be deleted and the words "fifteen shillings" shall be substituted.

**2.** This Act of Sederunt may be cited as the Act of Sederunt (Rules of Court Amendment No. 2) 1969, and shall come into operation on 1st April 1969.

And the Lords appoint this Act of Sederunt to be inserted in the Books of Sederunt.

*J. L. Clyde,*
I.P.D.

Edinburgh,
25th March 1969.

---

(a) 1895 c. 14.
(c) S.I. 1965/321 (1965 I, p. 803).

(b) 1933 c. 41.
(d) S.I. 1966/335 (1966 I, p. 778).

## SCHEDULE

### Fee-fund Dues

*Table of Fees Payable in the Court of Session and Offices Connected therewith*

346. Fees payable in the Court of Session and Offices connected therewith regulated by the Lords of Council and Session under the Act 58 and 59 Vict. cap. 14 with the approval of the Lords Commissioners of Her Majesty's Treasury.

## A. GENERAL DEPARTMENT

### I. Inner House

|  |  | £ | s. | d. |
|---|---|---|---|---|
| 1. | Appeals, or any other writ or step by which a clause or proceeding is originated, inclusive fee | 4 | 0 | 0 |
| 2. | Special cases, inclusive fee— | | | |
|  | (a) Where two parties only | 6 | 0 | 0 |
|  | (b) Each additional party, Subject to a maximum of £10 per case | 2 | 0 | 0 |
| 3. | Answers or other step by which a party first makes appearance in a cause or proceeding, inclusive fee | 2 | 0 | 0 |
| 4. | Certified copy interlocutor, each copy | 0 | 10 | 0 |
| 5. | Copies of Pleadings when certified by Clerk of Court | 0 | 10 | 0 |
| 6. | Certified copy of proceedings for appeal to the House of Lords | 4 | 0 | 0 |
| 7. | Captions— | | | |
|  | Making caption when ordered | 0 | 5 | 0 |
|  | Warrant for caption when issued | 0 | 5 | 0 |
| 8. | Letters of request to foreign Courts | 1 | 0 | 0 |
| 9. | Judges' opinions per sheet of writing or part thereof— | | | |
|  | (a) First copies | 0 | 4 | 0 |
|  | (b) Second and subsequent copies | 0 | 2 | 0 |

> NOTE. The inclusive fee will cover every other step of process not enumerated above.

### II. Outer House

| 1. | Summons or other writ or step by which a cause or proceeding is originated, inclusive fee | 4 | 0 | 0 |
|---|---|---|---|---|
| 2. | Defences, answers or other writ by which a party first makes appearance in a cause, inclusive fee | 4 | 0 | 0 |
| 3. | Minute by defender in consistorial cause | 1 | 0 | 0 |
| 4. | Certified copy interlocutor, each copy | 0 | 10 | 0 |
| 5. | Copies of pleadings certified by Clerk of Court | 0 | 10 | 0 |
| 6. | Captions— | | | |
|  | Marking caption when ordered | 0 | 5 | 0 |
|  | Warrant for caption when issued | 0 | 5 | 0 |
| 7. | Citation of each jury, to include outlays of sheriff-clerk in citing and countermanding | 1 | 0 | 0 |

> NOTE. The fee stamps to be affixed to precept before transmission to be sheriff-clerk. The precept to be issued not later than ten days previous to date fixed for trial.

|   |   | £ | s. | d. |
|---|---|---|---|---|

8. Letters of request to foreign Courts .. .. .. 1 0 0
9. Judges' opinions per sheet of writing or part thereof—
    (a) First copies .. .. .. .. .. 0 4 0
    (b) Second and subsequent copies .. .. .. 0 2 0
10. Certificate of divorce .. .. .. .. .. 0 15 0
    NOTE. The inclusive fee will cover every other step of process not enumerated above.

### III. EXCHEQUER CAUSES

1. Petition, Case, Appeal or Answers (Any other writ or step of procedure enumerated under Nos. I and II to be charged accordingly). .. .. .. .. 4 0 0

### B. PETITION DEPARTMENT

1. Petitions, petitions and complaints presented to Inner House, inclusive fee .. .. .. .. .. 4 0 0
2. Petitions in Inner House, not being first steps of process and Answers thereto .. .. .. .. 1 0 0
3. Petitions for sequestration .. .. .. .. 2 0 0
4. Answers or objections to No. I inclusive fee .. .. 4 0 0
5. Certified copies of petitions for sequestration and relative interlocutors, each .. .. .. .. 0 10 0
6. Every extract or certified copy of proceedings in or connected with sequestrations other than certified copies under No. 5, per sheet of writing or part thereof .. 0 4 0
7. Petitions and notes presented to the Outer House, being first steps of process and answers thereto inclusive fee .. 4 0 0
8. Petitions and notes in Outer House, not being first steps of process, and answers thereto .. .. .. 0 10 0
9. Petitions for suspension, suspension and interdict, or suspension and liberation, and answers thereto, inclusive fee .. 4 0 0
10. Caveats when lodged or renewed .. .. .. 0 5 0
11. Fiats .. .. .. .. .. .. 1 0 0
12. Petitions for loosing arrestments or recall of inhibitions, and answers thereto .. .. .. .. 0 10 0
13. Registering office copies of orders of English and Irish Courts .. .. .. .. .. 1 0 0
14. And, in addition, for each sheet of writing beyond four sheets 0 5 0
15. Authentication by judge of act and warrant, in terms of section 70 of the Bankruptcy (Scotland) Act, 1913 .. 0 10 0
16. Certified copy interlocutors, each .. .. .. 0 10 0
17. Copies of proceedings other than those above specified certified by Clerk of Court .. .. .. .. 0 10 0
18. Extracts of decrees, and of bonds of caution .. .. 1 0 0
19. And, in addition, for each sheet of writing beyond four sheets .. .. .. .. .. .. 0 5 0
20. Certified copy of proceedings for appeal to the House of Lords .. .. .. .. .. .. 4 0 0
21. Captions—
    Marking caption when ordered .. .. .. 0 5 0
    Warrant for caption when issued .. .. .. 0 5 0

## C. REGISTRATION APPEAL COURT AND VALUATION APPEAL COURT

|  |  | £ | s. | d. |
|---|---|---|---|---|
| 1. | Cases on appeal, inclusive fee ..   ..   ..   .. | 4 | 0 | 0 |
| 2. | Answers,     — do —     ..   ..   .. | 4 | 0 | 0 |

## D. COURT OF TRIAL OF ELECTION PETITIONS

|  |  | £ | s. | d. |
|---|---|---|---|---|
| 1. | Petitions against return of Members of Parliament   .. | 4 | 0 | 0 |
| 2. | Statement of matters ..   ..   ..   ..   .. | 1 | 0 | 0 |
| 3. | Any other petitions, applications, answers or objections submitted to the judges   ..   ..   ..   .. | 2 | 0 | 0 |
| 4. | Certificate of judgment   ..   ..   ..   .. | 1 | 10 | 0 |

## E. TAXATION OF EXPENSES

For taxing accounts of expenses incurred in judicial proceedings remitted to the Auditor for taxation—

|  | £ | s. | d. |
|---|---|---|---|
| Under £50   ..   ..   ..   ..   .. | 1 | 0 | 0 |
| For every additional sum of £50, or part of £50   .. | 1 | 0 | 0 |

NOTE. These fees to be collected by Clerks of Court.

## F. EXTRACTS

|  |  | £ | s. | d. |
|---|---|---|---|---|
| 1. | Extract of decree in absence— | | | |
|  | (a) Pronounced on consideration of summons or petition without any prior remit, or proof, or other procedure   ..   ..   ..   .. | 1 | 0 | 0 |
|  | (b) Pronounced on consideration of summons or petition after proof, remit or other procedure   .. | 1 | 10 | 0 |
|  | (c) Pronounced in proceedings under Entail Acts, or in liquidations under Companies Acts, or in application for power to complete title, or borrow money, or sell heritable or moveable estate, or to exercise other special powers ..   ..   .. | 1 | 10 | 0 |
| 2. | Extract of decree in foro,   ..   ..   ..   .. | 1 | 10 | 0 |

NOTE. The above fees are payable only on the first extract issued. When decree is extracted in duplicate, triplicate, etc. only copying fees under No. 6 of this part of the Table of Fees shall be charged.

|  |  | £ | s. | d. |
|---|---|---|---|---|
| 3. | Extract of admission as a solicitor   ..   ..   .. | 1 | 0 | 0 |
| 4. | Extract of protestation   ..   ..   ..   .. | 1 | 0 | 0 |
| 5. | Certificate under Judgments Extension Act, 1868   .. | 0 | 10 | 0 |
| 6. | Engrossment of extract, record copy, and certificate, each, per sheet of 250 words   ..   ..   ..   .. | 0 | 4 | 0 |

Figured work 2s. extra per sheet.

### G.  SIGNET OFFICE

1.  To signet any writ—

    (*a*)  Presented during office hours, viz. from 2.15 to 3.30 daily, except Saturday, on which day, from 10.30 to 11.00, the office being shut on public holidays    0  10  0

    (*b*)  Presented out of office hours, viz. on Monday, Tuesday, Wednesday, Thursday and Friday, even though holidays—

      From 10.00 a.m. to 2.15 p.m.             1  0  0

      From 7.00 p.m. to 8.00 p.m. ..           1  10  0

      On Saturday, even though holiday—
      From 2.00 p.m. to 3.00 p.m. ..           1  10  0

    (NOTE.  The above fees are prescribed by the Court, but the extra hours, during which the officers of the Signet are allowed to signet any writ, are fixed, and may be varied at any time, by the Keeper of the Signet.  In the event of such variation, the fees charged shall be as herein prescribed for hours before and after the ordinary office hours respectively.)

### H.  EDICTAL CITATIONS

1.  For access to and liberty to make excerpts or copies of writs, etc., from any record, for each year of record inspected    0  5  0

2.  For extracts or copies, per sheet of 250 words ..     0  5  0

---

### EXPLANATORY NOTE

*(This Note is not part of the Act of Sederunt.)*

This Act of Sederunt prescribes a new table of Fee-fund Dues in the Court of Session and makes consequential amendments to the Rules of Court.  It applies only to actions commenced on or after 1st April 1969.

## 1969 No. 479

## PENSIONS

## The Increase of Pensions (Teachers' Family Benefits) Regulations 1969

|  |  |
|---|---|
| *Made* - - - | *26th March* 1969 |
| *Laid before Parliament* | *31st March* 1969 |
| *Coming into operation* | *1st April* 1969 |

The Secretary of State for Education and Science, with the consent of the Minister for the Civil Service, in exercise of the power conferred on him by paragraph 12 of Schedule 2 to the Pensions (Increase) Act 1969(a), hereby makes the following Regulations:—

*Citation and Commencement*

**1.** These Regulations may be cited as the Increase of Pensions (Teachers' Family Benefits) Regulations 1969 and shall come into operation on 1st April 1969.

*Interpretation*

**2.**—(1) In these Regulations—

"the Act" means the Pensions (Increase) Act 1969;

"the Regulations" means the Teachers' Superannuation (Family Benefits) Regulations 1966(b), as amended by the Teachers' Superannuation (Family Benefits) (Amending) Regulations 1967(c) and the Teachers' Superannuation (Family Benefits) (Amending) Regulations 1968(d) (which Regulations, as so amended, have effect as if made under section 7 of the Teachers' Superannuation Act 1967(e) by virtue of paragraph 5(2) of Schedule 3 to that Act).

(2) A reference in these Regulations to a regulation shall, unless the context otherwise requires, be construed as a reference to a regulation of the Regulations.

(3) The Interpretation Act 1889(f) shall apply for the interpretation of these Regulations as it applies for the interpretation of an Act of Parliament.

*Exceptions from the Act*

**3.** In relation to pensions payable under the Regulations section 1(1) of the Act shall apply subject to the exception therefrom of—

    (*a*)  a short service widow's pension payable under regulation 48; and

    (*b*)  a children's pension payable under Regulation 51.

*Widow's Minimum Pension*

**4.**—(1) In relation to a widow's pension payable under regulation 45 of which the annual rate is either—

---

(a) 1969 c. 7.    (b) S.I. 1966/357 (1966 I, p. 813).    (c) S.I. 1967/1856 (1967 III, p. 4975).
    (d) S.I. 1968/1914 (1968 III, p. 5069).    (e) 1967 c. 12.    (f) 1889 c. 63.

(a) the minimum sum of £115 by reason of regulation 46(1); or

(b) a proportion of the minimum sum of £115 by reason of regulation 46(1) as affected by regulation 54

section 1(1) of the Act shall apply subject to the modifications specified in paragraphs (2) and (3) below.

(2) In a case to which sub-paragraph (a) of paragraph (1) above applies the amount of the increase shall be the amount, if any, of the excess over £115 of the aggregate of—

(a) the annual rate of the pension if it were determined under paragraph (2) or (3) of regulation 46; and

(b) the amount of the increase of the annual rate so determined if section 1 (1) and (2) of the Act were applicable thereto.

(3) In a case to which sub-paragraph (b) of paragraph (1) above applies the amount of the increase shall be the amount, if any, of the excess over the annual rate of the pension of the aggregate of—

(a) the annual rate of the pension if it were determined under paragraph (2) or (3) of regulation 46 and were subject to regulation 54; and

(b) the amount of the increase of the annual rate so determined if section 1(1) and (2) of the Act were applicable thereto.

Given under the Official Seal of the Secretary of State for Education and Science on 26th March 1969.

(L.S.)                                          **Edward Short,**
Secretary of State for Education
and Science.

Consent of the Minister for the Civil Service given under his Official Seal on 26th March 1969.

(L.S.)                                          **J. E. Herbecq,**
Authorised by the Minister for the
Civil Service.

## EXPLANATORY NOTE

*(This Note is not Part of the Regulations.)*

These Regulations except from increase under the Pensions (Increase) Act 1969 pensions payable under the Teachers' Superannuation (Family Benefits) Regulations 1966 to 1968 to the widow of a teacher with less than ten years' service and the children of a teacher.

They also provide that where a widow's pension is the minimum of £115 a year (or, in the case of a teacher with service in Scotland, Northern Ireland, the Isle of Man or the Channel Islands, a proportion of that minimum) the increase shall be limited to the amount (if any) by which the total of the pension and increase, if both were determined by the normal methods, would exceed £115 (or, if such is the case, the proportion of that sum being paid).

## 1969 No. 481

## DESIGNS

### The Designs (Amendment) Rules 1969

| | |
|---|---|
| *Made* - - - | *27th March* 1969 |
| *Laid before Parliament* | *14th April* 1969 |
| *Coming into Operation* | |
| *Rule* 4 - - | *15th April* 1969 |
| *Rule* 3 - - | *21st June* 1969 |

The Board of Trade, in pursuance of the powers conferred upon them by sections 36 and 40 of the Registered Designs Act 1949(a), as amended by the Patents and Designs (Renewals, Extensions and Fees) Act 1961(b), and of all other powers enabling them in that behalf, and with the consent of the Treasury, hereby make the following Rules:—

**1.** These Rules may be cited as the Designs (Amendment) Rules 1969 and shall come into operation as respects Rule 4 on 15th April 1969 and as respects Rule 3 on 21st June 1969.

**2.** The Interpretation Act 1889(c) shall apply to the interpretation of these Rules as it applies to the interpretation of an Act of Parliament and as if these Rules and the Rules hereby revoked were Acts of Parliament.

**3.** The fee payable by virtue of Rule 3 of the Designs Rules 1949(d), as amended(e), in respect of any of the matters specified in the schedule hereto shall on and after 21st June 1969 be the appropriate fee so specified and, accordingly, on that date—

(i) for Schedule 1 to the said Rules there shall be substituted the Schedule hereto; and

(ii) the Designs (Amendment No. 2) Rules 1964(f), and Rule 1(2) of, and Schedule 1 to, the Designs (Amendment) Rules 1965(g), shall be revoked.

**4.** Where on or after 15th April 1969 but before 21st June 1969, an application is made for an extension of the period of copyright in any registered design in respect of which the period of copyright current is due to expire after 20th June 1969, the fee payable shall be that which would be payable if the application was made on or after 21st June 1969.

*Edmund Dell,*
Minister of State,
Board of Trade.

27th March 1969.

We consent to the making of these Rules.

*Joseph Harper,*
*J. McCann,*
Two of the Lords Commissioners
of Her Majesty's Treasury.

26th March 1969.

---

(a) 1949 c. 88.　　(b) 1961 c. 25.　　(c) 1889 c. 63.　　(d) S.I. 1949/2368 (1949 I, p. 1417).
(e) The relevant amending instruments are S.I. 1964/229, 1336, 1965/1551 (1964 I, p. 428; 1964 II, p. 3045; 1965 II, p. 4528).
(f) S.I. 1964/1336 (1964 II, p. 3045).　　　　(g) S.I. 1965/1551 (1965 II, p. 4528).

## SCHEDULE

### LIST OF FEES PAYABLE

| Subject or Proceeding | Amount £ s. d. | Corresponding Form |
|---|---|---|
| 1. On application to register one design to be applied to a single article not being textile articles ... ... ... ... ... ... | 5 0 0 | Designs No. 2 or 3. |
|     If made of lace ... ... ... ... | 15 0* | „   „   „ |
| 2. On application to register one design to be applied to a set of articles not being textile articles ... ... ... ... ... ... | 10 0 0 | Designs No. 4 or 5. |
|     If made of lace ... ... ... ... | 1 10 0* | „   „   „ |
| 2A. On application to register one design to be applied to a set of textile articles:— | | |
|     Not being checks or stripes ... ... ... | 10 0 0 | Designs No. 4 or 5. |
|     Checks or stripes ... ... ... ... | 1 10 0* | „   „   „ |
| 3. On application to register one design to be applied to a textile article (not being checks or stripes) ... ... ... ... ... ... | 5 0 0 | Designs (Manchester) No. 1 or 3. |
| 4. On application to register one design to be applied to a textile article (checks or stripes) ... | 15 0* | Designs (Manchester) No. 2 or 3. |
| 5. On application for a copy of certificate of registration ... ... ... ... ... | 15 0 | Designs No. 6. |
| 6. On application to Registrar to state grounds of decision and materials used under Rule 31 ... | 3 0 0* | Designs No. 7. |
| 7. On request for extension of time within which an application for registration of a design may be completed:— | | |
|     Not exceeding one month ... ... ... | 2 0 0* | Designs No. 8. |
|     „    „    two months ... ... ... | 4 0 0* | „   „ |
|     „    „    three months ... ... ... | 6 0 0* | „   „ |
| 8. On application for extension of copyright under section 8(2) for second period ... ... | 10 0 0 | Designs No. 9. |
| 9. On application for extension of copyright under section 8(2) for third period ... ... | 20 0 0 | Designs No. 10. |
| 10. On request for enlargement of time for payment of fee for extension of copyright:— | | |
|     Not exceeding one month ... ... ... | 2 0 0* | Designs No. 11. |
|     „    „    two months ... ... ... | 4 0 0* | „   „ |
|     „    „    three months ... ... ... | 6 0 0* | „   „ |
|     „    „    four months ... ... ... | 8 0 0* | „   „ |
|     „    „    five months ... ... ... | 10 0 0* | „   „ |
|     „    „    six months ... ... ... | 12 0 0* | „   „ |
| 11. On application to enter subsequent proprietorship, &c. under Rule 39 made within six months from date of acquisition of proprietorship, &c.:— | | |

| Subject or Proceeding | Amount | Corresponding Form |
|---|---|---|
| | £ s. d. | |
| 11.—*contd.* | | |
| In respect of one design ... ... ... | 1 5 0* | Designs No. 12 or 13. |
| Made after six but within twelve months from date of acquisition of proprietorship, &c.:— | | |
| In respect of one design ... ... ... | 3 15 0 | „ „ „ |
| Made after expiration of twelve months from the date of acquisition of proprietorship, &c.:— | | |
| In respect of one design ... ... ... | 4 10 0 | Designs No. 12 or 13. |
| On application covering more than one design, for each additional design similarly acquired ... ... ... ... ... ... | 4 0 | — |
| 12. On application for entry of notification of document in the register made within six months of date of document:— | | |
| In respect of one design ... ... ... | 1 5 0* | Designs No. 14. |
| Made after six but within twelve months from date of document:— | | |
| In respect of one design ... ... ... | 3 15 0 | „ „ |
| Made after expiration of twelve months from date of document:— | | |
| In respect of one design ... ... ... | 4 10 0 | „ „ |
| On application covering more than one design, for each additional design referred to in the same document as the first design... ... | 4 0 | — |
| 13. On application of mortgagee, licensee, or other person for entry that he no longer claims such interest:— | | |
| In respect of one design ... ... ... | 15 0 | Designs No. 15. |
| For each additional design ... ... ... | 4 0 | — |
| 14. On application to enter change of name or nationality of registered proprietor in the register:— | | |
| In respect of one design ... ... ... | 15 0 | Designs No. 16. |
| For each additional design ... ... ... | 4 0 | — |
| 15. On application for alteration of address or address for service in the register:— | | |
| In respect of one design ... ... ... | 8 0 | Designs No. 17. |
| For each additional design ... ... ... | 1 0* | — |
| 16. On request under section 21 to correct error | 1 5 0* | Designs No. 18. |
| 17. On application by proprietor for cancellation | 8 0 | Designs No. 19. |
| 18. On request for search under section 23 when registration number is supplied ... ... | 12 6* | Designs No. 20. |
| 19. On request for search under section 23 when registration number is not supplied ... ... | 1 5 0* | Designs No. 21. |
| 20. On application for search under Rule 48 ... | 1 5 0* | Designs No. 22. |
| 21. On request for certificate of Registrar for use in obtaining registration in a foreign country or for use in legal proceedings or other special purpose ... ... ... ... ... ... | 15 0 | Designs No. 23. |

| Subject or Proceeding | Amount | Corresponding Form |
|---|---|---|
| | £ s. d. | |
| 22. On request for certificate of Registrar for use in obtaining registration in part of Her Majesty's dominions outside the United Kingdom ... ... ... ... ... ... | 8 0 | Designs No. 24. |
| 23. On application for compulsory licence under section 10 ... ... ... ... ... | 5 0 0* | Designs No. 25. |
| 24. On application for cancellation of registration under section 11(2) ... ... ... ... | 3 0 0* | Designs No. 26. |
| 25. On notice that hearing of an application for cancellation or compulsory licence will be attended ... ... ... ... ... ... | 2 10 0* | Designs No. 27. |
| 26. On application for entry of Order of Court in register ... ... ... ... ... ... | 15 0 | Designs No. 28. |
| 27. Inspection of register or design where inspection is permitted other than inspection under the second paragraph of section 22(2) ... | 2 6* | — |
| 28. Photographic copy of design or documents | Cost according to agreement | — |
| 29. Office copy of documents, every 100 words... | 1 0* (but never less than 2s.*) | — |
| 30. For certifying Office copies ... ... ... | 4 0 | — |

The fees to be paid on any proceeding at the Manchester Branch shall be the same as for the similar proceeding at the Office.

## EXPLANATORY NOTE

*(This Note is not part of the Rules.)*

These Rules further amend the Designs Rules 1949.

With the exceptions indicated by asterisk, the fees payable under the Rules are increased.

The new fees become payable on or after 21st June 1969 except in the case of fees for the extension of the copyright period in a design paid in advance. Such fees in respect of any period beginning on or after 21st June 1969 are increased on 15th April 1969.

## STATUTORY INSTRUMENTS

### 1969 No. 482

### PATENTS

### The Patents (Amendment) Rules 1969

| | |
|---|---|
| *Made* - - - | 27th March 1969 |
| *Laid before Parliament* | 14th April 1969 |
| *Coming into Operation* | |
| *Rule 4* | 15th April 1969 |
| *Rule 3* | 21st June 1969 |

The Board of Trade, in pursuance of the powers conferred upon them by sections 94 and 99 of the Patents Act 1949(a), as amended by the Patents Act 1957(b), the Patents and Designs (Renewals, Extensions and Fees) Act 1961(c) and the Patents (Fees Amendment) Order 1961(d) and of all other powers enabling them in that behalf, and with the consent of the Treasury, hereby make the following Rules :—

**1.** These Rules may be cited as the Patents (Amendment) Rules 1969 and shall come into operation as respects Rule 4 on 15th April 1969 and as respects Rule 3 on 21st June 1969.

**2.** The Interpretation Act 1889(e) shall apply to the interpretation of these Rules as it applies to the interpretation of an Act of Parliament.

**3.** The fee payable by virtue of Rule 3 of the Patents Rules 1968(f), as amended(g), in respect of any of the items specified in the Schedule hereto shall on and after 21st June 1969 be the appropriate fee so specified and, accordingly, on that date for Schedule 1 to the said Rules there shall be substituted the Schedule hereto.

**4.** Where on or after 15th April 1969 but before 21st June 1969 an application is made for a certificate of payment of a patent renewal fee in respect of any year beginning after 20th June 1969, the fee payable upon such application by virtue of Rule 3 of the said Patents Rules shall be that which would be payable if the application was made on or after 21st June 1969.

---

(a) 1949 c.87.                     (b) 1957 c.13.
(c) 1961 c.25.                     (d) S.I. 1961/1499 (1961 II, p. 3050).
(e) 1889 c.63.                     (f) S.I. 1968/1389 (1968 II, p.3958).
(g) The amending Rules are not relevant to the subject matter of these Rules.

*Edmund Dell.*
Minister of State.
Board of Trade.

27th March 1969.

We consent to the making of these Rules.

*Joseph Harper,*
*J. McCann,*
Two of the Lords Commissioners of
Her Majesty's Treasury.

26th March 1969.

## SCHEDULE

### List of Fees Payable

| | £ | s. | d. | Corresponding Form |
|---|---|---|---|---|
| 1. On application for a patent ... ... ... | 1 | 0 | 0* | Patents Form No. 1 or Schedule 3 Form 1A. |
| 2. On Convention application for a patent:— In respect of each application for protection in a Convention country ... ... | 1 | 0 | 0* | Patents Form No. 1 Con. or Schedule 3 Form 1B. |
| 3. On filing specification:— | | | | |
| Provisional ... ... ... ... | | | — | Patents Form No. 2. |
| Complete ... ... ... ... ... | 14 | 0 | 0* | Patents Form No. 3. |
| 4. On application for grant of patent of addition in lieu of an independent patent ... ... | 6 | 0 | 0* | Patents Form No. 1 Add. |
| 5. Declaration of inventorship of invention disclosed in complete specification ... | | | — | Patents Form No. 4. |
| 6. For extension of the period for filing complete specification ... ... ... | 3 | 10 | 0* | Patents Form No. 5. |
| 7. On request for the post-dating of an application under section 6(3) ... ... ... | 3 | 10 | 0* | Patents Form No. 6. |
| 8. For extension of time under Rule 30 or 33 or 50:— | | | | |
| Not exceeding one month ... ... | 1 | 5 | 0* | Patents Form No. 7. |
| Each succeeding month ... ... ... | 1 | 5 | 0* | „ „ „ |
| 9. On application for result of search made under sections 7 and 8 ... ... ... | | 1 | 0* | Patents Form No. 8. |
| 10. On application under section 9(2) for deletion of reference ... ... ... | 1 | 10 | 0 | Patents Form No. 9. |
| 11. For extension of the period for putting an application in order:— | | | | |
| Up to one month after the period allowed by section 12(1) ... ... | 3 | 0 | 0 | Patents Form No. 10. |
| Up to two months ... ... ... | 6 | 0 | 0 | „ „ „ |
| Up to three months ... ... ... | 9 | 0 | 0 | „ „ „ |
| 12. For postponement of acceptance of complete specification:— | | | | |
| Up to 13 months from date of filing of complete specification ... ... ... | 3 | 0 | 0 | Patents Form No. 11. |
| From 13 months to 14 months ... ... | 3 | 0 | 0 | „ „ „ |
| From 14 months to 15 months ... ... | 3 | 0 | 0 | „ „ „ |
| 13. On notice of opposition to grant of patent. By opponent ... ... ... ... | 2 | 10 | 0* | Patents Form No. 12. |
| 14. On hearing by Comptroller. By each party ... | 3 | 0 | 0 | Patents Form No. 13. |
| 15. On a request under section 16(3) ... ... | 1 | 5 | 0* | Patents Form No. 14. |
| 16. On a claim under section 16(4) ... ... | 1 | 5 | 0* | Patents Form No. 15. |
| 17. On an application for extension of the period under section 16(5) ... ... ... ... | 1 | 5 | 0* | Patents Form No. 16. |
| 18. On an application for a certificate under section 16(8) ... ... ... ... | 2 | 10 | 0* | Patents Form No. 17. |
| 19. On a claim under section 17(1) for application to proceed in name of claimants ... | 2 | 10 | 0* | Patents Form No. 18. |
| 20. On application for directions under section 17(5) ... ... ... ... ... ... | 7 | 10 | 0 | Patents Form No. 19. |

|  |  |  |  | Corresponding Form |
|---|---|---|---|---|
|  | £ | s. | d. |  |
| 21. On a request for sealing of a patent... ... | 3 | 0 | 0* | Patents Form No. 20. |
| 22. On application for extension of the period for requesting the sealing of a patent under section 19(3):— |  |  |  |  |
|   Not exceeding one month ... ... | 3 | 0 | 0 | Patents Form No. 21. |
|   „   „   two months ... ... | 6 | 0 | 0 | „   „   „ |
|   „   „   three months ... ... | 9 | 0 | 0 | „   „   „ |
| 23. On application for extension of the period for requesting the sealing of a patent under section 19(4):— |  |  |  |  |
|   Not exceeding one month ... ... | 1 | 10 | 0 | Patents Form No. 22. |
|   Each succeeding month ... ... ... | | 15 | 0 | „   „   „ |
| 24. On application under section 20 for amendment of a patent ... ... ... ... | 6 | 0 | 0* | Patents Form No. 23. |
| 25. †On application for certificate of payment of renewal fee:— |  |  |  |  |
|   Before the expiration of the 4th year from the date of the patent and in respect of the 5th year... ... ... | 8 | 0 | 0 | Patents Form No. 24. |
|   Before the expiration of the 5th year from the date of the patent and in respect of the 6th year ... ... ... | 9 | 0 | 0 | „   „   „ |
|   Before the expiration of the 6th year from the date of the patent and in respect of the 7th year... ... ... | 12 | 0 | 0 | „   „   „ |
|   Before the expiration of the 7th year from the date of the patent and in respect of the 8th year... ... ... | 13 | 0 | 0 | „   „   „ |
|   Before the expiration of the 8th year from the date of the patent and in respect of the 9th year... ... ... | 14 | 0 | 0* | „   „   „ |
|   Before the expiration of the 9th year from the date of the patent and in respect of the 10th year ... ... | 17 | 0 | 0* | „   „   „ |
|   Before the expiration of the 10th year from the date of the patent and in respect of the 11th year ... ... | 20 | 0 | 0* | „   „   „ |
|   Before the expiration of the 11th year from the date of the patent and in respect of the 12th year ... ... | 22 | 0 | 0* | „   „   „ |
|   Before the expiration of the 12th year from the date of the patent and in respect of the 13th year | 24 | 0 | 0* | Patents Form No. 24. |
|   Before the expiration of the 13th year from the date of the patent and in respect of the 14th year ... ... | 26 | 0 | 0* | „   „   „ |
|   Before the expiration of the 14th year from the date of the patent and in respect of the 15th year ... ... | 28 | 0 | 0* | „   „   „ |
|   Before the expiration of the 15th year from the date of the patent and in respect of the remainder of the term of the patent ... ... ... ... | 30 | 0 | 0* | „   „   „ |

†One half only of these fees payable on patents endorsed "Licences of Right".

| | £ s. d. | Corresponding Form |
|---|---|---|
| 26. On extension of the period for payment of renewal fees:— | | |
|     Not exceeding one month   ...   ... | 3 0 0 | Patents Form No. 25. |
|     „   „   two months   ...   ... | 6 0 0 | „   „   „ |
|     „   „   three months   ...   ... | 9 0 0 | „   „   „ |
|     „   „   four months   ...   ... | 12 0 0 | „   „   „ |
|     „   „   five months   ...   ... | 15 0 0 | „   „   „ |
|     „   „   six months   ...   ... | 18 0 0 | „   „   „ |
| 27. Certificate of payment of renewal fee   ... | — | Patents Form No. 26. |
| 28. On application under section 24 or 25 for extension of term of patent   ...   ... | 6 0 0* | Patents Form No. 27. |
| 29. On opposition to application for extension of term of patent   ...   ...   ... | 2 10 0* | Patents Form No. 28. |
| 30. On application for restoration of a patent ... | 4 10 0 | Patents Form No. 29. |
| 31. On notice of opposition to application for restoration of patent   ...   ...   ... | 2 10 0* | Patents Form No. 30. |
| 32. Additional fee on restoration of patent   ... | 15 0 0 | Patents Form No. 31. |
| 33. On application under section 28 for sealing of patent   ...   ...   ...   ... | 4 10 0 | Patents Form No. 32. |
| 34. On opposition to application under section 28 | 2 10 0* | Patents Form No. 33. |
| 35. Additional fee for sealing under section 28 ... | 15 0 0 | Patents Form No. 34. |
| 36. On application to amend specification after acceptance:— | | |
|     Up to sealing. By applicant   ...   ... | 3 10 0* | Patents Form No. 35. |
|     After sealing. By patentee   ...   ... | 6 0 0* | „   „   „ |
| 37. On notice of opposition to amendment. By opponent   ...   ...   ...   ... | 2 10 0* | Patents Form No. 36. |
| 38. On application to amend specification not yet accepted ...   ...   ...   ... | 2 10 0* | Patents Form No. 37. |
| 39. On application to amend an application for a patent...   ...   ...   ...   ... | 2 10 0* | Patents Form No. 38. |
| 39a. Application for the conversion of an application for a patent to a Convention application under Rule 94(2)   ...   ... | — | Patents Form No. 38 Con. |
| 40. On application for revocation of a patent under section 33   ...   ...   ... | 3 10 0* | Patents Form No. 39. |
| 41. On offer to surrender a patent under section 34   ...   ...   ...   ...   ... | — | Patents Form No. 40. |
| 42. On notice of opposition to surrender of a patent...   ...   ...   ...   ... | 2 10 0* | Patents Form No. 41. |
| 43. On application for endorsement of patent "Licences of Right"...   ...   ...   ... | 1 10 0 | Patents Form No. 42. |
| 44. On application for settlement of terms of licence under patent endorsed "Licences of Right"   ...   ...   ...   ... | 7 10 0 | Patents Form No. 43. |
| 45. On application by patentee for cancellation of endorsement of patent "Licences of Right"   ...   ...   ...   ... | 3 0 0 | Patents Form No. 44. |
| 46. On application for cancellation of endorsement "Licences of Right" ...   ... | 3 0 0 | Patents Form No. 45. |
| 47. On notice of opposition to cancellation of endorsement of patent "Licences of Right" | 3 0 0 | Patents Form No. 46. |
| 48. On application under section 37 for grant of compulsory licence or endorsement of a patent "Licences of Right"   ...   ... | 7 10 0 | Patents Form No. 47. |

|  |  |  |  | Corresponding Form |
|---|---|---|---|---|
|  | £ | s. | d. |  |
| 49. On application under section 40(1) for endorsement of patent "Licences of Right" or grant of licence ... ... ... | 7 | 10 | 0 | Patents Form No. 48. |
| 50. On application under section 40(3) for Order of Comptroller ... ... ... ... | 7 | 10 | 0 | Patents Form No. 49. |
| 51. On application under section 42 for revocation ... ... ... ... ... ... | 7 | 10 | 0 | Patents Form No. 50. |
| 52. On opposition to application under section 37, 40, 41 or 42 ... ... ... ... | 3 | 0 | 0 | Patents Form No. 51. |
| 53. On application for licence under section 41 ... | 7 | 10 | 0 | Patents Form No. 52. |
| 54. On application under section 55(1) for directions of Comptroller ... ... ... | 7 | 10 | 0 | Patents Form No. 53. |
| 55. On application under section 55(2) for directions of Comptroller ... ... ... | 7 | 10 | 0 | Patents Form No. 54. |
| 56. On application under section 56(1) to determine dispute ... ... ... ... | 7 | 10 | 0 | Patents Form No. 55. |
| 57. On reference of dispute to Comptroller under section 67(1) ... ... ... ... | 7 | 10 | 0 | Patents Form No. 56. |
| 58. For altering name or nationality or address or address for service in register, for each patent... ... ... ... ... ... | | 8 | 0 | Patents Form No. 57. |
| 59. On application for entry of name of subsequent proprietor in the register if made within six months from date of acquisition of proprietorship:— | 1 | 10 | 0 | Patents Form No. 58 or 60. |
| If made after the expiration of six months but within twelve months from the date of acquisition of proprietorship | 3 | 15 | 0 | „   „   „ |
| If made after expiration of twelve months from date of acquisition of proprietorship ... ... ... ... ... | 4 | 10 | 0 | „   „   „ |
| On each application covering more than one patent, the devolution of title being the same as in the first patent. For each additional patent ... ... | | 4 | 0 | „   „   „ |
| 60. On application for entry of notice of a mortgage or licence in the register, if made within six months from date of acquisition of interest or the sealing of the patent (whichever is the later) ... ... ... ... | 1 | 10 | 0 | Patents Form No. 59 or 61. |
| If made after expiration of six months but within twelve months from date of acquisition of interest or the sealing of the patent (whichever is the later) ... | 3 | 15 | 0 | „   „   „ |
| If made after expiration of twelve months from date of acquisition of interest or the sealing of the patent (whichever is the later) ... ... ... ... | 4 | 10 | 0 | „   „   „ |
| On each application covering more than one patent, the devolution of title being the same as in the first patent. For each additional patent... ... ... | | 4 | 0 | Patents Form No. 59 or 61. |

|  |  |  |  | Corresponding Form |
|---|---|---|---|---|
|  | £ | s. | d. |  |
| 61. On application for entry of notification of a document in the register, if made within six months from date of document or the sealing of the patent (whichever is the later):— | 1 | 10 | 0 | Patents Form No. 62. |
| If made after expiration of six months but within twelve months from date of document or the sealing of the patent (whichever is the later) ... ... | 3 | 15 | 0 | „ „ „ „ |
| If made after expiration of twelve months from date of document or the sealing of the patent (whichever is the later)... | 4 | 10 | 0 | „ „ „ „ |
| On each application covering more than one patent, for each additional patent referred to in the same document as the first patent ... ... ... ... | | 4 | 0 | „ „ „ „ |
| 62. On application for entry in the register of claim to a licence under a patent extended under section 23, 24 or 25 ... ... ... | 1 | 10 | 0 | Patents Form No. 63. |
| 63. On request to Comptroller to correct a clerical error:— | | | | |
| Up to sealing ... ... ... ... | | 15 | 0 | Patents Form No. 64. |
| After sealing ... ... ... ... | 1 | 10 | 0 | „ „ „ |
| 64. On notice of opposition to the correction of a clerical error ... ... ... ... ... | 1 | 10 | 0 | Patents Form No. 65. |
| 65. For certificate of Comptroller under section 77(1) ... ... ... ... ... ... | | 15 | 0 | Patents Form No. 66. |
| 66. On request for information as to a matter affecting a patent or an application therefor | 1 | 5 | 0* | Patents Form No. 67. |
| 67. For duplicate of patent ... ... ... | 3 | 10 | 0* | Patents Form No. 68. |
| 68. On notice of Order of Court ... ... ... | | 15 | 0 | Patents Form No. 69. |
| 69. On inspection of register or supply of an extract from register, or on inspection of original documents (other than provisional specifications), samples or specimens ... | | 2 | 6* | |
| 70. For typewritten office copies (every 100 words) (but never less than two shillings)... ... | | 1 | 0* | |
| 71. For photographic office copies and office copies of drawings | Cost according to agreement | | | |
| 72. For office copy of patent ... ... ... | | 6 | 0 | |
| 73. For certifying office copies, MSS., printed or photographic... ... ... ... each | | 4 | 0 | |
| 74. On written enquiry as to whether a patent or patents is or are in force; for each patent ... ... ... | | 1 | 0 | |

# EXPLANATORY NOTE

*(This Note is not part of the Rules.)*

These Rules further amend the Patents Rules 1968.

With the exceptions indicated by asterisk, the fees payable under the Rules are increased.

The new fees become payable on or after 21st June 1969 except in the case of renewal fees paid in advance. Renewal fees in respect of any year beginning on or after 21st June 1969 are increased on 15th April 1969.

STATUTORY INSTRUMENTS

## 1969 No. 483

# EDUCATION, ENGLAND AND WALES

## The Provision of Milk and Meals Regulations 1969

| | |
|---|---|
| Made - - - - | 27th March 1969 |
| Laid before Parliament | 2nd April 1969 |
| Coming into Operation | 7th April 1969 |

The Secretary of State for Education and Science, in exercise of the powers conferred upon him by section 49 of the Education Act 1944(a) as amended by the Secretary of State for Education and Science Order 1964(b) and section 3 of the Public Expenditure and Receipts Act 1968(c), hereby makes the following regulations :—

*Citation, commencement and interpretation*

**1.**—(1) These regulations may be cited as the Provision of Milk and Meals Regulations 1969 and shall come into operation on 7th April 1969.

(2) The Interpretation Act 1889(d) shall apply for the interpretation of these regulations as it applies for the interpretation of an Act of Parliament.

*Revocation*

**2.** The regulations specified in schedule 2 are hereby revoked.

*Duty of local education authority*

**3.**—(1) It shall be the duty of every local education authority (in these regulations called " authority "), subject to and in accordance with these regulations, to provide so far as is reasonably practicable such milk, meals and other refreshment as are required by day pupils in attendance at schools maintained by them.

(2) The duty imposed by paragraph (1) above shall include the duty to provide such premises, equipment and transport and such incidental and ancillary facilities and services as appear to the authority to be necessary ; and for the purposes of this regulation the duty to provide premises shall include the duty to make alterations to the school buildings, including such consequential alterations as are necessary to secure that the school premises conform to the prescribed standards.

*Provision of milk*

**4.**—(1) On every school day one third of a pint of milk shall be provided for every pupil in every primary school and special school and for every junior pupil in every school which is a primary school by virtue of section 114(3) of the Education Act 1944.

(2) On any school day a further third of a pint of milk may be provided in any special school for any delicate pupil within the meaning of the Handicapped Pupils and Special Schools Regulations 1959(e) as amended(f).

---

(a) 1944 c. 31.  (b) S.I. 1964/490 (1964 I, p. 800).  (c) 1968 c. 14.
(d) 1889 c. 63.  (e) S.I. 1959/365 (1959 I, p. 1024).
(f) The amending Regulations are not relevant to the subject matter of these Regulations.

(3) The authority shall provide milk—

(a) which is pasteurised or ultra heat treated or, if no such milk is obtainable, designated for sale as untreated ; and

(b) from sources and of a quality approved for the purposes of these regulations by the medical officer of health for the area of the authority after consultation with the medical officer of health for any county district concerned and the school medical officer.

(4) If it is not reasonably practicable for the authority to comply with the requirements of paragraph (3)(b) above, they shall provide full-cream dried milk prepared for drinking or milk tablets.

### Provision of meals and other refreshment

**5.**—(1) On every school day there shall be provided, and on any other day there may be provided, for every pupil as a midday dinner a meal suitable in all respects as the main meal of the day.

(2) On any school day there may be provided such other meals and refreshment as the authority consider appropriate.

### Exceptions and saving

**6.**—(1) The authority shall not be under any duty to provide milk under regulation 4(1) or as the case may be a meal under regulation 5(1) for any pupil who takes it so rarely or irregularly that unreasonable expense is involved in catering for him.

(2) These regulations shall be without prejudice to the exercise by the head teacher of a school, under the articles of government or rules of management for the school, of any function relating to the internal discipline of the school.

### Duties of managers and governors

**7.** The managers or governors of every school shall afford to the authority such facilities as are required by the authority to enable them to carry out their duties under these regulations and for that purpose shall allow the authority to make such use of the premises and equipment of the school, and to make such alterations to the school buildings, as the authority consider necessary.

### Organisers of school meals

**8.** The duties of the authority with respect to the appointment of officers shall include the duty of appointing a fit person to be the organiser of school meals.

### Supervision of pupils

**9.** The authority shall ensure that suitable arrangements are made for the supervision and social training of pupils during meals.

### Expenses

**10.**—(1) Subject to the provisions of this regulation, the expense incurred in providing milk, meals and other refreshment under these regulations shall be defrayed by the authority.

(2) The authority shall make arrangements for the payment by the parent of—

(a) a charge of 1s. 6d. for every meal provided in a county or voluntary school under regulation 5(1) ;

(b) such a charge (if any) as they consider appropriate for any meal provided in a special school under regulation 5(1) ; and

(c) such charges as they consider appropriate for meals and refreshment provided under regulation 5(2).

(3) The arrangements made by the authority under paragraph (2) above shall include provision for the remission of the charge in the case of any parent who satisfies them that he is unable to pay it without hardship.

(4) For the purposes of paragraph (3) above, a parent who is in receipt of a supplementary pension or a supplementary allowance under section 4 of the Ministry of Social Security Act 1966(a) shall be treated as unable to pay the charge without hardship ; and in the case of the charge under paragraph (2)(a) above, the question whether any parent not in receipt of such benefit is so unable to pay shall be determined in accordance with schedule 1.

*Inspection*

**11.** All the facilities (including buildings and equipment) provided under these regulations shall be open to inspection by any person authorised by the Secretary of State for that purpose.

Regulation 10(4)　　　　　　　SCHEDULE 1

DETERMINATION OF FINANCIAL HARDSHIP

*Net income scale*

1. Where the net weekly income of the parent of a family of any size specified in Part A of the following table is less than any amount shown in the corresponding entry in Part B, the number of children in respect of whom the charge shall be remitted is the number at the head of the column in Part B in which there appears the lowest amount in that entry which exceeds his income.

Part A.　　　　　　　　　　　　　　Part B.

| Size of family | Net weekly income in shillings | | | | | | | | | |
|---|---|---|---|---|---|---|---|---|---|---|
| | 1 | 2 | 3 | 4 | 5 | 6 | 7 | 8 | 9 | 10 |
| 1 | 195 | | | | | | | | | |
| 2 | 240 | 232 | | | | | | | | |
| 3 | 285 | 277 | 269 | | | | | | | |
| 4 | 330 | 322 | 314 | 306 | | | | | | |
| 5 | 375 | 367 | 359 | 351 | 343 | | | | | |
| 6 | 420 | 412 | 404 | 396 | 388 | 380 | | | | |
| 7 | 465 | 457 | 449 | 441 | 433 | 425 | 417 | | | |
| 8 | 510 | 502 | 494 | 486 | 378 | 470 | 462 | 454 | | |
| 9 | 555 | 547 | 539 | 531 | 523 | 515 | 507 | 499 | 491 | |
| 10 | 600 | 592 | 584 | 576 | 568 | 560 | 552 | 544 | 536 | 528 |

For larger families, in respect of each child—

(a) 45s. is to be added at each incremental point in every additional line ; and

(b) 8s. is to be subtracted at each incremental point in every additional column.

For the purposes of this paragraph the expression " size of family " means the number of dependent children in the family who have not attained the age of 19.

(a) 1966 c. 20.

*Calculation of net income*

2. In calculating the net income of the parent there shall be taken into account his income (reduced by income tax and national insurance contributions but including any benefit in kind other than a dwelling) from all sources, but there shall be disregarded the resources specified in paragraph 3 below and a deduction shall be made in respect of the expenses specified in paragraph 4 below.

*Resources to be disregarded*

3.—(1) 40s. of the income consisting of any one or more of the following—

(a) workmen's compensation ;

(b) disablement benefit ;

(c) disability pension ;

(d) the amount by which—
   (i) a war widow's pension ;
   (ii) a widow's pension under section 19(3) of the National Insurance (Industrial Injuries) Act 1965(a) or an analogous payment—

exceeds the rate of pension payable under schedule 3 of the National Insurance Act 1965(b).

(2) 20s. of any income other than any earnings or any of the following—

(a) benefit under the National Insurance Acts 1965 and 1966(c) ;

(b) industrial injury benefit under the National Insurance (Industrial Injuries) Acts 1965 and 1966 ;

(c) family allowances ;

(d) payments for maintenance (including any marriage allowance) ;

(e) any rent received in respect of accommodation whether let furnished or unfurnished ;

(f) any amount received as a contribution towards the expenses of the household from any other member of, or person living with, the family :

provided that the amount disregarded under this sub-paragraph shall not, together with the amount disregarded under sub-paragraph (1) above, exceed 40s.

(3) 40s. of the earnings of a mother or female guardian.

(4) 20s. of the casual earnings of an unemployed father or male guardian.

(5) Any maternity grant under section 23 of the National Insurance Act 1965.

(6) Any death grant under section 39 of the National Insurance Act 1965.

(7) Any payment in respect of a pupil under the Regulations for Scholarships and Other Benefits 1945(d) as amended(e).

(8) 25s. of any income if one parent is blind.

(9) 40s. of any income if both parents are blind.

(10) One-tenth of the rent received in respect of accommodation let unfurnished.

(11) One-quarter of the rent received in respect of accommodation let furnished.

(12) Nineteen-twentieths of any amount up to £3, and three quarters of any amount in excess of £3, received as a contribution towards the expenses of the household from any other member of, or person living with, the family.

*Expenses to be deducted*

4.—(1) The amount of any premium on a policy of assurance on the life of either parent.

---

(a) 1965 c. 52.       (b) 1965 c. 51.       (c) 1965 c. 51; 1966 c. 6.
       (d) S.R. & O. 1945/666 (Rev. VI, p. 378: 1945 I, p. 340).
(e) S.I. 1948/688, 2223 (Rev. VI, p. 378: 1948 I, p. 754; 1948 I, p. 755), S.I. 1964/1294 (1964 II, p. 2974).

(2) Any expenses reasonably incurred in the provision of necessary household assistance and necessary day care for a child below compulsory school age where—

(a) the parent is widowed, divorced or permanently separated from the other party to the marriage ;

(b) either parent is incapacitated ;

(c) the parent is an unmarried women.

(3) Any expenses necessarily incurred in the course of the parent's employment, including travelling expenses, trade union subscriptions and superannuation contributions.

(4) The amount of any rent, general and water rates and mortgage payments in respect of the home and of any hire purchase payments in respect of any caravan or houseboat which is the permanent home of the family.

(5) Any payment made—

(a) for the maintenance of a former wife or her child ;

(b) under an affiliation order ;

(c) under a contribution order in respect of a child in the care of a local authority.

(6) 12s. 6d. of the cost of any special diet prescribed by a registered medical practitioner.

Regulation 2 | **SCHEDULE 2**

**REVOCATIONS**

| Regulations Revoked | References |
| --- | --- |
| The Provision of Milk and Meals Regulations 1945. | S.R. & O. 1945/698 (Rev. VI, p. 380: 1945 I, p. 366). |
| The Provision of Milk and Meals Amending Regulations 1959. | S.I. 1959/409 (1959 I, p. 1029). |
| The Provision of Milk and Meals Amending Regulations 1965. | S.I. 1965/308 (1965 I, p. 771). |
| The Provision of Milk and Meals Amending Regulations 1968. | S.I. 1968/534 (1968 I, p. 1280). |
| The Provision of Milk and Meals (Amendment No. 2) Regulations 1968. | S.I. 1968/1251 (1968 II, p. 3381). |

Given under the Official Seal of the Secretary of State for Education and Science on 27th March 1969.

(L.S.)

*Alice Bacon,*
**Minister of State for Education and Science.**

## EXPLANATORY NOTE

*(This Note is not part of the Regulations.)*

These regulations consolidate with amendments the regulations which impose upon local education authorities the duty to provide milk, meals and other refreshment for pupils attending schools maintained by them. The principal amendments are—

(*a*) the provisions for determining the parent's capacity to pay the charge for school dinner (regulation 10 (4) and schedule 1) ; and

(*b*) the omission of the provision for the remission of that charge in respect of children belonging to large families.

## STATUTORY INSTRUMENTS

### 1969 No. 487 (S.42)

### ROAD TRAFFIC

### The Local Authorities' Traffic Orders (Procedure) (Scotland) Regulations 1969

| | |
|---|---|
| *Made* - - - - | *27th March* 1969 |
| *Laid before Parliament* | *3rd April* 1969 |
| *Coming into Operation* | *20th April* 1969 |

The Secretary of State (in relation to all matters other than orders under section 15 or 33 of the Road Traffic Regulation Act 1967(a)) and the Minister of Transport (in relation to orders under the said section 15 or 33) in exercise of their powers under section 84C of, and Schedule 8 to, the said Act, as amended by Part IX of the Transport Act 1968(b) and as read with section 32 of the Countryside Act 1968(c), and (for regulation 1(2) below only) the Secretary of State in exercise of his powers under sections 4, 26 and 32 of the said Act of 1967, and of all other enabling powers, after consultation with representative organisations in accordance with section 107(2) of the said Act of 1967 hereby make the following regulations:—

### PART I

### GENERAL

*Citation, commencement and revocation*

**1.**—(1) These regulations may be cited as the Local Authorities' Traffic Orders (Procedure) (Scotland) Regulations 1969, and shall come into operation on 20th April 1969.

(2) The Traffic Regulation Orders (Procedure) (Scotland) Regulations 1961(d), the Parking Places Orders (Procedure) (Scotland) Regulations 1961(e) and the Street Playgrounds Orders (Procedure) (Scotland) Regulations 1961(f) are hereby revoked.

*Interpretation*

**2.**—(1) In these regulations the following expressions have the meanings hereby respectively assigned to them:—

"the Act" means the Road Traffic Regulation Act 1967 as amended by Part IX of the Transport Act 1968 and as read with section 32 of the Countryside Act 1968;

---

(a) 1967 c. 76.
(b) 1968 c. 73.
(c) 1968 c. 41.
(d) S.I. 1961/669 (1961 I, p. 1407).
(e) S.I. 1961/505 (1961 I, p. 1145).
(f) S.I. 1961/1322 (1961 II, p. 2545).

"the appropriate Minister", in relation to any order under section 15 or 33 of the Act, means the Minister of Transport, and in relation to any other order to which these regulations apply, means the Secretary of State.

"the authority", in relation to any order, means the local authority making, or proposing to make, the order under the Act;

"consolidation order" means an order which revokes provisions of two or more existing orders and reproduces the unspent provisions of those orders without any change in substance;

"council" means a county council or a town council;

"Crown road" and "the appropriate Crown authority" have the same meanings as in section 32 of the Countryside Act 1968;

"the notice of proposals" and "the notice of making", in relation to an order, mean respectively the notices required to be published under regulations 5 and 17 of these regulations;

"the objection period" means the period within which objections to an order may be made in accordance with regulation 6 of these regulations;

"the order" means, in relation to anything occurring or falling to be done before its making, the order as proposed to be made and in relation to anything occurring or falling to be done on or after its making, the order as made; and

"relevant map", in relation to an order, means the map required to be prepared and kept in connection with that order by regulation 14 of these regulations.

(2) Any reference in these regulations to an order under any particular section of the Act includes a reference to an order varying or revoking an order made, or having effect as if made, under that section.

(3) Any reference in these regulations to any enactment shall be construed as a reference to that enactment as amended by or under any subsequent enactment.

(4) The Interpretation Act 1889(a) shall apply for the interpretation of these regulations as it applies for the interpretation of an Act of Parliament.

*Application of regulations*

**3.**—(1) These regulations apply to orders made or proposed to be made by a local authority under any of the following provisions of the Act, that is to say, sections 1(1) to (7), 5, 9, 15, 26, 28, 31, 33, 35, 36, 37(2) and (3), 73(3) and 74.

(2) Except where otherwise stated, each regulation applies to every such order.

(3) Except where otherwise stated, these regulations apply to an order under any of the above-mentioned provisions of the Act made or proposed to be made by such a local authority in pursuance of a direction of the appropriate Minister under section 84A(1) of the Act in the same way as it applies to an order in relation to which no such direction has been given.

(4) Where in connection with any order to which these regulations apply some, but not all, of the necessary procedural steps have been taken before the coming into operation of these regulations, then the remaining procedural steps in connection with that order shall be determined by, and carried out in accordance with, these regulations, as nearly as may be.

---

(a) 1889 c. 63.

## Part II

## PROCEDURE BEFORE MAKING THE ORDER

*Procedure of consultation*

**4.**—(1) Before making the order the authority shall:—

(a) where they are not the highway authority for any road to which the order relates, consult with the highway authority for that road, and

(b) where the order relates to a Crown road, consult with the appropriate Crown authority for that road, and

(c) in all cases consult with one or more organisations representing persons who use any road to which the order relates or are likely to be otherwise affected by any provisions of the order, unless it appears to the authority that there is no such organisation which can appropriately be consulted.

(2) The consultations referred to in paragraph (1) of this regulation are additional to the consultation with the chief constable required by section 84C(1) of the Act and any other consultation required by the Act.

(3) This regulation has effect subject to regulation 18 below.

*Publication of proposals*

**5.**—(1) After the consultation with the chief constable required by section 84C(1) of the Act and any other consultation required by the Act or by Regulation 4 above but before making the order the authority shall:—

(a) publish once at least in a local newspaper circulating in the area in which any road or other place to which the order relates is situated a notice of proposals containing the particulars specified in Part I of Schedule 1 to these regulations;

(b) publish a similar notice in the Edinburgh Gazette;

(c) comply with the relevant requirements of Schedules 2 and 3 to these regulations as to the notices to be displayed in each road or other place to which the order relates and as to the availability of documents for inspection.

(2) This regulation has effect subject to regulations 18 and 19 below.

*Objections*

**6.**—(1) The period during which objections to the order can be made shall begin not earlier than the date on which the authority have complied with the requirements of paragraph (1)(a) and (b), and have begun to display the notices required by paragraph (1)(c), of the last foregoing regulation, and shall continue for not less than 21 days.

(2) Any person desiring to object to the authority's proposal to make the order shall send within the period, and to the address, specified in the notice of proposals published as required by the last foregoing regulation a written statement of his objection and of the grounds thereof.

(3) This regulation has effect subject to regulations 18 and 19 below.

*Hearing of objections*

**7.**—(1) Before making any order to which these regulations apply the authority may hold a public hearing in connection with objections made to that order in accordance with regulation 6 above and the authority shall hold such a hearing before making the order in the following cases:—

(*a*) where the order is:—

    (i) an order under section 1, 5 or 35 of the Act which contains a provision for prohibiting the loading or unloading of vehicles in any road, or

    (ii) an order under section 9 of the Act which contains a provision for prohibiting the loading or unloading of vehicles in any road and which is proposed to be made within 6 months of the date on which a previous order under section 9 of the Act containing a similar provision as respects that road ceased to be in force,

    and an objection to that provision is made by any person in accordance with regulation 6 and is not withdrawn;

(*b*) where the order is:—

    (i) an order under section 1, 5 or 35 of the Act which contains a provision for requiring vehicular traffic generally, or vehicular traffic of any class, to proceed on a road in a specified direction, or for prohibiting such traffic from so proceeding, or

    (ii) an order under section 9 of the Act which contains a provision for requiring vehicular traffic generally, or vehicular traffic of any class, to proceed on a road in a specified direction, or for prohibiting such traffic from so proceeding, and which is proposed to be made within 6 months of the date on which a previous order under section 9 of the Act containing a similar provision as respects that road ceased to be in force,

    and an objection to that provision is made in accordance with regulation 6 above by a person who provides a service of stage or express carriages on any road to which the order relates, and is not withdrawn; and

(*c*) where the order is one which requires the consent of the appropriate Minister under section 84B of the Act, or under paragraph 17 of Schedule 8 to the Act, and that Minister has notified the authority that he will not be willing to give his consent to the making of the order until a public hearing has been held by the authority in connection with objections made and not withdrawn.

(2) Hearings may be held by the council or by a committee or sub-committee thereof or, if the authority so decide, by an independent person.

(3) If the authority decide that objectors shall be heard by an independent person the authority shall appoint for the purpose a suitable person, not being a member of the council or of any committee or sub-committee thereof or a person in the employment of the authority.

(4) Any hearing shall be held in public.

*Notice of public hearing*

**8.**—(1) Where a hearing is to be held in accordance with the provisions of this Part of these regulations the authority shall forthwith give notice in writing to any person by whom objection has been made informing him that, if within such period, not being less than 14 days, as is specified in the notice, he intimates that he so desires, an opportunity will be afforded him of being heard in support of his objection.

(2) If any objector given such notice intimates his desire to be heard the authority shall notify him in writing of the arrangements for the hearing not less than 21 days before the date on which the hearing is to take place and, where the hearing is to take place before the council or a committee or sub-committee thereof, the notice of any meeting of the said council, committee or sub-committee at which an objection is to be heard in pursuance of this regulation shall specify the hearing as an item of business.

(3) Where a hearing is to take place before an independent person in accordance with the provisions of this Part of these regulations the authority shall, in addition, not less than 21 days before the date on which the hearing is due to begin—

    (*a*) publish once at least in a local newspaper circulating in the area in which any road or other place to which the order relates is situated a notice of the hearing containing the particulars specified in Part II of Schedule 1 to these regulations;

    (*b*) publish a similar notice in the Edinburgh Gazette; and

    (*c*) comply with the relevant requirements of Schedules 2 and 3 to these regulations as to the display of notices in each road or other place to which the order relates and as to the availability of documents for inspection.

*Procedure at public hearing*

**9.**—(1) Where a hearing takes place in accordance with the provisions of this Part of these regulations any objector afforded an opportunity of being heard or, where the hearing is held before an independent person, any person interested in the subject matter of the hearing may be heard either in person or by counsel, solicitor or agent.

(2) Any person so interested may, whether or not he proposes to appear at the hearing, send to the independent person appointed to hold the hearing such written representations as he may wish to make with a view to their consideration by that person at the hearing.

(3) The council, committee or sub-committee, or the independent person, as the case may be, may refuse to hear any person or allow to be put forward for consideration at the hearing any objection, if they are or he is satisfied that the views of that person are or the objection is frivolous or such views have been adequately stated at the hearing by some other person.

*Manner of submission of orders for consent of appropriate Minister*

**10.** Where the order is one which under section 84B of, or under paragraph 17 of Schedule 8 to, the Act requires the consent of the appropriate Minister, the authority's application for such consent shall be accompanied by copies of such of the documents specified in Schedule 4 to these regulations as may be applicable.

*Consideration of objections*

**11.** Before making an order the authority shall consider all objections duly made in accordance with regulation 6 above and not withdrawn and where a hearing has taken place in accordance with the provisions of this Part of these regulations shall further consider—

(a) any representations in respect thereof which have been heard by the council, or

(b) any report or recommendation made by a committee or sub-committee of the council or by an independent person.

*Modifications*

**12.**—(1) The authority shall not make the order with modifications where:—

(a) any of the modifications would involve a departure from the order in the form to which the appropriate Minister or Crown authority have given their consent, or

(b) in a case where under section 84A(1) of the Act the appropriate Minister has directed the authority to make the order, any of the modifications would involve a departure from the form in which that Minister has directed the order to be made, or

(c) in a case where the consent of the appropriate Minister is not required by or under section 84B of, or under paragraph 17 of Schedule 8 to, the Act, any of the modifications would extend the application of the order or increase the stringency of any prohibition or restriction contained in it,

but subject as aforesaid the authority may make the order with modifications, whether in consequence of any objections or otherwise.

(2) Where the appropriate Minister proposes to consent to the order with modifications which appear to him substantially to affect the character of the order as submitted to him, the authority shall, before making the order, take such steps as the Minister may require for informing the persons likely to be concerned of the effect of the modifications, for giving to those persons an opportunity to make representations in connection therewith and for ensuring that any such representations are duly considered by the authority and (if the appropriate Minister so requests) by that Minister.

*Special provisions for transmission of documents to Secretary of State in certain cases*

**13.** Where the order is one in connection with which the holding of a public hearing is required by regulation 7(1)(a) or (b) above and the authority decide to make the order in a form which includes any provision at variance with the recommendations of the committee, sub-committee or independent person who held the hearing they shall:—

(a) before making the order, send to the Secretary of State a copy of the order as proposed to be made, a copy of the relevant map, a copy of the report and recommendations made following the hearing and a statement of the authority's reasons for not accepting the relevant recommendations;

(b) at the same time as they send to the Secretary of State the documents specified above, give written notification of this fact to each person who has duly objected to the order in accordance with regulation 6 above and has not withdrawn his objection;

(*c*) not make the order before the expiration of one month from the date on which the said documents were sent to the Secretary of State unless the Secretary of State gives the authority earlier notification that he has no observations to make about the order.

## PART III

## THE FORM OF THE ORDER

*The relevant map*

**14.**—(1) The authority shall prepare and keep in connection with the order a map on a scale of not less than 6 inches to 1 mile which clearly indicates by distinctive colours, symbols or markings:—

 (*a*) each road to which the order relates,

 (*b*) in a case where any provision of the order prohibits the use of a road by all vehicles, or by all vehicles of a particular class, the alternative route available for the vehicles to which the provision applies, and

 (*c*) in a case where the order does not relate to a road, the location of the site or other place to which the order applies and the relationship of that site or place to adjacent roads and premises.

(2) Except in the case of an order under section 33 of the Act it shall not be obligatory for the text of the order to make any specific reference to the relevant map or for that map to be made a part of the order.

(3) Where the relevant map is neither specifically referred to in the text of the order nor made a part of the order, the map shall be for purposes of illustration only and the matter indicated on it shall not prevail over the actual text of the order in the event of any discrepancy between the map and the text.

(4) None of the foregoing paragraphs of this regulation applies to:—

 (*a*) an order which provides only for the revocation of the provisions of any previous order, or

 (*b*) an order which relates only to a parking place and provides only for the variation of any one or more of the following matters, namely—

  (i) the charges for the use of the parking place,

  (ii) the time limits applicable to such use,

  (iii) the classes of vehicle which may use the parking place, and

  (iv) the conditions applicable to the use of the parking place by vehicles.

*Operative date of order*

**15.**—(1) The order shall specify the date on which it comes into operation or, in a case where different operative dates are provided for different provisions of the order, each of the dates on which a provision of the order comes into operation.

(2) No date on which an order, or a provision of an order, comes into operation shall be earlier than the date on which the notice of the making of the order is published in the local newspaper under regulation 17 below.

## Part IV

### MAKING THE ORDER AND SUBSEQUENT PROCEDURE

*Making the order*

**16.** Subject to the foregoing provisions of these regulations the authority may make the order and the order as made shall be signed and sealed in accordance with the provisions of section 342 of the Local Government (Scotland) Act 1947(a).

*Notice of making the order*

**17.**—(1) When the authority have made the order, they shall:—

(a) forthwith give notice in writing of the making of the order to the chief constable of the police area in which any road or other place to which the order relates is situated;

(b) notify in writing each person who has duly objected to the order in accordance with regulation 6 above and has not withdrawn his objection, of the authority's reasons for making the order in spite of the objection;

(c) within 14 days of the making of the order publish once in a local newspaper circulating in the area in which any road or other place to which the order relates is situated a notice of the making of the order containing the particulars specified in Part III of Schedule 1 to these regulations;

(d) within the same period publish a similar notice in the Edinburgh Gazette;

(e) comply with the relevant requirements of Schedule 3 to these regulations as to the availability of documents for inspection;

(f) where the order relates to any road, forthwith take such steps as are necessary to secure:—

(i) the erection on or near the road of such traffic signs in such positions as the authority may consider requisite for the purpose of securing that adequate information as to the effect of the order is given to persons using the road, and

(ii) in a case where the order contains provision for revoking, or altering the application of, a previous order, such removal or replacement of existing traffic signs as the authority may consider requisite for the purpose of avoiding confusion to users of the road or the continuance of traffic signs in incorrect positions,

but where the road is a Crown road only after consultation with the appropriate Crown authority.

(2) This regulation has effect subject to regulation 18 below.

## Part V

### SPECIAL PROCEDURAL PROVISIONS FOR CERTAIN ORDERS

*Special provisions for consolidation orders*

**18.**—(1) Regulations 4(1)(a) and (c), 5 and 6 above shall not apply to a consolidation order and regulation 17 above shall have effect in relation to such an order with the following modifications, namely, that the particulars to be contained in the notice of the making of the order shall consist only of:—

---

(a) 1947 c. 43.

    (i) the name of the authority;

    (ii) the title of the order;

    (iii) a statement of the titles of the orders the provisions of which are reproduced in the consolidation order;

    (iv) the operative date or dates of the order; and

    (v) the items numbered 7 and, if appropriate, 8 in Part III of Schedule 1 to these regulations.

(2) A consolidation order shall be framed so as to come into operation on a date not less than 14 days after the first publication in the local newspaper of the notice of the making of the order.

*Special provisions for certain experimental traffic orders*

**19.**—(1) This regulation applies to the following orders, that is to say—

    (*a*) an order under section 9(1) of the Act which provides only for one or more of the following matters:—

        (i) the revocation of an order made, or having effect as if made, under the said section 9(1);

        (ii) the variation of an order made, or having effect as if made, under the said section 9(1) so as to reduce the extent of its application or the stringency of any prohibition or restriction imposed by it;

    (*b*) an order under section 9(3) of the Act.

(2) Regulations 5 and 6 above shall not apply to any order to which this regulation applies.

Given under the seal of the Secretary of State for Scotland on 26th March 1969.

*William Ross,*
One of Her Majesty's Principal
Secretaries of State.

Given under the Official Seal of the Minister of Transport the 27th March 1969.

*Richard Marsh,*
Minister of Transport.

## SCHEDULE 1

### PARTICULARS TO BE INCLUDED IN PRESS NOTICES

### PART I—PARTICULARS TO BE INCLUDED IN THE NOTICE OF PROPOSALS

1. The name of the authority.

2. The title of the order.

3. A statement of the general nature and effect of the order.

4. Where the order relates to any road, the name or other brief description of the road and, in a case where the order is an order under section 73(3) or 74 of the Act, a statement of the appropriate length of that road to which the order will apply.

5. Where the order relates to an off-street parking place, a brief description of that place and of its location.

6. Where the order relates to a parking place, a statement of all the charges (if any) proposed to be made for the use of the parking place and of the time limits and the classes of vehicle for which the parking place will be available.

7. Each address at which a copy of the order, as drafted, a copy of the relevant map, and a copy of the authority's statement of reasons for proposing to make the order can be inspected, and the times when inspection can take place at each such address.

8. The period during which, and the address to which, objections to the order can be made, and a statement that all objections must be made in writing and must specify the grounds thereof.

## Part II—Particulars to be Included in the Notice of a Public Hearing Before an Independent Person.

1. The name of the authority.

2. The title of the order.

3. A statement which refers to the published notice of proposals for the order and which indicates that a public hearing will be held in connection with the order.

4. A brief statement of the general nature and effect of the order and of the name or other brief description of any road or other place to which the order will apply.

5. The date, time and place of the hearing and the name of the person appointed to hold the hearing.

6. Each address at which a copy of the order, as drafted, a copy of the relevant map, and a copy of the authority's statement of reasons for proposing to make the order can be inspected, and the times when inspection can take place at each such address.

## Part III—Particulars to be Included in the Notice of Making the Order.

1. The name of the authority.

2. The title of the order.

3. A statement of the general nature and effect of the order and of its operative date or dates.

4. Where the order relates to any road, the name or other brief description of the road.

5. Where the order relates to an off-street parking place, a brief description of that place and of its location.

6. Where the order relates to a parking place, a statement of all the charges (if any) proposed to be made for the use of the parking place and of the time limits and the classes of vehicle for which the parking place will be available.

7. Each address at which a copy of the order, as made, and a copy of the relevant map can be inspected, and the times when inspection can take place at each such address.

8. In the case of an order under section 1, 5, 9, 15, 28, 33 or 35 of the Act, a statement that any person who desires to question the validity of the order or of any provision contained in the order on the ground that it is not within the powers of the relevant section of the Act or on the ground that any requirement of that section or of section 84A, 84B or 84C of the Act or any regulations made under the said section 84C has not been complied with in relation to the order, may, within 6 weeks of the date on which the order is made, such date being stated in the notice, make application for the purpose to the Court of Session.

## SCHEDULE 2

### REQUIREMENTS AS TO NOTICES TO BE DISPLAYED IN A ROAD OR OTHER PLACE

### PART I—PARTICULARS TO BE INCLUDED IN THE NOTICE

1. The name of the authority.

2. The title of the order.

3. A brief statement of the effect of the order in relation to the road or other place where it is displayed.

4. An address at which a copy of the order, a copy of the relevant map and a copy of the authority's statement of reasons for proposing to make the order can be inspected, and the times when such inspection can take place.

5. Where the notice is a notice of proposals, the address to which, and the period during which, objections to the order can be made, and a statement that all objections must be made in writing and must specify the grounds thereof.

6. Where the notice announces the holding of a public hearing by an independent person, the date, time and place of the hearing and the name of the person appointed to hold the hearing.

### PART II—OTHER REQUIREMENTS AS TO THE DISPLAY OF THE NOTICE

1. Where the order relates to any road, the notice shall be displayed in a prominent position at or near each end of the road and in such other positions as the authority think requisite for securing that adequate information about the subject matter of the notice is given to persons using the road.

2. Where the order relates to an off-street parking place, the notice shall be displayed in one or more prominent positions in the road or roads giving access to the parking place, and, where the parking place is in public use, in the parking place itself.

3. The notice shall first be displayed as aforseaid at the same time as the corresponding notice is first published in the local newspaper and the authority shall take all reasonable steps to ensure that it remains in a legible condition and continues to be so displayed:—

    (a) in the case of a notice of proposals, until the end of the objection period;

    (b) in the case of a notice announcing a public hearing before an independent person, until the date on which the hearing begins.

## SCHEDULE 3

### REQUIREMENTS AS TO THE AVAILABILITY OF DOCUMENTS FOR INSPECTION

1. There shall be available for inspection at the authority's offices during normal office hours, and (if the authority think fit) at such other places within the authority's area and during such times respectively at those places as the authority may determine, the following documents:—

(*a*) a copy of the order as drafted or made, as the case may be;

(*b*) a copy of the relevant map;

(*c*) in the case of an order which varies or revokes a previous order, a copy of that order and of its relevant map;

(*d*) in the case of a proposed order, a copy of a statement setting out the authority's reasons for proposing to make the order; and

(*e*) in the case of an order made after the holding of a public hearing, a copy of the report and recommendations (if any) of the council, committee, sub-committee or independent person who held the hearing.

2. The said documents shall be made available as aforesaid on the date of the first publication in the local newspaper of the notice in connection with which they are required to be made available, and they shall continue to be so available:—

(*a*) where the notice is a notice of proposals, until the end of the objection period;

(*b*) where the notice is one announcing the holding of a public hearing by an independent person, until the date on which the hearing begins, and

(*c*) where the notice is a notice of making the order, until the end of 6 weeks from the date on which the order is made.

## SCHEDULE 4

### DOCUMENTS TO ACCOMPANY THE APPLICATION FOR THE APPROPRIATE MINISTER'S CONSENT

1. The order as proposed to be made.

2. The relevant map.

3. The statement of the authority's reasons for proposing to make the order.

4. The issues of each local newspaper and of the Edinburgh Gazette containing the notice of proposals.

5. Each unwithdrawn objection or, in a case where there are no objections or no unwithdrawn objections, a statement to this effect.

6. Copies of the reply or replies sent to each objector.

7. A list of the persons and organisations consulted by the authority and a statement of the views (if any) expressed by each such person or organisation.

8. In a case where a public hearing has been held, a copy of the report and recommendations (if any) made following the hearing.

9. In a case where the order relates to a Crown road, the consent of the appropriate Crown authority.

10. In a case where the order relates to a Crown road and will apply to persons or vehicles in the service of the Crown, particulars of the Crown authority or authorities whose persons and vehicles are known to be involved.

# EXPLANATORY NOTE

*(This Note is not part of the Regulations).*

These Regulations lay down the procedure to be followed by local authorities in Scotland in connection with the making by them of the main types of traffic and parking place orders under the Road Traffic Regulation Act 1967, as amended by Part IX of the Transport Act 1968. The Regulations replace the Traffic Regulation Orders (Procedure) (Scotland) Regulations 1961 (S.I. No. 669), the Parking Places Orders (Procedure) (Scotland) Regulations 1961 (S.I. No. 505) and the Street Playgrounds Orders (Procedure) (Scotland) Regulations 1961 (S.I. No. 1322), all of which are revoked.

Regulation 3 specifies the orders to which the Regulations apply. These include traffic regulation orders, experimental traffic orders, orders relating to the use of roads by public service vehicles, street playgrounds orders, orders relating to parking places both on and off the highway (including bus station and parking meter orders) and orders relating to speed limits.

Regulations 4 to 13 lay down the procedure to be followed before the order is made. They provide for preliminary consultations (Regulation 4), publication of proposals (Regulation 5), objections to the order (Regulations 6 and 11), public hearings (Regulations 7 to 9), the modifications of proposals (Regulation 12) and for certain cases where the appropriate Minister's consent is required or where the Secretary of State has to be notified of the local authority's proposals (Regulations 10 and 13).

Regulations 14 and 15 contain certain requirements about the order itself, in particular about the use of a map to illustrate the order and about the operative date of the order.

Provisions as to the manner of making the order and as to the giving notice of its making are contained in Regulations 16 and 17.

Certain of the above requirements are modified in relation to consolidation orders and some experimental traffic orders by Regulations 18 and 19.

Schedules 1 to 3 contain particulars of the details to be included in the press notices of an order, of the requirements as to display of notices of an order in the road itself, and of the requirements about making documents relating to an order available for public inspection. Schedule 4 lists the documents which must accompany an application for the appropriate Minister's consent.

## STATUTORY INSTRUMENTS

### 1969 No. 488 (C.12)

## BETTING AND GAMING
## The Gaming Act 1968 (Commencement No. 2) Order 1969

*Made* - - - *28th March* 1969

In pursuance of section 54(4) of the Gaming Act 1968(**a**), I hereby make the following Order :—

**1.** This Order may be cited as the Gaming Act 1968 (Commencement No. 2) Order 1969.

**2.** Section 27(6) of and Schedule 6 to the Gaming Act 1968 shall come into operation on 1st May 1969.

**3.** Subject, as regards section 27(6), to Article 2 of this Order, sections 26, 27, 28, 29, 38(1), (2) and (12) and (for the purposes of those subsections of section 38) 39(1) of the Gaming Act 1968 shall come into operation on 1st April 1970.

*James Callaghan,*
One of Her Majesty's Principal
Secretaries of State.

Home Office,
 Whitehall.
28th March 1969.

---

### EXPLANATORY NOTE
(*This Note is not part of the Order.*)

This Order brings into force, with effect from 1st April 1970, those provisions of the Gaming Act 1968 which prohibit, with certain exceptions, the supply or maintenance of slot-machines for playing games of chance by persons other than those who have obtained a certificate or permit from the Gaming Board for Great Britain.

Article 2 brings into force, with effect from 1st May 1969, the provisions for the grant of the necessary certificates and permits.

This Order also brings into force, with effect from 1st April 1970, those provisions of the Act which prohibit, with certain exceptions, the supply and maintenance of such machines on profit-sharing terms.

---

(**a**) 1968 c. 65.

## STATUTORY INSTRUMENTS

## 1969 No. 493 (S.44)

## POLICE

## The Police Cadets (Scotland) Amendment Regulations 1969

|  |  |
|---|---|
| *Made* - - - | 26th March 1969 |
| *Laid before Parliament* | 3rd April 1969 |
| *Coming into Operation* | 4th April 1969 |

In exercise of the powers conferred on me by section 27 of the Police (Scotland) Act 1967(a), and of all other powers enabling me in that behalf, and after consulting the Police Council for Great Britain in accordance with section 26(8) of the said Act, I hereby make the following regulations :—

*Citation*

**1.** These regulations may be cited as the Police Cadets (Scotland) Amendment Regulations 1969.

*Interpretation*

**2.** In these regulations any reference to the principal regulations is a reference to the Police Cadets (Scotland) Regulations 1968(b).

*Operation and effect*

**3.**—(1) These regulations shall come into operation on 4th April 1969 and, subject to paragraph (2) of this regulation, shall have effect :—

    (*a*) for the purposes of regulation 4 thereof, as from 1st September 1968 ;

    (*b*) for the purposes of regulation 5 thereof, as from 4th April 1969 ;

    (*c*) for the purposes of regulation 6 thereof, as from 1st January 1969.

(2) A travel allowance payable to a police cadet under regulation 15 of the principal regulations in respect of a return journey made on or after 1st January 1969 but before 4th April 1969 shall be calculated in accordance with the said regulation 15 as originally made or as amended by regulation 6 of these regulations, whichever is the more favourable in his case.

*Pay*

**4.** For the Table in Schedule 1 to the principal regulations (which contains scales of pay) there shall be substituted the following Table :—

---

(a) 1967 c.77.           (b) S.I. 1968/208 (1968 I, p.557).

"TABLE

| Age | Annual Pay |
|---|---|
| Under 17 years | £390 |
| 17 years | £425 |
| 18 years | £470 |
| 19 years | £505 |

"

*Charge for board and lodging*

**5.** In Schedule 2 to the principal regulations (which relates to charges for board and lodging) there shall be substituted "£93 10s." for "£90".

*Travel allowances*

**6.** For regulation 15(2) of the principal regulations (which relates to the amount of the travel allowance) there shall be substituted the following paragraph :—

"(2) An allowance payable under this regulation shall not in any case exceed the lesser of the two following amounts, namely : —

(*a*) the reasonable cost of the return journey actually made ;

(*b*) the reasonable cost of a return journey to the parent's or guardian's usual place of abode ;

and, without prejudice to the said limitation, an allowance payable in respect of a return journey to a place outside the British Isles shall not exceed £15.

In computing the amount referred to in sub-paragraphs (*a*) and (*b*) of this paragraph, any question as to reasonable cost shall be determined by the police authority."

*William Ross,*
One of Her Majesty's Principal
Secretaries of State.

St. Andrew's House,
Edinburgh, 1.
26th March 1969.

---

## EXPLANATORY NOTE
### (*This Note is not part of the Regulations.*)

These Regulations amend the Police Cadets (Scotland) Regulations 1968. Regulation 4 increases the pay of a police cadet by £15 or £20 a year, depending on his age.

Regulation 5 increases charges for board and lodging by £3 10s. 0d. a year.

Regulation 6 makes new provision as regards the maximum amount of a travel allowance when a police cadet visits a parent or guardian who lives outside the British Isles.

By virtue of Regulation 3(1)(*a*) and (*c*) the increases in pay have effect from 1st September 1968 and the changes in the maximum amount of a travel allowance have effect from 1st January 1969. This is provided in exercise of the power conferred by section 27(2) of the Police (Scotland) Act 1967. Regulation 3(2) contains a safeguard against any retrospective reduction in a travel allowance.

## STATUTORY INSTRUMENTS

## 1969 No. 500

## PATENTS

## The Patents Appeal Tribunal (Amendment) Rules 1969

| | | |
|---|---|---|
| *Made* - - - | *20th March* 1969 |
| *Coming into Operation* | *15th April* 1969 |

The Honourable Mr. Justice Lloyd-Jacob, a Judge of the High Court nominated by the Lord Chancellor to be the Appeal Tribunal under section 85(2) of the Patents Act 1949(**a**), hereby makes the following Rules by virtue of the power conferred on him by section 85(8) of that Act:—

1.—(1) These Rules may be cited as the Patents Appeal Tribunal (Amendment) Rules 1969 and shall come into operation on 15th April 1969.

(2) The Interpretation Act 1889(**b**) shall apply to the interpretation of these Rules as it applies to the interpretation of an Act of Parliament.

2. In Rule 5A of the Patents Appeal Tribunal Rules 1950(**c**), as amended(**d**), after the words "notice of appeal" there shall be inserted the words "or such further time as the Appeal Tribunal may direct".

Dated 20th March 1969.

*G. H. Lloyd-Jacob.*

---

### EXPLANATORY NOTE

*(This Note is not part of the Rules.)*

These Rules enable the Patents Appeal Tribunal to extend the respondent's time for lodging notice of his intention to support the decision appealed against on additional grounds.

---

(**a**) 1949 c. 87.     (**b**) 1889 c. 63.     (**c**) S.I. 1950/392 (1950 II, p. 201).
(**d**) The relevant amending instrument is S.I. 1961/1016 (1961 II, p. 1965).

STATUTORY INSTRUMENTS

## 1969 No. 501

## CHILDREN AND YOUNG PERSONS

### The Approved Schools (Contributions by Local Authorities) Regulations 1969

Made - - - -                31st March 1969

Coming into Operation        1st April 1969

In pursuance of the power conferred upon me by section 90(1) of the Children and Young Persons Act 1933(a), I, the Right Honourable James Callaghan, one of Her Majesty's Principal Secretaries of State, hereby make the following Regulations:—

**1.** These Regulations may be cited as the Approved Schools (Contributions by Local Authorities) Regulations 1969 and shall come into operation on 1st April 1969.

**2.** The Interpretation Act 1889(b) shall apply to the interpretation of these Regulations as it applies to the interpretation of an Act of Parliament.

**3.** In Regulation 1 of the Approved Schools (Contributions by Local Authorities) Regulations 1962(c), as amended(d) (which provides that the contributions to be made by the local authority named in an approved school order to the expenses of the managers of an approved school throughout the time, except in certain specified circumstances, during which the person to whom the order relates is under the care of the said managers, shall be at the rate of twelve pounds fifteen shillings and sixpence a week) for the words "twelve pounds fifteen shillings and sixpence" there shall be substituted the words "fourteen pounds".

**4.** The Approved Schools (Contributions by Local Authorities) Regulations 1968(d) are hereby revoked.

*James Callaghan,*
One of Her Majesty's Principal
Secretaries of State.

Home Office,
  Whitehall.
31st March 1969.

---

### EXPLANATORY NOTE

(*This Note is not part of the Regulations.*)

These Regulations raise from £12 15s. 6d. a week to £14 a week the contributions to be made by the local authority named in an approved school order towards the expenses of the managers of the school in respect of the person to whom the order relates during the time when that person is under the care of those managers.

---

(a)1933 c. 12.          (b) 1889 c. 63.          (c) S.I. 1962/623 (1962 I, p. 612).
(d) S.I. 1968/407 (1968 I, p. 1087).

## STATUTORY INSTRUMENTS

## 1969 No. 505 (S. 45)

## POLICE

### The Police (Scotland) Amendment (No. 2) Regulations 1969

| | |
|---|---|
| Made - - - - | 27th March 1969 |
| Laid before Parliament | 10th April 1969 |
| Coming into Operation | 1st July 1969 |

In exercise of the powers conferred on me by section 26 of the Police (Scotland) Act 1967(a) and of all other powers enabling me in that behalf, and after consulting (i) the Police Advisory Board for Scotland in accordance with section 26(9) of the said Act, and (ii) the Police Council for Great Britain in accordance with section 26(8) of the said Act, I hereby make the following regulations:—

### PART I

1. These regulations may be cited as the Police (Scotland) Amendment (No. 2) Regulations 1969 and shall come into operation on 1st July 1969.

2. The Police (Scotland) Regulations 1968(b) (hereinafter referred to as "the principal regulations") shall have effect subject to the amendments specified in Part II of these regulations.

### PART II

3. For paragraph (2) of regulation 18 of the principal regulations (which relates to duties of constables) there shall be substituted the following paragraph:—

"(2) Without prejudice to any enactment laying specific duties on constables, the following are duties which constables shall not be required to perform:—

(a) collection and recovery of monies due under decrees of affiliation and aliment and decrees for aliment;

(b) acting as theatre or public hall attendant;

(c) collection of market tolls;

(d) inspection of markets;

(e) inspection of cleansing;

(f) inspection of lighting;

(g) inspection of beach trading;

(h) inspection of licensed boats;

(i) inspection of common lodging houses;

(j) inspection of domestic servants' registries;

(k) inspection of theatrical agencies and employers;

(l) inspection of pet shops;

(m) inspection and registration of places of public refreshment;

(n) inspection and procuring samples under the Food and Drugs (Scotland) Act 1956(c) and the Fertilizers and Feeding Stuffs Act 1926(d);

(o) duties of inspector under the Shops Act 1950(e)

(p) inspection of weights and measures;

(q) inspection of premises under the Celluloid and Cinematograph Film Act 1922(f);

(r) inspection of premises for the purposes of the Petroleum (Consolidation) Act 1928(g)

---

(a) 1967 c. 77.   (b) S.I. 1968/716 (1968 II, p. 2024).   (c) 1956 c. 30.   (d) 1926 c. 45.
(e) 1950 c. 28.   (f) 1922 c. 35.   (g) 1928 c. 32.

(s) issue of licences relating to employment and premises;
(t) inspection of fire appliances."

**4.** For regulation 55 of the principal regulations (which relates to extra duty allowance) there shall be substituted the following regulation:—

"55.—(1) A constable required to undertake any of the following extra duties may receive an extra duty allowance, to be payable by the authority for which the duties are undertaken, if the police authority are satisfied that the performance of such extra duties causes, either regularly or on recurring occasions, a material addition to his normal hours of duty—

(a) duties of inspector under the Diseases of Animals Act 1950 (a), and making of returns in relation thereto;

(b) inspection of premises for the purposes of the Explosives Acts 1875 and 1923 (b).

(2) In respect of all other extra duties, no allowance shall be payable other than the allowance or payment (if any) to which a constable would normally be entitled as provided in these regulations."

*William Ross,*
One of Her Majesty's Principal
Secretaries of State.

St. Andrew's House,
Edinburgh 1.
27th March 1969.

## EXPLANATORY NOTE

*(This Note is not part of the regulations.)*

These Regulations amend the Police (Scotland) Regulations 1968 to provide for additions to the list of duties which constables shall not be required to perform, with consequential amendment to the list of duties for which a constable may receive an extra duty allowance.

(a) 1950 c. 36.          (b) 1875 c. 17; 1923 c.17.

## STATUTORY INSTRUMENTS

## 1969 No. 506 (S.46)

## EDUCATION, SCOTLAND

### The Grant-Aided Secondary Schools (Scotland) Grant (Amendment) Regulations 1969

| | |
|---|---|
| Made - - - | *26th March* 1969 |
| *Laid before Parliament* | 10*th April* 1969 |
| *Coming into Operation* | 1*st May* 1969 |

In exercise of the powers conferred upon me by sections 75(3) and (4)(*e*) and 76(1) of the Education (Scotland) Act 1962(a), and of all other powers enabling me in that behalf, and after causing a draft of the regulations to be published and sending a copy thereof to every education authority and having regard to the representations made in accordance with the provisions of section 144(2) of the said Act I hereby make the following regulations :—

*Citation, commencement and interpretation*

**1.**—(1) These regulations may be cited as the Grant-Aided Secondary Schools (Scotland) Grant (Amendment) Regulations 1969 and shall come into operation on 1st May 1969.

(2) These regulations shall be construed as one with the Grant-Aided Secondary Schools (Scotland) Grant Regulations 1959(b) (in these regulations referred to as "the principal regulations") and with the Grant-Aided Secondary Schools (Scotland) Grant (Amendment) Regulations 1968(c) (in these regulations referred to as "the Amendment Regulations of 1968").

*Amendment of the principal regulations*

**2.** The principal regulations shall be amended as follows :—
(1) in regulation 4 thereof there shall be substituted for paragraph (1) the following paragraph :—

"(1) Subject to the conditions prescribed in these regulations the Secretary of State may pay to the Managers of a recognised secondary school in aid of their approved expenditure on the maintenance of the school—

(*a*) in respect of the financial year of the school beginning after 1st April 1968 and ending before 1st January 1970 a grant of the amount specified in column (2) of the Schedule to these regulations opposite the name of the school in column (1) of that Schedule, and

(*b*) in respect of each financial year of the school beginning after 1st April 1969 a grant of the amount specified in column (3) of the

---

(a) 1962 c.47.      (b) S.I. 1959/833 (1959 I, p. 1104).
(c) S.I. 1968/449 (1968 I, p. 1161).

said Schedule opposite the name of the school in column (1) of that Schedule:

Provided that if the Secretary of State considers that the circumstances of any particular case justify him in so doing he may in lieu of the amount specified in column (2) or column (3) of the said Schedule pay such sum as he may determine being a sum not exceeding the sum whereby the said approved expenditure exceeds the income of the Managers from sources other than grants after deduction from the said income of any sums approved as being required for purposes other than the maintenance of the school." ;

(2) the Schedule to these regulations shall be substituted for the Schedule to the principal regulations as amended by the Amendment Regulations of 1968.

*William Ross,*
**One of Her Majesty's Principal
Secretaries of State.**

St. Andrew's House,
Edinburgh, 1.

26th March 1969.

Regulation 2

## SCHEDULE

| Column (1)<br>Name of School | Column (2)<br>Grant<br>(£) | Column (3)<br>Grant<br>(£) |
|---|---|---|
| Albyn School for Girls | 44,675 | 42,120 |
| Convent of the Sacred Heart Secondary School | 23,215 | 21,885 |
| Robert Gordon's College | 101,115 | 95,335 |
| St. Margaret's School | 28,430 | 26,805 |
| High School of Dundee | 95,670 | 90,200 |
| Merchant Company Schools:<br>    Daniel Stewart's College<br>    Mary Erskine School for Girls<br>    George Watson's College<br>    George Watson's Ladies' College | 363,510 | 342,735 |
| George Heriot's School | 101,010 | 95,240 |
| John Watson's School | 29,635 | 27,940 |
| Melville College | 37,770 | 35,615 |
| St. Mary's Cathedral Choir School | 4,685 | 4,415 |
| Craigholme School | 45,605 | 42,995 |
| Hutchesons' Grammar School for Boys<br>Hutchesons' Grammar School for Girls | 145,950 | 137,610 |
| Kelvinside Academy | 42,425 | 40,000 |
| Laurel Bank School | 54,640 | 51,515 |
| St. Aloysius' College | 63,860 | 60,210 |
| Westbourne School | 43,695 | 41,195 |
| Troon, Marr College | 80,805 | 76,185 |
| Dollar Academy | 83,480 | 78,710 |
| Benedictine Convent School | 15,405 | 14,520 |
| St. Joseph's College | 29,775 | 28,070 |
| Morrison's Academy for Boys<br>Morrison's Academy for Girls | 83,240 | 78,480 |
| Girls' School Company Limited:<br>    The Park School, Glasgow<br>    St. Bride's School, Helensburgh<br>    St. Columba's School, Kilmacolm | 126,435 | 119,210 |

# EXPLANATORY NOTE

*(This Note is not part of the Regulations.)*

These regulations amend the provisions of the Grant-Aided Secondary Schools (Scotland) Grant Regulations 1959, empowering the Secretary of State to pay to the Managers of secondary schools not managed by education authorities grants in aid of their expenditure on the maintenance of the schools. The regulations provide that the amount of grant specified in the schedule to the 1968 amendment regulations against each school, or group of schools, may be paid to the school Managers only in respect of the financial year of that school, or group of schools, beginning after 1st April 1968 ; they specify a reduced amount of grant which may be paid to the said Managers in respect of the financial year of the school, or group of schools, beginning after 1st April 1969 and subsequent years.

## STATUTORY INSTRUMENTS

### 1969 No. 507 (C.13)

### TRANSPORT

## The Transport Act 1968 (Commencement No. 2) Order 1969

*Made -   -   -   -   27th March* 1969

The Minister of Transport and the Secretary of State acting jointly, and the Minister of Transport acting separately, as shown in the Schedule to this Order, hereby make this Order in exercise of their powers under section 166 of the Transport Act 1968**(a)** and of all other enabling powers:—

**1.** This Order may be cited as the Transport Act 1968 (Commencement No. 2) Order 1969.

**2.** The provisions of the Transport Act 1968 (hereinafter referred to as "the Act") specified in the Schedule to this Order shall come into force on the 21st April 1969.

Sealed with the Official Seal of the Minister of Transport the 27th March 1969.

(L.S.)

*Richard Marsh,*
Minister of Transport.

Given under the seal of the Secretary of State for Scotland on 27th March 1969.

(L.S.)

*William Ross,*
One of Her Majesty's Principal
Secretaries of State.

Dated the 27th March 1969.

*George Thomas,*
One of Her Majesty's Principal
Secretaries of State.

### SCHEDULE

PROVISIONS COMING INTO FORCE ON THE 21ST APRIL 1969

A.  *Provisions brought into force by the Minister of Transport and the Secretary of State acting jointly*

*In Part IX of the Act*
Sections 126 to 129.
Section 130 in so far as it was not brought into force by the Transport Act 1968 (Commencement No. 1) Order 1968**(b)**.

*In the Schedules to the Act*
Schedule 14 in so far as it was not brought into force by the Transport Act 1968 (Commencement No. 1) Order 1968.

---

(a) 1968 c. 73.          (b) S.I. 1968/1822 (1968 III, p. 4830).

B. *Provisions brought into force by the Minister of Transport*

*In Part X of the Act*
Section 165 so far as it relates to those provisions of Schedule 18 to the Act specified below.

*In the Schedules to the Act*
In Schedule 18—

(a) The whole of Part II of that Schedule (REPEALS IN ROAD TRAFFIC REGULATION ACT act 1967 (1967 c. 76)) except the repeal of the words "left or parked" in section 80(1)(a) of that Act.

(b) In Part III of that Schedule—the following MISCELLANEOUS REPEALS

| Chapter | Short Title | Extent of Repeal |
|---------|-------------|------------------|
| 1967 c.xx. | The Greater London Council (General Powers) Act 1967. | Section 26. |

## EXPLANATORY NOTE

*(This Note is not part of the Order.)*

This Order brings into operation on the 21st April 1969 those provisions of Part IX (Regulation of Road Traffic) of the Transport Act 1968 (except section 131) which were not brought into operation by the Transport Act 1968 (Commencement No. 1) Order 1968. It also brings into operation on the same date all the provisions of Schedule 14 to the Act which were not brought into operation by the above-mentioned Commencement No. 1 Order, all the provisions of Part II of Schedule 18 to the Act (except for one repeal which is associated with section 131) and the repeal by Part III of Schedule 18 to the Act of section 26 of the Greater London Council (General Powers) Act 1967 (a repeal which is consequential on the bringing into operation of the above-mentioned provisions of Part IX of the Transport Act 1968).

## STATUTORY INSTRUMENTS

## 1969 No. 510

## CIVIL AVIATION

## The Civil Aviation (Navigation Services Charges) (Third Amendment) Regulations 1969

| | |
|---|---|
| *Made* - - - | *1st April 1969* |
| *Laid before Parliament* | *9th April 1969* |
| *Coming into Operation* | *1st May 1969* |

The Board of Trade in exercise of their powers under section 4 of the Civil Aviation (Eurocontrol) Act 1962(a) as having effect by virtue of the Transfer of Functions (Civil Aviation) Order 1966(b) and of all other powers enabling them in that behalf, and with the consent of the Treasury, hereby make the following Regulations:—

**1.** These Regulations may be cited as the Civil Aviation (Navigation Services Charges) (Third Amendment) Regulations 1969, and shall come into operation on 1st May 1969.

**2.** The Interpretation Act 1889(c) applies for the purpose of the interpretation of these Regulations as it applies for the purpose of the interpretation of an Act of Parliament.

**3.** The Civil Aviation (Navigation Services Charges) Regulations 1964 (d), as amended(e), shall be further amended as follows:—
    In Regulation 2, in paragraph (1) for the definition of "the standard charge" there shall be substituted the following definition:—
    " "the standard charge" means—

(*a*) in the case of an aircraft other than a helicopter, for each complete 1,000 lb. of the maximum total weight authorised of the aircraft in respect of which the charge is made and for each fraction of 1,000 lb. not being less than 500 lb., a charge

  (i) for services provided in connection with the use of London (Heathrow), London (Gatwick), Stansted or Prestwick aerodromes, of three shillings;

  (ii) for services provided in connection with the use of any of the other aerodromes to which these Regulations apply, of four shillings and sixpence;

(*b*) in the case of a helicopter, a charge equal to one half of the amount which, in the circumstances, would be the standard charge in the case of an aircraft other than a helicopter."

*W. T. Rodgers,*
Minister of State,
Board of Trade.

31st March 1969.

(a) 1962 c. 8.  (b) S.I. 1966/741 (1966 II, p. 1732).
(c) 1889 c. 63.  (d) S.I. 1964/1071 (1964 II, p. 2367).
(e) S.I. 1966/465, 1968/423 (1966 I, p. 982; 1968 I, p. 1109).

We consent to the making of these Regulations.

*Joseph Harper,*
*J. McCann,*
Lords Commissioners of
Her Majesty's Treasury.

1st April 1969.

## EXPLANATORY NOTE

(*This Note is not part of the Regulations.*)

These Regulations amend the Civil Aviation (Navigation Services Charges) Regulations 1964 as amended. They increase the standard charge at the aerodromes in respect of which the Regulations apply, other than Heathrow, Gatwick, Stansted and Prestwick, by 50 per cent.

## STATUTORY INSTRUMENTS

### 1969 No. 511

### AGRICULTURE

#### AGRICULTURAL GRANTS, GOODS AND SERVICES

## The Bacon Curing Industry Stabilisation Scheme 1969

*Laid before Parliament in draft*

|                          |     |     |     |                    |
|--------------------------|-----|-----|-----|--------------------|
| Made                     | -   | -   | -   | 31st March 1969    |
| Coming into Operation    |     |     |     | 1st April 1969     |

The Minister of Agriculture, Fisheries and Food and the Secretary of State acting jointly in exercise of the powers conferred on them by sections 38, 39 and 51 of the Agriculture (Miscellaneous Provisions) Act 1968(a) and of all other powers enabling them in that behalf, it appearing to them appropriate to make a scheme under the said section 38 for the purpose of avoiding undue fluctuations in income arising from carrying on the business of curing bacon in the United Kingdom, hereby, with the approval of the Treasury, make the following scheme a draft whereof has been laid before Parliament and approved by each House of Parliament :—

*Extent, citation, commencement and cessation*

**1.** This scheme, which applies throughout the United Kingdom, may be cited as the Bacon Curing Industry Stabilisation Scheme 1969 ; shall come into operation on the day after it is made and shall, unless previously revoked, cease to have effect on the expiration of the period of eighteen months beginning with the date on which it is made.

*Interpretation*

**2.**—(1) In this Scheme, unless the context otherwise requires—

"the Act" means the Agriculture (Miscellaneous Provisions) Act 1968 ;

"bacon" means the pigmeat product commonly known as bacon or as ham, which comprises any part of the carcase of a pig, consisting principally of meat (other than the feet and the hocks, when separated from the leg, and other than the head, including the chaps and the chawls), if such part of the carcase has been cured by salting or by pickling or by any similar process so as to alter the character of the meat, but does not include pickled pork ;

"bacon curer" means a producer of bacon to which this scheme applies ; and "registered bacon curer" means a bacon curer whose name is for the time being entered in the register kept by the Minister in accordance with paragraph 4 of this scheme ;

"fatstock guarantee payment" means any payment payable under the provisions of the Fatstock (Guarantee Payments) Order 1964(b) as amended (c) or any order further amending or replacing it ;

"the Minister" means the Minister of Agriculture, Fisheries and Food ;

---

(a) 1968 c. 34.    (b) S.I. 1964/463 (1964 I, p. 746).
(c) S.I. 1968/398 (1968 I, p. 1078).

"the Ministers" means the Minister of Agriculture, Fisheries and Food and the Secretary of State acting jointly.

(2) The Interpretation Act 1889(a) shall apply to the interpretation of this scheme as it applies to the interpretation of an Act of Parliament.

### Application

**3.** The provisions of this scheme apply only as respects bacon produced during the period beginning with the day on which this scheme comes into operation and ending with the 30th September 1969.

### Register of bacon curers

**4.**—(1) The Minister shall keep a register of bacon curers and shall enter therein the names and addresses of persons who carry on business as bacon curers and who apply to the Minister in writing to be registered.

(2) If the Minister is satisfied that any person entered in the register has ceased to be a bacon curer he may remove the name of such person from the register.

### Registration of bacon curers

**5.**—(1) Every person who becomes a bacon curer after the commencement of this scheme shall apply in writing to the Minister to be registered.

(2) Where two or more persons jointly carry on business as bacon curers they shall, for the purpose of registration, be treated as constituting a single person.

### Returns and information

**6.** The Minister may by notice in writing served on any bacon curer require him for the purposes of this scheme—

(a) to keep or cause to be kept, such records as are specified in the notice ;

(b) to furnish such returns and other information relating to his bacon curing activities as may be so specified.

### Production of records

**7.**—(1) Every bacon curer shall produce for inspection on demand by an authorised officer of the Minister or, in Northern Ireland, of the Ministry of Agriculture in Northern Ireland any records of his bacon curing activities kept by him and within his possession or control.

(2) In the application of this paragraph to Scotland, the "Minister" means the Secretary of State.

### Stabilising payments

**8.** The Minister may, if he thinks fit, make stabilising payments to registered bacon curers of sums in respect of bacon produced by them if the Ministers, having regard to the prices of pigmeat, of bacon and of offal, any fatstock guarantee payment which is payable and any other considerations which appear to them to be relevant, consider that the return from the sale of such bacon is not sufficient to cover the cost of bacon production.

### Levy payments

**9.** The Minister may require registered bacon curers to make levy payments to him in respect of bacon produced by them if the Ministers, having regard

(a) 1889 c. 63.

to the prices of pigmeat, of bacon and of offal, any fatstock guarantee payment which is payable and any other considerations which appear to them to be relevant, consider that the return from the sale of such bacon is more than sufficient to cover the cost of bacon production.

*Determination of rates*

**10.** The Ministers shall determine the rates of payments or levies as the case may be, week by week, having taken into account the price of pigmeat, the price of bacon, the price of offal and the fatstock guarantee payments and any other considerations which appear to them to be relevant.

*Estimation of levy*

**11.** The Ministers may estimate the amount of any levy payments payable by a bacon curer who, in the opinion of the Ministers, has failed to furnish any information necessary to enable that amount to be properly determined and to treat the estimated amount as the amount which is payable under the provisions of this scheme.

*Recovery of levy*

**12.** Any levy payment under paragraph 9 hereof which is required to be paid by any bacon curer shall be paid by him to the Minister and in the event of any default in any such payment it shall be recoverable by the Minister as a debt.

*Service of Notices*

**13.**—(1) Any notice authorised by this scheme to be served on any person shall be sufficiently served if it is delivered to him personally or left at his last known place of abode or business or sent to him by post in a letter addressed to him at the aforesaid place of abode or business.

(2) Any notice authorised by this scheme to be served on an incorporated company or body shall be sufficiently served if given to or served on the secretary or clerk of the company or body. For the purposes of this scheme and of section 26 of the Interpretation Act 1889, the proper address of such secretary or clerk shall be that of the registered or principal office of the company or body.

In Witness whereof the Official Seal of the Minister of Agriculture, Fisheries and Food is hereunto affixed on 27th March 1969.

(L.S.)                 *Cledwyn Hughes,*
           Minister of Agriculture, Fisheries and Food.

Given under the Seal of the Secretary of State for Scotland on 27th March 1969.

(L.S.)                 *William Ross,*
           Secretary of State for Scotland.

We approve.
31st March 1969.

                 *B. K. O'Malley,*
                 *Walter Harrison,*
      Two of the Lords Commissioners of
            Her Majesty's Treasury.

# EXPLANATORY NOTE

*(This Note is not part of the Scheme.)*

This scheme, which applies throughout the United Kingdom, authorises the Minister of Agriculture, Fisheries and Food to make stabilising payments to registered bacon curers in respect of bacon produced by them during the period from the commencement of this scheme until the 30th September 1969 if he and the Secretary of State consider that the return from the sale of bacon is not sufficient to cover the costs of producing bacon.

Similarly, the Minister of Agriculture, Fisheries and Food may require registered bacon curers to make levy payments in respect of bacon produced by them during the same period if he and the Secretary of State consider that the costs of producing bacon are more than covered by the return from the sale of bacon.

The Scheme also provides for the registration of bacon curers, the keeping of appropriate records and for the making of returns. It also authorises the Ministers to determine the rates of payment or of levies each week according to relevant criteria.

## STATUTORY INSTRUMENTS

### 1969 No. 512

## LONDON GOVERNMENT

### The Greater London Council (Sewerage Area) Order 1969

| | |
|---|---|
| *Made* - - - - | *31st March* 1969 |
| *Coming into Operation* | *1st April* 1969 |

The Minister of Housing and Local Government, in exercise of his powers under section 39(1)(b) and (2) of the London Government Act 1963(a) and of all other powers enabling him in that behalf, hereby makes the following order:

**1.**—(1) This order may be cited as the Greater London Council (Sewerage Area) Order 1969, and shall come into operation on 1st April 1969.

(2) The Greater London Council (Sewerage Area) Order 1965(b) and this order may be cited together as the Greater London Council (Sewerage Area) Orders 1965 and 1969.

**2.** The Interpretation Act 1889(c) applies to the interpretation of this order as it applies to the interpretation of an Act of Parliament.

**3.**—(1) On and from 1st April 1969, the sewerage area of the Greater London Council comprises the areas within the lines shown coloured red on the relevant boundary maps, other than the areas within the lines shown coloured green thereon.

(2) In this article—

"the relevant boundary maps" mean such of the boundary maps (as defined in the Greater London Council (Sewerage Area) Order 1965) as are marked with the numbers 1 to 13, 18, 19, 25 to 36, and 44 to 52, together with the boundary maps prepared in duplicate, sealed with the official seal of the said Minister and marked "Boundary Map of the Greater London Council (Sewerage Area) Order 1969", which maps are respectively marked with the numbers 14A, 17A, 20A, 21A, 22A, 23A, 24A, 37A, 41A, 43A and 53 to 63.

"the relevant index map" means the index map to the revelant boundary maps, prepared and sealed as aforesaid and marked "Index map of the Greater London Council (Sewerage Area) Order 1969".

(3) One set of the relevant boundary maps and the relevant index map is deposited and available for inspection at the offices of the Greater London Council and the other at the offices of the said Minister.

Given under the official seal of the Minister of Housing and Local Government on 31st March 1969.

(L.S.)

*J. E. Beddoe,*
Under Secretary,
Ministry of Housing and Local Government.

---

(a) 1963 c. 33.        (b) S.I. 1965/439 (1965 I, p. 1191).        (c) 1889 c.63.

# EXPLANATORY NOTE

*(This Note is not part of the Order.)*

This Order redefines the sewerage area of the Greater London Council for the purposes of the London Government Act 1963 from and including 1st April 1969. Section 39(3) of the Act of 1963 requires the Greater London Council to keep a map or other document showing the extent for the time being of the sewerage area, and that map or other document is to be open to inspection by members of the public.

# STATUTORY INSTRUMENTS

## 1969 No. 513

## TRUSTEES

## The Public Trustee (Fees) Order 1969

| | |
|---|---|
| Made - - - - | 1st *April* 1969 |
| *Coming into Operation* | 21st *April* 1969 |

The Treasury, in pursuance of the provisions of section 9 of the Public Trustee Act 1906(**a**), as amended by section 1 of the Public Trustee (Fees) Act 1957(**b**) and modified by section 2(1) of the Administration of Justice Act 1965(**c**), and with the sanction of the Lord Chancellor, hereby makes the following Order: —

### PRELIMINARY

*Citation, Commencement and Revocation*

**1.**—(1) This Order may be cited as the Public Trustee (Fees) Order 1969 and shall come into operation on 21st April 1969.

(2) The Public Trustee (Fees) Order 1957(**d**), as amended(**e**), is hereby revoked.

*Interpretation*

**2.**—(1) The Interpretation Act 1889(**f**), shall apply to the interpretation of this Order as it applies to the interpretation of an Act of Parliament.

(2) In this Order, unless the context otherwise requires: —

" The Act " means the Public Trustee Act 1906 ;

" The Act of 1957 " means the Public Trustee (Fees) Act 1957 ;

" Acceptance Fee valuation date " of any trust property means the date on which it is valued in accordance with paragraph 12 of this Order ;

" Common investment scheme " means a scheme made under section 1 of the Administration of Justice Act 1965 ;

" Fund " means a fund established under a scheme ; and " accounting date " means, in relation to a fund, a date appointed as such by a scheme ;

" Financial year " means the year ending 31st March ;

" Gross capital value " means the value of the trust property (excluding any annuity or other terminable payment purchased by any person in the name of, transferred to, or covenanted to be paid to, the Public Trustee for the benefit of some other person) and without deduction for debts, incumbrances, funeral expenses or estate duty ;

" Statutory owner " and " tenant for life " have the same meaning as in the Settled Land Act 1925(**g**) ;

---

(a) 1906 c. 55.　　(b) 1957 c. 12.　　(c) 1965 c. 2.　　(d) S.I. 1957/485 (1957 II, p. 2578).
(e) S.I. 1959/961, 1960/630, 1962/562, 1963/523, 1965/1743, 1967/284 (1959 II, p. 2704; 1960 III, p. 3310; 1962 I, p. 536; 1963 I, p. 584; 1965 III, p. 4932; 1967 I, p. 1009).
　　　　(f) 1889 c. 63.　　　　　　　　(g) 1925 c. 18.

" Trust " includes an executorship or administratorship, and also includes the administration of an estate in pursuance of section 3 of the Act, and any reference to the acceptance of a trust or to trust property shall be construed accordingly ;

" Will " includes any testamentary disposition.

## PART I

### GENERAL

*Classification of Fees*

**3.** The following Fees shall be charged in respect of the duties of the Public Trustee other than his duties under Common investment schemes—

(*a*) an Acceptance Fee ;

(*b*) an Administration Fee ;

(*c*) a Withdrawal Fee ;

(*d*) Fees for special services.

*Incidence*

**4.** Such Fees shall be paid out of capital, except the following which shall be paid out of income—

(*a*) fees which the Public Trustee directs to be paid out of income by virtue of section 1(3) of the Act of 1957 ;

(*b*) the Administration Fee in cases to which paragraph 16 (Annuities) applies ;

(*c*) the Insurance Fee to which paragraph 19 applies ;

(*d*) the Registration and Enquiry Fees to which paragraph 21 applies, where they relate to a person entitled to income ;

(*e*) the fee in respect of income tax and surtax work payable in accordance with paragraph 22 ; and

(*f*) the Income Collection Fee to which paragraph 25 applies.

*Calculation*

**5.** In ascertaining the amount payable in respect of any fee the Public Trustee—

(*a*) shall take the value of any trust property to be the price which he estimates that that property would fetch in the open market ; and

(*b*) may treat the value of any trust property as being that multiple of £10 which is nearest to his estimate of the exact value.

*Time of Payment*

**6.** The Public Trustee may, if it appears just and reasonable in any case, agree to the postponement of any payment due in respect of any fee.

*Commutation*

**7.** Liability to pay all or any sums which may become due in respect of any fee or any part of those sums may be commuted by the Public Trustee in consideration of a payment which seems to him to represent the capital value of that liability after taking into account—

(*a*) interest accruing thereon at the rate of 4 per cent. annually ; and

(*b*) any circumstances likely to affect that liability but for the commutation.

*Power to remit fees and settle disputes*

**8.**—(1) The Public Trustee may remit so much as appears equitable of a fee payable in relation to any trust where the whole or any part of the trust property is subject to another trust in which he is acting.

(2) With the approval of the Treasury, the Public Trustee may—

(*a*) compromise any dispute about his right to a fee or about the amount due ; and

(*b*) remit so much as appears equitable of a fee payable in relation to any trust where—

(i) his duties have been or are likely to be exceptionally simple ; or

(ii) the trust is otherwise of an exceptional character.

## PART II
### ACCEPTANCE FEE

*When Payable*

**9.** An Acceptance Fee shall be payable, in accordance with the provisions of this Part of this Order, upon acceptance by the Public Trustee of any trust other than one consisting entirely of an annuity or other terminable payment purchased by any person in the name of, transferred to or covenanted to be paid to the Public Trustee for the benefit of some other person.

*Property subsequently coming into Trust*

**10.** If additional property becomes subject to a trust which is administered by the Public Trustee and is not an accumulation of the income of the property already subject to the trust, an Acceptance Fee shall be payable in respect of the gross capital value of the additional property on its Acceptance Fee valuation date of such amount as would have been payable in respect of that value if—

(*a*) that value had formed part of the value of the property comprised in the trust at the date of acceptance of the trust ; and

(*b*) this Order had been in force at that date.

*Postponement of payment*

**11.**—(1) When an Acceptance Fee becomes payable in accordance with either of the preceding paragraphs in respect of any trust property, part or all of which is not in possession or is not readily realisable, the Public Trustee may charge an additional fee of £1.

(2) Where the Public Trustee charges an additional fee in accordance with this paragraph—

(*a*) he shall exclude the value of the property which is not in possession or is not readily realisable from the value of the trust property for the purpose of ascertaining the amount of the Acceptance Fee then payable ; and

(*b*) shall, when the property so excluded falls into possession or is realised, as the case may be, charge an Acceptance Fee of such amount as would have been payable in respect thereof if—

(i) the gross capital value of the excluded property at the date when it falls into possession or is realised had been treated as part of the value of the trust property at the date of acceptance of the trust ; and

(ii) this Order had been then in force.

*Amount of Fee*

**12.** The Acceptance Fee shall be calculated, in accordance with the provisions of this paragraph, as a percentage of the gross capital value of the trust property on the date of acceptance or on any other date, being no more than 6 months before or after that date, as seems to the Public Trustee to be convenient—

(*a*) where the Public Trustee is acting : —

    (i) as executor or administrator,

    (ii) as executor or administrator and as trustee,

    (iii) as original trustee of a will,

    (iv) as substituted or additional trustee,

    (v) as administrator of a small estate under section 3 of the Act,

    (vi) as trustee of land held in undivided shares and vested in him upon trust for sale pursuant to Part IV of the First Schedule to the Law of Property Act 1925(**a**),

    (vii) as trustee of an open space of land held in undivided shares and vested in him pursuant to Part V of the First Schedule to the Law of Property Act 1925 ; or

    (viii) as trustee of a trust created by an estate owner for the purpose of overreaching an equitable interest or power, appointed pursuant to section 2 (2) of the Law of Property Act 1925, or to section 21 of the Settled Land Act 1925 : —

| | |
|---|---|
| In respect of the first £25,000 ... ... | 1 per cent. |
| In respect of any excess over £25,000 up to £50,000 ... ... ... ... | 4/5 per cent. |
| In respect of any excess over £50,000 up to £75,000 ... ... ... ... | 2/5 per cent. |
| In respect of any excess over £75,000 up to £100,000 ... ... ... ... | 1/5 per cent. |
| In respect of any excess over £100,000 ... | 1/10 per cent. |
| Minimum fee ... ... ... ... | £15 |

Provided that—

    (*aa*) where the sale of land vested in the Public Trustee pursuant to Part IV of the First Schedule to the Law of Property Act 1925, is completed within one year of the date of acceptance of the trust and the proceeds are distributable absolutely, he shall remit so much of the fee as he thinks equitable, so however, that not less than £1 remains payable ;

    (*bb*) where the Public Trustee is acting as personal representative of a deceased tenant for life or of a statutory owner of a settlement under the Settled Land Act 1925, and is not acting otherwise in the trust, a fee of £15 only shall be payable.

(*b*) where the Public Trustee is acting—

    (i) as original trustee of a trust created *inter vivos* (other than a declaration of trust in favour of one beneficiary only) ; or

(a) 1925 c. 20.

    (ii) as trustee of a superannuation scheme: —

| | |
|---|---|
| In respect of the first £25,000 ... ... | ½ per cent. |
| In respect of any excess over £25,000 up to £50,000 ... ... ... ... | 2/5 per cent. |
| In respect of any excess over £50,000 up to £75,000 ... ... ... ... | 1/5 per cent. |
| In respect of any excess over £75,000 up to £100,000 ... ... ... ... | 1/10 per cent. |
| In respect of any excess over £100,000 ... | 1/20 per cent. |
| Minimum fee ... ... ... ... | £15 |

(c) where the Public Trustee is acting—

    (i) under a declaration of trust in favour of one beneficiary only,

    (ii) as original, substituted or additional trustee of property to which an infant is absolutely entitled under a will or on an intestacy: —

| | |
|---|---|
| In respect of the first £25,000 ... ... | ¼ per cent. |
| In respect of any excess over £25,000 ... | 1/10 per cent. |
| Minimum fee ... ... ... ... | £5 |

    Provided that no Acceptance Fee shall be charged in respect of property to which this sub-paragraph applies, if that property is already subject to a trust in which the Public Trustee is acting.

(d) where the Public Trustee is acting exclusively as custodian trustee, the fee shall be one half of the fee which would have been payable under this paragraph if he had then been appointed managing trustee of the same trust, save that not less than the appropriate minimum fee shall be charged in any case.

## PART III

### ADMINISTRATION FEE

*When payable*

**13.** An Administration Fee shall be payable, in accordance with the provisions of this part of this Order, at the commencement of each financial year, and—

    (a) shall be payable in full notwithstanding that the Public Trustee ceases to act in any trust or part of a trust in the course of the financial year;

    (b) shall not be payable in respect of the period between the date of the acceptance of any trust or part of a trust, as the case may be, and the commencement of the next financial year.

*Amount of Fee*

**14.**—(1) The Administration Fee shall be calculated as a percentage of that multiple of £100 which is nearest to the net capital value of a trust as certified by the Public Trustee after it has been estimated in accordance with the provisions of this paragraph.

    (2) The net capital value of a trust shall be $A + B - C$ where—

    $A$ is the aggregate value on the appropriate valuation date of all the property subject to the trust other than interests not in possession and annuities or other terminable payments to which paragraph 16 of this part of this Order applies;

*B* is the value (ascertained in accordance with the terms of the next following sub-paragraph) of any additional property which has become or becomes subject to the trust during the relevant period ;

*C* is such sum as the Public Trustee considers to be a reasonable deduction in respect of any property of the trust distributed or disbursed by him during the relevant period ;

the " appropriate valuation date " means whichever of the following dates next precedes the date on which the fee is payable—

(i) initially, 1st October 1968 in the case of any trust in which he was then acting, or in the case of any other trust, its Acceptance Fee valuation date ; and

(ii) subsequently, 1st October 1971 and each succeeding third anniversary thereof ; and

the " relevant period " means the period between the appropriate valuation date and the date on which the fee is payable.

(3) Where additional property becomes subject to a trust or where an interest already subject to a trust falls into possession—

(i) the initial valuation thereof shall be made by reference to the values prevailing on its Acceptance Fee valuation date ; and

(ii) the subsequent valuation thereof shall be made by reference to values prevailing on the next appropriate valuation date in accordance with the foregoing sub-paragraph.

(4) In valuing any property in accordance with this paragraph, no deduction shall be made for any debt specifically charged upon it.

**15.** For each financial year the Administration Fee shall be charged at the rate of ¼ per cent. of the net capital value of each trust:

Provided that, where the Public Trustee is acting exclusively—

(*a*) as custodian trustee, the rate shall be 3/40 per cent. ;

(*b*) as trustee of a Settlement under the Settled Land Act 1925, the rate shall be 3/40 per cent. in respect of any part of the trust property which at the appropriate valuation date is represented by land, and ⅛ per cent. in respect of any part of the trust property which at the appropriate valuation date is represented by capital moneys arising under the said Act ;

(*c*) as trustee of a Superannuation Scheme, the rate shall be ⅛ per cent. ;

(*d*) as trustee under a Declaration of Trust for one beneficiary only, the rate shall be ⅛ per cent.

*Annuities*

**16.** Where trust property includes an annuity or other terminable payment, purchased by any person in the name of, transferred to or covenanted to be paid to the Public Trustee for the benefit of some other person, the Administration Fee in respect of that annuity or payment shall be charged at the rate of 2 per cent. of the gross income without deduction of income tax or other outgoings, and no other fee shall be payable in respect thereof under this part of this Order.

## PART IV

### WITHDRAWAL FEE

*When payable*

**17.** A Withdrawal Fee shall be payable upon the Public Trustee ceasing to act in any trust, whether upon retirement or otherwise, or upon the withdrawal or distribution therefrom of any part of the trust property, except where—

(a) trust property held under a declaration of trust in favour of one beneficiary only is withdrawn for the purpose of transfer to a new trust accepted by the Public Trustee ;

(b) trust property is withdrawn for the purpose of paying any fees prescribed by this Order.

*Amount of Fee*

**18.**—(1) The Withdrawal Fee shall be calculated, in accordance with the provisions of this paragraph, as a percentage of the value of the property withdrawn.

(2) Subject to sub-paragraph (3) hereof, the Withdrawal Fee shall be charged : —

(a) where the property is withdrawn before the expiration of 3 complete financial years following that in which the trust was accepted by the Public Trustee, at the rate of 1 per cent. ;

(b) where the property is withdrawn after the expiration of 3 complete financial years following that in which the trust was accepted by the Public Trustee, at the rate of $1\frac{1}{2}$ per cent.

(3) Where the Public Trustee is acting in any case to which paragraph 12 (c) applies the Withdrawal Fee shall be charged at the rate of $\frac{1}{2}$ per cent.

## PART V

### FEES FOR SPECIAL SERVICES

*Insurance Fee*

**19.** Upon effecting or renewing any policy of insurance a fee shall be payable equal to the amount of any commission allowed thereon.

*Stockbroker's Commission Fee*

**20.** Upon any dealing in securities a fee shall be payable equal to the amount of any commission refunded by a broker.

*Registration and Enquiry Fees*

**21.**—(1) Where the Public Trustee, in compliance with a request, gives information for the purpose of any dealing with a beneficial interest, a fee of £3 shall be payable by the person to whom he gives information in respect of each dealing.

(2) Where the Public Trustee receives notice of any dealing with a beneficial interest in any trust in which he is acting or of the exercise or release of any power relating to any such trust, and he registers the same, a fee of £2 shall be payable by the person who gives such notice.

(3) Where the Public Trustee produces for inspection by a person, other than one who is beneficially interested in a trust or is a co-trustee of a trust, any deeds or documents relating to that trust, a fee of £2 shall be payable.

*Fee for tax work*

**22.** The following fees shall be payable for work undertaken by the Public Trustee :—

(a) upon the recovery by the Public Trustee, whether by way of repayment or set-off, of any United Kingdom income tax or any foreign tax of a similar character, such fee as may previously have been agreed with the beneficiary or beneficiaries for whose benefit the recovery is made or, in the absence of such an agreement, a fee of £1 or such fee not exceeding 10 per cent. of the tax recovered as the Public Trustee may determine ;

(b) for supplying or preparing returns, statements or computations in respect of :—

   (i) income tax or surtax where the Public Trustee recovers no income tax or surtax ; or

   (ii) Capital Gains Tax work,

a fee of such an amount not exceeding £25 as the Public Trustee may determine in each particular case.

*Investment Fee*

**23.** Upon a sale or purchase of any stocks, funds, shares, securities or land or upon an advance on mortgage a fee shall be payable at the rate of $\frac{3}{8}$ per cent. of the amount realised or invested :

Provided that where the Public Trustee is acting under the direction of a tenant-for-life or statutory owner of settled land, or where the Public Trustee is custodian trustee only, the fee shall be charged at one-half of the rate prescribed in this paragraph.

*Audit Fee*

**24.** Upon the performance by the Public Trustee of all his duties under section 13 of the Public Trustee Act 1906 a fee of £25 shall be payable.

*Income Collection Fee*

**25.**—(1) Subject to the provisions of this paragraph, an Income Collection Fee shall be payable annually, at such time or times as the Public Trustee may direct, in respect of the gross annual income of any trust which is received by him on or after 21st April 1969.

(2) The fee so payable shall be charged at the following rates—

(a) in respect of the first £2,500 of such income ...　　... 1½ per cent.

(b) in respect of any such income over £2,500 up to £5,000 ... ... ... ... ... ... ... ¾ per cent.

(c) in respect of any such income over £5,000 ... ... nil.

(3) Where in any trust there are two or more distinct funds, each of them shall be treated, for the purpose of calculating the Income Collection Fee, as a separate trust :

Provided that, if the whole of the income of such funds is payable to the same person, the fee payable under this paragraph shall not exceed the amount that would be payable if that income were derived from a single fund.

(4) Where the Public Trustee is acting exclusively as—

(a) a custodian trustee,

(b) a trustee of a superannuation scheme, or

(c) a trustee acting under a declaration of trust for one beneficiary only,

the Income Collection Fee shall be payable at one-half of the rate prescribed by sub-paragraph (2) of this paragraph.

(5) No fee shall be payable under this paragraph in respect of an annuity or terminable payment to which paragraph 16 applies.

(6) The Public Trustee may remit so much as appears equitable of the amount payable under this paragraph where—

(a) his duties have been or are likely to be exceptionally simple ; or

(b) the circumstances are otherwise exceptional.

PART VI

FEES IN RESPECT OF COMMON INVESTMENT SCHEMES

*Management fee*

**26.**—(1) A management fee (calculated in accordance with sub-paragraph (3) of this paragraph) shall be payable in respect of each fund and shall be charged on the income of the fund to which it relates.

(2) The management fee shall be payable in respect of each half-year during which the fund is in existence and shall become due on the accounting date terminating such half-year :

Provided that, for the purpose of calculating the fee payable under this paragraph, the period beginning with the establishment of the fund and ending with the first accounting date shall, irrespective of its length, be treated as a half-year.

(3) The management fee shall vary in accordance with the capital value of the fund on the relevant accounting date and shall be calculated as follows : —

(i) where such value does not exceed £2,000,000, at a rate of $\frac{1}{8}$ per cent. thereof ;

(ii) where such value exceeds £2,000,000 but does not exceed £3,000,000, at a flat rate of £2,500 ;

(iii) where such value exceeds £3,000,000, at a rate equal to the aggregate of £2,500 and 1/12 per cent. of such excess.

*Stockbroker's commission fee*

**27.** Upon any dealing in securities comprised in a fund, a fee shall be payable equal to the amount of any commission refunded by a broker.

Dated 1st April 1969.

*Joseph Harper,*
*J. McCann,*
Two of the Lords Commissioners
of Her Majesty's Treasury.

Dated 1st April 1969.

*Gardiner,* C.

## EXPLANATORY NOTE

*(This Note is not part of the Order.)*

This Order consolidates the Public Trustee (Fees) Orders with amendments. The principal amendments are:—

(*a*) The Public Trustee is given power to adopt a valuation made for another purpose when valuing property subsequently coming into a trust administered by him in order to determine the Acceptance Fee payable in respect of such property (paragraph 10).

(*b*) The rates at which fees are payable are expressed in fractions instead of shillings and pence in advance of decimalisation (paragraphs 12, 15, 18 and 23).

(*c*) The Administration Fee is to be fixed in accordance with the formula prescribed in paragraph 14 and the Public Trustee is given power to adopt a valuation made for another purpose in determining it (paragraph 14).

(*d*) New fees are introduced for tax work. The fee where income tax or any similar foreign tax is recovered is to be fixed by prior agreement or, in default thereof, at £1 or such fee not exceeding 10 per cent. of the tax recovered as the Public Trustee may determine. The fee for preparing returns, statements or computations in respect of income tax or surtax where no tax is recovered or in respect of capital gains tax work is to be such sum not exceeding £25 as the Public Trustee may determine (paragraph 22).

## STATUTORY INSTRUMENTS

## 1969 No. 517

## EXCHANGE CONTROL

## The Exchange Control (Authorised Dealers and Depositaries) Order 1969

| | |
|---|---|
| *Made* - - - | *2nd April* 1969 |
| *Coming into Operation* | *9th April* 1969 |

The Treasury, in exercise of the powers conferred upon them by sections 36(5) and 42(1) of the Exchange Control Act 1947(a), hereby make the following Order:—

1.—(1) This Order may be cited as the Exchange Control (Authorised Dealers and Depositaries) Order 1969.

(2) The Interpretation Act 1889(b) shall apply for the interpretation of this Order as it applies for the interpretation of an Act of Parliament.

(3) This Order shall come into operation on 9th April 1969.

2. Offices in the United Kingdom or the Channel Islands of the persons specified in Schedules 1 and 2 to this Order are authorised to act for the purposes of the said Act as authorised dealers in relation to gold.

3. Offices in the United Kingdom or the Channel Islands of the persons specified in Schedule 2 to this Order are authorised to act for the purposes of the said Act as authorised dealers in relation to all foreign currencies.

4. The following are authorised to act as authorised depositaries for the purposes of Part III of the said Act:—

(a) the Bank of England, and the Quotations Department of the Stock Exchange, London;

(b) offices in the United Kingdom or the Channel Islands of the persons specified in Schedule 2 to this Order;

(c) the persons specified in Schedule 3 to this Order.

5. The Orders specified in Schedule 4 to this Order are hereby revoked.

6. This Order shall extend to the Channel Islands, and any reference in this Order to the Exchange Control Act 1947 includes a reference to that Act as extended by the Exchange Control (Channel Islands) Order 1947(c).

*Joseph Harper,*
*J. McCann,*
Two of the Lords Commissioners
of Her Majesty's Treasury.

2nd April, 1969.

---

(a) 1947 c. 14.  (b) 1889 c. 63.
(c) S. R. & O. 1947/2034 (Rev. VI, p. 1001: 1947 I, p. 660).

## SCHEDULE 1

### Authorised Dealers in Gold

The Bank of England.
Mocatta & Goldsmid Ltd.
Sharps, Pixley & Co. Ltd.


## SCHEDULE 2

### Authorised Dealers in Gold and in all Foreign Currencies and Authorised Depositaries

Afghan National Bank Ltd.
African Continental Bank Ltd.
Algemene Bank Nederland N.V.
American Express International Banking Corporation.
Anglo-Israel Bank Ltd.
Anglo-Portuguese Bank Ltd.
Ansbacher & Co. Ltd., Henry.
Arbuthnot Latham & Co., Ltd.
Australia and New Zealand Bank Ltd.
Baer International Ltd., Julius.
Banco de Bilbao.
Banco Español en Londres, S.A.
Bangkok Bank Ltd.
Bank Melli Iran.
Bank of Adelaide.
Bank of America National Trust & Savings Association.
Bank of Baroda, Ltd.
Bank of Ceylon.
Bank of China.
Bank of Cyprus (London) Ltd.
Bank of India, Ltd.
Bank of Ireland.
Bank of Kobe, Ltd., The.
Bank of London & South America Ltd.
Bank of Montreal.
Bank of New South Wales.
Bank of New York, The.
Bank of New Zealand.
Bank of Nova Scotia.
Bank of Scotland.
Bank of Tokyo Ltd., The.
Bankers Trust Company.
Banque Belge Ltd.
Banque Belgo-Congolaise S.A.
Banque de l'Indochine.
Banque de Paris et des Pays-Bas Ltd.
Banque Italo-Belge S.A.
Barclays Bank D.C.O.
Barclays Bank Ltd.
Barclays Bank (London and International) Ltd.
Baring Brothers & Co., Ltd.
Belfast Banking Company, Ltd.
Brandt's Sons & Co., Ltd., Wm.
British and Continental Banking Company Ltd.
British and French Bank Ltd.
British Bank of the Middle East, The.
British Linen Bank.
Brown, Shipley & Co. Ltd.
Burston & Texas Commerce Bank Ltd.
Canadian Imperial Bank of Commerce.

Central Bank of India, Ltd.
Chartered Bank, The.
Charterhouse Japhet & Thomasson Ltd.
Chase Manhattan Bank N.A., The.
Chemical Bank New York Trust Company.
City National Bank of Detroit.
Clydesdale Bank Ltd.
Commercial Bank of Australia, Ltd.
Commercial Bank of the Near East Ltd.
Commercial Banking Company of Sydney, Ltd.
Commonwealth Trading Bank of Australia.
Continental Illinois National Bank and Trust Company of Chicago.
Co-operative Wholesale Society Ltd.
County Bank Ltd.
Coutts & Co.
Crédit Industriel et Commercial.
Crédit Lyonnais.
Crocker-Citizens National Bank.
Dai-Ichi Bank, Ltd., The.
Daiwa Bank Ltd., The.
Detroit Bank & Trust Company, The.
Discount Bank (Overseas) Ltd.
District Bank Ltd.
Eastern Bank, Ltd., The.
English, Scottish and Australian Bank, Ltd.
First National Bank of Boston, The.
First National Bank of Chicago, The.
First National City Bank.
First Pennsylvania Banking and Trust Company, The.
First Wisconsin National Bank of Milwaukee.
French Bank of Southern Africa Ltd.
Fuji Bank Ltd., The.
Ghana Commercial Bank.
Gibbs & Sons, Ltd., Antony.
Girard Trust Bank.
Glyn, Mills & Co.
Guinness Mahon & Co. Ltd.
Habib Bank (Overseas) Ltd.
Hambros Bank Ltd.
Hambros (Guernsey) Ltd.
Hambros (Jersey) Ltd.
Hibernian Bank Ltd.
Hill, Samuel & Co. (Guernsey) Ltd.
Hill, Samuel & Co. (Jersey) Ltd.
Hill, Samuel & Co. Ltd.
Hoare & Co., C.
Hongkong & Shanghai Banking Corporation, The.
International Commercial Bank Ltd.
Ionian Bank Ltd.
Irving Trust Company.
Isle of Man Bank Ltd.
Israel-British Bank (London) Ltd.
Johnson Matthey (Bankers) Ltd.
Joseph & Sons, Ltd., Leopold.
Keyser Ullmann Ltd.
Kleinwort, Benson (Channel Islands) Ltd.
Kleinwort, Benson (Guernsey) Ltd.
Kleinwort, Benson Ltd.
Lazard Brothers & Co., Ltd.
Lloyds Bank Europe Ltd.
Lloyds Bank Ltd.
Manufacturers Hanover Trust Company.

Marine Midland Grace Trust Company of New York.
Martins Bank Ltd.
Mellon National Bank and Trust Company.
Mercantile Bank Ltd.
Midland and International Banks Ltd.
Midland Bank Ltd.
Mitsubishi Bank, Ltd., The.
Mitsui Bank, Ltd., The.
Montagu & Co., Ltd., Samuel.
Morgan Grenfell & Co. Ltd.
Morgan Guaranty Trust Company of New York.
Moscow Narodny Bank, Ltd.
Munster and Leinster Bank Ltd.
National and Grindlays Bank Ltd.
National Bank Ltd.
National Bank of Australasia, Ltd.
National Bank of Commerce of Seattle, The.
National Bank of Detroit.
National Bank of Greece.
National Bank of Ireland Ltd., The.
National Bank of New Zealand, Ltd., The.
National Bank of Nigeria Ltd.
National Bank of Pakistan.
National Commercial & Glyns Ltd.
National Provincial & Rothschild (International) Ltd.
National Provincial Bank Ltd.
Netherlands Bank of South Africa Ltd.
Nippon Kangyo Bank Ltd., The.
Northern Bank Ltd.
Ottoman Bank.
Overseas Union Bank Ltd.
Provincial Bank of Ireland Ltd.
Rafidain Bank.
Ralli Brothers (Bankers) Ltd.
Rea Brothers Ltd.
Reserve Bank of Australia.
Rodo International Ltd.
Rothschild & Sons, N.M.
Rothschild & Sons (C.I.) Ltd., N.M.
Royal Bank of Canada, The.
Royal Bank of Scotland Ltd., The.
Sanwa Bank Ltd., The.
Sassoon Banking Co., Ltd., E.D.
Schroder, Wagg & Co. Ltd., J. Henry.
Scottish Co-operative Wholesale Society Ltd.
Singer & Friedlander Ltd.
Société Centrale de Banque.
Société Générale pour favoriser le développement du Commerce et de l'Industrie
    en France.
Standard Bank C.I. Ltd.
Standard Bank Ltd., The.
Standard Bank of West Africa Ltd.
State Bank of India.
Sumitomo Bank, Ltd., The.
Swiss Bank Corporation.
Swiss-Israel Trade Bank.
Tokai Bank, Ltd., The.
Toronto-Dominion Bank, The.
Trade Development Bank.
Ulster Bank Ltd.
Union Bank of Switzerland.
United Bank Ltd.

United Bank of Kuwait Ltd., The.
United California Bank.
United Commercial Bank Ltd.
Warburg & Co., Ltd., S.G.
Western American Bank (Europe) Ltd.
Westminster Bank Ltd.
Westminster Foreign Bank Ltd.
Williams Deacon's Bank Ltd.
Yorkshire Bank Ltd.
Zivnostenska Banka National Corporation.

## SCHEDULE 3
### AUTHORISED DEPOSITARIES

1. Members in the United Kingdom or the Channel Islands of:—
The Stock Exchange, London.
The Scottish Stock Exchange.
The Midlands & Western Stock Exchange.
The Northern Stock Exchange.
The Belfast Stock Exchange.
The Provincial Brokers' Stock Exchange.
The Association of Stock and Share Dealers.
The London Discount Market Association.
The Association of Canadian Investment Dealers and Members of the Toronto and Montreal Stock Exchanges in Great Britain.
The Association of New York Stock Exchange Member Firms having Representation in the United Kingdom.
The Issuing Houses Association.
The Association of Investment Trust Companies.
The British Insurance Association.

2. Solicitors practising in the United Kingdom, advocates practising in the Isle of Man, and advocates and écrivains of the Royal Courts of Jersey and Guernsey practising in the Channel Islands.

3. The Public Trustee and the Accountant General of the Supreme Court.

4. Persons in the United Kingdom not included in paragraphs 1, 2 or 3 of this Schedule who are holders of a principal's licence or are exempted (whether by definition, class or name) for the purposes of the Prevention of Fraud (Investments) Act 1958(a) or the Prevention of Fraud (Investments) Act (Northern Ireland) 1940(b), and the offices in the Channel Islands of such persons.

## SCHEDULE 4
### ORDERS REVOKED

| | |
|---|---|
| The Exchange Control (Authorised Dealers and Depositaries) Order 1968. | S.I. 1968/1634 (1968 III, p. 4457). |
| The Exchange Control (Authorised Dealers and Depositaries) (Amendment) (No. 4) Order 1968. | S.I. 1968/2019 (1968 III, p. 5482). |
| The Exchange Control (Authorised Dealers and Depositaries) (Amendment) Order 1969. | S.I. 1969/129 (1969 I, p. 356). |
| The Exchange Control (Authorised Dealers and Depositaries) (Amendment) (No. 2) Order 1969. | S.I. 1969/278 (1969 I, p. 757). |

(a) 1958 c. 45.                    (b) 1940 c. 9. (N.I.).

# EXPLANATORY NOTE

(*This Note is not part of the Order.*)

This Order, which supersedes (with amendments) the 1968 Order, as amended, lists:—

(*a*) the banks and other persons authorised under the Exchange Control Act 1947 to deal in gold and foreign currency; and

(*b*) those who are entitled to act as authorised depositaries for the purpose of the deposit of securities as required by that Act.

# STATUTORY INSTRUMENTS

## 1969 No. 518

## HOUSING, ENGLAND AND WALES
## HOUSING, SCOTLAND

### The Housing Corporation Advances (Increase of Limit) Order 1969

*Laid before the House of Commons in draft*

| | | |
|---|---|---|
| *Made* - - - | | *2nd April* 1969 |
| *Coming into Operation* | | *16th April* 1969 |

The Minister of Housing and Local Government and the Secretary of State, acting jointly in exercise of their powers under section 9(2) of the Housing Act 1964(a), and of all other powers enabling them in that behalf, hereby make the following order in the terms of a draft approved by resolution of the Commons House of Parliament :—

**1.** This order may be cited as the Housing Corporation Advances (Increase of Limit) Order 1969 and shall come into operation on 16th April 1969.

**2.** The Interpretation Act 1889(b) shall apply for the interpretation of this order as it applies for the interpretation of an Act of Parliament.

**3.** Advances made to the Housing Corporation under section 9(1) of the Housing Act 1964 shall not together exceed £75,000,000.

Given under the official seal of the Minister of Housing and Local Government on 2nd April 1969.

(L.S.)

*Anthony Greenwood,*
Minister of Housing and Local Government.

---

(a) 1964 c. 56.        (b) 1889 c. 63.

Given under the Seal of the Secretary of State for Scotland on 2nd April 1969.

(L.S.)
*William Ross,*
**Secretary of State for Scotland.**

*George Thomas,*
**One of Her Majesty's Principal Secretaries of State.**

**Welsh Office.**

2nd April 1969.

---

## EXPLANATORY NOTE

*(This Note is not part of the Order.)*

Under section 9 of the Housing Act 1964 the three Ministers respectively may make advances to the Housing Corporation to enable the Corporation to exercise and perform their functions. The total amount which may be advanced to the Corporation is limited to £50,000,000 or such greater sum, not exceeding £100,000,000, as the three Ministers jointly may by order specify. This order specifies that the total amount which may be so advanced shall not exceed £75,000,000.

## STATUTORY INSTRUMENTS

## 1969 No. 519 (L.7)

## COMPANIES

### WINDING-UP

## The Companies (Board of Trade) Fees Order 1969

| | |
|---|---|
| *Made* - - - - | 1*st April* 1969 |
| *Coming into Operation* | 1*st May* 1969 |

The Lord Chancellor and the Treasury, in exercise of the powers conferred on them by section 365(3) of the Companies Act 1948(a) and sections 2 and 3 of the Public Offices Fees Act 1879(b), hereby make, sanction and consent to the following Order:—

**1.**—(1) This Order may be cited as the Companies (Board of Trade) Fees Order 1969 and shall come into operation on 1st May 1969.

(2) The Companies (Board of Trade) Fees Order 1929(c), (in this Order referred to as "the 1929 Order"), the Companies (Board of Trade) Fees Order 1930(d), the Companies (Board of Trade) Fees Order 1949(e), the Companies (Board of Trade) Fees Order 1952(f) and the Companies (Board of Trade) Fees Order 1963(g) are hereby revoked.

**2.** The fees and percentages to be charged for and in respect of proceedings in the winding-up of companies shall be those set out in Tables A and B in the Schedule to this Order.

**3.** Where the head office of the company being wound up is situated out of England, and the liquidation takes place partly in England and partly elsewhere, or where the court has sanctioned a reconstruction of the company or a scheme of arrangement of its affairs, or where for any other reason the Official Receiver satisfies the Board of Trade that the fees in the said Table B would be excessive, such reduction may be made in the said fees as may, on the application of the Board of Trade, be sanctioned by the Treasury.

**4.**—(1) The fees set out in Table A shall be taken by adhesive or impressed stamps.

(2) The fees and percentages set out in Table B shall be taken in cash.

---

(a) 1948 c. 38.                (b) 1879 c. 58.
(c) S.R. & O. 1929/831 (Rev. IV, p. 749:1929, p. 352).
(d) S.R. & O. 1930/1064 (Rev. IV, p. 749:1930, p. 287).
(e) S.I. 1949/850 (1949 I, p. 930).      (f) S.I. 1952/2117 (1952 I, p. 624).
(g) S.I. 1963/467 (1963 I, p. 529).

**5.**—(1) An impressed stamp denoting payment of a fee shall be an impressed judicature fee stamp and the party presenting the document for stamping shall inform the stamping officer, by means of an indication on the document or otherwise, that the fee relates to a proceeding for or in the winding-up of a company.

(2) An adhesive stamp denoting payment of a fee shall be an adhesive fee stamp on which the words "Companies Winding-up" have been printed.

**6.**—(1) In any case where, on the coming into operation of this Order, any audit has become due or has taken place, but where the statement of affairs has not yet been lodged, a fee equal to Fee No. II(b) (2) of Table B of the 1929 Order shall be charged on the lodgment of the statement of affairs.

(2) In any case where, on the coming into operation of this Order, any sum has already been charged in respect of Fee No. II(b) (2) of Table B of the 1929 Order, or where a fee is charged under the last foregoing sub-paragraph, the amount thereof shall be deducted from any sum payable in respect of Fee No. 2(2) (ii) of Table B of this Order.

Dated 31st March 1969.

*Gardiner,* C.

Dated 1st April 1969.

*Joseph Harper,*
*J. McCann,*
Two of the Lords Commissioners of
Her Majesty's Treasury.

## SCHEDULE

### TABLES OF FEES

### TABLE A.

| Description of Proceeding | Amount |
|---|---|

| | £ s. d. |
|---|---|
| 1. On an application to the Board of Trade for a special bank account ... | 3 0 0 |
| 2. On an order of the Board of Trade for a special bank account ... | 5 0 0 |
| 3. On an application by a liquidator to an Official Receiver acting as a committee of inspection ... ... ... ... ... ... ... | 2 0 0 |

4. On an application to the Board of Trade—

    (i) under section 15 of the Companies (Winding Up) Act 1890(a), section 224 of the Companies (Consolidation) Act 1908(b), section 285 of the Companies Act 1929(c) or section 343 of the Companies Act 1948(d) for payment of money out of the Companies Liquidation Account or

    (ii) for the re-issue of a lapsed cheque, money order or payable order in respect of moneys standing to the credit of that account—

| | Amount |
|---|---|
|     (a) where the amount applied for does not exceed £5 ... ... | 2 6 |
|     (b) where the amount applied for exceeds £5 ... ... ... | 5 0 |
| 5. On a bond ... ... ... ... ... ... ... ... ... | 1 0 0 |
| 6. On an affidavit other than a proof of debts ... ... ... ... | 5 0 |
| 7. On the insertion in the *London Gazette* of a notice relating to a company which is being wound up by the court ... ... ... ... | 10 0 |

### TABLE B

| Description of Proceeding | Amount |
|---|---|

1. On the audit of the Official Receiver's or liquidator's accounts by the Board of Trade, a fee according to the following scale on the amount brought to credit, including the produce of calls on contributories, but after deducting (1) the amount spent out of the money received in carrying on the business of the company and (2) amounts paid by the Official Receiver or liquidator to secured creditors (other than debenture holders)—

| | £ s. d. |
|---|---|
|     (i) on every £100 or fraction of £100 up to £5,000... ... ... | 3 0 0 |
|     (ii) on every further £100 or fraction of £100 up to £100,000 ... | 2 0 0 |
|     (iii) on every further £100 or fraction of £100 up to £500,000 ... | 1 0 0 |
|     (iv) on every further £100 or fraction of £100 up to £1,000,000 ... | 10 0 |
|     (v) on every further £100 on excess of £1,000,000 ... ... | 5 0 |

(a) 1890 c. 63.               (b) 1908 c. 69.
(c) 1929 c. 23.               (d) 1948 c. 38.

TABLE B—continued

| Description of Proceeding | Amount |
|---|---|

£ s. d.

2. Where the Official Receiver acts as provisional liquidator only—

(1) where no winding-up order is made upon the petition, or where a winding-up order is rescinded, or all further proceedings are stayed prior to the summoning of the statutory meetings of creditors and contributories:—

such amount as the court may consider reasonable to be paid by the petitioner or by the company as the court may direct, in respect of the services of the Official Receiver as provisional liquidator;

(2) where a winding-up order is made, but the Official Receiver is not continued as liquidator after the statutory meetings of creditors and contributories—

(i) for all official stationery, printing, postage and telephones (except trunk calls)—

    (a) for a number of members and creditors not exceeding 20    11   0   0

    (b) for a number exceeding 20 but not exceeding 30    ...   15   0   0

    (c) for every additional 10 members or creditors or part thereof   3   10   0

Provided that where the net assets of the company, including uncalled capital, are estimated in the statement of affairs not to exceed £500, three-fifths only of the above fee shall be taken.

(ii) at the due date for audit of the accounts of a liquidator, other than the Official Receiver, on the net assets (including produce of calls on contributories) realised or brought to credit by the said liquidator after deducting any sums paid to secured creditors in respect of their securities and the sums spent out of the money received in carrying on the business of the company—

    (a) on the first £100,000 or fraction thereof      per cent. ...   3   0   0

    (b) on the next £150,000 or fraction thereof      per cent. ...   2   0   0

    (c) on all further sums      per cent. ...   1   0   0

3. Where the Official Receiver acts as liquidator of the company and a special manager is appointed (to include the Official Receiver's services as provisional liquidator):—

such amount as the court, on the application of the Official Receiver, with the sanction of the Board of Trade, may consider reasonable.

4. In all other cases where the Official Receiver acts as liquidator of the company (to include his services as provisional liquidator)—

(1) for all official stationery, printing, postage and telephones (except trunk calls)—

    (i) for a number of members and creditors not exceeding 20    ...   16   10   0

    (ii) for every additional 10 members or creditors or part thereof:   5   10   0
Provided that where the net assets of the company, including uncalled capital, do not exceed £500, three-fifths only of the above fee shall be taken.

TABLE B—continued

| Description of Proceeding | Amount |
|---|---|

| | £ s. d. |
|---|---|

4. (2) On the net assets, including produce of calls on contributories,
(cont) realised or brought to credit by the Official Receiver, after deducting
the sums on which amounts are payable under Fee No. 5 of this Table,
and the sums spent out of the money received in carrying on the
business of the company—

| | | £ s. d. |
|---|---|---|
| (i) on the first £2,500 or fraction thereof | per cent. ... | 12 0 0 |
| (ii) on the next £7,500 or fraction thereof | per cent. ... | 8 0 0 |
| (iii) on the next £90,000 or fraction thereof | per cent. ... | 4 0 0 |
| (iv) on all further sums | per cent. ... | 2 0 0 |

(3) On the sum distributed in dividends or paid to contributories,
preferential creditors and debenture holders by the Official Receiver, half the amount prescribed for that sum in paragraph (2) of
this Fee.

5. Where the Official Receiver collects calls or realises property for
debenture holders:—the amounts payable under Fee No. 4 (2) and
(3) of this Table, to be paid out of the proceeds of such calls or
property.

6. Where the Official Receiver realises property for secured creditors
other than debenture holders:—the amounts payable under Fee No.
4(2) of this Table, to be paid out of the proceeds of such property.

7. Where the Official Receiver collects calls or realises property as
liquidator under section 239(e) of the Companies Act 1948—the
amounts payable under Fee No. 4(2) and (3) of this Order.

8. For travelling, keeping possession, legal costs and other reasonable
expenses of the Official Receiver, the amount disbursed.

9. On payments of money out of the Companies Liquidation Account
under section 15 of the Companies (Winding Up) Act 1890, section
224 of the Companies (Consolidation) Act 1908 or section 343 of the
Companies Act 1948, on each pound or fraction of a pound—

| | £ s. d. |
|---|---|
| (1) where the money consists of unclaimed dividends, of each dividend paid out ... ... ... ... ... ... ... | 0 0 3 |

(2) where the money consists of undistributed funds or balances—

| | £ s. d. |
|---|---|
| (i) of the first £5,000 ... ... ... ... ... ... ... | 0 0 3 |
| (ii) of all further sums ... ... ... ... ... ... | 0 0 1½ |

Provided that—

(a) the total fee payable in any liquidation shall not exceed £500 and

(b) any payment of money out of the Companies Liquidation Account
in respect of the amount payable to the Board of Trade under
paragraph (2) of this Fee shall be disregarded in calculating that amount.

10. Where the Official Receiver performs any duty not provided for in
the foregoing Tables:—

such amount as the court, on the application of the Official Receiver,
with the sanction of the Board of Trade, may consider reasonable.

# EXPLANATORY NOTE

*(This Note is not part of the Order.)*

This Order replaces the Companies (Board of Trade) Fees Order 1929 and increases fees taken by the Board of Trade in proceedings for the winding-up of companies.

# STATUTORY INSTRUMENTS

## 1969 No. 520 (L.8)

## BANKRUPTCY, ENGLAND

## The Bankruptcy Fees (Amendment) Order 1969

| Made | - | - | - | 1st April 1969 |
|---|---|---|---|---|
| Coming into Operation | | | | 1st May 1969 |

The Lord Chancellor and the Treasury, in exercise of the powers conferred on them by section 133 of the Bankruptcy Act 1914(a) and sections 2 and 3 of the Public Offices Fees Act 1879(b), hereby make, sanction and consent to the following Order :—

**1.**—(1) This Order may be cited as the Bankruptcy Fees (Amendment) Order 1969 and shall come into operation on 1st May 1969.

(2) In this Order, a fee referred to by number shall mean a fee so numbered in Table B in the Schedule to the Bankruptcy Fees Order 1965(c).

(3) The Interpretation Act 1889(d) shall apply to the interpretation of this Order as it applies to the interpretation of an Act of Parliament.

**2.** The Bankruptcy Fees Order 1965 shall have effect subject to the following amendments :—

(1) In Fee No. 3, for the figures "£10 0 0", "£5 0 0" and "£2 10 0" there shall be substituted the figures "£12 0 0", "£8 0 0" and "£4 0 0" respectively.

(2) In Fee No. 5, for the figures "£5 0 0", "£2 10 0" and "£1 5 0" there shall be substituted the figures "£6 0 0", "£4 0 0" and "£2 0 0" respectively.

(3) In Fee No. 7(i), for the figures "£10 0 0", "£13 10 0" and "£3 0 0" there shall be substituted the figures "£11 0 0", "£15 0 0" and "£3 10 0" respectively.

(4) In Fee No. 7(ii), for the figures "£15 0 0" and "£5 0 0" there shall be substituted the figures "£16 10 0" and "£5 10 0" respectively.

(5) For Fee No. 10 there shall be substituted the following new fee:—
   "At the due date for audit of the accounts of a trustee in bankruptcy, other than the Official Receiver, on the net assets realised or brought to credit by such trustee after deducting any sums paid to secured creditors in respect of their securities and the sums spent out of money received in carrying on the business of the debtor—

| | | |
|---|---|---|
| (a) on the first £100,000 or fraction thereof per cent. | £3 | 0 0 |
| (b) on the next £150,000 or fraction thereof per cent. | £2 | 0 0 |
| (c) on all further sums per cent. | £1 | 0 0" : |

Provided that where an audit has become due before the coming into operation of this Order, this fee shall be charged at the time of the audit.

(6) In Fee No. 11, for the figures "£2 10 0" and "£1 5 0" there shall be substituted the figures "£3 0 0" and "£2 0 0" respectively.

---

(a) 1914 c. 59.       (b) 1879 c. 58.
(c) S.I. 1965/1622 (1965 II, p.4651).       (d) 1889 c. 63.

Dated 31st March 1969.

*Gardiner*, C.

Dated 1st April 1969.

*Joseph Harper,*
*J. McCann,*
Two of the Lords Commissioners
of Her Majesty's Treasury.

## EXPLANATORY NOTE

*(This Note is not part of the Order.)*

This Order increases certain fees taken by the Board of Trade in bankruptcy cases. It amends one fee to conform with the corresponding fee to be taken on the winding-up of a company and empowers the court to fix a fee in certain cases where a receiving order has been rescinded.

## STATUTORY INSTRUMENTS

### 1969 No. 521

### PLANT HEALTH

## The Importation of Potatoes (Health) (Great Britain) (Amendment) Order 1969

| | |
|---|---|
| *Made* - - - | *2nd April* 1969 |
| *Laid before Parliament* | *16th April* 1969 |
| *Coming into Operation* | *17th April* 1969 |

The Minister of Agriculture, Fisheries and Food and the Secretary of State, by virtue and in exercise of the powers vested in them respectively by section 2 of the Plant Health Act 1967(a) and of every other power enabling them in that behalf, order as follows :—

*Citation, extent and commencement*

**1.**—(1) This Order may be cited as the Importation of Potatoes (Health) (Great Britain) (Amendment) Order 1969, and the Importation of Potatoes (Health) (Great Britain) Order 1964(b) (hereinafter referred to as "the principal Order"), the Importation of Potatoes (Health) (Great Britain) (Amendment) Order 1968(c) and this Order may be cited together as the Importation of Potatoes (Health) (Great Britain) Orders 1964 to 1969.

(2) This Order shall apply to England and Wales and Scotland and shall come into operation on 17th April 1969.

*Interpretation*

**2.** The Interpretation Act 1889(d) shall apply to the interpretation of this Order as it applies to the interpretation of an Act of Parliament.

*Amendment of principal Order*

**3.** In column 1 of Schedule 3 to the principal Order, as amended by the Importation of Potatoes (Health) (Great Britain) (Amendment) Order 1968, for the words "Lower Saxony, north of latitude 53° North", appearing in the entry relating to the Federal Republic of Germany, there shall be substituted the words "of Lower Saxony except for the areas of that province south of the Mittelland Canal".

---

(a) 1967 c.8.
(c) S.I. 1968/165 (1968 I, p. 397).

(b) S.I. 1964/409 (1964 I, p. 674).
(d) 1889 c. 63.

In Witness whereof the official seal of the Minister of Agriculture, Fisheries and Food is hereunto affixed on 1st April 1969.


(L.S.)                                        *Cledwyn Hughes,*
                                        Minister of Agriculture, Fisheries and Food.


Given under the seal of the Secretary of State for Scotland on 2nd April 1969.


(L.S.)                                        *William Ross,*
                                        Secretary of State for Scotland.

---

## EXPLANATORY NOTE

*(This Note is not part of the Order.)*

This Order amends the Importation of Potatoes (Health) (Great Britain) Order 1964, as previously amended, by permitting the importation into Great Britain of potatoes, other than seed potatoes, from the Federal German province of Lower Saxony except for the areas of that province lying to the south of the Mittelland Canal, instead of from the parts of that province lying to the north of latitude 53° North. The importation of potatoes from the province of Schleswig-Holstein remains unaffected.

# STATUTORY INSTRUMENTS

## 1969 No. 522

## TRADE MARKS

## The Trade Marks (Amendment) Rules 1969

| | |
|---|---|
| *Made* - - - | *3rd April* 1969 |
| *Laid before Parliament* | *16th April* 1969 |
| *Coming into Operation* | |
| *Rules* 4 and 5 | *21st April* 1969 |
| *Rule* 3 | *21st June* 1969 |

Whereas, in pursuance of the requirements of section 40(3) of the Trade Marks Act 1938(a), the Board of Trade have, before making the following Rules under that Act, published notice of their intention to make such Rules and of the place where copies of the draft Rules might be obtained by advertising such notice in the Trade Marks Journal and the Official Journal (Patents) on the 26th February 1969 and 5th March 1969, being the manner which the Board considered most expedient so as to enable persons affected to make representations to the Board before the Rules were finally settled:

Now, therefore, the Board of Trade, in pursuance of the powers conferred on them by sections 40 and 41 of the Trade Marks Act 1938 and of all other powers enabling them in that behalf, and with the sanction of the Treasury, hereby make the following Rules :—

**1.** These Rules may be cited as the Trade Marks (Amendment) Rules 1969 and shall come into operation as respects Rules 4 and 5 on 21st April 1969 and as respects Rule 3 on 21st June 1969.

**2.** The Interpretation Act 1889(b) shall apply to the interpretation of these Rules as it applies to the interpretation of an Act of Parliament and as if these Rules and the Rules hereby revoked were Acts of Parliament.

**3.** The fee payable by virtue of Rule 3 of the Trade Marks Rules 1938(c), as amended (d), in respect of any of the matters specified in the Schedule hereto shall on and after 21st June 1969 be the appropriate fee so specified and, accordingly, on that date—

    (i) for Schedule 1 to the said Rules there shall be substituted the Schedule hereto ; and

    (ii) the Trade Marks (Amendment No. 2) Rules 1964(e) and the Trade Marks (Amendment) Rules 1967(f) shall be revoked.

---

(a) 1938 c. 22.                (b) 1889 c. 63.
(c) S.R. & O. 1938/661 (Rev. XXIII, p. 3: 1938 II, p. 3257).
(d) The relevant amending instruments are S.I. 1964/227, 1835, 1967/1366 (1964 I, p. 408; 1964 III, p. 3993; 1967 III, p. 4035).      (e) S.I. 1964/1835 (1964 III, p. 3993).
(f) S.I. 1967/1366 (1967 III, p. 4035).

**4.** Where on or after 21st April 1969 but before 21st June 1969 Form TM—No. 11 is filed in respect of the renewal of registration of a trade mark or a series of trade marks the last registration of which mark or series of marks is due to expire after 20th June 1969, the fee payable in respect of such renewal shall be that which would be payable if the said form were filed on or after 21st June 1969.

**5.** Where on or after 21st April 1969 but before 21st June 1969 Form Cotton—No. 6 is filed to secure the continued inclusion of a mark in the collection of refused marks pursuant to Rule 102 of the Trade Marks Rules 1938 in a case in which the relevant period of 14 years mentioned in that Rule is due to expire after 20th June 1969, the continuance fee payable shall be that which would be payable if the said form were filed on or after 21st June 1969.

*Edmund Dell,*
Minister of State,
Board of Trade.

3rd April 1969.

We sanction the making of these Rules.

*J. McCann,*
*Joseph Harper,*
Two of the Lords Commissioners
of Her Majesty's Treasury.

27th March 1969.

## SCHEDULE

### LIST OF FEES PAYABLE

| Matter or Proceeding | Amount | Corresponding Form |
|---|---|---|
| | £ s. d. | |
| 1   On application not otherwise charged to register a trade mark for a specification of goods included in one class ...   ... | 6   0   0 | T.M.–No. 2<br>Textile–No. 2 |
| 1a On application to register a series of trade marks under section 21(2) for a specification of goods included in one class ... | 6   0   0 | T.M–No. 2<br>Textile–No. 2 |
| 1b On application to register a defensive trade mark for a specification of goods included in one class   ...   ... | 7   0   0 | T.M–No. 32 |
| 1c On application under section 37 to register a certification trade mark for a specification of goods included in one class   ...   ...   ...   ...   ... | 6   0   0 | T.M–No. 6 |
| 1d On applications made at the same time under section 37 to register one certification trade mark for specifications of goods not all included in one class—<br>    In respect of every class   ...   ...<br>    Total fee in no case to exceed £120 for any number of classes. | 6   0   0 | T.M–No. 6 |

| Matter or Proceeding | Amount | Corresponding Form |
|---|---|---|
| | £  s.  d. | |
| 2  On a request to the Registrar to state grounds of decision relating to an application to register a trade mark and materials used ...  ...  ...  ... | 3  10  0* | T.M–No. 5 |
| 3  On notice of opposition before the Registrar under section 18, for each application opposed, by opponent  ... | 3  10  0* | T.M–No. 7 |
| 3a  On lodging a counter-statement in answer to a notice of opposition under section 18, for each application opposed, by the applicant; or in answer to an application under any of the sections 26, 27, 32 and 33, by the proprietor in respect of each trade mark; or in answer to a notice of opposition under section 35 or section 36, for each application or conversion opposed, by the proprietor... | 2  10  0* | T.M–No. 8 |
| 3b  On the hearing of each opposition under section 18, by applicant and by opponent respectively; or on the hearing of an application under any of the sections 26, 27, 32 and 33, by applicant and by proprietor respectively; or on the hearing of an opposition under section 35 or section 36, by proprietor and by opponent respectively  ...  ...  ... | 3  10  0* | T.M–No. 9 |
| 3c  On notice of opposition before the Board of Trade under paragraph 2(2) of Schedule 1 to the Act, for each application opposed, by the opponent...  ... | 3  10  0* | T.M–No. 37 |
| 3d  On lodging a counter-statement in answer to a notice of opposition before the Board of Trade under paragraph 2(2) of Schedule 1 to the Act, for each application opposed, by the applicant...  ... | 2  10  0* | T.M–No. 38 |
| 3e  On the hearing of each opposition before the Board of Trade under paragraph 2(2) of Schedule 1 to the Act, by applicant and by opponent respectively  ... | 3  10  0* | T.M–No. 39 |
| 4  For one registration of a trade mark not otherwise charged for a specification of goods included in one class  ...  ... | 6  0  0 | T.M–No. 10 |
| 4a  For one registration of a series of trade marks under section 21(2) for a specification of goods included in one class— | | |
| For the first mark  ...  ...  ... | 6  0  0 | T.M–No. 10 |
| And for every other mark of the series | 0  8  0 | |

| Matter or Proceeding | Amount | Corresponding Form |
|---|---|---|
| | £   s.   d. | |
| 4b For registration under section 37 of a certification trade mark for a specification of goods included in one class   ... | 6   0   0 | T.M–No. 10 |
| 4c For registration upon applications made at the same time of one certification trade mark, under section 37, for specifications of goods not all included in one class— | | |
|     In respect of every class   ...   ... | 6   0   0 | T.M–No. 10 |
|     Total fee in no case to exceed £120 for any number of classes. | | |
| 4d For one registration of a defensive trade mark for a specification of goods included in one class   ...   ...   ... | 7   0   0 | T.M–No. 10 |
| 5   Upon each addition to the registered entry of a trade mark of a note that the mark is associated with a newly registered mark   ...   ...   ...   ... | 0   6   0* | T.M–No. 10 |
| 5a On an application to dissolve the association between registered trade marks   ... | 3   0   0 | T.M–No. 19 |
| 6   On application to register a registered user of a registered trade mark in respect of goods within the specification thereof ... | 4   0   0* | T.M–No. 50 |
| 6a On application to register the same registered user of more than one registered trade mark of the same registered proprietor in respect of goods within the respective specifications thereof and subject to the same conditions and restrictions in each case— | | |
|     For the first mark   ...   ...   ... | 4   0   0* | T.M–No. 50 |
|     And for every other mark of the proprietor included in the application and statement of case   ...   ... | 0   5   0* | |
| 6b On application by the proprietor of a single trade mark under section 28(8)(a) to vary the entry of a registered user thereof   ...   ...   ...   ...   ... | 5   0   0* | T.M–No. 51 |
| 6c On application by the proprietor of more than one trade mark under section 28(8)(a) to vary the entries of a registered user thereof— | | |
|     For the first mark   ...   ...   ... | 5   0   0* | T.M–No. 51 |
|     And for every other mark of the proprietor for which the same user is registered, included in the application   ...   ...   ...   ... | 0   6   0* | |

| Matter or Proceeding | Amount | Corresponding Form |
|---|---|---|
| | £ s. d. | |
| 6d On application by the proprietor or registered user of a single trade mark under section 28(8)(*b*), for cancellation of the entry of a registered user thereof ... | 3 0 0 | T.M–No. 52 |
| 6e On application by the proprietor or registered user of more than one trade mark under section 28(8)(*b*), for cancellation of the entries of a registered user thereof— | | |
| For the first mark ... ... ... | 3 0 0 | T.M–No. 52 |
| And for every other mark of the proprietor for which the same user is registered, included in the application ... ... ... ... ... | 0 3 0 | |
| 6f On application under section 28(8)(*c*), to cancel the entry of a registered user of a single trade mark ... ... ... | 3 0 0 | T.M–No. 53 |
| 6g On application under section 28(8)(*c*), to cancel the entries of a registered user of more than one trade mark— | | |
| For the first mark ... ... ... | 3 0 0 | T.M–No. 53 |
| And for every other mark of the same proprietor for which the same user is registered, included in the application ... ... ... ... ... | 0 3 0 | |
| 6h On notice under section 28(9) and Rule 112, of intention to intervene in one proceeding for the variation or cancellation of entries of a registered user of trade marks ... ... ... ... ... | 1 5 0* | T.M–No. 54 |
| 7 On request to enter in the register and advertise a certificate of validity, under section 47 and Rule 88— | | |
| For the first registration certified ... | 1 10 0 | T.M–No. 49 |
| And for every other registration certified in the same certificate ... | 0 2 0 | |
| 7a On application under section 29(4) and Rule 76 for extension of time for registering a corporation as subsequent proprietor of trade marks on one assignment— | | |
| Not exceeding two months ... ... | 1 10 0 | T.M–No. 14 |
| Not exceeding four months ... ... | 3 0 0 | T.M–No. 14 |
| Not exceeding six months ... ... | 4 10 0 | T.M–No. 14 |
| 8 On application for certificate of the Registrar, under section 22(5) and Rule 79— For the first mark proposed to be assigned ... ... ... ... | 5 0 0* | T.M–No. 40 |
| And for every other mark of the same proprietor included in that assignment ... ... ... ... ... | 0 6 0* | |

| Matter or Proceeding | Amount | Corresponding Form |
|---|---|---|
| | £ s. d. | |
| 8a On application for approval of the Registrar, under section 22(6) or paragraph 2 of Schedule 3 of the Act, and Rule 79— | | |
| For the first mark ... ... ... | 5 0 0* | T.M–No. 41 or 42 |
| And for every other mark of the same proprietor included in the same transfer ... ... ... ... | 0 6 0* | |
| 8b On application for directions by the Registrar for advertisement of assignment of trade marks in use, without goodwill— | | |
| For one mark assigned ... ... | 2 10 0* | T.M–No. 43 |
| And for every other mark assigned with the same devolution of title ... | 0 6 0* | |
| 8c On application for extension of time for applying for directions for advertisement of assignment of trade marks in use, without goodwill, in respect of one devolution of title— | | |
| Not exceeding one month ... ... | 1 10 0 | T.M–No. 44 |
| Not exceeding two months ... ... | 3 0 0 | T.M–No. 44 |
| Not exceeding three months ... ... | 4 10 0 | T.M–No. 44 |
| 9 On application to register a subsequent proprietor in a case of assignment or transmission of a single trade mark— | | |
| If made within six months from the date of acquisition of proprietorship ... ... ... ... ... | 5 0 0* | T.M–No. 15 or 16 |
| If made after expiration of six months but within twelve months from the date of acquisition of proprietorship | 5 10 0* | ,, |
| If made after expiration of twelve months from the date of acquisition of proprietorship ... ... ... | 6 0 0* | ,, |
| 9a On application to register a subsequent proprietor of more than one trade mark standing in the same name, the devolution of title being the same in each case— | | |
| If made within six months from the date of acquisition of proprietorship | | |
| For the first mark ... ... | 5 0 0* | T.M–No. 15 or 16 |
| And for every other mark ... | 0 6 0* | |
| If made after expiration of six months but within twelve months from the date of acquisition of proprietorship | | |
| For the first mark ... ... | 5 10 0* | ,, |
| And for every other mark ... | 0 6 0* | |
| If made after expiration of twelve months from the date of acquisition of proprietorship— | | |
| For the first mark ... ... | 6 0 0* | ,, |
| And for every other mark ... | 0 6 0* | |

| Matter or Proceeding | Amount | Corresponding Form |
|---|---|---|
| | £ s. d. | |
| 10 On application to change the name or description of a proprietor or a registered user of a single trade mark where there has been no change in the proprietorship or in the identity of the user ... ... | 1 5 0* | T.M–No. 21 |
| 10a On application to change the name or description of a proprietor or a registered user of more than one trade mark standing in the same name, where there has been no change in the proprietorship or in the identity of the user, the change being the same in each case— | | |
| For the first mark ... ... ... | 1 5 0* | T.M.–No. 21 |
| And for every other mark ... ... | 0 3 0 | |
| 11 For renewal of registration of a trade mark at expiration of last registration ... | 15 0 0 | T.M–No. 11 |
| 11a For renewal of registration of a series of trade marks under section 21(2) at expiration of last registration— | | |
| For the first mark of the series ... | 15 0 0 | T.M–No. 11 |
| And for every other mark of the series | 0 6 0* | |
| 11b For renewal of registrations of the same certification trade mark with the same date for goods in more than one class— | | |
| In respect of every class ... ... | 15 0 0 | T.M–No. 11 |
| Total fee in no case to exceed £300 for any number of classes. | | |
| 11c Additional fee under Rule 67 ... ... | 1 10 0 | T.M–No. 12 |
| 11d Restoration fee under Rule 68 ... ... | 5 0 0* | T.M–No. 13 |
| 12 On an application to the Registrar for leave to add to or alter a single registered trade mark ... ... ... ... | 5 0 0* | T.M–No. 25 |
| 12a On an application to the Registrar for leave to add to or alter more than one registered trade mark of the same proprietor, being identical marks, the addition or alteration to be made in each case being the same— | | |
| For the first mark ... ... ... | 5 0 0* | T.M–No. 25 |
| And for every other mark ... ... | 2 10 0* | |
| 12b On notice of opposition to application for leave to add to or alter registered trade marks, for each application opposed ... | 3 10 0* | T.M–No. 47 |

| Matter or Proceeding | Amount | Corresponding Form |
|---|---|---|
| | £ s. d. | |
| 13 For altering one or more entries of the trade or business address of a registered proprietor or a registered user of a trade mark where the address in each case is the same and is altered in the same way (unless exempted from fee under Rule 81)— | | |
| For the first entry ... ... ... | 1 5 0* | T.M–No. 18 |
| And for every other entry ... ... | 0 3 0 | |
| 14 For every entry in the register of a rectification thereof or an alteration therein, not otherwise charged ... ... ... | 2 10 0* | T.M–No. 48 |
| 15 For cancelling the entry or part of the entry of a trade mark upon the register on the application of the registered proprietor of the trade mark ... ... | 0 15 0 | T.M–No. 22 or 23 |
| 16 On application under any of the sections 26, 27, 32 and 33, for rectification of the register or removal of trade mark from the register ... ... ... ... | 6 0 0* | T.M–No. 26 |
| 16a On application for leave to intervene in proceedings under any of the sections 26, 27, 32 and 33, for rectification of the register or removal of trade mark from the register ... ... ... ... | 3 10 0* | T.M–No. 27 |
| 17 On request, not otherwise charged, for correction of clerical error or for permission to amend application ... ... | 1 5 0* | T.M–No. 20 |
| 18 On request by registered proprietor of a trade mark for entry of disclaimer or memorandum in the register ... ... | 1 5 0* | T.M–No. 24 |
| 19 On application to the Board of Trade under Rule 93 to expunge or vary the registration of a certification trade mark or to vary the deposited regulations of a certification trade mark or of certification trade marks of the same registered proprietor where the regulations are substantially the same ... ... ... | 4 10 0 | T.M–No. 36 |
| 19a On request to the Board of Trade by the registered proprietor of a certification trade mark to permit alteration of the deposited regulations thereof— | | |
| For the regulations of one such registration ... ... ... ... | 2 10 0* | T.M–No. 35 |
| For the same or substantially the same regulations of each other registration proposed to be altered in the same way and included in the same request | 0 6 0* | |

| Matter or Proceeding | Amount | Corresponding Form |
|---|---|---|
| | £ s. d. | |
| 20 On application by registered proprietor under Rule 6, for conversion of specification ... ... ... ... ... | 0 12 6* | T.M–No. 45 |
| 20a On notice of opposition to a conversion of the specification or specifications of a registered trade mark or registered trade marks— | | |
| For one mark ... ... ... | 3 10 0* | T.M–No. 46 |
| For every other mark of the same proprietor having the same specification ... ... ... ... | 0 6 0* | |
| 21 On appeal from the Registrar to the Board of Trade, in respect of each decision appealed against, by Appellant... ... | 5 0 0* | T.M–No. 30 |
| 22 For a search under Rule 127 in respect of one class— | | |
| Without application for the Registrar's advice under Rule 20 ... ... | 1 10 0* | T.M–No. 28 |
| With application for the Registrar's advice under Rule 20 ... ... | 2 0 0* | T.M–No. 28 |
| 23 On request for the Registrar's preliminary advice under Rule 20, for each trade mark submitted in respect of one class ... | 0 10 0* | T.M–No. 29 |
| 24 For certificate of the Registrar (other than certificate under section 19(2)) of the registration of a trade mark ... ... | 0 15 0 | T.M–No. 31 |
| 24a For certificate of the Registrar (other than certificate under section 19(2)) of the registration of a series of trade marks under section 21(2) ... ... ... | 1 10 0 | T.M–No. 31 |
| 25 For certificate of the Keeper of an entry in the Manchester Record relating to one trade mark ... ... ... ... | 0 15 0 | Textile–No. 5 |
| 25a For certificate of the Keeper of an entry in the Manchester Record relating to a series of trade marks under section 21(2) | 1 10 0 | Textile—No. 5 |
| 26 For the continuance of a Cotton Mark in the Collection of Refused Marks— | | |
| For each mark in each class at the end of each period of fourteen years after date of application ... ... | 2 10 0* | Cotton–No. 6 |
| 27 For cancelling or making one or more entries of an address for service of a registered proprietor or a registered user of a trade mark where the address in each case is the same, on application made after the registration in each case— | | |
| For the first entry ... ... ... | 0 12 6* | T.M–No. 33 |
| And for every other entry included in the application ... ... ... | 0 2 6* | |

| Matter or Proceeding | Amount | Corresponding Form |
|---|---|---|
| | £ s. d. | |
| 27a For altering one or more entries of an address for service in the register included in one application for alteration, where the address and the alteration in each case are the same— | | T.M–No. 33 |
| For the first entry ... ... ... | 0 12 6* | |
| And for every other entry ... ... | 0 2 6* | |
| Total fee in no case to exceed £62-10-0 for any number of entries. | | |
| 28 For inspecting register or Manchester Record, or notice of opposition, counterstatement or decision in connection with any opposition or application for rectification of the register relating to any particular trade mark, for every quarter of an hour ... ... ... ... | 0 2 6* | — |
| 29 For permission to search amongst the classified representations of trade marks, for every quarter of an hour ... ... | 0 2 6* | — |
| 30 For office copy of documents, for every 100 words ... ... ... ... | 0 1 0* but never less than 2s.* | — |
| 31 For photographic copy of documents ... | Cost according to agreement | — |
| 32 For certifying office copies M.S. or photographic or printed matter ... ... | 0 15 0 | — |
| 33 For extra space in the Journal advertisement, in cases where the printing block for the trade mark exceeds 2 inches in breadth or depth, or in breadth and depth— | | |
| For every inch or part of an inch over 2 inches in breadth ... ... ... | 0 6 0 | — |
| For every inch or part of an inch over 2 inches in depth ... ... ... | 0 6 0 | — |

The fees to be paid on any proceeding at the Manchester Branch and at the office of the Cutlers' Company shall be the same as for the similar proceeding at the Office.

For the purpose of these fees (except as specially provided above) every mark of a series under section 21, or any preceding similar enactment, shall be deemed to be a mark separately registered.

# EXPLANATORY NOTE
*(This Note is not part of the Rules.)*

These Rules further amend the Trade Marks Rules 1938.

With the exceptions indicated by asterisk, the fees payable under the Rules are increased.

The new fees become payable generally on or after 21st June 1969, except in the case of renewal fees and continuance fees paid in advance. Such fees in respect of any period beginning on or after 21st June 1969 are increased on 21st April 1969.

## STATUTORY INSTRUMENTS

### 1969 No. 532

## LAND COMMISSION

## The Betterment Levy (Waiver of Interest) (No. 2) (Amendment) Regulations 1969

| | |
|---|---|
| *Made* - - - - - - - | *3rd April* 1969 |
| *Laid before the House of Commons* | *15th April* 1969 |
| *Coming into Operation* - - - | *16th April* 1969 |

The Minister of Housing and Local Government and the Secretary of State, acting jointly, being for the purposes of these regulations the appropriate Ministers in relation to Great Britain, in exercise of the powers conferred on them by sections 51(4) and 98 of the Land Commission Act 1967(a), and of all other powers enabling them in that behalf, hereby make the following regulations:—

*Citation, extent, commencement and interpretation*

**1.**—(1) These regulations, which may be cited as The Betterment Levy (Waiver of Interest) (No. 2) (Amendment) Regulations 1969, apply to Great Britain and shall come into operation on 16th April 1969.

(2) The Interpretation Act 1889(b) applies to the interpretation of these regulations as it applies to the interpretation of an Act of Parliament.

*Further waiver of interest payable to the Commission on levy*

**2.** The following regulation shall be inserted in the Betterment Levy (Waiver of Interest) (No. 2) Regulations 1967(c) as amended(d), after regulation 3 of those regulations.

" **4.** Where a notice of assessment has resulted in an operative assessment of levy, and the principal amount of levy payable in accordance with the assessment does not exceed £1,000, any interest which on the date of the coming into operation of the Betterment Levy (Waiver of Interest) (No. 2) (Amendment) Regulations 1969 is, or would apart from this regulation thereafter become, payable to the Commission on the principal amount of levy, or any part thereof, in accordance with the provisions of section 51 of the Act, shall be waived."

Given under the official seal of the Minister of Housing and Local Government on 2nd April 1969.

(L. S.)                      *Anthony Greenwood,*
Minister of Housing and Local Government.

Given under the seal of the Secretary of State for Scotland on 3rd April 1969.

(L. S.)                      *William Ross,*
Secretary of State for Scotland.

---

(a) 1967 c. 1.     (b) 1889 c. 63.     (c) S.I. 1967/1715 (1967 III, p. 4637).
(d) S.I. 1968/131 (1968 I, p. 351).

## EXPLANATORY NOTE
*(This Note is not part of the regulations.)*

The Betterment Levy (Waiver of Interest) Regulations 1967 (S.I. 1967/338 (1967 I, p. 1158)) and the Betterment Levy (Waiver of Interest) (No. 2) Regulations 1967 provide for the waiver of interest on betterment levy in certain cases specified in the regulations.

These regulations add a further case to those so specified. They make provision for the waiver of all outstanding interest on amounts of betterment levy where the original amount of levy charged did not exceed £1,000.

The regulations apply to Great Britain.

## STATUTORY INSTRUMENTS

### 1969 No. 535

## INCOME TAX

## The Income Tax (Interest on Unpaid Tax) Order 1969

| | |
|---|---|
| *Made* - - - - - - | 10*th April* 1969 |
| *Laid before the House of Commons* | 15*th April* 1969 |
| *Coming into Operation* - - - | 19*th April* 1969 |

The Treasury, in exercise of the powers conferred on them by section 40(2) of the Finance Act 1967(a), hereby make the following Order:—

1.—(1) This Order may be cited as the Income Tax (Interest on Unpaid Tax) Order 1969, and shall come into force on 19th April 1969.

(2) The Interpretation Act 1889(b) shall apply for the interpretation of this Order as it applies for the interpretation of an Act of Parliament.

2. The rate of interest prescribed by Section 40(1) of the Finance Act 1967 (which relates to interest on unpaid tax) shall be increased, for the purposes of Section 495(1) of the Income Tax Act 1952(c) and Section 8 of the Finance (No. 2) Act 1947(d) as extended in accordance with Section 40(6) of the Finance Act 1967, from 4 per cent per annum to 6 per cent per annum.

*Harold Wilson,*

*Roy Jenkins,*

Two of the Lords Commissioners of
Her Majesty's Treasury.

10th April 1969.

### EXPLANATORY NOTE

(*This Note is not part of the Order.*)

This Order increases from 4 per cent to 6 per cent per annum the rate of interest chargeable on overdue income tax (including surtax), corporation tax, capital gains tax, profits tax, excess profits tax and excess profits levy (other than tax charged for the purpose of making good to the Crown a loss attributable to fraud, wilful default or neglect). The increase applies from 19th April 1969, whether or not interest runs from before that date.

(a) 1967 c. 54.  (b) 52 & 53 Vict. c. 63.  (c) 15 & 16 Geo. 6 & 1 Eliz. 2 c. 10.
(d) 11 & 12 Geo. 6 c. 9.

## STATUTORY INSTRUMENTS

### 1969 No. 536

## LAND COMMISSION
### The Betterment Levy (Rate of Interest) (No. 2) Order 1969

| | |
|---|---|
| *Made* - - - - - - | *10th April* 1969 |
| *Laid before the House of Commons* | *15th April* 1969 |
| *Coming into Operation* - - - | *19th April* 1969 |

The Treasury, in exercise of the powers conferred upon them by section 51(2) of the Land Commission Act 1967(a) and of all other powers enabling them in that behalf, hereby make the following Order:—

**1.** This Order may be cited as the Betterment Levy (Rate of Interest) (No. 2) Order 1969, and shall come into operation on 19th April 1969.

**2.** The Interpretation Act 1889(b) shall apply for the interpretation of this Order as it applies for the interpretation of an Act of Parliament.

**3.** The rate of interest for the purposes of section 51 of the Land Commission Act 1967 shall be 6 per cent. per annum.

**4.** The Betterment Levy (Rate of Interest) Order 1969(c) is hereby revoked.

*Harold Wilson,*
*Roy Jenkins,*

Two of the Lords Commissioners
of Her Majesty's Treasury.

10th April 1969.

### EXPLANATORY NOTE
(*This Note is not part of the Order.*)

Section 51 of the Land Commission Act 1967 provides that interest shall be paid on unpaid or overpaid betterment levy. This Order decreases the rate of interest from 8 per cent. to 6 per cent. per annum and revokes the Betterment Levy (Rate of Interest) Order 1969.

| | | |
|---|---|---|
| (a) 1967 c. 1. | (b) 1889 c. 63. | (c) S.I. 1969/440. (1969 I, p. 1296). |

# STATUTORY    INSTRUMENTS

## 1969 No. 537

## AGRICULTURE

## The Price Stability of Imported Products (Rates of Levy No. 8) Order 1969

| | | |
|---|---|---|
| *Made* - - - - | | 10*th April* 1969 |
| *Coming into Operation* | | 11*th April* 1969 |

The Minister of Agriculture, Fisheries and Food, in exercise of the powers conferred upon him by section 1(2), (4), (5) and (6) of the Agriculture and Horticulture Act 1964(a) and of all other powers enabling him in that behalf, hereby makes the following order :—

**1.** This order may be cited as the Price Stability of Imported Products (Rates of Levy No. 8) Order 1969 ; and shall come into operation on 11th April 1969.

**2.**—(1) In this order—

" the Principal Order " means the Price Stability of Imported Products (Levy Arrangements) Order 1966(b), as amended by any subsequent order and if any such order is replaced by any subsequent order the expression shall be construed as a reference to such subsequent order ;

AND other expressions have the same meaning as in the Principal Order.

(2) The Interpretation Act 1889(c) shall apply to the interpretation of this order as it applies to the interpretation of an Act of Parliament.

**3.** In accordance with and subject to the provisions of Part II of the Principal Order (which provides for the charging of levies on imports of certain specified commodities) the rate of general levy for such imports into the United Kingdom of any specified commodity as are described in column 2 of the Schedule to this order in relation to a tariff heading indicated in column 1 of that Schedule shall be the rate set forth in relation thereto in column 3 of that Schedule.

In Witness whereof the Official Seal of the Minister of Agriculture, Fisheries and Food is hereunto affixed on 10th April 1969.

(L.S.)

*R. J. E. Taylor,*
Assistant Secretary.

---

(a) 1964 c. 28.        (b) S.I. 1966/936 (1966 II. p. 2271).        (c) 1889 c. 63.

## SCHEDULE

| 1.<br>Tariff<br>Heading | 2.<br>Description of Imports | 3.<br>Rate of<br>General Levy |
|---|---|---|
| | | per ton<br>£  s.  d. |
| 11.02 | Imports of :—<br>Cereal meal—<br>of barley     ..     ..     ..     ..     ..     .. | 5  10  0 |

## EXPLANATORY NOTE

### (*This Note is not part of the Order.*)

This order, which comes into operation on 11th April 1969, fixes a rate of general levy at 110*s.* per ton on imports of barley meal.

## 1969 No. 541

## BORROWING AND SECURITIES

### The Savings Certificates (Amendment) Regulations 1969

|  |  |  |
|---|---|---|
| *Made* - - - - | 15*th April* 1969 |
| *Laid before Parliament* | 17*th April* 1969 |
| *Coming into Operation* | 18*th April* 1969 |

The Treasury, in exercise of the powers conferred upon them by section 12 of the National Debt Act 1958(**a**) and of all other powers enabling them in that behalf, hereby make the following Regulations:—

**1.** These Regulations may be cited as the Savings Certificates (Amendment) Regulations 1969, and shall come into operation on 18th April 1969.

**2.** The Interpretation Act 1889(**b**) shall apply for the interpretation of these Regulations as it applies for the interpretation of an Act of Parliament.

**3.** Regulation 4 of the Savings Certificates Regulations 1933(**c**), as substituted by Regulation 1 of the Savings Certificates (Amendment) Regulations 1966(**d**) and amended by the Savings Certificates (Amendment) Regulations 1968(**e**), shall be further amended by substituting for the figures " 1,000 " in paragraph (1)(*g*) of the said Regulation the figures " 1,500 ".

**4.** The Savings Certificates (Amendment) Regulations 1968 are hereby revoked.

*J. McCann,*

*Walter Harrison,*

Two of the Lords Commissioners of
Her Majesty's Treasury.

15th April 1969.

---

### EXPLANATORY NOTE

(*This Note is not part of the Regulations.*)

These Regulations further amend Regulation 4 of the Savings Certificates Regulations 1933, as substituted by Regulation 1 of the Savings Certificates (Amendment) Regulations 1966. They increase the maximum permitted holding of National Savings Certificates of the Twelfth Issue from 1,000 unit certificates (purchase price £1,000) to 1,500 unit certificates (purchase price £1,500) as from 18th April 1969.

---

(**a**) 1958 c. 6 (7 & 8 Eliz. 2. c. 6).　　　(**b**) 1889 c. 63.
(**c**) S.R. & O. 1933/1149 (Rev. XV, p. 309: 1933, p. 1406).
(**d**) S.I. 1966/216 (1966 I, p. 419).　　(**e**) S.I. 1968/425 (1968 I, p. 1113).

STATUTORY INSTRUMENTS

## 1969 No. 542

## INCOME TAX

## The Ulster and Colonial Savings Certificates (Income Tax Exemption) (Amendment) Regulations 1969

Made - - - - 15th April 1969

Coming into Operation 18th April 1969

The Treasury, in exercise of the powers conferred upon them by section 193 of the Income Tax Act 1952(a) and of all other powers enabling them in that behalf, hereby make the following Regulations:—

**1.** These Regulations may be cited as the Ulster and Colonial Savings Certificates (Income Tax Exemption) (Amendment) Regulations 1969, and shall come into operation on 18th April 1969.

**2.** The Interpretation Act 1889(b) shall apply for the interpretation of these Regulations as it applies for the interpretation of an Act of Parliament.

**3.** Regulation 3 of the Ulster and Colonial Savings Certificates (Income Tax Exemption) Regulations 1956(c), as substituted by Regulation 1 of the Ulster and Colonial Savings Certificates (Income Tax Exemption) (Amendment) Regulations 1967(d) and amended by the Ulster and Colonial Savings Certificates (Income Tax Exemption) (Amendment) Regulations 1968(e), shall be further amended by substituting for the figures " 1,000 " in paragraph (g) of the said Regulation the figures " 1,500 ".

**4.** The Ulster and Colonial Savings Certificates (Income Tax Exemption) (Amendment) Regulations 1968 are hereby revoked.

*J. McCann,*

*Walter Harrison,*

Two of the Lords Commissioners of
Her Majesty's Treasury.

15th April 1969.

---

### EXPLANATORY NOTE

*(This Note is not part of the Regulations.)*

These Regulations further amend Regulation 3 of the Ulster and Colonial Savings Certificates (Income Tax Exemption) Regulations 1956, as substituted by Regulation 1 of the Ulster and Colonial Savings Certificates (Income Tax Exemption) (Amendment) Regulations 1967. They increase, by the addition of a further 500 unit certificates issued on or after 28th March 1966, the maximum holding of Ulster, Colonial and certain other Savings Certificates, the interest on which is in certain circumstances exempt from income tax under section 193 of the Income Tax Act 1952.

---

(a) 1952 c. 10.　　　　　　　　　　(b) 1889 c. 63.
(c) S.I. 1956/715 (1956 I, p. 1086).　　(d) S.I. 1967/579 (1967 I, p. 1787).
(e) S.I. 1968/428 (1968 I, p. 1129).

STATUTORY INSTRUMENTS

## 1969 No. 544

## PRICES AND INCOMES

## The Awards and Settlements (Temporary Continuation of Standstill) (No. 1) Order 1969

| | |
|---|---|
| *Made* - - - | 15*th April* 1969 |
| *Laid before Parliament* | 18*th April* 1969 |
| *Coming into Operation* | 19*th April* 1969 |

Whereas by virtue of a Reference to the National Board for Prices and Incomes under section 2(1) of the Prices and Incomes Act 1966(a) (the text whereof was published on 24th December 1968 in the Edinburgh Gazette) the implementation of the agreement described in Article 2 hereof relating to the pay of certain workers employed by members of the Electrical Contractors' Association of Scotland was forbidden by section 15(2) of that Act ;

And whereas before the said implementation ceased to be so forbidden a Report of the Board on the said Reference was published on 20th March 1969(b) with a recommendation adverse to the implementation of the said agreement ;

And whereas by virtue of the said recommendation and subsections (1) and (2)(a) of section 1 of the Prices and Incomes Act 1967(c) the said section 15(2) continued to apply to the implementation of the said agreement as it applied up to the date of publication of the said Report :

Now, therefore, the Secretary of State, having given notice under section 1(2)(a) of the said Act of 1967 within a period of ten days after the date of the said publication, of a proposal to make this Order, and having taken into consideration representations duly made in pursuance of the said notice, in exercise of the powers conferred on her by section 1(2)(b) of the said Act of 1967, as amended by section 3(2) of the Prices and Incomes Act 1968(d), and of all other powers enabling her in that behalf, hereby makes the following Order :—

1.—(1) This Order, which may be cited as the Awards and Settlements (Temporary Continuation of Standstill) (No. 1) Order 1969, shall come into operation on 19th April 1969.

(2) The Interpretation Act 1889(e) shall apply for the interpretation of this Order as it applies for the interpretation of an Act of Parliament.

2. The Secretary of State hereby directs that section 15(2) of the Prices and Incomes Act 1966 shall continue to apply to forbid the implementation up to and including 23rd November 1969 of the agreement made on 18th December 1968 between the Electrical Contractors' Association of Scotland and the

---

(a) 1966 c. 33.
(b) Report No. 108 entitled "Pay and conditions in the Electrical Contracting Industry in Scotland" (Cmnd. 3966).     (c) 1967 c. 53.
(d) 1968 c. 42.     (e) 1889 c. 63.

Electrical and Electronic Trades Union providing, with effect from 18th December 1968, for increases in the hourly rates of wages of chargehands, journeymen electricians, journeymen armature winders and apprentices employed by members of the said Association.

15th April 1969.

*Barbara Castle,*
First Secretary of State and
Secretary of State for Employment and Productivity.

## EXPLANATORY NOTE

*(This Note is not part of the Order.)*

This Order, which has effect from 19th April 1969, provides for the further continuation until 23rd November 1969 of the standstill on the implementation of an agreement relating to the pay of certain workers employed by members of the Electrical Contractors' Association of Scotland.

STATUTORY INSTRUMENTS

## 1969 No. 546

## WAGES COUNCILS

## The Wages Regulation (Aerated Waters) (Scotland) Order 1969

| Made | - | - | - | 14th April 1969 |
|---|---|---|---|---|
| Coming into Operation | | | | 5th May 1969 |

Whereas the Secretary of State has received from the Aerated Waters Wages Council (Scotland) the wages regulation proposals set out in the Schedule hereto ;

Now, therefore, the Secretary of State in exercise of her powers under section 11 of the Wages Councils Act 1959(a), and of all other powers enabling her in that behalf, hereby makes the following Order :—

**1.** This Order may be cited as the Wages Regulation (Aerated Waters) (Scotland) Order 1969.

**2.**—(1) In this Order the expression "the specified date" means the 5th May 1969, provided that where, as respects any worker who is paid wages at intervals not exceeding seven days, that date does not correspond with the beginning of the period for which the wages are paid, the expression "the specified date" means, as respects that worker, the beginning of the next such period following that date.

(2) The Interpretation Act 1889(b) shall apply to the interpretation of this Order as it applies to the interpretation of an Act of Parliament and as if this Order and the Order hereby revoked were Acts of Parliament.

**3.** The wages regulation proposals set out in the Schedule hereto shall have effect as from the specified date and as from that date the Wages Regulation (Aerated Waters) (Scotland) Order 1968(c) shall cease to have effect.

Signed by order of the Secretary of State.
14th April 1969.

*A. A. Jarratt,*
Deputy Under Secretary of State,
Department of Employment and Productivity.

(a) 1959 c. 69.  (b) 1889 c.63.
(c) S.I. 1968/751 (1968 II, p.2122).

Article 3                           SCHEDULE

The following minimum remuneration shall be substituted for the statutory minimum remuneration fixed by the Wages Regulation (Aerated Waters) (Scotland) Order 1968 (Order A.S. (64)).


### STATUTORY MINIMUM REMUNERATION

#### PART I

#### GENERAL

1. The minimum remuneration payable to a worker to whom this Schedule applies for all work except work to which a minimum overtime rate applies under Part III, is—

    (1) in the case of a time worker, the hourly general minimum time rate payable to the worker under Part II of this Schedule;

    (2) in the case of a worker employed on piece work, piece rates each of which would yield, in the circumstances of the case, to an ordinary worker at least the same amount of money as the hourly general minimum time rate which would be payable to the worker under Part II of this Schedule if he were a time worker.


#### PART II

#### GENERAL MINIMUM TIME RATES

#### ALL WORKERS EXCEPT WORKERS IN THE ORKNEY OR SHETLAND ISLANDS

2. The general minimum time rates payable to all workers except workers in the Orkney or Shetland Islands are as follows:—

|  | Per hour | | Per week of *41 hours* | |
|---|---|---|---|---|
|  | s. | d. | s. | d. |
| **(1) Male workers aged:—** | | | | |
| 21 years or over | 5 | 1½ | 210 | 1½ |
| 20 and under 21 years | 4 | 1¼ | 168 | 3¼ |
| 19 „  „  20  „ | 3 | 9½ | 155 | 5½ |
| 18 „  „  19  „ | 3 | 3½ | 134 | 11½ |
| 17 „  „  18  „ | 2 | 9½ | 114 | 5½ |
| 16 „  „  17  „ | 2 | 4 | 95 | 8 |
| Under 16 years | 1 | 10¾ | 77 | 9 |
| **(2) Female workers aged:—** | | | | |
| 19 years or over | 3 | 9½ | 155 | 5½ |
| 18 and under 19 years | 3 | 2½ | 131 | 6½ |
| 17 „  „  18  „ | 2 | 9¼ | 113 | 7½ |
| 16 „  „  17  „ | 2 | 3¼ | 93 | 1½ |
| Under 16 years | 1 | 10½ | 76 | 10½ |


#### WORKERS IN THE ORKNEY OR SHETLAND ISLANDS

3. The general minimum time rates payable to male or female workers in the Orkney or Shetland Islands are, in each case, 1d. per hour less than the general minimum time rates specified in paragraph 2.

## Part III

### OVERTIME AND WAITING TIME
### MINIMUM OVERTIME RATES

4.—(1) Minimum overtimes rates are payable to a worker to whom this Schedule applies as follows:—

(*a*) on a Sunday or a customary holiday, for all time worked...    DOUBLE TIME

(*b*) in any week, exclusive of any time in respect of which an overtime rate is payable under the provisions of (*a*) of this sub-paragraph, for all time worked in excess of *41 hours*...    ...    TIME-AND-A-HALF

(2) In this Part of this Schedule—

(*a*) the expressions "time-and-a-half" and "double time" mean respectively:—

  (i) in the case of a time worker, one and a half times and twice the hourly general minimum time rate otherwise payable to the worker;

  (ii) in the case of a worker employed on piece work, one and a half times and twice the piece rates otherwise payable to the worker under paragraph 1(2);

(*b*) the expression "customary holiday" means—

1st and 2nd January (or, if either of these days falls on a Sunday, 3rd January shall be substituted for such day); the local Spring holiday, the local Summer holiday and the local Autumn holiday, each to be allowed on a Monday fixed by the employer and notified to the worker not less than three weeks before the holiday; and Christmas Day (or, if Christmas Day falls on a Sunday, 26th December shall be substituted).

### WAITING TIME

5.—(1) A worker is entitled to payment of the minimum remuneration specified in this Schedule for all time during which he is present on the premises of his employer unless he is present thereon in any of the following circumstances:—

(*a*) without the employer's consent, express or implied;

(*b*) for some purpose unconnected with his work and other than that of waiting for work to be given to him to perform;

(*c*) by reason only of the fact that he is resident thereon;

(*d*) during normal meal times in a room or place in which no work is being done, and he is not waiting for work to be given to him to perform.

(2) The minimum remuneration payable under sub-paragraph (1) of this paragraph to a piece worker when not engaged on piece work is that which would be applicable if he were a time worker.

### Part IV

### APPLICABILITY OF STATUTORY MINIMUM REMUNERATION

6. This Schedule applies to workers in relation to whom the Aerated Waters Wages Council (Scotland) operates, that is to say, workers employed in Scotland in the trade specified in the Schedule to the Trade Boards (Aerated Waters Trade, Scotland) (Constitution and Proceedings) Regulations 1939(a), namely:—

The manufacture, wherever carried on, of mineral or aerated waters, non-alcoholic cordials, flavoured syrups, unfermented sweet drinks, and other similar beverages, and the manufacture in unlicensed premises of brewed liquors, including:—

(*a*) the operations of bottle washing, bottling and filling, and all other operations preparatory to the sale of any of the aforesaid liquors in bottles, jars, syphons, casks, or other similar receptacles;

(a) S.R. & O. 1939/1367 (1939 II, p.3178).

and including also:—

    (*b*) the operations of bottle washing, bottling and filling, and all subsidiary operations preparatory to the sale in bottles, jars or other similar receptacles of cider, ale, stout, porter and other alcoholic beers, where all or any of such last-mentioned operations are, or is, conducted or carried on in association with or in conjunction with all or any of the operations specified under (*a*) above so as to form a common or interchangeable form of employment for workers, and whether the two sets of operations or any of them are, or is, carried on simultaneously or not.

---

## EXPLANATORY NOTE

*(This Note is not part of the Order.)*

This Order, which has effect from 5th May 1969, sets out the statutory minimum remuneration payable in substitution for that fixed by the Wages Regulation (Aerated Waters) (Scotland) Order 1968 (Order A.S. (64)), which Order is revoked.

New provisions are printed in italics.

## 1969 No. 547

## WAGES COUNCILS

### The Wages Regulation (Aerated Waters) (Scotland) (Holidays) Order 1969

| | | | |
|---|---|---|---|
| *Made* | - - - | 14*th April* 1969 |
| *Coming into Operation* | | 5*th May* 1969 |

Whereas the Secretary of State has received from the Aerated Waters Wages Council (Scotland) the wages regulation proposals set out in the Schedule hereto ;

Now, therefore, the Secretary of State in exercise of her powers under section 11 of the Wages Councils Act 1959(**a**), and of all other powers enabling her in that behalf, hereby makes the following Order :—

**1.** This Order may be cited as the Wages Regulation (Aerated Waters) (Scotland) (Holidays) Order 1969.

**2.**—(1) In this Order the expression "the specified date" means the 5th May 1969, provided that where, as respects any worker who is paid wages at intervals not exceeding seven days, that date does not correspond with the beginning of the period for which the wages are paid, the expression "the specified date" means, as respects that worker, the beginning of the next such period following that date.

(2) The Interpretation Act 1889(**b**) shall apply to the interpretation of this Order as it applies to the interpretation of an Act of Parliament and as if this Order and the Order hereby revoked were Acts of Parliament.

**3.** The wages regulation proposals set out in the Schedule hereto shall have effect as from the specified date and as from that date the Wages Regulation (Aerated Waters) (Scotland) (Holidays) Order 1968(**c**) shall cease to have effect.

Signed by order of the Secretary of State.

*A. A. Jarratt,*
Deputy Under Secretary of State,
Department of Employment and Productivity.

14th April 1969.

---

(**a**) 1959 c. 69.            (**b**) 1889 c.63.
(**c**) S.I. 1968/752 (1968 II, p.2126).

Article 3    SCHEDULE

The following provisions as to holidays and holiday remuneration shall be substituted for the provisions as to holidays and holiday remuneration set out in the Wages Regulation (Aerated Waters) (Scotland) (Holidays) Order, 1968 (hereinafter referred to as "Order A.S. (65)").

PART I

APPLICATION

1. This Schedule applies to every worker for whom statutory minimum remuneration has been fixed.

PART II

CUSTOMARY HOLIDAYS

2.—(1) An employer shall allow to every worker in his employment to whom this Schedule applies a holiday (hereinafter referred to as a "customary holiday") in each year on the days specified in the following sub-paragraph, provided that the worker has been in his employment for a period of not less than four weeks immediately preceding the holiday, and (unless excused by the employer or absent by reason of the proved illness of, or accident to, the worker) has worked for the employer throughout the last three working days on which work was available to him immediately preceding the customary holiday.

(2) The said customary holidays are:—

1st and 2nd January (or, if either of these days falls on a Sunday, 3rd January shall be substituted for such day);
the local Spring holiday,
the local Summer holiday and
the local Autumn holiday,
each to be allowed on a Monday fixed by the employer and notified to the worker not less than three weeks before the holiday; and
Christmas Day (or, if Christmas Day falls on a Sunday, 26th December shall be substituted).

(3) Notwithstanding the preceding provisions of this paragraph, an employer may (except where in the case of a woman or young person such a requirement would be unlawful) require a worker who is otherwise entitled to any customary holiday under the foregoing provisions of this Schedule to work thereon, and, in lieu of any such holiday on which he so works, the worker shall be entitled to be allowed a day's holiday (hereinafter referred to as a "holiday in lieu of a customary holiday") on a weekday on which he would normally work within the period of 28 days next ensuing, provided that where a worker is required to work on the customary holiday fixed in respect of the local Spring, Summer or Autumn holiday, the holiday in lieu of the customary holiday shall be allowed on a Monday.

(4) A worker who is required to work on a customary holiday shall be paid:—

(a) for all time worked thereon at the minimum rate then appropriate to the worker for work on a customary holiday; and

(b) in respect of the holiday in lieu of the customary holiday, holiday remuneration in accordance with paragraph 8.

PART III

ANNUAL HOLIDAY AND LONG SERVICE ANNUAL HOLIDAY

3.—(1) Subject to the provisions of this paragraph and of paragraph 4, in addition to the holidays specified in Part II of this Schedule, an employer shall between the date on which the provisions of this Schedule become effective and 31st October 1969 and in each succeeding year between 1st April and 31st October allow a holiday (hereinafter referred to as an "annual holiday") to every worker in his employment to whom this Schedule applies who has been employed by him during the 12 months immediately preceding the commencement of the holiday season in that year for any of the periods of employment (calculated in accordance with the provisions of paragraph 12) set out in the Table below and the duration of the annual holiday shall in the case of each such worker be related to that period as follows:—

| Period of employment | Duration of holiday for workers with a normal working week of— | | | |
|---|---|---|---|---|
| | Six days | Five days | Four days | Three days or less |
| Column 1 | Column 2 | Column 3 | Column 4 | Column 5 |
| At least 48 weeks ... ... | 12 days | 10 days | 8 days | 6 days |
| „ „ 44 „ ... ... | 11 „ | 9 „ | 7 „ | 5 „ |
| „ „ 40 „ ... ... | 10 „ | 8 „ | 6 „ | 5 „ |
| „ „ 36 „ ... ... | 9 „ | 7 „ | 6 „ | 4 „ |
| „ „ 32 „ ... ... | 8 „ | 6 „ | 5 „ | 4 „ |
| „ „ 28 „ ... ... | 7 „ | 5 „ | 4 „ | 3 „ |
| „ „ 24 „ ... ... | 6 „ | 5 „ | 4 „ | 3 „ |
| „ „ 20 „ ... ... | 5 „ | 4 „ | 3 „ | 2 „ |
| „ „ 16 „ ... ... | 4 „ | 3 „ | 2 „ | 2 „ |
| „ „ 12 „ ... ... | 3 „ | 2 „ | 2 „ | 1 day |
| „ „ 8 „ ... ... | 2 „ | 1 day | 1 day | 1 „ |
| „ „ 4 „ ... ... | 1 day | 1 „ | — | — |

(2) Notwithstanding the provisions of the foregoing sub-paragraph:—

(a) The number of days of annual holiday which an employer is required to allow to a worker in any holiday season shall not exceed in the aggregate twice the number of days constituting the worker's normal working week.

(b) The duration of the worker's annual holiday in the holiday season ending on 31st October 1969, shall be reduced by any days of annual holiday duly allowed to him by the employer under the provisions of Order A.S. (65) between 1st April 1969 and the date on which the provisions of this Schedule become effective.

(3) In this Schedule the expression "holiday season" means in relation to the year 1969 the period commencing on 1st April 1969 and ending on 31st October 1969, and, in each succeeding year, the period commencing on 1st April and ending on 31st October of the same year.

4. An annual holiday shall be allowed on consecutive working days, being days on which the worker is normally called upon to work for the employer, and days of annual holiday shall be treated as consecutive, notwithstanding that some other holiday intervenes:

Provided that—

(1) Where the duration of an annual holiday to which a worker is entitled exceeds the period constituting the worker's normal working week the holiday may be allowed in two separate periods of consecutive working days, and in that event, notwithstanding the foregoing provisions of this Schedule, the worker shall be allowed the annual holiday as follows:—

(a) as to one period, not being less than the period constituting the worker's normal working week, during the holiday season, and

(b) as to the other period either during the holiday season or within the period ending on 31st March immediately following the holiday season.

(2) One day of annual holiday may be allowed on a non-consecutive working day falling within the holiday season (or after the holiday season in the circumstances specified in proviso (1)(*b*) of this paragraph) where the said annual holiday or, as the case may be, such separate period, is allowed immediately after a customary holiday or so that a customary holiday intervenes.

5. *Subject to the provisions of this paragraph, in addition to the holidays specified in paragraphs 2 and 3 an employer shall in the year commencing on 1st April 1969 and commencing on 1st April in each succeeding year allow an additional annual holiday (hereinafter referred to as a "long service annual holiday") amounting to the worker's normal working week to every worker to whom this Schedule applies whose contract of employment shall have existed continuously for five years or more at each 1st April.*

6. *Where a worker becomes entitled to a long service annual holiday in accordance with the provisions of paragraph 5, the holiday shall be allowed in one period of consecutive working days at a time to be fixed by the employer which need not be within the holiday season.*

7. An employer shall give to a worker reasonable notice of the commencing date or dates and of the duration of his annual holiday, *and of the commencing date of his long service annual holiday.* Such notice may be given individually to the worker or by the posting of a notice in the place where the worker is employed.

Part IV

## HOLIDAY REMUNERATION

### A—CUSTOMARY HOLIDAYS

8.—(1) Subject to the provisions of this paragraph, for each day of holiday to which a worker is entitled under Part II of this Schedule he shall be paid by the employer holiday remuneration equal to the appropriate statutory minimum remuneration to which he would have been entitled if the day had not been a day of holiday and he had been employed on work to which statutory minimum remuneration applies for the time usually worked by him on that day of the week:

Provided, however, that payment of the said holiday remuneration is subject to the condition that the worker (unless excused by the employer or absent by reason of the proved illness of, or accident to, the worker) presents himself for employment at the usual starting hour on each of the first two working days following the holiday.

(2) The holiday remuneration in respect of any customary holiday shall be paid by the employer to the worker on the pay day on which the wages for the second working day following the holiday are paid.

(3) The holiday remuneration in respect of any holiday in lieu of a customary holiday shall be paid on the pay day on which the wages are paid for the second working day following the holiday in lieu of a customary holiday:

Provided that the said payment shall be made immediately upon the termination of the worker's employment in the case where he ceases to be employed before being allowed a holiday in lieu of a customary holiday to which he is entitled, and in that case the condition specified in sub-paragraph (1) of this paragraph shall not apply.

### B—ANNUAL HOLIDAY AND LONG SERVICE ANNUAL HOLIDAY

9.—(1) Subject to the provisions of paragraph 10, a worker entitled to be allowed an annual holiday *or a long service annual holiday* under this Schedule shall be paid by his employer, on the last pay day preceding such holiday, one day's holiday pay (as defined in paragraph 14) in respect of each day thereof.

(2) Where under the provisions of paragraph 4, the annual holiday is taken in more than one period the holiday remuneration shall be apportioned accordingly.

10. Where any accrued holiday remuneration has been paid by the employer to the worker (in accordance with paragraph 11 of this Schedule or with Order A.S. (65) in respect of employment during any of the periods referred to in that paragraph or that Order respectively, the amount of holiday remuneration payable by the employer in respect of any *long service annual holiday* or annual holiday for which the worker has qualified by reason of employment during any of the said periods shall be reduced by the amount of the said accrued holiday remuneration unless that remuneration has been deducted from a previous payment of holiday remuneration made under the provisions of this Schedule or of Order A.S. (65).

### ACCRUED HOLIDAY REMUNERATION PAYABLE ON TERMINATION OF EMPLOYMENT

11. Subject to the provisions of this paragraph, if a worker ceases to be employed before being entitled to be allowed an annual holiday *or long service annual holiday* or before being allowed the whole of any annual holiday to which he is entitled under this Schedule, the employer shall, immediately on the termination of the employment (hereinafter referred to as "the termination date"), pay to the worker as accrued holiday remuneration:—

(1) in respect of any period of employment occuring before 1st April immediately preceding the termination date, an amount equal to the holiday remuneration to which the worker would have been entitled under the provisions of paragraph 9 if he had been allowed an annual holiday in respect of that period of employment at the termination date, LESS any holiday remuneration already paid for any day or days of annual holiday allowed subsequently to 1st April aforesaid in respect of that period of employment and,

(2) in respect of any period of employment since 31st March immediately preceding the termination date, an amount equal to one day's holiday pay (as defined in paragraph 14) multiplied by the number of days of annual holiday to which the worker would have been entitled under the provisions of paragraph 3 if by virtue of such period of employment he could have taken an annual holiday at the termination date, LESS any accrued holiday remuneration already paid by the employer to the worker in accordance with this paragraph or in accordance with the provisions of Order A.S. (65) in respect of that period *and,*

(3) *in respect of a long service annual holiday for which the worker may have qualified at 1st April immediately preceding the termination date and which he has not been allowed, an amount equal to one day's holiday pay (as defined in paragraph 14) multiplied by the number of days constituting the worker's normal working week at said 1st April:*

Provided that no worker shall be entitled to the payment by his employer of accrued holiday remuneration if he is dismissed on the grounds of misconduct and is so informed by the employer at the time of dismissal.

### Part V

### GENERAL

12. For the purposes of calculating any period of employment entitling a worker to an annual holiday or to any accrued holiday remuneration under this Schedule, the worker shall be treated:—

(1) as if he were employed for a week in respect of any week in which—

(a) he has worked for the employer for not less than 24 hours and has performed some work to which statutory minimum remuneration applies; or

(b) he has been absent throughout the week by reason of proved illness or accident (provided that the number of weeks which may be treated as weeks of employment for such reason shall not exceed eight in any such period as aforesaid); or

(c) he has been suspended throughout the week owing to shortage of work (provided that the number of weeks which may be treated as weeks of employment for such reason shall not exceed eight in any such period as aforesaid, and the number of consecutive weeks so treated shall not exceed two at any one time); and

(2) as if he were employed on any day of holiday allowed under the provisions of this Schedule, and for the purpose of the provisions of sub-paragraph (1) of this paragraph a worker who is absent on such a holiday shall be treated as having worked thereon for the employer for the number of hours ordinarily worked by him on that day of the week on work to which statutory minimum remuneration applies.

13. Where any day of annual holiday *or long service annual holiday* allowed to any worker under this Schedule falls upon a day of holiday or half-holiday to which the worker may be entitled under any enactment other than the Wages Councils Act 1959, the annual holiday shall be in addition to the said day of holiday but the said half-holiday shall be treated as part of the annual holiday.

14. In this Schedule, unless the context otherwise requires, the following expressions have the meanings hereby respectively assigned to them, that is to say:—

"Normal working week" means the number of days on which it has been usual for the worker to work in a week while in the employment of the employer during the 12 months immediately preceding the commencement of the holiday season, or, where under paragraph 11, accrued holiday remuneration is payable on the termination of the employment during the 12 months immediately preceding the termination date *where accrued holiday remuneration is due in respect of annual holiday, and during the 12 months immediately preceding 1st April where accrued holiday remuneration is due in respect of a long service annual holiday:*
Provided that—

(1) part of a day shall count as a day;

(2) no account shall be taken of any week in which the worker did not perform any work for which statutory minimum remuneration has been fixed.

"One day's holiday pay" means the appropriate proportion of the worker's weekly remuneration, that is to say,

where the worker's normal working week is six days—one sixth
where the worker's normal working week is five days—one-fifth
where the worker's normal working week is four days—one-quarter
where the worker's normal working week is three days—one-third
where the worker's normal working week is two days—one-half
where the worker's normal working week is one day—the whole,

and in this definition, "weekly remuneration" means the remuneration which the worker would be entitled to receive from the employer at the date of the holiday or, where accrued holiday remuneration is payable, at the termination date, for one week's work

(a) if working his normal working week and the daily number of hours normally worked by him (exclusive of overtime); and

(b) if paid at the appropriate rate of statutory minimum remuneration for work to which statutory minimum remuneration applies and at the same rate for any work for the same employer to which such remuneration does not apply.

"Statutory minimum remuneration" means minimum remuneration (other than holiday remuneration) fixed by a wages regulation order made by the Secretary of State to give effect to proposals submitted to her by the Wages Council.
"Week" means "pay week".

15. The provisions of this Schedule are without prejudice to any agreement for the allowance of any further holidays with pay or for the payment of additional holiday remuneration.

# EXPLANATORY NOTE

*(This Note is not part of the Order.)*

This Order, which has effect from 5th May 1969, sets out the holidays which an employer is required to allow to workers and the remuneration payable for these holidays, in substitution for the holidays and holiday remuneration fixed by the Wages Regulation (Aerated Waters) (Scotland) (Holidays) Order 1968 (Order A.S. (65)), which Order is revoked.

New provisions are printed in italics.

## STATUTORY INSTRUMENTS

### 1969 No. 549 (C.14)

### BETTING AND GAMING
### The Gaming Act 1968 (Commencement No. 3) Order 1969

*Made* - - - 15*th April* 1969

In pursuance of section 54(4) of the Gaming Act 1968(**a**), I hereby make the following Order :—

**1.** This Order may be cited as the Gaming Act 1968 (Commencement No. 3) Order 1969.

**2.** The following provisions of the Gaming Act 1968 shall come into operation on 1st May 1969, that is to say—

(*a*) sections 11(2) and 49 ;

(*b*) for the purposes of Schedules 3 and 4, those provisions of Schedule 2 which are referred to in Schedules 3 and 4 respectively ;

(*c*) Schedules 3 and 4 ; and

(*d*) paragraph 2 of Schedule 10.

*James Callaghan,*
One of Her Majesty's Principal
Secretaries of State.

Home Office,
Whitehall.
15th April 1969.

---

### EXPLANATORY NOTE
(*This Note is not part of the Order.*)

This Order brings into force, with effect from 1st May 1969, those provisions of the Gaming Act 1968 which relate to the machinery of registration of members' clubs and miners' welfare institutes for the purposes of Part II of that Act.

---

(**a**) 1968 c. 65.

## STATUTORY INSTRUMENTS

## 1969 No. 550

## BETTING AND GAMING

### The Gaming Act (Registration under Part II) Regulations 1969

|  |  |
|---|---|
| *Made* - - - - | 15*th April* 1969 |
| *Laid before Parliament* | 24*th April* 1969 |
| *Coming into Operation—* | |
| *Regulation* 4 - - - | 1*st May* 1969 |
| *Regulations* 2 *and* 3 *in accordance with Regulation* | 1(5) *and* (6) |

In pursuance of sections 13(2), 14(2) and 51 of the Gaming Act 1968(a), and after consultation with the Gaming Board for Great Britain, I hereby make the following Regulations:—

1.—(1) These Regulations may be cited as the Gaming Act (Registration under Part II) Regulations 1969.

(2) The Interpretation Act 1889(b) applies for the interpretation of these Regulations as it applies for the interpretation of an Act of Parliament.

(3) In these Regulations, "the Act" means the Gaming Act 1968.

(4) Nothing in these Regulations shall have effect in relation to any premises, or any part of any premises, in respect of which a licence under the Act is for the time being in force.

(5) Regulation 2 of these Regulations shall come into operation on the day to be appointed under section 54(4) of the Act for the purposes of section 13 of the Act.

(6) Regulation 3 of these Regulations shall come into operation on the day to be appointed under section 54(4) of the Act for the purposes of section 14 of the Act.

(7) Subject to paragraphs (5) and (6) above, these Regulations shall come into operation on 1st May 1969.

(8) These Regulations shall not extend to Scotland.

2.—(1) Section 13(1) of the Act (which prohibits bankers' games) shall not have effect in relation to the games of pontoon and chemin de fer when played on premises in respect of which a club or miners' welfare institute is for the time being registered under Part II of the Act.

(2) The reference in this Regulation to the game of pontoon does not include a reference to the game of blackjack, or to any other form of the game of pontoon

---

(a) 1968 c. 65.     (b) 1889 c. 63.

whose rules do not provide for the right to hold the bank to pass amongst the players in certain events arising in the course of play.

**3.**—(1) Where, on any day, gaming takes place on premises in respect of which a club or miners' welfare institute is for the time being registered under Part II of the Act, one or more charges (which, apart from this Regulation, would be prohibited by section 3 as applied by section 14(1) of the Act) may be made in respect of a person taking part in the gaming on that day, if the amount of the charge, or (in the case of more than one charge being made) of the charges in aggregate, does not exceed one pound in respect of that person for that day.

(2) In this Regulation, the reference to a day is a reference to the period between midday on one day and midday on the next.

**4.**—(1) An application for registration, renewal of registration or cancellation of registration under Part II of the Act shall be made in writing, in the appropriate form set out in Schedule 1 to these Regulations, by lodging the application with the clerk to the licensing authority for the petty sessions area in which the relevant premises are situated.

(2) A certificate of registration or renewal of registration under Part II of the Act shall be in the appropriate form set out in Schedule 2 to these Regulations.

(3) The register to be kept under paragraph 2 of Schedule 10 to the Act for the purposes of registration under Part II of the Act shall be in the form set out in Schedule 3 to these Regulations.

(4) Any reference in this Regulation to a form includes a reference to a form to the like effect with any variations which the circumstances may require.

*James Callaghan,*
One of Her Majesty's Principal
Secretaries of State.

Home Office,
　　Whitehall.
15th April 1969.

## SCHEDULE 1

Regulation 4(1)

*Application for registration under Part II of the Gaming Act 1968 of a Members' Club*

To the Clerk to the Gaming Licensing Committee for [the petty sessions area of in the county of ].

I, A.B. of hereby apply for the registration under Part II of the Gaming Act 1968 of the club named as follows:—

in respect of the premises consisting of:—
(*Give description sufficient to identify the premises precisely and in case of difficulty attach a plan of them*)

situated at the following address:—

The club is a bona fide members' club and is not carried on for any purpose other than those mentioned below. In particular it is not carried on for the private advantage of anyone other than its members generally. It has not less than 25 members, and is not of a merely temporary character.

The purposes of the club are as follows:—

*The club has not previously been registered under Part II of the Act in respect of these or any other premises.

*The club has previously been registered under Part II of the Act. No such registration has been cancelled (otherwise than by relinquishment). Renewal of such a registration has never been refused.

I am the [chairman] [secretary] of the club and am duly authorised to make this application on its behalf.

*Delete one or other of these paragraphs or (if both) give particulars on a sheet to be attached.

I understand that while the registration continues in force the officers of the club will be responsible to see that no one takes part in gaming of any kind (apart from slot-machines) on the premises AT ANY TIME who is not genuinely a member of the club or a guest of a member (Gaming Act 1968, ss. 12 & 23).

Dated the of 19 .

(*Signature*) A.B.

### NOTES

A copy of the application must be sent to the chief officer of police for the area, to the Collector of Customs and Excise for the area, and to the secretary of the Gaming Board for Great Britain not later than 7 days after it is sent to the licensing authority.

Notice of the application must be advertised, and a copy of the advertisement sent to the clerk to the licensing authority—see paragraph 3 of Schedule 3 to the Gaming Act 1968 and the paragraphs of Schedule 2 there referred to.

*Application for registration under Part II of the Gaming Act 1968 of a Miners' Welfare Institute*

To the Clerk to the Gaming Licensing Committee for [the petty sessions area of in the county of ].

I, A.B. of hereby apply for the registration under Part II of the Gaming Act 1968 of the miners' welfare institute (as defined in section 52(2) of that Act) named as follows:—

in respect of the premises consisting of:—
(*Give description sufficient to identify the premises precisely and in case of difficulty attach a plan of them*)

situated at the following address:—

*The institute has not previously been registered under Part II of the Act in respect of these or any other premises.

*The institute has previously been registered under Part II of the Act. No such registration has been cancelled (otherwise than by relinquishment). Renewal of such a registration has never been refused.

I am the [chairman] [secretary] of the institute and am duly authorised to make this application on its behalf.

I understand that while the registration continues in force the officers of the institute will be responsible to see that no one takes part in gaming of any kind (apart from slot-machines) on the premises AT ANY TIME who is not genuinely a member of the institute or a guest of a member (Gaming Act 1968, ss. 12 & 23).

Dated the                 of                 19  .

(*Signature*) A.B.

## NOTES

A copy of the application must be sent to the chief officer of police for the area, to the Collector of Customs and Excise for the area, and to the secretary of the Gaming Board for Great Britain not later than 7 days after it is sent to the licensing authority.

Notice of the application must be advertised, and a copy of the advertisement sent to the clerk to the licensing authority—see paragraph 3 of Schedule 3 to the Gaming Act 1968 and the paragraphs of Schedule 2 there referred to.

*Application for renewal of registration under Part II of the Gaming Act 1968*

To the Clerk to the Gaming Licensing Committee for [the petty sessions area of
                                    in the county of                                    ].

I,          A.B.          of

hereby apply for the renewal for a period of     years* of the registration under Part II of the Gaming Act 1968 of the club or miners' welfare institute named as follows:—

in respect of the premises specified in the register and situated at the following address:—

I am the [chairman] [secretary] of the club or institute and am duly authorised to make this application on its behalf.

I understand that while the registration continues in force the officers of the club or institute are responsible to see that no one takes part in gaming of any kind (apart from slot-machines) on the premises AT ANY TIME who is not genuinely a member of the club or institute or a guest of a member (Gaming Act 1968, ss. 12 & 23).

Dated the                 of                 19  .

(*Signature*) A.B.

*Application for cancellation of the registration under Part II of the Gaming Act 1968 of a club or institute*

To the Clerk to the Gaming Licensing Committee for [the petty sessions area of
                                    in the county of                                    ].

I,          A.B.          of

hereby apply for the cancellation of the registration under Part II of the Gaming Act 1968 of the club or institute named as follows:—

in respect of the premises situated at the following address:—

This application is made on the grounds specified in the statement of which two copies are attached.

Dated the                 of                 19  .

(*Signature*) A.B.

## SCHEDULE 2 Regulation 4(2)

*Certificate of registration under Part II of the Gaming Act* 1968

In the [petty sessions area of        in the county of        ].

Before the Gaming Licensing Committee

The [club] [miners' welfare institute] named as follows:—

is registered under Part II of the Gaming Act 1968 in respect of the premises consisting of:—

situated at the following address:—

[Restrictions have been imposed limiting gaming (which is not gaming by means of a machine to which Part III of the Act applies) to those parts of the premises specified in the Schedule to this Certificate.]

Unless renewed, the registration expires (subject to Schedule 3 (§ 22) to the Act) at the end of May 19 .

Dated the        of        19 .

C.D.
[Member of] [Clerk to] the Gaming
Licensing Committee

### SCHEDULE

*Parts of premises to which gaming is restricted*
[Not applicable]

*Certificate of renewal of registration under Part II of the Gaming Act* 1968

In the [petty sessions area of        in the county of        ].

Before the Gaming Licensing Committee

The registration under Part II of the Gaming Act 1968 of the club or miners' welfare institute named as follows:—

in respect of the premises specified in the register kept under paragraph 2 of Schedule 10 to the Act and situated at the following address:—

has been renewed.

[On renewal of the registration, restrictions were imposed limiting gaming (which is not gaming by means of a machine to which Part III of the Act applies) to those parts of the premises specified in the Schedule to this Certificate.]

Unless renewed, the registration expires (subject to Schedule 3 (§ 22) to the Act) at the end of May 19 .

Dated the        of        19 .

C.D.
[Member of] [Clerk to] the Gaming
Licensing Committee

### SCHEDULE

*Parts of premises to which gaming is restricted*
[Not applicable]

## SCHEDULE 3 Regulation 4(3)

*Register of Premises registered under Part II of the Gaming Act* 1968

Name of Club or Institute:—

Description of premises:—

Address of premises:—

Parts of premises to which gaming was restricted on date indicated below:—

No. 1

Brief description of the purposes of club (*or in case of miners' welfare institute, state that it is such*):—

| Date of issue or renewal | Period of validity | Restriction No. (*see above*) | Name and Address of Chairman or Secretary | Remarks (including details of refusal of renewal, cancellation or relinquishment) | |
|---|---|---|---|---|---|
| | | | | Date | Details |
| | | | | | |

## EXPLANATORY NOTE

(*This Note is not part of the Regulations.*)

These Regulations relate to the registration of members' clubs and miners' welfare institutes under Part II of the Gaming Act 1968, and make provision in relation to gaming on premises so registered.

Regulation 2 allows the games of pontoon and chemin de fer to be played on registered premises notwithstanding the general prohibition upon the playing of bankers' games. Regulation 3 allows charges to be made for gaming at a rate not exceeding £1 a person a day. These Regulations come into force with the sections of the Act to which they relate.

Regulation 4 prescribes the forms necessary for registration under Part II of the Act, including the form of register.

STATUTORY INSTRUMENTS

## 1969 No. 551

## INDUSTRIAL TRAINING

### The Industrial Training Levy (Electricity Supply) Order 1969

| | |
|---|---|
| *Made* - - - | *15th April* 1969 |
| *Laid before Parliament* | *25th April* 1969 |
| *Coming into Operation* | *7th May* 1969 |

The Secretary of State after approving proposals submitted by the Electricity Supply Industry Training Board for the imposition of a further levy on employers in the electricity supply industry and in exercise of her powers under section 4 of the Industrial Training Act 1964(a) and of all other powers enabling her in that behalf hereby makes the following Order :—

*Title and Commencement*

**1.** This Order may be cited as the Industrial Training Levy (Electricity Supply) Order 1969 and shall come into operation on 7th May 1969.

*Interpretation*

**2.**—(1) In this Order unless the context otherwise requires :—
  (*a*) "activities of the electricity supply industry" means any activities which, subject to the provisions of paragraph 2 of Schedule 1 to the industrial training order, are specified in paragraph 1 of that Schedule as activities of the electricity supply industry ;

  (*b*) "an appeal tribunal" means an industrial tribunal established under section 12 of the Industrial Training Act 1964 ;

  (*c*) "assessment" means an assessment of an employer to the levy ;

  (*d*) "emoluments" means all emoluments assessable to income tax under Schedule E (other than pensions), being emoluments from which tax under that Schedule is deductible, whether or not tax in fact falls to be deducted from any particular payment thereof ;

  (*e*) "employer" means any of the following employers in the electricity supply industry, that is to say—
   (i) the Electricity Council ;
   (ii) the Central Electricity Generating Board ;
   (iii) an Area Electricity Board ;
   (iv) the North of Scotland Hydro-Electric Board ;
   (v) the South of Scotland Electricity Board ;
   (vi) the London Transport Board ;

  (*f*) "the fourth base period" means the period of twelve months that commenced on 1st April 1967 ;

(a) 1964 c. 16.

(g) "the fourth levy period" means the period commencing with the day on which this Order comes into operation and ending on 31st March 1970 ;

(h) "the Industrial Training Board" means the Electricity Supply Industry Training Board ;

(i) "the industrial training order" means the Industrial Training (Electricity Supply Board) Order 1965(a) ;

(j) "the levy" means the levy imposed by the Industrial Training Board in respect of the fourth levy period ;

(k) "notice" means a notice in writing.

(2) The Interpretation Act 1889(b) shall apply to the interpretation of this Order as it applies to the interpretation of an Act of Parliament.

*Imposition of the Levy*

3.—(1) The levy to be imposed by the Industrial Training Board on employers in respect of the fourth levy period shall be assessed in accordance with the provisions of this Article.

(2) The levy shall be assessed by the Industrial Training Board in respect of each employer.

(3) The amount of the levy imposed on an employer shall be a sum equal to 0·035 per cent. of the emoluments of all persons employed by the employer in activities of the electricity supply industry in the fourth base period, the said sum being rounded down to the nearest £1.

*Assessment Notices*

4.—(1) The Industrial Training Board shall serve an assessment notice on every employer.

(2) An assessment notice shall state the Industrial Training Board's address for the service of a notice of appeal or of an application for an extension of time for appealing.

(3) An assessment notice may be served on an employer by sending it by post to the employer's principal office.

*Payment of the Levy*

5.—(1) Subject to the provisions of this Article and of Articles 6 and 7, the amount of an assessment appearing in an assessment notice served by the Industrial Training Board shall be payable by the employer to the Board in four equal instalments, and the said instalments shall be due respectively one, four, seven and ten months after the date of the notice.

(2) An instalment of an assessment shall not be recoverable by the Industrial Training Board until there has expired the time allowed for appealing against the assessment by Article 7(1) of this Order and any further period or periods of time that the Industrial Training Board or an appeal tribunal may have allowed for appealing under paragraph (2) or (3) of that Article or, where an appeal is brought, until the appeal is decided or withdrawn.

---

(a) S.I. 1965/1256 (1965 II, p. 3548).                    (b) 1889 c. 63.

*Withdrawal of Assessment*

**6.**—(1) The Industrial Training Board may, by notice served on the employer in the same manner as an assessment notice, withdraw an assessment if the employer has appealed against that assessment under the provisions of Article 7 of this Order and the appeal has not been entered in the Register of Appeals kept under the appropriate Regulations specified in paragraph (4) of that Article.

(2) The withdrawal of an assessment shall be without prejudice to the power of the Board to serve a further assessment notice on the employer.

*Appeals*

**7.**—(1) An employer assessed to the levy may appeal to an appeal tribunal against the assessment within one month from the date of the service of the assessment notice or within any further period or periods of time that may be allowed by the Industrial Training Board or an appeal tribunal under the following provisions of this Article.

(2) The Industrial Training Board by notice may for good cause allow an employer assessed to the levy to appeal to an appeal tribunal against the assessment at any time within the period of four months from the date of the service of the assessment notice or within such further period or periods as the said Board may allow before such time as may then be limited for appealing has expired.

(3) If the Industrial Training Board shall not allow an application for extension of time for appealing, an appeal tribunal shall upon application made to the tribunal by the employer assessed to the levy have the like powers as the said Board under the foregoing paragraph.

(4) An appeal or an application to an appeal tribunal under this Article shall be made in accordance with the Industrial Tribunals (England and Wales) Regulations 1965(**a**) as amended by the Industrial Tribunals (England and Wales) (Amendment) Regulations 1967(**b**), except where the employer is the North of Scotland Hydro-Electric Board or the South of Scotland Electricity Board in which case the appeal or application shall be made in accordance with the Industrial Tribunals (Scotland) Regulations 1965(**c**) as amended by the Industrial Tribunals (Scotland) (Amendment) Regulations 1967(**d**).

(5) The powers of an appeal tribunal under paragraph (3) of this Article may be exercised by the President of the Industrial Tribunals (England and Wales) or by the President of the Industrial Tribunals (Scotland) as the case may be.

*Evidence*

**8.**—(1) Upon the discharge of an employer's liability under an assessment the Industrial Training Board shall if so requested issue to the employer a certificate to that effect.

(2) The production in any proceedings of a document purporting to be certified by the Secretary of the Industrial Training Board to be a true copy

---

(a) S.I. 1965/1101 (1965 II, p. 2805).     (b) S.I. 1967/301 (1967 I, p. 1040).
(c) S.I. 1965/1157 (1965 II, p. 3266).     (d) S.I. 1967/302 (1967 I, p. 1050).

of an assessment or other notice issued by the Board or purporting to be a certificate such as is mentioned in the foregoing paragraph of this Article shall, unless the contrary is proved, be sufficient evidence of the document and of the facts stated therein.

15th April 1969.

*Barbara Castle,*
First Secretary of State and Secretary
of State for Employment and Productivity.

---

## EXPLANATORY NOTE
*(This Note is not part of the Order.)*

This Order which is made by the Secretary of State for Employment and Productivity gives effect to proposals submitted by the Electricity Supply Industry Training Board for the imposition of a further levy on employers in the electricity supply industry for the purpose of raising money towards the expenses of the Board.

The levy is to be imposed in respect of the fourth levy period commencing with the date on which this Order comes into operation and ending on 31st March 1970. The levy will be assessed by the industrial training board and there will be a right of appeal against an assessment to an industrial tribunal.

## 1969 No. 552 (S.50)

## BETTING AND GAMING

## The Gaming Act (Registration under Part II) (Scotland) Regulations 1969

| | | |
|---|---|---|
| Made - - - | 15th April 1969 |
| Laid before Parliament | 24th April 1969 |
| Coming into Operation | |
| Regulation 4 | 1st May 1969 |

Regulations 2 and 3 in accordance with Regulations 1(5) and (6)

In exercise of the powers conferred upon me by sections 13(2), 14(2), and 51 of the Gaming Act 1968(a), and of all other powers enabling me in that behalf, and after consultation with the Gaming Board for Great Britain, I hereby make the following regulations :—

1.—(1) These Regulations may be cited as the Gaming Act (Registration under Part II) (Scotland) Regulations 1969.

(2) The Interpretation Act 1889(b) applies for the interpretation of these regulations as it applies for the interpretation of an Act of Parliament.

(3) In these regulations, "the Act" means the Gaming Act 1968.

(4) Nothing in these regulations shall have effect in relation to any premises, or any part of any premises, in respect of which a licence under the Act is for the time being in force.

(5) Regulation 2 of these regulations shall come into operation on the day to be appointed under section 54(4) of the Act for the purposes of section 13 of the Act.

(6) Regulation 3 of these regulations shall come into operation on the day to be appointed under section 54(4) of the Act for the purposes of section 14 of the Act.

(7) Subject to paragraphs (5) and (6) above, these regulations shall come into operation on 1st May 1969.

2.—(1) Section 13(1) of the Act (which prohibits bankers' games) shall not have effect in relation to the games of pontoon and chemin de fer when played on premises in respect of which a club or miners' welfare institute is for the time being registered under Part II of the Act.

(2) The reference in this Regulation to the game of pontoon does not include a reference to the game of blackjack, or to any other form of the game of pontoon whose rules do not provide for the right to hold the bank to pass amongst the players in certain events arising in the course of play.

(a) 1968 c. 65.    (b) 1889 c. 63.

**3.**—(1) Where, on any day, gaming takes place on premises in respect of which a club or miner's welfare institute is for the time being registered under Part II of the Act, one or more charges (which, apart from this Regulation, would be prohibited by section 3 as applied by section 14(1) of the Act) may be made in respect of a person taking part in the gaming on that day, if the amount of the charge, or (in the case of more than one charge being made) of the charges in aggregate, does not exceed one pound in respect of that person for that day.

(2) In this regulation, the reference to a day is a reference to the period between midday on one day and midday on the next.

**4.**—(1) An application for registration, renewal of registration or cancellation of registration under Part II of the Act shall be made in writing, in the appropriate form set out in Schedule 1 to these regulations, by lodging the application with the sheriff clerk for the county or other area in which the relevant premises are situated.

(2) A certificate of registration or renewal of registration under Part II of the Act shall be in the appropriate form set out in Schedule 2 to these regulations.

(3) The register to be kept under paragraph 2 of Schedule 10 to the Act for the purposes of registration under Part II of the Act shall be in the form set out in Schedule 3 to these regulations.

(4) Any reference in this regulation to a form includes a reference to a form to the like effect with any variations which the circumstances may require.

*William Ross,*
One of Her Majesty's Principal
Secretaries of State.

St. Andrew's House,
Edinburgh, 1.
15th April 1969.

SCHEDULE 1

Regulation 4(1)

*Application for registration under Part II of the*
*Gaming Act* 1968 *of a Members' Club*

To the Sheriff Clerk, Sheriff Clerk's Office [                 ]

I,      A.B.      of

hereby apply for the registration under Part II of the Gaming Act 1968 of the club named as follows: —

in respect of the premises consisting of: —

(*Give description sufficient to identify the premises precisely and in case of difficulty attach a plan of them*)

situated at the following address: —

The club is a bona fide members' club and is not carried on for any purpose other than those mentioned below. In particular it is not carried on for the private advantage of anyone other than its members generally. It has not less than 25 members, and is not of a merely temporary character. It is not established for the principal purpose of gaming other than bridge or whist or both bridge and whist.

The purposes of the club are as follows: —

*The club has not previously been registered under Part II of the Act in respect of these or any other premises.

*The club has previously been registered under Part II of the Act. No such registration has been cancelled (otherwise than by relinquishment). Renewal of such a registration has never been refused.

*Delete one or other of these paragraphs or (if both) give particulars on a sheet to be attached.

I am the [chairman] [secretary] of the club and am duly authorised to make this application on its behalf.

I understand that while the registration continues in force the officers of the club will be responsible to see that no one takes part in gaming of any kind (apart from gaming by means of slot-machines) on the premises AT ANY TIME who is not genuinely a member of the club or a guest of a member (Gaming Act 1968, ss 12 & 23).

Dated the       of                    19  .

(*Signature*) A.B.

## NOTES

A copy of the application must be sent to the chief constable for the area, to the Collector of Customs and Excise for the area, and to the secretary of the Gaming Board for Great Britain not later than 7 days after it is sent to the sheriff clerk.

Notice of the application must be advertised, and a copy of the advertisement sent to the sheriff clerk—see paragraph 5 of Schedule 4 to the Gaming Act 1968 and paragraph 10 of Schedule 2 there referred to.

*Application for registration under Part II of the Gaming Act 1968 of a Miners' Welfare Institute*

To the Sheriff Clerk, Sheriff Clerk's Office [                                    ]

I,       A.B.       of

hereby apply for the registration under Part II of the Gaming Act 1968 of the miners' welfare institute (as defined in section 52(2) of that Act) named as follows: —

in respect of the premises consisting of: —

(*Give description sufficient to identify the premises precisely and in case of difficulty attach a plan of them*)

situated at the following address: —

*The institute has not previously been registered under Part II of the Act in respect of these or any other premises.

*The institute has previously been registered under Part II of the Act.

No such registration has been cancelled (otherwise than by relinquishment). Renewal of such a registration has never been refused.

*Delete one or other of these paragraphs or (if both) give particulars on a sheet to be attached.

I am the [chairman] [secretary] of the institute and am duly authorised to make this application on its behalf.

I understand that while the registration continues in force the officers of the institute will be responsible to see that no one takes part in gaming of any kind (apart from gaming by means of slot-machines) on the premises AT ANY TIME who is not genuinely a member of the institute or a guest of a member (Gaming Act 1968, ss 12 & 23).

Dated the       of                    19  .

(*Signature*) A.B.

## NOTES

A copy of the application must be sent to the chief constable for the area, to the Collector of Customs and Excise for the area, and to the secretary of the Gaming Board for Great Britain not later than 7 days after it is sent to the licensing authority.

Notice of the application must be advertised, and a copy of the advertisement sent to the sheriff clerk—see paragraph 5 of Schedule 4 to the Gaming Act 1968 and paragraph 10 of Schedule 2 there referred to.

### Application for renewal of registration under Part II of the Gaming Act 1968

To the Sheriff Clerk, Sheriff Clerk's Office [                                    ]

*not more*
*than ten.*

I,       A.B.       of

hereby apply for the renewal for a period of       years of the registration under Part II of the Gaming Act 1968 of the club or miners' welfare institute named as follows: —

in respect of the premises specified in the register and situated at the following address: —

I am the [chairman] [secretary] of the club or institute and am duly authorised to make this application on its behalf.

I understand that while the registration continues in force the officers of the club or institute are responsible to see that no one takes part in gaming of any kind (apart from gaming by means of slot-machines) on the premises AT ANY TIME who is not genuinely a member of the club or institute or a guest of a member (Gaming Act 1968, ss 12 & 23).

Dated the       of       19  .

*(Signature)* A.B.

### Appication for cancellation of the registration under Part II of the Gaming Act 1968 of a club or institute

To the Sheriff Clerk, Sheriff Clerk's Office [                                    ]

I,       A.B.       of

hereby apply for the cancellation of the registration under Part II of the Gaming Act 1968 of the club or institute named as follows: —

in respect of the premises situated at the following address: —

This application is made on the grounds specified in the statement of which two copies are attached.

Dated the       of       19  .

*(Signature)* A.B.

## SCHEDULE 2

Regulation 4(2)

### Certificate of registration under Part II of the Gaming Act 1968

In the Sheriff Court of [                    ] at [                            ]

Before Sheriff [                                    ]

The [club] [miners' welfare institute] named as follows: —
is registered under Part II of the Gaming Act 1968 in respect of the premises
consisting of: —

situated at the following address: —

[Restrictions have been imposed limiting gaming (which is not gaming by
means of a machine to which Part III of the Act applies) to those parts of the
premises specified in the Schedule to this Certificate.]

Unless renewed, the registration expires (subject to Schedule 4 § 20 to
the Act) at the end of December 19 .

Dated the          of                          19 .

C.D.
Sheriff Clerk

## SCHEDULE

*Parts of premises to which gaming is restricted*
[Not applicable]

*Certificate of renewal of registration under*
*Part II of the Gaming Act 1968*

In the Sheriff Court of [                    ] at [                              ]
Before Sheriff [                                    ]
The registration under Part II of the Gaming Act 1968 of the club or
miners' welfare institute named as follows: —
in respect of the premises specified in the register kept under paragraph 2 of
Schedule 10 to the Act and situated at the following address: —
has been renewed.

[On renewal of the registration, restrictions were imposed limiting gaming
(which is not gaming by means of a machine to which Part III of the Act
applies) to those parts of the premises specified in the Schedule to this Cer-
tificate].

Unless renewed, the registration expires (subject to Schedule 4 (§ 20) to
the Act) at the end of December 19 .
Dated the          of                          19 .

C.D.
Sheriff Clerk

## SCHEDULE

*Parts of premises to which gaming is restricted*
[Not applicable]

## SCHEDULE 3

Regulation 4(3)

*Register of Premises registered under*
*Part II of the Gaming Act 1968*

Name of Club or Institute: —
Description of premises: —
Address of premises: —
Parts of premises to which gaming was restricted on date indicated below: —
No. 1

Brief description of the purposes of club (*or in case of miners' welfare institute, state that it is such*):—

| Date of issue or renewal | Period of Validity | Restriction No. (*see above*) | Name and Address of Chairman or Secretary | Remarks (including details of refusal of renewal, cancellation or relinquishment) | |
|---|---|---|---|---|---|
| | | | | Date | Details |
| | | | | | |

## EXPLANATORY NOTE

### (*This Note is not part of the Regulations.*)

These Regulations relate to the registration in Scotland of members' clubs and miners' welfare institutes under Part II of the Gaming Act 1968, and makes provision in relation to gaming on premises so registered.

Regulation 2 allows the games of pontoon and chemin de fer to be played on registered premises notwithstanding the general prohibition upon the playing of bankers' games. Regulation 3 allows charges to be made for gaming at a rate not exceeding £1 a person a day. These Regulations come into force with the sections of the Act to which they relate.

Regulation 4 prescribes the forms necessary for registration under Part II of the Act, including the form of the register.

S T A T U T O R Y   I N S T R U M E N T S

## 1969 No. 553

## PENSIONS

## The Overseas Service (Pensions Supplement) Regulations 1969

|  |  |
|---|---|
| Made - - - - | *15th April* 1969 |
| *Laid before Parliament* | *23rd April* 1969 |
| *Coming into Operation* | *24th April* 1969 |

In exercise of the powers conferred on me by section 3 of the Pensions (Increase) Act 1962(**a**), article 2 of the Minister of Overseas Development (No. 1) Order 1964(**b**), sections 3(3) and 5(2) of the Pensions (Increase) Act 1965(**c**) and section 2(2) of, and paragraphs 9 and 10 of Schedule 2 to, the Pensions (Increase) Act 1969(**d**) and with the approval of the Minister for the Civil Service, I hereby make the following Regulations: —

### PART I

CITATION, COMMENCEMENT AND INTERPRETATION

**1.** These Regulations may be cited as the Overseas Service (Pensions Supplement) Regulations 1969 and shall come into operation on 24th April 1969.

**2.**—(1) In these Regulations, unless the context otherwise requires, the following expressions have the meanings hereby respectively assigned to them, that is to say: —

" basic pension " means the overseas pension awarded with effect from the date of the officer's retirement from overseas service (or if it commenced after that date, which would have been so awarded), or in the case of a pension in respect of the services of any person other than the pensioner, the pension first awarded less the amount of any increase, bonus or other allowance howsover authorised which may have been included in the amount of the award by virtue of the pension having been determined by reference to conditions existing prior to any specified date ;

" dependent pensioner " means (1) a person in receipt of an overseas pension in respect of the service of an overseas officer which is payable either by the Government of an overseas territory or in accordance with an enactment, scheme or other instrument specified in Schedule 2 to these Regulations as having been approved for the purposes of section 3 of the Act of 1962, or (2) a person in receipt of a pension payable under section 5(1) of the Superannuation (Miscellaneous Provisions) Act, 1967(**e**) in respect of the service of an officer under the government of the former mandated territory of Palestine :

" the Minister " means the Minister of Overseas Development ;

" notional pension " means the pension which would have been awarded under the Oversea Superannuation Scheme to a person to whom Part III of these Regulations applies if the pensionable emoluments taken into

---

(**a**) 1962 c. 2.          (**b**) S.I. 1964/1849 (1964 III, p. 4032).
(**c**) 1965 c. 78.     (**d**) 1969 c. 7.        (**e**) 1967 c. 28.

account under the Scheme had not been reduced in accordance with the provisions of Regulation 21(2) of the Oversea Superannuation Scheme (Consolidation) Regulations 1963 or, in the case of a person in receipt of a pension awarded under any previous Regulations made by the Secretary of State under the Oversea Superannuation Scheme, in accordance with the corresponding provision of those previous Regulations ;

" overseas increase " means any addition to the amount of basic pension, or the aggregate of two or more such additions, paid by the authority by whom the pension is payable and includes any increase, bonus or allowance so paid in respect of that pension howsoever authorised ;

" overseas territory " has the same meaning as in the Act of 1962 ;

" the Regulations " in part III of these Regulations means the Oversea Superannuation Scheme (Consolidation) Regulations 1963 and a reference to any provision of those Regulations shall, in the case of a person in receipt of a pension awarded under any previous Regulations made by the Secretary of State under the Oversea Superannuation Scheme, be construed as a reference to the corresponding provision of those previous Regulations ;

" the Act of " any specified year means the Pensions (Increase) Act of that year.

(2) Unless the context otherwise requires, any reference in these Regulations to any enactment shall be construed as a reference to that enactment as amended, extended or applied by or under any other enactment.

(3) The Interpretation Act 1889(a) shall apply for the interpretation of these Regulations as it applies for the interpretation of an Act of Parliament and as if these Regulations and the Regulations hereby revoked were Acts of Parliament.

## PART II

### SUPPLEMENTS IN RESPECT OF OFFICERS' PENSIONS

**3.** This Part of these Regulations shall apply to any person in receipt of a pension described in Schedule 3 to the Act of 1962 in respect of his own service who is certified as having been an overseas officer in respect of that service in accordance with section 3(2) of the Act of 1962, and to any person in receipt of a pension in respect of his own service payable under section 5(1) of the Superannuation (Miscellaneous Provisions) Act 1967.

**4.** Subject to the provisions of section 3 of the Act of 1962 and of these Regulations, the supplement payable to a person to whom this Part of these Regulations applies and—

(a) who is in receipt of a pension determined by reference to emoluments payable prior to the date specified in the first column of Schedule 1 to these Regulations in relation to the country from which he finally retired or, in the case of a person who retired from service under the United Kingdom Government or the Crown Agents for Oversea Governments and Administrations or the Central Office of the Oversea Audit Department, payable prior to 1st April 1947 ; or

(a) 1889 c. 63.

(b) who retired from the service of the Egyptian Government,

may be of such an amount that when aggregated with any overseas increase paid to such person corresponds with the aggregate of the amounts which would be payable—

(i) under section 1 of the Act of 1944(a) if his basic pension were specified in the First Schedule to that Act and had been determined by reference to a rate of emoluments received prior to 1st April 1947 ; and

(ii) under section 1 of the Act of 1952(a) if his basic pension were specified in the First Schedule to that Act and had begun before 1st April 1948 ; and

(iii) under section 1 of the Act of 1956(a) if his basic pension were specified in the First Schedule to that Act and had begun before 1st January 1948 ; and

(iv) under section 1 of the Act of 1959(a) if his basic pension were specified in the Schedule to that Act and had begun before 2nd April 1952 ; and

(v) under sections 1 and 2 of the Act of 1962(a) if his basic pension were specified in the Schedule to the Act of 1959 and had begun before 2nd April 1956 ; and

(vi) under section 1 of the Act of 1965(a) if his basic pension were specified in Schedule 1 to that Act and had begun before 2nd April 1957 ; and

(vii) under section 1 of the Act of 1969(a) if his basic pension were specified in Schedule 1 to that Act and had begun before 2nd July 1955:

Provided that—

(1) where a pension began before 16th August 1920, the amount of increase payable under the Act of 1920(a) if that pension had been specified in section 1(2) of that Act shall be added to the aggregate of the amounts payable under the Acts of 1944, 1952, 1956, 1959, 1962, 1965 and 1969, as determined in accordance with this regulation and shall also be taken into account in determining the relevant increase for the purposes of the Acts of 1944, 1959, 1962, 1965 and 1969 ; and

(2) in the case of a pension payable to an officer who retired from the Sudan Civil Service during 1950, the following proportion of the amount of increase payable under the Act of 1944 if the pension had been specified in the First Schedule to that Act shall be added to the aggregate of the amounts payable under the Acts of 1952, 1956, 1959, 1962, 1965 and 1969 as determined in accordance with this regulation:

|  |  |  |  |
|---|---|---|---|
| (i) Retirement in January 1950 ... | ... | ... | 11/12ths |
| (ii) Retirement in February 1950 | ... | ... | 10/12ths |
| (iii) Retirement in March 1950 ... | ... | ... | 9/12ths |
| (iv) Retirement in April 1950 | ... | ... | 8/12ths |
| (v) Retirement in May 1950 | ... | ... | 7/12ths |
| (vi) Retirement in June 1950 | ... | ... | 6/12ths |
| (vii) Retirement in July 1950 | ... | ... | 5/12ths |
| (viii) Retirement in August 1950 ... | ... | ... | 4/12ths |
| (ix) Retirement in September 1950 | ... | ... | 3/12ths |
| (x) Retirement in October 1950 ... | ... | ... | 2/12ths |
| (xi) Retirement in November 1950 | ... | ... | 1/12th |

(a) See footnotes to Schedule 3.

**5.** Subject to the provisions of section 3 of the Act of 1962 and of these Regulations, the supplement payable to a person to whom this Part of these Regulations applies and whose pension is determined by reference to emoluments payable on or after the date specified in the first column and prior to the date specified in the seventh column of Schedule 1 to these Regulations in relation to the country from which he finally retired, or by reference to emoluments payable by the Government of the Federation of Rhodesia and Nyasaland may be of such an amount that when aggregated with any overseas increase paid to him corresponds with the aggregate of the amounts, if any, which would be payable under the Acts of 1952, 1956, 1959, 1962, 1965 and 1969 if his basic pension were a pension specified in the appropriate Schedule to each of these Acts and had begun—

(a) on the day immediately following the effective date of the latest general revision of salaries authorised by the Government of the overseas territory from which he retired which was taken into account in determining the amount of that pension ; or

(b) in the case of retirement from service under the United Kingdom Government or the Crown Agents for Oversea Governments and Administrations or the Central Office of the Oversea Audit Department, on the date on which the corresponding pension (as defined in regulation 11(1) of these Regulations) awarded in respect of such service would be deemed to begin in accordance with the provisions of paragraph 1 of Schedule 2 to the Act of 1969.

**6.** No supplement shall be payable to a person to whom this Part of these Regulations applies in respect of any pension determined by reference to emoluments payable on or after the date specified in the seventh column of Schedule 1 to these Regulations in relation to the country from which that person finally retired.

### PART III

#### ADDITIONAL SUPPLEMENT IN RESPECT OF PENSIONS OF OFFICERS WHO WERE SPECIAL CONTRIBUTORS TO THE OVERSEA SUPERANNUATION SCHEME

**7.** This Part of these Regulations shall apply to any person in receipt of a pension payable under the Oversea Superannuation Scheme in respect of his own service who—

(a) is eligible for the payment of a supplement under the provisions of Part II of these Regulations in respect of that pension ;

(b) was a special contributor to the Oversea Superannuation Scheme as provided in Regulation 21 of the Regulations ; and

(c) has ceased to contribute to the superannuation scheme operated under the Federated Superannuation System for Universities or such other scheme of a like nature as may have been approved under the provisions of Regulation 21(1) of the Regulations, and has become eligible for benefit under that scheme.

**8.** The Minister may pay to any person to whom this Part of these Regulations applies a special supplement of an amount which when aggregated with the supplement payable under Part II of these Regulations in respect of his pension under the Oversea Superannuation Scheme is equal to the supplement which would have been payable under the said Part II if he had been entitled to a pension of the same amount as his notional pension.

## PART IV

### SUPPLEMENTS IN RESPECT OF PENSIONS OF DEPENDENT PENSIONERS

**9.**—(1) Subject to the provisions of section 3 of the Act of 1962 and of these Regulations, the supplement payable to a dependent pensioner whose pension is determined by reference to a rate of contributions paid by, and the age of, an officer from time to time, may be of such an amount that when aggregated with any overseas increase paid to such pensioner corresponds with the aggregate of the amounts, if any, which would be payable under the Acts of 1920 to 1969 as determined in accordance with subheads (i) to (vii) of and the proviso to regulation 4 if Part II of these Regulations had applied to such pensioner.

(2) The amount ascertained in accordance with the provisions of paragraph (1) of this regulation shall be reduced in respect of any case specified in paragraphs (3), (4), (5), (6), (7), (8) or (9) of this regulation in the proportion provided for in such paragraphs in relation to that case.

(3) Where the officer in respect of whose service under the Government of an overseas territory the pension is payable left such service, or died while in such service, after 16th August 1920, not having completed the full period of contributions prior to that date, the amount payable under Section 1 of the Act of 1920 as determined in accordance with the proviso to regulation 4 shall be reduced :—

(a) in the case of an officer who completed the full period of contributions prior to leaving such service or to his death while in such service, in the same proportion that the number of years in respect of which he contributed prior to 16th August 1920 bears to the total number of years in respect of which he contributed ; and

(b) in the case of an officer who died while in such service before completing the full period of contributions, in the same proportion that the number of years in respect of which he contributed prior to 16th August 1920 bears to the total number of years in respect of which he would have contributed had he continued to contribute until he had completed the full period of contributions ; and

(c) in any other case, in the same proportion that the number of years in respect of which he contributed prior to 16th August 1920 bears to the number of years in respect of which he contributed during his service under the said Government.

(4) Where the officer in respect of whose service under the Government of an overseas territory the pension is payable left such service, or died while in such service, after the date (hereinafter referred to as the " first date ") specified in the first column, or in the case of a pension in respect of service in the Gambia, Gold Coast, Nigeria or Sierra Leone the second column, of Schedule 1 to these Regulations in relation to that overseas territory, not having completed the full period of contributions prior to the first date, the amount payable under section 1 of the Act of 1944 as determined in accordance with sub-head (i) of regulation 4 shall be reduced—

(a) in the case of an officer who completed the full period of contributions prior to leaving such service or to his death while in such service, in the same proportion that the number of years in respect of which he contributed prior to the first date bears to the total number of years in respect of which he contributed ; and (*b*) in the case of an officer who died while in such service before completing the full period of contributions, in the same proportion that the number of years in respect of which he contributed prior to the first date bears to the total number of years in respect of which he would have contributed had he continued to contribute until he had completed the full period of contributions ; and

(*c*) in any other case, in the same proportion that the number of years in respect of which he contributed prior to the first date bears to the number of years in respect of which he contributed during his service under the said Government.

(5) Where the officer in respect of whose service under the Government of an overseas territory the pension is payable left such service, or died while in such service, after the date (hereinafter referred to as the "second date") specified in the second column of Schedule 1 to these Regulations in relation to that overseas territory, not having completed the full period of contributions prior to the second date, the amount payable under section 1 of the Act of 1952 and section 1 of the Act of 1956 as determined in accordance with sub-heads (ii) and (iii) respectively of regulation 4 shall be reduced—

(*a*) in the case of an officer who completed the full period of contributions prior to leaving such service or to his death while in such service, in the same proportion that the number of years in respect of which he contributed prior to the second date bears to the total number of years in respect of which he contributed ; and

(*b*) in the case of an officer who died while in such service before completing the full period of contributions, in the same proportion that the number of years in respect of which he contributed prior to the second date bears to the total number of years in respect of which he would have contributed had he continued to contribute until he had completed the full period of contributions ; and

(*c*) in any other case, in the same proportion that the number of years in respect of which he contributed prior to the second date bears to the number of years in respect of which he contributed during his service under the said Government.

(6) Where the officer in respect of whose service under the Government of an overseas territory the pension is payable left such service, or died while in such service, after the date (hereinafter referred to as the "third date") specified in the third column of Schedule 1 to these Regulations in relation to that overseas territory, not having completed the full period of contributions prior to the third date, the amount payable under section 1 of the Act of 1959 as determined in accordance with sub-head (iv) of regulation 4 shall be reduced—

(*a*) in the case of an officer who completed the full period of contributions prior to leaving such service or to his death while in such service, in the same proportion that the number of years in respect of which he contributed prior to the third date bears to the total number of years in respect of which he contributed ; and

(*b*) in the case of an officer who died while in such service before completing the full period of contributions, in the same proportion that the number of years in respect of which he contributed prior to the third date bears to the total number of years in respect of which he would have contributed had he continued to contribute until he had completed the full period of contributions ; and

(c) in any other case, in the same proportion that the number of years in respect of which he contributed prior to the third date bears to the number of years in respect of which he contributed during his service under the said Government.

(7) Where the officer in respect of whose service under the Government of an overseas territory the pension is payable left such service, or died while in such service, after the date (hereinafter referred to as the " fourth date ") specified in the fourth column of Schedule 1 to these Regulations in relation to that overseas territory, not having completed the full period of contributions prior to the fourth date, no account shall be taken of section 2 of the Act of 1962 and the amount payable under section 1 of that Act as determined in accordance with sub-head (v) of regulation 4 shall be reduced—

(a) in the case of an officer who completed the full period of contributions prior to leaving such service or to his death while in such service, in the proportion that the number of years in respect of which he contributed prior to the fourth date bears to the total number of years in respect of which he contributed ; and

(b) in the case of an officer who died while in such service before completing the full period of contributions, in the same proportion that the number of years in respect of which he contributed prior to the fourth date bears to the total number of years in respect of which he would have contributed had he continued to contribute until he had completed the full period of contributions ; and

(c) in any other case, in the same proportion that the number of years in respect of which he contributed prior to the fourth date bears to the number of years in respect of which he contributed during his service under the said Government.

(8) Where the officer in respect of whose service under the Government of an overseas territory the pension is payable left such service, or died while in such service, after the date (hereinafter referred to as the " fifth date ") specified in the fifth column of Schedule 1 to these Regulations in relation to that overseas territory, not having completed the full period of contributions prior to the fifth date, the amount payable under section 1 of the Act of 1965 as determined in accordance with sub-head (vi) of regulation 4 shall be reduced—

(a) in the case of an officer who completed the full period of contributions prior to leaving such service or to his death while in such service, in the proportion that the number of years in respect of which he contributed prior to the fifth date bears to the total number of years in respect of which he contributed ; and

(b) in the case of an officer who died while in such service before completing the full period of contributions, in the same proportion that the number of years in respect of which he contributed prior to the fifth date bears to the total number of years in respect of which he would have contributed had he continued to contribute until he had completed the full period of contributions ; and

(c) in any other case, in the same proportion that the number of years in respect of which he contributed prior to the fifth date bears to the number of years in respect of which he contributed during his service under the said Government.

(9) Where the officer in respect of whose service under the Government of an overseas territory the pension is payable left such service, or died while in such service, after the date (hereinafter referred to as the "sixth date") specified in the sixth column of Schedule 1 to these Regulations in relation to that overseas territory, not having completed the full period of contributions prior to the sixth date, the amount payable under the Act of 1969 as determined in accordance with sub-head (vii) of regulation 4 shall be reduced—

(a) in the case of an officer who completed the full period of contributions prior to leaving such service or to his death while in such service, in the proportion that the number of years in respect of which he contributed prior to the sixth date bears to the total number of years in respect of which he contributed ; and

(b) in the case of an officer who died while in such service before completing the full period of contributions, in the same proportion that the number of years in respect of which he contributed prior to the sixth date bears to the total number of years in respect of which he would have contributed had he continued to contribute until he had completed the full period of contributions ; and

(c) in any other case, in the same proportion that the number of years in respect of which he contributed prior to the sixth date bears to the number of years in respect of which he contributed during his service under the said Government.

(10) Notwithstanding anything contained in the preceding paragraphs of this regulation, if the period of contributions commenced on or after—

(a) the first date, no account shall be taken of the Act of 1944 ;

(b) the second date, no account shall be taken of the Acts of 1952 and 1956 ;

(c) the third date, no account shall be taken of the Act of 1959 ;

(d) the fourth date, no account shall be taken of the Act of 1962 ;

(e) the fifth date, no account shall be taken of the Act of 1965 ; or

(f) the sixth date, no account shall be taken of the Act of 1969.

(11) In this regulation the expression "period of contributions" means the period during which the officer was required to contribute under any law authorising the payment of the pension to the dependent pensioner in order that such pensioner shall qualify for the maximum pension payable under that law.

**10.**—(1) Subject to the provisions of section 3 of the Act of 1962 and of these Regulations, the supplement payable to a dependent pensioner whose pension is determined by reference to emoluments received by an officer during any period of service under the Government of an overseas territory, or which would be so determined apart from any provision specifying a fixed sum as the minimum rate of pension, shall be the amount which would have been payable had Part II of these Regulations applied to such pensioner.

(2) (a) No supplement shall be payable to or in respect of a dependent pensioner being a child of the officer in respect of whose service the pension is payable when, if the pension were a children's pension as described in section 52 of the Superannuation Act 1965(a), such pension would not be

(a) 1965 c. 74.

payable solely by reason of the fact that the dependent pensioner was not in his period of childhood and full-time education as specified in section 84 of the said Act.

(b) For the purposes of this paragraph a child of the officer means a child, stepchild, illegitimate child or adopted child of the officer in respect of whose service the pension is payable or of a wife of such officer.

## PART V
### PERSONS IN RECEIPT OF MORE THAN ONE PENSION

**11.**—(1) In this regulation the expression "corresponding pension" means:—

(a) any pension which may be increased under Section 1 of the Act of 1969 ;

(b) a service pension as defined in Schedule 2 of the Act of 1962 which would be taken into account in accordance with the provisions of that Schedule for the purpose of determining the authorised increase of a relevant pension ;

(c) any pension granted in respect of service under the Central Office of the Oversea Audit Department ;

(d) any other pension in respect of which an increase is payable under any scheme (wherever in force and whether or not authorised by or under any enactment) which has been determined by the Minister for the Civil Service to be similar to the provisions of the Acts of 1944, 1952, 1956, 1962, 1965 or 1969.

(2)—(a) Where a person is in receipt of more than one pension in respect of service under any of the Governments of the overseas territories specified in Schedule 1 to these Regulations:

(i) the supplements payable shall not in the aggregate exceed the amount which would be payable if he were in receipt of a single basic pension at a rate equal to the aggregate of his basic pensions and beginning at the time when the earliest of them began, together with an overseas increase at a rate equal to the aggregate of the overseas increases awarded in respect of those pensions: Provided that for the purposes of determining the amounts which would be payable under any of the Acts of 1920 to 1969 in respect of the aforesaid single basic pension the aggregate of his basic pensions shall not include any basic pension which began at a time when, if it were the only basic pension eligible for benefit under these Regulations, it would not have attracted any increase under that Act ; and

(ii) where the aggregate of the supplements in respect of each of his basic pensions as ascertained apart from this paragraph would exceed the maximum amount authorised under sub-paragraph (a)(i) of this paragraph the supplement payable in the case of each of such pensions shall be of such amount as, when aggregated with the overseas increase paid in respect of that pension, shall bear the same proportion to the aggregate increases which would be payable under the Pensions (Increase) Acts 1920 to 1969 in respect of the aggregate basic pensions as the basic pension bears to such aggregate: Provided that where the aggregate of the supplements so determined in respect of all the basic pensions, whether or not such pensions attract benefit under these Regulations, exceeds the maximum amount payable under the provisions of sub-paragraph (a)(i) of this paragraph each such supplement shall be reduced by an amount bearing the same proportion to that supplement as the excess bears to that aggregate.

(b) In this paragraph any reference to the basic pensions of a person shall be construed as including a reference to any pension in respect of service under any of the Governments of the overseas territories specified in Schedule 1 to these Regulations, whether or not those pensions are overseas pensions as described in Schedule 3 to the Act of 1962 and whether or not they are eligible for benefit under these Regulations.

(3) Subject to the provisions of this regulation, where a person who is in receipt of an overseas pension is also in receipt of a corresponding pension or pensions, paragraph (2) of this regulation shall apply for the purpose of determining the supplement payable in respect of the overseas pension as if any corresponding pension was a pension in respect of service under the Government of an overseas territory specified in Schedule 1 to these Regulations:

Provided that—

(a) no account shall be taken of any service pension, as defined in paragraph (1)(b) of this regulation, in relation to the Act of 1956, and

(b) for the purpose of determining the supplement under Part II of these Regulations the amount of any comparable relevant increases in the overseas pensions shall not exceed an amount which when added to the comparable relevant increases in the corresponding pensions is equal to the relevant increase which would have been payable in respect of the single basic pension at a rate equal to the aggregate of his basic pensions and beginning at a time when the earliest of them began apart from any basic pension which began at a time when if it were the only basic pension eligible for benefit under these Regulations, it would not have attracted any such relevant increase, such relevant increase being apportioned among the overseas pensions in the same proportion as the comparable relevant increase in the overseas pension bears to the aggregate of the comparable relevant increases in the overseas pensions, and

(c) in the application of paragraph (2) of this regulation, sub-paragraph (a)(i) shall be disregarded.

(4) In the application of this regulation to any person who is in receipt of a pension determined in accordance with section 2 of the Governors' Pensions Act 1957(a), as amended by the Superannuation (Miscellaneous Provisions) Act 1967, any pension in respect of service in the overseas civil service taken into account for the purposes of section 2(2)(b) of the said Act shall be regarded—

(a) as beginning on the same date as the Governor's pension granted under the Act, and

(b) as being the basic pension granted for that service notwithstanding that it may include an addition made in accordance with an enactment, scheme, or other instrument providing for the increase of pensions, but the amount of any such addition which is so included shall not be taken into account in determining the overseas increases in respect of that pension.

---

(a) 1957 c. 62.

(5) Where a person is in receipt of more than one pension to which the provisions of regulation 9 of these Regulations apply, the periods during which the officer in respect of whose service the pensions are payable contributed in respect of those pensions shall be aggregated for the purpose of determining the maximum supplement payable under the provisions of paragraph (2)(*a*) of this regulation:

Provided that where contributions were made in respect of more than one such pension in relation to the same period of service that period shall not be taken into account more than once.

(6) Where a person who is in receipt of a pension to which the provisions of regulation 9 of these Regulations apply is also in receipt of a pension to which those provisions do not apply, the supplements payable under these Regulations shall not in the aggregate exceed the amount which would be payable if he were in receipt of a single basic pension equal to the aggregate of his basic pensions, together with a single overseas increase at a rate equal to the aggregate of his overseas increases, and if such single basic pension were regarded as a pension to which the provisions of regulation 9 apply and which was determined by reference to the period of contributions made in respect of the pension actually payable to which the provisions of regulation 9 apply:

Provided that in determining the supplement in respect of the aforesaid single basic pension the amount of any relevant increase to that pension shall not exceed an amount which, when added to the comparable relevant increases in his corresponding pensions, is equal to the relevant increase which would have been payable in respect of the single basic pension at a rate equal to the aggregate of his basic pensions and beginning at a time when the earliest of them began apart from any basic pension which began at a time when, if it were the only basic pension eligible for benefit under these Regulations, it would not have attracted any such relevant increase, such relevant increase being apportioned among the overseas pensions in the same proportion as the comparable relevant increase in the overseas pension bears to the aggregate of the comparable relevant increases in the overseas pensions.

## PART VI

### GENERAL AND SUPPLEMENTAL PROVISIONS

**12.** Subject to the provisions of these Regulations, in the application of the Acts of 1920 to 1969 for the purpose of determining the supplement payable under these Regulations regard shall be had to the provisions of these Acts as they would be applied to a pension payable under the Superannuation Acts 1965 and 1967:

Provided that—

(*a*) in the case of any Act specified in the first column of Schedule 3 to these Regulations no account shall be taken of those provisions specified in the second column of that Schedule, and

(*b*) paragraph (i) of the definition of " the relevant date " in section 1(1) of the Act of 1956 and paragraph 2 of the Second Schedule thereof shall apply as if the date mentioned therein were the 1st January 1950.

**13.** Whenever, for the purpose of ascertaining any supplement payable under these Regulations, it is necessary to convert into sterling a basic pension or an overseas increase initially payable in a currency other than sterling, the rate of exchange to be taken for the purpose of any such conversion shall be the rate of exchange between that currency and sterling in force on 1st January 1963:

Provided that where an overseas increase is converted by the paying authority into any other currency at the official rate of exchange at the time of payment, and the amount of such increase in terms of sterling is less than it would have been if the overseas increase had been converted into sterling at the official rate of exchange on 1st January 1963 between the currency in which the overseas increase was initially payable and sterling, then the rate of exchange to be taken for the purpose of these Regulations shall be the official rate of exchange between such currency and sterling at the time of payment of the overseas increase.

**14.**—(1) In any case where an overseas increase which has been taken into account in determining any supplement payable under these Regulations is revised with retrospective effect such supplement shall be revised accordingly with similar effect and any overpayment made to the pensioner as a result of the revision may be recovered from him.

(2) Where any refund of overpayment as required by paragraph (1) of this regulation is not made within one month of notification no further supplements shall be payable to the pensioner until the amount of the refund so required has been made.

**15.** Application for a supplement under these Regulations shall be made to the Minister of Overseas Development who may require proof that any person applying for such supplement, or any person on behalf of whom such an application is made, is alive and eligible for such supplement, and no payment shall be made until such proof is furnished.

**16.** The Overseas Service (Pensions Supplement) Regulations 1966 and 1968(a), and the Overseas Service (Pensions Supplement) (Special Provisions) Regulations 1966(b) are hereby revoked.

**17.** Supplements of pensions payable by virtue of these Regulations may take effect from 1st April 1969.

*R. E. Prentice,*
Minister of Overseas Development.

14th April 1969.

I approve

Given under the official seal of the Minister for the Civil Service on 15th April 1969.

(L.S.)

*J. E. Herbecq,*
Authorised by the Minister for
the Civil Service.

---

(a) S.I. 1966/159, 1968/745 (1966 I, p. 280; 1968 II, p. 2119).
(b) S.I. 1966/564 (1966 II, p. 1213).

# SCHEDULE 1

Regulations 4, 5, 6 and 9

DATES SPECIFIED IN RELATION TO OVERSEAS TERRITORIES FOR THE
PURPOSES OF REGULATIONS 4, 5, 6 OR 9

| Overseas Territories | Col. 1 44/47 | Col. 2 52/56 | Col. 3 59 | Col. 4 62 | Col. 5 65 | Col. 6 69 | Col. 7 |
|---|---|---|---|---|---|---|---|
| Aden<br>Federation of South Arabia<br>Protectorate of South Arabia<br>People's Republic of Southern Yemen | 1. 1.46 | 1. 4.53 | 1. 7.56 | 1. 7.60 | 18. 1.63 | 1. 4.65 | 1. 7.67 |
| Antigua | 1. 1.45 | 1. 1.52 | 1. 1.56 | 1. 4.60 | 1. 4.61 | 1. 1.65 | 1. 7.67 |
| Bahamas | 1. 1.52 | 1. 1.52 | 1. 1.56 | 1. 1.59 | 1. 4.61 | 1. 7.64 | 1. 7.67 |
| Barbados | 1. 4.48 | 1. 4.52 | 1. 4.56 | 1. 4.61 | 1. 4.66 | 1. 7.67 | 1. 7.67 |
| Bermuda | 1. 1.52 | 1. 1.52 | 1. 7.56 | 1. 7.60 | 1. 4.61 | 1. 1.67 | 1. 7.67 |
| Botswana<br>Bechuanaland | 1. 1.47 | 1. 7.54 | 1. 8.58 | 1. 4.61 | 1.10.64 | 1. 7.67 | 1. 7.67 |
| British Antarctic Territory | — | — | — | 1. 7.61 | 1. 7.63 | 1. 7.67 | 1. 7.67 |
| British Solomon Islands Protectorate | 1. 1.46 | 1. 1.54 | 1. 4.58 | 1. 4.61 | 1.10.65 | 1. 4.67 | 1. 7.67 |
| Brunei | 1. 7.46 | — | — | — | — | — | 1. 7.67 |
| Ceylon | 1. 1.63 | 1. 7.67 | 1. 7.67 | 1. 7.67 | 1. 7.67 | 1. 7.67 | 1. 7.67 |
| Cyprus | 1. 1.45 | 1. 1.53 | 1. 7.55 | 1. 7.67 | 1. 7.67 | 1. 7.67 | 1. 7.67 |
| Dominica | 1. 1.45 | 1. 1.52 | 1. 1.56 | 1. 4.60 | 1. 4.61 | 1. 1.65 | 1. 7.67 |
| East African Community<br>East African Common Services Organisation<br>East Africa High Commission | 1. 1.46 | 1. 1.54 | 1. 7.56 | 1. 4.60 | 1. 7.67 | 1. 7.67 | 1. 7.67 |
| East African Railways and Harbours Administration<br>Kenya and Uganda Railways and Harbours Administration | 1. 1.46 | 1. 1.54 | 1. 7.56 | 1. 4.60 | 1. 7.67 | 1. 7.67 | 1. 7.67 |
| Eastern Nigeria<br>Eastern Region of Nigeria | 1. 1.46 | 1. 4.52 | 1.10.54 | 1. 4.60 | 1. 7.67 | 1. 7.67 | 1. 7.67 |
| Employing Authorities under the Oversea Superannuation Scheme | 1. 4.47 | — | — | — | — | — | 1. 7.67 |
| Falkland Islands | 1.12.46 | 1. 4.53 | 1. 1.57 | 1. 7.61 | 1. 7.63 | 1. 1.66 | 1. 7.67 |
| Federation of Malaysia<br>Federation of Malaya<br>Federated Malay States<br>Malayan Establishment<br>Malayan Union<br>Unfederated Malay States | 1. 8.47 | 1. 1.52 | 1. 1.55 | 1. 7.67 | 1. 7.67 | 1. 7.67 | 1. 7.67 |
| Federal Republic of Nigeria<br>Federation of Nigeria<br>Nigeria | 1. 1.46 | 1. 4.52 | 1.10.54 | 1. 9.59 | 1. 7.67 | 1. 7.67 | 1. 7.67 |
| Fiji | 1. 1.46 | 1. 1.50 | 1. 1.54 | 1. 4.61 | 1. 4.65 | 1. 4.67 | 1. 7.67 |
| The Gambia | 1. 1.46 | 1.12.53 | 1. 4.56 | 1. 1.60 | 1.11.63 | 1. 7.67 | 1. 7.67 |
| Ghana<br>Gold Coast | 1. 1.46 | 1. 4.52 | 1. 7.57 | 1. 7.67 | 1. 7.67 | 1. 7.67 | 1. 7.67 |
| Gibraltar | 1. 4.46 | 1. 1.50 | 1. 1.56 | 1. 1.60 | 1. 8.63 | 1. 7.67 | 1. 7.67 |

| Overseas Territories | Col. 1 44/47 | Col. 2 52/56 | Col. 3 59 | Col. 4 62 | Col. 5 65 | Col. 6 69 | Col. 7 |
|---|---|---|---|---|---|---|---|
| Gilbert and Ellice Islands | 1. 1.46 | 1. 1.50 | 1. 1.54 | 1. 4.61 | 1.10.65 | 1. 4.67 | 1. 7.67 |
| Grenada | 1. 1.45 | 1. 1.52 | 1. 1.56 | 1. 4.60 | 1. 4.61 | 1. 1.65 | 1. 7.67 |
| Guyana British Guiana | 1. 1.49 | 1. 1.54 | 1. 1.54 | 1. 4.61 | 1. 1.64 | 1. 7.67 | 1. 7.67 |
| Hong Kong | 1. 1.47 | 1. 4.51 | 1.10.53 | 1. 7.59 | 1. 7.63 | 1. 4.65 | 1. 7.67 |
| Jamaica | 1.10.50 | 1.10.50 | 1. 4.55 | 1. 4.58 | 1. 4.61 | 1. 7.67 | 1. 7.67 |
| Kenya | 1. 1.46 | 1. 1.54 | 1. 7.56 | 1. 4.60 | 1. 7.67 | 1. 7.67 | 1. 7.67 |
| Leeward Islands | 1. 1.45 | 1. 1.52 | 1. 1.56 | 1. 4.60 | 1. 4.61 | 1. 1.65 | 1. 7.67 |
| Lesotho Basutoland | 1. 1.47 | 1. 7.54 | 1. 8.58 | 1. 4.61 | 1.10.64 | 1. 7.67 | 1. 7.67 |
| Malawi Nyasaland | 1. 1.46 | 1. 5.53 | 1. 7.55 | 1. 4.61 | 1. 4.63 | 1. 1.66 | 1. 7.67 |
| Malta | 1. 4.48 | 1.10.53 | 1. 6.55 | 1. 4.59 | 1. 7.67 | 1. 7.67 | 1. 7.67 |
| Mauritius | 1. 7.47 | 1. 7.50 | 1. 1.57 | 1. 4.61 | 1. 1.64 | 1. 7.67 | 1. 7.67 |
| Montserrat | 1. 1.45 | 1. 1.52 | 1. 1.56 | 1. 4.60 | 1. 4.61 | 1. 1.65 | 1. 7.67 |
| Northern Nigeria Northern Region of Nigeria | 1. 1.46 | 1. 4.52 | 1.10.54 | 1. 9.59 | 1. 7.67 | 1. 7.67 | 1. 7.67 |
| Palestine | 1. 4.46 | 1. 7.67 | 1. 7.67 | 1. 7.67 | 1. 7.67 | 1. 7.67 | 1. 7.67 |
| Sabah North Borneo | 15. 7.46 | 1. 1.52 | 1. 1.56 | 1. 4.61 | 1. 7.67 | 1. 7.67 | 1. 7.67 |
| St. Christopher, Nevis and Anguilla | 1. 1.45 | 1. 1.52 | 1. 1.56 | 1. 4.60 | 1. 4.61 | 1. 1.65 | 1. 7.67 |
| St. Helena | 1. 1.52 | 1. 1.52 | 1. 4.58 | 1. 4.61 | 1. 7.65 | 1. 7.67 | 1. 7.67 |
| St. Lucia | 1. 1.45 | 1. 1.52 | 1. 1.56 | 1. 4.60 | 1. 4.61 | 1. 1.65 | 1. 7.67 |
| St. Vincent | 1. 1.45 | 1. 1.52 | 1. 1.56 | 1. 4.60 | 1. 4.61 | 1. 1.65 | 1. 7.67 |
| Sarawak | 1. 7.46 | 1. 1.52 | 1.10.54 | 1. 4.61 | 1. 7.67 | 1. 7.67 | 1. 7.67 |
| Seychelles | 1. 7.47 | 1. 1.54 | 1. 1.58 | 1. 4.61 | 1. 5.66 | 1. 7.67 | 1. 7.67 |
| Sierra Leone | 1. 1.46 | 1. 3.53 | 1. 2.55 | 1. 4.57 | 1. 7.67 | 1. 7.67 | 1. 7.67 |
| Singapore Straits Settlements | 1. 8.47 | 1. 1.52 | 16. 6.53 | 1. 4.61 | 1. 7.67 | 1. 7.67 | 1. 7.67 |
| Somali Republic Somaliland Protectorate | 1. 1.46 | 1.10.53 | 1.10.56 | 1. 7.67 | 1. 7.67 | 1. 7.67 | 1. 7.67 |
| Sudan | 1. 1.50 | — | — | — | — | — | 1. 7.67 |
| Swaziland | 1. 1.47 | 1. 7.54 | 1. 8.58 | 1. 4.61 | 1.10.64 | 1. 7.67 | 1. 7.67 |
| Tanzania Tanganyika Zanzibar | 1. 1.46 | 1. 1.54 | 1. 7.56 | 1. 4.60 | 1. 7.67 | 1. 7.67 | 1. 7.67 |
| The West Indies Federation | 1. 1.46 | — | — | — | — | — | 1. 7.67 |
| Tonga | 1.10.49 | — | — | — | — | — | 1. 7.67 |
| Trinidad and Tobago | 1. 1.49 | 1. 1.54 | 1. 1.59 | 1. 4.61 | 1. 1.66 | 1. 7.67 | 1. 7.67 |
| Turks and Caicos | 1.10.50 | 1.10.50 | 1. 4.55 | 1. 4.58 | 1. 4.61 | 1. 7.67 | 1. 7.67 |
| Uganda | 1. 1.46 | 1. 1.54 | 1. 7.56 | 1. 4.60 | 1. 7.67 | 1. 7.67 | 1. 7.67 |
| Western Nigeria Western Region of Nigeria | 1. 1.46 | 1. 4.52 | 1.10.54 | 1. 4.59 | 1. 7.67 | 1. 7.67 | 1. 7.67 |
| Western Pacific High Commission | 1. 1.46 | 1. 1.50 | 1. 1.54 | 1. 4.61 | 1.10.65 | 1. 4.67 | 1. 7.67 |
| Zambia Northern Rhodesia | 1. 1.46 | 1.10.51 | 1. 1.57 | 1. 4.61 | 1. 4.63 | 1. 7.67 | 1. 7.67 |

## SCHEDULE 2

Regulation 2

ENACTMENTS, SCHEMES AND INSTRUMENTS APPROVED FOR THE
PURPOSES OF SECTION 3 OF THE ACT OF 1962

Aden Widows' and Orphans' (United Kingdom) Pensions Scheme.
Bahamas Widows' and Orphans' Pension Fund.
Basutoland Widows' and Orphans' Pension Fund.
Bechuanaland Widows' and Orphans' Pension Fund.
British Guiana Widows' and Orphans' Pension Fund.
Ceylon Widows' and Orphans' Pension Fund.
East African Railways and Harbours Administration Superannuation Fund.
Gold Coast Widows' and Orphans' (Overseas Officers) Pension Fund.
Mauritius Widows' and Orphans' Pension Fund.
North Borneo Widows' and Orphans' Pension Fund.
Northern Rhodesia Widows' and Orphans' Pension Fund.
Oversea Superannuation Scheme.
Sarawak Widows' and Orphans' Pension Fund.
Seychelles Widows' and Orphans' Pension Fund.
Sierra Leone Widows' and Orphans' Pension Fund.
Somaliland Protectorate Widows' and Orphans' Pension Fund.
Swaziland Widows' and Orphans' Pension Fund.

## SCHEDULE 3

Regulation 12

MODIFICATIONS OF THE ACTS OF 1920 TO 1969

| Enactment | Provision to be disregarded |
|---|---|
| Pensions (Increase) Act 1920(a) ... | Sub-paragraph (3) of paragraph 1 of the Schedule. |
| Pensions (Increase) Act 1944(b) ... | Section 2; Subsection (2) of section 3; Subsection (1) of section 8; Paragraphs 7 and 8 of the Second Schedule. |
| Pensions (Increase) Act 1947(c) ... | Subsection (4) of section 2; In subsection (2) of section 3 the words from " or by reference " to " forty-six "; Subsection (3) of section 3. |
| Pensions (Increase) Act 1952(d) ... | Subsection (1) of section 4; Paragraphs 4 to 6 and 8 to 10 of the Second Schedule. |
| Pensions (Increase) Act 1956(e) ... | Paragraph (a) of the proviso to subsection (1) of section 1; Subsection (3) of section 3; Subsection (1) of section 9; Paragraphs 3 to 7 of the Second Schedule. |
| Pensions (Increase) Act 1962(f) ... | The whole of Schedule 2. |
| Pensions (Increase) Act 1969(g) ... | Paragraph 1 of Schedule 2. |

(a) 1920 c. 36.    (b) 1944 c. 21.    (c) 1947 c. 7.    (d) 1952 c. 45.
(e) 1956 c. 39.    (f) 1962 (11 & 12 Eliz. c. 2.) c. 2.    (g) 1969 c. 7.

## EXPLANATORY NOTE

*(This Note is not part of the Regulations.)*

These Regulations, which replace the Overseas Service (Pensions Supplement) Regulations 1966 and 1968 and the Overseas Service (Pensions Supplement) (Special Provisions) Regulations 1966, provide for the payment of supplements on pensions paid to or in respect of overseas civil servants.

Part II of these Regulations provides for the payment to an officer of a supplement which together with any increase or supplement otherwise payable on his pension corresponds as nearly as may be with the increases which would be payable on a similar pension under the Pensions (Increase) Acts 1920 to 1969. Similar provision for the dependants of officers is made in Part IV of the Regulations.

Part III of the Regulations provides for the payment of an additional supplement where a pension paid to an officer under the Oversea Superannuation Scheme is of a reduced amount because the contributions to that Scheme in respect of his overseas service were reduced by virtue of his continuing contributions to the Federated Superannuation System for Universities or other similar approved scheme during that overseas service.

The provisions of Regulation 13 ensure that the calculation of supplements is unaffected by changes in rates of exchange since the 1st January 1963 i.e. the effective date of the Pensions (Increase) Act 1962. Under the proviso to Regulation 13, however, an overseas increase cannot be deemed to be larger than it is in terms of sterling for the purposes of these regulations.

In accordance with section 3(3) of the Pensions (Increase) Act 1962, section 3(4) of the Pensions (Increase) Act 1965 and paragraphs 9 and 10 of Schedule 2 to the Pensions (Increase) Act 1969, the supplements are retrospectively payable from 1st April 1969.

## STATUTORY INSTRUMENTS

## 1969 No. 554

## EDUCATION, ENGLAND AND WALES

### The State Awards (Amendment) Regulations 1969

| | |
|---|---|
| *Made* - - - | *15th April* 1969 |
| *Laid before Parliament* | *24th April* 1969 |
| *Coming into Operation* | *25th April* 1969 |

The Secretary of State for Education and Science, in exercise of the powers conferred upon him by section 3 of the Education Act 1962(a) as amended by the Secretary of State for Education and Science Order 1964(b), hereby makes the following regulations:—

*Citation, commencement and interpretation*

**1.**—(1) These regulations may be cited as the State Awards (Amendment) Regulations 1969 and shall come into operation on 25th April 1969.

(2) The Interpretation Act 1889(c) shall apply for the interpretation of these regulations as it applies for the interpretation of an Act of Parliament.

*Effect of regulations*

**2.** The State Awards Regulations 1963(d) (in these regulations called "the principal regulations") shall, as respects any course beginning after 31st August 1969 to which these regulations apply, have effect subject to these regulations.

*State Bursaries*

**3.** In regulation 2 of the principal regulations the word "and" at the end of paragraph (*a*) shall be omitted and at the end of the regulation there shall be added—

"and

(*c*) State Bursaries, being awards to persons in respect of their attendance at such courses at universities, colleges or other institutions, whether in England or Wales or elsewhere, as are designated under regulation 3."

*Courses designated for State Studentships*

**4.** In regulation 3 (1) of the principal regulations—

(*a*) for the expression "Arts and Social Studies" in both places where it occurs there shall be substituted the expression "the Humanities";

(*b*) for sub-paragraph (*a*) there shall be substituted—
"(*a*) at a university or other institution in England or Wales in preparation for a doctorate, a master's degree or a degree of bachelor of letters or of bachelor of philosophy";
and

(*c*) sub-paragraph (*b*) shall be omitted.

---

| | |
|---|---|
| (a) 1962 c. 12. | (b) S.I. 1964/490 (1964 I, p. 800). |
| (c) 1889 c. 63. | (d) S.I. 1963/1223 (1963 II, p. 2035). |

### Courses designated for State Bursaries

**5.** In regulation 3 of the principal regulations there shall be added as a new paragraph (3)—

"(3) The courses designated for the purposes of paragraph (c) of regulation 2 shall be such full-time courses (not being courses designated for the purposes of paragraph (a) of regulation 2), being postgraduate courses or comparable to postgraduate courses, at universities, colleges or other institutions in the United Kingdom, as the Secretary of State may from time to time designate under this paragraph."

### Parental contribution

**6.** In determining the amount of grant to the holder of a State Bursary the Secretary of State may take account of any income of the holder's parent and accordingly the references in the proviso to regulation 6 and in regulation 7(1) of the principal regulations to the holder's dependants shall, in their application to State Bursaries, be construed as including references to his parent.

Given under the Official Seal of the Secretary of State for Education and Science on 15th April 1969.

*Edward Short,*
(L.S.)                                        Secretary of State
for Education and Science.

---

## EXPLANATORY NOTE

*(This Note is not part of the Regulations.)*

These regulations extend the powers of the Secretary of State for Education and Science to make State Awards so as to include State Bursaries, which will be awarded in respect of postgraduate courses designated under the regulations. Regulation 4 makes minor amendments to the State Awards Regulations 1963.

# STATUTORY INSTRUMENTS

## 1969 No. 562

## WAGES COUNCILS

## The Wages Regulation (Perambulator and Invalid Carriage) Order 1969

| | |
|---|---|
| *Made* - - - - - | 16*th April* 1969 |
| *Coming into Operation* | 12*th May* 1969 |

Whereas the Secretary of State has received from the Perambulator and Invalid Carriage Wages Council (Great Britain) the wages regulation proposals set out in Schedules 1 and 2 hereof;

Now, therefore, the Secretary of State in exercise of her powers under section 11 of the Wages Councils Act 1959(a), and of all other powers enabling her in that behalf, hereby makes the following Order:—

**1.** This Order may be cited as the Wages Regulation (Perambulator and Invalid Carriage) Order 1969.

**2.**—(1) In this Order the expression "the specified date" means the 12th May 1969, provided that where, as respects any worker who is paid wages at intervals not exceeding seven days, that date does not correspond with the beginning of the period for which the wages are paid, the expression "the specified date" means, as respects that worker, the beginning of the next such period following that date.

(2) The Interpretation Act 1889(b) shall apply to the interpretation of this Order as it applies to the interpretation of an Act of Parliament and as if this Order and the Order hereby revoked were Acts of Parliament.

**3.** The wages regulation proposals set out in Schedules 1 and 2 hereof shall have effect as from the specified date and as from that date the Wages Regulation (Perambulator and Invalid Carriage) Order 1967(c) shall cease to have effect.

Signed by order of the Secretary of State.

*A. A. Jarratt*,
Deputy Under Secretary of State,
16th April 1969.　　　　　　　　　Department of Employment and Productivity.

### SCHEDULE 1　　　　　　　　　　　　Article 3

The following minimum remuneration shall be substituted for the statutory minimum remuneration fixed by the Wages Regulation (Perambulator and Invalid Carriage) Order 1967 (Order I. (78)).

(a) 1959 c. 69.　　　　　　　　　　(b) 1889 c. 63.
(c) S.I. 1967/988 (1967 II, p.3008).

## STATUTORY MINIMUM REMUNERATION

### PART I

### GENERAL

1. Subject to the provisions of this Schedule, the minimum remuneration payable to a worker to whom this Schedule applies for all work except work to which a minimum overtime rate applies under Part IV is:—

(1) in the case of a time worker, the general minimum time rate applicable to the worker under Part II of this Schedule;

(2) in the case of a worker employed on piece work, piece rates each of which would yield, in the circumstances of the case, to an ordinary worker at least the same amount of money as the piece work basis time rate applicable to the worker under Part III of this Schedule.

### PART II

### GENERAL MINIMUM TIME RATES

2. Subject to the provisions of paragraphs 3, 4 and 5, the general minimum time rates applicable in any week to the workers specified in Column 1 of the next following Table, employed on time work, are the rates set out in Column 2 as follows:—

| Column 1 | Column 2 | |
|---|---|---|
| Class of Workers | Males Per hour | Females Per hour |
| | s. d. | s. d. |
| **MALE OR FEMALE WORKERS—** <br> (1) aged 21 years or over | | |
| A. Class A workers, i.e., workers in the occupations specified in (1) to (7) below who have had not less than four years' experience in any trade in the branch of the work on which they are engaged and who in the case of wood-working machinists sharpen and set their own tools and in the case of metallic platers are able to make and to maintain plating solutions... ... ... ... ... | 6 2¼ | 4 5¼ |
| (1) woodworking machinists; ... <br> (2) makers of complete wooden bodies for perambulators and invalid carriages; <br> (3) blacksmiths, forging or working in hot metals including setting and trueing; <br> (4) metallic platers on metal deposition; <br> (5) fitters and turners; <br> (6) varnishers or fine liners of wood or metal bodies; <br> (7) upholsterers. | | |
| B. Class B workers, i.e., workers in the occupations specified in (1) to (12) below (not being Class A workers) who have had not less than two years' experience in any trade in the branch of work on which they are engaged and who in the case of woodworking machinists do not sharpen and set their own tools and in the case of metallic platers are unable to make and to maintain plating solutions ... ... ... ... ... ... | 6 0 | 4 4¼ |

| Column 1 | Column 2 | |
|---|---|---|
| Class of Workers | Males<br>Per hour | Females<br>Per hour |
| | s. d. | s. d. |
| (1) woodworking machinists; | | |
| (2) wood body makers other than those specified in Class A(2) above; | | |
| (3) body painters by brush or spray engaged on body painting (other than priming, filling-in coats or dipping) and finishers by brush or spray (other than stove enamellers) or fine liners of chassis and wheels; | | |
| (4) metal polishers and finishers and metallic platers on metal deposition; | | |
| (5) rubber tyre workers (perambulator and invalid carriage tyres only); | | |
| (6) hand welders (either arc or gas welding); | | |
| (7) fitters and turners; | | |
| (8) sewing machinists, hood coverers and cutters; | | |
| (9) upholsterers; | | |
| (10) workers employed on cold strip spring bending, setting and trueing; | | |
| (11) workers employed on the operations of assembling, mounting and finishing the same perambulator or bed-folder throughout; | | |
| (12) wheel hand truers who use nipple keys. | | |
| C. Class C workers, i.e., workers in the occupations specified in (1) to (20) below (not being Class A or Class B workers) ... ... ... ... ... ... ... | 5 9¼ | 4 3¼ |
| (1) workers employed on cold bending (other than cold spring bending), riveting and striking; | | |
| (2) capstan operators; | | |
| (3) workers engaged on processes of painting, i.e., priming and filling-in coats, dipping and spray painting except those in occupations specified in Class A(6) or Class B(3); | | |
| (4) wheel lacers or wheel jig truers; | | |
| (5) automatic, spot or butt welders; | | |
| (6) workers employed on rim rolling, rim cutting, rim punching, rim grinding or rim welding; | | |
| (7) tyre fitters and jointers; | | |
| (8) spoke roll threaders; | | |
| (9) power and hand-press workers; | | |
| (10) power machine drillers; | | |
| (11) stove enamellers, spray or dip; | | |
| (12) metal polishers; | | |
| (13) workers employed on wiring and racking in plating shop; | | |
| (14) sewing machinists, hood coverers and cutters; | | |
| (15) workers employed on cushion filling, banding or studding; | | |
| (16) workers employed on any one of the operations of assembling, mounting and finishing perambulators or bed-folders other than those specified in Class B(11); | | |

| Column 1 | Column 2 | |
|---|---|---|
| Class of Workers | Males Per hour | Females Per hour |
| | s. d. | s. d. |
| (17) workers employed on the operations of assembling, mounting and finishing the same push-car throughout; | | |
| (18) warehouse and stores workers; | | |
| (19) packers and case makers (both export and home trade); | | |
| (20) any other class of worker not specified in Class A or Class B or in paragraph 3 below. | | |
| (2) aged 20 and under 21 years ... ... ... | 4 9¾ | 3 9¼ |
| " 19 " " 20 " ... ... ... | 4 6 | 3 8¾ |
| " 18 " " 19 " ... ... ... | 4 2½ | 3 7¾ |
| " 17 " " 18 " ... ... ... | 3 6¼ | 3 2¾ |
| " 16 " " 17 " ... ... ... | 3 1¼ | 2 11¾ |
| under 16 years ... ... ... ... | 2 10¾ | 2 8½ |

3. This paragraph does not apply to a worker engaged in any occupation where having regard to his experience a rate would apply to him under A or B of paragraph 2, but save as aforesaid, and subject to the provisions of paragraph 4, where a general minimum time rate specified in paragraph 2 (hereafter in this paragraph referred to as "the full rate") would apply to a worker aged 21 years or over if he possessed the appropriate experience therein mentioned, the general minimum time rate applicable to a worker not possessing such experience shall be as follows:—

(1) where the appropriate experience is 4 years—

(*a*) if the worker has not more than 2 years' experience before the age of 21 years, or if he enters the trade for the first time at or over that age

(i) during the first 12 months' experience after the age of 21 years, the full rate reduced by 2d. per hour;

(ii) during the second 12 months' experience after the age of 21 years, the full rate reduced by 1d. per hour;

(iii) thereafter, the full rate.

(*b*) if the worker has more than 2 but less than 4 years' experience before the age of 21 years

(i) during any period which completes the third year's experience, the full rate reduced by 2d. per hour;

(ii) during the fourth year's experience, or such period as completes it, the full rate reduced by 1d. per hour.

(2) where the appropriate experience is 2 years—

(*a*) if the worker has not more than 1 year's experience before the age of 21 years, or if he enters the trade for the first time at or over that age

(i) during the first 6 months' experience after the age of 21 years, the full rate reduced by 2d. per hour;

(ii) during the second 6 months' experience after the age of 21 years, the full rate reduced by 1d. per hour;

(iii) thereafter, the full rate.

(*b*) if the worker has more than 1 but less than 2 years' experience before the age of 21 years

    (i) during any period which completes the third 6 months' experience, the full rate reduced by 2d. per hour;

    (ii) during the fourth 6 months' experience, or such period as completes it, the full rate reduced by 1d. per hour:

Provided that the general minimum time rate applicable to the worker shall in no case be less than the general minimum time rate which would be applicable to him under paragraph 2(2) or paragraph 5 if he were aged 20 and under 21 years.

4. In the application of paragraphs 2 and 3 the following provisions shall apply:—

(1) for the purpose of determining the rate applicable to a worker, other than a worker of Class A(6), any period of experience as a worker in any of the Classes A, B and C shall count as experience in any other class in the same section of work;

(2) a worker employed in any week on work entitling him to be treated as a worker of more than one of the Classes A, B and C shall be entitled to a rate applicable to the highest class in respect of all work upon which he is employed in that week.

5. Notwithstanding the provisions of (2) of the Table to paragraph 2,

(1) the general minimum time rate applicable to a worker who is aged not less than 18 but less than 21 years and has had less than 2 years' employment in the trade shall be:—

    (a) during the worker's first year of employment in the trade 1d. per hour less than the general minimum time rate otherwise applicable to the worker under (2) of the said Table;

    (b) during the worker's second year of employment in the trade ½d. per hour less than the said general minimum time rate otherwise applicable;

(2) where a worker is employed in any occupation of any of the classes of worker specified in (1) of the Table to paragraph 2 (other than (18), (19) or (20) of Class C) and has completed 3 years' experience in one of the said occupations the general minimum time rate otherwise applicable to the worker under (2) of the said Table shall be increased by ½d. per hour.

PART III

PIECE WORK BASIS TIME RATES

6.—(1) Subject to sub-paragraph (2) of this paragraph, the piece work basis time rate applicable to any male or female worker employed on piece work is the rate applicable to that worker, specified in Column 2 of the Table in this sub-paragraph (hereinafter called "his appropriate rate"), increased by 20 per cent.:—

| Column 1 | Column 2 | |
| --- | --- | --- |
| | Males Per hour | Females Per hour |
| | s. d. | s. d. |
| (a) Male or female workers aged 21 years or over, of the classes specified in paragraph 2(1) of this Schedule: | | |
|     Class A ... ... ... ... ... ... | 5 4 | 4 0 |
|     Class B ... ... ... ... ... ... | 5 1¾ | 3 11 |
|     Class C ... ... ... ... ... ... | 4 11 | 3 10 |
| (b) Male or female workers being | | |
|     aged 20 and under 21 years ... ... ... | 4 1¼ | 3 4½ |
|     ,, 19 ,, ,, 20 ,, ... ... ... ... | 3 9¾ | 3 4 |
|     ,, 18 ,, ,, 19 ,, ... ... ... ... | 3 6¼ | 3 3 |
|     ,, 17 ,, ,, 18 ,, ... ... ... ... | 3 0 | 2 10¾ |
|     ,, 16 ,, ,, 17 ,, ... ... ... ... | 2 7¾ | 2 7¾ |
|     under 16 years ... ... ... ... ... | 2 5½ | 2 5 |

(2) In respect of any worker to whom this paragraph applies the provisions of paragraphs 3, 4 or 5 shall apply, as if he were a time worker, to reduce or, as the case may be, to increase his appropriate rate.

## PART IV

### OVERTIME AND WAITING TIME
### MINIMUM OVERTIME RATES

7. Minimum overtime rates are payable to a worker to whom this Schedule applies as follows:—

(1) on any day other than a Saturday, Sunday or customary holiday—

for the first 2 hours worked in excess of 8 hours ... time-and-a-quarter

thereafter ... ... ... ... ... ... time-and-a-half

Provided that where the employer normally requires the worker's attendance on 5 days only in the week, the said minimum overtime rates of time-and-a-quarter and time-and-a-half shall be payable after 9 hours' and 11 hours' work respectively.

(2) on a Saturday, not being a customary holiday—

(a) where the employer normally requires the worker's attendance on 6 days in the week—

for all time worked in excess of 4 hours ... ... time-and-a-half

(b) where the employer normally requires the worker's attendance on 5 days only in the week—

for the first 2 hours worked ... ... ... time-and-a-quarter

thereafter ... ... ... ... ... ... time-and-a-half

(3) on a Sunday or a customary holiday—

for all time worked ... ... ... ... ... double time

(4) in any week exclusive of any time in respect of which any minimum overtime rate is payable under the foregoing provisions of this paragraph—

for all time worked in excess of 40 hours ... ... time-and-a-quarter

8. In this Schedule,

(1) the expressions "time-and-a-quarter", "time-and-a-half" and "double time" mean respectively:—

(a) in the case of a time worker one and a quarter times, one and a half times and twice the general minimum time rate otherwise applicable to the worker;

(b) in the case of a worker employed on piece work:—

(i) a time rate equal respectively to one quarter, one half and the whole of the general minimum time rate which would be applicable to the worker if he were a time worker and a minimum overtime rate did not apply, and, in addition thereto,

(ii) piece rates each of which would yield, in the circumstances of the case, to an ordinary worker at least the same amount of money as the piece work basis time rate otherwise applicable to the worker.

(2) the expression "customary holiday" means—

(a) (i) In England and Wales:—

Christmas Day (or, if Christmas Day falls on a Sunday, such weekday as may be appointed by national proclamation, or, if none is so appointed, the next following Tuesday), Boxing Day, Good Friday, Easter Monday, Whit Monday (or where another day is substituted therefor by national proclamation, that day), August Bank Holiday, any day proclaimed as an additional bank holiday or as a public holiday and *three* other days (being days on which the worker normally works for the employer) in the course of a calendar year, to be fixed by the employer and notified to the worker not less than three weeks before the holiday;

(ii) In Scotland:—

New Year's Day (or, if New Year's Day falls on a Sunday, the following Monday), the local Spring holiday, the local Autumn holiday, any day proclaimed as an additional bank holiday or as a public holiday; and *six* other days (being days on which the worker normally works for the employer) in the course of a calendar year, to be fixed by the employer and notified to the worker not less than three weeks before the holiday;

or (*b*) in the case of each of the said days, a day substituted by the employer therefor, being a day recognised by local custom as a day of holiday in substitution for the said day.

## WAITING TIME

9.—(1) A worker is entitled to payment of the minimum remuneration specified in this Schedule for all the time during which he is present on the premises of the employer, unless he is present thereon in any if the following circumstances, that is to say:—

(*a*) without the employer's consent, express or implied;

(*b*) for some purpose unconnected with his work and other than that of waiting for work to be given to him to perform;

(*c*) by reason only of the fact that he is resident thereon, or

(*d*) during normal meal times in a room or place in which no work is being done, and he is not waiting for work to be given to him to perform.

(2) The minimum remuneration payable under sub-paragraph (1) of this paragraph to a piece worker when not engaged on piece work is:—

(*a*) in respect of the first two hours of waiting time on any working day, the appropriate rate specified in Column 2 of the Table to paragraph 6; and

(*b*) thereafter, the rate which would be applicable to him if he were a time worker.

## PART V

## APPLICATION

10. This Schedule applies to workers in relation to whom the Perambulator and Invalid Carriage Wages Council (Great Britain) operates, that is to say, workers employed in Great Britain in the trade specified in the Schedule to the Trade Boards (Perambulator and Invalid Carriage Trade, Great Britain) (Constitution and Proceedings) Regulations 1938(a), which Schedule reads as follows:—

"1. Subject to the provisions of this Schedule the following operations shall be operations of the Perambulator and Invalid Carriage Trade:—

(*a*) the making, wherever carried on, of perambulators, invalid carriages, folding push-cars, and the wheels or axles therefor;

(*b*) the making of the following articles for perambulators, invalid carriages, or folding push-cars when such making—

(i) is done in association or in conjunction with the making mentioned in sub-paragraph (*a*) above, or

(ii) constitutes the main business of the establishment, branch, or department, or

(iii) is done in a Toy-making establishment,

that is to say:—springs, tubular undercarriages, hood frames, bodies (including cane or wicker bodies), canopy frames, levers of all kinds, aprons, hood and canopy covers;

_____

(a) S.R. & O. 1938/810 (1938 II, p. 3244).

(c) the making of motor-cycle side-car bodies when done in an establishment, branch or department in which the main business is any of the making mentioned in sub-paragraphs (a) and (b) above;

(d) the making of fittings or accessories for perambulators, invalid carriages, or folding push-cars when done (a) in association or in conjunction with any of the making specified above, or (b) in a Toy-making establishment;

(e) the repair of any of the articles, the making of which is an operation of the trade herein specified, when done in association with or in conjunction with such making.

2. All operations of packing, warehousing, despatching, stock-taking, and other similar operations and all operations of crate making when such operations are incidental to any of the operations referred to in the preceding paragraphs hereof shall be deemed to be operations of the Perambulator and Invalid Carriage Trade.

3. Notwithstanding anything in this Schedule the following operations shall not be operations of the Perambulator and Invalid Carriage Trade:—

(a) the manufacture of self-propelled chain or lever-driven or mechanically propelled invalid carriages or parts thereof;

(b) operations included in the Trade Boards (Toy) Order 1920(a), or any amendment or variation thereof.

4. For the purposes of this Schedule—

(a) the expression 'invalid carriages' shall include spinal carriages;

(b) the expression 'perambulators' shall not include Toy perambulators;

(c) the making of hood and canopy covers shall include the covering or re-covering of hoods and canopies;

(d) 'Toy-making establishment' means an establishment, branch or depart-ment, in which the main business is the work specified in the Trade Boards (Toy) Order 1920, or any amendment or variation thereof."

Article 3                                        SCHEDULE 2

HOLIDAYS AND HOLIDAY REMUNERATION

The Wages Regulation (Perambulator and Invalid Carriage) (Holidays) Order 1965(b) (Order I. (76)) shall have effect as if in the Schedule thereto for sub-paragraph (2)(a) of paragraph 2, which relates to customary holidays, there were substituted the following:—

"(2) The said customary holidays are:—

(a) (i) In England and Wales—
Christmas Day (or, if Christmas Day falls on a Sunday, such weekday as may be appointed by national proclamation, or, if none is so appointed, the next following Tuesday), Boxing Day, Good Friday, Easter Monday, Whit Monday, (or where another day is substituted therefor by national proclamation, that day), August Bank Holiday, any day proclaimed as an additional bank holiday or as a public holiday and *three* other days (being days on which the worker normally works for the employer) in the course of a calendar year to be fixed by the employer and notified to the worker not less than three weeks before the holiday;

(ii) In Scotland—
New Year's Day (or, if New Year's Day falls on a Sunday, the following Monday);
the local Spring holiday;
the local Autumn holiday;
any day proclaimed as an additional bank holiday or as a public holiday; and *six* other days (being days on which the worker normally works for the employer) in the course of a calendar year to be fixed by the employer and notified to the worker not less than three weeks before the holiday;"

(a) S.R. & O. 1920/470 (1920 II, p. 792).     (b) S.I. 1965/2090 (1965 III, p. 6146).

# EXPLANATORY NOTE

*(This Note is not part of the Order.)*

This Order has effect from 12th May 1969. Schedule 1 sets out the statutory minimum remuneration payable in substitution for that fixed by the Wages Regulation (Perambulator and Invalid Carriage) Order 1967 (Order I.(78)), which Order is revoked. Schedule 2 amends the Wages Regulation (Perambulator and Invalid Carriage) (Holidays) Order 1965 (Order I.(76)), by providing for two additional days of customary holiday.

New provisions are printed in italics.

## 1969 No. 567

## PENSIONS

## The Increase of Pensions (Police and Fire Services) Regulations 1969

| | |
|---|---|
| *Made* - - - | *17th April* 1969 |
| *Laid before Parliament* | *25th April* 1969 |
| *Coming into Operation* | *1st May* 1969 |

In exercise of the powers conferred on me by section 1(4) of the Pensions (Increase) Act 1969(**a**) and paragraph 12 of Schedule 2 thereto, I hereby, with the consent of the Minister for the Civil Service, make the following Regulations :—

*Citation*

**1.** These Regulations may be cited as the Increase of Pensions (Police and Fire Services) Regulations 1969.

*Operation and effect*

**2.** These Regulations shall come into operation on 1st May 1969 and the increases authorised thereby shall take effect as from 1st April 1969.

*Interpretation*

**3.**—(1) Any reference in these Regulations to any enactment or instrument shall be construed as including a reference to that enactment or instrument as amended by or under any other enactment or instrument.

(2) In these Regulations—

(*a*) the expression "pension" includes an allowance, and

(*b*) the expression "principal Act" means the Pensions (Increase) Act 1969.

*Police, special constabulary and fire service pensions*

**4.**—(1) This Regulation shall apply to a pension payable—

(*a*) under the Police Pensions Act 1948(**b**) ;

(*b*) under section 34 of the Police Act 1964(**c**) or section 26 of the Police (Scotland) Act 1967(**d**) ; or

---

| | |
|---|---|
| (**a**) 1969 c. 7. | (**b**) 1948 c. 24. |
| (**c**) 1964 c. 48. | (**d**) 1967 c. 77. |

(c) in accordance with any scheme in force under section 26 of the Fire Services Act 1947(a),

being a pension which is reduced in amount or is not payable on account of the payment of some additional benefit.

(2) In relation to a pension to which this Regulation applies the definition of the expression "adjusted rate" in paragraph 2 of Schedule 2 to the principal Act shall have effect, subject to paragraph (4) of this Regulation, as if it were provided therein that the aggregate annual rate of the pension should be calculated as if no additional benefit were payable.

(3) Where the permitted reduction in the amount of a pension to which this Regulation applies exceeds the adjusted rate of that pension, within the meaning of the principal Act as modified by these Regulations, section 1(1) of the principal Act shall have effect, subject to paragraph (4) of this Regulation, as if it were provided therein that the increase payable thereunder should be reduced by that excess.

(4) If the modifications of the principal Act contained in paragraphs (2) and (3) of this Regulation would result in the increase of a pension under section 1 of that Act being less than it would have been but for those modifications, neither of the said modifications shall apply for the purpose of the calculation of the said increase.

(5) In this Regulation the expression "additional benefit" means—

(a) any benefit payable under the National Insurance Act 1965(b) together with any supplement thereto payable under section 2 of the National Insurance Act 1966(c) ;

(b) any benefit payable under the National Insurance (Industrial Injuries) Act 1965(d) together with any supplement payable therewith under the said section 2 ;

(c) any armed forces pension payable in pursuance of any Royal Warrant or other instrument ;

(d) any family allowances payable under the Family Allowances Act 1965(e) ; or

(e) any payment of whatever nature, other than a pension payable as mentioned in paragraph (1) of this Regulation, which is made to the pensioner by a fire authority, by any other local authority or by a Minister of the Crown,

and the expression "permitted reduction" means the amount (expressed as an annual rate) by which a pension would fall to be reduced on account of the payment of additional benefit if the reduction were not limited by the size of the pension.

## Police pensions

5.—(1) This Regulation shall apply where a pensioner is entitled to both a supplemental pension and some other pension under the Police Pensions Act 1948.

(2) In the circumstances mentioned in the preceding paragraph—

(a) notwithstanding anything in the Police Pensions Regulations, the relevant provisions of the principal Act and the provisions of Regulation 4 of these Regulations shall have effect as though the pensions mentioned in that paragraph constituted separate awards ; and

---

(a) 1947 c. 41.　　　　　　　　　　(b) 1965 c. 51.
(c) 1966 c. 6.　　　　　　　　　　　(d) 1965 c. 52.
(e) 1965 c. 53.

(b) without prejudice to Regulation 4(2) of these Regulations, the definition of "adjusted rate" in paragraph 2 of Schedule 2 to the principal Act shall have effect in relation to those pensions as if any relevant increase within the meaning of the Pensions (Increase) Act 1969 in the combined pensions were apportioned between those pensions as follows, that is to say, for the purpose of the said definition, so much of the combined increase as would have been payable had the pensioner not been entitled to a supplemental pension shall be treated as an increase in the other pension and the balance of the combined increase shall be treated as an increase in the supplemental pension.

(3) In this Regulation the expression "the Police Pensions Regulations" means the regulations for the time being in force under the Police Pensions Act 1948 and the expression "supplemental pension" has the same meaning as in those Regulations.

*Fire service pensions*

**6.**—(1) This Regulation shall apply to a pension calculated otherwise than by reference to a rate or average rate of emoluments received by the person in respect of whose service it is payable.

(2) In relation to a pension to which this Regulation applies payable, in respect of whole-time or part-time service, in accordance with—

(a) the Firemen's Pension Scheme 1952(a);

(b) the Firemen's Pension Scheme 1956(b);

(c) the Firemen's Pension Scheme 1964(c); or

(d) the Firemen's Pension Scheme 1966(d);

being a pension which began for the purposes of the principal Act after 1st July 1955, section 1(2) of the principal Act shall apply as though the pension so began not later than that date.

(3) In relation to a pension to which this Regulation applies payable to a widow in accordance with the Firemen's Pension Scheme 1966 and calculated in accordance with paragraph 2(1), as modified by paragraph 2(2), of Part I of Schedule 2 thereto, the definition of the expression "adjusted rate" in paragraph 2 of Schedule 2 to the principal Act shall have effect as if it were provided therein that the annual rate of the pension should be calculated as if the modifications set out in paragraph 2(2) of Part I of Schedule 2 to the said Scheme of 1966 did not apply.

*James Callaghan,*
One of Her Majesty's Principal
Secretaries of State.

15th April 1969.

Consent of the Minister for the Civil Service given under his Official Seal on 17th April 1969.

(L.S.)

*J. E. Herbecq,*
Authorised by the Minister
for the Civil Service.

(a) *See* S.I. 1952/944 (1952 I, p.1003).   (b) *See* S.I. 1956/1022 (1956 I, p.953).
(c) *See* S.I. 1964/1148 (1964 II, p.2574).   (d) *See* S.I. 1966/1045 (1966 II, p.2504).

# EXPLANATORY NOTE

*(This Note is not part of the Regulations.)*

These Regulations provide that specified provisions of the Pensions (Increase) Act 1969 shall apply in relation to certain police, special constabulary and fire service pensions subject to modifications and adaptations. Regulation 4 provides that in calculating the aggregate annual rate of a pension (by reference to which the amount of an increase under the 1969 Act is determined) no account shall be taken of reductions in the pension made on account of the payment of certain additional benefits but that, in certain cases, the increase is to be abated on account of such payment. Regulation 5 provides that where a police award comprises a supplemental and some other pension, those pensions are to be increased separately under the 1969 Act. Regulation 6 relates to certain flat rate fire pensions ; it provides, first, that certain such pensions shall be treated for the purpose of determining entitlement to, and the amount of, increases, as having begun at times other than those at which they are deemed under the 1969 Act to have begun and, secondly, that in calculating the aggregate annual rate of certain such pensions no account shall be taken of specified provisions (which relate to the widow of a fireman with at least ten years' service).

Regulation 2 provides that the Regulations shall take effect as from 1st April 1969, the date from which increases under the 1969 Act are payable.

# STATUTORY INSTRUMENTS

## 1969 No. 568

## AGRICULTURE

### LIVESTOCK INDUSTRIES

## The Pig Industry Development Authority (Dissolution) Order 1969

*Made* - - - *17th April* 1969

The Minister of Agriculture, Fisheries and Food and the Secretary of State concerned with agriculture in Scotland, acting jointly in exercise of the powers conferred on them by section 22(3) of the Agriculture Act 1967(a) and of all other powers enabling them in that behalf, being satisfied that the requirements of section 28 of the Agriculture Act 1957(b) (annual report and accounts) have been complied with on the part of the Pig Industry Development Authority in respect of years down to and including their financial year which was current on the date of the coming into force of the said section 22 and which, by virtue of that section, was deemed to end on that date, hereby make the following order :—

**1.** This order may be cited as the Pig Industry Development Authority (Dissolution) Order 1969.

**2.** The Pig Industry Development Authority established under Part III of the Agriculture Act 1957 is hereby dissolved.

In Witness whereof the Official Seal of the Minister of Agriculture, Fisheries and Food is hereunto affixed on 16th April 1969.

(L.S.)                                    *Cledwyn Hughes,*
                    Minister of Agriculture, Fisheries and Food.

Given under the Seal of the Secretary of State for Scotland on 17th April 1969.

(L.S.)                                    *William Ross,*
                    Secretary of State for Scotland.

### EXPLANATORY NOTE

*(This Note is not part of the order.)*

This order dissolves the Pig Industry Development Authority which was established under Part III of the Agriculture Act 1957 and whose assets,

(a) 1967 c. 22.                    (b) 5 & 6 Eliz. 2. c. 57.

liabilities and obligations were transferred to the Meat and Livestock Commission by virtue of section 22(1) of the Agriculture Act 1967 on the coming into force of that section on 1st October 1968.

By virtue of section 75 and Schedule 7 of the Agriculture Act 1967, the repeals of Part III, section 34 and Schedule 3 of the Agriculture Act 1957 and of the reference to the Pig Industry Development Authority in Part II of Schedule 1 of the House of Commons Disqualification Act 1957 take effect on the coming into force of this order.

## 1969 No. 571

## AGRICULTURE

### The Price Stability of Imported Products (Rates of Levy No. 9) Order 1969

| | | |
|---|---|---|
| *Made* - - - - | 18*th April* 1969 |
| *Coming into Operation* | 19*th April* 1969 |

The Minister of Agriculture, Fisheries and Food, in exercise of the powers conferred upon him by section 1(2), (4), (5), (6) and (7) of the Agriculture and Horticulture Act 1964(a) and of all other powers enabling him in that behalf, hereby makes the following order :—

1. This order may be cited as the Price Stability of Imported Products (Rates of Levy No. 9) Order 1969 ; and shall come into operation on 19th April 1969.

2.—(1) In this order—

" the Principal Order " means the Price Stability of Imported Products (Levy Arrangements) Order 1966(b), as amended by any subsequent order and if any such order is replaced by any subsequent order the expression shall be construed as a reference to such subsequent order ;

AND other expressions have the same meaning as in the Principal Order.

(2) The Interpretation Act 1889(c) shall apply to the interpretation of this order as it applies to the interpretation of an Act of Parliament and as if this order and the orders hereby revoked were Acts of Parliament.

3. In accordance with and subject to the provisions of Part II of the Principal Order (which provides for the charging of levies on imports of certain specified commodities)—

(a) the rate of general levy for such imports into the United Kingdom of any specified commodity as are described in column 2 of Part I of the Schedule to this order in relation to a tariff heading indicated in column 1 of that Part shall be the rate set forth in relation thereto in column 3 of that Part;

(b) the rate of country levy for such imports into the United Kingdom of any specified commodity as are described in column 2 of Part II of the Schedule to this order in relation to a tariff heading indicated in column 1 of that Part shall be the rate set forth in relation thereto in column 3 of that Part.

4. The Price Stability of Imported Products (Rates of Levy No. 7) Order 1969(d) and the Price Stability of Imported Products (Rates of Levy No. 8) Order 1969(e) are hereby revoked.

In Witness whereof the Official Seal of the Minister of Agriculture, Fisheries and Food is hereunto affixed on 18th April 1969.

(L.S.)

*R. J. E. Taylor,*
Assistant Secretary.

---

(a) 1964 c. 28.   (b) S.I. 1966/936 (1966 II, p. 2271).   (c) 1889 c. 63.
(d) S.I. 1969/473 (1969 I, p. 1358).   (e) S.I. 1969/537 (1969 I, p. 1465).

# SCHEDULE

## Part I

| 1.<br>Tariff<br>Heading | 2.<br>Description of Imports | 3.<br>Rate of<br>General Levy |
|---|---|---|
| | | per ton<br>£  s.  d. |
| | Imports of:— | |
| 10.01 | Denatured wheat    ..    ..    ..    .. | 10  0 |
| 10.01 | Any wheat (other than seed wheat the value of which is not less than £34 per ton, denatured wheat and durum wheat) for which a minimum import price level is prescribed    ..    ..    ..    ..    .. | 15  0 |
| 10.03 | Barley ..    ..    ..    ..    ..    ..    .. | 1  0  0 |
| 11.02 | Cereal meals— | |
| | of barley    ..    ..    ..    ..    .. | 5 10  0 |
| | of maize    ..    ..    ..    ..    .. | 5 10  0 |
| 11.02 | Rolled, flaked, crushed or bruised cereals—<br>barley ..    ..    ..    ..    ..    ..    .. | 5 15  0 |

## Part II

| 1.<br>Tariff<br>Heading | 2.<br>Description of Imports | 3.<br>Rate of<br>Country Levy |
|---|---|---|
| | | per ton<br>£  s.  d. |
| | Imports of:— | |
| 10.01 | Denatured wheat which has been grown in and consigned to the United Kingdom from Belgium, the French Republic, the Kingdom of the Netherlands or the Kingdom of Sweden..    ..    ..    .. | 10  0 |
| 10.01 | Any wheat (other than seed wheat the value of which is not less than £34 per ton, denatured wheat and durum wheat) for which a minimum import price level is prescribed and which is grown in and consigned to the United Kingdom from the French Republic or the Kingdom of the Netherlands    .. | 15  0 |
| 10.03 | Barley which has been grown in and consigned to the United Kingdom from Canada    ..    ..    .. | 1  0  0 |
| 10.03 | Barley which has been grown in and consigned to the United Kingdom from the Commonwealth of Australia    ..    ..    ..    ..    ..    .. | 15  0 |
| 10.03 | Barley which has been grown in and consigned to the United Kingdom from Belgium, the Kingdom of Denmark, Finland, the French Republic, the Kingdom of the Netherlands or the Kingdom of Sweden    ..    ..    ..    ..    ..    .. | 5  0 |

## EXPLANATORY NOTE

*(This Note is not part of the Order.)*

This order, which comes into operation on 19th April 1969, re-enacts with amendments the Price Stability of Imported Products (Rates of Levy No. 7) Order 1969 and incorporates the Price Stability of Imported Products (Rates of Levy No. 8) Order 1969.

It:—

(a) reduces to 10s. per ton the general levy on imports of denatured wheat;

(b) reduces to 10s. per ton the country levy on imports of denatured wheat which has been grown in and consigned to the United Kingdom from Belgium, France, the Netherlands or Sweden;

(c) reduces to 15s. per ton the general levy on wheat (other than seed wheat the value of which is not less than £34 per ton, denatured wheat and durum wheat);

(d) reduces to 15s. per ton the country levy on such wheat which is grown in and consigned to the United Kingdom from France or the Netherlands;

(e) reduces to 5s. per ton the country levy on imports of barley which has been grown in and consigned to the United Kingdom from Belgium, Denmark, Finland, France, the Netherlands or Sweden; and

(f) reimposes unchanged the other rates of general and country levy prescribed by the above-mentioned orders.

STATUTORY   INSTRUMENTS

# 1969 No. 572

## CUSTOMS AND EXCISE

# The Import Duties (Temporary Exemptions) (No. 2) Order 1969

| | |
|---|---|
| *Made* - - - - - - - | *21st April* 1969 |
| *Laid before the House of Commons* | *25th April* 1969 |
| *Coming into Operation* - - - | *1st May* 1969 |

The Lords Commissioners of Her Majesty's Treasury, by virtue of the powers conferred on them by sections 3(6) and 13 of the Import Duties Act 1958(a), and of all other powers enabling them in that behalf, on the recommendation of the Board of Trade hereby make the following Order:—

1.—(1) This Order may be cited as the Import Duties (Temporary Exemptions) (No. 2) Order 1969.

(2) The Interpretation Act 1889(b) shall apply for the interpretation of this Order as it applies for the interpretation of an Act of Parliament.

(3) This Order shall come into operation on 1st May 1969.

2.—(1) Until the beginning of 1st January 1970 or, in the case of goods in relation to which an earlier day is specified in Schedule 1 to this Order, until the beginning of that day, any import duty which is for the time being chargeable on goods of a heading of the Customs Tariff 1959 specified in that Schedule shall not be chargeable in respect of goods of any description there specified in relation to that heading.

(2) The period for which the goods of the headings of the Customs Tariff 1959 and descriptions specified in Schedule 2 to this Order are exempt from import duty shall be extended until the beginning of 1st January 1970 or, in the case of goods in relation to which an earlier day is specified in that Schedule, until the beginning of that day.

(3) Any entry in column 2 in Schedule 1 or 2 to this Order is to be taken to comprise all goods which would be classified under an entry in the same terms constituting a subheading (other than the final subheading) in the relevant heading in the Customs Tariff 1959.

(4) For the purposes of classification under the Customs Tariff 1959, in so far as that depends on the rate of duty, any goods to which paragraph (1) or (2) above applies shall be treated as chargeable with the same duty as if this Order had not been made.

*E. Alan Fitch,*

*J. McCann,*

Two of the Lords Commissioners of
Her Majesty's Treasury.

21st April 1969.

(a) 1958 c. 6.    (b) 1889 c. 63.

## SCHEDULE 1
### GOODS TEMPORARILY EXEMPT FROM IMPORT DUTY

| Tariff heading | Description |
|---|---|
| 28.18 | Magnesium oxide, dead-burned but not fused, of a purity not less than 96 per cent., containing (a) a total of not more than $1 \cdot 0$ per cent. by weight of aluminium compounds and iron compounds expressed as $Al_2O_3$ and $Fe_2O_3$, (b) a total of not more than $3 \cdot 5$ per cent. by weight of calcium compounds and silicon compounds expressed as CaO and $SiO_2$, the weight of silicon compounds being not less than $1 \cdot 5$ times and not more than 3 times the weight of calcium compounds; and (c) of which not less than 50 per cent. by weight is retained by a sieve having a nominal width of aperture of $\frac{3}{16}$ inch (until 3rd July 1969) |
| 29.03 | Methanesulphonic acid |
| 29.10 | 1,1-Diethoxyethane (until 4th September 1969) |
| 29.14 | 2,4-Dichlorobenzoyl chloride (until 3rd July 1969) |
| 29.22 | N-n-Butylaniline (until 3rd July 1969) |
| 29.24 | N-2,3-Epoxypropyltrimethylammonium chloride (until 3rd July 1969) |
| 29.25 | Procainamide hydrochloride (until 4th September 1969) |
| 29.26 | Guanidinium carbonate |
| 29.31 | 4-(Methylthio)-3,5-xylyl methylcarbamate |
| 29.35 | 2-[2-(4-Benzhydrylpiperazin-1-yl)ethoxy]ethanol 4,4'-methylenedi-(3-hydroxy-2-naphthoate) 4-Hydroxy-3-(1,2,3,4-tetrahydro-1-naphthyl)coumarin |
| 29.39 | Methylprednisolone Methylprednisolone 21-acetate |
| 29.44 | Natamycin (until 3rd July 1969) |
| 68.13 | Asbestos paper, rubber impregnated, in rolls, being not less than $0 \cdot 75$ millimetre and not more than $0 \cdot 85$ millimetre in thickness, weighing not less than $0 \cdot 71$ kilogramme and not more than $0 \cdot 78$ kilogramme per square metre, and which, when heated to a temperature of $1,000°$ centigrade, has a loss in weight of not less than 28 per cent. and not more than 32 per cent. (until 3rd July 1969) |
| 73.06 | Iron or steel ingots, blocks, lumps and similar forms, other than those manufactured entirely from pig iron smelted wholly with charcoal (until 3rd July 1969) |
| 73.07 | Iron or steel blooms, billets, slabs and sheet bars (until 3rd July 1969) |
| 73.08 | Iron or steel coils for re-rolling (until 3rd July 1969) |

## SCHEDULE 2
### GOODS FOR WHICH EXEMPTION FROM IMPORT DUTY EXTENDED

| Tariff heading | Description |
|---|---|
| 05.15 | Sand eels (ammodytes) |
| 29.04 | Tridecyl alcohol, mixed isomers (until 3rd July 1969) |
| 29.06 | 2-secButylphenol (until 6th November 1969) |
| 29.14 | Chloroacetyl chloride (until 3rd July 1969) |
| 29.22 | 1,2-Diaminoethane (until 3rd July 1969) Diethylenetriamine (until 3rd July 1969) Tetraethylenepentamine (until 3rd July 1969) Triethylenetetramine (until 3rd July 1969) |

| *Tariff heading* | *Description* |
|---|---|
| 29.23 | NN-Di-(2-hydroxy-n-propyl)aniline (until 3rd July 1969)<br>p-Phenetidine (until 4th September 1969) |
| 29.31 | n-Dodecane-1-thiol (until 3rd July 1969) |
| 29.35 | 2,3,5,6-Tetrahydro-6-phenylimidazo[2,1-b]thiazole hydrochloride |
| 29.44 | Rifamycin B diethylamide, monosodium derivative |
| 37.01 | Diazo film in sheets, being film which is capable, when developed by heating at between 105° and 135° centigrade, of producing a positive image consisting of light-scattering cavities in an otherwise transparent coating (until 4th September 1969) |
| 37.02 | Diazo film in rolls, being film which is capable, when developed by heating at between 105° and 135° centigrade, of producing a positive image consisting of light-scattering cavities in an otherwise transparent coating (until 4th September 1969) |
| 37.03 | Diazo paper, unexposed, being paper which is capable, when developed by heating at between 105° and 135° centigrade, of producing a positive image consisting of light-scattering cavities in an otherwise transparent coating (until 4th September 1969) |
| 39.03 | Scrap exposed X-ray film |
| 51.01 | Yarn wholly of polytetrafluoroethylene (until 4th September 1969) |
| 51.02 | Monofil wholly of fluorocarbon polymer (until 3rd July 1969) |
| 70.18 | Optical glass in the form of sheets, slabs or moulded lens blanks, having, with reference to the D line of sodium, a refractive index ($n_D$) not less than 1·5625 and not greater than 1·5650 and a dispersive power ($\nu_D$) not less than 60·0 and not greater than 61·5 (until 4th September 1969)<br>Optical glass in the form of sheets, slabs or moulded lens blanks, having, with reference to the D line of sodium, a refractive index ($n_D$) not less than 1·612 and not greater than 1·615 and a dispersive power ($\nu_D$) not less than 43·5 and not greater than 45·0; having also at a wavelength of 400 nanometres a light transmission for a 25 millimetres path of not less than 83 per cent.; and which acquires no visible stain when kept for 15 minutes at a temperature of 25° centigrade in contact with a buffered sodium acetate solution having a pH value of 4·6 (until 4th September 1969) |
| 73.19 | Hot rolled seamless circular steel tubes of an outside diameter of not less than $19\frac{1}{2}$ inches and not more than $24\frac{1}{2}$ inches, and of a wall thickness of not less than $\frac{7}{16}$ inch and not more than $\frac{5}{8}$ inch (until 4th September 1969) |
| 76.03 | Aluminium discs of a minimum value of 8s. per lb., not less than 6 inches nor more than 18 inches in diameter and not less than 0·033 inch nor more than 0·036 inch in thickness and which, when either face is placed on a flat surface, do not deviate from the flat by more than 0·010 inch at any point (until 4th September 1969) |
| 81.04 | Manganese metal of a purity not less than 96 per cent. and not more than 99·5 per cent. and containing not more than 1·0 per cent. by weight of carbon and not more than 3·0 per cent. by weight of iron (until 4th September 1969) |
| 85.15 | Loran receivers incorporating direct reading indicators, designed to operate only on frequencies of 1,700 kilocycles per second or more |
| 90.17 | Endoradiosondes for the measurement of pH; and specialised receiving and recording apparatus therefor (until 3rd July 1969) |

## EXPLANATORY NOTE

*(This Note is not part of the Order.)*

This Order provides that the goods listed in Schedule 1 shall be temporarily exempt from import duty, and those listed in Schedule 2 shall continue to be exempt from import duty, both until 1st January, 1970, except for items for which an earlier day is specified.

# STATUTORY INSTRUMENTS

## 1969 No. 573

## CUSTOMS AND EXCISE

### The Import Duties (Temporary Exemptions) (No. 3) Order 1969

| | |
|---|---|
| Made - - - - | 21st April 1969 |
| Laid before the House of Commons - - - | 25th April 1969 |
| Coming into Operation | 1st May 1969 |

The Lords Commissioners of Her Majesty's Treasury, by virtue of the powers conferred on them by section 13 of the Import Duties Act 1958(a) and of all other powers enabling them in that behalf, on the recommendation of the Board of Trade hereby make the following Order:—

1.—(1) This Order may be cited as the Import Duties (Temporary Exemptions) (No. 3) Order 1969.

(2) The Interpretation Act 1889(b) shall apply for the interpretation of this Order as it applies for the interpretation of an Act of Parliament.

(3) This Order shall come into operation on 1st May 1969.

2. Schedule 1 to the Import Duties (Temporary Exemptions) (No. 1) Order 1969(c) (which lists the goods temporarily exempted from import duty by virtue of Article 2(1) of the Order, and contains an entry for certain goods of heading 29.08 of the Customs Tariff 1959) shall be amended by omitting from that entry " 1,4-Di-(2-hydroxyethoxy)benzene ".

*B. K. O'Malley,*
*Joseph Harper,*
Two of the Lords Commissioners of
Her Majesty's Treasury.

21st April 1969.

### EXPLANATORY NOTE

*(This Note is not part of the Order.)*

This Order revokes the temporary exemption from import duty of 1,4-Di-(2-hydroxyethoxy)benzene.

(a) 1958 c. 6.　　(b) 1889 c. 63.　　(c) S.I. 1969/232 (1969 I, p. 620).

## STATUTORY INSTRUMENTS

## 1969 No. 575

## RIGHTS OF WAY

## The Town and Country Planning (Public Path Orders) Regulations 1969

| | |
|---|---|
| *Made* - - - - | *21st April* 1969 |
| *Laid before Parliament* | *28th April* 1969 |
| *Coming into Operation* | *1st May* 1969 |

The Minister of Housing and Local Government in exercise of his powers under sections 96(4) and 104 and paragraphs 1(1), 5 and 6 of Schedule 7 of the Town and Country Planning Act 1968(a) and section 217 of the Town and Country Planning Act 1962(b) and all other powers enabling him in that behalf and the Secretary of State in relation to Wales in exercise of his powers under sections 96(4) and 104 and paragraph 5 of Schedule 7 of the said Act of 1968 and section 217 of the said Act of 1962 and all other powers enabling him in that behalf, hereby make the following regulations:—

## PART I

### GENERAL

**1.** These regulations may be cited as the Town and Country Planning (Public Path Orders) Regulations 1969 and shall come into operation on 1st May 1969.

**2.**—(1) In these regulations, unless the context otherwise requires—

"the Act" means the Town and Country Planning Act 1968;

"the Minister" means except as respects Wales the Minister of Housing and Local Government and as respects Wales the Secretary of State for Wales;

"a public path order" means an order made under section 94 or 95 of the Act and includes an order revoking or varying any such order;

"Wales" includes Monmouthshire.

(2) The Interpretation Act 1889(c) shall apply to the interpretation of these regulations as it applies to the interpretation of an Act of Parliament.

## PART II

### FORM OF ORDER

**3.** A public path order shall be in the appropriate form (or substantially in the appropriate form) set out in Schedule 1 hereto with such modifications as the circumstances may require.

---

(a) 1968 c. 72.          (b) 1962 c. 38.          (c) 1889 c. 63.

**4.** The map required to be contained in a public path order shall be on a scale of not less than twenty-five inches to one mile or 1/2,500 or on such smaller scale as the Minister may in any particular case authorise.

**5.** In the case of any conflict between the map and the particulars contained in a schedule to a public path order, the schedule shall prevail.

## PART III

### PROCEDURE

**6.**—(1) A public path order shall be made in duplicate, and where the order is submitted to the Minister for confirmation shall be accompanied by two copies of the order and a copy of any notice published before the submission as required by paragraph 1 of Schedule 7 to the Act together with any representations or objections which have been duly made with respect to such order and not withdrawn and a statement by the authority by whom such order was made of the grounds on which the authority consider that such order should be confirmed.

(2) Where a public path order provides for extinguishing a right of way over land under, in, over, along or across which there is any apparatus belonging to or used by statutory undertakers for the purpose of their undertaking the consent of the undertakers shall also be sent to the Minister when the order is submitted to him for confirmation.

**7.** After a public path order has been confirmed by the Minister, the authority by whom such order was made shall, as soon as the requirements of paragraph 6 of Schedule 7 to the Act have been complied with, furnish to the Minister a certificate to that effect, and a copy of the notice required by that paragraph to be published.

**8.** After a public path order has been confirmed, the authority by whom the order was made shall send a copy of the order as confirmed to the Ordnance Survey and to every council (as defined by paragraph 1(3) of Schedule 7 to the Act) on whom notice was served under the provisions of paragraph 1(2) of that Schedule and where the whole or any part of the land to which the confirmed order relates is situate in a rural parish to the Council of that parish or, in the case of a rural parish not having a parish council, to the chairman of the parish meeting.

**9.** Any notice required to be given, served or displayed under Schedule 7 to the Act by an authority by whom a public path order is made shall be in the appropriate form (or substantially in the appropriate form) set out in Schedule 2 hereto.

SCHEDULE 1　　　　　　　　　　　　　　　Regulation 3

FORMS OF ORDERS

Form No. 1　　　　　　Public Path [Stopping-Up] [Diversion] Order

Town and Country Planning Act 1968, Section 94

(*Title of Order*)

Whereas the (*name of order-making authority*) are satisfied that it is necessary to [stop-up] [divert] the [footpath] [bridleway] to which this order relates in order to enable development to be carried out [in accordance with planning permission granted under

Part III of the Town and Country Planning Act 1962 or the enactments replaced by that Part of that Act] [by a government department].

Now, therefore, the (*name of order-making authority*) in pursuance of the powers in that behalf conferred by section 94 of the Town and Country Planning Act 1968 hereby make the following order:—

1. The [footpath] [bridleway] over the land situate at                    shown by a bold black line on the map annexed hereto and described in Part I of the Schedule hereto shall be [stopped-up] [diverted] as provided by this order.

[2. There shall be created to the reasonable satisfaction of (*name of order-making authority*) an alternative highway for use as a replacement for the [footpath] [bridleway] referred to in Article 1 above as specified in, and over the land described in, Part II of the Schedule hereto and shown by bold black dashes on the map contained in this order.] or

[2. The highway over the land situate at                    described in Part III of the Schedule hereto and shown hatched black on the map contained in this order shall be improved to the reasonable satisfaction of (*name of order-making authority*) as follows: (*description of improvement*)                    ].

3. The [stopping-up] [diversion] of the [footpath] [bridleway] referred to in Article 1 above shall have effect [on the date on which it is certified by (*name of order-making authority*) that the provisions of Article 2 above have been complied with.] [on the confirmation of this order].

[4. The following works [may] [shall] be carried out in relation to the highway described in Part [I] [II] [III] of the Schedule hereto, that is to say: (*description of works*)                    ].

[5. (*Name of person*) is hereby required to [pay] [make the following contributions in respect of] the cost of carrying out the above-mentioned works [that is to say: (*details of contributions*)                    ].                    .]

[6. Where immediately before the date on which a highway is [stopped-up] [diverted] in pursuance of this order there is apparatus on, under or over that highway belonging to statutory undertakers for the purpose of carrying on their undertaking, the undertakers shall continue to have the same rights in respect of the apparatus as they then had.]

[7.] This order may be cited as the (*name of order-making authority and name or reference of path or way*) Public Path [Stopping-Up] [Diversion] Order 19  .

## SCHEDULE

### PART I

Description of site of existing path or way.

(*Describe position and width, where necessary in sections, A-B, B-C, etc., as indicated on map.*)

### PART II

Description of site of alternative highway.

(*Describe position and width, where necessary in sections, D-E, E-F, etc., as indicated on map.*)

### PART III

Description of existing highway to be improved.

NOTE:—Omit words in square brackets where inappropriate.

Form No. 2                     Public Path Extinguishment Order

Town and Country Planning Act 1968, Section 95

(*Title of Order*)

Whereas the (*name of order-making authority*) (hereinafter called "the Council") [acquired] [appropriated] for planning purposes the land situate at
described in Part I of the Schedule hereto which is subject to the public right of way to which this order relates and the said land is held by the Council for the purposes for which it was [acquired] [appropriated];

And whereas the Council are satisfied that [an alternative right of way [has been] [will be] provided] [the provision of an alternative right of way is not required]:

Now, therefore, the Council in pursuance of the powers in that behalf conferred by section 95 of the Town and Country Planning Act 1968 hereby make the following order:—

1. The public right of way over the [footpath] [bridleway] situate at
shown by a bold black line on the map annexed hereto and described in the Schedule hereto shall be extinguished [on the confirmation of this order] [at the expiration of
days from the date of confirmation of this order].

2. This order may be cited as the (*name of order-making authority and name or reference of path or way*) Extinguishment Order 19  .

SCHEDULE

Description of site of path or way extinguished.

(*Describe position and width, where necessary in sections, A-B, B-C, etc., as indicated on map.*)

NOTE:—Omit words in square brackets where inappropriate.

SCHEDULE 2                                              Regulation 9

FORMS OF NOTICES

Form No. 1                     Notice of Public Path Order

Town and Country Planning Act 1968, Section [94] [95]

(*Name of authority by whom the order is made*)

(*Title of Order*)

(1) [To:
of                                      ].

The above-named order (hereinafter referred to as "the order") made on the
day of                   19   is about to be submitted to the [Minister of Housing and Local Government] [Secretary of State for Wales] for confirmation or to be confirmed by the (*name of order-making authority*) as an unopposed order.

The effect of the order, if confirmed without modification, will be to [extinguish the public right of way running from                          to                          [and create an alternative highway in lieu] ] [divert the public right of way running from
to                          to a line running from
to                   ].

A copy of the order and the map contained in it has been deposited at
and may be inspected free of charge at                       between the hours of
a.m. and          p.m. on                       .

Any representation or objection with respect to the order may be sent in writing to the (*name and address of order-making authority*) not later than (2)                   19
and should state the grounds on which it is made.

If no representations or objections are duly made, or if any so made are withdrawn, the (*name of order-making authority*) may, instead of submitting the order to the [Minister of Housing and Local Government] [Secretary of State for Wales] for confirmation, themselves confirm the order as an unopposed order. If the order is submitted to the [Minister] [Secretary of State] for confirmation any representations and objections which have been duly made and not withdrawn will be sent to the [Minister] [Secretary of State] with the order.

(1) [If you wish to be notified if the order is confirmed, and to have a copy of the order as confirmed, you should write to (*name and address of order-making authority*), giving your name and the address to which these documents may be sent].

Dated                                                      19  .

NOTES:—General: Omit words in square brackets where inappropriate.
      (1) Insert only in personal notices.
      (2) Insert date not less than 28 days from the date of first publication of this notice.

Form No. 2          Notice of Confirmation of Public Path Order
Town and Country Planning Act 1968, Section [94] [95]
(*Name of authority by whom order was made*)
(*Title of Order*)
(1) [To:
of                                             .]

On                     19     the [Minister of Housing and Local Government] [Secretary of State for Wales] [(*name of authority by whom the order was made*)] confirmed (2) [with modifications] the above-named order.

The effect of the order as confirmed is to [extinguish the public right of way running from                     to                     [and create an alternative highway in lieu]] [divert the public right of way running from                     to to a line running from                     to                     ].

A copy of the confirmed order and the map contained in it has been deposited at and may be inspected free of charge at                     between          a.m. and p.m. on                .

This order becomes operative as from                          but if any person aggrieved by the order desires to question the validity thereof or of any provision contained therein on the grounds that it is not within the powers of the Town and Country Planning Act 1968, or on the ground that any requirement of that Act or any regulation made thereunder has not been complied with in relation to the confirmation of the order, he may under section 178 of the Town and Country Planning Act 1962 within six weeks from (*date on which notice is first published as required by paragraph 6 of Schedule 7 to the Town and Country Planning Act 1968*) make application for the purpose to the High Court.

Dated                                                      19  .

NOTES:—General: Omit words in square brackets where inappropriate.
      (1) Insert only in personal notices.
      (2) Applicable only to confirmation by a Minister.

Given under the official seal of the Minister of Housing and Local Government on 18th April 1969.

(L.S.)                                          *Anthony Greenwood,*
Minister of Housing and Local Government.

*George Thomas,*
One of Her Majesty's
Principal Secretaries of State,
21st April 1969.                                          Welsh Office.

# EXPLANATORY NOTE

*(This Note is not part of the Regulations.)*

These regulations prescribe the forms and notices for, and deal with the making, submission (where necessary) to the Minister of Housing and Local Government or Secretary of State for Wales and confirmation of, (1) orders made by local authorities under section 94 of the Town and Country Planning Act 1968 stopping up or diverting public footpaths or bridleways to enable development to be carried out in accordance with planning permission or by a government department, and, (2) orders made by local authorities under section 95 of that Act stopping up footpaths or bridleways over land held by such local authorities for planning purposes.

## STATUTORY INSTRUMENTS

### 1969 No. 583

### CIVIL AVIATION

### The Air Navigation (General) (Second Amendment) Regulations 1969

| | |
|---|---|
| *Made* - - - | *22nd April* 1969 |
| *Coming into Operation* | 1*st May* 1969 |

The Board of Trade, in exercise of their powers under Articles 7(3) and 8(4) of the Air Navigation Order 1966(a), as amended(b), and of all other powers enabling them in that behalf, hereby make the following Regulations.

**1.** These Regulations may be cited as the Air Navigation (General) (Second Amendment) Regulations 1969, and shall come into operation on 1st May 1969.

**2.** The Interpretation Act 1889(c) applies for the purpose of the interpretation of these Regulations as it applies for the purpose of the interpretation of an Act of Parliament.

**3.** The Air Navigation (General) Regulations 1966(d), as amended(e), shall be further amended as follows:—

(1) In Regulation 11 in the list of prescribed countries:

(*a*) After "Dominica" there shall be inserted "Ghana";

(*b*) After "Kenya" there shall be inserted "Kuwait";

(*c*) After "St. Vincent" there shall be inserted "Singapore";

(*d*) "Southern Rhodesia" shall be deleted;

(*e*) For "United Republic of Tanzania and Zanzibar" there shall be substituted "United Republic of Tanzania";

(2) In the first sentence of the Schedule, for "(9)" there shall be substituted "(10)".

*Robert Burns,*
A Second Secretary
of the Board of Trade.

22nd April 1969.

(a) S.I. 1966/1184 (1966 III, p. 3073).  (b) There is no relevant amending instrument.
(c) 1889 c. 63.  (d) S.I. 1966/1256 (1966 III, p. 3411).
(e) S.I. 1966/1376 (1966 III, p. 3700).

# EXPLANATORY NOTE

*(This Note is not part of the Regulations.)*

These Regulations amend the Air Navigation (General) Regulations 1966, as previously amended.

In addition to correcting two minor errors, these Regulations add Ghana, Kuwait and Singapore to, and delete Southern Rhodesia from, the list of countries prescribed by Regulation 11 whose licensed maintenance engineers may issue certificates of maintenance and compliance for the purposes of the Air Navigation Order 1966.

# STATUTORY INSTRUMENTS

## 1969 No. 584

## PENSIONS

## The Increase of Pensions (Injury Warrant Pensions) Regulations 1969

| | |
|---|---|
| *Made* - - - | *22nd April* 1969 |
| *Laid before Parliament* | *29th April* 1969 |
| *Coming into Operation* | *30th April* 1969 |

The Minister for the Civil Service, in exercise of the powers conferred on him by paragraph 7 of Schedule 2 to the Pensions (Increase) Act 1956(a), section 3(2) of the Pensions (Increase) Act 1959(b), that section as applied by section 8(2) of the Pensions (Increase) Act 1962(c) and section 5(2) of the Pensions (Increase) Act 1965(d), and paragraphs 12 and 14 of Schedule 2 to the Pensions (Increase) Act 1969(e), and of all other powers enabling him in that behalf, hereby makes the following Regulations :—

*Citation and commencement*

**1.** These Regulations may be cited as the Increase of Pensions (Injury Warrant Pensions) Regulations 1969. and shall come into operation on 30th April 1969.

*Interpretation*

**2.**—(1) In these Regulations the expression "the Act of" a specified year means the Pensions (Increase) Act of that year.

(2) Any reference in these Regulations to the provisions of any enactment or instrument shall be construed, unless the context otherwise requires, as a reference to those provisions as amended or re-enacted by any other enactment or instrument.

(3) The Interpretation Act 1889(f) shall apply for the interpretation of these Regulations as it applies for the interpretation of an Act of Parliament.

*Pensions to which the Regulations apply*

**3.** These Regulations shall apply to any pension payable under the Injury Warrants 1952 to 1967(g), being a pension which is reduced by virtue of paragraph 16 or paragraph 25(1)(b) or (c) of the Injury Warrant 1952 or paragraph 10 of the Injury Warrant 1965 (which paragraphs provide for reduction by reason of other benefits).

---

(a) 1956 c.39.      (b) 1959 c.50.
(c) 1962 c.2 (11 & 12 Eliz.2).      (d) 1965 c.78.
(e) 1969 c.7.      (f) 1889 c.63.
(g) S.I. 1952/60, 1957/1354, 1965/1024, 1967/876 (1952 II, p.2400; 1957 II, p.1758; 1965 I, p. 2496; 1967 II, p.2614).

*Method of calculating adjusted rate of pensions*

**4.**—(1) In relation to any pension to which these Regulations apply, paragraph 2 of Schedule 2 to the Act of 1969 (meaning of "adjusted rate") shall apply subject to the modification specified in paragraph (2) of this Regulation.

(2) In calculating, in accordance with the said paragraph 2 of Schedule 2, the adjusted rate of a pension to which these Regulations apply, any reduction in such pension by virtue of paragraph 16 or paragraph 25(1)(*b*) or (*c*) of the Injury Warrant 1952 or paragraph 10 of the Injury Warrant 1965 shall be disregarded.

*Limit on total amount of increases under Pensions (Increase) Acts*

**5.**—(1) In relation to any pension to which these Regulations apply, section 1(1) of, and Schedule 2 to, the Act of 1956, section 1(1) of the Act of 1959, sections 1 and 2 of the Act of 1962, section 1 of the Act of 1965 and section 1(1) and (2) of the Act of 1969 shall apply subject to the modification specified in paragraph (2) of this Regulation.

(2) The aggregate of—

> (*a*) any increases by virtue of the Act of 1956, the Act of 1959 and the Act of 1962, as modified by Regulations 1, 2 and 3 of the Increase of Pensions (Modification) (No. 1) Regulations 1963(a),

> (*b*) any increase by virtue of the Act of 1965, as modified by Regulation 2 of the Increase of Pensions (Injury Warrant Pensions) Regulations 1966(b), and

> (*c*) any increase by virtue of the Act of 1969, as modified by Regulation 4 of these Regulations,

of a pension to which these Regulations apply shall not exceed the amount (if any) by which the aggregate of—

> (i) the adjusted rate of such pension calculated in accordance with paragraph 2 of Schedule 2 to the Act of 1969, as modified by Regulation 4 of these Regulations, and

> (ii) the increase thereof which would, apart from this paragraph, be payable by virtue of the Act of 1969, as modified by Regulation 4 of these Regulations,

exceeds the rate of the benefits in respect of which such pension is reduced by virtue of paragraph 16 or paragraph 25(1)(*b*) or (*c*) of the Injury Warrant 1952 or paragraph 10 of the Injury Warrant 1965.

(3) Regulation 3 of the Increase of Pensions (Injury Warrant Pensions) Regulations 1966 (which is superseded by paragraphs (1) and (2) of this Regulation) shall cease to have effect on the coming into operation of these Regulations.

*Effective date of increase*

**6.** Any increase authorised by these Regulations shall be payable in respect of any period beginning on or after 1st April 1969.

---

(a) S.I. 1963/677 (1963 I, p.833).          (b) S.I. 1966/24 (1966 I, p.34).

Given under the official seal of the Minister for the Civil Service on 22nd April 1969.

(L.S.)

J. E. Herbecq,
Authorised by the Minister
for the Civil Service.

## EXPLANATORY NOTE

*(This Note is not part of the Regulations.)*

Under the Injury Warrants 1952-1967 allowances are paid to Civil Servants and other persons employed by the Government who are injured on duty, and to the dependants of those who have died as a result of their injuries. These allowances are reduced by the value of certain social security benefits under the National Insurance Act 1965, the National Insurance (Industrial Injuries) Act 1965 and the Family Allowances Act 1965, as amended. These Regulations provide for pensions increase under the Pensions (Increase) Act 1969 to be calculated on the gross amount of the allowance (including any increases under the Pensions (Increase) Acts of 1956, 1959, 1962 and 1965) before the reduction for other benefits is made. The pensions increase so calculated is restricted in order to ensure that the allowances paid to beneficiaries under the Injury Warrants plus pensions increase will not exceed the amount (if any) by which the gross amount of the Warrant allowance plus pensions increase thereon exceeds the value of the social security benefits in respect of which the Warrant allowance is reduced.

STATUTORY INSTRUMENTS

## 1969 No. 585 (L. 9)

## COUNTY COURTS

### PROCEDURE

## The County Court (Amendment) Rules 1969

| | |
|---|---|
| *Made* - - - - | *21st April* 1969 |
| *Coming into Operation* | *23rd June* 1969 |

**1.**—(1) These Rules may be cited as the County Court (Amendment) Rules 1969.

(2) In these Rules an Order and Rule referred to by number means the Order and Rule so numbered in the County Court Rules 1936(a), as amended(b), and a Form referred to by number means the Form so numbered in Appendix A to those Rules.

(3) The Interpretation Act 1889(c) shall apply for the interpretation of these Rules as it applies for the interpretation of an Act of Parliament.

**2.** Order 2, Rule 1, shall be amended as follows:—

(1) The following paragraph shall be inserted after paragraph (3):—

"(4) Where the plaintiff's claim is founded on tort and the defendant or each of the defendants does not reside or carry on business in England or Wales, paragraph (1)(*a*) of this Rule shall have effect as if for the words 'the defendant or one of the defendants' there were substituted the words 'the plaintiff or one of the plaintiffs'."

(2) Paragraph (4) shall stand as paragraph (5).

**3.** Order 8, Rule 41, shall be amended as follows:—

(1) After paragraph (*e*) there shall be inserted the following paragraph:—

"(*f*) the claim is founded on a tort committed in England or Wales, or"

(2) Paragraphs (*f*) and (*g*) shall stand as paragraph (*g*) and (*h*) respectively.

**4.** Order 11 shall be amended as follows:—

(1) After Rule 3 there shall be inserted the following Rule:—

"**4.**—(1) Where a payment under Rule 1 of this Order is made by a defendant who makes a counterclaim against the plaintiff, it shall be accompanied by a notice stating, if it be the case, that in making the payment the defendant has taken into

Payment by defendant counter-claiming.

---

(a) S.R. & O. 1936/626 (1936 I, p. 282).

(b) The relevant amending instruments are S.R. & O. 1938/18, 731, 1475, 1939/815, S.I. 1950/1231, 1953/1728, 1955/1799, 1956/471, 1243, 1957/174, 1136, 1958/2226, 1960/1275, 1962/1293, 1964/353, 1974, 1965/2147, 1967/276 (1938 I, pp. 977, 986, 990; 1939 I, p. 469; 1950 I, p. 400; 1953 I, p. 404; 1955 I, p. 530; 1956 I, pp. 539, 541; 1957 I, pp. 512, 517; 1958 I, p. 372; 1960 I, p. 809; 1962 II, p. 1383; 1964 I, p. 543; III, p. 4477; 1965 III, p. 6292; 1967 I, p. 990).

(c) 1889 c. 63.

account and intends to satisfy the counterclaim or, as the case may be, such of the causes of action joined in the counterclaim as may be specified in the notice.

(2) For the purposes of Rule 2 of this Order a notice referred to in the foregoing paragraph shall be deemed to be such a notice as is mentioned in that Rule.

(3) Where a plaintiff elects to accept an amount paid into court in satisfaction of his claim or the cause or causes of action to which the payment relates and the payment was accompanied by such a notice as is referred to in paragraph (1) of this Rule, then, if the proceedings on the claim are stayed under Rule 7 or 9 of this Order, the proceedings on the counterclaim or, as the case may be, such of the causes of action joined in the counterclaim as are specified in the notice shall also be stayed."

(2) In Rule 14 for the words "Rules 1 to 3, 5 and 6" there shall be substituted the words "Rules 1 to 6".

**5.** Order 15 shall be amended as follows :—

(1) In Rule 2 for the words "only on the service of the process on him" there shall be substituted the words "on the date of the amendment".

(2) Rule 3 shall stand as paragraph (1) of that Rule and the following paragraph shall be added at the end :—

"(2) Where an application for an amendment is made after any relevant period of limitation has expired since the issue of the originating process, the court may nevertheless allow the amendment if it is such as the High Court would have power to allow in a like case".

(3) In the marginal note to Rule 5 for the word "unliquidated" there shall be substituted the word "amended".

**6.** In Order 16, Rule 13(1), for the words "send to" there shall be substituted the word "notify", and the words "notice in Form 97" and the marginal note "Form 97" shall be omitted.

**7.** Order 25, Rule 68(1), shall be amended as follows :—

(1) After the words "if the order is" there shall be inserted the words "for the oral examination of a judgment debtor or".

(2) The following paragraph shall be added at the end :—

"For the purposes of this paragraph a notice in Form 140 shall be treated as being indorsed on a copy of an order if it is incorporated in the same document as the copy".

**8.** In Order 35, Rule 11(1), for the words "on the main mast or on the single mast of the ship" there shall be substituted the words "on any mast of the ship or on the outside of any suitable part of the ship's superstructure".

**9.** Order 37, Rule 4, shall be amended as follows :—

(1) For the marginal note there shall be substituted the words "Non-compliance with Rules".

(2) For paragraph (1) there shall be substituted the following paragraph:—

"(1) Where there has been a failure to comply with any requirement of these Rules, the failure shall be treated as an irregularity and shall not nullify the proceedings, but the court may set aside the proceedings wholly or in part or exercise its powers under these Rules to allow such amendments, if any, and to give such directions, if any, as it thinks fit ".

(3) The following paragraph shall be added at the end of the Rule :—

" (4) The expression ' proceedings ' in paragraph (1), and where it first occurs in paragraph (2), includes any step taken in the proceedings and any document, judgment or order therein ".

**10.** Order 46 shall be amended as follows :—

(1) The following sub-paragraph shall be added to Rule 10(3) :—

" (c) Where such an offer as is mentioned in sub-paragraph (b) is made on Form 18A but the plaintiff elects not to accept it, the court may, if the hirer does not attend the hearing, treat the form as evidence of the facts stated therein for the purposes of sections 35(4)(b) and 36(1) of the Act ".

(2) Rule 17 shall be amended as follows :—

(a) The following paragraph shall be inserted after paragraph (1):—

" (1A) An application for the registration of a maintenance order in a magistrates' court or for an attachment of earnings order may be heard and determined by the registrar."

(b) In paragraph (2) for the words from " shall be made " to " the office of that court" there shall be substituted the words " may be made—

(a) on the making of the maintenance order or an order varying the maintenance order, or

(b) at any other time by lodging in the office of the court in which the order was made."

(c) Sub-paragraphs (a) to (f) of paragraph (2) shall stand as sub-paragraphs (i) to (vi) respectively.

(d) In paragraph (2) the word " and " shall be deleted at the end of sub-paragraph (v) and inserted at the end of sub-paragraph (vi) and the following sub-paragraph shall be added:—" (vii) the date of birth of each child named in the order ".

(e) In paragraph (3)(b) after the words " the applicant's affidavit " there shall be inserted the words " if any ".

(f) In paragraphs (8) and (9) the words " to the judge or, with the leave of the judge, to the registrar " shall be omitted.

**11.** Order 47 shall be amended as follows :—

(1) In Rule 17 the following provisions shall be omitted :—

(1) Paragraph (2) and the figure " (1) " at the beginning of the Rule.

(2) The words " or registrar " in the marginal note.

(2) In Rule 38(1) for the words "one clear day's notice" there shall be substituted the words "3 clear days' notice".

(3) The following Rule shall be substituted for Rule 40:—

Taxation
between
solicitor
and client.

"40.—(1) In this Rule references to a taxation of costs as between solicitor and client include references to—

(*a*) taxation of a solicitor's bill to his own client, and

(*b*) taxation on the common fund basis, that is to say, taxation as between solicitor and client where the costs are to be paid out of a common fund in which the client and others are interested.

(2) Where an order has been made for the taxation of costs as between solicitor and client, the solicitor shall lodge his bill within 14 days of the making of the order and Rule 38(4) of this Order (except paragraph (*b*)) shall apply as if for the reference therein to paragraph (1) of that Rule there were substituted a reference to this paragraph.

(3) On receipt of the bill the registrar shall fix a time and place for proceeding with the taxation and shall give to the applicant and any other party entitled to be heard on the taxation not less than 3 clear days' notice of the time and place so fixed.

(4) Subject to paragraphs (5) and (6) of this Rule, the costs as between solicitor and client in an action for the recovery of a sum of money only may be taxed on the scale applicable to the amount claimed.

(5) Rules 8 and 9 of this Order shall apply with the necessary modifications to the determination of the costs as they apply to the determination of costs as between party and party.

(6) Where there is a claim for a sum of money only and a counterclaim for a sum of money only, the costs of and subsequent to the filing of the counterclaim may be taxed on the scale applicable to the claim or that applicable to the counterclaim, whichever is the higher:

Provided that the costs of work done solely in connection with the claim shall not be on a scale higher than that applicable to the claim and the costs of work done solely in connection with the counterclaim shall not be on a scale higher than that applicable to the counterclaim.

(7) In garnishee proceedings the costs as between solicitor and client may be taxed on the scale applicable to the amount claimed by the judgment creditor.

(8) The judge by whom any order is made for the taxation of costs as between solicitor and client may, after affording to the solicitor an opportunity of making any representations that he desires to make,—

(*a*) determine the scale on which the costs are to be taxed under the preceding paragraphs of this Rule, and

(*b*) exercise any discretion, whether as to scale or any other matter, give any direction and grant any certificate that the judge could have exercised, given or granted in relation to costs as between party and party.

(9) On a taxation of costs as between solicitor and client the registrar shall not be bound to follow any determination of the

judge or registrar in relation to the costs as between party and party and accordingly, subject to any determination made under paragraph (8), the registrar may—

(a) exercise any of the powers conferred on the judge by that paragraph;

(b) allow items disallowed as between party and party, and

(c) allow a higher sum in respect of any item than the sum allowed as between party and party, not exceeding the maximum sum prescribed for that item in the scale on which the costs are being taxed.

(10) The costs of a taxation under the Solicitors Act 1957 shall be dealt with by the registrar in accordance with the provisions of that Act and shall be added to or deducted from the amount certified to be due."

1957 c. 27.

(4) The following Rule shall be added after Rule 48:—

"49. Subject to the provisions of this Order and to section 73(4) of the Solicitors Act 1957, Order 62, Rules 28, 29 and 31, of the Rules of the Supreme Court shall apply, with the necessary modifications, to the taxation of costs in the county court as they apply to the taxation of costs in the High Court".

Bases of taxation.

**12.** In each of the following provisions for the words "fold it as indicated, stamp it, and post it" there shall be substituted the words "send it by prepaid post":—

(a) paragraph (4) of the Instructions on Form 18,

(b) paragraph (4) of the Instructions on Form 19,

(c) paragraph (2) of the Instructions on Form 20,

(d) paragraph (2) of the Instructions on Form 21(1),

(e) paragraph (3) of the Instructions on Form 21(2), and

(f) paragraph (4) of the Instructions on Form 22.

**13.** Form 18A shall be amended as follows:—

(1) In the first Note the words "as to your means" shall be omitted.

(2) In the sentence beginning "*Add, in an action*" for the words "*applies* I understand that" there shall be substituted the following words:—

"*applies*—

6. Are the goods in your possession?............................. I understand that".

**14.** In paragraph 2(e) of Form 35 for the words "by posting the same on the previous day" there shall be substituted the words "by posting the same by first class mail on the previous day [or by second class mail on the        day of            19  ]".

**15.** At the end of paragraph (1) of Form 61 there shall be inserted the following words:—

"The defendant states that the goods are [not] in his possession".

**16.** In Form 65 after the first paragraph there shall be inserted the following paragraph:—

"[In making this payment the defendant has taken into account and intends to satisfy his counterclaim] [or his cause of action for            ]".

**17.** Form 97 shall be revoked.

**18.** The following form shall be substituted for Form 150:—

"150

### ORDER FOR ORAL EXAMINATION OF JUDGMENT DEBTOR

[*General Title—Form* 1]

Order 25,
Rules 2(3),
68(1).

Seal

To

of

WHEREAS the Plaintiff obtained a judgment [*or* order] against the above-named Defendant      in this Court [*or as the case may be*] on the     day of     19  , for the payment of £   :   : for debt [*or* damages] and costs, of which £   :   :   still remains unpaid.

YOU ARE HEREBY ORDERED to attend before the Registrar at the office of this Court at     on     day the     day of 19  , at   o'clock [*or* before the Registrar of the     County Court at such time and place as he may appoint], and be orally examined as to any and what debts are owing to you and whether you have any and what other property or means of satisfying the said judgment [*or* order], and to produce at such time and place any books or documents in your possession or power containing particulars relating to your property or means.

AND IT IS FURTHER ORDERED that the costs of this application and of the examination thereunder be in the discretion of the said Registrar.

AND TAKE NOTICE that unless you obey the directions contained in this order you will be guilty of contempt of Court and will be liable to be committed to prison.

Dated this      day of      19  .

                               **Registrar**

This order was made on the application of

         of

[solicitor[s] for ] the Plaintiff

*Travelling expenses to be paid or tendered to the said*

                         *Defendant*    £   :   :

---

[I appoint     day, the     day of     19  , at   o'clock, at the office of the      County Court at       for this examination.

            Registrar of the        County Court]."

**19.** Notwithstanding anything in Rule 12, the Forms mentioned in that Rule may continue to be used in the form hitherto prescribed until the Lord Chancellor otherwise directs.

We, the undersigned members of the Rule Committee appointed by the Lord Chancellor under section 102 of the County Courts Act 1959(a), having by virtue of the powers vested in us in this behalf made the foregoing Rules, do hereby certify the same under our hand and submit them to the Lord Chancellor accordingly.

> *Owen Temple-Morris.*
> *D. O. McKee.*
> *S. Granville Smith.*
> *Connolly H. Gage.*
> *Hugh Mais*
> *W. Ralph Davies*
> *E. A. Everett.*
> *Brian D. Bush.*
> *Arthur Figgis.*
> *A. F. Stapleton Cotton.*
> *D. A. Marshall.*

I allow these Rules, which shall come into force on 23rd June 1969.

Dated 21st April 1969.

> *Gardiner,* C.

---

## EXPLANATORY NOTE

### (*This Note is not part of the Rules.*)

These Rules amend the County Court Rules so as—

(1) to give the county court power to allow process to be served out of the jurisdiction where the claim is founded on a tort committed in England or Wales (Rules 2 and 3);

(2) to permit a counterclaiming defendant who pays money into court in satisfaction of the plaintiff's claim to state that he has taken his counterclaim into account in calculating the amount of the payment (Rules 4 and 16);

(3) to provide that a person ordered to be added or substituted as a defendant shall become a party on the date of amendment and to enable the county court to allow certain amendments, notwithstanding that any relevant period of limitation has expired (Rule 5);

(4) to prescribe a new form of order for the oral examination of a judgment debtor (Rules 7 and 18);

(5) to regulate the effect of non-compliance with any requirement of the Rules (Rule 9);

(6) to enable the court in an action for the recovery of goods under the Hire-Purchase Act 1965 to treat the hirer's form of admission as evidence that the goods are in his possession (Rules 10(1), 13 and 15);

(7) to modify the procedure under the Maintenance Orders Act 1958 (Rule 10(2));

---

(a) 1959 c. 22.

(8) to make fresh provision for the taxation of costs as between solicitor and client and as to the bases of taxation (Rule 11);

(9) to make minor alterations with regard to the service of process and other matters (Rules 6, 8, 12, 14 and 17).

## STATUTORY INSTRUMENTS

### 1969 No. 586 (S.52)

### EDUCATION, SCOTLAND

### The Teaching Council (Scotland) Act 1965
### (Amendment of Constitution of the Council) Order 1969

| | | | | |
|---|---|---|---|---|
| *Made -* | *-* | *-* | *-* | 21*st April* 1969 |
| *Coming into Operation* | | | | 30*th April* 1969 |

In the exercise of the powers conferred on me by paragraph 6 of Schedule 1 to the Teaching Council (Scotland) Act 1965**(a)** and of all other powers enabling me in that behalf, and after consultation with the General Teaching Council and other bodies who appear to me to be concerned, I hereby make the following order:—

**1.** This order may be cited as the Teaching Council (Scotland) Act 1965 (Amendment of Constitution of the Council) Order 1969 and shall come into operation on 30th April 1969.

**2.** In Schedule 1 to the Teaching Council (Scotland) Act 1965:—

    (*a*) in paragraph 4(1) there shall be added at the end:—
"save that in respect of the initial membership of the Council the period of office shall be four years six months."; and

    (*b*) in paragraph 5(3) after the word "years" there shall be inserted:—
"or, as the case may be, four years six months".

*William Ross,*
One of Her Majesty's Principal
Secretaries of State.

St. Andrew's House,
  Edinburgh, 1.
21st April 1969.

### EXPLANATORY NOTE
(*This Note is not part of the Order.*)

This Order extends the period of office of the initial membership of the General Teaching Council for Scotland from four years to four years six months.

(a) 1965 c. 19.

## STATUTORY INSTRUMENTS

### 1969 No. 588

### SUGAR

### The Sugar (Rates of Surcharge and Surcharge Repayments) (No. 4) Order 1969

| | | |
|---|---|---|
| *Made* - - - | | *22nd April* 1969 |
| *Laid before Parliament* | | *24th April* 1969 |
| *Coming into Operation* | | *25th April* 1969 |

The Minister of Agriculture, Fisheries and Food, in exercise of the powers conferred on him by sections 7(4), 8(6) and 33(4) of the Sugar Act 1956(a) having effect subject to the provisions of section 3 of, and Part II of Schedule 5 to, the Finance Act 1962(b), and section 58 of the Finance Act 1968 (c) and of all other powers enabling him in that behalf, with the concurrence of the Treasury, on the advice of the Sugar Board, hereby makes the following order:—

1.—(1) This order may be cited as the Sugar (Rates of Surcharge and Surcharge Repayments) (No. 4) Order 1969; and shall come into operation on 25th April 1969.

(2) The Interpretation Act 1889(d) shall apply for the interpretation of this order as it applies for the interpretation of an Act of Parliament.

2. Notwithstanding the provisions of Article 2 of the Sugar (Rates of Surcharge and Surcharge Repayments) (No. 3) Order 1969(e), the rates of surcharge payable under and in accordance with the provisions of section 7 of the Sugar Act 1956, having effect as aforesaid, in respect of sugar and invert sugar imported or home produced or used in the manufacture of imported composite sugar products shall on and after 25th April 1969 be those rates specified in Schedule 1 to this order.

3. For the purpose of section 8(3)(*b*) of the Sugar Act 1956, having effect as aforesaid, the rates of surcharge repayments in respect of invert sugar produced in the United Kingdom from materials on which on or after 25th April 1969 sugar duty has been paid or, by virtue of paragraph 1 of Part II of Schedule 5 to the Finance Act 1962, is treated as having been paid shall, notwithstanding the provisions of Article 3 of the Sugar (Rates of Surcharge and Surcharge Repayments) (No. 3) Order 1969 be those specified in Schedule 2 to this order.

---

(a) 1956 c. 48.  (b) 1962 c. 44.
(c) 1968 c. 44.  (d) 1889 c. 63.
(e) S.I. 1969/362 (1969 I, p. 997).

In Witness whereof the Official Seal of the Minister of Agriculture, Fisheries and Food is hereunto affixed on 22nd April 1969.

(L.S.)                                           *R. P. Fraser,*

                                              Authorised by the Minister.

We concur.

22nd April 1969.

                                              *E. Alan Fitch,*

                                              *Walter Harrison,*

                              Two of the Lords Commissioners of
                                      Her Majesty's Treasury.


## SCHEDULE 1

### PART I

#### SURCHARGE RATES FOR SUGAR

| Polarisation | | | | Rate of Surcharge per cwt. | |
|---|---|---|---|---:|---:|
| | | | | s. | d. |
| Exceeding— | | | | | |
| 99° ... ... ... | | | | 16 | 4·0 |
| 98° but not exceeding 99° ... | | | ... ... ... | 15 | 4·8 |
| 97° ,, ,, ,, 98° ... | ... | ... ... | ... ... | 15 | 0·3 |
| 96° ,, ,, ,, 97° ... | ... | ... | ... ... | 14 | 7·6 |
| 95° ,, ,, ,, 96° ... | ... | ... | ... ... | 14 | 2·9 |
| 94° ,, ,, ,, 95° ... | ... | ... | ... ... | 13 | 10·2 |
| 93° ,, ,, ,, 94° ... | ... | ... | ... ... | 13 | 5·5 |
| 92° ,, ,, ,, 93° ... | ... | ... | ... ... | 13 | 0·8 |
| 91° ,, ,, ,, 92° ... | ... | ... | ... ... | 12 | 8·0 |
| 90° ,, ,, ,, 91° ... | ... | ... | ... ... | 12 | 3·3 |
| 89° ,, ,, ,, 90° ... | ... | ... | ... ... | 11 | 10·6 |
| 88° ,, ,, ,, 89° ... | ... | ... | ... ... | 11 | 5·9 |
| 87° ,, ,, ,, 88° ... | ... | ... | ... ... | 11 | 2·0 |
| 86° ,, ,, ,, 87° ... | ... | ... | ... ... | 10 | 10·1 |
| 85° ,, , ,, 86° ... | ... | ... | ... ... | 10 | 6·6 |
| 84° ,, ,, ,, 85° ... | ... | ... | ... ... | 10 | 3·0 |
| 83° ,, ,, ,, 84° ... | ... | ... | ... ... | 9 | 11·5 |
| 82° ,, ,, ,, 83° ... | ... | ... | ... ... | 9 | 8·0 |
| 81° ,, ,, ,, 82° ... | ... | ... | ... ... | 9 | 4·8 |
| 80° ,, ,, ,, 81° ... | ... | ... | ... ... | 9 | 1·7 |
| 79° ,, ,, ,, 80° ... | ... | ... | ... ... | 8 | 10·6 |
| 78° ,, ,, ,, 79° ... | ... | ... | ... ... | 8 | 7·4 |
| 77° ,, ,, ,, 78° ... | ... | ... | ... ... | 8 | 4·3 |
| 76° ,, ,, ,, 77° ... | ... | ... | ... ... | 8 | 1·2 |
| Not exceeding 76° ... | ... | ... | ... ... | 7 | 10·5 |

## PART II

### SURCHARGE RATES FOR INVERT SUGAR

| Sweetening matter content by weight | Rate of Surcharge per cwt. |
|---|---|
| | s. d. |
| 70 per cent. or more ... ... ... ... ... ... ... | 10 4 |
| Less than 70 per cent. and more than 50 per cent. ... ... ... | 7 5 |
| Not more than 50 per cent. ... ... ... ... ... ... | 3 8 |

## SCHEDULE 2

### SURCHARGE REPAYMENT RATES FOR INVERT SUGAR

| Sweetening matter content by weight | Rate of Surcharge Repayment per cwt. |
|---|---|
| | s. d. |
| More than 80 per cent. ... ... ... ... ... ... ... | 12 3 |
| More than 70 per cent. but not more than 80 per cent. ... ... | 10 4 |
| More than 60 per cent. but not more than 70 per cent. ... ... | 7 5 |
| More than 50 per cent. but not more than 60 per cent. ... ... | 5 11 |
| Not more than 50 per cent. and the invert sugar not being less in weight than 14 lb. per gallon ... ... ... ... ... | 3 8 |

## EXPLANATORY NOTE

(*This Note is not part of the Order.*)

This order prescribes—

(*a*) reductions equivalent to 2s. 4d. per cwt. of refined sugar in the rates of surcharge payable on sugar and invert sugar which become chargeable with surcharge on or after 25th April 1969;

(*b*) correspondingly reduced rates of surcharge repayment in respect of invert sugar produced in the United Kingdom from materials on which surcharge has been paid.

## 1969 No. 589

## SUGAR

### The Composite Sugar Products (Surcharge and Surcharge Repayments—Average Rates) (No. 4) Order 1969

|  |  |  |  |  |  |
|---|---|---|---|---|---|
| *Made* | - | - | - | - | *22nd April* 1969 |
| *Laid before Parliament* | | | | | *24th April* 1969 |
| *Coming into Operation* | | | | | *25th April* 1969 |

Whereas the Minister of Agriculture, Fisheries and Food (hereinafter called " the Minister ") has on the recommendation of the Commissioners of Customs and Excise (hereinafter called " the Commissioners ") made an order(a) pursuant to the powers conferred upon him by sections 9(1) and 9(4) of the Sugar Act 1956(b), having effect subject to the provisions of section 3 of, and Part II of Schedule 5 to, the Finance Act 1962(c), to the provisions of section 52(2) of the Finance Act 1966(d), and to the provisions of Section 58 of the Finance Act 1968(e), providing that in the case of certain descriptions of composite sugar products surcharge shall be calculated on the basis of an average quantity of sugar or invert sugar taken to have been used in the manufacture of the products, and that certain other descriptions of composite sugar products shall be treated as not containing any sugar or invert sugar, and that in the case of certain descriptions of goods in the manufacture of which sugar or invert sugar is used, surcharge repayments shall be calculated on the basis of an average quantity of sugar or invert sugar taken to have been so used:

Now, therefore, the Minister, on the recommendation of the Commissioners and in exercise of the powers conferred upon him by sections 9(1), 9(4) and 33(4) of the Sugar Act 1956, having effect as aforesaid, and of all other powers enabling him in that behalf, hereby makes the following order:—

**1.**—(1) This order may be cited as the Composite Sugar Products (Surcharge and Surcharge Repayments—Average Rates) (No. 4) Order 1969; and shall come into operation on 25th April 1969.

(2) The Interpretation Act 1889(f) shall apply for the interpretation of this order as it applies for the interpretation of an Act of Parliament.

**2.** Surcharge payable on or after 25th April 1969 under and in accordance with the Sugar Act 1956, having effect as aforesaid, in respect of sugar and invert sugar used in the manufacture of the descriptions of imported composite sugar products specified in column 2 of Schedule 1 to this order shall, notwithstanding the provisions of the Sugar (Rates of Surcharge and Surcharge Repayments) (No. 4) Order 1969(g) and the Composite Sugar Products (Surcharge and Surcharge Repayments—Average Rates) (No. 3) Order 1969(a), be calculated by reference to the weight or value, as the case may be, of the products at the rates specified in relation thereto in column 3 of the said Schedule.

(a) S.I. 1969/363 (1969 I, p. 1000).    (b) 1956 c. 48.    (c) 1962 c. 44.
(d) 1966 c. 18.    (e) 1968 c. 44.    (f) 1889 c. 63.
(g) S.I. 1969/588 (1969 I, p. 1560).

**3.** Imported composite sugar products other than those of a description specified in Schedules 1 and 2 to this order shall be treated as not containing any sugar or invert sugar for the purposes of surcharge payable on or after 25th April 1969.

**4.** Surcharge repayments payable on and after 25th April 1969 under and in accordance with the provisions of section 8 of the Sugar Act 1956, having effect as aforesaid, in respect of sugar and invert sugar used in the manufacture of the descriptions of goods specified in column 1 of Schedule 3 to this order shall, notwithstanding the provisions of the Sugar (Rates of Surcharge and Surcharge Repayments) (No. 4) Order 1969(a) and the Composite Sugar Products (Surcharge and Surcharge Repayments—Average Rates) (No. 3) Order 1969(b), be calculated by reference to the quantity of the goods at the rates specified in relation thereto in column 2 of the said Schedule.

In Witness whereof the Official Seal of the Minister of Agriculture, Fisheries and Food is hereunto affixed on 22nd April 1969.

(L.S.)　　　　　　　　　　　　　　　　　　*R. P. Fraser,*
　　　　　　　　　　　　　　　　Authorised by the Minister.

SCHEDULE 1

In this Schedule:—

" Tariff heading " means a heading or, where the context so requires, a subheading of the Customs Tariff 1959 (see paragraph (1) of Article 1 of the Import Duties (General) (No. 4) Order 1968(c)).

" Per cent." means, where it occurs in relation to any rate of surcharge, per cent. of the value for customs duty purposes of the product to which it relates.

| Tariff heading | Description of Imported Composite Sugar Products | Rate of Surcharge |
|---|---|---|
| | | per cwt.<br>s.　d. |
| 04.02 ...　　... | Milk and cream, preserved, concentrated or sweetened, containing more than 10 per cent. by weight of added sweetening matter　...　... | 7　3 |
| 17.02 (B) (2) and 17.05 (B) | Syrups containing sucrose sugar, whether or not flavoured or coloured, but not including fruit juices containing added sugar in any proportion:—<br>containing 70 per cent. or more by weight of sweetening matter　...　...　...　... | 10　4 |
| | containing less than 70 per cent., and more than 50 per cent., by weight of sweetening matter... | 7　5 |
| | containing not more than 50 per cent. by weight of sweetening matter　...　...　...　... | 3　8 |

(a) S.I. 1969/588 (1969 I, p. 1560).　　(b) S.I. 1969/363 (1969 I, p. 1000).
(c) S.I. 1968/679 (1968 I, p. 1519).

| Tariff heading | Description of Imported Composite Sugar Products | Rate of Surcharge |
|---|---|---|
| | | per cwt. |
| | | s.   d. |
| 17.02 (F) ... | Caramel:— | |
| | Solid ...   ...   ...   ...   ...   ...   ... | 16   4 |
| | Liquid   ...   ...   ...   ...   ...   ... | 11   5 |
| 17.04 ...   ... | Sugar confectionery, not containing cocoa ...   ... | 13   3 |
| 18.06 ...   ... | Chocolate and other food preparations containing cocoa:— | |
| | Chocolate couverture not prepared for retail sale; chocolate milk crumb, liquid ...   ... | 7   3 |
| | Chocolate milk crumb, solid   ...   ...   ... | 8   11 |
| | Solid chocolate bars or blocks, milk or plain, with or without fruit or nuts; other chocolate confectionery consisting wholly of chocolate or of chocolate and other ingredients not containing added sugar, but not including such goods when packed together in retail packages with goods liable to surcharge at a higher rate | 7   4 |
| | Other   ...   ...   ...   ...   ...   ... | 9   6 |
| | | per cent. |
| 19.08 ...   ... | Pastry, biscuits, cakes and other fine bakers' wares containing added sweetening matter:— | |
| | Biscuits   ...   ...   ...   ...   ...   ... | $3\frac{1}{2}$ |
| | Other   ...   ...   ...   ...   ...   ... | $2\frac{1}{10}$ |
| 20.01 ...   ... | Vegetables and fruit, prepared or preserved by vinegar or acetic acid, containing added sweetening matter | $4\frac{9}{10}$ |
| 20.03 ...   ... | Fruit preserved by freezing, containing added sugar | $1\frac{3}{4}$ |
| | | per cwt. |
| | | s.   d. |
| 20.04 ...   ... | Fruit, fruit-peel and parts of plants, preserved by sugar (drained, glacé or crystallised)   ...   ... | 10   9 |
| 20.05 ...   ... | Jams, fruit jellies, marmalades, fruit purée and fruit pastes, being cooked preparations, containing added sweetening matter   ...   ...   ...   ... | 10   3 |
| | | per cent. |
| 20.06 ...   ... | Fruit otherwise prepared or preserved, containing added sweetening matter:— | |
| | Ginger   ...   ...   ...   ...   ...   ... | 7 |
| | Other   ...   ...   ...   ...   ...   ... | $1\frac{3}{4}$ |

## SCHEDULE 2

| Tariff heading | Description of Imported Composite Sugar Products |
|---|---|
| 17.05 (A) and (B) | Sugar and invert sugar, flavoured or coloured. |

## SCHEDULE 3

| Description of goods | Rate of surcharge repayment per bulk barrel of 36 gallons |
|---|---|
| Lager ... ... ... ... ... | 8·1d. |
| All beer other than lager ... ... | 7·3d. |

## EXPLANATORY NOTE

*(This Note is not part of the Order.)*

This order provides for reductions on and after 25th April 1969 in the average rates of surcharge payable on imported composite sugar products of the descriptions specified in Schedule 1 and in the average rates of surcharge repayment in respect of exported goods of the descriptions specified in Schedule 3. These correspond to the reductions in surcharge rates effected by the Sugar (Rates of Surcharge and Surcharge Repayments) (No. 4) Order 1969 (S.I. 1969/588). Provision is also made for certain imported composite sugar products to be treated as not containing any sugar or invert sugar.

STATUTORY INSTRUMENTS

## 1969 No. 590

## CARIBBEAN AND NORTH ATLANTIC TERRITORIES

### The Bahama Islands (Constitution) Order 1969

| | |
|---|---|
| Made - - - - - | 23rd April 1969 |
| Laid before Parliament | 29th April 1969 |
| Coming into Operation | On a day to be appointed under Section 1(2). |

At the Court at Windsor Castle, the 23rd day of April 1969

Present,

The Queen's Most Excellent Majesty in Council

Whereas at a conference held in London in September 1968 between representatives of Her Majesty's Government in the United Kingdom and representatives of the Bahama Islands it was agreed that it was desirable that a new Constitution for the Bahama Islands embodying certain changes from the existing Constitution should be conferred and that the Bahama Islands should be known as the Commonwealth of the Bahama Islands :

Now, therefore, Her Majesty, by virtue and in exercise of the powers vested in Her in that behalf by section 1 of the Bahama Islands (Constitution) Act 1963(a) and of all other powers enabling Her in that behalf, is pleased, by and with the advice of Her Privy Council, to order, and it is hereby ordered, as follows : —

**1.**—(1) This Order may be cited as the Bahama Islands (Constitution) Order 1969.

(2) This Order shall come into operation on such day as the Governor, acting in his discretion, may, by proclamation published in the Gazette, appoint, which day shall not be earlier than 30th April 1969.

*Citation and commencement.*

**2.**—(1) In this Order—

" the appointed day " means the day appointed under section 1(2) of this Order ;

" the Constitution " means the Constitution set out in the Schedule to this Order ;

" the existing Constitution " means the Constitution set out in the Schedule to the Bahama Islands (Constitution) Order in Council 1963(b) as amended by the Bahama Islands (Constitution) (Amendment) Order 1964(c) ;

*Interpretation.*

---

(a) 1963 c. 56.  (b) S.I. 1963/2084 (1963 III, p. 4403).
(c) S.I. 1964/2041 (1964 III, p. 5125).

" the existing laws " means any laws made before the appointed day by any legislature for the time being constituted as the legislature of the Bahama Islands and having effect as part of the law of the Bahama Islands immediately before the appointed day (whether or not they have then come into operation) and any rules, regulations, orders or other instruments made in pursuance of such laws and having such effect.

(2) The provisions of section 130 of the Constitution shall apply for the purpose of interpreting sections 2 to 10 of this Order and otherwise in relation thereto as they apply for the purpose of interpreting and in relation to the Constitution.

Establishment of Constitution.

**3.** With effect from the appointed day—

(*a*) the Bahama Islands shall be known as the Commonwealth of the Bahama Islands ;

(*b*) the Constitution shall come into force in the Bahama Islands ; and

(*c*) the Bahama Islands (Constitution) Order in Council 1963, the Bahama Islands Royal Instructions 1963 and the Bahama Islands (Constitution) (Amendment) Order 1964 are revoked.

Existing laws.

**4.**—(1) Subject to the provisions of this section, the existing laws shall have effect on and after the appointed day as if they had been made in pursuance of the Constitution and shall be construed with such modifications, adaptations, qualifications and exceptions as may be necessary to bring them into conformity with the Constitution.

(2) Where any matter that falls to be prescribed or otherwise provided for the purposes of the Constitution by the Legislature or by any other authority or person is prescribed or provided for by or under any existing law (including any adaptation or modification of any such law made under this section) or is otherwise prescribed or provided for immediately before the appointed day by or under the existing Constitution, that prescription or provision shall, as from the appointed day, have effect as if it had been made for those purposes by the Legislature or, as the case may be, by the other authority or person.

(3) The Governor may, by order published in the Gazette, at any time within six months after the appointed day make such adaptations or modifications to any existing law as may appear to him to be necessary or expedient for bringing that law into conformity with the provisions of the Constitution or otherwise for giving effect or enabling effect to be given to those provisions ; and any existing law shall have effect accordingly from such day (not being earlier than the appointed day) as may be specified in the order.

(4) An order made under this section may be amended or revoked by the Legislature or, in relation to any existing law affected thereby, by any other authority having power to amend, repeal or revoke that existing law.

(5) The provisions of this section shall be without prejudice to any powers conferred by the Constitution or by any other law upon any person or authority to make provision for any matter, including the amendment or repeal of any existing law.

**5.**—(1) Any person who immediately before the appointed day holds or is acting in any office to which this section applies shall be deemed as from that day to have been appointed to or to act in that office or the corresponding office in accordance with the provisions of the Constitution:

Existing Governor, Ministers, judges and other officers.

Provided that any person who under the existing Constitution or any existing law would have been required to vacate his office at the expiration of any period shall vacate his office at the expiration of that period.

(2) This section applies to the offices of the Governor, the Premier, any other Minister, any judge of the Supreme Court, any judge of the Court of Appeal, the Secretary to the Cabinet, any whole-time member of the Public Service Commission and any member of the Police Service Commission, to the offices constituting the personal staff of the Governor and to any public office.

(3) Any person who becomes the holder of the office of Prime Minister or any other Minister by virtue of subsection (1) of this section and who immediately before the appointed day is charged with responsibility for any matter or any department of government shall, as from the appointed day, be deemed to have been charged with responsibility for that matter or department under section 70(1) of the Constitution, and any designation of the style by which any such Minister is to be known having effect immediately before the appointed day shall, as from that day, be deemed to have been made under that section.

(4) The provisions of this section shall be without prejudice to any powers conferred by or under the Constitution upon any authority or person to abolish any office or to remove from office any person holding or acting in any office.

(5) Any person who holds or is acting in any office by virtue of subsection (1) of this section and who, before the appointed day, has made any oath or affirmation required to be taken by him before assuming the functions of his office shall be deemed to have made any like oath or affirmation so required by the Constitution or any other law.

**6.**—(1) As soon as practicable on or after the appointed day the Governor shall proceed under section 30 of the Constitution to the appointment of Senators.

The Legislature.

(2) The persons who immediately before the appointed day are members of the House of Assembly established by the existing Constitution (in this section referred to as " the existing House ") shall as from that day be members of the House of Assembly established by the Constitution as if they had been elected thereto in pursuance of the Constitution and, subject to subsections (3) and (4) of this section, shall hold their seats in that House in accordance with the provisions of the Constitution.

(3) If any person who becomes a member of the House of Assembly by virtue of subsection (2) of this section does not possess Bahamian status on the appointed day he shall be deemed for the purposes of paragraph (*d*) of section 39(1) of the Constitution to have ceased to possess that status on the expiration of one month after the appointed day if he does not then possess that status.

(4) If any person who becomes a member of the House of Assembly by virtue of subsection (2) of this section is on the appointed day interested in any government contract for the purposes of paragraph (f) of section 39(1) of the Constitution and if he is still so interested on the expiration of one month after the appointed day he shall be deemed for the purposes of that paragraph to have become interested in that contract on the expiration of that period.

(5) The persons who immediately before the appointed day are the Speaker and Deputy Speaker of the existing House shall as from that day be the Speaker and Deputy Speaker respectively of the House of Assembly established by the Constitution as if they had been elected as such in pursuance of the Constitution and shall hold their offices in accordance with the provisions of the Constitution.

(6) The Rules of Procedure of the Senate established by the existing Constitution and of the existing House as in force immediately before the appointed day shall, except as may be otherwise provided under section 44 of the Constitution, have effect on and after that day as if they had been made under that section, but shall be construed with such modifications, adaptations, qualifications and exceptions as may be necessary to bring them into conformity with the Constitution.

(7) Any person who becomes a member of the House of Assembly by virtue of subsection (2) of this section and who, since he was last elected as a member of the existing House, has made an oath or affirmation of allegiance in accordance with section 43 of the existing Constitution, shall be deemed to have complied with the requirements of section 45 of the Constitution relating to the making of such an oath or affirmation.

(8) Notwithstanding anything contained in section 57(2) of the Constitution (but subject to section 58 of the Constitution) the Governor shall dissolve the Legislature, unless it has been sooner dissolved under section 57(1) of the Constitution, at the expiration of five years from the date when the existing House first met after the general election of members thereof last preceding the appointed day.

(9) For the purposes of section 62(1) of the Constitution the first period of five years shall be deemed to have commenced on 27th November 1967.

**Legal proceedings.** **7.**—(1) All proceedings commenced or pending immediately before the appointed day before the Supreme Court or the Court of Appeal established by the existing Constitution may continue on and after that day before the Supreme Court or the Court of Appeal, as the case may be, established by the Constitution.

(2) Any decision given before the appointed day by the Supreme Court or the Court of Appeal established by the existing Constitution shall, for the purposes of its enforcement or of any appeal therefrom, have effect on and after that day as if it were a decision of the Supreme Court or the Court of Appeal, as the case may be, established by the Constitution.

**Emergency laws.** **8.**—(1) Until such time as provision is made by a law enacted by the Legislature conferring upon the Governor—

(a) power to make a proclamation declaring that a state of public emergency exists in the Bahama Islands for the purposes of that law ; and

(b) power to make, during any period when such a proclamation is in force, such laws for the Bahama Islands, to have effect notwithstanding the provisions of any other law of the Legislature, as may appear to the Governor to be necessary or expedient for securing the public safety, the defence of the Islands or the maintenance of public order or for maintaining supplies and services essential to the life of the community,

the Emergency Powers Order in Council 1939(a), as amended(b), shall have effect as if the Islands were a territory specified in the First Schedule to that Order.

(2) The powers conferred upon the Governor by the Emergency Powers Order in Council 1939, as amended, shall be exercised by him after consultation with the Prime Minister :

Provided that if in the judgment of the Governor it is impracticable for him to consult with the Prime Minister, those powers shall be exercised by the Governor, acting in his discretion.

(3) The references in subsection (1) of this section to powers conferred upon the Governor by provision made as therein mentioned are references to powers which are exercisable by him in the same manner as the powers conferred upon him by the Emergency Powers Order in Council 1939 are exercisable by virtue of the provisions of subsection (2) of this section.

**9.**—(1) Any regulations made by the Governor under section 15 of the Bahama Islands (Constitution) Order in Council 1963 and in force immediately before the appointed day shall continue in force on and after that day and may be amended or revoked by subsequent regulations as if subsection (1) of that section had not been revoked, and any such regulations shall have effect notwithstanding the provisions of Part VI of the Constitution and shall not be a pensions law for the purposes of section 113 of the Constitution. *(Regulations for retirement, compensation, etc.)*

(2) All sums required for the payment of compensation under any such regulations are hereby charged upon the Crown Lands Fund for Development and, notwithstanding anything contained in section 115 of the Constitution, shall be paid out of that Fund upon the authority of a warrant under the hand of the Governor, acting in his discretion.

(3) Any compensation, gratuity, grant or allowance payable under any such regulations shall, if it is so provided in any such regulations, be exempt from tax under any law in force in the Bahama Islands relating to the taxation of incomes or imposing any other form of taxation.

**10.**—(1) Any direction having effect immediately before the appointed day under section 97 or section 103(1A) of the existing Constitution shall have effect on and after that day as if it had been made under section 99 or, as the case may be, section 107(3) of the Constitution. *(Delegation of certain powers, and proceedings before Commissions.)*

(2) Any proceedings commenced or pending immediately before the appointed day before any Commission established by Part VI of the existing Constitution may continue on and after that day before the appropriate Commission established by Part VI of the Constitution.

*W. G. Agnew.*

(a) See S.I. 1952 I at p. 621.    (b) The relevant amending instruments are S.I. 1956/731, 1963/88, 1633 (1956 I, p. 512; 1963 I, p. 105; III, p. 3084).

# THE SCHEDULE TO THE ORDER

# THE CONSTITUTION OF THE COMMONWEALTH OF THE BAHAMA ISLANDS

## ARRANGEMENT OF SECTIONS

### PART I

#### PROTECTION OF FUNDAMENTAL RIGHTS AND FREEDOMS OF THE INDIVIDUAL

### PART II

#### THE GOVERNOR

### PART III

#### THE LEGISLATURE

##### *General*

## PART IV

### THE EXECUTIVE

## PART V

### THE JUDICIARY

#### The Supreme Court

#### The Court of Appeal

## PART VI

### THE PUBLIC SERVICE

#### The Public Service Commission

#### Public Service Board of Appeal

# PART VII

## FINANCE

# PART VIII

## MISCELLANEOUS

# THE SCHEDULE TO THE CONSTITUTION

Forms of Oaths and Affirmations.

# PART I

## PROTECTION OF FUNDAMENTAL RIGHTS AND FREEDOMS OF THE INDIVIDUAL

Fundamental rights and freedoms of the individual.

**1.** Whereas every person in the Bahama Islands is entitled to the fundamental rights and freedoms of the individual, that is to say, has the right, whatever his race, place of origin, political opinions, colour, creed or sex, but subject to respect for the rights and freedoms of others and for the public interest, to each and all of the following, namely—

(a) life, liberty, security of the person and the protection of the law;

(b) freedom of conscience, of expression and of assembly and association ; and

(c) protection for the privacy of his home and other property and from deprivation of property without compensation,

the subsequent provisions of this Part shall have effect for the purpose of affording protection to the aforesaid rights and freedoms subject to such limitations of that protection as are contained in those provisions, being limitations designed to ensure that the enjoyment of the said rights and freedoms by any individual does not prejudice the rights and freedoms of others or the public interest.

Protection of right to life.

**2.**—(1) No person shall be deprived intentionally of his life save in execution of the sentence of a court in respect of a criminal offence of which he has been convicted.

(2) A person shall not be regarded as having been deprived of his life in contravention of this section if he dies as the result of the use, to such extent and in such circumstances as are permitted by law, of such force as is reasonably justifiable—

(a) for the defence of any person from violence or for the defence of property ;

(b) in order to effect a lawful arrest or to prevent the escape of a person lawfully detained ;

(c) for the purpose of suppressing a riot, insurrection or mutiny ; or

(d) in order to prevent the commission by that person of a criminal offence,

or if he dies as a result of a lawful act of war.

Protection from inhuman treatment.

**3.**—(1) No person shall be subjected to torture or to inhuman or degrading treatment or punishment.

(2) Nothing contained in or done under the authority of any law shall be held to be inconsistent with or in contravention of this section to the extent that the law in question authorises the infliction of any description of punishment that was lawful in the Bahama Islands immediately before 7th January 1964.

Protection from slavery and forced labour.

**4.**—(1) No person shall be held in slavery or servitude.

(2) No person shall be required to perform forced labour.

(3) For the purposes of this section, " forced labour " does not include—

(a) any labour required in consequence of the sentence or order of a court ;

(b) any labour required of a member of a disciplined force in pursuance of his duties as such or, in the case of a person who has conscientious objections to service in a naval, military or air force, any labour which that person is required by law to perform in place of such service ;

(c) labour required of any person while he is lawfully detained which, though not required in consequence of the sentence or order of a court, is reasonably necessary in the interests of hygiene or for the maintenance of the place in which he is detained ; or

(d) any labour required during a period of public emergency (that is to say, a period to which section 15 of this Constitution applies) or in the event of any other emergency or calamity that threatens the life or well-being of the community, to the extent that the requiring of such labour is reasonably justifiable, in the circumstances of any situation arising or existing during that period or as a result of that other emergency or calamity, for the purpose of dealing with that situation.

**5.**—(1) No person shall be deprived of his personal liberty save as may be authorised by law in any of the following cases— <sup></sup>

Protection from arbitrary arrest or detention.

(a) in execution of the sentence or order of a court, whether established for the Bahama Islands or some other country, in respect of a criminal offence of which he has been convicted or in consequence of his unfitness to plead to a criminal charge or in execution of the order of a court on the grounds of his contempt of that court or of another court or tribunal ;

(b) in execution of the order of a court made in order to secure the fulfilment of any obligation imposed upon him by law ;

(c) for the purpose of bringing him before a court in execution of the order of a court ;

(d) upon reasonable suspicion of his having committed, or of being about to commit, a criminal offence ;

(e) in the case of a person who has not attained the age of twenty-one years, for the purpose of his education or welfare ;

(f) for the purpose of preventing the spread of an infectious or contagious disease or in the case of a person who is, or is reasonably suspected to be, of unsound mind, addicted to drugs or alcohol, or a vagrant, for the purpose of his care or treatment or the protection of the community ;

(g) for the purpose of preventing the unlawful entry of that person into the Bahama Islands or for the purpose of effecting the expulsion, extradition or other lawful removal from the Bahama Islands of that person or the taking of proceedings relating thereto.

(2) Any person who is arrested or detained shall be informed as soon as is reasonably practicable, in a language that he understands, of the reasons for his arrest or detention.

(3) Any person who is arrested or detained in such a case as is mentioned in subsection (1)(c) or (d) of this section and who is not released shall be brought without undue delay before a court ; and if any person arrested or detained in such a case as is mentioned in the

said paragraph (*d*) is not tried within a reasonable time he shall (without prejudice to any further proceedings that may be brought against him) be released either unconditionally or upon reasonable conditions, including in particular such conditions as are reasonably necessary to ensure that he appears at a later date for trial or for proceedings preliminary to trial.

(4) Any person who is unlawfully arrested or detained by any other person shall be entitled to compensation therefor from that other person.

Provisions to secure protection of law.

**6.**—(1) If any person is charged with a criminal offence, then, unless the charge is withdrawn, the case shall be afforded a fair hearing within a reasonable time by an independent and impartial court established by law.

(2) Every person who is charged with a criminal offence—

(*a*) shall be presumed to be innocent until he is proved or has pleaded guilty ;

(*b*) shall be informed as soon as reasonably practicable, in a language that he understands and in detail, of the nature of the offence charged ;

(*c*) shall be given adequate time and facilities for the preparation of his defence ;

(*d*) shall be permitted to defend himself before the court in person or, at his own expense, by a legal representative of his own choice or by a legal representative at the public expense where so provided by or under a law in force in the Bahama Islands ;

(*e*) shall be afforded facilities to examine in person or by his legal representative the witnesses called by the prosecution before the court, and to obtain the attendance and carry out the examination of witnesses to testify on his behalf before the court on the same conditions as those applying to witnesses called by the prosecution ;

(*f*) shall be permitted to have without payment the assistance of an interpreter if he cannot understand the language used at the trial of the charge ; and

(*g*) shall, when charged on information in the Supreme Court, have the right to trial by jury ;

and except with his own consent the trial shall not take place in his absence unless he so conducts himself in the court as to render the continuance of the proceedings in his presence impracticable and the court has ordered him to be removed and the trial to proceed in his absence.

(3) When a person is tried for any criminal offence, the accused person or any person authorised by him in that behalf shall, if he so requires and subject to payment of such reasonable fee as may be prescribed by law, be given within a reasonable time after judgment a copy for the use of the accused person of any record of the proceedings made by or on behalf of the court.

(4) No person shall be held to be guilty of a criminal offence on account of any act or omission that did not, at the time it took place, constitute such an offence, and no penalty shall be imposed for any

criminal offence that is severer in degree or description than the
maximum penalty that might have been imposed for that offence at the
time when it was committed.

(5) No person who shows that he has been tried by a competent
court for a criminal offence and either convicted or acquitted shall
again be tried for that offence or for any other criminal offence of
which he could have been convicted at the trial for that offence,
save upon the order of a superior court in the course of appeal or
review proceedings relating to the conviction or acquittal.

(6) No person shall be tried for a criminal offence if he shows that
he has been pardoned for that offence.

(7) No person who is tried for a criminal offence shall be compelled
to give evidence at the trial.

(8) Any court or other adjudicating authority prescribed by law
for the determination of the existence or extent of any civil right
or obligation shall be established by law and shall be independent
and impartial ; and where proceedings for such a determination are
instituted by any person before such a court or other adjudicating
authority, the case shall be given a fair hearing within a reasonable
time.

(9) All proceedings instituted in any court for the determination
of the existence or extent of any civil right or obligation, including
the announcement of the decision of the court, shall be held in public.

(10) Nothing in subsection (9) of this section shall prevent the court
from excluding from the proceedings persons other than the parties
thereto and their legal representatives to such extent as the court—

(a) may be empowered by law so to do and may consider necessary
or expedient in circumstances where publicity would prejudice
the interests of justice, or in interlocutory proceedings or in the
interests of public morality, the welfare of persons under the
age of eighteen years or the protection of the private lives of
persons concerned in the proceedings ;

(b) may be empowered or required by law to do so in the interests
of defence, public safety or public order ; or

(c) may be empowered or required to do so by rules of court and
practice existing immediately before 7th January 1964 or by any
law made subsequently to the extent that it makes provision
substantially to the same effect as provision contained in any such
rules.

(11) Nothing contained in or done under the authority of any law
shall be held to be inconsistent with or in contravention of—

(a) subsection (2)(a) of this section to the extent that the law in
question imposes upon any person charged with a criminal offence
the burden of proving particular facts ;

(b) subsection (2)(e) of this section to the extent that the law in
question imposes conditions that must be satisfied if witnesses
called to testify on behalf of an accused person are to be paid
their expenses out of public funds ;

(c) subsection (5) of this section to the extent that the law in question authorises a court to try a member of a disciplined force for a criminal offence notwithstanding any trial and conviction or acquittal of that member under the disciplinary law of that force, so, however, that any court so trying such a member and convicting him shall in sentencing him to any punishment take into account any punishment awarded him under that disciplinary law.

(12) In this section, " legal representative " means a person entitled to practise in the Bahama Islands as counsel and attorney of the Supreme Court.

Protection for privacy of home and other property.

**7.**—(1) Except with his consent, no person shall be subjected to the search of his person or his property or the entry by others on his premises.

(2) Nothing contained in or done under the authority of any law shall be held to be inconsistent with or in contravention of this section to the extent that the law in question makes provision—

(a) which is reasonably required—

(i) in the interests of defence, public safety, public order, public morality, public health, town and country planning, the development of mineral resources, or the development or utilisation of any other property in such a manner as to promote the public benefit ; or

(ii) for the purpose of protecting the rights and freedoms of other persons ;

(b) to enable an officer or agent of the Government of the Bahama Islands, a local government authority or a body corporate established by law for public purposes to enter on the premises of any person in order to inspect those premises or anything thereon for the purpose of any tax, rate or due or in order to carry out work connected with any property that is lawfully on those premises and that belongs to that Government, authority or body corporate, as the case may be ; or

(c) to authorise, for the purpose of enforcing the judgment or order of a court in any civil proceedings, the search of any person or property by order of a court or the entry upon any premises by such order,

except so far as that provision or, as the case may be, the thing done under the authority thereof is shown not to be reasonably justifiable in a democratic society.

Protection of freedom of conscience.

**8.**—(1) Except with his consent, no person shall be hindered in the enjoyment of his freedom of conscience, and for the purposes of this section the said freedom includes freedom of thought and of religion, freedom to change his religion or belief and freedom, either alone or in community with others, and both in public and in private, to manifest and propagate his religion or belief in worship, teaching, practice and observance.

(2) Except with his consent (or, if he is a person who has not attained the age of twenty-one years, the consent of his guardian) no person attending any place of education shall be required to receive religious

instruction or to take part in or attend any religious ceremony or observance if that instruction, ceremony or observance relates to a religion other than his own.

(3) No religious body or denomination shall be prevented from or hindered in providing religious instruction for persons of that body or denomination in the course of any education provided by that body or denomination whether or not that body or denomination is in receipt of any government subsidy, grant or other form of financial assistance designed to meet, in whole or in part, the cost of such course of education.

(4) No person shall be compelled to take any oath which is contrary to his religion or belief or to take any oath in a manner which is contrary to his religion or belief.

(5) Nothing contained in or done under the authority of any law shall be held to be inconsistent with or in contravention of this section to the extent that the law in question makes provision which is reasonably required—

(a) in the interests of defence, public safety, public order, public morality or public health ; or

(b) for the purpose of protecting the rights and freedoms of other persons, including the right to observe and practise any religion without the unsolicited interference of members of any other religion,

and except so far as that provision or, as the case may be, the thing done under the authority thereof is shown not to be reasonably justifiable in a democratic society.

**9.**—(1) Except with his consent, no person shall be hindered in the enjoyment of his freedom of expression, and for the purposes of this section the said freedom includes freedom to hold opinions, to receive and impart ideas and information without interference, and freedom from interference with his correspondence.

*Protection of freedom of expression.*

(2) Nothing contained in or done under the authority of any law shall be held to be inconsistent with or in contravention of this section to the extent that the law in question makes provision—

(a) which is reasonably required—

(i) in the interests of defence, public safety, public order, public morality or public health ; or

(ii) for the purpose of protecting the rights, reputations and freedoms of other persons, preventing the disclosure of information received in confidence, maintaining the authority and independence of the courts, or regulating telephony, telegraphy, posts, wireless broadcasting, television, public exhibitions or public entertainments ; or

(b) which imposes restrictions upon persons holding office under the Crown or upon members of a disciplined force,

and except so far as that provision or, as the case may be, the thing done under the authority thereof is shown not to be reasonably justifiable in a democratic society.

Protection of freedom of assembly and association.

**10.**—(1) Except with his consent, no person shall be hindered in the enjoyment of his freedom of peaceful assembly and association, that is to say, his right to assembly freely and associate with other persons and in particular to form or belong to political parties or to form or belong to trade unions or other associations for the protection of his interests.

(2) Nothing contained in or done under the authority of any law shall be held to be inconsistent with or in contravention of this section to the extent that the law in question makes provision—

(a) which is reasonably required—

(i) in the interests of defence, public safety, public order, public morality or public health ; or

(ii) for the purpose of protecting the rights and freedoms of other persons ; or

(b) which imposes restrictions upon persons holding office under the Crown or upon members of a disciplined force,

and except so far as that provision or, as the case may be, the thing done under the authority thereof is shown not to be reasonably justifiable·in a democratic society.

Protection of freedom of movement.

**11.**—(1) Except with his consent, no person shall be hindered in the enjoyment of his freedom of movement, and for the purposes of this section the said freedom means the right to move freely throughout the Bahama Islands, the right to reside in any part thereof, the right to enter the Bahama Islands and immunity from expulsion therefrom.

(2) Nothing contained in or done under the authority of any law shall be held to be inconsistent with or in contravention of this section to the extent that the law in question makes provision—

(a) which is reasonably required—

(i) in the interests of defence, public safety, public order, public morality, public health, town and country planning or the prevention of plant or animal diseases ; or

(ii) for the purpose of protecting the rights and freedoms of other persons,

and except so far as that provision or, as the case may be, the thing done under the authority thereof is shown not to be reasonably justifiable in a democratic society ;

(b) for the removal of a person from the Bahama Islands to be tried outside the said Islands for a criminal offence or to undergo imprisonment in some other country in respect of a criminal offence of which he has been convicted ;

(c) for the imposition of restrictions upon the movement or residence within the Bahama Islands of public officers or members of a disciplined force that are reasonably required for the purpose of the proper performance of their functions ; or

(d) for the imposition of restrictions on the movement or residence within the Bahama Islands of any person who does not possess Bahamian status or the exclusion or expulsion therefrom of any such person.

(3) Any restriction on a person's freedom of movement which is involved in his lawful detention shall not be held to be inconsistent with or in contravention of this section.

(4) For the purposes of paragraph (*c*) of subsection (2) of this section, " law " in that subsection includes directions in writing regarding the conduct of public officers generally or any class of public officer issued by the Government of the Bahama Islands.

**12.**—(1) Subject to the provisions of subsections (4), (5) and (8) of this section, no law shall make any provision which is discriminatory either of itself or in its effect.

*Protection from discrimination on the grounds of race, etc.*

(2) Subject to the provisions of subsections (6), (8) and (9) of this section, no person shall be treated in a discriminatory manner by any person acting by virtue of any written law or in the performance of the functions of any public office or any public authority.

(3) In this section, the expression " discriminatory " means affording different treatment to different persons attributable wholly or mainly to their respective descriptions by race, place of origin, political opinions, colour or creed whereby persons of one such description are subjected to disabilities or restrictions to which persons of another such description are not made subject or are accorded privileges or advantages which are not accorded to persons of another such description.

(4) Subsection (1) of this section shall not apply to any law so far as that law makes provision—

(*a*) for the appropriation of revenues or other funds of the Bahama Islands or for the imposition of taxation (including the levying of fees for the grant of licences) ; or

(*b*) with respect to the entry into or exclusion from, or the employment, engaging in any business or profession, movement or residence within, the Bahama Islands of persons who do not possess Bahamian status ; or

(*c*) with respect to adoption, marriage, divorce, burial, devolution of property on death or other matters of personal law ; or

(*d*) whereby persons of any such description as is mentioned in subsection (3) of this section may be subjected to any disability or restriction or may be accorded any privilege or advantage which, having regard to its nature and to special circumstances pertaining to those persons or to persons of any other such description, is reasonably justifiable in a democratic society ; or

(*e*) for authorising the granting of licences or certificates permitting the conduct of a lottery, the keeping of a gaming house or the carrying on of gambling in any of its forms subject to conditions which impose upon persons who possess Bahamian status disabilities or restrictions to which other persons are not made subject.

(5) Nothing contained in any law shall be held to be inconsistent with or in contravention of subsection (1) of this section to the extent that it requires a person to possess Bahamian status or to possess any other qualification (not being a qualification specifically relating to race, place of origin, political opinions, colour or creed) in order to be eligible for service as a public officer or as a member of a disciplined force or for the service of a local government authority or a body corporate established by law for public purposes.

(6) Subsection (2) of this section shall not apply to anything which is expressly or by necessary implication authorised to be done by any such provision of law as is referred to in subsection (4) or (5) of this section.

(7) Subject to the provisions of subsection (4)(*e*) and of subsection (8) of this section, no person shall be treated in a discriminatory manner in respect of access to any of the following places to which the general public have access, namely, shops, hotels, restaurants, eating-houses, licensed premises, places of entertainment or places of resort.

(8) Nothing contained in or done under the authority of any law shall be held to be inconsistent with or in contravention of this section to the extent that the law in question makes provision whereby persons of any such description as is mentioned in subsection (3) of this section may be subjected to any restriction on the rights and freedoms guaranteed by sections 7, 8, 9, 10 and 11 of this Constitution, being such a restriction as is authorised by section 7(2)(*a*), 8(5), 9(2), 10(2) or 11(2)(*a*), as the case may be.

(9) Nothing in subsection (2) of this section shall affect any discretion relating to the institution, conduct or discontinuance of civil or criminal proceedings in any court that is vested in any person by or under this Constitution or any other law.

Protection from deprivation of property.

**13.**—(1) No property of any description shall be compulsorily taken possession of, and no interest in or right over property of any description shall be compulsorily acquired, except where the following conditions are satisfied, that is to say—

(*a*) the taking of possession or acquisition is necessary in the interests of defence, public safety, public order, public morality, public health, town and country planning or the development or utilisation of any property in such manner as to promote the public benefit or the economic well-being of the community ; and

(*b*) the necessity therefor is such as to afford reasonable justification for the causing of any hardship that may result to any person having an interest in or right over the property ; and

(*c*) provision is made by a law applicable to that taking of possession or acquisition—

(i) for the prompt payment of adequate compensation ; and

(ii) securing to any person having an interest in or right over the property a right of access to the Supreme Court, whether direct or on appeal from any other authority, for the determination of his interest or right, the legality of the taking of possession or acquisition of the property, interest or right, and the amount of any compensation to which he is entitled, and for the purpose of obtaining prompt payment of that compensation ; and

(*d*) any party to proceedings in the Supreme Court relating to such a claim is given by law the same rights of appeal as are accorded generally to parties to civil proceedings in that Court sitting as a court of original jurisdiction.

(2) Nothing in this section shall be construed as affecting the making or operation of any law so far as it provides for the taking of possession or acquisition of property—

(*a*) in satisfaction of any tax, rate or due ;

(*b*) by way of penalty for breach of the law, whether under civil process or after conviction of a criminal offence under the law of the Bahama Islands ;

(c) as an incident of a lease, tenancy, mortgage, charge, bill of sale, pledge or contract ;

(d) upon the attempted removal of the property in question out of or into the Bahama Islands in contravention of any law ;

(e) by way of the taking of a sample for the purposes of any law ;

(f) where the property consists of an animal upon its being found trespassing or straying ;

(g) by way of the vesting or administration of trust property, enemy property or the property of persons adjudged or otherwise declared bankrupt or insolvent, persons of unsound mind, deceased persons, bodies corporate or unincorporate in the course of being wound up, or defunct companies that have been struck off the Register of Companies ;

(h) in the execution of judgments or orders of courts ;

(i) by reason of its being in a dilapidated or dangerous state or injurious to the health of human beings, animals or plants ;

(j) in consequence of any law making provision for the validation of titles to land or (without prejudice to the generality of the foregoing words) the confirmation of such titles, or for the extinguishment of adverse claims, or with respect to prescription or the limitation of actions ; or

(k) for so long only as may be necessary for the purposes of any examination, investigation, trial or inquiry or, in the case of land, the carrying out thereon—

    (i) of work of reclamation, drainage, soil conservation or the conservation of other natural resources ; or

    (ii) of agricultural development or improvement that the owner or occupier of the land has been required, and has, without reasonable and lawful excuse, refused or failed to carry out.

(3) Nothing in this section shall be construed as affecting the making or operation of any law for the compulsory taking of possession in the public interest of any property, or the compulsory acquisition in the public interest of any interest in or right over property, where that property, interest or right is held by a body corporate established by law for public purposes in which no moneys have been invested other than moneys provided by the Legislature.

**14.**—(1) If any person alleges that any of the provisions of sections 2 to 13 (inclusive) of this Constitution has been, is being or is likely to be contravened in relation to him then, without prejudice to any other action with respect to the same matter which is lawfully available, that person may apply to the Supreme Court for redress. *Enforcement of fundamental rights.*

(2) The Supreme Court shall have original jurisdiction—

(a) to hear and determine any application made by any person in pursuance of subsection (1) of this section ; and

(b) to determine any question arising in the case of any person which is referred to it in pursuance of subsection (3) of this section,

and may make such orders, issue such writs and give such directions as it may consider appropriate for the purpose of enforcing or securing the enforcement of any of the provisions of the said sections 2 to 13 (inclusive) to the protection of which the person concerned is entitled :

Provided that the Supreme Court shall not exercise its powers under this subsection if it is satisfied that adequate means of redress are or have been available to the person concerned under any other law.

(3) If, in any proceedings in any court established for the Bahama Islands other than the Supreme Court or the Court of Appeal, any question arises as to the contravention of any of the provisions of the said sections 2 to 13 (inclusive), the court in which the question has arisen shall refer the question to the Supreme Court.

(4) No law of the Legislature shall make provision with respect to rights of appeal from any determination of the Supreme Court in pursuance of this section that is less favourable to any party thereto than the rights of appeal from determinations of the Supreme Court that are accorded generally to parties to civil proceedings in that Court sitting as a court of original jurisdiction.

(5) A law of the Legislature may confer upon the Supreme Court such additional or supplementary powers as may appear to be necessary or desirable for enabling the Court more effectively to exercise the jurisdiction conferred upon it by subsection (2) of this section and may make provision with respect to the practice and procedure of the Court while exercising that jurisdiction.

Provisions for time of war or emergency.

**15.**—(1) This section applies to any period when—

(a) Her Majesty is at war ; or

(b) there is in force a proclamation (in this section referred to as a " proclamation of emergency ") made by the Governor and published in the Gazette declaring that a state of public emergency exists for the purposes of this section.

(2) Nothing contained in or done under the authority of any law shall be held to be inconsistent with or in contravention of section 5, any provision of section 6 other than subsection (4) thereof, or any provision of sections 7 to 12 (inclusive) of this Constitution to the extent that the law in question makes in relation to any period to which this section applies provision, or authorises the doing during any such period of anything, which is reasonably justifiable in the circumstances of any situation arising or existing during that period for the purpose of dealing with that situation.

(3) Where any proclamation of emergency has been made, copies thereof shall as soon as is practicable be laid before both chambers of the Legislature, and if for any cause those chambers are not due to meet within five days the Governor shall, by proclamation published in the Gazette, summon them to meet within five days and they shall accordingly meet and sit upon the day appointed by the proclamation and shall continue to sit and act as if they had stood adjourned or prorogued to that day :

Provided that if the proclamation of emergency is made during the period between a dissolution of the Legislature and the next ensuing general election—

(a) the chambers to be summoned as aforesaid shall be the chambers referred to in section 58 of this Constitution unless the Governor is satisfied that it will be practicable to hold that election within seven days of the making of the proclamation of emergency ; and

(b) if the Governor is so satisfied, he shall (instead of summoning the chambers so referred to to meet within five days of the making of the proclamation) summon the chambers of the new Legislature to meet as soon as practicable after the holding of that election.

(4) A proclamation of emergency shall, unless it is sooner revoked by the Governor, cease to be in force at the expiration of a period of fourteen days beginning on the date on which it was made or such longer period as may be provided under subsection (5) of this section, but without prejudice to the making of another proclamation of emergency at or before the end of that period.

(5) If at any time while a proclamation of emergency is in force (including any time while it is in force by virtue of the provisions of this subsection) a resolution is passed by each chamber of the Legislature approving its continuance in force for a further period, not exceeding three months, beginning on the date on which it would otherwise expire, the proclamation shall, if not sooner revoked, continue in force for that further period.

(6) Where any person who is lawfully detained in pursuance only of such a law as is referred to in subsection (2) of this section so requests at any time during the period of that detention not earlier than six months after he last made such a request during that period, his case shall be reviewed by an independent and impartial tribunal established by law and presided over by a person appointed by the Chief Justice.

(7) On any review by a tribunal in pursuance of this section of the case of a detained person, the tribunal may make recommendations concerning the necessity or expediency of continuing his detention to the authority by which it was ordered but, unless it is otherwise provided by law, that authority shall not be obliged to act in accordance with such recommendations.

(8) The powers of the Governor under this section shall be exercised by him after consultation with the Prime Minister:

Provided that if in the judgment of the Governor it is impracticable for him to consult with the Prime Minister, those powers shall be exercised by the Governor acting in his discretion.

**16.**—(1) In this Part of this Constitution, unless it is otherwise Interpretation. expressly provided or required by the context—

"contravention" in relation to any requirement includes a failure to comply with that requirement, and cognate expressions shall be construed accordingly ;

"court" means any court of law in the Bahama Islands other than a court constituted by or under disciplinary law :

Provided that—

   (a) in sections 2, 4, 5, subsections (2), (3), (5), (9) and (10) of section 6, section 12 and section 14(3), "court" includes, in relation to an offence against disciplinary law, a court constituted by or under disciplinary law ; and

   (b) in sections 4 and 5, "court" includes, in relation to an offence against disciplinary law, an officer of a disciplined force ;

"disciplinary law" means a law regulating the discipline of any disciplined force ;

" disciplined force " means—

    (*a*) a naval, military or air force ;

    (*b*) the Police Force of the Bahama Islands ;

    (*c*) the Prison Service of the Bahama Islands ;

" member " in relation to a disciplined force includes any person who, under the law regulating the discipline of that force, is subject to that discipline.

(2) Any reference in sections 2, 5, 11 and 13 of this Constitution to a criminal offence shall be construed as including an offence against disciplinary law, and any such reference in subsections (2) to (7) (inclusive) of section 6 of this Constitution shall, in relation to proceedings before a court constituted by or under disciplinary law, be construed in the same manner.

(3) In relation to any person who is a member of a disciplined force raised under a law of any country other than the Bahama Islands and lawfully present in the Bahama Islands, nothing contained in or done under the authority of the disciplinary law of that force shall be held to be inconsistent with or in contravention of any of the provisions of this Part.

## PART II

### THE GOVERNOR

The Governor.

**17.**—(1) There shall be a Governor and Commander-in-Chief of the Bahama Islands who shall be appointed by Her Majesty by Commission under Her Sign Manual and Signet and shall hold office during Her Majesty's pleasure.

(2) The Governor shall have such powers and duties as are conferred or imposed on him by or under this Constitution or any other law and such other powers as Her Majesty may from time to time be pleased to assign to him, and, subject to the provisions of this Constitution and of any law by which any such powers or duties are conferred or imposed, shall do and execute all things that belong to his office (including the exercise of any powers with respect to which he is empowered by this Constitution to act in his discretion) according to such instructions, if any, as Her Majesty may from time to time see fit to give him under Her Sign Manual and Signet or through a Secretary of State:

Provided that the question whether or not the Governor has in any matter complied with any such instructions shall not be inquired into in any court of law.

(3) A person appointed to the office of Governor shall, before entering upon the functions of that office, make oaths or affirmations of allegiance and for the due execution of that office in the forms set out in the Schedule to this Constitution.

Office of Deputy Governor.

**18.**—(1) There shall be a Deputy Governor who shall be appointed by the Governor in pursuance of instructions given by Her Majesty through a Secretary of State and shall hold office during Her Majesty's pleasure.

(2) If the office of Deputy Governor is vacant or the person holding that office is acting in the office of Governor under section 19 of this Constitution or is for any other reason unable to perform the functions of the office of Deputy Governor, then the Governor, acting in his discretion, may appoint a person to act as Deputy Governor and any such person shall continue to act until his appointment is revoked by the Governor, acting in his discretion.

**19.**—(1) During any period when the office of Governor is vacant Acting or the Governor is absent from the Bahama Islands or is for any Governor. other reason unable to perform the functions of his office—

(a) the Deputy Governor ; or

(b) if the office of Deputy Governor is vacant or the Deputy Governor is absent from the Bahama Islands or is for any other reason unable to perform the functions of the office of Governor, such person as Her Majesty may designate in that behalf by instructions given through a Secretary of State (in this section referred to as " the person designated "),

shall, during Her Majesty's pleasure, act in the office of Governor and perform the functions of that office accordingly.

(2) Before assuming the functions of the office of Governor, the Deputy Governor or the person designated shall make the oaths or affirmations directed by section 17(3) of this Constitution to be made by the Governor.

(3) The Deputy Governor shall not continue to act in the office of Governor after the Governor has notified him that he is about to assume or resume the functions of that office and the person designated shall not continue to act in that office after the Governor or Deputy Governor has so notified him.

(4) The Governor or, if the Deputy Governor has assumed the functions of the office of Governor under this section, the Deputy Governor may, if he has occasion to be absent from the Bahama Islands for a period that in his opinion will be of short duration, direct by notice published in the Gazette that, notwithstanding his absence from the Bahama Islands, he will continue to perform the functions of the office of Governor.

(5) For the purposes of subsection (1) of this section :—

(a) so long as any direction given by the Governor or, as the case may be, the Deputy Governor under subsection (4) of this section is in force, he shall not be regarded as absent from the Bahama Islands or as unable to perform the functions of the office of Governor by reason only that he is in, or is in passage to or from, any place outside the Bahama Islands ; and

(b) the Governor or the Deputy Governor shall not be regarded as absent from the Bahama Islands or as unable to perform the functions of the office of Governor by reason only that he is in passage from one part of the Bahama Islands to another.

(6) In this section " the Governor " means the person holding the office of Governor and " the Deputy Governor " means the person holding the office of Deputy Governor.

**Authority of Deputy Governor.**

**20.**—(1) The Governor, acting in his discretion, may by writing under his hand, authorise the Deputy Governor to exercise for and on behalf of the Governor, subject to such exceptions and conditions as the Governor may from time to time specify, any or all of the functions of the office of Governor.

(2) The powers and authority of the Governor shall not be affected by any authority of the Deputy Governor under subsection (1) of this section and, subject to the provisions of this Constitution and of any law by which any function which the Deputy Governor is authorised to exercise is conferred, the Deputy Governor shall comply with such instructions relating to the exercise of that function as the Governor, acting in his discretion, may from time to time address to him :

Provided that the question whether or not the Deputy Governor has in any matter complied with any such instructions shall not be enquired into in any court of law.

(3) Any authority given under subsection (1) of this section may at any time be varied or revoked by Her Majesty by instructions given through a Secretary of State or by the Governor, acting in his discretion, by writing under his hand.

(4) In subsection (1) of this section the reference to any functions of the office of Governor does not include a reference to—

(*a*) the functions conferred upon the Governor by this section ; or

(*b*) any functions conferred upon the Governor by any Act of the Parliament of the United Kingdom or by any Order of Her Majesty in Council or other instrument made under any such Act other than the Bahama Islands (Constitution) Act 1963.

**Salary and duty allowance of Governor and Acting Governor.**

**21.**—(1) The Governor shall receive such salary and (save when some other person is performing the functions of his office under section 19 of this Constitution) such duty allowance as, subject to subsection (3) of this section, may be prescribed by any law of the Legislature.

(2) During any period when any person is performing the functions of the office of Governor under section 19 of this Constitution that person shall receive a salary calculated at the rate of ninety-five per centum of the salary of the Governor and such duty allowance as would otherwise be payable to the Governor and shall not be entitled to receive during that period any salary in respect of any other office payable out of the revenues of the Bahama Islands.

(3) The salary, duty allowance and other conditions of service of the Governor or any other person performing the functions of the office of Governor under section 19 of this Constitution shall not be altered to his disadvantage during his continuance in the office of Governor or while he continues to perform the functions of that office, as the case may be, and the said salary and duty allowance are hereby charged on, and shall be paid out of, the Consolidated Fund.

**Personal staff and expenditure of the Governer**

**22.**—(1) The Legislature may, by law, prescribe the offices that are to constitute the personal staff of the Governor, the salaries and allowances that are to be paid to the members of that staff and the other sums that are to be paid in respect of the expenditure attaching to the office of Governor.

(2) Any salaries, allowances or other sums prescribed under the subsection (1) of this section are hereby charged on, and shall be paid out of, the Consolidated Fund.

(3) Subject to the provisions of subsection (4) of this section, the power to make appointments to the offices for the time being prescribed under subsection (1) of this section as being offices constituting the personal staff of the Governor, and to remove and to exercise disciplinary control over persons holding or acting in such offices, shall vest in the Governor, acting in his discretion.

(4) The Governor, acting in his discretion, may appoint to any of the offices prescribed under subsection (1) of this section such public officer as he may select from a list submitted by the Public Service Commission, but—

(a) the provisions of subsection (3) of this section shall apply in relation to any officer so appointed as respects his service on the personal staff of the Governor but not as respects his service as a public officer ;

(b) an officer so appointed shall not, during his continuance on the personal staff of the Governor, perform the functions of any public office ; and

(c) an officer so appointed may at any time be appointed by the Governor, acting in his discretion, if the Public Service Commission so requests, to assume or resume the functions of a public office and shall thereupon vacate his office on the personal staff of the Governor, but the Governor may, acting in his discretion, decline to release the officer for that appointment.

(5) All offices prescribed under subsection (1) of this section as offices that are to constitute the personal staff of the Governor shall be deemed to be public offices for the purposes of sections 97, 102, 104, 111, 112 and 113 of this Constitution.

**23.**—(1) In the exercise of his functions the Governor shall, subject to the provisions of this section, obtain and act in accordance with the advice of the Cabinet or of a Minister acting under the general authority of the Cabinet.

*Exercise of Governor's functions.*

(2) Subsection (1) of this section shall not apply to the exercise by the Governor of—

(a) any function relating to any of the matters for which he is responsible under section 72 or 73(1) of this Constitution ;

(b) any function conferred upon him by this Constitution which is expressed to be exercisable by him in his discretion, or on or in accordance with the recommendation or advice of, or with the concurrence of, or after consultation with, any person or authority other than the Cabinet ; or

(c) any function conferred upon him by any other law which is expressed to be exercisable by him in his discretion or which he is otherwise authorised by such law to exercise without obtaining the advice of the Cabinet.

(3) Where the Governor is by this Constitution or any other law directed to exercise any function on the recommendation of any person or authority, he shall (subject, in the case of any recommendation

referred to in section 101(1) of this Constitution, to the provisions of that section) exercise that function in accordance with such recommendation:

Provided that—

(a) before he acts in accordance therewith, he may, acting in his discretion, once refer that recommendation back for reconsideration by the person or authority concerned ; and

(b) if that person or authority, having reconsidered the original recommendation under the preceding paragraph, substitutes therefor a different recommendation, the provisions of this subsection shall apply to that different recommendation as they apply to the original recommendation.

(4) Where the Governor is by this Constitution or any other law directed to exercise any function after consultation with any person or authority he shall not be obliged to exercise that function in accordance with the advice of that person or authority.

(5) Where the Governor has obtained the advice of the Cabinet or a Minister on any matter in pursuance of subsection (1) of this section, he may act otherwise than in accordance with that advice if in his judgment it is necessary or expedient so to act for the purposes of any matter for which he is responsible under section 72 or 73(1) of this Constitution.

(6) Where any function is vested by any law other than this Constitution in any person or authority other than the Governor (not being a court of law), the Governor may exercise that function in such circumstances and to such extent as he may consider necessary or expedient for the purposes of any matter for which he is responsible as aforesaid.

(7) Where any function conferred upon the Governor by this Constitution or any other law is expressed to be exercisable by him in his discretion, he shall exercise that function according to his own deliberate judgment.

(8) Where the Governor is by this Constitution or any other law directed to exercise any function in his discretion or on or in accordance with the recommendation or advice of, or with the concurrence of, or after consultation with, any person or authority, the question whether he has so exercised that function shall not be inquired into in any court of law.

**Powers to dispose of land.**

24. Subject to the provisions of this Constitution and any law for the time being in force in the Bahama Islands, the Governor, in Her Majesty's name and on Her Majesty's behalf, may, under the Public Seal, make grants and dispositions of any lands or other immovable property in the Bahama Islands or any interests in such property that are vested in Her Majesty or the Governor on behalf of Her Majesty as the property of the Crown for the beneficial interest of the said Islands and may exercise in relation to such property or interests any other powers that are lawfully exercisable by Her Majesty.

**Powers to constitute offices and make appointments, etc.**

25. Subject to the provisions of Part VI of this Constitution and of any other law for the time being in force in the Bahama Islands, the Governor, in Her Majesty's name and on Her Majesty's behalf, may—

(a) constitute offices for the Bahama Islands and make appointments, to be held during Her Majesty's pleasure, thereto ; and

(b) remove any person so appointed or take such other disciplinary action in relation to him as the Governor may think fit.

**26.**—(1) The Governor may, in Her Majesty's name and on Her Majesty's behalf— Powers of pardon, etc.

(a) grant to any person convicted of an offence against any law for the time being in force in the Bahama Islands, a pardon, either free or subject to lawful conditions ;

(b) grant to any person a respite, either indefinite or for a specified period, from the execution of any punishment imposed on that person for such an offence ;

(c) substitute a less severe form of punishment for that imposed by any sentence for such an offence ; or

(d) remit the whole or any part of any sentence passed for such an offence or any penalty or forfeiture otherwise due to Her Majesty on account of such an offence.

(2) The powers of the Governor under subsection (1) of this section shall be exercised by him in accordance with the advice of such Minister as may for the time being be designated in that behalf by the Governor, acting in accordance with the advice of the Prime Minister.

**27.**—(1) There shall be an Advisory Committee on the Prerogative of Mercy (in this and the next following section referred to as "the Committee ") which shall consist of— Establishment and procedure of Advisory Committee.

(a) the Attorney-General ; and

(b) not less than three nor more than five other members who shall be appointed by the Governor.

(2) A member of the Committee appointed under subsection (1) (b) of this section shall hold his seat thereon for such period as may be specified in the instrument by which he was appointed :

Provided that his seat shall become vacant—

(a) in the case of a person who, at the date of his appointment was a Minister, if he ceases to be a Minister ; or

(b) if the Governor, by writing under his hand, so directs.

(3) The Minister for the time being designated under section 26(2) of this Constitution shall attend and preside at any meeting of the Committee.

(4) No business shall be transacted at any meeting of the Committee unless there are at least three members present, of whom one shall be the Attorney-General.

(5) Subject to subsection (4) of this section, the Committee shall not be disqualified for the transaction of business by reason of any vacancy in its membership or the absence of any member and the validity of the transaction of business by the Committee shall not be affected by reason only of the fact that some person who was not entitled to do so took part in its proceedings.

(6) In the exercise of his functions under this section the Governor shall act in accordance with the advice of the Prime Minister.

**Functions of Advisory Committee.**

**28.**—(1) Where any person has been sentenced to death (otherwise than by a court-martial) for an offence, the Minister for the time being designated under section 26(2) of this Constitution (in this section referred to as " the Minister ") shall cause a written report of the case from the trial judge, together with such other information derived from the record of the case or elsewhere as he may require, to be taken into consideration at a meeting of the Committee ; and after obtaining the advice of the Committee he shall decide in his own deliberate judgment whether to advise the Governor to exercise any of his powers under section 26(1) of this Constitution.

(2) The Minister shall consult with the Committee before advising the Governor to exercise any of his powers under section 26(1) of this Constitution in any case not falling within subsection (1) of this section unless in any particular case he considers the matter to be too urgent to permit such prior consultation.

(3) In any case not falling within subsection (1) of this section the Minister may consult with the Committee either by summoning a meeting of the Committee for the purpose or by sending to each of the other members of the Committee such information as the Minister considers relevant to the matter and by giving each such member a reasonable time, not being less than seven days from the sending of the information, to inform the Minister of his advice as to the advice which the Minister should tender to the Governor :

Provided that if any member within such time requests the Minister to summon a meeting of the Committee to consider the case, the Minister shall comply with that request.

(4) Where the Minister consults with the Committee in pursuance of subsection (2) of this section he shall not be obliged to act in accordance with any advice given to him by the Committee.

## PART III

### THE LEGISLATURE

#### General

**Establishment of Legislature.**

**29.** There shall be a Legislature for the Bahama Islands which shall consist of Her Majesty, a Senate and a House of Assembly.

#### The Senate

**Composition of Senate.**

**30.**—(1) The Senate shall consist of sixteen members (in this Constitution referred to as " Senators ") who shall be appointed by the Governor by instrument under the Public Seal in accordance with the provisions of this section.

(2) Of the sixteen Senators—

(a) nine shall be appointed by the Governor acting in accordance with the advice of the Prime Minister ;

(b) four shall be appointed by the Governor acting in accordance with the advice of the leader of the opposition ; and

(c) three shall be appointed by the Governor acting after consultation with the Prime Minister and such other persons as the Governor, acting in his discretion, may decide to consult.

**31.** Subject to the provisions of section 32 of this Constitution, a person shall be qualified to be appointed as a Senator if, and shall not be qualified to be appointed unless, he— *Qualifications for appointment as Senator.*

(a) is a British subject of the age of thirty years or upwards ;

(b) possesses Bahamian status ; and

(c) has been ordinarily resident in the Bahama Islands for a period of not less than five years immediately prior to his appointment.

**32.**—(1) No person shall be qualified to be appointed as a Senator who— *Disqualifications for appointment as Senator.*

(a) is, by virtue of his own act, under any acknowledgment of allegiance, obedience or adherence to a foreign power or state ;

(b) is disqualified for membership of the Senate by any law of the Legislature enacted in pursuance of subsection (2) of this section ;

(c) is a member of the House of Assembly ;

(d) has been adjudged or otherwise declared bankrupt under any law in force in the Bahama Islands and has not been discharged ;

(e) is a person certified to be insane or otherwise adjudged to be of unsound mind under any law in force in the Bahama Islands ;

(f) is under sentence of death imposed on him by a court in any part of the Commonwealth, or is serving a sentence of imprisonment (by whatever name called) exceeding twelve months imposed on him by such a court or substituted by competent authority for some other sentence imposed on him by such a court, or is under such a sentence of imprisonment the execution of which has been suspended ;

(g) is disqualified for membership of the House of Assembly by virtue of any law of the Legislature by reason of his having been convicted of any offence relating to elections ; or

(h) is interested in any government contract and has not disclosed to the Governor the nature of such contract and of his interest therein.

(2) The Legislature may by law provide that, subject to such exceptions and limitations (if any) as may be prescribed therein, a person shall be disqualified for membership of the Senate by virtue of—

(a) his holding or acting in any office or appointment specified (either individually or by reference to a class of office or appointment) by such law ;

(b) his belonging to any of the armed forces of the Crown specified by such law or to any class of person so specified that is comprised in any such force ; or

(c) his belonging to any police force specified by such law or to any class of person so specified that is comprised in any such force.

(3) For the purposes of subsection (1)(f) of this section—

(a) two or more sentences of imprisonment that are required to be served consecutively shall be regarded as separate sentences if none of those sentences exceeds twelve months, but if any one of such sentences exceeds that term they shall be regarded as one sentence ; and

(b) no account shall be taken of a sentence of imprisonment imposed as an alternative to or in default of the payment of a fine.

**Tenure of seats of Senators.**

**33.**—(1) A Senator shall vacate his seat in the Senate—

(a) upon a dissolution of the Legislature ;

(b) if he resigns it by writing under his hand addressed to the President of the Senate, or, if the office of President is vacant or the President is absent from the Bahama Islands, to the Vice-President ;

(c) if he is absent from the sittings of the Senate for such period and in such circumstances as may be prescribed in the Rules of Procedure of the Senate ;

(d) if, with his consent, he is nominated as a candidate for election to the House of Assembly ;

(e) if he ceases to be a British subject or to possess Bahamian status ;

(f) subject to subsection (2) of this section, if any circumstances arise that, if he were not a Senator, would cause him to be disqualified for appointment as such by reason of paragraph (a), (b), (d), (e), (f) or (g) of section 32(1) of this Constitution ; or

(g) if he becomes interested in any government contract:

Provided that a Senator shall not vacate his seat under this paragraph if before or as soon as practicable after he becomes interested in the contract the nature of the contract and of his interest therein is disclosed to the Senate in such manner as may be prescribed by the Rules of Procedure of the Senate and if the Senate by resolution exempts him from vacating his seat under this paragraph.

(2) If circumstances such as are referred to in subsection (1)(f) of this section arise because a Senator is under sentence of death or imprisonment, declared bankrupt, adjudged to be of unsound mind or convicted of an offence relating to elections and if it is open to the Senator to appeal against the decision (either with the leave of a court or other authority or without such leave), he shall forthwith cease to perform his functions as a Senator but, subject to subsection (3) of this section, he shall not vacate his seat until the expiration of a period of thirty days thereafter:

Provided that the President of the Senate may, at the request of the Senator, from time to time extend that period for further periods of thirty days to enable the Senator to pursue an appeal against the decision, so, however, that extensions of time exceeding in the aggregate one hundred and fifty days shall not be given without the approval, signified by resolution, of the Senate.

(3) If, on the determination of any appeal, such circumstances continue to exist and no further appeal is open to the Senator, or if, by reason of the expiration of any period for entering an appeal or notice thereof or the refusal of leave to appeal or for any other reason, it ceases to be open to the Senator to appeal, he shall forthwith vacate his seat.

(4) If at any time before the Senator vacates his seat such circumstances as aforesaid cease to exist, his seat shall not become vacant

on the expiration of the period referred to in subsection (2) of this section and he may resume the performance of his functions as a Senator.

**34.**—(1) When the Senate first meets after this Constitution comes into operation or after any general election and before it proceeds to the despatch of any other business, the Senate shall, in accordance with such procedure as may be prescribed by the Rules of Procedure of the Senate, elect a Senator to be President of the Senate ; and, if the office of President falls vacant at any time, the Senate shall, as soon as practicable, proceed in like manner to fill the vacant office.

President and Vice-President.

(2) When the Senate first meets after this Constitution comes into operation or after any general election and before it proceeds to the despatch of any other business except the election of the President, it shall elect a Senator to be Vice-President of the Senate ; and if the office of Vice-President falls vacant at any time, the Senate shall, as soon as practicable, elect a Senator to that office.

(3) The Senate shall not elect a Senator who is a Minister or Parliamentary Secretary to be the President or Vice-President of the Senate.

(4) A person shall vacate the office of President or Vice-President of the Senate—

(a) if he ceases to be a Senator ;

(b) if he is appointed to be a Minister or Parliamentary Secretary ;

(c) if he announces the resignation of his office to the Senate or if, by writing under his hand addressed, in the case of the President, to the Clerk of the Senate and, in the case of the Vice-President, to the President (or, if the office of President is vacant or the President is absent from the Bahama Islands, to the Clerk), he resigns that office ; or

(d) in the case of the Vice-President, if he is elected to be President.

(5) If, by virtue of section 33(2) of this Constitution, the President or Vice-President is required to cease to perform his functions as a Senator he shall also cease to perform his functions as President or Vice-President, as the case may be, and those functions shall, until he vacates his seat in the Senate or resumes the performance of the functions of his office, be performed—

(a) in the case of the President, by the Vice-President or, if the office of Vice-President is vacant or the Vice-President is required to cease to perform his functions as a Senator by virtue of section 33(2) of this Constitution, by such Senator (not being a Minister or Parliamentary Secretary) as the Senate may elect for the purpose ;

(b) in the case of the Vice-President, by such Senator (not being a Minister or Parliamentary Secretary) as the Senate may elect for the purpose.

(6) If the President or Vice-President resumes the performance of his functions as a Senator in accordance with the provisions of section 33(4) of this Constitution, he shall also resume the performance of his functions as President or Vice-President, as the case may be.

**Determination of questions as to membership**

**35.**—(1) The Supreme Court shall have jurisdiction to hear and determine any question whether—

(a) any person has been validly appointed as a Senator ; or

(b) any Senator has vacated his seat or is required under section 33(2) of this Constitution to cease to perform his functions as a Senator.

(2) Subject to the following provisions of this section, the Legislature may by law make, or provide for the making of, provision with respect to—

(a) the institution of proceedings for the determination of any question referred to in subsection (1) of this section ; and

(b) the powers, practice and procedure of the Supreme Court in relation to any such proceedings.

(3) Proceedings for the determination of any question referred to in subsection (1) of this section shall not be instituted except with the leave of a judge of the Supreme Court.

(4) No appeal shall lie from the decision of a judge of the Supreme Court granting or refusing leave to institute proceedings in accordance with subsection (3) of this section.

## House of Assembly

**Composition of House of Assembly.**

**36.** The House of Assembly shall consist of thirty-eight members (in this Constitution referred to as " Representatives ") who, being qualified for election as Representatives in accordance with the provisions of this Constitution, have been elected in the manner provided by or under any law for the time being in force in the Bahama Islands :

Provided that no person shall be permitted to cast more than one vote in any election of Representatives.

**Qualifications for election as a Representative.**

**37.** Subject to the provisions of section 38 of this Constitution, a person shall be qualified to be elected as a Representative if, and shall not be qualified to be so elected unless, he—

(a) is a British subject of the age of twenty-one years or upwards ;

(b) possesses Bahamian status ;

(c) has ordinarily resided in the Bahama Islands for a period of, or periods amounting in the aggregate to, not less than five years before the date of his nomination for election ; and

(d) has ordinarily resided in the Bahama Islands for a period of not less than six months immediately before the date of such nomination.

**Disqualifications for election as a Representative.**

**38.**—(1) No person shall be qualified to be elected as a Representative who—

(a) is, by virtue of his own act, under any acknowledgment of allegiance, obedience or adherence to a foreign power or state ;

(b) is disqualified for membership of the House of Assembly by any law of the Legislature enacted in pursuance of subsection (2) of this section ;

(c) has been adjudged or otherwise declared bankrupt under any law in force in the Bahama Islands and has not been discharged ;

(*d*) is a person certified to be insane or otherwise adjudged to be of unsound mind under any law in force in the Bahama Islands ;

(*e*) is under sentence of death imposed on him by a court in any part of the Commonwealth, or is serving a sentence of imprisonment (by whatever name called) exceeding twelve months imposed on him by such a court or substituted by competent authority for some other sentence imposed on him by such a court, or is under such a sentence of imprisonment the execution of which has been suspended ;

(*f*) is disqualified for membership of the House of Assembly by any law of the Legislature by reason of his holding, or acting in, any office the functions of which involve—

(i) any responsibility for, or in connection with, the conduct of any election ; or

(ii) any responsibility for the compilation or revision of any electoral register ;

(*g*) is disqualified for membership of the House of Assembly by virtue of any law of the Legislature by reason of his having been convicted of any offence relating to elections ;

(*h*) is a Senator ; or

(*i*) is interested in any government contract and has not disclosed the nature of such contract and of his interest therein by publishing a notice in the Gazette within one month before the day of election.

(2) The Legislature may by law provide that, subject to such exceptions and limitations (if any) as may be prescribed therein, a person shall be disqualified for membership of the House of Assembly by virtue of—

(*a*) his holding or acting in any office or appointment specified (either individually or by reference to a class of office or appointment) by such law ;

(*b*) his belonging to any of the armed forces of the Crown specified by such law or to any class of person so specified that is comprised in any such force ; or

(*c*) his belonging to any police force specified by such law or to any class of person so specified that is comprised in any such force.

(3) For the purposes of subsection (1)(*e*) of this section—

(*a*) two or more sentences of imprisonment that are required to be served consecutively shall be regarded as separate sentences if none of those sentences exceeds twelve months, but if any one of such sentences exceeds that term they shall be regarded as one sentence ; and

(*b*) no account shall be taken of a sentence of imprisonment imposed as an alternative to or in default of the payment of a fine.

**39.**—(1) A Representative shall vacate his seat in the House of Assembly— *Tenure of office of Representatives.*

(*a*) upon a dissolution of the Legislature ;

(*b*) if he resigns it by writing under his hand addressed to the Speaker or, if the office of Speaker is vacant or the Speaker is absent from the Bahama Islands, to the Deputy Speaker ;

(c) if he is absent from the sittings of the House for such period and in such circumstances as may be prescribed in the Rules of Procedure of the House ;

(d) if he ceases to be a British subject or to possess Bahamian status ;

(e) subject to the provisions of subsection (2) of this section, if any circumstances arise that, if he were not a Representative, would cause him to be disqualified for election as such by virtue of paragraph (a), (b), (c), (d), (e), (f) or (g) of section 38(1) of this Constitution ; or

(f) if he becomes interested in any government contract:

Provided that a Representative shall not vacate his seat under this paragraph if before or as soon as practicable after he becomes interested in the contract the nature of the contract and of his interest therein is disclosed to the House of Assembly in such manner as may be prescribed by the Rules of Procedure of the House and if the House by resolution exempts him from vacating his seat under this paragraph.

(2) If circumstances such as are referred to in subsection (1)(e) of this section arise because any Representative is under sentence of death or imprisonment, declared bankrupt, adjudged to be of unsound mind or convicted of an offence relating to elections and it is open to the Representative to appeal against the decision (either with the leave of a court or other authority or without such leave), he shall forthwith cease to perform his functions as a Representative, but, subject to subsection (3) of this section, he shall not vacate his seat until the expiration of a period of thirty days thereafter:

Provided that the Speaker may, at the request of the Representative, from time to time extend that period for further periods of thirty days to enable the Representative to pursue an appeal against the decision, so, however, that extensions of time exceeding in the aggregate one hundred and fifty days shall not be given without the approval, signified by resolution, of the House of Assembly.

(3) If, on the determination of any appeal, such circumstances continue to exist and no further appeal is open to the member, or if, by reason of the expiration of any period for entering an appeal or notice thereof or the refusal of leave to appeal or for any other reason, it ceases to be open to the Representative to appeal, he shall forthwith vacate his seat.

(4) If at any time before the Representative vacates his seat such circumstances as aforesaid cease to exist, his seat shall not become vacant on the expiration of the period referred to in subsection (2) of this section and he may resume the performance of his functions as a Representative.

**Speaker and Deputy Speaker.**    **40.**—(1) When the House of Assembly first meets after any general election and before it proceeds to the despatch of any other business, the House shall, in accordance with such procedure as may be prescribed by the Rules of Procedure of the House, elect from among the Representatives who are not Ministers or Parliamentary Secretaries one Representative to be the Speaker of the Assembly and another Representative to be Deputy Speaker ; and, if the office of Speaker or Deputy Speaker falls vacant at any time before the next dissolution of the House of Assembly, the House shall, as soon as practicable, proceed in like manner to fill the vacant office.

(2) A person shall vacate the office of Speaker or Deputy Speaker—

(a) if he ceases to be a Representative:

Provided that the Speaker shall not vacate his office by reason only that he has ceased to be a Representative on a dissolution of the Legislature, until the House of Assembly first meets after that dissolution ;

(b) if he is appointed to be a Minister or Parliamentary Secretary ;

(c) if he announces the resignation of his office to the House of Assembly or if, by writing under his hand addressed, in the case of the Speaker, to the Clerk of the House and, in the case of the Deputy Speaker, to the Speaker (or, if the office of Speaker is vacant or the Speaker is absent from the Bahama Islands, to the Clerk), he resigns that office ; or

(d) in the case of the Deputy Speaker, if he is elected to be Speaker.

(3) If by reason of section 39(2) of this Constitution the Speaker or Deputy Speaker is required to cease to perform his functions as a member of the House of Assembly, he shall also cease to perform his functions as Speaker or Deputy Speaker and those functions shall, until he vacates his seat in the House or resumes the performance of the functions of his office, be performed—

(a) in the case of the Speaker, by the Deputy Speaker or, if the office of Deputy Speaker is vacant or the Deputy Speaker is required to cease to perform his functions as a member of the House of Assembly by virtue of section 39(2) of this Constitution, by such Representative (not being a Minister or Parliamentary Secretary) as the House may elect for the purpose ;

(b) in the case of the Deputy Speaker, by such Representative (not being a Minister or Parliamentary Secretary) as the House may elect for the purpose.

(4) If the Speaker or Deputy Speaker resumes the performance of his functions as a Representative in accordance with the provisions of section 39(4) of this Constitution, he shall also resume the performance of his functions as Speaker or Deputy Speaker, as the case may be.

**41.**—(1) An Election Court, consisting of two judges of the Supreme Court appointed by the Governor acting in his discretion or, if for any reason two such judges are not available, one such judge and a Chief Magistrate or Stipendiary and Circuit Magistrate appointed by the Governor acting in his discretion, shall have jurisdiction to hear and determine any question whether— *Determination of questions as to membership*

(a) any person has been validly elected as a Representative ; or

(b) any Representative has vacated his seat or is required, under the provisions of section 39(2) of this Constitution, to cease to perform his functions as a Representative.

(2) Subject to the following provisions of this section, the Legislature may by law make, or provide for the making of, provision with respect to—

(a) the institution of proceedings for the determination of any question referred to in subsection (1) of this section ; and

(b) the powers, practice and procedure of an Election Court in relation to any such proceedings.

(3) The determination by an Election Court of any question referred to in subsection (1) of this section shall be final.

(4) Proceedings for the determination of any question referred to in subsection (1) of this section shall not be instituted except with the leave of a judge of the Supreme Court.

(5) An appeal shall lie to the Court of Appeal on a point of law from the decision of a judge of the Supreme Court granting or refusing leave to institute proceedings in accordance with this section ; but, subject as aforesaid, that decision shall be final.

### *Powers and Procedure*

Power to make laws.

**42.** Subject to the provisions of this Constitution, the Legislature may make laws for the peace, order and good government of the Bahama Islands.

Mode of exercise of power to make laws.

**43.**—(1) Subject to the provisions of sections 51 and 52 of this Constitution, the power of the Legislature to make laws shall be exercised by bills passed by both chambers, either without amendment or with such amendments only as are agreed to by both chambers, and assented to by Her Majesty or by the Governor on behalf of Her Majesty.

(2) When a bill is presented to the Governor for assent, he shall signify that he assents or that he withholds assent or that he reserves the bill for the signification of Her Majesty's pleasure :

Provided that, unless he has been authorised by a Secretary of State to assent thereto, the Governor shall reserve for the signification of Her Majesty's pleasure any bill which appears to him, acting in his discretion—

(*a*) to be inconsistent with any subsisting obligation imposed on Her Majesty by any treaty, convention or agreement or arrangement relating to any country or international or similar organisation outside the Bahama Islands ;

(*b*) to be likely to prejudice the Royal prerogative ;

(*c*) to be in any way repugnant to or inconsistent with the provisions of this Constitution ;

(*d*) to be inconsistent with any subsisting obligation (other than an obligation relating to the entry of persons into or the maintenance of internal security in the Bahama Islands) contained in any agreement entered into by the Government of the Bahama Islands under authority especially conferred on the Government for the purpose by a law enacted by the Legislature ;

(*e*) to affect external affairs, defence, internal security or the Police Force.

(3) A bill assented to by Her Majesty shall become a law when the Governor has signified such assent by proclamation published in the Gazette.

(4) In every bill presented to the Governor for assent, other than a bill presented under section 51 or 52 of this Constitution, the words of enactment shall be as follows :—

" Be it enacted by The Queen's Most Excellent Majesty, by and with the advice and consent of the Senate and the House of

Assembly of the Commonwealth of the Bahama Islands, and by the authority of the same, as follows: —".

(5) In every bill presented to the Governor for assent under section 51 or section 52 of this Constitution the words of enactment shall be as follows: —

" Be it enacted by The Queen's Most Excellent Majesty, by and with the advice and consent of the House of Assembly of the Commonwealth of the Bahama Islands in accordance with the provisions of section 51 (or section 52, as the case may be) of the Constitution of the Commonwealth of the Bahama Islands, and by the authority of the same, as follows: —".

(6) Any alteration of the words of enactment of a bill in consequence of the provisions of subsection (5) of this section shall not be deemed to be an amendment of the bill.

**44.**—(1) Subject to the provisions of this Constitution, each chamber of the Legislature may from time to time make, amend or revoke Rules of Procedure for the regulation and orderly conduct of its own proceedings and the despatch of business, and the passing, intituling and numbering of bills and the presentation of the same to the Governor for assent. *Rules of Procedure.*

(2) The Legislature may provide that any resolution for the suspension, amendment or revocation of any Rule of Procedure of a chamber of the Legislature shall not be passed unless it is supported by the votes of all, or a specified number or proportion, of the members of the chamber present and voting on the resolution.

**45.** No member of either chamber of the Legislature shall be permitted to take part in the proceedings of that chamber (other than proceedings necessary for the purposes of this section) until he has made and subscribed before that chamber an oath or affirmation of allegiance in the form set out in the Schedule to this Constitution: *Oath of allegiance.*

Provided that the election of a President of the Senate or the election of a Speaker of the House of Assembly may take place before the members of the Senate or the House of Assembly, as the case may be, have made such oath or affirmation.

**46.** A chamber of the Legislature shall not be disqualified for the transaction of business by reason of any vacancy in the membership thereof (including any vacancy not filled when the chamber is first constituted or is reconstituted at any time), and any proceedings therein shall be valid notwithstanding that some person who was not entitled so to do sat or voted in the chamber or otherwise took part in the proceedings. *Validity of proceedings.*

**47.**—(1) The President of the Senate or, in his absence, the Vice-President or, if they are both absent, a Senator (not being a Minister or Parliamentary Secretary) elected by the Senate for that sitting shall preside at each sitting of the Senate. *Presiding in the Senate and House of Assembly.*

(2) The Speaker or, in his absence, the Deputy Speaker or, if they are both absent, a Representative (not being a Minister or Parliamentary Secretary) elected by the House for that sitting shall preside at each sitting of the House.

(3) References in this section to circumstances in which the President, Vice-President, Speaker or Deputy Speaker is absent include references to circumstances in which the office of President, Vice-President, Speaker or Deputy Speaker is vacant.

**Quorum.**

48.—(1) If at any sitting of either chamber of the Legislature any member of the chamber who is present draws the attention of the member presiding at the sitting to the absence of a quorum and, after such interval as may be prescribed in the Rules of Procedure of the chamber, the member presiding at the sitting ascertains that a quorum of the chamber is still not present, the chamber shall be adjourned.

(2) For the purposes of this section—

(*a*) a quorum of the Senate shall consist of six Senators ;

(*b*) a quorum of the House of Assembly shall consist of ten Representatives ;

(*c*) the member presiding at the sitting of either chamber shall be included in reckoning whether there is a quorum of that chamber present.

**Voting.**

49.—(1) Save as otherwise provided in this Constitution, all questions proposed for decision in either chamber of the Legislature shall be determined by a majority of the votes of the members thereof present and voting.

(2) The President or other member presiding in the Senate and the Speaker or other member presiding in the House of Assembly shall not vote unless on any question the votes are equally divided, in which case he shall have and exercise a casting vote.

**Restrictions with regard to certain financial measures.**

50.—(1) The Senate shall not—

(*a*) proceed upon any bill other than a bill sent from the House of Assembly that, in the opinion of the member presiding, makes provision for any of the following purposes : —

(i) for the imposition, repeal or alteration of taxation ;

(ii) for the imposition of any charge upon the Consolidated Fund or any other fund of the Government of the Bahama Islands ;

(iii) for the payment, issue or withdrawal from the Consolidated Fund or any other fund of the Government of the Bahama Islands of any moneys not charged thereon or any alteration in the amount of such a payment, issue or withdrawal ; or

(iv) for the composition or remission of any debt due to the Government of the Bahama Islands ;

(*b*) proceed upon any amendment to any bill that, in the opinion of the member presiding, is an amendment that makes provision for any of those purposes or an amendment to any provision for any of those purposes contained in the bill ;

(*c*) proceed upon any motion (including any amendment to a motion) the effect of which, in the opinion of the member presiding, would be to make provision for any of those purposes ; or (*d*) receive any petition that, in the opinion of the member presiding, requests that provision be made for any of those purposes.

(2) Nothing in subsection (1)(*b*) of this section shall be construed as preventing the Senate from returning any bill to the House of Assembly with a message recommending any amendment to the bill that the Senate may consider desirable.

(3) Except on the recommendation or with the consent of the Governor signified by a Minister, the House of Assembly shall not—

(*a*) proceed upon any bill (including any amendment to a bill) that, in the opinion of the member presiding, makes provision for any of the following purposes : —

    (i) for the imposition of taxation or the alteration of taxation otherwise than by reduction ;

    (ii) for the imposition of any charge upon the Consolidated Fund or any other fund of the Government of the Bahama Islands or the alteration of any such charge otherwise than by reduction ;

    (iii) for the payment, issue or withdrawal from the Consolidated Fund or any other fund of the Government of the Bahama Islands of any moneys not charged thereon or any increase in the amount of such a payment, issue or withdrawal ; or

    (iv) for the composition or remission of any debt due to the Government of the Bahama Islands ;

(*b*) proceed upon any motion (including any amendment to a motion) the effect of which, in the opinion of the member presiding, would be to make provision for any of those purposes ; or

(*c*) receive any petition that, in the opinion of the member presiding, requests that provision be made for any of those purposes.

**51.**—(1) This section applies to any money bill which is not a taxation bill.

Restriction on powers of Senate as to money bills other than taxation bills.

(2) If any bill to which this section applies, having been passed by the House of Assembly and sent to the Senate at least two months before the end of the session, is not passed by the Senate without amendment within two months after it is sent to the Senate, the bill shall, unless the House of Assembly otherwise resolves, be presented to the Governor for assent notwithstanding that the Senate has not consented to the bill.

(3) There shall be inserted in any bill that is presented to the Governor for assent in pursuance of subsection (2) of this section any amendments to it that are certified by the Speaker to have been recommended by the Senate and agreed to by the House of Assembly.

(4) There shall be endorsed on every bill to which this section applies—

(*a*) when it is sent to the Senate, the certificate of the Speaker signed by him that it is a money bill which is not a taxation bill ; and (*b*) if it is presented to the Governor for assent in pursuance of subsection (2) of this section, the certificate of the Speaker signed by him that it is a money bill which is not a taxation bill and that the provisions of subsections (1) and (2) of this section have been complied with.

**Restriction on powers of Senate as to other bills.**

**52.**—(1) This section applies to any bill other than a bill to which section 51 of this Constitution applies.

(2) If any bill to which this section applies is passed by the House of Assembly in two successive sessions (whether or not the Legislature is dissolved between those sessions) and, having been sent to the Senate in each of those sessions at least one month before the end of the session, is rejected by the Senate in each of those sessions, that bill shall, on its rejection for the second time by the Senate, unless the House of Assembly otherwise resolves, be presented to the Governor for assent notwithstanding that the Senate has not consented to the bill:

Provided that the foregoing provisions of this subsection shall not have effect unless at least nine months have elapsed between the date on which the bill is passed by the House of Assembly in the first session and the date on which it is passed by that House in the second session.

(3) For the purposes of this section, a bill shall be deemed to be rejected by the Senate if—

(*a*) in the case of a taxation bill, it is not passed by the Senate without amendment ; or

(*b*) in the case of any other bill, it is not passed by the Senate without amendment, or it is passed by the Senate with any amendment which is not agreed to by the House of Assembly.

(4) There shall be endorsed on every taxation bill when it is sent to the Senate the certificate of the Speaker signed by him that it is a taxation bill.

(5) For the purposes of this section, a bill that is sent to the Senate in any session shall be deemed to be the same bill as a former bill sent to the Senate in the preceding session if, when it is sent to the Senate, it is identical with the former bill or contains only such alterations as are certified by the Speaker to be necessary owing to the time that has elapsed since the date of the former bill or to represent any amendments which have been made or recommended by the Senate in the former bill in the preceding session and agreed to by the House of Assembly.

(6) The House of Assembly may, if it thinks fit, on the passage through that House of a bill that is deemed to be the same bill as a former bill sent to the Senate in the preceding session, suggest any amendments without inserting the amendments in the bill, and any such amendments shall be considered by the Senate, and, if agreed to by the Senate, shall be treated as amendments made by the Senate and agreed to by the House of Assembly ; but the exercise of this power by the House of Assembly shall not affect the operation of this section in the event of the rejection of the bill in the Senate.

(7) There shall be inserted in any bill that is presented to the Governor for assent in pursuance of this section any amendments to it

that are certified by the Speaker to have been made or recommended by the Senate in the second session and agreed to by the House of Assembly.

(8) There shall be endorsed on any bill that is presented to the Governor for assent in pursuance of this section the certificate of the Speaker signed by him that it is a bill to which this section applies and that the provisions of this section have been complied with.

**53.**—(1) In sections 51 and 52 of this Constitution " money bill " means a public bill which, in the opinion of the Speaker subject to the provisions of subsection (6) of this section, contains only provisions dealing with all or any of the following matters, that is to say— *Provisions relating to sections 51 and 52.*

(a) the imposition, repeal, remission, alteration or regulation of taxation ;

(b) the imposition, for the payment of debt or other financial purposes, of charges on public money, or the variation or repeal of any such charges ;

(c) the grant of money to the Crown or to any authority or person, or the variation or revocation of any such grant ;

(d) the appropriation, receipt, custody, investment, issue or audit of accounts of public money ;

(e) the raising or guarantee of any loan or the repayment thereof, or the establishment, alteration, administration or abolition of any sinking fund provided in connection with any such loan ; or

(f) subordinate matters incidental to any of the matters aforesaid.

(2) In sections 51 and 52 of this Constitution " taxation bill " means a money bill which, in the opinion of the Speaker subject to the provisions of subsection (6) of this section, contains provisions for the imposition of an income tax, a capital gains tax, a capital levy or estate duty or makes provision for the cesser, remission, suspension, alteration or regulation of any such tax, levy or duty.

(3) Whenever the office of Speaker is vacant or the Speaker is for any reason unable to perform any function conferred upon him by subsection (1) or (2) of this section or by section 51 or 52 of this Constitution, that function may be performed by the Deputy Speaker.

(4) If, in respect of a bill passed by the House of Assembly and certified by the Speaker to be a money bill which is not a taxation bill or, as the case may be, a taxation bill and sent to the Senate, the Senate passes a resolution declaring that it dissents from the Speaker's certificate, the bill shall be referred back to the Speaker by the Senate.

(5) Thereupon the Speaker shall refer the matter forthwith to the Attorney-General for his advice.

(6) On receiving the advice of the Attorney-General, the Speaker shall, in accordance with that advice, endorse forthwith on the bill a further certificate signed by him that the bill is a money bill which is not a taxation bill or, as the case may be, a taxation bill and the bill so endorsed shall be returned to the Senate.

(7) The period between the date on which the bill is referred back to the Speaker and the date on which it is returned to the

Senate shall not be taken into account in computing the period of two months referred to in section 51(2) of this Constitution in a case where the further certificate is that the bill is a money bill which is not a taxation bill, or in computing the period of nine months referred to in section 52(2) of this Constitution in a case where the further certificate is that the bill is a taxation bill.

(8) Subject to the provisions of subsections (4) and (5) of this section, any certificate given by the Speaker or Deputy Speaker under section 51 or 52 of this Constitution or this section shall be conclusive for all purposes and shall not be questioned in any court.

Power of disallowance in respect of laws relating to Bahamas Government stock.

**54.**—(1) Any law enacted by the Legislature which has been assented to by the Governor and which appears to Her Majesty's Government in the United Kingdom to alter, to the injury of the stockholder, any provision relating to any stock to which this section applies or to involve a departure from the original contract in respect of any such stock, may be disallowed by Her Majesty through a Secretary of State.

(2) Whenever such a law has been disallowed by Her Majesty the Governor shall cause notice of such disallowance to be published in the Gazette and the law shall be annulled with effect from the date of publication of that notice.

(3) On the annulment of any law under this section any enactment repealed or amended by or in pursuance of that law shall have effect as from the date of the annulment as if that law had not been made ; and, save as provided in the foregoing provisions of this subsection, the provisions of section 38(2) of the Interpretation Act 1889(a) shall apply to that annulment as they apply to the repeal of an Act of Parliament.

(4) The stock to which this section applies is stock forming the whole or any part of the public debt of the Bahama Islands—

(a) in which a trustee might at any time have invested by virtue of section 2 of the Colonial Stock Act 1900(b) ; or

(b) by the conditions of issue of which it is provided that this section shall apply to it.

Privileges of chambers.

**55.** The Legislature may by law determine and regulate the privileges, immunities and powers of either chamber of the Legislature and the members thereof, but no such privileges, immunities or powers shall exceed those of the Commons House of Parliament of the United Kingdom or of the members thereof.

*Summoning, Prorogation and Dissolution*

Sessions of the chambers.

**56.**—(1) Subject to the provisions of this Constitution, the sessions of the chambers of the Legislature shall be held in such places and shall commence at such times as the Governor may appoint by proclamation published in the Gazette :

Provided that the sessions of the two chambers shall commence on the same day.

(2) There shall be a session of each chamber from time to time so that a period longer than twelve months does not intervene between the last sitting in one session and the first sitting in the next session.

---

(a) 1889 c. 63.                    (b) 1900 c. 62.

**57.**—(1) The Governor may at any time prorogue or dissolve the Legislature by proclamation published in the Gazette.

(2) The Governor shall dissolve the Legislature at the expiration of five years from the date when the House of Assembly first meets after any general election of Representatives unless the Legislature has been sooner dissolved under the powers conferred by subsection (1) of this section.

(3) In the exercise of the powers conferred upon him by subsection (1) of this section, the Governor shall act in accordance with the advice of the Prime Minister:

Provided that—

(*a*) if the Prime Minister advises the Governor to dissolve the Legislature and the Governor considers that the government of the Bahama Islands can be carried on without a dissolution and that a dissolution would not be in the interests of the Bahama Islands, the Governor, acting in his discretion, may refuse to dissolve the Legislature ; and

(*b*) if the office of Prime Minister is vacant and the Governor considers that' there is no prospect of his being able to appoint a person who can command the support of the majority of the Representatives to that office within a reasonable time, the Governor, acting in his discretion, may dissolve the Legislature.

*Prorogation and dissolution of the Legislature.*

**58.**—(1) Subject to the provisions of subsection (2) of this section, the Governor may, between a dissolution of the Legislature and the next ensuing general election, by proclamation published in the Gazette, summon the two chambers of the Legislature as constituted immediately before the said dissolution, and that Legislature shall thereupon be deemed (except for the purposes of section 59(1) of this Constitution) not to have been dissolved but shall be deemed (except as aforesaid) to be dissolved on the day on which the next ensuing general election is held.

(2) If the Governor is of the opinion that an emergency has arisen of such a nature that it is necessary to exercise the power conferred by this section he may exercise that power after consultation with the Prime Minister ; and if the Prime Minister is of the opinion that such an emergency has arisen and so advises the Governor, the Governor shall exercise that power in accordance with the advice of the Prime Minister.

*Recalling dissolved Legislature in case of emergency.*

**59.**—(1) A general election of Representatives shall be held at such time within three months after every dissolution of the Legislature as the Governor shall appoint by proclamation published in the Gazette.

(2) Whenever any person vacates his seat as a Representative for any reason other than a dissolution of the Legislature, an election to fill the vacancy shall be held within two months after the occurrence of the vacancy or, where the question whether a vacancy has occurred is determined under section 41 of this Constitution, after that determination unless the Legislature is sooner dissolved or the date by which the Legislature will be dissolved under the provisions of section 57(2) of this Constitution is less than four months after the occurrence of the vacancy or, as the case may be, that determination.

*General elections, bye-elections and appointments to Senate.*

(3) As soon as practicable after every general election the Governor shall proceed under section 30 of this Constitution to the appointment of Senators.

(4) Whenever any person vacates his seat as a Senator for any reason other than a dissolution of the Legislature, the Governor shall, as soon as practicable, appoint a person to fill the vacancy under the same paragraph of section 30(2) of this Constitution as the person whose seat has become vacant was appointed.

### Delimitation of Constituencies

**Division of Bahama Islands into single-member constituencies.**

**60.**—(1) The Bahama Islands shall be divided into thirty-eight electoral areas (hereinafter referred to as " constituencies ") of which not less than sixteen nor more than twenty shall be in the Island of New Providence and not less than eighteen nor more than twenty-two shall be in the remainder of the Bahama Islands.

(2) Subject to subsection (1) of this section, the boundaries of constituencies shall be determined in accordance with the provisions of section 62 of this Constitution.

(3) Each constituency shall return one member to the House of Assembly in accordance with the law for the time being in force relating to elections.

**Constituencies Commission.**

**61.**—(1) There shall be a Constituencies Commission for the Bahama Islands (in this and the next following section referred to as " the Commission ").

(2) The members of the Commision shall be—

(a) the Speaker who shall be Chairman ;

(b) a judge of the Supreme Court who shall be Deputy Chairman and shall be appointed by the Governor acting after consultation with the Chief Justice ;

(c) two members of the House of Assembly who shall be appointed by the Governor acting in accordance with the advice of the Prime Minister ; and

(d) one member of the House of Assembly who shall be appointed by the Governor acting in accordance with the advice of the leader of the opposition.

(3) The office of a member of the Commission shall become vacant—

(a) if he ceases to be the Speaker, a judge of the Supreme Court or a member of the House of Assembly, as the case may be ; or

(b) in the case of a member appointed under paragraph (b), (c) or (d) of subsection (2) of this section, if his appointment is revoked by the Governor.

(4) If the office of a member of the Commission, appointed under paragraph (b), (c) or (d) of subsection (2) of this section is vacant or any such member is for any reason unable to perform the functions of his office the Governor may appoint a person qualified for appointment under the said paragraph (b), (c) or (d), as the case may be, to act in the office of that member and any person so appointed may continue so to act until his appointment is revoked.

(5) In revoking the appointment of a member of the Commission under subsection (3)(*b*) of this section, and in making or revoking an appointment to act in the office of a member of the Commission under subsection (4) of this section, the Governor shall act in the same manner as he would act if he were making an appointment to the office of that member under subsection (2) of this section.

(6) Any decision of the Commission shall require the concurrence of not less than three members of the Commission.

(7) Subject to the provisions of subsection (6) of this section, the Commission may act notwithstanding a vacancy in its membership, and no proceedings of the Commission shall be invalidated by reason only that some person not entitled to do so has taken part in them.

**62.**—(1) Subject to the provisions of section 60(1) of this Constitution, the Commission shall, at intervals of not more than five years, review the boundaries of the constituencies and submit to the Governor a single report either— Procedure for review of constituencies.

(*a*) stating that, in the opinion of the Commission, no change is required ; or

(*b*) recommending the changes in those boundaries specified in the report,

and the Governor shall cause such report to be laid before the House of Assembly forthwith.

(2) In carrying out a review for the purposes of this section, the Commission shall be guided by the general consideration that the number of voters entitled to vote for the purposes of electing every member of the House of Assembly shall, so far as is reasonably practicable, be the same and the need to take account of special considerations such as the needs of sparsely populated areas, the practicability of elected members maintaining contact with electors in such areas, size, physical features, natural boundaries, local government areas, geographical isolation and inadequacy of communications.

(3) When the Commission intends to proceed under subsection (1) of this section, it shall, by notice in writing, inform the Prime Minister, who shall cause a copy of that notice to be published in the Gazette.

(4) As soon as may be after the Commission has submitted a report recommending changes in the boundaries of any constituencies the Prime Minister shall lay before the House of Assembly for its approval a draft of an order by the Governor for giving effect, whether with or without modifications, to the recommendations contained in the report, and that draft may make provision for any matters which appear to the Prime Minister to be incidental to or consequential upon the other provisions of the draft.

(5) Where any draft order laid under this section would give effect to any such recommendations with modifications, the Prime Minister shall lay before the House of Assembly together with the draft a statement of the reasons for the modifications.

(6) If the motion for the approval of any draft order laid under this section is rejected by the House of Assembly, or is withdrawn by leave of that chamber, an amended draft shall be laid without undue delay by the Prime Minister before the House of Assembly.

(7) If any draft order laid under this section is approved by resolution of the House of Assembly, the Prime Minister shall submit it to the Governor who shall make an order (which shall be published in the Gazette) in terms of the draft ; and that order shall come into force on such day as may be specified therein and, until revoked by a further order made by the Governor in accordance with the provisions of this section, shall have the force of law in the Bahama Islands :

Provided that the coming into force of any such order shall not affect any election to the House of Assembly until a proclamation is made by the Governor appointing the date for the holding of a general election of Representatives or affect the constitution of the House of Assembly then in being.

(8) The question of the validity of any order by the Governor purporting to be made under this section and reciting that a draft thereof has been approved by resolution of the House of Assembly shall not be inquired into in any court of law.

# PART IV

## THE EXECUTIVE

Executive authority.

**63.**—(1) The executive authority of the Bahama Islands is vested in Her Majesty.

(2) Subject to the provisions of this Constitution, the executive authority of the Bahama Islands may be exercised on behalf of Her Majesty by the Governor, either directly or through officers subordinate to him, but nothing in this subsection shall operate so as to prejudice the provisions of any law for the time being in force in the Bahama Islands whereby functions are conferred on persons or authorities other than the Governor.

The Cabinet.

**64.**—(1) There shall be a Cabinet for the Bahama Islands which, subject to the provisions of this Constitution, shall have the general direction and control of the government of the Bahama Islands and shall be collectively responsible therefor to the Legislature.

(2) The Cabinet shall consist of the Prime Minister and not less than eight other Ministers, who shall be appointed in accordance with the provisions of section 65 of this Constitution.

Appointment of Ministers.

**65.**—(1) The Governor, acting in his discretion, shall appoint as Prime Minister the Representative who, in his judgment, is best able to command the confidence of a majority of the Representatives and who is willing to accept the office of Prime Minister.

(2) The Ministers other than the Prime Minister shall be such persons as the Governor, acting in accordance with the advice of the Prime Minister, shall appoint from among the Senators and the Representatives :

Provided that at least one and not more than three of such Ministers shall be appointed from among the Senators.

(3) If occasion arises for making an appointment of a Minister between a dissolution of the Legislature and the next following general election, the preceding provisions of this section shall have effect for the purpose as if the Legislature had not been dissolved.

(4) Appointments made under this section shall be made by instrument under the Public Seal.

**66.**—(1) The Prime Minister shall vacate his office—

(a) if he ceases to be a Representative for any reason other than a dissolution of the Legislature ;

(b) if, under the provisions of section 39(2) of this Constitution, he is required to cease to perform his functions as a Representative ;

(c) if he is absent from the Bahama Islands for a period exceeding forty-eight hours without having given the Governor prior notice of such absence ; or

(d) if the Governor revokes his appointment as Prime Minister in accordance with the provisions of subsection (2) or (3) of this section.

Tenure of office of Prime Minister.

(2) If the House of Assembly by the affirmative votes of a majority of all the Representatives passes a resolution that it has no confidence in the Government of the Bahama Islands, the Governor shall, by instrument under the Public Seal, revoke the Prime Minister's appointment:

Provided that before so doing the Governor shall consult with the Prime Minister and shall not revoke the Prime Minister's appointment if he dissolves the Legislature under section 57 of this Constitution.

(3) The Governor, acting in his discretion, may by instrument under the Public Seal revoke the appointment of the Prime Minister if at any time between the holding of a general election and the first sitting of the House of Assembly thereafter the Governor considers that, in consequence of the changes in the House of Assembly resulting from that election, the Prime Minister will not be the Representative best able to command the support of a majority of the Representatives.

**67.**—(1) A Minister, other than the Prime Minister, shall vacate his office—

(a) whenever a person is appointed to the office of Prime Minister ;

(b) if his appointment to his office is revoked by the Governor by instrument under the Public Seal ;

(c) if, for any reason other than a dissolution of the Legislature, he ceases to be a member of the chamber of which he was a member at the date of his appointment as a Minister or if he is not a member of that chamber when it first meets after a dissolution of the Legislature ; or

(d) if, under the provisions of section 33(2) or, as the case may be, 39(2), of this Constitution, he is required to cease to perform his functions as a Senator or Representative.

Tenure of office of Ministers other than the Prime Minister.

(2) The powers of the Governor under subsection (1)(b) of this section shall be exercised by him in accordance with the advice of the Prime Minister unless the Cabinet, upon the appointment of any person as Prime Minister, signifies its desire that, during the tenure by that person of the office of Prime Minister, the powers should be exercised in accordance with the advice of the Cabinet.

**Performance of functions of Prime Minister in certain events.**

**68.**—(1) Whenever the Prime Minister is absent from the Bahama Islands or is unable by reason of illness to perform the functions conferred upon him by this Constitution, the Governor may, by directions in writing, authorise any other Minister who was appointed from among the Representatives temporarily to perform the functions conferred on the Prime Minister by this Constitution (other than the functions conferred upon him by subsection (2) of this section) and that member may perform those functions until his authority is revoked by the Governor.

(2) The powers conferred upon the Governor by this section shall be exercised by him acting in his discretion if the office of Prime Minister is vacant or if, in his judgment, it is impracticable to obtain the Prime Minister's advice owing to his illness or absence, and in any other case shall be exercised in accordance with the advice of the Prime Minister.

**Temporary Ministers.**

**69.**—(1) Whenever a Minister other than the Prime Minister is unable, by reason of his illness or absence from the Bahama Islands or absence from his duties on leave, to perform the functions of his office, the Governor may, in writing, appoint a person who is a member of the same chamber of the Legislature as that Minister to be a temporary Minister:

Provided that if occasion arises for the making of an appointment between a dissolution of the Legislature and the next following general election, the preceding provisions of this section shall have effect for the purpose as if the Legislature had not been dissolved.

(2) Subject to the provisions of section 67 of this Constitution, a temporary Minister shall hold office until he is notified by the Governor in writing that the Minister on account of whose inability to perform the functions of his office he was appointed is again able to perform those functions or that Minister vacates his office.

(3) The powers conferred on the Governor by this section shall be exercised by him in accordance with the advice of the Prime Minister.

**Allocation of portfolios to Ministers.**

**70.**—(1) Subject to the provisions of this Constitution, the Governor, acting in accordance with the advice of the Prime Minister, may by directions in writing charge any Minister with responsibility for any matter or any department of government and designate the style by which any Minister so charged shall be known:

Provided that a Minister appointed from among the Representatives shall be charged with responsibility for finance and shall be styled " Minister of Finance ".

(2) Nothing in this section shall empower the Governor to confer on any Minister authority to exercise any power or discharge any duty that is conferred or imposed by this Constitution or any other law on the Governor or any person or authority other than a Minister.

(3) Without prejudice to the generality of subsection (2) of this section, except for the purpose of submitting questions relating to such matters to the Cabinet and conducting government business relating to such matters in either chamber of the Legislature, a Minister shall not be charged under this section with responsibility for—

(a) any matter for which the Governor is responsible under section 72 or 73(1) of this Constitution ;

(b) the discharge by the courts of the Bahama Islands of their judicial functions ;

(c) the initiation, conduct and discontinuance of criminal proceedings ;

(d) the audit of the accounts of the Bahama Islands ;

(e) the making of appointments (including appointments on promotion, appointments on transfer and the confirmation of appointments) to public offices, the removal or disciplinary control (including the withholding of increments of salary) of persons holding or acting in such offices and the grant of any benefits in relation to pensions and gratuities in pursuance of section 113 of this Constitution.

(4) For the purposes of subsection (3)(e) of this section, the office of a judge of the Supreme Court or Court of Appeal or a member of the personal staff of the Governor shall be deemed to be a public office.

(5) Subject to the provisions of this Constitution, where any Minister has been charged with the responsibility for a matter or department of government in pursuance of this section, he shall exercise general direction and control over the work relating to that matter and over that department and, subject to such direction and control by the Minister, the work and the department shall be under the supervision of a public officer (in this Constitution referred to as a permanent secretary) appointed for the purpose:

Provided that for the purposes of this subsection a permanent secretary may be appointed to supervise the work relating to several matters and departments.

**71.**—(1) Without prejudice to the powers of Her Majesty's Government in the United Kingdom to regulate the external affairs of the Bahama Islands, the Government of the Bahama Islands shall have such authority to conduct external affairs as may from time to time be entrusted to the Government of the Bahama Islands by Her Majesty's Government in the United Kingdom. <sub>Authority of Government of Bahama Islands to conduct external affairs.</sub>

(2) The scope of the authority that is entrusted to the Government of the Bahama Islands under subsection (1) of this section shall be such as may be defined by, and that authority shall be exercised in accordance with, the terms of such communications as may from time to time be made to the Government of the Bahama Islands by Her Majesty's Government in the United Kingdom, and every communication made in pursuance of this subsection shall be published in the Gazette.

**72.** The Governor, acting in his discretion, shall be responsible for the following matters— <sub>Governor's special responsibility for external affairs and defence.</sub>

(a) such matters relating to external affairs as may be specified in any instructions given to him by Her Majesty under Her Sign Manual and Signet or through a Secretary of State ; and

(b) defence, including the armed forces.

**73.**—(1) Responsibility for internal security and all matters relating to the Police Force is vested in the Governor ; but the Governor shall by instrument under his hand (in this section referred to as " the instrument of entrustment ") entrust the designated Minister with authority to discharge that responsibility. <sub>Governor's special responsibility for internal security and the Police Force and entrustment thereof.</sub>

(2) The instrument of entrustment shall contain such directions as the Governor may think fit with respect to—

(a) the exercise by the designated Minister of the authority entrusted to him ;

(b) the relationship between the Commissioner of Police and the Governor and between the Commissioner of Police and the designated Minister ;

(c) the provision of information to the Governor and the Security Council by the designated Minister.

(3) The entrustment made in pursuance of subsection (1) of this section shall not prejudice the right of the Governor himself to take action, if he considers it necessary so to do, for the purpose of discharging the responsibility vested in him by that subsection.

(4)—(a) If at any time he considers it necessary so to do in the interests of the matters for which responsibility is vested in him by subsection (1) of this section, the Governor may, by notice addressed to the Prime Minister, suspend the operation of the instrument of entrustment ; and during any period when the operation of the instrument is so suspended the designated Minister shall have no authority to discharge the responsibility referred to in subsection (1) of this section.

(b) Before suspending the operation of the instrument of entrustment the Governor shall consult the Security Council unless in his judgment it is impracticable for him to do so.

(5) The instrument of entrustment may be varied by a supplementary instrument made in like manner or may be revoked and replaced by a new instrument.

(6) In the foregoing provisions of this section—

(a) references to the Governor are references to the Governor acting in his discretion ;

(b) " the designated Minister " means the Minister for the time being designated for the purposes of this section by the Governor acting in accordance with the advice of the Prime Minister ;

(c) " matters relating to the Police Force " does not include matters so relating for which provision is made by Part VI of this Constitution ; and

(d) " the Security Council " means the Council established by section 74 of this Constitution.

(7) The entrustment made in pursuance of subsection (1) of this section shall not have the effect of conferring or imposing on the designated Minister any power, authority or duty that is conferred or imposed by any provision of this Constitution (other than subsection (1) of this section) or by any other law upon the Governor or any person or authority other than the designated Minister.

**Security Council.** 74.—(1) There shall be a Security Council which shall consist of—

(a) the Governor, as Chairman ;

(b) the Prime Minister ;

(c) such other Minister as may for the time being be designated in that behalf by the Governor acting in accordance with the advice of the Prime Minister ;

(d) such other persons as may be appointed by the Governor acting after consultation with the Prime Minister.

(2) A member of the Security Council appointed under subsection (1)(d) of this section shall vacate his seat on the Council if the Governor, acting after consultation with the Prime Minister, so directs by writing under his hand.

(3) The functions of the Security Council shall be to consult together and exchange information on questions of policy relating to external affairs, defence, internal security and the Police Force.

(4) Without prejudice to the generality of subsection (3) of this section—

(a) the Governor shall consult with the Security Council and keep the Council informed with respect to any matter for which he is responsible under section 72 of this Constitution that may involve the political, economic or financial interests of the Bahama Islands or the enactment of laws by the Legislature ;

(b) the Security Council shall consider any question relating to internal security or the Police Force on which it is reported to the Council by the Governor, acting in his discretion, or by any Minister for the time being entrusted with any responsibility under section 73 of this Constitution that a difference of opinion exists between them ; and

(c) the Security Council may tender advice to the Governor with respect to the discharge by the Governor of his responsibility under section 73(1) of this Constitution.

(5) Nothing in subsections (3) and (4) of this section shall be construed as requiring the Governor to obtain or act in accordance with the advice of the Security Council in the discharge of his responsibility under the said section 73(1).

(6) The Governor, acting in his discretion, may summon a meeting of the Security Council whenever he considers it desirable to do so and shall summon such a meeting whenever the Prime Minister requests him to do so.

(7) The Governor, acting after consultation with the Prime Minister, may summon any person who is not a member of the Security Council to attend any meeting of the Council whenever he considers it desirable to do so.

(8) Subject to the provisions of this section, the Security Council may regulate its own procedure.

**75.** The Governor shall, for the due exercise of his functions, be entitled to all papers which are available to the Cabinet and to any other information concerning the government of the Bahama Islands which is so available. *Governor entitled to information.*

**76.**—(1) The Governor, acting in accordance with the advice of the Prime Minister, may appoint Parliamentary Secretaries from among the members of the two chambers of the Legislature to assist Ministers in the performance of their functions. *Parliamentary Secretaries.*

(2) If occasion arises for making an appointment of a Parliamentary Secretary between a dissolution of the Legislature and the next following general election, subsection (1) of this section shall have effect for the purpose as if the Legislature had not been dissolved.

(3) The provisions of section 67 of this Constitution shall apply to Parliamentary Secretaries as they apply to Ministers other than the Prime Minister.

Oaths.

**77.** A Minister or Parliamentary Secretary shall, before entering upon the duties of his office, make before the Governor an oath or affirmation of allegiance and an oath or affirmation for the due execution of his office in the forms set out in the Schedule to this Constitution.

Leave of absence for Ministers and Parliamentary Secretaries.

**78.** The Governor, acting in accordance with the advice of the Prime Minister, may grant leave of absence from his duties to any Minister or Parliamentary Secretary.

Summoning of Cabinet.

**79.** The Governor, acting in his discretion, may summon a special meeting of the Cabinet whenever he thinks fit, but, subject thereto, the Cabinet shall not be summoned except by the authority of the Prime Minister.

Presiding in Cabinet.

**80.** The Prime Minister shall, so far as is practicable, attend and preside at all meetings of the Cabinet and in his absence such other Minister shall preside as the Prime Minister shall appoint :

Provided that whenever the Governor is present at any meeting of the Cabinet which he has summoned under the provisions of section 79 of this Constitution he shall preside.

Quorum of Cabinet.

**81.**—(1) No business shall be transacted at any meeting of the Cabinet if there are present at the meeting less than a majority of the members for the time being of the Cabinet.

(2) Subject to subsection (1) of this section, the Cabinet shall not be disqualified for the transaction of business by reason of any vacancy in the membership of the Cabinet (including any vacancy not filled when the Cabinet is first constituted or is reconstituted at any time) and the validity of the transaction of business in the Cabinet shall not be affected by reason only of the fact that some person who was not entitled so to do took part in those proceedings.

Summoning of persons to Cabinet.

**82.** The Prime Minister or, in the case of a meeting summoned under section 79 of this Constitution, the Governor, acting in his discretion, may summon any public officer to a meeting of the Cabinet whenever, in the opinion of the Prime Minister or, as the case may be, the Governor, the business before the Cabinet renders the presence of the officer desirable.

Secretary to Cabinet.

**83.**—(1) The office of Secretary to the Cabinet is hereby constituted and appointments to that office shall be made by the Governor, acting in accordance with the advice of the Prime Minister.

(2) The Secretary to the Cabinet shall be removable from that office by the Governor, acting in accordance with the advice of the Prime Minister.

(3) The office of Secretary to the Cabinet shall, for the purposes of sections 97, 99, 102, 104, 111, 112, and 113 of this Constitution, be deemed to be a public office.

(4) A person who is a public officer may, without ceasing to hold office in the public service, be appointed, in accordance with the provisions of this section, to the office of Secretary to the Cabinet, but—

(a) before the Prime Minister advises the Governor to make such appointment, the Prime Minister shall consult with the Public Service Commission ;

(b) an officer so appointed shall not, during his continuance in office as Secretary to the Cabinet, perform the functions of any public office ; and

(c) an officer so appointed may at any time be appointed by the Governor, acting on the recommendation of the Public Service Commission, to assume or resume the functions of a public office and he shall thereupon vacate his office as Secretary to the Cabinet, but no appointment under this paragraph shall be made without the concurrence of the Prime Minister.

(5) The Secretary to the Cabinet shall have charge of the Cabinet Office and shall be responsible, in accordance with such instructions as may be given to him by the Prime Minister, for arranging the business for, and keeping the minutes of, the meetings of the Cabinet and for conveying the decisions of the Cabinet to the appropriate person or authority, and shall have such other functions as the Prime Minister may from time to time direct.

(6) The Secretary to the Cabinet shall—

(a) transmit to the Governor copies of all papers submitted for consideration by the Cabinet at the same time as those papers are transmitted to Ministers ;

(b) inform the Governor of the summoning of any meeting of the Cabinet and of the matters to be discussed at that meeting at the same time as Ministers are so informed ; and

(c) furnish the Governor, as soon as practicable after each meeting of the Cabinet, with a copy of the record of the proceedings at that meeting showing the matters discussed and the conclusions reached by the Cabinet at that meeting.

**84.**—(1) There shall be an Attorney-General for the Bahama Islands whose office shall be a public office and who shall be appointed by the Governor, acting on the recommendation of the Judicial and Legal Service Commission.

Attorney-
General.

(2) If the office of Attorney-General is vacant or the holder thereof is for any reason unable to perform the functions of his office, the Governor, acting on the recommendation of the Judicial and Legal Service Commission, may appoint a person to act in that office, and any person so appointed may continue so to act until a person is appointed to hold that office and assumes the functions thereof or, as the case may be, the holder thereof resumes those functions or until his appointment is revoked by the Governor, acting on the recommendation of the Judicial and Legal Service Commission.

(3) The Legislature may by law prescribe qualifications for appointment to hold the office of Attorney-General :

Provided that a person who has been appointed to hold that office may continue in office notwithstanding that such qualifications are subsequently so prescribed or varied.

(4) The Attorney-General shall receive such salary and allowances as, subject to subsection (5) of this section, may from time to time be prescribed by any law of the Legislature, and the said salary and allowances are hereby charged on, and shall be paid out of, the Consolidated Fund.

(5) The salary of the Attorney-General and his conditions of service other than allowances shall not be altered to his disadvantage during his continuance in office.

**Tenure of office of Attorney-General.**

**85.**—(1) Subject to the provisions of subsections (2) to (6) (inclusive) of this section, a person holding the office of the Attorney-General shall vacate office when he attains the age of sixty years :

Provided that the Governor, acting in his discretion, may permit an Attorney-General who has attained the age of sixty years to continue in office until he has attained such later age, not exceeding sixty-five years, as may (before the Attorney-General has attained the age of sixty years) have been agreed between them.

(2) The Attorney-General may be removed from office only for inability to discharge the functions thereof (whether arising from infirmity of body or mind or any other cause) or for misbehaviour, and shall not be so removed except in accordance with the provisions of subsection (3) of this section.

(3) The Attorney-General shall be removed from office by the Governor by instrument under the Public Seal if the question of his removal from office has been referred to a tribunal appointed under subsection (4) of this section and the tribunal has recommended to the Governor that he ought to be removed from office for inability as aforesaid or for misbehaviour.

(4) If the Governor, acting in his discretion, considers that the question of removing the Attorney-General from office for inability as aforesaid or for misbehaviour ought to be investigated, or if the Prime Minister or the Chief Justice after consultation with the Prime Minister represents to the Governor that that question ought to be investigated, then—

(a) the Governor shall appoint a tribunal, which shall consist of a Chairman and not less than two other members, selected by the Governor, acting in his discretion, from among persons who hold or are qualified to hold or have held high judicial office ; and

(b) that tribunal shall inquire into the matter and report on the facts thereof to the Governor and recommend to the Governor whether the Attorney-General ought to be removed from office for inability as aforesaid or for misbehaviour.

(5) The provisions (excluding sections 2 and 7(2)) of the Commissions of Inquiry Act(a) of the Bahama Islands as in force imme-

---

(a) Statute Law of the Bahama Islands 1965, Ch. 180.

diately before the coming into operation of this Constitution shall, subject to the provisions of this section, apply as nearly as may be in relation to tribunals appointed under subsection (4) of this section or, as the context may require, to the members thereof as they apply in relation to Commissions or Commissioners appointed under that Act and for that purpose shall have effect as if they formed part of this Constitution.

(6) If the question of removing the Attorney-General from office has been referred to a tribunal under subsection (4) of this section, the Governor, acting in his discretion, may suspend the Attorney-General from performing the functions of his office and any such suspension may at any time be revoked by the Governor, acting in his discretion, and shall in any case cease to have effect if the tribunal recommends to the Governor that the Attorney-General should not be removed from office.

**86.**—(1) The Attorney-General shall have power, in any case in which he considers it desirable so to do— *Powers of Attorney-General.*

    (a) to institute and undertake criminal proceedings against any person before any civil court established for the Bahama Islands in respect of any offence alleged to have been committed by that person ;

    (b) to take over and continue any criminal proceedings as aforesaid that have been instituted or undertaken by any other person or authority ; and

    (c) to discontinue, at any stage before judgment is delivered, any criminal proceedings as aforesaid instituted or undertaken by himself or any other person or authority.

(2) The powers of the Attorney-General under subsection (1) of this section may be exercised by him in person or by officers subordinate to him acting under and in accordance with his general or special instructions.

(3) The powers conferred upon the Attorney-General under subsection (1)(b) and (c) of this section shall be vested in him to the exclusion of any other person :

Provided that where any other person or authority has instituted criminal proceedings, nothing in this subsection shall, save when the Attorney-General has exercised his powers under subsection (1)(b) of this section, prevent the withdrawal of those proceedings by or at the instance of that person or authority and with the leave of the court.

(4) For the purposes of this section, any appeal from any determination in any criminal proceedings before any court, or any case stated or question of law reserved for the purpose of any such proceedings, to any other court established for the Bahama Islands or to Her Majesty in Council shall be deemed to be part of those proceedings.

(5) In the exercise of the powers conferred on him by this section and by section 53(5) of this Constitution, the Attorney-General shall not be subject to the direction or control of any other person or authority.

# PART V

## THE JUDICIARY

### The Supreme Court

Constitution of Supreme Court.

**87.**—(1) There shall be a Supreme Court for the Bahama Islands having such powers and jurisdiction as may be provided by any law for the time being in force in the Bahama Islands.

(2) The judges of the Supreme Court shall be a Chief Justice and such number of Puisne Judges as the Legislature may by law prescribe:

Provided that the office of a judge of the Supreme Court shall not, without his consent, be abolished during his continuance in office.

(3) The Chief Justice of the Supreme Court shall be a person qualified for appointment under subsection (5) of this section and shall be appointed by the Governor, by instrument under the Public Seal, after consultation with the Prime Minister.

(4) The Puisne Judges of the Supreme Court shall be persons qualified as aforesaid and shall be appointed by the Governor, by instrument under the Public Seal, after consultation with the Chief Justice.

(5) The qualifications for appointment as a judge of the Supreme Court shall be such as may be prescribed by any law for the time being in force in the Bahama Islands:

Provided that a person who has been appointed as a judge of the Supreme Court may continue in office notwithstanding any subsequent variation in the qualifications so prescribed.

Tenure of office of judges of Supreme Court.

**88.**—(1) Subject to the following provisions of this section, a judge of the Supreme Court shall vacate his office when he attains the age of sixty-five years:

Provided that a judge who has attained that age may continue in office for such period as may be necessary to enable him to deliver judgment or to do any other thing in relation to any proceeding commenced before him before he attained that age.

(2) A judge of the Supreme Court may be removed from office only for inability to discharge the functions of his office (whether arising from infirmity of body or mind or any other cause) or for misbehaviour, and shall not be so removed except in accordance with the provisions of subsection (3) of this section.

(3) A judge of the Supreme Court shall be removed from office by the Governor by instrument under the Public Seal if the question of the removal of that judge from office has, at the request of the Governor, made in pursuance of subsection (4) of this section, been referred by Her Majesty to the Judicial Committee of Her Majesty's Privy Council under section 4 of the Judicial Committee Act 1833(a) or any other enactment enabling Her Majesty in that behalf, and the Judicial Committee has advised Her Majesty that the judge ought to be removed from office for inability as aforesaid or misbehaviour.

(a) 1833 c. 41.

(4) If the Governor considers that the question of removing a judge of the Supreme Court from office for inability as aforesaid or misbehaviour ought to be investigated, then—

(a) the Governor shall appoint a tribunal, which shall consist of a Chairman and not less than two other members, selected by the Governor from among persons who hold or have held high judicial office ;

(b) the tribunal shall inquire into the matter and report on the facts thereof to the Governor and recommend to the Governor whether he should request that the question of the removal of that judge should be referred by Her Majesty to the Judicial Committee ; and

(c) if the tribunal so recommends, the Governor ·shall request that the question should be referred accordingly.

(5) The provisions (excluding sections 2 and 7(2)) of the Commissions of Inquiry Act of the Bahama Islands as in force immediately before the coming into operation of this Constitution shall, subject to the provisions of this section, apply as nearly as may be in relation to tribunals appointed under subsection (4) of this section or, as the context may require, to the members thereof as they apply in relation to Commissions or Commissioners appointed under that Act and for that purpose shall have effect as if they formed part of this Constitution.

(6) If the question of removing a judge of the Supreme Court from office has been referred to a tribunal under subsection (4) of this section the Governor may suspend the judge from performing the functions of his office, and any such suspension may at any time be revoked by the Governor, and shall in any case cease to have effect—

(a) if the tribunal recommends to the Governor that he should not request that the question of the removal of the judge from office should be referred by Her Majesty to the Judicial Committee ; or

(b) if the Judicial Committee advises Her Majesty that the judge ought not to be removed from office.

(7) The powers conferred upon the Governor by this section shall be exercised by him acting in his discretion.

**89.**—(1) If the office of Chief Justice is vacant, or if the holder thereof is for any reason unable to perform the functions of his office, then, until some other person has been appointed to, or has been appointed to act in, and has assumed the functions of, that office, or until the holder thereof has resumed those functions, as the case may be, such one of the Puisne Judges as the Governor, acting after consultation with the Prime Minister, may appoint for that purpose shall act in the office of Chief Justice. *Acting judges of Supreme Court.*

(2) If the office of a Puisne Judge is vacant, or if any such Judge is acting as Chief Justice, or is for any reason unable to perform the functions of his office the Governor, acting after consultation with the Chief Justice, may appoint a person possessing such legal qualifications and experience as he may deem appropriate to act as a Puisne Judge of the Supreme Court :

Provided that a person may be so appointed notwithstanding that he has attained the age of sixty-five years.

(3) Any person appointed under this section to act as a Puisne Judge of the Supreme Court may continue so to act until his appointment is revoked by the Governor, acting after consultation with the Chief Justice.

**Salaries of judges of Supreme Court.**

**90.**—(1) The judges of the Supreme Court shall receive such salaries and allowances as, subject to subsection (2) of this section, may from time to time be prescribed by any law of the Legislature, and the said salary and allowances are hereby charged on, and shall be paid out of, the Consolidated Fund.

(2) The salary of a judge of the Supreme Court and his conditions of service other than allowances shall not be altered to his disadvantage during his continuance in office.

**Oaths to be taken by judges of Supreme Court.**

**91.** Before entering upon the functions of his office, every judge of the Supreme Court shall make and subscribe before the Governor, or some other person authorised in that behalf by the Governor, oaths or affirmations of allegiance and for the due execution of his office in the forms set out in the Schedule to this Constitution.

## The Court of Appeal

**Constitution of Court of Appeal.**

**92.**—(1) There shall be a Court of Appeal for the Bahama Islands having such powers and jurisdiction as may be provided by any law for the time being in force in the Bahama Islands.

(2) The judges of the Court of Appeal shall be a President and such number of Justices of Appeal, not being less than two, as the Legislature may by law prescribe:

Provided that the office of a Justice of Appeal shall not, without his consent, be abolished during his continuance in office.

(3) The judges of the Court of Appeal shall be persons qualified for appointment under subsection (4) of this section and shall be appointed by the Governor, acting after consultation with the Prime Minister, by instrument under the Public Seal for such period as may be specified in their respective instruments of appointment.

(4) A person shall be qualified to be appointed as a judge of the Court of Appeal if, and shall not be qualified to be so appointed unless, he holds or has held high judicial office.

(5) Any power exercisable by a single judge of the Court of Appeal may, at any time when there is no such judge present in the Bahama Islands and able to perform the functions of his office, be exercised by a judge of the Supreme Court as if that judge were a judge of the Court of Appeal.

**Tenure of office of judges of Court of Appeal.**

**93.**—(1) Subject to the following provisions of this section, the office of a judge of the Court of Appeal shall become vacant upon the expiration of the period of his appointment to that office.

(2) A judge of the Court of Appeal may be removed from office only for inability to discharge the functions of his office (whether arising from infirmity of body or mind or any other cause) or for misbehaviour, and shall not be so removed except in accordance with the provisions of subsection (3) of this section.

(3) A judge of the Court of Appeal shall be removed from office by the Governor by instrument under the Public Seal if the question of the removal of that judge from office has, at the request of the Governor, made in pursuance of subsection (4) of this section, been referred by Her Majesty to the Judicial Committee of Her Majesty's Privy Council under section 4 of the Judicial Committee Act 1833 or any other enactment enabling Her Majesty in that behalf, and the Judicial Committee has advised Her Majesty that the judge ought to be removed from office for inability as aforesaid or misbehaviour.

(4) If the Governor considers that the question of removing a judge of the Court of Appeal from office for inability as aforesaid or misbehaviour ought to be investigated, then—

(a) the Governor shall appoint a tribunal, which shall consist of a Chairman and not less than two other members, selected by the Governor from among persons who hold or have held high judicial office ;

(b) the tribunal shall inquire into the matter and report on the facts thereof to the Governor and recommend to the Governor whether he should request that the question of the removal of that judge should be referred by Her Majesty to the Judicial Committee ; and

(c) if the tribunal so recommends, the Governor shall request that the question should be referred accordingly.

(5) The provisions (excluding sections 2 and 7(2)) of the Commissions of Inquiry Act of the Bahama Islands as in force immediately before the coming into operation of this Constitution shall, subject to the provisions of this section, apply as nearly as may be in relation to tribunals appointed under subsection (4) of this section or, as the context may require, to the members thereof as they apply in relation to Commissions or Commissioners appointed under that Act and for that purpose shall have effect as if they formed part of this Constitution.

(6) If the question of removing a judge of the Court of Appeal from office has been referred to a tribunal under subsection (4) of this section the Governor may suspend the judge from performing the functions of his office, and any such suspension may at any time be revoked by the Governor, and shall in any case cease to have effect—

(a) if the tribunal recommends to the Governor that he should not request that the question of the removal of the judge from office should be referred by Her Majesty to the Judicial Committee ; or

(b) if the Judicial Committee advises Her Majesty that the judge ought not to be removed from office.

(7) The powers conferred upon the Governor by this section shall be exercised by him acting in his discretion.

**94.**—(1) If the office of the President is vacant, or if the holder thereof is for any reason unable to perform the functions of his office, then, until some other person has been appointed to, or has been appointed to act in, and has assumed the functions of, that office, or until the holder thereof has resumed those functions, as the case may

Acting judges of Court of Appeal.

be, such one of the Justices of Appeal as the Governor, acting after consultation with the Prime Minister, may appoint for that purpose shall act in the office of President.

(2) If the office of a Justice of Appeal is vacant, or if any Justice of Appeal is acting as the President, or is for any reason unable to perform the functions of his office the Governor, acting after consultation with the Prime Minister, may appoint a person possessing such legal qualifications and experience as he, after consultation with the President, may deem appropriate to act as a Justice of Appeal.

(3) Any person appointed under this section to act as a Justice of Appeal may continue so to act until his appointment is revoked by the Governor, acting in his discretion.

Salaries of judges of Court of Appeal.

**95.**—(1) The judges of the Court of Appeal shall receive such salaries and allowances as, subject to subsection (2) of this section, may from time to time be prescribed by any law of the Legislature, and the said salary and allowances are hereby charged on, and shall be paid out of, the Consolidated Fund.

(2) The salary of a judge of the Court of Appeal and his conditions of service other than allowances shall not be altered to his disadvantage during his continuance in office.

Oaths to be taken by judges of Court of Appeal.

**96.** Before entering upon the functions of his office every judge of the Court of Appeal shall make and subscribe before the Governor, or some other person authorised in that behalf by the Governor, oaths or affirmations of allegiance and for the due execution of his office in the forms set out in the Schedule to this Constitution.

## PART VI

### THE PUBLIC SERVICE

#### *The Public Service Commission*

Composition of Public Service Commission.

**97.**—(1) There shall be a Public Service Commission for the Bahama Islands which shall consist of a Chairman and not less than two nor more than four other members appointed by the Governor, by instrument under the Public Seal, for such period, being not less than three nor more than six years, as may be specified in their respective instruments of appointment.

(2) A person shall be disqualified for appointment as a member of the Public Service Commission if he is a member of either chamber of the Legislature or a public officer.

(3) A person shall not, while he holds or is acting in the office of a member of the Public Service Commission or within a period of five years commencing with the date on which he last held or acted in that office, be eligible for appointment to or to act in any public office.

(4) The office of a member of the Public Service Commission shall become vacant—

(a) at the expiration of the period specified in the instrument by which he was appointed ;

(b) if he becomes a member of either chamber of the Legislature ; or

(c) if he is removed from office in accordance with subsection (5) of this section.

(5) A member of the Public Service Commission shall be removed from office by the Governor, by instrument under the Public Seal, if the Governor is satisfied that he ought to be removed from office for inability to discharge the functions thereof (whether arising from infirmity of body or mind or any other cause) or for misbehaviour.

(6) Whenever the office of the Chairman of the Public Service Commission is vacant or the holder thereof is for any reason unable to perform the functions of his office, such one of the other members of the Public Service Commission as the Governor shall appoint may act in the office of the Chairman.

(7) If the office of a member of the Public Service Commission other than the Chairman is vacant or the holder thereof is acting as the Chairman or is for any reason unable to perform the functions of his office, the Governor may appoint a person who is qualified for appointment as a member of the Commission to act as such a member ; and any person so appointed may, subject to the provisions of subsection (4) of this section, continue to act until he is notified by the Governor that the circumstances giving rise to the appointment have ceased to exist.

(8) The members of the Commission shall receive such salaries and allowances as, subject to subsection (9) of this section, may from time to time be prescribed by any law of the Legislature and the said salaries and allowances are hereby charged on, and shall be paid out of, the Consolidated Fund.

(9) The salary of a member of the Commission and his conditions of service other than allowances shall not be altered to his disadvantage during his continuance in office.

(10) The powers conferred upon the Governor by this section shall be exercised by him acting after consultation with the Prime Minister.

**98.**—(1) Subject to the provisions of this Constitution, power to make appointments to public offices, and to remove or exercise disciplinary control over persons holding or acting in such offices, is vested in the Governor, acting on the recommendation of the Public Service Commission.

*Appointments, etc. of public officers.*

(2) This section shall apply in relation to the office of teacher in the Department of Education and of officer of the medical establishment, and to any person holding or acting in either of such offices, as it applies to other public offices and to persons holding or acting in those offices.

(3) Before the Public Service Commission recommends to the Governor the appointment of a person to be a permanent secretary or the head of a department of government (or to be the holder of any such other office of similar status as the Governor may, after consultation with the Prime Minister, specify by notice in the Gazette) the Commission shall consult the Prime Minister.

(4) The Public Service Commission may have such other functions in relation to public offices and public officers as may be prescribed by any law of the Legislature or regulations made by the Governor.

(5) Notwithstanding the preceding provisions of this section, power to make appointments to any office of permanent secretary on transfer from another such office carrying the same salary is vested in the Governor, acting on the recommendation of the Prime Minister.

(6) The power to make appointments under subsection (1) of this section shall not extend to postings or transfers between duty posts in the same grade or scale within a department of government of public officers in that department, and the power to make such postings or transfers is vested in the head of that department.

**Delegation of Governor's powers.**
**99.** The Governor, acting on the recommendation of the Public Service Commission, may by directions given by instrument under the Public Seal delegate, to such extent and subject to such conditions as may be specified in those directions, the powers vested in him by section 98(1) of this Constitution (other than powers to make appointments to the offices referred to in section 98(3) and to remove or exercise disciplinary control over persons holding or acting in such offices) to such public officers as may be so specified.

## Public Service Board of Appeal

**Composition of Public Service Board of Appeal.**
**100.**—(1) There shall be a Public Service Board of Appeal for the Bahama Islands which shall consist of the following members, who shall be appointed by instrument under the Public Seal,—

(a) a Chairman appointed by the Governor, acting in his discretion, from among persons who hold or have held high judicial office or are qualified to hold high judicial office ;

(b) one member appointed by the Governor, acting in accordance with the advice of the Prime Minister ; and

(c) one member appointed by the Governor, acting in accordance with the advice of the appropriate representative body.

(2) A person shall be disqualified for appointment as a member of the Board if he is a member of either chamber of the Legislature.

(3) The office of a member of the Board shall become vacant—

(a) at the expiration of three years from the date of his appointment ;

(b) if he becomes a member of either chamber of the Legislature ; or

(c) if he is removed from office in accordance with the following provisions of this section.

(4) A member of the Board may be removed from office only for inability to exercise the functions of his office (whether arising from infirmity of body or mind or any other cause) or for misbehaviour and shall not be so removed except in accordance with the following provisions of this section.

(5) A member of the Board shall be removed from office by the Governor by instrument under the Public Seal if the question of his removal from office has been referred to a tribunal appointed under

subsection (6) of this section and the tribunal has recommended to the Governor that he ought to be removed from office for inability as aforesaid or for misbehaviour.

(6) If the Governor, acting in his discretion, considers that the question of removing a member of the Board under this section ought to be investigated, then—

(a) the Governor shall appoint a tribunal which shall consist of a chairman and not less than two other members, selected by the Chief Justice from among persons who hold or have held or are qualified to hold high judicial office ; and

(b) the tribunal shall enquire into the matter and report on the facts thereof to the Governor and recommend to him whether the member ought to be removed under this section.

(7) If the question of removing a member of the Board has been referred to a tribunal under this section, the Governor, acting in his discretion, may suspend that member from performing the functions of his office and any such suspension may at any time be revoked by the Governor, acting as aforesaid, and shall in any case cease to have effect if the tribunal recommends to the Governor that that member should not be removed from office.

(8) Subsections (5), (6) and (7) of this section shall not apply in relation to a member of the Board who is a judge of the Supreme Court or a judge of the Court of Appeal, and his removal from, or suspension from performing the functions of his office as a judge under section 88 or 93, as the case may be, of this Constitution shall have the like effect in relation to him as a member of the Board.

(9) (a) If the office of any member of the Board is vacant or the holder thereof is for any reason unable to perform the functions of his office, the Governor may appoint a person who is qualified to be appointed to that office to act in that office, and any person so appointed may, subject to the provisions of subsection (3)(b) and of subsections (4) to (8) (inclusive) of this section, continue so to act until he is notified by the Governor that the circumstances giving rise to the appointment have ceased to exist.

(b) In the exercise of the powers conferred by paragraph (a) of this subsection the Governor shall act in the same manner as he would act if he were making an appointment under subsection (1) of this section to the office concerned.

(10) In this section " the appropriate representative body " means such body representing the interests of public officers as the Governor may, by order, prescribe.

**101.**—(1) Subject to the provisions of this section, an appeal shall lie to the Public Service Board of Appeal at the instance of the officer in respect of whom the recommendation is made against any recommendation made by the Public Service Commission to the Governor that any public officer should be removed from office or that any penalty should be imposed on him by way of disciplinary control. *Appeals in disciplinary cases.*

(2) Before the Governor acts in accordance with any recommendation of the Public Service Commission in respect of which an appeal lies to the Public Service Board of Appeal, he shall inform the said officer

of that recommendation and if the officer then appeals to the Public Service Board of Appeal the Governor shall not act in accordance with that recommendation pending the determination of the appeal:

Provided that the Governor, acting on the recommendation of the Public Service Commission, may nevertheless suspend the officer from performing the functions of any public office pending the determination of the appeal.

(3) Upon any appeal to the Public Service Board of Appeal under the provisions of this section the Board shall consider the case and advise the Governor what action should be taken in respect of that officer, and the Governor shall then act in accordance with that advice.

(4) The Governor may by regulations provide that an appeal shall not lie to the Public Service Board of Appeal against recommendations of the Public Service Commission—

(a) in respect of officers holding public offices the emoluments of which do not exceed such amounts as may be prescribed by the regulations ; and

(b) for the imposition of such penalties (other than removal from office) as may be so prescribed.

(5) Any decision of the Public Service Board of Appeal shall require the concurrence of at least two members of the Board.

(6) Subject to the provisions of this section, the Public Service Board of Appeal may make rules with respect to—

(a) the procedure in appeals to the Board, including the manner in which and the time within which appeals shall be submitted to the Board ; and

(b) the procedure of the Board.

(7) Rules made under subsection (6) of this section may, with the consent of the Prime Minister, confer powers or impose duties on any public officer or any authority of the Government of the Bahama Islands for the purpose of the exercise of the functions of the Board.

(8) Subject to the provisions of this section and of its rules of procedure, the Board may act notwithstanding any vacancy in its membership or the absence of any member, and the validity of the transaction of any business by the Board shall not be affected by reason only of the fact that some person who was not entitled to do so took part in its proceedings.

(9) Subject to subsection (7) of this section, in the exercise of its functions under this Constitution the Board shall not be subject to the direction or control of any other person or authority.

## The Judicial and Legal Service Commission

Composition of Judicial and Legal Service Commission.

**102.**—(1) There shall be a Judicial and Legal Service Commission for the Bahama Islands.

(2) The members of the Commission shall be—

(a) the Chief Justice, who shall be Chairman of the Commission ;

(b) the Attorney-General ;

(c) the Chairman of the Public Service Commission ; and

(*d*) a person appointed by the Governor, acting after consultation with the Chief Justice, by instrument under the Public Seal.

(3) A person shall not be qualified to be appointed as a member of the Commission under subsection (2)(*d*) of this section unless he holds or is qualified to hold or has held high judicial office ; and a person shall be disqualified for appointment as such if he is a member of either chamber of the Legislature or a public officer.

(4) The office of the member of the Commission appointed under subsection (2)(*d*) of this section shall become vacant—

(*a*) at the expiration of three years from the date of his appointment ;

(*b*) if he becomes a member of either chamber of the Legislature or a public officer ; or

(*c*) if he is removed from office in accordance with subsection (5) of this section.

(5) The member of the Commission appointed as aforesaid shall be removed from office by the Governor by instrument under the Public Seal if the Governor, acting after consultation with the Chief Justice, is satisfied that he ought to be removed from office for inability to discharge the functions thereof (whether arising from infirmity of body or mind or any other cause) or for misbehaviour :

Provided that if such person is a judge of the Supreme Court or a judge of the Court of Appeal, he shall not be so removed unless, in accordance with the provisions of section 88 or 93, as the case may be, of this Constitution, he is removed from his office as a judge and his suspension from performing the functions of his office as a judge under section 88 or 93, as the case may be, shall have the like effect in relation to him as a member of the Commission.

(6) If the office of the member of the Commission appointed under subsection (2)(*d*) of this section is vacant or the holder thereof is for any reason unable to perform the functions of his office, the Governor, acting after consultation with the Chief Justice, may appoint a person who is qualified for appointment as that member to act in the office of that member ; and any person so appointed may, subject to the provisions of subsection (4) of this section, continue to act until he is notified by the Governor, acting as aforesaid, that the circumstances giving rise to the appointment have ceased to exist.

(7) A person who is acting in the office of Attorney-General shall not take part in any proceedings of the Commission relating to the exercise of its functions under section 84 of this Constitution.

**103.**—(1) Power to make appointments to the offices to which this section applies and to remove and to exercise disciplinary control over persons holding or acting in such offices, is vested in the Governor, acting on the recommendation of the Judicial and Legal Service Commission. Appointments, etc. of judicial and legal officers.

(2) Subsection (1) of this section applies to the offices of Solicitor-General, Chief Magistrate, Stipendiary and Circuit Magistrate, Registrar of the Supreme Court, Registrar General, Crown Counsel and Legal Draftsman, and such other public offices as may, by notice in the Gazette, be prescribed by the Governor.

### The Police Service Commission

Composition
of Police
Service
Commission.

**104.**—(1) There shall be a Police Service Commission for the Bahama Islands which shall consist of a Chairman and two other members appointed by the Governor by instrument under the Public Seal.

(2) A person shall be disqualified for appointment as a member of the Police Service Commission if he is a member of either chamber of the Legislature or a public officer.

(3) A person shall not, while he holds or is acting in the office of a member of the Police Service Commission or within a period of five years commencing with the date on which he last held or acted in that office, be eligible for appointment to or to act in any public office.

(4) The office of a member of the Police Service Commission shall become vacant—

(a) at the expiration of five years from the date of his appointment or such earlier time as may be specified in the instrument by which he was appointed ;

(b) if he becomes a member of either chamber of the Legislature ; or

(c) if he is removed from office in accordance with subsection (5) of this section.

(5) A member of the Police Service Commission shall be removed from office by the Governor by instrument under the Public Seal if the Governor is satisfied that he ought to be removed from office for inability to discharge the functions thereof (whether arising from infirmity of body or mind or any other cause) or for misbehaviour.

(6) Whenever the office of the Chairman of the Police Service Commission is vacant or the holder thereof is for any reason unable to perform the functions of his office, such one of the other members of the Police Service Commission as the Governor shall appoint may act in the office of Chairman.

(7) If the office of a member of the Police Service Commission other than the Chairman is vacant or the holder thereof is acting as Chairman or is for any reason unable to perform the functions of his office, the Governor may appoint a person who is qualified for appointment as a member of the Commission to act as such a member ; and any person so appointed may, subject to the provisions of subsection (4) of this section, continue to act until he is notified by the Governor that the circumstances giving rise to the appointment have ceased to exist.

(8) The members of the Commission shall receive such salary and allowances as, subject to subsection (9) of this section, may be prescribed by any law of the Legislature, and the said salaries and allowances are hereby charged on, and shall be paid out of, the Consolidated Fund.

(9) The salary of a member of the Commission and his conditions of service other than allowances shall not be altered to his disadvantage during his continuance in office.

(10) The powers conferred upon the Governor by this section shall be exercised by him acting after consultation with the Prime Minister.

**105.** Power to make appointments to the offices of Commissioner of Police and Deputy Commissioner of Police and to remove and to exercise disciplinary control over any person holding or acting in either of those offices is vested in the Governor, acting after consultation with the Police Service Commission.

Appointments, etc. of Commissioner and Deputy Commissioner of Police.

**106.**—(1) Save as provided is section 105 of this Constitution, power to make appointments to offices in the Police Force of or above the rank of Inspector is vested in the Governor, acting on the recommendation of the Police Service Commission.

Appointments of other officers in the Police Force.

(2) Power to make appointments to offices in the Police Force below the rank of Inspector is vested in the Commissioner of Police.

(3) There shall be in the Police Force such number of Police Promotion Boards, each consisting of officers in the Police Force above the rank of Inspector, as may be prescribed by regulations made under subsection (5) of this section.

(4) In the exercise of the powers to make appointments to offices in the Police Force vested in him, the Commissioner of Police may refer any question relating to the promotion of an officer in the Police Force to a rank below that of Inspector to a Police Promotion Board for their advice, but he shall not be obliged to act in accordance with the advice given him by any such Board.

(5) The Governor may by regulations make provision for all or any of the following matters—

(a) the number of Police Promotion Boards which shall be established for the Police Force ;

(b) the composition of any Police Promotion Board and the method of appointment and tenure of office of the members thereof ; and

(c) the manner in which a Police Promotion Board shall perform its functions.

(6) The power to make appointments under subsection (1) of this section shall not extend to postings or transfers within the Police Force of officers in that Force, and the power to make such postings and transfers is vested in the Commissioner of Police.

**107.**—(1) Save as provided in section 105 of this Constitution and subsection (2) of this section, power to remove and to exercise disciplinary control over persons holding or acting in offices in the Police Force is vested in the Governor, acting on the recommendation of the Police Service Commission.

Removal and discipline of members of Police Force.

(2) The following powers are vested in the Commissioner of Police—

(a) in respect of officers of or above the rank of Assistant Superintendent, the power to administer reprimands ;

(b) in respect of Inspectors, the power to exercise disciplinary control other than removal or reduction in rank ; and

(c) in respect of officers below the rank of Inspector, the power to exercise disciplinary control including the power of removal.

(3) The Commissioner of Police may, by directions in writing, and subject to such conditions as he thinks fit, delegate to any officer of the Police Force of or above the rank of Inspector any of his powers

under subsection (2)(c) of this section other than the power of removal ; but an appeal from any award of punishment by such an officer shall lie to the Commissioner.

(4) The Legislature may by law provide that an appeal shall lie to the Governor from a decision of the Commissioner of Police to remove or exercise disciplinary control over persons holding or acting in offices in the Police Force in such cases as may be prescribed by such law, and in determining any such appeal the Governor shall act on the recommendation of the Police Service Commission.

**Right of Commissioner to tender advice.**

**108.**—(1) The Police Service Commission shall permit the Commissioner of Police to express his views in its presence on any matter that is before the Commission for its consideration, except when the matter is an appeal from a decision of the Commissioner of Police:

Provided that the Commission may, if it sees fit, invite the Commissioner of Police to appear before it in relation to any such appeal.

(2) Nothing in this Part of this Constitution shall affect or be construed as affecting any right of the Commissioner of Police to tender his own advice to the Governor on any question.

## General

**Proceedings of Commissions.**

**109.**—(1) No business shall be transacted at any meeting of a Commission to which this section applies unless a quorum of that Commission is present ; and for the purposes of this subsection—

(a) a quorum of the Public Service Commission shall consist of two members at any time when there are not more than three members of the Commission holding office by virtue of appointments made under section 97(1) of this Constitution and shall consist of three members at any other time ;

(b) a quorum of the Judicial and Legal Service Commission shall consist of three members, of whom one shall be the Chairman of the Commission ;

(c) a quorum of the Police Service Commission shall consist of two members.

(2) Any question proposed for decision at any meeting of a Commission to which this section applies shall be determined by a majority of the votes of the members present and voting, and if on any such question the votes are equally divided the member presiding shall have and exercise a casting vote.

(3) Subject to the provisions of subsection (1) of this section, a Commission to which this section applies may act notwithstanding a vacancy in its membership ; and no proceedings of such a Commission shall be invalidated by reason only that some person not entitled to do so has taken part in them.

(4) Subject to the provisions of this Constitution, the Governor, after consultation with the Prime Minister and a Commission to which this section applies, may by regulations provide for any of the following matters, that is to say :—

(a) the appointment, tenure of office and terms of service of staff to assist the Commission in the performance of its functions ;

(b) the protection and privileges of members of the Commission in respect of the performance of their functions and the privilege of communications to and from the Commission and its members in case of legal proceedings ;

(c) the definition and trial of offences connected with the functions of the Commission and the imposition of penalties for such offences :

Provided that no such penalty shall exceed a fine of fifteen hundred dollars or imprisonment for a term of one year or both such a fine and such imprisonment ;

(d) requiring persons to attend before the Commission to answer questions relating to any inquiry held by the Commission or to any business of the Commission ; and

(e) conferring powers and imposing duties on any public officer or any authority of the Government of the Bahama Islands for the purpose of facilitating the performance by the Commission of its functions.

(5) Subject to the provisions of this Constitution, a Commission to which this section applies may regulate its own procedure.

(6) Unless it is otherwise provided or required by the context, references in this section to a Commission to which this section applies are references to the Public Service Commission, the Judicial and Legal Service Commission, or the Police Service Commission, as the case may be.

**110.** The question whether—

(a) a Commission established under this Part of this Constitution has validly performed any function vested in it by or under this Constitution ;

(b) any person or Police Promotion Board has validly performed any function delegated to or vested in such person or Board by or in pursuance of the provisions of section 99 or, as the case may be, section 106, 107 or 108 of this Constitution ; or

(c) any member of such Commission or any other person has validly performed any other function in relation to the work of the Commission or in relation to any such function as is referred to in paragraph (b) of this section,

shall not be inquired into in any court.

*Protection of Commissions, etc. from legal proceedings.*

**111.**—(1) Subject to the provisions of section 113 of this Constitution, the law applicable to the grant and payment to any officer, or to his widow, children, dependants or personal representatives, of any pension, gratuity or other like allowance (in this section and sections 112 and 113 of this Constitution referred to as an " award ") in respect of the service of that officer in a public office shall be that in force on the relevant day or any later law not less favourable to the person concerned.

*Applicability of pensions law.*

(2) For the purposes of this section the relevant day is—

(a) in relation to an award granted before the date on which this Constitution comes into operation, the day on which the award was granted ;

(b) in relation to an award granted or to be granted on or after the date on which this Constitution comes into operation to or in respect of a person who was a public officer before that date, the day immediately before that date ;

(c) in relation to an award granted or to be granted to or in respect of a person who first becomes a public officer on or after the date on which this Constitution comes into operation, the day on which he becomes a public officer.

(3) For the purposes of this section, in so far as the law applicable to an award depends on the option of the person to or in respect of whom it is granted or to be granted, the law for which he opts shall be taken to be more favourable to him than any other law for which he might have opted.

(4) For the purposes of this section and of sections 112 and 113 of this Constitution, the office of a judge of the Supreme Court or of the Court of Appeal and the office of a member of the Public Service Commission, the Public Service Board of Appeal, the Judicial and Legal Service Commission or the Police Service Commission shall be deemed to be a public office.

Pensions, etc. charged on the Consolidated Fund.

**112.** Awards granted under any law for the time being in force in the Bahama Islands are hereby charged on, and shall be paid out of, the Consolidated Fund.

Grant and withholding of pensions, etc.

**113.**—(1) The power to grant any award under any pensions law for the time being in force in the Bahama Islands (other than an award to which, under that law, the person to whom it is payable is entitled as of right) and, in accordance with any provisions in that behalf in any such law, to withhold, reduce in amount or suspend any award payable under any such law shall vest in the Governor.

(2) The power vested in the Governor by subsection (1) of this section shall be exercised by him—

(a) in the case of an award payable in respect of the services of any person who, having been a public officer, was, immediately before the date on which he ceased to hold public office, serving as—

(i) Deputy Governor ;

(ii) a judge of the Supreme Court ;

(iii) a judge of the Court of Appeal ;

(iv) a member of the Public Service Commission, the Public Service Board of Appeal, the Judicial and Legal Service Commission or the Police Service Commission ;

(v) Attorney-General ;

(vi) Auditor ;

(vii) Commissioner of Police or Deputy Commissioner of Police ; or

(viii) a member of the personal staff of the Governor (other than a person referred to in section 22(4) of this Constitution),

in his discretion ;

(b) in the case of an award payable in respect of the services of any person who, having been a public officer, was, immediately before the date aforesaid, serving in any office to which section 103 of this Constitution applies at the date of the exercise of the power, on the recommendation of the Judicial and Legal Service Commission ;

(c) in the case of an award payable in respect of the services of any person who, having been a public officer, was, immediately before the date aforesaid, serving in any office in the Police Force, other than the office of Commissioner of Police or Deputy Commissioner of Police, on the recommendation of the Police Service Commission ; and

(d) in the case of an award payable in respect of the services of any other person, on the recommendation of the Public Service Commission.

(3) In this section, " pensions law " means any law relating to the grant to any person, or to the widow, children, dependants or personal representatives of that person, of an award in respect of the services of that person in a public office, and includes any instrument made under any such law.

## PART VII

### FINANCE

**114.**—(1) Save as provided in subsection (2) of this section, there shall be in and for the Bahama Islands a Consolidated Fund into which, subject to the provisions of any law for the time being in force in the Bahama Islands, shall be paid all revenues of the Bahama Islands.

<small>Consolidated Fund.</small>

(2) Any moneys received in respect of any grant or disposition made in pursuance of section 24 of this Constitution of any land, property or interest referred to in that section shall be paid into a special fund to be known as the Crown Lands Fund for Development.

**115.**—(1) No money shall be withdrawn from the Consolidated Fund or other public funds of the Bahama Islands except upon the authority of a warrant under the hand of the Minister of Finance :

<small>Withdrawal of money from the Consolidated Fund or other public funds.</small>

Provided that where, in the opinion of the Governor, acting in his discretion, moneys are required to enable him to discharge his responsibilities for internal security and the Police Force, such moneys may be withdrawn from the Consolidated Fund either—

(a) upon the authority of a warrant under the hand of the Minister of Finance ; or

(b) upon the authority of a warrant (hereinafter referred to as " a Governor's warrant ") under the hand of the Governor, acting in his discretion.

(2) No warrant shall be issued by the Minister of Finance for the purpose of meeting any expenditure unless—

(a) the expenditure has been authorised for the financial year during which the withdrawal is to take place—

(i) by an Appropriation Act ; or

(ii) by a supplementary estimate approved by resolution of the House of Assembly ; or

(b) the expenditure has been authorised in accordance with the provisions of section 116(4), 117 or 118 of this Constitution ; or

(c) it is statutory expenditure :

Provided that no such warrant shall be issued for the purpose of meeting expenditure from the Crown Lands Fund for Development unless the expenditure has been authorised by a law enacted by the Legislature or, in the case of expenditure for purposes of capital development, by resolution of the House of Assembly.

Authorisation of expenditure.

**116.**—(1) The Minister of Finance shall cause to be prepared and laid before the House of Assembly before or not later than sixty days after the commencement of each financial year estimates of the revenues and expenditure of the Bahama Islands for that year.

(2) The heads of expenditure contained in the estimates (other than statutory expenditure) shall be included in a bill to be known as an Appropriation Bill which shall be introduced into the House of Assembly to provide for the issue from the Consolidated Fund or other public funds of the Bahama Islands of the sums necessary to meet that expenditure and the appropriation of those sums for the purposes specified therein.

(3) If in respect of any financial year it is found that the amount appropriated by the Appropriation Act for any purpose is insufficient or that a need has arisen for expenditure for a purpose for which no amount has been appropriated by that law, a supplementary estimate showing the sums required shall be laid before and voted on by the House of Assembly.

(4) Where in respect of any financial year the Minister of Finance considers it necessary to authorise expenditure for any purpose in excess of the amount appropriated for that purpose by the Appropriation Act, or for a purpose for which no amount has been appropriated by that law, he may, subject to the Rules of Procedure of the House of Assembly in that regard, authorise, with the prior approval of the Cabinet, such expenditure by special warrant and shall, at least at quarterly intervals, prepare statements of such excess expenditure to be laid before and voted on by the House of Assembly.

(5) Where in respect of any financial year moneys have been withdrawn from the Consolidated Fund upon the authority of a Governor's warrant by virtue of proviso (b) to section 115(1) of this Constitution, the Minister of Finance shall, if the circumstances of the case so require, prepare in respect of such moneys a statement of expenditure to be laid before the House of Assembly.

(6) Where in respect of any financial year supplementary estimates or statements of excess expenditure have been approved by the House of Assembly in accordance with the provisions of subsection (3) or (4) of this section, a supplementary Appropriation Bill shall be introduced into the House of Assembly in the financial year next following the financial year to which such estimates or statements relate, providing for the appropriation of the sums so approved for the purposes specified in those estimates or statements.

(7) Statutory expenditure shall not be voted on by the House of Assembly but, without further authority of the Legislature, shall be paid out of the Consolidated Fund by warrant under the hand of the Minister of Finance.

**117.** If the Appropriation Act in respect of any financial year has not come into operation by the beginning of that financial year, the House of Assembly by resolution may empower the Minister of Finance to authorise the withdrawal of moneys from the Consolidated Fund or other public funds of the Bahama Islands for the purpose of meeting expenditure necessary to carry on the public services until the expiration of four months from the beginning of that financial year or the coming into operation of the Appropriation Act, whichever is the earlier.

*Authorisation of expenditure in advance of appropriation.*

**118.** Where at any time the Legislature has been dissolved before any provision or any sufficient provision is made under this Part of this Constitution for the carrying on of the government of the Bahama Islands, the Minister of Finance may issue a warrant for the payment out of the Consolidated Fund or other public funds of the Bahama Islands of such sums as he may consider necessary for the continuance of the public services until the expiry of a period of three months commencing with the date on which the House of Assembly first meets after that dissolution, but a statement of the sums so authorised shall, as soon as practicable, be laid before and voted on by the House of Assembly and the aggregate sums so voted shall be included, under the appropriate heads, in the next Appropriation Bill.

*Delay in the Appropriation Act owing to dissolution.*

**119.** The public debt of the Bahama Islands, including the interest thereon, sinking fund payments in respect of that debt and the costs, charges and expenses incidental to the management of that debt, is hereby charged on the Consolidated Fund, the general revenues and on the other public funds and assets of the Bahama Islands.

*Public debt.*

**120.**—(1) There shall be an Auditor for the Bahama Islands whose office shall be a public office and who shall be appointed by the Governor, acting on the recommendation of the Public Service Commission.

*Auditor.*

(2) If the office of Auditor is vacant or the holder thereof is for any reason unable to perform the functions of his office, the Governor, acting on the recommendation of the Public Service Commission, may appoint a person to act in that office, and any person so appointed may, subject to the provisions of section 121 of this Constitution, continue to act until he is notified by the Governor, acting on the recommendation of the Public Service Commission, that the circumstances giving rise to the appointment have ceased to exist.

(3) The Legislature may by law prescribe qualifications for appointment to hold the office of Auditor :

Provided that a person who has been appointed to hold that office may continue in office notwithstanding that such qualifications are subsequently so prescribed or varied.

(4) The Auditor shall receive such salary and allowances as, subject to subsection (5) of this section, may be prescribed by any law of the Legislature and the said salary and allowances are hereby charged on, and shall be paid out of, the Consolidated Fund.

(5) The salary of the Auditor and his conditions of service other than allowances shall not be altered to his disadvantage during his continuance in office.

Tenure of office of Auditor.

**121.**—(1) Subject to the provisions of subsection (3) of this section, the Auditor shall vacate his office when he attains the age of sixty years :

Provided that the Governor, acting after consultation with the Prime Minister and the Public Service Commission, may permit an Auditor to continue in office for a period not exceeding six months after his attainment of that age.

(2) The Auditor may be removed from office only for inability to discharge the functions of his office (whether arising from infirmity of body or mind or any other cause) or for misbehaviour and shall not be so removed except in accordance with the provisions of subsection (3) of this section.

(3) The Auditor shall be removed from office by the Governor by instrument under the Public Seal if the Governor, acting in his discretion, is satisfied that he ought to be removed from office for inability as aforesaid or misbehaviour.

Functions of Auditor.

**122.**—(1) The accounts of the Supreme Court and the courts subordinate thereto, the Court of Appeal, all departments and offices of the Government of the Bahama Islands, the offices of the Clerk of the Senate and the Clerk of the House of Assembly, the Public Service Commission, the Public Service Board of Appeal, the Judicial and Legal Service Commission and the Police Service Commission shall be audited and reported on annually by the Auditor and for that purpose the Auditor or any person authorised by him shall at all times be entitled to have access to all books, records, returns and other documents relating to such accounts.

(2) The Auditor shall submit his reports made under subsection (1) of this section to the Speaker of the House of Assembly who shall cause them to be laid before the House ; and he shall also send a copy of each report to the Governor and to the President of the Senate and the President shall cause the copy sent to him to be laid before the Senate.

(3) In the exercise of his functions under the provisions of this section, the Auditor shall not be subject to the direction or control of any other person or authority.

(4) Nothing in this section shall prevent the performance by the Auditor of—

(a) such other functions in relation to the accounts of the Government of the Bahama Islands and the accounts of other public authorities and other bodies administering public funds in the Bahama Islands as may be prescribed by or under any law for the time being in force in the Bahama Islands ; or

(b) such other functions in relation to the supervision and control of expenditure from public funds in the Bahama Islands as may be so prescribed.

**123.** Subject to the provisions of this Part of this Constitution, the Governor may by regulations provide for any of the following matters—

*Legislation relating to public finance*

(a) the management of the Consolidated Fund ;

(b) the supervision, control and direction of the financial business and affairs of the Government of the Bahama Islands ;

(c) the preparation of estimates ;

(d) the opening and operation of banking accounts ;

(e) the system of Government accounting ;

(f) the financial control and supervision of self accounting units and statutory bodies performing public functions.

**124.** In this Part of this Constitution—

*Interpretation.*

" financial year " means the twelve months ending on the 31st December in any year or on such other date as may from time to time be prescribed by any law of the Legislature ;

" statutory expenditure " means expenditure charged on the Consolidated Fund or on the general revenues and assets of the Bahama Islands by virtue of any of the provisions of this Constitution or by virtue of any provision of any other law for the time being in force in the Bahama Islands.

## PART VIII

### MISCELLANEOUS

**125.**—(1) Save as otherwise provided in sections 33(1)(b), 34(4)(c), 39(1)(b) and 40(2)(c) of this Constitution, any person who is appointed to or to act in any office established by this Constitution may resign from that office by writing under his hand addressed to the person by whom he was appointed.

*Resignations.*

(2) The resignation of any person from any such office (including any seat in a chamber of the Legislature) by writing under his hand addressed in accordance with this Constitution to any other person shall take effect when the writing signifying the resignation is received by that other person.

**126.**—(1) Where any person has vacated any office (including any seat in a chamber of the Legislature) established by this Constitution, he may, if qualified, again be appointed or elected or otherwise selected to hold that office in accordance with the provisions of this Constitution.

*Re-appointments and concurrent appointments.*

(2) When the holder of any office constituted by or under this Constitution is on leave of absence pending relinquishment of that office the person or authority having power to make appointments to that office may appoint another person thereto.

(3) Where two or more persons are holding the same office by reason of an appointment made in pursuance of subsection (2) of this section, then—

(a) for the purposes of any function conferred upon the holder of that office ; and

(b) for the purposes of any reference in this Constitution to the absence, illness or inability to perform the functions of his office of the holder of that office,

the person last appointed to the office shall be deemed to be the sole holder of the office.

**Provisions relating to government contracts.**

**127.** For the purposes of sections 32, 33, 38 and 39 of this Constitution—

(a) " government contract " means, subject to such exceptions as the Legislature may by law prescribe, any contract made with the Government of the Bahama Islands or with a department of that Government or with an officer of that Government contracting as such ; and

(b) a person shall be deemed to be interested in a government contract if—

(i) subject to such exceptions as the Legislature may by law prescribe, he is a party to such a contract or a partner in a firm or director or manager of a company which is a party to such a contract ; or

(ii) he is otherwise interested in such a contract in such manner as the Legislature may by law prescribe.

**Bahamian Status.**

**128.** For the purposes of this Constitution, a person shall possess Bahamian status if—

(a) he is a British subject and was born in the Bahama Islands ; or

(b) he is a British subject and was born outside the Bahama Islands of a father or mother who was born in the Bahama Islands ; or

(c) he is a person who possesses Bahamian status under the provisions of any law for the time being in force in the Bahama Islands ; or

(d) he has obtained the status of a British subject by reason of the grant by the Governor of a certificate of naturalisation under the British Nationality and Status of Aliens Act 1914(a) or the British Nationality Act 1948(b) ; or

(e) she is the wife of a person to whom any of the foregoing paragraphs of this section applies not living apart from such person under a decree of a court or a deed of separation ; or

(f) such person is the child, stepchild or lawfully adopted child under the age of eighteen years of a person to whom any of the foregoing paragraphs of this section applies.

**Jurisdiction of Court of Appeal in relation to Turks and Caicos Islands.**

**129.** The Court of Appeal shall have jurisdiction to hear and determine such appeals (including cases stated and questions of law reserved) from the courts of the Turks and Caicos Islands as may be prescribed by or under any law for the time being in force in the Turks and Caicos Islands ; and the powers, practice and procedure of the Court when exercising the jurisdiction referred to in this section and the powers

---

(a) 1914 c. 17.     (b) 1948 c. 56.

and duties of other persons or authorities in connection with the exercise of that jurisdiction shall be such as may be prescribed by or under any such law.

130.—(1) In this Constitution, unless it is otherwise provided or required by the context—

    " chamber " means either the Senate or the House of Assembly as the context may require ;

    " the Commonwealth " means the United Kingdom, Canada, Australia, New Zealand, India, Pakistan, Ceylon, Ghana, Malaysia, Nigeria, Cyprus, Sierra Leone, Tanzania, Jamaica, Trinidad and Tobago, Uganda, Kenya, Malawi, Malta, Zambia, The Gambia, Singapore, Guyana, Lesotho, Botswana, Barbados, Mauritius, Swaziland and any dependency of any such country ;

    " election " means an election of a member or members of the House of Assembly ;

    " the Gazette " means the Official Gazette of the Bahama Islands ;

    " the Governor " means the Governor and Commander-in-Chief of the Bahama Islands ;

    " high judicial office " means the office of judge of a court having unlimited jurisdiction in civil and criminal matters in some part of the Commonwealth or a court having jurisdiction in appeals from any such court ;

    " the leader of the opposition " means the member of the House of Assembly who in the judgment of the Governor, acting in his discretion, is best able to command the support of a majority of those members who do not support the Government or, if there is no such person, the member of the House who, in his judgment, commands the support of the largest single group of such members who are prepared to support one leader ;

    " the Legislature " means the Legislature established by this Constitution ;

    " Minister " includes a temporary Minister appointed under section 69 of this Constitution except in sections 64, 65, 68 and 80 of this Constitution ;

    " the Police Force " means the Police Force established in and for the Bahama Islands and maintained under the provisions of the Police Act 1965(a) of the Bahama Islands or any law amending or replacing that Act ;

    " public office " means, subject to the provisions of subsection (5) of this section, any office of emolument in the public service ;

    " public officer " means the holder of any public office and includes any person appointed to act in any such office ;

    " the public service " means the service of the Crown in a civil capacity in respect of the government of the Bahama Islands ;

    " session " means, in relation to a chamber of the Legislature, the sittings of that chamber commencing when it first meets after this Constitution comes into operation or after any general election or prorogation of the Legislature and terminating when the Legislature is prorogued or is dissolved without having been prorogued ;

*Interpretation.*

(a) No. 29 of 1965.

" sitting " means, in relation to a chamber of the Legislature, a period during which that chamber is sitting continuously without adjournment and includes any period during which the chamber is in committee.

(2) In this Constitution, unless it is otherwise provided or required by the context—

(a) any reference to the date on which this Constitution comes into operation shall be construed as a reference to the appointed day referred to in section 1(2) of the Order in Council to which this Constitution is scheduled ;

(b) any reference to a law of the Legislature shall be construed as including a reference to a law of any Legislature established for the Bahama Islands at any time before this Constitution comes into operation and to any instrument having the force of law made in exercise of a power conferred by a law of the Legislature ;

(c) any reference to power to make appointments to any office shall be construed as including a reference to power to make appointments on promotion and transfer to that office and to power to appoint a person to act in that office during any period during which it is vacant or the holder thereof is unable (whether by reason of absence or of infirmity of body or mind or any other cause) to perform the functions of that office ;

(d) any reference to the holder of an office by a term designating or describing his office shall be construed as including a reference to any person for the time being acting in that office or, to the extent of his authority, otherwise authorised to perform the functions of that office.

(3) In this Constitution, unless it is otherwise provided or required by the context, references to the functions of the Governor shall be construed as references to his powers and duties in exercise of the executive authority of the Bahama Islands and to any other powers or duties conferred or imposed on him as Governor by or under this Constitution or any other law in force in the Bahama Islands.

(4) Where by this Constitution any person is directed, or power is conferred on any person or authority to appoint a person, to act in or otherwise to perform the functions of an office if the holder thereof is unable to perform the functions of that office, the validity of any performance of those functions by the person so directed or of any appointment made in exercise of that power shall not be called in question in any court on the ground that the holder of the office is not unable to perform the functions of the office.

(5) For the purposes of this Constitution, a person shall not be considered to hold a public office by reason only that he is in receipt of a pension or other like allowance in respect of public service, and references to a public office shall not be construed as including—

(a) references to the office of Minister, Parliamentary Secretary, President or Vice-President of the Senate, Senator, Speaker or Deputy Speaker of the House of Assembly or Representative or member of the Constituencies Commission or the Advisory Committee on the Prerogative of Mercy ;

(b) except as otherwise expressly provided, references to the office of a judge of the Supreme Court or Court of Appeal, a member of the Public Service Commission, the Public Service Board of Appeal, the Judicial and Legal Service Commission or the Police Service Commission, the Secretary to the Cabinet or an office on the personal staff of the Governor ;

(c) references to any office in the Department of Tourism ;

(d) references to the office of a member of any board, committee or other similar body (whether incorporated or not) established by any law for the time being in force in the Bahama Islands.

(6) References in this Constitution to the power to remove a public officer from his office shall be construed as including references to any power conferred by any law to require or permit that officer to retire from the public service.

(7) Any provision of this Constitution that vests in any person or authority power to remove any public officer from his office shall be without prejudice to the power of any person or authority to abolish any office or to any law providing for the compulsory retirement of public officers generally or any class of public officer on attaining an age specified therein.

(8) If any circumstances arise that, under the provisions of this Constitution, require the Governor to remove a judge of the Supreme Court or the Court of Appeal or the Attorney-General or the Auditor from office for inability to discharge the functions of his office, the Governor, acting in his discretion, may carry out such removal either by dismissing that officer or by requiring him to retire.

(9) Any power conferred by any law to permit any officer mentioned in subsection (8) of this section to retire before the date on which, under the provisions of this Constitution, he is required to vacate his office shall vest in the Governor acting in his discretion.

(10) Where any power is conferred by this Constitution to make any proclamation, order, rules or regulations or to give any direction, the power shall be construed as including a power exercisable in like manner to amend or revoke any such proclamation, order, rules, regulations or directions.

(11) The Interpretation Act 1889(a) shall apply, with the necessary adaptations, for the purpose of interpreting this Constitution and otherwise in relation thereto as it applies for the purpose of interpreting and in relation to Acts of Parliament of the United Kingdom.

(a) 1889 c. 63.

## THE SCHEDULE TO THE CONSTITUTION
(Sections 17(3), 45, 77, 91 and 96)

### FORMS OF OATHS AND AFFIRMATIONS

1. *Oath of Allegiance*

I, ....................................., do swear that I will be faithful and bear true allegiance to Her Majesty Queen Elizabeth the Second, Her Heirs and Successors, according to law. So help me God.

2. *Affirmation of Allegiance*

I, ....................................., do solemnly and sincerely affirm and declare that I will be faithful and bear true allegiance to Her Majesty Queen Elizabeth the Second, Her Heirs and Successors, according to law.

3. *Oath for the due execution of the office of Governor and Commander-in-Chief*

I, ....................................., do swear that I will well and truly serve Her Majesty Queen Elizabeth the Second in the office of Governor and Commander-in-Chief. So help me God.

4. *Affirmation for the due execution of the office of Governor and Commander-in-Chief*

I, ....................................., do solemnly and sincerely affirm and declare that I will well and truly serve Her Majesty Queen Elizabeth the Second in the office of Governor and Commander-in-Chief.

5. *Oath for the due execution of the office of Prime Minister or other Minister or Parliamentary Secretary*

I, ....................................., being appointed Prime Minister/Minister/Parliamentary Secretary, do swear that I will to the best of my judgment, at all times when so required, freely give my counsel and advice to the Governor (or any other person for the time being lawfully performing the functions of that office) for the good management of the public affairs of the Bahama Islands, and I do further swear that I will not on any account, at any time whatsoever, disclose the counsel, advice, opinion or vote of any particular Minister or Parliamentary Secretary and that I will not, except with the authority of the Cabinet and to such extent as may be required for the good management of the affairs of the Bahama Islands, directly or indirectly reveal the business or proceedings of the Cabinet or the nature or contents of any documents communicated to me as a Minister/Parliamentary Secretary or any matter coming to my knowledge in my capacity as such and that in all things I will be a true and faithful Prime Minister/Minister/Parliamentary Secretary. So help me God.

6. *Affirmation for the due execution of the office of Prime Minister or other Minister or Parliamentary Secretary*

I, ....................................., being appointed Prime Minister/Minister/Parliamentary Secretary, do solemnly and sincerely affirm and declare that I will to the best of my judgment, at all times when so required, freely give my counsel and advice to the Governor (or any other person for the time being lawfully performing the functions of that office) for the good management of the public affairs of the Bahama Islands, and I do further solemnly and sincerely affirm and declare that I will not on any account, at any time whatsoever, disclose the counsel, advice, opinion or vote of any particular

Minister or Parliamentary Secretary and that I will not, except with the authority of the Cabinet and to such extent as may be required for the good management of the affairs of the Bahama Islands, directly or indirectly reveal the business or proceedings of the Cabinet or the nature or contents of any documents communicated to me as a Minister/Parliamentary Secretary or any matter coming to my knowledge in my capacity as such and that in all things I will be a true and faithful Prime Minister/Minister/Parliamentary Secretary.

## 7. *Judicial Oath*

I, .................................., do swear that I will well and truly serve Her Majesty Queen Elizabeth the Second, Her Heirs and Successors, in the office of ................................ and will do right to all manner of people after the laws and usages of the Bahama Islands without fear or favour, affection or ill will. So help me God.

## 8. *Judicial Affirmation*

I, .........................................., do solemnly and sincerely affirm and declare that I will well and truly serve Her Majesty Queen Elizabeth the Second, Her Heirs and Successors, in the office of ............................. and will do right to all manner of people after the laws and usages of the Bahama Islands without fear or favour, affection or ill will.

---

## EXPLANATORY NOTE

### (*This Note is not part of the Order.*)

This Order provides a new constitution for the Bahama Islands, conferring internal self-government. The Constitution makes provision with respect to the fundamental rights and freedoms of the individual, the office of Governor, the Legislature (which includes two chambers called the Senate and the House of Assembly), the Cabinet, the Judiciary, the Public Service and finance. It provides for the Governor to have responsibility for certain matters relating to external affairs and for defence, internal security and the Police Force but to entrust to a Minister authority to discharge the responsibility for internal security and the Police Force, and establishes a Security Council with consultative functions with respect to external affairs, defence, internal security and the Police Force.

## 1969 No. 591

## CARIBBEAN AND NORTH ATLANTIC TERRITORIES

### The Turks and Caicos Islands (Constitution) (Amendment) Order 1969

|  |  |
|---|---|
| Made - - - - | 23rd April 1969 |
| Laid before Parliament | 29th April 1969 |
| Coming into Operation | As provided in section 1(2). |

At the Court at Windsor Castle, the 23rd day of April 1969

Present,

The Queen's Most Excellent Majesty in Council

Her Majesty, by virtue of the powers conferred upon Her by section 5 of the West Indies Act 1962(a) and of all other powers enabling Her in that behalf, is pleased, by and with the advice of Her Privy Council, to order, and it is hereby ordered, as follows:—

**Citation, construction and commencement.** 1.—(1) This Order may be cited as the Turks and Caicos Islands (Constitution) (Amendment) Order 1969 and shall be construed as one with the Turks and Caicos Islands Constitution Orders 1965 to 1968(b).

(2) This Order shall come into operation on the day appointed under section 1(2) of the Bahama Islands (Constitution) Order 1969(c) for the coming into operation of that Order.

**Amendment of section 2(1) of Constitution.** 2. Section 2(1) of the Constitution of the Turks and Caicos Islands is amended by the deletion of the definition of " Governor " (inserted by paragraph 1 of Schedule 2 to the Turks and Caicos Islands (Constitution) Order 1965) and the substitution therefor of the following definition :—

' " Governor " means the person for the time being holding the office of Governor and Commander-in-Chief of the Bahama Islands and includes any person for the time being acting in that office save when any such person is so acting by reason of the absence of the holder of the office for the purpose of visiting the Turks and Caicos Islands ; ".'

**Revocation of section 2B of Constitution.** 3. Section 2B of the Constitution of the Turks and Caicos Islands (inserted by paragraph 2 of Schedule 2 to the Turks and Caicos Islands (Constitution) Order 1965) is revoked.

---

(a) 1962 c. 19.　　　　　(b) S.I. 1965/1861, 1967/977, 1139, 1968/728
(1965 III, p. 5609; 1967 II, p. 2960, p. 3370; 1968 II, p. 2107).
(c) S.I. 1969/590 (1969 I, p. 1567).

**4.** Section 49(1) of the Constitution of the Turks and Caicos Islands (as set out in paragraph 15 of Schedule 2 to the Turks and Caicos Islands (Constitution) Order 1965) is amended by the deletion of the words "established by the Constitution of the Bahama Islands set out in the Schedule to the Bahama Islands (Constitution) Order in Council 1963".

Amendment of section 49(1) of Constitution.

*W. G. Agnew.*

## EXPLANATORY NOTE

### *(This Note is not part of the Order.)*

This Order makes certain minor amendments to the Constitution of the Turks and Caicos Islands that are consequential upon the provisions of the Bahama Islands (Constitution) Order 1969.

## STATUTORY INSTRUMENTS

## 1969 No. 592

## CIVIL AVIATION

## The Civil Aviation Act 1949 (Overseas Territories) Order 1969

| | |
|---|---|
| *Made* - - - - | 23rd April 1969 |
| *Laid before Parliament* | 29th April 1969 |
| *Coming into Operation* | 30th April 1969 |

At the Court at Windsor Castle, the 23rd day of April 1969

Present,

The Queen's Most Excellent Majesty in Council

Her Majesty, by virtue and in exercise of the powers in that behalf by section 66 of the Civil Aviation Act 1949(a) or otherwise in Her Majesty vested, is pleased, by and with the advice of Her Privy Council, to order, and it is hereby ordered, as follows :—

1.—(1) This Order may be cited as the Civil Aviation Act 1949 (Overseas Territories) Order 1969.

(2) This Order shall come into operation on 30th April 1969.

(3) The Orders set out in Schedule 1 to this Order are revoked in so far as they form part of the law of the territories specified in Schedule 3 to this Order :

Provided that nothing in this paragraph shall affect the operation of section 13 of the Civil Aviation Act 1949 as extended to the said territories by the Colonial Civil Aviation (Application of Act) Order 1952(b), which section is, for the sake of convenience, reproduced in paragraph 5 of Schedule 2 to this Order.

(4) Nothing in paragraph (3) of this Article shall affect—

(a) any Order in Council made under any enactment revoked by this Order ;

(b) any instrument or other thing made or done or having effect under any of the enactments revoked by this Order or under any such Order as is mentioned in subparagraph (a) of this paragraph ;

but any such Order or instrument or thing aforesaid shall, if and so far as in force immediately before the coming into force of this Order, continue in force (subject however, to any Order in Council or instrument or thing made or done after the coming into force of this Order) and so far as it could have been made or done under this Order shall have effect as if made or done under this Order.

---

(a) 1949 c. 67.  (b) S.I. 1952/868 (1952 I, p. 565).

(5) In this Article "instrument" includes any order, regulation, direction, instruction, rule or other requirement, any notice and any certificate, licence, validation or other authority.

(6) Any document referring to any enactment revoked by this Order shall be construed as referring to this Order or to the corresponding enactment in this Order.

2.—(1) In this Order unless the context otherwise requires—

" Central and Southern Line Islands " means the islands of Malden, Starbuck, Vostock, Caroline and Flint ;

" Colony " means any of the colonies, protectorates or other territories mentioned in Schedule 3 to this Order, and includes the dependencies of a colony ;

" Chicago Convention " means the Convention on International Civil Aviation signed on behalf of the Government of the United Kingdom at Chicago on the seventh day of December 1944 ;

" Government Aerodrome " means an aerodrome under the control of the Governor and a naval, military or air force aerodrome ;

" Governor " means the officer for the time being administering the Government of the Colony.

(2) In this Order references to " Her Majesty's dominions " shall be construed as though British protectorates and protected states and trust territories administered by the Government of any part of Her Majesty's dominions, formed part of Her Majesty's dominions.

(3) The Interpretation Act 1889(a) shall apply, with the necessary adaptations, for the purpose of interpreting this Order and otherwise in relation thereto as it applies for the purpose of interpreting and in relation to Acts of Parliament.

3. The provisions of sections 8, 9, 10, 11, 14, 27, 38, 40, 41, 51, 53, 57, 58, 59, 60, 61, 62 and 63 of the Civil Aviation Act 1949, adapted and modified as set out in Schedule 2 hereto, are hereby extended to the territories mentioned in Schedule 3 hereto.

*W. G. Agnew.*

SCHEDULE 1        Article 1(3).

ORDERS REVOKED

| Order | Reference |
| --- | --- |
| The Colonial Civil Aviation (Application of Act) Order 1952. | S.I. 1952/868 (1952 I, p. 565). |
| The Colonial Civil Aviation (Application of Act) (Amendment) Order 1953. | S.I. 1953/591 (1953 I, p. 275). |
| The Colonial Civil Aviation (Application of Act) (Amendment) (No. 2) Order 1953. | S.I. 1953/1669 (1953 I, p. 277). |
| The Colonial Civil Aviation (Application of Act) (Amendment) Order 1954. | S.I. 1954/830 (1954 I, p. 463). |

(a) 1889 c. 63.

| Order | Reference |
|-------|-----------|
| The Colonial Civil Aviation (Application of Act) (Amendment) Order 1955. | S.I. 1955/709 (1955 I, p. 458). |
| The Colonial Civil Aviation (Application of Act) (Amendment) Order 1958. | S.I. 1958/1514 (1958 I, p. 303). |
| The Colonial Civil Aviation (Application of Act) (Amendment) Order 1959. | S.I. 1959/1052 (1959 I, p. 684). |
| The Colonial Civil Aviation (Application of Act) (Amendment) Order 1961. | S.I. 1961/2317 (1961 III, p. 4271). |
| The Colonial Civil Aviation (Application of Act) (Amendment) Order 1965. | S.I. 1965/980 (1965 I, p. 2419). |

Article 3.

SCHEDULE 2

## CIVIL AVIATION ACT 1949

### PART II

#### REGULATION OF CIVIL AVIATION

##### General

Power to give effect to Chicago Convention and regulate air navigation.

1. Section 8.—(1) Her Majesty may by Order in Council make such provision as appears to Her to be requisite or expedient—

(a) for carrying out the Chicago Convention, any Annex thereto relating to international standards and recommended practices (being an Annex adopted in accordance with the Convention) and any amendment of the Convention or any such Annex made in accordance with the Convention ; or

(b) generally for regulating air navigation.

(2) Her Majesty may by Order in Council make provision—

(a) as to the registration of aircraft in the Colony ;

(b) for prohibiting aircraft from flying unless certificates of airworthiness issued or validated under the Order are in force with respect to them and except upon compliance with such conditions as to maintenance or repair as may be specified either in the Order or by the Governor ;

(c) for the licensing, inspection and regulation of aerodromes, for access to aerodromes and places where aircraft have landed, for access to aircraft factories for the purpose of inspecting work therein carried on in relation to aircraft or parts thereof and for prohibiting or regulating the use of unlicensed aerodromes ;

(d) for prohibiting persons from engaging in, or being employed in or (except in the maintenance at unlicensed aerodromes of aircraft not used for or in connection with commercial, industrial or other gainful purposes) in connection with, air navigation in such capacities as may be specified either in the Order or by the Governor except in accordance with provisions in that behalf contained in the Order, and for the licensing of those employed at aerodromes licensed under the Order in the inspection or supervision of aircraft ;

(e) as to the conditions under which, and in particular the aerodromes to or from which, aircraft entering or leaving the Colony may fly, and as to the conditions under which aircraft may fly from one part of the Colony to another ;

(f) as to the conditions under which passengers and goods may be carried by air and under which aircraft may be used for other commercial, industrial or gainful purposes, and for prohibiting the carriage by air of goods of such classes as may be specified either in the Order or by the Governor ;

(g) for minimizing or preventing interference with the use or effectiveness of apparatus used in connection with air navigation, and for prohibiting or regulating the use of such apparatus as aforesaid and the display of signs and lights liable to endanger aircraft ;

(h) generally for securing the safety, efficiency and regularity of air navigation and the safety of aircraft and of persons and property carried therein, for preventing aircraft endangering other persons and property and, in particular, for the detention of aircraft for any of the purposes specified in this paragraph ;

(i) for requiring persons engaged in, or employed in or in connection with, air navigation to supply meteorological information for the purposes of air navigation ;

(j) for regulating the making of signals and other communications by or to aircraft and persons carried therein ;

(k) for regulating the use of the civil air ensign and any other ensign established by Her Majesty in Council for purposes connected with air navigation ;

(l) for prohibiting aircraft from flying over such areas in the Colony as may be specified either in the Order or by the Governor ;

(m) for applying, adapting or modifying, or enabling the Governor to apply, adapt or modify, the enactments relating to customs in relation to aerodromes and to aircraft and to persons and property carried therein and for preventing smuggling by air, and for permitting, or enabling the Governor to permit, in connection with air navigation, subject to such conditions as appear to Her Majesty in Council, or to the Governor, as the case may be, to be requisite or expedient for the protection of the revenue, the importation of goods into the Colony without payment of duty ;

(n) as to the manner and conditions of the issue, validation, renewal, extension or variation of any certificate, licence or other document required by the Order (including the examinations and tests to be undergone), and as to the form, custody, production, cancellation, suspension, endorsement and surrender of any such document ;

(o) for regulating, or enabling the Governor to regulate, the charges that may be made for the use of aerodromes licensed under the Order and for services provided at such aerodromes ;

(p) for prescribing, or enabling the Governor to prescribe, the fees to be paid in respect of the issue, validation, renewal, extension or variation of any certificate, licence or other document or the undergoing of any examination or test required by, or in pursuance of, the Order and in respect of any other matters in respect of which it appears to Her Majesty in Council, or to the Governor, to be expedient for the purpose of the Order to charge fees ;

(q) for exempting from the provisions of the Order or any of them any aircraft or persons or classes of aircraft or persons.

(3) An Order in Council under this section may make different provision with respect to different classes of aircraft, aerodromes, persons or property and with respect to different circumstances and with respect to different parts of the Colony but shall, so far as practicable, be so framed as not to discriminate in like circumstances between aircraft registered in the Colony operated on charter terms by one air transport undertaking and such aircraft so operated by another such undertaking.

(4) An Order in Council under this section may, for the purpose of securing compliance with the provisions thereof, provide for the imposition of penalties not exceeding a fine of two hundred pounds and imprisonment for a term of six months, and, in the case of any provision having effect by virtue of paragraph (*l*) of subsection (2) of this section, may also for that purpose provide for the taking of such steps (including firing on aircraft) as may be specified in the Order.

(7) Part VI of this Act applies to this section.

**Control of aviation in time of war or emergency.**    2. Section 9.—(1) In time of war, whether actual or imminent, or of great national emergency, the Governor may by order regulate or prohibit, either absolutely or subject to such conditions as may be contained in the order, the navigation of all or any descriptions of aircraft over the Colony or any portion thereof; and may by order provide for taking possession of and using for the purposes of Her Majesty's naval, military or air forces any aerodrome, or any aircraft in the Colony, or any machinery, plant, material or things found in or on any such aerodrome or such aircraft, and for regulating or prohibiting the use, erection, building, maintenance or establishment of any aerodrome, or flying school, or any class or description thereof.

(2) An order under this section may make, for the purposes of the order, such provision as an Order in Council under section 8 of this Act may by virtue of subsection (4) of that section make for the purpose of securing compliance with provisions thereof having effect by virtue of paragraph (*l*) of subsection (2) of that section.

(3) Any person who suffers direct injury or loss, owing to the operation of an order of the Governor under this section, shall be entitled to receive compensation from the Governor, from such public funds as he may lawfully apply for the purpose, the amount thereof to be fixed, in default of agreement, by an arbitrator to be agreed upon or failing agreement to be appointed by the Chief Justice or other chief judicial officer of the Colony:

Provided that no compensation shall be payable by reason of the operation of a general order under this section prohibiting flying in the Colony or any part thereof.

(6) Part VI of this Act applies to this section.

**Investigation of accidents.**    3. Section 10.—(1) The Governor may make regulations providing for the investigation of any accident arising out of or in the course of air navigation, and either occurring in or over the Colony or occurring elsewhere to British aircraft registered in the Colony.

(2) Regulations under this section may contain provisions—

(*a*) requiring notice to be given of any such accident as aforesaid in such manner and by such persons as may be specified;

(*b*) applying, with or without modification, for the purpose of investigations held with respect to any such accidents any of the provisions of any law in force in the Colony relating to the investigation of deaths or accidents;

(*c*) prohibiting, pending investigation, access to or interference with aircraft to which an accident has occurred, and authorising any person, so far as may be necessary for the purposes of an investigation, to have access to, examine, remove, take measures for the preservation of, or otherwise deal with, any such aircraft;

(*d*) authorising or requiring the cancellation, suspension, endorsement or surrender of any licence or certificate granted in the Colony under this Part of this Act or any Order in Council or order made under this Part of this Act, or the withdrawal or suspension of any validation conferred in the Colony of a licence granted by a duly competent authority elsewhere, where it appears on an investigation that the licence or certificate ought to be cancelled, suspended, endorsed or surrendered, or the validation withdrawn or suspended, as the case may be, and requiring the production of any such licence or certificate for the purpose of being so dealt with:

Provided that nothing in this section shall limit the powers of any authority under sections 530 to 537 of the Merchant Shipping Act 1894(a) or any enactment amending those sections.

(3) If any person contravenes or fails to comply with any regulations under this section, he shall be liable, on summary conviction, to a fine not exceeding fifty pounds or to imprisonment for a term not exceeding three months.

(5) Part VI of this Act applies to this section.

4. Section 11.—(1) Where an aircraft is flown in such a manner as to **Dangerous** be the cause of unnecessary danger to any person or property on land **flying.** or water, the pilot or the person in charge of the aircraft, and also the owner thereof unless he proves to the satisfaction of the court that the aircraft was so flown without his actual fault or privity, shall be liable on summary conviction to a fine not exceeding two hundred pounds or to imprisonment for a term not exceeding six months or to both such fine and such imprisonment.

In this section the expression " owner " in relation to an aircraft includes any person by whom the aircraft is hired at the time of the offence.

(2) The provisions of this section shall be in addition to and not in derogation of the powers conferred on Her Majesty in Council by section 8 of this Act.

(3) Part VI of this Act applies to this section.

5. Section 13.—(1) The Governor may, with the approval of a Secretary **Licensing of** of State, make regulations—
    **air transport** **and commer-**
(a) to secure that aircraft shall not be used in the Colony by any **cial flying.** person—
   (i) for plying, while carrying passengers or goods for hire or reward, on such journeys or classes of journeys (whether beginning and ending at the same point or at different points) as may be specified in the regulations, or
   (ii) for such flying undertaken for the purpose of any trade or business as may be so specified,
except under the authority of, and in accordance with, a licence granted to the said person by the licensing authority specified in the regulations ;
(b) as to the circumstances in which a licence under the regulations may or shall be granted, refused, revoked or suspended, and in particular as to the matters to which the licensing authority specified in the regulations is to have regard in deciding whether to grant or refuse such a licence ;
(c) as to appeals from the licensing authority by persons interested in the grant, refusal, revocation or suspension of any licence under the regulations ;
(d) as to the conditions which may be attached to such a licence (including conditions as to the fares, freight or other charges to be charged by the holder of the licence), and for securing compliance with any conditions so attached ;

(a) 1894 c. 60.

6

(e) as to the information to be furnished by an applicant for, or the holder of, such a licence to such authorities as may be specified in the regulations ;

(f) prescribing the fees to be paid in respect of the grant of any licence under the regulations, or enabling such fees to be prescribed by any person or authority specified in that behalf by the regulations ;

and such regulations may make different provision as respects different classes of aircraft and different classes of licences.

(2) Regulations made under this section may, for the purpose of securing compliance with the regulations, provide for the imposition of the following penalties, namely—

(a) in the case of a first offence against the regulations, a fine not exceeding five hundred pounds or imprisonment for a term not exceeding three months or both such fine and such imprisonment ; and

(b) in the case of a second or subsequent offence against the regulations, a fine not exceeding five thousand pounds or imprisonment for a term not exceeding two years or both such fine and such imprisonment.

(3) Part VI of this Act applies to this section.

**Information as to air transport undertakings and use of customs aerodromes.**

6. Section 14.—(1) The Governor may, with the approval of a Secretary of State, make regulations—

(a) requiring any person—

(i) who carries on the business of carrying passengers or goods in aircraft for hire or reward on such journeys or classes of journeys (whether beginning and ending at the same point or at different points) as may be specified in the regulations, or

(ii) who is the holder of a licence in respect of a customs aerodrome,

to furnish to such authorities as may be specified in the regulations such information relating to the use of aircraft for the purpose of his said business and to the persons employed in connection with that use, or, as the case may be, relating to the use of the aerodrome and to the persons employed in aircraft arriving thereat or departing therefrom, as may be prescribed by the regulations ;

(b) requiring the owner, or the pilot or other person in charge, of any aircraft arriving at, or departing from, any customs aerodrome to furnish to the holder of the licence in respect of that aerodrome such information as may be necessary to enable the holder of the said licence to comply with such of the provisions of the regulations as relate to him ;

(c) prescribing the times at which, and the form and manner in which, any information required under the regulations is to be furnished:

Provided that a person carrying on such a business as is mentioned in sub-paragraph (i) of paragraph (a) of this subsection shall not be required to furnish information relating to the use of aircraft on journeys wholly outside the Colony, or relating to persons exclusively employed outside the Colony, unless the person carrying on the business is either a British subject or a British protected person resident in the Colony or a citizen of the Republic of Ireland resident in the Colony or a body corporate incorporated under the law of the Colony.

(2) Regulations under this section may provide for imposing on any person who contravenes or fails to comply with any provision of the regulations such penalties (not exceeding a fine of twenty pounds and a further fine of five pounds for every day on which the contravention or non-compliance continues after conviction therefor) as may be specified in the regulations.

(3) No information with respect to any particular undertaking which has been obtained by virtue of regulations under this section shall, without the consent of the person carrying on that undertaking, be disclosed otherwise than in connection with the execution of such regulations, and if any person discloses any such information in contravention of this subsection, he shall be liable, on summary conviction, to imprisonment for a term not exceeding three months or to a fine not exceeding fifty pounds or to both such fine and such imprisonment or, on conviction on indictment, to imprisonment for a term not exceeding two years or to a fine not exceeding one hundred pounds or to both such fine and such imprisonment.

Nothing in this subsection shall apply to the disclosure of any information for the purposes of any legal proceedings which may be taken by virtue of this subsection or of regulations made under this section, or for the purpose of any report of any such proceedings, but, save as aforesaid, the restriction imposed by this subsection shall, in relation to any legal proceedings (including arbitrations), extend so as to prohibit and prevent any person who is in possession of any such information so obtained from disclosing, and from being required by any court or arbitrator to disclose, that information (whether as a witness or otherwise) except with the consent of the person carrying on the undertaking to which the information relates.

(4) In this section the expression " customs aerodrome " means an aerodrome for the time being appointed as a place of landing or departure of aircraft for the purposes of the enactments relating to customs.

(5) Part VI of this Act applies to this section.

## PART III

### AERODROMES AND OTHER LAND

7. Section 27.—(1) If the Governor is satisfied, with respect to any building, structure or erection in the vicinity of an aerodrome to which this section applies that, in order to avoid danger to aircraft flying in that vicinity in darkness or conditions of poor visibility, provision ought to be made (whether by lighting or otherwise) for giving to such aircraft warning of the presence of that building, structure or erection, he may by order authorise (subject to any conditions specified in the order) the proprietor of the aerodrome, and any person acting under the proprietor's instructions,— *Indication of presence of obstructions near aerodromes.*

(a) to execute, instal, maintain, operate, and, as occasion requires, to repair and alter, such works and apparatus as may be necessary for enabling such warning to be given in the manner specified in the order, and

(b) so far as may be necessary for exercising any of the powers conferred by the order to enter upon and pass over (with or without vehicles) any such land as may be specified in the order:

Provided that no such order shall be made in relation to any building, structure or erection if it appears to the Governor that there have been made, and are being carried out, satisfactory arrangements for the giving of such warning as aforesaid of the presence of the building, structure or erection.

(2) The Governor shall, before making any such order as aforesaid, cause to be published, in such manner as he thinks best for informing persons concerned, notice of the proposal to make the order and of the place where copies of the draft order may be obtained free of charge, and take into consideration any representations with respect to the order which may, within such period not being less than two months after the publication of the notice as may be specified therein, be made to him by any

person appearing to him to have an interest in any land which would be affected by the order ; and at the end of that period the order may, subject to the provisions of this section, be made with such modifications (if any) of the original draft as the Governor thinks proper.

(3) Every such order as aforesaid shall provide—

(a) that, except in a case of emergency, no works shall be executed on any land in pursuance of the order, unless, at least fourteen days previously, the proprietor of the aerodrome to which the order relates has served in the manner prescribed by the order on the occupier of that land, and on every other person known by the proprietor to have an interest therein, a written notice containing such particulars of the nature of the proposed works, and the manner in which and the time at which it is proposed to execute them, as may be prescribed by or in accordance with the order ; and

(b) that if, within fourteen days after service of the said notice on any person having such an interest, the proprietor of the aerodrome receives a written intimation of objection on the part of that person to the proposals contained in the notice, being an intimation which specifies the grounds of objection, then, unless and except in so far as the objection is withdrawn, no steps shall be taken in pursuance of the notice without the specific sanction of the Governor ;

and shall also provide for requiring the proprietor of the aerodrome to which the order relates to pay to any person having an interest in any land affected by the order such compensation for any loss or damage which that person may suffer in consequence of the order as may, in default of agreement, be determined from time to time by a single arbitrator appointed by the Chief Justice or other chief judicial officer of the Colony ; and, for the purposes of this subsection, any expense reasonably incurred in connection with the lawful removal of any apparatus installed in pursuance of such an order, and so much of any expense incurred in connection with the repair, alteration, demolition or removal of any building, structure or erection to which such an order relates as is attributable to the operation of the order, shall be deemed to be loss or damage suffered in consequence of the order.

(4) The ownership of anything shall not be taken to be affected by reason only that it is placed in, or affixed to, any land in pursuance of such an order as aforesaid ; and (subject to the provisions of the next following subsection) so long as any such order in respect of an aerodrome is in force, no person shall, except with the consent of the proprietor of the aerodrome, wilfully interfere with any works or things which, to the knowledge of that person, are works or things executed or placed, in, on or over any land in pursuance of the order.

If any person contravenes the foregoing provisions of this subsection, he shall be liable, on summary conviction, to imprisonment for a term not exceeding six months or to a fine not exceeding two hundred pounds or to both such fine and such imprisonment ; and every person who wilfully obstructs a person in the exercise of any of the powers conferred by such an order as aforesaid shall be liable, on summary conviction, to a fine not exceeding fifty pounds.

(5) Nothing in this section shall operate, in relation to any building, structure or erection, so as to restrict the doing of any work for the purpose of repairing, altering, demolishing or removing the building, structure or erection:

Provided that—

(a) notice of the doing of that work is given as soon as may be to the proprietor of the aerodrome ; and (*b*) the giving of warning of the presence of the building, structure or erection in the manner provided by any order under this section in force in relation thereto is not interrupted.

(7) In this section—

(*a*) the expression " aerodrome to which this section applies " means a Government aerodrome or any premises which, by virtue of an Order in Council made under section 8 of this Act, are for the time being licensed as an aerodrome for public use ; and

(*b*) the expression " proprietor of the aerodrome " means, in relation to any premises used or appropriated for use as an aerodrome, the person carrying on or entitled to carry on the business of an aerodrome in those premises or, in the case of a Government aerodrome, the officer in charge of the aerodrome.

(8) Part VI of this Act applies to this section.

8. Section 38.—(1) If any person trespasses on any land forming part of a Government aerodrome or an aerodrome licensed in pursuance of an Order in Council under section 8 of this Act, he shall be liable, on summary conviction, to a fine not exceeding five pounds : *Trespassing on aerodromes.*

Provided that no person shall be liable to any penalty under this section unless it is proved that, at the material time, notices warning trespassers of their liability under this section were posted so as to be readily seen and read by members of the public, in such positions on or near the boundary of the aerodrome as appear to the court to be proper.

(2) Part VI of this Act applies to this section.

## Part IV

### Liability for Damage, etc., caused by Aircraft

9. Section 40.—(1) No action shall lie in respect of trespass or in respect of nuisance, by reason only of the flight of an aircraft over any property at a height above the ground, which, having regard to wind, weather and all the circumstances of the case, is reasonable, or the ordinary incidents of such flight so long as the provisions of Part II and this Part of this Act and any Order in Council or order made in pursuance of Part II or this Part of this Act, being provisions which extend to the Colony, are duly complied with. *Liability of aircraft in respect of trespass, nuisance and surface damage.*

(2) Where material loss or damage is caused to any person or property on land or water by, or by a person in, or an article or person falling from, an aircraft while in flight, taking off or landing, then unless the loss or damage was caused or contributed to by the negligence of the person by whom it was suffered, damages in respect of the loss or damage shall be recoverable without proof of negligence or intention or other cause of action, as if the loss or damage had been caused by the wilful act, neglect, or default of the owner of the aircraft :

Provided that where material loss or damage is caused as aforesaid in circumstances in which—

(*a*) damages are recoverable in respect of the said loss or damage by virtue only of the foregoing provisions of this subsection ; and

(*b*) a legal liability is created in some person other than the owner to pay damages in respect of the said loss or damage ;

the owner shall be entitled to be indemnified by that other person against any claim in respect of the said loss or damage.

(3) Part VI of this Act applies to this section.

| | |
|---|---|
| Nuisance caused by aircraft on aerodromes. | 10. Section 41.—(1) An Order in Council under section 8 of this Act may provide for regulating the conditions under which noise and vibration may be caused by aircraft on aerodromes and may provide that subsection (2) of this section shall apply to any aerodrome as respects which provision as to noise and vibration caused by aircraft is so made. |

(2) No action shall lie in respect of nuisance by reason only of the noise and vibration caused by aircraft on an aerodrome to which this subsection applies by virtue of an Order in Council under section 8 of this Act, as long as the provisions of any such Order in Council are duly complied with.

(3) Part VI of this Act applies to this section.

## Part V

### Miscellaneous

| | |
|---|---|
| Application of law of wreck and salvage to aircraft. | 11. Section 51.—(1) Any services rendered in assisting, or in saving life from, or in saving the cargo or apparel of, an aircraft in, on or over the sea or any tidal water, or on or over the shores of the sea or any tidal water, shall be deemed to be salvage services in all cases in which they would have been salvage services if they had been rendered in relation to a vessel ; and where salvage services are rendered by an aircraft to any property or person, the owner of the aircraft shall be entitled to the same reward for those services as he would have been entitled to if the aircraft had been a vessel. |

The foregoing provisions of this subsection shall have effect notwithstanding that the aircraft concerned is a foreign aircraft, and notwithstanding that the services in question are rendered elsewhere than within the limits of the territorial waters adjacent to any part of Her Majesty's dominions.

(2) The Governor may by regulations direct that any provisions of any law of the Colony for the time being in force which relate to wreck, to salvage of life or property or to the duty of rendering assistance to vessels in distress shall, with such exceptions, adaptations and modifications, if any, as may be specified in the regulations, apply in relation to aircraft as those provisions apply in relation to vessels.

(3) For the purposes of this section, any provisions of any law of the Colony which relate to vessels laid by or neglected as unfit for sea service shall be deemed to be provisions relating to wreck.

(4) Part VI of this Act applies to this section.

| | |
|---|---|
| Exemption of aircraft and parts thereof from seizure on patent claims. | 12. Section 53.—(1) Any lawful entry into the Colony or any lawful transit across the Colony, with or without landings, of an aircraft to which this section applies shall not entail any seizure or detention of the aircraft or any proceedings being brought against the owner or operator thereof or any other interference therewith by or on behalf of any person in the Colony, on the ground that the construction, mechanism, parts, accessories or operation of the aircraft is or are an infringement of any patent, design or model. |

(2) The importation into, and storage in, the Colony of spare parts and spare equipment for an aircraft to which this section applies and the use and installation thereof in the repair of such an aircraft shall not entail any seizure or detention of the aircraft or of the spare parts or spare equipment or any proceedings being brought against the owner or operator of the aircraft or the owner of the spare parts or spare equipment or any

other interference with the aircraft by or on behalf of any person in the Colony on the ground that the spare parts or spare equipment or their installation are or is an infringement of any patent, design or model:

Provided that this subsection shall not apply in relation to any spare parts or spare equipment which are sold or distributed in the Colony or are exported from the Colony for sale or distribution.

(3) This section applies—

(*a*) to an aircraft, other than an aircraft used in military, customs or police services, registered in any country or territory in the case of which there is for the time being in force a declaration made by Her Majesty by Order in Council, with a view to the fulfilment of the provisions of the Chicago Convention to which this section relates, that the benefits of those provisions apply to that country or territory, and

(*b*) to such other aircraft as Her Majesty may by Order in Council specify.

(5) Part VI of this Act applies to this section.

# PART VI

## SUPPLEMENTAL

13. Section 57.—(1) Any Order in Council, order or regulation made under any of the enactments to which this Part of this Act applies or this Part of this Act, or any order or regulation made, or instructions given, by the Governor thereunder, may contain such incidental and supplementary provisions as appear to Her Majesty in Council, or to the Governor, as the case may be, to be necessary or expedient for the purposes of the Order in Council, order, regulations or instructions; and any such Order in Council may authorise the Governor to make orders, regulations or to give instructions for the purposes of the Order in respect of such matters as may be specified in the Order.

*Orders in Council.*

(2) An Order in Council made under any of the enactments to which this Part of this Act applies or this Part of this Act shall be subject to annulment in pursuance of a resolution of either House of Parliament and may be revoked or varied by a subsequent Order in Council.

(3) Any reference in the enactments to which this Part of this Act applies or this Part of this Act to the provisions of an Order in Council shall include a reference to the provisions of any order or regulation made, or instructions given, under the Order in Council.

14. Section 58. Any Order in Council, order or regulations made under any enactment to which this Part of this Act applies or this Part of this Act in relation to aircraft may provide for the detention of aircraft to secure compliance with the Order in Council, order or regulations, as the case may be, or with any enactment to which this Part of this Act applies in connection with which the Order in Council, order or regulations is or are made, and may make such further provision as appears to Her Majesty in Council or to the Governor, as the case may be, to be necessary or expedient for securing such detention.

*Detention of aircraft.*

15. Section 59.—(1) Notwithstanding that an Order in Council made by virtue of any enactment to which this Part of this Act applies or this Part of this Act or an order or a regulation made by virtue of any such enactment by the Governor has effect only as part of the law of the Colony, no provision contained in the Order in Council, order or regulation shall,

*Extra-territorial effect.*

on the ground that it would have extra-territorial operation, be deemed to be invalid in so far as it applies to British aircraft registered in the Colony, wherever they may be, or prohibits, requires or regulates—

(a) the doing of anything by persons in, or any of the personnel of, such British aircraft as aforesaid, wherever they may be, or

(b) the doing of anything in relation to such British aircraft as aforesaid by other persons being British subjects, British protected persons or citizens of the Republic of Ireland, wherever they may be.

For the purposes of this subsection the personnel of an aircraft shall be deemed to include the commander or other person in charge of the aircraft, and all other members of the crew of the aircraft.

Nothing in this subsection shall affect subsection (1) of section 3 of the British Nationality Act 1948(a) (which limits the criminal liability of certain persons who are not citizens of the United Kingdom and Colonies).

(2) Her Majesty may by Order in Council direct that any of the following provisions, that is to say—

(a) any enactment to which this Part of this Act applies ; or

(b) any enactment in this Part of this Act ; or

(c) any provision of any Order in Council, order or regulations made by virtue of any such enactment ;

being a provision which has extra-territorial operation in relation to British aircraft registered in the Colony, shall, subject to such exceptions, adaptations and modifications, if any, as may be specified in the Order made under this subsection, have such operation also in relation to British aircraft registered in the United Kingdom or any territory, other than the Colony, mentioned in subsection (1) of section 66 of this Act or registered in the Isle of Man or the Channel Islands.

Offences.    16. Section 60. Any offence under any enactment to which this Part of this Act applies or under an Order in Council or order or regulation made under either any such enactment or this Part of this Act shall, for the purpose of conferring jurisdiction, be deemed to have been committed in any place where the offender may for the time being be.

Savings.    17. Section 61.—(1) Neither this Part of this Act nor any enactment to which this Part of this Act applies shall apply to aircraft belonging to or exclusively employed in the service of Her Majesty:

Provided that Her Majesty may, by Order in Council, apply to any such aircraft, with or without modification, any of the said enactments or any Orders in Council, orders or regulations made thereunder.

(2) Nothing in, or in any instrument made under, the enactments to which this Part of this Act applies or this Part of this Act, shall prejudice or affect the rights, powers or privileges of any general or local lighthouse authority.

## PART VII

### GENERAL

Jurisdiction.    18. Section 62.—(2) The Governor may, by regulations, make provision as to the courts in which proceedings may be taken for enforcing any claim in respect of aircraft, and in particular may provide for conferring jurisdiction in any such proceedings on any court exercising Admiralty jurisdiction and for applying to such proceedings any rules of practice or procedure applicable to proceedings in Admiralty.

(3) Part VI of this Act applies to this section.

(a) 1948 c. 56.

19. Section 63.—(1) In this Act, except where the context otherwise Interpreta-
requires, the following expressions have the meanings hereby respectively tion.
assigned to them, that is to say—

" aerodrome " means any area of land or water designed, equipped,
set apart or commonly used for affording facilities for the landing and
departure of aircraft ;

" British aircraft " means aircraft registered in any part of Her Majesty's
dominions ;

" land " includes any estate or other interest in land and any easement ;

(2) Any reference in this Act to the carrying out of works on land
shall be construed as including a reference to the making of excavations
on the land or to the carrying out of levelling operations on the land,
and references to the maintenance of works or to interference with works
shall be construed accordingly.

(3) For the avoidance of doubt it is hereby declared that in this Act
the expression " loss or damage " includes in relation to persons, loss of
life and personal injury.

(4) Any reference in this Act to goods or articles shall be construed
as including a reference to mails or animals.

(5) Any reference in this Act to any country or territory shall, unless
the context otherwise requires, be construed as including a reference to
the territorial waters, if any, adjacent to that country or territory.

(6) Any power conferred by this Act shall be in addition to and not
in derogation of any other power so conferred.

(8) Any power conferred by this Act to make any Order in Council,
order or regulation shall be construed as including a power exercisable in
the like manner and subject to the like conditions, if any, to vary or
revoke the Order in Council, order or regulation.

(9) References in this Act to any enactment shall, except in so far as
the context otherwise requires, be taken as referring to that enactment as
amended by or under any other enactment.


## SCHEDULE 3 Article 3.

### TERRITORIES TO WHICH THIS ORDER APPLIES

Bahamas
Bermuda
British Antarctic Territory
British Honduras
British Indian Ocean Territory
British Solomon Islands Protectorate
Cayman Islands
Central and Southern Line Islands
Falkland Islands (Colony and Dependencies)
Fiji
Gibraltar
Gilbert and Ellice Islands Colony
Hong Kong
Montserrat
St. Helena and its Dependencies
St. Vincent
Seychelles
Sovereign Base Areas of Akrotiri and Dhekelia
Turks and Caicos Islands
Virgin Islands.

## EXPLANATORY NOTE

*(This Note is not part of the Order.)*

The legislation relating to Civil Aviation (other than the Carriage by Air Act 1932 and legislation concerned with the constitutions and functions of the state controlled Airways Corporations) was consolidated in the Civil Aviation Act 1949, which was applied, with the necessary modifications and adaptations, to overseas dependent territories by the Colonial Civil Aviation (Application of Act) Order 1952. That Order has been amended several times to take account of the many changes of status and constitution which have occurred in relation to dependent territories and former dependent territories. It has also been amended by the Tokyo Convention Act 1967 (Overseas Territories) Order 1968 (S.I. 1968/1844).

The present Order consolidates the previous Orders and also takes account of the repeals contained in the Civil Aviation Act 1968 (c. 61) and the attainment of independence by certain territories ; it excludes from its purview Antigua, Dominica, Grenada, St. Christopher, Nevis and Anguilla, and St. Lucia, which have become Associated States under the provisions of the West Indies Act 1967 (c. 4).

STATUTORY INSTRUMENTS

## 1969 No. 593

## UNITED NATIONS

## The Southern Rhodesia (United Nations Sanctions) (Dominica) Order 1969

| | |
|---|---|
| Made - - - - | 23rd April 1969 |
| Laid before Parliament | 29th April 1969 |
| Coming into Operation | On a day to be appointed under Article 1. |

At the Court at Windsor Castle, the 23rd day of April 1969

Present,

The Queen's Most Excellent Majesty in Council

Whereas under Article 41 of the Charter of the United Nations the Security Council of the United Nations has, by a resolution passed on 29th May 1968, called upon Her Majesty's Government in the United Kingdom and other Members of the United Nations to take certain measures in relation to Southern Rhodesia, including measures relating to trade and dealings in, and the carriage of, goods, the operation of airlines and aircraft, entry into their territories of persons connected with Southern Rhodesia and the promotion of emigration to Southern Rhodesia ;

And Whereas the said resolution reaffirmed, to the extent that it did not supersede, the resolution passed on 16th December 1966 by which the Security Council of the United Nations so called upon Her Majesty's Government in the United Kingdom and other Members of the United Nations to take certain measures in relation to Southern Rhodesia, including measures relating to undertakings in Southern Rhodesia for the manufacture or assembly or aircraft and motor vehicles :

Now, therefore, Her Majesty, in exercise of the powers conferred on Her by section 1 of the United Nations Act 1946(a), is pleased, by and with the advice of Her Privy Council, to order, and it is hereby ordered, as follows :—

*Citation and commencement*

**1.** This Order may be cited as the Southern Rhodesia (United Nations Sanctions) (Dominica) Order 1969, and shall come into operation on such day as the Governor may appoint, which day shall not be earlier than 30th April 1969.

*Importation of certain goods into Dominica*

**2.**—(1) Except under the authority of a licence granted by the Governor, all goods that are exported from Southern Rhodesia after the commencement of this Order are prohibited to be imported into Dominica.

(2) Any person who imports any goods into Dominica in contravention of paragraph (1) of this Article shall be guilty of an offence against this Order.

(a) 1946 c. 45.

(3) Nothing in this Article shall be construed so as to prejudice any other provision of law prohibiting or restricting the importation of goods into Dominica.

*Exportation of goods from Southern Rhodesia*

**3.**—(1) Except under the authority of a licence granted by the Governor, no person shall export any goods from Southern Rhodesia.

(2) Except under such authority as aforesaid no person shall—

(*a*) make or carry out any contract for the exportation of any goods from Southern Rhodesia after the commencement of this Order ; or

(*b*) make or carry out any contract for the sale of any goods which he intends or has reason to believe that another person intends to export from Southern Rhodesia after the commencement of this Order ; or

(*c*) do any act calculated to promote the exportation of any goods from Southern Rhodesia.

(3) Except under such authority as aforesaid, no person shall deal in any goods that have been exported from Southern Rhodesia in contravention of paragraph (1) of this Article, that is to say, shall, by way of trade or otherwise for gain, acquire or dispose of such goods or of any property or interest in them or any right to or charge upon them or process them or do any act calculated to promote any such acquisition, disposal or processing by himself or any other person.

(4) Any person who contravenes the foregoing provisions of this Article shall be guilty of an offence against this Order and, in the case of a person who—

(*a*) is a citizen of the United Kingdom and Colonies or a British subject without citizenship or a British protected person ; or

(*b*) is a citizen of Southern Rhodesia ; or

(*c*) is a body incorporated or constituted under the law of Dominica, Southern Rhodesia, or any country or territory mentioned in Schedule 1 to this Order,

shall be guilty of such an offence wherever the contravention takes place.

(5) Nothing in this Article shall be construed so as to prejudice any other provision of law prohibiting or restricting the exportation of goods from Southern Rhodesia or acts incidental or related thereto.

*Exportation of certain goods from Dominica*

**4.**—(1) Except under the authority of a licence granted by the Governor, all goods are prohibited to be exported from Dominica to Southern Rhodesia.

(2) Any person who exports any goods from Dominica in contravention of paragraph (1) of this Article shall be guilty of an offence against this Order.

(3) Nothing in this Article shall be construed so as to prejudice any other provision of law prohibiting or restricting the exportation of goods from Dominica.

*Supply of goods to Southern Rhodesia*

**5.**—(1) Except under the authority of a licence granted by the Governor, no person shall—

(*a*) supply or deliver or agree to supply or deliver to or to the order of any person in Southern Rhodesia any goods that are not in that country ;

(b) supply or deliver or agree to supply or deliver any such goods to any person, knowing or having reasonable cause to believe that they will be supplied or delivered to or to the order of a person in Southern Rhodesia or that they will be used for the purposes of any business carried on in or operated from Southern Rhodesia ; or

(c) do any act calculated to promote the supply or delivery of any goods in contravention of the foregoing provisions of this paragraph.

(2) Any person who contravenes the foregoing provisions of this Article shall be guilty of an offence against this Order and, in the case of a person who—

(a) is a citizen of the United Kingdom and Colonies or a British subject without citizenship or a British protected person ; or

(b) is a citizen of Southern Rhodesia ; or

(c) is a body incorporated or constituted under the law of Dominica, Southern Rhodesia, or any country or territory mentioned in Schedule 1 to this Order,

shall be guilty of an offence wherever the contravention takes place.

*Carriage of certain goods exported from or destined for Southern Rhodesia*

**6.**—(1) Without prejudice to the generality of Article 3 of this Order, no ship or aircraft to which this Article applies and no land transport vehicle within Dominica shall be used for the carriage of any goods if those goods are being or have been exported from Southern Rhodesia in contravention of Article 3(1) of this Order.

(2) Without prejudice to the generality of Articles 4 and 5 of this Order, no ship or aircraft to which this Article applies and no land transport vehicle within Dominica shall be used for the carriage of any goods if the carriage is, or forms part of, carriage from any place outside Southern Rhodesia to any destination therein or to any person for the purposes of any business carried on in or operated from Southern Rhodesia.

(3) This Article applies to British ships registered in Dominica or any country or territory mentioned in Schedule 1 to this Order, to aircraft so registered or registered in Southern Rhodesia and to any other ship or aircraft that is for the time being chartered to any person who is—

(a) a citizen of the United Kingdom and Colonies or a British subject without citizenship or a British protected person ; or

(b) a citizen of Southern Rhodesia ; or

(c) a body incorporated or constituted under the law of Dominica, Southern Rhodesia, or any country or territory mentioned in Schedule 1 to this Order.

(4) If any ship, aircraft or land transport vehicle is used in contravention of paragraph (1) of this Article, then—

(a) in the case of a British ship registered in Dominica or any country or territory mentioned in Schedule 1 to this Order or any aircraft so registered or registered in Southern Rhodesia, the owner and master of the ship or, as the case may be, the operator and the commander of the aircraft ; or

(b) in the case of any other ship or aircraft, the person to whom the ship or aircraft is for the time being chartered and, if he is such a person as is referred to in sub-paragraph (a) or sub-paragraph (b) or sub-paragraph (c) of paragraph (3) of this Article, the manager or the master of the ship or, as the case may be, the operator or the commander of the aircraft ; or

(c) in the case of a land transport vehicle, the operator of the vehicle,

shall be guilty of an offence against this Order unless he proves that he did not know and had no reason to suppose that the goods were being or had been exported from Southern Rhodesia in contravention of Article 3(1) of this Order.

(5) If any ship, aircraft or land transport vehicle is used in contravention of paragraph (2) of this Article, then—

(a) in the case of a British ship registered in Dominica or any country or territory mentioned in Schedule 1 to this Order or any aircraft so registered or registered in Southern Rhodesia, the owner and the master of the ship or, as the case may be, the operator and the commander of the aircraft ; or

(b) in the case of any other ship or aircraft, the person to whom the ship or aircraft is for the time being chartered and, if he is such a person as is referred to in sub-paragraph (a) or sub-paragraph (b) or sub-paragraph (c) of paragraph (3) of this Article, the manager or the master of the ship or, as the case may be, the operator or the commander of the aircraft ; or

(c) in the case of a land transport vehicle, the operator of the vehicle,

shall be guilty of an offence against this Order unless he proves that he did not know and had no reason to suppose that the carriage of the goods in question was, or formed part of, carriage from any place outside Southern Rhodesia to any destination therein or to any person for the purposes of any business carried on in or operated from Southern Rhodesia.

(6) Nothing in this Article applies to any goods in so far as those goods are being carried for the purposes of the doing of any thing which, by virtue of the grant of any licence or permission, is not prohibited by this Order.

(7) Nothing in this Article shall be construed so as to prejudice any other provision of law prohibiting or restricting the use of ships, aircraft or land transport vehicles.

*Manufacture or assembly in Southern Rhodesia of aircraft or motor vehicles*

**7.**—(1) Except under the authority of a licence granted by the Governor, no person shall—

(a) operate or use any undertaking in Southern Rhodesia, whether established before or after the commencement of this Order, as an undertaking to which this Article applies ; or

(b) authorise any undertaking in Southern Rhodesia to be operated or used by any other person as an undertaking to which this Article applies or give his consent to or connive in or by his neglect contribute to such operation or use.

(2) Except under such authority as aforesaid, no person shall—

(a) establish in Southern Rhodesia any undertaking to which this Article applies ; or

(b) convert any undertaking in Southern Rhodesia into an undertaking to which this Article applies ; or

(c) dispose (whether absolutely or for any lesser interest) of any undertaking in Southern Rhodesia to any other person if he knows or has reasonable cause to believe that that other person intends to use it as an undertaking to which this Article applies ; or

(*d*) acquire (whether absolutely or for any lesser interest) any undertaking in Southern Rhodesia with the intention of using it as an undertaking to which this Article applies ; or

(*e*) dispose (whether absolutely or for any lesser interest) of any property or assets of or forming part of any undertaking in Southern Rhodesia to which this Article applies to any other person otherwise than in the ordinary course of the business of that undertaking or acquire any such property or assets disposed of as aforesaid.

(3) No person shall—

(*a*) make or carry out any contract for any of the following transactions, that is to say :—

    (i) the use or operation of any undertaking or the authorisation of, or the giving of consent to, the use or operation of any undertaking ; or

    (ii) the establishment, conversion, disposal or acquisition of any undertaking ; or

    (iii) the disposal or acquisition of the property or assets of or forming part of any undertaking,

if that transaction would be in contravention of the foregoing provisions of this Article ; or

(*b*) do any other act calculated to promote any such transaction.

(4) The undertakings to which this Article applies are undertakings for the manufacture or assembly of aircraft or motor vehicles.

(5) Any person who contravenes the foregoing provisions of this Article shall be guilty of an offence against this Order and, in the case of a person who—

(*a*) is a citizen of the United Kingdom and Colonies or a British subject without citizenship or a British protected person ; or

(*b*) is a citizen of Southern Rhodesia ; or

(*c*) is a body incorporated or constituted under the law of Dominica or any country or territory mentioned in Schedule 1 to this Order,

shall be guilty of such an offence wherever the contravention takes place.

*Investigation, etc. of suspected British ships and aircraft*

**8.**—(1) Where any authorised officer, that is to say, any such officer as is referred to in section 692(1) of the Merchant Shipping Act 1894(a), has reason to suspect that any British ship registered in Dominica or any country or territory mentioned in Schedule 1 to this Order has been or is being or is about to be used in contravention of paragraph (1) or paragraph (2) of Article 6 of this Order, he may (either alone or accompanied and assisted by persons under his authority) board the ship and search her and, for that purpose, may use or authorise the use of reasonable force, and he may request the master of the ship to furnish such information relating to the ship and her cargo and produce for his inspection such documents so relating and such cargo as he may specify ; and an authorised officer (either there and then or upon consideration of any information furnished or document or cargo produced in pursuance of such a request) may, in the

---

(a) 1894 c. 60.

case of a ship that is reasonably suspected of being or of being about to be used in contravention of Article 6(2) of this Order, exercise the following further powers with a view to the prevention of the commission (or the continued commission) of any such contravention or in order that enquiries into the matter may be pursued, that is to say, he may either direct the master to refrain, except with the consent of an authorised officer, from landing at any port specified by the officer any part of the ship's cargo that is so specified or request the master to take any one or more of the following steps : —

(a) to cause the ship not to proceed with the voyage on which she is then engaged or about to engage until the master is notified by any authorised officer that the ship may so proceed ;

(b) if the ship is then in a port in Dominica or any country or territory mentioned in Schedule 1 to this Order, to cause her to remain there until the master is notified by any authorised officer that the ship may depart ;

(c) if the ship is then in any other place, to take her to any such port specified by the officer and to cause her to remain there until the master is notified as mentioned in sub-paragraph (b) of this paragraph ; and

(d) to take her to any other destination that may be specified by the officer in agreement with the master ;

and the master shall comply with any such request or direction.

(2) Without prejudice to the provisions of paragraph (8) of this Article, where a master refuses or fails to comply with a request made under this Article that his ship shall or shall not proceed to or from any place or where an authorised officer otherwise has reason to suspect that such a request that has been so made may not be complied with, any such officer may take such steps as appear to him to be necessary to secure compliance with that request and, without prejudice to the generality of the foregoing, may for that purpose enter upon, or authorise entry upon, that ship and use, or authorise the use of, reasonable force.

(3) Where the Governor or any person authorised by him for that purpose either generally or in a particular case has reason to suspect that any aircraft registered in Dominica, Southern Rhodesia or any country or territory mentioned in Schedule 1 to this Order has been or is being or is about to be used in contravention of paragraph (1) or paragraph (2) of Article 6 of this Order or of Article 9 of this Order, the Governor or that authorised person may request the operator and the commander of the aircraft or either of them to furnish such information relating to the aircraft and its cargo and produce for his inspection such documents so relating and such cargo as he may specify, and that authorised person may (either alone or accompanied and assisted by persons under his authority) board the aircraft and search it and, for that purpose, may use or authorise the use of reasonable force ; and, if the aircraft is then in Dominica, the Governor or any such authorised person (either there and then or upon consideration of any information furnished or document or cargo produced in pursuance of such a request) may further request the operator and the commander or either of them to cause the aircraft to remain in Dominica until notified that the aircraft may depart ; and the operator and the commander shall comply with any such request.

(4) Without prejudice to the provisions of paragraph (8) of this Article, where the Governor or any person authorised by him, as aforesaid has reason to suspect that any request that an aircraft should remain in Dominica

that has been made under paragraph (3) of this Article may not be complied with, the Governor or that authorised person may take such steps as appear to him to be necessary to secure compliance with that request and, without prejudice to the generality of the foregoing, may for that purpose—

(a) enter, or authorise entry, upon any land and upon that aircraft ;

(b) detain, or authorise the detention of, that aircraft ; and

(c) use, or authorise the use of, reasonable force.

(5) A person authorised by or under the authority of the Governor to exercise any power for the purposes of paragraph (3) or paragraph (4) of this Article shall, if requested to do so, produce evidence of his authority before exercising that power.

(6) No information furnished or document produced by any person in pursuance of a request made under this Article shall be disclosed except—

(a) with the consent of the person by whom the information was furnished or the document was produced :

> Provided that a person who has obtained information or is in possession of a document only in his capacity as servant or agent of another person may not give consent for the purposes of this subparagraph but such consent may instead be given by any person who is entitled to that information or to the possession of that document in his own right ; or

(b) to any person who would have been empowered under this Article to request that it be furnished or produced or to any person holding or acting in any office under or in the service of the Crown in respect of the Government of Dominica or under or in the service of the Government of any country or territory mentioned in Schedule 1 to this Order ; or

(c) with the concurrence of the Government of the United Kingdom, to any organ of the United Nations or to any person in the service of the United Nations or of the Government of any other country for the purpose of assisting the United Nations or that Government in securing compliance with or detecting evasion of measures in relation to Southern Rhodesia decided upon by the Security Council of the United Nations ; or

(d) with a view to the institution of, or otherwise for the purposes of, any proceedings for an offence against this Order or for an offence against any provision of law with respect to similar matters that is for the time being in force in any country or territory mentioned in Schedule 1 to this Order.

(7) Any power conferred by this Article to request the furnishing of information or the production of a document or of cargo for inspection shall include a power to specify whether the information should be furnished orally or in writing and in what form and to specify the time by which and the place in which the information should be furnished or the document or cargo produced for inspection.

(8) The following persons shall be guilty of an offence against this Order, that is to say :—

(a) a master of a ship who disobeys any direction given under paragraph (1) of this Article with respect to the landing of any cargo ; or

(b) a master of a ship or an operator or a commander of an aircraft who without reasonable excuse, refuses or fails within a reasonable time to comply with any request made under this Article by any person empowered to make it or who wilfully furnishes false information or produces false documents to such a person in response to such a request ; or

(c) a master or a member of the crew of a ship or an operator or a commander or a member of the crew of an aircraft who wilfully obstructs any such person (or any person acting under the authority of any such person) in the exercise of his powers under this Article.

(9) Nothing in this Article shall be construed so as to prejudice any other provision of law conferring powers or imposing restrictions or enabling restrictions to be imposed with respect to ships or aircraft.

### Restrictions on the use of certain aircraft

9.—(1) Except under the authority of a licence granted by the Governor no aircraft to which this Article applies shall fly on any flight between any place that is within Southern Rhodesia and any place, whether within or outside Dominica, that is outside Southern Rhodesia for the purpose of carrying passengers or cargo between those places.

(2) The aircraft to which this Article applies are—

(a) aircraft registered in Dominica or any country or territory mentioned in Schedule 1 to this Order ;

(b) aircraft that are not so registered but that are operated by or on behalf of a body incorporated or constituted under the law of any country or territory referred to in sub-paragraph (a) of this paragraph ; and

(c) any other aircraft that is for the time being chartered to any person who is—

    (i) a citizen of the United Kingdom and Colonies or a British subject without citizenship or a British protected person ; or

    (ii) a citizen of Southern Rhodesia ; or

    (iii) a body incorporated or constituted under the law of Dominica or any country or territory mentioned in Schedule 1 to this Order.

(3) If any aircraft is flown in contravention of paragraph (1) of this Article, then—

(a) in the case of an aircraft such as is referred to in sub-paragraph (a) of paragraph (2) of this Article, the operator and the commander of the aircraft ; or

(b) in the case of an aircraft such as is referred to in sub-paragraph (b) of paragraph (2) of this Article, the operator of the aircraft and, if he is a citizen of the United Kingdom and Colonies or a British subject without citizenship or a British protected person or a citizen of Southern Rhodesia, the commander of the aircraft ; or

(c) in the case of an aircraft such as is referred to in sub-paragraph (c) of paragraph (2) of this Article, the person to whom the aircraft is for the time being chartered and, if he is such a person as aforesaid, the operator or the commander of the aircraft,

shall be guilty of an offence against this Order.

### Restrictions on certain air service linking arrangements

10.—(1) Except under the authority of a licence granted by the Governor, no person shall, whether alone or together with any other person or body, make or carry out any arrangement or agreement to which this Article applies.

(2) This Article applies to any arrangement or agreement—

(*a*) for co-ordinating any air transport service provided by means of an aircraft to which Article 9 of this Order applies and which is not a Southern Rhodesian aircraft with any air transport service provided by means of a Southern Rhodesian aircraft ; or

(*b*) whereby a person operating an air transport service by means of an aircraft to which Article 9 of this Order applies and which is not a Southern Rhodesian aircraft provides any civil aviation facility for or on behalf of, or in collaboration or association with, a person operating an aircraft transport service by means of a Southern Rhodesian aircraft, or for the purposes of or in connection with a civil aviation facility provided by any such last-mentioned person.

(3) In this Article—

(*a*) " air transport service " means any carriage of passengers or cargo by air, whether or not for reward, and whether organised on regular schedules or for one or more specific occasions ;

(*b*) " civil aviation facility " means any facility or service provided for the purposes of or in connection with the carriage of passengers or cargo by air or for the purposes of or in connection with the operation of aircraft therefor ; and

(*c*) an aircraft is deemed to be a Southern Rhodesian aircraft if, and only if, it is an aircraft to which Article 9 of this Order applies and—

    (i) it is registered in Southern Rhodesia ; or

    (ii) it is operated by or on behalf of a body incorporated or constituted under the law of Southern Rhodesia ; or

    (iii) it is for the time being chartered to such a body.

(4) Any person who contravenes paragraph (1) of this Article shall be guilty of an offence against this Order and, in the case of a person who—

(*a*) is a citizen of the United Kingdom and Colonies or a British subject without citizenship or a British protected person ; or

(*b*) is a citizen of Southern Rhodesia ; or

(*c*) is a body incorporated or constituted under the law of Dominica or any country or territory mentioned in Schedule 1 to this Order,

shall be guilty of such an offence wherever the contravention takes place.

*Restrictions on entry into Dominica*

**11.**—(1) This Article applies to the following persons, that it is say—

(*a*) any person who, on seeking to enter Dominica, tenders to an immigration officer a document being or purporting to be a current passport or other document establishing a person's identity or nationality issued by, or in the name of, or on behalf of, or under the authority of, the Government of Southern Rhodesia, or the Governor or any Minister of Southern Rhodesia, or any persons or body of persons in Southern Rhodesia exercising or claiming to exercise any governmental functions in relation to that country, by whatever name described (including any person or body of persons claiming to be the Government of that country or to be a Minister or Ministers or any officer of such a Government or otherwise to exercise authority on behalf of such a Government) ; and

(*b*) any person whom the Governor has reason to believe—

    (i) to be ordinarily resident in Southern Rhodesia ; and

    (ii) to have furthered or encouraged or to be likely to further or encourage any unconstitutional action in Southern Rhodesia or any action calculated to evade or contravene or to facilitate the evasion or contravention of this Order or of the Orders revoked by this Order or of any provision of law with respect to similar matters from time to time in force in any country or territory mentioned in Schedule 1 to this Order.

(2) Subject to paragraph (3) of this Article, an immigration officer may, in the case of a person to whom this Article applies who seeks to enter Dominica—

(i) refuse to admit him to Dominica (which refusal shall remain in force until expressly revoked) ; or

(ii) admit him to Dominica subject to a condition restricting the period for which he may remain there, with or without conditions for restricting his employment or occupation.

(3) The power to refuse admission conferred by paragraph (2) of this Article shall not be exercised on any occasion in respect of a person who—

(a) being a woman, satisfies an immigration officer that she is the wife of a person who is resident in Dominica or of a person who enters or seeks to enter Dominica with her ; or

(b) satisfies an immigration officer that he is under the age of sixteen and that at least one of his parents is resident in Dominica or is entering or seeking to enter Dominica with him ;

and the references in this paragraph to a person entering or seeking to enter Dominica shall be construed as not including a person who, on the occasion in question, is refused admission to Dominica.

(4) If any person to whom this Article applies—

(a) enters or remains within Dominica, otherwise than in accordance with the directions or under the authority of an immigration officer, while a refusal of admission under paragraph (2) of this Article is in force in relation to him ; or

(b) contravenes or fails to comply with any conditions imposed on him under that paragraph,

he shall be guilty of an offence and shall be liable on summary conviction to a fine not exceeding 1,000 dollars or to imprisonment for a term not exceeding three months or to both ; and a person convicted of such an offence shall be deemed to be a prohibited immigrant and may be removed from Dominica in accordance with, and subject to the restrictions contained in, the law of Dominica relating to the removal of prohibited immigrants.

(5) Nothing in this Article shall apply to any person who is regarded as belonging to Dominica for the purposes of Chapter I of the Constitution of Dominica ; and nothing in this Article shall be construed as derogating from the powers conferred by any other provision of law in relation to restrictions on the entry to or remaining in Dominica of any person to whom this Article applies.

(6) In this Article—

" immigration officer " means any person who under the law of Dominica is, or has the powers of, an immigration officer and includes any person appointed by the Governor to be an immigration officer for the purposes of this Article ;

" prohibited immigrant " means a person belonging to a category, however described, the members of which are, under the law of Dominica, declared to be prohibited from entry into Dominica (whether or not the prohibition may be raised) and to be liable to deportation from Dominica.

*Restrictions on certain activities promoting emigration to Southern Rhodesia*

**12.**—(1) Except under the authority of a licence granted by the Governor, no person shall—

(a) publish, or be a party to the publication of, any advertisement or any public notice or announcement soliciting or encouraging other persons to take up employment or residence in Southern Rhodesia ; or

(b) do any other act calculated to solicit or encourage members of the public generally or members of any particular class of the public to take up such employment or residence.

(2) Any person who contravenes paragraph (1) of this Article shall be guilty of an offence against this Order unless, in the case of a person who publishes, or is a party to the publication of, an advertisement or a public notice or announcement of such a character as is described in sub-paragraph (a) of that paragraph, he proves that he did not know and could not with reasonable diligence have ascertained that the advertisement, notice or announcement was of that character.

(3) Nothing in paragraph (1)(b) of this Article shall be construed as prohibiting the publication of factual accounts of actions, events, places or things.

*Obtaining of evidence and information*

**13.** The provisions of Schedule 2 to this Order shall have effect in order to facilitate the obtaining, by or on behalf of the Governor, of evidence and information for the purpose of securing compliance with or detecting evasion of this Order and in order to facilitate the obtaining, by or on behalf of the Governor, of evidence of the commission of an offence against this Order.

*Penalties and Proceedings*

**14.**—(1) Any person guilty of an offence against this Order shall be liable—

(a) on conviction before the High Court of the West Indies Associated States to imprisonment for a term not exceeding two years or to a fine or to both ; or

(b) on summary conviction to imprisonment for a term not exceeding six months or to a fine not exceeding 2,500 dollars or to both.

(2) Where any body corporate is guilty of an offence against this Order and that offence is proved to have been committed with the consent or connivance of, or to be attributable to any neglect on the part of, any director, manager, secretary or other similar officer of the body corporate or any person who was purporting to act in any such capacity, he, as well as the body corporate, shall be guilty of that offence and shall be liable to be proceeded against and punished accordingly.

(3) Summary proceedings for an offence against this Order, being an offence alleged to have been committed outside Dominica, may be commenced at any time not later than twelve months from the date on which the person charged first enters Dominica after committing the offence.

(4) Proceedings for an offence against this Order may be taken, and the offence may for all incidental purposes be treated as having been committed, in any place in Dominica where any person charged with that offence is for the time being.

(5) Proceedings for an offence against this Order shall not be instituted in Dominica except by, or with the consent of, the Attorney-General of Dominica :

Provided that this paragraph shall not prevent the arrest, or the issue or execution of a warrant for the arrest, of any person in respect of such an offence, or the remanding in custody or on bail, of any person charged with such an offence, notwithstanding that the necessary consent to the institution of proceedings for the offence has not been obtained.

(6) Nothing in this Article shall apply in respect of an offence under Article 11 of this Order or proceedings for such an offence.

## Exercise of powers of the Governor

**15.**—(1) The Governor may, to such extent and subject to such restrictions and conditions as he may think proper, delegate or authorise the delegation of any of his powers under this Order (other than the power to give authority under Schedule 2 to this Order to apply for a search warrant) to any person, or class or description of persons, approved by him, and references in this Order to the Governor shall be construed accordingly.

(2) Any licences granted under this Order may be either general or special, may be subject to or without conditions, may be limited so as to expire on a specified date unless renewed and may be varied or revoked by the authority that granted them.

## Interpretation

**16.**—(1) In this Order the following expressions have the meanings hereby respectively assigned to them, that is to say:—

" commander ", in relation to an aircraft, means the person designated as commander of the aircraft by the operator thereof, and includes any person who is for the time being in charge or command of the aircraft ;

" dollars " means dollars in the currency of Dominica ;

" Governor " means the Governor or other officer administering the government of Dominica ;

" land transport vehicle " includes a barge ;

" master ", in relation to a ship, includes any person (other than a pilot) for the time being in charge of the ship ;

" operator ", in relation to an aircraft or to a land transport vehicle, means the person for the time being having the management of the aircraft or the vehicle ;

" owner ", in relation to a ship, includes any person for the time being having the management of the ship and any person to whom it is chartered ; and

" person in Southern Rhodesia " includes any body constituted or incorporated under the law of Southern Rhodesia and any body carrying on business (whether within Southern Rhodesia or not) which is controlled by persons or bodies resident in Southern Rhodesia or constituted or incorporated as aforesaid.

(2) In this Order any reference to the holder of an office by a term designating or describing his office shall be construed as including, to the extent of his authority, a reference to any person for the time being authorised to perform the functions of that office.

(3) Any provision of this Order which relates to goods exported from Southern Rhodesia (or to the exportation of goods from Southern Rhodesia) shall not have effect in respect of goods exported (or the exportation of goods) which have only passed through Southern Rhodesia in transit and have not been the subject of any transaction there other than a transaction

relating solely to their transportation ; and any provision of this Order which relates to the exportation of goods to Southern Rhodesia, the supply or delivery of goods to or to the order of any person in Southern Rhodesia or the importation of goods into Southern Rhodesia shall not have effect in relation to goods which are intended only to pass through Southern Rhodesia in transit and not to be the subject of any transaction there other than a transaction relating solely to their transportation.

(4) For the purposes of this Order, the entry into Southern Rhodesia of a vehicle shall not be regarded as constituting the supply or delivery of that vehicle to or to the order of any person in Southern Rhodesia or as constituting its importation into Southern Rhodesia if the entry is merely for the purpose of the vehicle transporting persons into, out of or across Southern Rhodesia or transporting goods across Southern Rhodesia and is not part of or associated with a transaction involving a transfer of the ownership of the vehicle or of any interest therein.

(5) This Order applies to or in relation to any ship or aircraft or any body corporate that purports to be registered in any particular place or, as the case may be, that purports to be incorporated or constituted under the law of that place as it applies to or in relation to any ship or aircraft that is so registered or any body corporate that is so incorporated or constituted.

(6) Any provision of this Order which prohibits the doing of a thing except under the authority of a licence granted by the Governor shall not have effect in relation to any such thing done outside Dominica provided that it is so done under the authority of a licence granted in accordance with any law in force in the United Kingdom (being a law substantially corresponding to the relevant provision of this Order) by the authority competent in that behalf under that law ; and any such provision as aforesaid of this Order shall also not have effect in relation to any such thing—

(a) done in any country or territory (other than the United Kingdom) mentioned in Schedule 1 to this Order ; or

(b) done elsewhere outside Dominica by a person who is ordinarily resident in, or by a body incorporated or constituted under the law of, a country or territory referred to in sub-paragraph (a) of this paragraph,

provided that it is so done under the authority of a licence or with permission granted in accordance with any law in force in that country or territory (being a law substantially corresponding to that provision) by the authority competent in that behalf under that law.

(7) The Interpretation Act 1889(a) shall apply, with the necessary adaptations, for the purpose of interpreting this Order and otherwise in relation thereto as it applies for the purpose of interpreting and in relation to Acts of Parliament.

*Revocation and transitional*

**17.**—(1) The Southern Rhodesia (Prohibited Trade and Dealings) (Overseas Territories) Order 1967(b) and the Southern Rhodesia (Prohibited Trade and Dealings) (Overseas Territories) (Amendment) Order 1967(c) (hereinafter referred to as " the existing Orders ") are revoked in so far as they are part of the law of Dominica.

(2) Without prejudice to the provisions of section 38 of the Interpretation Act 1889 as applied by Article 16 of this Order, references to this Order, or to a particular provision thereof, in Articles 8 and 13 (together with Schedule

---

(a) 1889 c. 63.     (b) S.I. 1967/18 (1967 I, p. 10).     (c) S.I. 1967/248 (1967 I, p. 952).

2) of this Order shall be construed as including references to the existing Orders or, as the case may require, to the corresponding provision of any of the existing Orders.

(3) The references in Articles 3(3) and 6 of this Order to goods that have been exported from Southern Rhodesia in contravention of Article 3(1) of this Order shall be deemed to include references to goods which have been exported from Southern Rhodesia in contravention of Article 4(1) of the Southern Rhodesia (Prohibited Trade and Dealings) (Overseas Territories) Order 1967.

*W. G. Agnew.*

Articles 3, 5, 6, 7, 8, 9 and 10     **SCHEDULE 1**

The United Kingdom.
The Channel Islands.
Isle of Man.
Antigua.
Bahama Islands.
Bahrain.
Bermuda.
British Honduras.
British Solomon Islands Protectorate.
British Virgin Islands.
Brunei.
Cayman Islands.
Cyprus: Sovereign Base Areas of Akrotiri and Dhekelia.
Falkland Islands.
Fiji.
Gibraltar.
Gilbert and Ellice Islands Colony.
Grenada.
Hong Kong.
Montserrat.
New Hebrides.
Qatar.
Seychelles.
Swaziland.
St. Christopher, Nevis and Anguilla.
St. Helena.
St. Lucia.
St. Vincent.
Tonga.
The Trucial States.
Turks and Caicos Islands.

Articles 13 and 15          **SCHEDULE 2**
EVIDENCE AND INFORMATION

1.—(1) Without prejudice to any other provision of this Order, or any provision of any other law, the Governor (or any person authorised by him for that purpose either generally or in a particular case) may request any person in or resident in Dominica to furnish to the Governor (or to that authorised person) any information in his possession or control, or to produce to the Governor (or to that authorised person) any document in his possession or control, which the Governor (or that authorised person) may require for the purpose of securing compliance with or detecting evasion of this Order; and any person to whom such a request is made shall comply with it within such time and in such manner as may be specified in the request.

(2) Nothing in the foregoing sub-paragraph shall be taken to require any person who has acted as counsel or solicitor for any person to disclose any privileged communication made to him in that capacity.

(3) Where a person is convicted before the High Court of the West Indies Associated States for failing to furnish information or produce a document when

requested so to do under this paragraph, the court may make an order requiring him, within such period as may be specified in the order, to furnish the information or produce the document.

(4) The power conferred by this paragraph to request any person to produce documents shall include power to take copies of or extracts from any document so produced and to request that person, or, where that person is a body corporate, any other person who is a present or past officer of, or is employed by, the body corporate, to provide an explanation of any of them.

2.—(1) If any judge of the High Court of the West Indies Associated States, magistrate or justice of the peace is satisfied by information on oath given by a person authorised by the Governor to act for the purposes of this paragraph either generally or in a particular case—

(a) that there is reasonable ground for suspecting that an offence against this Order has been or is being committed and that evidence of the commission of the offence is to be found on any premises specified in the information, or in any vehicle, vessel or aircraft so specified ; or

(b) that any documents which ought to have been produced under paragraph 1 of this Schedule and have not been produced are to be found on any such premises or in any such vehicle, vessel or aircraft,

he may grant a search warrant authorising any police officer, together with any other persons named in the warrant and any other police officers, to enter the premises specified in the information or, as the case may be, any premises upon which the vehicle, vessel or aircraft so specified may be, at any time within one month from the date of the warrant and to search the premises, or, as the case may be, the vehicle, vessel or aircraft.

(2) A person authorised by any such warrant as aforesaid to search any premises or any vehicle, vessel or aircraft may search every person who is found in, or whom he has reasonable ground to believe to have recently left or to be about to enter, those premises or that vehicle, vessel or aircraft and may seize any document or article found on the premises or in the vehicle, vessel or aircraft or on such person which he has reasonable ground to believe to be evidence of the commission of any offence against this Order or any documents which he has reasonable ground to believe ought to have been produced under paragraph 1 of this Schedule or to take in relation to any such article or document any other steps which may appear necessary for preserving it and preventing interference with it:

Provided that no female shall, in pursuance of any warrant issued under this paragraph, be searched except by a female.

(3) Where, by virtue of this paragraph, a person is empowered to enter any premises, vehicle, vessel or aircraft he may use such force as is reasonably necessary for that purpose.

(4) Any documents or articles of which possession is taken under this paragraph may be retained for a period of three months or, if within that period there are commenced any proceedings for an offence against this Order to which they are relevant, until the conclusion of those proceedings.

3. A person authorised by the Governor to exercise any power for the purposes of this Schedule shall, if requested to do so, produce evidence of his authority before exercising that power.

4. No information furnished or document produced (including any copy or extract made of any document produced) by any person in pursuance of a request made under this Schedule and no document seized under paragraph 2(2) of this Schedule shall be disclosed except—

(a) with the consent of the person by whom the information was furnished or the document was produced or the person from whom the document was seized :

Provided that a person who has obtained information or is in possession of a document only in his capacity as servant or agent of another person may not give consent for the purpose of this sub-paragraph but such consent may instead be given by any person who is entitled to that information or to the possession of that document in his own right ; or

(*b*) to any person who would have been empowered under this Schedule to request that it be furnished or produced or to any person holding or acting in any office under or in the service of the Crown in respect of the Government of Dominica or under or in the service of the Government of any country or territory mentioned in Schedule 1 to this Order ; or

(*c*) with the concurrence of the Government of the United Kingdom, to any organ of the United Nations or to any person in the service of the United Nations or to the Government of any other country for the purpose of assisting the United Nations or that Government in securing compliance with or detecting evasion of measures in relation to Southern Rhodesia decided upon by the Security Council of the United Nations ; or

(*d*) with a view to the institution of, or otherwise for the purposes of, any proceedings for an offence against this Order or for an offence against any provision of law with respect to similar matters that is for the time being in force in any country or territory mentioned in Schedule 1 to this Order.

5. Any person who—

(*a*) without reasonable excuse, refuses or fails within the time and in the manner specified (or, if no time has been specified, within a reasonable time) to comply with any request made under this Schedule by any person who is empowered to make it ; or

(*b*) wilfully furnishes false information or a false explanation or otherwise wilfully obstructs any person in the exercise of his powers under this Schedule ; or

(*c*) with intent to evade the provisions of this Schedule, destroys, mutilates, defaces, secretes or removes any document,

shall be guilty of an offence against this Order.

---

## EXPLANATORY NOTE
### (*This Note is not part of the Order.*)

This Order, made under the United Nations Act 1946, revokes the Southern Rhodesia (Prohibited Trade and Dealings) (Overseas Territories) Order 1967 as respects Dominica and replaces, with modifications, the provisions of that Order. It also introduces certain further restrictions and confers certain further powers in connection with Southern Rhodesia.

The Order restricts the importation into Dominica of goods exported from Southern Rhodesia and the exportation from Dominica of goods intended for Southern Rhodesia. It also imposes restrictions on the exportation of goods from Southern Rhodesia and the supply of goods to Southern Rhodesia as well as certain related activities and dealings, including the carriage of goods in British ships or aircraft. The Order imposes restrictions with respect to undertakings in Southern Rhodesia for the manufacture or assembly of aircraft or motor vehicles. It restricts the use of certain aircraft operating to or from Southern Rhodesia and certain related civil aviation transactions. It authorises restrictions upon the entry into Dominica of certain persons connected with Southern Rhodesia and it prohibits certain advertisements and similar activities aimed at encouraging emigration to Southern Rhodesia.

The Order also makes provision for the investigation of ships and aircraft that are suspected of contravening the Order and it confers powers to obtain evidence and information for the purposes of the Order.

# STATUTORY INSTRUMENTS

## 1969 No. 594

## CIVIL AVIATION

## The Civil Aviation Act (Isle of Man) Order 1969

| | |
|---|---|
| *Made* - - - | *23rd April* 1969 |
| *Laid before Parliament* | *29th April* 1969 |
| *Coming into Operation* | *1st May* 1969 |

At the Court at Windsor Castle, the 23rd day of April 1969

Present,

The Queen's Most Excellent Majesty in Council

Her Majesty, in pursuance of the powers conferred upon Her by section 67 of the Civil Aviation Act 1949(a), is pleased, by and with the advice of Her Privy Council, to order, and it is hereby ordered, as follows:—

**1.** This Order may be cited as the Civil Aviation Act (Isle of Man) Order 1969 and shall come into operation on 1st May 1969.

**2.** In Part II of the Schedule to the Civil Aviation Act (Isle of Man) Order 1952(b) (which Schedule specifies the exceptions, adaptations and modifications subject to which the Civil Aviation Act 1949 is extended to the Isle of Man by that Order)—

(a) after paragraph 2 there shall be inserted the following paragraph:—

'2A. In section 8(2)(p) the words "subject to the consent of the Treasury" shall be omitted.';

(b) in paragraph 12 for the words "or the Governor" there shall be substituted the words "or the Manx Board"; and

(c) at the end of paragraph 14(1)(c) there shall be inserted the following sub-paragraph:—

"(d) after the said definition there shall be inserted the following definition:—

' "Manx Board" means the Isle of Man Airports Board;' ".

*W. G. Agnew.*

---

(a) 1949 c. 67.        (b) S.I. 1952/1032 (1952 I, p. 561).

## EXPLANATORY NOTE

*(This Note is not part of the Order.)*

This Order amends the Civil Aviation Act (Isle of Man) Order 1952, which extended the Civil Aviation Act 1949 to the Isle of Man, by removing the requirement of Treasury consent to the prescribing by an Order in Council under the Act of fees to be paid there and by substituting the Isle of Man Airports Board for the Governor as the authority who (in addition to the Board of Trade) may make regulations under such Orders in Council.

# STATUTORY INSTRUMENTS

## 1969 No. 595

## CIVIL AVIATION

## The Air Navigation (Isle of Man) Order 1969

| | |
|---|---|
| *Made* - - - | *23rd April* 1969 |
| *Laid before Parliament* | *29th April* 1969 |
| *Coming into Operation—* | |
| *for making regulations* | *1st May* 1969 |
| *for all other purposes* | *1st June* 1969 |

At the Court at Windsor Castle, the 23rd day of April 1969

Present,

The Queen's Most Excellent Majesty in Council

Her Majesty, in exercise of the powers conferred upon Her by sections 8, 41, 57, 58 and 61 of the Civil Aviation Act 1949(a), as extended to the Isle of Man by the Civil Aviation Act (Isle of Man) Order 1952(b) and the Civil Aviation Act (Isle of Man) Order 1969(c), and of all other powers enabling Her in that behalf, is pleased, by and with the advice of Her Privy Council, to order, and it is hereby ordered, as follows:—

**1.**—(1) This Order may be cited as the Air Navigation (Isle of Man) Order 1969.

(2) This Order shall come into operation—

(*a*) on 1st May 1969, for the purpose of enabling regulations to be made thereunder, and

(*b*) on 1st June 1969, for all other purposes.

**2.**—(1) The Interpretation Act 1889(d) shall apply for the purpose of the interpretation of this Order as it applies for the purpose of the interpretation of an Act of Parliament.

(2) In this Order the expression "Manx Board" means the Isle of Man Airports Board.

**3.**—(1) The Air Navigation Order 1966(e), as amended by the Air Navigation (Amendment) Order 1966(f), the Air Navigation (Second Amendment) Order 1967(g) and the Air Navigation (Third Amendment) Order 1968(h), shall apply in relation to the Isle of Man with the exceptions, modifications and adaptations specified in the Schedule to this Order.

(2) Any certificate, licence or other document issued under, validated by or otherwise in force under the said Order of 1966 shall be deemed to have been issued or validated or to be otherwise in force under that Order as hereby applied in relation to the Isle of Man.

*W. G. Agnew.*

---

(a) 1949 c. 67.
(b) S.I. 1952/1032 (1952 I, p. 561).
(c) S.I. 1969/594 (1969 I, p. 1681).
(d) 1889 c. 63.
(e) S.I. 1966/1184 (1966 III, p. 3073).
(f) S.I. 1966/1408 (1966 III, p. 3769).
(g) S.I. 1967/1678 (1967 III, p. 4592).
(h) S.I. 1968/1857 (1968 III, p. 4883).

SCHEDULE

### EXCEPTIONS, MODIFICATIONS AND ADAPTATIONS OF THE AIR NAVIGATION ORDER 1966 AS AMENDED

1. Any reference to the Civil Aviation Act 1949 shall be construed as a reference to that Act as extended to the Isle of Man by the Civil Aviation Act (Isle of Man) Order 1952 as amended.

2.—(1) Subject to any express substitution made by this Schedule and to sub-paragraph (2) below, any reference to the United Kingdom shall be construed as a reference to the Isle of Man.

(2) The references to the United Kingdom which are not to be so construed are references to Her Majesty's Government in the United Kingdom, to aircraft registered in, or in a country other than, or outside, the United Kingdom, and to a country or state other than the United Kingdom, and references in Article 81(2), in the definitions in Article 83(1) of "the Commonwealth", "Contracting State" and "notified", and in Schedules 9 and 10.

3. Article 2 shall be omitted.

4. In Article 22, at the end of paragraph (3), there shall be added the following words:—

"If the operator has his principal place of business in the Isle of Man, references in the first sentence of this paragraph to the Board shall include the Manx Board".

5. In Article 26(1) for the word "Board" there shall be substituted the words "Manx Board".

6. In Article 36(1)(b) after the word "Board" there shall be inserted the words "or of the Manx Board".

7. In Article 47(7) after the word "Board" there shall be inserted the words "or of the Manx Board".

8. At the end of Article 56 there shall be added the following paragraph:—

"(5) The foregoing provisions of this Article shall apply in relation to aerodrome licences granted by the Manx Board under Article 64 of this Order as if for references to the Board there were substituted references to the Manx Board.".

9.—(1) In Article 59(3) paragraph (b) shall be omitted.

(2) In Article 59(4) for the words from "to the competent authority" to the end there shall be substituted the words "to the Manx Board".

(3) After Article 59(5) there shall be added the following paragraph:—

"(6) The foregoing provisions of this Article shall apply in relation to Rules of the Air and Air Traffic Control in the Isle of Man as if for the reference to the Board in paragraph (1) there were substituted a reference to the Manx Board."

10. At the end of Article 60 there shall be added the following paragraph:—

"(3) The foregoing provisions of this Article shall apply in relation to areas or routes in the Isle of Man as if for references to the Board there were substituted references to the Manx Board.".

11. In Article 61(1) for the word "Board" there shall be substituted the words "Manx Board".

12. In Article 64 for the word "Board" wherever it occurs there shall be substituted the words "Manx Board".

13. In Article 65 for the word "Board" in both places where it occurs there shall be substituted the words "Manx Board".

14. In Article 66 for the word "Board" wherever it occurs there shall be substituted the words "Manx Board".

15. In Article 68 for the word "Board" in both places where it occurs there shall be substituted the words "Manx Board".

16. In Article 70(2) and (4) after the word "Board" wherever it occurs there shall be inserted the words "or the Manx Board".

17.—(1) In Article 71(1) for the word "Board" there shall be substituted the word "Governor", the words "with the concurrence of the Commissioners of Customs and Excise and" shall be omitted and for the word "they" there shall be substituted the word "he".

(2) In Article 71(2) for the word "Board" there shall be substituted the word "Governor" and the words "with the concurrence of the Commissioners of Customs and Excise" shall be omitted.

18. In Article 73 for the word "Board" wherever it occurs there shall be substituted the words "Manx Board".

19. In Article 74 after the word "Board" there shall be inserted the words "the Manx Board".

20. In Article 76 after the word "Board" there shall be inserted the words "by the Manx Board".

21. In Article 77 for the words "The Board may, with the consent of the Treasury," there shall be substituted the words "The Manx Board may".

22. For Article 80 and the heading thereto there shall be substituted the following heading and Article:—

"*Extent of the Order*

80. The provisions of this Order shall apply to all aircraft within the Isle of Man.".

23. In Article 82 for the reference to the Board there shall be substituted a reference to the Manx Board in relation to any provision of this Order where the Manx Board is substituted for the Board by this Order.

24. In Article 83, in paragraph (1)—

(*a*) in the definition of "Air traffic control unit" for the word "Board" there shall be substituted the words "Manx Board";

(*b*) in the definition of "Authorised person" after the word "Board" there shall be inserted the words "the Manx Board or the Governor";

(*c*) after the definition of "Government aerodrome" there shall be inserted the following definition:—

' "Governor" means the Governor, Lieutenant Governor, Deputy Governor, Deputy Lieutenant Governor and acting Governor or acting Lieutenant Governor of the Isle of Man for the time being;';

(*d*) in the definition of "Prescribed" after the word "Board" there shall be inserted the words "or by the Manx Board";

(*e*) after the definition of "Special VFR flight" there shall be inserted the following definition:—

' "Summary conviction" means conviction subject to and in accordance with the Summary Jurisdiction Acts 1927 to 1960, being Acts of Tynwald, and any Acts amending or consolidating those Acts;'.

25. For Article 86(1) there shall be substituted the following paragraph:—

"(1) Subject to the following provisions of this Article, the following Orders, in so far as they apply to the Isle of Man, are hereby revoked, that is to say:—

The Air Navigation (Consolidation) Order 1923(a),
The Air Navigation (Amendment) Order 1925(b),
The Air Navigation (Amendment) Order 1927(c),
The Air Navigation (Amendment) Order 1928(d),
The Air Navigation (Amendment) (No. 2) Order 1928(e),
The Air Navigation (Amendment) (No. 3) Order 1928(f),
The Air Navigation (Amendment) (No. 4) Order 1928(g),
The Air Navigation (Amendment) (No. 2) Order 1929(h),
The Air Navigation (Amendment) (No. 3) Order 1929(i),
The Air Navigation (Amendment) Order 1930(j),
The Air Navigation (Amendment) (No. 2) Order 1930(k),
The Air Navigation (Amendment) (No. 3) Order 1930(l),
The Air Navigation (Amendment) Order 1931(m),
The Air Navigation (Amendment) Order 1932(n),
The Air Navigation (Amendment) (No. 2) Order 1932(o),
The Air Navigation (Amendment) Order 1933(p),
The Air Navigation (Amendment) Order 1934(q),
The Air Navigation (Amendment) (No. 2) Order 1934(r),
The Air Navigation (Amendment) (No. 3) Order 1934(s),
The Air Navigation (Amendment) Order 1935(t),
The Air Navigation (Amendment) Order 1936(u),
The Air Navigation (Isle of Man) (Amendment) Order 1937(v),
The Air Navigation Acts (Extension to the Isle of Man) Order 1938(w),
The Air Navigation (Amendment) (Ministry of Civil Aviation) Order 1945(x)."

26. Article 87(2) shall be omitted.

27. In Schedule 2 (and its heading) the references to Article 2(8) shall be omitted.

28. In Schedule 11 the reference to the Wireless Telegraphy Act 1949(y) shall be construed as a reference to that Act as extended to the Isle of Man by the Wireless Telegraphy (Isle of Man) Order 1952(z).

---

## EXPLANATORY NOTE

### (*This Note is not part of the Order.*)

This Order provides that the provisions of the Air Navigation Order 1966 as amended shall apply, with certain exceptions, adaptations and modifications, to the Isle of Man.

---

(a) S.R. & O. 1923/1508 (1923, p. 13).
(b) S.R. & O. 1925/1260 (1925, p. 4).
(c) S.R. & O. 1927/263 (1927, p. 4).
(d) S.R. & O. 1928/36 (1928, p. 20).
(e) S.R. & O. 1928/588 (1928, p. 26).
(f) S.R. & O. 1928/591 (1928, p. 28).
(g) S.R. & O. 1928/900 (1928, p. 32).
(h) S.R. & O. 1929/984 (1929, p. 59).
(i) S.R. & O. 1929/1001 (1929, p. 60).
(j) S.R. & O. 1930/334 (1930, p. 31).
(k) S.R. & O. 1931/84 (1931, p. 19).
(l) S.R. & O. 1931/85 (1931, p. 21).
(m) S.R. & O. 1931/419 (1931, p. 23).
(n) S.R. & O. 1932/585 (1932, p. 67).
(o) S.R. & O. 1932/851 (1932, p. 77).
(p) S.R. & O. 1933/743 (1933, p. 346).
(q) S.R. & O. 1934/712 (1934 I, p. 123).
(r) S.R. & O. 1934/905 (1934 I, p. 128).
(s) S.R. & O. 1934/1102 (1934 I, p. 130).
(t) S.R. & O. 1935/513 (1935, p. 100).
(u) S.R. & O. 1936/571 (1936 I, p. 61).
(v) S.R. & O. 1937/1065 (Rev. I, p. 1165: 1937, p. 102).
(w) S.R. & O. 1938/1329 (Rev. I, p. 1197: 1938 I, p. 29).
(x) S.R. & O. 1945/1637 (Rev. I, p. 1184: 1945 I, p. 9).
(y) 1949 c. 54.
(z) S.I. 1952/1899 (1952 III, p. 3418).

# STATUTORY INSTRUMENTS

## 1969 No. 596

## CIVIL AVIATION

### The Tokyo Convention Act 1967 (Guernsey) Order 1969

| | |
|---|---|
| *Made* - - - | *23rd April* 1969 |
| *Coming into Operation* | *1st May* 1969 |

At the Court at Windsor Castle, the 23rd day of April 1969

Present,

The Queen's Most Excellent Majesty in Council

Her Majesty, in exercise of the powers conferred upon Her by section 8 of the Tokyo Convention Act 1967(**a**) and of all other powers enabling Her in that behalf, is pleased, by and with the advice of Her Privy Council, to order, and it is hereby ordered, as follows :—

**1.** This Order may be cited as the Tokyo Convention Act 1967 (Guernsey) Order 1969 and shall come into operation on 1st May 1969.

**2.** In this Order the expression "Guernsey" shall mean the Bailiwick of Guernsey and the territorial waters thereof.

**3.** The Interpretation Act 1889(**b**) shall apply for the purpose of the interpretation of this Order as it applies for the purpose of the interpretation of an Act of Parliament.

**4.** Sections 1(1) and (3), 3, 4, 5(1) to (3) and (5), 6(1), 7, 8 and 9(1) and (2) of the Tokyo Convention Act 1967 shall extend to Guernsey with the exceptions, adaptations and modifications specified in the Schedule to this Order.

*W. G. Agnew.*

### SCHEDULE

EXCEPTIONS, ADAPTATIONS AND MODIFICATIONS IN THE
TOKYO CONVENTION ACT 1967

1.—(1) Any reference to the Civil Aviation Act 1949(**c**) shall be construed as a reference to that Act as extended to Guernsey by the Civil Aviation Act (Channel Islands) Order 1953(**d**) and the Civil Aviation (Channel Islands) Order 1966(**e**).

---

(**a**) 1967 c. 52.      (**b**) 1889 c. 63.
(**c**) 1949 c. 67.      (**d**) S.I. 1953/393 (1953 I, p. 270).
(**e**) S.I. 1966/688 (1966 II, p. 1546).

(2) Any reference to the Civil Aviation (Licensing) Act 1960(a) shall be construed as a reference to that Act as extended to Guernsey by the Civil Aviation (Licensing) Act 1960 (Channel Islands) Order 1961(b) and brought into force, as so extended, by the Civil Aviation (Licensing) Act 1960 (Channel Islands) (Commencement) Order 1964(c).

2. In section 1 for the words "the United Kingdom" wherever those words occur there shall be substituted the word "Guernsey".

3.—(1) In section 3(1) for the words "the United Kingdom" there shall be substituted the word "Guernsey".

(2) In section 3(5)(b) for sub-paragraphs (i) and (ii) there shall be substituted the following sub-paragraphs:—

"(i) in Guernsey, to an officer of police or immigration officer ; or

(ii) in any other country which is a Convention country, to an officer having functions corresponding to the functions in Guernsey either of an officer of police or of an immigration officer.".

(3) In section 3(6) for the words "the United Kingdom" in the first two places where those words occur there shall be substituted the word "Guernsey" ;

and for sub-paragraph (i) of paragraph (b) there shall be substituted the following sub-paragraph:—

"(i) where the country in question is Guernsey to an officer of police or immigration officer or, in the case of any other country, to an officer having functions corresponding to the functions in Guernsey either of an officer of police or of an immigration officer ;".

4. In section 4 for the words "the United Kingdom" there shall be substituted the word "Guernsey".

5. In section 5(1) for the words "the United Kingdom" except where those words last occur there shall be substituted the word "Guernsey".

6. In section 6(1) in paragraph (a) after the words "any such Order in Council," there shall be inserted the words "or by the States Board of Administration" and the words "and in Scotland sufficient evidence" shall be omitted.

7.—(1) In section 7(1)—

(i) in paragraph (b)(ii) of the definition of the expression "British-controlled aircraft" for the words "the United Kingdom" there shall be substituted the word "Guernsey" ;

(ii) after the definition of the expression "military aircraft" there shall be inserted the following additional definition:—

"officer of police" means—

(a) in relation to Guernsey, Herm and Jethou, a member of the salaried police force of the Island of Guernsey and, within the limit of his jurisdiction, a member of the special constabulary of the Island of Guernsey ;

(b) in relation to Alderney, a member of the said police force and a member of any police force which may be established by the States of Alderney ; and

(c) in relation to Sark, the Constable, the Vingtenier and a member of the said police force of Guernsey ;".

---

(a) 1960 c. 38.  (b) S.I. 1961/574 (1961 I, p. 1260).
(c) S.I. 1964/1117 (1964 II, p. 2508).

(2) In section 7(2) for the words "the United Kingdom" there shall be substituted the word "Guernsey" and for the words "a constable" there shall be substituted the words "an officer of police".

(3) In section 7(3) for the words "the United Kingdom" in both places where they occur there shall be substituted the word "Guernsey".

(4) For section 7(5) there shall be substituted the following subsection:—

"(5) Any regulations or order made by the Board of Trade under this Act shall not come into force in Guernsey until registered by the Royal Court.".

8. For section 9(2) there shall be substituted the following subsection:—

"(2) This Act and the Civil Aviation Acts 1949 and 1960 may be cited together as the Civil Aviation Acts 1949 to 1967.".

## EXPLANATORY NOTE

*(This Note is not part of the Order.)*

This Order extends the Tokyo Convention Act 1967 to the Bailiwick of Guernsey with exceptions, adaptations and modifications (apart from section 2 (provisions as to extradition) which applies of its own force).

## STATUTORY INSTRUMENTS

### 1969 No. 597

### CIVIL AVIATION

## The Tokyo Convention Act 1967 (Isle of Man) Order 1969

| | |
|---|---|
| *Made* - - - - | *23rd April* 1969 |
| *Coming into Operation* | *1st May* 1969 |

At the Court at Windsor Castle, the 23rd day of April 1969

Present,

The Queen's Most Excellent Majesty in Council

Her Majesty, in exercise of the powers conferred upon Her by section 8 of the Tokyo Convention Act 1967(a) and of all other powers enabling Her in that behalf, is pleased, by and with the advice of Her Privy Council, to order, and it is hereby ordered, as follows:—

**1.** This Order may be cited as the Tokyo Convention Act 1967 (Isle of Man) Order 1969 and shall come into operation on 1st May 1969.

**2.** The Interpretation Act 1889(b) shall apply for the purpose of the interpretation of this Order as it applies for the purpose of the interpretation of an Act of Parliament.

**3.** Sections 1, 3, 4, 5(1) to (3) and (5), 6(1), 7, 8 and 9(1) and (2) of the Tokyo Convention Act 1967 shall extend to the Isle of Man with the exceptions, adaptations and modifications specified in the Schedule to this Order.

*W. G. Agnew.*

### SCHEDULE

EXCEPTIONS, ADAPTATIONS AND MODIFICATIONS IN THE
TOKYO CONVENTION ACT 1967

1.—(1) Any reference to the Civil Aviation Act 1949(c) shall be construed as a reference to that Act as extended to the Isle of Man by the Civil Aviation Act (Isle of Man) Order 1952(d).

(2) Any reference to the Civil Aviation (Licensing) Act 1960(e) shall be construed as a reference to that Act as extended to the Isle of Man by the Civil Aviation (Licensing) Act 1960 (Isle of Man) Order 1961(f) and brought into force, as so extended, by the Civil Aviation (Licensing) Act 1960 (Isle of Man) (Commencement) Order 1964(g).

2.—(1) In section 1(1) for the words "United Kingdom" wherever those words occur there shall be substituted the words "Isle of Man" and the words "or in a part of" and "or in that part of" shall be omitted.

---

(a) 1967 c. 52.
(b) 1889 c. 63.
(c) 1949 c. 67.
(d) S.I. 1952/1032 (1952 I, p. 561).
(e) 1960 c. 38.
(f) S.I. 1961/575 (1961 I, p. 1262).
(g) S.I. 1964/1118 (1964 II, p. 2509).

(2) In section 1(2) for the words "United Kingdom" in both places where those words occur there shall be substituted the words "Isle of Man", the words "or in a part of" shall be omitted and for the words from "or the Civil Aviation (Eurocontrol) Act 1962" to "for Northern Ireland" there shall be substituted the words "shall be instituted except by or with the consent of the Attorney General for the Isle of Man".

(3) In section 1(3) for the words "United Kingdom" in both places where those words occur there shall be substituted the words "Isle of Man" and the words "or in a part of" and "(or, as the case may be, in that part thereof)" shall be omitted.

3.—(1) In section 3(1) for the words "United Kingdom" there shall be substituted the words "Isle of Man".

(2) In section 3(5)(b) for sub-paragraphs (i) and (ii) there shall be substituted the following sub-paragraphs:—
   "(i) in the Isle of Man, to a constable or immigration officer; or
   (ii) in any other country which is a Convention country, to an officer having functions corresponding to the functions in the Isle of Man either of a constable or of an immigration officer.".

(3) In section 3(6) for the words "United Kingdom" in the first two places where those words occur there shall be substituted the words "Isle of Man";
and for sub-paragraph (i) of paragraph (b) there shall be substituted the following sub-paragraph:—
   "(i) where the country in question is the Isle of Man to a constable or immigration officer or, in the case of any other country, to an officer having functions corresponding to the functions in the Isle of Man either of a constable or of an immigration officer;".

4. In section 4 for the words "United Kingdom" there shall be substituted the words "Isle of Man".

5. In section 5(1) for the words "United Kingdom" except where those words last occur there shall be substituted the words "Isle of Man".

6. In section 6(1) in paragraph (a) after the words "any such Order in Council," there shall be inserted the words "or by the Lieutenant Governor or the Isle of Man Airports Board" and the words "and in Scotland sufficient evidence" shall be omitted.

7.—(1) In section 7(1) in paragraph (b)(ii) of the definition of the expression "British-controlled aircraft" for the words "United Kingdom" there shall be substituted the words "Isle of Man".

(2) In section 7(2) for the words "United Kingdom" there shall be substituted the words "Isle of Man".

(3) In section 7(3) the words from "and references to a part" to the end of the subsection shall be omitted.

(4) Section 7(5) shall be omitted.

8. For section 9(2) there shall be substituted the following subsection:—
   "(2) This Act and the Civil Aviation Acts 1949 and 1960 may be cited together as the Civil Aviation Acts 1949 to 1967.".

---

## EXPLANATORY NOTE

*(This Note is not part of the Order.)*

This Order extends the Tokyo Convention Act 1967 to the Isle of Man with exceptions, adaptations and modifications (apart from section 2 (provisions as to extradition) which applies of its own force).

# STATUTORY INSTRUMENTS

## 1969 No. 598

## CIVIL AVIATION

## The Tokyo Convention Act 1967 (Jersey) Order 1969

| | |
|---|---|
| *Made* - - - | *23rd April* 1969 |
| *Coming into Operation* | *1st May* 1969 |

At the Court at Windsor Castle, the 23rd day of April 1969

Present,

The Queen's Most Excellent Majesty in Council

Her Majesty, in exercise of the powers conferred upon Her by section 8 of the Tokyo Convention Act 1967(a) and of all other powers enabling Her in that behalf, is pleased, by and with the advice of Her Privy Council, to order, and it is hereby ordered, as follows :—

**1.** This Order may be cited as the Tokyo Convention Act 1967 (Jersey) Order 1969 and shall come into operation on 1st May 1969.

**2.** In this Order the expression "Jersey" shall mean the Bailiwick of Jersey and the territorial waters thereof.

**3.** The Interpretation Act 1889(b) shall apply for the purpose of the interpretation of this Order as it applies for the purpose of the interpretation of an Act of Parliament.

**4.** Sections 1(1) and (3), 3, 4, 5(1) to (3) and (5), 6(1), 7, 8 and 9(1) and (2) of the Tokyo Convention Act 1967 shall extend to Jersey with the exceptions, adaptations and modifications specified in the Schedule to this Order.

*W. G. Agnew.*

---

(a) 1967 c. 52.  (b) 1889 c. 63.

## SCHEDULE

EXCEPTIONS, ADAPTATIONS AND MODIFICATIONS IN THE

TOKYO CONVENTION ACT 1967

1.—(1) Any reference to the Civil Aviation Act 1949(a) shall be construed as a reference to that Act as extended to Jersey by the Civil Aviation Act (Channel Islands) Order 1953(b) and the Civil Aviation (Channel Islands) Order 1966(c).

(2) Any reference to the Civil Aviation (Licensing) Act 1960(d) shall be construed as a reference to that Act as extended to Jersey by the Civil Aviation (Licensing) Act 1960 (Channel Islands) Order 1961(e) and brought into force, as so extended, by the Civil Aviation (Licensing) Act 1960 (Channel Islands) (Commencement) Order 1964(f).

2. In section 1 for the words "the United Kingdom" wherever those words occur there shall be substituted the word "Jersey" and the words "or in a part of" (in both places), "or in that part of" and "(or, as the case may be, in that part thereof)" shall be omitted.

3.—(1) In section 3(1) for the words "the United Kingdom" there shall be substituted the word "Jersey".

(2) In section 3(5)(b) for sub-paragraphs (i) and (ii) there shall be substituted the following sub-paragraphs:—

"(i) in Jersey, to a police officer or aliens officer ; or

(ii) in any other country which is a Convention country, to an officer having functions corresponding to the functions in Jersey either of a police officer or of an aliens officer.".

(3) In section 3(6) for the words "the United Kingdom" in the first two places where those words occur there shall be substituted the word "Jersey" ;

and for sub-paragraph (i) of paragraph (b) there shall be substituted the following sub-paragraph:—

"(i) where the country in question is Jersey to a police officer or an aliens officer or, in the case of any other country, to an officer having functions corresponding to the functions in Jersey either of a police officer or of an aliens officer ;".

4. In section 4 for the words "the United Kingdom" there shall be substituted the word "Jersey".

5. In section 5(1) for the words "the United Kingdom" except where those words last occur there shall be substituted the word "Jersey".

6. In section 6(1) in paragraph (a) after the words "any such Order in Council," there shall be inserted the words "or by the Harbours and Airports Committee" and the words "and in Scotland sufficient evidence" shall be omitted.

7.—(1) In section 7(1) in paragraph (b)(ii) of the definition of the expression "British-controlled aircraft" for the words "the United Kingdom" there shall be substituted the word "Jersey".

(2) In section 7(2) for the words "the United Kingdom" there shall be substituted the word "Jersey" and for the words "a constable" there shall be substituted the words "a police officer".

---

(a) 1949 c. 67.
(b) S.I. 1953/393 (1953 I, p. 270).
(c) S.I. 1966/688 (1966 II, p. 1546).
(d) 1960 c. 38.
(e) S.I. 1961/574 (1961 I, p. 1260).
(f) S.I. 1964/1117 (1964 II, p. 2508).

(3) In section 7(3) the words from "and references to a part" to the end of the subsection shall be omitted.

(4) For section 7(5) there shall be substituted the following subsection:—

"(5) Any regulations or order made by the Board of Trade under this Act shall not come into force in Jersey until registered by the Royal Court.".

8. For section 9(2) there shall be substituted the following subsection:—

"(2) This Act and the Civil Aviation Acts 1949 and 1960 may be cited together as the Civil Aviation Acts 1949 to 1967.".

---

# EXPLANATORY NOTE

*(This Note is not part of the Order.)*

This Order extends the Tokyo Convention Act 1967 to the Bailiwick of Jersey with exceptions, adaptations and modifications (apart from section 2 (provisions as to extradition) which applies of its own force).

# STATUTORY INSTRUMENTS

## 1969 No. 599

## INCOME TAX

## The Double Taxation Relief (Taxes on Income) (Portugal) Order 1969

*Laid before the House of Commons in draft*

*Made - - - -*          *23rd April* 1969

At the Court at Windsor Castle, the 23rd day of April 1969

Present,

The Queen's Most Excellent Majesty in Council

Whereas a draft of this Order was laid before the Commons House of Parliament in accordance with the provisions of section 347(6) of the Income Tax Act 1952(a), and an Address has been presented to Her Majesty by that House praying that an Order may be made in the terms of this Order:

Now, therefore, Her Majesty, in exercise of the powers conferred upon Her by section 347(1) of the said Income Tax Act 1952, as amended by section 17 of the Finance Act 1961(b) and by section 39 and section 64 of the Finance Act 1965(c), and of all other powers enabling Her in that behalf, is pleased, by and with the advice of Her Privy Council, to order, and it is hereby ordered, as follows:—

**1.** This Order may be cited as the Double Taxation Relief (Taxes on Income) (Portugal) Order 1969.

**2.** It is hereby declared—

   (*a*) that the arrangements specified in the Convention set out in the Schedule to this Order have been made with the Government of Portugal with a view to affording relief from double taxation in relation to income tax, corporation tax or capital gains tax and taxes of a similar character imposed by the laws of Portugal; and

   (*b*) that it is expedient that those arrangements should have effect.

*W. G. Agnew.*

---

(a) 15 & 16 Geo. 6 & 1 Eliz. 2. c. 10.     (b) 9 & 10 Eliz. 2. c. 36.     (c) 1965 c. 25.

## SCHEDULE

CONVENTION BETWEEN THE UNITED KINGDOM OF GREAT BRITAIN AND NORTHERN IRELAND AND PORTUGAL FOR THE AVOIDANCE OF DOUBLE TAXATION AND THE PREVENTION OF FISCAL EVASION WITH RESPECT TO TAXES ON INCOME

The United Kingdom of Great Britain and Northern Ireland and Portugal;
Desiring to conclude a Convention for the avoidance of double taxation and the prevention of fiscal evasion with respect to taxes on income;
Have agreed as follows:

### ARTICLE 1

### Persons Covered

This Convention shall apply to persons who are residents of one or both of the Contracting States.

### ARTICLE 2

### Taxes Covered

(1) The taxes which are the subject of this Convention are:—

(a) In the United Kingdom of Great Britain and Northern Ireland:
  (i) the income tax (including surtax);
  (ii) the capital gains tax; and
  (iii) the corporation tax
  (hereinafter referred to as "United Kingdom tax").

(b) In Portugal:
  (i) the property tax (contribuição predial);
  (ii) the agricultural tax (imposto sobre a indústria agrícola);
  (iii) the industrial tax (contribuição industrial);
  (iv) the tax on income from movable capital (imposto de capitais);
  (v) the professional tax (imposto profissional);
  (vi) the complementary tax (imposto complementar);
  (vii) the tax for overseas defence and development (imposto para a defesa e valorização do Ultramar);
  (viii) the tax on capital gains (imposto de mais-valias);
  (ix) any surcharges on the preceding taxes; and
  (x) other taxes charged by reference to the taxes referred to in heads (i) to (viii) for the benefit of local authorities and the corresponding surcharges (hereinafter referred to as "Portuguese tax").

(2) The Convention shall also apply to any identical or substantially similar future taxes which are imposed in addition to, or in place of, the existing taxes by either Contracting State.

### ARTICLE 3

### General Definitions

(1) In this Convention, unless the context otherwise requires:
  (a) the term "United Kingdom" means Great Britain and Northern Ireland, including any area outside the territorial sea of the United Kingdom which, in accordance with international law, has been or may hereafter be designated, under the laws of the United Kingdom concerning the Continental Shelf, as an area within which the rights of the United Kingdom with respect to the sea bed and sub-soil and their natural resources may be exercised;
  (b) the term "Portugal" means European Portugal comprising the continental territory and the archipelagoes of Azores and Madeira and includes any area outside the territorial sea of Portugal which, in accordance with international law, has been or may hereafter be designated, under the laws of Portugal concerning the Continental Shelf, as an area within which the rights of Portugal with respect to the sea bed and sub-soil and their natural resources may be exercised;

(c) the terms "a Contracting State" and "the other Contracting State" mean the United Kingdom or Portugal as the context requires;

(d) the term "competent authority" means, in the case of the United Kingdom, the Commissioners of Inland Revenue or their authorized representative; in the case of Portugal, the Director-General of Taxation (*Director-Geral das Contribuições e Impostos*) or his authorized representative;

(e) the term "tax" means United Kingdom tax or Portuguese tax as the context requires;

(f) the term "person" comprises an individual, a company and any other body of persons;

(g) the term "company" means any body corporate or any entity which is treated as a body corporate for tax purposes;

(h) the terms "enterprise of a Contracting State" and "enterprise of the other Contracting State" mean respectively an enterprise carried on by a resident of a Contracting State and an enterprise carried on by a resident of the other Contracting State;

(i) the term "international traffic" includes any voyage of a ship or aircraft other than a voyage solely between places in the Contracting State which is not the Contracting State of which a person deriving the profits of the operation of a ship or aircraft is a resident.

(2) Where under the Convention a person is entitled to exemption or relief from tax in a Contracting State on certain income if (with or without further conditions) he is subject to tax in the other Contracting State in respect thereof and he is subject to tax there by reference to the amount of that income which is remitted to, or received in, that other Contracting State the amount of that income on which exemption or relief is to be allowed in the first-mentioned Contracting State shall be limited to the amount so remitted or received.

(3) As regards the application of the Convention by a Contracting State any term not otherwise defined shall, unless the context otherwise requires, have the meaning which it has under the laws of that Contracting State relating to the taxes which are the subject of the Convention.

## ARTICLE 4

### Residence

(1) For the purposes of this Convention, the term "resident of a Contracting State" means any person who, under the law of that State, is liable to taxation therein by reason of his domicile, residence, place of management or any other criterion of a similar nature, and the terms "resident of the United Kingdom" and "resident of Portugal" shall be construed accordingly.

(2) Where by reason of the provisions of paragraph (1) an individual is a resident of both Contracting States, then his status shall be determined in accordance with the following rules:

(a) he shall be deemed to be a resident of the Contracting State in which he has a permanent home available to him. If he has a permanent home available to him in both Contracting States, he shall be deemed to be a resident of the Contracting State with which his personal and economic relations are closest (centre of vital interests);

(b) if the Contracting State in which he has his centre of vital interests cannot be determined, or if he has not a permanent home available to him in either Contracting State, he shall be deemed to be a resident of the Contracting State in which he has an habitual abode;

(c) if he has an habitual abode in both Contracting States or in neither of them, he shall be deemed to be a resident of the Contracting State of which he is a national;

(*d*) if he is a national of both Contracting States or of neither of them, the competent authorities of the Contracting States shall settle the question by mutual agreement.

(3) Where by reason of the provisions of paragraph (1) a person other than an individual is a resident of both Contracting States, then it shall be deemed to be a resident of the Contracting State in which its place of effective management is situated.

## ARTICLE 5

### Permanent Establishment

(1) For the purposes of this Convention, the term "permanent establishment" means a fixed place of business in which the business of the enterprise is wholly or partly carried on.

(2) The term "permanent establishment" shall include especially:

(*a*) a place of management;

(*b*) a branch;

(*c*) an office;

(*d*) a factory;

(*e*) a workshop;

(*f*) a mine, quarry or other place of extraction of natural resources;

(*g*) a building site or construction or assembly project which exists for more than twelve months.

(3) The term "permanent establishment" shall not be deemed to include:

(*a*) the use of facilities solely for the purpose of storage, display or delivery of goods or merchandise belonging to the enterprise;

(*b*) the maintenance of a stock of goods or merchandise belonging to the enterprise solely for the purpose of storage, display or delivery;

(*c*) the maintenance of a stock of goods or merchandise belonging to the enterprise solely for the purpose of processing by another enterprise;

(*d*) the maintenance of a fixed place of business solely for the purpose of purchasing goods or merchandise, or for collecting information, for the enterprise;

(*e*) the maintenance of a fixed place of business solely for the purpose of advertising, for the supply of information, for scientific research or for similar activities which have a preparatory or auxiliary character, for the enterprise.

(4) A person acting in a Contracting State on behalf of an enterprise of the other Contracting State—other than an agent of an independent status to whom paragraph (5) applies—shall be deemed to be a permanent establishment in the first-mentioned State if he has, and habitually exercises in that State, an authority to conclude contracts in the name of the enterprise, unless his activities are limited to the purchase of goods or merchandise for the enterprise.

(5) An enterprise of a Contracting State shall not be deemed to have a permanent establishment in the other Contracting State merely because it carries on business in that other State through a broker, general commission agent or any other agent of an independent status where such persons are acting in the ordinary course of their business.

(6) The fact that a company which is a resident of a Contracting State controls or is controlled by a company which is a resident of the other Contracting State, or which carries on business in that other State (whether through a permanent establishment or otherwise), shall not of itself constitute either company a permanent establishment of the other.

## ARTICLE 6

### Income from Immovable Property

(1) Income from immovable property may be taxed in the Contracting State in which such property is situated.

(2) (a) The term "immovable property" shall, subject to sub-paragraph (b) below, be defined in accordance with the law of the Contracting State in which the property in question is situated.

(b) The term "immovable property" shall in any case include property accessory to immovable property, livestock and equipment used in agriculture and forestry, rights to which the provisions of general law respecting landed property apply, usufruct of immovable property and rights to variable or fixed payments as consideration for the working of, or the right to work, mineral deposits, sources and other natural resources; ships and aircraft shall not be regarded as immovable property.

(3) The provisions of paragraph (1) shall apply to income derived from the direct use, letting, or use in any other form of immovable property. Those provisions shall also apply to income from property which, under the law of the Contracting State in which the property in question is situated, is assimilated to income from immovable property.

(4) The provisions of paragraphs (1) to (3) shall also apply to the income from immovable property of an enterprise and to income from immovable property used for the performance of professional services.

## ARTICLE 7

### Business Profits

(1) The industrial or commercial profits of an enterprise of a Contracting State shall be taxable only in that State unless the enterprise carries on business in the other Contracting State through a permanent establishment situated therein. If the enterprise carries on business as aforesaid, the industrial or commercial profits of the enterprise may be taxed in the other State but only so much of them as is attributable to that permanent establishment.

(2) Where an enterprise of a Contracting State carries on business in the other Contracting State through a permanent establishment situated therein, there shall in each Contracting State be attributed to that permanent establishment the industrial or commercial profits which it might be expected to make if it were a distinct and separate enterprise engaged in the same or similar activities under the same or similar conditions and dealing at arm's length with the enterprise of which it is a permanent establishment.

(3) In the determination of the profits of a permanent establishment, there shall be allowed as deductions expenses which are incurred for the purposes of the permanent establishment including executive and general administrative expenses so incurred, whether in the State in which the permanent establishment is situated or elsewhere, excluding expenses which would not be deductible if the permanent establishment were a separate enterprise.

(4) No profits shall be attributed to a permanent establishment by reason of the mere purchase by that permanent establishment of goods or merchandise for the enterprise.

(5) The term "industrial or commercial profits" means income derived by an enterprise from the conduct of a trade or business, including income derived by an enterprise from the furnishing of services of employees or other personnel and dividends, interest or royalties effectively connected with a trade or business carried on through a permanent establishment which an enterprise of a Contracting State has in the other Contracting State, but the term does not include dividends, interest or royalties not so connected; nor does it include remuneration for personal (including professional) services.

## ARTICLE 8

### Shipping and Air Transport

(1) Profits which a resident of a Contracting State derives from the operation of ships or aircraft in international traffic shall be taxable only in that Contracting State.

(2) The Agreement between the Contracting States for the Avoidance of Double Taxation on Income derived from Sea and Air Transport, signed at Lisbon on 31st July, 1961, shall, in relation to any tax for any period for which the present Convention has effect as respects that tax, cease to have effect so far as it exempts from United Kingdom tax or Portuguese tax, profits derived from the operation of ships or aircraft by, respectively, Portuguese undertakings or United Kingdom undertakings as therein defined.

## ARTICLE 9

### Associated Enterprises

Where

(a) an enterprise of a Contracting State participates directly or indirectly in the management, control or capital of an enterprise of the other Contracting State, or

(b) the same persons participate directly or indirectly in the management, control or capital of an enterprise of a Contracting State and an enterprise of the other Contracting State,

and in either case conditions are made or imposed between the two enterprises in their commercial or financial relations which differ from those which would be made between independent enterprises, then any profits which would, but for those conditions, have accrued to one of the enterprises, but, by reason of those conditions, have not so accrued, may be included in the profits of that enterprise and taxed accordingly.

## ARTICLE 10

### Dividends

(1) Dividends paid by a company which is a resident of a Contracting State to a resident of the other Contracting State may be taxed in that other State.

(2) Dividends paid by a company which is a resident of one Contracting State to a resident of the other Contracting State who is subject to tax in that other State in respect thereof, may be taxed in the first-mentioned State and according to the law of that State but the tax so charged shall not exceed:

(a) 10 per cent of the gross amount of the dividends if:
  (i) the recipient is a company which is a resident of Portugal which controls directly at least 25 per cent of the voting power in the company paying the dividends; or
  (ii) the recipient is a company which is a resident of the United Kingdom which holds directly at least 25 per cent of the capital of the company paying the dividends;

(b) in all other cases, 15 per cent of the gross amount of the dividends.

(3) The term "dividends" as used in this Article means income from shares, "jouissance" shares or "jouissance" rights, mining shares, founders' shares or other rights, not being debt-claims, participating in profits, as well as income from other corporate rights assimilated to income from shares by the taxation law of the State of which the company making the distribution is a resident and, in the case of the United Kingdom, includes any item (other than interest or royalties relieved from United Kingdom tax under Article 11 or Article 12 of this Convention) which under the law of the United Kingdom is treated as a distribution of a company and, in the case of Portugal includes, in addition to profits attributed to members of a partnership, profits attributed under an arrangement for participation in profits (conta em participação).

(4) If the recipient of dividends does not bear tax at a rate exceeding 20 per cent in respect thereof in the Contracting State of which it is a resident and owns 10 per cent or more of the class of shares in respect of which the dividends are paid then paragraph (2) shall not apply to the dividends to the extent that they can have been paid only out of profits which the company paying the dividends earned or other income which it received in a period ending twelve months or more before the relevant date. For the purposes of this paragraph the term "relevant date" means the date on which the recipient of the dividends became the owner of 10 per cent or more of the class of shares in question. Provided that this paragraph shall not apply if the shares were acquired for bona fide commercial reasons and not primarily for the purpose of securing the benefit of this Article.

(5) The provisions of paragraphs (1) and (2) shall not apply if the recipient of the dividends, being a resident of a Contracting State, has in the other Contracting State, of which the company paying the dividends is a resident, a permanent establishment with which the holding by virtue of which the dividends are paid is effectively connected. In such a case, the provisions of Article 7 shall apply.

(6) Where a company which is a resident of a Contracting State derives profits or income from the other Contracting State, that other State may not impose any tax on the dividends paid by the company to persons who are not residents of that other State, or subject the company's undistributed profits to a tax on undistributed profits, even if the dividends paid or the undistributed profits consist wholly or partly of profits or income arising in such other State.

## ARTICLE 11

### Interest

(1) Interest arising in a Contracting State and paid to a resident of the other Contracting State may be taxed in that other State.

(2) However, such interest may be taxed in the Contracting State in which it arises, and according to the law of that State; but where the resident of the other Contracting State is subject to tax there in respect thereof, the tax so charged in the first-mentioned State shall not exceed 10 per cent of the amount of the interest.

(3) The term "interest" as used in this Article means income from Government securities, bonds or debentures, whether or not secured by mortgage and whether or not carrying a right to participate in profits, and debt-claims of every kind as well as all other income assimilated to income from money lent by the taxation law of the State in which the income arises.

(4) The provisions of paragraphs (1) and (2) shall not apply if the recipient of the interest, being a resident of a Contracting State, has in the other Contracting State in which the interest arises a permanent establishment with which the debt-claim from which the interest arises is effectively connected. In such a case, the provisions of Article 7 shall apply.

(5) Interest shall be deemed to arise in a Contracting State when the payer is that State itself, a local authority or a resident of that State. Where, however, the person paying the interest, whether he is a resident of a Contracting State or not, has in a Contracting State a permanent establishment in connection with which the indebtedness on which the interest is paid was incurred, and such interest is borne by such permanent establishment, then such interest shall be deemed to arise in the Contracting State in which the permanent establishment is situated.

(6) Where, owing to a special relationship between the payer and the recipient or between both of them and some other person, the amount of the interest paid, having regard to the debt-claim for which it is paid, exceeds the amount which would have been agreed upon by the payer and the recipient in the absence of such relationship, the provisions of this Article shall apply only to the last-mentioned amount. In that case, the excess part of the payments shall remain taxable according to the law of each Contracting State, due regard being had to the other provisions of this Convention.

ARTICLE 12

**Royalties**

(1) Royalties arising in a Contracting State and paid to a resident of the other Contracting State may be taxed in that other State.

(2) However, such royalties may be taxed in the Contracting State in which they arise, and according to the law of that State; but where the resident of the other Contracting State is subject to tax there in respect thereof, the tax so charged in the first-mentioned State shall not exceed 5 per cent of the gross amount of the royalties.

(3) The term "royalties" as used in this Article means payments of any kind received as a consideration for the use of, or the right to use, any copyright of literary, artistic or scientific work (including cinematograph films and films or tapes for radio or television broadcasting), any patent, trade mark, design or model, plan, secret formula or process, or for the use of, or the right to use, industrial, commercial, or scientific equipment, or for information concerning industrial, commercial or scientific experience and shall include gains derived from the sale or exchange of any right or property giving rise to such royalties.

(4) The provisions of paragraphs (1) and (2) shall not apply if the recipient of the royalties, being a resident of a Contracting State, has in the other Contracting State in which the royalties arise a permanent establishment with which the right or property giving rise to the royalties is effectively connected. In such a case, the provisions of Article 7 shall apply.

(5) Royalties shall be deemed to arise in a Contracting State when the payer is that State itself, a local authority or a resident of that State. Where, however, the person paying the royalties, whether he is a resident of a Contracting State or not, has in a Contracting State a permanent establishment in connection with which the obligation to pay the royalties was incurred, and the royalties are borne by the permanent establishment, then the royalties shall be deemed to arise in the Contracting State in which the permanent establishment is situated.

(6) Where, owing to a special relationship between the payer and the recipient or between both of them and some other person, the amount of the royalties paid, having regard to the use, right or information for which they are paid, exceeds the amount which would have been agreed upon by the payer and the recipient in the absence of such relationship, the provisions of this Article shall apply only to the last-mentioned amount. In that case, the excess part of the payments shall remain taxable according to the law of each Contracting State, due regard being had to the other provisions of this Convention.

ARTICLE 13

**Capital Gains**

(1) Gains from the alienation of immovable property, as defined in paragraph (2) of Article 6, may be taxed in the Contracting State in which such property is situated.

(2) Gains from the alienation of movable property forming part of the business property of a permanent establishment which an enterprise of a Contracting State has in the other Contracting State or of movable property pertaining to a fixed base available to a resident of a Contracting State in the other Contracting State for the purpose of performing professional services, including such gains from the alienation of such a permanent establishment (alone or together with the whole enterprise) or of such a fixed base, may be taxed in the other State.

(3) Notwithstanding paragraph (2) of this Article, gains from the alienation of ships and aircraft operated in international traffic and movable property pertaining to the operation of such ships and aircraft shall be taxable only in the Contracting State of which the alienator is a resident.

(4) Gains from the alienation of any property other than those mentioned in paragraphs (1) and (2), shall be taxable only in the Contracting State of which the alienator is a resident.

## ARTICLE 14

### Independent Personal Services

(1) Income derived by a resident of a Contracting State in respect of professional services or other independent activities of a similar character shall be taxable only in that State unless he has a fixed base regularly available to him in the other Contracting State for the purpose of performing his activities. If he has such a fixed base, the income may be taxed in the other Contracting State but only so much of it as is attributable to that fixed base.

(2) The term "professional services" includes, especially independent scientific, literary, artistic, educational or teaching activities as well as the independent activities of physicians, lawyers, engineers, architects, dentists and accountants.

## ARTICLE 15

### Employments

(1) Subject to the provisions of Article 17, salaries, wages and other similar remuneration (other than remuneration to which Article 18 applies) derived by a resident of a Contracting State in respect of an employment shall be taxable only in that State unless the employment is exercised in the other Contracting State. If the employment is so exercised, such remuneration as is derived therefrom may be taxed in that other State.

(2) Notwithstanding the provisions of paragraph (1), remuneration derived by a resident of a Contracting State in respect of an employment exercised in the other Contracting State shall be taxable only in the first-mentioned State if:

(a) the recipient is present in the other State for a period or periods not exceeding in the aggregate 183 days in the fiscal year concerned, and

(b) the remuneration is paid by, or on behalf of, an employer who is not a resident of the other State, and

(c) the remuneration is not borne by a permanent establishment or a fixed base which the employer has in the other State.

(3) Notwithstanding the preceding provisions of this Article, remuneration in respect of an employment exercised aboard a ship or aircraft in international traffic may be taxed in the Contracting State in which the place of effective management of the enterprise is situated.

## ARTICLE 16

### Artistes and Athletes

Notwithstanding the provisions of Articles 14 and 15, income derived by public entertainers, such as theatre, motion picture, radio or television artistes, and musicians, and by athletes, from their personal activities as such may be taxed in the Contracting State in which these activities are exercised.

## ARTICLE 17

### Pensions

(1) Any pensions and other similar remuneration (other than pensions or remuneration to which Article 18 applies) paid in consideration of past employment to a resident of a Contracting State and any annuity paid to such a resident shall be taxable only in that State.

(2) The term "annuity" means a stated sum payable periodically at stated times during life or during a specified or ascertainable period of time under an obligation to make the payments in return for adequate and full consideration in money or money's worth.

## ARTICLE 18

### Governmental Functions

(1) (*a*) Subject to the provisions of sub-paragraph (*b*) of this paragraph, remuneration or pensions paid out of public funds of the United Kingdom or Northern Ireland or of the funds of any local authority in the United Kingdom to any individual in respect of services rendered to the Government of the United Kingdom or Northern Ireland or a local authority in the United Kingdom in the discharge of functions of a governmental nature, shall be taxable only in the United Kingdom.

(*b*) Where the individual is a Portuguese national without also being a United Kingdom national, sub-paragraph (*a*) of this paragraph shall not apply, but the remuneration or pension shall, for the purposes of Article 22, be deemed to be income from a source within the United Kingdom.

(2) (*a*) Subject to the provisions of sub-paragraph (*b*) of this paragraph, remuneration or pensions paid by, or out of funds created by, Portugal or a local authority thereof to any individual in respect of services rendered to Portugal or a local authority thereof, in the discharge of functions of a governmental nature, shall be taxable only in Portugal.

(*b*) Where the individual is a national of the United Kingdom without also being a Portuguese national, sub-paragraph (*a*) of this paragraph shall not apply, but the remuneration or pension shall, for the purposes of Article 22, be deemed to be income from a source within Portugal.

(3) The provisions of paragraphs (1) and (2) shall not apply to remuneration or pensions in respect of services rendered in connection with any trade or business.

## ARTICLE 19

### Students

(1) Payments which a student or business apprentice who is or was immediately before visiting one of the Contracting States a resident of the other Contracting State and who is present in the first-mentioned Contracting State solely for the purpose of his education or training receives for the purpose of his maintenance, education or training shall not be taxed in the first-mentioned State, provided that such payments are made to him from sources outside that State.

(2) Students attending a university, higher educational establishment or establishment for technical instruction in a Contracting State who take employment in the other Contracting State in order to obtain practical experience directly related to their studies shall not be taxed in that other State on income from that employment unless the duration of that employment exceeds 183 days.

## ARTICLE 20

### Income Not Expressly Mentioned

Items of income of a resident of a Contracting State who is subject to tax there in respect thereof being income of a class or from sources not expressly mentioned in the foregoing Articles of this Convention shall be taxable only in that State. Provided that this Article shall not be construed as affecting the taxation of income attributable to a permanent establishment which a resident of one Contracting State has in the other Contracting State.

## ARTICLE 21

### Personal Allowances

(1) Subject to paragraph (3) of this Article, individuals who are residents of Portugal shall be entitled to the same personal allowances, reliefs and reductions for the purposes of United Kingdom taxation as British subjects not resident in the United Kingdom.

(2) Subject to paragraph (3) of this Article, individuals who are residents of the United Kingdom shall be entitled to the same personal allowances, reliefs and reductions for the purposes of Portuguese tax as Portuguese nationals (other than Portuguese State employees) resident in the United Kingdom.

(3) Nothing in this Convention shall entitle an individual who is a resident of a Contracting State and whose income from the other Contracting State consists solely of dividends, interest or royalties (or solely of any combination thereof) to the personal allowances, reliefs and reductions of the kind referred to in this Article for the purposes of taxation in that other Contracting State.

### ARTICLE 22
### Elimination of Double Taxation

(1) Subject to the provisions of the law of the United Kingdom regarding the allowance as a credit against United Kingdom tax of tax payable in a territory outside the United Kingdom (which shall not affect the general principle hereof), Portuguese tax payable under the laws of Portugal and in accordance with this Convention, whether directly or by deduction, on profits, income or chargeable gains from sources within Portugal (excluding, in the case of a dividend, tax payable in respect of the profits out of which the dividend is paid) shall be allowed as a credit against any United Kingdom tax computed by reference to the same profits, income or chargeable gains by reference to which the Portuguese tax is computed.

(2) For the purposes of paragraph (1) of this Article, the term "Portuguese tax payable" shall be deemed to include any amount which would have been payable as Portuguese tax but for the exemption or reduction of tax granted under—

(a) any of the following provisions, that is to say:
  (i) **Agricultural Tax Code (Decree Law 45104 of 1st July, 1963)**
      Article 350
  (ii) **Industrial Tax Code (Decree Law 45103 of 1st July, 1963)**
      Articles 14 Heads 21 and 22
             18 Heads 8 and 9
             20
             83
  (iii) **Code of the Tax on Income from Movable Capital (Decree Law 44561 of 10th September, 1962)**
      Articles 21 Head 2
             22
  (iv) **Complementary Tax Code (Decree Law 45399 of 30th November, 1963)**
      Articles 8 Sub-head (1) (q)
             35
             85 Head 15
  (v) **Decree Law 46492 of 18th August, 1965**
      Article 27
      so far as they were in force on, and have not been modified since, the date of signature of this Convention, or have been modified only in minor respects so as not to affect their general character;

(b) any other provision which may subsequently be made granting an exemption or reduction which is agreed by the competent authorities of the Contracting States to be of a substantially similar character, if it has not been modified thereafter or has been modified only in minor respects so as not to affect its general character. Provided that relief from United Kingdom tax shall not be given by virtue of this sub-paragraph in respect of income from any source if the income arises in a period starting more than ten years after the exemption from, or reduction of, Portuguese tax was first granted in respect of that source.

(3) United Kingdom tax payable under the laws of the United Kingdom and in accordance with this Convention, whether directly or by deduction, on income or capital gains derived from sources within the United Kingdom by a resident of Portugal

shall be allowed as a deduction from the Portuguese tax payable in respect of that income but the deduction shall not however exceed the smaller of:

(a) the fraction of the United Kingdom tax corresponding to the fraction of such income or capital gains charged to Portuguese tax; or

(b) the proportion of the Portuguese tax before any such deduction which the amount of such income or capital gains charged to Portuguese tax bears to the total income or capital gains chargeable to Portuguese tax.

(4) Where profits on which an enterprise of a Contracting State has been charged to tax in that State are also included in the profits of an enterprise of the other Contracting State and the profits so included are profits which would have accrued to that enterprise of the other Contracting State if the conditions made between each of the enterprises had been those which would have been made between independent enterprises, the amount of such profits included in the profits of both enterprises shall be treated for the purpose of this Article as income from a source in the other Contracting State of the enterprise of the first-mentioned Contracting State and credit shall be given accordingly in respect of the extra tax chargeable in the other Contracting State as a result of the inclusion of the said amount.

(5) For the purposes of this Article, profits or remuneration for personal (including professional) services performed in one of the Contracting States shall be deemed to be income from sources within that State, and the services of an individual whose services are wholly or mainly performed in ships or aircraft shall be deemed to be performed in the Contracting State in which is situated the place of the effective management of the enterprise operating the ships or aircraft.

## ARTICLE 23

### Non-Discrimination

(1) The nationals of a Contracting State shall not be subjected in the other Contracting State to any taxation or any requirement connected therewith which is other or more burdensome than the taxation and connected requirements to which nationals of that other State in the same circumstances are or may be subjected.

(2) The term "nationals" means:

(a) in relation to the United Kingdom:

(i) all citizens of the United Kingdom and Colonies other than those citizens who derive their status as such from connection with any territory to which this Convention may be extended under Article 27 but has not been so extended;

(ii) all legal persons and associations deriving their status as such from the laws of the United Kingdom or any territory for whose international relations the United Kingdom is responsible to which this Convention is extended under Article 27;

(b) in relation to Portugal: all individuals possessing the nationality of Portugal and all legal persons and associations deriving their status as such from the laws of Portugal.

(3) The taxation on a permanent establishment which an enterprise of a Contracting State has in the other Contracting State shall not be less favourably levied in that other State than the taxation levied on enterprises of that other State carrying on the same activities.

(4) Enterprises of a Contracting State, the capital of which is wholly or partly owned or controlled, directly or indirectly, by one or more residents of the other Contracting State, shall not be subjected in the first-mentioned Contracting State to any taxation or any requirement connected therewith which is other or more burdensome than the taxation and connected requirements to which other similar enterprises of that first-mentioned State are or may be subjected.

(5) Nothing contained in this Article shall be construed as obliging either Contracting State to grant to individuals not resident in that State any of the personal allowances, reliefs and reductions for tax purposes which are granted to individuals so resident, nor as restricting the right of either Contracting State to tax in accordance with Article 10 dividends paid to a company which is a resident of the other Contracting State.

## ARTICLE 24

### Mutual Agreement

(1) Where a resident of a Contracting State considers that the actions of one or both of the Contracting States result or will result for him in taxation not in accordance with this Convention, he may, notwithstanding the remedies provided by the national laws of those States, present his case to the competent authority of the Contracting State of which he is a resident.

(2) The competent authority shall endeavour, if the objection appears to it to be justified and if it is not itself able to arrive at an appropriate solution, to resolve the case by mutual agreement with the competent authority of the other Contracting State, with a view to the avoidance of taxation not in accordance with the Convention.

(3) The competent authorities of the Contracting States shall endeavour to resolve by mutual agreement any difficulties or doubts arising as to the interpretation or application of the Convention.

(4) The competent authorities of the Contracting States may communicate with each other directly for the purpose of reaching an agreement in the sense of the preceding paragraphs or for the purpose of giving effect to the provisions of the Convention.

## ARTICLE 25

### Exchange of Information

(1) The competent authorities of the Contracting States shall exchange such information as is necessary for the carrying out of this Convention and of the domestic laws of the Contracting States concerning taxes covered by this Convention insofar as the taxation thereunder is in accordance with this Convention. Any information so exchanged shall be treated as secret and shall not be disclosed to any persons or authorities other than those (including a court or administrative body) concerned with the assessment or collection of, or prosecution in respect of, or the determination of appeals in relation to, the taxes which are the subject of the Convention.

(2) In no case shall the provisions of paragraph (1) be construed so as to impose on one of the Contracting States the obligation:

(a) to carry out administrative measures at variance with the laws or the administrative practice of that or of the other Contracting State;

(b) to supply particulars which are not obtainable under the laws or in the normal course of the administration of that or of the other Contracting State;

(c) to supply information which would disclose any trade, business, industrial, commercial or professional secret or trade process, or information, the disclosure of which would be contrary to public policy (*ordre public*).

(3) The competent authorities of the Contracting States shall notify to each other any changes which have been made in their respective taxation laws.

## ARTICLE 26

### Diplomatic and Consular Officials

Nothing in this Convention shall affect the fiscal privileges of diplomatic or consular officials under the general rules of international law or under the provisions of special agreements.

ARTICLE 27

**Territorial Extension**

(1) This Convention may be extended, either in its entirety or with any necessary modifications, to any territory for whose international relations the United Kingdom is responsible or to any part of Portugal which is implicitly excluded from the application of the Convention where, in either case, taxes are imposed substantially similar in character to those to which the Convention applies. Any such extension shall take effect from such date and subject to such modifications and conditions, as may be specified and agreed between the Contracting States in notes to be exchanged through diplomatic channels.

(2) Unless otherwise agreed by both Contracting States, the denunciation of the Convention by one of them under Article 29 shall terminate, in the manner provided for in that Article, the application of the Convention to any territory or part to which it has been extended under this Article.

ARTICLE 28

**Entry into Force**

(1) This Convention shall be ratified and the instruments of ratification shall be exchanged at London as soon as possible.

(2) The Convention shall enter into force upon the exchange of instruments of ratification(a) and its provisions shall have effect:

(a) In the United Kingdom:

    (i) as respects income tax, surtax and capital gains tax for any year of assessment beginning on or after 6th April in the calendar year next following that in which the Convention enters into force;

    (ii) as respects corporation tax for any financial year beginning on or after 1st April in the calendar year next following that in which the Convention enters into force.

(b) In Portugal:

    as respects Portuguese tax on profits, income or capital gains arising on or after 1st January in the calendar year next following that in which the Convention enters into force.

ARTICLE 29

**Termination**

This Convention shall remain in force until denounced by one of the Contracting States. Either Contracting State may denounce the Convention, through diplomatic channels, by giving notice of termination at least six months before the end of any calendar year after the year 1968. In such event, the Convention shall cease to have effect:

(a) In the United Kingdom:

    (i) as respects income tax, surtax and capital gains tax for any year of assessment beginning on or after 6th April in the calendar year next following that in which the notice is given;

    (ii) as respects corporation tax for any financial year beginning on or after 1st April in the calendar year next following that in which the notice is given.

(b) In Portugal:

    as respects Portuguese tax on profits, income or capital gains arising on or after 1st January in the calendar year next following that in which the notice is given.

(a) Instruments of ratification were exchanged on 17th January 1969.

In witness whereof the undersigned, being duly authorized thereto, have signed this Convention.

Done in duplicate at Lisbon, this 27th day of March 1968, in the English and Portuguese languages, both texts being equally authoritative.

For the United Kingdom of Great Britain and
    Northern Ireland:

ANTHONY LAMBERT

For Portugal:

A. FRANCO NOGUEIRA

---

# EXPLANATORY NOTE
## (*This Note is not part of the Order.*)

Under the Convention with Portugal scheduled to this Order, shipping and air transport profits, certain trading profits not arising through a permanent establishment, pensions (other than Government pensions) and the earnings of temporary business visitors are (subject to certain conditions) to be taxed only in the country of the taxpayer's residence. Capital gains arising from the disposal of movable property are to be taxed only in the country of the taxpayer's residence unless they arise from the disposal of the assets of a permanent establishment which the taxpayer has in the other country. Government salaries and pensions are normally to be taxed by the paying Government only. Payments made for the maintenance, etc., of visiting students are (subject to certain conditions) to be exempt in the country visited.

The rate of tax in the source country on income flowing from one country to the other is, in general, not to exceed 15 per cent in the case of dividends from portfolio investment, 10 per cent in the case of dividends from direct investment and interest, and 5 per cent in the case of royalties.

Where income continues to be taxable in both countries, the country of the taxpayer's residence will relieve the double taxation by giving a credit for the other country's tax. The credit to be given by the United Kingdom includes credit for Portuguese tax which would have been payable but for relief granted under certain provisions of the Portuguese law in order to encourage development there.

There are provisions safeguarding nationals and enterprises of one country against discriminatory taxation in the other country and for the exchange of information and consultation between the taxation authorities of the two countries.

The Convention is to take effect in the United Kingdom for income tax, surtax, corporation tax and capital gains tax in the year following that in which the instruments of ratification are exchanged.

## STATUTORY INSTRUMENTS

### 1969 No. 610

## WAGES COUNCILS

## The Wages Regulation (Coffin Furniture and Cerement-making) Order 1969

| | |
|---|---|
| *Made* - - - | *23rd April* 1969 |
| *Coming into Operation* | 16*th May* 1969 |

Whereas the Secretary of State has received from the Coffin Furniture and Cerement-making Wages Council (Great Britain) the wages regulation proposals set out in the Schedule hereto ;

Now, therefore, the Secretary of State in exercise of her powers under section 11 of the Wages Councils Act 1959(a), and of all other powers enabling her in that behalf, hereby makes the following Order :—

**1.** This Order may be cited as the Wages Regulation (Coffin Furniture and Cerement-making) Order 1969.

**2.**—(1) In this Order the expression "the specified date" means the 16th May 1969, provided that where, as respects any worker who is paid wages at intervals not exceeding seven days, that date does not correspond with the beginning of the period for which the wages are paid, the expression "the specified date" means, as respects that worker, the beginning of the next such period following that date.

(2) The Interpretation Act 1889(b) shall apply to the interpretation of this Order as it applies to the interpretation of an Act of Parliament and as if this Order and the Order hereby revoked were Acts of Parliament.

**3.** The wages regulation proposals set out in the Schedule hereto shall have effect as from the specified date and as from that date the Wages Regulation (Coffin Furniture and Cerement-making) Order 1966(c) shall cease to have effect.

Signed by order of the Secretary of State.

23rd April 1969.

*A. A. Jarratt,*
Deputy Under Secretary of State,
Department of Employment and Productivity.

---

(a) 1959 c. 69.          (b) 1889 c. 63.          (c) S.I. 1966/637 (1966 II, p. 1424).

SCHEDULE Article 3

The following minimum remuneration shall be substituted for the statutory minimum remuneration fixed by the Wages Regulation (Coffin Furniture and Cerement-making) Order 1966 (Order U. (74)).

## STATUTORY MINIMUM REMUNERATION

### PART I

### GENERAL

1. Subject to the provisions relating to guaranteed weekly remuneration set out in paragraph 11, the minimum remuneration payable to a worker to whom this Schedule applies is as follows, that is to say:—

(1) for all work except work to which a minimum overtime rate applies under Part IV—

  (a) in the case of a time worker, the general minimum time rate payable to the worker under the provisions of Part II or Part III of this Schedule,

  (b) in the case of a worker employed on piece work, piece rates each of which would yield, in the circumstances of the case, to an ordinary worker at least the same amount of money as the piece work basis time rate applicable to the worker under the provisions of Part II or Part III of this Schedule;

(2) for all work to which a minimum overtime rate applies under Part IV of this Schedule, that rate.

2. In this Schedule—

  (1) "the coffin furniture section" means that section of the trade specified in paragraph 13 in which there is carried on the manufacture of coffin furniture from any metal by any process, including the operations of packing, warehousing, despatching or other operations incidental to or appertaining to the manufacture of such coffin furniture;

  (2) "the cerement-making section" means that section of the trade specified in paragraph 13 in which there is carried on the manufacture of cerements, including shrouds, face curtains, face cloths, sidecloths, winding sheets, pillow covers, coffin pads, sleeves or frilling, including the operations of folding, packing, warehousing, despatching or other operations incidental to or appertaining to the manufacture of any of the said articles.

### PART II

### COFFIN FURNITURE SECTION

### GENERAL MINIMUM TIME RATES

### MALE WORKERS

3. The general minimum time rates payable to male workers (other than engravers or engravers' assistants) employed in the coffin furniture section are as follows:—

|  | Per hour |
|---|---|
|  | s.   d. |

(1) Workers aged 21 years or over and employed as:—

  (a) Dressers, Planishers (including Wheelers), Platers, Polishers,

  Pressure Die Casters or Stampers—

| | | | | | | | | s. | d. |
|---|---|---|---|---|---|---|---|---|---|
| Grade I | ... | ... | ... | ... | ... | ... | ... | ... | 4 | 11 |
| Grade II | ... | ... | ... | ... | ... | ... | ... | ... | 5 | 1½ |
| Grade III | ... | ... | ... | ... | ... | ... | ... | ... | 5 | 6½ |

Per hour
s.  d.

(b) Gravity Die Casters, Press Workers, Pressure Die Casters' Assistants, Platers' Assistants or Sprayers ... ... ...  4 11

(c) Assemblers, Despatchers, Packers or Warehousemen ... ...  4 10½

(2) All other workers aged 21 years or over (other than engravers or engravers' assistants as aforesaid) ... ... ... ... ... ...  4 10

(3) Workers aged under 21 years, being—

Aged  20 and under 21 years  ... ... ... ... ... ...  3 10½
  „  19  „  „  20  „  ... ... ... ... ... ...  3 8
  „  18  „  „  19  „  ... ... ... ... ... ...  3 5
  „  17  „  „  18  „  ... ... ... ... ... ...  3 1½
  „  16  „  „  17  „  ... ... ... ... ... ...  2 9½
  „  under 16 years  ... ... ... ... ... ...  2 7½

## FEMALE WORKERS

4. The general minimum time rates payable to female workers (other than engravers or engravers' assistants) employed in the coffin furniture section are as follows:—

Per hour
s.  d.

(1) Workers aged 21 years or over, being—

(a) Polishers, Blackers, Die Casters, Heavy Hand Press Workers, Power Press Workers, Heavy Machine Workers, Lace Cutters, Platers, Spray Painters and Lacquerers or Stampers ... ...  4 2

(b) Assemblers, Drillers, Fettlers, Light Hand Press Workers, Light Machine Workers, Packers, Platers' Assistants, Tappers, Viewers, or Warehouse and Despatch Workers ... ... ... ...  3 11½

(2) Workers aged under 21 years, being—

Aged  20 and under 21 years  ... ... ... ... ... ...  3 10
  „  19  „  „  20  „  ... ... ... ... ... ...  3 8½
  „  18  „  „  19  „  ... ... ... ... ... ...  3 5
  „  17  „  „  18  „  ... ... ... ... ... ...  2 11½
  „  16  „  „  17  „  ... ... ... ... ... ...  2 8½
  „  under 16 years  ... ... ... ... ... ...  2 6½

Provided that the general minimum time rate payable during her first six months' work in the said section to a worker who enters, or has entered, the section for the first time at or over the age of 18 years shall be 1d. per hour less than the rate otherwise payable under (1) or (2) of this paragraph.

## PIECE WORK BASIS TIME RATE

## MALE OR FEMALE WORKERS

5. The piece work basis time rate applicable to a male or female worker (other than an engraver or an engraver's assistant) employed on piece work in the coffin furniture section is a rate which is equal to the general minimum time rate which would be payable if the worker were a time worker, increased by 15 per cent.

## Part III

## CEREMENT-MAKING SECTION

### GENERAL MINIMUM TIME RATES

### FEMALE WORKERS

6. The general minimum time rates payable to female workers employed in the cerement-making section are as follows:—

|  | Per hour |
|---|---|
|  | s.   d. |

(1) Workers other than Pinkers or Choppers, being—

| | Per hour |
|---|---|
| Aged 21 years or over ...   ...   ...   ...   ...   ... | 3   11½ |
| „   20 and under 21 years   ...   ...   ...   ...   ... | 3   10 |
| „   19 „    „ 20 „   ...   ...   ...   ...   ... | 3   8½ |
| „   18 „    „ 19 „   ...   ...   ...   ...   ... | 3   5 |
| „   17 „    „ 18 „   ...   ...   ...   ...   ... | 2   11½ |
| „   16 „    „ 17 „   ...   ...   ...   ...   ... | 2   8½ |
| „   under 16 years   ...   ...   ...   ...   ... | 2   6½ |

(2) Pinkers or Choppers—the rate appropriate to the worker's age under (1) of this paragraph increased by 10 per cent.:

Provided that the general minimum time rate payable during her first six months' work in the said section to a worker who enters, or has entered, the section for the first time at or over the age of 18 years shall be 1d. per hour less than the rate otherwise payable under (1) or (2) of this paragraph.

### PIECE WORK BASIS TIME RATE

### FEMALE WORKERS

7. The piece work basis time rate applicable to a female worker employed on piece work in the cerement-making section is a rate equal to the general minimum time rate which would be payable if the worker were a time worker, increased by 15 per cent.

## Part IV

## OVERTIME AND WAITING TIME IN BOTH SECTIONS OF THE TRADE

### MINIMUM OVERTIME RATES

8. Subject to the provisions of this Part of this Schedule, minimum overtime rates are payable to any worker as follows:—

(1) On any day in the week other than a Saturday, Sunday or customary holiday—

| | |
|---|---|
| (a) for the first 2 hours worked in excess of *8 hours* ... | time-and-a-quarter |
| (b) for the next 2 hours so worked   ...   ...   ... | time-and-a-half |
| (c) thereafter ...   ...   ....   ...   ...   ... | double time |

(2) On a Saturday, not being a customary holiday—

| | |
|---|---|
| for the first 2 hours worked   ...   ...   ... | time-and-a-quarter |
| for the next 2 hours   ...   ...   ...   ... | time-and-a-half |
| thereafter   ...   ...   ...   ...   ... | double time |

(3) On a Sunday or a customary holiday—

| | |
|---|---|
| for all time worked   ...   ...   ...   ... | double time |

Provided that where the employer normally requires the worker's attendance on Sunday and not on Saturday (except where in the case of a woman or young person such attendance on Sunday is unlawful) for the purposes of this Part of this Schedule Saturday shall be treated as a Sunday and Sunday as a Saturday.

9. In this Part of this Schedule—

(1) The expression "customary holiday" means—

    (a)  (i) In England and Wales—

Christmas Day (or, if Christmas Day falls on a Sunday, such weekday as may be appointed by national proclamation, or, if none is so appointed, the next following Tuesday), Boxing Day, Good Friday, Easter Monday, Whit Monday, August Bank Holiday and two other days (being days on which the worker normally works) in the course of a calendar year, to be fixed by the employer and notified to the worker not less than three weeks before the holiday;

       (ii) in Scotland—

New Year's Day (or, if New Year's Day falls on a Sunday, the following Monday);

the local Spring holiday;

the local Autumn holiday; and

five other days (being days on which the worker normally works) in the course of a calendar year, to be fixed by the employer and notified to the worker not less than three weeks before the holiday;

or (b) in the case of each of the said days (other than a day fixed by the employer and notified to the worker as aforesaid) a day substituted therefor, being either a day recognised by local custom as a day of holiday in substitution for the said day or a day fixed by agreement between the employer and the worker or his representative.

(2) The expressions "time-and-a-quarter", "time-and-a-half" and "double time" mean respectively—

    (a) in the case of a time worker, one and a quarter times, one and a half times and twice the general minimum time rate otherwise payable to the worker;

    (b) in the case of a worker employed on piece work—

      (i) a time rate equal respectively to one quarter, one half and the whole of the general minimum time rate which would be payable to the worker if he were a time worker, and a minimum overtime rate did not apply, and, in addition thereto,

      (ii) the piece rates otherwise applicable to the worker under paragraph 1(1)(b).

## WAITING TIME

10.—(1) A worker is entitled to payment of the minimum remuneration specified in this Schedule for all time during which he is present on the premises of the employer, unless he is present thereon in any of the following circumstances, that is to say:—

    (a) without the employer's consent, express or implied;

    (b) for some purpose unconnected with his work and other than that of waiting for work to be given to him to perform;

    (c) by reason only of the fact that he is resident thereon; or

    (d) during normal meal times in a room or place in which no work is being done, and he is not waiting for work to be given to him to perform.

(2) The minimum remuneration payable under sub-paragraph (1) of this paragraph to a piece worker when not engaged on piece work is that which would be payable if he were a time worker.

## Part V

## GUARANTEED WEEKLY REMUNERATION

11.—(1) This paragraph applies to a worker who ordinarily works for the employer for at least 34 hours weekly on work to which statutory minimum remuneration applies under the provisions of this Schedule.

(2) Notwithstanding the foregoing provisions of this Schedule, where in any week

(a) no remuneration is payable to the worker under the foregoing provisions of this Schedule, or by way of holiday remuneration under any wages regulation order made by the Secretary of State to give effect to the proposals of the Council,

or

(b) the total amount of any such remuneration is less than the guaranteed weekly remuneration provided for by this Part of this Schedule,

the minimum remuneration payable to that worker for that week, in lieu of any amount aforesaid, shall, subject to the provisions of this paragraph, be the guaranteed weekly remuneration.

(3) The amount of the guaranteed weekly remuneration is 34 hours' pay calculated at the general minimum time rate ordinarily payable to the worker.

(4) Payment of the guaranteed weekly remuneration in any week is subject to the condition that the worker throughout the period of his ordinary employment in that week, excluding any day allowed to him as a holiday, is—

(a) capable of and available for work; and

(b) willing to perform such duties outside his normal occupation as the employer may reasonably require if his normal work is not available to him in the establishment in which he is employed.

(5) The guaranteed weekly remuneration shall not be payable to a worker

(a) in any week in which work is not available to him by reason of a strike or lock-out; or

(b) in any week in which the worker has been dismissed on the grounds of serious misconduct; or

(c) if at any time in the week the worker is absent from work by reason of sickness; or

(d) if at any time in the week or during the preceding four weeks the worker has been otherwise absent from work without the leave of the employer.

(6) The amount of the guaranteed weekly remuneration applicable to a piece worker shall be the sum to which he would be entitled if he were a time worker.

## Part VI

## INTERPRETATION

12.—(1) In paragraph 3 the expressions "Grade I", "Grade II" and "Grade III" have the following meanings:—

(a) in the case of a Dresser—

"Grade I" means a worker employed on dressing who is not of Grade II or III.

"Grade II" means a worker who has not had less than one year's experience as a dresser and who turns, screws inside and out, files flat and squares at the vice and finishes his work throughout.

"Grade III" means a worker who has had more than three years' experience as a dresser and who, in addition to fulfilling the conditions of Grade II, is an expert in all processes, or is a charge hand responsible for all work and order in the shop.

(*b*) in the case of a Planisher or Wheeler—

"Grade I" means a worker employed on planishing or wheeling who is not of Grade II or III.

"Grade II" means a worker who has had not less than one year's experience as a planisher or wheeler and is an expert in all processes and is able to do good class work.

"Grade III" means a worker who has had more than three years' experience as a planisher or wheeler and who, in addition to fulfilling the conditions of Grade II, is employed in making mitred breast plates or handle plates of any design.

(*c*) in the case of a Plater—

"Grade I" means a worker employed as a plater who is not of Grade II or III.

"Grade II" means a worker who has had not less than one year's experience as a plater and is able to work vats satisfactorily without supervision or is skilled in oxydising and relieving.

"Grade III" means a worker who has had more than three years' experience as a plater and who, in addition to fulfilling the conditions of Grade II, is qualified to make up his own solutions and is an expert in all processes, or is a charge hand responsible for all work and order in the shop.

(*d*) in the case of a Polisher—

"Grade I" means a worker employed as a polisher who is not of Grade II or III.

"Grade II" means a worker who has had not less than one year's experience as a polisher and is expert in all processes of any class of common work and can emery-bob and mop best work.

"Grade III" means a worker who has had more than three years' experience as a polisher and who, in addition to fulfilling the conditions of Grade II, is an expert in all processes of both common and best work, or is a charge hand responsible for all work and order in the shop.

(*e*) in the case of a Pressure Die Caster—

"Grade I" means a worker employed on pressure die casting who is not of Grade II or III.

"Grade II" means a worker who has had not less than one year's experience as a pressure die caster and is able to work correctly any modern type of die casting machine and to insert and remove his own dies.

"Grade III" means a worker who has had more than three years' experience as a pressure die caster and who, in addition to fulfilling the conditions of Grade II, is an expert in all processes without supervision, or is a charge hand responsible for all work and order in the shop.

(*f*) in the case of a Stamper—

"Grade I" means a worker employed on stamping who is not of Grade II or III.

"Grade II" means a worker who has had not less than one year's experience as a stamper and is an expert in all processes and undertakes all classes of work of all strengths of metal used.

"Grade III" means a worker who has had more than three years' experience as a stamper and, in addition to fulfilling the conditions of Grade II, is an expert in all classes of stamping, pressing and cutting out by hand, or is a charge hand responsible for all work and order in the shop.

(2) For the purposes of paragraph 4:—

(*a*) "a heavy hand press worker" is a worker employed on hand press work on any blank of which the largest diameter is 7 inches or over and the thickness of the material 48/1000ths of an inch or over;

(*b*) "a light hand press worker" is a worker employed on any other hand press work.

(3) For the purposes of paragraphs 3 and 4:—

(a) "plater" means a worker employed in a plating shop who works with plating solutions;

(b) "plater's assistant" means a worker employed in a plating or spraying department who is normally employed in wiring up or jigging and who does not work with plating solutions.

## APPLICABILITY OF STATUTORY MINIMUM REMUNERATION

13. This Schedule does not apply to any worker employed in engraving or in assisting a worker so employed or to a male worker employed in the cerement-making section of the trade, but, save as aforesaid, this Schedule applies to workers in relation to whom the Coffin Furniture and Cerement-making Wages Council (Great Britain) operates, that is to say, workers employed in Great Britain in the Coffin Furniture and Cerement-making trade specified in the Regulations with respect to the Constitution and Proceedings of the Trade Board for the Coffin Furniture and Cerement-making Trade (Great Britain) made by the Minister of Labour and dated 16th December 1919(a), that is to say:—

(a) the manufacture wherever carried on of Coffin Furniture from any metal by any process;

(b) the manufacture of Cerements, including shrouds, face curtains, face cloths, sidecloths, winding sheets, pillow covers, coffin pads, sleeves or frilling;

including:

(c) the operations of folding, packing, warehousing, despatching or other operations incidental to or appertaining to the manufacture of any of the above-mentioned articles.

---

## EXPLANATORY NOTE

*(This Note is not part of the Order.)*

This Order, which has effect from 16th May 1969, sets out the statutory minimum remuneration payable in substitution for that fixed by the Wages Regulation (Coffin Furniture and Cerement-making) Order 1966 (Order U. (74)), which Order is revoked.

New provisions are printed in italics.

---

(a) S.R. & O. 1919/2222 (1919 II, p. 544).

# STATUTORY INSTRUMENTS

## 1969 No. 611

## WAGES COUNCILS

## The Wages Regulation (Coffin Furniture and Cerement-making) (Holidays) Order 1969

| | |
|---|---|
| *Made* - - - | *23rd April* 1969 |
| *Coming into Operation* | *16th May* 1969 |

Whereas the Secretary of State has received from the Coffin Furniture and Cerement-making Wages Council (Great Britain) the wages regulation proposals set out in the Schedule hereto ;

Now, therefore, the Secretary of State in exercise of her powers under section 11 of the Wages Councils Act 1959(a), and of all other powers enabling her in that behalf, hereby makes the following Order :—

**1.** This Order may be cited as the Wages Regulation (Coffin Furniture and Cerement-making) (Holidays) Order 1969.

**2.**—(1) In this Order the expression "the specified date" means the 16th May 1969, provided that where, as respects any worker who is paid wages at intervals not exceeding seven days, that date does not correspond with the beginning of the period for which the wages are paid, the expression "the specified date" means, as respects that worker, the beginning of the next such period following that date.

(2) The Interpretation Act 1889(b) shall apply to the interpretation of this Order as it applies to the interpretation of an Act of Parliament and as if this Order and the Order hereby revoked were Acts of Parliament.

**3.** The wages regulation proposals set out in the Schedule hereto shall have effect as from the specified date and as from that date the Wages Regulation (Coffin Furniture and Cerement-making) (Holidays) Order 1966(c) shall cease to have effect.

Signed by order of the Secretary of State.

23rd April 1969.

*A. A. Jarratt,*
Deputy Under Secretary of State,
Department of Employment and Productivity.

Article 3        SCHEDULE

The following provisions as to holidays and holiday remuneration shall be substituted for the provisions as to holidays and holiday remuneration set out in the Wages Regulation (Coffin Furniture and Cerement-making) (Holidays) Order 1966 (hereinafter referred to as "Order U. (75)").

---

(a) 1959 c. 69.             (b) 1889 c. 63.

(c) S.I. 1966/638 (1966 II, p. 1433).

Part I

## APPLICATION

1. This Schedule applies to every worker (other than an out-worker) for whom statutory minimum remuneration has been fixed.

Part II

## CUSTOMARY HOLIDAYS

2.—(1) An employer shall allow to every worker to whom this Schedule applies a holiday (hereinafter referred to as a "customary holiday") in each year on the days specified in the following sub-paragraph, provided that the worker has been in his employment for a period of not less than eight weeks immediately preceding the customary holiday and has worked for the employer during the whole or part of that period and (unless excused by the employer or absent by reason of the proved illness of the worker) has worked for the employer throughout the last working day on which work was available to him immediately prior to the customary holiday.

(2) The said customary holidays are:—

(a) (i) in England and Wales—
Christmas Day (or, if Christmas Day falls on a Sunday, such weekday as may be appointed by national proclamation, or, if none is so appointed, the next following Tuesday), Boxing Day, Good Friday, Easter Monday, Whit Monday, August Bank Holiday and two other days (being days on which the worker normally works) in the course of a calendar year, to be fixed by the employer and notified to the worker not less than three weeks before the holiday;

(ii) in Scotland—
New Year's Day (or, if New Year's Day falls on a Sunday, the following Monday);
the local Spring holiday;
the local Autumn holiday; and
five other days (being days on which the worker normally works) in the course of a calendar year, to be fixed by the employer and notified to the worker not less than three weeks before the holiday; or

(b) in the case of each of the said days (other than a day fixed by the employer and notified to the worker as aforesaid) a day substituted therefor, being either a day recognised by local custom as a day of holiday in substitution for the said day, or a day agreed between the employer and the worker or his representative.

(3) Notwithstanding the preceding provisions of this paragraph, an employer may (except where in the case of a woman or young person such a requirement would be unlawful) require a worker who is otherwise entitled to any customary holiday under the foregoing provisions of this Schedule to work thereon and, in lieu of any customary holiday on which he so works, the employer shall allow to the worker a day's holiday (hereinafter referred to as a "holiday in lieu of a customary holiday") on a weekday on which he would normally work for the employer, within the period of four weeks next ensuing.

(4) A worker who is required to work on a customary holiday shall be paid:—

(a) for all time worked thereon at the minimum rate then appropriate to the worker for work on a customary holiday; and

(b) in respect of the holiday in lieu of the customary holiday, holiday remuneration in accordance with paragraph 6.

## Part III

## ANNUAL HOLIDAY

3.—(1) Subject to the provisions of paragraph 4, in addition to the holidays specified in Part II of this Schedule an employer shall between *6th April 1969* and 30th September 1969, and between *6th April* and 30th September in each succeeding year, allow a holiday (hereinafter referred to as an "annual holiday") to every worker in his employment to whom this Schedule applies who has been employed by him during the 12 months immediately preceding the commencement of the holiday season for any of the periods set out in the table below and the duration of the annual holiday shall in the case of each such worker be related to his period of employment during that 12 months as follows:—

| Period of employment | | Duration of annual holiday for workers with a normal working week of: | |
|---|---|---|---|
| | | Five days | Four days or less |
| At least 48 weeks .. .. .. .. .. | | 10 days | 8 days |
| „ „ 44 „ .. .. .. .. .. .. | | 9 „ | 7 „ |
| „ „ 40 „ .. .. .. .. .. .. | | 8 „ | 6 „ |
| „ „ 36 „ .. .. .. .. .. .. | | 7 „ | 6 „ |
| „ „ 32 „ .. .. .. .. .. .. | | 6 „ | 5 „ |
| „ „ 28 „ .. .. .. .. .. .. | | 5 „ | 4 „ |
| „ „ 24 „ .. .. .. .. .. .. | | 5 „ | 4 „ |
| „ „ 20 „ .. .. .. .. .. .. | | 4 „ | 3 „ |
| „ „ 16 „ .. .. .. .. .. .. | | 3 „ | 2 „ |
| „ „ 12 „ .. .. .. .. .. .. | | 2 „ | 2 „ |
| „ „ 8 „ .. .. .. .. .. .. | | 1 day | 1 day |
| „ „ 4 „ .. .. .. .. .. .. | | 1 „ | — |

(2) Notwithstanding the provisions of the last foregoing sub-paragraph the number of days of annual holiday which an employer is required to allow to a worker in any holiday season shall not exceed in the aggregate twice the number of days constituting the worker's normal working week.

(3) The duration of the worker's annual holiday in the holiday season in 1969 shall be reduced by any days of annual holiday duly allowed to him by the employer under the provisions of Order U.(75) between 6th April 1969 and the date on which the provisions of this Schedule become effective.

(4) In this Schedule the expression "holiday season" means in relation to an annual holiday during the year 1969, the period commencing on *6th April 1969*, and ending on 30th September 1969, and in relation to each subsequent year the period commencing on *6th April* and ending on 30th September in that year.

4.—(1) An annual holiday under the Schedule shall be allowed on consecutive working days, being days on which the worker is normally called upon to work for the employer, and days of annual holiday shall be treated as consecutive notwithstanding that a customary holiday on which the worker is not required to work for the employer, a holiday in lieu of a customary holiday or a day upon which the worker is not normally called upon to work for the employer intervenes:

Provided that where the duration of an annual holiday which an employer is required to allow to a worker exceeds the number of days constituting the worker's normal working week the said holiday may be allowed in two separate periods of such consecutive working days, and in that event, notwithstanding the foregoing provisions of this Schedule, the annual holiday shall be allowed as follows:—

(*a*) as to one period which, together with any day of customary holiday allowed at the same time, shall not be less than the number of days constituting the worker's normal working week, during the holiday season;

(b) as to the other period, during the holiday season or before *6th April* immediately following the holiday season;

(c) where either period of holiday includes a day of customary holiday, and the total number of days of holiday is equal to the number of days constituting the worker's normal working week, one day of annual holiday may be allowed on a non-consecutive working day during the holiday season or before *6th April*, as the case may be.

(2) Subject to the provisions of sub-paragraph (1) of this paragraph, any day of annual holiday under this Schedule may be allowed on a day on which the worker is entitled to a day of holiday or to a half-holiday under any enactment other than the Wages Councils Act 1959.

5. An employer shall give to a worker reasonable notice of the commencing date or dates and duration of the period or periods of his annual holiday. Such notice shall be given at least 28 days before the first day of the holiday and may be given individually to the worker or by the posting of a notice in the place where the worker is employed.

PART IV

HOLIDAY REMUNERATION

A—CUSTOMARY HOLIDAYS AND HOLIDAYS IN LIEU OF
CUSTOMARY HOLIDAYS

6.—(1) For each day of holiday to which a worker is entitled under Part II of this Schedule he shall be paid by the employer holiday remuneration equal to the appropriate statutory minimum remuneration to which he would have been entitled as a time worker if the day had not been a day of holiday and he had been employed on work for which statutory minimum remuneration is payable as follows:—

(a) where the worker is normally employed for more than 30 hours a week, for 8 hours, or

(b) where the worker is normally employed for 30 hours a week or less, for 4 hours:

Provided, however, that payment of the said holiday remuneration is subject to the condition that the worker presents himself for employment not later than half an hour after the usual starting hour on the first working day following the holiday, and works his normal hours of work on that day or, if he fails to do so, failure is by reason of the proved illness of the worker or with the consent of the employer.

(2) Where a worker normally works on every weekday in the week except Saturday, he shall be paid the sum equivalent to the holiday remuneration in respect of any Saturday in respect of which he would have been entitled to a holiday under Part II of this Schedule if it had been a day on which he had normally worked:

Provided, however, that payment of the said sum is subject to the condition that the worker presents himself for employment not later than half an hour after the usual starting hour on the first working day following that Saturday, and works his normal hours of work on that day or, if he fails to do so, failure is by reason of the proved illness of the worker or with the consent of the employer.

(3) The holiday remuneration in respect of any customary holiday shall be paid by the employer to the worker not later than the pay day on which the wages for the pay week including the first working day following the customary holiday are paid.

(4) The holiday remuneration in respect of any holiday in lieu of a customary holiday shall be paid not later than the pay day on which the wages for the pay week including the first working day following the holiday in lieu of a customary holiday are paid:

Provided that the said payment shall be made immediately upon the termination of the worker's employment in the case where he ceases to be employed before being allowed a holiday in lieu of a customary holiday to which he is entitled, and in that case the proviso contained in sub-paragraph (1) of this paragraph shall not apply.

## B—ANNUAL HOLIDAY

7.—(1) Subject to the provisions of paragraph 8, a worker qualified to be allowed an annual holiday under this Schedule shall be paid as holiday remuneration by his employer on the last pay day preceding such annual holiday or preceding each period of such annual holiday:—

(a) *in the case of male piece workers aged 21 years or over employed in the coffin furniture section of the trade as dressers, planishers (including wheelers), platers, polishers, pressure die casters or stampers in Grades I, II or III; gravity die casters, press workers, pressure die casters' assistants, platers' assistants or sprayers; or assemblers, despatchers, packers or warehousemen in respect of each day of annual holiday:—*

*one day's holiday pay as defined in paragraph 11 but as if the words "increased by fifty per cent" were inserted after the words "appropriate rate of statutory minimum remuneration", and*

(b) *in the case of all other workers, whichever of the following amounts is the greater:—*

(i) *an amount equal to two fifty-seconds of the total remuneration paid by the employer to the worker during the twelve months ended on 5th April immediately preceding the holiday, or*

(ii) one day's holiday pay (as defined in paragraph 11) in respect of each day of annual holiday.

(2) Where under the provisions of paragraph 4 an annual holiday is allowed in more than one period the holiday remuneration shall be apportioned accordingly.

8. Where any accrued holiday remuneration has been paid by the employer to the worker in accordance with paragraph 9 of this Schedule or in accordance with the provisions of Order U.(75), in respect of employment during any of the periods referred to in that paragraph or that Order respectively, the amount of holiday remuneration payable by the employer in respect of any annual holiday for which the worker has qualified by reason of employment during the said period shall be reduced by the amount of the said accrued holiday remuneration unless that remuneration has been deducted from a previous payment of holiday remuneration made under the provisions of this Schedule or of Order U.(75).

## ACCRUED HOLIDAY REMUNERATION PAYABLE ON TERMINATION OF EMPLOYMENT

9. Where a worker ceases to be employed after the provisions of this Schedule become effective, the employer shall, immediately on the termination of the employment, pay to the worker as accrued holiday remuneration:—

(1) in respect of employment in the 12 months *up to and including the immediately preceding 5th April*, a sum equal to the holiday remuneration for any days of annual holiday for which he has qualified, except days of annual holiday which he has been allowed or has become entitled to be allowed before leaving the employment; and

(2) in respect of any employment since the *said 5th April*, a sum equal to the holiday remuneration which would have been payable to him if he could have been allowed an annual holiday in respect of that employment at the time of leaving it.

## PART V

## GENERAL

10. For the purpose of calculating any period of employment qualifying a worker for an annual holiday or for any accrued holiday remuneration under this Schedule, the worker shall be treated:—

(1) as if he were employed for a week in respect of any week in which—

(a) he has worked for the employer and has performed some work for which statutory minimum remuneration is payable;

(b) he has been absent throughout the week solely by reason of the proved illness of, or accident to, the worker, provided that the number of weeks which may be treated as weeks of employment for such reason shall not exceed eight in the aggregate in the period of 12 months immediately preceding the commencement of the holiday season;

(c) he is absent from work throughout the week owing to suspension due to shortage of work, provided that the number of weeks which may be treated as weeks of employment for such reason shall not exceed eight in the aggregate in any such period as aforesaid;

(2) as if he were employed on any day of holiday allowed under the provisions of this Schedule, and for the purposes of the provisions of sub-paragraph (1) of this paragraph, a worker who is absent on such a holiday shall be treated as having worked thereon for the employer for the number of hours ordinarily worked by him on that day of the week on work for which statutory minimum remuneration is payable.

11. In this Schedule, unless the context otherwise requires, the following expressions have the meanings hereby respectively assigned to them, that is to say:—

"normal working week" means the number of days on which it has been usual for the worker to work in a week in the employment of the employer during the 12 months immediately preceding the commencement of the holiday season or, where under paragraph 9 accrued holiday remuneration is payable on the termination of the employment, during the 12 months immediately preceding the date of the termination of the employment:

Provided that—

(1) part of a day shall count as a day;

(2) no account shall be taken of any week in which the worker did not perform any work for which statutory minimum remuneration has been fixed.

"one day's holiday pay" means the appropriate proportion of the remuneration which the worker would be entitled to receive from his employer at the date of the annual holiday (or where the holiday is allowed in more than one period at the date of each period) or at the termination date, as the case may require, for one week's work if working his normal working week and the number of daily hours normally worked by him (exclusive of overtime) and if paid as a time worker at the appropriate rate of statutory minimum remuneration for work for which statutory minimum remuneration is payable and at the same rate for any work for which such remuneration is not payable, and in this definition "appropriate proportion" means—

where the worker's normal working week is five days     ...     one-fifth
where the worker's normal working week is four days or less ...     one-quarter.

"statutory minimum remuneration" means minimum remuneration (other than holiday remuneration) fixed by a wages regulation order made by the Secretary of State to give effect to proposals submitted to her by the Council.

*"total remuneration"* means any payments paid or payable to the worker under his contract of employment for time worked or piece work done by him, holiday remuneration, any productivity, long service or other bonus payable to the worker on a weekly, fortnightly or monthly basis and merit payments so payable but does not include any other payments.

"week" in paragraphs 3 and 10 means "pay week".

12. The provisions of this Schedule are without prejudice to any agreement for the allowance of any further holidays with pay or for the payment of additional holiday remuneration.

---

# EXPLANATORY NOTE

*(This Note is not part of the Order.)*

This Order, which has effect from 16th May 1969, sets out the holidays which an employer is required to allow to workers and the remuneration payable to such workers for those holidays in substitution for the holidays and holiday remuneration fixed by the Wages Regulation (Coffin Furniture and Cerement-making) (Holidays) Order 1966 (Order U. (75)), which Order is revoked.

New provisions are printed in italics.

## STATUTORY INSTRUMENTS

## 1969 No. 618

## EDUCATION, ENGLAND AND WALES

## The Remuneration of Teachers (Primary and Secondary Schools) Order 1969

| | | |
|---|---|---|
| *Made* - - - - - | | *29th April* 1969 |
| *Coming into Operation* | | *30th April* 1969 |

Whereas—

(1) in pursuance of section 2(2) of the Remuneration of Teachers Act 1965(a) (hereinafter referred to as "the Act") the Committee constituted under section 1 of the Act for the purpose of considering the remuneration of teachers in primary and secondary schools maintained by local education authorities (hereinafter referred to as "the Committee") have transmitted to the Secretary of State for Education and Science (hereinafter referred to as "the Secretary of State") recommendations agreed on by them with respect to the remuneration of such teachers;

(2) in pursuance of section 2(3) of the Act, the Secretary of State has prepared a draft document setting out the scales and other provisions required for determining the remuneration of teachers of the description aforesaid in the form in which, in his opinion, those scales and provisions should be so as to give effect to those recommendations;

(3) the Secretary of State, as required by section 2(4) of the Act, has consulted the Committee with respect to the draft document and made such modifications thereof as were requisite for giving effect to representations made by the Committee; and

(4) the Secretary of State has arranged for a document setting out the requisite scales and other provisions in the form of the draft as modified as aforesaid to be published by Her Majesty's Stationery Office on 28th April 1969 under the title "SCALES OF SALARIES FOR TEACHERS IN PRIMARY AND SECONDARY SCHOOLS, ENGLAND AND WALES, 1969".

Now therefore the Secretary of State, in pursuance of section 2(4) of the Act, hereby orders as follows:—

### Citation and Commencement

**1.** This Order may be cited as the Remuneration of Teachers (Primary and Secondary Schools) Order 1969 and shall come into operation on 30th April 1969.

(a) 1965 c. 3.

*Interpretation*

**2.** The Interpretation Act 1889(a) shall apply for the interpretation of this Order as it applies for the interpretation of an Act of Parliament.

*Remuneration of Teachers*

**3.** The remuneration payable from 1st April 1969 to teachers in primary and secondary schools maintained by local education authorities shall be determined in accordance with the scales and other provisions set out in the document published by Her Majesty's Stationery Office as aforesaid.

*Revocation*

**4.** The Remuneration of Teachers (Primary and Secondary Schools) Order 1967(b), the Remuneration of Teachers (Primary and Secondary Schools) Amending Order 1968(c) and the Remuneration of Teachers (Primary and Secondary Schools) (Amendment No. 2) Order 1968(d) are hereby revoked and section 38(2) of the Interpretation Act 1889 (which relates to the effect of repeals) shall have effect in relation to those Orders as if they were enactments repealed by an Act.

Given under the Official Seal of the Secretary of State for Education and Science on 29th April 1969.

    (L.S.)                            *Edward Short,*
                            Secretary of State for Education and Science.

---

### EXPLANATORY NOTE

*(This Note is not part of the Order.)*

This Order brings into operation the scales and other provisions relating to the remuneration of teachers in primary and secondary schools maintained by local education authorities set out in a document published by Her Majesty's Stationery Office. This document contains the recommendations of the Committee constituted under the Remuneration of Teachers Act 1965 for the purpose of considering the remuneration of such teachers.

The Order has effect from 1st April 1969 by virtue of section 7(3) of the Act.

---

(a) 1889 c. 63.                (b) S.I. 1967/1305 (1967 III, p. 3916).
(c) S.I. 1968/375 (1968 I, p. 1029).     (d) S.I. 1968/1799 (1968 III, p. 4813).

## 1969 No. 619

## SOCIAL SECURITY

## The National Insurance (Industrial Injuries) (Prescribed Diseases) Amendment Regulations 1969

|  |  |
|---|---|
| *Made -  -  -  -* | *29th April* 1969 |
| *Laid before Parliament* | *2nd May* 1969 |
| *Coming into Operation* | *26th May* 1969 |

The Secretary of State for Social Services, in exercise of his powers under sections 56 and 85 of the National Insurance (Industrial Injuries) Act 1965(**a**) and section 57 of that Act as modified by section 8 of the National Insurance Act 1966(**b**) and of all other powers enabling him in that behalf, after reference to the Industrial Injuries Advisory Council, hereby makes the following regulations : —

*Citation, interpretation and commencement*

**1.** These regulations, which may be cited as the National Insurance (Industrial Injuries) (Prescribed Diseases) Amendment Regulations 1969, shall be read as one with the National Insurance (Industrial Injuries) (Prescribed Diseases) Regulations 1959(**c**), as amended(**d**) (hereinafter referred to as " the principal regulations "), and shall come into operation on 26th May 1969.

*Amendment of Part I of Schedule 1 to the principal regulations*

**2.** Part I of Schedule 1 to the principal regulations, shall be amended by the addition at the end of the first and second columns thereof, respectively, of the disease, hereinafter referred to as " nasal adeno-carcinoma ", specified in the first column of the Schedule hereto and of the occupations set against the said disease in the second column of that Schedule.

*Transitional provisions*

**3.**—(1) Where a person, who has been employed on or at any time after 5th July 1948 in insurable employment in any occupation referred to in the second column of the Schedule hereto, is, as the result of nasal adeno-carcinoma, either incapable of work or suffering from a loss of faculty on the date on which these regulations come into operation, and the disease is due to the nature of the employment, the provisions of regulation 6 of the principal regulations (which relates to the date of development) shall be applied subject to the modification that the date on which these regulations come into operation shall be treated as the first day on which he was incapable of work or, as the case may be, as the day on which he first suffered from the relevant loss of faculty, and the date of development shall be determined accordingly.

(2) Where a person to · whom the last foregoing paragraph applies is awarded disablement benefit in respect of nasal adeno-carcinoma and claims

(**a**) 1965 c. 52.      (**b**) 1966 c. 6.      (**c**) S.I. 1959/467 (1959 II, p. 1943).
(**d**) The relevant amending instruments are S.I. 1965/1264; 1966/987 (1965 II, p. 3596; 1966 II, p. 2366).

an increase of that benefit under section 14 of the National Insurance (Industrial Injuries) Act 1965 (which section relates to increases of disablement pension in cases of special hardship) then, if at any time after having been employed as aforesaid but before the date on which these regulations come into operation that person has abandoned any occupation as a result of the disease, the fact that he has abandoned that occupation shall be disregarded in determining his regular occupation for the purposes of the said section 14.

Signed by authority of the Secretary of State for Social Services.

*David Ennals,*
Minister of State,
Department of Health and Social Security.

29th April 1969.

Regulation 2                            SCHEDULE

| Description of disease or injury | Nature of occupation |
|---|---|
| 45. Adeno-carcinoma of the nasal cavity or associated air sinuses. | Any occupation involving: attendance for work in or about a building where wooden furniture is manufactured. |

## EXPLANATORY NOTE

*(This Note is not part of the Regulations.)*

These Regulations, by making an addition to the diseases prescribed in Part I of Schedule 1 to the National Insurance (Industrial Injuries) (Prescribed Diseases) Regulations 1959, extend insurance under the National Insurance (Industrial Injuries) Act 1965 to adeno-carcinoma of the nasal cavity or associated air sinuses in the case of persons insurably employed in certain occupations connected with the manufacture of wooden furniture.

The Regulations also contain transitional provisions relating to persons who are already suffering from the disease on the date when these Regulations come into operation.

STATUTORY INSTRUMENTS

## 1969 No. 620

## INDUSTRIAL TRAINING

## The Industrial Training Levy (Civil Air Transport) Order 1969

| | |
|---|---|
| *Made* - - - | *24th April* 1969 |
| *Laid before Parliament* | *6th May* 1969 |
| *Coming into Operation* | *14th May* 1969 |

The Secretary of State after approving proposals submitted by the Civil Air Transport Industry Training Board for the imposition of a further levy on employers in the civil air transport industry and in exercise of her powers under section 4 of the Industrial Training Act 1964(a) and of all other powers enabling her in that behalf hereby makes the following Order :—

*Title and commencement*

**1.** This Order may be cited as the Industrial Training Levy (Civil Air Transport) Order 1969 and shall come into operation on 14th May 1969.

*Interpretation*

**2.**—(1) In this Order unless the context otherwise requires :—

(*a*) "Air Corporation" means the British Overseas Airways Corporation or the British European Airways Corporation, and includes B.O.A.C. Associated Companies Limited and BEA Helicopters Limited ;

(*b*) "an appeal tribunal" means an industrial tribunal established under section 12 of the Industrial Training Act 1964 ;

(*c*) "assessment" means an assessment of an employer to the levy ;

(*d*) "average" in relation to any numbers means the average of such numbers calculated to the lowest whole number ;

(*e*) "the Board" means the Civil Air Transport Industry Training Board ;

(*f*) "business" means any activities of industry or commerce ;

(*g*) "civil air transport establishment" means an establishment in Great Britain engaged wholly or mainly in the civil air transport industry for a total of twenty-seven or more weeks in the period of twelve months that commenced on 1st April 1968 or, being an establishment that commenced to carry on business in the said period, for a total number of weeks exceeding one-half of the number of weeks in the part of the said period commencing with the day on which business was commenced and ending on the last day thereof ;

(a) 1964 c. 16.

(*h*) "the civil air transport industry" means any one or more of the activities which, subject to the provisions of paragraph 2 of Schedule 1 to the industrial training order, are specified in paragraph 1 of that Schedule as the activities of the civil air transport industry ;

(*i*) "employer" (except in Article 3(7)(*b*) of this Order) means a person who is an employer in the civil air transport industry at any time in the second levy period ;

(*j*) "the industrial training order" means the Industrial Training (Civil Air Transport Board) Order 1967(**a**) ;

(*k*) "the levy" means the levy imposed by the Board in respect of the second levy period ;

(*l*) "notice" means a notice in writing ;

(*m*) "the relevant dates" means 31st July 1968 and 31st January 1969 ;

(*n*) "the second levy period" means the period commencing with the day on which this Order comes into operation and ending on 31st March 1970 ;

(*o*) other expressions have the same meaning as in the industrial training order.

(2) Any reference in this Order to an establishment that commences to carry on business or that ceases to carry on business shall not be taken to apply where the location of the establishment is changed but its business is continued wholly or mainly at or from the new location, or where the suspension of activities is of a temporary or seasonal nature.

(3) The Interpretation Act 1889(**b**) shall apply to the interpretation of this Order as it applies to the interpretation of an Act of Parliament.

*Imposition of the Levy*

**3.**—(1) The levy to be imposed by the Board on employers in respect of the second levy period shall be assessed in accordance with the provisions of this Article.

(2) The levy shall be assessed by the Board separately in respect of each civil air transport establishment of an employer, not being an Air Corporation, the British Airports Authority or an employer who is exempted from the levy by virtue of paragraph (8) of this Article, but in agreement with the employer one assessment may be made in respect of any number of such establishments in which case those establishments shall be deemed for the purposes of that assessment to constitute one establishment.

(3) Subject to the provisions of this Article, the levy assessed in respect of a civil air transport establishment shall be the amount obtained by multiplying the sum of £8 by the number that is equal to the average of the numbers of all persons employed, or deemed under the provisions of the next following paragraph to have been employed, at or from the establishment by the employer on each of the relevant dates.

---

(**a**) S.I. 1967/263 (1967 I, p. 968).      (**b**) 1889 c. 63.

(4) In the case where a civil air transport establishment is taken over (whether directly or indirectly) by an employer in succession to, or jointly with, another person, a person employed at or from the establishment on either or both of the relevant dates by a person other than the employer carrying on the establishment on the day upon which this Order comes into operation shall be deemed for the purposes of this Article to have been so employed by the last mentioned employer.

(5) The amount of the levy imposed in respect of a civil air transport establishment that ceases to carry on business in the second levy period shall be in the same proportion to the amount that would otherwise be due under paragraph (3) of this Article as the number of days between the commencement of the said levy period and the date of cessation of business (both dates inclusive) bears to the number of days in the said levy period.

(6) The levy shall be assessed by the Board in respect of each Air Corporation and of the British Airports Authority, and the amount of the levy shall, subject to the provisions of this Article, be the amount obtained by multiplying the sum of £8 by the number that is equal to the average of the numbers of all persons employed on each of the relevant dates by such Corporation or Authority, as the case may be.

(7) For the purposes of this Article, no regard shall be had to any person employed as follows :—

(a) by a local authority in—

   (i) the manufacture, installation, testing, inspection or repair of any articles (being certain articles made wholly or mainly from metal or metal and plastics material) to which paragraph 2(b)(iv) of Schedule 1 to the industrial training order applies ;

   (ii) any operations (being certain building work or civil engineering work) specified in paragraph 2(b)(viii) of the said Schedule ;

   (iii) any activities specified in paragraph 1(g) or 1(h) of that Schedule, not being activities mentioned in head (ii) or head (iv) of paragraph 3(o) thereof ; or

   (iv) the repair of motor vehicles, including the carrying out of running repairs or of minor adjustments thereto ;

(b) as a member of the crew of an aircraft that is operated by an employer having his sole or principal place of business outside Great Britain ; or

(c) wholly in the supply of food or drink for immediate consumption, except where such person is a member of the crew of an aircraft.

(8) There shall be exempt from the levy every employer in whose case the average of the numbers of the persons employed (or deemed under the provisions of paragraph (4) of this Article to have been employed) by him in the civil air transport industry on each of the relevant dates was less than eleven.

*Assessment Notices*

**4.**—(1) The Board shall serve an assessment notice on every employer assessed to the levy, but one notice may comprise two or more assessments.

(2) An assessment notice shall state the Board's address for the service of a notice of appeal or of an application for an extension of time for appealing.

(3) An assessment notice may be served on the person assessed to the levy either by delivering it to him personally or by leaving it, or sending it to him by post, at his last known address or place of business in the United Kingdom or, if that person is a corporation, by leaving it, or sending it by post to the corporation, at such address or place of business or at its registered or principal office.

## Payment of the Levy

**5.**—(1) Subject to the provisions of this Article and of Articles 6 and 7, the amount of each assessment appearing in an assessment notice served by the Board shall be payable to the Board in two equal instalments.

(2) The first of the said instalments shall be due one month after the date of the assessment notice, and the second instalment shall be due one month after the date (not being earlier than three months after the date of the assessment notice) of a notice requiring payment of that instalment, which notice shall be served by the Board on the person assessed to the levy in the same manner as an assessment notice.

(3) An instalment of an assessment shall not be recoverable by the Board until there has expired the time allowed for appealing against the assessment by Article 7(1) of this Order and any further period or periods of time that the Board or an appeal tribunal may have allowed for appealing under paragraph (2) or (3) of that Article or, where an appeal is brought, until the appeal is decided or withdrawn.

## Withdrawal of Assessment

**6.**—(1) The Board may, by a notice served on the person assessed to the levy in the same manner as an assessment notice, withdraw an assessment if that person has appealed against that assessment under the provisions of Article 7 of this Order and the appeal has not been entered in the Register of Appeals kept under the appropriate Regulations specified in paragraph (5) of that Article.

(2) The withdrawal of an assessment shall be without prejudice to the power of the Board to serve a further assessment notice in respect of any establishment or, as the case may be, persons to which that assessment related and, where the withdrawal is made by reason of the fact that an establishment has ceased to carry on business in the second levy period, the said notice may provide that the whole amount payable thereunder in respect of the establishment shall be due one month after the date of the notice.

## Appeals

**7.**—(1) A person assessed to the levy may appeal to an appeal tribunal against the assessment within one month from the date of the service of the assessment notice or within any further period or periods of time that may be allowed by the Board or an appeal tribunal under the following provisions of this Article.

(2) The Board by notice may for good cause allow a person assessed to the levy to appeal to an appeal tribunal against the assessment at any time within the period of four months from the date of the service of the assessment notice or within such further period or periods as the Board may allow before such time as may then be limited for appealing has expired.

(3) If the Board shall not allow an application for extension of time for appealing, an appeal tribunal shall upon application made to the tribunal by the person assessed to the levy have the like powers as the Board under the foregoing paragraph.

(4) In the case of an establishment that ceases to carry on business in the second levy period on any day after the date of the service of the relevant assessment notice the foregoing provisions of this Article shall have effect as if for the period of four months from the date of the service of the assessment notice mentioned in paragraph (2) of this Article there were substituted the period of six months from the date of the cessation of business.

(5) An appeal or an application to an appeal tribunal under this Article shall be made in accordance with the Industrial Tribunals (England and Wales) Regulations 1965(**a**) as amended by the Industrial Tribunals (England and Wales) (Amendment) Regulations 1967(**b**) except where the assessment relates to an establishment that is wholly in Scotland in which case the appeal or application shall be made in accordance with the Industrial Tribunals (Scotland) Regulations 1965(**c**) as amended by the Industrial Tribunals (Scotland) (Amendment) Regulations 1967(**d**).

(6) The powers of an appeal tribunal under paragraph (3) of this Article may be exercised by the President of the Industrial Tribunals (England and Wales) or by the President of the Industrial Tribunals (Scotland) as the case may be.

**8.**—(1) Upon the discharge by a person assessed to the levy of his liability under an assessment the Board shall if so requested issue to him a certificate to that effect.

(2) The production in any proceedings of a document purporting to be certified by the Secretary of the Board to be a true copy of an assessment or other notice issued by the Board or purporting to be a certificate such as is mentioned in the foregoing paragraph of this Article shall, unless the contrary is proved, be sufficient evidence of the document and of the facts stated therein.

24th April 1969.

*Barbara Castle,*
First Secretary of State and
Secretary of State for Employment and Productivity.

---

## EXPLANATORY NOTE
*(This Note is not part of the Order.)*

This Order gives effect to proposals submitted by the Civil Air Transport Industry Training Board to the Secretary of State for Employment and Productivity for the imposition of a further levy upon employers in the civil air transport industry for the purpose of raising money towards the expenses of the Board.

The levy is to be imposed in respect of the second levy period commencing on the day upon which this Order comes into operation and ending on 31st March 1970. The levy will be assessed by the Board and there will be a right of appeal against an assessment to an industrial tribunal.

---

(**a**) S.I. 1965/1101 (1965 II, p. 2805).     (**b**) S.I. 1967/301 (1967 I, p. 1040).
(**c**) S.I. 1965/1157 (1965 II, p. 3266).     (**d**) S.I. 1967/302 (1967 I, p. 1050).

STATUTORY INSTRUMENTS

## 1969 No. 628

## SEA FISHERIES

### BOATS AND METHODS OF FISHING

## The Fishing Nets (Northwest Atlantic) Order 1969

| | |
|---|---|
| *Made* - - - - | *28th April* 1969 |
| *Laid before Parliament* | *7th May* 1969 |
| *Coming into Operation* | *8th May* 1969 |

The Minister of Agriculture, Fisheries and Food and the Secretary of State for Scotland and the Home Department (being the Secretaries of State respectively concerned with the sea fishing industry in Scotland and Northern Ireland) in exercise of the powers conferred upon them by sections 3 and 15 of the Sea Fish (Conservation) Act 1967(a) and of all other powers enabling them in that behalf, hereby make the following Order:—

*Citation and commencement*

**1.** This Order may be cited as the Fishing Nets (Northwest Atlantic) Order 1969, and shall come into operation on 8th May 1969.

*Interpretation*

**2.**—(1) In this Order—

"British sea-fishery officer" means any person who is for the time being a British sea-fishery officer by virtue of section 11(2) of the Sea Fisheries Act 1883(b) as amended or extended by or under any subsequent enactment;

"fishing boat" means a vessel of whatever size, and in whatever way propelled, which is for the time being employed in sea fishing or the sea fishing service;

"net" means any net constructed to take fish whilst being towed or hauled at or near the bottom of the sea by or from a fishing boat;

"sub-area 1" means that area forming part of the waters in relation to which this Order has application which lies to the north and east of a rhumb line from a point in 75° north latitude and 73° 30′ west longitude to a point in 69° north latitude and 59° west longitude; east of 59° west longitude; and to the north and east of a rhumb line from a point in 61° north latitude and 59° west longitude to a point in 52° 15′ north latitude and 42° west longitude;

"sub-area 2" means that area forming part of the waters in relation to which this Order has application which lies to the south and west of sub-area 1 and to the north of the parallel of 52° 15′ north latitude;

"sub-area 3" means that area forming part of the waters in relation to which this Order has application lying south of the parallel of 52° 15′ north latitude

---

(a) 1967 c.84.  (b) 1883 c.22.

and to the east of a line extending due north from Cape Bauld on the north coast of Newfoundland to a point in 52° 15′ north latitude; to the north of the parallel 39° north latitude and to the east and north of a rhumb line extending in a northwesterly direction which passes through a point in 43° 30′ north latitude, 55° west longitude, in the direction of a point in 47° 50′ north latitude, 60° west longitude, until it intersects a straight line connecting Cape Ray on the coast of Newfoundland with Cape North on Cape Breton Island; thence in a northeasterly direction along the said line to Cape Ray;

"division 3 N/P" means those waters forming part of sub-area 3 which lie south of the Newfoundland coast, west of a line from Cape St. Mary to a point 46° north latitude, 54° 30′ west longitude, south of a line drawn eastwards along the parallel 46° north latitude to meet the meridian 46° 30′ west longitude; and west of a line due south to meet the parallel 39° north latitude;

"sub-area 4" means that area forming part of the waters in relation to which this Order has application lying to the west of sub-area 3 and to the east of a line described as follows:—beginning at the terminus of the international boundary between the United States of America and Canada in Grand Manan Channel, at a point 44° 46′ 35.34″ north latitude, 66° 54′ 11.23″ west longitude, thence due south to the parallel of 43° 50′ north latitude; thence due west to the meridian of 67° 40′ west longitude; thence due south to the parallel of 42° 20′ north latitude; thence due east to a point in 66° west longitude; thence along a rhumb line in a south easterly direction to a point in 42° north latitude, 65° 40′ west longitude; thence due south to the parallel of 39° north latitude;

"sub-area 5" means that area forming part of the waters in relation to which this Order has application lying to the west of the western boundary of sub-area 4;

(2) The Interpretation Act 1889(a) shall apply for the interpretation of this Order as it applies for the interpretation of an Act of Parliament, and as if this Order and the Order hereby revoked were Acts of Parliament.

*Revocation of previous Order*

**3.** The Fishing Nets (Northwest Atlantic) Order 1959(b) is hereby revoked.

*Waters in relation to which this Order has application*

**4.** This Order has application in relation to those waters, except territorial waters, bounded by a line drawn due south from the coast of Rhode Island along 71° 40′ west longitude to 39° north latitude; thence due east to 42° west longitude; thence due north to 59° north latitude; thence due west to 44° west longitude; thence due north to the coast of Greenland; thence along the west coast of Greenland to 78° 10′ north latitude; thence southward to a point in 75° north latitude and 73° 30′ west longitude; thence along a rhumb line to a point in 69° north latitude and 59° west longitude; thence due south to 61° north latitude; thence due west to 64° 30′ west longitude; thence due south to the coast of Labrador; thence in a southerly direction along the coast of Labrador to the southern terminus of its boundary with Quebec; thence in a westerly direction along the coast of Quebec, and in an easterly and southerly direction along the coasts of New Brunswick, Nova Scotia, and Cape Breton Island to Cabot Strait; thence along the coasts of Cape Breton Island, Nova Scotia,

---

(a) 1889 c.63.          (b) S.I. 1959/1226 (1959 II, p.2469).

New Brunswick, Maine, New Hampshire, Massachusetts, and Rhode Island
to the point of beginning; and which waters comprise the sub-areas 1 to 5 as
defined for the purposes of this Order.

*Sizes of Mesh of Nets*

**5.**—(1) Except as hereinafter provided, there shall not be carried in any
British fishing boat registered in the United Kingdom any net or part of a net
of a description specified in Column 2 of Schedule 1 to this Order for the purpose
of fishing in any of the sub-areas forming part of the waters to which this Order
has application and specified in Column 1 of the Schedule for fish of a description
specified in relation to that sub-area unless it has in all its parts meshes of such
a size that when any mesh is stretched diagonally lengthwise of the net a flat
gauge 2 mm. thick and of the width specified in Column 3 of the said Schedule 1
opposite to the reference to that description of net and that sub-area, will pass
easily through the mesh whether the net is wet or dry.

(2) For the purposes of the last foregoing paragraph the reference to fish
of a description specified in relation to any sub-area shall be construed as a
reference to fish of a description specified in relation to that sub-area in Schedule
2 to this Order.

*Obstruction of Nets*

**6.**—(1) Except as hereinafter provided, there shall not be carried in any
British fishing boat registered in the United Kingdom for the purpose of fishing
in any of the sub-areas forming part of the waters to which this Order has
application for fish of any description specified in Schedule 2 to this Order in
relation to that sub-area any net or part of a net having a covering of canvas
or any other material attached to it or in respect of which any artifice may have
been employed in such manner that the mesh in any part of the net is obstructed
or otherwise diminished in effect.

(2) Nothing in this Order shall be deemed to prohibit the attachment to the
underside of the cod-end of any net, of canvas, netting or other material for the
purpose of preventing or reducing wear and tear.

*Topside Chafers*

**7.**—(1) There shall not be carried in any British fishing boat registered in
the United Kingdom any net to which a topside chafer is attached unless the
net is a trawl net, the attachment is made for the purpose of fishing in waters in
relation to which this Order has application and the chafer complies with one
of the following specifications:—

    (*a*) a piece of netting, rectangular in shape, having in all its parts meshes
        the dimensions of which are not less than those of the meshes of the
        cod-end whether the netting and the cod-end respectively be wet or dry;
        being in width at least one and a half times the width of the part of the
        cod-end which is covered by it, (such widths being measured at right
        angles to the long axis of the cod-end); and fastened to the cod-end only
        along the forward and lateral edges of the piece of netting in such a way
        that—

        (i) if there is a splitting strop, the piece of netting begins at a distance
            of not more than four of the meshes to which it is attached forward
            of the splitting strop and ends at a distance of not less than four
            of such meshes forward of the cod-line mesh, or

    (ii) if there is no splitting strop, the piece of netting extends for not more than one-third of the length of the cod-end and ends at a distance of not less than four of the meshes of the net to which it is attached forward of the cod-line mesh; or

  (b) pieces of netting having in all their parts meshes the dimensions of which are not less than those of the meshes of the cod-end whether the netting and the cod-end respectively be wet or dry; each piece being—

    (i) fastened by its forward edge only across the cod-end at right angles to the long axis of the cod-end;

    (ii) of a width of at least the width of the cod-end (such width being measured at right angles to the long axis of the cod-end at the point of attachment), and

    (iii) of not more than ten meshes long; and the said pieces having an aggregate length when so attached not exceeding two-thirds of the length of the cod-end; or

  (c) a piece of netting made of the same material as the cod-end, having in all its parts meshes whereof the dimensions are twice the dimensions of the meshes of the cod-end, whether the netting and the cod-end respectively be wet or dry, and fastened to the cod-end along the forward, lateral and rear edges only of the netting, in such a way that each mesh of the piece of netting coincides with four meshes of the cod-end.

(2) In this article "topside chafer" means a piece of netting attached to the upperside of the cod-end of a net for the purpose of preventing or reducing wear and tear.

(3) The provisions of this Article shall be without prejudice to the provisions of Article 7 of the Fishing Nets (North-East Atlantic) Order 1968(a) and the carrying of any net to which a topside chafer is attached in accordance with the provisions of that Article shall be deemed not to be a contravention of the provisions of this Article.

## Defences

8.—(1) In any proceedings in respect of a contravention of Article 5 of this Order it shall be a sufficient defence to prove in relation to any net to which the proceedings relate being a net carried for the purpose of fishing in sub-area 3 that the net was being carried on a voyage undertaken solely for the purpose of fishing in division 3 N/P primarily for redfish (Sebastes);

Provided that the provisions of this paragraph shall not apply in any case where the fishing boat on which the net was carried has on board during the voyage a quantity of—

  (a) cod (Gadus morhua); or

  (b) haddock (Melanogrammus aeglefinus); or

  (c) sea fish of any other description specified in relation to sub-area 3 in said Schedule 2 (excluding redfish (Sebastes))

any of which exceeds 5,000 lbs. (2,268 Kgs.) or one-tenth of the total weight of all fish on board whichever is the greater.

---

(a) S.I. 1968/2075 (1968 III, p. 5610).

(2) In any proceedings in respect of a contravention of Article 5 of this Order it shall be a sufficient defence to prove in relation to any net to which the proceedings relate being a net carried for the purpose of fishing in sub-area 4 that the net was being carried on a voyage undertaken solely for the purpose of fishing in sub-area 4 primarily for sea fish of a description other than the descriptions of sea fish specified in relation to sub-area 4 in Schedule 2 to this Order;

Provided that the provisions of this paragraph shall not apply in any case where the fishing boat on which the net was carried has on board during the voyage a quantity of—

 (a) cod (Gadus morhua); or
 (b) haddock (Melanogrammus aeglefinus); or
 (c) sea fish of any other description specified in relation to sub-area 4 in said Schedule 2

any of which exceeds 5,000 lbs (2,268 Kgs.) or one-tenth of the total weight of all the fish on board whichever is the greater.

(3) In any proceedings in respect of a contravention of Article 5 of this Order it shall be a sufficient defence to prove in relation to any net to which the proceedings relate being a net carried for the purpose of fishing in sub-area 5 that the net was being carried on a voyage undertaken solely for the purpose of fishing in sub-area 5 primarily for any description of sea fish other than cod (Gadus morhua) or haddock (Melanogrammus aeglefinus);

Provided that the provisions of this paragraph shall not apply in any case where the fishing boat on which the net was carried has on board during the voyage a quantity of such cod or of such haddock exceeding in either case 5,000 lbs. (2,268 Kgs.) or one-tenth in weight of the total weight of all fish on board whichever is the greater.

**9.** For the purpose of enforcing the provisions of this Order a British sea-fishery officer may exercise, with respect to any British fishing boat registered in the United Kingdom, any of the following powers:—

 (1) he may go on board the boat;

 (2) he may examine all fishing implements belonging to the boat;

 (3) he may make any examination or enquiry which he deems necessary to ascertain whether any contravention of the provisions of this Order has been committed.

In witness whereof the Official Seal of the Minister of Agriculture, Fisheries and Food is hereunto affixed on 14th April 1969.

 (L.S.)            *Cledwyn Hughes,*
               Minister of Agriculture,
                 Fisheries and Food.

Given under the seal of the Secretary of State for Scotland on 16th April 1969.

 (L.S.)             *William Ross,*
              Secretary of State for Scotland.

Given under the Hand of the Secretary of State for the Home Department on 28th April 1969.

                *James Callaghan,*
               Secretary of State for the
                 Home Department.

## SCHEDULE 1

Article 5

### PRESCRIPTION OF SIZE OF MESH

| Column 1 | Column 2 | Column 3 |
|---|---|---|
| Sub-area | Description of net | Width of flat gauge |
| 1. | (1) Seine net ... ... ... ... ... | 110 millimetres |
| | (2) Such part of any trawl net as is made of cotton, hemp, polyamide fibres or polyester fibres ... ... ... ... ... | 120 millimetres |
| | (3) Such part of any trawl net as is made of manila or any other material not mentioned in (2) above ... ... ... ... ... | 130 millimetres |
| 2. | (1) Seine net ... ... ... ... ... | 100 millimetres |
| 3. | (2) Such part of any trawl net as is made of cotton, hemp, polyamide fibres or polyester fibres ... ... ... ... ... | 105 millimteres |
| 4. | | |
| 5. | (3) Such part of any trawl net as is made of manila or any other material not mentioned in (2) above ... ... ... ... ... | 114 millimetres |

Articles 5 and 6 SCHEDULE 2

## SPECIFICATION OF DESCRIPTIONS OF FISH IN RELATION TO SUB-AREAS

| Sub-area 1 | Sub-area 2 | Sub-area 3 | Sub-area 4 | Sub-area 5 |
|---|---|---|---|---|
| cod (Gadus morhua) | cod (Gadus morhua) | cod (Gadus morhua) | cod (Gadus morhua) | cod (Gadus morhua) |
| haddock (Melanogrammus aeglefinus) | haddock (Melanogrammus aeglefinus) | haddock (Melanogrammus aeglefinus) | haddock (Melanogrammus aeglefinus) | haddock (Melanogrammus aeglefinus) |
| redfish (Sebastes) | redfish (Sebastes) | redfish (Sebastes) | witch (Glyptocephalus cynoglossus) | |
| halibut (Hippoglossus hippoglossus) | halibut (Hippoglossus hippoglossus) | halibut (Hippoglossus hippoglossus) | yellowtail flounder (Limanda ferruginea) | |
| witch (Glyptocephalus cynoglossus) | witch (Glyptocephalus cynoglossus) | witch (Glyptocephalus cynoglossus) | winter flounder (Pseudopleuronectes americanus) | |
| American plaice (Hippoglossoides platessoides) | American plaice (Hippoglossoides platessoides) | yellowtail flounder (Limanda ferruginea) | American plaice (Hippoglossoides platessoides) | |
| Greenland halibut (Reinhardtius hippoglossoides) | Greenland halibut (Reinhardtius hippoglossoides) | American plaice (Hippoglossoides platessoides) | | |
| | | Greenland halibut (Reinhardtius hippoglossoides) | | |
| | | pollock (Pollachius virens) | | |
| | | white hake (Urophycis tenuis) | | |

## EXPLANATORY NOTE

### (This Note is not part of the Order.)

The Order regulates the sizes of mesh of seine and trawl nets carried by registered British fishing boats for the purpose of fishing in five defined areas of the Northwest Atlantic for sea fish specified in the Order. It supersedes the Fishing Nets (Northwest Atlantic) Order 1959.

The new Order introduces minimum mesh sizes for sub-areas 1 and 2 and increases the mesh size for sub-area 3; extends the provisions permitting the use of small mesh nets in catching certain species of fish; and makes certain changes in relation to topside chafers.

# STATUTORY INSTRUMENTS

## 1969 No. 630 (C.15)

## REPRESENTATION OF THE PEOPLE

## The Representation of the People Act 1969 (Commencement) Order 1969

| | | |
|---|---|---|
| *Made* - - - | *29th April* 1969 |
| *Laid before Parliament* | *9th May* 1969 |
| *Coming into Operation* | *12th May* 1969 |

In exercise of the powers conferred on me by section 27(3) of the Representation of the People Act 1969(a), I hereby make the following Order :—

**1.** This Order may be cited as the Representation of the People Act 1969 (Commencement) Order 1969 and shall come into operation on 12th May 1969.

**2.** The provisions of the Representation of the People Act 1969 specified in the Schedules to this Order shall come into force, in so far as they are not brought into operation by virtue of section 27(1) of that Act, on the dates mentioned in the headings of those Schedules, but the provisions mentioned in any one of the said Schedules shall not have effect in relation to any election notice of which has been published before the date mentioned in the heading of that Schedule.

*James Callaghan,*

One of Her Majesty's Principal
Secretaries of State.

Home Office,
  Whitehall.
29th April 1969.

---

(a) 1969 c. 15.

## SCHEDULE 1

PROVISIONS COMING INTO FORCE ON 12TH MAY 1969

| Provisions of the Act | Subject matter of provisions |
|---|---|
| Section 7(1) and (3) | Preparation of register. |
| Section 19 | Expenses of returning officers, etc. at or in connection with local government elections. |
| Section 20 | Refunds to local authorities of additional superannuation contributions for returning officers. |
| Section 21 | Summary prosecutions of offences at local elections. |
| Section 22 | References, in connection with election petitions, to offices of profit under the Crown. |
| Section 23(4) | Consequential provision as to ward elections in the City of London. |
| Section 24(1) and (4) | Consequential and supplementary amendments, and repeal. |
| Section 25 | Expenses. |
| Section 26 | Construction with Representation of the People Act 1949(a), and printing of that Act with insertions. |
| Section 27 | Commencement. |
| Section 28 | Citation. |
| Schedule 2, paragraphs 2(2), 12 and 38. | Consequential and supplementary amendments of Representation of the People Act 1949. |
| Schedule 3, Part I | Repeals (spent or unnecessary enactments). |
| So much of Part II of Schedule 3 as is set out in the Appendix hereto. | Repeals (consequential repeals). |
| Schedule 4 | Insertions authorised in Representation of the People Act 1949 in revised edition of Statutes. |

---

(a) 1949 c. 68.

APPENDIX TO SCHEDULE 1

REPEALS TAKING EFFECT ON 12TH MAY 1969

| Chapter | Short Title | Extent of Repeal |
|---|---|---|
| 12, 13 & 14 Geo. 6. c. 68. | The Representation of the People Act 1949. | Section 38.<br><br>Section 46(4) proviso.<br><br>Section 115(2) from the words "or holds" onwards.<br><br>In section 159(5) the words "by the Director of Public Prosecutions or his assistant", and the words from "For the purposes" onwards.<br><br>In section 165(3) the words "thirty-eight".<br><br>In Schedule 4, paragraph 5(2) from the beginning of paragraph (*a*) to the words "duty, and" in paragraph (*b*). |

## SCHEDULE 2

PROVISIONS COMING INTO FORCE ON 1ST AUGUST 1969

| Provisions of the Act | Subject matter of provisions |
|---|---|
| Section 8(1) to (3) | Limit on election expenses. |
| Section 9 | Broadcasting during elections. |
| Section 10 | Bands of music, torches, flags and banners. |
| Schedule 2, paragraphs 16 and 20. | Consequential and supplementary amendments of Representation of the People Act 1949. |
| So much of Part II of Schedule 3 as is set out in the Appendix hereto. | Repeals (consequential repeals). |

APPENDIX TO SCHEDULE 2

REPEALS TAKING EFFECT ON 1ST AUGUST 1969

| Chapter | Short Title | Extent of Repeal |
|---|---|---|
| 12, 13 & 14 Geo. 6. c. 68 | The Representation of the People Act 1949. | In section 65(2) in paragraph (a) the words "polling agents", and in paragraph (i) of the proviso the words "polling agent". <br><br> Section 97. |

SCHEDULE 3

PROVISIONS COMING INTO FORCE ON 16TH FEBRUARY 1970

| Provisions of the Act | Subject matter of provisions |
|---|---|
| Section 4 | Disfranchisement of offenders in prison, etc. |
| Section 5 | Extension for married persons of right to vote by proxy or by post. |
| Section 6 | Other amendments as to proxy and postal voting. |
| Section 7(2) | Correction of registers of electors. |
| Section 8(4) to (6) | Declaration and publication of election expenses. |
| Section 11 | Election agents and polling agents. |
| Section 12 | Description of candidate in nomination paper and on ballot paper. |
| Section 13 | Death of candidate. |
| Section 14 | Miscellaneous amendments of elections rules. |
| Section 15 | Property qualification in local government. |
| Section 16 | Date of qualification of candidate at local government election. |
| Section 17 | Filling of regular and casual vacancies at uncontested ordinary election. |
| Section 18(2) to (5) | Timing of elections, and of steps at elections. |
| Section 23(3) | Consequential provision as to ward elections in the City of London. |

## SCHEDULE 3—continued

| Provisions of the Act | Subject matter of provisions |
|---|---|
| Section 24(2), (3) and (5). | Consequential and supplementary amendments, and repeal. |
| Schedule 1, Part I and Part II, paragraphs 1, 2, 3 and 5 to 13. | Miscellaneous amendments of parliamentary and local elections rules. |
| Schedule 2, paragraphs 5, 7, 8, 9, 13(2), 14, 15, 18, 19, 22, 23(2), 24, 25, 26, 27, 29, 30, 31, 32, 34, 35 and 39. | Consequential and supplementary amendments of Representation of the People Act 1949. |
| So much of Part II of Schedule 3 as is set out in the Appendix hereto. | Repeals. |

APPENDIX TO SCHEDULE 3

REPEALS TAKING EFFECT ON 16TH FEBRUARY 1970

| Chapter | Short Title | Extent of Repeal |
|---|---|---|
| 23 & 24 Geo. 5. c. 51. | The Local Government Act 1933. | Section 57(b). |
| | | Section 67(5)(b). |
| 12, 13 & 14 Geo. 6. c. 68. | The Representation of the People Act 1949. | In section 12, in subsection (2) the word "either" and the words from "or" at the end of paragraph (a) onwards, and subsection (5). |
| | | In section 23, in subsection (2) from the word "unless" onwards, in subsection (3) the words "and not otherwise", and subsection (5). |
| | | In section 25, in subsection (4) the words "for a service voter" and the words "for an elector", and in subsection (6) the words "In relation to service voters and their proxies". |

APPENDIX TO SCHEDULE 3—continued

| Chapter | Short Title | Extent of Repeal |
|---|---|---|
| 12, 13 & 14 Geo. 6. c. 68 (contd.) | The Representation of the People Act 1949. | Section 57(2).<br><br>In section 70, in subsection (1) and in subsection (2), the words "before a justice of the peace".<br><br>In Schedule 2, in the parliamentary elections rules, in rule 1 the note at the end of the time-table; rule 7(4); rule 24; and rule 55(2).<br><br>In Schedule 2, in the local elections rules, in rule 7(1) proviso the words "in the case of an election to fill a casual vacancy"; rule 19(2)(e); and rule 20.<br><br>In Schedule 3, in rule 7, the words "paragraph 7 of rule 5, or"; rule 18; and rule 46(2). |

## EXPLANATORY NOTE

### (*This Note is not part of the Order.*)

This Order brings into force on various dates the provisions of the Representation of the People Act 1969 set out in the Schedules to the Order. The only provisions of the Act not brought into force are section 18(1) (ordinary day of election at certain local government elections) and Schedule 1, Part II, paragraph 4 (official mark).

# APPENDIX
# OF CERTAIN INSTRUMENTS
# NOT REGISTERED AS S.I.

## Orders in Council,
## Letters Patent
## and Royal Instructions

relating to the Constitutions etc. of
Overseas Territories or to appeals to the Judicial
Committee,

## Royal Proclamations, etc.

# HONG KONG

## The Hong Kong Additional Instructions 1969

Dated: 11th March 1969.                     *ELIZABETH R.*

ADDITIONAL INSTRUCTIONS to Our Governor and Commander-in-Chief in and over Our Colony of Hong Kong and its Dependencies or other Officer for the time being Administering the Government of Our said Colony and its Dependencies.

We do hereby direct and enjoin and declare Our will and pleasure as follows:—

Citation, construction and commencement.

**1.**—(1) These Instructions may be cited as the Hong Kong Additional Instructions 1969 and shall be construed as one with the Hong Kong Royal Instructions 1917 as amended (hereinafter called "the principal Instructions ").

(2) The Hong Kong Royal Instructions 1917 to 1967(a) and these Instructions may be cited together as the Hong Kong Royal Instructions 1917 to 1969.

Amendment of clause II of principal Instructions.

**2.** Clause II of the principal Instructions is amended by substituting for the words " Secretary for Chinese Affairs " the words " Secretary for Home Affairs ".

Amendment of clause X of principal Instructions.

**3.** Clause X of the principal Instructions is amended by inserting after the words " excepting only " the words " in cases relating to the appointment, disciplinary control or removal from office of a public officer or ".

Amendment of clause XIII of principal Instructions.

**4.** Clause XIII of the principal Instructions is amended by substituting for the words " Secretary for Chinese Affairs " the words " Secretary for Home Affairs ".

Amendment of clause XIX of principal Instructions.

**5.** Clause XIX of the principal Instructions is amended by substituting for the words " five Members " the words " ten Members ".

Amendment of clause XXIV of principal Instructions.

**6.** Clause XXIV of the principal Instructions is amended by deleting the words " , if seconded by any other Member,".

Given at Our Court at St. James's this eleventh day of March 1969 in the Eighteenth year of Our Reign.

---

(a) S.I. 1964 II, p. 3119; 1965 III, p. 6452; 1967 III, p. 5417.

# *Modifications to Legislation*

| Year and Number (or date) | Act or instrument | How affected |
|---|---|---|
| **1871** *Instrt. not S.I.* 29 June | Trial of the Pyx O. in C. 1871 (Rev. IV, p. 537) | **am.,** 1969/148 |
| **1898** | Merchant Shipping (Mercantile Marine Fund) Act 1898 (c. 44) | sch. 2— scale of payments **replaced,** 1969/386 rules 1, 7 proviso. **a.m.,** 1969/386 exemptions **am.,** 1969/386 |
| **1913** | Ancient Monuments Consolidation and Amdt. Act 1913 (c. 32) | functions transfd. *see* 1969/388 |
| **1917** *Instrt. not S.I.* 14 Feb. | Hong Kong R. Instructions 1917 ... | **am.,** Addnl. Instructions 10.2.69 |
| **1919** | Ministry of Health Act 1919 (c. 21) ... | functions transfd. *see* 1969/388 s. 5 rep. 1969/388 |
| **1923** | Salmon and Freshwater Fisheries Act 1923 (c. 16) | functions transfd. *see* 1969/388 |
| **1927** 1184 | Supreme Ct. Funds Rules 1927 (1927, p. 1638) | **am.,** 1969/206 |
| **1929** 831 | Companies (Bd. of Trade) Fees O. 1929 (Rev. IV, p. 749) | **r.,** 1969/519 |
| **1930** | Land Drainage Act 1930 (c. 44) ... | functions transfd. *see* 1969/388 |
| 1064 | Companies (Bd. of Trade) Fees O. 1930 (Rev. IV, p. 749) | **r.,** 1969/519 |
| **1931** | Ancient Monuments Act 1931 (c. 16) | functions transfd. *see* 1969/388 |

| Year and Number (or date) | Act or instrument | How affected |
|---|---|---|
| **1932** | Destructive Imported Animals Act 1932 (c. 12) | functions transfd. *see* 1969/388 |
| 560 | Agricultural Marketing (Facilities Ctee.) Regs. 1932 (Rev. I, p. 160) | functions transfd. *see* 1969/388 |
| 715 | Agricultural Marketing (Consumers Ctee.) Regs. 1932 (Rev. I, p. 158) | functions transfd. *see* 1969/388 |
| **1933** | | |
| 789 | Milk Marketing Scheme (Approval) O. 1933 (Rev. I, p. 224) | functions transfd. *see* 1969/388 |
| 1149 | Savings Certificates Regs. 1933 (Rev. XV, p. 309) | **am.,** 1969/541 |
| **1935** | Herring Industry Act 1935 (c. 9)    ... | functions transfd. *see* 1969/388 |
| **1936** | | |
| 626 | County Ct. Rules 1936 (1936 I, p. 282) | **am.,** 1969/585 |
| **1937** | Agriculture Act 1937 (c. 70) ...    ... | functions transfd. *see* 1969/388 |
| 1226 | Indian Military Service Family Pension Fund Rules 1937 (Rev. X, p. 632) | **am.,** 1969/400 |
| **1938** | Herring Industry Act 1938 (c. 42)  ... | functions transfd. *see* 1969/388 |
| 661 | Trade Marks Rules 1938 (Rev. XXIII, p. 3) | **am.,** 1969/522 |
| **1940** | Agriculture (Miscellaneous War Provns.) Act 1940 (c. 14) | functions transfd. *see* 1969/388 |
| **1941** | Agriculture (Miscellaneous Provns.) Act 1941 (c. 50) | functions transfd. *see* 1969/388 |
| **1944** | Agriculture (Miscellaneous Provns.) Act 1944 (c. 28) | functions transfd. *see* 1969/388 |
| **1945** | | |
| 698 | Provision of Milk and Meals Regs. 1945 (Rev. VI, p. 380) | **r.,** 1969/483 |
| **1946** | Acquisition of Land (Authorisation Procedure) Act 1946 (c. 49) | functions transfd. *see* 1969/388 |
| | Hill Farming Act 1946 (c. 73)    ... | functions transfd. *see* 1969/388 |
| | National Health Service Act 1946 (c. 81) | functions transfd. *see* 1969/388 |

| Year and Number (or date) | Act or instrument | How affected |
|---|---|---|
| **1946** | | |
| 137 | Family Allowances (Making of Claims and Payments) Regs. 1946 (Rev. VII, p. 616) | am., 1969/288 |
| 138 | Family Allowances (Qualifications) Regs. 1946 (Rev. VII, p. 607) | r., 1969/212 |
| **1947** | Agriculture Act 1947 (c. 48) ...    ... | functions transfd. *see* 1969/388 |
| 1421 | Trial of the Pyx O. 1947 (Rev. IV, p. 541) | r., 1969/148 |
| 1778 | Double Taxation Relief (Taxes on Income) (Seychelles) O. 1947 (Rev. X, p. 486) | am., 1969/379 |
| **1948** | Radioactive Substances Act 1948 (c. 37) | ss. 3, 4, 12 am., 1968/388 |
| | Agricultural Holdings Act 1948 (c. 63) | functions transfd. *see* 1969/388 |
| 60 | National Health Service (Functions of Regional Hospital Bds. etc.) Regs. 1948 (Rev. XV, p. 541) | r., 1969/297 |
| 167 | Is. of Scilly (National Health Service) O. 1948 (Rev. XV, p. 807) | am., 1969/355 |
| 594 | National Health Service (Functions of Regional Hospital Bds.) (S.) Regs. 1948 (Rev. XV, p. 841) | am., 1969/437 |
| 944 | Teachers Pensions (National Insurance Mod.) (S.) Regs. 1948 (Rev. VI, p. 823) | am., 1969/77 |
| 1041 | National Insurance (Claims and Payments) Regs. 1948 (Rev. XVI, p. 313) | am., 1969/289, 339 |
| 1390 | National Health Service (Appointment of Medical and Dental Officers) (S.) Regs. 1948 (Rev. XV, p. 854) | am., 1969/257 |
| **1949** | National Health Service (Amdt.) Act 1949 (c. 93) | functions transfd. *see* 1969/388 |
| 850 | Companies (Bd. of Trade) Fees O. 1949 (1949 I, p. 930) | r., 1969/519 |
| 2058 | County Cts. Districts O. 1949 (1949 I, p. 955) | am., 1969/295 |
| 2368 | Designs Rules 1949 (1949 I, p. 1417) ... | am., 1969/481 |
| 2452 | Agricultural Marketing (Ctee. of Investigation) Regs. 1949 (1949 I, p. 32) | functions transfd. *see* 1969/388 |
| **1950** | | |
| 392 | Patents Appeal Tribunal Rules 1950 (1950 II, p. 201) | am., 1969/500 |

| Year and Number (or date) | Act or instrument | How affected |
|---|---|---|
| **1950** 1869 | Agricultural Marketing (Re-organisation Commn.) Regs. 1950 (1950 I, p. 16) | functions transfd. *see* 1969/388 |
| **1951** | Sea Fish Industry Act 1951 (c. 30) | functions transfd. *see* 1969/388 |
| | National Health Service Act 1951 (c. 31) | functions transfd. *see* 1969/388 |
| **1952** | Agriculture (Fertilisers) Act 1952 (c. 15) | functions transfd. *see* 1969/388 |
| | National Health Service Act 1952 (c. 25) | functions transfd. *see* 1969/388 |
| | Agriculture (Ploughing Grants) Act 1952 (c. 35) | functions transfd. *see* 1969/388 |
| | Agriculture (Calf Subsidies) Act 1952 (c. 62) | functions transfd. *see* 1969/388 |
| 868 | Colonial Civil Aviation (Application of Act) O. 1952 (1952 I, p. 565) | **r.** (certain territories), 1969/592 |
| 900 | Public Service Vehicles (Licences and Certificates) Regs. 1952 | **am.,** 1969/32 |
| 1032 | Civil Aviation Act (Is. of Man) O. 1952 (1952 I, p. 561) | **am.,** 1969/594 |
| 1457 | Family Allowances (Conditions for Increase of Allowances) Regs. 1952 (1952 I, p. 996) | **am.,** 1969/212 |
| 1999 | Family Allowances (Qualifications) Amdt. Regs. 1952 (1952 I, p. 1001) | **r.,** 1969/212 |
| 2117 | Companies (Bd. of Trade) Fees O. 1952 (1952 I, p. 624) | **r.,** 1969/519 |
| **1953** | White Fish and Herring Industries Act 1953 (c. 17) | functions transfd. *see* 1969/388 |
| | Historic Buildings and Ancient Monuments Act 1953 (c. 49) | functions transfd. *see* 1969/388 |
| 591 | Colonial Civil Aviation (Application of Act) (Amdt.) O. 1953 (1953 I, p. 275) | **r.** (certain territories), 1969/592 |
| 1059 | Family Allowances (Qualifications) (Amdt.) Regs. 1953 (1953 I, p. 746) | **r.,** 1969/212 |
| 1669 | Colonial Civil Aviation (Application of Act) (Amdt.) (No. 2) O. 1953 (1953 I, p. 277) | **r.** (certain territories), 1969/592 |
| 1671 | Aliens O. 1953 (1953 I, p. 94) ... | **am.,** 1969/388 |
| **1954** | Protection of Birds Act 1954 (c. 30) ... | functions transfd. *see* 1969/388 |
| | Pests Act 1954 (c. 68) ...    ...    ... | functions transfd. *see* 1969/388 |

| Year and Number (or date) | Act or instrument | How affected |
|---|---|---|
| **1954** | | |
| 224 | National Health Service (Executive Councils) Regs. 1954 (1954 I, p. 1270) | r., 1969/352 |
| 641 | National Insurance and Industrial Injuries (Switzerland) O. 1954 (1954 I, p. 1422) | r., 1969/384 |
| 830 | Colonial Civil Aviation (Application of Act) (Amdt.) O. 1954 (1954 I, p. 463) | r. (certain territories), 1969/592 |
| **1955** | Fisheries Act 1955 (c. 7)     ...     ... | functions transfd. *see* 1969/388 |
| 709 | Colonial Civil Aviation (Application of Act) (Amdt.) O. 1955 (1955 I, p. 458) | r. (certain territories), 1969/592 |
| **1956** | Therapeutic Substances Act 1956 (c. 25) | ss. 4, 8, 9 **am.**, 1969/388 |
| | Finance Act 1956 (c. 54)     ...     ... | functions transfd. *see* 1969/388 |
| 715 | Ulster and Colonial Savings Certificates (Income Tax Exemption) Regs. 1956 (1956 I, p. 1086) | **am.**, 1969/542 |
| 1048 | Conveyance in Harbours of Govt. Explosives and Explosives of Visiting Forces Regs. 1956 (1956 I, p. 841) | r., 1969/18 |
| 1049 | Conveyance by Rail of Govt. explosives and Explosives of Visiting Forces Regs. 1956 (1956 I, p. 886) | r., 1969/19 |
| 1050 | Conveyance by Road of Govt. Explosives and Explosives of Visiting Forces Regs. 1956 (1956 I, p. 896) | r., 1969/20 |
| 1075 | National Health Service (Executive Councils) Amdt. Regs. 1956 (1956 I, p. 1552) | r., 1969/352 |
| 1077 | National Health Service (Service Ctees. and Tribunals) Regs. 1956 (1956 I, p. 1554) | am., 1969/354 |
| 1078 | National Health Service (Supplementary Ophthalmic Services) Regs. 1956 (1956 I, p. 1524) | am., 1969/351 |
| 1793 | National Health Service (Functions of Regional Hospital Bds. etc.) Amdt. Regs. 1956 (1956 I, p. 1512) | r., 1969/297 |
| **1957** | White Fish and Herring Industries Act 1957 (c. 22) | functions transfd. *see* 1969/388 |
| | Dentists Act 1957 (c. 28)     ...     ... | sch. 1 para. 14 **am.**, 1969/388 |
| | Agriculture Act 1957 (c. 57) ...     ... | functions transfd. *see* 1969/388 |
| | Coal-Mining (Subsidence) Act 1957 (c. 59) | functions transfd. *see* 1969/388 |

| Year and Number (or date) | Act or instrument | How affected |
|---|---|---|
| **1957** | | |
| 356 | Teachers (Superannuation) (S.) Regs. 1957 (1957 I, p. 733) | r., 1969/77 |
| 485 | Public Trustee (Fees) O. 1957 (1957 II, p. 2578) | r., 1969/513 |
| 2224 | Judicial Ctee. Rules 1957 (1957 I, p. 1205) | am., 1969/365 |
| **1958** | Agricultural Marketing Act 1958 (c. 47) | functions transfd. *see* 1969/388 |
| 426 | Federation of Malaya (Appeals to Privy Council) O. in C. 1958 (1958 I, p. 1322) | am., 1969/369 |
| 1514 | Colonial Civil Aviation (Application of Act) (Amdt.) O. 1958 (1958 I, p. 303) | r. (certain territories), 1969/592 |
| 1595 | Teachers (Superannuation) (S.) (Amdt. No. 1) Regs. 1958 (1958 I, p. 1077) | r., 1969/77 |
| **1959** | Agriculture (Small Farmers) Act 1959 (c. 12) | functions transfd. *see* 1969/388 |
| | Agricultural Improvement Grants Act 1959 (c. 31) | functions transfd. *see* 1969/388 |
| | Weeds Act 1959 (c. 54) ... ... | functions transfd. *see* 1969/388 |
| 277 | Milk and Dairies (General) Regs. 1959 (1959 I, p. 1351) | functions transfd. *see* 1969/388 |
| 364 | Schools Regs. 1959 (1959 I, p. 1584) ... | am., 1969/231 |
| 366 | Special Schools and Establishments (Grant) Regs. 1959 (1959 I, p. 1051) | am., 1969/410 |
| 393 | Further Education (Local Education Authies.) Regs. 1959 (1959 I, p. 1577) | r., 1969/403 |
| 394 | Further Education (Grant) Regs. 1959 (1959 I, p. 1041) | r., 1969/403 |
| 409 | Provision of Milk and Meals Amdg. Regs. 1959 (1959 I, p. 1029) | r., 1969/483 |
| 467 | National Insurance (Industrial Injuries) (Prescribed Diseases) Regs. 1959 (1959 II, p. 1943) | am., 1969/619 |
| 476 | Abolition of the Education (S.) Fund (Consequential Provns.) Regs. 1959 (1959 I, p. 1095) | am., 1969/77 |
| 833 | Grant-Aided Secondary Schools (S.) Grant Regs. 1959 (1959 I, p. 1104) | am., 1969/506 |
| 890 | Standards for School Premises Regs. 1959 (1959 I, p. 1006) | am., 1969/433 |
| 961 | Public Trustee (Fees) O. 1959 (1959 II, p. 2704) | r., 1969/513 |

| Year and Number (or date) | Act or instrument | How affected |
|---|---|---|
| **1959** | | |
| 1052 | Colonial Civil Aviation (Application of Act) (Amdt.) O. 1959 (1959 I, p. 684) | **r.** (certain territories), 1969/592 |
| 1169 | Family Allowances (Qualifications) Amdt. Regs. 1959 (1959 I, p. 1276) | **r.**, 1969/212 |
| 1226 | Fishing Nets (Northwest Atlantic) O. 1959 (1959 II, p. 2469) | **r.**, 1969/628 |
| 2245 | Public Path Orders Regs. 1959 (1959 II, p. 2343) | **r.**, 1969/269 |
| **1960** | Horticulture Act 1960 (c. 22) ...     ... | functions transfd. *see* 1969/388 |
| | Professions Supplementary to Medicine Act 1960 (c. 66) | sch. 1 para. 1 **am.**, 1969/388 |
| 250 | Cycle Racing on Highways Regs. 1960 (1960 III, p. 3047) | **am.** (*temp.*), 1969/111, 161 |
| 630 | Public Trustee (Fees) O., 1960 (1960 III, p. 3310) | **r.**, 1969/513 |
| 870 | Detention Centre (S.) Rules 1960 (1960 I, p. 1176) | **am.**, 1969/253 |
| 1064 | National Insurance (Switzerland) O. 1960 (1960 II, p. 2340) | **r.**, 1969/384 |
| 1240 | National Health Service (Functions of Regional Hospital Bds. etc.) Amdt. Regs. 1960 (1960 II, p. 2072) | **r.**, 1969/297 |
| 1444 | Conveyance in Harbours of Govt. Explosives and Explosives of Visiting Forces (Amdt.) Regs. 1960 (1960 I, p. 1385) | **r.**, 1969/18 |
| 1445 | Conveyance by Rail of Govt. Explosives and Explosives of Visiting Forces (Amdt.) Regs. 1960 (1960 I, p. 1390) | **r.**, 1969/19 |
| 1446 | Conveyance by Road of Govt. Explosives and Explosives of Visiting Forces (Amdt.) Regs. 1960 (1960 I, p. 1396) | **r.**, 1969/20 |
| 1505 | Goods Vehicles (Licences and Prohibitions) Regs. 1960 (1960 III, p. 3020) | **am.**, 1969/420 |
| 1695 | National Insurance (Non Participation—Teachers Superannuation) (S.) Regs. 1960 (1960 II, p. 2281) | **r.**, 1969/77 |
| **1961** | National Health Service Act 1961 (c. 19) | functions transfd. *see* 1969/388 |
| 34 | National Health Service (Functions of Regional Hospital Bds. etc.) Regs. 1961 | **r.**, 1969/297 |

| Year and Number (or date) | Act or instrument | How affected |
|---|---|---|
| **1961** | | |
| 209 | Motor Vehicles (Tests) (Exemption) Regs. 1961 | r., 1969/419 |
| 411 | Parking Places Orders (Procedure) (E. and W.) Regs. 1961 | r., 1969/463 |
| 471 | National Insurance (Non-Participation—Teachers Superannuation) (S.) Regs. 1961 | r., 1969/77 |
| 505 | Parking Places Orders (Procedure) (S.) Regs. 1961 | r., 1969/487 |
| 669 | Traffic Regulation Orders (Procedure (S.) Regs. 1961 | r., 1969/487 |
| 1242 | Street Playground Orders (Procedure) (E. and W.) Regs. 1961 | r., 1969/463 |
| 1322 | Street Playgrounds Orders (Procedure) (S.) Regs. 1961 | r., 1969/487 |
| 1582 | Further Education (Local Education Authies.) Amdg. Regs. 1961 | r., 1969/403 |
| 2108 | Motor Vehicles (Tests) (Exemptions) (Amdt.) Regs. 1961 | r., 1969/419 |
| 2317 | Colonial Civil Aviation (Application of Act) (Amdt.) O. 1961 | r. (certain territories), 1969/592 |
| **1962** | Commonwealth Immigrants Act 1962 (c. 21) | s. 16 am., 1969/388 |
| | Health Visiting and Social Work (Training) Act 1962 (c. 33) | s. 7 am., 1969/388 |
| 25 | Family Allowances (Qualifications) Amdt. Regs. 1962 | r., 1969/212 |
| 347 | Drainage Charges (Forms) Regs. 1962 | r., 1969/469 |
| 562 | Public Trustee (Fees) O. 1962       ... | r., 1969/513 |
| 623 | Approved Schools (Contribution by Local Authies.) Regs. 1962 | am., 1969/501 |
| 1127 | Motor Vehicles (Production of Test Certificates) Regs. 1962 | r., 1969/418 |
| 1669 | Salmon and Migratory Trout (Prohibition of Drift-net Fishing) O. 1962 | am., 1969/167 |
| **1963** | Agriculture (Miscellaneous Provisions) Act 1963 (c. 11) | functions transfd. *see* 1969/388 |
| | Weights and Measures Act 1963 (c. 31) | s. 10 am., 1969/388 |
| | Water Resources Act 1963 (c. 38)   ... | functions transfd. *see* 1969/388 |
| 133 | Act of Sederunt (Alteration of Sheriff Ct. Fees) 1963 | am., 1969/464 |
| 382 | Wages Regulation (Brush and Broom) (Holidays) O. 1963 | r., 1969/209 |
| 467 | Companies (Bd. of Trade) Fees. O. 1963 | r., 1969/519 |
| 523 | Public Trustee (Fees) O. 1963       ... | r., 1969/513 |
| 569 | Eggs (Guaranteed Prices) O. 1963    ... | r., 1969/401 |

| Year and Number (or date) | Act or instrument | How affected |
|---|---|---|
| **1963** | | |
| 709 | Town and Country Planning General Development O. 1963 | am., 1969/276 |
| 1017 | National Health Service (Functions of Regional Hospital Bds. etc.) Regs. 1963 | r., 1969/297 |
| 1026 | Motor Vehicles (Driving Licences) Regs. 1963 | am., 1969/252 |
| 1223 | State Awards Regs. 1963 ... ... | am., 1969/554 |
| 1571 | Milk (Special Designation) Regs. 1963 | functions transfd. *see* 1969/388 |
| 1710 | Weights and Measures Regs. 1963 ... | am., 1969/81 |
| 2084 | Bahama Is. (Constitution) O. in C. 1963 | r. (*prosp.*), 1969/590 |
| 2111 | National Insurance (Mod. of Teachers Superannuation) (S.) Regs. 1963 | r., 1969/77 |
| *Instrt. not S.I.* | | |
| 20 Dec. | Bahama Is. R. Instructions 1963 (1963 III, p. 4840) | r. (*prosp.*), 1969/590 |
| | | |
| **1964** | Agriculture and Horticulture Act 1964 (c. 28) | functions transfd. *see* 1969/388 |
| | Harbours Act 1964 (c. 40) ... ... | functions transfd. *see* 1969/388 |
| 73 | National Insurance (Industrial Injuries) (Claims and Payments) Regs. 1964 | am., 1969/291 |
| 81 | Weights and Measures (Equivalents for dealing with drugs) Regs. 1964 | r. (*prosp.*), 1969/101 |
| 359 | Motor Vehicles (Approved Driving Instructors) Regs. 1964 | r., 1969/85 |
| 409 | Importation of Potatoes (Health) (G.B.) O. 1964 | am., 1969/521 |
| 462 | Eggs (Guaranteed Prices) (Amdt.) O. 1964 | r., 1969/401 |
| 1071 | Civil Aviation (Navigation Services Charges) Regs. 1964 | am., 1969/510 |
| 1144 | Weights and Measures (Equivalents for dealings with drugs) Amdt. Regs. 1964 | r. (*prosp.*), 1969/101 |
| 1309 | Further Education (Local Education Authies.) Amdg. Regs. 1964 | r., 1969/403 |
| 1310 | Further Education (Grant) Amdg. Regs. 1964 | r., 1969/403 |
| 1336 | Designs (Amdt. No. 2) Rules 1964 ... | r., 1969/481 |
| 1382 | Town and Country Planning (General) Regs. 1964 | r., 1969/286 |
| 1514 | Further Education (Grant) Second Amdg. Regs. 1964 | r., 1969/403 |
| 1515 | Further Education (Local Education Authies.) Second Amdg. Regs. 1964 | r., 1969/403 |

| Year and Number (or date) | Act or instrument | How affected |
|---|---|---|
| **1964** | | |
| 1771 | London Govt. (Executive Councils) O. 1964 | **am.,** 1969/353 |
| 1835 | Trade Marks (Amdt. No. 2) Rules 1964 | **r.,** 1969/522 |
| 2041 | Bahama Is. (Constitution) (Amdt.) O. 1964 | **r.** (*prosp.*), 1969/590 |
| **1965** | Cereals Marketing Act 1965 (c. 14) ... | functions transfd. *see* 1969/388 |
| | Teaching Councils (S.) Act 1965 (c. 19) | sch. 1 **am.,** 1969/586 |
| | Finance Act 1965 (c. 25) ... ... | functions transfd. *see* 1969/388 |
| | National Insurance Act 1965 (c. 51) | s. 49 **am.,** 1969/289 |
| | National Health Service Contributions Act 1965 (c. 54) | s. 1 **am.,** 1969/388 |
| | Superannuation Act 1965 (c. 74) ... | sch. 8 **am.,** 1969/349 |
| 2 | Further Education (Local Education Authies.) Amdg. Regs. 1965 | **r.,** 1969/403 |
| 308 | Provision of Milk and Meals Amdg. Regs. 1965 | **r.,** 1969/483 |
| 321 | (A.S. Rules of Court., consolidation and amdt.) 1965 | **am.,** 1969/474, 475 |
| 499 | Town and Country Planning General (Amdt.) Regs. 1965 | **r.,** 1969/286 |
| 516 | Income Tax (Employments) Regs. ... | **am.,** 1969/170 |
| 527 | National Health Service (Regional Hospital Areas) O. 1965 | **am.,** 1969/451 |
| 542 | River Authies. (Precepts) Regs. 1965... | **r.,** 1969/438 |
| 621 | London Authies. (Superannuation) O. 1965 | **am.,** 1969/413 |
| 980 | Colonial Civil Aviation (Application of Act) (Amdt.) O. 1965 | **r.** (certain territories), 1969/592 |
| 1105 | Merchant Shipping (Life-Saving Appliances) Rules 1965 | **am.,** 1969/409 |
| 1164 | National Health Service (Functions of Regional Hospital Bds. etc.) Amdt. Regs. 1965 | **r.,** 1969/297 |
| 1166 | Teachers (Superannuation) (S.) (Amdt.) Regs. 1965 | **r.,** 1969/77 |
| 1167 | Teachers (Superannuation) (S.) Rules 1965 | **r.,** 1969/77 |
| 1400 | Motor Vehicles (Competitions and Trials) (E.) Regs. 1965 | **r.,** 1969/414 |
| 1414 | Motor Vehicles (Competitions and Trials) (W.) Regs. 1965 | **r.,** 1969/414 |
| 1500 | County Ct. Funds Rules 1965 ... | **am.,** 1969/204 |
| 1551 | Designs (Amdt.) Rules 1965 ... ... | **am.,** 1969/481 |
| 1590 | Town and Country Planning General (Amdt. No. 2) Regs. 1965 | **r.,** 1969/286 |
| 1622 | Bankruptcy Fees O. 1965 ... ... | **am.,** 1969/520 |

| Year and Number (or date) | Act or instrument | How affected |
|---|---|---|
| **1965** | | |
| 1707 | Mayor's and City of London Ct. Funds Rules 1965 | am., 1969/205 |
| 1743 | Public Trustee (Fees) O. 1965 ... | r., 1969/513 |
| 1815 | Measuring Instruments (Intoxicating Liquor) Regs. 1965 | am., 1969/67 |
| 1823 | Nuclear Installations (Insurance Certificates) Regs. 1965 | am., 1969/64 |
| 1861 | Turks and Caicos Is. (Constitution) O. 1965 | am. (*prosp.*), 1969/591 |
| 2090 | Wages Regulation (Perambulator and Invalid Carriage) (Holidays) O. 1965 | am., 1969/562 |
| **1966** | Mines (Working Facilities and Support) Act 1966 (c. 4) | functions transfd. *see* 1969/388 |
| | National Health Service 1966 (c. 8) ... | functions transfd. *see* 1969/388<br>s. 4 am., 1969/388 |
| | Sea Fisheries Regulation Act 1966 (c. 38) | functions transfd. *see* 1969/388 |
| 10 | Witnesses' Allowances Regs. 1966 ... | am., 1969/214 |
| 11 | Coroners (Fees and Allowances) Rules 1966 | am., 1969/213 |
| 24 | Increase of Pensions (Injury Warrant Pensions) Regs. 1966 | am., 1969/584 |
| 159 | Overseas Service (Pensions Supplement) Regs. 1966 | r., 1969/553 |
| 188 | Aircraft (Exemption from Seizure on Patent Claims) O. 1966 | r., 1969/150 |
| 479 | Eggs (Guaranteed Prices) (Amdt.) O. 1966 | r., 1969/401 |
| 564 | Overseas Service (Pensions Supplement) (Special Provns.) Regs. 1966 | r., 1969/553 |
| 569 | National Health Service (Appointment of Consultants) Regs. 1966 | r., 1969/163 |
| 637 | Wages Regulation (Coffin Furniture and Cerement-making) O. 1966 | r., 1969/610 |
| 638 | Wages Regulation (Coffin Furniture and Cerement-making) (Holidays) O. 1966 | r., 1969/611 |
| 1065 | Supplementary Benefit (General) Regs. 1966 | am., 1969/294 |
| 1067 | Supplementary Benefit (Claims and Payments) Regs. 1966 | am., 1969/293 |
| 1069 | Motor Vehicles (Competitions and Trials) (S.) Regs. 1966 | r., 1969/414 |
| 1174 | Botswana (Procedure in Appeals to Judicial Ctee. of Privy Council) O. 1966 | am., 1969/376 |

| Year and Number (or date) | Act or instrument | How affected |
|---|---|---|
| **1966** 1176 | Lesotho (Procedure in Appeals to Judicial Ctee. of Privy Council) O. 1966 | **am.,** 1969/368 |
| 1182 | Republic of Singapore (Appeals to Judicial Ctee.) O. 1966 | **am.,** 1969/370 |
| 1210 | National Health Service (General Medical and Pharmaceutical Services) Regs. 1966 | **am.,** 1969/217 |
| 1229 | National Insurance (Mod. of Teachers Superannuation) (S.) Amdt. Regs. 1966 | **r.,** 1969/77 |
| 1233 | National Health Service (General Medical and Pharmaceutical Services) (S.) Regs. 1966 | **am.,** 1969/254 |
| 1240 | Motor Vehicles (Tests) (Exemption) (Amdt.) Regs. 1966 | **r.,** 1969/419 |
| 1256 | Air Navigation (General) Regs. 1966 ... | **am.,** 1969/583 |
| 1257 | Rules of the Air and Air Traffic Control Regs. 1966 | **r.,** 1969/216 |
| 1288 | Motor Vehicles (Construction and Use) Regs. 1966 | **r.,** 1969/321 |
| 1289 | Motor Vehicles (Authorisation of Special Types) General O. 1966 | **r.,** 1969/344 |
| 1377 | Rules of the Air and Air Traffic Control (Amdt.) Regs. 1966 | **r.,** 1969/216 |
| 1432 | Further Education (Local Education Authies) Amdg. Regs. 1966 | **r.,** 1969/403 |
| 1449 | National Health Service (General Dental Services) (S.) Regs. 1966 | **am.,** 1969/254, 436 |
| 1519 | Wages Regulation (Retail Newsagency Tobacco and Confectionery) (E. and W.) O. 1966 | **r.,** 1969/35 |
| **1967** | Agriculture Act 1967 (c. 22) ... ... | functions transfd. *see* 1969/388 |
|  | National Health Service (Family Planning) Act 1967 (c. 39) | functions transfd. *see* 1969/388 |
|  | Finance Act 1967 (c. 54) ... ... | s. 40 **am.,** 1969/535 |
|  | Sea Fisheries (Shellfish) Act 1967 (c. 83) | functions transfd. *see* 1969/388 |
|  | Abortions Act 1967 (c. 87) ... ... | s. 2 **am.,** 1969/388 |
| 18 | Southern Rhodesia (Prohibited Trade and Dealings) (Overseas Territories) O. 1967 | **r.** (Dominica) (*prosp.*), 1969/593 |
| 176 | Motor Vehicles (Competitions and Trials) (W.) (Amdt.) Regs. 1967 | **r.,** 1969/414 |
| 248 | Southern Rhodesia (Prohibited Trade and Dealings) (Overseas Territories) (Amdt.) O. 1967 | **r.** (Dominica) (*prosp.*), 1969/593 |

| Year and Number (or date) | Act or instrument | How affected |
|---|---|---|
| **1967** | | |
| 261 | Motor Vehicles (Tests) (Exemption) (Amdt.) Regs. 1967 | **r.,** 1969/419 |
| 278 | National Health Service (Executive Councils) Amdt. Regs. 1967 | **r.,** 1969/352 |
| 284 | Public Trustee (Fees) O. 1967 ... | **r.,** 1969/513 |
| 330 | National Insurance (Unemployment and Sickness Benefit) Regs. 1967 | **am.,** 1969/292 |
| 363 | Rate Support Grant Regs. 1967 ... | **am.,** 1969/105 |
| 415 | Motor Vehicles (Competitions and Trials) (E.) (Amdt.) Regs. 1967 | **r.,** 1969/414 |
| 439 | Motor Vehicles (Competitions and Trials) (W.) (Amdt.) (No. 2) Regs. 1967 | **r.,** 1969/414 |
| 467 | Rate Support Grant (Pooling Arrangements) Regs. 1967 | **am.,** 1969/403 |
| 489 | Teachers' Superannuation Regs. 1967 | **am.,** 1969/80 |
| 533 | Rules of the Air and Air Traffic Control (Second Amdt.) Regs. 1967 | **r.,** 1969/216 |
| 628 | Wages Regulation (Rubber Proofed Garment) (Holidays) O. 1967 | **am.,** 1969/131 |
| 640 | Wages Regulation (Boot and Shoe Repairing) O. 1967 | **r.,** 1969/428 |
| 641 | Wages Regulation (Boot and Shoe Repairing) (Holidays) O. 1967 | **am.,** 1969/428 |
| 643 | Rules of the Air and Air Traffic Control (Third Amdt.) Regs. 1967 | **r.,** 1969/216 |
| 706 | Motor Vehicles (Competitions and Trials) (S.) (Amdt.) Regs. 1967 | **r.,** 1969/414 |
| 815 | Commonwealth Countries and Republic of Ireland (Immunities) (No. 2) O. 1967 | **am.,** 1969/142 |
| 901 | Teachers Superannuation (Family Benefits) (S.) Regs. 1967 | **r.,** 1969/78 |
| 937 | National Health Service (General Dental Services) Regs. 1967 | **am.,** 1969/217, 399 |
| 988 | Wages Regulation (Perambulator and Invalid Carriage) O. 1967 | **r.,** 1969/562 |
| 1018 | Army Terms of Service Regs. 1967 ... | **am.,** 1969/245 |
| 1078 | Sausage and Other Meat Product (S.) Regs. 1967 | **am.,** 1969/327 |
| 1079 | Canned Meat Product (S.) Regs. 1967 | **am.,** 1969/326 |
| 1081 | Rules of the Air and Air Traffic Control (Fourth Amdt.) Regs. 1967 | **r.,** 1969/216 |
| 1087 | Control of Office Development (Exemption Limit) O. 1967 | **am.,** 1969/174 |
| 1162 | Teachers (Education, Training and Registration) (S.) Regs. 1967 | **am.,** 1969/77 |

| Year and Number (or date) | Act or instrument | How affected |
|---|---|---|
| **1967** | | |
| 1188 | Wages Regulation (Retail Newsagency, Tobacco and Confectionery) (E. and W.) (Amdt.) O. 1967 | r., 1969/35 |
| 1241 | Town and Country Planning General (Amdt.) Regs. 1967 | r., 1969/286 |
| 1270 | Motor Vehicles (Construction and Use) (Amdt.) Regs. 1967 | r., 1969/321 |
| 1305 | Remuneration of Teachers (Primary and Secondary Schools) O. 1967 | r., 1969/618 |
| 1330 | London Authies. (Superannuation) (Amdt.) O. 1967 | am., 1969/413 |
| 1366 | Trade Marks (Amdt.) Rules 1967 ... | r., 1969/522 |
| 1556 | Rules of the Air and Air Traffic Control (Fifth Amdt.) Regs. 1967 | r., 1969/216 |
| 1570 | National Insurance (Determination of Claims and Questions) (No. 2) Regs. 1967 | am., 1969/290 |
| 1653 | National Health Service (Functions of Regional Hospital Bds. etc.) Regs. 1967 | r., 1969/297 |
| 1665 | Motor Vehicles (Construction and Use) (Amdt.) (No. 2) Regs. 1967 | r., 1969/321 |
| 1666 | Motor Vehicles (Construction and Use) (Amdt.) (No. 3) Regs. 1967 | r., 1969/321 |
| 1683 | Carriage of Goods by Road (Parties to Convention) O. 1967 | am., 1969/385 |
| 1715 | Betterment Levy (Waiver of Interest) (No. 2) Regs. 1967 | am., 1969/532 |
| 1736 | Teachers Superannuation (S.) (Amdt.) Regs. 1967 | r., 1969/77 |
| 1753 | Motor Vehicles (Construction and Use) (Amdt.) (No. 4) Regs. 1967 | r., 1969/321 |
| 1759 | Wages Regulation (Brush and Broom) O. 1967 | am., 1969/208, 209 |
| 1806 | Wages Regulation (Rubber Proofed Garment) (No. 2) O. 1967 | r., 1969/131 |
| 1819 | Registration of Births (Amdt.) Regs. 1967 | am., 1969/203 |
| 1853 | Acquisition of Land (Rate of Interest after Entry) (S.) (No. 3) Regs. 1967 | r., 1969/459 |
| 1854 | Acquisition of Land (Rate of Interest after Entry) (No. 3) Regs. 1967 | r., 1969/458 |
| 1855 | Opencast Coal (Rate of Interest on Compensation) (No. 4) O. 1967 | r., 1969/460 |
| 1898 | Wages Regulation (Boot and Shoe Repairing) (Amdt.) O. 1967 | r., 1969/428 |

| Year and Number (or date) | Act or instrument | How affected |
|---|---|---|
| **1968** | New Town (S.) Act 1968 (c. 16) ... | ss. 38, 39 **am.**, 1969/453 |
| | Agriculture (Miscellaneous Provns) Act 1968 (c. 34) | functions transfd. *see* 1969/388 |
| | Health Services and Public Health Act 1968 (c. 46) | functions transfd. *see* 1969/388 |
| | | ss. 59, 61 **am.**, 1969/388 |
| | Medicines Act 1968 (c. 67) ... ... | ss. 1, 5 **am.**, 1969/388 |
| | Town and Country Planning Act 1968 (c. 72) | functions transfd. *see* 1969/388 |
| | Customs (Import Deposits) Act 1968 (c. 74) | sch. 1 **am.**, 1969/240 |
| | Sea Fisheries Act 1968 (c. 77) ... | functions transfd. *see* 1969/388 |
| 25 | Police Cadets Regs. 1968 ... ... | **am.**, 1969/408 |
| 26 | Police Regulations 1968 ... ... | **am.**, 1969/137 |
| 172 | Traffic Regulation Orders (Procedure) (E. and W.) Regs. 1968 | **r.**, 1969/463 |
| 196 | Approved Schools (Contributions by Education Authies.) (S.) Regs. 1968 | **r.**, 1969/224 |
| 208 | Police Cadets (S.) Regs. 1968 ... ... | **am.**, 1969/493 |
| 296 | Foreign Compensation (Financial Provns.) O. 1968 | expired (24.3.69) |
| 344 | Land Registration (District Registries) O. 1968 | **r.**, 1969/115 |
| 362 | Motor Vehicles (Construction and Use) (Amdt.) Regs. 1968 | **r.**, 1969/321 |
| 375 | Remuneration of Teachers (Primary and Secondary Schools) Amdg. O. 1968 | **r.**, 1969/618 |
| 400 | Sugar Beet (Research and Education) O. 1968 | expired (31.3.69) |
| 407 | Approved Schools (Contribution by Local Authies.) Regs. 1968 | **r.**, 1969/501 |
| 425 | Savings Certificates (Amdt.) Regs. 1968 | **r.**, 1969/541 |
| 426 | Motor Vehicles (Construction and Use) (Amdt.) (No. 2) Regs. 1968 | **r.**, 1969/321 |
| 428 | Ulster and Colonial Savings Certificates (Income Tax Exemption) (Amdt.) Regs. 1968 | **r.**, 1969/542 |
| 438 | Motor Vehicles (Authorisation of Special Types) (Amdt.) O. 1968 | **r.**, 1969/344 |
| 443 | National Health Service (General Dental Services) Amdt. Regs. 1968 | **r.**, 1969/217 |
| 523 | Motor Vehicles (Construction and Use) (Amdt.) (No. 3) Regs. 1968 | **r.**, 1969/321 |
| 534 | Provision of Milk and Meals Amdg. Regs. 1968 | **r.**, 1969/483 |
| 580 | Merchant Shipping (Light Dues) O. 1968 | **r.**, 1969/386 |

| Year and Number (or date) | Act or instrument | How affected |
|---|---|---|
| **1968** | | |
| 601 | Goods Vehicles (Plating and Testing) Regs. 1968 | **am.,** 1969/322 |
| 602 | Motor Vehicles (Construction and Use) (Amdt.) (No. 4) Regs. 1968 | **r.,** 1969/321 |
| 679 | Import Duties (General) (No. 4) O. 1968 | **am.** (*temp.*), 1969/232, 572, 573 |
| 716 | Police (S.) Regs. 1968 ... ... ... | **am.,** 1969/137, 505 |
| 745 | Overseas Service (Pensions Supplement) (Amdt.) Regs. 1968 | **r.,** 1969/553 |
| 751 | Wages Regulation (Aerated Waters) (S.) O. 1968 | **r.,** 1969/546 |
| 752 | Wages Regulation (Aerated Waters) (S.) (Holidays) O. 1968 | **r.,** 1969/547 |
| 839 | Motor Vehicles (Authorisation of Special Types) (Amdt.) (No. 2) O. 1968 | **r.,** 1969/344 |
| 1235 | White Fish and Herring Subsidies (U.K.) Scheme 1968 | **am.,** 1969/471 |
| 1248 | Motor Vehicles (Construction and Use) (Amdt.) (No. 5) Regs. 1968 | **r.,** 1969/321 |
| 1251 | Provision of Milk and Meals (Amdt. No. 2) Regs. 1968 | **r.,** 1969/483 |
| 1389 | Patents Rules 1968 ... ... ... | **am.,** 1969/482 |
| 1591 | Betterment Levy (Rate of Interest) (No. 2) O. 1968 | **r.,** 1969/440 |
| 1632 | Motor Vehicles (Construction and Use) (Amdt.) (No. 6) Regs. 1968 | **r.,** 1969/321 |
| 1634 | Exchange Control (Authorised Dealers and Depositories) O. 1968 | **r.,** 1969/517 |
| 1799 | Remuneration of Teachers (Primary and Secondary Schools) (Amdt. No. 2) O. 1968 | **r.,** 1969/618 |
| 1837 | Rules of the Air and Air Traffic Control (Sixth Amdt.) Regs. 1968 | **r.,** 1969/216 |
| 1885 | Anti-Dumping (Provisional Charge to Duty) O. 1968 | **r.,** 1969/60 |
| 1939 | Price Stability of Imported Products (Rates of Levy No. 13) O. 1968 | **r.,** 1969/45 |
| 1948 | Import Duties (Temporary Exemptions) (No. 6) O. 1968 | **am.,** 1969/315 |
| 1986 | Eggs (Protection of Guarantees) O. 1968 | **r.,** 1969/187 |
| 2019 | Exchange Control (Authorised Dealers and Depositories) (Amdt.) (No. 4) O. 1968 | **r.,** 1969/517 |
| 2049 | Registration of Births, Deaths and Marriages Regs. 1968 | **mod. (W.),** 1969/203 |
| 2050 | Birth Certificate (Shortened Form) Regs. 1968 | **mod. (W.),** 1969/203 |

| Year and Number (or date) | Act or instrument | How affected |
|---|---|---|
| **1968** | | |
| 2052 | Justices (Supplemental List) Rules 1968 | **am.,** 1969/76 |
| 2070 | Rules of the Air and Air Traffic Control (Seventh Amdt.) Regs. 1968 | **r.,** 1969/216 |
| | | |
| **1969** | | |
| 45 | Price Stability of Imported Products (Rates of Levy No. 1) O. 1969 | **r.,** 1969/211 |
| 52 | Motor Vehicles (Construction and Use) (Amdt.) Regs. 1969 | **r.,** 1969/321 |
| 129 | Exchange Control (Authorised Dealers and Depositories) (Amdt.) O. 1969 | **r.,** 1969/517 |
| 211 | Price Stability of Imported Products (Rates of Levy No. 2) O. 1969 | **r.,** 1969/314 |
| 278 | Exchange Control (Authorised Dealers and Depositories) (Amdt.) (No. 2) O. 1969 | **r.,** 1969/517 |
| 314 | Price Stability of Imported Products (Rates of Levy No. 3) O. 1969 | **r.,** 1969/329 |
| 318 | Price Stability of Imported Products (Rates of Levy No. 4) O. 1969 | **r.,** 1969/329 |
| 329 | Price Stability of Imported Products (Rates of Levy No. 5) O. 1969 | **r.,** 1969/407 |
| 407 | Price Stability of Imported Products (Rates of Levy No. 6) O. 1969 | **r.,** 1969/473 |
| 440 | Betterment Levy (Rate of Interest) O. 1969 | **r.,** 1969/536 |
| 473 | Price Stability of Imported Products (Rates of Levy No. 7) O. 1969 | **r.,** 1969/571 |
| 537 | Price Stability of Imported Products (Rates of Levy No. 8) O. 1969 | **r.,** 1969/571 |

# Index to Part I

Page

Page

SBN 11 840030 4